The Safe Hiring Manual

The Complete Guide to Employment Screening Background Checks for Employers, Recruiters, and Job Seekers

2nd Edition

By Lester S. Rosen

Facts
ON DEMAND
PRESS

©2012 by BRB Publications, Inc.
Facts on Demand Press
PO Box 27869
Tempe, AZ 85285
800-929-3811
www.brbpublications.com

Facts
ON DEMAND
▶ PRESS

The Safe Hiring Manual

The Complete Guide to Employment Screening Background Checks for Employers, Recruiters, and Job Seekers

Second Edition

©2012 By BRB Publications, Inc.
PO Box 27869 • Tempe, AZ 85285 • 800.929.3811
ISBN13: 978-1-889150-59-8 • ISBN10: 1-889150-59-2

Written by Lester S. Rosen
Edited by Thomas Ahearn, Courtney M. Nock, and Michael Sankey
Cover Design by Robin Fox & Associates

Cataloging-in-Publication Data
(Provided by Quality Books, Inc.)

Rosen, Lester S.
 The safe hiring manual : the complete guide to
employment screening background checks for employers,
recruiters, and job seekers / by Lester S. Rosen. -- 2nd
ed.
 p. cm.
 Includes index.
 ISBN 978-1-889150-59-8

 1. Employee screening. 2. Employee selection.
I. Title.

HF5549.5.E429R67 2012   658.3'112
                      QBI12-600172

Praise for
The Safe Hiring Manual

"The Safe Hiring Manual is "the source" and its author, Les Rosen, is "the authority" on background screening applicants, whether employees or volunteers...Given the complexity of federal and state laws that regulate background screening, you need to be very careful in threading the legal needle. That's why we rely on Les and that's why you need the Safe Hiring Manual, the most comprehensive and up-to-date book on background screening."
Ralph Yanello | CEO-Founder-Lawyer
Shield the Vulnerable, a service of LawRoom

"The update of The Safe Hiring Manual is very timely because the practice of conducting background checks is facing many challenges with the EEOC's focus on credit checks, education verifications and issuance of their New Guidance on use of Criminal Background Checks as well as many special interest groups advocating for previously incarcerated persons rights. From 'Ban the Box' to expanded expungement of criminal records rights employers are facing an affront on getting information they believe will help them provide a safe workplace, reduce theft, embezzlement, fraud , identify theft, other crimes and to assess overall employee trustworthiness. In this edition of his landmark book Les Rosen provides an insightful mosaic of information that provides clear guidance and every person involved in hiring people needs to read this book."
W. Barry Nixon, SPHR
Executive Director
National Institute for Prevention of Workplace Violence, Inc.

"If you are in charge of talent acquisition or in the business of hiring, this is a must read! The book gives you easy access to set up secure hiring practices and reinforces the importance of checking out candidates, before its too late. Do your due diligence and read this book - before you hire your next candidate.
Brenda Gilchrist, SPHR
The HR Matrix, LLC

"Hiring employees has never been riskier than it is today. Employers must comply with a myriad of employment and other laws in order to stay compliant and out of court. Once again, Les Rosen, one of the preeminent experts in background searches and accompanying laws hits it out the park with the only book you will ever need to guide you on safe hiring practices. Packed with practical advice in an easy to read format, this book provides you policies, forms, tips to help you understand the data you collect and guidance along the way to make sure you are legally compliant with all avenues of your background checks. Your lawyers will thank you for getting this book!"
Allison West, Esq., SPHR
Trainer/Speaker/Investigator/ HR Consultant
Employment Practices Specialists

" . . .an extraordinarily detailed and complete book on how HR Depts. can be used to help protect a company from criminal acts and civil liability. . . . Security professionals will benefit from this book in several ways. First, it is an invaluable resource on protecting an organization from a bad hire and it can help security depts. make the case for better screening to senior management. Second, it shows how organizations that ignore due diligence in hiring are leaving themselves exposed to liability. Third, anyone auditing the hiring process, will learn what is legal, what is not, and what is considered best practice."
Security Management
Sept. 2005 (about first edition)

"The Safe Hiring Manual is a densely informational and comprehensive guide of almost every bit of datum HR departments need to know - and this reviewer cannot think of an iota not addressed for those firms caring enough to conduct due diligence."
Pat Beltrante
Beltrante & Associates

"This book is an invaluable resource for any company concerned about potential losses due to fraud. Companies of all sizes should use the techniques and methods in this book as their first line of defense against fraud and embezzlement."
John D. Gill, J.D., CFE
General Counsel
Association of Certified Fraud Examiners

"… a comprehensive reference for the critically-important area of applicant/employee background checking/verification in this era of privacy protection and legal liability for bad hiring decisions. The chapters on using proper applications and employment history, by themselves, more than justify purchasing this book and using it to guide during every hiring decision."
Craig Pratt, SPHR
Human Resource Consultant
Craig Pratt and Associates

"The Safe Hiring Manual is a great volume for your professional reference collection, and an even better giveaway for your clients. How often are you trying to explain the legal and diligence searches that are possible for pre-employments? Or the fall-out that occurs when they don't do a background check. The timeliness of this work is seen in the coverage of topics such as FCRA, International background checks, drug checks, identity theft and terrorist searches."
Cynthia Hetherington
www.hetheringtongroup.com/publishing.shtml
Hetherington Information Services, LLC

Table of Contents

Section 5: Criminal Records & Employment Screening

Section 6: Additional Tools for Employment Screening

18. Education and Credentials Verifications   397

The Need for Verification of Education Credentials, The Verification Process, How to Verify if a School is Accredited, The Use of Fake Diplomas is a Real Problem, About Distance Learning (Online) Schools, Verifying High School and GED Diplomas, Occupational Licensing and Vocational Verifications, Conclusion — Educational Credentials Checking, Additional Education Verification Resources

19. Social Media Background Checks   413

The Social Media Explosion, Research Shows How Employers Use Internet for Screening, Landmines and Traps with Social Media Background Checks, Legal Risks for Employers Using Social Media for Employment Screening, Solutions if Using Social Media Background Checks, Bottom Line with Social Media Background Checks: Proceed with Caution, Setting a Company Policy

20. Other Background Screening Tools for Employers   437

Driving Records, Workers' Compensation Records, Using Civil Court Case Files, Judgments, Liens & Bankruptcies, Sexual Offender Databases, Military Records, Security Clearances, Merchant Databases, National Wants and Warrants, Specialty Databases - Government, Specialty Databases - Private

21. International Background Checks   457

Introduction, Statistics Supporting the Use of International Background Screening, Two Types of International Background Checks: Screening vs. Investigation, Why Employers Cannot Assume Government Screens Workers from Abroad, The Basic Components and Challenges of International Background Screening, Additional Challenges Specific to International Criminal Checks, International Education Verifications, International Employment Verifications, Other Resources and Tips for International Screening Due Diligence, Legal Implications for Employers Doing International Background Checks, Privacy and Data Protection in International Background Screening, A Comparison of Privacy Laws in the U.S. and the EU, About Canada's Strict Privacy Laws — PIPEDA, Recommendations for International Background Screening Programs, Additional Resource Links

22. Terrorist Database Searches and The Patriot Act   485

The Post 9/11 World and Terrorist Search Procedures for Employers, Terrorist Searches and U.S. Vital Industries, Terrorist Databases — the Good and the Bad, Use All the Tools, Past Employment Verification — The Key to Protecting Vital Industries from Terrorists, Conclusion

23. Drug Testing in the U.S.   501

Introduction, Studies Show Drugs in Workplace Cost Employers Billions, The ABC's of Drug Testing, Setting Drug Testing Policies and Procedures, What is Tested? – DOT Drug Tests and Non-DOT Drug Tests, How Does the Drug Test Work?, Pros and Cons of Testing Methods, Drug Testing Costs, Legal Issues and Drug Testing, Is Drug Testing Covered by the Fair Credit Reporting Act?, Recommended Drug Testing Information Resources

Section 7: Managing Unique Issues that Surface when Screening

24. Dealing With Fraud, Embezzlement, and Integrity   519

Screening for Honesty and Morality, Eight Tools to Encourage Future Honesty, How to Avoid Hiring an Embezzler, Corporate Fraud and Sarbanes-Oxley, Psychological Testing for Honesty and Integrity

25. Workplace Violence 535

What is Workplace Violence?, Examples and Studies of Violence in the Workplace, The Economic Cost of Workplace Violence, What Causes Workplace Violence?, Defining the Circumstance, Three Severity Levels of Workplace Violence Behavior, Preventing Workplace Violence, Other Important Resources for Workplace Violence

26. Additional Issues and Trends for Employers 549

Employers Come in All Sizes, Frequently Asked Questions about Small Business, Special Challenges Faced by Small Businesses, Large Employer Issues, Special Problems with Large Hourly, Seasonal, Temporary Contract Workforces, Using Instant Online Databases for Quick Hiring Decisions, Special Issues When Hiring in a Labor Shortage, Special Issues with Safe Hiring and Job Boards, Special Issues with Safe Hiring and Recruiters, Electronic Signatures and Applicant Consents, Candidates Presenting Their Own Verified Credentials, Looking Toward the Future – Background Screening and the Creation of a Human Capital Database, Top Ten Trends in Background Checks for 2012, Useful Human Resource Sites for Employers

27. Screening Temps, Vendors, Consultants, Independent Contractors & Volunteers 573

Screening Essential Non-Employees, The Duty of Due Diligence, Screening and Special Issues Concerning Independent Contractors, Screening Staffing Firms and Temporary Workers, Screening Volunteers, Screening Home Workers

28. Employer Issues with IDs, ID Theft, and Privacy 591

The Problem of 'Who is Really Who', Identity in America, Identification Criteria Used by Employers, Tools Employers Can Use to Avoid Fraudulent Identification in the Workplace, Identity Verification Before or After the Hire, Employee Privacy Rights, Privacy and Data Protection in Background Check Screening Reports, FTC Report on Protecting Consumer Privacy Recommends Businesses Adopt Best Privacy Practices

29. Form I-9, E-Verify, and "After the Hire" Issues 605

Introduction to "After the Hire" Issues, "Form I-9" Employment Eligibility Verification Compliance, "E-Verify" Electronic Employment Eligibility Verification, Employment "At Will" and Probationary Periods, Confidentiality Agreements and Ethics Policy, Maintaining Employment Screening Records, Employees May Have the Right to Inspect Their Personnel Files, Screening Current Employees, "Continuous Screening" or "Re-Screening", If Screening Results Lead to Possible Termination Issues, Employee Misconduct Issues, Ongoing Training, Performance Reviews and Ongoing Monitoring, Responding to Employee Complaints, Termination Procedures, Exit Interviews, Maintaining Documents after Separation, E-Verify History and Milestones

Section 8: What Job Seekers Need to Know About Background Checks

30. Job Seeker Questions and Concerns about Background Checks 629

Introduction, A Job Seeker's Guide to Background Checks, Job Applicants and Credit Reports, Criminal Records and Getting Back Into the Workforce — Six Critical Steps for Ex-Offenders Trying to Get a Job,

Section 9: Conclusion

The Appendix   671

The Index   717

Acknowledgments

First and foremost, this book is dedicated to my wife Donna for her unending support and everything that she does, and daughter Alex.

The book is also dedicated to the memory of Carl R. Ernst, a legendry visionary and early pioneer in the area of Public Records and the application of the FCRA to background checks.

This book in particular owes a large debt of gratitude to two extremely talented individuals: Michael Sankey, CEO of BRB Publications, and Thomas Ahearn, News Editor at Employment Screening Resources. The book would not have been possible without their dedication, commitment, and contributions.

I would also like to thank Courtney Nock and Heather M. Garcia for invaluable editing and research.

My gratitude also extends to a number of people who contributed directly to this edition of the Safe Hiring Manual or to my understanding of the area. They include (in alphabetical order) Kerstin Bagus, Tim Baxter, Robert R. Belair, Brue Berg, Craig Bertschi, Wendy Bliss, Ron S. Brand, Arthur J. Cohen, Eyal Ben Cohen, Dennis DeMay, Pamela Devata, Rod M. Fliegal, Beth Givens, Larry Henry, Derek Hinton, Stephen J. Hirschfeld, Brad Landin (President of Employment Screening Resources), Jennifer L. Mora, W. Barry Nixon, Barbra de Oddone, Kendra Paul, and Dr. John Schinnerer.

I would also like to acknowledge and thank two important people that have contributed to previous editions of the Safe Hiring Manual and whose work carries over into this edition, Greg Pryor and Esther Lynn Dobrin.

To everyone at Employment Screening Resources (ESR) and to our key advisor, Stanley Abrams, I thank you for your dedication and professionalism.

In a larger sense, I would like to thank all of the employers, human resources professionals, security and risk management professionals, and members of the screening industry that I have spent time with over the years who have contributed to my understanding of the subject of safe hiring. Especially critical have been the active members and board members past and present of the National Association of Professional Background Screeners (www.NAPBS.com) who have raised the degree of professionalism in the screening industry that has created an environment where a book such as this can make a contribution.

You have all made this book possible.

Les Rosen

October 2012

Introduction to 'The Safe Hiring Manual'

Who Benefits from this Book?

The Safe Hiring Manual benefits anyone who hires or wants to be hired. More broadly, this book applies to any type of work engagement, including employees, volunteers, independent contractors, temporary workers, and contingent workers.

This book is written for employers who desire to hire the highest quality applicants and to maintain a safe and profitable workplace for everyone's benefit. It is also written to help job applicants understand the processes employers must endure to avoid the legal and financial nightmare of even one bad hiring decision. After all, job applicants do not wish to work in an environment where the co-workers represent a safety risk.

Human Resources and Security professionals will find these pages contain the needed tools and best practices to obtain and use the needed accurate and actionable information vital to the hiring process. Recruiters and staffing vendors, as well as volunteer, youth, and faith based organizations, will also gain knowledge and benefit.

As you will learn, it is not enough for an organization to merely obtain relevant and accurate information on applicants. The critical point is that the information be obtained, protected, and used legally. The whole area of hiring – and background checks in particular – is heavily controlled by legislation, litigation, and governmental regulation.

And this arena can change quickly. For example, in April 2012 the Equal Employment Opportunity Commission (EEOC) issued a new Enforcement Guidance on criminal records that will certainly impact the manner of how employers hire. A new federal agency in Washington DC, the Consumer Financial Protection Bureau (CFPB), is now involved in regulating background checks. There are new developments almost weekly such as lawsuits, proposed legislation, or new regulations. Readers who want to stay on top of this area can do so by following the blog at: www.esrcheck.com/wordpress.

Background checking firms will also find this book invaluable. While *The Safe Hiring Manual* is not intended to be an the encompassing "how-to" manual for screening firms, it does present the essential tools, facts, and methodology practices that every background screening firm needs to know.

Don't Fall Victim to the "Parade of Horribles"

The process of matching the right person to the right job is a subject that affects nearly everyone – employers, employees, job applicants, and professionals in human resources, security, staffing, and recruiting, as well as the general public – when visiting a business or when a serviceperson enters a home.

The following true stories concern "bad hires" – employees who did not undergo proper background screening and who were too unfit, unqualified, and dangerous for their jobs – who caused financial loss, severe damage, and death. These stories also show negative outcomes which may have been prevented with proper pre-employment background checks:

✓   A carpet-cleaning firm in California hired its new employees on the "warm body theory." If the employer needed to hire someone quick and the person applying claimed he had relevant experience — and the applicant looked good to the hiring manager — then no background checking was performed. In 1998, a newly hired employee was immediately sent into homes to clean carpets. Within a month, a horrible event occurred — the new employee committed a brutal murder. The victim was a woman who was having her carpets cleaned. As the facts came out, it became apparent this employee's past-employment claims were false. He had been convicted of a violent crime and had been in prison for the past ten years. If the employer had just taken two minutes to pick up the phone and call the supposed past employment references, then the employer would have immediately discovered the applicant's fraudulent past employment claims. Had the employer done a simple background check, it would have raised red flags. A brief phone call or a simple record check would have saved a life. The victim's husband sued the company. The case went to trial and a jury awarded the victim's family $9.38 million in 2002. After an appeal by the company, the parties eventually settled out of court for an undisclosed amount. *('How to Avoid Hiring Mishaps'* *http://securitymanagement.com/article/how-avoid-hiring-mishaps-005529)*.

✓ In 2001, a woman was raped and beaten to death in her suburban Florida home, which her killer then set on fire with the intent of destroying any evidence. Six months before her violent death, the victim had contracted with a major department store to have the air ducts in her home cleaned. Unknown to her, both men sent on the service call had criminal records. One of the men, a twice-convicted sex offender on parole, returned to the home six months later to rape and kill her. The tragedy inspired the victim's sister to start 'Sue Weaver C.A.U.S.E. – Consumer Awareness of Unsafe Service Employment' to honor her murdered sister. C.A.U.S.E.'s national awareness campaign educates consumers, employers, and legislators on the necessity of proper annual criminal background checks on workers entering homes or working with vulnerable populations. The Sue Weaver C.A.U.S.E. website is at www.sueweavercause.org. *('Could You or a Loved One End Up Like Elizabeth Smart?' 5/3/10, www.huffingtonpost.com/janet-kinosian/could-you-or-a-loved-one_b_559526.htm.).*

✓ A proper "integrity" background check for a C-level executive could have saved investors $340 million they invested in a start-up firm that went bankrupt due to a dysfunctional CEO who was only minimally background checked. The firm that was developing 'pay by touch' machines for biometric payment at checkout lost $137 million on $600,000 in revenues in 2007 after the CEO engaged in drug abuse, partying, and other excesses, such as instructing his staff to give jobs and shares of stock to women he met. Smart investors, including two billionaires and venture capitalists, were among the people hoodwinked into investing millions of dollars. A nationally known wealth management investment firm continued to ensnare investors, including NFL players, even after the firm was in trouble and even though it did not do a background check. There was plenty in the CEO's past which would have demonstrated that no sensible person would have invested in this endeavor. The San Francisco Chronicle uncovered civil judgments and other run-ins that would have been big red flags for rational investors. *(How 'visionary' raised - and lost - a fortune* 12/7/2008 www.sfgate.com/cgi-bin/article.cgi?f=/c/a/2008/12/06/MNIK147QU3.DTL)

"Parade of Horribles" Defined

As a rhetorical device, a "Parade of Horribles" is used to argue against taking or avoiding a certain course of action by listing a number of unpleasant predictions of extremely undesirable events which will result from the action.

Source: http://en.wikipedia.org/wiki/Parade_of_horribles

Employment Screening Background Checks

The purpose of this book is to compile all the information an employer needs to keep a workplace safe and profitable. There are many numbers of books aimed at helping employers find the ideal candidate for a position. The critical topic, where information is harder to come by, is how to determine who NOT to hire, and why. The book assumes that an employer has already identified a finalist through whatever processes are used, and is now at the point of making a final hiring decision. At that point, the question becomes: Is there any reason NOT to hire this candidate?

This book is geared to help employers identify candidates who pose a risk to the employer, co-workers, or the public and how to protect a workplace from hiring a person with an unsuitable criminal record, false credentials, or a person intent on harming this country. No employer wants to hire someone that is unqualified, unsafe, dangerous, or dishonest. This book is a guide on how to avoid that.

The tools, skills, knowledge, and resources aimed at keeping an unqualified person from the workplace falls under the general term "safe hiring." Putting everything together in a comprehensive program to exercise "due diligence" in hiring is referred to as a "Safe Hiring Program" or "SHP."

A number of themes recur throughout this book:

- ✓ From the employer's point of view, one consistent theme is the old adage "an ounce of prevention is worth a pound of cure." When an employer fails to exercise due diligence in hiring and just one bad hire slips through, the results can be disastrous. Since 9/11, safe hiring and employment screening have become a greater factor of American life. Just as everyone who goes into an airport is screened to ensure everyone's safety, safe hiring and pre-employment screening protects employers, employees, and the general public alike.
- ✓ Another critical theme is that due diligence and safe hiring are not signs that Big Brother has arrived or that privacy and civil liberties are being sacrificed for the sake of security for a few. An essential theme in this book is, as Americans, we need to balance our needs for security in the workplace with fundamental American notions of privacy, and fairness and giving people a second chance. Balance! To quote Benjamin Franklin: "They that can give up essential liberty to obtain a little temporary safety deserve neither liberty nor safety."
- ✓ We will look at privacy considerations as well as the proper use of information in a legal and non-discriminatory fashion. A Safe Hiring Program is conducted with the consent of job applicants. You will also learn about criminal records — specifically that a criminal record may not be used automatically to deny employment without a job-related justification to do so. As a society, we want ex-offenders to have jobs in order to become law abiding and tax paying citizens. However, not every ex-offender is a good fit for every job. Chapter 30 contains advice for ex-offenders on how to deal with a past criminal record during the job-hunting process.

Employers have long recognized that many employee problems are caused by problem employees. The goal of this book is to help an employer to not hire a problem employee in the first place. By using this book, you will gain new tools, skills, knowledge, and resources that can be used to implement the very best Safe Hiring Program.

Employers Must Know Whom They Are Hiring

Ask any labor lawyer, human resource manager, or security professional whether an employer should engage in pre-employment screening. Their response: it is an absolute necessity. The exercise of due diligence is a must in today's environment, and proper due diligence includes verifications, background checks — a complete pre-employment screening.

How Ridiculous is the Following?

✓ On a busy downtown street, you look for a person walking by that appears to be "reasonable" — based upon whatever criteria you wish to use for "reasonable."

✓ You have a five-minute conversation with this person who proceeds to tell you all about himself/herself.

✓ Since this person still appears to be "reasonable," you say to him/her: "Here are the keys to my house. Come over and walk inside anytime, day or night — my house is your house."

Now, compare that to the current system in place in America for hiring a great many workers:

✓ A worker sends in a resume, which is merely a marketing device whereby an applicant tells an employer only what the applicant chooses to reveal.

✓ The applicant comes in for an interview and talks about himself or herself.

✓ The interviewer makes a judgment about the person based upon whatever criteria the interviewer is using. If the judgment is positive, within a short period of time a hiring decision is made.

Once a worker is hired, this person literally has the keys to your economic house. This person now has access to your assets, clients, co-workers, money, reputation, and even your very existence. If you make a bad-hiring decision, the results can be devastating. At the root of the problem is the fact that one of the most utilized hiring tools in America is simply the use of "gut instinct."

The Economic Fallout from a Bad Hire

With the recent upheaval in the U.S. economy, hiring the right person for the job has become even more crucial for both employers and employees alike. For almost every firm in the United States, the direct cost associated with labor is either the first or second largest line item in a budget; this includes revenues spent for pay, benefits, recruiting, and training. If firms add in the cost of managing employees, the figure is even greater. It has been estimated by CFO Research Services that companies spend about 36 percent of their revenues on "human capital." That figure was even higher in some industries, such as financial services or the pharmaceutical industry.

Yet many employers spend more time and effort choosing a copier or deciding between competing brands of laptops than they do in selecting employees.

The following statistics circulated by Automatic Data Processing, Inc. (ADP®), a payroll processing firm, are compiled by their employment screening division:

✓ 30% of all business failures are due to employee theft and related forms of dishonesty.
✓ The direct and indirect average cost of employee turnover is equal to 150% of the annual salary.
✓ 51% of all resumes, applications, and references provided by applicants contain inaccurate information.
✓ 7% of applicants have had a criminal record within the last seven years.

2011 ADP Annual Screening Index

The ADP Annual Screening Index from Automatic Data Processing, Inc. (ADP®) charts hiring risks in the workplace and helps employers assess the value of their own background screening programs. The 2011 Annual Screening Index, based on more than 6.5 million individual background checks completed by ADP in the 2010 calendar year, revealed the following:

- ✓ 46% of employment, education and/or reference checks showed a difference in information between what the applicant provided and what the source reported.

- ✓ 45% of credit records showed a judgment, lien, bankruptcy, or referral to a collection agency.

- ✓ 36% of driving records showed "one or more violations or convictions."

- ✓ 9% of background checks disclosed some form of adverse record (such as a criminal history, credit or driving records, etc.)

- ✓ 6% of criminal background checks revealed a criminal record within the last seven years – with 24% of those having two or more adverse records.

- ✓ 6% of background checks revealed a previous worker's compensation claim.

In addition, a review of background checks across eight industries – automotive, business services, construction, healthcare, hospitality, manufacturing, retail, and transportation – revealed the following:

- ✓ Business Services industry screened records had the lowest number of previous workers' compensation claims (2%) and negative reference responses (1%).

- ✓ Automotive dealers continued to have the highest percentage of driver records showing one or more violations (44%) and four or more violations (9%), year over year.

- ✓ Hospitality (65%) and Automotive dealer (64%) records had the highest percentage of reference checks reflecting variances between what an applicant provided and what a source reported.

- ✓ Transportation industry records continued to reflect the most accurate reference data.

- ✓ Construction, Hospitality, and Retail had the highest percentage of records that reflected a criminal record in the last seven years (each 9%, respectively), while the Healthcare industry had the lowest rate at 4%, and Business Services and Transportation records, each 5%, respectively.

The ADP Screening Index also revealed that screened records for companies with 1,000+ employees were among the highest for personal reference information variances (46%) while the under 50-employee segment recorded twice the number of previous workers' compensation claims than records in the 1,000+ tier. The highest percentage of prior criminal records (7%) was in the 50-999 employee segment, while the under-50 employee grouping had lowest (4%).

ADP is one of the world's largest providers of business outsourcing solutions. To download a copy of ADP's 2011 Screening Index, visit www.adp.com/tools-and-resources/calculators-and-tools/adp-annual-screening-index.aspx.

Source: Automatic Data Processing, Inc. (ADP®) 2011 ADP Annual Screening Index

© Copyright 2011 ADP, Inc.

Another survey, conducted in 2004, supports the conclusion that employers face serious issues when hiring. According to an online survey by the Society for Human Resource Management (SHRM) in May 2004, a random sample of email responses showed that 88% of employers found some degree of inconsistencies in resumes. Only 2% never found inconsistencies and just 9% said they do not investigate the backgrounds of applicants. For employers, human resource professionals, and security managers, these figures are certainly something to think about.

AUTHOR TIP

Even the United States Supreme Court has Recognized the Value and Need for Background Checks

In *NASA v. Nelson (2011)*, a group of NASA scientists objected to government background checks as a violation of a constitutional right to privacy. The U.S. Supreme Court, in an 8-0 decision, rejected the employees' constitutional challenge, holding that even assuming a constitutional right of "informational privacy" exists (a question the Court did not decide), the background investigation inquiries are reasonable and would not violate any such privacy right. As the Court noted:

"The questions respondents challenge are part of a standard background check of the sort used by millions of private employers. The Government has been conducting employment investigations since the Republic's earliest days, and the President has had statutory authority to assess an applicant's fitness for the civil service since 1871. Standard background investigations similar to those at issue became mandatory for federal civil-service candidates in 1953, and the investigations challenged here arose from a decision to extend that requirement to federal contract employees. This history shows that the Government has an interest in conducting basic background checks in order to ensure the security of its facilities and to employ a competent, reliable workforce (emphasis added) to carry out the people's business. The interest is not diminished by the fact that respondents are contract employees."

In response to an objection about questions on drug use, the Court notes that:

"(q)uestions are reasonably aimed at identifying capable employees who will faithfully conduct the Government's business. Asking an applicant's designated references broad questions about job suitability is an appropriate tool for separating strong candidates from weak ones. The reasonableness of such questions is illustrated by their pervasiveness in the public and private sectors."

See: www.supremecourt.gov/opinions/10pdf/09-530.pdf.

Replacement Costs and Damage Control

The direct economic cost of replacing a single bad hiring decision can be very expensive. Staffing industry sources estimate the cost of a single bad hire can range from twice the yearly salary to a much higher amount, depending upon the position. The time, money, and energy spent recruiting, hiring, and training is wasted, not to mention the amount of time lost between the date a bad hire is identified to when a suitable replacement is trained and in place.

An employer must also consider costs that are hard to quantify such as loss of productivity, knowledge, know how, and disruption to the workflow. With a 10% turnover rate, a firm will spend a substantial amount of its revenue on employee replacements.

Even more difficult to measure are other intangible costs that should also be taken into consideration when calculating the long-term fallout from a bad hiring decision:

✓ Lost customers or business causing damage to a firm's credibility.
✓ Damage to employee morale.
✓ Brand destruction.
✓ Litigation.

Firms spend millions of dollars to brand their products or services. One bad hire can create irrevocable brand destruction. A fast food worker can contaminate food or a hotel worker can assault a guest. With just one highly publicized incident, millions of dollars spent building brand identification is lost.

Termination lawsuits, harassment claims, negligent hiring lawsuits, and customer dissatisfaction all undermine a company's finances and reputation. The financial costs to defend these suits can be staggering, and the damage these suits can cause to relationships with customers and employees may cause the business to fail.

Litigation and Attorneys' Fees for Bad Hires

If the matter turns into litigation, then the legal fees stemming from a single incident can easily soar into six-figures, and jury awards can be astounding. Employers have a duty of due diligence in hiring, and if their hiring practices cause harm to co-workers or members of the public, an employer can be sued for *negligent hiring*. Employees can be sued for *negligent retention* when they fail to terminate, discipline, or properly supervise another employee after learning this person is dangerous or unfit. Even the bad employee may sue, claiming wrongful termination.

According to the Insurance Information Network of California, lawsuits for negligent hiring, retention, and out-of-court settlements in California due to workplace violence averaged over $500,000 each; jury verdicts in these cases averaged about $3 million. In another study quoted in The Reish & Luftman Practical Guide to Employment Law (October, 2002), employers in California in 1999 lost sixty percent of negligent hiring cases. There is no reason to believe the figures are significantly different in other states or has changed significantly since the study was done.

According to a very detailed legal article on negligent hiring lawsuits:

> "One of the fastest growing areas of tort litigation involves the imposition of liability upon third parties for intentional or criminal acts committed by one person against another." *29 Am Jur Trials, Sec. 1*

This in-depth article was written for the purpose of assisting lawyers who are either suing employers or defending employers in negligent hiring lawsuits. The fact that how-to books are written expressly for lawyers about negligent hiring cases should be a wake-up call to employers. Safe Hiring is a priority for employers who want to stay out of court.

An example of just how dramatic jury verdicts can be was demonstrated by the 1998 Massachusetts case of *Ward, et al. v. Trusted Health Resources, Inc.* A health care facility failed to check the background of ex-felon Jesse Rogers. The facility had hired Rogers to care for a 32-year-old quadriplegic with cerebral palsy and his 77-year-old grandmother. Weeks after he was removed from the assignment due to failure to consistently show up for work, Rogers murdered both the patient and the grandmother formerly in his care. A jury awarded a $26.5 million dollar verdict.

Believe it or not, the Ward case is not the highest amount awarded in a negligent hiring case. In 2001, a New Jersey jury awarded $40 million in damages to the estate of a home health care patient stabbed to death in her own home by an employee of a home health care provider. This health care provider had not performed a background check even though the attacker told his employer he had a criminal record. If a background check had been performed, then the employer would have also uncovered the soon-to-be murderer's history of mental problems.

Negligent hiring cases are not limited to just health care. Firms from all industries have been subject to lawsuits and claims of negligent hiring stemming from not only acts of violence, but also workplace theft and embezzlement. A firm can be sued for hiring employees who steal confidential information for the purpose of fraud or identity theft, or sued for hiring a person who harasses his or her co-workers.

These jury verdicts and settlements underscore the legal duty of employers to exercise due diligence in hiring.

Once litigation starts, HR and security managers will find that in addition to their normal duties they now have a second, nearly full-time job — dealing with the discovery process, the learning curve accompanying the litigation process, and managing the ensuing organizational fallout.

> **AUTHOR TIP** A cartoon on the author's wall shows a terminated employee being escorted out of the building with his box of personal items. As he is leaving, the escort says: "Don't worry. If it is any conciliation, we are also going to fire the idiot who hired you."
>
> Unfortunately, a bad hiring decision can also have negative career repercussions for the hiring manager. The HR or security manager can come under fire even if not involved in the hiring decision. One of the goals of this book is to supply the tools so you will not be that "idiot."

Workers with Criminal Records and the Cost of Workplace Violence

Statistics maintained by firms that perform pre-employment screening and background checks unanimously agree — unless a firm engages in due diligence in hiring, **it is a statistical certainty that the firm will eventually hire someone with an unsuitable criminal record.** These industry statistics show that as much as ten percent of the applicants who are screened have criminal records. Of course, not all ten percent would necessarily be dangerous or disqualified from being hired. Some of the criminal matters can be for minor acts, or the record may have already been disclosed to the employer. Rules concerning the proper use of criminal records in hiring are discussed in Chapter 16.

The impact of violence on the American workplace is staggering. The cost in lost wages alone is $55 million dollars per year, according to the Bureau of Justice Statistics. That figure does not take into account the human suffering associated with workplace violence or the economic and legal fallout.

Experts who study workplace violence have concluded it is difficult to predict ahead of time who will be violent. However, experts have also found there is an important common denominator when it comes to workplace violence — a history of past violence. Given the reluctance that many employers have in giving a reference that may reveal past violence, a criminal background check is often the most recommended method to help avoid workplace violence in the first place.

Effects of Resume Fraud

Industry statistics, such as the ADP Study, clearly demonstrate that resume fraud is as high as 40%. In other words, in 2 of every 5 resumes an employer receives, there are material misstatements or omissions that go beyond the acceptable bounds of puffing up a resume. These resumes venture into the world of fantasy, make-believe and deception. Every applicant has the right to put a best foot forward in a resume, but when the applicant is untruthful, there is a problem.

An example of resume fraud can be as simple as claiming to have worked at a job for a longer period than is accurate. There can be outright distortions such as an overstatement of title or inaccurate claims of promotion, e.g. claiming to be a supervisor when the position is really a file clerk. In more extreme instances, some applicants go so far as to entirely make up jobs, degrees, and credentials. There have been high profile examples of false credentials in resumes, including:

- ✓ Scott Thompson, former CEO of Yahoo!, falsely claimed a Bachelor's degree in accounting and computer science from Stonehill College but his degree was in accounting only.
- ✓ Ram Kumar, Research Director of Institutional Shareholder Services, falsely claimed a law degree.
- ✓ Kenneth Lonchar, former CFO of Veritas, falsely claimed an MBA from Stanford.
- ✓ Ron Zarrella, CEO of Bausch & Lomb, falsely claimed an MBA from New York University.
- ✓ Bryan Mitchell, Chairman of MCG Capital, falsely claimed a BA in economics from Syracuse University.

The resume fraud issue has also surfaced in the sports world. George O'Leary lost his job as football coach at a major university because he claimed he had an advanced degree that he did not earn.

Potential Shareholders' Suits, Corporate Fraud and Honesty Issues, and Sarbanes-Oxley

It is only a matter of time before publicly-traded firms are the subjects of shareholder lawsuits for loss of value as a result of negligent hiring. A California-based software firm failed to perform a simple background check on its CFO. When it was revealed that the CFO did not in fact have an MBA as he claimed, the stock's value plummeted fifteen percent, and a major analyst lowered his rating on the firm's stock from "out-perform" to "neutral." How can a publicly-traded company not justify spending a few minutes and a few dollars in order to make sure there was a qualified, truthful person running their finances?

In the current business climate, corporate honesty and integrity are also emerging as critical issues. Spectacular corporate and financial fraud cases such as those involving Tyco, Enron, and WorldCom have placed a new emphasis on honesty as a critical element of corporate life. Under the Sarbanes-Oxley Act, publicly-held corporations are now held to a standard of exercising proper control over their financials, which means knowing whom they are hiring. Without a Safe Hiring Program, a firm is at increased risk of finding itself the main subject of the next negative headline.

Employee Theft and Fraud

Another reason why employers need to be very concerned about who they hire is employee theft and fraud. Consider these startling facts and figures from the 2012 Report to the Nations on Occupational Fraud and Abuse from the Association of Certified Fraud Examiners (ACFE):

- ✓ The study estimates that the typical organization loses five percent of its revenues to occupational fraud each year and that this figure translates to a potential projected global fraud loss of more than $3.5 trillion applied to the estimated 2011 Gross World Product.
- ✓ The study also found that the median loss caused by the occupational fraud cases was $140,000, and more than one-fifth of these cases caused losses of at least $1 million.

The ACFE 2012 Report to the Nations, which will be discussed more in detail in Chapter 23, is available at: www.acfe.com/RTTN/.

Another reason for concern is embezzlement. As discussed in detail in Chapter 23, embezzlers are typically difficult to spot once hired. They often come disguised as the perfect employee. In order to obtain a position of trust, this employee often makes himself or herself indispensable and highly regarded. In order to prevent the embezzlement from being discovered, the embezzler must typically go through extraordinary steps to prevent anyone from finding out what he or she is doing. If an embezzler were to take a vacation or miss a day of work, an employer may discover something amiss.

According to research cited in an article called *Getting Wise to Lies* found in the May 1, 2006 issue of Time Magazine, there is "a lot of evidence that those who cheat on job applications also cheat in school and in life." That was the opinion of Dr. Richard Griffith, director of the industrial and organizational psychology program at the Florida Institute of Technology. Dr. Griffith is the editor of a book on job applicant faking, titled <u>A Closer Examination of Applicant Faking Behavior</u> (2007). He is concerned that if an applicant fakes a degree, how can the employee be trusted to tell the truth when it comes to financial statements?

These observations confirm what many employers, security and human resources professionals already know – that if an applicant lies in order to get into a job, there is no way of knowing what lies or acts of dishonesty will occur when they are working for you. What is the best strategy to keep embezzlers, liars, and cheats out of your workplace? Due diligence in safe hiring!

The Cost of Firing and the Importance of Documentation

If a firm determines it must terminate an individual, the firm may risk litigation for wrongful termination regardless of the reason for the termination. There will be attorney fees. This explains why some employers have a fear of firing. Consider the following scenario experienced by many firms:

First, an employer takes steps to avoid the necessity of firing the person. The employer may move the person into a different position, trying to find a position where the employee will do the least harm, or perhaps the employer will place the employee on a 90-day improvement plan. When the employer finally realizes that the employee is not going to work out, the employee is let go. Afterwards, the HR or legal department discovers the firm did not sufficiently document the reasons for termination. The next week the former employee files a lawsuit for wrongful termination.

Once a firm recognizes an employee will be terminated, it must begin the process of documenting the reasons. Merely saying, "It just didn't work out," is usually not a sound basis for termination. If the employee happens to be a member of a protected classification under discrimination laws, it is even more critical to be able to document a bona fide business reason for the termination. The lesson is take steps to avoid hiring a problem employee in the first place.

Employee Problems are Caused by Problem Employees

One of the most frequently asked questions by employers is: "Why perform background checks?" The short answer is that employee screening is one critical way to keep problem employees out of the workplace. As any employer or human resources professional knows, a great deal of time is spent dealing with employee problems. As advised in the very first edition of 'The Safe Hiring Manual' back in 2005: "Problem employees usually cause employee problems." Employers certainly would be wise if they can try to minimize problem employees in the first place with background checks.

Background Checks Occur at Intersection of Security and Rehabilitation

In August 2010, two news stories about background checks from very different angles appeared in two major media outlets – CNN and the Wall Street Journal (WSJ) – on the same day:

✓ The CNN story investigated why British Petroleum (BP) and a company used to hire cleanup workers for the recent oil spill in the Gulf of Mexico did not perform basic background checks. According to the CNN story, this lack of background checks for oil cleanup workers led to a sex offender landing a job and then allegedly raping a co-worker. A CNN investigation into the incident revealed that basic background checks were not performed on those hired to remove oil from the beaches in Mississippi. A County Sheriff in Mississippi told CNN he learned from the head of BP security that no background checks were conducted on the cleanup workers. He stated he warned the BP official that BP risked the criminal element looking for jobs and they would not know who they were dealing with if they did not do background checks. The Sherriff also said that, if asked, his department would have performed the background checks for free. The 41-year-old suspect – who faces charges of sexual battery and failure to register as a sex offender – has a criminal history dating back to 1991. He was put on the national sex offender registry for a 1996 conviction for contributing to the delinquency of a minor and was also on probation after being convicted in 2003 for cruelty to children, CNN reports.

✓ While the CNN story showed the need for background checks for security reasons, a WSJ blog asked if employers can disqualify job applicants simply for having a criminal past and finds the answer may not be so clear cut. The Equal Employment Opportunity Commission (EEOC) argues that the practice of employers disqualifying applicants with criminal records or bad credit history may be discrimination since those applicants are "disproportionately black or Latino." The WSJ law blog also quoted an AP story to show that employers using a blanket refusal to hire applicants with criminal records could risk going against federal employment law: If criminal histories are taken into account, the EEOC says employers must also consider the nature of the job, the seriousness of the offense and how long ago it occurred. For example, it may make sense to disqualify a bank employee with a past conviction for embezzlement, but not necessarily for a DUI. The AP also reported that the EEOC filed a class-action discrimination lawsuit against a Dallas-based events planning firm in 2009, alleging that the firm "used credit history and criminal records to discriminate against blacks, Hispanics, and males."

The two news stories read back to back – one in which the failure to do a background check possibly led to a preventable crime, the other questioned if background checks using credit histories and criminal records are discriminatory. These articles could leave employers wondering how much background checking is too much and how much is too little. These two stories – appearing on the same day from major news organizations but with vastly different angles – underscore the point that **background checks occur at the intersection of two fundamental American values: security and giving people a second chance**. On the one hand, background checks can promote safety, security, and honesty while lessening the chance for workplace violence or the hiring of unqualified workers with fake credentials. On the other hand, employers using background checks should be concerned with issues of fairness and privacy while combating discrimination, as well as the need to give ex-offenders a second chance so that they can become law abiding tax paying citizens, which requires a job. Otherwise, as a society we will build more jails and prisons and less schools and hospitals. These are concepts addressed in later chapters. The solution for employers is reaching the right balance in their background check program.

Background Check Bashing – Either Too Much or Too Little

The news headlines in recent years dealing with background checks demonstrate that to some extent, Americans are conflicted about the whole topic of background checks.

On one hand, discrimination and privacy advocates feel that background checks are too intrusive and unfair. The Equal Employment Opportunity Commission (EEOC) has filed a test case alleging that a large national employer used credit report and criminal records to unfairly discriminate against members of protected groups. As of the time this book went to press, eight U.S. states have placed restrictions on the use of credit reports by employers for employment decisions. Scientists from the Jet Propulsion Laboratory (JPL) in Southern California succeeded in taking their complaints all the way to the United States Supreme Court that government mandated security checks revolving around background checks and entry into facilities are overly intrusive and an invasion of privacy. A recent study conducted at a major university suggested that after a relatively short period of time, criminal records are not a predictor of future misconduct.

Conversely, the tragic shootings at University of Alabama-Huntsville and Ohio State University in Spring 2010 have led to many to question if background checks should be even more in-depth. Those shootings had horrific impacts on the victim's families and the communities involved and questions have been raised if even more background checks should have been done.

In the case of the Ohio State University workplace violence, a top notch and highly respected background screening firm performed what appeared to be a standard entry level criminal record search and found what any screening firm would likely have found, which was no record. However, critics note that a 30 year old conviction for receiving stolen property should have been unearthed, even though old records have been destroyed, and there was some confusion about the date of birth that should have been used.

Of course, to find a thirty year old prison record under those circumstances would normally require an employer to retain private investigators at the cost of many hundreds of dollars for each and every potential new hire, as opposed to public record background screenings. And ironically, even if the screening firm had located the 30 year old criminal record for a non-violent offense and was able to establish the record belonged to the shooter, any use of it would have been soundly criticized as unfair and discriminatory. It seems that employers cannot win either way.

As it turns out, in the Ohio State University case a past employment verifications may have raised the red flags that would have alerted the employer to take a closer look at the hiring decision. It underscores that employers need to use a number of overlapping tools to evaluate a potential hire, and that no one tool, such as a criminal background check, can be used to make hiring decisions. In addition, background checks are just one component of an overall workplace violence prevention strategy.

The bottom-line is that background screening occurs at the intersection of competing and compelling societal interests. On one hand, no one wants to see workplace violence, or to have unqualified people get jobs with fake credentials. Safety, security and honesty are core values. On the other hand, society is also rightly concerned with fairness and privacy and as well as efforts to combat discrimination. The issue is reaching the right balance.

It is interesting that nearly every time there is an objection because there is too much screening, there is also often a call for even more screening after it is revealed that some crime or offenses occurred or where an inappropriate applicant was hired without a sufficient background check. With all due respects to the JPL scientists, one would assume their position may be different if it ever turned out that a failure to perform background checks resulted in a terrorist hurting the U.S., someone with fake credentials getting hired and obtaining access, or workplace violence occurring that could have been prevented.

What Can Employers Do?

Given the enormous price tag of a bad hiring decision, it is no surprise that employers of all sizes are looking to various tools in hopes of boosting the effectiveness of the hiring process. However, the good news is that employers do not need to live through this "Parade of Horribles." There is something employers can do — institute a Safe Hiring Program.

Keep in mind that due diligence and background checks are aimed at telling employers who NOT to hire rather than who to hire. This book is not about how to identify, recruit, hire, or retain the best qualified candidates. There are numerous outstanding resources to help employers do that. Rather, the processes in this book assume an employer is looking for the best hire, and wants to ensure there is no reason NOT to hire. A background check, for example, typically occurs at the end of the hiring process after a finalist has (or finalists have) been identified and an employer is about to make an offer. However, many of the processes in this book help an employer exercise due diligence earlier during the selection process, so as the employer is whittling down a large pool of applicants to find the finalist, dishonest or unsafe applicants may be eliminated from the final pool.

Chapter 1

Due Diligence and Negligent Hiring

Inside This Chapter:

- ✓ Due Diligence and Negligent Hiring Defined

- ✓ How Negligent Hiring Lawsuits Start

- ✓ A Safe Hiring Program Shows Due Diligence

- ✓ Avoiding a Negligent Hiring Lawsuit

- ✓ Proving Negligent Hiring

- ✓ Defenses against Negligent Hiring Lawsuits

- ✓ Due Diligence After Hiring

- ✓ Additional Examples of Negligent Hiring Cases

- ✓ Summary of Defenses That Do and Do Not Work in Negligent Hiring Cases

- ✓ Take the Safe Hiring Test

Due Diligence and Negligent Hiring Defined

Every employer carries around a large invisible burden when hiring workers. That burden is the obligation — the duty — to exercise reasonable care for the safety of others. The legal description of the duty of care is called **"due diligence."** The employer's duty to exercise due diligence means the employer must consider if a potential new employee represents a risk to others in view of the nature of the job.

> **Question:** What is a term that can be used to describe an employer who fails to exercise due diligence in the hiring process?

> **Answer:** The term **"defendant,"** as in a party who is sued for damages in a civil lawsuit for failure to perform a legal duty.

When an employer fails to exercise due diligence and a person is harmed by an employee, that employer can be sued. The name of the legal action is called "**negligent hiring**," sometimes referred to as "**the negligent hiring doctrine.**"

Negligent hiring is the flip side of due diligence. If an employer hires someone who they either knew – or in the exercise of reasonable care *should have known* – was too dangerous, dishonest, unfit, or unqualified for the position, and it was foreseeable that some sort of injury could happen to someone as a result, then the employer can be sued for negligent hiring. This is called the *"knew or reasonably should have known"* standard.

Obviously, most employers will not hire someone they know is dangerous or unfit for a job. It is the "should have known" part that gets employers into difficulties. As a general rule, employers should assume that a jury may find if an employer COULD have known the applicant was unsafe, dangerous, unfit, or dishonest, the employer SHOULD have known. For many jurors, "could have known" is the same as "should have known."

The threat of being sued for negligent hiring is far from theoretical. As discussed in the Introduction, lawsuits for negligent hiring are one of the fastest growing areas of tort litigation. Employers are being hit with multi-million dollar jury verdicts and settlements as well as enormous attorneys' fees, and the odds seem to be against an employer.

Negligent Hiring Lawsuit Statistics

Employers have lost more than 79 percent of negligent hiring cases and the average settlement of a negligent hiring lawsuit is nearly $1 million. *(Sources: Fortune, 2/00 & Human Resources Management, 2008).*

Keep in mind usually if a negligent hiring case is brought, the plaintiff's attorney is likely working on a "contingency fee" basis, which means the attorney representing the injured party only gets paid if the plaintiff wins and receives a percentage of the award of damages. Consequently, the plaintiff's attorney has an incentive to only take serious cases with substantial monetary damages. That means the case will likely be about a serious injury or occurrence. In the most extreme case, the victim may not even be in court if he or she was killed as a result of some alleged failure on the part of the employer. In that case, the victim's family is normally the plaintiff in what is called a "wrongful death case."

In addition, the reality is that as an employer, an employer's case is not being decided by a jury of "peers" in the sense that it is unlikely that there will be 12 business owners, private investigators, or Human Resources professionals on the jury. The jury is likely to be composed primarily of men and women who have been employees, and anyone with any HR experience will likely be "thanked and excused" during the jury selection process. As a result, an employer will face a jury that may well believe that the employer had the resources, opportunity, staffing, and duty to conduct proper due diligence. Certainly, the victim of whatever crime or act that gave rise to the lawsuit had no opportunity to exercise due diligence.

In other words, if an employer is sued, that employer will have some explaining to do. In addition, an employer may find that an inordinate amount of time is used if in a lawsuit for negligent hiring. Not only may there be numerous requests for productions for all sorts of documents, but hours may be spent in having employees prepared for depositions and having depositions taken.

How Negligent Hiring Lawsuits Start

Assume you have an employee who is driving to an assignment and gets into an accident or, while on the job, an employee accidentally injures someone while trying to perform his or her duties. In these cases, most employers would agree an employer would expect to be liable. In fact, there is a legal theory called **Respondent Superior** which means literally that the Master must respond when their employee commits a wrongdoing while engaged in the scope and course of his duties. The law refers to this as *vicarious liability*.

What happens if an employee decides to beat up someone on the job? What happens if an employee meets someone on the premises, goes to that person's home, and commits a sexual assault or a theft?

In these scenarios, an employer may say: "Wait a minute, I have looked through the job descriptions and the job says nothing about assaults, thefts, or sexual offenses on or off the job. He was not doing those things in the performance of his duty. These were independent and intentional acts he committed."

The employer would be right to a point. Under the traditional legal theory of Respondent Superior, the employer likely could not be sued successfully. However, such a limitation would result in innocent victims being denied their day in court and negligent employers not being held responsible. As a result, the ability to bring a lawsuit for negligent hiring was developed in order to afford relief to victims injured by the negligent actions of an employer, where the negligence had foreseeable consequences and caused the injury.

The right to bring a lawsuit for negligent hiring as well as negligent supervision, training, or promotion is established primarily through case law and is legally recognized in the majority of states. As of November 2010, a fifty state survey revealed that all fifty states have judicially recognized the concept of negligent hiring or retention.

 The American Bar Association provides a state-by-state analysis of the torts of negligent hiring and negligent retention and the prima facie elements of each claim under state law at: http://abalel.omnibooksonline.com/2010/data/papers/087.pdf.

A Safe Hiring Program Shows Due Diligence

Understanding how due diligence is associated with liability for negligent hiring is critical for any employer. If a bad hire does something to force an employer to defend in court, then an employer must show how it took appropriate measures of due diligence.

Firms that do not perform due diligence are sitting ducks for litigation, including attorneys' fees and big damage awards. Employers that implement and follow a **Safe Hiring Program (SHP)** show due diligence measures that are a powerful legal protection. Fortunately for these employers, the cost of exercising due diligence through a SHP is very modest. Even if there is a cost involved, employers need to measure the risk of hiring blind with the considerable and near certain risk of litigation and attorney fees stemming from a single bad hiring decision. As the old saying goes, it is a matter of "paying now or paying later."

Conversely, a SHP protects the employer in case a bad hire slips through. Despite an employer's best efforts, there is always the possibility someone will be hired that causes harm. If an employer can convince a jury that the employer exercised due diligence and acted in a reasonable fashion, then the employer has a powerful defense against a lawsuit.

Proving Due Diligence When Using Inexpensive but Questionable Record Sources

When an employer obtains criminal records, the employer needs to carefully evaluate if the information obtained truly shows due diligence. For example, one "national" database service advertises they provide criminal conviction, sexual offender registry data, and incarceration record information from across the U.S. for a fee of only a few dollars per name searched. To an employer seeking a cost-effective due diligence solution, this search may seem like a good deal at first blush. Unfortunately, because of the nature of this sort of database search, there is a strong possibility a criminal record can be missed, especially since only 66% of criminal court records are online.

As explained in Chapter 14, database searches can be valuable secondary tools to supplement the more accurate on-site court search of public records. Databases can be problematic due to issues of timelines, completeness, accuracy, and coverage. A database search can create a false sense of security. The fact that a name is not in a criminal database search, despite the use of the term "national," does not mean a person does not have a record or is not a criminal. Conversely, just because a name is in a database does not mean the person is a criminal. If an employer relies primarily upon a $2.00 "national database search" and a criminal record is missed, the employer would have a challenging time convincing a jury that a $2.00 search demonstrates due diligence.

Avoiding a Negligent Hiring Lawsuit

What must an employer do to AVOID negligence in hiring? This is the million-dollar question. The answer is — it depends. What does it depend upon? Those topics will be discussed in the next several pages.

Non-Regulated Private Employers — A Moving Target

Some employers have obligations or standards created by law. However, for the vast majority of private employers, liability depends upon the jury's view of the facts in each particular case. Generally, due diligence is a moving target. Unless an employer is governed by federal or state statutes, there is no one thing an employer can do to makes itself 100% immune from being sued. In other words, with some limited exceptions discussed below, there is not a national standard of care that, if followed, insures an employer is not negligent as a matter of law.

Generally speaking, the employer's duty of care is commensurate with the reasonably anticipated risk to third parties. That is where a Safe Hiring Program comes in. The SHP consists of a number of overlapping tools and procedures that, when combined, create an ample defense against a negligent hiring lawsuit.

Public Employers Also Must be Concerned

Public entities, ranging from local school districts, counties, states, and the federal government, also hire employees. Although governmental entities enjoy immunity from being sued, there are tort claim acts that allow lawsuits in certain situations. For example, the Federal Tort Claims Act (FTCA) allows a person to bring a lawsuit against the U.S. government for personal injury, wrongful death, or property damage under the following four conditions:

- ✓ The injury must have been caused by a U.S. government employee acting negligently or wrongfully (but not intentionally).
- ✓ The employee must have been acting within the scope of his office or employment.
- ✓ The injured party must comply with the claims procedures, which include submitting a claim to the appropriate federal agency within two years from the date of injury.
- ✓ A lawsuit can only be filed if the agency either denies the claim or six months pass with no action, whichever comes first.

The federal law also excludes a number of possible causes of action such as injuries caused by a government contractor, or caused by government employees acting in accordance with the law or carrying out discretionary duties.

Although some protections and some procedural barriers exist when it comes to a public employer getting sued for negligent hiring, public employers need to exercise due diligence in their hiring as well.

Mandated Background Checks

Some private employers have obligations created by state or federal law to perform background checks or not hire individuals with certain criminal matters in their past. When determining what is proper due diligence, an employer must be aware of any rules or regulations affecting its particular industry. For example, every state has a myriad of laws requiring a criminal record background check before someone can be hired within a certain industry (heath care, child care, etc.), or be licensed by a state licensing board (nurse, private investigator, etc.).

Employers and boards regulated by a federal or state law will likely already be aware of that obligation by virtue of being in that industry. Many public positions also require background checks. It is beyond the scope of this book to attempt to summarize the vast number of specific state laws that require background checks. However, it is clear that any private or public employers who violate the rules on mandatory checks can be sued if their failure results in harm to a co-worker or third party.

Abiding by State Laws and Industry Standards

There can also be standards which encourage employers to practice due diligence. The legislatures in several states have created standards that provide strong incentives to use background checks as a means to avoid negligent hiring. Below are two examples.

- ✓ In accordance with **Fla. Stat. Ann**. § 768.096, a Florida employer who conducts a background investigation of an employee, including utilization of the Florida Crime Information Center system through the Florida Department of Law Enforcement (FDLE), is presumed not to have been negligent in the hiring of an employee. The election by an employer not to conduct an investigation under § 768.096 does not raise a presumption that an employer failed to use reasonable care in hiring an employee.
- ✓ A similar law went into effect in **Texas** in 2003. This law created an incentive for "in-home service" or "residential delivery" companies to perform background checks on their employees. If an employer runs a background check using the Texas online database and the report comes back clear, then the employer has the protection of a rebuttable presumption that the company did not act negligently. Texas Department of Public Safety (DPS) has established an internet site for criminal records, registered sex offenders, and deferred adjudications at http://records.txdps.state.tx.us.

Ohio Law Offers Protections for Employers Hiring Job Applicants with Criminal Records

The State of Ohio passed new laws that offerw protections for employers hiring job applicants with criminal records. The law, Senate Bill 337, took effect September 28, 2012, is an extensive reform of the collateral sanctions that impose employment restrictions and limitations on over 2 million Ohioans with misdemeanor and felony convictions. The law includes a provision for the sealing of one felony and one misdemeanor conviction, or two misdemeanor convictions. It also provides for the creation of a Certificate of Qualification for Employment that lifts automatic disqualification for certain state-issued occupational licenses and provides some protection for employers from negligent hiring lawsuits.

Other states with similar laws include Massachusetts and New York. For more information, see the white papers page at www.ESRcheck.com/Download.

> **Legal Presumption and Rebuttable Presumption Defined**
>
> A legal presumption is a fact the law assumes to be true. However, once a fact is assumed true, the other party can then offer evidence to "rebut" or disprove the presumption. The advantage to an employer when there is a "rebuttable presumption" of acting with due diligence is the employer starts off not having to prove anything. The suing party has the obligation of presenting evidence to disprove the employer's due diligence.

In addition, employers should consider general industry standards and guidelines, even if they are not mandatory. For example, in Chapter 22 on Terrorism, there is a discussion of certain rules the federal government has strongly suggested, but not mandated, for the food industry.

Finally, an employer may consider if a member of its industry has been sued for negligence in connection with hiring, and the outcome. Not only can an employer learn from what has happened to other firms, but a verdict can create an industry standard that other employers may be held to as well.

 The American Society for Industrial Security (ASIS) – www.asisonline.org – has published the **Pre-employment Background Screening Guideline (2009)** that: "Aids employers in understanding and implementing the fundamental concepts, methodologies, and related legal issues associated with the pre-employment background screening of job applicants." The author participated on the committee that formulated the Guideline. See: www.asisonline.org/guidelines/published.htm.

Proving Negligent Hiring

To prove negligent hiring, an injured party (or the surviving family members suing for a wrongful death claim in the event the victim died) must prove the following:

- ✓ **Injury.**
- ✓ **Existence of a duty of care owed toward the plaintiff.**
- ✓ **The employer breaches the duty of care.**
- ✓ **Causation between the negligent hiring and the injury.**

The following are detailed breakdowns about each of these four points proving negligent hiring.

1. Injury

For a lawsuit to be brought, the plaintiff must allege there is an injury. The injury can include injuries that are physical (assault, murder, sexual offenses), emotional or psychological (infliction of emotional distress), property loss or damage (theft, destruction), or even identity theft.

Examples of injuries in negligent hiring cases include:

- ✓ The plaintiff, Welsh Manufacturing, brought suit against the security guard company it hired, Pinkerton's, Inc. As a result of three major thefts resulting in losses in excess of $200,000, a security guard was found to have been a co-conspirator in connection with those thefts. *Welsh Mfg., Div. of Textron, Inc. v. Pinkerton's, Inc., 474 A.2d 436 (R.I. 1984).*
- ✓ The plaintiff, an industrial contractor, brought suit against the company it hired to perform janitorial services. A janitor stole cash from a desk on subsequent nights and burned down the building in order to cover up the theft. *Lou-Con, Inc. v. Gulf Building Services, Inc., 287 So.2d 192 (La.App. 4th Cir. 1973).*
- ✓ The plaintiff, a hitchhiker, brought suit against an employer of a truck driver. A rape was committed by the truck driver after he offered the plaintiff a ride in his truck. *Malorey v. B & L Motor Freight, Inc., 146 Ill. App. 3d 265 (1986).*

✓ The plaintiffs, the parents of a disabled minor daughter, brought suit against a home health care agency. A substitute home health aide provided by the agency injected the daughter with a large unauthorized insulin dose, causing a seizure. *Interim Healthcare of Fort Wayne, Inc. v Moyer ex rel. Moyer, 746 N.E.2d 429 (Ind. App. 2001).*

✓ The plaintiffs, parents of a murder victim, brought suit against their daughter's employer. A co-worker at her office murdered her at her own apartment after gaining access to her address at work. *Gaines v. Monsanto Co., 655 S.W.2d 568 (Mo.App. 1983).*

✓ The plaintiff, a female employee, brought suit against her employer. A co-employee harassed her using cruel practical jokes, obscene comments, behavior of a sexual nature, unwanted touching of employee's person, and veiled threats to her personal safety. *Watson v. Dixon, 502 S.E.2d 15 (N.C.App. 1998).*

✓ The plaintiff, a female former deputy sheriff, brought suit against the county. Another officer showed and sent to others a doctored photo of the deputy with her breasts exposed resulting in claims of defamation and invasion of privacy. *Kiesau v. Bantz, 686 N.W.2d 164 (Iowa 2004).*

Example of Large Award Negligent Hiring Case

In November 2011, the family of a truck driver killed in a 2008 accident in Arkansas was awarded $7 million in damages in a wrongful death lawsuit brought against a timber company and its truck driver in an Arkansas Federal Court. Lawyers serving as counsel for the family of the man killed in the accident argued that the timber company had negligently hired the truck driver who caused the accident without conducting a basic background search that would have quickly revealed a history of unsafe driving that included having his license revoked twice. The case involved the timber company truck driver's qualifications to drive a commercial vehicle and the timber company's failure to appropriately screen its drivers. Evidence was introduced at the trial that the timber company truck driver never should have been permitted to drive a tractor trailer since he had lied on his application and had received two license revocations, previous infractions that the timber company could have easily discovered with a simple background search that took only 15 minutes and cost $15. The deadly crash occurred only 19 days after the truck driver was negligently hired by the timber company for the driving job. The jury returned a unanimous verdict that awarded $7 million to the victim's family and found the timber company 75 percent liable and its driver 25 percent liable.

Source: *'Langdon & Emison obtains $7 million in truck accident verdict' 11/10/2011 http://pressreleases.kcstar.com/?q=node/70015).*

---

2. Existence of a Duty of Care Owed Toward the Plaintiff

The injured party must show there is some connection or relationship between itself and the employer, so the employer owes a **duty of care**. This can occur in numerous situations, such as a co-worker on the job, a member of the public in a location where customers are expected to have contact with employees, tenants in an apartment building injured by a maintenance worker, and other situations where the victim and the dangerous employee are expected to come into contact. In other words, an employer breaches a duty of care if it creates a situation where a third party is expected to be brought into contact with the employee who causes the injury, under conditions for which there is an opportunity for an injury to occur. It does not matter that the particular injury was foreseeable, just that any injury was foreseeable.

Certain employers have a **higher duty of care** because of the unique situations of the job. **An employer's duty of care will increase with the degree of risk involved with the position.** For example, consider the nature of the authority and position of trust a security guard holds. Many courts impose an even higher standard of care on a security guard business than other types of employers since there is a greater likelihood of harm to third parties. *Welsh Mfg., Div. of Textron, Inc. v. Pinkerton's, Inc., 474 A.2d 436 (R.I. 1984).* In other words, when the job enables a person to act under some color of authority, a greater risk is involved because a person can potentially abuse that authority.

Similarly, courts have held employers who send workers into people's homes to a higher standard. This is on the theory that when an employer hires an employee who is given a unique opportunity to commit a crime, the employer has a higher duty of care. Examples are firms that clean carpets, deliver or fix appliances, or perform pest control services in a home. An example is a homeowner who brought suit against the exterminating service she hired when one of its employees raped her in her home. *Smith v. Orkin Exterminating Co., Inc., 540 So.2d 363 (La.App. 1st Cir. 1989).*

Other examples of higher duties of care can be medical professionals, home health care agencies or childcare workers that serve a vulnerable population particularly at risk. An example is a prisoner whose estate brought suit against the prison for failure, as custodians, to take reasonable action to protect prisoners against the risk of self-inflicted physical harm. *Thomas v. County Com'rs of Shawnee County, 198 P.3d 182 (Kan.App. 2008).*

Another example is a worker hired in a call center who has access to sensitive financial information such as credit card numbers, or personal information such as SSNs. An example is an investor, who brought suit against a broker company when a dealer breached the duty of care it owed and used the investor's funds in a Ponzi scheme. *Dolin v Contemporary Financial Solutions, Inc., 622 F.Supp.2d 1077 (D.Colo. 2009).*

Examples Where Employers May Have an Increased Duty of Care

In deciding how extensively to perform background screening, employers need to consider the risks involved. Here are some examples:

✓ The workers have contact or responsibilities with groups at risk, such as the young, infirmed, or elderly.

✓ Jobs such as a security guard, where a person acts under a "color of authority." A person who wears a uniform is even a higher risk since a person may assume they have authority and may let their guard down.

✓ Jobs with special responsibilities such as an apartment manager who has the master key to all of the apartments.

✓ Jobs where a worker has access to sensitive consumer information, such as credit card numbers or Social Security numbers (SSNs).

✓ Jobs by statute where there is particular sensitivity, i.e. workers with safety sensitive positions at nuclear plants. Sarbanes-Oxley compliance is another area that may create a higher duty of care.

✓ Jobs where workers enter homes, or where other unique risks exist. A person in their own home can be extremely vulnerable since they are shielded from the public and cannot obtain help easily. In fact, as mentioned at the beginning of the book, an organization called the Sue Weaver CAUSE advocates greater due diligence where workers enter homes: www.sueweavercause.org/.

---

3. The Employer Breaches the Duty of Care

The employer breaches or violates the duty of care when an employer has either actual knowledge of the employee's unfitness or, in the exercise of reasonable care, would have knowledge the employee was dangerous, unfit, or not qualified. In other words, if the employer does not perform a reasonable background check, a jury could find the duty of care has been breached.

✓ In a case against the Episcopal Diocese of Pittsburgh, a court found the jury could find that defendants breached their duty to properly hire, train, and supervise a priest because they failed to discover he was not sufficiently trained and experienced in counseling, he had problems with alcohol and his personal life, and he had a propensity to engage in dual relationships with female communicants. *Podolinski v. Episcopal Diocese of Pittsburgh, 23 Pa. D. & C.4th 385, (Pa.Com.Pl. 1995).*

✓ In a Wisconsin case, a court held it is foreseeable that failing to properly train or supervise a loss prevention associate would subject shoppers to unreasonable risk, injury, or damage. If the defendant fails to properly hire, train, or supervise its employees, then it breaches its duty to shoppers at its store. The jury determined the defendant negligently hired, trained, or supervised its employees and therefore breached its duty to its patrons. *Miller v. Wal-Mart Stores, Inc., 580 N.W.2d 233 (Wis. 1998).*

✓ In a case involving a nightclub bouncer punching a patron, a court held that by the very nature of the job, a bouncer has significant interaction with the public and is routinely placed in confrontational situations with patrons. Therefore, hiring a bouncer who is known to have violent propensities would likely be a breach of the duty. *Hall v. SSF, Inc., 930 P.2d 94 (Nev. 1996).*

✓ In a Georgia case, a court held that a jury could find that a security company breached a duty when it failed to conduct a background check which would have revealed that a salesman had been convicted of burglary and kidnapping. *Underberg v. Southern Alarm, Inc., 643 S.E.2d 374 (Ga.App. 2007).*

The level of the duty of care an employer must use is determined by the mythical "reasonable person standard." No one has yet located that person, although many lawyers have spent considerable time looking for the "reasonable person." The following is how one leading legal textbook describes the degree of care an employer must exercise.

Employer's Duty of Care Explained in Legalese

"As a general rule it may be stated that the degree of care required to be exercised by an employer in selecting or retaining an employee is the degree of care that a person of ordinary prudence would use in view of the nature of the employment and the consequences of the employment of an incompetent person. Such degree of care should be commensurate with the nature and danger of the business and the grade of service for which the employee is intended, as well as to the hazard to which other employees would be exposed from the employment of a careless or incompetent person." *29 Am. Jur. Trials 267, §9 Duty owed plaintiff by employer – Employer's knowledge of employee's incompetence (1982).*

4. Causation Between the Negligent Hiring and the Injury

The plaintiff must show the negligence was the cause of the injury. That means the injuries were a logical consequence of the employer's misconduct or incompetence. If an employee attacks a victim and causes injuries, there is no question the attack was the actual or physical cause of the injury. However, see discussion below for a defense based upon a lack of causation.

Defenses against Negligent Hiring Lawsuits

There are defenses an employer can raise in a lawsuit for negligent hiring. In the real world, an employer cannot count on a defense being successful. It is much better not to get sued in the first place. When an injury occurs and a lawsuit is initiated, most employers would have paid anything to avoid it.

Some of the defenses listed below are intertwined and could be used in more than one category.

Investigation Would Not Have Revealed Anything Negative

Even with more investigation, the employer would not have discovered anything that was relevant to the injury. A New York court held that a grade school principal's failure to perform a background check on a person recommended as a volunteer art teacher before permitting him to work with students, including a student he later molested, could not serve as a basis for a cause of action for negligent hiring, in absence of any evidence the volunteer had a criminal history and where a routine background check would not have revealed his propensity to molest minors. *Koran I. v. New York City Board of Education, 683 N.Y.S.2d 228 (1998).*

A New York court held that there was no evidence that negative information would have been disclosed through an adequate background check of a nurse who allegedly sexually assaulted a patient while sedated. *Travis v. United Health Services Hospitals, Inc., 23 A.D.3d. 884 (2005).*

A Texas court held that, even though a nightclub did not discover a security guard's past violations of the peace officer manual and a prior reprimand for use of profanity to a member of the public, the information would not have been enough to put the club on notice that hiring the security guard posed a risk of harm to the public. *Fifth Club, Inc. v. Ramirez, 196 S.W.3d 788 (Tex. 2006).*

Lack of Foreseeability

The most successful defense has been the injury that occurred was not foreseeable. A successful foreseeability defense proves the knowledge gained through a proper background check in light of the hazards of the job would not indicate a given injury would occur. For example, information that a school bus driver had been terminated from his former position for tardiness did not demonstrate the subsequent employer should have known the driver posed a risk of engaging in sexual misconduct with children. *Giraldi by Giraldi v. Community Consol. School Dist. No. 62, 279 Ill.App.3d 679 (1996).*

In a California case, the owner of a beauty school hired an employee to manage and supervise student training. The employee met a minor who was the son of a student at the school. As a result of meeting the minor through the school, the employee met the minor outside of the school and engaged in an illegal sexual encounter. The employee had previously been convicted of sexual offenses against children. The court held that the beauty school was not liable because even if they did a background check, nothing would have been revealed related to managing a beauty school. The past offenses did not involve students or customers of a hairdressing establishment and there was no indication the employee posed a threat to minors he may encounter in the course of his work. The court further held that an employer is not responsible for guaranteeing the safety of everyone an employee may incidentally meet while on the job. *Federico v. Superior Court, 59 Cal. App. 4th 1207 (1997).*

In an Indiana case, a corporation that supplies traffic controllers to contractors hired an employee to flag traffic at a construction site. The employee left the job site during the middle of his shift without permission, got into his personal vehicle, drove several miles, broke into a private residence, and murdered two people. The court held that, because his job did not put him into personal contact with citizens, it did not provide access to people's homes or property, and it authorized the employee to do nothing more than stand on the street and control the flow of traffic, the victims and the harm that befell them was not reasonably foreseeable. *Clark v. Aris, Inc., 890 N.E.2d. 750 (Ind.App. 2008).*

Lack of Causation

An employer can argue there was no causal or factual connection between the failure to investigate and the injury. For a victim to sue, she must show "but for" the employer's act or omission, she would not have been injured. For example, in one case the plaintiff was injured when he was struck by a car driven by an intoxicated employee of a car repossession firm hired to repossess the car. The plaintiff alleged the firm was negligent in hiring the employee without a repossessor license. The court determined that not being licensed to repossess was insufficient to establish the employee's unfitness as a repossessor. Additionally, there was no evidence that being unlicensed to repossess cars caused the accident. *Jones v. Beker, 260 Ill.App.3d 481 (1994).*

In another case involving the issue of causation, a court held that a construction company was not liable to a plaintiff employee on theories of negligent hiring and supervision, where another employee of the construction company shot the plaintiff off the job site as a result of an altercation the previous night. Even though there was evidence the employee who did the shooting was aggressive and used drugs, the plaintiff failed to show the construction firm did anything more than hire the two employees to work at the same time so hence they knew each other. The plaintiff failed to show the defendant's alleged negligent hiring and supervision actually caused the shooting. *Escobar v. Madsen Constr. Co., 226 Ill App 3d 92 (1992).*

In a Texas case involving a vehicle that collided with a gravel truck, plaintiffs sought to introduce evidence that the driver had made misrepresentations about his immigration status to obtain his commercial driver's license and employment. The court held that the driver's immigration status did not cause the collision, and was not relevant to the negligent hiring claim. Even if the employer's failure to screen, and thus its failure to discover the driver's inability to work in the United States made the accident possible, the driver's status as an illegal alien or his use of a fake Social Security number to obtain a commercial driver's license did not create a foreseeable risk that he would negligently drive a gravel truck. *TXI Transportation Company, v. Hughes, 306 S.W.3d 230 (Tex. 2010).*

Superseding or Intervening Cause

Related to the causation and foreseeability issue is the issue of proximate cause. An employer can argue that its negligence in hiring was not the legal or "proximate" cause of the injury because there was a superseding or intervening cause that was unexpected or was not reasonably foreseeable. An employer may have started a chain of events that led to an injury by making a bad hire, but some courts have held that the result was so unexpected that the employer cannot be held liable.

For example, in a case in New Mexico the employee delivered a television to the victim's apartment. Three nights later the employee returned, entered the apartment without permission and raped the victim. Even though the employee would not have meet the victim "but for" being hired to deliver a television, the court ruled that at the time of the crime the employee was on his own time, was not acting within the scope of his employment, was not in the employer's business vehicle, and had no authority from the employer to enter the apartment. In addition, he did not enter the victim's apartment to repair an appliance and the offense did not occur in or near the business. The employer knew the employee had a prior criminal record and that a purse belonging to a rape victim had been found near its place of business. However, on those facts, the court held that the act of the employee was independent of the employer and too attenuated to be attributed to the employers. *F & T Co. v. Woods, 92 N.M. 697 (1979).*

However, employers should not assume that they avoid liability just because their employee acted on his or her own or committed an intentional act. The "superseding cause" defense is determined on a case-by-case basis and other courts have found employers liable for acts committed by employees where the employer should have known about the employee's dangerous propensities. In another New Mexico case, a hotel was found liable for the sexual assault of a minor guest by an employee on the hotel premises while the employee was working. The employee had consumed alcoholic beverages during working hours.

According to the court:

> "There was evidence from which a jury might find that defendant was aware or should have been aware that [the employee] had a drinking problem and a propensity for violence. Two incidents had occurred on hotel property shortly before the assault that gave rise to this lawsuit. [The employee] was terminated from his job as dishwasher for drinking prior to the incident that gave rise to this lawsuit. Shortly after that termination, [the employee] went to defendant's place of business to inquire about re-instatement. He was drunk, interfered with the kitchen's operation, and became violent when he was asked to leave the premises. He was forcibly subdued by defendant's security personnel and he left under threat of criminal prosecution. Further, defendant later rehired [the employee] as a steward. [the employee's] position as a steward required him to help in the preparation of banquets. He had some contact with customers and other invitees in this connection. He was not closely supervised and had access to alcoholic beverages, which he consumed with some regularity while on duty. Other employees were aware of [the employee's] behavior in this regard."

The court held the employer was on notice of the dangerous propensities and the behavior was foreseeable. *Pittard v. Four Seasons Motor Inn, Inc. 101 N.M. 723, 730-31 (Ct.App. 1984).*

In a Georgia case, two 14 year-old girls sued a landlord for hiring a manager who abused them. The landlord argued that anything the manager did was on the manager's own time. However, the court held the girls would not have met the manager in the first place if the landlord had not initially hired the manager. It was alleged that the landlord was on notice that the manager had dangerous tendencies, and that the landlord could be sued for creating an opportunity for abuse. *Harvey Freeman & Sons, Inc. v. Stanley, 378 S.E.2d 857 (Ga. 1989).*

In another case, a nine-year old girl was raped at a city playground by a city employee with a background of violent criminal behavior. He had been assigned to the children's playground generally alone and unsupervised. The City tried to defend on the basis the employee was not acting in the scope of employment, but the rape was an intervening and superseding cause breaking the chain of causation. The appellate court ruled the sole issue was in fact whether the city was negligent by allowing the employee access to the playground, and there was sufficient evidence for a jury to find that a violent assault was foreseeable when a violent employee was knowingly assigned to a children's park. *Haddock v. City of New York, 140 A.D.2d 91, 532 N.Y.S.2d 379 (1988).*

The guardian of a mentally handicapped store employee brought suit against the company that provided janitorial services to the store for a sexual assault committed on the store employee by a janitor. The janitor had no prior criminal history and had not received complaints of sexual harassment. The court found that the assault resulted from the janitor's independent criminal actions which were not reasonably foreseeable under the circumstances, and that his actions were an intervening superseding act relieving the janitorial company of liability. *Wood v. Safeway, Inc. 121 P.3d 1026 (Nev. 2005).*

An employee's mother brought suit on behalf of her son who was shot during a restaurant robbery to which a manager was connected. The court found that because neither of the manager's prior convictions (selling cocaine and nonpayment of child support) involved violence or theft, or indicated a propensity for violence the manager's participation in a robbery was not foreseeable. The court held that the manager's own criminal behavior, and that of his cohorts, was a superseding cause that precluded the employer's liability for the crimes. *Barton v Whataburger, Inc. 276 S.W.3d 456 (Tex.App. – Houston [1st Dist.] 2008).*

In reviewing these cases, the courts consider a number of factors such as the vulnerability of the victims, the existence of a special relationship or duty of care between the employer and the victim, what the employer either knew or reasonably should have known about the employee, the connection of the injury to the employer's businesses, and the foreseeability the employee may harm someone in a way that has some connection to the employer.

Industry Standard

Employers have asserted that when their background check follows industry practice or state procedure they cannot be liable for negligent hiring. However, neither compliance with an industry standard nor with state law alone insulates an employer from potential liability for negligent hiring. For example, in an Illinois case, the defendant was an investigative agency that responded to claims of insufficient background checks by asserting that it followed the industry standard. The court stated that compliance with what other firms do was no indication it had met its pre-employment screening obligations. It was inadequate to claim the defendant followed the industry standard because it is possible a whole industry could be reckless in performing background checks. *Easley v. Apollo Detective Agency, Inc., 69 Ill.App.3d 920 (1979).*

Cost

Although cost can be a consideration in a claim of negligence, it is unlikely to prevail as a defense to negligent hiring given the relatively low cost of a background check. In one case, an applicant for a truck driver position gave negative answers on his application to questions about criminal convictions and vehicular offenses. Later, a seventeen-year-old hitchhiker was raped and beaten by the truck driver. The employer had only verified the response to the questions about vehicular crimes. A criminal records check would have revealed convictions for violent sex crimes and an arrest for attacking two teenaged hitchhikers. The employer asserted a defense that imposing the requirement of doing criminal background checks was too costly a burden to place on employers. The court dismissed this defense because it considered the cost minor when compared to the possible harm not performing the check could cause. *Malorney v. B & L Motor*

Freight, Inc., 146 Ill.App.3d 265 (1986). Even small employers cannot claim that cost prevented them from exercising due diligence. As outlined in Chapter 26, small business are well able to implement due diligence at very little cost.

Worker was an Independent Contractor

An employer may try to contest liability by claiming the worker was an independent contractor. That would be an uphill battle. First, a court may well look at the real nature of the relationship, not what an employer chooses to label it. The fact that an employer classifies a worker as an independent contractor and issues a 1099 form at the end of the year instead of a W-2 is probably irrelevant. The IRS has published guidelines on how to differentiate between independent contractors and employees. The real issue of whether the worker was, in fact, an independent contractor or an employee is the degree of control the business can exercise over the worker. For more information, visit www.irs.gov/businesses/small/article/0,,id=99921,00.html or see additional discussion in Chapter 27.

Even if the individual was, in fact, an independent contractor, courts have found an employer may be liable for the negligent hiring of an independent contractor when the employer knew or should have known the independent contractor was not competent. A firm risks being sued for negligence for its own independent failure to adequately investigate the firm it hired, or to require that its contractor hire safely. If the task involved some peculiar risk of harm, the lawsuit may allege a failure to adequately supervise or train the contractor.

Courts have even found that a business can be held liable for negligent hiring when it hires an independent contractor that in turn negligently hires someone who causes an injury. In an Iowa case, a victim brought an action against both a cable television company and its independent contractor who employed a cable installer who raped her. The cable company argued it was not liable since the rapist worked for the contractor and was not employed by the cable company. The court held that both the cable company and its independent contractor could be held liable for the negligent hiring of the rapist. The independent contractor who employed the rapist could be liable under a general allegation of negligent hiring. The cable company had an independent duty towards its customers, and could not abandon that duty simply by hiring a contractor. *D.R.R. v. English Enterprises, 356 N.W.2d 580 (Iowa App. 1984).* For additional information about the responsibility of employers and independent contractors, see Chapter 27.

Due Diligence After Hiring

Liability does not end with the hiring process. In fact, employers can be sued for failure to exercise due diligence in retention, supervision, or promotion as well.

Negligent Retention

An employer may be liable for negligent retention when during the course of employment, the employer becomes aware or should have become aware of problems with an employee who indicated his unfitness, and the employer fails to take further action to prevent such conduct such as investigation, discharge, or reassignment. In a Minnesota case, the court ruled a church could be sued for negligent retention if the church knew or should have known about the propensity of a church pastor to engage in sexual misconduct with persons who sought spiritual or religious advice from him. *Olson v. First Church of Nazarene, 661 N.W.2d 254 (Minn.App. 2003).* In an action a co-employee brought after being assaulted, evidence that an employee had been fired previously after lunging with clenched fists at a supervisor was enough for a jury's conclusion the employer should have known of the employee's propensity to react violently when angry. Therefore, when the employee was rehired after he threatened to bring a racial discrimination claim, the defendant was liable for negligent rehiring and retention. *Tecumseh Products Co., Inc. v. Rigdon, 552 S.E.2d 910 (Ga. App. 2001).*

A customer who contracted for the installation of air-conditioning units brought a negligent retention action against an air-conditioning installation company after the employee stopped working on the installation several months into the project. The company had learned that the employee had, on two previous occasions, contracted side jobs in violation of company policy and never completed the projects. Upon discovering this, the company reprimanded the employee, but continued to employ him in the same service position. The court found that the company owed potential and existing customers a legal duty to protect them from the employee's conduct and that the customer's injury was a foreseeable consequence of the company's retention of the employee. *CoTemp, Inc. v. Houston West Corp. 222 S.W.3d 487 (Tex.App. – Houston [14th Dist.] 2007).*

Negligent Supervision

Under this theory, employers are subject to direct liability for the negligent supervision of employees when third parties are injured as a result of the tortuous acts of employees. The employer's liability rests upon proof the employer knew or, through the exercise of ordinary care, should have known the employee's conduct would subject third parties to an unreasonable risk of harm. Before the employer is held liable, there must be facts or occurrences that put the employer on notice that the supervised person poses a danger to third parties. In an Arkansas case helpful to employers, a retailer was sued for invasion of privacy and outrageous conduct when a store security officer conducted an investigation of theft from the store. The court found there was no evidence that put the employer on notice that the employee would be overzealous or aggressive in an investigation and the allegation was dismissed. *Addington v. Wal-Mart Stores, Inc., 105 S.W.3d 369 (Ark.App. 2003).*

In a South Dakota case, an underage employee was given unsupervised an unrestricted access to alcoholic beverages during his shifts as a drink runner at a racetrack and was not prevented from becoming intoxicated while at work. The court held that the employer had a duty to supervise its employees as to be aware of any problems with the free access to alcohol and that it was foreseeable that an unsupervised, underage employee afforded free reign to consume alcohol could lead to abuse, leaving work premises unfit to drive, and possibly injure a member of the public. *McGuire v Curry, 766 N.W.2d 501 (S.D. 2009).*

A New York employee brought an action against her employer alleging that it negligently supervised another employee allowing harassment to take place. The court held that anything that occurred prior to when the plaintiff complained about the other employee could not form the basis of a negligent supervision claim because the employer was not on notice about the employee's predatory behavior until specific enough complaints were brought to the employer's attention as to alert the employer of the employee's misbehavior. *Tainsky v. Clarins USA, Inc. 363 F.Supp.2d 578 (S.D.N.Y. 2005).*

Negligent Promotion

For someone to successfully recover damages, it must be proven the employer knew or should have known the employee was incompetent or unfit to perform the job to which he was promoted. As a matter of law it was not negligence for a garage owner to promote an employee to the position of night garage manager without making a detailed investigation at that time of his possible criminal past, because at the commencement of his employment more than three years earlier the employee was successfully bonded, his previous job checked out satisfactorily, and during the interim period of employment he performed exemplary service for the employer. *Abraham v. S. E. Onorato Garages, 50 Haw. 628 (1968).*

Negligent Failure to Warn

The duty of care can even extend to a duty to warn consumers that a former dangerous employee was terminated and no longer works for the employer. An electronics services company terminated an employee who the employer either knew or should have reasonably known had a propensity towards violence. The employee had entered the victim's home on various occasions for business reasons. After the employee was terminated, he gained entry into the victim's home by pretending he was there for business purposes and raped the victim. The court held that because the employee had been to the victim's home in the past on the employer's behalf, a special relationship had developed between the victim and the employer, and the employer had a duty to warn the victim the employee was no longer employed. *Coath v. Jones, 277 Pa.Super. 479 (1980).*

In a case helpful to employers, a Minnesota court held that a reference check is not a "special relationship" that would evoke an affirmative duty to warn of an employee's propensities. Even though a former employer would possess direct knowledge about its past employed not available to a prospective employer, the new employer is not deprived of normal opportunities of self-protection if the former employer refuses to disclose information about the employee's prior bad acts. *Grozdanich v. Leisure Hills Health Center, Inc., 25 F.Supp.2d 953 (D.Minn. 1998).*

Employer Unaware of Past Conduct or Employee Hides It

Claiming that an employer had no duty to conduct a background check because the employer was not aware of a criminal record, or that the applicant hid it or lied about it, was rejected in a case decided by the Fourth Circuit Court of Appeals in 2004. The Court held that a janitorial service that did not check backgrounds could be sued for negligent hiring when an employee attacked a college student, and a background check may have shown prior physical assault on a woman. The court rejected the defense that there was no duty to check since the applicant denied a criminal conviction on a previous application and there was nothing to put the employer on actual notice of a prior criminal history.

The janitorial firm was hired by a college on the condition that background checks were to be performed. The janitorial service failed to conduct a background check despite having employed the attacker on several different occasions before the attack. A lower court agreed with the janitorial service that the case should be dismissed because the employee had previously indicated no criminal record on an application and the janitorial service had no reason to suspect a criminal record.

The Appellate court reversed, and determined there was sufficient basis for the case to proceed to a jury trial. The Appellate Court, citing an earlier court decision, determined an employer can be liable for the acts of an employee on a theory of negligence when:

> "an employer in placing a person with known propensities, or propensities which should have been discovered by reasonable investigation, in an employment position in which, because of the circumstances of the employment, it should have been foreseeable that the hired individual posed a threat of injury to others."
> *Blair v. Defender Services, Inc., 386 F.3d 623, 629 (4th Cir. 2004)*

According to the Court, it was a jury issue if a background check may have revealed a criminal complaint filed in a neighboring county by a woman that the employee had previously attacked.

Increased Need for Employer Due Diligence

One impact of the recent recession is the greater likelihood of job applicant fraud, which means there is an increased need for employer due diligence. Fraudulent educational claims, or worthless diplomas from degree mills, are already familiar problem for employers, recruiters and HR professionals. However, resume fraud has taken on an added urgency with the advent of services that would actually create fake employment references from fake companies. The service apparently even included a phone number that an employer could call in order to reach a service that in fact would verify the fake employment. So it appears that some job applicants have been willing to resort to these extreme and dishonest measures to gain an advantage in the job market. In the long run, worthless diplomas bought over the internet or scams to create manufactured past employment will probably be unsuccessful for the most part, provided that employers exercise some due diligence. For fake education, a competent background firm will typically verify first if a school is legitimate. If the school does not appear on accepted lists of accredited institution, then a screening firm can review lists of known diploma mills and scams. Screening firms will also verify if the accreditation agency is for real, since fake schools have resorted to creating fake accreditation agencies.

Additional Examples of Negligent Hiring Cases

Here are some additional examples of negligent hiring cases that involved employers and former employees:

Difference Between Negligent Hiring and Direct Employer Vicarious Liability

A case decided by the California Supreme Court on June 23, 2011 graphically demonstrates the difference between allegations of negligent hiring as opposed to **"vicarious" liability** where an employer has direct responsibility for the acts of an employee.

In that case, the plaintiff was injured in a car accident when another driver tried to pass a truck in the middle lane. The driver ended up getting back into the middle lane but hit the truck, causing the car to spin and fly over the divider and hit the plaintiff's SUV. The plaintiff (the injured party) sued both drivers, including the truck driver on the theory that the truck driver should have been in the slow lane, should not have sped up to prevent passing, and should have avoided the collision by being aware of a car trying to pass. The trucking firm employing the truck driver was also sued under a theory of vicarious liability, which means the employer is liable for the acts of its employees committed in the scope and course of the employment. In the alternative, the plaintiff ALSO sued for negligent hiring and retention.

The basis of the negligent hiring and retention lawsuit was that the truck driver had two previous accidents, one of which he was at fault and sued and the other occurring 16 days before the events in this case. In addition, the driver was in the country illegally, had used a phony social security number, and was fired from or quit without good reason three of his last four driving jobs. Also, the only evaluation received by the truck driver's current employer was negative. In order to avoid such prejudicial evidence, the trucking firm offered to admit that it was vicariously liable for any negligent driving by its employee. Vicarious liability is based on a legal concept called "respondent superior," which means that an employer is liable for the act of its employees committed in the scope of employment. Such an admission would mean that a plaintiff would not have to prove that the employer was negligent in hiring or retaining. Just showing the employee was negligent while working for the employer is sufficient.

The trial court, however, allowed the plaintiff to introduce the evidence relating to negligent hiring and retention and the jury heard about the prior accidents and the apparent lack of due diligence in the selection process. As a result, the jury found the truck driver negligent and the trucking company was also negligent in hiring and retaining the driver.

The trucking company appealed on the basis that evidence of negligent hiring should not have been admitted where the trucking company was willing to accept liability vicariously for the acts of its employee, and that the admission of such unnecessary evidence was prejudicial. Furthermore, under California's complicated laws concerning allocation of fault between defendants, the trucking company argued that it was held liable for a larger portion of the damages than it otherwise would have.

The California Supreme Court ruled for the trucking firm, indicating that once an employer is willing to accept responsibility for an employee's act, the only issue is whether the employee was negligent. It is no longer relevant if, in addition, the employer was also negligent in hiring and/or retaining the worker. Adding evidence pertaining to negligent hiring and retention is prejudicial and in this case may well have altered the allocation of responsibility.

The case is <u>Diaz vs. Carcamo, 253 P.3d 535 (Cal. 2011)</u>. The case underscored the difference between negligent hiring and direct vicarious liability. The case Diaz vs. Carcamo, is available at: <u>http://scholar.google.com/scholar_case?case=6787332853309228079&q=Diaz+vs.+Carcamo&hl=en&as_sdt=2,5</u>.

Case Demonstrates Outer Limits to Negligent Hiring Exposure

The case involved a plumber that was hired in 1999, even though the plumbing company knew the person had been convicted of domestic violence and/or arson involving the plumber's ex-wife. Four years later, in 2003, the plumber performed a service call at the victim's home. The plumber and the victim started a relationship that eventually turned romantic in nature. About a month after the service call with the victim, the plumber was terminated for misuse of a company vehicle, drug and alcohol use, and an allegation of threatening a co-worker. By 2005, the victim apparently had enough and ended the relationship and applied for a restraining order against the plumber. The plumber shot and killed her and was convicted of her murder. The victim's daughter brought a lawsuit for negligent hiring against the plumbing company. The case was dismissed by the trial court on a motion for summary judgment, and it was appealed. The Appeals court upheld the dismissal, for two reasons:

✓ First, the court ruled that an employer no longer has liability for negligent hiring after terminating and the end of the employer-employee relationship.

✓ As an additional ground, the Court also ruled that there was insufficient causation between the employer hiring the plumber and the murder of the victim, so that the employer's hiring was not the proximate or legal cause of the murder.

In reaching its ruling, the court reviewed California law on negligent hiring. Essentially, an employer can be held liable when it hires someone that causes harm where the employer either knew, or reasonably should have known, that the person was dangerous or unfit, it was foreseeable that harm could occur, and the injury to victim was caused by the employer's act. In this case, the court determined that the duty of care does NOT extend to acts committed by a former employee AFTER terminating. The logic was that a reasonable person could not foresee that an ex-employee would injure a party two years after termination. The California Court found that:

> "Because the employer-employee relationship ends on termination of an employee's employment, we conclude an employer does not owe a plaintiff a duty of care in a negligent hiring and retention action for an injury or harm inflicted by a former employee on the plaintiff even though that former employee, as in this case, initially met the plaintiff while employed by the employer."

As additional support for its decision, the Court also relied on a lack of causation. The court noted that there must be some "nexus or casual connection between" the employer's negligence and the harm suffered. Without sufficient connation, there is a lack of proximate or legal cause, and therefore the employer would not be liable. The Court noted that the plumbing firm could not be the guarantor of the safety of all customers or other persons whom the employee incidentally meet while performing plumbing work, especially given that the relationship began outside of the plumber's duties, and the romantic relationship did not even start until AFTER the plumber was terminated.

However employers may not want to assume this case announces a firm rule that essentially creates immunity from negligent hiring lawsuits every time a bad hire is terminated. As the Court noted, the existence of a legal duty of care has to be analyzed in the particular factual situation in question. A different argument could be made for example if the employer had hired someone for a position where it was foreseeable that a work related relationship would continue even after termination. This could occur where the job entailed working with vulnerable patients. For example, where there is a higher duty of care it is foreseeable that once the introduction is made, ongoing relationships that are work related could be established. The case is *Phillips v. TLC Plumbing, Inc. (2009)172 Cal.App.4th 1133, 1144.*

About Defenses That Do and Do Not Work in Negligent Hiring Cases

If an employer is sued for negligent hiring on the basis that they hired someone that they either knew or – in the exercise of reasonable care – should have known was dangerous, unqualified, unfit or dishonest, and it was reasonably foreseeable that some of harm could occur, an employer can be sued for negligent hiring. That is the opposite of due diligence. If the subject of a legal action, employers do have some potential defenses in a court case, but they are far from a sure thing.

The Best Defense

The best defense is that the employer did in fact exercise due diligence and reasonable care, but despite those best efforts, a bad hire fell through the cracks. An employer would have to show they took a number of steps designed to avoid bad hires. An employer can review the adequacy of their hiring efforts by taking the Safe Hiring Audit (see the last chapter.)

Another defense that had been successful is that the crime or injury was too remote or unconnected from the employer's negligence or was not foreseeable. An example is the California case mentioned earlier where a plumber with a criminal record was hired, met a woman on the job that he started dating, was terminated by the employer, and then murdered the girlfriend two years later. The victim's family argued that but for the negligent hiring, the two would not have met in the first place and the murder would not have occurred. The court found that the murder two years later and long after termination was not sufficiently connected to the hiring to hold employer legally responsible.

Another defense is that a background check would have not have revealed anything anyway, so the employer's failure to conduct an adequate pre-screening was not the cause of the injury. As the old adage goes, "every dog has its first bite." If there was nothing for a background check to locate that was a potential a "Red Flag," that is also a defense.

Defenses that Do Not Work

Employers have not been very successful in defending lawsuits on the basis that due diligence and background checks cost too much, especially considering how inexpensive it is to screen. Another argument that may not go far with a jury is that the employer did what every other employer did in their industry. The fact that all employers in an industry engage in the same practice does not mean that the employer has meet the legal duty of due diligence, since a "standard practice" is not the same as a "standard of care." The least successful defense is the argument that the employer is also the victim as well, or they were victimized by an applicant lying. An employer who claims they too were the victim may not find a sympathetic jury where the victim has suffered some grave injury, or perhaps even death.

When a negligent hiring case goes to a jury, an employer does not have a jury of their peers in the sense that there are not twelve Human Resources or Security Directors in the jury box. More likely, most if not all of the jury members are also employees or retired employees. As a practical matter, a jury may well assume that the employer had the resources, duty, and opportunity to exercise due care. After all, the victim of a case involving negligent hiring probably had no say in who was hired. At the end of the day, when there are serious allegations of harm against an employer, the employer is going to have some explaining to do. The bottom line: stay out of the situation in the first place through due diligence.

In Conclusion

When an employer fails to conduct due diligence on an employee, and someone is harmed in a situation where damage was foreseeable, the employer cannot escape liability because it did not know about the hire's past criminal conduct. The fact that an applicant denies a criminal record or the employer does not know about it is not an excuse. To avoid liability, employers should be proactive in conducting background checks. Exercising due diligence in hiring and conducting background checks is a small price to pay to avoid the "Parade of Horribles" that can befall an employer that makes bad hiring decisions.

Take the Safe Hiring Test

The goal for any employer is to stay out of court, if possible, in the first place. Since anyone in the U.S. has the right to file a lawsuit against anyone else for just the cost of a filing fee, employers may have no choice in the matter. The next best thing an employer can do is to take steps to minimize the possibility of being sued for negligent employment related practices and, if sued, to maximize its ability to defend itself. An effective tool to control the risks associated with litigation is a Safe Hiring Program.

A 25-point Safe Hiring Test is presented in the very last chapter in *The Safe Hiring Manual*: Chapter 32. This test allows an employer to judge the effectiveness of its Safe Hiring Program and how well the program would stand-up in court if the employer is required to explain to a jury what precautions were taken. Below are several sample questions.

Sample Questions on the Safe Hiring Test
- ✓ Does your organization have written policies, practices, and procedures for safe hiring?
- ✓ Is there documented organizational responsibility for safe hiring with consequences of not following program spelled out?
- ✓ Are the safe hiring policies, practices, and procedures reviewed and updated every year for legal compliance?
- ✓ Is there a documented audit procedure at your company to ensure safe-hiring practices are followed?
- ✓ If screening is outsourced to a third-party firm, can the employer demonstrate Due Diligence and show procedures are in compliance with the federal Fair Credit Reporting Act (FCRA)?

Chapter 2

Discrimination and Privacy Laws

This chapter covers two major areas of legal concern for employers and recruiters: **discrimination** and **privacy**.

Inside This Chapter:

- ✓ Discrimination Laws
- ✓ Federal Discrimination Laws
- ✓ How to Avoid Age Discrimination
- ✓ The "E-RACE" Initiative
- ✓ Discrimination and Criminal Records
- ✓ Discrimination against Unemployed Job Applicants
- ✓ Privacy Laws and Employers
- ✓ Safe Hiring Programs and Privacy
- ✓ Privacy and the Trend of Offshoring Data and Call Centers
- ✓ Privacy and the Use of Home Operators
- ✓ Discrimination and Privacy — Conclusion

Discrimination Laws

The regulatory environment has a wide application to many facets of the employment relationship. As presented earlier, one of the core components of a Safe Hiring Program is "an awareness of the legal and regulatory environment surrounding safe hiring and compliance." The main emphasis deals with these elements of a SHP:

✓ The application stage.
✓ The interview stage.
✓ Reference questions.
✓ The use of records and information, particularly criminal convictions.
  (NOTE: Each of these stages is discussed in the appropriate chapter. This chapter examines overall issues related to discrimination.)

In order to evaluate the privacy and discrimination factors in the use of hiring tools, it is essential to understand that the hiring process occurs on a time line. Each step of the continuum carries its own set of legal implications. Matching your hiring tools to the proper stage of the time line is key to sorting out the best applicants, helping prevent a bad hire, and to avoid any practice that may even suggest an invasion of privacy or a discriminatory practice. The available tools of the hiring process can roughly be divided into seven stages as follows:

1. **Sourcing stage:** This is the process of gathering potential applicants through a variety of means that can include inbound applications from job boards, websites, newspapers, or outbound efforts, such as recruiters seeking passive candidates.

2. **Preliminary screening stage:** In order to narrow down the applicant pool, there is a preliminary screening primarily based upon the applicants' self-stated qualifications, conveyed by the resumes, applications, or newer tools such as video websites.

3. **Assessment stage:** This stage can include the interviewing process to further narrow down the field of candidates, as well as numerous other assessment tools, ranging from objective testing to references from past employers or supervisors, or various other testing methods.

4. **Decision process stage:** Here, the employer has narrowed the pool to one, two, or three finalists and is moving toward a conditional job offer based upon an internal decision-making process.

5. **Background checking stage:** At this point, either a conditional job offer has been made or is contemplated, and the employer needs to exercise due diligence, typically through a background screening firm, to determine if there is any reason NOT to hire the candidate. The emphasis of a background screening firm at this point is a factual verification of details such as job title and dates.

6. **The post offer/pre-hire stage:** This is where an employer is able for the first time, if they so choose, to address such areas as pre-employment physicals.

7. **The post hire/on boarding stage:** This is where an employer, for example, can complete the form I-9 process.

Federal and state anti-discrimination laws make it clear that decisions based on prohibited criteria are illegal. These criteria include race, color, national origin, religion, ancestry, medical condition, age, marital status, sex, or exercise of family care or medical leaves. These are prohibited criteria because they are not valid predictors of job performance or bona fide occupational qualifications (BFOQ). In the past, prohibited criteria have been found to cause unfair treatment and discrimination. This type of discrimination is called **"disparate treatment."** A person is being pre-judged based upon membership in a group or status instead of what he or she can accomplish as an individual. The word "prejudice" simply means to "pre-judge" a person based upon the color of the person's skin, country of origin, sex or some other criteria that has nothing to do with job performance.

The situation becomes complicated because information that appears neutral on its face can be utilized in a discriminatory way. This is called **"disparate impact"** and occurs when employer selection processes that appear fair on the surface actually result in a screening out of identifiable groups from employment. For example, credit reports and criminal records are perfectly legal for employers to obtain provided the methods used comply with various state and federal rules. However, the use of credit reports or criminal records can have a discriminatory impact if they are used in such a way that results in a disparate impact upon certain groups. The generally accepted limitations to the use of these records are discussed in later chapters and in the Appendix.

Employers need to have a basic understanding of the statutes, cases, and regulations on both the federal and state levels that affect how any employer can legally collect and utilize personal information about job applicants in order to make hiring decisions.

Federal Discrimination Laws

There are a number of federal laws that prohibit discrimination in employment. The Equal Employment Opportunity Commission (EEOC) enforces these laws at the federal level. The EEOC also provides oversight and coordination of all federal equal employment opportunity regulations, practices, and policies. According to the EEOC website at www.eeoc.gov/laws/statutes/index.cfm, these are the primary federal laws which prohibit job discrimination:

- ✓ **Title VII of the Civil Rights Act of 1964 (Title VII)** prohibits employment discrimination based on race, color, religion, sex, or national origin: www.eeoc.gov/laws/statutes/titlevii.cfm.
- ✓ **Equal Pay Act of 1963 (EPA)** protects men and women who perform substantially equal work in the same establishment from sex-based wage discrimination: www.eeoc.gov/laws/statutes/epa.cfm.
- ✓ **Age Discrimination in Employment Act of 1967 (ADEA)** protects individuals who are 40 years of age or older: www.eeoc.gov/laws/statutes/adea.cfm.
- ✓ **Title I and Title V of the Americans with Disabilities Act of 1990 (ADA)** prohibit employment discrimination against qualified individuals with disabilities in the private sector and in state and local governments: www.eeoc.gov/laws/statutes/ada.cfm.
- ✓ **Sections 501 and 505 of the Rehabilitation Act of 1973** prohibit discrimination against qualified individuals with disabilities who work in the federal government: www.eeoc.gov/laws/statutes/rehab.cfm.
- ✓ **Civil Rights Act of 1991** provides (among other things) monetary damages in cases of intentional employment discrimination: www.eeoc.gov/laws/statutes/cra-1991.cfm.
- ✓ **The Genetic Information Nondiscrimination Act of 2008 (GINA)** makes it illegal to discriminate against employees or applicants because of genetic information (Effective November 21, 2009): www.eeoc.gov/laws/statutes/gina.cfm.

The federal laws only affect employers above a certain size. For example, the Civil Rights and the Americans with Disabilities Act cover employers with fifteen or more employees based upon the number of employees during each working day of twenty or more calendar weeks of the current or preceding calendar year. However, the Age Discrimination Act utilizes twenty employees as the threshold. As a practical matter, even small employers who believe they fall below the federal limits are well advised to take these federal laws into consideration. First, it can be complicated to determine how many employees a small firm has for purposes of determining if the law applies. All employees including part time and temporary workers are counted. An employer may not count "independent contractors," but the possibility exists that the contractors may be counted if in fact they are really engaged in an employment type relationship, regardless of how the employer chooses to compensate them. If an employer has two or more separate businesses, there are circumstances where the businesses will be counted as one for purpose of determining the employee count.

The rules about counting employees to determine if a firm is large enough to meet the threshold for application of federal civil rights laws can also be very complex. In addition, there are states where state laws can be in effect even if a federal law technically does not apply. More importantly, if a small employer engages in any conduct that would have been a violation of federal law if they were larger, an aggrieved applicant or employee may still be able to go to court stating an alternative cause of action such as intentional infliction of emotional distress.

The **Title VII of the Civil Rights Act** and the **Americans with Disabilities Act (ADA)** are probably the two most well-known laws that apply to discriminatory hiring practices. These laws prohibit any non-job-related inquiry, either verbal or through the use of an application form, which directly or indirectly limits a person's employment opportunities because of race, color, religion, national origin, ancestry, medical condition, disability (including AIDS), marital status, sex (including pregnancy), age (40+), exercise of family care leave or leave for an employee's own serious health condition.

These laws generally prohibit any type of questions of applicants which:

✓ Identify a person on a basis covered by the Act; or,
✓ Results in the disproportionate screening out of members of a protected group; or,
✓ Are not a valid predictor (not a job-related inquiry) of potential successful job performance.

Griggs v. Duke Power Co.

Griggs v. Duke Power Co., 401 U.S. 424 (1971) was a groundbreaking United States Supreme Court case concerning the disparate impact theory of employment discrimination.

The Court ruled that the company's employment requirements did not relate to the applicants' ability to perform the job, and had the impact of discriminating against African-American employees, even though the company had not intended it to do so. In the 1950s, Duke Power's Dan River plant had a policy that African-Americans were allowed to work only in its Labor department, which constituted the lowest-paying positions in the company. In 1955, the company added the requirement of a high school diploma for its higher paid jobs. After the passage of the Civil Rights Act the company removed its racial restriction, but retained the high school diploma requirement, and added the requirement of an IQ test as well as the diploma. African American applicants, less likely to hold a high school diploma and averaging lower scores on the IQ tests, were selected at a much lower rate for these positions compared to White candidates. It was found that White people who had been working at the firm for some time, but met neither of the requirements, performed their jobs as well as those that did meet the requirements.

The Supreme Court ruled that under Title VII of the Civil Rights Act, if such tests disparately impact ethnic minority groups, businesses must demonstrate such tests are "reasonably related" to the job for which the test is required. As such, Title VII of the Civil Rights Act prohibits employment tests (when used as a decisive factor in employment decisions) that are not a "reasonable measure of job performance," regardless of the absence of actual intent to discriminate. Since the aptitude tests involved, and the high school diploma requirement, were broad-based and not directly related to the jobs performed, Duke Power's employee transfer procedure was found by the Court to be in violation of the Act.

More about the Americans with Disabilities Act (ADA)

This federal law regulates hiring of Americans with disabilities and has broad implications. In terms of background screenings, an employer may not use or obtain any information that violates the rights afforded under this law. The most obvious impact of the law relates to medical records, disabilities, and workers' compensation records. Employment screening firms may access and provide workers' compensation records, but only under the strict procedures mandated by the Americans with Disabilities Act.

The ADA can potentially have an impact on the timing of a background check. In *Leonel v. American Airlines, 400 F.3d 702 (9th Cir. 2005)*, the plaintiffs were seeking jobs with a major airline. They were issued conditional offers of employment contingent upon passing *both* their background check and medical examination. Their blood was drawn prior to the background checks being completed. According to the case, the airline then discovered a medical condition, and rescinded the job offers on the basis that the applicants did not disclose the medical condition during the medical exams.

The plaintiffs sued for a violation of the federal Americans with Disability Act and also under the California law governing employment discrimination, the California Fair Employment and Housing Act (FEHA). The plaintiffs alleged that under federal law and California law, before a medical test can be performed, there must first be a "real" job offer on the table. Since the background check was not yet completed before the medical information was obtained, the plaintiffs argued that the employer had not met federal and state standards and had conducted a medical test before there was a job offer.

The court accepted the argument, ruling that in order to conduct a "post-offer" medical exam, the employer must have first evaluated all relevant and available non-medical information. When the employer still has non-medical information to evaluate, such as a background check, it is premature to request a medical exam because there has not been a "job offer." The rule has two benefits for job applicants. First, it allows a job applicant to determine if they were rejected for medical reasons or some non-medical reason obtained in the background report. Secondly, it safeguards the applicant from having to reveal personal medical information prematurely. If the applicant is not offered the job, then they are not put in to a position of providing personal medical information for no reason.

One occasion where the ADA (and similar state laws) may raise a concern is for criminal convictions involving drugs or alcohol. Under the ADA, an employer cannot discriminate on the basis that an applicant is an alcoholic or a former drug user. However, the ADA and similar state laws do not protect a person who is currently using drugs or abusing alcohol. Where a person is otherwise qualified for a position, and the background screening reveals a drug or alcohol conviction, an employer should carefully review the totality of the circumstances involved before denying employment on that basis. Certainly, the current use of illegal drugs is not protected. The decision may also depend upon the position in question. For driving positions, for example, an employer may certainly evaluate driving-related convictions more seriously. Workers' compensation record searches are discussed in more detail in Chapter 30.

State and Local Discrimination Laws

To add to the complexity for employers, a number of states and local jurisdictions have their own rules governing discrimination. The federal Equal Employment Opportunity Commission website indicates over 100 state and local fair employment practice agencies, or FEPA's. Most states have their own Civil Rights Acts as well as an agency within state government that enforces these state laws. State laws can vary from the federal rules in terms of the size of the employer covered and what constitutes a violation. Even local jurisdictions and cities can regulate employers. For example, the City and County of San Francisco have the San Francisco Human Rights Commission which can investigate and mediate complaints of discrimination for employees of any San Francisco employer, regardless of size.

Here is where it gets even more complicated for employers—they are generally subject to the most stringent discrimination laws in their jurisdictions. For example, even though the Federal Civil Rights Act limits jurisdiction to employers with fifteen or more employees, a California employer is subject to the California Fair Employment and Housing Act (FEHA) that has jurisdiction starting at five employees. Other states apply the discrimination laws to all employers. Most states have websites for the agency that enforces civil rights and fair employment practices law. For example, see the site for the state of Michigan at www.michigan.gov/mdcr/. To access data concerning civil rights and discrimination laws for each state, see the CCH Business Owners Toolkit at www.toolkit.cch.com/text/P05_0160.asp.

Specific Issue for Employers – How to Avoid Previous Names and Marital Status Discrimination

One of the areas where the discrimination laws have an effect on safe hiring is the use of previous names in a criminal search. The issue arises because past names are a necessary identifying piece of information. For example, when searching for criminal records, researchers base the search on the last name. However, if an applicant at one time was known by a different name, a complete criminal search must be conducted under BOTH names. The most typical situation is in the case of a woman who has married and changed her name.

The problem is that by referring to a name as a maiden name, an applicant potentially is being identified on the basis of their marital status or sex, which can be a violation of federal and state discrimination laws. In California, for example, asking for an applicant's maiden name has been specifically labeled as an unacceptable question by the California Department of Fair Employment and Housing, the California agency charged with enforcing the California civil rights laws. Consequently, a previous name search should not be referred to as a "maiden name" search, since that clearly indicates that an employer is obtaining information on marital status, which is a prohibited basis upon which to make an employment decision. That is why any application or consent for background screening should always include the phrase "previous name" instead of "maiden name."

Is this an example of a distinction without a difference or political correctness going too far? No. Marital status has been a traditional basis for a woman to be the subject of discrimination. The fact is that whether a man or woman is married is simply not a valid basis to predict job performance. However, the reality has been that a woman applicant who is married may be the subject of discrimination based on a belief that she may leave the job to have a family. By phrasing it as a "previous name," the same information is obtained for purposes of a background check, but the application information is facially neutral. In addition, a female applicant is not discouraged from applying based upon an apprehension that by asking for a "maiden name" there is a likelihood of discrimination.

How to Avoid Age Discrimination

Using Date of Birth Information on the Job Application

Most authorities agree that any information tending to reveal age should not be requested on an application form or during an oral interview. Asking for date of birth during the selection process could violate the federal **Age Discrimination in Employment Act** as well as various state civil rights laws. Asking for date of birth tends to deter older applicants from applying. If the application material contains date of birth information, the inference is that a firm may be methodically denying consideration of older workers. Many states have rules which prohibit an employer, either directly or through an agent, from seeking or receiving information that reveals date of birth and age before an offer is made. For example, the California Pre-employment Inquiry Guidelines by the California Department of Fair Employment and Housing lists specific age questions that cannot be asked.

Special problems are faced when an applicant's date of birth is not available. When researching court records, the date of birth is probably the most important factor needed to identify an individual since many court records do not contain Social Security numbers. In fact, in some jurisdictions, a criminal search cannot be conducted without a date of birth. It is also needed in many states in order to obtain a driving record, thus the date of birth is a key piece of identifying data on DMV records.

Under the federal **Age Discrimination Act of 1967**, there is not an absolute prohibition against asking for date of birth or age. That is a common misconception among employers. In fact, the EEOC has specifically ruled that asking for date of birth or age is not automatically a violation of the act. However, the EEOC ruling indicated that any such request would be closely scrutinized to ensure that the request has a permissible purpose. The EEOC also indicated that the reason for asking for date of birth should be clearly disclosed so older applicants are not deterred from applying (See 29 Code of Federal Regulations §1625.4 – 1625.5). The following information is provided by the EEOC website at: http://eeoc.gov/eeoc/publications/age.cfm:

> **"Pre-Employment Inquiries**
>
> The ADEA (Age Discrimination in Employment Act) does not specifically prohibit an employer from asking an applicant's age or date of birth. However, because such inquiries may deter older workers from applying for employment or may otherwise indicate possible intent to discriminate based on age, requests for age information will be closely scrutinized to make sure that the inquiry was made for a lawful purpose, rather than for a purpose

prohibited by the ADEA. If the information is needed for a lawful purpose, it can be obtained after the employee is hired."

If a firm does screening in-house, then the firm may consider performing all screening and obtaining information **post-offer**. This provides maximum protection since there can be no inference that age played a role in the decision to hire or not hire.

Use of Date of Birth Information by the Employment Screening Company

What if an employer outsources background screening to a private firm? The screening firm will normally need date of birth to perform the service. There are several options.

First, with advancing technology, many screening firms are able to offer a paperless system, where the applicant fills out the forms online, including sensitive information such as date of birth. That way, an employer or Applicant Tracking System (ATS) is not obtaining or storing dates of birth. If working with a screening firm that does not have advanced technology, an employer can consider outsourcing to a screening firm only post-offer. If a conditional offer of employment is made that depends upon a background screening report, then asking for the date of birth post-offer is probably safe. The downside, however, is that it is an administrative burden for most employers to coordinate the process of giving offers, followed by collecting the date of birth, and finally transmitting it to a screening firm. Most employers have a practice of requiring all applicants to fill out a consent form for the background screening firm at the same time the original application is filled out, and the screening firm's forms will typically need date of birth information.

Another possible route is to only request the date of birth information on the screening firm's form and not on any employer form. Furthermore, the applicant release forms should not be made available to the person or persons with hiring authority in order to avoid any suggestion that age information was used in any step of the hiring process. Most employment screening companies recommend that employers keep the screening forms and reports separate from the employee's personnel file or application papers.

To additionally protect the employer, the form used for the screening company can have such additional language as:

✓ The information requested on the screening firm's form is for screening and verification of information only and has no role in the selection process.
✓ All federal and state rights are respected in the employer's screening process.
✓ The year of birth is optional on the form (although this can lead to delays).
✓ The information is used for identification only and without such information the screening process may be delayed.

Another option is an employer can require a screening firm to takes steps to remove all references to age and date of birth in its reports so that employers will not receive age information.

An option some employers have used is to setup a system that communicates the date of birth directly to the screening firm so that the data is never in the employer's possession. This can be done by establishing a special "800" phone number the applicants call to leave their date of birth or with a tear-off form that the applicant mails in. One downside to these types of workarounds is they will likely delay screening reports because of the extra steps involved.

Another option is to have someone in the office, such as a receptionist, physically separate the screening firm's form from the application so there is no question that a decision maker has not viewed the date of birth before the application is reviewed. Also there are new online options where an applicant can supply the date of birth as part of the application process, but only the screening firm will be able to see it.

Most employers choose the option of asking applicants to place date of birth on the screening company forms or system. For questions about a form's legality, an employer should consult their legal counsel, seek advice from their attorney, or contact the appropriate local or state authority or federal EEOC office.

The "E-RACE" Initiative

The Equal Employment Opportunity Commission has championed equal opportunity in employment since its inception shortly after the signing of Title VII of the Civil Rights Act of 1964. Although the EEOC has been successful in its enforcement efforts, race and color discrimination still exist in the workplace. In an effort to identify and implement new strategies to strengthen its enforcement of Title VII and advance the statutory right to a workplace free of race and color discrimination, EEOC has instituted the **E-RACE (Eradicating Racism And Colorism from Employment) Initiative**.

The E-RACE Initiative is designed to improve EEOC's efforts to ensure workplaces are free of race and color discrimination. Specifically, the EEOC will identify issues, criteria, and barriers that contribute to race and color discrimination, explore strategies to improve the administrative processing and the litigation of race and color discrimination claims, and enhance public awareness of race and color discrimination in employment. As a framework for implementing the E-RACE Initiative, EEOC developed a set of detailed E-RACE goals and objectives to be achieved within a five-year timeframe from FY 2008 to FY 2013.

E-RACE Goals

The five main goals of E-RACE are to:

- ✓ Improve data collection and data analysis in order to identify, track, investigate and prosecute allegations of discrimination.
- ✓ Improve quality and consistency in EEOC's Charge Processing and Litigation Program and improve federal sector systems.
- ✓ Develop strategies, legal theories, and training modules to address emerging issues of race and color discrimination.
- ✓ Enhance visibility of EEOC's enforcement efforts in eradicating race and color discrimination.
- ✓ Engage the public, employers, and stakeholders to promote voluntary compliance to eradicate race and color discrimination.

The EEOC also combines the objectives of E-RACE with existing EEOC initiatives to increase its outreach to human resource professionals and employer groups to address race and color discrimination in the workplace. For more information on E-RACE, visit: www.eeoc.gov/eeoc/initiatives/e-race/index.cfm.

The following article summarizes leading cases on discrimination and employment screening as well as the approach of the EEOC.

From Griggs to SEPTA: The EEOC's Increased Focus on Employment Screening

By Rod M. Fliegel and Jennifer L. Mora, Attorneys At Law

Littler Mendelson, P.C.

There has been a flurry of activity at the U.S. Equal Employment Opportunity Commission ("EEOC") over the past couple of years in which the EEOC's "systemic discrimination" unit has been investigating employer policies and/or practices that screen job applicants for employment based on criminal or credit records. In addition, plaintiffs' counsel have been filing lawsuits challenging employer practices in which African-American and/or Hispanic applicants are disqualified for employment based on criminal or credit records. Now more than ever, employers need to understand the EEOC's efforts in addressing the use of credit and criminal records for employment purposes and take proactive steps to ensure that, if challenged, their hiring policies will withstand scrutiny by the EEOC and the plaintiffs' bar.

Title VII of the Civil Rights Act of 1964 prohibits employers from discriminating against individuals because of, among other things, race, color or national origin. Title VII does not expressly prohibit employers from using criminal background reports for employment purposes. However, in developing regulatory guidance and pursuing litigation against employers based on their employment screening practices, the EEOC relies on Section 703(k) of Title VII, which states that if an otherwise neutral employment policy or practice has a "disparate impact" on a protected classification, the policy or practice violates Title VII. Disparate impact discrimination occurs when a uniformly applied neutral selection procedure disproportionately excludes people on the basis of a protected trait and the procedure is not "job related... and consistent with business necessity," or when the employer's business goals can be served in a less discriminatory way. 42 U.S.C. § 2000e-2(k)(1)(A)(i).

The Supreme Court's decision in *Griggs v. Duke Power Company*, 401 U.S. 424 (1971), was one of the first decisions to consider the legality of an employer's hiring practices under Title VII. In *Griggs*, the employer required applicants to have a high school diploma or pass a standardized general education test for employment purposes. The class action suit claimed that such a requirement had a disparate impact on African American workers. In concluding that the employer's hiring requirements violated Title VII, the Supreme Court held that in order to pass muster under Title VII, the practice must be "related to business necessity and/or job performance." The Supreme Court agreed that the employer violated Title VII's prohibition against unlawful disparate impact because Duke Power did not prove that its hiring requirements had any connection to the jobs at issue.

Thereafter, the EEOC issued its first "Policy Statement on Conviction Records" on February 4, 1987 ("1987 Policy Statement"). According to the 1987 Policy Statement, if an employer's policy or practice of excluding individuals from employment on the basis of their conviction records has an adverse impact on African Americans or Hispanics, the policy or practice is unlawful "in the absence of a justifying business necessity." In determining whether its policy is justified by business necessity, the 1987 Policy Statement stated that the employer must prove that it considered the following factors: the nature and gravity of the offense or offenses; the time that has passed since the conviction and/or completion of the sentence; and the nature of the job held or sought based on a conviction policy or practice.

The EEOC issued an additional policy statement on July 29, 1987, referred to as its "Policy Statement on the use of statistics in charges involving the exclusion of individuals with conviction records from employment." This supplemental policy statement reiterated its position that "an employer's policy or practice of excluding individuals from employment on the basis of their conviction records has an adverse impact on Blacks and Hispanics in light of statistics showing that they are convicted at a rate disproportionately greater than their representation in the population." However, the policy statement carved out an exception to its general rule, concluding that a "no cause" determination would be "appropriate" in circumstances where: (1) "the employer can present more narrowly drawn statistics showing either that Blacks and Hispanics are not convicted at a disproportionately greater rate;" or (2) "there is no adverse impact in its own hiring process resulting from the convictions policy."

Several years later, the EEOC issued its September 7, 1990 "Guidance Dealing With Arrest Records" ("1990 Guidance"). The 1990 Guidance discussed the extent to which the use of arrest records for employment purposes has an adverse impact on African Americans and Hispanics. According to the 1990 Guidance: "Since using arrests as a disqualifying criteria can only be justified where it appears that the applicant actually engaged in the conduct for which he/she was arrested and that conduct is job related, the Commission further concludes that an employer will seldom be able to justify making broad general inquiries about an employee's or applicant's arrests." The 1990 Guidance explains that an employer must focus on the conduct, not the arrest or conviction per se in relation to the job sought, to demonstrate unfitness for the position. Again, the EEOC underscored the importance of employers considering the three factors outlined in its 1987 Policy Statement and suggested that employers also consider whether "the alleged conduct was actually committed."

The EEOC has yet to update the 1987 Policy Statement or the 1990 Guidance. In the past few years, however, the EEOC has reaffirmed its long-standing position that, upon a showing of disparate impact, employers must be able to justify their conviction-based screening policies under Title VII's business necessity standard. In addition, the EEOC revisited the issue of criminal records during separate public meetings held on May 17, 2007 (focusing on employment testing and screening) and November 20, 2008 (focusing on arrest and conviction records).

The EEOC's interest in Title VII protections for job applicants with a criminal record was sparked at least in part by the Third Circuit Court of Appeals' opinion in *El v. Southeastern Pennsylvania Transportation Authority (SEPTA)*, 479 F.3d 232 (3d Cir. 2007). In El, the plaintiff was rejected for a job as a paratransit driver based on his 40-year old homicide conviction. The court of appeals affirmed judgment as a matter of law for SEPTA but ruled that, if an employer's conviction-based screening policy in fact causes a disparate impact, the employer must produce "empirical evidence" justifying its screening policy in order to establish business necessity. The court of appeals ruled that an employer must show specifically that its screening policy "accurately" distinguishes between job applicants posing an "unacceptable level of risk" and those who do not. The court of appeals seemed very skeptical of testimony from SEPTA's expert – leading criminologist Dr. Alfred Blumstein – that the plaintiff actually posed a greater crime-risk than a non-offender job applicant even though the plaintiff's conviction was from the 1960s, but explained that it had to rule for SEPTA because the plaintiff failed to offer any evidence to refute Dr. Blumstein's testimony. The court of appeals noted that, if the plaintiff had provided such evidence, it would have been a "different case."

The Third Circuit's analysis is markedly different from, and in fact criticized, the EEOC's historical enforcement guidance. As mentioned above, the EEOC has taken the position in its 1987 Policy Statement that, if an employer's conviction-based screening policy causes a disparate impact, the employer must show that it considered: (1) the "nature and gravity" of the applicant's offense; (2) the "time that has passed since the conviction and/or completion of sentence;" and (3) the "nature of the job held or sought." The distinction between the EEOC's historical enforcement guidance and El is material because the Third Circuit looked beyond the elements of SEPTA's screening policy to whether the results of SEPTA's screening process could be squared with the recidivism statistics and particularly with the statistics suggesting that the risk of recidivism declines as the time "clean" since release from incarceration increases.

It remains to be seen whether the EEOC and the other Circuit Courts will adopt the Third Circuit's holding that if a disparate impact is established, empirical evidence is required from the employer to sustain a conviction-based screening policy under Title VII's business necessity standard. In July 2011, the EEOC held another public meeting on the topic of protections for job applicants with arrest and conviction records under Title VII. Despite the fact that one of the Commissioners referenced at the hearing the Third Circuit's criticism of the EEOC's 1987 Policy, the EEOC did not reveal at the meeting whether it will update the 1987 Policy.

In its first post-July 2011 meeting advisory opinion letter, the EEOC's Office of Legal Counsel provided some insight into the Commission's current enforcement position. The advisory opinion letter was written in response to a request for comments from the Peace Corps about its proposed application for volunteer positions with its international service programs. The EEOC staff attorney noted at the outset that a pre-employment *inquiry* concerning criminal records "does not in itself violate Title VII because Title VII does not regulate inquiries by employers." However, the EEOC staff attorney further commented that the use of criminal record information as part of its screening process may violate Title VII if the employer intentionally and selectively enforces its screening policy against protected class members. The EEOC staff attorney further remarked that, *if* the employer's screening policy in fact has a disparate impact on protected class members, the policy must be "job related and consistent with business necessity." It is this statement by the EEOC staff attorney, which presupposes that proof of disparate impact is *required* rather than *presumed*, that suggests the Commission may not be prepared to adopt a presumption of disparate impact.

According to the advisory opinion letter, in order to exclude an applicant based on a criminal conviction, the criminal conduct should be "recent enough" and "sufficiently job-related to be predictive of performance in the position sought, given its duties and responsibilities." Given this framework, which implicitly incorporates the Third Circuit's analysis in *El*, the EEOC staff attorney was troubled by the Peace Corps' application because it asked about "all convictions regardless of when they occurred." Thus, the EEOC staff attorney recommended that the employer narrow its criminal history inquiry to focus on "convictions that are related to the specific positions in question, and that have taken place in the past seven years, consistent with the proposed provisions of the federal government's general employment application form." (In June 2011, the same EEOC staff attorney made a similar suggestion in an advisory opinion letter to the U.S. Census Bureau.)

Next, the EEOC staff attorney analyzed the employer's request that the applicant provide information about criminal arrests, noting: "[a]rrest records, by their nature, should be treated differently from conviction records." The EEOC staff attorney explained that, because the criminal justice system requires the highest degree of proof for a conviction (i.e., "beyond a reasonable doubt"), a conviction record can serve as a sufficient indication that the person in fact committed the offense. On the other hand, the EEOC staff attorney stated, arrest records are unreliable indicators of guilt because: (1) individuals are presumed innocent until proven guilty or charges may be dismissed and, therefore, an arrest record is not persuasive evidence that the person actually engaged in the conduct alleged; (2) an applicant's criminal history information may be incomplete and may not reflect that his or her arrest charges have been modified or dropped because some state criminal record repositories fail to report the final disposition of an arrest; and (3) arrest records may be inaccurate due to a variety of other factors (e.g., confusion regarding names and personal identifying information, misspellings, clerical errors, or because the individual provided inaccurate information at the time of arrest).

With this framework in mind, the EEOC staff attorney advised the employer to "consider whether its questions about arrests and charges will serve a useful purpose in screening applicants" and, if so, she recommended that the employer only ask about arrests and charges for offenses that are related to the position in question. In order to ensure that the employer relies on accurate arrest-related information when considering an individual for a volunteer position, the EEOC staff attorney recommended that the employer also give the applicant a reasonable opportunity to dispute the validity of any information showing that the applicant has an arrest record. (This varies somewhat from prior and impractical EEOC Guidance suggesting that an employer should make an effort to try to independently confirm whether the applicant in fact was guilty.)

In addition to the EEOC's Policy Statement, Guidance, and public meetings focusing on the use of criminal records for employment purposes, a handful of significant lawsuits have been initiated by the EEOC. On September 28, 2008, in *EEOC v. Peoplemark, Inc.*, the EEOC sued Peoplemark, Inc., alleging that Peoplemark's purported policy prohibiting the hiring of any person with a criminal record violated Title VII because it had a disparate impact on African American applicants. Based on certain procedural failures by the EEOC (i.e., the failure to timely identify an expert statistician) and most likely other concerns, the EEOC agreed to dismiss the case after 18 months of vigorous litigation. On March 31, 2011, the district court concluded that the EEOC's lawsuit against Peoplemark was frivolous and, therefore, ordered the EEOC to pay more than $750,000 in attorney's fees and expert costs. *EEOC v. Peoplemark, Inc.*, 2011 U.S. Dist. LEXIS 38696 (W.D. Mich., March 31, 2011) [Alternative citation: 112 FEP Cases 158 (W.D. Mich. 2011).].

The more recent and pending case of *EEOC v. Freeman*, Case No. RWT 09cv2573 [Alternative citation: 2010 WL 1728847 (D.Md. Apr. 26, 2010).], filed in federal district court in Maryland on September 30, 2009, alleges that an African American individual applied for a position with Freeman in August 2007, and was informed that she would be hired, contingent on passing a drug, criminal, and credit background check. Shortly thereafter, Freeman informed the applicant that she would not be offered a position. In the Complaint, the EEOC alleged that Freeman's hiring practices have a significant disparate impact against the protected groups and are not job related or justified by business necessity. The EEOC further asserted that there are appropriate, less-discriminatory alternative selection procedures available to Freeman.

Finally, in December 2010, the EEOC filed its pending lawsuit against Kaplan Higher Education Corp. in the federal district of Ohio, *EEOC v. Kaplan Higher Education Corp.,* (Case No. 1:10 CV 2882) [Alternative citation: 2011 WL 2115878 (N.D. Ohio May 27, 2011).], alleging that the company engaged in a pattern of discrimination against African American workers. Specifically, the lawsuit, which remains pending, claims that Kaplan's use of credit history for employment purposes is neither job-related nor justified by any business necessity. Kaplan, on the other hand, has publicly defended its hiring practices and denies that its use of credit history for employment purposes had any disparate impact on applicants.

These lawsuits show the EEOC's willingness to file lawsuits against some employers in order to promote its policy objectives. Not shown in the public filings, however, is the concerted effort by the EEOC's systemic discrimination unit to broadly investigate the use of criminal and credit information by employers in many different industries (e.g., transportation, information technology, retail, etc.). It seems evident that, likely as a result of the $750,000 award against the EEOC in the Peoplemark case, the EEOC is using its sweeping investigatory powers to try to line up lawsuits before filing them (or seeking conciliation). This, too, is not shown by the small number of active lawsuits, but is clear from the number of employers who have been, and are, responding to onerous and costly demands for documents and information from the EEOC. And all of this, of course, is against the backdrop of "hurry up and wait" for the EEOC's updated Enforcement Guidance – guidance that seems long overdue at this point.

In the meantime, it is prudent for employers to assess their background check programs with an eye towards the dynamic legal landscape, including not only the activity by the EEOC, but in the state legislatures and under related laws, such as the federal Fair Credit Reporting Act (where there has been a surge in class action lawsuits against employers).

Discrimination and Criminal Records

Under Title VII of the Civil Rights Act of 1964, the use of arrest and conviction records to deny employment can be illegal when it is not relevant for the job since it can limit the employment opportunities of applicants or workers based on their race or ethnicity. The EEOC has guidance and policy statements on the use of arrest and conviction records in employment that make the use of a blanket "no hire" policy that excludes job applicants with criminal records unlawful under Title VII of the Civil Rights Act of 1964 since it discriminates against minority groups with higher rates of criminal convictions.

Discrimination and criminal records are covered in greater detail in Chapters 15 and 16.

Discrimination against Unemployed Job Applicants

With the recent economic downturn, discrimination against unemployed job applicants has made the headlines recently. News stories indicate employers and staffing agencies have publicly advertised jobs in fields ranging from electronic engineers to restaurant and grocery managers to mortgage underwriters with the explicit restriction that only currently employed candidates will be considered. Some employers may use current employment as a signal of quality job performance, but such a correlation is decidedly weak. A blanket reliance on current employment serves as a poor proxy for successful job performance.

EEOC Public Meeting Examines Treatment of Unemployed Job Applicants by Employers

A U.S. Equal Employment Opportunity Commission public meeting held in February 2011 examined the impact of employers considering only those currently employed for job vacancies. According to the EEOC press release 'Out of Work? Out of Luck,' (www.eeoc.gov/eeoc/newsroom/release/2-16-11.cfm):

- ✓ The use of an individual's current or recent unemployment status as a hiring selection device is a troubling development in the labor market that may act as a negative counterweight to government efforts to get people back to work. Women, particularly older women and those in non-traditional occupations, are disproportionately affected by this restriction.
- ✓ Denying jobs to the already-unemployed can also have a disproportionate effect on certain racial and ethnic minority community members. Unemployment rates for African-Americans, Hispanics, and Native Americans are higher than those of whites. When comparing college-educated workers, the unemployment rate for Asians is also higher. Thus, restricting applications to the currently employed could place a heavier burden on people of color.
- ✓ The use of employment status to screen job applicants could also seriously impact people with disabilities. Excluding persons who are currently unemployed from applicant pools is real and can have a negative impact on persons with disabilities.
- ✓ Current national employment statistics show that African-Americans and Hispanics are overrepresented among the unemployed. Excluding the unemployed would be more likely to limit opportunities for older applicants as well as persons with disabilities.
- ✓ At a moment when everyone should be doing whatever they can to open up job opportunities to the unemployed, it is profoundly disturbing that the trend of deliberately excluding the jobless from work opportunities is on the rise.

In addition to presenting statistical evidence, some panelists recounted stories unemployed workers have shared where they were told that they would not be considered for employment due to being unemployed.

The EEOC meeting showed that the government is concerned that some companies may not be considering unemployed applicants for job openings and are excluding the jobless from applying. The EEOC press release 'Out of Work? Out of Luck' is at www.eeoc.gov/eeoc/newsroom/release/2-16-11.cfm. For additional information about the February 2011 EEOC meeting see www.eeoc.gov/eeoc/meetings/2-16-11/index.cfm.

AUTHOR TIP

There has been legislation proposed on both the federal and state level to prohibit discrimination on the basis of unemployment. The Federal Fair Employment Opportunity Act, introduced in 2011, is an example of the concern that federal lawmakers have on this issue.

New Jersey became the first state to enact a law to prohibit discrimination against job applicants who are unemployed: New Jersey Statutes, Title 34, Chap. 8B, § § 1-2-C.34B-1 to 34:8B-2 (A.3359/S.2388, approved March 29, 2011).

See www.njleg.state.nj.us/2010/Bills/PL11/40_.PDF.

The District of Columbia enacted The Unemployed Anti-Discrimination Act of 2012 which made it unlawful for all employers and employment agencies in the District to consider the unemployed status of an applicant in employment and hiring decisions. The new law took effect in May 2012. See: http://dcclims1.dccouncil.us/images/00001/20120308112351.pdf.

Another example is California Assembly Bill No. 1450 (AB 1450) that would fine CA employers and employment agencies who refuse to consider jobless applicants for job openings. See: www.leginfo.ca.gov/pub/11-12/bill/asm/ab_1401-1450/ab_1450_bill_20120105_introduced.pdf.

Briefing Paper on Hiring Discrimination against the Unemployed

A July 2011 briefing paper titled "Hiring Discrimination Against the Unemployed: Federal Bill Outlaws Excluding the Unemployed from Job Opportunities, as Discriminatory Ads Persist" from the National Employment Law Project (NELP), a national advocacy organization for employment rights of lower-wage and unemployed workers, found that hiring discrimination against the unemployed continued as employers and staffing firms posted job listings excluding unemployed jobseekers and expressly denied job opportunities to those workers hardest hit by the economic downturn.

NELP conducted its review over a four-week period from March 9, 2011 to April 5, 2011. A NELP researcher reviewed job postings during that period that appeared on four of the nation's most prominent online job posting websites: CareerBuilder.com, Indeed.com, Monster.com, and Craigslist.com. The online research sought information on both employers and staffing firms that were specifically identified by name (often, job listings are posted anonymously) while also seeking a diverse sample from across the United States. NELP's snapshot of jobs postings identified more than 150 ads that included exclusions based on current employment status, including 125 ads that identified specific companies by name. Below are several examples from the Briefing Paper:

Selected Employer Job Postings with Discriminatory Language*

Position/Job Type and Location	Discriminatory Language
Position for Licensed P&C Team Member in Huntsville, Alabama	*must be currently employed*
Paralegal position, Atlanta, Georgia	*must be currently employed*
Group Kitchen Manager position, San Francisco, California	*require current (or very recent) tenure*
IT Professional/Engineering, Maryland Heights, Missouri	*currently employed*
Restaurant/Food Service positions, Lubbock, Texas	*must be currently employed*
Professor position, Fresno, California	*must be currently employed*

*NELP Briefing Paper –*Hiring Discrimination Against the Unemployed: Federal Bill Outlaws Excluding the Unemployed from Job Opportunities, as Discriminatory Ads Persist* (July, 12, 2011)
www.nelp.org/page/-/UI/2011/unemployed.discrimination.7.12.2011.pdf?nocdn=1

The informal NELP survey of a number of job posting websites found numerous job ads stating that jobseekers "must be currently employed." The study claimed the "perverse catch-22" of job seekers not being able to get a job unless they already have a job was deepening our unemployment crisis:

> This perverse catch-22 is deepening our unemployment crisis by arbitrarily foreclosing job opportunities to many who are otherwise qualified for them. It dilutes the storehouse of talent in America, by casting aside an untold number of skilled and dedicated workers who have the misfortune of being unemployed in the worst downturn since the Great Depression. And it adds to the crisis that unemployed workers, their families and their communities face, as we try to crawl out of this deep recessionary hole.

The briefing paper from NELP, an advocacy group for the unemployed and low-wage workers, may be found at: www.nelp.org/page/-/UI/2011/unemployed.discrimination.7.12.2011.pdf?nocdn=1.

Privacy Laws and Employers

The second major area of legal concern for employers is privacy. Employers have a legal duty to respect the privacy of applicants and employees in a variety of areas, such as privacy limitation regarding what information an employer can obtain, how to protect the data, who else can see the data, and the rights of applicants and employees to discover what data has been obtained. Since the news media revelations in 2005 about the large-scale theft of data from firms who store large amounts of personal and identifiable data, maintaining privacy has become a very critical concern.

The subject matter of workplace privacy is very broad and spans a whole range of issues from electronic monitoring of email, searches of personal belongings, and physical surveillance to regulating workplace behavior and dress codes, off the job conduct, and the protection and dissemination of confidential information. For purposes of this book, the concern is focused on gathering, utilizing, and protecting information necessary for hiring and retention decisions. Privacy issues are also addressed in the following chapters:

- ✓ Privacy issues related to defamation are covered in Chapter 9 on The References Process.
- ✓ International privacy and data protection are addressed in Chapter 21 on International Background Checks.
- ✓ The employer's duty to protect confidential information, including employee files, is covered in Chapter 28 on Identity Theft.
- ✓ The duty of a pre-employment screening firm to protect the confidentiality of data is addressed in Chapter 3 on the Fair Credit Reporting Act and in Chapter 12 on Working with Screening Firms.
- ✓ Privacy and drug testing are addressed in Chapter 23 on Drug Testing.
- ✓ Privacy and the Internet and social media sites are covered in Chapter 19 dealing with social media searches and "Web 2.0."
- ✓ Privacy and data brokers are covered in Chapter 11.

The *right to privacy* from unwarranted governmental intrusion is guaranteed to every American citizen by the United States' Constitution. Although the federal constitutional protections do not extend to private employers dealing with job applicants and employees, most states have passed privacy legislation that recognizes a right to privacy to employees of private employers. Many states have passed privacy laws that cover specific situations, such as states that do not allow consideration or regulation by an employer of various forms of "off-duty" conduct.

There is a "common law" right to privacy in many states as well when it comes to employment matters. A common law right means a legal right created by precedents set by court cases, instead of laws created by a legislative body. Common law rights include:

- ✓ The right to avoid public disclosure of private information.
- ✓ The right to be protected from false or misleading statements being made in public.
- ✓ Unreasonable intrusion into private affairs, either physically (such as a polygraph test) or otherwise invading an area of personal privacy.
- ✓ Infliction of emotional distress by outrageous conduct

California has led the nation in issues involving employee privacy. A leading case is *Hill v. National Collegiate Athletic Association, 7 Cal.4th 1 (1994)*. The *Hill* case provides an excellent framework to analyze privacy claims. In the *Hill* case, the issue was whether a college athletic association could require student athletes to sign consent forms for drug testing. The California Supreme Court ruled that the drug testing requirement was an invasion of privacy because drug testing required an intrusion into bodily integrity. The court further held that the benefits did not outweigh the intrusion of rights, there were less intrusive means to accomplish the goal, and the NCAA failed to show the particular program it proposed furthered the intended goal. In its discussion, the Court in *Hill* discussed various privacy rights and wrote that: "A 'reasonable' expectation of privacy is an objective entitlement founded on broadly based and widely accepted community norms."

Privacy claims are typically a balancing test with different competing interests being examined and weighed. In analyzing an invasion of privacy claim in an employment context, courts will first look to see if the employer invaded an employee's or applicant's protected privacy rights. If the employer's action did intrude upon privacy rights, then the court will examine:

✓ Did the employer's action further a legitimate and socially beneficial aim?
✓ If so, did the purposes to be achieved outweigh any resulting invasion of privacy?
✓ Was there a less intrusive alternative that could have accomplished the same aim without invading privacy?

There are other privacy matters that are not a matter of balance but have been made illegal directly by statute. For example, in 1988, the U.S. Congress enacted the Employee Polygraph Protection Act (29 U.S.C. §§ 2001-2009). This act severely limits the ability of most private employers from using a polygraph or lie detector test for job applicants or current employees who are being investigated. Although there are some narrow exceptions, as a practical matter this law ended the use of lie detectors.

In a United States Supreme Court case concerning pornography, Justice Brennan famously wrote that hard-core pornography was hard to define, but that "I know it when I see it." Jacobellis v. Ohio, 378 U.S. 184 (1964).

Given all the complexities of piracy law, and the fact that privacy is also a cultural concept that can change from society to society, the same can be said about privacy as well. Privacy can be an issue in many different contexts and situations. However, this section is only focused on the narrow issue of privacy and hiring.

Safe Hiring Programs and Privacy

There is no reason why a well-designed Safe Hiring Program should violate any statute or common right to privacy. The processes outlined in this book are NOT intended to pry into an applicant's private life, turn employers into "big brothers," or turn hiring managers or HR professionals into the "hiring police." In fact, the type of information an employer obtains is job-related information about how a person has conducted themselves in their "public" lives — an area of their life that is visible to the public. For example, where a person has worked or attended school is generally not a confidential matter. Anyone who was interested could see where the applicant was working or studying. Those activities are done in the open. In addition, if a person has a criminal record, that too is a matter of public record. A Safe Hiring Program does not invade those areas that society generally keeps private and confidential. The one tool that comes closest to butting up against a reasonable expectation of privacy would be credit reports, which are discussed in Chapter 17.

In addition, all of the Safe Hiring techniques recommended in this book are done with an applicant's expressed consent. As outlined in Chapter 7 on Applications, a conscientious employer will require each applicant to consent to and authorize in writing a background screening. If pre-employment background screening is outsourced to a background screening firm pursuant to the Fair Credit Reporting Act (FCRA), then by federal law there must be written authorization and disclosure (an exception is for truck drivers, and even then there still must be authorization).

Of course, just because information may not be private does not mean it is not confidential. If an employer locates a criminal record, efforts must be made to limit that information to just those in the company with a need-to-know for purposes of making a hiring decision. Personal identifiable information such as a Social Security Number is confidential and must be safeguarded. The right to privacy extends to how information obtained in a Safe Hiring Program is stored in order to protect against unauthorized viewing or theft. Another consideration is computer security when applicant data is transmitted or stored over a network. Maintaining confidentiality and security is a critical employment screening task.

As mentioned throughout this book, employers who engage in a Safe Hiring Program do not find that good applicants feel their privacy rights are being violated provided there are safeguards and assurances in place to insure the information will be kept confidential and used for legal purposes. Honest candidates understand that background screening is a sound business practice that helps all concerned. Job applicants want to work with qualified and safe co-workers in a profitable, professional environment.

Supreme Court Ruling in NASA Case Limits Privacy Rights of Workers in Employment Background Checks

In a case pitting individual privacy rights of citizens against national security concerns of a country, the U.S. Supreme Court unanimously overturned a ruling limiting government inquiries about contract workers at a National Aeronautics and Space Administration (NASA) laboratory and ruled the federal government can ask employees about their drug treatment, medical conditions, or other personal matters during background checks and that the questions did not violate the constitutional privacy rights of employees. The case – *NASA v. Nelson, 131 S.Ct. 746 (2011)* –concerned contract workers who challenged the extensive background checks required at a NASA jet propulsion laboratory in Pasadena, CA as overly intrusive. The Supreme Court ruling overturned a federal appeals court ruling that said the government went too far in asking contract workers questions about drug treatment and suitability for employment and gave the government broad latitude to ask personal questions during backgrounds checks of contractors at government facilities. Federal employees have undergone standard background checks since 1953, and the government began background checks of contract employees in 2005 as part of the policies developed after the terrorist attacks of September 11, 2001. Supreme Court Justice Samuel Alito wrote for the court stating that: "The challenged portions of the forms consist of reasonable inquiries in an employment background check." However, the Court did not announce broad rules or a test for interpreting what questions were permissible, and according to some legal observers, future litigation is still possible. The Court did site several factors that made these inquiries permissible:

- Citizen employees (and citizen contractors) of the government fall under the hand of the government more than citizens not working for the Government.
- The questions are reasonable and sufficiently employment-related.
- Private employers as well as the government have long used background checks.

Information gathered in background checks would be confidential due to the federal Privacy Act on dissemination of employee and contractor information.

The U.S. Supreme Court recognized the value of background checks in the NASA privacy case. The Government has an interest in conducting basic employment background checks. Reasonable investigations of applicants and employees aid the Government in ensuring the security of its facilities and in employing a competent, reliable workforce. In the context of the case, it appears the same rule applies to private employers since the Court cited how private employers do similar searches.

The case NASA v. Nelson - 131 S.Ct. 746 (2011) is available at: http://supreme.justia.com/cases/federal/us/562/09-530/.

Privacy Considerations when Screening In-house or Outsourcing

In conducting pre-employment investigations, an employer essentially has two choices. The employer can either conduct the investigation in-house or outsource to a third party.

One advantage of outsourcing background screening is that screening companies must abide by the Fair Credit Reporting Act (FCRA), which is the "gold standard" of privacy. Under the FCRA, all background screening is done with the applicant's written authorization as well as a disclosure of rights. There are limits to what may be obtained and for what reasons and who can access the information. There are also rules about maximum accuracy and re-investigation. By following the FCRA, employers have less concern that an applicant can allege a violation of privacy since everything is done pursuant to federal law at the onset. How the FCRA protects privacy is specifically discussed in Chapter 3.

However, if an employer performs in-house applicant screening, then the employer no longer has the protection of the FCRA. In this situation, the employer's actions are governed by privacy law considerations. As a result, the employer needs to have an in-depth understanding of the privacy law framework within their jurisdiction or at the location where the job is being performed.

Essentially, an employer who does in-house screening or investigations must be aware of the general balancing test that attempts to reconcile the employer's need to have certain information with the privacy rights of job applicants and current employees. It is not unlawful for an employer to conduct its own background checks; however, considering the promulgation of more laws intended to preserve individual rights to privacy, employers can be at risk when performing screening in-house. To minimize risk, firms that do their own screening should act as though the FCRA applied.

Privacy and the Trend of Offshoring Data and Call Centers

A developing trend among larger U.S. firms is to send Personally Identifiable Information (PII) offshore to call centers and data centers in order to take advantage of low-cost foreign labor. The practice of American businesses "offshoring" PII of consumers outside of the United States for processing and beyond the reach of U.S. laws has increased concern over privacy and identity theft in foreign lands. Privacy advocates are concerned when these U.S. firms send sensitive information such as medical records and Social Security Numbers beyond the privacy protections of the U.S.

This practice is also occurring, often unbeknown to employers, within the pre-employment screening industry. There are no official statistics since background screening firms that engage in this practice do not want it publicized. However, within the background screening industry it is well-known fact there are large background screening firms that offshore PII in bulk on a daily basis. Thus depending on the screening firm used, job applicants and employers may not realize there is a measurable likelihood that their PII will end up outside the U.S. and its territories—and beyond U.S. privacy law— in a foreign call center or data processing location.

Although there has been talk at state and federal levels of implementing new acts or amending current ones regarding offshoring, there are no current U.S. laws that explicitly prevent companies from offshoring personal information. However, California recently passed a Disclosure Law. SB 909 requires a new disclosure and additions to a Consumer Reporting Agency's privacy policy to be made to consumers before their personally information such as Social Security Numbers (SSN) is sent offshore, overseas, and outside of the United States. Information about SB 909 is presented later in this chapter.

Groups and Advocates Against Offshoring

The American Transcription Association

Medical transcriptionists in the U.S. are bound by the Health Insurance Portability and Accountability Act (HIPAA), which protects the privacy of your medical records and sets strict standards for secure handling, transfer, and storage of files. However, U.S. law does not apply in foreign countries where many companies offshore their transcription work.

The American Transcription Association (ATA) and the ATA is against offshoring for two main reasons:

- ✓ Sending personal information outside of the country can lead to unsecured transfer of personal data and even information and identity theft; and
- ✓ Offshoring work means U.S.-based transcriptionists are losing jobs.

As a result, documented cases of offshore transcriptionists who have threatened to disclose personally identifying information from medical records – which would have been a breach of HIPAA – face little chance of being extradited and brought to justice in America, making foreign transcriptionists immune to prosecution for all intents and purposes.

While offshoring transcription work can be cheaper because wages are so much lower in some foreign countries than in the U.S., the ATA believes personal and sensitive information "should not be handled by the lowest bidder" and serious privacy, confidentiality, and security issues need to be addressed. Find out more about offshoring at the American Transcription Association website www.ataus.org.

Communications Workers of America

The December 2011 Communications Workers of America (CWA) Report 'Why Shipping Call Center Jobs Overseas Hurts Us Back Home' highlighted the linkage between the offshoring of call center jobs and a range of negative impacts on U.S. consumers and job seekers. Key findings of the CWA report include:

✓ Continued instances of fraud directly related to employees at overseas call centers;

✓ A lack of accountability and insufficient safeguards to protect consumer information from overseas security breaches; and

✓ The recent trend of sub-outsourcing in which foreign call centers located in places like India have outsourced to even cheaper labor markets, including countries such as Saudi Arabia and Egypt.

The CWA report is at http://files.cwa-union.org/national/News/Misc/20111215-offshore-callcenter.pdf.

White Paper on the Dangers of Offshoring

The 2012 white paper *'The Dangers of Offshoring Personally Identifiable Information (PII) Outside of United States'* by this book's author includes numerous instances of scams carried out by workers at foreign call centers targeting customers that raise legitimate concerns about the security of personal data being handled overseas:

✓ In March 2012, an undercover investigation discovered Indian call centers selling Britons' confidential personal data to criminals and marketing firms for as little as two pence. See: http://in.news.yahoo.com/indian-call-centres-accused-selling-britons-personal-data-045625037.html.

✓ In March 2009, a BBC investigation revealed a criminal gang selling UK credit card details stolen from Indian call centers for $10 a card. See: http://news.bbc.co.uk/1/hi/uk/7953401.stm.

✓ In April 2005, workers from an Indian call center were arrested for defrauding US bank customers out of $350,000 by charming PIN numbers out of customers and using them to transfer funds illegally. See: http://www.theregister.co.uk/2005/04/11/india_callcentre_fraud_arrests/.

✓ In October 2003, a California hospital outsourcing its medical transcribing had a Pakistani medical transcriber in a dispute with her employer about wages threaten to publish the medical records of thousands of Americans on the Internet. See: http://www.sfgate.com/cgi-bin/article.cgi?file=/c/a/2003/10/22/MNGCO2FN8G1.DTL.

Concerned CRAs

Concerned CRAs is a group of more than 125 Consumer Reporting Agencies (CRAs) dedicated to consumer protection. The group has endorsed to a set of standards that oppose offshoring PII of U.S. citizens outside the country to be processed beyond U.S. privacy laws. These standards are listed at www.concernedcras.com/no_offshoring.htm and are also represented below (as of August, 2012).

No Off-Shoring

In recent years, many states have taken measures to prevent the misuse of personal and identifiable information (PII) in order to fight the rising tide of identity theft. The federal government has also taken measures. The main federal protections are contained in Gramm-Leach-Bliley Act ("GLBA") and Health Insurance Portability and Accountability Act of 1996 ("HIPAA"). The federal Fair Credit Reporting Act (FCRA) was amended in 2003 to also provide additional measures to protect against identity theft.

Unfortunately, all such protections as a practical matter cease to exist once PII leaves the shores of the United States. Although some countries have extremely strong data and privacy protection laws, such as the European Union (EU) states, many places where information is sent off-shore for processing have very little if any protection. These countries are selected because they offer a way to cut costs. However, many of these counties have little or no practical data protection. In addition, as a practical matter, American job applicants have no ability to enforce their privacy rights overseas. In many counties, there is little practical or cost-effective access to courts and it is extremely difficult for an American consumer to contact a foreign police department to lodge a complaint or to obtain assistance. The lack of any meaningful protection once U.S. data is sent off-shore is a major gap in the effort to combat identity theft and to protect privacy. In some countries, for example, private data can be purchased very cheaply.

Of course, data theft can also occur in the U.S. However, in the U.S., there are legal protections, resources, and recourse mechanisms to help victims of identity theft. Once the data goes off-shore, that protection dissipates rapidly.

Although there are economic advantages to a screening firm to off-shore, a Consumer Reporting Agency (CRA) that chooses to display the "No Off-Shoring" seal subscribes to the belief that risking a consumer's personal and identifiable information to make more money is not justified by the risk to the consumer and the employer.

Furthermore, when PII is off-shored, it is typically done without the employer or the consumer being told it is happening, what country the data is going to, or what data protection is in place.

Some of the tasks being performed off-shore include:

1. Off-shore call centers calling US employers or schools to verify employment or education.

2. Off-shore centers entering orders into the screening firm's systems or other data entry tasks.

3. Off-shore data centers accessing databases to look up information about a consumer.

Each of these tasks is highly risky and can potentially place a consumer at risk.

A CRA that chooses to display the "No Off-Shoring" seal is self-certifying that they subscribe to the following standards:

1. Domestic Background Screening: Where a CRA is providing background screening services for consumers in the United States based upon information available in the U.S., a firm displaying this seal certifies it does not send data outside the U. S. or its territories for processing or preparation of a background report or for any other reason. All work is done in the U.S.

2. International Screening: Where there is an international background check for verification of employment education or a professional degree, or for a criminal record check, some information may have to go offshore by necessity since the information being sought is offshore. However, firms displaying this seal have taken measures to protect personal and confidential data:

    a. Documentation or information such as passport numbers or unique identification numbers and date of birth are not sent to anyone overseas other than the actual verification provider, e.g. employer or school registrar, whenever possible.

    b. Where it is necessary to utilize a local firm, the local firm will first be asked to provide local contact information so that the CRA can contact the foreign verifying party directly.

    c. If due to infrastructure or other issues in a foreign country a foreign research firm must perform the verification, then the CRA or its agent has properly vetted the local firm, and will redact any unnecessary information.

3. Where a CRA utilizes a third party service to perform domestic or international services in connection with providing background reports, firms that adopted this standard have made reasonable inquires to ensure that any provider is also following this standard.

4.   This is a self-certification standard. There is no process of enforcement or accreditation. Employers relying upon the seal should still take appropriate measures to ensure that consumer data is protected in the screening process.

5.   The exception to off-shoring data is where the CRA has clearly disclosed to the end-user employer that such off-shoring may occur along with a disclosure of the potential risks involved and the employer in turn clearly discloses to the consumer that their personal information may go offshore for processing along with a disclosure of the potential risks involved.

Survey Finds Offshoring IT Jobs Led to Dramatic Increases in Data Breaches

A survey of 350 IT managers quoted in *Security Management Magazine* demonstrates the risk to privacy and data protection when "offshoring." According to the survey conducted by Amplitude Research, 69 percent of all respondents said they thought outsourcing decreased network security while about half of IT managers working for companies that outsourced IT jobs to other countries said their security had been negatively impacted, and 61 percent said their company had experienced a data breach. The study noted data breaches occurred in just 35 percent of the companies that do not send IT jobs outside of the U.S. See: www.securitymanagement.com/article/outsourcing-risk-006564.

There are no official statistics on the number of background screening firms processing data offshore, since background screening firms that engage in this practice do not want it widely known. The practice of off shoring lowers operating costs and increase profits, but firms have to offshore PII in bulk on a daily basis.

The passage of California Senate Bill 909 is the first step in disclosing the offshoring habits of these firms.

California Senate Bill 909 (SB 909)

On September 29, 2010, Governor Arnold Schwarzenegger signed into law **California Senate Bill 909 (SB 909)**, which became the first law in the nation that addresses the issue of Personally Identifiable Information (PII) of consumers who are the subjects of background checks being sent "offshore" (i.e. outside the United States or its territories and beyond the protection of U.S. privacy and identity theft laws). Employers in California – and employers doing business in California – need to be aware of this new law which changed the way employers conduct background checks in the state.

Authored by State Senator Rod Wright (D – Inglewood), SB 909 amended the California Investigative Consumer Reporting Agencies Act (ICRA) that regulates background checks in California. SB 909 requires a new disclosure and additions to a Consumer Reporting Agency's privacy policy to be made to consumers before their personally information such as Social Security Numbers (SSN) is sent offshore overseas and outside of the United States. SB 909 is NOT a regulatory bill since the bill does not regulate or prohibit offshoring. **It is a disclosure bill** – meaning consumers must be made aware of the background screening agency's privacy practices, including whether the consumer's PII will be sent outside of the country. Below is a synopsis of SB 909. (Note: The author worked with Senator Wright's office in drafting language for SB 909.)

Notification to Consumers	CA SB 909 added language to Civil Code 1786.16 that requires a consumer must be notified as part of a disclosure before the background check of the web address where that consumer "may find information about the investigative reporting agency's privacy practices, including whether the consumer's personal information will be sent outside the United States or its territories." If a background screening firm does not have a web site, then the background screening firm must provide the consumer with a phone number where the consumer can obtain the same information. Language 1786.16 (vi) Notifies the consumer of the Internet Web site address of the investigative consumer reporting agency identified in clause (iv), or, if the agency has no Internet Web site

address, the telephone number of the agency, where the consumer may find information about the investigative reporting agency's privacy practices, including whether the consumer's personal information will be sent outside the United States or its territories and information that complies with subdivision (d) of Section 1786.20. This clause shall become operative on January 1, 2012.

CRA Privacy Practices on Web Site

Effective January 1, 2012, SB 909 additionally requires an investigative Consumer Reporting Agency (CRA) to "conspicuously post" on its primary Internet Web site information describing its privacy practices with respect to its preparation and processing of investigative consumer reports. If CRA does not have an Internet Web site, the CRA has to mail a written copy of the privacy statement to consumers upon request.

CRA Privacy Policies Online

The CRA's privacy policy must contain "information describing its privacy practices with respect to its preparation and processing of investigative consumer reports." Specifically, background screening firms in California (and firms that do business in California) must have a statement in their privacy policy entitled "Personal Information Disclosure: United States or Overseas" that indicates whether the personal information will be transferred to third parties outside the United States or its territories.

"Conspicuously Post"

The term "conspicuously post" is defined in California Business and Professions Code Section 22577:

(b) The term "conspicuously post" with respect to a privacy policy shall include posting the privacy policy through any of the following:

(1) A Web page on which the actual privacy policy is posted if the Web page is the homepage or first significant page after entering the Web site.

(2) An icon that hyperlinks to a Web page on which the actual privacy policy is posted, if the icon is located on the homepage or the first significant page after entering the Web site, and if the icon contains the word "privacy." The icon shall also use a color that contrasts with the background color of the Web page or is otherwise distinguishable.

(3) A text link that hyperlinks to a Web page on which the actual privacy policy is posted, if the text link is located on the homepage or first significant page after entering the Web site, and if the text link does one of the following:

(A) Includes the word "privacy."

(B) Is written in capital letters equal to or greater in size than the surrounding text.

(C) Is written in larger type than the surrounding text, or in contrasting type, font, or color to the surrounding text of the same size, or set off from the surrounding text of the same size by symbols or other marks that call attention to the language.

(4) Any other functional hyperlink that is so displayed that a reasonable person would notice it.

Third Parties

SB 909 defines "third parties" as including, but not being limited to:

A contractor,

Foreign affiliate,

Wholly owned entity, or

An employee of the investigative consumer reporting agency.

Separate Section on Privacy Policy

SB 909 also requires a "separate section that includes the name, mailing address, e-mail address, and telephone number of the investigative consumer reporting agency representatives who can assist a consumer with additional information regarding the investigative consumer reporting agency's privacy practices or policies in the event of a compromise of his or her information."

Damages

In the event a consumer is harmed by virtue of a background screening firm negligently preparing or processing data outside of the U.S., SB 909 provides for damages to the consumer in an amount equal to the sum of:

> Any actual damages sustained by the consumer as a result of the unauthorized access, AND the costs of the successful legal action together with reasonable attorney's fees, as determined by the court.

Language From 1786.20

1786.20(d) (1) An investigative consumer reporting agency doing business in [California] shall conspicuously post, as defined in subdivision (b) of Section 22577 of the Business and Professions Code, on its primary Internet Web site information describing its privacy practices with respect to its preparation and processing of investigative consumer reports. If the investigative consumer reporting agency does not have an Internet Web site, it shall, upon request, mail a written copy of the privacy statement to consumers. The privacy statement shall conspicuously include, but not be limited to, both of the following:

(A) A statement entitled "Personal Information Disclosure: United States or Overseas," that indicates whether the personal information will be transferred to third parties outside the United States or its territories.

(B) A separate section that includes the name, mailing address, e-mail address, and telephone number of the investigative consumer reporting agency representatives who can assist a consumer with additional information regarding the investigative consumer reporting agency's privacy practices or policies in the event of a compromise of his or her information.

Summary

By January 1, 2012, employers should have added the URL (Uniform Resource Locator) link to their privacy policy to their online forms (or comply with the provision for firms without web sites). Employers should have added the required information to their online privacy policy and the front page of their web site (or have material to mail to an applicant upon request). Note there is a civil liability of $10,000 per applicant for non-compliance by an employer or CRA, so it is important to make sure to be in compliance.

See www.leginfo.ca.gov/pub/09-10/bill/sen/sb_0901-0950/sb_909_bill_20100929_chaptered.pdf to view a copy of the bill.

Examples of "PII"

The following are examples of Personally Identifiable Information (PII) – which is also sometimes referred to as Personal and Identifiable Information and Personal Identifiable Information – used for the express purpose of distinguishing individual identity, and thus are clearly PII under the definition used by the U.S. Office of Management and Budget*:

- Full name.
- Birthday.
- Birthplace.
- Social Security number.

- Vehicle registration plate.
- Driver's license number.
- Credit card number.
- National identification number.
- IP (Internet Protocol) address.
- Face, fingerprints, or handwriting.
- Digital identity.
- Genetic information.

*http://en.wikipedia.org/wiki/Personally_identifiable_information#Examples

Privacy and the Use of Home Operators

Another issue related to offshoring is using home workers, some of whom would fall under the category of "offshore workers" as well. Using home-based operators to perform employment and education verifications often represents a financial advantage for background screening firms. The labor cost can be cheaper than employees. The concern for employers is that their applicants' personal data could be sent to home operators working from kitchen tables and dorm rooms across America. The following are key concerns regarding the use of home operators during the employment screening process:

✓ **Privacy:** A screening firm would be directly responsible for making private information viewable and printable on people's home computers.

✓ **Professionalism:** A screening firm would have difficulty accurately claiming that at-home researchers are "professionals" when they are unsupervised, unregulated, and acting as cheap substitutes for what is supposed to be a professional service. How does the sound of barking dogs, crying babies and television sets in the background strike those asked to provide verifications?

✓ **FCRA Defensibility:** A screening firm would have difficulty defending the practice of using at-home researchers against a claim under FCRA section 607(b) concerning reasonable procedures for accuracy.

✓ **IC Classification:** A screening firm cannot classify someone as an Independent Contractor (IC) when they work only for you, when you tell them exactly how to do their job, and when they are providing the same core services provided by your in-house staff.

✓ **Training/QC:** A screening firm cannot train and discuss production issues in real time. It is also difficult for at-home researchers to learn from each other when everyone is working in isolation. Furthermore, since everyone works alone it is harder to enforce quality rules across the entire organization.

✓ **Supervision:** Unsupervised at-home researchers are very difficult to supervise. In addition, since they are paid by the completed verification, they may be more tempted to fake orders since there is no one supervising them in real-time.

✓ **Reliability:** A screening firm would be dependent entirely on the researcher's priorities, which may not be your own. They may put a hair appointment ahead of the employer's forty new verifications that have to be called today. The employer wants load balancing to be under their control and not secondary to at-home researcher's personal schedules.

✓ **Hidden Costs:** There are hidden costs to managing and maintaining multiple remote researchers as opposed to a central pool of talent. Take, for instance, the time lost to the unreliable performance of at-home researcher's internet connections, home computers, and printers.

✓ **Due Diligence:** A screening firm and employer could face significant legal exposure if the at-home researcher's performance falls below a professional standard of care due to lack of training and supervision.

✓ **Disclosure:** Would the employer want to disclose to their applicants that the sensitive, personal data and professional service they've entrusted their employer with was being performed by unsupervised home workers?

A professional background screening company should not utilize any home based or offshore operators to provide critical employment and education verifications. All work should be done in a professionally supervised call center dedicated to the highest level of customer service, privacy, and accuracy.

Discrimination and Privacy — Conclusion

Legal limits and privacy/confidentiality are two important concepts presented in this chapter that will be revisited throughout this book and are intertwined with a Safe Hiring Program.

Legal limits are what an employer can and cannot find out about applicants. The primary law that affects this issue is equal employment opportunity law on the federal, state, and sometimes even the local level. The basic rule is that an employer can ask an applicant either directly on an application or interview — or find out indirectly through a past employment reference check — anything that is:

✓ A valid predictor of job performance.
✓ Not barred specifically by an equal employment law, such as questions concerning race ethnicity, religion, age, or sex.
✓ Not prohibited due to a disparate impact even though neutral on its face, such as the use of arrest records.
✓ Not prohibited by a specific statute, such as the prohibition on lie-detector machines.
✓ Not prohibited due to illegal procedures, such as failure to follow the FCRA.

The role of privacy rights and confidentiality is the second key point in a Safe Hiring Program. An employer who follows the FCRA should not run afoul of privacy rights.

Before selecting a background screening firm, employers should determine if that firm is processing information outside of the U.S. The risk is significant, even if the offshore facility is wholly owned or a subsidiary of a U. S. firm. An employer needs to have a full understanding of how data and privacy is protected once it leaves the U.S., and what duty is owed to job applicants in terms of notice that their data is going abroad.

Chapter 3

The Fair Credit Reporting Act (FCRA)

Inside This Chapter:

✓ A Basic Understanding of the FCRA

✓ FCRA Definitions — Important Terms Found in the FCRA

✓ The Four Groups Affected by the FCRA

✓ The Fair Credit Reporting Act (FCRA) in Four Easy Steps

- (Includes Sample Notice Letters)

✓ FAQs about Adverse Action Letters under FCRA and Employment Screening

✓ Other Important FCRA Provisions

✓ U. S. Supreme Court Case on "Willfulness" Under the FCRA

✓ The Fair and Accurate Credit Transactions (FACT) Act or FACTA – The 2003 FCRA Amendment

✓ FTC Staff Report on Fair Credit Reporting Act

✓ FTC Warns Background Check Mobile Apps May Violate FCRA

✓ Employment Screening Lawsuits Increase as Attorneys and Consumers Become Familiar with FCRA

✓ Dissecting Recent Lawsuits for FCRA Violations

✓ Does the FCRA Apply to Employers Who Perform Background Checks In-House?

✓ Sources of Information about the FCRA

A Basic Understanding of the FCRA

When an employer uses a third party to help conduct a background check, there is a critical federal law the employer must be familiar with and follow. The law is called the Fair Credit Reporting Act (FCRA). The FCRA establishes specific requirements and rules for a pre-employment background report, called a Consumer Report, which is usually much broader in scope than just a credit report.

A Consumer Report can include a wide variety of obtained information concerning job applicants, such as criminal and civil records, driving records, civil lawsuits, reference checks, and any other information obtained by a **Consumer Reporting Agency (CRA)**. Therefore, the FCRA fundamentally controls the information on applicants that is assembled, evaluated, or disseminated by certain third parties and used for employment purposes. In fact, for employment purposes, the wording "Fair Credit Reporting Act" is somewhat confusing since the report can also include items such criminal records, driving records, employment verification, education verification, and other types of reports in addition to a credit report.

When initially passed in 1970, the FCRA was meant primarily to promote confidentiality, privacy, accuracy, and relevancy regarding information gathered about consumers. The law was extensively amended in 1996 with changes effective September 30, 1997. That amendment substantially overhauled the use of consumer reports for employment purposes by providing greater protection to consumers. Other important amendments were made in 1998 and additional amendments were passed in 2003.

Who is in Charge, Anyway?

Since the passage of the FCRA, a federal agency called the **Federal Trade Commission (FTC)** has been in charge of interpreting and enforcing the FCRA. The FTC issued a report in 2011 called "Forty Years of Experience with the Fair Credit Reporting Act: An FTC Staff Report and Summary of Interpretations - The Federal Trade Commission (FTC)" that compiles and updates the agency's guidance on the Fair Credit Reporting Act (FCRA).

However, the role of the FTC may change in the future. An issue being decided in Washington D.C. as of the publication of this book is what role the new **Consumer Financial Protection Bureau (CFPB)** will have in issuing new rules concerning the FCRA. Also unclear is the relationship between the CFPB and the Federal Trade Commission (FTC) which has historically regulated and supervised background firms. The CFPB was created to protect consumers regarding financial products. The creation was part of the **Dodd–Frank Wall Street Reform and Consumer Protection Act** (Pub.L. 111-203, H.R. 4173) and was signed into law by President Barack Obama on July 21, 2010. The CFPB has rule making and enforcement powers over the FCRA. However, the CFPB does not have supervisory power over background firms. Congress specifically exempted background firms from being supervised by the CFPB since a background report is not a financial product. However, it is unclear what role the CFPB will play in the future. Since background firms are still supervised by the FTC under the new law, it remains to be seen if the CFPB attempts to extend their jurisdiction to backgrounds checks, or not, and the relationship between the two agencies. Obviously, there are a host of practical issues if the CFPB decides the rules and engages in enforcement, and the FTC is in charge of supervision. An example of the potential confusion surrounds forms discussed in this chapter that a background screening firm provides to both consumers and employers who utilize background screening services as well as furnishers of information. Historically, those forms were written by the FTC. However, the FCRA has been modified to reflect that under new law, the CFPB will provide the forms.

Consumer Financial Protection Bureau Adopts Rule to Supervise Larger Credit Reporting Companies

For the first time at the federal level, the Consumer Financial Protection Bureau (CFPB) has adopted a rule to begin supervising larger consumer reporting agencies (CRAs) – including the "big three" credit reporting companies Equifax, Experian, and TransUnion – effective September 30, 2012.

The rule 'Defining Larger Participants of the Consumer Reporting Market' states that the CFPB will supervise consumer reporting agencies with more than $7 million in annual receipts, which a press release from CFPB estimated to be 30 companies accounting for approximately 94 percent of the market's annual receipts.

The consumer reporting market includes: the largest credit reporting companies selling comprehensive consumer reports; consumer report resellers who buy consumer information from the largest agencies then typically provide further input on the report and resell; specialty consumer reporting companies that primarily collect and provide specific types of information such as on payday loans or checking accounts; and companies that analyze consumer report data.

It appears the rules do not extend to CRAs who are involved in the preparation of consumer reports for employment purposes.

The rule outlining the CFPB's supervision of larger consumer reporting agencies is available at: http://files.consumerfinance.gov/f/201207_cfpb_final-rule_defining-larger-participants-consumer-reporting.pdf. The CFPB press release 'Consumer Financial Protection Bureau to supervise credit reporting' is available at www.consumerfinance.gov/pressreleases/consumer-financial-protection-bureau-to-superivse-credit-reporting/.

FCRA Definitions — Important Terms Found in the FCRA

What is a Consumer Report? (FCRA Section 603(d))

A consumer report is a report prepared by a consumer reporting agency that consists of any written, oral, or other communication of any information pertaining to the applicant's or employee's credit worthiness, credit standing, credit capacity, character, general reputation, personal characteristics, or mode of living, if this information is used or expected to be used or collected for employment purposes.

What is an Investigative Consumer Report? (FCRA Section 603(e))

An Investigate Consumer Report is a special type of consumer report when the information is gathered through personal interviews (by phone calls or in person) of neighbors, friends, or associates of the employee or applicant reported on, or from other personal acquaintances or persons who may have knowledge about information bearing on the applicant's or employee's credit worthiness, credit standing, credit capacity, character, general reputation, personal characteristics, or mode of living, if this information is used or expected to be used or collected for employment purposes. The Investigative Consumer Report includes reference checks with former employers about job performance. However, a report would NOT be an Investigative Consumer Report if it were simply a verification of former employment limited to only factual matters such as the date started, date ended, salary, or job title. Once a reference checker asks about eligibility for rehire and job performance, then the report then becomes an Investigative Consumer Report. Per FCRA Section 606(d)(4), if the information is adverse to the consumer's interest, the CRA must either obtain confirmation of the information from an additional source with independent knowledge or ensure the person interviews is the best possible source of information.

What is a Consumer Reporting Agency (CRA)? (FCRA Section 603(f))

A Consumer Reporting Agency, or CRA, is any person or entity which, for monetary fees, dues, or on a cooperative nonprofit basis, regularly engages in whole or in part in the practice of assembling or evaluating consumer information or other information on consumers for the purposes of furnishing reports to third parties. It includes private investigators that "regularly" engage in pre-employment inquires.

What is Meant by Employment Purposes? (FCRA Section 603(h))

A report is prepared for employment purposes when the report is used for the purpose of evaluating an applicant or employee for employment, re-assignment, or retention. Under the FCRA, a Consumer Report for employment purposes is considered a "Permissible Purpose."

What is Meant by Adverse Action? (FCRA Section 603(k))

Adverse action in relationship to employment means a denial of employment or any other decision for employment purposes that adversely affects any current or prospective employee.

An Important Area NOT Covered by the FCRA

What if a business needs to investigate another business before entering into an economic relationship, such as investing, joint venturing, licensing agreements, merger or acquisition, a vendor check, or to just check out trade credit? A business may simply want to check out a competitor. The research may involve criminal or civil records, judgments, liens or bankruptcies, or even a business credit report such as a Dun and Bradstreet report. (To learn more about Dun and Bradstreet reports, visit www.dnb.com/us/.) None of these investigations are covered by the FCRA, even if done by a third party. This is because the investigation is not focused on an individual and the FCRA only protects individuals.

What if a business wanted information about the people behind the other business? Any business relationship ultimately depends upon the integrity of the people involved. All the agreements and lawyers in the world cannot protect you or your business if the people you are dealing with lack integrity. Even in that scenario, a firm or a third party working on their behalf may check public records and even call schools and employers as long as the purpose is NOT employment. Here are three important considerations:

1. Even if the investigation is for business due diligence, under no circumstances can the business or their agent pull a personal credit report on any individual involved without consent. A personal credit report is ALWAYS covered by the FCRA, and can only be pulled for FCRA approved purposes.

2. If the economic transaction really amounts to starting an employment relationship, such as the acquisition of a small corporation where the principal is going to work for the acquiring company, this could trigger the need for full FCRA compliance.

3. There may be other laws that apply as well. In some states, the investigation can only be conducted by a state licensed private investigator.

The Four Groups Affected by the FCRA

The FCRA addresses the rights and obligations of four groups. The descriptions below are focused on the groups as they relate to employment.

1. **Consumer Reporting Agencies (CRAs)**. Again, these are third parties such as background screening firms or private investigators that provide Consumer Reports.

2. **Users of Consumer Information**. These are primarily employers who hire CRA's to prepare Consumer Reports.

3. **Furnishers of Consumer Information**. Furnishers can include credit card companies that report payment histories to the three national credit collecting agencies, also past employers and schools — anyone who answers telephone calls from Consumer Reporting Agencies.

4. **Consumers**. The FCRA provides the consumers (applicants) with a host of rights in the process. These rights are discussed throughout this chapter and in Chapter 30.

AUTHOR TIP

Does FCRA Apply to Private Investigators?

Some private investigators have incorrectly assumed that the FCRA does not apply to them because they have a state license. Nothing can be further from the truth. Any P.I. who "regularly" does pre-employment screening is also a CRA and absolutely subject to the rules and regulations of the FCRA. There is no exact definition of the term "regularly," but any investigator who does more than one background screen for employment purposes must assume the FCRA applies. Basically, there is no P.I. exception to the FCRA.

Bad News and Good News about FCRA

There is bad news and good news about the FCRA. The bad news is that the FCRA is a very complex and convoluted law that makes little sense if an employer sits down and tries to read it. Anyone wanting to read the law can go to the website for the Federal Trade Commission (FTC), the federal agency charged with administering the law. Web links to review the law are available at the end of this chapter.

The good news is that there are only four basic steps an employer needs to know about the FCRA in order to begin a background screening program through an employment screening firm. These steps are explained in detail in the next section of this chapter.

Here is an important fact to keep in mind: The basic purpose of the law is to regulate what third parties do. The FCRA kicks in when a pre-employment background pre-screening is conducted by the Consumer Reporting Agency. Therefore, if an employer works with a professional pre-employment background firm, which is a CRA, the employer should select the firm based in part upon the background firm's knowledge of the FCRA. A competent background firm should know how to fully comply with legal requirements of the FCRA, including the preparation of all documents and forms needed for a fully compliant screening program.

AUTHOR TIP

Employers risk legal liability if the procedures utilized to check on applicants infringe on legally protected areas of privacy. By following the FCRA, an applicant's privacy rights are protected. For this reason, many legal experts advise employers to engage the services of an outside screening firm. See Chapter 10 for a discussion on the pros and cons of outsourcing.

When engaging the services of a CRA, both the employer and the CRA must understand how critical it is to follow the FCRA. Failure to do so can result in substantial legal exposures, including fines, damages, punitive damages, and attorney's fees. Below is a brief summary of the substantial penalties involved for NOT following the FCRA.

FCRA Sec.	Type of Non-Compliance	Maximum Possible Penalties
616	Willful failure to comply with FCRA — applies to both employer and CRA	Attorney's fees / Punitive damages / $1,000 nominal damages even if no actual damages- This section is used in class action lawsuits where the attorney for the class action does not seek to prove each individual's damages, but will alleged the $1,000 nominal damages per class member, in addition to seeking punitive damages and attorney's fees.
617	Negligent non-compliance — applies to both employer & CRA	Actual damages/attorney's fees (no punitive damages or nominal damages)
619	Obtaining a report under false pretense — applies to both employer and CRA	Fine and two years prison
620	Unauthorized disclosure of consumer information by CRA officer or employee	Fine and two years prison
621	Administrative enforcement against CRAs engaged in a pattern of violations	Civil penalties of $2,500 per violation.

The Fair Credit Reporting Act (FCRA) in Four Easy Steps

When engaging the services of a Consumer Reporting Agency, **both the employer and the CRA must follow certain steps to maintain compliance with the federal Fair Credit Reporting Act (FCRA)**. Failure to do so can result in substantial legal exposures, including fines, damages, punitive damages, and attorneys' fees. Private investigators who engage in the business of pre-employment background screening are also covered by the FCRA.

To utilize the services of a Consumer Reporting Agency, employers do not need to know all of the ins and outs of the FCRA. What is necessary for any employer is to understand the basic FCRA requirements in order to make sure that any supplier of hiring-related services is in compliance. Here are the four primary steps an employer needs to understand in order to make sure their program is in compliance.

Practice Pointer

The information below only covers the federal requirements under the FCRA. It is important to always keep in mind that there are a number of states with their own additional requirements. Some of the requirements are related to the FCRA, such as a number of "only in California" rules discussed in the next chapter. Other requirements may relate to a particular type of search, such as a New York notice that must be made if criminal records are being checked. The point is that an employer needs to take into account both federal and state rules.

Step 1 — Employer Certification

The FCRA created a unique self-policing system. Prior to receiving a **Consumer Report** – which is another term for a background check report – an employer must first certify to the Consumer Reporting Agency in writing that the employer will follow all the steps set forth in the FCRA. The employer certifies it will do the following:

✓ Use the information for employment purposes only, which is a permissible purpose under the FCRA.

✓ Not use the information in violation of any federal or state equal opportunity law.

✓ Obtain all the necessary disclosures and consents as required by the FCRA (steps 2 and 3 below).

✓ Give the appropriate notices in the event an adverse action is taken against an applicant based in whole or in part on the contents of the Consumer Report (see step 3 below).

✓ Give the additional information required by law if an Investigative Consumer Report is needed.

These requirements are explained further in a document prepared by the Federal Trade Commission titled 'NOTICE TO USERS OF CONSUMER REPORTS: OBLIGATIONS OF USERS UNDER THE FCRA.' The FCRA requires a Consumer Reporting Agency to provide a copy of this document to every employer who requests a background check report. This notice is available on the FTC website at www.ftc.gov/os/2004/11/041119factaapph.pdf and a copy of this notice is reprinted in the Appendix. FCRA Sections 604 and 606 apply to Step 1 – Employer Certification and also apply to Step 2 – Written Release and Disclosure.

Practice Notes

A CRA may include the required FCRA certification language in an agreement that also contains business terms. A CRA and an employer can certainly negotiate business terms but the fundamental requirements of the FCRA are not open to discussion for one simple reason--it is the law! For a discussion of business terms that are commonly discussed by CRAs and employers, see Chapter 12. In addition, a state may impose additional specific requirements regarding the employer certification of how an empoyer will utilize background reports. One such example is California.

Step 2 — Written Release and Disclosure

Before obtaining a consumer report from a Consumer Reporting Agency, the employer must obtain the applicant's written consent and also provide that applicant with a clear and conspicuous written disclosure that a background report may be requested. The disclosure must be provided in a separate, stand-alone document in order to prevent it from being buried in an employment application. The 1998 amendment to the FCRA clarified that the disclosure and the consent may be in the same document. However, the Federal Trade Commission, which enforces the FCRA, cautions that this form should not contain excessive information that may distract a consumer.

The requirement that the release and disclosure be in a separate and standalone document is critical. Otherwise if just part of the application, a consumer may not understand or even realize a consumer report is being prepared. Some labor attorneys recommend the background check forms not even be stapled to any other documents. Of course, as discussed in Chapter 12, the release and disclosure can also be provided electronically with an electronic signature.

A special procedure is necessary when the employer requests a Consumer Reporting Agency to obtain employment references. When the Consumer Reporting Agency is merely verifying factual matters such as the dates of employment, job title, or salary, this special procedure is not necessary. However, as mentioned previously, when the Consumer Reporting Agency asks for information on topics such as job performance, that falls into a special category of consumer report called an "Investigative Consumer Report." When an Investigative Consumer Report is used, there are some special procedures to follow:

✓ There must be a disclosure to the applicant where it is "clearly and accurately disclosed" that "an investigative consumer report" is being requested, along with certain specified language such as the report will include information concerning "character, general reputation, personal characteristics, and mode of living, whichever are applicable." Unless it is contained in the initial disclosure, the consumer must receive this additional disclosure within three days after the request is made.

✓ The disclosure must tell the applicant they have a right to request additional information about the nature and scope of the investigation.

✓ If the applicant makes a written request for more information, then the employer has five days to respond with additional information and must provide a copy of a document prepared by the Federal Trade Commission called *"A Summary of Your Rights Under the Fair Credit Reporting Act"* provided by the CRA. This form can also be provided to applicants who are subject to a "consumer report" that does not contain employment references.

As a practical matter, a Consumer Reporting Agency should handle all of these requirements for an employer as part of their services. Still, an employer should be aware there are legal issues involved in preparing a proper form. Not only is there required information that must be conveyed to applicants, but also wrong language or excessive language can put an employer at risk. There is also the issue on asking for date of birth, as discussed in the previous chapter.

Another concern is if a release or disclosure form contains a release of liability meant to protect the employer, the furnisher of information sources, or the screening firm. A release can potentially be contrary to public policy by requiring an applicant to give up rights. A release can also violate the rule against excessive verbiage on a form, which could detract from a consumer's clear understanding of the documents signed. In response to this issue, some firms use separate release forms and disclosure forms, while only placing the release of liability language on the release form. A good idea for firms who utilize release of liability language on a form is to consider adding the phrase, "to the extent permitted by law" after the release language.

The consent portion of an authorization form used for a background check should indicate the release is "valid for future screening for retention, promotion, or reassignment (unless revoked in writing)."

In 1998, Congress passed one exception to the FCRA rules concerning these various notices. The trucking industry has an exception allowing for telephonic or electronic communications from commercial drivers. The reason is that commercial drivers may be hired over the phone from truck stops, and there is not an opportunity to obtain a written release or give certain notices.

Where Does an Employer Obtain Forms?

To perform a background check legally under the FCRA the employer will need forms, such as the authorization and disclosure forms signed by the applicant, and the certification form an employer must sign. While there are no industry-accepted or official standardized forms in use, forms are available from a variety of sources. Nearly every background screening firm will provide forms. Part of selecting process of a screening firm is to determine the firm's ability to provide legally compliant forms. Since a background firm cannot practice law or give legal advice, the forms provided are based upon generally accepted industry standards. Many law firms provide forms to their business clients or will review forms proivded by a background screening firm. Some states have additional specific form requirements as well, as discussed in the next chapter.

Step 3 — Pre-Adverse Notice

When an employer receives a Consumer Report and intends not to hire the applicant based on the report, the applicant then has certain rights. If the "adverse action" is <u>intended</u> as a result of a Consumer Report, then the applicant is entitled to certain documents, see FCRA Section 604. **Before** taking the adverse action, the employer must provide the following information to the applicant:

- ✓ A copy of the consumer report.
- ✓ The document "A Summary of Your Rights Under the Fair Credit Reporting Act." This document is usually provided by the screening service.

The purpose of the notice is to give an applicant the opportunity to see the report with the information being used against them. If the report is inaccurate or incomplete, the applicant then has the opportunity to contact the Consumer Reporting Agency to dispute or explain what is in the report. Otherwise, applicants could be denied employment without knowing they were the victims of inaccurate or incomplete data.

In effect, the pre-adverse action and post-adverse action processes act as a release valve to help guard against any mistakes having an adverse impact on applicants due to incomplete or inaccurate records. Although no statistics are available, it appears that in the majority of cases when an employer receives a background report that results in a job offer not being made, or being rescinded, the applicant has little to complain about. If an applicant is caught making a material falsehood, or a falsehood by omission, most employers would not want to hire a dishonest person.

However, there can be times when an applicant is truly the victim of some sort of error. For example:

1. An applicant was the victim of identity theft and discovers through a background check for the first time that someone committed a crime using his identity

2. An applicant failed to make the final payment on a traffic ticket and did not realize there was a warrant for arrest issued for a failure to appear. This is easily resolved by the applicant going to court and taking care of the matter.

3. An applicant had a discrepancy in the employment dates. The applicant indicated they had worked for the past employer for 3 years but the employer's records only shows two years. In fact, the consumer was assigned there by a staffing company their first year and the staffing company paid the salary. So from the consumer's point of view, they had been on the job three years, but from the payroll department's vantage point, they only show the consumer as being on salary for two years.

4. A consumer had gone back to court and had a criminal matter judicially set aside. However, the court clerk did not update the files, so when the background firm checked for court reports, it still showed that the criminal record was current.

5. A court retriever just plain misreads the date of birth and reported a criminal record belonging to someone else with the same name and does not see it is a different date of birth. As with any endeavor involving human beings, mistakes can happen. The adverse action notice procedure gives the applicant an opportunity to have the mistake corrected sooner than later.

6. A consumer had earned two degrees, but the school's computer system was only capable of reporting one degree. At that point, the applicant is on notice that every time there is a background check, the school will only report one of the two degrees.

Pre-Adverse Notice Sample Letter

[DATE]
[COMPANY NAME]
[ADDRESS1]
[ADDRESS2]
[CITY][STATE][ZIP]

RE: PRE-ADVERSE ACTION NOTICE

Dear [FIRST NAME] [LAST NAME],

We are required to inform you that you may be denied the position you are seeking with our organization based in whole or in part on information received in a background investigation report from the following consumer reporting agency:

Employment Screening Resources ("ESR")

7110 Redwood Blvd, Suite C

Novato, CA 94945

888-999-4474

We attached a copy of the report provided to us, as well as a copy of "A Summary of Your Rights Under the Fair Credit Reporting Act" prepared by a governmental agency.

1. If you want to dispute any inaccurate or incomplete information in the report, please contact ESR directly without delay (see contact information above).

2. If you want to explain any items in the report that will help us make a final decision, please contact the person below without delay.

Sincerely,

[COMPANY NAME]
[USER FIRST NAME][USER LAST NAME]
Enclosures:
Copy of your background investigation report
A Summary of Your Rights Under the Fair Credit Reporting Act

An additional form can also be sent with the pre-adverse action letter if an employer plans on instituting a procedure for an **"Individualized Assessment."** This follows a best practice recommendation by the U.S. Equal Employment Opportunity Commission (EEOC) in their updated Enforcement Guidance on the Consideration of Arrest and Conviction Records in Employment Decisions Under Title VII of the Civil Rights Act of 1964 issued on April 25, 2012 (See: www.eeoc.gov/laws/guidance/arrest_conviction.cfm).

According to the EEOC, an "Individualized assessment generally means that an employer informs the individual that he may be excluded because of past criminal conduct; provides an opportunity to the individual to demonstrate that the exclusion does not properly apply to him; and considers whether the individual's additional information shows that the policy as applied is not job related and consistent with business necessity."

An applicant may show that either the background check report is incorrect or incomplete, or the background check report is true and complete but, there are reasons the criminal record is not disqualifying. If the consumer has a complaint about the accuracy of the background check, the consumer needs to contact the screening firm. If a consumer concedes the background report is accurate but still believes he or she should be considered, then the consumer needs to talk to the employer.

In addition to the pre-adverse action letter, a second letter should be sent advising the applicant that they may request an individualized assessment. It is a better practice to send two separate letters rather than combining the two, in order to demonstrate compliance with both the FCRA and the EEOC Guidance.

Below is a sample "Individualized Assessment" notice.

Sample "Individualized Assessment" Notice

[DATE]
[COMPANY NAME]
[ADDRESS1]
[ADDRESS2]
[CITY][STATE][ZIP]

REQUEST FOR INFORMATION REQUIRED FOR

INDIVIDUALIZED ASSESSMENT OF CRIMINAL RECORD HISTORY

Dear [FIRST NAME][LAST NAME],

This notice provides you with required information that is unrelated to any other communication you may have received regarding your application.

IF NO CRIMINAL HISTORY is found in your background check report (a copy was attached to the Pre-Adverse Action Notice sent to you today by separate email), you may disregard this notice and take no further action.

IF A CRIMINAL HISTORY is found in your background check report; you should immediately review the attached "Individual Assessment Factors" with respect to your criminal record(s) history. If you want to provide an explanation relating to one or more of identified factors, please send an email as soon as possible to the person listed below addressing the specific areas of additional information outlined in the attachment.

If you provide a timely response, we will consider the information and contact you directly if we need anything else or want to speak to you.

Sincerely,

[COMPANY NAME]
[USER FIRST NAME][USER LAST NAME]
Enclosure:

Individual Assessment Factors

The Individual Assessment Factors can be found in the April 25, 2012 EEOC Guidance reprinted in the Appendix.

Of course, if the applicant fails to respond to the letter about an "Individualized Assessment," an employer does not need to take any further action. If the applicant fails to respond to the pre-adverse action letter, the next step is the post adverse action notice.

As a practical matter, by the time an applicant is the subject of a Consumer Report, an employer has spent time, money, and effort in recruiting and hiring. An employer may well be vested in the applicant and at a minimum, a Human Resources department will want to know if and how an unqualified applicant got through them to the background check stage. Therefore, it is in the employer's best interest to give an applicant an opportunity to explain any adverse information before denying a job offer. If there was an error in the public records, giving the applicant the opportunity to explain or correct it could be to the employer's advantage.

Even if there are other reasons for not hiring an applicant in addition to matters contained in a consumer report, the adverse action notification procedures still apply. If the intended decision was based in whole or part on the Consumer Report, the applicant has a right to receive the report. In fact, these rights apply even if the information in the consumer report used against an applicant is not even negative on its face. For example, an applicant may have a perfect payment record on his or her credit report, but an employer may be concerned that the debt level is too high compared to the salary. The applicant still is entitled to a notice of pre-adverse action, because it is possible that the credit report is wrong about the applicant's outstanding debts. In a situation where the employer would have made an adverse decision anyway, regardless of the background report, following the adverse action procedures is still the best practice for legal protection.

The question that arises is how long an employer must wait before denying employment based upon information contained in a Consumer Report. The Fair Credit Reporting Act is silent on this point. However, many legal authorities advise that an employer should wait a reasonable period of time before making the final decision. According to an opinion letter from the Federal Trade Commission (FTC), a minimum period of five business days would be reasonable. See: www.ftc.gov/os/statutes/fcra/weisberg.shtm. However, an employer may consider a longer period just to be on the safe side. This period should be the time that would be needed for an applicant to meaningfully review the report and make known to the employer or the Consumer Reporting Agency any inaccurate or incomplete information in the Consumer Report. It is critical the applicant have an appropriate opportunity to review, reflect, and react before the employer takes the official adverse action.

A Consumer Reporting Agency should be able to assist employers in complying with the above requirements. This does not mean that an employer is required to hold the job open for a long period of time. After the first notice is given, and the applicant has had an appropriate opportunity to respond, an employer may either wait until there has been a re-investigation, or fill the position with another applicant. Most employers find as a practical matter that this provision of law does NOT impose any hardship or burden upon an employer. Even though in rare situations an employer may have questions on how to proceed, the clear advantages of a pre-employment screening program far outweigh any complications that can theoretically arise from non-compliance. This duty belongs to the employer, although it may be delegated to a background screening firm.

Step 4 — Notice must be given to Applicant after Adverse Action

If, after sending out the documents required in Step 3, the employer intends to make a final decision not to hire, the employer must take one more step. The employer must send the applicant a Notice of Adverse Action informing the job applicant that the employer has made a final decision and must provide a copy of the form "Summary of Your Rights under the Fair Credit Reporting Act."

Many employers find it difficult to believe that Congress intended an applicant be notified twice, both before an adverse action and after. The law clearly requires two notices. This is also the interpretation of the Federal Trade Commission staff. The purpose is to give job applicants the maximum opportunity to correct any incomplete or inaccurate reports that could affect their chances of employment.

A special problem arises when an employer brings a worker on premises before the background check is complete, only to later find the background report uncovers negative information that may have disqualified the person. An employer may be tempted to simply call the person in, hand them the report, a final paycheck, and both letters at the same time. However, this does not give the applicant a reasonable time to review, reflect, and respond to the report. If the background report was incomplete or incorrect, there is not a meaningful opportunity for the applicant to exercise their rights under the FCRA. The best procedure is to follow the FCRA by providing the worker with their report, a statement of rights, the first letter and an opportunity to offer any response. The second letter should be delayed until a reasonable time has passed for an applicant to respond. Although it is administratively more difficult than giving two letters at once, two letters at once may violate an applicant's rights.

Sample of Notice of Adverse Action Letter

[DATE]
[COMPANY NAME]
[ADDRESS1]
[ADDRESS2]
[CITY][STATE][ZIP]

Dear [FIRST NAME][LAST NAME],

We are required to inform you that you are no longer being considered for the position you were seeking with our organization. This decision was based in whole or in part on information in a background check report obtained from the following consumer reporting agency:

Employment Screening Resources ("ESR")

7110 Redwood Blvd, Suite C

Novato, CA 94945

888-999-4474

Employment Screening Resources had no role in the decision regarding your employment and cannot explain to you why the decision was made.

Pursuant to the Fair Credit Reporting Act, you have the following rights:

1. You may obtain an additional free copy of your report within sixty days of receipt of this notice by contacting Employment Screening Resources (see contact information above).

2. You may dispute any information contained in the report directly with Employment Screening Resources (see contact information above).

Sincerely,

[COMPANY NAME]

[USER FIRST NAME][USER LAST NAME]

Enclosures:

Copy of your background investigation report

A Summary of Your Rights Under the Fair Credit Reporting Act

See FCRA section 615 for more information on notice of adverse action. Attached in the Appendix is a copy of the summary of rights that should be given to a job applicant any time an employer sends either a pre-adverse action or a post-adverse action letter.

FAQs about Adverse Action Letters under FCRA and Employment Screening

Below are several frequently asked question dealing with the federal Fair Credit Reporting Act (FCRA) and the pre-adverse and post-adverse action notices.

Suppose an employer has two finalists for one position. The employer submits both names for background checks, and both candidates have clear background reports. The firm then decides to offer the job to one candidate over the other, purely based upon the belief that one candidate was a better fit than the other, with nothing to do with the background reports.

Question: *Should the employer still send the adverse action notices (both pre and post notices) to the rejected job candidate, even though the rejected candidate's background report played no part in the hiring decision?*

Answer: *Although a background screening firms cannot give legal advice, it can give a very lawyer-like answer, which is: It depends.*

Assuming the screening report is 100% not related to the decision, and it was entirely a fit issue, then theoretically an employer can bypass adverse action. Technically, adverse action notices are required only where a background report played a role, in whole or in part, in the employment decision. The idea is to give an applicant a meaningful opportunity to review, reflect, and act upon a report if the applicant feels it is incorrect or incomplete in any fashion.

Even if the background report played just a minimal part in the final decision, the adverse action notices would be required. However, if the employer merely decided to screen both finalists and found nothing in the screening report that impacted the final decision, then strictly speaking the adverse action notices would not be required.

Of course, as with most things involving employment decisions and background checks, nothing is ever quite that cut and dried. Here are some possible complications:

- The first issue is proof. The rejected applicant may claim that the fit argument was a pretext. This is especially risky if the candidate not hired is a member of a protected class and argues failure to hire due to discrimination. Invariably, the attorney for the plaintiff that chooses to sue would probably add on a cause of action for failure to follow the FCRA by not giving the rejected applicant a chance to correct a report. Plaintiff lawyers have become very sophisticated in their understanding of the FCRA, and employers and screening firms that violate it can well be targets of litigation.

- In addition, the subject of what is adverse can be tricky. Even if there is nothing derogatory on the face of the report, the rejected applicant can still claim that the report gave the wrong impression. For example, a job title may have been reported that was different than what the applicant used. Another example is a credit report if it was run as part of the background check. If the credit report came back and there was nothing derogatory, such as late payments, there still could be information that was incorrect. For example, some employers look to see how much debt an applicant is in and compare their monthly obligations to their salary. If the reported debt information was incorrect, the applicant can argue he/she was placed in a false light without a chance to correct it.

- Another problem is consistent administration of the adverse action rules. If an employer starts picking and choosing when to send or not send notices, an error can be made in other cases since it can be a judgment call to a certain extent as to whether there was anything negative that influenced the decision. Some employers choose to send the notice to any rejected applicant that was the subject of a background report and not hired to ensure full compliance. After all, employers usually only submit background check requests generally on finalists so the situation may not come up that often.

The bottom line is always about risk management. Providing adverse action notices are a quick clerical task that takes little time. Many employers decide to follow a consistent policy of always sending out adverse action notices, even if not strictly required so nothing falls through the cracks, and they don't need to justify anything later. If for some reason the lack of notices becomes an issue in an employment related litigation, it may be hard to convince a jury that in fact the report was 100% irrelevant to the decision.

If there is a particular case where an employer does not want to send out the adverse action notices, then the employer may want to prepare a memo to file clarifying that it was a fit issue only, and the screening report was not involved even one iota.

The next question deals with an existing employee.

Question: *What if the person is already employed, and the employer performs some additional check, such as a criminal check or credit report. Do we still need an adverse action period?*

Answer: *Details are everything if taking adverse action on a current employee due to a background check.*

A 2010 federal district court case demonstrates the importance of handling the adverse action process correctly when terminating an existing employee due to an unsatisfactory background check.

In the case decided on February 26, 2010 by the U.S. District Court for the Southern District of Ohio, *Burghy v Dayton Racquet Club, Inc.*, 695 F.Supp.2d 689 (S.D.Ohio 2010), an employer ran a credit check on all employees in the accounting department, including the plaintiff who had been working in the current location for seven years. For reasons not disclosed in the case, the employer decided to terminate the plaintiff due to the result of the credit report.

According to the plaintiff, a meeting was called on January 16, 2008 where she was told she would never work for the employer again and to go home. Shortly thereafter, she received a copy of the report as well as a letter stating that the information in the report may or may not affect employment. On January 23, 2008, she received a second letter indicating she was terminated.

The plaintiff sued on the basis that the FCRA requires that an employer provide a consumer with a copy of any consumer report and a statement of their rights BEFORE an adverse decision is made about employment. The plaintiff argued that she was both given the report and terminated all on the same day so she did not receive a pre-adverse action notice.

The employer disputed the account and argued that the first meeting did not constitute a termination; it only indicted an intention to terminate. In addition, the plaintiff was still paid for another week after the second letter, and there was some discussion about trying to get her job back.

The court ruled that since there was a disputed issue of fact, it was up to the jury to decide what happened, and the employer's motion to dismiss was denied. In other words, if the jury accepted the plaintiff's version of the facts, then the jury could find an FCRA violation.

This case illustrates the important point for employers **about terminating current employees.** As discussed in the preceding pages, under the FCRA, when an employer receives a Consumer Report and decides not to hire the applicant based upon the report in any way, the applicant has certain rights. Before taking the adverse action, the employer must provide certain information to the applicant. A second letter is required if the decision is to be made final.

In this case, where the consumer was already on the job, employers need to be much more careful. To avoid any misunderstandings, an employer should make it absolutely clear in writing (and with witnesses) that the first letter is NOT a final decision, and the consumer has the opportunity to review the report and make his or her objections known. The difficulty in this case was that the employer allegedly made it clear that the termination was final in the first meeting. Of course, the problem with an existing employee, especially one in a sensitive position such as accounting, is that an employer may not want them on premises if it turns out the decision becomes final.

In this case, the employer did send the plaintiff home with salary being paid but allegedly made the mistake of making the termination final immediately as opposed to the required waiting period.

This case again underscores the fact that employment screening is a highly regulated area of employment law that requires specialized skills and knowledge.

Court Finds Not Hiring Applicant Constitutes 'Adverse Action' under FCRA

In a Court opinion filed December 30, 2009, *Feldmann v. New York Life Ins. Co.*, 2011 WL 382201 (E.D.Mo. 2011), the U.S. District Court for the Eastern District of Missouri ruled that not getting hired is an 'adverse action' as defined by the federal Fair Credit Reporting Act (FCRA), the law that governs background checks. In that case, the plaintiff, who was representing himself, filed legal papers alleging that his report contained inaccurate/erroneous information that the employer and information providers knew would likely have an adverse impact on the plaintiff's ability to secure employment. The plaintiff further alleged that he was not notified he was not being hired based upon the contents of a consumer report.

One of the defendants filed a motion to dismiss on the basis that the plaintiff failed to state a claim showing that the plaintiff was entitled to relief under FCRA. Although the Court did note that the plaintiff's legal pleadings were not the model of clarity, that it was clear enough that the plaintiff was asking for relief based upon an inaccurate report and not being hired. The court stated that, the defendant should be on notice that the adverse action was that the defendant failed to hire the plaintiff. The Court declined to dismiss the case or to require the plaintiff to spell it any more clearly.

This case underscores the importance of employers following the adverse action rules have when performing background checks. A consumer is entitled to a pre-adverse notice, including a statement of their rights and a copy of the report, before any adverse decision is made. If the decision is made final, they are entitled to a second notice. The purposes of these rules to is to provide a consumer with a meaningful opportunity to be heard in case the consumer believes the background report is incomplete or incorrect.

Although background firms go to great lengths to provide accurate information, as with anything involving human beings, there is a possibility of an error. This notice process provides a valuable safety valve so that nothing adverse happens to a consumer before they have the chance to review the report and make any objections known. Where a consumer is the victim of identity theft, an employment screening report may be the first time they even know identity theft had occurred. (Source: www.esrcheck.com/wordpress/2010/02/08/court-finds-that-not-hiring-someone-constitutes-an-adverse-action-for-purposes-of-the-fair-credit-reporting-act-fcra/).

Other Important FCRA Provisions

In addition to the four steps for FCRA compliance mentioned earlier, a CRA has other obligations. Observance of these obligations may also become important when an employer selects a CRA to assist with background investigations.

✓ **A CRA must follow reasonable procedures concerning identity and proper use of information per FCRA 607(a).** Per the requirements of the FCRA, every consumer reporting agency shall maintain reasonable procedures designed to avoid violations of section 605 (relating to what may be reported) and to limit the furnishing of consumer reports to the purposes listed under section 604. These procedures require that prospective users of the information identify themselves, certify the purposes for which the information is sought, and certify that the information will be used for no other purpose. Every consumer reporting agency is required to make a reasonable effort to verify the identity of a new prospective user and for the uses certified by a prospective user prior to furnishing the user a consumer report. No consumer reporting agency may furnish a consumer report to any entity if it has reasonable grounds for believing that the consumer report will not be used for a purpose listed in section 604. *Lesson— A CRA must know the client and the limitations on what can be reported. These rules are of particular importance in view of well publicized incidents in 2005 of the theft of data from firms where criminals posed as legitimate users and were able to set-up accounts in order to steal personal information, using it to commit crimes.*

✓ **CRA must take measures to ensure accuracy of report (FCRA 607(b)).** Whenever a consumer reporting agency prepares a consumer report, it shall follow reasonable procedures to assure maximum possible accuracy of the information concerning the individual about whom the report relates. *Lesson— The CRA should have written procedures that are followed and enforced to ensure maximum accuracy.*

✓ **CRA must provide the employer with the form entitled "Notice to Users of Consumer Reports: Obligations of Users under the FCRA."** See FCRA Section 607(d). A copy of the notice is in the Appendix.

✓ **CRA must provide employer with the form entitled "Summary of Your Rights Under the Fair Credit Reporting Act" with every report.** See FCRA 604(b)(1)(B). A copy of the summary is in the Appendix.

AUTHOR TIP

Whose Forms Apply Anyway?

In addition to the forms **"Summary of Your Rights Under the Fair Credit Reporting Act"** and **"Notice to Users of Consumer Reports: Obligations of Users under the FCRA,"** there is a third form that in some situations a CRA must provide called **"Notice to Furnishers of Information: Obligations of Furnishers Under the FCRA."** This document is required in certain circumstances when an applicant requests a re-investigation, or where there is an issue of identity theft.

According to regulations from the Consumer Financial Protection Board (CFPB), these forms must be changed by January 1, 2013 to reflect that consumers can obtain information about their rights under the FCRA from the CFPB instead of the Federal Trade Commission (FTC). The three forms historically indicated the FTC as the agency consumers could contact with questions.

This new regulation is available online at: http://ecfr.gpoaccess.gov/cgi/t/text/text-idx?c=ecfr;sid=09558a8309d73086b9217fe5af1ce0ef;rgn=div5;view=text;node=12%3A8.0.2.14.16;idno=12;cc=ecfr#12:8.0.2.14.16.1.1.1.

✓ **A CRA may only include certain items of information in a consumer report.** FCRA Section 605 specifically limits certain information:

- Bankruptcy cases older than 10 years, from the date of entry of the order for relief or the date of adjudication, as the case may be. See Chapter 20 for limitations on bankruptcy as related to employment.
- Civil suits, civil judgments, and records of arrest older than seven years from date of entry. Due to the 1998 FCRA amendment, this section now only refers to a seven-year limitation on arrests, but not criminal convictions. There are no limits under the federal FCRA for reporting criminal convictions although there are some state limits.
- Paid tax liens older than seven years from date of payment.
- Accounts placed for collection or charged to profit and loss which are older than seven years.

- Any other adverse item of information, other than records of convictions of crimes, which are older than seven years. Note that criminal convictions are excluded from the limitations, which leaves a seven-year limitation on using arrests without dispositions.

The FCRA, however, provides that these exceptions do not apply to an individual whose annual salary is reasonably expected to equal $75,000 a year or more.

✓ **Communication with employers about arrests**. In a federal case, it was alleged that a national employment screening firm uncovered information that the applicant had an arrest record over seven years ago. There were no convictions, only arrests. The federal Fair Credit Reporting Act (FCRA) prohibits the reporting of an arrest older than seven years old unless the applicant is reasonably expected to make a salary of over $75,000 per year. In order to determine if the arrests were reportable, the screening firm sent a communication to the prospective employer indicating there was a criminal history over seven years old but was not a conviction, and it could only be reported if the applicant was going to make over the $75,000 yearly limit. The employer was told that if they wished to receive this information, they must confirm to the screening firm if the applicant met the salary threshold. The job applicant filed a lawsuit in the United States District Court for the Eastern District of Pennsylvania alleging damages for the practice of disclosing the existence of outdated arrest records. The basis of the lawsuit was that the manner in which the background firm asked about salary amounted to a notification that an applicant has an arrest record. The screening firm, among other arguments, suggested merely reporting the existence of old arrest records did not violate the FCRA since the background firm did not provide disclosure of the actual records. The court denied the screening firm's motion to dismiss and allowed the lawsuit to proceed. The Court ruled that even if the FCRA was ambiguous on what constitutes reporting an arrest record, the FCRA was clear that the general prohibition against reporting items of adverse information over seven years old was violated. By informing the employer there was such information in the process of establishing the applicant's salary, the screening firm ended up reporting something adverse that may have been prohibited.

✓ **Rules concerning accuracy in reporting adverse public records**. If a CRA reports items of information as matters of public record that are likely to have an adverse effect upon a consumer's ability to obtain employment, the CRA must maintain strict procedures designed to insure whenever such public record information is reported, it is complete and up to date. For purposes of this duty, items of public record relating to arrests, indictments, convictions, suits, tax liens, and outstanding judgments shall be considered up to date if the public record status of the item is current at the time it is reported. This means the best way to ensure that information is accurate is to look at the public record, such as the actual courthouse documents for a criminal record, and not rely solely upon assembled databases. See FCRA Section 613(a)(2). The duty to accurately report a criminal matter under FCRA section 613 is typically satisfied by a CRA sending a researcher directly to the courthouse to pull any public record to insure it is accurate, up to date, and to also look for identifiers. See FCRA section 613(a)(2). However, the FCRA does provide an alternative procedure under FCRA section 613(a)(1). Instead of going to the courthouse, a CRA can notify the consumer that public record information is being reported by the consumer reporting agency along with the name and address of the person to whom such information is being reported (See FCRA Section 613(a)(1)). However, arguably in some states there is the question: is this alternative procedure advisable? These states generally require whenever a criminal matter is reported, reasonable procedures be followed such as double-checking any database "hit" against the actual records at the courthouse. In California, for example, a background firm can only report a criminal conviction or other matters of public record for employment purposes if "it is complete and up to date," which is defined as checking the status at the time the matter is reported (See California Civil Code section 1786.28(b)). Double-checking a database "hit" at the courthouse certainly affords employees, applicants, and background firms the most protection and the highest degree of accuracy. The duty to deal with adverse information in a public record can have an important impact when using criminal record databases. This is discussed in-depth in Chapter 14.

Practice Note

FCRA section 613 allows for a "letter" option which means a CRA does not need to go to the courthouse to reconfirm the accuracy of the information. However, FCA section 607(b) discusses "reasonable procedures for maximum possible accuracy." See chapter 14 for a discussion on how these two sections would appear to apply to each other.

✓ **Re-investigation rule.** When a CRA prepares an investigative consumer report, no adverse information in the consumer report (other than information which is a matter of public record) may be included in a subsequent consumer report unless such adverse information has been verified during the process of making such subsequent consumer report, or the adverse information was received within the three-month period preceding the date the subsequent report is furnished. See FCRA Section 614. This only applies to matters that are adverse on its face. Employment or education verification is not adverse on its face, even if it becomes adverse in the context of the application, such as the information shows an applicant lied about job history.

✓ **Disclosure rules.** Upon request, a CRA must disclose to a consumer what is in the consumer's file, identify sources, identity everyone who procured a report for employment for the past two years, and comply with various rules, e.g. provide trained personnel who can explain to a consumer any information in the report. See FCRA Sections 609 and 610.

✓ **Duty to investigate.** If an applicant contests what is in the report, the CRA has an obligation to investigate and determine accuracy within 30 days, and to take appropriate actions. The CRA must give notice to the report furnisher within five days. Various other duties are dependent upon results of re-investigation. See FCRA Sections 611 and 612. The CRA must carefully follow a series of rules in terms of various notices and responses and have a FCRA compliance procedure in place.

✓ **Identity theft information.** FCRA Section 605A (g) sets out the duty of a CRA to give certain information to consumers if a consumer reports a suspicion that they have or are about to become a victim of identity theft including information on how to file an alert.

Federal Lawsuit Demonstrates What Employers Should NOT Do

An opinion issued by the U.S. District Court in Northern District of Illinois in 2003, *Socorro v. IMI Data Search, Inc., 2003 WL 1964269 (N.D.Ill. 2008),* provides a case study on what an employer and screening firm should NOT do when it comes to safe hiring.

According to the allegations filed in the case, the plaintiff was contacted by a major hotel and offered a position. On his first day, he completed several forms, including an employment application where he truthfully stated he had no criminal record.

The application contained an authorization for a background check that the plaintiff did not initial. There was no indication in the court's opinion that any separate disclosure was signed as required by the FCRA.

After employment began, the major hotel hired a screening firm to do a background check. The screening firm mistakenly reported the plaintiff had been convicted of a misdemeanor and served six months in jail. According to the court opinion, the plaintiff in fact did NOT have a criminal conviction. Neither the major hotel nor the background firm investigated the denial, and the plaintiff was terminated. To make matters worse, the plaintiff alleged after he was fired, the major hotel told third parties he was fired because he lied on his application and spent time in jail. The plaintiff eventually found a new job but at a substantially lower compensation.

Assuming all these facts are true, what mistakes did the major hotel and the background firm make? Some mistakes include:

- Failed to provide a separate Disclosure for the background check under the FCRA.
- Failed to comply with the adverse action rules under the FCRA. If the consumer applicant had the chance to explain, it could have been cleared up.
- Failed to re-investigate when told information was incorrect.

Although the reasons for the mistaken criminal records are not clear, the question arises if reasonable procedures were used in obtaining the background data.

U. S. Supreme Court Case on "Willfulness" Under the FCRA

A June 4, 2007 decision by U. S. Supreme Court on a case related to the application of the FCRA to certain insurance industry practices proved to have significant impact on employers regarding background checks. The case, *Safeco Ins. Co. of America v. Burr*, 127 S.Ct. 2201 (2007), dealt with the use of credit reports to set insurance rates and the obligation of insurers to send out adverse action notices to consumers whose rates were affected by their credit reports.

In this case, the U.S. Supreme Court broadened the definition of "willful" under the FCRA to also include "reckless conduct." Since under FCRA section 616 (15 U.S.C. 1681n) punitive damages are only allowed if there was "willful" non-compliance, this decision caused serious impact for employers and consumer reporting agencies.

The Court dealt with a split among lower federal courts on the interpretation of what the FCRA meant by "willfulness." Some federal courts had ruled that a willful violation of the FCRA meant a business had to have actual knowledge their conduct was in violation of the FCRA. However, in this case the Supreme Court ruled that a reckless disregard can be an action entailing an unjustifiably high risk of harm that is either known or *so obvious that it should be known*. Consequently, if a Consumer Reporting Agency (CRA) had an interpretation of its duties under the FCRA that was objectively unreasonable, then the CRA faced potential exposure for punitive damages.

The net effect is that it is now somewhat easier to sue an employer or screening firm for punitive damages. If a lawsuit is filed against screening firms or employers for FCRA violations, a request for punitive damages on a recklessness theory is now more likely. There is also an increased possibility of class action lawsuits based upon FCRA violations because of the loosened willfulness definition to include recklessness. As a practical matter, lawyers bringing lawsuits against employers or screening firms will try to allege, among other things, punitive damages.

The bottom line is a screening firm or employer is now held to a higher standard of compliance. Where the line will be drawn between mere negligence and recklessness in any particular case is always a difficult proposition. However, just because a screening firm or employer believes it is acting lawfully or is unaware it is acting unlawfully, it is NOT protected from an allegation of willful violation of the FCRA with an exposure to punitive damages. Since insurance coverage for a defendant typically does not cover punitive damages, a plaintiff in such a legal action generally has greater leverage. This issue again underscores the critical nature of legal compliance associated with background checks.

The Fair and Accurate Credit Transactions (FACT) Act or FACTA – The 2003 FCRA Amendment

On December 4, 2003, President George W. Bush signed into law H.R. 2622, known as the **Fair and Accurate Credit Transactions (FACT) Act or FACTA**. This amended the Fair Credit Reporting Act. This wide ranging law dealt with a number of topics such as identity theft, increased consumer access to their credit report, pre-emption of certain state financial laws by the federal law, and increased the accuracy of credit reports. The new law allows consumers to receive a fee credit report once a year from a "National Specialty Consumer Reporting Agency" (NSCRA), which includes not only credit bureaus, but other types of national firms collecting data on consumers (See Chapter 11 for more details on what constitutes a NSCRA). This is sometimes referred to as a "FACT Act Disclosure." The law also provides for fraud alerts to be placed in credit reports and the ability to block credit reports in certain situations.

For purposes of employment, these are some of the critical components of FACT:

✓ **Truncation of Social Security Number.** FCRA Section 609 was amended to allow consumers to request that the first five digits of his or her Social Security Number be deleted from any disclosure to the consumer. The purpose is to help combat identity theft, since identity theft often occurs at the consumer's mailbox.

✓ **Statute of limitations.** FCRA Section 618 sets the period of time someone may sue for a violation of the FCRA. The statute of limitations has been extended from two years from the date of violation, to two years from the date of the discovery of the violation by the consumer, and up to five years from the date of the actual violation. Consumer reporting agencies should plan on keeping records for at least six years to allow time for the statutory period plus the normal delay time experienced in receiving notice of a lawsuit.

✓ **Investigation of current employees.** Under FCRA Section 604, employers now have the ability to conduct third party investigations of current employees without disclosure or having to first get written authorization.

Fixing a Flaw — Investigation of Current Employees

This was probably the most critical issue the FACT amendment addressed for employers. A little history is in order here: When the 1997 amendments to the FCRA were first enacted, many security professionals, as well as labor attorneys and human resource professionals, had widely interpreted the notice and disclosure requirements as applying only to pre-employment hiring and not post-hire workplace investigations.

However, in 1999, attorney Judi Vail sent a letter to the FTC (the federal agency that enforces the FCRA) asking whether the FCRA applied to investigations of sexual harassment claims against current employees. The FTC staff had a practice from 1997 to 2001 of issuing staff opinion letters in response to inquiries. In what was commonly referred to as the Vail letter, the FTC flatly stated that investigation of current employees by third parties who regularly conduct such investigations are covered by the same FCRA rules used for pre-employment screening.

There are many situations when a firm may wish to use a third party to investigate a current employee. If there are allegations of sexual harassment, employers have a duty to conduct a thorough, prompt, and fair investigation, and is often done by hiring an outside professional. If there is suspicion of misconduct, such as theft, drug dealing, or other criminal conduct, then the expertise of an outside investigator may also be required.

However, when investigative secrecy is required, it is difficult to conduct an effective third-party investigation under FCRA ground rules as interpreted by the Vail letter. As soon as the target is tipped off, it is very easy to destroy evidence, influence witnesses, or attempt to derail the investigation.

Another problem was securing witness cooperation. The FCRA provides a mechanism for the object of the inquiry to obtain a copy of the report, thereby revealing information sources. The result is that witnesses cannot be promised anonymity, discouraging witnesses from assisting an investigation.

Before the FACT amendment, to comply with the FCRA, a third-party investigator had to obtain written authorization from the subject of the report. The employee also had to receive a stand-alone disclosure that a consumer report is being prepared.

A number of court cases whittled away at the Vail letter. Finally, the issue was put to rest by the FACT legislation. The FCRA was amended so that an employer would not need to obtain a written release and authorization in order to conduct investigation of current employees, where the investigation involved one of the following:

- ✓ Suspected misconduct relating to employment.
- ✓ Compliance with federal, state, or local laws and regulations.
- ✓ The rules of a self-regulating organization.
- ✓ Any pre-existing written policies of the employer.

> **AUTHOR TIP**
>
> **Future Consents**
>
> In order to protect the right to conduct future investigations when necessary, employers may consider adding the following language to their authorization forms— "This authorization and release will remain valid for future preparation of a consumer report or investigative consumer report for purposes of retention, promotion, or re-assignment unless revoked in writing." This is sometimes legally referred to as an "Evergreen" clause meaning it stays active in the future (although most likely not forever since that would not be reasonable to assume a consumer would consent forever). Because of the special notice requirements needed for an Investigative Consumer Report (ICR), such a clause would likely be best suited to public record check, such as a future criminal check. See Chapter 7 for more details.

Limitations Still Exist Even with FACT Act

First, the investigation cannot be made for the purpose of investigating a consumer's credit worthiness, credit standing, or credit capacity. A credit report is always covered by the FCRA. Second, the matter cannot be reported to an outside person or entity except for certain governmental agents and agencies.

Finally, there is still a procedure in place that must be followed if there are any adverse actions as a result of the investigation, such as termination or discipline. After taking any adverse action that was based in any part on the report, the employer must provide the consumer with a summary of the nature and substance of the investigation. However, there are limits on providing the source of the information.

FTC Staff Report on Fair Credit Reporting Act

In July 2011, the Federal Trade Commission issued a staff report that compiled and updated the agency's guidance on the FCRA. The report, **"Forty Years of Experience with the Fair Credit Reporting Act: An FTC Staff Report and Summary of Interpretations,"** provides a brief overview of the FTC's role in enforcing and interpreting the FCRA, includes a section-by-section summary of the agency's interpretations of the Act, and also withdraws the agency's 1990 Commentary on the FCRA, which has become partially obsolete since it was issued 21 years ago.

The 1990 Commentary that the FTC withdrew was comprised of a series of FTC statements about how it would enforce the various provisions of the FCRA. Since 1990, the FRCA has been updated several times, most significantly by the Consumer Credit Reporting Reform Act of 1996 and as mentioned previously, the Fair and Accurate Credit Transactions Act of 2003, also known as the FACT Act. Both updates expanded the provisions of the FCRA. The new staff report deletes several FTC interpretations in the 1990 Commentary that have since been repealed, amended, or have become obsolete or outdated. The report also adds several interpretations reflecting changes that Congress has made to the FCRA over the years, rules issued by the FTC and other agencies under the FACT Act, statements in numerous staff opinion letters, and the staff's experience from enforcement actions.

The section-by-section Staff Summary in the report contains the FTC staff's interpretations of the FCRA and includes many interpretations from the "Statement of General Policy or Interpretations" that the Commission published in May 1990. It includes informal guidance the staff has provided to the public in the ensuing years and their experience in enforcing the FCRA. In some cases, the Staff Summary – which should be used in conjunction with the text of the FCRA – includes a partial summary of the statute, rather than the full text, as a preamble to discussion of issues pertaining to various sections and subsections. These summary statements of the law should not be used as a substitute for the statutory text. The report is available at: http://ftc.gov/os/2011/07/110720fcrareport.pdf.

FTC Warns Background Check Mobile Apps May Violate FCRA

In February 2012, the Federal Trade Commission warned marketers of six background check mobile applications ("apps") they may be violating the FCRA. The FTC sent letters to three background check app marketers warning that they must comply with the FCRA if the background check reports they provide are being used for employment, housing, and credit purposes.

The FTC named the three background check mobile app marketers that received the warning letters and also provided links to copies of the warning letters. According to the letters, the FTC has made no determination whether the companies are violating the FCRA but encourages them to review their background check apps and their policies and procedures. A portion of the letters read:

> "At least one of your company's mobile applications involves background screening reports that include criminal histories. Employers are likely to use such criminal histories when screening job applicants. If you have reason to believe that your [background] reports are being used for employment or other FCRA purposes, you and your customers who are using your reports for such purposes must comply with the FCRA."

Under the FCRA, operations that assemble or evaluate such information to provide to third parties qualify as CRAs. Background check mobile apps marketers may qualify as CRAs under the Act since they assemble or evaluate similar information to provide to third parties. As CRAs, they must:

✓ Take reasonable steps to ensure the user of each report has a "permissible purpose" to use the report;
✓ Take reasonable steps to ensure the maximum possible accuracy of the information conveyed in its reports; and
✓ Provide users of its reports with information about their obligations under the FCRA, such as their obligation to provide notice to employees and applicants of any adverse action taken on the basis of a consumer report.

The press release 'FTC Warns Marketers That Mobile Apps May Violate Fair Credit Reporting Act' is available at: www.ftc.gov/opa/2012/02/mobileapps.shtm. A sample warning letter from the FTC to the mobile phone background screening apps marketers is available at: www.ftc.gov/os/2012/02/120206mobileappsletter.pdf.

White Paper Analysis

A 2011 white paper – **'Background Check Mobile Phone Apps and Instant Background Check Web Sites: Fast and Easy, But Are They Accurate?'** – also noted the same issues about FCRA compliance that the FTC warned of regarding background screening apps that allow users to perform instant background checks on anyone at any time from their mobile phones by searching publicly available records. Co-authored by Lester Rosen and Kerstin Bagus, the white paper examined the accuracy of background screening mobile apps and found that while these apps may be fast, cheap, and easy to use, the information they provide may not be entirely accurate. According to the authors, the instant background screening information "can lead to hasty and dangerous conclusions" in the hands of average users, including:

- ✓ **Reporting inaccurate information**. Since these apps typically return raw data not fully verified or confirmed with the original record source, they can include "false positives" with outdated results such as a conviction history that does not exist. Even worse, they can show "false negatives" with no criminal history when one actually does exist.
- ✓ **Returning information for the wrong person with the same name**. Since these services do not generally require identifiers such as dates of birth, they can return results that match the name entered, but do not necessarily match that exact person—an issue often referred to as "common names."
- ✓ **Creating a false sense of security**. Safety issues can quickly arise when a "clear" background check result is naively interpreted as a promise that the person being searched has no criminal record.
- ✓ **Privacy issues for the person being checked.** Since the average person is not knowledgeable about the proper usage of public records, there are no privacy controls in place for the individual being searched.
- ✓ **Reputational injuries.** The reputation of the individual being searched may be harmed if the information is not correct.
- ✓ **Misuse of information for employment or tenant purposes.** Employers and landlords who use results from these sites can find themselves in a legal and financial nightmare due to intense legal regulation surrounding the use of information for employment purposes from the FCRA as well as numerous state laws. While some of these services say that the data should not be used for employment or tenant screening or any FCRA purpose, these warnings are often buried in fine print. There are even sites that do not even mention the FCRA.

This complimentary white paper 'Background Check Mobile Phone Apps and Instant Background Check Web Sites: Fast and Easy, But Are They Accurate?' is available at: www.esrcheck.com/Download/.

Employment Screening Lawsuits Increase as Attorneys and Consumers Become Familiar with FCRA

A number of cases, class action suits are being utilized as the vehicle to bring legal actions against employers. It is anticipated that this trend towards lawsuits will continue. The lesson here is while employers need to be diligent in their hiring, at the same time they need to ensure they are following the FCRA rules that regulate the collection, dissemination, and use of consumer information, including consumer credit information. This means it is even more critical for employers to review policies and procedures to ensure accuracy and legal compliance given how heavily background checks are regulated.

One source of lawsuits occurs when certain vendor database searches produce inaccurate and incomplete information used for background checks. These databases should only be used for secondary research and not as the primary, sole source of information. Inexpensive and instant vendor database searches with unreliable results can miss criminal records and give both employers and consumers a false sense of security. As discussed later in this book, background checks based solely upon vendor databases have substantial issues in terms of timeliness, completeness, and accuracy.

Potential class members in a lawsuit, including employees and prospective employees, may be entitled to statutory damages of up to $1,000 for each violation in the case of willful non-compliance. Class action lawsuits also create exposure for large awards of attorneys' fees and the potential exposure to punitive damages. A United States Supreme Court case decided in June 2007, Safeco Ins. Co. of America v. Burr, 127 S.Ct.2201 (2007) substantially increased the risk of punitive damages under the FCRA by ruling that a reckless disregard of the FCRA could be sufficient to show "willful" non-compliance. The net effect is it is now easier to sue an employer or a background screening firm for punitive damages.

To be clear, the mere fact a lawsuit is filed and allegations are made by no means proves the validity of the claims, and filing of the lawsuit is merely the first step in the legal process. However, this uptick in lawsuits underscores the need for employers to carefully review background checking programs and to work with accredited background screening firms that can provide information to assist in compliance with the federal FCRA and various other federal and state laws concerning background checks.

Dissecting Recent Lawsuits for FCRA Violations

The following is a summary of some lawsuits involving alleged violations of the FCRA. This analysis is intended to provide valuable lessons for employers.

There are several key points to keep in mind. Where the matter is only in the allegation stage, and there has been no judicial determination as of the truthfulness of the charge, the parties are not identified beyond the named parties in the title for the lawsuit. To be clear, unless there was an appeal or a final judgment (such as Court or jury verdict or a motion in the favor of the plaintiff for a summary judgment), these civil claims are just allegations, and there have been no factual determinations. The mere fact that a lawsuit is filed and allegations are made by no means proves the validity of the claims, and filing of the lawsuit is merely the first step in the legal process. However, this sort of lawsuit underscores the need for employers to carefully review background checking programs and to work with accredited background screening firms that can provide information to assist in compliance with the federal Fair Credit Reporting Act (FCRA) and various other federal and state laws concerning background checks.

Class Action Lawsuit for Failure to Follow Fair Credit Reporting Act Settles for $4.3 Million

In a case that once again emphasizes the importance of employers following the FCRA for employment screening, attorneys for thousands of mass-transit drivers and school bus drivers announced approval of a class action settlement of 4.3 million dollars for failure to adhere to the requirements of the FCRA. The proposed settlement was approved by a federal Judge in Illinois stemming from a national class-action suit involving allegations of FCRA violations against sister companies that employed drivers. The suit alleged the two companies – both subsidiaries of a company in Great Britain – obtained criminal background checks on drivers and job applicants without their written authorization and, in some cases, denied them jobs without providing them a copy of their criminal background report in violation of the federal FCRA law. The FCRA requires that all background checks be conducted with consent and, in the case an adverse employment action occurs as a result of a background check, the applicant is entitled to certain notifications including a copy of the report. The overall settlement was for $5.9 million, with $4.3 million going to the class action and the court awarding an additional $1.6 million for court costs and attorneys' fees. According to a spokeswoman for the law firm that filed the suit, the settlement was the largest ever involving employment-related Fair Credit Reporting Act claims. Under the terms of the proposed settlement as reported in the press:

- ✓ Each worker terminated by either company based on an unauthorized criminal background check report could receive $2,000 to $4,000.
- ✓ Each worker terminated by either company based on a criminal background check report without first receiving a copy of that report will receive $750.
- ✓ Each worker who was the subject of an unauthorized criminal background report but who continued to work for either company will likely receive between $150 and $300.

According to the press release, the largest labor organization representing transit workers in the United States filed the two separate class actions in federal district courts in Illinois for violation of their legal rights under the Fair Credit Reporting Act. In each case, workers were dismissed from employment after the subsidiary companies hired a vendor to perform background checks on their employees and reported that the employee supposedly had a past criminal record. Under the Fair Credit Reporting Act, employers are obliged to notify consumers of any adverse actions as a result of a background check and to give the consumers a reasonable opportunity to dispute the accuracy of the reported information. The lawsuits sought relief for all employees similarly dismissed – and all applicants similarly refused employment – on the basis of a background check. This case once again demonstrates that the process of obtaining background checks is highly legally relegated and employers and background firms need to pay strict attention to all of the various legal rules affecting hiring, including the FCRA.

The Court document is available at: www.workplaceclassaction.com/First%20transit%20settlement%20agrement.pdf (Sources: 'Bus Drivers File Class Action Suits Against First Group' www.prnewswire.com/news-releases/bus-drivers-file-class-action-suits-against-first-group-63531807.html) & 'First Group affiliates pay $4.3M settlement' http://news.cincinnati.com/article/AB/20110317/BIZ01/103180324/First-Group-affiliates-pay-4-3M-settlement).

Employer Not Always Liable for Technical Violation of FCRA

The advantage of having policies and procedures in place to follow the FCRA was demonstrated in a ruling from a federal trial court. The ruling found a violation of the Fair Credit Reporting Act (FCRA) does not always mean an employer is liable for damages where the employer committed an inadvertent mistake that resulted in no damages to the consumer. See: *Lagrassa v. Jack Gaughen, LLC, 2011 WL 1257371 (M.D. Pa. 2011)*.

In the case, a consumer applied for a job, and the employer obtained a background check report from a Consumer Reporting Agency (CRA). Although the employer had procedures in place to obtain a consent and disclosure as required by the FCRA, the background check report was allegedly requested without obtaining the proper consent first.

The background check report was returned showing a criminal history. According to the case, the employer's own investigation revealed that the applicant had misrepresented work experience and licensure status. According to the court's decision, the employer terminated the consumer because: "[a]fter being given an opportunity to dispute the information, Plaintiff continued to provide false information and her dishonesty disqualified her from holding a sales-manager position."

The lawsuit alleged that the employer failed to comply with the FCRA in two critical ways:

✓ The employer failed to disclose that it may obtain a background check and failed to obtain an authorization in writing;
✓ Before taking adverse action, based on negative information in the background check report, the employer failed to provide a "pre-adverse" action letter which includes a copy of the report and a description of the consumer's rights prepared by the Federal Trade Commission (FTC).

The consumer sued under two theories:

✓ First, the consumer sued for negligent non-compliance under FCRA section 617, which requires that the consumer suffer some actual damages.
✓ Second, the consumer also sued for statutory damages for willful non-compliance under FCRA section 616, which can include punitive damages. Where statuary damages are sought, a consumer does not need to show any actual damages but that the employer or CRA acted willfully, which can include a knowing or reckless disregard of the FCRA. Both sections allow for attorney's fees. An action under FCRA Section 616 can create a large exposure to an employer or CRA since it exposes them to punitive damages and attorney's fees.

The court dismissed the claim of negligent non-compliance on the basis that the consumer admitted she suffered no actual damages, which the court ruled was required to prove negligent non-compliance.

As to the willful non-compliance cause of action, the court ruled that "a violation of the FCRA by itself does not amount to willful noncompliance." The court found there was no evidence that could demonstrate the employer's actions were knowing or reckless. As a result, that cause of action was also dismissed.

An additional aspect of the case was the plaintiff also sued the CRA. However, the court noted the background check report was "accurate, complete and up-to-date." Furthermore, the court noted the duty to provide pre-adverse action notice belonged to the employer and not the CRA. (NOTE: An employer can outsource that obligation to a background screening firm, but there was no mention in the court's decision of any such arrangement).

More information on this case may found at: http://docs.justia.com/cases/federal/district-courts/pennsylvania/pamdce/1:2009cv00770/76014/54/.

AUTHOR TIP For more information on the FCRA and staffing firms and volunteers, see Chapter 27.

Background Check Class Action against Employer for Violations of FCRA Survives Challenge

A class action was filed against a well-known pizza delivery chain alleging failure to comply with the requirements of the FCRA. In *Singleton v. Domino's Pizza, LLC 2012 WL 245965 (D.Md. 2012)*, the Court ruled that the plaintiffs had made a sufficient showing to deny a motion by the employer to dismiss. In addition, the court refused to strike allegations that the conduct was willful, which means the employer faces statutory damages as well as potential punitive damages.

The lawsuit contended that both plaintiffs were the subject of background checks, had started working, and later were terminated after the background check was completed. In both instances, the plaintiffs were not provided with a copy of the report or advised of any rights before the termination. In addition, both plaintiffs alleged that the background screening consent they signed included a release of liability for the background check on the form that was part of the application packet. The form was called a "Background Investigation Information and Consent" or BIIC. As a result, according to the complaint, the employer failed to meet the legal requirement for a "standalone" form since the BIIC contained extraneous information and was not separate.

FCRA section 604(b)(3)(A) requires that before taking any adverse action against a consumer, such as not hiring the consumer or termination if the background check is completed after hiring, the employer must provide certain information to the consumer, often referred to as a notice of pre-adverse action. This includes a copy of the background report as well as a statement of rights prepared by the Federal Trade Commission. The purpose is to provide a safety valve in the event the report is inaccurate or incomplete which can happen, for example, if a consumer is the victim of identity theft, and a crime is committed in his or her name or if a court record is inaccurate. The consumer then has an opportunity to set the record straight.

The second allegation was based on FCRA sections 604(b)(2)(A)(i)-(ii) which regulate disclosure of information to a consumer and the need for a written authorization, including a specific requirement the disclosure be "in a document that consists solely of the disclosure."

In this case, the lawsuit alleged that the disclosure contained a release of liability that purported to release the employer, as well as any provider of information, from any liability, claims, or causes of action related to the information obtained. The Court ruled that this could be the basis of a violation of the "standalone" document requirement by inserting unnecessary information on the release. In fact, two previous opinions letters from the staff of the FTC have indicated such a release of liability would not be consistent with the FCRA:

- ✓ In one letter, the FTC indicated such language would violate the FCRA because the form would not consist "solely" of the disclosure. (See the FTC Hauxwell letter at www.ftc.gov/os/statutes/fcra/hauxwell.shtm.)
- ✓ The second letter indicated the FCRA required a form that is not "encumbered by any other information… (in order) to prevent consumers from being distracted by other information side-by-side with the disclosure." (See the FTC Leathers letter at www.ftc.gov/os/statutes/fcra/leathers.shtm.) The Court did not address the allegation that merely having the disclosure form as part of the employment packet also violated the "standalone" rules.

Although the employer pointed out the FTC staff letters are not legally binding, the Court did note they were considered persuasive and would bear upon whether the employer willfully violated the FCRA. The Court noted that:

"Ultimately, both the statutory text and FTC advisory opinions indicate that an employer violates the FCRA by including a liability release in a disclosure document. Because the BIIC form contains such a release, [the defendant] has not shown, as a matter of law, that the form complies with the FCRA. Its attempt to have counts two and three dismissed on this ground must, therefore, fail."

In the motion to strike, the employer sought to avoid exposure to punitive damages by arguing that its actions did not amount to a willful violation of the FCRA, and the employer should not be subject to statutory damages under FCRA section 616. If an employer is merely negligent, then a plaintiff is only entitled to actual damages as well as reasonable attorney's fees and court costs. If an employer is willful, then the damages can be up to $1,000 a person regardless of actual damages. In a class action lawsuit, the class seeks to obtain $1,000 for every person subject to the violation, which can be a large number if a large employer is involved. The class action also seeks attorney's fees and, more importantly, punitive damages.

In this case, the Court ruled that defendant failed to show its interpretation of the FCRA was "not objectively unreasonable." At this stage of the case, the Court denied the motion to strike the punitive damages. This does not mean the Court determined the defendant engaged in any wrongful procedures but only that the allegations would not be thrown out.

This lawsuit confirms a trend that litigation for FCRA violations will increase, especially class actions alleging punitive damages. While at the time this book went to press there were no judicial findings, there are several important lessons for employers in this case:

- ✓ A disclosure form should not contain a release of liability clause. In fact, it is debatable whether such a release, even on another form, has value.
- ✓ An employer should consider keeping the background check form separate from any application package.
- ✓ An employer must absolutely understand and abide by the pre-adverse and post adverse action rules.
- ✓ Background screening is a critical task for any organization that wants to exercise due diligence and protect the public, its employees, and its assets. However, it is a highly legally regulated, and employers are well advised to only work with background screening firms that are familiar with the FCRA and have legal compliance expertise. Although a background screening firm cannot give legal advice, a knowledgeable screening firm can alert employers to industry standard information to assist with compliance. Employers can also choose to work with a background screening firm that is accredited by The National Association of Professional Background Screeners (NAPBS) Background Screening Credentialing Council (BSCC) for successfully proved compliance with the Background Screening Agency Accreditation Program (BSAAP).

The case is available at www.nka.com/wp-content/uploads/2011/07/DominosFCRAComplaint.pdf. (Source: www.prweb.com/releases/Dominos/FCRA_lawsuit/prweb9141109.htm.)

Class Action Lawsuit against Major Financial Institution for FCRA Violations Demonstrates Importance of Legal Compliance

A class action case filed against a large financial institution – one of the nation's top 10 banks – also centered around legal compliance in the background screening program. The lawsuit was filed on behalf of an employee who alleged violations of the federal Fair Credit Reporting Act (FCRA). According to a press release from the attorneys for the plaintiff, the lawsuit alleged the financial institution obtained background checks in violation of the FCRA and failed to provide required notices.

The lawsuit – filed in the United States District Court for the District of Maryland – alleged the financial institution violated the FCRA in two ways:

- ✓ The lawsuit alleged the financial institution's authorization form was flawed. The law imposes strict formatting requirements on companies who do background checks. The plaintiff alleges that by burying its background check authorization in a job application, including extraneous information, the financial institution violated the FCRA. The FCRA requires that a consumer receive a "clear and conspicuous" disclosure in a document that consists solely of the disclosure that a background report may be obtained for employment purposes.

✓ The lawsuit also alleged the financial institution failed to provide copies of the background reports when it used them to take adverse employment actions, such as refusing to hire an applicant, refusing to promote an employee, or terminating an employee. The FCRA requires employers to provide consumers with copies of their background checks if the employer intends to take adverse action that is based in any part on the background check report, along with a statement of rights prepared by the Federal Trade Commission (FTC), so consumers have an opportunity to contest any information they feel is inaccurate or incomplete. If the employer proceeds to take adverse action, a second post-adverse action notice is required.

Additional information about the case can be found at www.nka.com/capital-one and a case status update is available at www.nka.com/news/nichols-kaster-pllp-files-a-class-action-lawsuit-against-capital-one-on-behalf-of-employee-for-its-unauthorized-and-improper-use-of-consumer-reports/.

The lawsuit demonstrates how violations of the FCRA can create large potential liability. Potential class members, including employees and prospective employees, may be entitled to statutory damages of up to $1,000 for each violation in the case of willful non-compliance. Class action lawsuits also create exposure for large awards of attorneys' fees and the potential exposure to punitive damages under the SafeCo case.

Source: www.prweb.com/releases/2011/12/prweb9039707.htm.

FCRA Class Action Lawsuit for Failure to Follow Legal Requirements

In *Reardon v Closetmaid Corp. 2011 WL 1628041 (W.D.Pa. 2011)*, it was alleged that an employer committed two violations of the FCRA:

✓ The employer disqualified job applicants on the basis of information from a consumer report without appropriate disclosure forms from the applicant, and
✓ After disqualifying the applicant, the employer failed to give the applicant a reasonable period of time to dispute the information contained in the report before refusing to hire that applicant. In other words, the class action suit alleged a violation of the "pre-adverse action" requirements whereby an applicant must be given a reasonable time to review and dispute the background check report before a final action is taken to deny employment.

The attorneys for the plaintiff sought statutory damages and punitive damages. The FCRA also provided for attorneys' fees.

The case revolved around the federal rules for "certifying" a class so a class action can proceed. A class action suit allows the claims of numerous potential plaintiffs to be heard in one legal case, rather than separate legal actions each person would have to bring. In its decision, the Court engaged in a preliminary analysis to determine if the case had merit. The Court noted at the current stage of the litigation, the plaintiff had stated a claim sufficient for certification of the case as a class action.

The court reviewed the fact the FCRA requires an employer obtain a disclosure on a standalone document separate from the employment application. The purpose is to make it clear to an applicant a background check may be obtained. In this case, the court noted there was no dispute the application form signed by the plaintiff was not a "standalone form" but was contained in the form with more than one disclosure and more than one release.

Furthermore, the Court noted that under the FCRA, an applicant is entitled to a notice of "pre-adverse action" before a decision to not offer a job is made final, so an applicant can dispute the report. The plaintiff contended an applicant is entitled to at least five business days, which was the time period an opinion letter from the FTC found to be reasonable. (See the Weisberg letter at: www.ftc.gov/os/statutes/fcra/weisberg.shtm). If a decision is made final, an applicant is entitled to a second letter that contains a notification of certain rights.

In this case, the evidence showed the first letter sent advising the applicant of derogatory information in her background check report was sent December 18, 2006. The second letter notifying her that she would not be hired was dated December 22, 2006, which was four days later.

The employer argued the FCRA was silent as to the amount of time needed between letters, and the FTC opinion letter is not legally binding. However, the court ruled that an FTC opinion letter is entitled to "respect" and was sufficient at that point in the litigation to allow the plaintiff to state a claim the FCRA was violated. The Court found that although five days may not be required as a matter of law, it was the jury's decision whether or not the plaintiff was given reasonable time to dispute the information in the report.

Class Action Case Shows Importance of Background Screening Firms Following FCRA Accuracy Requirements when Reporting Sexual Offender Data

According to a civil complaint for damages, a background screening firm allegedly reported sexual offender data on applicants based solely upon a name match only, without making any effort whatsoever to confirm if the data belonged to the applicant. The suit alleged that such a practice violated the rule contained in FCRA section 607(b) that a screening firm must take reasonable procedure to assure maximum possible accuracy. (*Samuel M. Jackson v. Infotrack Information Services, No. 1:11-cv-5801, (N.D.Il. 2011)*).

In addition, the class action suit contended the screening firm "also reported public record information to employers without informing consumers that such information was being reported and without maintaining strict procedures to assure that the public information that it reported was complete and up to date" as required by FCRA section 613.

In this case, the lead plaintiff had a common name, and the screening firm reported seven possible sexual offender matches relating to three individuals with the same name. The first possible match was convicted when the plaintiff was four years old, had a different date of birth, and was of a different race. The second possible match belonged to a 66 year old person of a different race sentenced to life in prison also with a different date of birth. The third individual was also another race and had a different date of birth. The plaintiff contended he never lived in any of the states where the matches were reported and was not a sexual offender.

Based upon his allegations, it appears matching the records to the plaintiff would have demonstrated the sexual offender record did not belong to the plaintiff.

According to the case filed, when contacted by the plaintiff, the background screening firm advised him that the screening firm had a practice of routinely reporting all sexual offender matches based upon first and last name while making no effort to determine if the matter was applicable to a candidate. The suit contended the background screening firm told the lead plaintiff their practice often leads to problems. The suit alleged a background screening firm can use other information to insure accuracy, such a date of birth.

As a result, the suit alleged the background screening firm "creates and distributes grossly and obviously inaccurate consumer reports to employers by including sex offender information in its consumer reports without making sure that some aspect of the consumer's unique personal identifying information – such as a date of birth, middle initial, social security number, or even race information – matches its reported sex offender information."

The lawsuit alleged the background screening firm acted in reckless disregard of its duties and is seeking punitive damages on behalf of the class of individuals who have been wrongly identified as sex offenders by the screening firm as well as attorney's fees. Class action cases can create substantial exposure for defendants.

At the time this book went to print, only a complaint has been filed, which is merely an allegation, and no response has been filed or has there been any judicial determination made as to the accuracy of the allegations.

However, the seriousness of the allegations, if true, underscores the differences between professional background screening firms and mere data vendors. An accredited professional background screening firm would not report a person was possibly a sexual offender without taking appropriate steps per the FCRA to evaluate the data's accuracy.

FTC Fines Data Broker $800,000 Dollars to Settle Charges of Violating FCRA

In the first Federal Trade Commission (FTC) case to address the sale of Internet and social media data in the employment screening context, Spokeo, Inc. – a data broker that compiles and sells detailed information profiles on millions of consumers – agreed in June 2012 to pay a $800,000 fine to settle FTC charges that the company marketed profiles to companies in the human resources, background screening, and recruiting industries without taking steps to protect consumers required under the Fair Credit Reporting Act (FCRA).

The FTC charged that Spokeo operated as a Consumer Reporting Agency (CRA) and violated the FCRA by:

✓ Failing to make sure the information it sold would be used only for legally permissible purposes;
✓ Failing to ensure the information was accurate; and
✓ Failing to tell users of its consumer reports about their obligation under the FCRA, including the requirement to notify consumers if the user took an adverse action against the consumer based on information contained in the consumer report.

In addition to imposing the $800,000 civil penalty, the FTC's settlement order with Spokeo – which is available at www.ftc.gov/os/caselist/1023163/120612spokeoorder.pdf – bars the company from future violations of the FCRA.

According to the FTC:

> "Spokeo collects personal information about consumers from hundreds of online and offline data sources, including social networks. It merges the data to create detailed personal profiles of consumers. The profiles contain such information as name, address, age range, and email address. They also might include hobbies, ethnicity, religion, participation on social networking sites, and photos."

The FTC alleged that:

> "Spokeo marketed the profiles on a subscription basis to human resources professionals, job recruiters, and others as an employment screening tool. The company encouraged recruiters to "Explore Beyond the Resume." It ran online advertisements with taglines to attract employers, and created a special portion of the Spokeo website for recruiters. It created and posted endorsements of its services, representing those endorsements as those of consumers or other businesses."

More information about *The United States of America (For the Federal Trade Commission), Plaintiff, v. Spokeo, Inc., Defendant (United States District Court for the Central District of California) Case No. CV12-05001 FTC File No. 1023163* is available at: www.ftc.gov/os/caselist/1023163/index.shtm.

Source: www.ftc.gov/opa/2012/06/spokeo.shtm.

Background Screening Company to Pay $2.6 Million Penalty to Settle FTC Charges of Multiple FCRA Violations

Not only can a screening firm be sued, but federal regulators can also take action. In August 2012, a leading employment background screening firm that provides consumer reports to employers, without admitting any wrongdoing, agreed to pay a $2.6 million penalty to settle Federal Trade Commission (FTC) charges that it violated the Fair Credit Reporting Act (FCRA) multiple times. The case represented the first time the FTC charged an "employment" background screening company with violating the FCRA. The FTC charged the company violated the FCRA as required by law by failing to use reasonable procedures to assure the maximum possible accuracy of information it provided, failing to give consumers copies of their reports, and failing to reinvestigate consumer disputes. In addition to the $2.6 million civil penalty, the settlement also prohibits the company from continuing its alleged illegal practices. See: www.ftc.gov/opa/2012/08/hireright.shtm.

Class Actions Under the Fair Credit Reporting Act

By Craig Bertschi, Kilpatrick Townsend & Stockton LLP

Among the many threats facing the background screening industry today, one of the most serious is class action lawsuits. Over the last five years, there has been a dramatic increase in the number of class action lawsuits filed against background screening companies asserting claims under the Fair Credit Reporting Act ("FCRA"). Some of these suits have produced enormous, eight figure settlements and correspondingly rich awards of attorneys fees. These big settlements have incentivized plaintiffs and their lawyers to bring more lawsuits, perpetuating the cycle.

What is a class action lawsuit?

Although most people have heard of class action lawsuits, through the media or perhaps as a result of receiving a "class notice" in the mail, few people have more than rudimentary understanding of class action litigation. A class action is a lawsuit by proxy in which a single plaintiff or group of plaintiffs brings a lawsuit on their own behalf and on behalf of all other people who have suffered the same harm, e.g. smokers, people exposed to asbestos, purchasers of a particular model of car with defective brakes, etc. For a case to proceed as a class action, it is essential that the claims of the members of the class be similar, based on the same facts and legal theories and not dependent upon individualized proof. If the plaintiffs bringing the suit can convince a judge to "certify" a class, which means to allow the case to proceed as a class action, then the plaintiffs serve as "class representatives" and litigate the case on behalf of themselves and everyone in the class. The absent class members do not actively participate in the litigation; however, they do share in the proceeds of any judgment or settlement obtained in the case. Many times, the recovery for absent members of the class is trivial in comparison to the attorneys fees awarded to the attorneys representing the class, which has resulted in public skepticism about and justified criticism of these lawsuits.

Class actions under the FCRA

For plaintiffs' lawyers and their clients, the FCRA is a particularly attractive statute under which to bring a class action. This is true for many reasons.

First, background screeners and their clients, typically employers, tend to follow standardized procedures with respect to the creation and use of consumer reports. The same disclosure and authorization forms are given to all job applicants. Employers' pre- and post-adverse action procedures are usually set forth in a written policy that is followed each time a consumer report with negative or disqualifying information is obtained. And, background screeners generally follow standard procedures when compiling consumer reports, responding to consumer requests for disclosures and otherwise complying with their obligations under the FCRA. Because of this uniformity, it is often easy for plaintiffs to show that there are no (or few) individualized issues of fact and that litigating the case as a class action is appropriate. See Federal Rule of Civil Procedure 23(b)(3).

Second, the FCRA allows for the recovery of "statutory" damages upon proof of a willful violation of the statute. Under the FCRA, the damages that a plaintiff can recover depends upon whether the defendant has negligently or willfully violated some provision to the statute. For plaintiffs alleging a negligent violation under the statute, the only damages recoverable are "actual damages," which requires the plaintiff to prove that he actually suffered some injury as a result of the defendant's violation of the statute. 15 U.S.C. § 1681o. However, if the plaintiff is able to demonstrate that the defendant willfully violated the FCRA, then the plaintiff is entitled to recover statutory damages ranging from $100 to $1000 per violation. 15 U.S.C. § 1681n. And, the plaintiff does not have to prove that he was injured in any way as a result of the defendant's willful violation of the statute, but can recover statutory damages for mere technical violations of the FCRA. In the context of a class action, plaintiffs typically allege that the defendant has willfully violated the FCRA in order to avoid having to present evidence on the actual damages suffered by each individual member of the class. As the reasoning goes, individualized proof of damages is unnecessary if a willful violation is proven, and each member of the class is entitled to $100 to $1000, even if they have not been harmed by the defendant's alleged violation of the statute.

Of course, proving that the defendant willfully, as opposed to negligently, violated the FCRA is not a simple matter. While the plaintiff is not required to prove that the defendant had a subjective intent to violate the statute, he must nevertheless prove that the defendant either knew or should have known that its actions violated the FCRA. Put differently, the plaintiff must demonstrate that the defendant's interpretation of its obligations under the Statute and corresponding actions were "objectively unreasonable." *Safeco Ins. Co. of America v. Burr*, 551 U.S. 47 (2007). This is a high standard indeed and precludes a finding of willfulness when the plaintiff asserts novel claims under the FCRA.

Third, the FCRA does not contain a cap on the amount of damages that can be recovered by a plaintiff in a class action lawsuit. Other consumer protection statutes, like the Truth and Lending Act and the Fair Debt Collection Practices Act contain statutory damages caps. For example, under the Truth and Lending Act, plaintiffs can recover a maximum of $500 or 1% of a defendant's net worth, whichever is less. The same is true under the Fair Debt Collection Practices Act. Unfortunately, the Fair Credit Reporting Act does not contain a similar limitation on damages. Thus, from a plaintiff's perspective, "the sky is the limit."

Fourth, the Fair Credit Reporting Act expressly authorizes counsel for a prevailing plaintiff to recover attorneys' fees. 15 U.S.C. § 1681n and 1681o. In class actions, courts typically award attorneys fees ranging from 20 to 33% of the size of the amount paid by the defendant in settlement of a case. Thus, in the case of one of the larger, eight-figure settlements, attorneys' fees could be millions of dollars. Even in smaller cases, class counsel could recover hundreds of thousands of dollars in attorneys' fees.

Conclusion

In summary, FCRA lawsuits, when brought as class actions, are a particularly potent and lucrative tool for plaintiffs and their counsel. Background screening companies are well advised to insure that their procedures comply with the FCRA in order to minimize the risk that they become the next defendant in one of these suits.

Does the FCRA Apply to Employers Who Perform Background Checks In-House?

Employers with an in-house security department may decide to avoid the requirements of the FCRA by conducting their own investigations. On its face, the FCRA only applies to third parties and not in-house resources. With that in mind, many employers believe that if internal security or Human Resources perform the background checks, the FCRA mandates are not applicable. Unfortunately, these employers may still find their actions inadvertently trigger the FCRA compliance rules.

For example, suppose an in-house security department hires a court retrieval service or an investigator merely to go to a courthouse to pull criminal records. According to an opinion letter by the FTC legal staff (See the Slyter letter dated June

12, 1998, available at www.ftc.gov/os/statutes/fcra/slyter.htm), some court researching firms and private investigators can, in fact, be Consumer Reporting Agencies. If an employer happens to select a court researcher to obtain records who happens to qualify as a Consumer Reporting Agency, then what the employer thought was an in-house report suddenly turns into a Consumer Report. At this point, even though the investigation started out as an internal security procedure, hiring a consumer reporting agency can mean that all FCRA rules apply. This includes the need for written consent and disclosure and adverse action letters. Starting an in-house investigation without FCRA consent turns into an FCRA covered investigation.

Similarly, an employer who directly accesses an online database to obtain information about an applicant may also invoke the FCRA. In general, there are two types of databases an employer may access. If an employer accesses a public records database maintained by courts or other public entities, then the employer is not going through a third party, and the FCRA is probably not invoked (although additionally there may be state laws that apply). However, if an employer utilizes a commercial database service, such as an online "background check" that compiles public records, then the employer is performing a background check covered by the FCRA and the FCRA rules apply. An example is an online criminal record service that compiles millions of criminal records from public sources. The FCRA comes into play in this situation because an employer is accessing information assembled by third parties that bears upon an individual's character, general reputation personal characteristics, or mode of living as defined in the FCRA. In addition, some online commercial databases do not permit their data to be used for any FCRA-covered purpose, such as employment. These databases require a user to agree that the information can only be used as a source of "lead-generation" to conduct further investigation, such as going to the courthouse to confirm a criminal conviction. More information about the use of these databases is contained in Chapter 12.

The best advice for private employers who do in-house screening is: **Act as though the FCRA applies!**

Conducting Internal Background Checks

A policy least likely to trigger the FCRA is for an internal security department to only obtain records that any member of the general public can obtain and only to use their own internal employees to obtain the records. An example of the latter is a company sending its own employees to a courthouse to obtain criminal records.

Additionally, if the employer operates per the FCRA, the applicant would have the right to first review the report before any decision is finalized and to clarify any mistakes. If corporate security does not follow the FCRA, and the applicant is erroneously denied employment without a pre-adverse action letter and the opportunity to be heard, then the employer could be held liable for illegal employment practices if the rejected applicant pursues legal recourse.

When considering whether to conduct internal investigations, companies must also consider pertinent state laws. There are two sets of laws any employer must consider. The first set is the myriad of labor laws that apply to all information obtained by employers, regardless of who obtains it. Examples are the discrimination rules discussed in Chapter 2. The second set of laws to consider is state FCRA-type laws. If an employer accidentally triggers the federal FCRA, the employer may be sued under state law as well.

In addition, there is a new trend aimed at applying FCRA-type protections to applicants who are screened in-house. Many privacy advocates consider the fact that internal investigations are not regulated as a loophole in the FCRA. Here is the issue: Suppose an employer utilizes a screening firm and operates under the FCRA. If negative information is found, the applicant has a right to receive an adverse action letter and has the opportunity to review and respond before the action is made final. However, if an employer conducts the investigation, the employer does not have to follow the FCRA procedures – including the adverse action sections – since the FCRA only applies to outside agencies. An employer can simply deny employment and never tell the applicant. But there have been documented cases of employers getting the information wrong or there were errors in the public records, and the applicant never knew why they did not get the job.

The Story of Mr. Lewis

In a lawsuit filed by Scott Lewis in the Southern District of Ohio, Mr. Lewis alleged he suddenly lost his current job and had severe difficulty getting a new job. He could not figure out why suddenly no one wanted to talk to him. He reported on one occasion he called the employer back after believing he had a good interview and was told he was an unsavory character and if he contacted the employer again the employer would contact the police.

According to the case allegations:

> "Plaintiff states that, after months of searching for employment with no success, he engaged a private investigator to determine the reason for his repeated rejections. The investigator conducted a criminal background check on Plaintiff, which, according to Lewis, produced a record consisting of various felony convictions, including a 1996 murder conviction, all of which properly belong to Timothy Lockhart. Plaintiff contends that whomever entered Mr. Lockhart's arrest data entered the last four digits of his telephone number as the last four digits of his social security number. This error resulted in Mr. Lockhart's information being entered under Plaintiff's social security number. Thus, any third party who did a search using Plaintiff's social security number would retrieve Mr. Lockhart's criminal history."

> *— Lewis v. Ohio Professional Electronic Network LLC, 190 F.Supp.2d 1049, 1054 (S.D.Ohio 2002).*

The problem, according to Mr. Lewis, was private employers accessed a private database in Ohio and obtained information about applicants. If the information was erroneous, as it was in this situation, the applicant would never know because private employers had no FCRA duty to give the applicant a copy of the report or a chance to explain.

Essentially, a person could be "blackballed" and never know it.

Partly in response to the facts in the Lewis matter, **California** passed the nation's first law that attempted to regulate in-house employer investigations. Effective in 2002, the law required that information about public records obtained by an employer, even without the use of an outside agency, must be provided to an applicant, unless that applicant waived the right. California employers are required to follow a series of steps when they do an in-house investigation that gives FCRA type protection, including adverse action notices if public record is obtained and used adversely. *Cal. Civ. Code § 1786.53.*

AUTHOR TIP | **Beware Of Online Websites That Will Get You The Dirt On Anyone!**

Most internet search engines will reveal a number of websites offering to sell all sorts of data about anyone, and "do-it-yourself background checks" are a popular subject for spam email. Some of these sites advertise they have billions of records on Americans — all it takes is a credit card and supposedly anyone can find out anything about anyone. Putting aside the significant privacy issues, there is one important piece of advice for employers: ***Do not use these sites for employment unless you really know what you are doing***. Since the use of these sites is likely to fall under the FCRA if used for employment, an employer needs to proceed with caution. A clue is these sites either do not even mention the FCRA or mention it only briefly in passing. In a Safe Hiring Program, an employer needs to work one-to-one with a professional with an understanding of the FCRA. These do-it-yourself sites typically have no one to talk with who can give employers the professional assistance needed. An additional problem with these sites is employers may not know the source, accuracy, or integrity of the data. If an employer does an online criminal search, an employer may be getting a questionable "database search," which is subject to the limitations and issues discussed in Chapter 15.

Conclusion — online websites may be helpful for limited purposes, but employers need to proceed with extreme caution when using them.

Sources of Information about the FCRA

✓ "Forty Years of Experience with the Fair Credit Reporting Act: An FTC Staff Report and Summary of Interpretations" - The Federal Trade Commission (FTC) issued a staff report in July 2011 that compiles and updates the agency's guidance on the Fair Credit Reporting Act (FCRA), the 1970 law designed to protect the privacy of credit report information and ensure that the information supplied by credit reporting agencies (CRAs) is as accurate as possible. To see the report, visit http://ftc.gov/os/2011/07/110720fcrareport.pdf.

✓ The FTC's home page for the FCRA is at www.ftc.gov/os/statutes/fcrajump.shtm. The text of the FCRA is available online at www.ftc.gov/os/statutes/031224fcra.pdf.

✓ Following the 1997 amendments, the FTC staff wrote letters in response to questions that were published online. The staff letters are online. These letters do not carry the force of law, but they are persuasive. They may eventually form the basis of any commentary published by the FTC; See Cast letter, October 27, 1997, See www.ftc.gov/os/statutes/fcra/index.htm. These letters have been summarized by the author. See: www.backgroundchecktraining.com/file/FTC%20Staff%20Opinion%20letters%20summary%20by%20LSR.html#Section615

✓ Commentary for FCRA prior to amendments effective 1997 can be found in 16 CFR Ch. 1 (1-1-97 edition). Future FTC commentaries on the FCRA are likely.

✓ See resources listed at: www.esrcheck.com/services/research.php.

✓ FCRA required documents are also found on the FTC website and in the Appendix. These are:

- General Summary of Consumer Rights
- Notice of Furnisher Responsibilities
- Notice of User Responsibilities

✓ The Consumer Financial Protection Bureau (CFPB) web page 'Consumer Laws and Regulations: Fair Credit Reporting Act (FCRA)' at: www.consumerfinance.gov/guidance/supervision/manual/fcra-narrative.

✓ The Background Check Training and Education website at: www.backgroundchecktraining.com.

Chapter 4

State Laws for Background Checks

A number of states have their own rules and laws for regulating the background reports performed by Consumer Reporting Agencies.

Inside This Chapter:

- ✓ State Laws Controlling CRA Activities

- ✓ States That Restrict the Reporting of Records Based on Time Periods

- ✓ Background Checks in All Fifty States – Which State Law Applies?

- ✓ "Only in California" and other State Laws for Screening

- ✓ New York Rules

- ✓ Massachusetts Criminal Offender Record Information (CORI) Reform Law

- ✓ Other Special State Laws

State Laws Controlling CRA Activities

Along with the federal Fair Credit Reporting Act (FCRA), a number of states have their own rules and laws for regulating the background reports performed by Consumer Reporting Agencies (CRAs). It is important for employers to outsource their screening to a vendor who is fully familiar with the applicable state laws.

There may be situations where a CRA can legally report a criminal matter, but a specific state rule limits the employer's use of that same information. For example, under the FCRA and under many state laws, a CRA may report an arrest not resulting in a conviction. However, the employer may be under some separate state limitation on how the arrest is utilized. An employer needs to be aware there are potentially separate state rules that control what a CRA can transmit to an employer and separate state rules that control how the employer can use the information.

Subtle FCRA and State Law Differences

Differences between the FCRA and state laws can be very subtle. Here are examples:

- ✓ In **New Jersey**, a CRA must not only notify a consumer within five days that a dispute is considered frivolous (which is similar to FCRA 611) but must also state reasons why. *NJSA §56:11-36.*
- ✓ In **New York**, if an item of information is corrected or can no longer be verified, an agency must mail a corrected copy of the consumer's report to the consumer at no charge. A mailing is not required under FCRA § 611. *N.Y. Gen. Bus. Law § 380-f.*
- ✓ In **Massachusetts**, the final adverse action letter must be in minimum 10 point type, sent within 10 days, with specified language. *Mass. Gen. Laws ch. 93, §62.*
- ✓ In **Texas**, a CRA must mail a corrected copy to everyone who requested a consumer report in the past six months. *Tex. Bus. & Com. Code Ann. §20.06.*
- ✓ **California**, **Minnesota**, and **Oklahoma** have a "check the box" requirement where an applicant can check a box and is entitled to a copy of the report. *Cal. Civ. Code § 1785.20.5; Minn. Stat. § 13C.02; Okla. Stat. Ann. Tit. 24, § 148.* In addition, California has two other possible boxes to check — one for credit reports and one for employers who do their own background reports. See the section "Only in California" in later in this chapter.

 Some U.S. States have Stricter Background Check Rules than Others

At least twenty states arguably have stricter state FCRA rules. The twenty states are: Arizona, California, Colorado, Georgia, Kansas, Kentucky, Louisiana, Maine, Maryland, Massachusetts, Minnesota, Montana, New Jersey, New Hampshire, New Mexico, New York, Oklahoma, Rhode Island, Texas, and Washington. Also, state laws affecting background screening can change at any time.

Examples of Different State Rules

The following list of states and state rules are not intended to be a comprehensive or definitive statement of current state laws. These examples are only illustrations of some of the differences found in some states. Of course, this list is subject to change without notice due to legislative action in a state.

- ✓ Special rules concerning the notice and initial disclosure— **CA, MA, MN, NY, OK**.
- ✓ Rules for notice of Investigative Consumer Report (ICR) to consumers— **CA, ME, MA, MN, NJ, NY**.
- ✓ Rules for the Nature and Scope letter that is given to a consumer if they request more information about an ICR— **ME, NY**.
- ✓ Special rules for pre-adverse action and post-adverse action letters— **GA, KS, LA, ME, MD, MA, MN, MT, NH, RI, WA**.

✓ Right of applicant to know if report is requested— **ME, NY**.

✓ Disclosures to consumer by agency— **AZ, CA, CO, GA, ME, MD, NJ, RI**.

✓ Disputed accuracy rules— **AZ, CO, MA, ME, MD, NJ, NY, RI, TX**.

✓ Rules on timing of notice for ICR— **CA, ME, MA, MN, NJ, NY**.

✓ States that have separate rules just for credit reports where there is some complication about how and if the rules also apply to pre-employment reports— **CA, NM, NV, RI**

✓ States that have laws regulating the use of credit report checks of job applicants and current employees by employers for employment purposes—**CA, CT, HI, IL, MD, OR, VT, WA**.

✓ States that prohibit the CRA from utilizing arrests not resulting in convictions. This is a separate set of rules where the CRA itself is under a state mandate (as opposed to employers being under the mandate). Examples include **KY, NM, NY**.

✓ States that limit the use of arrest records not resulting in a convictions by employers—**AK, CA, CO, CT, GA, HI, ID, IL, KY, MA, ME, MI, MN, MS, MT, NV, NY, OH, OR, PA, RI, TX, UT, VA, WA, WV, WI.**

✓ States that have a seven-year limitation on reporting criminal convictions and impose that state law directly on a Consumer Reporting Agency. Even though the federal FCRA was amended in 1998 to do away with the seven-year limitation on reporting criminal convictions, some states still have a version of a seven-year limitation law—**CA, CO, KS, MD, MA, MT, NH, NM, NV, NY, TX, WA.**

AUTHOR TIP **How Does an Employer or Background Screening Firm Possibly Keep Up to Date on All 50 States?**

One answer is CRAHelpDesk.com. CRAHelpDesk.com is a resource for consumer reporting agencies and hiring managers. The State Rules Register product explains in detail the states' laws as well as restrictions placed over and above the FCRA. The State Rules Register describes state FCRA-type laws that affect Consumer Reporting Agencies (CRAs) and hiring managers:

1. Which public records can be reported by Consumer Reporting Agencies.

2. What restrictions are placed by states on the use of record information by employers and hiring managers.

3. The special state forms and specific, required wording that must be used on CRA or employer.

See www.crahelpdesk.com/home.aspx

States That Restrict the Reporting of Records Based on Time Periods

According to Derek Hinton and Larry Henry (from *The Criminal Records Manual 3rd Edition*, published in 2008 by Facts on Demand Press):

> "There is a big difference in a state law that restricts the use of a criminal record by employers and a state law that restricts what a vendor, i.e., consumer reporting agency, CRA, can report. Several states restrict what a vendor can report, i.e., they have different limitations than the federal FCRA based on time periods. However, there are many exceptions and many of the states are changing their laws to mirror the federal guidelines.

> States that still restricted vendor reporting of criminal conviction information to seven years are California, Colorado, Kansas, Maryland, Massachusetts, Montana, New Hampshire, New Mexico, New York, Texas, and Washington.

However, Kansas, Maryland Massachusetts, New Hampshire, and Washington waive the time limit if the applicant is reasonably expected to make $20,000 or more annually. In New York, the exception is $25,000. In Colorado and Texas, the figure is $75,000. Further, since Colorado and Texas enacted their FCRA analog statutes after September 30, 1996, they are arguably preempted by the FCRA 15 U.S.C. §1681t(b)(1)(E). California removed its $75,000 salary cap after September 30, 1996, and as such, at least that portion of the law is arguably preempted. An interesting argument could be made that the entire statute is preempted since it was amended after the cutoff date."

These facts leave employers with two immediate problems:

1. First, it is harder to create a workable national rule when some states have their own state-imposed limitation. So there is no issue in determining applicable state law, as a matter of practical convenience some screening firms simply adopt the seven-year rule nationwide. This has some logic since cases older than seven years could potentially be stale under EEOC standards. However, it can also lead to serious cases not being reported in states with no seven-year rule, and it can lead to situations where a CRA is aware that an applicant has a criminal conviction, but by law must keep it under wraps and sit on potentially important information.

2. The second problem is the question "When does the seven years begin?" The general rule is the seven years begins to run from the date the consumer is free of physical custody, regardless of whether the person was on parole or probation. However, if the consumer violates probation or parole and went back into custody even for one day, the clock would arguably start to run all over again. See the 'When Does the Seven Year Limit Begin?' section below.

The following examples are some further complexities associated with the seven-year rule imposed by states:

✓ It is arguable that some of these seven-year restrictions are not enforceable because they are "pre-empted" by the FCRA, meaning that the federal rules override the state limitations. However, that depends upon a complicated analysis of both federal and state law, as described later in this chapter. State laws cannot be ignored, especially if a state court has yet to acknowledge that a state rule has been pre-empted. On the other hand, if an analysis of the FCRA clearly shows a state law is pre-empted, an employer clearly cannot violate the FCRA either.

✓ The lack of a national rule when it comes to the seven-year rule also creates potential confusion when more than one state is involved. This confusion can occur if the applicant, the employer, the screening firm, or the job location are physically located in different states, and one of them has a seven-year rule.

✓ The state of Nevada also has a seven-year restriction but appears to only apply to a report issued for credit purposes and not employment. Nev. Rev. Stat. § 598C.150 does seem to apply to employment when read with Nev. Rev. Stat § 598C.060.

Expert Tip by FCRA Attorney Larry Henry: Nevada's Unique Seven Year Rule

According to noted FCRA authority Attorney Larry Henry of Rhodes Hieronymus, Nevada's statute is unique. First, it appears that a Consumer Report under Nevada law only applies to consumer reports that deal with: payment history, credit worthiness, credit standing, or credit history. (See NRS 589C.060.) CRAs are defined as those companies supplying consumer reports as defined above. (See NRS 589C.100.) Thus a CRA that does not supply credit reports is not a CRA in Nevada and it has no restrictions.

If a screening company does provide credit reports in Nevada and is a CRA under their statute, but the report does not relate to any of the credit related factors listed above, then arguably the seven year limitation on criminal records does not apply. Attorney Henry notes that the definitional language restricts the Nevada law to credit related matters only. They have no law covering non-credit types of consumer reports. He sees no cases in Nevada interpreting this statute. Obviously, the reference to the reporting of criminal records is a bit odd in a statute dealing with credit reports, but credit related reports can contain criminal information as well. The logical conclusion is if a CRA never provides a credit report in Nevada, the Nevada seven year rule does not apply.

However, once a CRA provides a Nevada credit report, then the seven year limitation may apply to all reports. This is a good example of how complex issues surrounding background reports can become and how background checks are no longer just about providing data but are an area subject to extensive legal regulation. Also keep in mind that Nevada takes the position that background checks are covered by the Nevada Private Investigator licensing laws, and that any CRA doing business in Nevada must have a valid P.I. license.

- ✓ The seven-year rule applies to what a background screening firm can report. This rule does not apply to employers who do their own criminal checks in-house.
- ✓ However, even an employer who does their own search in-house must still be aware if they utilize records older than seven years, they need to consider the EEOC implications. See Chapter 14 for a discussion of how the EEOC affects the use of older criminal records.
- ✓ If an employer does their own search to avoid the seven-year rule, the employer must be careful to use the same time period for all similarly situated applicants so no applicant can claim disparate treatment.
- ✓ An employer who does their own search in-house must be cautious about utilizing any outside researchers since that can trigger the application of the FCRA or state law versions of the FCRA. See the section 'Conducting Internal Investigations' on how an internal investigation can inadvertently trigger the FCRA.

When Does the Seven Year Limit Begin?

An ongoing question for employers, screening firms, and criminal record search firms is "When does the seven years begin?" The Federal Trade Commission published commentaries to the FCRA which are contained in the Code of Federal Regulations. The FTC commentaries are intended to be interpretations of the law and clarify how the FTC will construe the FCRA in light of congressional intent as reflected in the statute and legislative history. According to page 514 of the commentary, the reporting time period is calculated as follows: (NOTE: The Federal Trade Commission ("FTC" or "Commission") is rescinding its Statements of General Policy or Interpretations Under the Fair Credit Reporting Act ("FCRA"). Recent legislation transferred authority to issue interpretive guidance under the FCRA to the Consumer Financial Protection Bureau ("CFPB")). Effective Date: July 26, 2011:

> *The seven-year reporting period runs from the date of disposition, release or parole, as applicable. For example, if charges are dismissed at or before trial, or the consumer is acquitted, the date of such dismissal or acquittal is the date of disposition. If the consumer is convicted of a crime and sentenced to confinement, the date of release or placement on parole controls. (Confinement, whether continuing or resulting from revocation of parole, may be reported until seven years after the confinement is terminated.) The sentencing date controls for a convicted consumer whose sentence does not include confinement. The fact that information concerning the arrest, indictment, or conviction of crime is obtained by the reporting agency at a later date from a more recent source such as a newspaper or interview does not serve to extend this reporting period.*

(Source: Section 605(a)(5) of the FDIC Laws and Regulations www.fdic.gov/regulations/laws/rules/6500-2750.html).

The logical conclusion is the FCRA intends to not count as part of the seven years rule any time not spent in confinement. The seven years starts when a person is out of custody, even though he or she may still be on parole or probation.

However, nothing is as easy as it may seem. The difficulty is a court record will only indicate the date the sentence was imposed by the court and the length of the sentence. It is not always possible to tell from the docket or court record when the confinement actually ended since the release date from custody is often NOT contained in a public file. The date is actually contained in files maintained by the county jail or probation office for a county sentence or by the state Department of Corrections for a state prison sentence. Information from these offices is not easily accessible without a subpoena.

When a person is sentenced, the Court will indicate any credit the person will receive for time already served, such as time in custody awaiting trial if the person was not able to make bail. That would be part of the public record. With that information, a background firm may have a slightly better idea of when the person got out custody, but still, without knowing how much the sentence was reduced in jail or prison for "good time" or for some other factor, the actual get out of jail date is not a public record. In addition, a person may be released from physical custody when their sentence is coming to an end and placed in a half-way or re-entry house. However, in that situation, a person is still typically considered to be "in custody" and not released.

Also, criminal record reporting is not based upon simply counting back seven years. Assume a screening firm did a background check in California in 2012. California has a seven-year rule. Suppose the court docket shows the applicant was convicted of a serious crime in 2003, which is beyond the seven years, but received a 3-year prison sentence so that according to the sentence, the applicant would have likely been in custody during a portion of the past seven years. Under the FCRA, the criminal conviction is reportable because there is no limit on reporting convictions (although the EEOC rules may apply*). Is it reportable in a state such as California that has a seven-year reporting limit?* Based upon the sentence imposed, the consumer's sentence would have apparently gone into the seven-year period and is reportable. However, since custody information is generally not public record, in some situations, the date of release is both unknown and unattainable to an employer or CRA.

The background check firm is in a "Catch-22." If a background check agency did not report that, and the applicant was hired and re-offended on the job or harmed the public, the background check agency would have exposure to fault. If the background check firm reports it, there is a possibility the person was out of custody early and did not go within the seven years. Most CRA's, if they are concerned about the issues involved with legal compliance, will take the position that a determination must be made on the publicly available information, and assumptions cannot be made either way about early releases.

What happens if the person was released and was out of custody for seven years but was still on parole or probation? If the person was arrested for violation of parole or probation and spent any time in jail because of that fact, the better view is the seven year clock is reset and starts over again. The reason? The person was in custody for the offense with the seven years due to a parole or probation violation.

This demonstrates that even in states with a seven year limit, a CRA must go back further than seven years, since a case is still reportable that is older than seven years if a person was incarcerated during the past seven years due to the case. And a CRA cannot assume an older case is not reportable without further research since a case older than seven years is brought back into the seven years rule if a person is jailed for having violated probation or parole within the seven year period. The seven years starts over again.

The lesson—a screening firm or court researcher should not limit their research to the past seven years since reportable older cases can be missed.

Background Checks in All Fifty States – Which State Law Applies?

A recurring issue for larger employers with facilities in multiple states is 50-state legal compliance. As seen above, the rules for pre-employment background screening have become Balkanized, meaning many states have their own rules and regulations. This is similar to the early days of the railroads—one state had one type of rail, and the next state had a different rail, so at state borders things usually came to a halt. Compliance does become challenging for large employers trying to exercise due diligence across state lines, but challenging is not the same as impossible. Compliance just requires a little more work.

FACT Act, Pre-emption & National Standards

As mentioned previously, in late 2003, President Bush signed the Fair and Accurate Credit Transaction (FACT) Act. The primary thrust of FACT was to extend the FCRA federal pre-emption of conflicting state laws in the area of consumer credit. Congress and the financial industry were concerned that the FCRA allowed states to begin passing their own laws in 2004, undermining a uniform national credit reporting system. The FACT Act prevented that. The FACT Act also increased identity theft protection, provided for free yearly credit reports, and changed the rules concerning investigation of current employees.

Although the FACT Act established that the FCRA takes priority over state laws in areas involving credit reporting, the inter-relationship between federal and state law is still complicated regarding employment issues.

FCRA section 625 (as amended in the 2003 FACT Act) provides that, in certain areas, state laws that exist prior to September 30, 1996 could prevail over the FCRA. Any state limit in effect on reporting criminal convictions prior to that date would be valid, although under federal FCRA rules, there is no limit on how far back a background firm can go on reporting a criminal conviction.

For example, California had a seven year limit in place prior to September 30, 1996 that did not allow criminal records to be reported beyond seven years unless the applicant made over $30,000 a year. That was changed in 1998 to $75,000 a year, and, in 2002, California changed that limit to place a prohibition on reporting any convictions older than seven years regardless of salary *(See Cal. Civ. Code § 1786.18)*. The California law contains an exception if the investigative consumer report is to be used by an employer who is explicitly required by a governmental regulatory agency to check for criminal convictions older than seven years when the employer is reviewing a consumer's qualification for employment *(See Cal. Civ. Code § 1786(b)(2))*. An argument can be made that by changing the law, any California limitation is now null and void and is pre-empted since the current law was not passed prior to September 30, 1996, and California now falls under the federal rules, which have no limit on reporting convictions. To date, no one has stepped forward as a guinea pig to test this theory. Similarly, Texas has a statute with a $75,000 limit that was effective September 1, 1997 that arguably has no force and effect under the FCRA *(See Tex. Bus. & Com. Code Ann. § 20.05)*. In addition, many authorities argue that the Colorado and Texas seven year rule has also been pre-empted by the federal FCRA.

The Forms Issue

A major issue for multi-state employers is which form to use. A 50-state form would be a challenge due to the number of states with their own rules. If a form is written to accommodate all of the various state rules, it may be so long and convoluted that one could argue such a form would be improper as it violates the FCRA mandate "a clear and conspicuous disclosure has been made in writing to the consumer at any time before the report is procured or caused to be procured, in a document that consists solely of the disclosure..." *(See FCRA § 604(b)(2)(A))*. Opinion letters issued by the Federal Trade Commission warn employers that a form may be improper if it is "encumbered by any other information... [in order] to prevent consumer from being distracted by other information side-by-side with the disclosure." (See the FTC Leathers letter at www.ftc.gov/os/statutes/fcra/leathers.shtm.)

The biggest source of complexity comes from the use of disclosure forms that include "investigative consumer report" language to enable employers to go beyond factual matters such as dates of employment and job title and to gather quantitative reference information, such as job performance. Since a number of states have complex rules that cover that, a 50-state form would present particularly difficult. If an employer is just seeking public records, there are not as many exceptions to cover.

Multi-state employers should work with CRA's that understand each of the separate state rules discussed above. This understanding should not only include forms but also the different rights afforded to applicants at different stages of the process, as outlined in the previous sections.

A new solution is to use online processes to ensure the proper disclosures are used in the appropriate circumstances. An applicant can be asked to fill in a form online and also indicate the state where they live and the state where the job is to be performed. Software can then automatically display the appropriate state specific disclosures or language through a software solution. See an example at www.esrcheck.com/ESR-Assured-Compliance.php.

Which State Law(s) to Follow

In order to give applicants all of their rights under state law, the next issue is which state's laws apply.

Assume that a California resident is applying for a job in Ohio with a firm that is owned by a company in New York, and a California screening firm does the background check. Both California and New York have a seven-year restriction on criminal records, but Ohio does not. Even though the applicant would likely move to Ohio if he gets the job, at the time of the search he is still a California resident. If the candidate has a criminal record in California older than seven years, can it be reported for a job in Ohio by a California screening firm? Can the candidate sue in California or New York for reporting a conviction that was too old under California and New York law even though it would be permissible under the laws of Ohio?

> **AUTHOR TIP**
>
> ### Rule of Thumb for Deciding which State's Screening Laws to Follow
>
> The employer should first consider *the law of the state where the employment is to occur*. However, an employer or screening firm needs to understand where a consumer can possibly sue them and consider the laws of that state. For example, an applicant may sue a prospective employer or screening firm based upon the state where they are living at the time of the background check. If the laws are contradictory, then a choice must be made as to the state that would most likely have jurisdiction over a lawsuit.

There are several issues to also consider when deciding which state's laws to follow:

✓ The first issue is **which claims can be brought in what court**. This is sometimes referred to as "subject matter jurisdiction." This can be a complex issue since there are two court systems in the U.S. — federal courts and state courts. A legal action for violations of the FCRA may be brought in federal court since FCRA § 618 provides for federal jurisdiction. However, a consumer cannot bring claims in a federal FCRA lawsuit in the nature of defamation, invasion of privacy, or negligence since those are pre-empted by FCRA section FCRA 610(e) except as to information furnished with malice or willful intent to injure. However, there are state claims that can be litigated in federal court, such as violation of a state's civil rights statutes. To get around federal limitations on certain claims, a plaintiff may attempt to bring an action solely under state law in state court. An employer or screening firm sued in state court under state law may argue the claim is still pre-empted under federal law and ask for removal to federal court. However, one federal district court in the Eastern District of Kentucky ruled in 2006 that FCRA Section 610(e) does NOT prevent a consumer from suing for a state court claim for defamation because FCRA Section 610(e) only provides immunity for disclosures required under law but does not give immunity where a consumer report is inaccurate. *Poore v. Sterling Testing Systems, Inc., 410 F.Supp.2d. 557 (E.D.Ky.2006).* This can have important implications for background screening firms.

✓ The second issue is **venue**. Venue means a place where an act or injury occurred. It is the proper place, or forum, for the lawsuit.

✓ The third issue is **jurisdiction**. Jurisdiction means the ability of the court to exercise power over a business or a person. Just because the applicant may have been injured in Ohio does not automatically mean an Ohio court has any power over the New York employer or the California based CRA. For the applicant to go into an Ohio court and to file a lawsuit, the Ohio court must have personal jurisdiction over the parties. *(NOTE: This is different from choice of law or Conflict of Law. In general terms, Conflict of Law means which law a court should apply in a lawsuit where the case has a relationship to more than one state. Factors include the place where injury occurred, place where conduct occurred that caused injury, the domicile of the parties, and where the relationship between the parties is centered. Jurisdiction refers to the power of the court to even exercise control over the parties to the lawsuit in the first place.)*

New York Case Gives Potential Guidance on Issue of Which State Law Applies for Reporting Criminal Records: The IMPACT Rule

An ongoing issue for employers and background screening firms is the question of which law applies when a criminal record found in one state impacts an employment decision in another state. Since state reporting laws can vary widely, employers and screening firms are sometimes left without clear guidance whether a criminal record can be reported or utilized because it is not clear which state law to apply.

A case from New York – *Hoffman v. Parade Publications,15 N.Y.3d 285 (2010).* – provides some potential guidance on the issue of which state law applies for reporting criminal records. In this case, a New York-based publisher made the decision to close down their offices in Atlanta and to terminate the Atlanta employee. The terminated employee serviced accounts in ten states in the south and southeast but did NOT service any accounts in New York. The terminated employee brought a legal action in state court in New York City on the basis of age discrimination in violation of both New York City and State of New York civil rights laws. The publisher defended on the basis there was not subject matter jurisdiction because the plaintiff did not live in New York and, other than attending corporate meetings in New York, had no connection to New York.

The trial court agreed and dismissed the case on the basis there was no impact in New York even though the decision was made there. The Appellate court disagreed and ruled that making the decision in New York was sufficient to invoke New York law, even for an out of state resident. New York's highest court, in a split 4-3 decision, reversed again holding there had to be an "impact" in New York to apply New York laws to an out of state plaintiff. In other words, a person from out of state cold not utilize the courts of New York to pursue a claim of a violation of rights just because the decision was made in New York if there was no impact within the state. The Court noted any other rule could result in inconsistent and arbitrary results. On the other hand, a requirement that there be an impact in the state is relatively simple to follow and leads to predictable rules.

Although the case does not address background screening and criminal records directly, the logic of the case is very instructive in situations where multiple states may be involved. By following an impact rule, screening firms and employers are able to implement predictable rules that do not depend upon the happenstance of which state a person committed a crime or where the person now lives but instead focuses the impact on where the employment incurs.

This case by no means settles the debate, but it does demonstrate the advantages to a logical approach to the multiple state issues. However, there can still be complicated scenarios depending upon where the job is to be performed, where the consumer is living when the background check was performed, and even possibly the location of the screening firm (which in this case was California).

The bottom line is professional background screening is far from merely being a data retrieval service but is a professional endeavor that is highly regulated and requires a knowledgeable safe hiring partner.

Long Arm Statute

The topic of jurisdiction fills numerous law books. One of the key concepts is called a Long Arm Statute which allows a state to have a long reach when it comes to exercising personal jurisdiction over people and businesses. States can assume broad jurisdiction based on such concepts as minimum contacts or systemic and continuous activity in a state. Another basis for a state court to obtain jurisdiction is when a business intends to conduct business in that state.

For employers, the issue is generally very simple—the firm can generally be sued in any state where it does business, which is very broadly defined. Similar rules apply to screening firms. A screening firm can be sued in any state where it does business. Legal cases suggest if a screening firm has an interactive website where the screening firm conducts background checks, then that firm is doing business in all fifty states for purposes of personal jurisdiction. Additionally, the screening firm can likely be sued in any state where it solicits business or has clients.

Understanding where a lawsuit can be brought is the key to choosing which state laws to apply. In the example above, the issue is whether a California court would likely exercise jurisdiction in a lawsuit against a California screening firm and a New York employer when the criminal record was appropriate to report under Ohio law but not under California law.

What does all this mean? As a general rule, firms that hire in more than one state should first consider the law of the state where the employment occurs. However, the employer should also consider if other states may be likely to allow a consumer to sue for a violation of their state law. This can include the state where the consumer resides, the state where the employer is located, or the state where the consumer reporting agency has its place of business.

The result, of course, is employers and screening firms are occasionally left to take their best "guess" about which laws to apply since there is not a clear national rule. In addition, employers can find themselves in the position of having to apply different rules to different applicants. Until Congress pre-empts the area with a clear national rule, this will remain a confusing area for employers.

The next section examines three states with unique state laws affecting employers and employment screening.

"Only in California" and other State Laws for Screening

There are a number of states with their own special set of rules for background checks. The following is an example of just three states: California, New York, and Massachusetts. A qualified screening firm should be able to guide an employer in all fifty states.

Background Checks in California: Compliance with a Whole Different Set of Rules than the Rest of the Country

You have heard it said before many times in both positive and negative ways: California is different. This fact rings true regarding background checks. California has unique rules for background checks that go beyond the other 49 states and the FCRA. California employers must follow these rules to the letter since applicants can sue for up to $10,000 for any violation arguable regardless of damages!

And California even added more critical screening rules effective January 1, 2012. Senate Bill 909 (SB 909) and Assembly Bill 22 (AB 22) changed how employers conduct background checks in the state. SB 909 relates to the "offshoring" of Personally Identifiable Information (PII) of consumers who are the subjects of background checks outside of the United States and beyond the protection of U.S. privacy laws. AB 22 regulates the use of credit report checks of job applicants and current employees by employers for employment purposes.

As covered in detail in Chapter 2, SB 909 requires a consumer must be notified before the background check, as part of a disclosure, of the Web address where that consumer "may find information about the investigative reporting agency's privacy practices, including whether the consumer's personal information will be sent outside the United States or its territories." SB 909 also requires background check firms to conspicuously post on its primary Web site a statement in their privacy policy entitled "Personal Information Disclosure: United States or Overseas" that indicates whether the personal information will be transferred to third parties outside the U.S. In the event consumers are harmed by a background check firm negligently sending data outside of the U.S., SB 909 provides for damages to consumers.

AB 22 prohibits employers or prospective employers – with the exception of certain financial institutions – from obtaining a consumer credit report for employment purposes unless the position of the person for whom the report is sought is specified under the law. In addition, AB 22 requires the written notice informing the person for whom a consumer credit report is sought for employment purposes to also inform that person of the specific reason for obtaining the report. With the passage of AB 22, California in now one of eight states to pass laws restricting credit report checks of job applicants and current employees by employers for employment purposes. The other seven states are: Connecticut, Hawaii, Illinois, Maryland, Oregon, Vermont and Washington. More information about credit reports is available in Chapter 17.

In addition to the new laws SB 909 and AB 22, California has many existing rules for background checks in the state. Employers must understand the California Investigative Consumer Reporting Agencies (ICRA) Act, CA Labor Code, and the Regulations for the California Department for Fair Employment and Housing Act (FEHA).

 California uses different terminology than the FCRA. For example, in California all background checks are called Investigative Consumer Reports (ICR), as opposed to the FCRA language that uses the terms "Consumer Reports" and "Investigative Consumer Reports."

Employers face substantial civil exposure up to $10,000 for failure to follow the special rules for background checks that include the following:

- ✓ Special CA check the box rule for free report (similar to MN and OK). *Cal. Civ. Code § 1785.20.5*
- ✓ Second checkbox if employer obtains public records directly.
- ✓ Special CA rules for the Consent and Disclosure including name, address, and phone of CRA and right to obtain additional information.
- ✓ Special language on first page of each report about accuracy.
- ✓ Consent before each ICR.
- ✓ Special additional statements of California specific rights on the authorization form.
- ✓ Special rule for employer certification; employer needs to certify additional matters above and beyond FCRA certifications.
- ✓ Spanish Language Form if applicant requests more information.
- ✓ Seven-year limit on criminal records (unless governmental requirement), but math is tricky.
- ✓ California is a "No Arrest" state (but a pending case can be reported).
- ✓ Limitation on reporting diversion programs or arrest (with exception for certain hospitals).
- ✓ Placing the background firm's privacy policy on the forms.

Despite all of the special rules mentioned above, "due diligence" through background checks is still mission critical for California employers. Employees are typically a firm's greatest investment and largest cost, and each hire also represents a large potential risk. Every employer has the obligation to exercise due diligence in hiring since an employer that hires someone it either knew – or should have known through reasonable screening – was dangerous, unfit, or unqualified for the work can be sued for negligent hiring. The bottom line: California employers must maintain compliance with a whole different set of rules than the rest of the country when conducting due diligence background checks.

One significant difference between California and the rest of the states is the limitation on the use of criminal records that have not been verified at the courthouse. Under the federal FCRA, a Consumer Reporting Agency (CRA) has two choices. Upon locating a criminal record, a CRA can either send a letter notice to the applicant at the same time the criminal record is reported to the employer, or it can "maintain strict procedures designed to insure that whenever public record information which is likely to have an adverse effect on a consumer's ability to obtain employment is reported it is complete and up to date." This most often comes up in a situation where a screening firm utilizes a database.

- ✓ California law has a prohibition on the letter notice to an applicant. California instead requires that:
     "b) A consumer reporting agency which furnishes a consumer report for employment purposes and which for that purpose compiles, collects, assembles, evaluates, reports, transmits, transfers, or communicates items of information on consumers which are matters of public record and are likely to have an adverse effect upon a consumer's ability to obtain employment shall in addition maintain strict procedures designed to insure that whenever public record information which is likely to have an adverse effect on a consumer's ability to obtain employment is reported it is complete and up to date. For purposes of this paragraph, items of public record relating to arrests, indictments, convictions, suits, tax

liens, and outstanding judgments shall be considered up to date if the current public record status of the item at the time of the report is reported." *(CA Civil Code Section 1786.28(b))*

✓ California also placed limits on "do-it-yourself" background checks by employers. If an employer does their own investigation of an applicant or current employee without using the services of a background screening provider and collects public records such as criminal records, there are new rules that are in effect. Any information must be turned over to the applicant/employee within seven days unless the employer suspects misconduct or wrongdoing, in which case supplying the information may only be delayed. In addition, an employer who uses this procedure must provide a form to all applicants/employees with a checkbox that, if checked, permits a person to waive the right to receive the copy of any public record. If the investigation results in an adverse action, there are additional employer requirements as well. This procedure is only in effect if an employer does its own investigation.

Mr. Lewis & California Legislation

Remember the story about Scott Lewis in Chapter 3? He was the unfortunate victim of an error in a vendor's database. Mr. Lewis could not get a job because prospective new employers would not let him respond to an adverse background check. The California legislation was, in part, spurred by the Scott Lewis story.

Megan's Law and Registered Sexual Offenders – An "Only in California" Twist

The use of the California Sexual Registration listing, commonly known as Megan's Law, is widespread among employers. However, there is a little known provision in California that may actually limit an employer's legal use of that information in some situations.

Megan's Law is a Federal Act (HR 2137) first passed in 1996. Originally, information on sex offenders that register under California Penal Code Section 290 was only available by personally visiting police stations and sheriff's offices or by calling a 900 number. Unconstitutional / Preempted by People v Ruffin Cal. App. 5 Dist (2011).

The website at www.meganslaw.ca.gov was established by the California Department of Justice pursuant to a 2004 California law for the purpose of allowing "the public for the first time to use their personal computers to view information on sex offenders required to register with local law enforcement under California's Megan's Law."

The California version of Megan's law contains a provision which prohibits the information to be used in regards to insurance, loans, credit, employment, education, housing, or accommodation or benefits or privileges provided by any business. California Penal Code Section 290.4(d) (2).

However, there is an exception. According to California law, a person is authorized to use information disclosed pursuant to this section only to protect a person at risk. California Penal Code Section 290.4(d) (1).

The problem for employers who want to use this information is there is no legal definition for the term a "person at risk." Neither the California Penal code, the legislative history of the section, or the Megan's law website defines a "person at risk." Until a court provides a definition, employers are well advised to apply a common-sense approach by looking at risk factors associated with the nature of the job. For example, there is a widespread industry agreement that vulnerable individuals, such as the young, the aged, the infirmed, or the physically or mentally disabled, are at risk. In addition, people inside their own home are likely to be at greater risk, since it is harder to obtain help, so home workers may be considered a population segment that works with people at risk. Another category is workers who operate under some sort of badge or color of authority or who wear a uniform. In this situation, a person may let their guard down. Until a court makes a clear decision, employers should make an effort to determine if there is a good faith belief it is reasonably foreseeable that a member of a group at risk could be negatively impacted if a sexual offender was hired.

Of course, if the underlying criminal record is discovered and otherwise meets the many complicated rules governing the reporting and use of criminal records in California, then the "at risk" analysis may not be needed, and the employer can handle it like any other criminal record.

There are two other challenges for California employers using the Megan's law website:

✓ First, it is possible that a person may be registered as a sex offender, but the crime is beyond the 7 year California reporting provisions that restrict what a Consumer Reporting Agency can report. Although not yet tested in the Courts, the industry standard is for a screening firm to report the listing, on the basis that the background firm is reporting on the offender's current status as a registered sexual offender.

✓ The other issue is that there are large numbers of sex offenders that either do not register or abscond from the jurisdiction.

New York Rules

Additional Language for Criminal Background Checks to Help Ex-Offenders Have a Second Chance

In New York, *Article 23-A Licensure and Employment of Persons Previously Convicted of One or More Criminal Offenses,* which became effective September 2008, gives employers some additional protections against lawsuits for negligent hiring if they can show an applicant with a criminal record was hired after good faith consideration of the rules affecting the use of criminal convictions. Article 23-A states an employer is required to consider and balance various factors where an applicant has a criminal record (unless, of course, there is a statute that prohibits the employment of a person with certain convictions). The factors enumerated in section 753 of Article 23-A include such things as:

✓ The duties of the job.
✓ The relationship between the criminal offense and the job.
✓ How long ago the conviction occurred.
✓ The applicant's age at time of the crime.
✓ How serious the offense was.
✓ Information produced regarding the applicant's rehabilitation and good conduct.

Effective February 1, 2009, three additional laws went into effect in the State of New York also designed to give ex-offenders a second chance of entering the workforce. These laws affect both employers and background firms. When passing some of these laws, the New York legislature cited a 2007 study that found New York employees were largely not familiar with New York laws on utilizing past convictions or that a criminal record poses a significant barrier to employment. These three laws required the following effective February 1, 2009:

1. **Provide a copy of Article 23-A:** An employer must provide a copy of Article 23-A to all job applicants undergoing a background check. An employer may want to provide that notice at the same time the applicant signs a consent form and receives a disclosure form. A technical reading of the statute may suggest such a requirement is limited only to a situation where an employer is requesting a special type of background report called an 'Investigative Consumer Report' where information is obtained through interviews. However, the legislature in New York, based upon the legislative history, clearly intended this to apply to all consumer reports. As a best practice, employers should consider providing this notice regardless of the type of background report being conducted.

2. **Posting a copy of Article 23-A:** An employer must also post a copy of Article 23-A in 'a place accessible to his or her employees and in a visually conspicuous manner.' Employers can simply download the copy of 23-A linked in this article. The required notice was included in commercial labor posters that come out in 2009 for the state of New York.

3. **Provide additional copy of Article 23-A if a criminal record is found:** When a background report on an applicant contains information on a criminal conviction, the employer must again provide a copy of Article 23-A to the applicant.

As part of the legislative approach, New York employers that follow Article 23-A now have increased protection from lawsuits for negligent hiring. This protection applies where an employer hires someone that has a conviction history but the employer has made a reasonable and good faith determination that, due to the factors in Article 23-A, the applicant should still be hired. In that situation, there is a 'rebuttable presumption' that evidence of the employee's past criminal record cannot be admitted into evidence and be used against the employer.

A 'rebuttable presumption' is an assumption of fact accepted by the court until disproved by the other side. For example, evidence of the employee's past criminal record can only be used in a negligent hiring case if the plaintiff can overcome the presumption by showing there was not a reasonable and good faith determination by the employer under article 23-A. This new protection can potentially provide employers that do hire applicants with a criminal record protection from a lawsuit as long as the employer can document the employer discovered the criminal record and then applied the criteria in Article 23-A in a reasonable and good faith manner.

Article 23-A is available at http://public.leginfo.state.ny.us/menugetf.cgi?COMMONQUERY=LAWS under EXC - Executive.

Massachusetts Criminal Offender Record Information (CORI) Reform Law

In August 2010, Massachusetts Governor Patrick signed into law Chapter 256 of the Acts of 2010 – known as "CORI Reform." This law changed who has authorized access to CORI and how CORI could be accessed. While most of the new provisions went into effect on May 4, 2012, the CORI Reform law did prohibit employers from asking about criminal offender record information – which includes criminal charges, arrests, and incarceration – on "initial" written job applications effective November 4, 2010.

In May 2012, the Massachusetts Department of Criminal Justice Information Services (DCJIS) launched a new Criminal Offender Record Information (CORI) request service online called 'iCORI' to allow individuals and organizations to request and obtain Massachusetts criminal offender record information over the Internet. For more information about iCORI, one of the main provisions of the new CORI Reform law that took effect on May 4, 2012, visit the DCJIS web page at: http://www.mass.gov/eopss/agencies/dcjis/. The new CORI regulations are available at: http://www.mass.gov/eopss/crime-prev-personal-sfty/bkgd-check/cori/cori-regulations.html.

Since May 4, 2012, employers, volunteer organizations, landlords, and individuals can request, pay for, and receive CORI online using the iCORI online service. Employers have "Standard Access" to CORI data on any criminal charges pending as of the date of the request; felony or misdemeanor convictions; convictions that have not been sealed; and any murder, manslaughter, and sex offenses. Certain employers who must comply with statutory, regulatory, or accreditation requirements regarding employees' criminal records have "Required Access" to CORI for additional adult CORI information dating back to an individuals' 17th birthday. All users and organizations are required to register.

CORI Reforms that Took Effect November 4, 2010:

✓ **No Inquiry about Criminal History on Job Application ("Ban the Box"):** Bans questions about criminal history from initial written job application, unless conviction information is required for a particular job by federal or state law. (§101)

CORI Reforms that Took Effect May 4, 2012:

✓ **Access to CORI by Non-Statutorily Authorized Requestors:** Employers, landlords, and professional licensing authorities will have access to CORI (subject to content and time limits mentioned above) on the internet. (§21)

✓ **Conducting CORI Screening:** CORI checks are permitted only after a CORI Acknowledgement Form has been completed, and The CORI subject has signed an authorization from.

✓ **Verify a Subject's Identity:** If a criminal record is received from the DCJIS, the information is to be closely compared with the information on the CORI Acknowledgement Form and any other identifying information provided by the applicant to ensure the record belongs to the applicant. Also, if the information in the CORI record provided does not exactly match the identification information provided by the applicant, a determination is to be made by an individual authorized to make such determinations based on a comparison of the CORI record and documents provided by the applicant.

✓ **Provide Criminal Record before Asking Questions Related to them and in the Event of likely Adverse Decision:** An employer (or other decision-maker), must provide a copy of any criminal record information in the employer's possession before questioning an applicant about his/her record. (§19) Also, when an adverse decision is made based on a criminal record, the employer (or other decision-maker) must give the applicant a copy of the record the decision is based on. (§19)

✓ **Adverse Decisions Based on CORI:**
   • Where adverse action is contemplated based on the results of a criminal history background check (regardless of source), the applicant will be notified immediately.
   • The source(s) of the criminal history will also be revealed.
   • Subject must have an opportunity to dispute the accuracy of the CORI record.
   • Subjects shall be provided a copy of DCJIS' Information Concerning the Process for Correcting a Criminal Record. See: www.mass.gov/eopss/docs/chsb/cori-process-correcting-criminal-record.pdf.

✓ **Procedure to Correct Inaccurate Record:** CORI subjects have a right to inspect and obtain a copy of their own records. (§35) Also, the department of criminal justice information services will publish guidelines on how to correct inaccurate information and may work with other agencies to help individuals fix inaccurate records. (§35)

✓ **Limitations on Conviction Dissemination:**
   • Prohibits dissemination of convictions after a specified waiting period that begins after release from incarceration or custody. (§21) (10 years for felonies; 5 years for misdemeanors; Violations of domestic abuse orders will be treated as felonies.)
   • Prior records will remain available for as long as last conviction is still available to be disseminated. (§21)
   • Permanent access to convictions for murder, manslaughter, sex offenses. (§21)

✓ **Limitations on Non-Conviction Dissemination:**
   • Non-conviction (not guilty, dismissed cases) will not be disseminated to most requestors. (§21)
   • Pending cases will be disseminated. (§21)
   • CWOFs will be treated as pending cases until they are dismissed, after which they will be treated as non-convictions. (§21)
   • Only entities with specific statutory access can receive non-convictions.

✓ **Employer Negligent Hiring/Liability Protection:**
   • Employers that make decisions within 90 days of obtaining CORI from the state will not be held liable for negligent/discriminatory hiring practices by reason of reliance on the CORI. (§21)
   • No protection for employers using info from private companies.

✓ **Department of Criminal Justice Information Services (DCJIS) Model CORI Policy:** A 'DCJIS Model CORI Policy' available at www.mass.gov/eopss/docs/chsb/dcjis-model-cori-policy-may-2012.pdf shows the practices and procedures to be followed when Criminal Offender Record Information (CORI) and other criminal history checks may be part of a general background check for employment, volunteer work, licensing purposes.

✓ **Criminal Offender Record Information (CORI) Acknowledgment Form:** The 'CORI Acknowledgment Form' is required of organizations using a Consumer Reporting Agency (CRA) for CORI criminal background checks that is available at: www.mass.gov/eopss/docs/chsb/fillable-cori-acknowledgment-form-organizations-using-a-cra.pdf.

✓ **Information Concerning the Process in Correcting a Criminal Record:** Must be provided to subjects of background checks where adverse decisions are made on CORI. www.mass.gov/eopss/docs/chsb/cori-process-correcting-criminal-record.pdf.

Other Special State Laws

The issue of special state laws will also come into play in other areas examined as subject matter in additional chapters with in this publication. For example, there are specific state rules affecting:

✓ E-verify requirements
✓ Drug testing
✓ Credit History
✓ Internet and social media background checks
✓ "Ban the Box" rules regulating what can be asked in a job application form about past criminal history

These issues are discussed in the appropriate chapters through this book.

Chapter 5

The Safe Hiring Program (SHP)

A fact of business life is: *Employee problems are caused by problem employees.*

Each new hire represents an enormous investment and potential risk to an employer. Ironically, many employers spend more time, energy, and money shopping for a new piece of office equipment than they do on a new hire.

Despite inherent challenges in weeding out problem applicants, there are steps employers can and should take. The best way for employers to make one of the most critical decisions in their business is to institute a **Safe Hiring Program (SHP)**.

Inside This Chapter:

✓ Definition of a Safe Hiring Program

✓ Anatomy of a Safe Hiring Program

✓ The S.A.F.E. System

✓ Reasons Why Safe Hiring is Such a Challenge

✓ The Four Biggest Benefits of the SHP

✓ What the SHP Does NOT Do

✓ Risk Management Calculation for Safe Hiring

✓ The ROI of a Screening Program

✓ Answers to 10 Commonly Expressed Concerns of Employers

Definition of a Safe Hiring Program

A Safe Hiring Program (SHP) is a series of policies, practices, and procedures designed to minimize the probability of hiring dangerous, questionable, or unqualified candidates, while at the same time helping to identify those candidates who are capable, trustworthy, and best suited to the job requirements.

The SHP is part of the fabric of how a firm operates its businesses. The program:

- ✓ Dictates the types of precautions to be taken and sets limits for eligibility for employment.
- ✓ Incorporates screening and selection procedures, clearly stating qualifiers and disqualifiers.
- ✓ Utilizes a series of overlapping tools, recognizing that no one tool is perfect.
- ✓ Recognizes that due diligence requires multiple approaches.

Moreover, a Safe Hiring Program:

- ✓ Maps out the events in the hiring process.
- ✓ Dictates policy in order to ensure all candidates are treated equally and fairly.
- ✓ Establishes legally defensible practices for dealing with undesirable or potentially problematic applicants.

These practices are to be supported by documented procedures.

Yes, safe hiring is not something that occurs without some effort. Without a safe hiring program, it is a statistical certainty that an employer will eventually hire someone with an unsuitable criminal record or false credentials, creating a very real possibility of a legal and financial nightmare.

Anatomy of a Safe Hiring Program

Given the enormous price tag of a bad hiring decision, it is no surprise that employers of all sizes are looking to various tools in hopes of boosting the effectiveness of the hiring process. The tools used include honesty and skills testing, behavior-based testing, group interview techniques, criminal record checks, and verification of previous employment. Not one of these tools alone has proven 100% effective in weeding out bad candidates; each tool should be used in conjunction with all the tools documented in your overall Safe Hiring Program.

Five Core Areas of a Safe Hiring Program

A Safe Hiring Program consists of five core areas:

Core Competencies	Key Components
1. Organizational Infrastructure	Have organizational commitment and structure to a Safe Hiring Program. The *S.A.F.E System* sets in place the critical *Policies, Practices, and Procedures* necessary for a Safe Hiring Program.
2. Initial Screening Practices	The *AIR (Application, Interview, & References) Process* begins from the first job announcement or advertisement. It may also include an initial identification check.
3. In-Depth Screening Practices	These practices include a criminal record check and other tools described throughout the book.
4. Post-Hire Practices	Practices include a continuing commitment to a safe workplace even after an applicant has been hired.
5. Legal Compliance Practices	Practices include an awareness of the legal and regulatory environment surrounding safe hiring and compliance.

One gets started by deciding to incorporate the elements of the S.A.F.E. System into an overall Safe Hiring Program that is implemented on a company-wide basis. In this way, large organizations can ensure that hiring managers within different divisions, and even different physical locations, follow the same procedures.

The S.A.F.E. System

S.A.F.E. stands for:

S—Set-up a safe hiring program consisting of documented policies, practices, and procedures.

A—Acclimate and train all people with safe hiring responsibilities including hiring managers.

F—Facilitate and implement the safe hiring program.

E—Evaluate and audit the safe hiring program.

The "E" includes making sure people involved understand their own compensation and advancement is judged in part by the attention they pay to the hiring process. Organizations typically accomplish those things that are measured, audited, and rewarded — so do that in your hiring program. A detailed explanation of the S.A.F.E. system and how it is used to create a Safe Hiring Program is in Chapter 6.

 A key concept presented in this book is "pre-employment screening" or as it is sometimes called, "employment screening." This process is also referred to as "background checks." A Safe Hiring Program is NOT the same thing as pre-employment screening.

Pre-employment screening is only one part of the total approach to a Safe Hiring Program. Pre-employment screening is certainly a critical part, but there is much more to an SHP.

The background screen occurs when an employer or an outside professional firm assembles information such as criminal records, credit reports, or credentials verifications on an applicant.

Many employers make the mistake of believing that safe hiring is an event that is typically outsourced to a screening firm or investigator. This misconception is manifested because employers often feel they merely need to spend money to perform background checks and criminal record searches in order to show due diligence. These firms somewhat incorrectly view pre-employment screening as a process that begins after a hiring manager selects an applicant then submits the name to the firm's security or human resources department or chooses to outsource by calling in an employment screening firm for a background report or to conduct the screening tasks.

The key point to remember is in an effective SHP the primary tools are processes that occur **in-house** as part of a routine, documented hiring program. For example, one of the most effective tools for safe hiring is the application, interview, and reference checking process, also known as the AIR Process. This multi-step process, examined in detail in this book, is not only one of the best lines of defense against a bad hire, but the cost is right — virtually nothing. The only cost is a commitment to safe hiring.

Reasons Why Safe Hiring is Such a Challenge

Even though everyone agrees that safe hiring and due diligence are missions critical for any business, there are still numerous employers who find safe hiring to be a challenge. Sadly, there are many employers that either do nothing when it comes to due diligence or do way too little. Here are some of the issues that face employers:

Compliance with Hiring Laws

As discussed in earlier chapters, laws associated with employment screening have sought to achieve a balance between privacy and due diligence. Although a number of laws limit, prohibit, or regulate obtaining and using background information, there is a great deal of information an employer is entitled to obtain and use in making the best hiring decisions. Certainly, all citizens have a reasonable expectation to privacy and a right to be treated fairly, yet, at the same time, an employer has the right to make diligent and reasonable job-related inquiries into a person's background so that the company, its employees, and the public are not placed at risk.

Therefore, it is vital to keep the scope of reference checking and screening within specified legal boundaries. There are certain matters that are not valid predictors of job performance and delving into them can be considered discriminatory. This can include information about religion or race, national origin, marital status, age, medical condition, and so forth. An employer cannot ask reference questions or obtain background information on those subject areas that cannot legally be raised in an interview situation with an applicant face-to-face.

There is No Instant Database That Gives All the Answers

Unfortunately, there is no magic database in existence. There is no national credentials database where an employer can instantly confirm an applicant's past employment or education. There is no public record database where an employer can instantly find out if the applicant has a criminal record, a problematic driving record, or a job-related civil lawsuit.

Some employers have been given the legal authority to obtain government criminal records when filling positions involving security or access to groups at risk. In many states, for positions involving access to vulnerable patients or children, screeners for hospitals and school districts can submit applicant's fingerprints to be checked by the FBI or state authorities.

However, for most private employers, the challenge is more pressing because of the fact a criminal record check is not nearly as effective a tool as most employers might believe. Although certainly a criminal check is an essential part of any hiring program, it does not necessarily provide complete protection — there are over 10,000 courthouses in 3,500+ jurisdictions in the U.S.A. Since employers cannot search every jurisdiction, there is always the possibility of missing a criminal record from a court not searched. The possibility of errors is compounded by the fact the searches are conducted by human beings who enter names in computers, scan listings of names, or engage in some other activity that ultimately depends upon human intervention. There is always the possibility of error. Even official government "rap sheets" are subject to error, and the reasons for errors on government records are discussed in Chapter 15.

There are privately-assembled multi-jurisdictional databases, but these too can lead to false negatives — that is, a person with a criminal record comes up clean.

Confirming education credentials and past employment is equally labor intensive. Although some colleges and universities allow online record verifications and electronic transcripts, employers must still identify and individually go to each relevant school database. Past employers must be contacted, which is a process that presents its own difficulties.

There Are No Magical Tools That Find an "Honest" Person

In the wake of Enron, WorldCom, and what appears to be a general collapse of corporate ethics and morality, more emphasis is now placed on the age-old question asked by Greek philosopher Diogenes, *"How do you find an honest person?"*

Part of the challenge in safe hiring is that by definition, employers are seeking an elusive quality. Ultimately, the ability to find an honest person depends on the correct use of a number of overlapping tools. These include 1) a number of objective fact-finding tools (pre-employment screening and reference checks), 2) tools used to convince applicants to be self-revealing (applications and interviews), and 3) to a subjective extent, instinct and intuition. However, reliance only on instinct and intuition can be dangerous.

Consider this fact— for every dishonest person ever hired there was someone who sized up the person hired and concluded that this person would be good for the job.

There is no surefire test or method that will tell an employer if a particular person is an honest person, although Chapter 24 addresses ways to incorporate some effective honesty and integrity testing.

It is Almost Impossible to Spot Liars at Interviews

Even if Diogenes had found an honest person, there is a body of modern evidence that suggests it is difficult for anyone, from ancient philosophers to modern day employer, to use an interview to determine who is really who. Employers have a distinct challenge when it comes to spotting liars. Industry statistics suggest that as many as 30% of all job applicants falsify information about their credentials, but trying to spot liars at interviews is, well, difficult if not impossible.

There are lists of so-called "tell-tale signs" that a person is lying. For example, employers might observe if a person is avoiding eye contact, fidgeting, or hesitating before answering. Unfortunately, it can be a costly mistake for an interviewer to think lying can always be detected by such visual clues, "tells," or by relying upon one's own instinct or intuition since some of the so-called "visual clues" can simply be a sign of nervousness about the interview or stress and not an intent to lie. In fact, accomplished liars are more dangerous because they can disguise themselves as truthful and sincere. An experienced liar will often show no visible signs.

The problem is further complicated because many people feel they can detect who is lying and who is not. Studies have demonstrated that most people are poor judges of when they are being told the truth and when they are being deceived. Dr. Paul Ekman, a retired psychology professor in the Department of Psychiatry at the University of California Medical School in San Francisco, is the author of thirteen books, including *Telling Lies (W.W. Norton, 2001)*. Based upon extensive testing, Dr. Ekman concluded that without training, a person could only detect who was lying at 50% of the time. According to Dr. Ekman: "Most liars can fool most people most of the time."

Researchers Identify True Clues to Lying

Below is text from an article in the *New York Times* summarizing this area of study.

"One of the consistent findings of the new research, which is being conducted by psychologists at several universities, is that people think they are better detectors of lies than they really are. Dozens of studies have found that people's accuracy at detecting lies usually exceeds chance by very little. While guessing alone would give a rate of 50 percent accuracy, in the recent studies the best rate of accuracy for any group has never exceeded 60 percent, and is most often near chance.

This is true even for those in professions where lie detection is at a premium. In a study done at Cornell University, for example, customs inspectors proved no better than college students at guessing which people were trying to smuggle contraband. Likewise, a study at Auburn University in Alabama found that police detectives were no more successful in judging people lying about a mock crime than were students.

Another study found that a group of seasoned Federal law enforcement officers from the Secret Service and the Criminal Investigation Divisions of the armed forces were no more accurate in detecting deceit than were newly recruited officers who had just joined those agencies. The one difference between the groups, though, was that the seasoned officers, who averaged seven years of service, felt more confident of their ability to detect lying, even though they were no more accurate. Studies such as these have revealed that people are poor at detecting lies in large part because they base their judgment on the wrong clues. For example, in the study of customs inspectors, people were most often thought to be telling lies if they did such things as hesitating before answering questions, avoided meeting the eyes of their questioner or shifted their posture. None of these signs, though, were actually more common among those who lied than among those who did not. "

Source: www.nytimes.com/1985/02/12/science/reseachers-identify-true-clues-to-lying.html?pagewanted=all.

Another researcher at the same school as Paul Ekman, Dr. Maureen O'Sullivan, tested 13,000 people for the ability to detect deception. Using three different tests, only 31 subjects — nicknamed "wizards" — could *usually* tell whether a person was lying about an opinion, how someone is feeling, or about a crime. More information about these studies is available at www.paulekman.com.

Some interviewees tell lies they have ingrained in their life story. They have created identities and legends of their own and, when they tell their stories, they are not fabricating on the spot. They put "it" on their resumes, talk about "it," and tell their friends about "it". "It" becomes part of their personalities and personal histories because they have told "it" so often. "It" becomes second nature as they retell "it" again and again.

That does not mean some liars cannot be detected at interview. John E. Reid and Associates offers a one-day course specifically designed around interviewing of applicants. Information on John E. Reid and Associates one-day course specifically on interviewing applicants is at www.reid.com/training-interview-dates.html.

Employers, HR, and Security professionals should remember that as valuable as instinct may be, it does not substitute for factual verification of an applicant's credentials through background checks and other safe hiring techniques.

The Effects of Corporate Culture and Other Impediments

At some firms, efforts at safe hiring may be impeded by the simple fact that it has historically not been done. Pre-employment screening, reference checks, and criminal background checks are relatively new on the corporate scene. Although a 2010 study by the Society for Human Resource Management (SHRM) suggests the use of screening tools is on the rise with roughly three out of four employers performing background checks, there are still some employers who are still reluctant to engage in screening out of a concern that an applicant may find it insulting. There is even more reluctance to perform screening for higher-level positions, especially positions that have a C in the title such as CEO or CFO. The higher a person is in the organization, the more harm that person can do to that organization.

The Four Biggest Benefits of the SHP

Employers do not have to sit back and wait to be victimized. By addressing workplace problems at their main source – problem employees – employers can substantially lessen risks to their businesses.

To prevent the hire of potentially problematic individuals, businesses are responsible for taking appropriate steps toward the development of policies and countermeasures before the hiring process begins. All relevant departments and personnel must be familiar with – and committed to – their company Safe Hiring Program. Properly implemented, an SHP helps employers in four key ways—

1. Deterrence

Making it clear that screening is part of the hiring process can deter potentially problematic applicants and discourage applicants with something to hide. An applicant with serious criminal convictions or falsified information on his or her resume is less likely to apply at a firm that announces pre-employment background checks are part of the hiring process. Do not become the employer of choice for people with problems when simply having a screening program can deter those problem applicants.

2. Encourage Honesty

The goal of a safe hiring program is not to find only "perfect candidates." Many candidates who may have some blemish on their record may still be well-suited for employment. However, employers need to be fully informed when making a hiring decision. Having a Safe Hiring Program encourages applicants to be especially forthcoming in their interviews. Making it clear that background checks are part of the hiring process is strong motivation for applicants to reveal information about themselves they feel may be uncovered by a background check.

3. Fact-Finding

Although instincts play a large role in hiring, basing a decision on hard information is even better, and safer. Effective screening obtains factual information about a candidate in order to supplement the impressions obtained from an interview. It is also a valuable tool for judging the accuracy of a candidate's resume. Facts limit uncertainty in the hiring process.

4. Due Diligence

Implementing a Safe Hiring Program helps an employer practice due diligence in their hiring. Having an SHP is a powerful defense in the event of a lawsuit.

Ten Safe Hiring Tools

When recruiters, hiring managers, or human resources professionals need to fill a position, it is not enough to simply look for the proper skills set, experience, or a good fit. Employers must also determine if there are reasons not to hire the candidate.

Below are ten evaluation tools that can be used immediately at no cost. These techniques protect a firm, yet do not discourage good applicants. These ten tools cost nothing, can be implemented by employers almost immediately, and go a long ways towards avoiding workplace problems.

✓ Have each job applicant sign a consent form for a background check, including a check for criminal records, past employment and, education. Announcing that your firm checks backgrounds may discourage applicants with something to hide, and encourage applicants to be truthful and honest about mistakes they have made in the past.

✓ Employment applications should ask about criminal records in the broadest possible terms allowed by law and should not be limited to felonies. (However, see Chapter 16 on the new EEOC Guidance.)

✓ Towards the end of an interview, advise applicants that the firm will perform a criminal background and reference check as a standard business practice, and ask whether the applicant has any concerns to share. Good applicants will shrug off the question, while applicants with a problem may either reveal something or withdraw. (Note: Under the new 2012 EEOC Guidance on criminal records, an employer may want to modify this approach.)

✓ Applicants should also be asked during an interview what they think a former employer will say about them. For example, "If we were to contact past employers, how would they describe your job performance?" Since the applicant has signed a release and has been told such checks may occur, they may be more motivated to reveal information about past jobs.

✓ Applications must clearly state that any false or misleading statements or material omissions are grounds to terminate the hiring process or employment, regardless of when discovered. This is particularly important if a criminal record is found. Under current law, a criminal record may not be used to automatically disqualify an applicant unless there is a sound business reason. However, if an applicant has lied about a criminal matter, the falsehood can be the basis for an adverse decision.

✓ If employment begins before a background check is completed, state in writing that employment is conditioned upon a background report that is satisfactory to the employer.

✓ Verifying past employment is probably the single most important tool for an employer. Generally speaking, past job performance can be an important predictor of future success. Some employers make a costly mistake by not checking past employment because past employers may not give detailed information. However, even verification of dates of employment and job title is critical because an employer must be concerned about unexplained gaps in the employment history. Although there can be many reasons for a gap in employment, if an applicant cannot account for the past seven to ten years, that can be a red flag. It is also important to know where a person has been because of the way criminal records are maintained in the United States. Contrary to popular belief, there is not a national criminal database available to most employers. Searches must be conducted at each relevant courthouse, and there are over 10,000 courthouses in America. However, if an employer knows where an applicant has been, it increases the accuracy of a criminal search and decreases the possibility that an applicant has served time for a serious offense. Finally, documenting an attempt to obtain references can demonstrate due diligence.

✓ Obtain a listing of all past addresses for seven to ten years. This is also needed for a criminal search.

✓ Include future screenings in the consent language. This becomes important if a future investigation is required for some form of workplace misconduct.

✓ Check for criminal records. Since criminal records are public information, employers can check at the local courthouse. An employer may consider convictions or cases currently pending, but not arrests. Also, certain cases may not be legally used for employment decisions. There are services that can obtain such information from courthouses all over the United States, as well as provide other assistance.

What the SHP Does NOT Do

Although it is important to understand the benefits of a Safe Hiring Program, it is also important to be clear on what the SHP does not do. While a properly implemented program can considerably minimize the risk of hiring a problem employee, it is not a guarantee that every person with an undisclosed criminal record or false credential will be identified.

The world's experts on background screening and pre-employment investigations are probably the FBI and the CIA. They spend millions on pre-hiring investigations. Yet, from time to time, there are newspaper stories about how the FBI hires spies and the CIA hires crooks. If the world's experts do not have a 100% success rate with millions of dollars to spend and full access to governmental databases, what chance do private employers have?

As the term suggests, background screening is a large-scale process that operates on a cost/benefit basis. A firm is looking at confirming known information (such as past employment or education) or doing quick and cost-effective checks of readily available public documents such as criminal records.

Background screening is not meant to be a full investigation, where the investigator develops leads and intensely focuses on the individual. During an investigation the investigator is focused on one person (as opposed to a group) and is doing an in-depth examination (as opposed to using diagnostic tools) where the information is either hidden or not readily apparent. Thus, investigations are typically much more expensive than a background screening.

As a result, when performing a background screening, it is possible something will fall through the cracks. Given that screening is relatively inexpensive, employers cannot expect a foolproof process for the prices being charged. However, screening is extremely effective at keeping the workplace safe, productive, and reasonably trouble-free. Screening also demonstrates due diligence, which is important if a problem employee is hired and the employer needs to defend their hiring practices in a lawsuit.

Risk Management Calculation for Safe Hiring

Another way of analyzing the value of a Safe Hiring Program is to utilize risk-management analysis. Risk can be defined as *the possibility of suffering loss.* Risk management means *the systematic identification of the risks involved and determining the best course of action to avoid or minimize the risks.* It can also be thought of as a cost-benefit analysis.

The Federal Aviation Administration (FAA) has prepared an excellent introduction to risk management. According to the FAA:

> "Risk management…. is pre-emptive, rather than reactive. The approach is based on the philosophy that it is irresponsible and wasteful to wait for an accident to happen, then figuring out how to prevent it from happening again. We manage risk whenever we modify the way we do something to make our chances of success as great as possible, while making our chances of failure, injury or loss as small as possible. It is a commonsense approach to balancing the risks against the benefits to be gained in a situation and then choosing the most effective course of action."

One key principle of risk management is to Accept No Unnecessary Risk. According to the FAA:

> "Unnecessary risk is that which carries no commensurate return in terms of benefits or opportunities. Everything involves risk. The most logical choices for accomplishing an operation are those that meet all requirements with the minimum acceptable risk. The corollary to this axiom is "accept necessary risk" required to successfully complete the operation or task."

As a part of a risk management process, it is critical to fully identify all of the risks that can be encountered and to demonstrate the cost of avoiding the risks.

In the case of safe hiring, the risks are well known. As seen throughout this book, the cost of controlling the risks of a bad hire is marginal in comparison to the benefits gained. The most effective screening tools cost an employer very little. The portion of the Safe Hiring Program that involves utilizing outside professional services has a cost that is minimal compared to just one bad hire. Any risk-management analysis will come to one conclusion — a firm is taking an unnecessary risk when they do not engage in a safe hiring program.

See www.asy.faa.gov/Risk/SSHandbook/Chap15_1200.PDF for more information about the FAA materials on risk management.

The ROI of a Screening Program

Employers justify the costs associated with employment screening because of the clear Return on Investment — the ROI — these programs bring to the workplace.

There are two costs associated with a screening program. First is the cost of the in-house time and effort needed to pursue a Safe Hiring Program; second, the cost of any outsourced services. These costs will be covered in greater detail in a later section. In the meantime, let us assume as a general rule, the cost of a background screening is less than the cost of an employee's salary on his or her first day on the job. Of course, applicants may be screened at different levels so the cost is not the same for all candidates. A screening for a janitorial position may be less costly than a more in-depth screening used for an executive position. However, since the executive also gets paid more, the cost of a screening as a percentage of salary still works out as less than the new executive's first day salary.

Two Approaches to Calculating ROI

Because the purpose of background screening is to prevent harm, it is often difficult to quantify the ROI of events that did not happen. As seen in Chapter 1, a firm hit with even a single incident of workplace violence or related legal action immediately recognizes the advantages of a Safe Hiring Program.

Method One: Making a Judgment as to the Value of Avoiding the "Parade of Horribles"

Assume an average background check performed by a third party firm is $65, and during a twelve month period a firm submits 100 names to a screening firm. Keep in mind that most employers only screen finalists, not all who apply. The third-party costs of this service would be $6,500.

Given the fact that industry sources indicate that up to ten percent of all screened workers have criminal records, a firm would have to decide if it was worth $6,500 to avoid hiring ten workers with some sort of undisclosed criminal record. A judgment has to be made as to whether it is worth that cost in order to avoid hiring problem employees. Given the impact that even one "bad hire" can bring, it would appear to be a very small price to pay.

Method Two: Calculation of Benefit from Lack of Turnover

One way benefits of a Safe Hiring Program can be measured is by estimating the average costs associated with a single employee turnover. An easy way to consider these costs is by building a "turnover calculator" that breaks down all the costs associated with having and filling a vacancy on an item-by-item basis. When the expenses involved are broken down to basics, it is easy to see how such costs can add up to a sizeable figure. An example of a *Turnover Cost Calculator Form* appears in the Appendix.

Answers to 10 Commonly Expressed Concerns of Employers

Even with all of the advantages of a Safe Hiring Program, many employers have questions and concerns about implementing safe hiring and background checks. These are the ten most common concerns that employers express regarding safe hiring or a screening program.

1. Is a Safe Hiring Program Legal?

Employers have an absolute right to select the most-qualified candidate for a job. The only limitations on employers are the ones that employers already understand and abide by in all of their workplace policies. For example, employers must ensure that all selection procedures are non–discriminatory, based upon factors that are valid predictors of job performance, and do not invade privacy rights or other laws. A safe hiring program easily falls within these limitations. If a firm utilizes a pre-employment screening agency, then a federal law called the Fair Credit Reporting Act (FCRA) balances the right of an employer to know whom they hire with the applicant's rights of disclosure and privacy. Under this law, the employer first obtains the applicant's written consent to be screened. In the event negative information is found, the applicant must be given the opportunity to correct the record. Employers should set up a consistent policy so similarly situated applicants are treated the same. A qualified screening company will assist an employer with legal compliance issues.

2. Does Safe Hiring Invade Privacy?

No. Employers can find out about only those things an applicant has done in his or her "public" life. For example, checking court records for criminal convictions or calling past employers or schools does not invade a zone of personal privacy. Employers are looking only at information that is a valid and non-discriminatory predictor of future job performance. As a general rule, an employer will not ask for any information that an employer could not ask an applicant in a face-to-face interview. Employers should also take steps to maintain confidentiality within their organization, such as keeping reports in a separate file from the personnel files. To maintain privacy, most background firms offer internet systems with secured websites.

3. Is Safe Hiring Cost-Effective?

In a Safe Hiring Program, the cost to select one new employee will typically cost less than the cost of that new employee on his or her first day on the job. That is pocket change compared to the damage one bad hire can cause. In addition, if an employer utilizes an outside agency, the service is typically used only to screen an applicant if a decision has been made to extend a job offer. Not all applicants are screened. It is ironic that some firms will spend hours shopping for a computer bargain yet at the same time try to save money by not adequately checking out a job applicant, which represents an enormous investment. Problem employees usually cause employee problems, and money is well spent to avoid problems in the first place.

4. Does Safe Hiring Discourage Good Applicants?

Employers who engage in a safe hiring program do not find that good applicants are deterred. Job applicants have a desire to work with qualified and safe co-workers in a profitable environment. A good candidate understands background screening is a sound business practice. It is not an invasion of privacy or an intrusion.

5. Does Background Screening Delay Hiring?

No. Background screening is normally done in 48 to 72 hours. Most of the necessary information is obtained by going to courthouses or calling past employers or schools. Occasionally there can be delays beyond anyone's control such as previous employers who will not return calls, schools that are closed for vacation, or a court clerk who needs to retrieve a record from archive storage.

Furthermore, an organization that is careful in its hiring practices should find a lower rate of negative "hits" during background checks. As discussed in later chapters, there are a number of steps a firm should take to ensure safe hiring well before a name is submitted to a background screening company. These techniques include making it clear your firm does background checks in order to weed out bad applicants, knowing the "red flags" to look for in an application, and asking questions in interviews that will help filter out problem candidates.

6. Does Safe Hiring Have to be Outsourced to be Effective?

Not at all. In fact, the most effective safe hiring tools are completed in house and cost nothing. Firms that take time to thoroughly develop an application process, an interview process, and a reference checking process receive a great deal of protection. Many firms do outsource part of the task, such as criminal record checks, because of the specialized skills, knowledge, and resources that are involved in a correct check. Typically these tasks, although vital, are not part of a firm's core expertise and can be performed by a third party more quickly and efficiently.

7. If a Company Outsources The SHP, Is It Difficult to Implement?

Even for an overburdened HR, security, or risk management department already handling numerous tasks, outsourcing background screening can be done very quickly and effectively. A qualified pre-employment screening firm can set up the entire program and provide all the necessary forms in a short time. Many firms have internet-based systems that speed up the flow of information and allow an employer to track the progress of each applicant in real time.

8. How is a Background Check Service Provider Selected if All or Part of the SHP is Outsourced?

An employer should apply the same criteria they would use in selecting any other providers of critical professional services. An employer should look for a professional partner and not just an information vendor selling data at the lowest price. For example, if an employer were choosing a law firm for legal representation, it would not merely select the cheapest — the employer would clearly want to know it is selecting a firm that is competent, experienced, knowledgeable, as well as reputable and reasonably priced. The same criteria should also apply to critical HR services. A background screening firm should have an understanding of the legal implications of background checks, particularly the federal Fair Credit Reporting Act. A list of screening firms that have voluntarily agreed to an industry code of ethics by joining the National Association of Professional Background Screeners (NAPBS) is available at www.napbs.com.

Employers can also choose to select a background screening firm that has formally achieved accreditation from the NAPBS Background Screening Credentialing Council (BSCC) for successfully proving compliance with the Background Screening Agency Accreditation Program (BSAAP). How to select a background screening firm is discussed in more detail in Chapters 10 to 12.

9. Does a Company Risk Being Sued by an Applicant?

Unfortunately, anyone can go to the courthouse and sue anyone else. On a risk/management basis however, the advantage of performing pre-employment screening clearly outweighs the possibility that an applicant may sue. Statistics overwhelmingly show that employers do not need to be concerned, as a practical matter, about applicant lawsuits. On the other hand, it is an absolute certainty, without screening, an employer becomes the employer of choice for everyone with a problem and will hire unsuitable criminals and applicants with false credentials. An employer can be protected by following certain basic guidelines in a fair and legal screening program.

10. Is It Worth the Time and Energy to Even Think About Safe Hiring, Given Everything Else an Employer Has To Do?

Since the fundamental rule in running a business of any size is that employee problems stem from problem employees — it is time and money well spent to avoid hiring a problem in the first place. As outlined in the next chapter, if there is an incident of workplace violence or litigation due to a bad hire, then a firm would want to pay almost anything to avoid the bad hire in the first place. Use of a legally sound screening program can protect against the vast majority of employee issues.

Both employers and applicants have learned that pre-employment screening is an absolute necessity in today's business world. More importantly, we have learned due diligence in hiring is a way to keep firms safe and profitable in difficult economic times.

Chapter 6

The S.A.F.E. System

As we have learned, an effective Safe Hiring Program is much more than just pre-employment screening and background checks. This chapter examines how to set up and document your own Safe Hiring Program.

Inside This Chapter:

✓ The Elements of the S.A.F.E. System

✓ Example of a Safe Hiring Program Using the S.A.F.E. System - (Including Samples of Statements and Policies Employers Can Use)

- Sample # 1 – Safe Hiring Policy Statement
- Sample # 2 – Overall Practices to Carry out Employer's Safe Hiring Program
- Sample # 3 – Statement Implementing the Application, Interview & Reference Checking (AIR) Process
- Sample # 4 – The Application Process
- Sample # 5 – The Interview Process
- Sample # 6 – The Reference Checking Stage
- Sample # 7 – The Pre-employment Screening Process
- Sample # 8 – Standards for Screening
- Sample # 9 – Analysis of Information
- Sample # 10 – Criminal History Information

✓ The Sample Policies and the Matrix of Criminal Record Use

✓ Language About Background Screening in the Employee Manual

- Sample # 11 – Sample Policy to be Placed in Employee Manual

✓ Conclusion — Procedures for Implementing Your Safe Hiring Program

✓ The ABC Company Safe Hiring Checklist

The Elements of the S.A.F.E. System

As stated in the last chapter, the S.A.F.E. System is the creative driving force behind a Safe Hiring Program. S.A.F.E. stands for:

> **S**—Set-up a safe hiring program consisting of documented policies, practices, and procedures.
> **A**—Acclimate and train all people with safe hiring responsibilities including hiring managers.
> **F**—Facilitate and implement the safe hiring program.
> **E**—Evaluate and audit the safe hiring program.

By evaluating and auditing the Safe Hiring Program, organizations can make sure the people responsible understand their compensation and advancement is judged in part by the attention they pay to the hiring process. Organizations typically accomplish those things that are measured, audited, and rewarded. Let us take a look at each element:

S = Set-up a Program of Policies and Procedures to be Used throughout the Organization

This is done in four steps:

1. **Who is in charge** — For any program to succeed, someone in the organization must have both the responsibility and the authority to carry out the program. Unless someone is firmly accountable and holding others accountable, it is hard to succeed.
2. **Policies** — Have internal policies and procedures in place. A sample policy memorandum is contained at the end of this chapter.
3. **Set-up the elements for safe hiring** — The critical elements are the Application, Interview, and Reference Checking Process, also called the *AIR Process*. These are done within an organization and are a matter of training and commitment. Typically it is not a line item in the budget.
4. **Criminal check** — Once an applicant has gone through the AIR Process, then a criminal check program can be conducted.

A = Acclimate/Train All Persons with Safe Hiring Responsibilities, Especially Hiring Managers

It is recommended that each hiring manager go through training on the AIR Process. The program would include the importance of safe hiring and pre-employment screening, how to implement the AIR Process, and why it is personally a matter of importance to hiring mangers that due diligence be demonstrated in the hiring process. It is critical that all training be documented so there is no question in the event of a lawsuit that there was adequate training.

F = Facilitate/Implement the Program

In order to facilitate the program, it is recommended that each hiring manager be provided with a Safe Hiring checklist that goes into every applicant file. A sample checklist is attached at the end of this chapter. The elements on the checklist may vary for each firm. The checklist makes it easier for hiring managers to follow the program since it creates a routine and provides a clear audit trail.

E = Evaluate and Audit the Program

As a general rule, members of an organization accomplish those things that are measured, audited, and rewarded. As a result, a Safe Hiring Program will be most effective if hiring managers clearly understand they will be audited periodically on how well they implement and follow the system. Otherwise, the hiring manager may just assume the Safe Hiring Program is unimportant and no one will follow-up. If regional and division managers routinely ask to see a number of files in order to ensure the Safe Hiring checklists are in the file, then the hiring managers will quickly understand this is something they must do. Compliance with the system must be part of a hiring manager's evaluation for purposes of salary and promotion. In turn, the regional managers must be held accountable by their supervisors who make sure they are checking. The audit trail must go to the top. Only in that way will every member of the firm understand that safe hiring is, in fact, a priority.

Defining Key Terms: Policies, Practices & Procedures

Public records and screening expert Carl R. Ernst describes Policies, Practice, and Procedures:

Policy: A policy is a general statement of a principle according to which a company performs business functions. A company does not need to maintain policies in order to operate. However, practices and procedures that exist without the underpinnings of a consistent policy are continually in jeopardy of being changed for the wrong reasons, with unintended legal consequences.

Practice: A practice is a general statement of the way the company implements a policy. Good practices support policy. To implement the policy statement example above, your company could establish a practice of validating the existence and currency of the registered entity on the public record.

Procedure: A procedure documents an established practice. Use of forms is one of the useful ways procedures are documented. For a firm that has a practice of checking past court records for criminal records, the procedures would be the documentation on how it is done, as well as the documents showing it was done.

Policies, practices and procedures that are not in writing are worthless. To the extent that policies, practices and procedures are documented in writing, it is possible to independently verify from the procedure whether employees are conforming to the practice, and therefore to the policy. This kind of documentation makes it easy to perform reliable audits. However, if policies and practices are not documented in writing, the only documentation available is the results of actions of employees documented in paper output, such as copies of filings, search requests and search reports, and vendor invoices. In addition, it is also worthless having policies, practices and procedures unless an employer can also demonstrate with documentation that there was training, implementation, and auditing to ensure that programs were followed.

The Stages of Hiring

Safe Hiring practices may also depend upon the stage of the hiring process. Essentially, hiring is done in separate stages. The stages and available tools of the hiring process can roughly be divided as follows:

1. Sourcing Stage: This is the process of gathering potential applicants through a variety of means that can include inbound applications from job boards, websites, newspapers, or outbound efforts, such as recruiters seeking passive candidates;
2. Preliminary Screening Stage: In order to narrow down the applicant pool, there is a preliminary screening primarily based upon the applicants' self-stated qualifications, conveyed by the resumes or applications or newer tools such as video websites;
3. Assessment Stage: This stage can include the interviewing process to further narrow down the field of candidates, as well as numerous other assessment tools, ranging from objective testing, references from past employers or supervisors, or various other testing methods;
4. Decision Process Stage: Here, the employer has narrowed the pool to one, two, or three finalists and is moving toward a conditional job offer based upon an internal decision-making process;
5. Background Checking Stage: At this point, either a conditional job offer has been made or is contemplated, and the employer needs to exercise due diligence, typically through a background screening firm, to determine if there is any reason NOT to hire the candidate. The emphasis of a background screening firm at this point is a factual verification of details such as job title and dates;
6. The Post Offer/Pre-Hire Stage: This is where an employer is able for the first time, if they so choose, to address such areas as pre-employment physicals;
7. The Post Hire/On-Boarding Stage: This is where an employer, for example, can complete the form I-9 process.

Many tasks discussed in this book are performed in stages 1 through 4 with the AIR Process. Background checks are part of stage 5. Certain tasks can only be performed post-offer, such as a workers compensation records inquiry (See Chapter 20). Other tasks can only be performed post-hire (i.e. after the applicant has come onboard), such as the I-9 procedure (See Chapter 29).

The important point about background checks is that they do not tell employers who to hire. There are a number of tools that help employers seek and identify the best and most qualified applicants. Background checks are a due diligence task aimed at raising potential Red Flags that may be relevant to reasons NOT to hire someone.

Example of a Safe Hiring Program Using the S.A.F.E. System

Over the remainder of this chapter you will see a series of sample internal policy and procedure documents from a fictitious firm called the ABC Company. These documents cover the basics of their Safe Hiring Program and provide a hands-on example of how a S.A.F.E. System is implemented. An employer may wish to consider utilizing the services of a labor attorney or Human Resources consultant to draft a policy that is tailored for their firm. The following material is not given or intended to be used as legal advice.

> The author wishes to **acknowledge** the contributions made by attorneys and screening experts **Larry Henry** of Rhodes Hieronymus and **Arthur J. Cohen** for additional language that was added to the material on employer policies in this updated edition of *The Safe Hiring Manual*.

The first example is a General Policy Statement (called **The Safe Hiring Statement**) which summarizes the big picture.

This Safe Hiring Statement assumes the ABC Company is outsourcing the employment screening aspect of the Safe Hiring Program to a third party firm. However, if a company intends to perform those functions in-house, then the memo must be adjusted accordingly. Later in this chapter is a separate policy statement that an employer can utilize in their employee manual. In succeeding chapters, details of each element of the Safe Hiring Program are discussed. A safe hiring audit is provided in Chapter 32.

Sample # 1 – Safe Hiring Policy Statement

ABC Company Memo: Safe Hiring Policy Statement

Policy and Purpose

To ensure that individuals who join this firm are well qualified and have a strong potential to be productive and successful, and to further ensure that this firm maintains a safe and productive work environment that is free from any form of violence, harassment, or misconduct, it is the policy of this company to exercise appropriate practices to screen out applicants whose employment would be inconsistent with this policy.

In addition, if an employee changes positions in the Company, any additional required background checks for that position which have not previously been performed will be performed.

It is also the position of the company that all hiring practice be conducted in strict conformity with all applicable laws and regulations and that specifically, the company will not permit any hiring practice that result in any disparate treatment or a disparate impact on applicants.

To the extent possible and where permitted by law, these same policies also apply to non-employees who are paid by the company, such a workers form staffing firms, independent contractors or vendors.

General Statement

1. The employer maintains a Safe Hiring Program. This program includes certain procedures that occur prior to an offer being made, including the Application, Interview, and Reference checking process. In addition, this firm will perform pre-employment screening and credentials verification on applicants including criminal background checks.

2. A pre-employment background check is a sound business practice that benefits everyone. The fact that a candidate is subject to a pre-employment screening is not a reflection on any particular applicant and is not a sign of mistrust or suspicion. All finalists are subject to this procedure. The success of our firm depends upon our people and although we operate in an environment of trust, our firm still must verify that all employees are both qualified and safe. All finalists for any position at this firm are subject to the same policy.

3. All offers of employment are conditioned upon the firm's receipt of a pre-employment background screening investigation that is acceptable to the firm at the firm's sole discretion.

4. This firm relies upon the accuracy of information contained in the employment application as well as the accuracy of other data presented throughout the hiring process and employment, including any oral interviews. Any misrepresentations, falsifications, or material omissions in any of the information or data, no matter when discovered, may result in the firm's exclusion of the individual from further consideration for employment or, if the person has been hired, termination of employment. Applicants also are expected to provide references from their former employers as well as educational reference information that can be used to verify academic accomplishments and records. Background checks may include verification of information provided on the completed application for employment, the applicant's resume, or on other forms used in the hiring process. Information to be verified includes, but is not limited to, Social Security Number and previous addresses. Employer may also conduct a reference check and verify the applicant's education and employment background as stated on the employment application or other documents listed above.

5. The background check may also include a criminal record check. If a conviction is discovered, then the employer will closely scrutinize the conviction in view of our policy of ensuring a safe and profitable workplace. A criminal conviction does not necessarily automatically bar an applicant from employment. Before an employment decision is made, a determination will be made whether the conviction is job related and exclusion is consistent with business necessity would present safety or security risks, taking into account the nature and gravity of the act, the nature of the position, and the age of the conviction, in the manner set forth in the most current EEOC Guidance in effect on the proper use of a criminal record. Additional checks, such as a driving record or a credit report, may be made on applicants for particular job categories if appropriate and job-related. Employment screening assessments to determine an applicant's job fit may also be required of all applicants for employment. Skills tests related to the demands of the job may also be required.

6. All procedures will be reviewed by legal counsel to ensure they are in strict conformity with the Federal Fair Credit Reporting Act, the Americans with Disabilities Act, state and federal anti-discrimination laws, privacy laws, and all other applicable federal and state laws. All pre-employment background screenings are conducted by a third party to ensure privacy. All reports are kept strictly confidential and are only viewed by individuals in this firm who have direct responsibility in the hiring process. All screening reports are kept and maintained separately from employee personnel files. Under the Fair Credit Reporting Act (FCRA), all background screenings are done only after a person has signed a release and received a disclosure.

   [**NOTE**: Additionally, the disclosure should include language about the impact of state laws if the employer operates in more than one state. Also, the impact of any union contract should also be considered.]

7. If a criminal record is to be used as a basis to disqualify an applicant form employment, the employer's policy is to provide an opportunity for an individualized assessment for those candidates identified by criminal background checks to determine if the policy as applied to an applicant is job related and consistent with business necessity.

8. All pre-employment background screenings are conducted by a third party to ensure privacy. All reports are kept strictly confidential and are only viewed by individuals in this firm who have direct responsibility in the hiring process. All screening reports are kept and maintained separately from employee personnel files. Under the Fair Credit Reporting Act (FCRA), all background screenings are done only after a person has signed a release and received a disclosure. Additionally, the disclosure should include language about the impact of state laws if the employer operates in more than one state. Also, the impact of any union contract should also be considered. The specific components of a candidate's background check will depend on the job to be performed including the job duties, the essential functions of the job, and the circumstances and environment under which the job is to be performed.

9. Any offers of employment will conditioned upon the firm's receipt of a pre-employment background screening investigation that is acceptable to the firm at the firm's sole discretion.

10. Different jobs may be subject to a greater degree of screening deriving upon the risk factors and responsibilities associated with each job. However, it is the policy of this firm to treat similarly situated individuals in a similar fashion and, as a result, all final candidates for each job or job category will be screened in a consistent fashion.

11. It is the policy of the employer to not ask about criminal records in the initial application process. However, the employer will advise all applicants that before any employment is made final, there will be a background check including criminal records in accordance with this policy. This enables all applicants to have a full and fair understanding of the hiring process. However, any inquiry about criminal history will be asked in a way reasonable designed not deter or chill applicants with criminal histories from applying. In addition, at such time that an applicant is asked about a criminal record, the employer will undertake measures to reasonably limit any inquiries taking into account job relatedness and business necessity.

    [**NOTE:** Above is optional depending upon how an employer intends to comply with the new EEOC Guidance reviewed in chapter 16.]

12. It is the duty of all persons with decision-making responsibilities for hiring to understand and carry out the firm's policies regarding the Safe Hiring Program and the commitment that all law and regulation be followed, including federal, state, and local discrimination laws.

Disclaimers

It is not the purpose of this Policy to provide detailed information or descriptions of each individual pre-employment background check that can be performed. It is not the purpose of this Policy to provide detailed information how to make a final decision regarding the results of a pre-employment background check; every case must be decided on its own merits subject to the Company requirement that all candidates be treated equally and consistently. It is not the purpose of this Policy to provide detailed information of all applicable law. Questions about these subjects should be directed to the Human Resources or Legal Departments.

This Policy does not limit ABC Company's right to hire, discipline or terminate. This Policy does not create a contract of employment. All employment is at will unless contract or law applies to the contrary.

Sample # 2 – Overall Practices to Carry out Employer's Safe Hiring Program

In addition to having a Safe Hiring Policy Statement, the firm's actual practices need to be documented. As you will see noted throughout this chapter when applicable, please keep in mind that depending upon how an employer chooses to proceed in light of the new EEOC 2012 Guidance on the use of criminal records, the following may need to be altered.

The Safe Hiring Program for ABC Company

- The Safe Hiring Program will be coordinated by either the Human Resources Department or Security Department, hereinafter referred to as the Program Administrator.

- The Program Administrator is responsible for implementation of procedures to ensure that all steps in the Safe Hiring Program are documented.

- The Program Administrator is also in charge of implementing, training all managers with hiring responsibility, and auditing adherence to this program, including periodic assessments to measure and evaluate the effectiveness of the program, review potential improvements, and to ensure continuing legal compliance. The Program Administrator is also responsible for full documentation of the program and maintaining ongoing documentation of the program's operation, as well as all training. The Program Administrator will oversee training, keeping a record of who participated, dates of attendance, the training material, as well as monitoring of the effectiveness of the training.

- The Program Administrator is also responsible for maintaining confidentiality of any material containing Personally Identifiable Information (PII) or anything else of a confidential nature such as criminal records, and to ensure that any information collected on an applicant is only used for purposes of employment decisions.

- The Program Administrator is also responsible for maintaining and updating his or her knowledge of the legal and practical aspects of safe hiring and background checks.

- The Program Administrator will also maintain a record of consultations and research considered in crafting the policy and procedures, as well as any justifications for the policies and procedures.

Sample # 3 – Statement Implementing the Application, Interview & Reference Checking (AIR) Process

An important part of the Safe Hiring Program is what is called the **AIR Process – an acronym for the Application, Interview and Reference Checking Process.** The next three chapters of this book examine each of these processes in detail. The memo below outlines how the ABC Company acknowledges and implements these important functions.

Statement of Best Practices

The ABC Company will utilize the application, interview, and reference checking stages of the hiring process. The Program Administrator is responsible for developing procedures for the implementation of these practices. These duties include:

- Developing forms that must be completed and placed in each applicant's file before the employment decision is made final.

- Training all persons with hiring responsibility in these procedures and document the training.

- Institute and document procedures to ensure these practices are being followed.

Sample # 4 – The Application Process

Application Stage – Use and Carefully Review Application Forms

[**NOTE:** The subject of ascertaining and utilizing criminal records in the hiring process is covered later in Sample # 10 – Criminal History Information.]

1. Use an application form, not just resumes:

- Use of an employment application form is considered a best practice. Resumes are not always complete or clear. Applications ensure uniformity, include all needed information that is obtained, prevent employers from having impermissible information, and provide employers with a place for applicants to sign certain necessary statements.

- The application will include a statement that lack truthfulness or contain material omissions are grounds to terminate the hiring process or employment no matter when they are discovered. Candidates are expected to provide full, accurate, and complete information as part of the hiring process.

- The application will include additional statements that must be approved by the Human Resource department and legal counsel. These can include statements that employment is "at will," and "we are an equal opportunity employer, and our firm has an arbitration policy when it comes to disputes concerning employment, such as employment is at-will."

Optional (Required if using a third party background screening firm.)

2. Require a release for a background check in the application process.

- Each job applicant must sign a consent form for a background check including a check for criminal records, past employment, and education. Under the Federal Fair Credit Reporting Act, before a background check is requested from a Consumer Reporting Agency, there must be a disclosure on a separate stand-alone document.

3. The employer will review the application carefully for "red flags "that may indicate a need for further review, including but not limited to:

- Applicant does not sign application.

- Applicant does not sign consent to background screening.

- Applicant leaves criminal questions blank (Note: Only applies if an employer requests criminal information on the initial application form.)

- Applicant self-reports a criminal violation (taking into account that applicants can self-report matters incorrectly). (Note: Only applies if an employer requests criminal information on the initial application form.

- Applicant fails to explain why he or she left past jobs.

- Applicant fails to explain gaps in employment history.

- Applicant gives an explanation for an employment gap or for the reason leaving a previous job that does not make sense.

- Applicant uses excessive cross-outs and changes, as though making it up as they go along.

- Applicant fails to give complete information, i.e. insufficient information to identify a past employer, leaves out salary, etc.

- Applicant fails to indicate or cannot recall the name of a former supervisor.

- The application form is not internally consistent or conflicts with other information obtained about the applicant.

Sample # 5 – The Interview Process

The key here is to include the six questions that should always be asked during the "housekeeping stage" of the interview.

ABC Company Interview Stage

These six questions are to be asked at every interview. These questions give a candidate the opportunity to clarify any matter in their application form. The six questions are:

1. We do background checks on everyone to whom we make an offer. Do you have any concerns you would like to discuss? Good applicants will shrug off this question.

2. We also check for criminal convictions for all finalists consistent with all rules, law, and regulations concerning the legal and appropriate use of criminal records and discrimination. Are you aware of that? (By this point, the candidate has already been invited for an interview, and an employer may decide that the process is far enough along that a question about relevant past criminal conduct can now be asked consistent with the new EEOC Guidance of 2012, discussed in Chapter 16. However, the EEOC advises against open ended criminal questions. An employer may choose in view of the new EEOC Guidance, to only advise the applicant that a criminal check will be conducted on finalists.)

3. We contact all past employers. What do you think they will say?

4. Will a past employer tell us that you were tardy, did not perform well, etc.?

5. Also, use the interview to ask questions about any unexplained employment gaps and ask the applicant to confirm everything on the application.

6. Is everything in the application and everything you told us in the hiring process true, correct, and complete?

Sample # 6 – The Reference Checking Stage

ABC Company Reference Checking Standards

Check References and Look for Unexplained Employment Gaps

- All past employers for a period of 7-10 years must be contacted. All efforts to contact past employers as well as the results of any conversations must be noted and documented. Even if a past employer will not provide qualitative information about the applicant's potential performance, it is critical to verify, at a minimum, his or her start date, end date, and job titles.

- The Program Administrator will create forms that are to be used to assist in the process. These will include a call history to document who was called and when, as well as the results of the call.

- The Program Administrator will also ensure there is proper training on legal and illegal reference questions. The Hiring Manager will make the decision necessary to determine if a candidate should be offered a position. However, Human Resources or a third-party screening firm will call past employers to confirm dates of employment and job titles in order to ensure that all finalists have been subject to the same process and that no one is hired unless the firm has made reasonable efforts to confirm past employment.

- The firm will not contact the current employer without an authorization, but reserves the right to call the current employer after the applicant has begun employment or to ask the applicant for a copy of their paycheck stub to confirm current employment.

> **AUTHOR TIP** See Chapter 9 for additional information on past employment checks.

Verifying past employment is one of the single most important tools an employer has. It is as important as doing criminal checks. Why? Past job performance can be an important predictor of future success. Some employers make a costly mistake by not checking past employment because they believe past employers may not give detailed information. However, even verifying dates of employment and job titles are critical because an employer must be concerned about unexplained gaps in the employment history. Although there can be many reasons for a gap in employment, if an applicant cannot account for the past seven to ten years, that can be a red flag.

In addition, documenting the fact that an effort was made will demonstrate due diligence.

It is also critical to know where a person has been because of the way criminal records are maintained in the United States. There are over 10,000 courthouses in America. If an employer knows where an applicant has been as a result of past employment checks, it increases the accuracy of a criminal search and decreases the possibility an applicant has served time for a serious offense.

Sample # 7 – The Pre-employment Screening Process

This next sample outlines the pre-employment process, including standards that the ABC Company has put into place.

ABC Company Pre-Employment Screening Process

All pre-employment screening will be conducted through a third party Consumer Reporting Agency (CRA). The Program Administrator will:

- Administer and coordinate the pre-employment screening program.
- Approve all forms utilized in the process and ensure that all forms are utilized consistently.
- To the extent deemed necessary, have the employer's legal department or outside counsel approve all forms and procedures for compliance with all applicable federal, state, and local law and regulations.
- Submit names and background requests to the CRA.
- Receive reports from the CRA.
- Contact the CRA as necessary to review the report or receive additional information.
- Review all reports, and in the case of negative or derogatory information, take appropriate action by contacting the hiring manger.
- Ensure that in the event an adverse decision is intended, the firm will take appropriate measures under the Fair Credit Reporting Act. That includes providing an applicant with a copy of the Consumer Report and statement of rights prior to the adverse action. If the adverse action is final, then the Program Administrator shall also cause a second notice, required by the FCRA, to be sent. The Program Administrator may delegate these duties to the CRA.
- When an exception is made to hire an applicant despite negative or derogatory information, the administrator will ensure the file properly documents the reasons for the decision.
- Maintain the background reports in complete privacy and confidence ensure only individuals with hiring authority are made aware of report contents, and further ensure that all reports are only ordered and utilized for screening purposes.
- Supervise the storage of all release forms and screening reports in a secure area, separate from employee personnel files.

- Select a CRA to perform pre-employment screening services through a Request for Proposal (RFP) process, and approve all billing submitted by the CRA.

- Ensure the program is administered uniformly and consistently and in compliance with all applicable laws including the Fair Credit Reporting Act, state and federal discrimination laws, and laws regulating the gathering and use of information in the employment process.

- No information shall be requested, obtained, or utilized that would be in violation of any state or federal law, rule, or regulation.

- Perform such other tasks and duties in order to carry out the aims and purposes of the pre-employment screening policy.

Mechanics of the Screening Program

- All applications for employment will contain consent approved forms for pre-employment screening including appropriate FCRA disclosure forms and any forms required by state law that all applicants must sign and date when applications are returned, OR prior to a candidate being selected as a finalist or being offered employment, the candidate shall sign approved forms necessary for pre-employment background screening.

- All forms, including the original application and resume, shall be transmitted to the CRA by the Program Administrator.

- All offers of employment are conditional upon receipt of a background report that is satisfactory to the firm. In a situation where an offer is made prior to the receipt of the background report, the offer letter shall state, in writing—

    "This offer of employment is conditional upon the employer's receipt of a pre-employment background screening investigation that is acceptable to the employer at the employer's sole discretion."

- No employment will commence prior to the completion of the background report unless the Program Administrator and department head/Vice-President determines there is an exceptional circumstance. In that case, the employment will be conditional on a satisfactory report, as indicated above.

Sample # 8 – Standards for Screening

ABC Company Standards for Screening

The Program Administrator shall determine for each position, in consultation as necessary with the hiring manager, what level of pre-employment screening is required, taking into account the nature of the position, including duties and responsibilities, the essential functions of the position, the duties to be performed, and the environment in which the job is to be performed. [**NOTE:** The following factors are given as example and are not necessarily a complete statement of all factors an employer will take into account.]

- What are the essential functions of the job?
- What are the job duties?
- What are the circumstances under which the job is to be performed?
- What is the environment in which the job is to be performed (e.g. an office, a private home, etc.?)
- Does the position have access to money or assets?
- Does the position carry significant authority or fiduciary responsibility?

- Does the position carry access to trade secrets, confidential information, personal information of others, or any other information that can be considered confidential or private?
- Does the position have access to members of the public or co-workers so that any propensity to violence or dishonesty could foreseeably cause harm?
- What level of supervision does an employee have in the manner their job is to be performed?
- Would the position be difficult to replace in terms of recruitment, hiring and training?
- Would a new hire's falsification of skills, experience, or background put the firm at risk or lower the firm's productivity?
- Would a bad hire expose the firm to litigation or financial claims from the applicant, co-workers, customers, or the public, or other risks?
- Is there a statutory, licensing, or legal requirement for certain positions to be screened?
- Does the position involve driving?
- Does the new position involve unique or peculiar risk, such as access to children, the aged or the infirmed, work inside of a home or some other environment out of public view, or hold a position of authority?

Levels of Screening

The Program Administrator will designate which positions shall be screened at which level. Additional screening may be requested as necessary for a particular position by a hiring manager or the Program Administrator. All screenings will be done consistently and uniformly. Once it has been determined that a particular position requires a particular level of pre-employment screening, all finalists for that particular position will be screened at the same level.

[**Author's Note**: The four levels listed below are examples of screening that can be utilized:]

1. **Individual** — For casual or temporary labor. Recommended search: County criminal search in local county or county of residence and other individual reports such as a Social Security trace and driving record.

2. **Basic** — For entry-level employees, retail or manufacturing, or positions where the employer has internally checked references and education. Recommended search: A full seven year on-site criminal records check for felonies and misdemeanors, Credit Report or Social Security and identity check, and driver's license check.

3. **Standard** — For more responsible positions and permanent hire. Recommended search: The Basic search above plus verification of the last three employers (and references if available) and highest post high school education.

4. **Extended** — For positions involving increased responsibility or supervision of others. Recommended search: The Basic and Standard search above plus checking Superior Court civil cases in the last two relevant counties for litigation matters that may be job related.

[**Author's Note**: The Program Administrator may review other available tools such as a sexual offender or a criminal database search as long as it is used as a supplemental, and not a primary, source of information.]

Sample # 9 – Analysis of Information

ABC Company - Analysis of the Background Screen

General:

When a background check report is returned with derogatory or potentially negative information that would reasonably impact a hiring decision, the Program Administrator will contact the hiring manager or other appropriate person to review the information. The Program Administrator will normally provide a verbal summary rather than the actual written report in order to limit confidential material from circulating within the company. The Program Administrator will only convey the information that is necessary for the company to engage in a decision making process in order to maintain confidentially.

The following are general guidelines as to what information is considered potentially negative or derogatory. This list is not intended to be exhaustive or exclusive. There may be other factors which are appropriate for the position or the applicant under consideration. The decision to hire or not hire is not based upon any rigid matrix or pre-determined formula but is based upon a consideration of the totality of the circumstances. The same guidelines may also apply to decision impacting retention, promotion or reassignment. General guidelines include:

- In the event of a criminal record, in addition to any factors listed below, the employer will conduct an analysis pursuant to its Criminal History Information Policy. (See Sample #10 below.)

- The derogatory information is inconsistent with the nature of the job, taking into account the risk factors listed above under "Standards for Screening." (See Sample #8 above.)

- The applicant or employee is found to have engaged in dishonest, misleading, or untruthful conduct, including but not limited to misrepresentations or omission of material facts during the selection process. This can include but is not limited to discrepancies or falsehoods in self-reporting criminal records as well as past employment, education, and credentials, or in identification of the applicant.

- The applicant or employee is found to have engaged in violence, wrongdoing, or other conduct inappropriate in the workplace. The applicant is found to not have the necessary knowledge, skills, abilities, experience aptitude, or qualifications to successfully fulfill the job requirements.

- The information demonstrates that the applicant or employee has engaged in conduct that may be legally considered in the hiring process. That finding may preclude an applicant from effectively performing his or her job duties or may create a security or safety issue in the workplace.

- The derogatory information makes the applicant unable or ineligible to perform the essential job functions or creates a potential legal liability for the firm. For example, the applicant must drive a vehicle as part of the job responsibility and does not have a valid license or a clear driving record.

Process:

If the hiring manager, the Program Administrator, or management believes the information will form the basis of an adverse action or termination based upon the application of the guidelines reviewed above, then the Program Administrator will document the basis of the decision, including specifically the job-related basis for the adverse action or termination.

In the event of an intended adverse action or termination, the Program Administrator will also initiate the adverse action notification procedures required by the Fair Credit Reporting Act.

If the hiring manager believes the negative information should not preclude employment or promotion, the hiring manager will seek approval from the respective department head or Vice-President who will decide the issue in consultation with the Program Administrator and legal counsel, if appropriate. If the decision is to offer the position despite negative information, then the reasons for the decision shall be appropriately documented in writing and provided to the Program Administrator. The purpose is to protect the firm by showing the negative information was considered in light of all available information about the candidate and the position, and the firm exercised discretion only after a due diligence inquiry. The documentation is needed in the event the decision is challenged in the future. For example, an applicant with negative information may object to not being hired because a previous candidate with similar negative information did get hired. The previous candidate who was hired may have had excellent references or past work history that justified hiring despite negative information. In addition, if a person with adverse information is hired and that person commits an act resulting in harm to the firm or causes litigation, the fact the person was hired only after a screening process in which all facts were carefully considered would tend to establish due diligence.

In reviewing the background report or other material forming the basis of not hiring, retaining, promoting or reassigning a consumer, the Program Administrator will make all reasonable effort to protect the privacy of the consumer and the confidentiality of the information, including such processes as a not widely distributing the entire background checks, making the information only available to decision makers and only release information that is reasonably needed by decision makers.

Sample # 10 – Criminal History Information

(**NOTE:** The exact policy will depend upon how an employer chooses to comply with the EEOC Enforcement Guidance issued April 25, 2012 that is reviewed in Chapter 16. This is presented only as an example of how an employer may prepare a policy).

Criminal Convictions: As part of the employer's policy of maintaining a safe and productive workplace, an employer will also conduct a screening of criminal records for any individual prior to or at the time of employment. However, it is also this firm's policy that a criminal conviction does not automatically preclude a person from being hired. In the event this firm confirms the applicant has a criminal record, the hiring decision will be based upon a careful consideration of the factors outlined in the current EEOC Guidance in effect. The employer will, among other things, carefully review and balance the nature of the position in question, the nature and gravity of the offense, and the amount of time that has passed since the conviction, as set forth in the EEOC Guidance, to determine whether there is a job related business justification for not hiring the applicant. For these reasons, the firm will closely scrutinize the application of any candidate with such a criminal conviction or who is currently on probation or parole, consistent with the firm's policy of not automatically excluding any applicant with a criminal record consistent with the current EEOC Guidance in effect.

- A check for criminal records is conducted to determine whether a person is fit for a particular job. The firm recognizes that society has a vested interest in giving ex-offenders a chance to obtain gainful employment. However, the firm is under a due diligence obligation to make efforts to determine if a person is reasonably fit for a particular position.
- If a criminal record is found, then the firm will first determine if there is a business reason not to hire the person as set forth in the EEOC Enforcement Guidance issued on April 25, 2012.
- The firm will not consider any arrest that did not result in a conviction. However, the firm may consider the underling behavior associated with the arrest if it can be determined, and will also consider any explanation offered by the applicant. However, if an applicant has a pending or current charge that has not been resolved, the firm reserves the right to request that the applicant first obtain a disposition of the matter before progressing further with the application process.

- The firm will also take into account applicable state laws that place limitations on the use or consideration of criminal conduct

- The firm's employment application will not ask about criminal convictions. It will however include a criminal record check advisement that a criminal record check will be conducted at an appropriate time, pursuant to all federal and state rules and regulations including discrimination rules and guidances from the EEOC. The application will also state that a criminal record will not automatically disqualify an applicant. The advisement is not intended to chill or deter applicants with criminal records from applying but is only intended to fairly and accurately disclose the nature of the firm's hiring processes. This is important for EEOC compliance.

- The firm reserves the right to inquire of any applicant if he or she has a criminal record, either during an interview, post-interview or before making an offer. The firm will request that an applicant fully complete a form specifying if the applicant has a criminal record and relevant details about it.

- The firm will make reasonable efforts to limit any inquiry about past criminal conduct in a way reasonably designed to avoid requiring the revelation of information that is old or irrelevant.

- In the event a criminal matter is revealed by the applicant, the firm will not automatically act on such information without first going through the following process:

  1. The employer will first determine whether such criminal matter is relevant to the job. If the firm determines it is not relevant, then the inquiry will end.

  2. If the firm determines the inquiry is relevant to the job, the employer will then analyze the information in light of the job utilizing the three part test as set forth by the EEOC in its most recent Guidance.

  3. In the event that an analysis of the criminal record of an applicant pursuant to the three part test leads the firm to conclude that there is a job related business justification to not consider the applicant further, the firm will sent out appropriate pre- and adverse action notices pursuant to the Fair Credit Reporting Act.

  4. As part of the Adverse Action process, the firm's Program Administrator will also provide the applicant with an opportunity for an Individualized Assessment of the applicant pursuant to the 2012 EEOC Guidance on criminal records.

In a situation where an applicant makes a material false statement or a material omission about a past criminal record, and the firm determines that such falsehood or omission was intentional and reflects an act of deceit or dishonesty, then the firm may make a decision not to proceed with the application process on that basis since honesty and integrity are always an essential function of any position in this company.

Sample Policies and the Matrix of Criminal Record Use

The sample internal policy does not contain a "matrix" for the use of criminal records in the sense of outlining certain crimes or types of crimes that would eliminate a candidate from consideration. These are sometimes referred to as an "Adjudication Matrix," where a screening firm applies an employer's criteria to information found. These matrixes can go beyond criminal searches and include past employment, credit reports, driving records, and other searches. A number of attorneys, background firms, or employers have developed such matrixes or guidelines. For example, a criminal offense matrix could list the various crimes that would make an applicant ineligible for employment. These are typically organized around a red light, orange light, and green light system. A red light mean the person is not eligible based upon the nature of the offense. A green light means the applicant is clear, and the orange light means that the offense has not been included in the matrix or additional matters need consideration. (A related issue, discussed in Chapter 15, is criminal policies that may attempt to flatly exclude applicants with certain types of criminal records.)

Prior to the issuance of the EEOC Guidance on April 25, 2012, a criminal record matrix was generally considered a source of potential liability. The use of a matrix could lead to allegations of automated disqualification which would potentially run counter to the EEOC's position that each candidate with a criminal record be considered on their individual merits right then the make a decision solely on their status as an ex-offender. This is the precise problem that the EEOC has dealt with historically and was a critical factor for part of this new Guidance.

Because of the emphasis in the new Guidance on employers only asking criminal questions relevant to a job, as opposed to broad and opened ended questions, the use of a criminal matrix now may be something that employers need to consider. A matrix can assist in the development of the level of granular questions needed to only ask about relevant criminal matters. However, there is a critical difference between an exclusionary "red, yellow or green light" matrix and the type of matrix that may be needed for EEOC compliance.

A matrix for EEOC compliance does not represent a final decision. There are two potential uses for a matrix in terms of compliance with the EEOC Guidance,

First, as outlined in Chapter 16, a matrix is only a tool to permit analysis as to which crimes are relevant to which jobs in the first place. A matrix can help employers decide how to design and limit questions about past criminal conduct so that questions are not overly broad, and can be more closely tailored to h job.

Second, as part of EEOC compliance program, if an applicant admits to a criminal record, it does not lead to automatic exclusions. Rather, by use of a matrix, an employer can determine if the criminal matter is relevant or not. If not relevant, the inquiry ends. If the criminal matter is relevant, then the employer moves onto the next step of the analysis, which is the application of the three-part "Green" factors. Even if the three part-test leads to a conclusion that the criminal matter is job related and that exclusion is business necessity, the applicant under the EEOC Guidance would still be entitled to an "Individualized Assessment."

It should also be noted that in the event an employer wishes to engage is such a matrix in order to comply with the EEOC requirements, a background screening firm is only applying an employer's criteria to the data found. In other words, the screening firm is administering a clerical task (although it can also be done by intelligent software) by applying the employer's criteria and is not making an independent judgment.

Language About Background Screening in the Employee Manual

Many employers do not refer to pre-employment screening in their Employee Manuals. Even when employers screen current employees for purposes of promotion, reassignment, or retention, there are no legal requirements that compel employers to refer to "screening" in their handbooks. However, there is also no reason not to include screening in the employee handbook.

An Employee Manual is one of the most effective ways to communicate general policies and procedures to employees. A well-written manual helps avoid misunderstandings about policies or benefits, helps avoid lawsuits, and thereby enhances morale. Manuals also promote consistency of treatment and reduce the risk of charges of discrimination being made.

Using the Manual for Supplemental Background Checks

There are situations where an employer may need to perform a supplemental background check after a person is hired.

1. After the employee has been hired, an employer may need to conduct additional background checks to determine eligibility for promotion, re-assignment, or retention in the same manner as described above.

2. An employer may have to deal with specific job requirements imposed by a client, such as a background check of current employees assigned to the position. (See discussion in Chapter 29 on screening current employees.)

3. An employer may decide for due diligence reasons to conduct "on going" checks as part of a retention program (See discussion in Chapter 29 on screening current employees).

4. An employer may discover some sort of workplace misconnect or wrongdoing. Under the FACT Act, an employer can do background checks in such a situation without first obtaining a written authorization or providing a disclosure (See Chapter 3 on the Fair Credit Reporting Act).

5. An employer may have a policy requiring employees to advise an employer if they are arrested. If so, an employer many need to investigate the behavior underlying the arrest (See Chapters 15 and 16 concerning arrest records).

6. A firm may be acquired or merged with another firm, and the new owners wants background checks of existing employees (See discussion in Chapter 29 on screening current employees).

The sample policy on employment screening below is suggested language for an Employee Manual. The text can be modified as appropriate for firms that choose to include their employment screening policy in the employee handbook for current employees if there is post-hiring screening. Because no one handbook applies to all businesses or all situations, this language is a general suggestion.

Sample # 11 – Sample Policy to be Placed in Employee Manual

Sample Policy on Employment Background Screening

To ensure that individuals who join this firm are well qualified and have a strong potential to be productive and successful —and to further ensure that this firm maintains a safe and productive work environment free of any form of violence, harassment, or misconduct — it is the policy of this company to perform pre-employment screening and credentials verification on applicants who are offered and accept an offer of employment. A pre-employment background check is a sound business practice that benefits everyone. It is not a reflection on a particular job applicant.

Offers of employment are conditional upon the firm's receipt of a pre-employment background screening investigation that is acceptable to the firm at the firm's sole discretion. Any applicant who refuses to sign a background screening release form will not be eligible for employment.

[**Optional:** The firm also may conduct background checks as appropriate for purposes of retention, promotion, or re-assignment. All of the same rule and policies apply.]

To ensure privacy, all pre-employment background screenings are conducted by a third party. All screenings are conducted in strict conformity with the Federal Fair Credit Reporting Act (FCRA), the Americans with Disabilities Act (ADA), and state and federal anti-discrimination and privacy laws. All reports are kept strictly confidential and are only viewed by individuals in this firm who have direct responsibility in the hiring process. All screening reports are kept and maintained separately from your personnel file. Under the Fair Credit Reporting Act, all background screenings are done only after a person has received a disclosure and has signed a release. In addition, you have certain legal rights to discover and to dispute or explain any information prepared by the third party background-screening agency. If the employer intends to deny employment wholly or partly because of information obtained in an pre-employment check conducted by the company's consumer reporting agency, then the applicant will first be provided with a copy of the background report, a statement of rights, and the name, address, and phone number of the consumer reporting agency to contact about the results of the check or to dispute its accuracy.

The firm also reserves the right to conduct a background screening any time after the employee has been hired to determine eligibility for promotion, re-assignment, or retention in the same manner as described above.

Applicants also are expected to provide references from their former employers as well as educational reference information that can be used to verify academic accomplishments and records. Background checks may include verification of information provided on the completed application for employment, the applicant's resume, or on other forms used in the hiring process. Information to be verified includes, but is not limited to, Social Security Number and previous addresses. Employer may also conduct a reference check and verify the applicant's education and employment background as stated on the employment application or other documents listed above.

The background check may also include a criminal record check. If a conviction is discovered, then the employer will closely scrutinize the conviction in view of our policy of ensuring a safe and profitable workplace. A criminal conviction does not necessarily automatically bar an applicant from employment. Before an employment decision is made, a determination will be made whether the conviction is related to the position for which the individual is applying or would present safety or security risks, taking into account the nature and gravity of the act, the nature of the position, and the age of the conviction, as well as the most current EEOC Guidance in effect on the proper use of a criminal record.

Additional checks such as a driving record or a credit report may be made on applicants for particular job categories if appropriate and job-related. Employment screening assessments to determine an applicant's job fit may also be required of all applicants. Skills tests related to the demands of the job may also be required.

This firm relies upon the accuracy of information contained in the employment application as well as the accuracy of other data presented throughout the hiring process and employment, including any oral interviews. Any misrepresentations, falsifications, or material omissions in any of the information or data, no matter when discovered, may result in the firm's exclusion of the individual from further consideration for employment or, if the person has been hired, termination of employment.

Conclusion — Procedures for Implementing Your Safe Hiring Program

After formulating a general policy and outlining the practices the employer will utilize, the final step is to create the implementation procedures. A checklist such as the one below can be a handy tool to ensure that the practices are actually being followed and implemented. Each firm that implements a Safe Hiring Program will undoubtedly customize the procedural details to accommodate its particular needs. However, employers, at a minimum, should address the issues raised in this chapter. The last portion of the Safe Hiring Checklist is to be used to document the actual procedures used in the Safe Hiring Program.

The ABC Company Safe Hiring Checklist

To be completed for every new applicant before being hired.

Applicant: _____

Position: _____

Hiring Manager _____

Task	Yes/No/ NA	Date/ Initials	Notes/Follow-up
Application Process			
Did applicant sign the consent form?			
Is application complete?			
Did applicant sign and date application?			
Did applicant leave criminal questions blank? (Only applies if employer requests criminal information on initial application form.)			
Did applicant indicate a criminal record?			
Did applicant explain why left past jobs?			
Did applicant explain gaps in job history?			
Any excessive cross-outs or changes seen?			
Is the application internally consistent and consistent with other information in the employer's possessions?			
Interview Process			
Did applicant explain any excessive cross-outs/changes?			
Leaving past jobs: Did applicant explain?			
Leaving past jobs: Was verbal reason consistent with reason on written app?			
Employment Gaps: Did applicant explain?			
Employment Gaps: Are verbal explanations consistent with written app?			
Security Question. 1 – "Our firm has a standard policy of background checks and drug tests on all applicants. Do you have any concerns you would like to share with me about our procedures?"			Answer:
Security Question 2 – "We also do criminal background checks on finalists pursuant to all applicable rules and regulations including EEOC Guidance. Are you aware of that?"			Answer:

Security Question 3 – "If I were to contact past employers pursuant to the release you have signed, what do you think they would tell us about you?"			Answer:
Security Question 4 – "If I were to contact past employers pursuant to the release you have signed, would any of them tell us you were terminated or were disciplined?"			Answer:
Security Question 5 – "Please explain any gaps in employment."			Answer:
Security Question 6 – "Is everything in the application and everything you told us in the hiring process true, correct, and complete?"			Answer:
Reference Checks (performed by employer or by a third party)			
Have references been checked for at least last 5-10 years, regardless of whether past employers will give details?			
Have efforts been documented?			

Discrepancies between information located and what applicant reported in application:
  a. dates/title salary/job title
  b. reason for leaving			

Background Check			
Submitted for background check?			
Check completed?			
Background check reviewed for discrepancies/issues?			
If not CLEAR or SATISFACTORY, what action is taken per policy and procedures?			Describe:

Notes: Use back if necessary. Sign and date all entries

Chapter 7

AIR – The Application Process

When does the application process start? In a *Safe Hiring Program*, it starts before applications are printed or given out. It really starts when the job is first created.

Inside This Chapter:

- ✓ Application Process Starts BEFORE Application Is Filled Out

- ✓ Using the Application Form as a Hiring Tool

- ✓ Reasons Employers Should Not Rely on Resumes

- ✓ Ten Critical Items Every Application Needs

- ✓ Critical Areas and Questions Applications Must Avoid

- ✓ Applications and Disclosure of Criminal Records

- ✓ Final Step—Review the Application as a Whole

- ✓ Ten Sure Signs of a Lawsuit Waiting to Happen

- ✓ Review the Form with the Applicant

- ✓ Where to Find a Good Application Form

Application Process Starts BEFORE Application Is Filled Out

 The key walkaway point in the next three chapters is that a background check all by itself may not constitute due diligence. Due diligence really starts at the very beginning of the process. In general, screening firms find that firms that have a well thought out and implemented safe hiring program are much less likely to be surprised with derogatory or negative information.

First, an employer needs to create a **job description**. This is important for a number of reasons. Having a job description that clearly defines the essential function of the job and core competence not only helps identify and select the right candidate during recruitment, but also provides legal protection when it comes to claims of discrimination or compliance with the Americans with Disabilities Act (ADA). It is essential to have a job description in the event a criminal record is disclosed or discovered. This helps insure the employer is consistent with the requirements of the federal Equal Employment Opportunity Commission (EEOC), as explained in Chapter 2. As discussed in Chapter 19 on Social Media Background Checks, having a well-designed job description also helps employers utilize social media, if they choose, in a way that lessens the risks of discrimination complaints and lawsuits.

A job description should clearly indicate the levels of education and experience required of candidates. Those who do not have the required education or experience may be discouraged from applying. If a candidate misleads an employer about knowledge, skills, or experience, then the fact the requirements were clearly set forth in the job description will assist the employer in the event there is a rejection or termination. An employer can always take the position that dishonesty on an application is grounds for termination. However, the employer's position is buttressed when it is clear from a well-written job description there were certain requirements for the position, the job description was provided to the applicant, and the applicant misled the employer about his or her qualifications.

Numerous resources and websites, as well as commercially available software, can assist an employer in preparing job descriptions. One useful site, found at www.careerinfonet.org/jobwriter/default.aspx?nodeid=19, contains a job description writer feature. Employers may also use the job descriptions formulated by the National Academy of Science, Committee on Occupational Classification and Analysis. This organization created the *Dictionary of Occupational Titles* or DOT (which is not to be confused with the Department of Transportation and DOT drug testing). For an online dictionary of jobs, visit their web page at www.wave.net/upg/immigration/dot_index.html.

The job duties of a person in a management or supervisor position are also a critical consideration. Does part of the written job description indicate a manager's duty to "record, report, and address issues of workplace misconduct such as acts of workplace violence, or harassment, or drug abuse?" Placing these duties in the written job description of supervisors serves to re-enforce their role in workplace safety.

Inform the Applicant about the Background Check

As part of any recruitment effort, the employer is well-advised to place applicants on notice that the firm practices safe hiring with background checks. The goal is to get maximum advantage from safe hiring by discouraging applicants to hide something when applying. Employers can place a phrase in the job announcement, bulletin, classified advertisement, or internet site that indicates the firm requires background checks.

The most likely effect is that applicants with something to hide will go down the block to employers that do not exercise due diligence. Let a competitor be the employer of choice for people with problems. Announcing a company background check policy does not keep good applicants from employers any more than security checkpoints at airports stop people from flying.

In any discussion of an employment application an employer should keep in mind new guidelines issued by the EEOC on April 25, 2012 titled **Enforcement Guidance on the Consideration of Arrest and Conviction Records in**

Employment Decisions Under Title VII of the Civil Rights Act of 1964. The Guidance impacts how and when criminal records are considered, including questions on the application form about past criminal matters. The EEOC was clearly concerned with the ability of applicants with criminal records to obtain employment. As discussed in detail in Chapter 16, the new EEOC Guidance among other things suggests that an employer consider not asking an applicant about a criminal record in the initial application, although such a rule is not mandatory. A question about past criminal conduct on an application could potentially "chill" or "deter" a person with criminal record from even applying. In addition, the EEOC strongly suggests that if and when an inquiry is made about criminal conduct, there be some reasonably job related limitation so an employer is not asking a broad and open-ended question that spans the applicant's entire life. Such an inquiry could potentially result in what amounts to a lifetime ban or at least a significant barrier to employment opportunities.

If an employer follows this suggestion, then an employer may temper any comment about a criminal background check while noting the position is subject to an appropriate criminal background check consistent with current EEOC Guidelines prior to an applicant starting the new position.

AUTHOR TIP Here is a sample statement an employer may consider if questions about criminal records are removed from the application:

> "If the company determines an applicant is suitable for the position based on a job related evaluation of skills and experience that may also include an interview, prior to final selection and subsequent employment, an applicant will be subject to a background check that is appropriate to the job functions and business necessity. If related criminal records are revealed in the process, the applicant will not be disqualified automatically."

Such an approach may be a way for employers to balance the need to follow EEOC Guidelines, yet at the same time ensure a safe and productive workplace. For example, during the interview process an employer should not ask to show a right to work in the U.S. but may make statement that such proof will be required if a person begins work. The key point is to ensure all applicants have a fair chance to apply and to be considered on their own merits before being rejected due to a particular status that applies to them. Such a statement should not be a roundabout way to slam the door in the face of an ex-offender or to "chill" or deter an ex-offender from even applying. On the other hand, an employer must also be concerned that applicants understand that at some appropriate point an appropriate background check will occur. Arguably, it would be unfair to mislead someone into thinking that a background check will never be conducted.

Using the Application Form as a Hiring Tool

One of the most critical safe hiring tools is the application process. Done correctly, the application process protects the employer. Although it seems obvious, the most important aspect of the application process is to use a proper job application form. Consider it a best practice. A professionally reviewed, pre-printed job application should allow the employer to legally obtain the necessary information to begin the hiring process. Applications ensure uniformity and that all needed information is obtained. Also, applications protect employers from having impermissible information a resume may contain. Resumes, for example, may reveal membership in groups or organizations that may reveal that an applicant is a member of protected class, knowledge employers can do without. The application provides employers with a place for applicants to sign necessary statements that are part of the hiring process.

As a rule of thumb, resumes are not always complete or clear. If an employer insists upon using resumes, then the employer is well-advised to always use a standardized application form as well. Learn more about using resumes later in this chapter.

Revealing Negative Information

Negative information honestly disclosed and explained on an application or in an interview may very well have no effect, especially if the applicant otherwise has an excellent and verified work history. However, when an applicant has failed to honestly disclose negative information such as the existence of a criminal conviction, then the employer's concern turns to the lack of honesty involved. If the applicant is dishonest and negative information is first revealed by a background check, then the failure to hire may be justified. That is why it is important to have broad enough language in the application to cover all relevant offenses.

AUTHOR TIP **All applications should have this language:**

"The information provided by the applicant is true and correct, and any misstatements or omission of material facts in the application or the hiring process may result in discontinuing of the hiring process or termination of employment, no matter when discovered."

This allows the employer greater flexibility in dealing with a dishonest applicants. As discussed in Chapter 8, there is scientific evidence that demonstrates what employers already know — if a person was dishonest in the way they got the job, there is a likelihood they will be dishonest once in the job.

Reasons Employers Should Not Rely on Resumes

Some employers still hire based primarily upon a resume. This can be a major mistake from the viewpoint of safe hiring. A resume is a marketing tool for an applicant. Many resumes start by describing the type of job an applicant is looking for or a statement of skills and experience. In a resume, an applicant picks and chooses whatever information he or she wants to share.

Many job hunters use a resume writing service. While there is nothing wrong with using a service to prepare a professional looking resume, the service typically will attempt to enhance the applicant's experience. The service's goal is to get the applicant to the interview stage.

Employers, however, need facts in order to make hiring decisions. What are some of the dangers in using a resume?

Resumes May Have Information an Employer Should Not Have

For some reason, job applicants often feel compelled to reveal things about themselves that an employer does not need or legally should not know. Resumes often reveal volunteer affiliations, hobbies, interests, or memberships in groups that reveal such prohibited information as race, religion, ethnicity, sexual orientation, or age. For example, a resume may reveal a person does volunteer time with a church or belongs to a group that is clearly associated with a particular race or nationality. The problem is the federal EEOC and equivalent sets of individual state's rules prohibit an employer from obtaining or using such information. Having this information in the form of a resume in the employer's file is not a good practice in the event the employer is ever the subject of civil litigation or a government investigation into their hiring practices. By using an application form, an applicant cannot volunteer irrelevant information an employer should not possess.

In addition, it is much easier for an employer to prescreen candidates using a standardized application. An employer trying to screen a large number of resumes can more easily compare applicants. Another benefit to using a standard application is the advantages provided in compliance for employer subject to EEOC reporting rules including the Department of Labor, Office of Federal Contract Compliance Programs (OFCCP).

The Six Biggest Job Applicant Lies

Although statistics vary widely, there is widespread agreement that a substantial number of resumes and applications belong in the fiction section of the bookstore. The rate of fraud can be as high as 40% and higher according to different sources. Applicants certainly have the right to put their best foot forward, and puffing their qualifications is an American tradition. But when puffing crosses the line into fabrication, an employer needs to be concerned. When you hire an applicant who uses lies and fabrication to get hired, the issue is that the same type of dishonesty will continue once they have the job. What are the six most common fabrications claimed by job applicants?

✓ **Claiming a degree not earned:** Yes, believe it or not, applicants will make up a degree. Sometimes, they actually went to the school but never graduated. Some applicants may have had just a few credits to go, and decided to award themselves the degree anyway. On some occasions, an applicant will claim a degree from a school they did not even attend. The best practice for an employer is to state clearly on the application form that the applicant should list any school they want the employer to consider. In that way, if an applicant lies, the employer can act on the lack of truthfulness regardless of whether the educational requirement is part of the job requirements.

✓ **Diploma Mills or Fake Degree:** A related issue is diploma mills or fake degrees that can be purchased online. For those that actually attended classes, read books, wrote papers and took tests to earn a diploma, you apparently did it the old fashioned way. Now, getting a "degree" is as easy as going online and using your credit card. There are even websites that will print out very convincing, fake degrees from nearly any school in America. In fact, the author obtained a degree for his dog in Business Administration from the University of Arizona-and the dog had been dead for ten years. A transcript was even obtained and the dog got a "B" in English! Some sites will even provide a phone number so an employer can call and verify the fake degree. Some of the degree mills even have fake accreditation agencies with names similar to real accreditation bodies, in order to give a fake accreditation for a fake school.

✓ **Job Title:** Another area of faking is the job description or job title. Applicants can easily give their career an artificial boost by "promoting" themselves to a supervisor position, even if they never managed anyone.

✓ **Claiming Knowledge, Skills, Abilities, or Experience They Do Not Possess:** Employers normally hire based on a job description that will describe the knowledge, skills, and abilities (KSA) needed for a job as well as the experience required. These are exactly the areas, however, where employers often find a candidate has fibbed. (For more about the importance of identifying and describing the KSA associated with a job, see: www.va.gov/jobs/hiring/apply/ksa.asp.)

✓ **Dates of Employment:** Another concern for employers is applicants that cover up dates of employment in order to hide "employment gaps." For some applicants, it may be a seemingly innocent attempt to hide the fact that it has taken awhile to get a new job. In other cases, the date fabrication can be more sinister, such as a person that spent time in custody for a crime who may be trying to hide that fact.

✓ **Compensation:** A related issue is pay applicants have been known to exaggerate compensation in order to have a better negotiating position in the new job.

Verifying past employment is one of the single most important tools for an employer since, generally speaking, past job performance can be an important predictor of future success. The common denominator in all of these lies is that they can be all be discovered by a program of pre-employment screening. To quote a phrase popular in the 1980s: "Trust, but verify."

Resumes May Not Have Information an Employer Needs

As mentioned, resumes may amplify facts and experience. At the same time, resumes may not give an employer all the information needed to make an informed hiring decision. With a proper application, an applicant cannot skip over jobs he or she would rather not mention. An application can allow an employer to spot unexplained employment gaps. Also, job applicants typically do not self-reveal their criminal records in a resume.

Finally, an application form can contain critical elements that an employer may want to convey to the applicant or critical questions that an employer may want to ask, such as whether the applicant has a criminal record.

> **AUTHOR TIP**
>
> Because employment applications provide legal and practical advantages, some firms astutely reject resumes and may return them to applicants. Jobseekers are told they must fill out the company-approved application only or are told increasingly to use the employer's online job portal, often powered by an **Applicant Tracking System (ATS)**, as the exclusive means of applying for employment.
>
> There are many advantages to using ATS online systems, such as tracking legal compliance with the rules for the Office of Federal Contract Compliance Programs (OFCCP). (See: www.dol.gov/ofccp/).
>
> The same considerations in this chapter generally apply regardless of whether an employer uses a paper application or an online application.

Ten Critical Items Every Application Needs

It is much easier for an employer to prescreen candidates using a standardized application. An employer trying to screen a large number of resumes can more easily compare applicants. Ten critical things need to be addressed in every application as part of a Safe Hiring Program:

1. The application needs to clearly state that "there will be a background check" or "a background check will be performed." (See discussion above about the added complexities of such questions in view of the 2012 EEOC Guidance on criminal records.) A well-worded application form discourages applicants with something to hide and encourages applicants to be open and honest.

2. An application should state that "untruthfulness or material omissions are grounds to terminate the hiring process or employment, no matter when discovered." This is critical when an applicant is not truthful about a criminal conviction or some other important item of information in their application, especially if it is discovered after the person has been hired and onboarded.

3. The form should clarify that "a criminal conviction is not automatic grounds for rejection." As discussed later in Chapter 16, it could be a form of discrimination to automatically reject an applicant because of a criminal record. The keyword is "automatically." Without the statement that there is no automatic rejection, an applicant may be deterred from applying in the first place out of fear of being automatically rejected upon honestly answering the question. The chilling effect on an applicant could be a form of discrimination in itself, which is why this additional language is necessary. Conversely, if a person has lied about a criminal violation, then dishonesty may become the basis for disqualification. As is discussed in Chapter 16, an employer should very carefully consider if the application should ask about past criminal matters. If an employer wishes to avoid such a question at the application stage, the employer can give a "criminal advisement" informing the applicant that at some later stage relevant questions about past criminal matters will be asked.

4. The application form should indicate the applicant consents to "pre-employment background screening including verifying educational and professional credentials, past employment, and court records." Such a release may discourage an applicant with something to hide or encourage an applicant to be forthcoming in an interview. If

an employer uses an outside service to perform a pre-employment screening, the federal Fair Credit Reporting Act requires there must be a consent and disclosure form separate from the application.

5. The consent portion on any release form used for a background check must indicate the release is "valid for future screening for retention, promotion, or reassignment (unless revoked in writing)." This is sometimes referred to legally as an "Evergreen" clause meaning it stays active in the future (although most likely not forever since that would not be reasonable to assume a consumer would consent forever). This is helpful, for example, when an employer needs to conduct a post-employment investigation into allegations of sexual harassment or other workplace problems. Even though the Fair and Accurate Credit Transaction Act (FACT Act) of 2003 gives employers more flexibility to conduct investigations where there is suspicion of workplace misconduct or wrongdoing, such a clause provides an employer additional grounds. An employer may also want to check on information brought to its attention after the hiring occurred that may suggest dishonesty on the consumer's part or the existence of a criminal record, even though there is no current misconduct. At least one state, California, has a state law that suggests such a future release is not valid and a new one is always needed. California also has procedural requirements for any employer that obtains the information directly without the use of a screening firm. Employers may wish to consult their attorneys if there is ever a need to do additional checks after a person is hired.

6. The application form must ask for ALL employment for the past 5-10 years. This is critical. A standardized application form makes it easier to spot unexplained gaps in employment. This is an important step in the hiring process and a critical part of exercising due diligence. Even if an employer hires a background company to perform a pre-employment criminal check, records can be missed because there is no national criminal record resource available for use by private employers. Criminal checks must be done in each county where the applicant has lived, worked, or attended school. If a person has an uninterrupted job history, an employer may have more confidence that the applicant has not been in serious trouble over the years.

7. The form should ask about addresses for the last seven to ten years. This helps in determining the scope of any criminal record search.

8. The form should allow the applicant to indicate whether the current employer may be contacted for a reference.

9. The application should ask: "Please list all degrees or educational accomplishments that you wish to be considered by the employer in the employment decision." It puts job applicants on notice that any degree they list may be considered. This is helpful in situations where applicants are dishonest about their educational accomplishments even if the degree may not be a job requirement.

10. Finally, an employer can cover other standard matters. Examples include: the organization's "at will" policy; the employer is "a non-discriminatory employer;" uses mandatory arbitration in disputes; and requires applicants provide original documents to verify their identity and right to work in the United States.

An Example of an Application Language Law

Some states have limitations on asking about certain criminal matters. For example, an application generally should not ask about convictions that have been pardoned, sealed, erased or expunged (unless required by statute for a particular occupation or clearance). A good example is an Illinois law that was passed in 2004. The Illinois law requires employers to modify their employment applications to "contain specific language which states that the applicant is not obligated to disclose sealed or expunged records of conviction or arrest." This law also bars employers from asking "if an applicant has had records expunged or sealed." 20 ILCS 2630/12 (2004).

Other states with limitations include California, Georgia, Washington, Massachusetts and Utah. Still other states may have specific prohibitions on asking for other types of information as well.

A best practice is to contact a labor attorney with knowledge of your state, or Chamber of Commerce, HR Association (such as a local chapter of SHRM), or HR Consultant to ensure your form is consistent with state laws.

Critical Areas and Questions Applications Must Avoid

Federal and state laws prohibit any non-job related inquiry, either verbal or through the use of an application form, which directly or indirectly limits a person's employment opportunities because of race, color, religion, national origin, ancestry, medical condition, disability (including AIDS), marital status, sex (including pregnancy), age (40+), exercise of family care leave, or leave for an employee's own serious health condition. There are other areas that an employer may go into, but with limits, such as criminal records.

Employers want to avoid application questions and interview questions that directly identify a person as a member of a protected group. However, even questions that appear neutral on their face can be illegal if the question results in a disproportionate screening of members of a protected group or is not a valid predictor of job performance. Examples include application questions about arrests, which will be discussed in detail in later chapters on criminal investigations and criminal records.

As a rule of thumb, an employer cannot ask anything in an application that an employer cannot ask in a face-to-face personal interview. In Chapter 8 on interviews, there is an in-depth chart listing questions that are prohibited. These same rules apply to applications.

AUTHOR TIP Whenever there is an issue of a bad hire, the first step most attornies or experts take is to carefully examine the initial application form. In those situations, it is quite common to discover issues in the application that clearly suggest this was a problem just waiting to happen. The importance of a careful review of the application cannot be stressed enough. Failure to carefully review an application is one of the leading causes of hires that "do not work out."

Applications and Disclosure of Criminal Records

One of the most effective uses of an effective application form is it enables an employer to directly ask an applicant if he or she has a criminal record. As mentioned previously, per the 2012 EEOC Guidance, the suggestion is given, although it is not mandatory, that an employer not ask such a question upfront. See Chapter 16 for details.

Assuming an employer asks some sort of question on the topic, it has the advantage of discouraging applicants with something to hide and encouraging applicants to be open, honest, and truthful. The question is often in the form of a check box. Keep in mind that a number of cities, counties, and states have limitations on asking about criminal records too soon in the process on the basis that it discourages individuals with criminal records from applying for jobs. Society has in interest in giving ex-offenders a "second chance" so that they can become tax paying, law abiding citizens. This has led to a "Ban the Box" movement referring to the "box" asking about past criminal behavior. This is discussed in detail in Chapter 16 on Criminal Records.

Unfortunately, many employers use language in their applications that is too narrow, too broad, or too ambiguous. Each of these mistakes can put an employer in difficulty. Let us go over this language in detail.

Too Narrow

An example of a question that is too narrow is to only ask about felonies and not misdemeanors. Misdemeanors can be very serious. For example, most employers would want to know if an applicant had a conviction for offenses such as fighting with a police officer, illegal possession of weapons, spousal abuse or child abuse, commercial burglary, assault, and many other offenses. Yet in California, these can all be misdemeanors. Many serious offenses are plea-bargained down to misdemeanor offenses as well. Without the proper language, an applicant can honestly answer he or she has not been convicted of a felony even though there may be serious misdemeanor convictions an employer needs to know about. Key point: Employers need to keep in mind that conduct leading to a misdemeanor conviction is not always less serious than a felony conduct, as discussed in more detail in Chapter 14.

Too Broad

On the other hand, some employers ask questions that are so broad it improperly covers matters that are protected. For example, an employer should not ask "Have you ever been arrested or convicted for any crime?" or "Have you ever committed a criminal act?" There are a number of limitations under state and federal law concerning what an employer may legally ask about or "discover" concerning an applicant's or employee's criminal record. Many states have limitations on the use of arrest records or certain convictions that have been set aside, such as a pardon, expungement, or deferred adjudication. Federal and state equal opportunity laws can also be impacted if an applicant is forced to reveal old matters that are no longer relevant. In fact, it can be a misdemeanor in California for an employer to knowingly violate some of these rules. Furthermore, if an applicant is placed in a position where he is forced to reveal information about himself that he is legally entitled not to disclose, in some states an employer can actually be sued for "defamation by compelled self-publication." In other words, if forced to say something defamatory about himself, an applicant may be able to file a lawsuit against the employer for defamation.

Too Ambiguous

The third mistake is to ask an applicant, *"Have you ever been convicted of a felony or serious misdemeanor?"* or *"Have you ever been convicted of a crime of violence?"* or a similar question that calls for an opinion. The problem occurs when an applicant is called upon to make a judgment about his own offense. For example, if a misdemeanor is serious, this can call for a very complex legal and factual determination on which lawyers and even judges could disagree. By asking a question that is ambiguous and leaves waffle room, an applicant can argue that in his or her mind the offense was not serious and a "no" answer was truthful. That is why a question cannot contain any ambiguity. At times an applicant can be simply confused by court proceedings and may not understand the results or what they mean.

A California Example

Here are some of the limitations involved in California. Although not every state has rules as restrictive as California, employers in all states should be careful to ensure that their applications are legally compliant.

✓ An employer may NOT ask about arrests or detentions that did not result in a conviction.

✓ An employer may only consider convictions or pending cases.

✓ There are certain limitations on misdemeanors, crimes that have been sealed or otherwise expunged, cases where a person participated in pre-trial diversion, or certain minor marijuana convictions.

✓ An employer should NOT automatically deny employment due to a criminal conviction, but should consider the nature and gravity of the offense, whether it is job related, and when it occurred.

Below are examples of language that a California employer may consider using subject to the 2012 EEOC Guidance on criminal records. Again, keep in mind every state has its own rules, and an employer should check with an attorney in regards to state law.

Have you ever been convicted for a crime? (Exclude convictions for marijuana-related offenses for personal use more than two years old; convictions that have been sealed, expunged or legally eradicated, and misdemeanor convictions for which probation was completed and the case was dismissed) Yes_____ No___

Here is alternative wording to avoid the problems associated with certain minor convictions:

Have you ever been convicted of a felony, or a misdemeanor involving any violent act, use or possession of a weapon or act of dishonesty for which the record has not been sealed or expunged? If yes, please briefly describe the nature of the crime(s), the date and place of conviction and the legal disposition of the case.

This company will not deny employment to any applicant solely because the person has been convicted of a crime. The company however, may consider the nature, date and circumstances of the offense as well as whether the offense is relevant to the duties of the position applied for.

Are you currently out on bail, the subject of a current warrant for arrest, or released on your own recognizance pending trial? Yes ___ No ___

As mentioned previously, it is normally recommended the application contain language saying "the conviction of a crime will not automatically result in a denial of employment." Automatic disqualification could be a violation of state and federal discrimination laws. However, an employer may deny employment if the employer can establish a business-related reason for the refusal to hire. Refer to Chapter 2 for a detailed discussion on discrimination laws and safe hiring.

Cup of Coffee with that Criminal Conviction? Starbucks Case Underscores Importance of Well-Crafted Employment Application

A California appellate court case, *Starbucks Corporation v. Lord*, addressed the issue of how applicants are asked about criminal records on an application form. A class action was filed against Starbucks Corporation on behalf of 135,000 unsuccessful job applicants on the basis that the Starbuck "application contains an 'illegal question' about prior marijuana convictions that are more than two years old." The lawsuit was claiming $200 per applicant, which meant Starbucks was facing a potential exposure of $26 million dollars.

On the application form Starbucks asked, "Have you ever been convicted of a crime in the last seven (7) years?" It then states, "If Yes, list convictions that are a matter of public record (arrests are not convictions). A conviction will not necessarily disqualify you for employment."

On the reverse side of the application, just before the signature line, Starbucks clarified the criminal question with a disclaimer that reflects protections afforded job applicants under California Labor Code sections 432.7 and 432.8:

CALIFORNIA APPLICANTS ONLY: Applicants may omit any conviction for the possession of marijuana (except for convictions for the possession of marijuana on school grounds or possession of concentrated cannabis) that are more than two (2) years old, and any information concerning a referral to, and participation in, any pre-trial or post trial diversion program.

The disclaimer however, was the very last sentence in a 346 word paragraph that went into other areas, including employment being at will, release of information, misrepresentations in the application and even disclaimers about Maryland and Massachusetts.

The plaintiffs were concerned that since the disclaimer was physically separated from the question about past crimes and was essentially buried in the fine print, those applicants either would "overlook" the disclaimer, or would not want to go back and cross out their previous responses, or ask for a clear copy.

The Court agreed there was an issue of whether the "one-size-fits-all style" of applications used was ambiguous or not. However, the court also found that two of the plaintiffs in the case were not harmed by any ambiguity since they both testified they understood the question and had no drug history anyway. Because there was no one suing who had actually been harmed, the Court ruled in Starbuck's favor.

The Court discussed how allowing these kinds of suits by plaintiffs who were not actually harmed would potentially "create a whole new category of employment-professional job seekers, whose quest is to voluntarily find (and fill out) job applications which they know to be defective solely for the purpose of pursing litigation. This is not the law in California." Even though the employer prevailed, it was only because the plaintiffs were not in fact real applicants. This type of case should cause every employer to review their application form with their attorney or HR section for legal compliance.

Final Step—Review the Application as a Whole

A key walkaway point is there is no one tool tells an employer the entire story. An employer needs to review and cross-reference all the information they have. An employer needs to not only review each individual part of the application, but to also ask the question: does it make sense as a whole? For example, do past addresses seem to correlate to locations of past employers? Are there unexplained employment gaps? Do dates of graduation from a school or the date a license or certification was obtained make sense in terms of employment history and past addresses?

Ten Sure Signs of a Lawsuit Waiting to Happen

After going through the process of preparing an effective application and utilizing it instead of a resume, many employers make the fatal mistake of not reading the application carefully. This is a major mistake. Employee lawsuits often catch employers by surprise. Another way employers are bitten by their applications happens when, upon closer examination, the employee's application shows that the employer could have reasonably predicted they were hiring a lawsuit just waiting to happen. Per the 2012 EEOC Guidance, a recommended best practice is to NOT ask about criminal records on an application. If an employer adopts that practice, that could impact the suggestions below.

By looking for the following **ten danger signals**, an employer can avoid hiring a problem employee in the first place:

1. **Applicant does not sign application**. An applicant with something to hide may purposely not sign the application form so the applicant cannot later be accused of falsification.
2. **Applicant does not sign consent for background screening.** When a firm uses an outside agency to perform screening, federal law requires a separate disclosure and signed consent from the applicant. A background consent form protects employers in two ways: 1) it discourages applicants with something to hide and 2) encourages candid interviews. If a candidate fails to sign the consent, it is not a good sign.
3. **Applicant leaves criminal questions blank**. If the application asks about past criminal convictions, an applicant with a past problem may simply skip the questions about criminal records. The timing of when and how to ask about past convictions under the 2012 EEOC Guidance is covered in Chapter 16. Most jurisdictions only permit questions about convictions and pending cases. A criminal record can be either a felony or a misdemeanor; employers make a big mistake if they only ask about felonies since misdemeanors can be

extremely serious too. Although employment may not be denied automatically because of a criminal conviction, an employer may consider the nature and gravity of the offense, the nature of the job, and the age of the offense when evaluating whether there is a sound business reason not to employ someone with a criminal record. If an applicant lies about a criminal record, then the false application may be the reason to deny employment.

4. **Applicant self-reports a criminal violation.** Just because an applicant self-reports an offense does not eliminate the possibility other offenses exist, or the applicant may report it in a misleading way to lessen its seriousness. An employer is well-advised to check it out.

AUTHOR TIP

The first four points are sometimes referred to as the **"honest criminal syndrome."** A person may have had a criminal record in the past and does not want to be dishonest about it. On the other hand, the person may not want to be fully revealing either. That is why it is so critical to look at the application's criminal question carefully to ensure it is filled out. Self-reported offenses should be looked at extra carefully. For example, an applicant self-reported that he stole some beer from a store. He neglected to mention it was stolen at the point of a gun, which is robbery, a much more serious offense. Another applicant reported he was stopped by police when he was younger, and some recreational drugs he had were found under the car seat. A review of the court records revealed it was actually two pounds of cocaine — which is a lot of recreation.

Again, keep in mind that the 2012 EEOC Guidance on criminal records may cause employers to modify when and how they ask these questions.

5. **Applicant fails to explain gaps in employment history.** There can be many reasons for a gap in employment. For example, an applicant may have been ill, gone back to school, or had difficulty finding a new job. However, if an applicant cannot account for the past seven to ten years, that can be a red flag. It could potentially mean he or she was in custody for a criminal offense. It is also important to know where a person has been because of the way criminal records are maintained in the United States. Contrary to popular belief, there is not a national criminal database available to most employers. Searches must be conducted at each relevant courthouse, and there are over 10,000 courthouses in the U.S. However, if an employer knows where an applicant has been, it increases the accuracy of a criminal search and decreases the possibility that an applicant has served time for a serious offense. If there is an unexplained gap, an employer may not know where to search and can miss a criminal record.

6. **Explanations for employment gaps or reasons for leaving past jobs do not make sense.** If there were employment gaps reported by the applicant, do the reasons for the gaps make sense? A careful review of this section of the application is needed and anything that does not make sense must to be cleared up in the interview.

7. **Applicant fails to give sufficient information to identify a past employer for reference checks.** This is another sign of possible trouble. Verifying past employment is a critical and important tool for safe hiring. Some employers make a costly mistake of not checking past employment because past employers historically tend not to give detailed information. However, even if a reference check only reveals dates of employment and job titles, this critical information eliminates employment gaps. In addition, documenting the fact an effort was made will demonstrate due diligence.

8. **Applicant fails to explain reason for leaving past jobs.** Past job performance can be an important predictor of future success.

9. **Applicant fails to indicate or cannot recall the name of a former supervisor.** Another red flag. Past supervisors are important in order to conduct past employment checks.

10. **Excessive cross-outs and changes.** This can be an indication an applicant is making it up as he/she goes along.

These ten danger signs all assume that an employer is using an application form, not a resume.

Review the Form with the Applicant

One way to avoid making these mistakes is to go through the application with the jobseeker, checking to be certain the applicant filled out the forms completely. Rehash the question with the applicant if he or she has shown questionable answers. The process is not intended to necessarily ensure accuracy but to determine with certainty that the applicant stands behind what he or she has stated on the application form.

> **AUTHOR TIP** The author testified as an expert witness in a case where a school district hired a teacher who had been convicted in another state of a felony charge —sex with a minor. The offense made the person ineligible to teach. On the employment application where it asked if the applicant had ever been convicted of a crime, the applicant put a slash mark in between the Yes and the No. The school district has a policy of reviewing the application with the applicant to clarify what the applicant meant. A school district employee asked the applicant which box he meant to check, and the applicant then clearly indicated "Yes." Unfortunately, after being on notice there was a criminal offense in the applicant's background, the school district failed to follow through and investigate the offense. After the applicant was hired, he was accused of inappropriate behavior with female students at the school. Under legal scrutiny, the failure to follow through after being put on notice of a past crime was found to be negligent hiring.

Where to Find a Good Application Form

Application forms are available from a number of sources:

- ✓ The local or state Chamber of Commerce may have forms available.
- ✓ A firm's business or labor attorney will normally have a new employee package available with an application form.
- ✓ Human resources consultants and HR organizations may have forms.
- ✓ Office supply stores sell basic business forms including application forms.
- ✓ Books about running a business are available from local book stores and may have sample forms.
- ✓ There are firms that specialize in selling employment related forms and products on the Internet.

Many firms design their own employment forms to reflect the particular needs of their firm or industry.

One word of caution: Many states have unique rules regarding what can and cannot be on an application. Some of these rules concern what an employer may ask about past criminal convictions. It is beyond the scope of this book to review the requirements for all fifty states, however, an employer is well-advised to consult with a labor attorney for every state they hire within to review the legality of their application forms.

Chapter 8

AIR – The Interview Process

Interviews must be conducted in a manner that not only assures the employer of finding the best candidate for the position but also is legal, and does not put the employer in harm's way. In this chapter let us examine the job interview as in integral part of a Safe Hiring Program.

Inside This Chapter:

- ✓ The Importance of Interviews

- ✓ Advantages of a Structured Interview

- ✓ The Integrity Interview

- ✓ Six Questions That Should Be Asked In Every Interview

- ✓ The Questions Not to Ask — and Why

- ✓ Pre-Employment Inquiry Guidelines Chart

- ✓ Looking for "Red Flag" Behavior

- ✓ Additional Integrity Questions

The Importance of Interviews

The interview is the first opportunity for an employer to meet face-to-face with applicants who may literally and figuratively hold the keys to future business success in their hands. During the interview process, an employer practicing safe hiring must take steps to protect the workforce and ensure the best and most qualified candidates are hired.

Within a Safe Hiring Program, an interview can accomplish three goals:

1. **Convey critical information to the applicant in order to discourage bad applicants and to encourage honesty**. Applicants need to understand clearly the firm has a Safe Hiring Program. Use the interview to convey the message to all applicants. Since at the same time an employer is recruiting qualified employees who will adopt the firm's values and become loyal and hardworking, the safe hiring process cannot be accomplished in an overbearing fashion. Think of the interview as an opportunity to reinforce the message already communicated in company application forms and job announcements — your firm practices safe hiring!

2. **Allow for the transfer of information from the applicant to the employer**. The interview is a time when an employer has an opportunity to fill in any gaps. Also, the employer has a chance to ask the additional penetrating questions if the candidate seems to have attempted to conceal or lie about unfavorable information.

3. **Permit an assessment of the candidate**. Even though a Safe Hiring Program is based upon the premise that instinct and intuition alone are not enough, the interview still provides the employer an opportunity to assess the knowledge, skills, and abilities of the applicant in person. Of course good candidates can come across poorly, and bad candidates can come across well. The assessment is just one of many tools used in the calculus of a hiring decision.

Given these three goals, how does an organization ensure that positive results happen? This chapter examines the needed tools.

Advantages of a Structured Interview

An interview is typically accomplished using a written set of questions selected ahead of time by the employer and provided to the hiring managers conducting the interviews. There are literally thousands of potential interview questions that can be asked. Questions can also depend upon the particular industry, the needs of the firm, and the position being filled. An employer needs to review all potential questions and select a set of questions that would be the most useful for selecting the best employees. That does not mean that everyone is always asked the exact same questions. Different positions may require that certain portions of an interview require customized questions. This can be done by a supplemental question set that is position-specific. However, the interview should assure all similarly situated candidates have the same question set.

A structured interview is defined as an interview format used across an organization. Structured interview questions are usually pre-printed on forms. The advantages for an employer using a structured interview are significant.

- ✓ First, it ensures uniformity in the interview process and protects against claims of discrimination or disparate treatment.
- ✓ Second, it helps to keep hiring managers on track by using legally defensible questions. By giving interviewers a script to follow, it helps an employer's efforts at training interviewers not to ask prohibited questions. A discussion and chart of permissible and impermissible questions is presented later in this chapter.
- ✓ Third, and most critical from the aspect of a Safe Hiring Program, the structured interview ensures the employer that certain essential "integrity questions" are asked of all candidates. Some of these questions are covered below.

At the same time, the process does not mean the interviewers are simply clerical robots, going through the motions and recording responses in a rote fashion. Penetrating follow-up questions and keen observations of the applicants are still critical to make sure all required areas are covered.

AUTHOR TIP Another helpful hiring tool is a preliminary telephone screen. After an employer has reviewed and narrowed down a possible list of candidates, doing a telephone screen will help narrow down the list even further and save an employer valuable time. A phone screen is accomplished by calling each potential candidate and asking the same list of questions. If the candidate appears to meet the initial criteria, then an interview can be immediately scheduled. If a message is left and the applicant does not call back, then that applicant can be eliminated from consideration. A sample telephone screen script can be found in the Appendix. Also keep in mind that in order to develop job-related interview questions, an employer first needs a written job description so that meaningful questions can be developed.

Behavior-Based Questions Should be Used

An essential part of a Safe Hiring Program is to question applicants carefully about their knowledge, skills, abilities, and experience. Part of the interview is designed to determine if the applicant will be a good fit, taking into account the work environment and the team the person will work with.

Interview techniques where the applicant is merely told to "tell me about yourself" have not proved altogether effective. In order to obtain more insight employers may ask hypothetical questions such as "what would you do if..." The "if" could be anything ranging from working with difficult people to completing assignments under deadlines. However, that still does not tell an employer about how the person actually did in the past.

Behavior-based interviewing is one of the newest and most effective methods for establishing if a person is a good fit for both the job and the organization. In a "behavior-based interview," a person is asked to accurately describe real situations they have encountered and what they did to resolve the issue or problem. The method is based on the concept that the most accurate predictor of how a candidate will perform in the future is how he or she performed in the past in a similar situation. The question could be about a time when a person faced a typical workforce problem. This type of interview question may typically start with the phrase, "Tell me about a time when..."

There are numerous books, resources, and websites that offer suggestions on behavior-based interview questions. Here are sample questions to demonstrate the format:

- ✓ Tell me about a time when you had to coordinate several different people to achieve a goal. What were the challenges involved, and how did you overcome them?
- ✓ Tell me about the most difficult business related decisions you have had to make in the past six months. Describe the situation and what made it difficult. How did you resolve it?
- ✓ Give me an example of when you had to work with someone who was very difficult to get along with, and how you handled that situation.

Don't Interview Before Hiring? Maybe Not as Ridiculous as it Sounds

The June 2009 issue of *Fast Company* magazine ran an article that suggested that employers may get better results if they hire without doing an interview. The story was by Dan Heath and Chip Heath, authors of *Made to Stick-Why Some Ideas Survive and Others Don't*.

The apparent radical suggestion was based upon a substantial body of empirical evidence that shows interviews are not nearly as predictive of job performance on future jobs as other tools, such as work sample, job-knowledge tests, and peer ratings of past job performance. The authors cite a study where a medical school admitted based upon interviews. After the class was selected, the school was told to admit another 50 students. Since the best remaining students had gone elsewhere, the school was forced to take 50 "dregs." The result—there was no difference between those that interviewed well and those that did not in terms of academic achievement or even in the first year internship, where social skill could arguably play a role. The authors compare the idea that a short interview can tell an employer if an applicant is a good hire to a baseball manager that ignores batting statistics and instead takes a prospect out for a beer to judge "fit."

The authors concluded that the reason an interview is relied on so heavily is that employers think they are good at interviews. Studies have demonstrated that most people are poor judges of when they are being told the truth and when they are being deceived. Paul Ekman, a psychology professor in the Department of Psychiatry at the University of California Medical School in San Francisco, is the author of thirteen books, including *Telling Lies*. Ekman has tested about 6,000 people who are professionals trained to spot liars, including police officers, lawyers, judges, psychiatrists, and agents of the FBI, the CIA and the Drug Enforcement Administration, to determine if they can tell if someone is lying. According to his research, most people are not very accurate in judging if a person is lying. The average accuracy in studies is rarely above 60%, while chance is 50%. Even among professional lie catchers, the ability to detect liars is not much better than 50%. In one study, customs agents who interviewed people at customs stations did not do any better than college students.

The *Fast Company* article concluded that job tests is one of the most effective means of hiring, and cites as an example, asking a sales applicant sell you something, or having a graphic designer design something.

This advice is exactly in line with the author has been suggesting to employers for many years—trust but verify. Industry statistics suggest that as many as 30% of all job applicants falsify information about their credentials. Trying to rely on interviews gives little protection. Some interviewees tell lies they have ingrained in their life story. They have created identities and legends of their own and, when they tell their stories, they are not fabricating on the spot. They put "it" on their resumes and talk about it and tell their friends about it. It becomes part of their personalities and personal histories because they have told it so often. It becomes second nature as they retell it again and again.

There are lists of so-called "tell-tale signs" that a person is lying. For example, employers might observe if a person is avoiding eye contact, fidgeting, or hesitating before answering. Unfortunately, it can be a costly mistake for an interviewer to think lying can always be detected by such visual clues by relying upon one's own instinct or intuition, since some of the so-called "visual clues" can simply be a sign of nervousness about the interview, or stress, and not an intent to lie. In fact, accomplished liars are more dangerous because they can disguise themselves as truthful and sincere. An experienced liar may show no visible signs.

Employers, HR, and Security professionals should remember that as valuable as instinct may be, it does not substitute for factual verification of an applicant's credentials through techniques such as employment screening background checks and skills tests.

The Integrity Interview

For organizations that hire people for extremely sensitive or high-risk positions, the firm can conduct a full "integrity interview" to determine if a person is a good fit. Also, the same questions can be used to help detect if there is any reason NOT to hire the person.

Integrity questions are used to explore:

- ✓ Does the applicant really have the knowledge, skills, abilities, and experience claimed?
- ✓ Is the applicant really who he says he is, or she is?
- ✓ Has the applicant left any material out of the application process?

✓ Has the applicant misstated any qualifications in the application process?
✓ Is there any reason to think the applicant's moral rudder is not set straight?
✓ In other words, is the applicant an honest person?

A good interviewer creates a comfortable and professional environment but also stresses the need for complete honesty. Consider the following specific questions:

It is not unusual to exaggerate in an application or resume. However, we need complete and accurate information concerning certain areas.

Is there anything in your employment application that you want to change or correct? This is the time.

If we checked with your former employers, would any of them report that you were asked to leave?

If the interviewer wished to cover potential security issues such as criminal record or drug and alcohol use, then this question could be asked:

If we were to check court records, would we find any convictions or outstanding warrants?

AUTHOR TIP One way to accomplish an integrity interview is to retain the services of a professional interviewer from outside your office. This professional can conduct an in-depth interview covering a full employment history and also address security concerns such as terminations, drug and alcohol use, and criminal record. In the case of a large firm, the interview could be completed by another person within the organization such as personnel in security or loss prevention departments.

Open-Ended Questions and Follow-Up Questions

A proven technique of an integrity interview is the use of "open-ended" and "follow-up" questions. A key to using this technique is for the interview not to rely upon information given beforehand.

Let us say the interviewer starts with questions about a person's job history. If the interviewer does not have a resume or application, every question is "open-ended," meaning the interviewee supplies all the information and no part of the answer is suggested by the question. This is the opposite of a "leading question" where the question itself suggests an answer.

For example, if an interviewer says, "I see you left Acme Industries due to a lay-off." That is a leading question. It suggests the answer, allowing the applicant to merely expand on that theme. An example of an open-ended question is "How long was your employment with Acme?" or "Why did that employment end?"

It is critical to ask follow-up questions when the answers do not make sense. If an applicant says something illogical, the interviewer should not hesitate to ask the applicant to review the answer. Sometimes it helps to ask the same question in a different way. For example, ask the applicant to describe in detail what occurred leading up to or after the event. If the applicant is making something up, that may be obvious. If an applicant gives a non-answer or an answer that is too fast and too pat, then a follow-up question would be helpful. For example, if an applicant says, "We already covered that," the interviewer, simply says, "I must have missed it. Can we review that again?"

As a practical matter, company managers and HR professionals are not expected to give every applicant the third degree. However, interviewers should be trained so they are not so glued to the questioning process that they do not pay attention to how the answers are given.

Six Questions That Should Be Asked In Every Interview

In order to help hiring managers have a better understanding of a candidate and to weed out those who are unacceptable risks, it can be very effective to empower interviewers with some key "standard questions." Asking standard questions has several advantages. They allow for a consistent process so that all applicants are subjected to the same questions. Standard questions create a more comfortable environment for the interviewers. They do not have the pressure of having to remember every question they asked because the questions are written out for them. If the questions on safe hiring issues feel uncomfortable, then the interviewer can simply indicate that these questions are asked of everyone and they are required due to standard company policy.

There are six suggested, critical interview questions every employer or hiring manager should be trained to ask. Of course, an employer would not want to get the interview off on the wrong foot with questions aimed at past criminal conduct or negative employment experiences. One of the goals of an interview is to help foster a talking environment where a potential employee understands and accepts the goals and direction of the organization. However, every interview does have a "housekeeping" portion where standard questions are asked. That would be a good time for the following six questions.

1.   *Our firm has a standard policy of conducting background checks on all hires before an offer is made or finalized. You have already signed a release form. Do you have any concerns about that?*

This is a general question about screening. Since the applicant has signed a release form, there is a powerful incentive to be honest and reveal any issues.

2.   *We also check for criminal convictions for all finalists. Do you have any concerns about that?*

This question goes from the general to the specific. Be sure to ask the question in a form that is legally permissible in your state. It is important NOT to ask a question that is so broadly worded that it may lead to an applicant revealing more information than allowed by law. Again, make sure the applicant understands that he or she has signed a release and this process is standard company policy.

One caveat — The 2012 EEOC Guidance suggested: "As a best practice, and consistent with applicable laws, the Commission recommends that employers not ask about convictions on job applications and that, if and when they make such inquiries, the inquiries be limited to convictions for which exclusion would be job related for the position in question and consistent with business necessity."

Presumably, the idea was that an employer may automatically toss in the trash can any application from anyone who admitted a criminal conviction. The question then becomes whether an interview would be an appropriate place to ask that question. On one hand, it can be argued that since the applicant is now in the interview state, the process is far enough along to ask a criminal question. That is because the applicant has advanced based upon his or her qualifications and experience as it relates to the position. However, the counter argument is that a question asking an applicant to reveal a criminal past, even at the interview stage, can potentially be discriminatory. However, as reviewed in Chapter 16, at some point in the process, an employer needs to ask a finalist about criminal records. Since the Guidance is so new, there is obviously no case law or legislation with an answer. However, if the language, tone, and tenor of the comment make it clear that a "yes" answer becomes a "knock out" at this stage of the hiring process, the EEOC or a plaintiff could argue that it amounts to an automatic rejection based upon a criminal record without consideration of whether the past criminal conviction is job related. A more conservative approach may be to just notify the applicant that a criminal check appropriate to the position will be conducted before the job starts and perhaps even make it a condition of any job offer. Again, be sure to state that any conditional offer is contingent upon a background check that is *acceptable to the employer.*

Even if an employer determines that the interview is an appropriate stage, recall that the EEOC is concerned about overly broad questions that can elicit old or irrelevant information not reasonably related to the job. The concern is that an old or irrelevant record can in effect become a lifetime ban to employment. See Chapter 16 for more information on when and how to ask about past criminal conduct.

3. *When we talk to your past employers, what do you think they will say?*

   Note the questions begins: "When we contact your past employers…" Thus the applicant is given notice past employers will be contacted. This general question again provides a powerful incentive to be very accurate.

4. *Will your past employers tell us that there were any issues with tardiness, meeting job requirements, etc.?*

   This question goes again to a specific area. Ask detailed questions about matters that are expressly relevant to the job opening.

5. *Can you tell me about any unexplained gaps in your employment history?*

   If there are any unexplained employment gaps, it is imperative to ask about them.

6. *Is everything in the application and everything you told us in the interview true, correct, and complete?*

   This is the critical final question. It sends a clear message to an applicant that the employer takes the process seriously and that the applicant needs to be completely open, honest, and truthful. An interview can add an advisement that if there is anything the applicant wants to change on the application, now is the time to do it.

Since applicants have signed consent forms and believe the firm is doing background checks, applicants have a powerful incentive to be truthful. These questions are the equivalent of a "New Age" lie detector test. Employers can no longer administer actual lie detector tests and probably would not want to even if they could. However, these questions serve a valuable function by providing a strong motivation for applicants to be self-revealing. It also takes advantage of the natural human trait to want to have some control over what others say about you. If an applicant believes a future employer may hear negative information from a past employer, the applicant may want to be able to set the record straight before the future employer has the chance to hear negative information from someone else.

Good applicants will shrug the questions off, and applicants with something to hide may reveal vital information. Applicants with something to hide may react in a number of different ways. Some applicants may tough it out during the first question. However, the questions are designed to go from the general to the specific. By the second question, an applicant may well begin to express concerns or react in some way that raises a red flag. An applicant may object to the questions by asking if the questions invade their privacy rights. If an applicant raises such an objection, then simply indicate that these are standard job-related questions asked of all applicants.

Why Checking Employment Gaps Is So Important

An employer related the following story. The applicant was just perfect for the computer job. He had all of the right qualifications. During the interview, the interviewer asked the usual questions. While taking a last look at the resume, the interviewer happened to notice a two–year gap in the employment and education history. Out of curiosity, the interviewer asked about the gap.

The applicant explained that he had decided to go back to go school and retrain so he could join the computer age. The interviewer was merely curious about the classes because he wanted to find some good classes for other employees. Where was it? Oh, it was a state-sponsored job-retraining program. Where was the program based?

With just a few questions it finally came out. The so-called computer school where the courses were taken was actually classes offered at a state prison. Of course, the applicant did have a perfect attendance record.

This story illustrates two key points:

✓ Look at the resume or application for unexplained gaps.

✓ Use the interview to ask the applicant about any gaps.

Actually, the criminal record by itself would not have disqualified the computer technician. The real problem was that the job the applicant interviewed for required a person to go inside state prisons to fix computers — and prisons may not care to have former inmates come back in a professional capacity.

The Questions Not to Ask — and Why

As mentioned at the outset of this chapter, a true Safe Hiring Program means the job interview process must be conducted in a legal manner. Just as there are troublesome, improper areas or questions to be avoided on an employment application, the same is true for job interviews. If certain questions are asked or if questions are asked in a certain way, then an employer may be exposed to a variety of discrimination charges and lawsuits.

Pre-Employment Inquiry Guidelines

By Barbara S. de Oddone, an Attorney specializing in labor law.

In order to avoid claims that you have not compared candidates equitably based solely on job-related criteria, you should have an outline of job-pertinent questions (open-ended, not "yes" or "no" questions) that you ask of every candidate seeking a particular position. In order to provide documentary evidence of your questions and the candidates' answers, you should make brief notes of the answers on your interview outline. Avoid keeping any notes that are not related to the job in question.

One particular category of pre-employment inquiries deserves special caution: inquiries that may reveal that the applicant is a person with a disability. It is impermissible to ask a question that will elicit information about a disability or medical condition, including workers' compensation history. See the Pre-Employment Inquiry Guidelines Chart on the following pages. On the other hand, if it is obvious that an applicant is a person with a disability, such as an applicant who uses a wheelchair, it is permissible to ask whether the applicant will need a reasonable accommodation to proceed through the application process and, if employed, to perform the essential functions of the job. The Federal Equal Employment Opportunity Commission (EEOC) states:

✓ [when] an employer could reasonably believe that an applicant will need reasonable accommodation to perform the functions of the job, the employer may ask that applicant certain limited questions. Specifically, the employer may ask whether s/he needs reasonable accommodation and what type of reasonable accommodation would be needed to perform the functions of the job.

The EEOC describes the permissible circumstances for this inquiry as follows:

✓ [when] the employer reasonably believes the applicant will need reasonable accommodation because of an obvious disability;

✓ [when] the employer reasonably believes the applicant will need reasonable accommodation because of a hidden disability the applicant has voluntarily disclosed to the employer; or

✓ [when] an applicant has voluntarily disclosed to the employer that s/he needs reasonable accommodation to perform the job.

Remember: Keep all information gathered about applicants confidential. It is important to maintain all job applicant information in confidential locked files and refrain from disclosing information to any but those who need to know.

Pre-Employment Inquiry Guidelines Chart

Mr. Rod Fliegel, an attorney and shareholder with Littler Mendelson, P.C., has graciously supplied us with the following chart, an excellent guide to use for protecting a Safe Hiring Program's application and interview processes. Mr. Fliegel has extensive experience defending national and local employers in state, federal, and administrative litigation, including high-stakes class actions. He also has special compliance and litigation expertise concerning the intersection of the federal and state background check laws.

Mr. Fliegel also notes that the relationship between a screening firm and the employer is an "agency" relationship with legal ramifications. Both parties must be aware of this. Simply put, when an employer outsources aspects of its hiring process to a screening firm, such as pre-employment background or reference checks, the employer is trusting the screening firm to act on its behalf and in compliance with all applicable federal, state, and local legal constraints. Take for sake of example pre-employment disability-related inquiries. The EEOC's "Technical Assistance Manual" or "TAM" expressly states: "If an employer uses an outside firm to conduct background checks, the employer should assure that this firm complies with the ADA's prohibitions on pre-employment inquiries. Such a firm is an agent of the employer. The employer is responsible for actions of its agents and may not do anything through a contractual relationship that it may not itself do directly." (The TAM is available at: https://askjan.org/links/ADAtam1.html#X.)

A number of states have their own published guidelines as well. For example, *The Pre-Employment Inquiry Guidelines Chart* below is adapted from "Employment Inquiries," California Department of Fair Employment & Housing, http://www.dfeh.ca.gov/res/docs/publications/dfeh-161.pdf .

The excerpt below is from Littler Mendelson, P.C., *The National Employer* Ch. 11 (LexisNexis 2012-2013 ed.) attributed to Rod M. Fliegel and Jennifer L. Mora, Attorneys At Law, Littler Mendelson, P.C.

	You May Ask:	**You Should Not Ask:**
ADDRESS/ RESIDENCE	"Can you be reached at this address? If not, would you care to leave another?" "Can you be reached at these telephone numbers? If not, would you care to leave another?"	"Do you own your home or rent?" "Do you live with your spouse?" "With whom do you live?"
AGE	Only questions that verify non-minor status; *i.e.*, "Are you over 18?" "If hired can you show proof of age?" "If under 18, can you after employment submit a work permit?"	"How old are you?" "What is your date of birth?" "What is your age?" "When were you born?" Dates of attendance or completion of elementary or high school. Any questions that imply a preference for persons under 40 years of age.

	You May Ask:	**You Should Not Ask:**
AIDS/HIV	"Are you able to perform the essential functions of the job applied for either with or without a reasonable accommodation? Yes or No?"	Any question that is likely to illicit information regarding whether an applicant (or current employee) has AIDS/ HIV.
ARRESTS & CONVICTIONS	"Have you ever been convicted of a criminal offense? Do not include convictions that were sealed, eradicated or expunged, or convictions that resulted in referral to a diversion program." (Note: Convictions will not necessarily disqualify you from employment. Factors such as the age and time of the offense, the seriousness and nature of the violation, and rehabilitation will be considered when making any employment decisions). Employers should check state law with respect to restrictions on criminal history inquiries.	Any question regarding an arrest that did not result in a conviction. Any question regarding criminal records that have been sealed, eradicated or expunged.
CITIZENSHIP/ BIRTHPLACE	"Are you authorized to work in the U.S.? If hired, you will be required to submit verification of your legal right to work in the United States." BUT ask this of all applicants, not only persons appearing to the interviewer to speak a primary language other than English or be foreign-born.	"Are you a United States citizen?" "Where were you born?" Or any questions regarding birthplace or citizenship status of applicant, applicant's spouse, parents or other relatives.
COLOR OR RACE	Statement that photograph may be required after employment.	Any questions concerning race or color of skin, eyes, hair, etc. Should not require applicant to affix a photograph to application nor should applicant be given the option of attaching a photograph.
COURT RECORDS (see also "Arrests & Convictions," above)	"Has a court, jury or government agency ever made a finding you committed unlawful harassment or discrimination?"	"Have you ever filed for bankruptcy?" "Have you ever sued or filed claims or complaints against your employer?" "Have you ever been a plaintiff in a lawsuit?"
PHYSICAL OR MENTAL CONDITION,	"Can you, with or without reasonable accommodation, perform the essential	"Do you have any physical disabilities or handicaps?"

	You May Ask:	**You Should Not Ask:**
DISABILITY	duties of the job(s) for which you are applying (see attached job description)?" "Are you currently able to perform the essential duties of the job(s) for which you are applying?" If the disability is obvious, or disclosed, you may ask about accommodations. Statement by employer that offer may be contingent on applicant's passing a job-related physical examination.	Questions regarding applicant's general medical condition, state of health, or illnesses. "Are you disabled?" An employer MAY NOT make any medical inquiry or conduct any medical examination prior to making a conditional offer of employment. "Have you ever filed for or received workers' compensation?" What medical problems the applicant may have. The amount of sick time or medical leave taken at last job.
DRUG USE	Current use of illegal drugs. Recent use of illegal drugs.	Questions about past addictions. Questions about use of prescription drugs or frequency of alcohol use.
EDUCATION	"Are you presently enrolled or do you intend to enroll in school?" "What subjects did you excel in at school?" "Did you participate in extracurricular activities?" "What did you select as your major?" "Did you work an outside job while attending school? Doing what? What did you like/ dislike about your part-time job during school?" "Are you interested in continuing your education? Why? When? Where?" "Did your education prepare you for the job you are seeking with us? In what ways?"	"Who paid for your educational expenses while you were in school?" "Did you go to school on a scholarship?" "Do you still owe on student loans taken out during school?" "When did you graduate from high school?"
EXPERIENCE, SKILLS & ACTIVITIES	"Do you have any special skills or knowledge?" "Are your skills recent?" "When did you last use a computer (or any other specific program, machine or skill)?" "Do you enjoy being active in community affairs?"	"Does your physical condition make you less skilled?"

	You May Ask:	You Should Not Ask:
	"Are there any activities which have provided you with experience, training, or skills which you feel would be helpful to a position with us?" "How will your involvement in [activity] affect your work here?"	
FAMILY	"Do you have any commitments that would prevent you from working regular hours?" "Can you work overtime, if needed?" "Are you now or do you expect to be engaged in any other business or employment? If 'yes,' what kind of business or employment is it? How much time does it require?"	"How many children do you have?" "Who takes care of your children while you are working?" "Do your children go to day care?" "What does your husband (or wife) think about your working outside the home?" "What does your husband (or wife) do?" "What is your husband's (or wife's) salary?" Name of spouse or children of applicant. Is your spouse the same gender as you?
MARITAL STATUS	"Please state the name(s) of any relatives already employed by this company or a competitor." "Whom should we contact in case of an emergency?"	"Is it Mrs. or Miss?" "Are you single? Married? Divorced? Separated? Engaged? Widowed?" "Do you have a domestic partner?" "What is your maiden name?" Identity of applicant's spouse.
MILITARY SERVICE	"Have you served in the U.S. military?" "Did your military service and training provide you with skills you could put to use in this job?"	"Have you served in the army of a foreign country?" "What type of discharge did you receive from the U.S. military service?" "Can you provide discharge papers?"
NAME	"Have you ever used another name?" or, "Is any additional information relative to change of name, use of an assumed name, or nickname necessary to enable a check on your work and educational record? If yes, please explain."	"What is your maiden name?"
NATIONAL ORIGIN	In order to comply with the Federal Immigration Reform and Control Act of 1986, you may ask: "Are you prevented from being employed in the United States because of your visa or immigration status?"	"What is your national origin?" "Where were you born?" "What is the origin of your name?" "What is your native language?" "What country are your ancestors from?"

	You May Ask:	**You Should Not Ask:**
		"Do you read, write, or speak Korean (or another foreign language)?" (unless based on job requirements) How applicant acquired the ability to read, write or speak a foreign language. Or any other questions as to nationality, lineage, ancestry, national origin, descent or parentage of applicant, applicant's parents or spouse.
NOTICE IN CASE OF EMERGENCY	Name and address of *person* to be notified in case of accident or emergency.	Name and address of *relative* to be notified in case of accident or emergency.
ORGANIZATIONS	About any organization memberships, excluding any organization of which the name or character indicates the race, color, creed, sex, marital status, religion, national origin, or ancestry of its members: "Do you enjoy being active in community affairs?"	For a list of all organizations, clubs, societies, and lodges to which the applicant belongs.
PHOTOGRAPHS	For a photograph after hiring for identification purposes.	Any applicant to submit a photograph whether mandatory or optional before hiring.
PREGNANCY	"How long do you plan to stay on the job?" "Are you currently able to perform the essential duties of the job(s) for which you are applying?"	"Are you pregnant?" "When was your most recent pregnancy terminated?" "Do you plan to become pregnant?" Any questions about medical history concerning pregnancy and related matters.
PRIOR EMPLOYMENT	"How did you overcome problems you faced there?" "Which problems frustrated you the most?" "Of the jobs indicated on your application, which did you enjoy the most, and why?" "What were your reasons for leaving your last job?" "Have you ever been discharged from any position? If so, for what reason?"	"How many sick days did you take at your old job?" "Did you file any claims against your former employer?" "Have you sustained any work-related injury?"

	You May Ask:	**You Should Not Ask:**
	"Can you meet the attendance requirements of the job?"	
REFERENCES	"By whom were you referred for a position here?" Names of persons willing to provide professional and/or character references for applicant.	Questions put to applicant's former employers or acquaintances that the employer would be prohibited from asking the applicant, such as questions that elicit information specifying the applicant's race, color, religion, national origin, disability, age or sex.
RELIGION OR CREED	Statement by employer of regular days, hours or shifts to be worked. "Are you available to work on weekends?" (if there is a legitimate business reason for this question)	"What is your religion?" "What church do you go to?" "What are your religious holidays?" "Does your religion prevent you from working weekends or holidays?"
SEXUAL ORIENTATION		"Are you a gay/lesbian/bisexual?" "Do you have a domestic partner?" "What is your view regarding same-sex partner benefits?"

Looking for "Red Flag" Behavior

A savvy interviewer will be able to spot red flags that indicate further questions may be needed. Many of these tip-offs are non-verbal in nature. Of course, a perfectly honest and capable candidate may exhibit these red flags, while a practiced liar may not exhibit any at all! Therefore, this standard list of non-verbal clues is certainly not to be used as a basis for a hiring decision but could be used as a basis to ask more questions. The list below is by no means complete, since many additional behaviors could be added. In addition, as recounted in Chapter 5, scientific studies have shown that interviewers, even trained law enforcement professionals, can have difficulty detecting who is lying. However, the following list may be helpful:

- ✓ Non-responsive answers such as answering a question other than the question asked.
- ✓ Answering your question with a question or repeating your question.
- ✓ Answers do not make sense or are inconsistent.
- ✓ Becoming inappropriately defensive.
- ✓ Breaking eye contact.
- ✓ Clearing throat, stuttering, voice changing pitch, speed, or volume.
- ✓ Shifting body position or defensive body language such as crossing arms, shrugging shoulders.
- ✓ Hesitation before answering.
- ✓ Inability to remember dates and details.
- ✓ Loss of previous cooperative behavior.
- ✓ Making excuses before asked.

✓ Nervous hand movements such as wringing or tightly gripping hands, repeated fluttering, brushing of lint, or moving documents.

✓ Not remembering something when applicant has remembered other events in detail.

✓ Protesting too much that they made the choice to leave a company.

Summing It Up — An Interesting Story

Below is an interesting story by Dr. Marty Nemko. Dr. Nemko is co-author of *Cool Careers for Dummies*. He is a career and small business counselor in Oakland, California. His writings can be found at www.martynemko.com.

How it Works — A Story by Dr. Marty Nemko

Chester the Molester is looking through the Chronicle's employment ads. He finds an ad that sounds good — assistant manager of Pooh's Corner Children's Bookstore. On the bottom of the ad he reads, "We conduct background checks." He thinks, "Whoops, better look elsewhere."

Then Chester figures, "Ah, what the heck. They probably don't really do background checks."

So he applies, sending that resume and cover letter he so cleverly concocted. For example, "2000-2002: state-sponsored education program." Translation: Two years in San Quentin.

"I mean, I did learn a lot there!" he rationalizes. His cover letter and resume make Chester sound like a cross between T. Berry Brazelton and Maria from The Sound of Music.

The ruse works and Chester gets a call from Happy Chappy. They want him to come in for an interview! In his Mr. Rogers get-up, Chester saunters in, but he is in for a surprise. The receptionist says, "Before your interview, would you complete this application form and sign at the bottom authorizing the background screening?" He replies, "Sure, no problem," but he is thinking, "Uh-oh."

Chester shows for the interview, handing the application to the interviewer, Sally Savvy. Most of the questions are those standard simulations. Chester is so slick at BS'ing questions such as "What would you do if a child throws a tantrum?" Then Sally asks, "Before offering you the position, we would do a background check. Any objection to that?" Chester's heart starts to race, but he forces himself to look calm. "Not at all," he lies.

Sally continues: "As part of that check, we look to see if you have a criminal record. I notice on the application form, you didn't answer the question, 'In the past seven years, have you been convicted of a crime?' " Chester responds, "Oh, I forgot. I'll answer it now." He writes "No." His heart pounds through his chest wall.

Sally is relentless: "Oh, and of course, we contact your previous employers. Is there anything negative they're likely to say about you?" Beads of sweat form above his upper lip, like Richard Nixon in the 1960 presidential debate. "Well, uh, no." Chester manages to keep his voice calm sounding but he cannot control his eyes and forehead. The perceptive Sally knows he is nervous.

"Oh, and one more question. Because this job will require you to handle customers' money,

we will be conducting a credit check. Do you have any objections?" This is the last straw—Chester's debts greatly exceed the job's salary. Now he cannot even control his voice.

"Be my guest," he squeaks.

The interview ends and Chester thinks, "I don't want this stupid job anyway." Sally thinks, "There's something wrong with this guy." Even if she had planned to offer him the position, she would have first done a background check. That would likely have revealed Chester's criminal record and that his previous employer fired him for inappropriately touching children.

Additional Integrity Questions

Below are additional questions that can be used during an in-depth integrity interview.

- ✓ Tell me every job you have had in the past 10 years, including start and end date, salary, job title when started and ended, and supervisor, including names, addresses, and telephone numbers.
- ✓ Are there any falsifications on your application?
- ✓ Did you leave any jobs off your application?
- ✓ How will your previous employers describe your attendance? …Excellent? …O.K.? …Poor?
- ✓ How many days have you missed in the last year?
- ✓ How many verbal/written reprimands for your attendance did you receive in the past 2 years?
- ✓ How many tardiness days were recorded in your personnel file in the last year / job?   Why?
- ✓ How many disciplinary actions in the past 3 years?
- ✓ Where have you been suspended?   Why?
- ✓ Where have you been fired or asked to resign?   Why?
- ✓ Will any of your previous employers say they let you go or fired you?
- ✓ Where will you receive your best evaluation? The worst evaluation?
- ✓ Where have you suspected or had knowledge of co-workers or supervisors stealing?
- ✓ What have you taken?
- ✓ What will be found when your criminal record is checked? Note: convictions will not necessarily disqualify any applicant from employment.
- ✓ What does your current driving record show in the way of violations?
- ✓ Can you describe your best work related qualities?
- ✓ What is the worst thing any former employer will say about you?
- ✓ Whom do you know at the place of employment you are applying at?
- ✓ When was the last time in possession of illegal drugs?
- ✓ Currently, or within the past six months, what is your use of any controlled substance? …Marijuana? …Cocaine? …Speed? …PCP? …LSD? …Hashish? …Other?
- ✓ What is your current use of alcohol?
- ✓ Has the use of alcohol ever interfered with your work?
- ✓ To what extent do you gamble? Has gambling ever been a problem for you?
- ✓ Have you ever been the subject of, or a witness in, any type of investigation at work?

Free Interview Generator Guide Creates Standardized Questions for Human Resources and Hiring Managers

Employment Screening Resources (ESR) has created a free web based Interview Generator Guide to help employers build printed interview forms for any position. The tool allows employers to select from generic interview questions or to create their own questions and then create a printed form that can be saved or modified. The tool also gives employers the flexibility of adding their own question to different sections of the interview guide.

The free tool solves several issues for employers. It helps employers and HR professionals produce a printed structured interview guide and focus on developing relevant questions for each position. Printed interview forms also help employers ensure that interviewers are asking the right questions every time, in the right way. It helps to ensure that all applicants for a position are treated fairly and uniformly. Using a "structured interview" guide helps employers ask permissible questions in a consistent fashion for all applicants for a position. An employer should only choose those questions that are valid predictors of job performance for a particular position.

The tool can be found at: www.esrcheck.com/Interviewgenerator.php.

AUTHOR TIP

In a situation where a candidate is persistent in wanting to know why he or she was not hired, HR needs to strike a delicate balance between giving too much or too little information.

If the decision not to hire was based in anyway upon a background check, then of course the FCRA pre- and post-adverse action rules apply and an employer should engage in an individualized assessment (see Chapter 16) if a criminal record was involved. If the persistent applicant did not even get as far as a background check, but still cannot accept "No" for an answer, an employer or HR professional should still be careful how they handle the situation.

There may be a temptation to help the applicant by engaging in a conversation about why he or she was not a good fit or as qualified for the position. It is worth keeping in mind the old adage that no good deed goes unpunished. The unfortunate fact is sometimes job candidates are insistent on knowing why they were not hired in order to gather ammunition to file a lawsuit or discrimination complaint. Since there is never an obligation to engage in a debate with a candidate over hiring, it is not to the advantage of HR to get into a prolonged discussion. Keep in mind that even if the employer is trying to offer some friendly help, an unhappy applicant may not understand or recall what was said and, in a later court proceeding, may have a very different recollection of any conversation.

Conversely, an impersonal dismissal also carries potential consequences. First, it potentially damages an employer's "branding" in terms of recruitment. In addition, a reason disgruntled applicants may visit an attorney to explore whether any legal action is available is that they felt demeaned in some fashion, or they were dismissed as a human being.

Short, direct, and honest is the key, all while maintaining the dignity of the candidate. However, under no circumstances should an employer try to sugar coat the fact that someone else was a better match or more qualified, or debate the details of the decision. The best approach may be to just indicate that the employer decided to forward with a different candidate based upon experience and qualifications, and to thank them for their interest. Some employers indicate the applicant may reapply or that applications are kept on file for a certain period.

Chapter 9

AIR – The Reference Process

Inside This Chapter:

✓ Verification Checks are Critical

✓ The Importance of the Reference Check

✓ How Far Back Should Reference Checks Go?

✓ Procedures Employers Need to Implement for Quality Reference Checking

✓ Other Effective Reference Techniques

✓ Use Reference Questions that are 100% Legal

✓ Who Should Make the Past Employment Calls?

✓ Why Employers Won't Give References

✓ A New Assessment Tool – Automated Reference Checks

✓ Suggestions on How to Deal with Requests for References

Before reading further, it is important to understand the distinction between certain terms:

1. **A Past Employment Verification** refers to verifying **factual data** such as start date, end date, and job title.
2. **A Reference Check** of past employment means obtaining qualitative information about the person's performance such as how well the person did or where improvements are needed or if the person would be rehired.
3. **A Supervisor Reference** occurs when larger firms provide verifications through a Human Resources, staffing, or payroll department, or through someone else who does not actually know the applicant but is familiar with the firm. The verifier has the applicant's history of dates of employment and job titles. A reference, by comparison, is typically given by someone who actually knew the applicant, such as a former supervisor.
4. **A Personal Reference** comes from someone familiar with the applicant in a context other than employment.

The first part of this chapter examines the importance and use of the verification as part of a Safe Hiring Program.

Verification Checks are Critical

Trust, but Verify
At the height of the Cold War, during negotiations with the Soviet Bloc on weapons reductions, a popular phase was "Trust, but Verify." Good advice, especially today!

Even if all an employer gets is "name, rank, and serial number," it can be argued that verifying past employment is one of the most critical components an employer can undertake in the hiring process. Ideally, these checks provide specifics about past job performance that could be used as likely predictors of future success. Some employers make the costly error of not checking references. They know many organizations have policies against giving out detailed information about current or former employees. Employers might assume the effort is worthless because all they will get is "name, rank, and serial number," if anything at all. However, here is the critical point:

Even if all you get is verification of dates of employment and job titles, past employer phone calls are still vital for safe hiring.

Why is this so important? There are actually five essential reasons why a Safe Hiring Program requires calling past employers regardless of whether the past employer limits the information to start date, end date, and job title.

1. Eliminates Unexplained Employment Gaps

If you do not know where a person has been, then you are hiring a stranger. If you hire a stranger, then you have a substantial risk of being the victim of the legal and economic fallout of a bad hire.

As covered in previous chapters, if there are unexplained employment gaps in an application or resume, the employer cannot eliminate the possibility that the person's "absence" from the work force was involuntary, such as in being incarcerated for a criminal offense. By eliminating any gap in employment over the past five to ten years, it lessens the possibility the applicant spent time in custody for a significant criminal offense

AUTHOR TIP   The issue is not whether a person has gaps in his or her employment, but whether any gaps are *unexplained.* Not everyone has an uninterrupted employment history. Employment gaps can have very reasonable explanations, such as time off to go to school or for a sabbatical, or for personal and family reasons. Sometimes it can take a person time to find a new job. Gaps can indicate negative things too, such as a prison or jail stay.

Keep in mind that finding no gaps does not completely eliminate the possibility an applicant spent time in jail for some lesser offense. In many jurisdictions, a person convicted of a misdemeanor, such as a DUI, can fulfill a jail sentence in alternative ways — community service program, weekend custody, etc. In some jurisdictions, lesser offenders are eligible for a "bracelet" program, where they wear an electronic bracelet programmed to send a signal if they are not home by curfew. Also called the "commit a crime, go to your room program," this allows them to leave the house during specified hours to go to work.

Remember the story in Chapter 1 about the carpet cleaner? If the carpet cleaner had served time in a federal prison, the background check may not have revealed there was a criminal record. Therefore, the only way the employer could have uncovered the prison stay was to call the bogus past employers on the application or resume. A quick telephone call would have revealed a falsified application.

The importance of looking for unexplained gaps is underscored by the requirements imposed by the Federal Aviation Authority (FAA). When jobs fall under their authority, such as at airports and airlines, everyone hired must have a complete, validated ten-year history. If there is a gap, then the gap must be explained.

2. Indicates Where to Search for Criminal Records

There is no national database of criminal records that private employers can legally access. Criminal record searches must be conducted at each relevant courthouse, and there are over 10,000 courthouses covering some 3,500+ state and federal jurisdictions. However, when an employer knows where an applicant has been, then "the knowing where to look" increases the accuracy of a criminal search. If an employer does not know where to search (see Chapter 14), then he can easily miss a court where an applicant had a significant criminal act, and thereby inadvertently hire a person with a serious criminal record.

3. Allows an Employer to Hire Based Upon Facts, Not Just Instinct

The pitfalls of using the "warm body theory" of hiring have been demonstrated in earlier chapters. Although the use of instinct is valuable in the hiring process, there is simply no substitute for factual verifications. Given the statistics that up to one-third of all resumes contain material falsehoods, the need to verify statements in a resume or application is critical. Just knowing with certainty that the applicant did in fact have the jobs and position claimed goes a long way towards a solid hiring decision.

4. Allows an Employer to Demonstrate Due Diligence

Here is the critical point—if something goes wrong, an employer needs to be able to convince a jury that the **employer made reasonable efforts**, given the situation, to engage in safe hiring. Documentation for each person hired shows that an employer made reasonable steps by contacting past employers to confirm job information and to ask questions. This is powerful evidence an employer was not negligent. As stated before, an employer is not expected to be 100% successful in their hiring. No one is. Any employer is expected to act in good faith and to take diligent efforts to hire safe and qualified people. This cannot be done without demonstrating that the employer made the effort, which means documenting that he or she picked up the phone and tried.

What constitutes a reasonable effort? Taking reasonable care means attempting to obtain employer references and documenting those attempts. To a degree, the level of reasonable inquiry depends upon the nature of the job and the risk to third parties. A higher standard of care may be required for hiring an executive than a food service worker. Regardless, every employer has a legal obligation to exercise appropriate care in the selection and retention of employees. The law does not require that an employer be successful in obtaining references. It is clear that an employer must at least try.

5. Potential Employer May Receive Valuable Information

Many employers assume when they call a past employer they will get a "No comment," or "We do not give references." However, there is a significant percentage of time when both a verification and reference is possible. Sometimes this occurs when a firm has not been strongly counseled by their employment attorney not to give a reference, such a smaller employers who may not have been trained by a lawyer not to give references. Also, the previous employer may feel morally obliged to give references. Successful reference calls can also occur when the person calling has excellent communication skills, is professional, and is able to start some dialogue. There are many HR and security professionals who have developed the ability to obtain references, even from the most reluctant sources. Techniques on how to obtain references are given later in this chapter.

The Importance of the Reference Check

As mentioned earlier, doing a reference check of past employment means obtaining qualitative information about the person's performance, including past performance, improvements needed, and recommendation for rehire.

Employers, HR, and security professionals seeking to obtain references face a substantial challenge. Sometimes it may not be possible to obtain references because the previous employer has an established policy against giving references. Other times the challenge may be how to locate an actual supervisor or former supervisor who is willing to talk about the applicant. Many firms refer all reference questions to payroll or accounting, where a staff member can only give the basic information. The new "900 number" reference services do not even allow for a discussion with a live human being — it is all completed by computer.

Here is a fundamental rule— when you need to know something, there is always someone who knows what you need. The old adage "when there is a will, there is a way" also applies to reference checking. The challenge is finding that person and convincing him or her to give you the information. Sometimes, it requires more effort. Is it worth the additional effort of extensive attempts at checking? For an executive position, the extra effort may be worth it. For a position that can be more accurately described as "rank and file," or where there is a large scale hiring program, the real world limitation on time and budget may dictate setting up a program where a reasonable effort is made to satisfactorily demonstrate due diligence.

> **Job Applicants Can Be Anything They Want to Be with a New Fraudulent Service that Creates Fake Jobs at Fake Companies**
>
> To help some frustrated jobseekers succeed in the current job market, one company is offering false job references – complete with job titles, start dates and end dates, and salary – to people seeking employment who are willing to pay a fee plus a monthly subscription. This company offers phony references from real "Reference Providers" and work histories from "Virtual Companies." According to the company's website at www.careerexcuse.com, the company is "The World's Largest Network of Job Reference Providers" that can help jobseekers with bad references, weak resumes, and who have been fired. The company acts as a jobseeker's past employer with operators standing by to give "great" references, a work history, and pay range. This company will act as a jobseeker's "very own human resource department and supervisor" using a "virtual" company to verify a jobseeker's name, job title, job description, and work dates, as well as answer any questions with a positive reference in a professional manner.
>
> Of course, this service is not free. Jobseekers visiting the website can choose from three packages, ranging from a Basic Voicemail Plan for one professional reference that costs $65 followed by $20 monthly subscription, up to a Premium Package Plan for $195 plus a $50 monthly subscription. For the Premium plan, a reference script is assigned to three Reference Providers who act as a phony Human Resource Manager, phony Immediate Supervisor, and phony Secondary Supervisor. These Reference Providers are also subscribers to the service and are paid $50 for each reference they provide while acting as supervisors and HR departments.

> While it is true some jobseekers will stop at nothing to land a job, providing false past employment reference information is not the best way for a prospective employee to begin a business relationship with a potential employer. When jobseekers offer false past employment information to employers, they may end up being hired for jobs they are too unfit, unqualified, dishonest, or dangerous to complete. Meanwhile, honest jobseekers are overlooked for being more truthful with their references.

How Far Back Should Reference Checks Go?

How many years back should one go when checking previous employers? The answer can depend upon the applicant's relevant work history, the sensitivity of the position, and the availability of information. Some applicants may only have had one employer in the past ten years. Others may have had a large number. If a person is an hourly worker, then it is possible the person has held numerous past jobs. A young worker may not have a work history to check.

As a general guideline, employers should go back a minimum of five years, although seven to ten is much better. If the employer is in an industry where there is a great deal of turnover, then it may not be practical to go back even five years, if the five-year span represents a large number of previous employers. Employers should utilize a rule of reason, but also keep in mind that an employer should be internally consistent so that all similarly situated applicants are treated in a similar fashion. If an employer goes back five years for an administrative assistant, then all candidates who have reached the stage where references are conducted should also have their references checked going back five years.

Procedures Employers Need to Implement for Quality Reference Checking

A successful, in-house system of reference checking is possible. Here are ten important steps every employer should know about the mechanics of obtaining past references.

1. Set up a physical system to make and track calls, and monitor your progress by using a Past Employment Worksheet

Effective reference checking requires a system; otherwise it is nearly impossible to track who has been called, the status of each call, and who else needs to be called.

This is especially true in a large company environment. In a typical large company reference-checking situation, a checker may be given a number of applicants to check references. Assume HR is given five applicants to check. Also assume that each applicant has on the average three past employers, making a total of 15 needed calls. Chances are that the percentage of successful first time calls will be limited. A successful call means getting through to the right person and getting as much information as the person can give you. The reality is most calls will result in an "incomplete," meaning that a call back is needed. Perhaps the caller had to leave a message on a voicemail, the phone number did not work or is busy, or the past employer needs "a release" from the applicant. All of these situations require that HR note the outcome and schedule a follow-up. As the HR person is calling on the third candidate, past employers may be calling back in response to earlier messages. Sometimes a round or two of "phone-tag" is involved. Obviously, a tracking system is a necessity. Here are suggestions to make the work flow easier:

✓ Have a prepared Past Employment Worksheet ready to go for each candidate. For each applicant, the reference checker needs to fill out the name and contact information for each past employer as well as any standard reference questions. A sample Past Employer Worksheet is found in the Appendix.

✓ Use the Past Employer Worksheet to track all phone calls, including who was called and the results. The information is worth its weight in gold should an employer ever be called upon to demonstrate due diligence in court. Even if the reference attempt was unsuccessful, a completed worksheet showing each call — including the date, time, phone number, person called, and the result — is the best possible proof that an employer exercised due diligence.

✓ In advance, it is helpful to place the essential information reported by the applicant on the Past Employment Worksheet. Now, during a call, the reference checker can write down what the past employer reports, providing an easy-to-read side-by-side comparison.

✓ If specific job-related questions are being asked relevant to the Knowledge, Skill, and Abilities (KSA) related to a particular position, then make sure those questions are ready. This may mean having the application easily accessible for a quick reference.

✓ Using a Past Employer Worksheet also insures you are asking the same questions for similarly situated candidates. A critical function of a reference-checking program is to treat all candidates fairly. Treat similarly situated candidates the same way!

2. Independently confirm the existence and phone number for the past employer

It may not happen very often, but many HR and Security Professionals have heard of situations where an applicant set-up a fake reference on a resume by providing a friend's telephone number, with the friend standing by to answer, posing as a past employer. When the prospective employer makes the phone call, the friend gives a glowing and professorial reference. Or, an applicant bent on a "fake reference" can use other alternatives such as setting up a voicemail service, leaving a message indicating the voice mail box belongs to a supposed reference, and later have a friend return the call posing as a past supervisor. Cases are reported of applicants attempting to act as their own reference. With cell phones, call forwarding and internet phone services, such trickery is now easier than ever.

To avoid the possibility of a fake reference, it is recommended that a verifier independently establish the past employer is legitimate and to locate a valid phone number by use of an internet service or local phone book. There are a number of websites where phone numbers can be found very quickly. They typically have the same data that dialing "411" information would have, except the internet services are free. Any legitimate firm will have a listed phone number. The chance of an applicant going to the trouble of creating a legal entity just to get a listed phone number is, well, not likely.

Here are some websites where employer phone numbers can be located:

- www.infousa.com
- www.city-yellowpages.com
- www.switchboard.com
- www.superpages.com
- www.infospace.com
- www.411.com

In addition, verifiers can also research the past employer by running the name on the Internet search engine at www.google.com. There may be times when a firm is not listed. That can happen if the firm has moved, merged, changed names, or gone out of business. In that situation, the new employer may well have to talk further with the applicant to find someone who can verify an employment.

An employer or screening firm can go even further and verify the legitimacy of the past employer by looking up the employer on a secretary of state website's search of valid registered business entities, or do an online search of Fictitious Business Names sites. An employer can even use one of the commercial services, such as Dunn and Bradstreet, Hoovers, or Manta to name a few.

Of course, a verifier must also use good judgment. If the phone is not answered in a professional manner, or there are the sounds of traffic and children in the background, then something is not right.

Finally, if there is any suspicion of a set-up or fake reference, it may be necessary to verify if the person giving the reference was, in fact, employed by the past employer. That may even require, in some situations, calling HR or payroll to make sure the person the verifier is talking with was in fact employed there.

3. Be careful when contacting an applicant's current employer

A recurring issue in any past employment check is sensitivity about contacting the current employer. A current employer should NOT be contacted unless the applicant specifically gives permission.

The reason is there are some employers who, upon learning a current employee is looking to leave, will immediately take steps to terminate the employee. This is especially true for positions of greater responsibility where the applicant may have access to customer lists or trade secrets. In some industries, within minutes of learning an employee is actively looking for a new position, the current employer will have the Security Department box up the employee's personal items, confiscate all computers and disks, turn off all access to any computer systems, de-activate the parking permit and building access code, and have the person physically escorted off premises with a last paycheck.

If such a hasty departure is caused by a phone call by the prospective new employer, and the job offer does not come through, then the applicant is left without a job and free to contemplate whether they should visit a lawyer. In order to avoid this, here is a simple two-step program:

- ✓ On the application, in large letters, make sure there is a box someplace asking an applicant "May we contact your current employer?"
- ✓ Do NOT call the current employer unless the applicant has clearly marked the "Yes" Box. If the applicant failed to check either box, then do not call until that is clarified. Anything other than a clear indication of YES can create problems.

If the employer still needs to verify current employment, there are three options for doing so:

- ✓ Ask the applicant for the name of a past supervisor or co-worker who is no longer working with the applicant at the current place of employment. Again, if there is any question about the authenticity of the supplied name, the employer can call and verify the ex-employee did in fact work at the current workplace.
- ✓ Ask the applicant to bring in W-2's for each year of work, or at least the full past year.
- ✓ Wait until after the employee is hired before calling the past employer; providing the new hire is subject to a written offer letter clearly stating "continued employment is conditional upon a background screening report that is satisfactory to the employer." Once the new employee is working there can be a final phone call. By making current employment part of the written offer letter, an applicant has a powerful incentive to be accurate about the current employment situation, since any false or misleading statements or omissions will have serious consequences. It is important to include the phrase "satisfactory to the employer" in order to avoid a debate with an applicant/new hire about what is or is not a good screening report.

4. Use "Soft Sell Techniques"

If a verifier faces resistance to a reference, the best approach is usually a soft sale. Here are some techniques that may help convince a past employer to give the information you need:

- ✓ Do not start right off asking for an employment reference. That will immediately make an employer defensive and create a barrier to effective communication.
- ✓ Explain the purpose and try to convince the past employer to be of assistance. How? By finding a common ground. For example, explain that your applicant cannot be employed without some additional information, or that getting some information would be a great benefit.
- ✓ Start with a non-controversial request, such as start date, end date, or job title.
- ✓ Before asking reference questions, segue into the subject with non-controversial questions such as "What was the nature of the job?" If you are told the person's job title was "project manager," then ask the past employer what that job entails. It is then a short trip to ask "How did the applicant perform the job?"
- ✓ If your state has a statute that protects an employer who gives an employment reference, then you may explain that to a reference.

✓ Offer to send a release. A release gives a past employer a great comfort level. It demonstrates the new employer, in fact, has a valid business reason for requesting the information, and the past employer has permission to give it. Keep in mind, however, a release is not a blank check for the past employer to say anything they want. Even with a release, the past employer must be careful to limit the information to those items that are job-related and factual.

5. Be careful about the "Eligible for Rehire" question

If nothing else works, a firm can at least be asked if the previous employer would rehire the applicant, or whether the applicant is eligible for rehire. This has become a standard reference question. Even firms with a "name, rank, and serial number" policy are comfortable with answering this question. In reality, the past employer is being asked the ultimate question, which is "knowing what you know about the person," and assuming you are also a highly trained, competent and motivated HR manager, "Would you want the person back?"

However, there are several problems with the "Eligible for Rehire" question. First, if a firm in fact has a no reference policy, then they are technically violating their policy if they answer. They are essentially giving a qualitative evaluation of the person. If they answer "No," that potentially could be a form of defamation.

Second, a real issue with the question is the answer is often meaningless. Here is why. Suppose a past employer is called and asked about "eligible for rehire," and the past employer says, "Yes." What does that mean? It could mean that technically the person is "eligible" to be rehired because there is no notation on the personnel file that indicates there is a prohibition against accepting that application. However, in truth and in fact, that past employer would never consider rehiring that person, they just won't say so.

Conversely, a "No" answer could mean the particular employer has a policy against rehiring anyone who left, even though the applicant was the best worker they could ever hope for.

The wording of the question that is most helpful is the following: "Knowing what you know about Mr. Smith, if you were in a position to rehire him for the same job he left, would you want him back?"

In order to interpret that answer, the verifier must understand the assumptions being made. They are assuming that the person who is giving the answer has a similar interest to the new employer and is capable of making a meaningful judgment. In other words, in order to give the answer meaning, the verifier has to make assumptions about the knowledge and judgment of the person giving the information.

If an HR professional giving the information is someone who the verifier happens to know and the verifier has respect for the experience and judgment of this HR professional, then the answer is extremely valuable. If the verifier is talking to a stranger, then it is really a judgment call as to the value of the information. It really comes down to the old rule–information from a trusted source is the best information.

 AUTHOR TIP If your organization has been instructed not to answer reference questions but to verify information only, then the "rehire question" is really a reference question. In fact, "Would you rehire?" is the ultimate reference question since employer 1 is asking employer 2's ultimate judgment about whether a new employer should hire their former employee.

6. Send a faxed request — It is harder to ignore than voicemail

Often times a verifier cannot get through to a live person and must leave a voicemail. As everyone knows in this busy world, it is easy to ignore voicemail. By the time the verifier leaves the third voicemail, it becomes less likely the past employer intends to respond. Assuming the verifier has verified that the reference person is not away on a leave or vacation, and it is the right person, the verifier needs a way to get through.

Short of physically going over to the past employers office and demanding time (not very practical, of course) the next best thing is to send a fax request. For some reasons, a piece of paper demands attention — people feel they need to do something with a piece of paper but they can ignore voicemail. A fax to a former employer can also include the information to be verified, along with a return fax number, of course.

If all else fails, a faxed request at least shows a due diligence effort to get the information. The fax to the past employer should be maintained in the file as proof of the efforts made.

Another technique is to mail a written request. This technique is only effective for verification of factual information. How much meaning should be put on past employers answers to faxed or mailed reference questions? That is difficult to say.

7. Use other sources such as former co-workers or supplied references

Depending on the importance of the position and the time and resources available, the verifier may attempt to talk with a professional reference the applicant has supplied. This is known as a "supplied reference."

One technique is to ask a supplied reference for another person who may know the applicant. This is known as talking with a developed reference. A "developed reference" is a source of information the verifier has developed on his or her own, without input from the candidate.

Talking to a developed reference can be a very valuable source of information. The verifier can get information from someone who was not told in advance he or she would be contacted, which increases the probability of a truly spontaneous and non-rehearsed conversation leading to additional insights about the candidate.

8. Use professional networking when possible

HR professionals can sometimes engage in **professional networking** to obtain reference information. Sometime just "reading between the lines" can be of assistance. A previous employer may be unwilling to give specific information but may be willing to convey a sense about or opinion about the applicant or communicate in some other "unofficial" manner.

It should be noted there is no such thing as an "off the record comment." Should a matter ever go to litigation and a deposition is taken, an HR manager or employer would have a legal obligation to reveal all the details of a conversation, if directly asked.

There is, however, an ethical issue to consider. If an HR or security professional knows that a colleague works at a firm that has a strict policy against giving references, then a request for information is really asking another professional to violate a firm's policy. The fact that such a conversation may be "off the record" may not help.

9. Use other procedures if the former employer is out of business, bankrupt, moved, merged, or cannot be located

For a number of reasons a previous employer may not be available for a past employment check. First, a verifier may have trouble obtaining information if a firm has merged or been acquired, and no one can locate the personnel records. In this situation, a verifier has two options. One is to contact the applicant to locate a former co-worker or supervisor; however, that requires the verifier to confirm the credibility of the former employee, since there would be no way to verify the source of information from the former employer. The second option is to contact the applicant and request a copy of the W-2 (if the applicant was on the payroll) or a 1099 (if the applicant was a contractor). To help confirm employment, an employer can also "Google" the applicant or use a new service available at www.zoominfo.com to see if there are any references on the internet.

A verifier can also run into difficulties if given insufficient information about the past employer. It is critical to require any applicant to completely identify the past employer by name, city, and state in order to facilitate a telephone call. Using an applicant-supplied phone number can be a source of difficulty; not only must the verifier be alert to the possibility of a "fake or set-up reference," but often, the phone number an applicant recalls was the number for a division or branch, not the number needed for that firm's past employment verifications.

10. If a past employer says there is no record, then a verifier needs to go one step further

What if a past employer tells a verifier there is no record of an applicant having worked there? Before jumping to the conclusion the applicant has lied, a verifier should dig deeper. There can be reasonable explanations for apparent discrepancies. An applicant may have worked at the previous company as a temporary worker, under contract, or was actually employed by a third-party employer organization.

Many companies utilize the services of a Professional Employer Organization (PEO) to act as the employer of record although the work is performed at the company workplace under the company's direction and control. In these situations, the previous company's records will show that no such person worked there, though their facility was the physical location where the applicant worked. Since the applicant physically worked at the firm's premises, the applicant may well report that business as the employer. The applicant may not be certain who actually issued the check.

It is also important to ask the employer to double-check their records under the applicant's Social Security Number and any other names the applicant may have used.

AUTHOR TIP

Automated Third Party Verification Services

Some employers utilize outsourced third party services to handle past employment verification calls. The third party service will download all employment information so that verifiers, such as employers or screening firms, call the third party service instead of the employer directly. This saves the employer time and money since they do not need to respond to phone calls, faxes, or emails. The verification is typically completed by the verifier online or through an interface. Examples are uConfirm or The Work Number for Everyone (WNFE) found at www.talx.com. If there is concern about the accuracy of data about an individual applicant, these sites provide an email address for questions. One drawback is that the information is typically limited to dates, title, and possibly salary, and there is no one to talk to in order to locate additional information.

YOU NEED TO KNOW

A Case in Point

An applicant reported a two-year employment history. However, a telephone call to the past employer showed the applicant only worked there for a year and a half. On the surface, it appeared the applicant lied about the time period of employment. Since honesty and integrity are integral to any employment relationship, the employer was about to terminate the hiring process and rescind the offer. However, the employer could not believe that such a good prospect actually lied and took the extra step of asking the applicant about the apparent discrepancy. Upon further investigation, it turned out the applicant started off working for the past employer as an unpaid intern for six months, then was hired full-time. From the applicant's point of view, he had worked there for two years — employment records for the company reflected only a year and a half. If the employer had not gone the extra step, then all of the time, energy, and expense of recruiting the prospect would have been wasted. On the other hand, if the person had lied, the extra time spent confirming the facts would also have protected the employer in the event of any adverse legal action.

Other Effective Reference Techniques

The Appendix provides a list of sample reference questions. Some suggestions made by experts include:

✓ Use of questions showing behavior – e.g. "Can you give me a specific example of how he (or she) was a great team player?"

✓ Ask a targeted question – e.g. "The candidate states he (or she) implemented a sales training program. Can you tell me about their contribution?"

✓ Read the candidate's resume to the past employer and ask for a reaction to the resume content.

✓ Use open-ended questions to inspire narrative answers.

Human Resources consultant and expert on hiring and reference questions Wendy Bliss gives the following tips on effective reference techniques. More information on this topic is available in her book *Legal, Effective References: How to Give and Get Them*, published by the Society for Human Resource Management in 2001.

Mission Possible: 10 Tips for Effective Telephone Reference Checks

By Wendy Bliss, J.D., SPHR

Author of *Legal, Effective References*

www.wendybliss.com

Due to the popularity of the "name, rank and serial number" approach to reference requests, it is often challenging to uncover useful, in-depth information about job applicants during telephone reference checks. However, it is by no means impossible! With practice and persistence, you can greatly increase the quantity and quality of information obtained in conversations with reference sources. On your next reference-checking mission, use the following tips:

✓ **Create a powerful script.** Do not "wing it" when calling references. Develop a written outline that includes questions and comments that will enable you to: 1) establish rapport with reference contacts; 2) minimize potential opposition to your inquiries; 3) obtain relevant, detailed information about the applicant; and 4) follow up with the source as needed. Tips 2 through 9 below provide techniques for accomplishing each of these objectives. To build skill and consistency, use your reference check script for every reference check.

✓ **Open the door for effective communication in the first sixty seconds.** When contacting a reference, your initial goal is to make a positive connection and set the stage for a candid conversation. Identify yourself by name and position. Share general information about your company and the specific opening there for which the applicant is being considered. Let the reference contact know that you have the applicant's permission to call, assuming that is the case. (If the applicant has not given your organization prior written consent to do so, it is inadvisable to conduct any reference checks.) After sharing this introductory information, making a complimentary statement about the source, such as "Betty made favorable comments about your guidance and supervision during her interviews with us," may predispose the source to sharing full and frank feedback with you.

✓ **Avoid the "R" word.** The mere mention of the word "reference," particularly in the initial stage of a reference check call, may arouse worries about defamation and other legal claims in the mind of the person you have contacted. So, you should set the stage for cooperation. Explain the purpose for the call and the potential benefits of sharing candid information by taking a future focus. For instance, stating that "An important reason for my call is to gain information that will help our company most effectively supervise Richard in the event we hire him" emphasizes the developmental benefit of answering your questions fully.

✓ **Ask the right questions, in the right order.** After establishing rapport with the source, climb the ladder of reference inquiries to gain a thorough understanding of the applicant's employment history, qualifications, job performance, and past problems on the job. Start by asking the most innocuous and easily answered questions first, including confirmation of dates of employment, positions held and salary history. Next, move up the ladder of inquiry to gather information about the applicant's job duties, performance, work habits, and his or her suitability for the open position at your company. Finally, inquire about the most sensitive topics including reasons for leaving, and incidents of misconduct or dangerous behaviors. This three-tiered approach to questioning — saving the toughest topics for last — usually leads to at least partial cooperation from reference sources.

✓ **Ask open-ended questions, and give prompters.** Questions about the applicant that begin with the words "what," "how," or "why" invite detailed responses. Other phrases that encourage full and specific disclosure begin with phrases such as "Give me an example of the applicant's ability to . . .,"or "Describe a time when the applicant . . ." Follow up questions or statements such as "Can you elaborate on that?" or "That's interesting. Please tell me more about that," to prompt the source to give more details.

✓ **Listen carefully for vocal clues.** Many reference sources who are reluctant to share negative information will tip off reference checkers to potential problems with the applicant through a variety of signals. Is the source's tone of voice guarded? Does he or she sound cautious or reluctant to answer even basic fact verification questions? Reference checkers should also be on the alert for unusually long pauses, throat-clearing, or "umms" and "ahs" that may indicate hesitancy to give information candidly, particularly if these occur in response to a sensitive question.

✓ **Dig deep when you get shallow responses.** When a reference source gives a vague answer, carefully rehearsed, or inconsistent, probe for more useful information. In such situations, politely ask for more details with remarks such as "I am not sure I understood what you meant when you said . . . Can you clarify that for me?" Another technique that may help you discover the truth when you are being stonewalled is to ask very direct questions that require a "yes" or "no" response. For example, ask "Was Pat fired?" or "Was Chris ever disciplined for poor performance or misconduct while employed at your company?" These pinpointed questions probe non-answers about an applicant's reasons for leaving a prior job, or provide clues about his or her performance and conduct with the previous employer.

✓ **Be prepared for reluctant references.** While the above techniques will increase your overall success in obtaining useful information during reference checks, you will undoubtedly still encounter stiff resistance from some reference sources. When this occurs, offer to fax the source a copy of the reference authorization form signed by the applicant. This will be particularly helpful if your reference authorization form includes a waiver of liability that protects anyone who provides a reference about the applicant. You can also explain that the applicant will not be hired without satisfactory information about the applicant's performance in past jobs, which is an effective way to encourage sources having positive information about the applicant to go ahead and do the right thing. Additionally, you can inquire as to whether the source's unwillingness to share information about the applicant is an indication of problems with the applicant. If all else fails, contact a different source at the same organization – such as a higher level manager, another supervisor, or even a colleague – who worked directly with the applicant. It is very possible that a different source in the same organization will be willing to give you the information you seek.

✓ **When closing a call, leave the door open to get more information.** At the end of your reference check discussions, thank the source for his or her time. Ask for permission to contact the source again if you have additional questions. Finally, ask if the source knows of any other people inside or outside the source's organization who would have knowledge of the applicant's background, job performance or others matters relevant to the applicant's suitability to work at your organization.

✓ **Use good form in documenting calls.** All telephone reference check attempts and calls should be documented using a standardized form. This form can be developed internally, or can be obtained from books on reference checking such as my book *Legal Effective References: How to Give and Get Them.*

Use Reference Questions that are 100% Legal

Remember the same standards that apply to reference checking also apply to interview questions — all questions must be specifically job-related. Never ask any question of a reference you would not ask the candidate face-to-face. Focus on skills and accomplishments as well as performance issues that apply specifically to your job opening, such as ability to meet deadlines or to work well with others on a team project. See Chapter 8 for a list of questions that can and cannot be asked of an applicant in an interview. Again, these questions are also applicable when interviewing a past employer.

Who Should Make the Past Employment Calls?

There are three different groups who can do past employment checks:

- ✓ The actual hiring managers
- ✓ Human Resources
- ✓ An outsourced third party, such as a background firm

Here are the pros and cons of each group:

Hiring Manager

Advantages: The manager knows the job and knows what talents and skills are needed. Also, the hiring manager is the person who has to live with the decision. For sensitive or critical positions, the manager may want to receive input directly from previous employers. Even if the previous employer has a "no comment" policy, there may still be an advantage in talking personally to the previous employer and attempting to glean what information is available "between the lines."

Disadvantages: There is much less control over the process in terms of whether the hiring manager is asking legal questions or treating candidates in a similar fashion. In addition, many hiring managers may be tempted to make fewer calls and may settle for just one completed call before making a decision. Hiring managers may not be as concerned about the need to establish a full employment history or look for employment gaps. Although these drawbacks can be lessened with written procedures, training, and auditing of hiring files, they are still sources of concern.

Human Resources

Advantages: Any reference check done by human resources more likely will be done thoroughly, properly, and legally with proper documentation and consistency.

Disadvantages: The human resources department does not know the job requirements nearly as well as the hiring manager. In addition, even for a firm with a fully staffed Human Resources department, employment reference checking is a time consuming task. The difficulty with performing employment reference checks in-house is not the time the actual interview takes; it is the constant interruptions of returned phone calls throughout the day, tracking the progress of each candidate, and making repeated attempts when there is not a callback. It can also take time to locate former employers and phone numbers as well.

Background Checking Firm

Advantages: By outsourcing, a firm knows that nothing will fall through the cracks, since a background firm can be counted on to methodically contact all past employers. In addition, the fees charged by screening firms are typically very modest.

Disadvantages: A verifier employed by a screening firm typically knows little about the employer or the job. Screening firms often do employment checks in high volume and are unlikely to ask in-depth, pertinent questions. In addition, given the prices charged by screening firms, the verifiers are not HR professionals but rather have skills that are closer to a professional call center.

Who Makes the Call? — Conclusion

The answer is to recognize the difference between *reference checks used to determine if a person should be offered the position* in the first place and *due diligence of past employment checks* utilized to ensure an employer has confirmed dates and details of past employment and subjected all finalists to the same process.

In order to make sure nothing falls through the cracks, HR or a background screening firm may be called upon to do a check, just to make sure all the bases have been covered. The worst that can happen is some former employer may be called twice — once by the hiring manager and again by HR or a background screening firm.

Many organizations encourage the hiring manager to make whatever employment checks are needed to help decide if the person is a good fit — to form an opinion as to whether or not to make a job offer in the first place. Of course, employers are well advised to make sure a hiring manager is trained, so that only legal and permissible questions are asked.

Survey Reveals 98 Percent of Businesses Conduct Reference Background Checks on Some or All Job Candidates

A 2010 survey from the Society for Human Resource Management (SHRM) comprised from a sample of over 400 randomly selected Human Resources professionals from SHRM's membership revealed that approximately three out of four U.S. businesses performed – 76 percent – of organizations conducted reference background checks for all job candidates while 22% did so on selected job candidates, meaning 98 percent of organizations conducted reference checks on some or all job candidates as part of their pre-employment screening programs.

For the purpose of this research, the phrase "reference background checks" referred to any verification of information provided by a job applicant (e.g., employment history), or communication with people regarding the job applicant (e.g., former supervisor or co-worker). When asked which category of job candidates they conducted reference checks on, the organizations surveyed answered as follows:

✓   76 percent said job candidates who will have access to highly confidential employee information.

✓   72 percent said job candidates for positions with fiduciary and financial responsibility.

✓   62 percent said job candidates who will have access to company or other people's property.

✓   59 percent said job candidates for senior executive positions such as CEO and CFO.

When asked for the primary reasons for conducting reference checks on job candidates, the organizations surveyed answered as follows:

✓   55 percent said to reduce legal liability for negligent hiring.

✓   35 percent said to determine that credentials were accurately represented by the job candidate.

✓   27 percent said to assess past performance and predict future performance.

✓   19 percent said to ensure a safe work environment for employees and also to comply with applicable state laws requiring background checks.

The SHRM Poll *'Conducting Reference Background Checks'* is available at:
www.shrm.org/Research/SurveyFindings/Articles/Pages/ConductingReference

Why Employers Won't Give References

The current system of employment reference checks makes no sense. Even though everyone agrees that past employment checking is an essential part of the hiring process, many employers, on advice of legal counsel, have a "no comment policy," allowing only verification of basic information such as start and end dates and job title. Some companies will not even release salary information — salaries coming under the heading of "competitive intelligence," thus protected — even when presented with a signed release.

The results are not only illogical but also run counter to the best interest of employers and well-deserving job applicants. Good prospects are sometimes unable to get the recommendations they deserve, while applicants with a negative history can go on to victimize new and unsuspecting employers, with their history safely hidden behind them. In fact, the only beneficiaries of this upside-down system are the very job applicants that employers want to avoid.

Adding to the confusion is the fact that oftentimes the very employer or HR professional who is attempting to get a reference will turn around on the same day and refuse to give out a reference on one of their own past employees. Despite the fact that employers, labor lawyers, HR, and security professionals all agree that past employment checks should be conducted, it is also a well-known fact that most employers will not give any information beyond "name, rank, and serial number."

What is happening here? What is the reason for this completely illogical system?

It is the fear of being SUED!

Employers who give negative references can be sued for defamation. When the defamation is in oral form (such as over the phone) it is called slander. When in written form (such as a negative letter of recommendation) it is called libel.

For example, what if an applicant had a history with previous employers that showed he was often late, did not get along with others, was not productive, did not meet goals, or was disciplined for inappropriate workplace conduct? These are all critical items of information a new employer would want and need to know.

Yet, few former employers are willing to convey this information. Labor lawyers repeatedly instruct employers NOT to give out anything but "name, rank, and serial number."

If there is no question that misconduct occurred, such as a criminal conviction, then the former employer is probably on safer grounds. However, in situations where the former employee can dispute the accusation, an employer should be concerned about a lawsuit. Suppose a former employee was accused of harassment, and an internal company investigation indicated the harassment did occur. If the company reveals this about the applicant to the new employer, the previous employer could still face a lawsuit. An internal company investigation does not carry weight of law, thus it may be defamation.

To make matters even worse, employers can be sued, believe it or not, by giving a POSITIVE reference. This can happen where the employer gave a good reference letter but withheld negative information for fear of being sued for defamation. If the resulting recommendation created a false impression, and as the result of the misrepresentation it is foreseeable that someone can be injured, the past employer can be sued. And why not? They lied.

Liability for a False Positive Reference – the School District Case

In a 1997 California case, the State Supreme Court ruled that a school district could be liable for damages when it gave a very positive job recommendation and left out important negative information. A school administrator was accused of inappropriate sexual misconduct towards a 13-year-old girl. The named victim not only sued the administrator, but also sued former schools that gave him favorable employment recommendations even though the former schools were aware of similar allegations of sexual misconduct at previous schools. The favorable recommendations included statements such as—

✓ He had "genuine concern" for students and had "outstanding rapport" with everyone.

✓ "I wouldn't hesitate to recommend (him) for any position."

✓ He was "an upbeat, enthusiastic administrator who related well to the students."

✓ He was "in a large part" responsible for making the school "a safe, orderly and clean environment for students and staff."

The Court ruled that a former employer providing a recommendation owes a duty to protect employers and third parties, and cannot misrepresent the qualifications and character of an ex-employee where there is a substantial risk of physical injury. In other words, an employer could not portray a former employee in a false light by only giving the good and not the bad. Having written a letter that they knew would be used to gain employment at other schools where there were potential victims, the schools had an obligation tell the whole truth. See *Randi W vs. Muroc Joint Unified School District*, (14 Cal.4th 1066)(1997)

So, here is the situation. If a past employer gives a negative reference, the past employer can be sued for defamation by the applicant. If the employer gives a positive reference, a victim of misconduct can potentially sue the past employer for giving a false reference if negative information is left out.

The law arguably places employers who give recommendations in a "Catch-22." If an employer fails to disclose an accusation because of insufficient credible evidence, then the employer risks being sued by third party victims. However, if the employer does mention an accusation, the ex-employee can arguably sue for defamation.

Interesting Facts about Defamation Lawsuits

According to facts contained on the website for the National Workrights Institute, the threat of defamation lawsuits are grossly over-exaggerated.

"The reality of the threat of defamation from employer references is often well exaggerated. The truth is that very few employers are ever sued for defamation and almost none are found liable. In 1997 there were only 13 cases in the United States in which employees sued ex-employers for defamation in the context of reference giving. Of those cases, only four were successful and only once was a plaintiff's award of damages upheld. In 1998 there were four cases with not one successful plaintiff and in 1999 there were five cases with only one plaintiff succeeding."

Source: www.workrights.org/issue_other/oi_reference_check.html.

Still, hesitation to give references exists despite protection given under many state laws. Forty states currently have some sort of employer immunity statute. These statutes are designed to promote good faith communication of job related information between employers. For example, California Civil Code Section 47(c) was amended in 1994 to add a section to protect employers from defamation lawsuits when giving an employment reference to another employer. The code states:

> *This subdivision applies to and includes a communication concerning the job performance or qualifications of an applicant for employment, based upon credible evidence, made without malice, by a current or former employer of the applicant, to and upon request of the prospective employer.*

What does this mean in plain English? Essentially it means that if a new prospective employer contacts a former employer, the former employer has a "qualified privilege" to give information, as long as the information is:

✓ Job related;
✓ Based upon credible evidence; and
✓ Made without malice.

Unfortunately, it is difficult to gauge whether these laws have actually encouraged employers to free up the flow of necessary information. For the most part, these laws merely put into a statute what has already been the case law, or "common law," in most jurisdictions — that good faith communication between interested parties has some protection. However, even with this protection, many legal sources argue that the risk of a defamation claim outweighs any benefit to an employer from giving reference information. For one thing, applicants can still sue for defamation if they contend the reference was given in "bad faith." Further, what constitutes, "credible evidence," or what is "job related," can be open to interpretation.

One more consideration must be added to the mix. Generally, an employer has no obligation to say anything at all. If a firm was considering the application of Jack D. Ripper and called up a past employer, that past employer can legally say "No comment." In other words, past employers have no duty to warn. The exception of course may be if the employer only gives the "good stuff" and leaves out the bad, as in the California School case.

If employers had a duty to warn, it would potentially put an impossible task on employers. Why? Because employers would be placed in the untenable position of being sued every time one of their ex-employees would get a new position. It would create an incredible burden if every time an employer was called up for a reference, they had to choose between being sued by the applicant for defamation or being sued by the new employer or a victim for failure to warn or for giving a negligent reference.

A Tale of Two References – One Makes You Liable for Damages and the Other Does Not

In a 2008 federal appeals case, *Kadlec Medical vs. Lakeview, 527 F.3d 412 (5th Cir. 2008)*, two past medical employers gave past employment information for the same anesthesiologist. After the anesthesiologist moved on to yet another hospital, he botched a routine 15 minute procedure, leaving a patient in a permanent vegetative state allegedly due to the anesthesiologist's own addiction to drugs.

The new hospital and its insurance company settled with the victim and in turn sued the previous two medical organizations for misrepresentations in the past employment information given to the new hospital. The allegation was based upon misrepresentations since the new hospital claimed it hired the anesthesiologist because the defendants did not give accurate information by withholding information about misconduct and drug use.

The first defendant was a medical group that was fully aware that the anesthesiologist had a drug abuse issue. After giving the anesthesiologist a second chance, he continued to misuse drugs. The anesthesiologist was terminated for that reason.' However, the first defendant gave the anesthesiologist a glowing recommendation. The court noted that:

> *...if an employer makes a misleading statement in a referral letter about the performance of its former employees, the former employer may be liable for its statements if the facts and circumstances*

warrant. Here, defendants (medical group) were recommending an anesthesiologist, who had the lives of patients in his hands every day. Policy considerations dictate that the defendants had a duty to avoid misrepresentations in their referral letters if they mislead plaintiffs into thinking that (the anesthesiologist) was an excellent anesthesiologist, where they had information that he was a drug addict.

The situation with the second defendant, the hospital, however, was more complicated. The hospital knew that the anesthesiologist was a potential danger, but yet chose to say nothing, hiding behind a claim that they were too busy to provide more details.

The Court noted that it found no Louisiana case, or cases outside of Louisiana, that imposed a requirement that a past employer reveal negative past information, absent a situation where the past employer made some sort of affirmative misrepresentation. In other words, the first hospital did not have a legal duty to voluntarily step up and give negative information, as long as it limited its report to just factual employment data such as dates and job title. The court noted:

And although the (hospital) might have had an ethical obligation to disclose their knowledge of (the anesthesiologist's) drug problems, they were also rightly concerned about a possible defamation claim if they communicated negative information about (the anesthesiologist).

The Court noted that if such an obligation were imposed upon employers, there would not only be privacy concerns, but it would create a burden if employers had to investigate each time if negative matters about a past employee was the type that had to be disclosed. As a result, the employer that gave a glowing recommendation where it was obviously not true could be liable. The employer that kept its mouth shut was not liable, even though it knew the truth and kept it to itself. The bottom line: if an employer limits itself to just dates of employment and job title, it has no obligation to warn of future dangerousness, provided the employer did not falsely mislead the new employer.

That is why so many employers choose to not say anything either way and limit verifications to dates of employment and job title. A practice has developed essentially that if you do not have something good to say, then don't say anything at all. Another interesting aspect to this story is that some 40 states have laws that give employers some variation of immunity for statements about past employers that are made in good faith in response to a request from a potential new employer, and are factual and non-malicious. Even with this protection, labor lawyers still often caution employers to stick to the facts only (name and dates of employment) since it can still be murky as to what is "factual."

A Conclusion about Past Employer References

Because of these complications, and the fact that an employer has no obligation to give a reference, many lawyers advise the "no comment" policy. That is the reason why many employers will only give "name, rank, and serial number." Unfortunately, if everyone followed this policy, then all companies would be placed in jeopardy because it becomes very difficult to know whom you are hiring.

A New Assessment Tool – Automated Reference Checks

Online automated reference checks and assessment tools are new pre-hire resources. An example is the services offered by www.Checkster.com, a company founded by a veteran in the talent management sector. Job candidates select references, such as former supervisions and co-workers, who then receive an email assessment request to fill out and return by email. This self-service eliminates time spent making phone calls and waiting for and tracking responses. The questionnaire itself is a scientifically designed assessment instrument designed to give a fresh look at the applicant and contains a number of state-of-the-art validation tools. The results are communicated back to a recruiter or hiring manager in a graphical and intuitive report. Although there are others competing in the same space, Checkster clearly has thought through and designed the process from both the assessment and talent management point of view.

The employer obtains a quick, candid assessment because the person giving the reference is advised that the actual scores are confidential. The email evaluations provide a scientific assessment of what is "under the candidate's hood" – thus increasing the employer's odds of making a job offer to the best candidate.

However, the question has arisen from some hiring managers: "Can services like Checkster replace the type of employment verifications performed by background firms?" The short answer is no.

Traditional background checks and Checkster type services do complement each other, but they serve different purposes. Although services from these firms can be extremely valuable, they are different tools for different functions. Automated reference checks occur in the talent sourcing and selection stages to help can help to eliminate some preliminary candidates from consideration. By comparison, background checks occur AFTER a tentative decision has been reached. In other words, automated type services are used to decide who to focus on out of a pool of candidates, while a background check seeks to assist an employer in exercising due diligence by examining if there is any reason NOT to hire someone that an employer has potentially targeted for employment. Thus there is a fundamental difference between an email-based reference service and the role of a background firm.

A huge advantage for an employer utilizing traditional background checking techniques is in the event of a lawsuit for negligent hiring the employer has a powerful argument in front of a jury that they excised due diligence. The whole idea behind due diligence as a legal defense is independent factual verification. For example, background firms do not take the applicant's word for whether the past employer even existed. A background firm will typically independently verify that the past employer existed as well as verify the phone number is real, independent of what the applicant contends. Even if past references are contacted for evaluation purposes by email, the task of verifying the truthfulness and accuracy of the employment history still requires a screening firm to independently obtain information from past employers, one of the most important and powerful due diligence tools in the employment process.

There is also the possibility of a fake or set-up reference or an applicant creating a fake identity and having the bogus ones "verified." Automated reference checks provide statements indicating they take steps to minimize the possibility of fraud through analysis of the results. However, the final analysis is there is no substitute for the hand work of manual checks. By manually verifying the existence of past employers, and verifying dates of employment to reveal gaps in employment, an employer is taking the final due diligence steps needed for making a hiring decision final.

There are also potential FCRA complications depending on the details on how and when used. These services encourage responses by telling reference sources that all replies are aggregated and that applicants will not know which particular person gave which core. However, if the use of these tools triggers the FCRA, then such promises of anonymity could not be kept, since the FCRA requires transparency and individual scoring would likely need to be reveled at some point.

The bottom-line conclusion is risk management. Although these email assessment tools are an excellent means of providing an in-depth assessment about a candidate during the decision-making stage, the traditional background check complements them for the final candidates and provides the demonstrable due diligence that can be used as a legal defense if there is a negligent hire lawsuit.

Suggestions on How to Deal with Requests for References

Employers concerned about obtaining references will undoubtedly find themselves in the position of being asked for references. Employers and Human Resource professionals have responded in various ways, as we have outlined. So what are the best ways to handle incoming reference checks?

The Following Guidelines Should be Considered When Giving Reference Information

✓ A firm should have a written policy and procedure for giving references.

✓ All information should go through a central source. This gives a firm consistency and reduces the chances that a manager may give out information that is contrary to company policy. As a practical matter, many organizations understand that even though there may be such a policy, there is in reality a practice of individual managers giving information. When that is the case, an alternative policy is to allow managers to do so under a strict program with procedures, training, and consequences for failing to follow procedures.

✓ Clearly document who is requesting the information, for what purpose, and exactly what is provided. Former employees have been known to have friends or paid "reference checkers" contact previous employers.

✓ Clearly document who in the company is giving the information because this can be important in order to trace who-exactly-said-what in a reference check. Keep in mind that staff members may leave a company and, without a written record of a staffer's account, an employer may not be able to defend their reference actions.

✓ If the information requested goes beyond dates and job title, a company may ask for a copy of a written release. This also provides some protection against defamation lawsuits.

✓ If an ex-employee has filed a discrimination charge or lawsuit against the company, then no information should be given beyond job dates and job title without contacting your legal department.

If the employer intends to give negative information, the following may be helpful:

✓ Remember that employees most often seek the advice of an attorney when they are surprised, and imagine an applicant's surprise when he or she hears for the first time from some new potential employer they are getting a negative reference from a past employer. If negative references may be an issue, what the past employer intends to say should be handled and documented at the time the employee leaves during the exit interview.

✓ Disclose only factual information. Make sure everything has been documented. For example, if the former employee was convicted of a crime, a past employer can simply report the public record. A past employer's evaluations of the employee can be a good source of information. The employee has already seen the performance evaluations and in most cases signed them.

✓ Avoid conclusions and give facts instead. For example, avoid saying a former employee "had a bad attitude." Instead, convey facts showing a failure to get along with team members. Let the facts speak for themselves.

✓ Include favorable facts about the employee. That demonstrates an employer is even-handed.

✓ Make sure the personnel file is factually correct. That is something HR may do when an employee leaves.

In the event the former employee has a pending claim against the company for any reason (e.g. workers compensation, lawsuit), an employer should strictly limit any comment to only the basic data such as start date, end date, and job title.

There is another reason to be very careful about giving references. There are a number of firms that offer private references checking services on behalf of job applicants who want to find out if a past employer is giving a negative reference. In fact, there is one firm that hires court reporters to call past employers on behalf of job applicants. The court reporters transcribe the conversation exactly as it occurs. In many states a tape recording would be illegal, but a court always accepts a court reporter's transcript as accurate. The court reporter calls a past employer and tells them they are doing an employment reference. They just don't happen to mention that it is on behalf of the past employee fishing for material for a defamation lawsuit.

What Is Pre-Employment Screening and Who Does It?

Inside This Chapter:

- ✓ The Pre-employment Screening Process

- ✓ When the Pre-employment Screening Process Occurs

- ✓ The Basics of Screening

- ✓ Pros and Cons of Employers Performing Background Screening or Outsourcing

- ✓ Private Investigator or Background Screening Company?

The Pre-employment Screening Process

In the broadest sense, the term "pre-employment screening" is shorthand for the process of assessing applicants for an employer's particular job or category of job. The assessment is performed according to employer policies and is based upon the nature of the job category and applicable laws; all of which are designed to reveal fully-qualified applicants.

These policies are implemented according to practices which are designed to reasonably separate those applicants who are qualified for the particular job from those who may not be qualified due to (1) lack of experience or credentials or (2) other personal factors that may pose an unacceptable risk to the employer, other employees, or those using the employer's services. Practices are documented through procedures that methodically assemble standardized types of information concerning applicants. Above all, the approach and assessment a firm takes to implement these pre-employment screening practices are integral to the success of a firm's Safe Hiring Program.

The ultimate purpose of a Safe Hiring Program?

✓ Get the best person for the job so the company can prosper.
✓ Do not get sued by either a victim or an applicant. Keep in mind that hiring and background checks are increasingly regulated by legislation, regulation, and litigation.

A core component of a Safe Hiring Program is performing in-depth screening of applicants. A number of procedures and tools are used to screen applicants before these applicants come on the premises as employees. Consider the following definition:

> *Pre-employment screening is an assessment of a group of applicants for employment by means of methodically assembling standardized types of information concerning qualifications and behavior that, when obtained and applied in a legal fashion, is considered relevant to the potential job in order to reasonably detect those applicants that are either not qualified or have risk factors that need further consideration.*

No One Definition of a Background Check

The term "background check" has become a common phrase in today's business vocabulary. There are numerous news stories about the need for background checks or efforts made by various organizations, such as churches, charities, or businesses to obtain "background checks." However, there is one significant problem: There is simply no one definition as to what constitutes a background check.

A "background check" can vary from a one county criminal check all the way to an in-depth FBI-type investigation that costs thousands of dollars. Employers and consumers can be misled into making certain assumptions about a person because they have been the subject of a "background check." The biggest assumption is that the person must be safe or qualified because they passed a "background check."

Unfortunately, nothing may be further from the truth. Employers, consumers, and online daters should not be lulled into a false sense of security just because some site has performed a "background check" unless you know exactly what was checked, how it was checked, and when.

When the Pre-employment Screening Process Occurs

Background checks occur at the point of the process where an employer has a candidate in mind, and the employer has made, or is about to make, a job offer. Occasionally, an employer may have two finalists and will perform a background check on more than one finalist to help whittle it down, but that is less common. It is important to note that a background check is generally NOT used to help an employer decide who to hire—rather it's used to help decide if there is any reason NOT to hire someone that has gone through the hiring process and is now a finalist. Employers have a number of other tools to help select the best qualified hire—assessments, 360 interviewing, and so forth. Background checks are generally not a tool to pick the candidate. However, once the finalist is selected is where due diligence and background screening comes into play.

By now you probably are fully aware of why pre-employment screening is a necessary process for employers. But to quickly review, employers typically engage in pre-employment screening for four reasons:

1. To discourage applicants with something to hide. Simply having a prescreening program discourages job applicants with a criminal background or falsified credentials.
2. To eliminate uncertainty in the hiring process. Many employers have discovered the hard way that relying on instinct alone is not enough. Hard information is also an important part of the hiring process.
3. To demonstrate Due Diligence. All employers have a reasonable duty of care in the hiring process. This means an employer must take reasonable steps to determine whether an employee is fit for a particular job. For example, if an employer hires a bus driver and does not take reasonable efforts to determine whether the bus driver has a criminal record, the employer could be found liable if that driver assaults a passenger, and a reasonable background check would have discovered the prior assaults.
4. To encourage honesty in the application and interview process. Employers find that just having a background program will encourage applicants to be more forthcoming about their history.

Performing background screenings is certainly not a guarantee that every bad applicant will be discovered. For the prices charged by prescreening firms, employers cannot expect an in-depth and exhaustive FBI-type investigation. However, just engaging in a prescreening program demonstrates due diligence and provides an employer with a great deal of legal protection.

It is also important to understand that a prescreening program is aimed at how a person has performed in the public aspect of their lives. Items such as criminal records or previous job performance reflect how a person behaved towards others or discharged his/her obligations or responsibilities. Screening is NOT an invasion of privacy, a sign of mistrust, or an act of "Big Brother."

What Are These Tools and Procedures?

The next several chapters discuss in detail elements involved in the screening process including proper procedures, documentation, and related legal compliance issues. Below is a partial list of these elements. Keep in mind that a few of these elements may be optional in your Safe Hiring Program:

✓ Civil Lawsuits, Judgments, Liens
✓ Credit Report
✓ Criminal History
✓ Education and Credentials Verification
✓ International searches
✓ Merchant Databases
✓ Motor Vehicle Report (driving record)
✓ Past Employment References
✓ Security Clearances
✓ Social Security Number Trace
✓ Worker's Compensation Records

It is important to note that a background screen is NOT the same thing as an in-depth investigation of each applicant. The term "investigation" refers to a more focused look at each candidate and can include seeking to develop information unknown to the investigator. For example, in an investigation, the investigator may not know the past employers and schools and may have to locate that information. In a background screening, the employer is seeking to verify the past employment and school information given. In addition, an investigator may look for all property and assets owned by a subject, and this detailed of an approach is normally not appropriate for pre-employment screening.

Screening is not going to detect every potential problem of an applicant, and neither may an investigation.

Given that a background check is performed on a number of applicants and that cost considerations are always present, even the best screening program can result in a "bad apple" getting through. However, reasonable steps are taken to try to limit and discourage bad hires and to demonstrate due diligence.

Employers Screening Versus Investigation – Not the Same Thing

The difference between "screening" and "investigations" is analogous to the difference between giving cholesterol tests to a large number of consumers for a medical risk factor for heart disease versus doing an exploratory surgical procedure one patient at a time. Obviously an exploratory procedure is much more reliable, but it is also intrusive, time consuming, and expensive. On the other hand, when giving merely a cholesterol test instead of performing exploratory surgery, it is possible that someone with a serious condition might slip through the cracks and have a more serious condition than indicated. However, the cost must be weighed against the benefit of faster, less-expensive, and less-intrusive procedures that have an excellent detection rate on a greater number of people.

Think of screening as working with what you see. *Investigation* is digging for what is not seen.

Importance of Consistency and Scope

Critical in nearly every area of employee screening, similarly situated people should be treated in a similar fashion. Proper pre-employment screening does not mean all applicants must be screened exactly the same. What it does mean is that all applicants who are finalists for a particular job opening should receive the same level of scrutiny. A firm may choose to screen in more detail candidates for a vice president's position than those applying to be on the maintenance crew. All vice presidential applicants should be screened in the same way, while all maintenance worker candidates should be screened like all other maintenance worker candidates.

All applicants do not have to be submitted for review by an outside agency performing background screening. An employer might elect only to utilize those services for a finalist or finalists. Regardless, each similarly situated finalist should be screened in the same fashion. Similarly, if background checks are handled in-house, it is acceptable only to perform the courthouse searches for those individuals that you have narrowed down to be potential new hires, acceptable as long as it is done consistently.

The degree of scrutiny for any particular category of jobs is determined by a number of factors, such as access to money or assets, the level of authority over others the position carries, or access to the public or co-workers. Also, employers should take into account the difficulty faced in replacing the new hire if he or she does not work out or the damage that could be done to the organization's productivity if an incompetent person is hired in that position.

Once an employer has determined how intensively the position should be researched, then all finalists for this job level should receive consistent treatment. There are laws working against you if you don't.

The Basics of Screening

The following acronym summarizes the core concocts behind background checks. These basics of screening will be expanded upon in other chapters throughout *The Safe Hiring Manual*.

- **S – Sources** of information are public information (e.g. criminal records) and private records, such as verification of credentials. The key point is that a background check covers those areas of a person's life conducted in the public sphere.
- **C – Consent** must be in writing under Fair Credit Reporting Act (FCRA) and state laws.
- **R – Rationale** – Pre-employment screening discourages applicants with something to hide, encourages honesty, demonstrates due diligence, and helps to hire based upon facts and not just instinct.

- **E – Even-handed** – Similarly situated people must be treated similarly.
- **E – Effectiveness** – No single tool can be relied upon but need series of overlapping tools.
- **N – Not** an FBI check or "Big Brother" watching but a valuable due diligence employment tool.

These basics of screening will be expanded upon in other chapters throughout *The Safe Hiring Manual*.

AUTHOR TIP Of particular importance is the fact that no one single item of information all by itself tells the whole story. From the point of view of an employer, it may be helpful if the employer can go to a web site, put in the person's name and last four digits of the social security number, and get a thumbs up or thumbs down. Of course, the real world does not work that way. Data is not gathered neatly in one place, and even if it was, there would be large privacy concerns. An employer needs to establish the big picture by utilizing many sources of information. Background screening firms also do not simply push a button and get results. As can be seen throughout *The Safe Hiring Manual*, each type of search has many moving and complicated parts, all with substantial legal considerations.

Surveys Show Employment Screening Continues to Rise in 21st Century

In 2010, a series of background checking surveys from the Society for Human Resource Management (SHRM) looked at policies for conducting reference, criminal, and credit background checks on job candidates.

The SHRM Poll 'Conducting Reference Background Checks' asked: *"Does your organization, or an agency hired by your organization, conduct reference background checks for any job candidates?"*

✓ 76 percent of organizations surveyed said *reference background checks* were conducted on all job candidates.

✓ 22 percent of organizations surveyed said *reference background checks* were conducted on selected job candidates.

✓ 2 percent of organizations surveyed said they did not conduct *reference background checks* for any job candidates.

✓ Overall, 98 percent of organizations surveyed said they conducted *reference background checks* on some or all job candidates.

The SHRM Poll 'Conducting Criminal Background Checks' asked: *"Does your organization, or an agency hired by your organization, conduct criminal background checks for any job candidates?"*

✓ 73 percent of organizations surveyed said *criminal background checks* were conducted on all job candidates.

✓ 19 percent of organizations surveyed said *criminal background checks* were conducted on selected job candidates.

✓ 7 percent of organizations surveyed said they did not conduct *criminal background checks* for any job candidates.

✓ Overall, 92-93 percent of organizations surveyed said they conducted *criminal background checks* on some or all job candidates.

The SHRM Poll 'Conducting Credit Background Checks' asked: *"Does your organization, or an agency hired by your organization, conduct credit background checks for any job candidates?"*

✓ 13 percent of organizations surveyed said *credit background checks* were conducted on all job candidates.

✓ 47 percent of organizations surveyed said *credit background checks* were conducted on selected job candidates.

✓ 40 percent of organizations surveyed said they did not conduct *credit background checks* for any job candidates.

✓ Overall, 60 percent of organizations surveyed said they conducted *credit background checks* on some or all job candidates.

The 2010 SHRM surveys reveal an increase in the percentage of firms that conduct pre-employment screening when compared to a SHRM survey reported in the September, 2004 edition of HR Executive magazine. In that 2003 study 82 percent of the respondents indicated they conducted some degree of screening of potential employees, up from 66 percent in a 1996 survey. The two screening tools with the largest increase in usage were criminal records (80 percent in 2003 compared to 51 percent in 1996) and credit reports (35 percent in 2003 compared to 19 percent in 1996).

With the 2010 SHRM surveys revealing that nearly all employers (98 percent) conduct reference checks and almost as many (92-93 percent) performing criminal checks on some or all candidates, the statistics shows employment screening has risen dramatically since the events of 9/11/2001, and continues to rise into the 21st century.

Sources:

www.shrm.org/Research/SurveyFindings/Articles/Pages/ConductingReferenceBackgroundChecks.aspx

www.shrm.org/Research/SurveyFindings/Articles/Pages/BackgroundCheckCriminalChecks.aspx

www.shrm.org/Research/SurveyFindings/Articles/Pages/BackgroundChecking.aspx

Pros and Cons of Employers Performing Background Screening or Outsourcing

Every employer faces an important choice in their Safe Hiring Program — what services should be performed in-house, and what services should be outsourced?

There are numerous tasks an employer could certainly perform in-house — verifying professional licenses or contacting past employers. In fact, as discussed in Chapter 9, there are advantages to employers doing the initial reference phone calls in-house because only the employer can determine if an applicant is an appropriate fit.

However, some employers find it more efficient to outsource certain screening tasks even if they have sufficient staffing to do it themselves. Most employers do not clean their own office windows or build their own office furniture just because they can. Deciding who will do screening tasks — in-house or outsource — comes down to economics and "focus on core competency."

There are six points to consider when deciding what part of the screening program an employer should perform in-house and what should be outsourced to a professional screening firm.

1. Is it a better use of time and energy to outsource?

Human resources and security departments realize there are only so many functions an in-house department can provide, and it makes sense to identify those tasks that can be efficiently outsourced to a third party. Many firms find it an inefficient use of their time and energy to attempt to perform services that a third-party specialist can provide efficiently and cost-effectively. As a result, many firms outsource their screening tasks to professional pre-employment screening firms, and this allows HR and security departments to devote more time and resources to the function of managing people and delivery of vital HR services to employees.

2. Does the employer have the required expertise to perform background screening in-house?

Sometimes it is not practical for an employer to attempt to perform many of the tasks involved in pre-employment screening because of the highly specialized knowledge and resources required. To do prescreening in-house, an employer would have to learn how professional applicant screening is accomplished. The employer would have to learn the many complicated state and federal laws governing what information they can and cannot access. Furthermore, the employer would have to find cost-effective sources for the information such as criminal record checks.

3. Is outsourcing more cost-effective than in-house processing?

Consider the cost to devote staff time and resources to the physical management of the process, including computers and implementing a software solution to manage and track all applicants being screened including each applicant's current status. A typical report from a screening firm should cost less than the first day's salary paid to the new employee. This is called the "Less than One Day's Pay Rule." Considering the cost of a bad hire, this is a very minimal investment. Of course, firms may do more in-depth screening for higher paying positions. However, even if the position is paid more, the "Less than One Day's Pay Rule" usually holds true.

For larger employers, deep discounts from screening vendors are often available with volume. Even with such discounts, some employers look at the total spent on screening as a line item on the budget and are concerned with the total amount. However, even for large firms hiring thousands of employees, screening costs are still likely to be less than the cost of just one lawsuit.

Let us add up real in-house screening costs, including "soft-costs" and associated overhead costs. Take the employer who feels it is less costly to do educational verifications in-house than to pay a screening firm, but this logic fails to take into account all the associated costs including training, supervision, the infrastructure costs; the administrative cost of maintaining employees; the cost of other tasks not being done; and all of the other costs associated with employees. One reality is verification phone calls are typically not completed on the first attempt; chances are an employer makes four calls but only one will get through. Leave a message? Quite often those verification targets call back up to 48 hours later. During the day, the employer will be continually interrupted with return calls. In the end, the true cost of an in-house verification process is usually much higher than most employers' first estimates.

4. Can the employer effectively manage the outsource process in terms of quality and performance levels?

When using a software/internet-based system, does the employer have appropriate and prioritized controls over the outsourced work? If an employer retains the services of a firm that utilizes an internet software tracking system, then employers have a high degree of control over timeliness and quality since these systems usually allow the employer to privately monitor in real-time the exact status of all reports. Will an employer have an in-house system with the same performance benefits? Perhaps, but it may be costly to set up.

5. Are there legal advantages to outsourcing?

The fifth consideration is legal compliance. By outsourcing screening tasks, employers enjoy the protection of the Fair Credit Reporting Act (FCRA). As explained in Chapter 3, this federal law governs the activities of screening companies and third party agencies in a way to provide both employers and job applicants significant legal protection.

When an employer performs these services in-house, care must be taken to not unduly invade an applicant's privacy. Employers that do perform any screening in-house are well advised to conduct the program under the rules of the FCRA, which includes:

✓ A disclosure to the applicant that a screening is being conducted,
✓ Obtaining a written consent, and

✓ Giving an applicant an opportunity to correct any information before it is used as a basis not to hire.

There are additional special circumstances employers need to be aware of. In states where there is a seven-year limitation on a background screening firm reporting criminal information, an employer who does their own criminal investigation is not subject to the limitation.

6. Are there organizational advantages to outsourcing?

As a matter of corporate culture, many organizations do not want new applicants to feel as though the other company employees are conducting an investigation into their background. By outsourcing the task to an independent third party, there is a greater sense of privacy. Job applicants understand that background screening is a necessary business practice, but many feel relieved if others in the same organization are not doing the investigation. In addition, why should an applicant's first contact with the HR Department be a background screening? That is a negative. Human resource managers have found there is a substantial advantage to advising applicants that a professional outside agency conducts the screening.

The Advantages of a Management Fee Model

For organizations that do substantial hiring, there are advantages to using a management fee model. In this program, management retains a screening firm as a management consultant. For a fixed percentage fee, the screening firm helps set-up procedures, provides software, and negotiates prices with information provider sources. This gives the large enterprise employers the same economic advantages enjoyed by an outside screening firm. Instead of the employer paying the screening firm for data, the employer pays for information services at a wholesale level. Of course, the employer pays all overhead and labor when using its own employees and facilities. The big advantage for the employer is the total control over the process and the fact there is complete transparency in the pricing model. With a standard vendor relationship, the employer has no idea as to the mark-up of data or the profit level. The employer has no control over what profit margin the screening firm is taking or how much the screening firm is spending on qualified labor. Conversely, under the management fee model, the employer has direct control over all costs and is only paying for expertise.

When deciding if a management fee model is right for them, employers should consider the following factors:

✓ The employer's hiring volume is so large there is significant cost savings by setting up its own screening program.
✓ Safe hiring is such an integral part of its business that having internal control is a crucial business need.
✓ The firm operates in a number of states and jurisdictions, so a centralized office can contend with each jurisdiction, helping the firm to meet national screening and hiring standards.

Research Finds Companies Using Employment Background Checks Experience 60 Percent Better Quality of Hire Compared to Companies without Screening

A study published in 2010 on employment background screening determined that organizations using automated tools for background checking, employment and education verification, and reference checking experienced 60 percent better quality of hire compared to those without employment background screening solutions in place. The report from Aberdeen Group, a Harte-Hanks Company – *"Employment Screening: Mitigating Risk, Driving Down Cost"* (September 2010) – was based on over 400 survey respondents to Aberdeen's 2010 Talent Acquisition Strategies Study. It looked at the components of employment background screening that are most widely used and how these components impact hiring performance.

The report found that employment background screening is fundamental to best-in-class performance. When asked what kinds of technology they currently used as part of their talent acquisition process, over three-quarters (78 percent) of survey respondents cited the use of employment background screening solutions. The report also found that companies using employment background screening were 43 percent more likely to achieve "Best-in-Class" companies, which Aberdeen Group defines as the top 20 percent of performers along the following categories:

✓   First year retention of hires.

✓   Percentage of new-hires that were the top-choice candidate.

✓   Average year-over-year decrease in time-to-fill vacant positions.

Overall, the research revealed that among Best-in-Class companies the most utilized employment screening technology was employment background screening, with 83 percent using employment screening such as background checks and drug testing. Results for surveying the most common aspects and elements of an employment background screening solution included:

✓   88 percent performed domestic criminal background checks.

✓   87 percent performed previous employment/education verification.

✓   72 percent performed reference checking.

✓   60 percent performed drug screening.

The Aberdeen Group survey also showed these two employment background screening elements – criminal background checks and employment/education verifications – are even more important in the financial services, healthcare, and public sector environments:

✓   Financial services: 93 percent performed criminal background checks and 97 percent performed employment/education verifications.

✓   Healthcare: 94 percent performed criminal background checks and 94 percent performed employment/education verifications.

✓   Public sector: 100 percent performed criminal background checks and 83 percent performed employment/education verifications.

On questions regarding on reasons for choosing a screening company, the Aberdeen Group survey found the speed with which the process was completed (62 percent of respondents) and the accuracy of the results (54 percent of respondents) were far and away the top criteria.

The report is available at: www.aberdeen.com/Aberdeen-Library/6812/RA-background-employment-screening.aspx.

Screening Firm Pricing

Although it is important to obtain competitive pricing, it is usually not advisable to choose the lowest cost provider. As the old saying goes, you get what you pay for.

Since there are many screening firms, some even advertising their pricing on the internet, there are a wide variety of pricing options available to employers. As a general rule, an employer should expect to pay no more than the new hire's first day salary. The reason this rule works is that the higher the position, the more screening an employer may do. A lower position in terms of salary would likely require less screening.

Some firms offer packages with bundled services, but many screening firms also sell services a la carte. Essentially, data is a commodity. Many employers base their cost comparisons on the price of a criminal record searched at the county level. Looking at internet advertisers, the average cost of a one-county criminal search is in the $18-22 range, although some firms advertise as low as $15 per county. Pricing also depends greatly on volume. Generally speaking, background screening is a low-margin, high-volume business. Larger employers would expect to receive substantially lower prices, and usually do.

Within a relatively narrow range, most firms have similar costs of data. The real price differential is the cost of labor and business efficiencies. Firms can offer low cost by utilizing cheap labor to process background reports. The disadvantage to an employer is that they are not dealing with knowledgeable people. Firms can lower costs by sheer economies of scales or technology. A low quote could also be the result of a firm trying to "buy" market share by undercutting market costs or using screening services as a "loss leader" to sell other services.

Employers always need to make certain they are comparing "apples to apples." For example, if a bid for a criminal record check is extremely low, the employer needs to be certain they are getting a search for both felonies and misdemeanors and not just a felony search. An employer also needs to confirm if criminal searches are being conducted at the courthouses or if low-cost database-only searches are actually being used instead of the real thing — a courthouse search. Although databases are a valuable secondary tool, they are subject to limitations described in Chapter 14.

Private Investigator or Background Screening Company?

Screening and investigation are two separate endeavors. A number of states have statutes to license private investigators. Whether screening firms also need to have a PI license is unclear in many states. State statutes that regulate private investigators normally exempt those other entities that regularly examine public records, otherwise anyone who utilized public records — from real estate agents to genealogists — would be in violation of state PI laws. Some confusion has been caused by the fact that the FCRA labels certain screening activity as an "Investigative Consumer Report." This applies when a Consumer Reporting Agency calls a past employer and asks about past job performance. Because the word "Investigative" is used, the argument has been made that when a screening firm does an "investigative consumer report," a PI license is necessary. On the other hand, many professional investigators do not consider making routines phone calls from a call-center environment to past employers an investigation, and many pre-employment screening firms do not possess PI licenses because they do not consider their work to be investigative.

The best advice is that an employer should determine if, in their state, a private investigator license is required for employment screening firms.

However, the bottom-line is that there is no FCRA exception for a private investigator. Even the Transportation Security Agency (TSA), a branch of the federal government, must abide by the FCRA. The FCRA clearly states in section 603(f) that:

> "The term "consumer reporting agency" means any person which, for monetary fees, dues, or on a cooperative nonprofit basis, regularly engages in whole or in part in the practice of assembling or evaluating consumer credit information or other information on consumers for the purpose of furnishing consumer reports to third parties, and which uses any means or facility of interstate commerce for the purpose of preparing or furnishing consumer reports."

That means that a PI who regularly engages in background checks must follow the FCRA and their status as a licensed investigator has no bearing on their FCRA obligations. Of course, an investigator may argue that the first background check they do does not fall under the FCRA because it is not done on a regular basis, but if a PI holds him or herself out as doing background checks, then that is a risky argument.

The next chapter examines the background screening industry.

Chapter 11

The Background Screening Industry

Many employers outsource their background screening needs to professional background screening service providers. A background screening company is a private enterprise firm and, as emphasized throughout this publication, is classified as a Consumer Reporting Agency per the Fair Credit Reporting Act (FCRA). This chapter provides an overview of this industry.

Inside This Chapter:

✓ Background Screening is a Multi-Billion Dollar Industry

✓ Role of Pre-Employment Screening Industry in the American Economy

✓ How Pre-Employment Screening Companies Perform Their Tasks

✓ How the Background Check Industry has Changed Since 2000

✓ NAPBS – The Background Screening Industry Trade Association

✓ A Brief History of NAPBS

✓ The NAPBS Accreditation Program

✓ NAPBS Background Screening Agency Accreditation Program (BSAAP) Standards for Consumer Reporting Agencies (CRA)

Background Screening is a Multi-Billion Dollar Industry

With the advances in technology spurring widespread data availability, the pre-employment background screening industry has grown substantially in the past 30 years. The size of the employment background screening industry is currently estimated to be anywhere between two to five billion dollars.

Although there is no exact count of the number of firms that provide employment screening services, industry observers estimate there are literally thousands of firms involved in some level of background screening. Firms range from large, publicly held companies to retired police officers and other one-person services. Using an Internet search engine to look up the keyword "employment screening" or "background checks" will take an employer to literally thousands of web pages. Of course, many firms are in adjacent industries, such as security, human resources, drug or psychological testing, or payroll, and offer screening as a secondary service.

The Different Sizes of Screening Firms

The firms in the industry can be roughly broken down into four tiers distinguished in terms of revenues and assets:

1. **Tier One:** These are the biggest firms, with annual revenues of usually 50 million dollars or more. Many tier one firms have a substantial advantage in terms of technology, branding, breadth of services, resources, and the ability to provide large-scale, cost-effective solutions for large employers.

2. **Tier Two:** While substantial in size and revenue, tier twos are not as large as the tier one players. Tier two firms can roughly be placed in the 10 million to 50 million dollar sales range. Tier two firms are also characterized by large investments in technology and deep resources, and like the tier ones, tier twos have the ability to service large employers.

> ### Sign of the Times
>
> In the 2007 edition of *The Safe Hiring Manual*, five tier one firms were identified. With one exception, all have changed ownership. In alphabetical order, the 2007 list was: Avert (part of ADP), ChoicePoint, First Advantage, Kroll, and United States Information Services (USIS).
>
> ChoicePoint was purchased by LexisNexis, and USIS and Kroll were rolled into a new firm with HireRight, operating under the HireRight name. First Advantage was also sold but still operates under the same name. Due to acquisitions and consolidation in the industry, and since most firms are privately held which means revenue information is not public, it is difficult to accurately identify all the current members of tiers one and two.

3. **Tier Three:** These are smaller firms with revenues roughly in the 1 million to 10 million dollar range. Typically, tier three firms have strong regional footprints as well as some national presence. Sometimes considered "boutique" firms, tier threes can compete in the screening marketplace by virtue of some niche service or a high level of customer service particularly within their geographical footprint. Many tier threes have begun offering technology solutions like their tier one and tier two competitors. A tier three's emphasis is less on being a low cost "data vendor" and more on customer service. With a tier 3 firm, an employer is more likely to have an account executive they become familiar with that can help to provide a professional service.

4. **Tier Four:** These are very small firms or sole practitioners that primarily serve a small local area. Tier four firms are typically private investigators, retired law enforcement, franchisees or agents of larger firms, or one and two person offices. Challenges for these firms include keeping up with advancing technology and staying on top of legal compliance issues.

There are Different Types of CRAs

As mentioned, a background screening firm is considered to be a CRA – Consumer Reporting Agency. However, there are different types of CRAs.

First, a traditional background screening firm is typically not a data broker (although it is possible a firm may do both). A data broker aggregates large amounts of data on Americans for resale and other use. There are numerous websites where consumers are told they can do a background check on anyone, many of which do not even mention the FCRA rule, or if it is mentioned, is buried in the fine print. Data brokers are sometimes erroneously lumped in other with discussions about the background screening industry. In fact the FTC has proposed in March of 2012 that the practices of data brokers be regulated. See: www.ftc.gov/os/2012/03/120326privacyreport.pdf.

Second, a CRA can be a National Specialty Consumer Reporting Agency (NSCRA). FCRA Section 603(w) defines the term NSCRA as a "consumer reporting agency that compiles and maintains files on consumers on a nationwide basis relating to:

- Medical records or payments;
- Residential or tenant history;
- Check writing history;
- Employment history; or
- Insurance claims."

A traditional background screening firm will typically acquire data for a one-time use only, and does not maintain a database of consumer data that is used again in the future. A CRA may "re-sell" data it acquires from a NSCRA, such as employment history information where the data has been compiled in a database for purposes of re-sale, but that does not make a CRA a NSCRA. A CRA that resells data is also referred to as a "reseller," since a CRA obtains data from a number of sources.

For example under the FACT Act of 2003 that amended the FCRA, consumers were given the right to obtain a free copy of his or her consumer file from a National Specialty Consumer Reporting Agency once during a 12 month period. (FCRA Section 612) Many CRAs who are NOT a National Specialty Consumer Reporting Agency have also offered such a choice purely as a convenience to consumers, even though they are not a NSCRA.

Role of Pre-Employment Screening Industry in the American Economy

The background screening industry provides a critical service in the U.S. As a whole, the screening industry:

- ✓ Helps employers comply with the legal hiring standards set by state and federal law.
- ✓ Plays a critical part in helping public and private employers to comply with legal hiring standards in order to avoid legal exposure for negligent hiring.
- ✓ Makes a safer workplace for customers and employees and helps employers avoid the nightmares associated with workplace violence, theft, hiring based upon fraudulent credentials, or hiring terrorists.
- ✓ Plays a critical part in the homeland security effort by acting as a private sector version of law enforcement but highly regulated by federal and state laws.
- ✓ Improves both the profitability and productivity of American business by helping employers make better hiring decisions and lowering the high cost associated with employee turnover.

The screening process ultimately works to appropriately prevent employment in those cases where:

- ✓ Someone lies on an employment application or during the interview process,

✓ The applicant or employee has criminal violations that may have serious consequences with respect to the integrity of job performance, or

✓ Does not have the claimed credentials needed for the position sought.

This helps the U.S. economy and makes the U.S. a safe place to work. Employers depend upon pre-employment reports to make safe hiring decisions (and to show due diligence to avoid litigation) and help make the U.S. a safe environment. Screening firms provide a crucial public function in a highly-regulated environment where consumers have a full array of rights and remedies.

The Functionality Issues Screening Companies Face

When providing background reports, screening firms do not work in an *inappropriate* manner to prevent employment for applicants with minor violations or misdemeanors unrelated to the work to be performed. As part of the hiring process, applicants have the opportunity up front to disclose minor violations and provide an explanation about such incidents.

The screening process ultimately works to *appropriately* prevent employment in those cases where:

✓ Someone lies on an employment application or during the interview process,

✓ The applicant or employee has criminal violations that may have serious consequences with respect to the integrity of job performance, or

✓ Does not have the claimed credentials needed for the position sought.

The Compliance Issues Screening Companies Face

The Fair Credit Reporting Act (FCRA), which is the gold standard of privacy and consumer protection, controls the operations of background screening firms. Screening firms only obtain information on "consumers" who have given their full written authorization and have received an extensive written disclosure. Background reports are governed by detailed procedures designed to provide accuracy, transparency, and accountability.

Rules for the screening industry also include an extensive procedure to give consumers notice of any adverse information and recourse in the event a consumer considers any information contained in a consumer report to be inaccurate or incomplete. Consumers have a right to obtain reports and to have anything re-investigated that they disagree with. Furthermore, consumers are protected by the rules of the Equal Employment Opportunities Commission (EEOC) as well as numerous state laws.

The Government Data Source Issues Screening Companies Face

It is critical for employers, legislators, the courts, and public officials to understand that background screening is not in the same category as "data miners" and other entities who are "data profiteers."

Unreasonable restrictions on screening firms have only served to harm employers and taxpaying citizens seeking employment. When a public record-holder deletes dates of birth from files and the public index, they have inadvertently removed the primary identification – the date of birth – used by a screening firm to make a determination if a record belongs to a particular applicant. Although it is understandable that courts would desire to protect Social Security Numbers, masking a date of birth does not promote privacy or consumer protection, but only serves to delay employment decisions. This delay can ultimately hurt the very consumer who has signed a consent form and wants the potential employer to have the information. Other government restrictions and impediments that serve to hurt employers and job applicants are lengthy delays in providing access to public records and excessive court fees.

Public officials need to understand:

✓ Background checks by a CRA are normally only conducted when a consumer has received (or is about to receive) a job offer, and the consumer has authorized the background check in writing. Both the applicant and the employer want the report completed to the extent possible within 72 hours, which is the industry standard.

✓ Any delay in a CRA's ability to complete reports in a timely manner works to the determent of consumers. Consumers want a CRA to have fast access to criminal records.

✓ A CRA can only access criminal records with the express written authorization of a job applicant pursuant to the federal Fair Credit Reporting Act (FCRA) and applicable state laws.

✓ The researchers who go to courthouses across the U.S. for background screening firms do NOT make any decision as to what is or is not reportable. One of the services provided by a CRA is that they filter out any information that is non-reportable with reference to applicable federal and state rules.

✓ Background screening is an intensely regulated task, subject to not only to the FCRA and state laws, but also other laws including civil rights laws and privacy laws. In addition, background screening is subject to regulation by the Federal Trade Commission (FTC) and the Equal Employment Opportunity Commission (EEOC). There is also a substantial body of case law on subjects such as accuracy in reporting criminal records.

✓ Unless expressly authorized by an act of Congress or a state legislature, a private employer cannot utilize the Federal Bureau of Investigation (FBI) database or state criminal database for a "LiveScan" background check. The vast majority of private employers need to utilize the services of a background screening firm to perform a background check

Some courts and public officials have attempted in recent years to limit screening firms' access to public records in the mistaken belief that such restrictions protect privacy and serve the public good. Nothing could be less accurate.

Conclusion

Employers depend upon pre-employment reports to make safe hiring decisions and to show due diligence to avoid litigation. Unreasonable restrictions to access public records (pursuant to the signed consent and authorization of an applicant) only work to the benefit of criminals, terrorists, and cheaters, and to the detriment of employers, employees, honest citizens, and taxpayers.

How Pre-Employment Screening Companies Perform Their Tasks

Although there is no standard industry terminology, two separate terms can be used — PROFILE and ORDER. The term PROFILE refers to all information about an applicant. The term ORDER means a particular search, such as a search in Santa Clara County, California, for a criminal record, or contacting the University of Kansas to verify a former student's past education. *One profile may contain a number of orders.*

When assembling and evaluating data on applicants, background firms fundamentally perform tasks in six areas:

1. Accept Requests from Employers

After a screening firm has determined that a business requesting a background check is legitimate and has a permissible purpose under the FCRA, the business needs to transmit its requests to the screening firm. Current technology provides employers with a number of options. Before the widespread use of the Internet, employers would need to fax a request of a check. That gradually gave way to online systems where employers could go to a secured web site and enter in the information themselves. However, employer data entry is now a thing of the past as well and has given way to paperless online systems where an applicant receives an email initiated by the employer with a user name and password that takes the applicant to a secured online form where the applicant imputes his or her own data. Even more advanced options include seamless integration with Applicant Tracking Systems (ATS) where an employer can facilitate the entire workflow of the ATS at the click of a mouse. (See Chapter 12 for more details.)

This not only relieves an employer from tedious data entry, but also provides a workaround on the thorny issue of employers possessing date of birth and Social Security number too soon in the process. At least one state, Utah, has passed legislation prohibiting employers from having personal information such as date of birth and Social Security number until there has been a job offer, or a background check is requested.

Employers using an online system generally must certify to the background screening firm, pursuant to the FCRA, that the employer has and will retain the applicant's written FCRA authorization and disclosure. If the online request also includes an order for an employment or education verification, then a written consent form may still be necessary in order to allow the background firm to contact those schools or employers who require consent. However, screening firms are also able to offer electronic signatures, so that paper truly becomes a thing of the past. (See section on E-sign and electronic signatures in Chapter 12.)

2. Engage in Various Workflows to Fulfill the Requests

Once a request for a screening is put into progress, each order must be routed to the proper source in order to obtain the information. For firms with a software system, the orders are normally routed automatically to the proper source. For background firms without a software system, some delays can occur.

The following is a brief description of some of the workflows involved:

✓ **Criminal records from state courts**

When a screening firm receives an order for a criminal search, the order is normally transmitted to the researcher who specializes in that specific court. Available to background firms is an entire industry — a virtual subculture — of court researchers covering every court in America, typically providing a turnaround time within 48 hours for record search requests. Some of the larger background firms have their own employee networks or hire court researchers to work for them. In most cases, court researchers work for multiple background firms. Again, employers may find that their report requests are subject to delay if they use screening firms that do not utilize web-enabling software.

As mentioned previously, background firms must sometimes deal with county or state court officials who do not understand background checks and try to impede the efforts of a screening firm to get information on the misguided premise they are "protecting an applicant." Nothing can be further from the truth.

Another important issue is determining who is in charge of reporting criminal hits to employers. Employers need to be certain that any criminal hit is reviewed by a knowledgeable member of the screening firm's staff. The complicated legal and factual determinations of what is and is not reportable should not be made by court researchers who are from all walks of life, including PIs, genealogists, and abstractors who have gone into the public record retrieval business. They are typically not lawyers, paralegals, or HR professionals. Their expertise is in looking for names and understanding court record indices. They are generally not experienced in the immensely complicated and highly regulated legal ramifications to the end users.

✓ **Driving records, credit reports, and Social Security number (SSN) trace reports**

For the most part, background firms use online access to obtain these reports in a matter of moments and can quickly pass results electronically to their clients by using a seamless business to business interface.

Although there are a few states where driving records cannot be obtained instantly, the majority of states do have instant access. Credit reports, if ordered online, offer immediate results. (However, see chapter 17 for detailed discussions on the challenges involved in obtaining and using credit reports). A Social Security trace can be immediate also, although it may entail additional time and workflow if an employer is using the trace to determine where to search for criminal records. Some background screening firms offer enhanced software features that will automatically place orders for these specialty reports.

✓ **Credentials verification – employment, education, and licenses**

When an employer requests a Credentials Verification, the background firm must typically route the request to the specific company employee, department, or vendor handling these requests. These searches are subject to delays out of the control of a screening firm, such as schools that are closed for vacation or holidays, or employers that will not call back, or have moved, merged, or gone bankrupt. These are disused in more details in the chapters on employment and education verification. Again, a firm with software systems is in a better position to track and manage the process. Firms without software systems must manually handle papers and files which can take longer.

3. Track the Status of All Orders and Manage Handling Delays

While the orders are being processed in various workflows, a screening firm must be able to track in real time the status of each order and keep the employer informed. Background firms with online systems give employers an advantage — the employer goes online to see the exact progress of each order and the likely time of completion. If there is a delay, then the employer is told exactly what is causing the delay.

Background screening firms not using an online system to manage the workflow generally use a paper-based system where all work is monitored manually. A physical file is maintained for each applicant. The screening firm must wait to receive back information on each order and then enter the results into a written report to present to the employer. Each manual step adds time to the overall process and increases the possibility of clerical errors. The use of technology allows a screening firm to track all progress electronically, saving valuable time in the process.

It is important to understand that, for certain searches, there may be delays beyond the control of anyone. Hiring famous detective Sam Spade would not get results any sooner. Sources of delays can be:

- ✓ Where courthouses require that the researcher give the county clerk a list of names to search and the county clerk in turn gives the researcher an estimated turnaround time. When there is a possible "hit," then the clerk needs to pull the file. No one has control over how long a court clerk takes to provide information. Court delays can be caused by the courthouse being closed for a holiday.
- ✓ The date of birth is required to obtain or verify some information and has not been provided.
- ✓ On employment verifications, an employer may not return calls despite repeated attempts, or a past employer cannot be located, has no records, has moved, or is no longer in business. After three attempts it is unlikely an employer will respond.
- ✓ On education verification, school record checks can be delayed where the school is closed or on break, verification can only be done by mail, or advanced fee prepayment is required.

The critical issue for employers is they need real-time updates and status reports on any source of delays. They need to know the report is being worked on and when the information is expected back.

4. Assemble Orders into an Applicant Profile

From the screening firm's point of view, each aspect of the order must be monitored and usually completed within 72 hours. From the point of view of the employer, individual orders are not as relevant as obtaining the entire profile as soon as possible so a hiring decision can be made.

The profiling function requires a screening firm to reassemble each order into a comprehensive report. Firms with more advanced software are able to assemble each of the components into a report automatically and quickly. If assembling reports becomes a manual process, then expect some lag time.

5. Provide the Profile Report to the Employer

How fast and how efficiently the employer receives the entire applicant profile is what separates the good screening companies from the not so good. Firms with sophisticated software programs that automatically send updates and final reports may provide a time advantage, but the real issue of concern to employers is— does the screening firm review what is being sent or does the screener's software merely send raw data automatically to the employer? Firms that tend to be essentially data vendors simply dispense completed reports without review or "flag" potential areas of concern.

6. Handling Data "Exceptions"

The majority of consumer reports come back "clear." When there is a "hit," the employer may need assistance. A "hit" means the screening firm has located information potentially derogatory or adverse. This information may be derogatory on its face alone, such as a criminal record. There can be other instances when information only becomes derogatory when it is compared to other data. For example, if the screening firm reports the applicant was employed for a two-year period, this information alone is not derogatory. If the applicant falsely claims he or she was at the job for four years, then the report data could be adverse.

It is important for an employer to clearly understand how their screening firm operates regarding data exceptions. Some screening firms operate solely on the data vendor approach, giving employers whatever they find as a data pass, without regard to the limitations of federal or state laws or without making any attempt at flagging potential discrepancies or providing any assistance regarding the use of the data. Other firms, though, follow a service model that has a policy of not providing employers with information they cannot legally possess.

Even though a screening firm cannot give legal advice, an employer may at least expect general industry guidance and some advice on the issues to consider. If the employer decides not to hire the applicant, then the employer may need assistance with the adverse action procedures; see Chapter 3 on adverse action procedures under the FCRA.

 Chapter 12 contains more information on how to find and choose a background screening firm, including a sample form employers can use to request a bid for services from screening companies. The form is called an RFP – Request For Proposal.

The Growth of the Industry – An Eyewitness Account

The pre-employment screening industry is relatively new. Industry consultant Bruce Berg has been involved in the screening industry since 1990. The article below gives the history of the employment screening industry from his point of view.

Background Checks – From an Afterthought to a Real Industry

By Bruce Berg, Berg Consulting, www.bergconsultinggroup.com

For twenty years as an executive for several Fortune 500 companies, I always would challenge my Human Resource Manager with the question "Isn't there some way we could have checked out this loser before we hired him!?" The response was always a blank stare. HR just had not been taught about background checks. Their job was to fill the position with the best candidate. The problem was they had to judge the candidate mostly on feelings because there was no easy way to verify that the candidate was, in fact, who they claimed to be.

In 1990, I was looking for a business opportunity and found a tiny company that was doing just this. They could check criminal, credit, address history, prior employment, education, workers' comp history, and professional licenses. For me this was a "Wow" — a company offering these "application verification" services actually existed! I thought this would be a slam-dunk business success. What company wouldn't want this information? So I jumped into the screening industry.

What I very quickly learned was that while the security and loss prevention people understood the concept, it was an anathema to the HR side. Screening firms had to educate the profession as they improved their ability to provide relevant information. Industry software was developed that allowed customers to manage their search requests. All this time screening firms kept educating HR professionals through marketing, trade shows, and advertising in industry publications such as HR Magazine, HR Executive Magazine, and Security Management Magazine.

In 1995 the industry experienced heavy growth. What made it all happen? The increased demand for services came from a combination of things, including more and more negligent hiring lawsuits, big stories in the general press about people who were harmed by ex-cons who worked for companies that did not know the employee's past. Better and quicker access to county criminal data via the local court researcher networks was developed, violence and safety in the workplace became issues along with drug-free workplace programs, education sessions at SHRM and ASIS conferences — and more and more companies began offering these services. The "big boys" in the industry in the '80s and early '90s were doing background checks as a sideline. A number of small firms that jumped in and specialized in background checks helped to create an industry.

In 1997 the changes to the Federal Fair Credit Reporting Act defined us as Consumer Reporting Agencies and, while we were all at first uncomfortable operating under this law, once implemented, it really did tend to further legitimize the industry and create some much needed standards. It also brought a lot of national press to hiring issues and the need for pre-employment screening.

The screening industry grew dramatically between 1991 and 1998. Such fast growth attracted investor attention and the consolidation in the industry went into full swing. At the same time, because of the increased demand, more and more companies got into the business all serving to educate the end-user regarding the need and the value of screening. After 9/11, the words "background checks" were on everyone's lips. In 2002, at a pre-employment screeners conference, a grass roots call was made for a professional organization. As a result, the National Association of Professional Background Screeners was formed by some very dedicated members of the industry.

Now we are a full-fledged industry with estimated annual sales of $4-5 billion. There are about 1800 companies offering background checks to employers, from the smallest one-person company through mid-sized and even very large-sized companies, some of them public firms. These companies have an established industry infrastructure with half a dozen suppliers of ready-made software from which to choose. There are now several information wholesalers selling county criminal checks, prior employment verifications, education verifications, and even an instant, though limited, multi-state database of criminal convictions. The end user can order checks via the web, modem, fax, phone, or email. They can order a single search or submit the entire application to the background checking company, or simply send their candidates to the vendor for screening. The end user can receive back the results in various formats, including the actual details of the background check, a summary narrative, a "hire-no hire decision" or even a numeric score. Candidates can now pay to have his background pre-screened and certified via the web before even applying for a job.

The latest impact on the industry developed over the past ten years has come from new sources of data aggregation. For example, private firms have developed the so-called "National Criminal Databases." Because these databases are NOT comprehensive but do contain records that might not otherwise be found through traditional search methods, these have become an important routine adjunct search.

Tools have also been developed for Identity Fraud via access to both private and government databases, including E-verify and the Social Security Administration (pre-employment Consent Based SSN Verification and post-employment SSN verification). Finally, Applicant Tracking Systems (ATS) have had an impact on the way firms not only find candidates and hire, but in the manner in which background checks are processed. The ATS is used by recruiters to sort through all their applicants and when ready to do the background check, they click a button on their ATS and the background search request is communicated to their background screening company with the results coming back into their ATS.

Today the HR manager and employer have a quick, easy, comprehensive outsourcing avenue to screen out the adverse employee. This is not just common practice; it has become a key tool in the pre-hire process — so key, in fact, that many HR departments have progressed to doing a preliminary screen on their applicants even before they invest their time in the interview process. Forewarned is forearmed.

How the Background Check Industry has Changed Since 2000

The background check industry has changed much in recent years since the beginning of the 21st century. Below are comparisons of the industry from 2000 and 2012 in six critical areas that have changed in the industry:

1. Number of Employers Performing Background Checks:

✓ **2000:** An estimated 50 percent of companies conduct background checks on their employees according to the 1996 Society for Human Resource Management (SHRM) Workplace Violence Survey.

✓ **2012:** A series of surveys from SHRM in 2010 reveals that approximately three out of four U.S. businesses perform some type of background check as part of their pre-employment screening programs, with 76 percent conducting reference background checks and 73 percent conducting criminal background checks.

2. Industry Standards for Background Checks:

✓ **2000:** There is no national trade association, industry standards, or definitive publications on background screening.

✓ **2012:** The industry now has a non-profit trade association, the National Association of Professional Background Screeners (NAPBS), representing the interests of background check companies. In 2004, the first comprehensive book on employment screening (the first edition of this book) is published - *The Safe Hiring Manual – The Complete Guide to Keeping Criminals, Terrorists, and Imposters Out of Your Workplace*' by Lester Rosen. In 2010 the Background Screening Credentialing Council (BSCC) of NAPBS launches the Background Screening Agency Accreditation Program (BSAAP) for a singular background check industry standard representing a background check company's commitment to excellence, accountability, and professionalism.

3. Sources for Background Check Information:

✓ **2000:** Background check information is primarily limited to traditional sources such as criminal records, driving records, verifications, and reference checks.

✓ **2012:** With the advent of new Internet technology – and new media such as blogs, videos on YouTube, and social networking sites like Facebook in particular – there are many more potential outlets from which employers may gather information about job applicants. There is also widespread availability of database searches such as government sanctions, terrorist lists, and other records.

4. The Need for International Background Checks:

✓ **2000:** Before the rise of outsourcing, much of the workforce is perceived to have lived, worked, and been educated inside of the United States, so the idea of international background checks for job applicants seems expensive and unnecessary to most companies. There are also limited resources available for such background checks.

✓ **2012:** According to recent U.S. government statistics, there are 38.5 million foreign-born U.S. residents representing 12.5 percent of the population, more than 1.1 million persons became Legal Permanent Residents (LPRs) of the United States in 2009, and the unauthorized immigrant population living in the U.S. reached an estimated 10.8 million in January 2009 and grew 27 percent between 2000 and 2009. Given these facts, U.S. companies must be prepared to perform international background checks on job applicants with global backgrounds. Numerous resources are now available for background screening firms to conduct international background checks, as well as resources concerning international privacy and data protection.

5. Compliance Issues Concerning Background Checks:

✓ **2000:** Background check companies must comply with the federal Fair Credit Reporting Act (FCRA), originally passed in 1970, that regulates the collection, dissemination, and use of consumer information and is enforced by the Federal Trade Commission (FTC).

✓ **2012:** Background screening has become an intensely legally regulated endeavor. Background check companies must comply with a myriad of industry regulations in addition to FCRA requirements such as the Fair And

Accurate Credit Transaction Act (FACT Act) of 2003 (which amended the FCRA), Sarbanes-Oxley, the Patriot Act, E-Verify employment eligibility verification, Equal Employment Opportunity Commission (EEOC) discrimination issues against protected classes pertaining to the use of criminal records and credit reports for employment purposes, and new consumer data privacy protections regulations such as "Safe Harbor" and privacy laws that protect the Personally Identifiable Information (PII) of consumers. There are now an abundance of state laws regulating credit reports and criminal records. California, for example, completely revamped its background screening laws in 2002 and added new requirements in 2010 for when PII is sent offshore beyond the protection of U.S. privacy laws. Many states have their own version of the FCRA.

6. Technology Used in Background Screening:

✓ **2000:** Most employers are required to fax orders to a background check firm. The idea of entering orders into an online system or making information available in online in real time as to the status of a report is only in the beginning stages.

✓ **2012:** Technology in the background check industry increased substantially with the use of online processes to not only enter orders, but also with paperless systems with electronic signatures. An applicant can enter their own information, along with integrations into Applicant Tracking Systems (ATS) so background checks can be ordered with the click of a mouse. With the advent of Web 2.0, employers may expect to see more advances in the technology for the background screening process. Firms are able to build in legal compliance into the software programs. The downside, however, is that Internet entrepreneurs have seized upon background checks as a way to make quick money and in some instances are playing off the fears of Americans by offering cheap and instant checks based upon using databases never intended to be a substitute for a background check.

Much has changed in the background check industry in the years spanning 2000 to 2012, and many more changes are sure to come in the years ahead. Both background screeners and the employers they serve need to keep pace with advancements in the many changes regarding background screening.

NAPBS – The Background Screening Industry Trade Association

One of the most exciting developments in the pre-employment screening industry was the emergence of the first industry non-profit trade association in 2003. Called the National Association of Professional Background Screeners, or NAPBS, the new association attracted nearly 300 of the nation's leading pre-employment screening companies. The association's website is found at www.NAPBS.com.

Per the website, the mission of NAPBS is:

"The National Association of Professional Background Screeners (NAPBS®) exists to promote ethical business practices, promote compliance with the Fair Credit Reporting Act and foster awareness of issues related to consumer protection and privacy rights within the background screening industry.

The Association provides relevant programs and training aimed at empowering members to better serve clients and to maintain standards of excellence in the background screening industry.

The Association is active in public affairs and provides a unified voice on behalf of members to local, state, and national lawmakers about issues impacting the background screening industry."

AUTHOR TIP It is highly recommended that any employer who engages the services of a background screening firm ensure that the firm is a member of NAPBS. Although membership does not guarantee any particular level of knowledge or service, it is a valuable indicator that the firm has a commitment to the industry organization that is promoting professional standards and has promulgated a code of conduct.

A Brief History of NAPBS

The NAPBS began through the efforts of many people. Steve Brownstein, the editor of *The Background Investigator* (www.search4crime.com), a newspaper devoted to the screening industry, held the nation's first screening industry conference in Long Beach, CA in April, 2002. Brownstein encouraged the attendees to think in terms of a national association in order to promote and protect the screening industry. Sandra Burns agreed to head a committee to look into the possibility of forming an association. In November, 2002, Brownstein and *The Background Investigator* sponsored a large national conference in Tampa, Florida, attended by over 175 screening professionals. At this meeting, there was widespread support for the formation of an association. Michael Sankey of BRB Publications joined Sandra Burns as a member of the interim board along with Bill Brudenell, Charlotte O'Neill, Jack Wallace, author Les Rosen, and Mike Cool.

Les Rosen was designated chairperson of the steering committee that formed NAPBS. The interim board, along with other interested members of the screening industry, met in Arizona in January, 2003 and again in Washington D.C. in April, 2003. The interim Membership and Ethics committee met in Dallas, Texas in the Spring of 2003.

A membership drive was held in the last half of 2003, resulting in over 200 members. In order to provide seed money for the group, in early 2003, several screening firms stepped forward and generously donated the necessary funds to launch the association and to retain the services of a professional management firm.

First NAPBS Board of Directors

The NAPBS began its first full year of operations with an elected Board of Directors in 2004. There are now over 500 NAPBS members. The first elected NAPBS Board of Directors consisted of the following people:

- ✓ Les Rosen, Co-chairman
- ✓ David Hein, Co-chairman
- ✓ Jason B. Morris, Co-chair elect
- ✓ Mary Poquette, Co-chair elect
- ✓ Katherine Bryant, Secretary
- ✓ Barry Nadell, Co-treasurer
- ✓ Catherine Aldrich, Co-treasurer
- ✓ Kevin G. Connell
- ✓ Ann Lane
- ✓ Larry Henry
- ✓ Michael Sankey

The original operating, standing committees included:

- ✓ Ethics/Accreditation
- ✓ Finance
- ✓ Membership
- ✓ Provider Advisory
- ✓ Best Practices and Compliance
- ✓ Government Relations
- ✓ Public Awareness and Communications
- ✓ Resources Library

The First NAPBS Conference

The first NAPBS conference was held in Scottsdale, Arizona in 2004. Below is a press release announcement according to the NAPBS website:

> Scottsdale, AZ, March 30, 2004— On March 29 and 30 more than 225 individuals representing over 175 companies converged on Scottsdale, AZ for the inaugural Annual Conference of the National Association of Professional Background Screeners (NAPBS).
>
> NAPBS was formed to promote a greater awareness among employers nationwide of the growing importance of conducting background and reference checks. According to David Hein, NAPBS Board Co-chair, "It is estimated that fewer than 35% of employers are currently screening their applicants. Yet every day headlines across the country highlight the sometimes dire consequences that may result when prospective employees' backgrounds aren't thoroughly checked."
>
> The Association's members are companies from across the country who provide pre-employment/background screening, court records research, and tenant screening services. Employers can be assured they are dealing with a screening firm that subscribes to the organization's goals and standards if the NAPBS logo appears in the screening firms collateral or on their website.
>
> Among its many missions, NAPBS will help develop and coordinate training and other relevant programs to enable its members to better serve their clients, to promote and maintain the highest standards of excellence and ethics in the background screening industry, to ensure compliance with the Fair Credit Reporting Act, and to foster awareness of issues related to consumer protection and privacy rights within the industry.
>
> Joining the Association requires prospective members to abide by a Code of Ethics. Additionally, NAPBS is developing membership accreditation criteria to further insure member companies meet the high standards the Association has established.
>
> For additional information concerning NAPBS, or for a list of Association members, call their offices at 1-888-686-2727.
>
> The day-to-day activities of NAPBS are managed by an association management company which provides NAPBS with a professional staff dedicated to fulfilling the mission of the organization. NAPBS headquarters is located in Durham, NC.

In the years following the first conference in 2004, the NAPBS has held an annual industry conference every year in different cities around the United States. Attendance has grown every year, with the 2011 Conference attracting more than 525 attendees, according to the NAPBS website. Below are the NAPBS Annual Conference locations:

- ✓ 2004: Scottsdale, AZ
- ✓ 2005: San Antonio, TX
- ✓ 2006: Nashville, TN
- ✓ 2007: Austin, TX
- ✓ 2008: New Orleans, LA
- ✓ 2009: St. Louis, MO
- ✓ 2010: San Antonio, TX
- ✓ 2011: Denver, CO
- ✓ 2012: Nashville, TN
- ✓ 2013: Scottsdale, AZ

The NAPBS Accreditation Program

The Need for Increased Emphasis on Professionalism in Background Screening Industry

When the National Association of Professional Background Screeners (NAPBS®) was formed in 2003, the idea of an accreditation process was simply an idea, but an idea that was a central driving force in order to demonstrate that background screening was a professional endeavor. Every profession has to have standards, and NAPBS accreditation represents the standards for the screening industry.

Before the NAPBS accreditation program, employers were largely on their own when selecting a background screening firm. Background screening is a critical function subject to intense legal regulation, and so the stakes are high. With hundreds upon hundreds of background screening firms to choose from, employers faced a confusing landscape of competing screening providers that made it hard to distinguish one background screening provider from another. Some background screening firms had ISO (International Organization for Standardization) certification while others had "commercial" rankings published by private "for-profit" publications, which only added to the confusion.

Background of Accreditation Program

In April 2009, in conjunction with its Annual Conference, the NAPBS launched the Background Screening Agency Accreditation Program (BSAAP) to serve as the industry's primary vehicle for quality assurance, self-regulation, and public accountability. The NAPBS also formed a governing body for its new accreditation program – the Background Screening Credentialing Council (BSCC) – to ensure firms seeking accreditation would meet a measurable standard of competence. The BSAAP advances professionalism in the background screening industry through the promotion of best practices, awareness of legal compliance, and development of standards that protect consumers.

Over the years, it took a lot of hard work from many very dedicated people who put the NAPBS accreditation program together on their own time, and the screening industry owes a debt of gratitude to all of those people who made the accreditation program a reality.

Currently, NAPBS accreditation is quickly becoming a requirement of many employers when considering a background screening provider since it is the only practical means of third party verification of the professionalism and competency of a particular screening firm.

How the Accreditation Program Works

Governed by a set of 58 clauses divided into six sections, the BSAAP recognizes a screening company's commitment to excellence, accountability, professional standards, and continued institutional improvement. Accreditation has become a widely recognized "seal of approval" that brings national recognition to background screening organizations. To become accredited, background screening firms must pass a rigorous audit of policies and procedures related to six critical areas:

- ✓ Consumer protection;
- ✓ Legal compliance;
- ✓ Client education;
- ✓ Product standards;
- ✓ Service standards; and
- ✓ General business practices.

The BSCC oversees the application process and ensures all organizations seeking accreditation meet or exceed a measurable standard of competence in these six areas. The accreditation program is open to any U.S.-based background screening company, and the process takes approximately six months from submission to completion. Companies are accredited for five years, and the program also includes an interim surveillance audit after three years.

A copy of the Standards list is presented later in this chapter.

Benefits & Challenges of Accreditation Program

The benefits of NAPBS accreditation are two fold, both external and internal.

Externally, accreditation is proof positive to an employer that a background screening firm meets the accreditation guidelines. Also it is very important for this industry to show it is self-regulating before government agencies seek to over control the industry. Accreditation is a big part of demonstrating the industry can police itself.

Internally, the accreditation process reinforces the standards needed to document policies, practices, and procedures for the auditor. Once a background screening firm makes the commitment of time and energy to undergo a third party audit though NAPBS accreditation, it is actually a very exciting process to review each standard and document compliance. It's also a tremendous training opportunity for the company to educate all employees.

> **AUTHOR TIP** Accreditation is a goal that is within reach of any background firm that feels it is important to demonstrate their professionalism and competency. There are even third party expert consultants that can assist a background firm in achieving accreditation, such as www.CRAzoom.com headed by Derek Hinton, a background screening industry veteran.

While every business has a number of pressing shorter term priorities, it is critical to think long term and strategically about what the future holds. In the background screening industry, the "writing is on the wall" so to speak that accreditation will be nothing less than a business necessity for a professional screening company competing in the current economic environment.

NAPBS Background Screening Agency Accreditation Program (BSAAP) Standards for Consumer Reporting Agencies (CRA)

Below is a copy of the Standards. This document below is printed with the permission of the National Association of Professional Background Screeners (NAPBS®). Source:

www.napbs.com/files/public/Consumer_Education/Accreditation/NAPBS_Standard_with_Audit_Criteria_030209.pdf.

NAPBS Background Screening Agency Accreditation Program (BSAAP) Standards for Consumer Reporting Agencies (CRA)

Introductory
This Standard is applicable only to Consumer Reporting Agencies providing Consumer Reports for employment purposes.

Definitions
For purposes of this standard, the terms and acronyms below shall have the following definitions.

1. **"Consumer report"** has the meaning given to it in § 603(d) of the federal FCRA.
2. **"CRA"** means a consumer reporting agency as defined in § 603(f) of the federal FCRA.
3. **"Federal FCRA"** means the Fair Credit Reporting Act, 15 U.S.C. § 1681 *et seq.*
4. **"Investigative consumer report"** has the meaning given to it in § 603(e) of the federal FCRA.
5. **"Policy"** means a written directive that is required to be followed by the entity.
6. **"Procedure"** means a written description of how a policy is implemented and followed by the entity. (Procedures may be referred to within the entity as "standard operating procedures," "SOPs," "operating guidelines" or other names.
7. **"Worker"** means any individual who performs services for CRA and who has access to CRA premises or systems. The word "worker" encompasses employees as well as temporary workers, interns, contractors and others who perform work for the CRA.

8. "**Public Record Researcher**" means any person or entity contracted or employed by a CRA, other than another CRA providing consumer reports in pursuant to FCRA Sec. 607(e), who searches for and/or retrieves information that is currently in the custody of a government entity such as a court, state agency or other government repository.

9. "**Consumer Information**" means any information about an individual consumer provided to the CRA by the consumer, client, or other parties in the course of compiling a consumer report.

10. "**FTC**" means **Federal Trade Commission**.

Section 1: Consumer Protection

1.1 Information Security Policy
CRA shall have a Written Information Security Policy (WISP). CRA shall designate one or more individuals within the organization who are responsible for implementing, managing and enforcing the information security policy.

1.2 Data Security
CRA shall have procedures in place to protect consumer information under the control of the CRA from internal and external unauthorized access. These procedures shall include specifications for the securing of information in both hard copy and electronic form, including information stored on portable and/or removable electronic devices.

1.3 Intrusion, Detection and Response
CRA shall have procedures in place to detect, investigate and respond to an information system intrusion, including consumer notification where warranted.

1.4 Stored Data Security
CRA shall have procedures in place to ensure backup data is stored in an encrypted or otherwise protected manner.

1.5 Password Protocol
CRA shall require strong password protocol pursuant to current security best practices.

1.6 Electronic Access Control
CRA shall have procedures in place to control access to all electronic information systems and electronic media that contain consumer information. CRA shall have procedures in place to administer access rights. Users shall only be given the access necessary to perform their required functions. Access rights shall be updated based on personnel or system changes.

1.7 Physical Security
CRA shall have procedures in place to control physical access to all areas of CRA facilities that contain consumer information.

1.8 Consumer Information Privacy Policy
CRA shall have a Consumer Information Privacy Policy detailing the purpose of the collection of consumer information, the intended use, and how the information will be shared, stored and destroyed. The CRA shall post this policy on its Web site, if it has one, and will make said policy available to clients and/or consumers upon request in at least one other format.

1.9 Unauthorized Browsing
CRA shall have a procedure that prohibits workers from searching files and databases unless they have a bona fide business necessity.

1.10 Record Destruction
When records are to be destroyed or disposed of, CRA shall follow FTC regulations and take measures to ensure that all such records and data are destroyed and unrecoverable.

1.11 Consumer Disputes
CRA shall have procedures in place for handling and documenting a consumer dispute that comply with the federal FCRA.

1.12 Sensitive Data Masking
CRA shall have a procedure to suppress or truncate Social Security numbers and other sensitive data elements as required by law.

1.13 Database Criminal Records
When reporting potentially adverse criminal record information derived from a non-government owned or non-government sponsored/supported database pursuant to the federal FCRA, the CRA shall either: A) verify the information directly with the venue that maintains the official record for that jurisdiction prior to reporting the adverse information to the client; or B) send notice to the consumer at the time information is reported.

Section 2: Legal Compliance

2.1 Designated Compliance Person(s)
The CRA shall designate an individual(s) or position(s) within the organization responsible for CRA's compliance with all sections of the federal FCRA that pertain to the consumer reports provided by the CRA for employment purposes.

2.2 State Consumer Reporting Laws
The CRA shall designate an individual(s) or position(s) within the organization responsible for compliance with all state consumer reporting laws that pertain to the consumer reports provided by the CRA for employment purposes.

2.3 Driver Privacy Protection Act (DPPA)
The CRA shall designate an individual(s) or position(s) within the organization responsible for compliance with the DPPA that pertain to the consumer reports provided by the CRA for employment purposes, if the CRA furnishes consumer reports that contain information subject to the DPPA.

2.4 State Implemented DPPA Compliance
If the CRA furnishes consumer reports that contain information subject to the DPPA-implementing statutes in a particular state(s), the CRA shall designate an individual(s) or position(s) within the organization responsible for compliance with state implementations of the DPPA that pertain to the products and services provided by the CRA for employment purposes.

2.5 Integrity
CRA shall not engage in bribery or any other fraudulent activity to obtain preferential treatment from a public official.

2.6 Prescribed Notices
CRA shall provide client all federal FCRA-required, FTC-prescribed documents which the federal FCRA mandates be provided to client by the CRA.

2.7 Certification from Client
Before providing consumer reports to clients, CRA shall obtain a signed agreement from client (referred to as "user" in federal FCRA) in which client agrees to meet the requirements of the federal FCRA, and applicable state and federal laws.

Section 3: Client Education

3.1 Client Legal Responsibilities
CRA shall have procedures in place to inform client that they have legal responsibilities when using consumer reports for employment purposes. CRA shall recommend that client consult their legal counsel regarding their specific legal responsibilities.

3.2 Client Required Documents
CRA shall provide sample documents or inform client of specific documents which are needed to meet legal requirements regarding employer's procurement and use of consumer reports.

3.3 Truth in Advertising
CRA shall communicate to clients the nature of the original source, limitations, variables affecting the information available and scope of information provided by each consumer reporting product offered by the CRA.

3.4 Adverse Action
CRA shall inform client that there are legal requirements imposed by the federal FCRA and, in some instances, state consumer reporting laws, regarding taking adverse action against a consumer based on a consumer report. CRA shall recommend to client that they consult with counsel to develop a legally compliant adverse action policy.

3.5 Legal Counsel

CRA shall communicate to client that they are not acting as legal counsel and cannot provide legal advice. CRA shall communicate to client the importance of working with counsel to develop an employment screening program specific to their needs. CRA shall also communicate to client the necessity to work with counsel to ensure that client's policies and procedures related to the use of CRA-provided information is in compliance with applicable state and federal laws.

3.6 Understanding Consumer Reports

CRA shall provide guidance to client on how to order, retrieve, read and understand the information provided in consumer reports provided by the CRA.

3.7 Information Protection

CRA shall provide information to client regarding (1) the sensitive nature of consumer reports, (2) the need to protect such information and (3) the consumer report retention and destruction practices as outlined in the federal FCRA and the DPPA.

Section 4: Researcher and Data Product Standards

4.1 Public Record Researcher Agreement

CRA shall require a signed agreement from all non-employee public record researchers. The agreement shall clearly outline the scope of services agreed to by CRA and researcher, including jurisdictions covered, search methodology, depth of search, disclosure of findings, methodology and time frame for communication and completion of requests, methodology for confirming identity of subject of record(s), confidentiality requirements, and reinvestigation requirements.

4.2 Vetting Requirement

CRA shall have procedures in place to vet or qualify new public record researchers.

4.3 Public Record Researcher Certification

CRA shall require public record researcher to certify in writing that they will conduct research in compliance with all applicable local, state and federal laws, as well as in the manner prescribed by the jurisdiction which maintains the official record of the court; never obtain information through illegal or unethical means; and utilize document disposal and/or destruction methods pursuant to the federal FCRA.

4.4 Errors and Omissions Coverage

CRA shall obtain proof of public record researcher's Errors and Omissions Insurance. If public record researcher is unable to provide proof of insurance, CRA shall maintain coverage for uninsured and/or underinsured public record researcher.

4.5 Information Security

CRA shall provide a secure means by which public record researcher will receive orders and return search results.

4.6 Auditing Procedures

CRA shall maintain auditing procedures for quality assurance in regard to their active public record researchers.

4.7 Identification Confirmation

CRA shall follow reasonable procedures to assure maximum possible accuracy when determining the identity of a consumer who is the subject of a record prior to reporting the information. CRA shall have procedures in place to notify client of any adverse information that is reported based on a name match only.

4.8 Jurisdictional Knowledge

The CRA shall designate a qualified individual(s) or position(s) within the organization responsible for understanding court terminology, as well as the various jurisdictional court differences if CRA reports court records.

Section 5: Verification Service Standards

5.1 Verification Accuracy

CRA shall maintain reasonable procedures to assure maximum possible accuracy when obtaining, recording and reporting verification information.

5.2 Current Employment

CRA shall have procedures in place to contact consumer's current employer directly only when authorized by client and/or consumer.

5.3 Diploma Mills

When attempting educational verifications from known or suspected diploma mills, CRA shall have reasonable procedures in place to advise client of such.

5.4 Procedural Disclosures

CRA shall provide full disclosure to clients about general business practices regarding number of attempts to verify information, what constitutes an "attempt," locate fees, fees charged by the employer or service provider and standard question formats prior to providing such services.

5.5 Verification Databases

If CRA compiles and stores employment or education verification information for sale, CRA shall have procedures in place to ensure that data is accurate at the time information is provided to end user and have procedures in place for handling consumer disputes.

5.6 Use of Stored Data

If CRA provides investigative consumer reports from stored data, CRA shall have procedures in place to ensure the CRA does not provide previously reported adverse information unless it has been re-verified within the past three months, or for a shorter time if required by state or local law.

5.7 Documentation of Verification Attempts

CRA shall have procedures in place to document all verification attempts made and the result of each attempt, in completing all verification services.

5.8 Outsourced Verification Services

CRA shall require a signed agreement from all providers of outsourced verification services. The agreement shall clearly outline the scope of services to be provided, verification methodology, documentation of verification efforts, disclosure of findings, time frame for communication and completion of requests, confidentiality requirements, reinvestigation requirements and other obligations as furnishers of information under the federal FCRA.

5.9 Conflicting Data

Should CRA receive information from the verification source subsequent to the delivery of the consumer report, and as a direct result of the initial inquiry, that conflicts with originally reported information, and that new information is received within 120 days of the initial report, (or as may be required by law), CRA shall have procedures in place to notify client of such information.

5.10 Professional Conduct

CRA shall train all employees engaged in verification work on procedures for completing verifications in a professional manner.

5.11 Authorized Recipient

If CRA is requesting verification by phone, fax, email or mail, CRA shall have procedures in place to confirm that verification request is directed to an authorized recipient.

Section 6: General Business Practices

6.1 Character

Owners, officers, principals and employees charged with the enforcement of company policy must consent to undergo a criminal records check and be found free of convictions for any crimes involving dishonesty, fraud or moral turpitude.

6.2 Insurance

CRA shall maintain errors and omissions insurance. If CRA does not maintain errors and omission insurance, CRA must self-insure in a manner compliant with its state's insurance requirements.

6.3 Client Credentialing

CRA shall have a procedure to identify and authenticate all clients prior to disclosing consumer reports or other consumer information. The procedure shall require the CRA to maintain written records regarding the qualification of each client who receives consumer reports or other consumer information.

6.4 Vendor Credentialing

CRA shall have a procedure to identify and authenticate all vendors prior to disclosing consumer information. The procedure shall require the CRA to maintain written records regarding the qualification of each vendor who receives consumer information.

6.5 Consumer Credentialing

CRA shall develop and implement requirements for what information consumers shall provide as proof of identity prior to providing file disclosure to the consumer. The CRA shall maintain procedures to document the information used to identify each consumer to whom file disclosure is provided.

6.6 Document Management

CRA shall have a written record retention and destruction policy pursuant to the federal FCRA.

6.7 Employee Certification

CRA shall require all workers to certify they will adhere to the confidentiality, security and legal compliance practices of the CRA.

6.8 Worker Training

CRA shall provide training to all workers on confidentiality, security and legal compliance practices of the CRA.

6.9 Visitor Security

CRA shall utilize a visitor security program to ensure visitors do not have access to consumer information.

6.10 Employee Criminal History

CRA shall conduct a criminal records check on all employees with access to consumer information when such searches can be conducted without violating state or federal law. These searches shall be conducted at least once every two years for the duration of their employment. Criminal offenses shall be evaluated to determine initial or continued employment based upon their access to consumer information and state and federal laws.

6.11 Quality Assurance

CRA shall have procedures in place to reasonably ensure the accuracy and quality of all work product.

6.12 Certification

CRA shall have on staff one person designated to oversee and administer the certification process and future compliance by the CRA, including enforcement of the standard by all concerned. This person shall be vested with the responsibilities and authority attendant to this task, and shall be the CRA contact for the auditor and certification related matters for NAPBS®.

The next chapter examines how to choose a screening firm and the best way for employers to work with a screening firm.

This chapter closes with an interview of this book's author. The interview was published in the November/December 2011 issue of the *NAPBS Journal*.

NAPBS Accredited Member Spotlight:

Employment Screening Resources (ESR)

Attorney Lester Rosen, Founder and CEO of Employment Screening Resources (ESR), who also served as chairperson of the steering committee that founded NAPBS and served as its first co-chair, recently shared his thoughts on the accreditation process.

Choice to Become Accredited

In ESR's view, NAPBS accreditation will become a requisite by a great number of employers when considering a screening provider, as it's the only practical means of third party verification as to the professionalism and competency of a particular firm. Without the accreditation program, employers have no real way of differentiating between providers of screening services. With accreditation as a baseline requirement, employers have a level of assurance that a background screening firm meets the stringent accreditation standards. It is just a **matter of time** before most employers will only want to deal with accredited screening firms.

Benefits of Accreditation

The benefits of NAPBS accreditation are two fold, both external and internal. Externally, accreditation is proof positive to an employer that a background screening firm meets the accreditation guidelines. Internally, our going through the accreditation process was educational and reinforced the standards that ESR already upheld. Also, since the NAPBS mission relates to professionalism in the screening industry, and with most other professions having some sort of accreditation or licensing process, it is very important for our industry to show that we are self-regulating before government agencies seek to over control the industry – accreditation is a big part of demonstrating that we police ourselves.

Challenges of Accreditation

The main challenge of accreditation is that it requires a real commitment to spend the time needed to document your policies, practices, and procedures for the auditor. However, once a background screening firm makes the commitment of time and energy to undergo a third party audit though NAPBS accreditation, it is actually a very exciting process to review each standard and document compliance. It's also a tremendous training opportunity for all members of the team.

Auditor Experience

The auditor who conducted both the 'desk review' and 'onsite audit' was extremely professional and very pleasant to work with. Even though the amount of ESR's accreditation material made Tolstoy's novel "War and Pace" look like a short story, the auditor was obviously familiar with the material and all of the details giving us confidence as we went through the process.

Accreditation Advice

Every business has a number of pressing shorter term priorities, and in addition to performing against these, it is critical to think strategically about what the future holds. In the background screening industry, ESR thinks the "writing is on the wall" so to speak that accreditation will be nothing less than a business necessity for a professional screening company competing in the current economic environment. Also, keep in mind that there is nothing about the accreditation process or standards that would prevent a professional firm from achieving accreditation. It may be a lot of work, but it's very doable for any size firm. There are even consulting firms that will now help a background screening firm through the process.

Other Thoughts

When the NAPBS was founded back in 2002 and 2003, the idea of an accreditation process was a central driving force in order to demonstrate that background screening was a professional endeavor. The thought was that as an industry we needed to create standards, or risk outside regulation. Every profession has to have standards, and NAPBS accreditation represents the standards for our industry. Over the years, it took a lot of hard work from many very dedicated people who put the accreditation program together on their own time, and the results have been nothing short of tremendous. The screening industry owes a debt of gratitude to all of those people who made the accreditation program a reality.

Originally Published in NAPBS® JOURNAL for November-December 2011

Selecting & Working with a Background Screening Company

This chapter provides the tools an employer can use when selecting a pre-employment screening firm and also how an employer should work with screening firm after selection.

Inside This Chapter:

- ✓ Introduction

- ✓ Factors to Consider when Choosing a Background Screening Firm

- ✓ Traps for the Unwary when Choosing a Screening Firm

- ✓ Questions to Ask a Background Screening Firm

- ✓ Sample Request for Proposal (RFP) for Screening Services

- ✓ How to Work with a Background Screening Company

Introduction

A first decision an employer faces about background screening is whether to perform the screening in-house or to outsource. There are some tasks an employer could certainly perform in-house, such as local criminal record checks; however, a growing trend among profitable and efficient organizations is outsourcing services that, although vital, do not represent the company's core strength. But many firms realize it is an inefficient use of their time and energy to attempt to perform background-check services that a third-party specialist can provide quality services efficiently and in a cost-effective manner. Furthermore, the employer would have to learn the many complicated state and federal laws governing what information they can and cannot access, and acquire specialized software and information sources.

The first part of this chapter will greatly assist in the selection process.

Factors to Consider when Choosing a Background Screening Firm

Since there are scores of companies that offer employment pre-screening services, some cautionary advice is in order with respect to making a choice.

- ✓ First, an employer should look for a professional partner and not just an information vendor selling data at the lowest price.

- ✓ Second, an employer should apply the same criteria that it would use in selecting any other provider of critical professional services. For example, if an employer were choosing a law firm for legal representation, it would not simply choose the cheapest law firm.

- ✓ Although cost is always a consideration, the employer would clearly want to know it is selecting a law firm that is competent, experienced and knowledgeable, reputable and reasonably priced.

- ✓ Above all, an employer would want to know that it is dealing with a firm with integrity. The same criteria should be used for selecting any provider of a professional service. A screening service must have the proven ability and knowledge to provide this professional service. A review of the company's Web site and materials as well as contacting the firm's current clients for a professional reference should be helpful in establishing the firm's qualifications.

- ✓ An employer should verify if a firm has joined the National Association of Professional Background Screeners (NAPBS). Membership in NAPBS demonstrates a commitment to professionalism and an industry-wide code of conduct. Employers should also see if a background screening firm is accredited by the NAPBS Background Screening Credentialing Council (BSCC) for successfully proving compliance with the Background Screening Agency Accreditation Program (BSAAP). NAPBS accreditation is covered in more detail in Chapter 11.

- ✓ Also refer to the sample Request for Proposal (RFP) later in this chapter.

The following specific suggestions are offered for any organization choosing to use a pre-employment screening firm.

Consider a Screener's Overall Expertise

A screening service must have the proven ability and knowledge to provide this professional service. A review of the background screening company's website and materials as well as contacting the firm's current clients for a professional reference should be helpful in establishing the firm's qualifications.

Another aspect of a firm's expertise concerns representations made on the firm's website and literature. Here are some examples of "red flags."

- ✓ Does the firm discuss applicable federal and state law such as the Fair Credit Reporting Act and discrimination laws? If not, an employer should be very concerned with the issue of legal compliance.

✓ Does a firm express an understanding that a so-called "national criminal" database search is "only a secondary screening tool and cannot be relied upon generally as a primary source of information"? If not, that is a red flag!

✓ If a firm advertises a bankruptcy search as a tool for hiring, then an employer may be concerned since bankruptcy is generally impermissible for employment purposes.

✓ If a firm offers to provide employers other records such as property ownership, or reveal the names of friends and associates, then the employer needs to question it that firm understands screening and employment law. Those two searches are not likely to be a valid predictor of job performance, and that can be discriminatory.

✓ Another danger signal occurs if a screening firm represents that a Social Security trace "verifies" a person's Social Security Number. Although a valuable tool, a Social Security trace is not an official government record.

✓ Does the firm have a commitment to accuracy, and does it have polices, practices. and procedures to ensure the quality of its work products.

A discussion of each of these "red flags" follows in later chapters.

AUTHOR TIP | **Background Screening Firms "Traffic in the Reputations" of People**

A 2007 federal case described Consumer Reporting Agencies as firms "that traffic in the reputations of ordinary people." That case dealt with a court matter that was misreported in a credit report. After the plaintiff asked for a re-investigation, a subsequent court record check also resulted in a court researcher making an error. The need for firms that research court files to exercise reasonable diligence in understanding court files is critical since an error can have profound repercussions. The Court went on to say that a CRA must "train its employees to understand the legal significance of the documents they rely upon." This underscores that background screening is simply not a data supply business but rather a professional service that requires substantial expertise and experience. See: *Dennis v. BEH-1* 520 F.3d 1066 (9th Cir. 2008).

Source: http://caselaw.findlaw.com/us-9th-circuit/1006393.html.

Legal Compliance Expertise

It is imperative that a screening service understand the laws surrounding pre-employment screening and hiring, and they make a commitment to provide an employer with only the information the employer may legally possess.

As mentioned previously, the Federal Fair Credit Reporting Act (FCRA) defines a background screening company as a Consumer Reporting Agency (CRA). There are four levels of inquiry an employer needs to make when analyzing the legal compliance abilities of a CRA.

✓ Does the CRA clearly understand which laws regulate what a CRA must do and cannot do? A CRA must have a deep understanding of the FCRA and applicable state laws that control everything from the forms needed and what is legal to report, to how to respond to a consumer inquiry or complaint. It is not enough that a CRA understands the federal law; does the CRA understand the laws in all fifty states?

✓ Does the CRA have a commitment to keep its clients posted on all of the rules and regulatory changes of concern? As discussed throughout this book, there are numerous regulations affecting employers. For keeping up to date on legal matters, an employer should determine how much assistance to expect from their CRA.

✓ Does the CRA have fifty-state legal knowledge since state laws are as critical as federal law?

✓ In order to protect the employer from having impermissible data, does the CRA make any effort to review specific reports or data before handing them over to the employer? Some CRAs will make the commitment to review all reports to make sure that clients only receive what they can legally possess. For example, in California there are numerous rules, regulations, and restrictions on the employer's use of criminal records. Some CRAs take the position that this is not their department and just forward whatever they find. The result is that employers can very quickly find themselves in legal hot water. Other CRAs make it part of their service to review all negative data and scrub out anything that is clearly not reportable per state regulations.

(**NOTE:** Although a screening firm is not giving legal advice, a firm can follow standard industry guidelines and practices in making these determinations. There are some CRAs who actually have their field researchers write the "hit reports" when a criminal record is located and forward the reports directly to an employer. The difficulty, of course, is that field researchers are seldom lawyers or HR professionals. They are court runners who come from all walks of life, but generally have no training in determining what is or is not reportable. An employer needs to know who actually fills out the hit reports, be it a knowledgeable background specialist who works for the CRA, or some anonymous file retriever. An employer must be clear on this when retaining the services of a data vendor or any firm providing professional document retrieval or screening services.)

Focus on Legal Compliance

Because of the mosaic of overlapping federal and state laws, employment screening is increasingly becoming a legal compliance industry. Not only are there specific laws intended to regulate the activities of screening firms but screening also intersects with the immense complexities of federal and state employment and discrimination laws. KPMG Corporate Finance LLC – a leading provider of investment banking and strategic advisory services globally, closely follows the screening industry, and in an industry report released in Fall, 2003, KPMG observed:

> "There is likely to be an increased focus on compliance and legal issues in background screening. Compliance with the constantly evolving maze of state and federal regulations covering consumer information and background screening is challenging. Many employers and background screening companies are not focused on the issue, cannot afford the investment required to stay compliant, or choose not to make the investment as a calculated risk of doing business. We believe that the increased visibility of background screening and the sensitivity of the information involved are likely to lead to increased litigation and scrutiny of the process. The burden of compliance will continue to emerge as an important barrier to entry for the industry, and it is another factor that favors larger firms that can better leverage the required investment."

The full report is at www.kpmgcorporatefinance.com/us/pdf/bkgd_screen.pdf.

A Screening Firm's Personal Service, Consulting & Training

It is critical to keep in mind that pre-employment screening is much more than just providing raw data. The HR department should expect immediate assistance on any special situations that arise or if further applicant background investigation is required. A service provider should be able to work directly with the human resources department and conduct whatever training and orientation is necessary.

Also, of importance to choose a firm that is familiar with any special needs of your industry. For example, the health care industry has special concerns and requirements — unique licensing standards and disciplinary actions — so a health provider should ensure that their screening firm is familiar with those needs.

Pricing

Some employers make the mistake of believing that all background screening is done the same way, so often selection ends up depending upon price. Employers need to compare apples to apples and analyze the pricing model. Firms may cut corners by restricting how far back they conduct criminal searches or save money by hiring the cheapest possible labor to process crucial information Some background firms can use cost saving techniques that leave employers vulnerable. For example, firms use "at-home" operators or sending confidential data off shore to places like to India for processing may place encounter data privacy risks.

Unfortunately, employers who make a decision based upon price alone can find out the hard way that they did not get what they thought they were paying for.

Performance Criteria for Information Providers

Keep in mind no screening firm can ever guarantee when information will be available. In fact, there are times when information is simply not available, even if the employer were to hire Sam Spade and money was no object.

Examples of situations where there can be delays beyond one's control are:

- ✓ **Criminal records.** Records are generally returned in 72 hours. There can be a delay if there is a possible match and the researcher asks a court clerk to pull the file for verification. A screening firm has no control whatsoever when the court clerk will make the information available. In some counties, budgets and staffing can cause delays.
- ✓ **Education.** The school can be closed during holidays or vacations. If an employer wants to verify a degree over Winter or Spring break, then short of breaking into the school or hacking their computer, there is no physical way for that search to be completed until school is back in session. More and more schools are making verification available via internet inquiry, particularly if you have a student's username and password.
- ✓ **Past employment.** As noted in Chapter 9, there are a number of instances when the most conscientious background firm will not be able to obtain a timely employment verification. This can happen if an employer refuses to call back, or is out of business, or has moved or merged or has not retained employment records. If an employer refuses to call back despite repeated attempts, there is little that can be done short of sending a "bouncer-type" to physically sit in the employer's office until the past employer complies.

Software and Internet Options

A service provider should also be able to provide reports and related services with an internet access option in addition to conventional media methods of fax, email, mail. One big advantage to internet software is the ability to track a report, seeing when the various screening components are completed.

YOU NEED TO KNOW

Beware of Bells and Whistles

How critical is technology in selecting a service provider? During the dot.com boom, some background screening firms touted all sorts of Internet-based features as significant advantages for employers. Now, when selecting a screening firm, technology is a given. However, what differentiates screening companies today is often measurable by the value added with knowledge and service. Although a firm may devise new features and tout them as unique, it is not difficult for other firms to eventually match such services.

With the evolution of the HR-XML standard, ATS (Applicant Tracking Systems), and ASP (Application Service Providers) software, even small local screening firms have access to technology that is every bit as good as the larger national players. Large firms may have more resources to provide customized solutions for employers at the enterprise level. However, this advantage is quickly dissipating as technology advances. Employers should question the screener's investment of time and energy in developing the knowledge, experience, and customer service needed to help employers navigate the various ins and outs of safe hiring. Screening firms must react quickly to assist employers in responding to a criminal "hit" or to applicants who claim their report is wrong. Chapter 26 contains an in-depth discussion of the HR-XML standard and Applicant Tracking Systems.

Screening firms that invest in technology and focus on the "enterprise" or Fortune 500 level may provide a distinct advantage regarding a seamless interface with a current HR system. In addition, some of the larger screening firms can provide interfaces to related services such as drug testing or various pre-employment assessment tools. Such integration will be commonplace in the near future among all sizes of background screening firms. If every screening firm has similar technology, then the issues for employers once again become service and knowledge.

For most employers, screening and safe hiring is ultimately a professional service and not just a commodity where screening firms merely compete to sell data cheaper. Although one may predict a few large national screening firms will emerge in the future, a substantial number of regional screening firms will likely thrive. The regional firms can provide greater levels of customer service, support and knowledge that large enterprise-level screening firms are traditionally not able to deliver.

Data Security & Safeguarding Privacy

Although the information in a background report is not secret, the reports by their nature are sensitive and confidential. By law, the reports must be restricted to those individuals who are directly involved in the hiring process. To preserve confidentiality, a screening firm should have policies and procedures in place to ensure confidentiality — and should work with an employer to assist in keeping these matters private.

Here are suggested practical guidelines to maximize confidentiality:

- ✓ Look for a privacy and security policy on the screening firm's website or in their literature.
- ✓ Ask about how information is gathered. As mentioned above, a firm that uses home operators is a potential red flag. Unsupervised home operators create quality control issues, as well as privacy concerns. Employers may want to think carefully before utilizing a service that sends an applicant's personal data such as a Social Security Number or data of birth, to home workers in an unsupervised environment.
- ✓ If a report is to be faxed (which is now very old technology), the screening firm must clearly determine if the fax machine is a private or secured machine. If not, the screening company needs to have a "call before fax" policy so only the intended recipient will receive the report.
- ✓ The front page of a printed version of a screening report should not contain any confidential information, and should clearly establish that the report is a confidential matter only.
- ✓ A screening company should advise an employer to set up the following procedure to safeguard privacy. These can include:
  - All reports go directly to the designated HR or security manager that is in charge of the program and will remain only in that person's possession.
  - If a report raises issues that need to be discussed with others in the company, the person in charge of the background program should maintain physical custody of the actual report, unless there are more appropriate measures aimed at maintaining confidentiality. Background reports should not be sent through the office mail, or left lying on a supervisor's desk.
- ✓ Reports should be maintained securely and separately from an employee's personnel file. After someone is hired, there is no reason why a supervisor or anyone else should have access to the report. For example, an employer would not want a supervisor reviewing a confidential report that might bias an individual's routine performance appraisal.
- ✓ If the report is transmitted through an internet or Intranet system or by email, then the employer should ask for assurance from a background firm that they are following appropriate security procedures for maintaining confidentiality.

- Does the firm have appropriate firewalls and internet security in place, with reports being sent in a secured and encrypted manner?
- Are there adequate password protection and policies in place to allow only the appropriate individuals to order and view reports?

✓ Adapt other appropriate measures to ensure that only authorized individuals will receive information — periodically change passwords, or audit who has access to the company Intranet system.

✓ Firms with advanced technology are able to provide employers with a completely paperless system, so screening reports need not be printed. That saves the employer from having to download or print reports. That lessens the possibility of paper reports being viewed by individuals who do not have a permissible purpose. Some screening firms are able to retain reports for employers indefinitely.

Under the National Association of Professional Background Screeners (NAPBS®) Background Screening Agency Accreditation Program (BSAAP), an NAPBS accredited background screening firm must prove compliance with a strict professional standard composed of requirements and measurements regarding protection of privacy of consumers. These standards are show in the prior chapter.

An example of how screening companies can protect personal information of individuals undergoing background checks is by following the strict data privacy and security regulations '201 CMR 17.00: STANDARDS FOR THE PROTECTION OF PERSONAL INFORMATION OF RESIDENTS OF THE COMMONWEALTH' passed by Massachusetts. The following went into effect in 2010 to protect the personal information of Massachusetts residents.

Massachusetts Data Privacy Protection Law

The Massachusetts Offices of Consumer Affairs and Business Regulations (OCABR) passed strict data privacy and security regulations '201 CMR 17.00: STANDARDS FOR THE PROTECTION OF PERSONAL INFORMATION OF RESIDENTS OF THE COMMONWEALTH' that went into effect March 1, 2010 to protect the personal information of Massachusetts residents by requiring businesses to have a multitude of safeguards including a comprehensive Written Information Security Policy (WISP).

The Massachusetts law 201 CMR 17.00 covers any business that "receives, stores, maintains, processes, or otherwise has access to personal information in connection with the provision of good or services or in connection with employment." The rules define "personal information" as a Massachusetts resident's name combined with financial, bank, or credit card account, driver's license, or social security numbers. The regulations also applied to third parties and required that there be contracts to ensure that the regulations are implemented and maintained, although the contracts did not need to be updated before March 1, 2012. Massachusetts rules apply to out of state firms that handle personal information as well.

The Massachusetts regulations required companies handling personal information to adopt several administrative, technical, and physical safeguards, including computer system security requirements that involve encryption of personal information on laptops and other portable devices as well as data transmitted across public networks or wirelessly. Businesses regulated by these rules must also implement a comprehensive WISP that included the following elements:

- Designation of Employee(s) to Maintain the WISP Program.
- Identification and Assessment of Internal and External Risks.
- Restricting Physical or Electronic Access to Personal Information.
- Verifying Third-Party Service Providers can Protect Personal Information.
- Collection, Access, and Retention Standards for Personal Information.
- Access, Storage, Use, and Disclosure of Personal Information.

- Review, Responsive Action, and Documentation of Responsive Action.
- Destruction of Personal Information No Longer Needed.
- Employee Training on WISP Program.
- Monitoring the WISP Program.
- Review of WISP Program.

The Massachusetts law has been described as the toughest in the nation, and should go a long ways toward improving privacy and data security and fighting identity theft.

A text of the regulations '201 CMR 17.00: STANDARDS FOR THE PROTECTION OF PERSONAL INFORMATION OF RESIDENTS OF THE COMMONWEALTH' can be viewed at: www.mass.gov/ocabr/docs/idtheft/201cmr1700reg.pdf.

References

As with any provider of a professional service, an employer wants to check the provider's references. Just as a screening company should advise an employer to carefully screen each applicant before he or she is hired, an employer should exercise the same due diligence when retaining a screening company.

For more information on pre-employment background checks, see the following resources:

✓ The National Association of Professional Background Screeners (NAPBS) – www.napbs.com.
✓ The ASIS Pre-employment Background Screening Guidelines 2006 – www.asisonline.org/guidelines/guidelinespreemploy.pdf.

Traps for the Unwary when Choosing a Screening Firm

Trap #1: Lack of Data and Privacy Protection

Remember the discussion in Chapter 2 about privacy and the trend of offshoring data – where a great deal of Personal and Identifiable Information (PII) is sent offshore for processing where there is no real protection? Despite significant attention in the U.S. on data and privacy protection, many American consumers are not aware of offshoring. When Personal and Identifiable Information (PII) is on a U.S. resident is sent abroad, the data is beyond the protection of U.S. privacy laws and there is very little, if any, protection for the consumer.

A couple of years ago, there was a news story about a California hospital that outsourced its medical transcribing, and the work ended up in Pakistan. A medical transcriber in Pakistan got into a dispute with her employer about wages and threatened to publish the medical records of thousands of Americans on the Internet. Needless to say, the hospital suffered through a great deal of negative publicity and the privacy and confidentially of medical records for numerous Americans was endangered because their personal information was sent offshore, beyond the reach of U.S. privacy laws. Of course, even after the matter was settled with appropriate payments, no one knows for sure what information the offshore worker may have decided to keep or for what reason.

Some background firms save money by sending information offshore for data processing, or use foreign operators to contact past employers or schools in the U.S. The offshore agent is completely beyond U.S. privacy rules and there is little control over how the data is handled. As the California hospital learned, sending private data abroad for processing is risky business. Recent news articles have revealed that call center workers in foreign countries are actively engaged in the theft of consumer information from call centers in order to commit identity theft. When data is stolen, a U.S. resident has no practical means of contacting a foreign police department or obtaining the services of a foreign attorney to file a lawsuit.

The bottom-line: protection of PII is mission critical for any screening firm. Any employer that is concerned about the privacy of their applicants' personal information should ask their background firm if data is being sent outside of the U.S. for processing, and if so, what information is being sent, what country is involved and what protections are in place.

Trap #2: The Lack of Standardization of Packages

Another aspect of background screening that can confuse employers is the fact there is no standardization as to what background firms are offering. Unfortunately, it can be very difficult to compare offerings from different background firms without an insider's knowledge of how screening works.

For example, some screening firms may offer a "package" to do an "unlimited" amount of criminal searches for a fixed fee. But what is truly included? To an employer who does not understand how this works, there may be a temptation to simply choose the firm offering the cheapest price or the best package. Below are legitimate questions to ask before blindly assuming that a cheap "package" price is a good deal:

- ✓ First, are the counties being searched "derived" or "developed?" A "derived" search means that the screening firm is simply looking at addresses and jurisdictions that come up in some sort of social security trace report. A "developed" search means a screening firm also adds in those counties where a person has worked. Obviously, firms that do a "developed" search are likely doing more searches and giving more protection. Firms trying to save money at an employer's expense will do a "derived" search only, and the employer will be none the wiser.
- ✓ Second, an employer needs to understand what databases the screening firm is using to establish past addresses. A screening firm utilizing only a credit bureau's social trace is likely to produce less address information and thus do fewer searches for the employer. On the other hand, the employer has less protection. An employer is may be better off using a screening firm utilizing an address information manager that incorporates more jurisdictions and a wider to search.
- ✓ A third consideration is how the criminal records are checked. If the screening firm is only using an inexpensive, supplemental database in order to save money, there is a real possibility relevant information will be missed or incorrect information reported. Although these databases can be valuable because they can lead to the discovery of information and additional places to search, they are inherently not as accurate as court searches. Databases do not cover all jurisdictions, do not always contain identifiers, such as date of birth, and are not always updated with the latest information. These facts are covered in detail in a later chapter.

As with anything else, if a deal is too good to be true, it may not be the real thing. Employers may get baited into an "unlimited" seven year search, and switched into a search that does not protect them.

Trap #3: The Use of Home Operators

Another issue similar to offshoring is the use of "home workers." (Some of whom would fall under the category of "offshore workers" as well.) Some screening firms use home based operators to perform employment and education verifications. This can represents a huge financial savings for the screening firm by classify them as independent contractors and not paying taxes or workers' compensation or other costs associated with employees.

Any PII put into the hands of a home worker can loses most, if not all, of the protections it would have in a business facility with requisite access controls along with physical and technical security protocols. This is not to suggest that all home workers are not perfectly capable workers, but must be examined carefully given the sensitive nature of the work and privacy issues.

Below are the top 10 reasons NOT to utilize a background firm sending applicants' personal data to home operators working from kitchen tables and dorm rooms across America.

1. **Privacy:** A screening firm would be directly responsible for making private information viewable and printable on people's home computers.
2. **Professionalism:** A screening firm would have difficulty accurately claiming that at-home researchers are "professionals" when they are unsupervised, unregulated and acting as cheap substitutes for what is supposed to be

a professional service. Ask yourself how the sound of barking dogs, crying babies and television sets in the background may strike those asked to provide verifications.

3. **FCRA Defensibility:** A screening firm would have difficulty defending the practice of using at-home researchers against a claim under FCRA section 607(b) concerning reasonable procedures for accuracy.

4. **IC Classification:** A screening firm cannot classify someone as an Independent Contractor (IC) when they work only for you, when you tell them exactly how to do their job, and when they are providing the same core services provided by your in-house staff.

5. **Training/QC:** A screening firm cannot train and discuss production issues in real time. It is also difficult for at-home researchers to learn from each other when everyone is working in isolation. Furthermore, since everyone works alone it is harder to enforce quality rules across the entire organization.

6. **Supervision:** Unsupervised at-home researchers are very difficult to supervise. In addition, since they are paid by the completed verification, they may be more tempted to fake orders since there is no one supervising them in real-time.

7. **Reliability:** A screening firm would be dependent entirely on the researcher's priorities, which may not be your own. They may put a hair appointment ahead of your forty new verifications that have to be called today. You want load balancing to be under your control and not secondary to at-home researcher's personal schedules.

8. **Hidden Costs:** There are hidden costs to managing and maintaining multiple remote researchers as opposed to a central pool of talent. Take, for instance, the time lost to the unreliable performance of at-home researcher's internet connections, home computers and printers.

9. **Due Diligence:** A screening firm and employer could face significant legal exposure if the at-home researcher's performance falls below a professional standard of care due to lack of training and supervision.

10. **Disclosure:** Would you want to disclose to your applicants that the sensitive, personal data and professional service they have entrusted you with was being performed by unsupervised home workers?

The employer should ask for status of protection and risk management from the screening firm regarding any home workers. The CRA should be called upon to give factual information about what data is in the home and if they have insurance to cover any identity thefts.

Questions to Ask a Background Screening Firm

The *40 Questions to Ask a Pre-Employment Background Screening Firm* below is a master checklist of questions to draw from to find a Safe Hiring Partner (SHP). The checklist can help employers identify quality background firms offering professional background checks and to avoid firms offering a "knock-off service" where the employer is not receiving the professional services they should receive.

The use of this checklist may depend on the employer's technical level and size.

40 Questions to Ask a Pre-Employment Background Screening Firm

✓ Does your background screening firm have legal staff and help desk with expertise on pre-employment screening and the Fair Credit Reporting Act (FCRA), and also provide written documentation and resources on safe hiring, due diligence, and legal compliance issues?

✓ Does your background screening firm have state of the art web-based system that requires NO SOFTWARE to purchase and provides state of the art security and data privacy protection?

✓ Is exact information about your applicants available on the web 24/7, including real time status complete with notes?

✓ Does your background screening system track the real-time status of every search so that nothing falls through the cracks?

✓ Can your background screening firm archive all records so an employer can have paperless systems?

✓ Does your background screening firm operate on a platform that is HR-XML certified and can be integrated seamlessly into HRIS and ATS systems?

✓ Can your background screening firm provide control features so an employer can set-up multiple sub-accounts, so that the Administrator can view all accounts, but each sub-account can only view their own reports?

✓ Is all work done in the USA to protect privacy and control quality -- i.e., nothing sent offshore to India or other "cheaper places" that puts data privacy and quality control at risk?

✓ Are all employment and education checks conducted by professionals in a controlled, call center type environment, so that nothing is sent to cheaper at-home workers, where data privacy and the quality of work is at risk?

✓ Are all employees with your background screening firm subject to an intensive training when they are hired, and attend documented training weekly?

✓ For employment verifications, are anti-fraud procedures in place, such as verifications of all past employer phone numbers instead of relying upon an applicant supplied number?

✓ For Education verifications, are steps taken to verify if a college or university is accredited and to watch out for Diploma Mills?

✓ Do you have a policy of NO set-up fee/no monthly obligations?

✓ Do you offer 24/7 ordering online that gives an employer total control over the ordering process and speeds up turnaround time?

✓ Do you offer flexible options to receive reports (fax, e-mail, or online)?

✓ Are your background screening reports easy to read, with important information summarized at the top for ease of use?

✓ Are criminal searches conducted using the most accurate means which normally means onsite (no cheap database substitutes)?

✓ Do you search for both felonies and misdemeanors when available?

✓ When a criminal hit is reported, does knowledgeable person in your background screening firm report the findings (as opposed to having the information entered by some unknown court researcher)?

✓ When there is a criminal hit, are you proactive in calling the client to advise them there is a potential problem?

✓ Does your background screening firm take measures to ensure that ALL legal and relevant criminal records are searched, as opposed to just going back "seven" years, which can leave an employer exposed?

✓ Do you accurately describe the pros and cons of criminal databases, and ensure clients are informed that databases are research tools only and are subject to false negatives and false positives?

✓ If a client orders a "multi-jurisdictional" database, do you re-verify any criminal "hit" at the courthouse for maximum accuracy, instead of relying on merely notifying the applicant of a potential hit?

✓ Do you provide clients with all necessary FCRA forms and procedures?

✓ Do you notify your clients of changes in the FCRA and other applicable laws?

✓ Is a member of your background screening firm a nationally recognized writer and speaker on safe hiring and the FCRA?

✓ Does the President of your background screening firm have an open door policy for any customer issues or questions?

✓ Is your average turnaround time 72 hours less?

✓ If there is a delay for reasons that are out of your control, do you notify us online with in-depth notes and the ETA?

✓ Does your background screening firm have large clients with nationally recognized names?

✓ Do you partner with leading web sites and HR service providers?

✓ Regarding customer service, will there be someone assigned to our account and familiar with our needs?

✓ Does your background screening firm provide free training programs?

✓ Do you offer ordering options such as customized packages or individual searches and competitive pricing?

✓ Do you provide a guide or interactive U.S. map showing the significant rules for all 50 states when it comes to screening?

✓ Has your background screening firm published information on background checks and safe hiring such as books, blogs, articles, white papers, legal updates, newsletters, pamphlets, etc. to show its knowledge of the screening industry?

✓ Does your background screening firm have extensive international capabilities?

✓ Is your background screening firm "Safe Harbor" certified to perform screenings in the EU?

✓ Is your background screening firm a member of the background screening trade association - National Association of Professional Background Screeners (NAPBS®) - and does your firm actively participate and support professionalism in the screening industry?

✓ Is your background screening firm accredited by the National Association of Professional Background Screeners (NAPBS®) Background Screening Credentialing Council (BSCC) for successfully proving compliance with the Background Screening Agency Accreditation Program (BSAAP)?

Hint: Hopefully, all of the answers to the questions above are YES.

Sample Request for Proposal (RFP) for Screening Services

This is a Sample Request for Proposal (RFP) to assist employers, Human Resources, and Security Professionals in selecting a provider for employment screening services. This document can also be found at the author's web page at www.esrcheck.com/backgroundscreeningrfp.php.

Sample Request for Proposal (RFP)

Dear Service Provider,

You are invited to submit a proposal for providing our firm with pre-employment background screening services. Please submit all responses directly to the following address: *{Place your contact person, company name, company address and telephone number here}*

Please note the following:

☐ All proposals must be received by the following date: _____

☐ All bids must be submitted in writing. Faxes are not accepted.

☐ Employer reserves the right to accept or reject any bid in its sole discretion and is not obligated to choose to lowest bid.

☐ Proposals must remain valid for a period of 180 days.

☐ Please direct all questions and comments to the person indicated above only.

☐ Communication with any other individual may be considered grounds for disqualification.

☐ The bid will be evaluated based upon the following criteria:

> Price
>
> Proven Ability to meet needs
>
> Turnaround time commitment
>
> Customer service
>
> Supplier Personal
>
> Understanding of legal requirements
>
> Infrastructure, including the system for tracking and reporting
>
> Ease of reading screening reports
>
> Additional services provided
>
> Quality and completeness of product provided
>
> Knowledge of the process involved

Sample Request for Proposal For Screening Services

I.   Services Offered

☐ Indicate if you provide following services, describe them and your methodologies:

> County felony and misdemeanor records
>
> Credit Reports
>
> Social Security traces
>
> Driving records
>
> Federal Records
>
> Employment verification
>
> Education verification
>
> Professional license
>
> Sexual Offender search
>
> Terrorist databases
>
> International criminal searches
>
> International employment and education verification
>
> Others

☐ Do you utilize the services of any subcontractors to fulfill criminal record searches, or any other search? If so, identify the methods used including quality control procedures.

☐ Do you use databases for any searches? If so, please describe:

> The nature of the database

> Any limitations on the usage of the database
>
> Any legal compliance issues, such as FCRA Section 613

- ☐ Please describe any quality control procedures you follow to insure accuracy in your reporting of results.
- ☐ Does your firm have national capabilities? Describe.
- ☐ Does your firm have international capabilities? Describe.
- ☐ Describe your quality control procedures.

II. Turnaround Time

- ☐ What is your turnaround time for each of the services above?
- ☐ Describe your methodology to ensure turnaround time of reports.
- ☐ Are you able to generate turnaround time reports for each order that is placed and for each search conducted? Do you notify employers if there is a delay and how long?
- ☐ Is there a performance guarantee?

III. Reporting Format and Technology

- ☐ Describe the software or online system utilized by your firm.
- ☐ How does an employer send an order to your firm?
- ☐ How is an employer informed of results?
- ☐ How is an employer kept advised of status?
- ☐ What protection do you provide to keep customers limited to their candidate's data only.
- ☐ Please describe your ability to integrate with Applicant Tracking Systems or HR Information Systems.
- ☐ Please describe your ability to accept online candidate consents.
- ☐ Please provide a sample report.

IV. Legal Compliance

- ☐ Describe your understanding of the laws that govern pre-employment screening and your methodology for compliance with those laws.
- ☐ How does your firm keep updated on applicable federal and state laws affecting employment screening?
- ☐ Do you maintain a guide to applicable laws in all 50 states?
- ☐ Describe what assistance you will give us, if any, in legal compliance.
- ☐ Describe how you keep your clients updated on important legal changes.
- ☐ If there is a criminal case found, who determines if it is reportable and describe the methodology used to determine whether it is reportable?

V. Privacy and Security

- ☐ Does your firm have a Privacy and Data Security policy? If so, please provide.
- ☐ Describe your security and data protection practices, including any third party certifications
- ☐ Does your firm send Personal and Identifiable Information (PII) outside of the United States for either for domestic or international screening? If so, please describe in detail.

☐ How do you vet new clients to ensure your services are in compliance with the FCRA? Does your firm utilize any home based workers who have access to (PII) about an applicant? If so, describe the process and describe how personal and identifiable applicant information is protected.

☐ Does your firm utilize home operators to complete employment and education verifications? If so, describe the process and describe how personal and identifiable applicant information is protected.

VI. Customer Service

☐ Do you provide any customer training or continuing education? If so, please describe.

☐ Do you provide an account executive that will handle our account?

☐ Do you have an internal trouble ticket system? If so, describe how it works.

☐ If there is not a trouble ticket system, describe your internal methodology to insure that customer service issues are addressed in a timely manner and that there is follow-through.

☐ Describe your problem escalation procedures in the event of a service issue.

VII. About Your Firm

☐ Please describe the background and experience of your firm.

☐ Please provide a short biography of the principals of your firm.

☐ Do you require a contract?

☐ Describe your account set-up procedures.

☐ Are there set-up fees?

☐ Can we set up a customized screening program?

☐ How do you handle billing an employer with multiple locations, or different departments?

☐ Do you have errors and omissions (E & O) issuance? Describe.

☐ Please list representative clients.

☐ Please list three references. To the extent possible, choose references that have needs similar to our firm. Please provide full contact information.

☐ Is your firm a member of the trade association for background firms, the National Association of Professional Background Screeners (NAPBS)? If not a member, do you certify that you adopt and agree with their goals and standards?

☐ Has your firm been accredited by the NAPBS Background Screening Credentialing Council (BSCC) for proving compliance with the Background Screening Agency Accreditation Program (BSAAP)? If not, are you currently in the process of obtaining an NAPBS accreditation?

☐ If your firm is not accredited by NAPBS, is your firm in compliance with the NAPBS Accreditation guidelines? If not, please indicate in detail the steps being taken to be in compliance with NAPBS accreditation.

☐ Describe how you train your employees.

☐ Describe how you keep your employees updated on legal issues effecting screening.

VIII. Pricing

☐ Please provide pricing for each item listed above.

☐ Do you have any package plans? Please describe.

☐   Are there any other costs or expenses we should know about?

IX. Other advantages

☐   Are there any other advantages in selecting your firm to provide pre-employment background screening services?

☐   There are many firms that provide this service. Why should we choose you?

Source: www.esrcheck.com/backgroundscreeningrfp.php

How to Work with a Background Screening Company

The next portion of this chapter outlines the complete mechanics of how to working a background screening firm, once a firm is chosen per the criteria above. The twenty questions frequently asked by employers about this process are followed by corresponding answers considered to be best practices.

1. How does an employer start the screening process with a CRA?

Initially, an employer needs to sign a Certification Form with the CRA. This is required by the Fair Credit Reporting Act (FCRA), and explained in detail in Chapter 3. Certification means the employer will utilize the information provided according to law. A typical certification form indicates:

✓   The employer understands the information can be used for employment purposes only,
✓   That all information must remain confidential,
✓   That information will not be used to discriminate unlawfully, and
✓   The employer will follow the rules contained in the FCRA for the use of consumer reports.

Under the FCRA, a background firm is required to provide two documents to an employer (both documents are available in the Appendix:

✓   The first document is the "Notice to Users of Consumer Reports: Obligations of Users under the FCRA."
✓   The second document is "A Summary of Your Rights under the Fair Credit Reporting Act," directed at job applicants.

Note that California has additional special certification rules that must be followed, contained in the California Investigative Consumers Reporting Agencies Act - Civil Code section 1786 et. seq. Any background firm or employer doing business in California, hiring in California, or using the consumer report in connection with a California resident or California employment location must be familiar with and follow the special California requirements.

2. What forms does an applicant need to sign or receive?

A Disclosure Form

It is critical that employers utilize forms that are legally compliant under both federal law and state law. Although a CRA may provide an employer with forms, it is still the employer's responsibility to ensure the forms are legal in their state. A number of states have state-specific requirements. As of September 30, 1997, the FCRA says the Disclosure Form is necessary for any background check report whether or not it involves a credit report. Previously, release forms were contained in the back of employment applications. Congress was concerned that applicants were not made aware that a report might be prepared. As a result of the FCRA amendments effective in 1997, a separate stand-alone document is required to perform background checks. The amended FCRA requires an employer "make a clear and conspicuous written disclosure to the consumer before the report is obtained, in a document that consists solely of the disclosure, that a consumer report may be obtained." Under the FCRA, applicants do not necessarily sign the form, but that would be a best practice in order to show compliance.

Release and Authorization Form

The Release Form serves several purposes. First, it is the release of information so a CRA may obtain background information under the FCRA. Second, it is the place where the job applicant provides the necessary identifying information to the CRA to obtain public records. Third, this release may be needed when a former employer or school requests a release before information is given. Also, it can be used to reassure a job applicant that all of his rights are protected, and that screening is a sound business practice that is not to be taken personally. Whether or not it can be combined with the disclosure form depends upon how much information an employer wants to have in their release form. Too much information can violate the rule that the disclosure for cannot have excess verbiage that distracts from the plain meaning of the disclosure.

The Release and Authorization typically does ask for the date of birth. The correct date of birth will be needed for positive identification (See Chapter 2 for a discussion of the "date of birth issue"). If an employer does not want to have date of birth on the release form, then arrangements need to be made with a CRA to obtain it separately. The employer needs to be aware that without date of birth, there is likely to be delays. See Chapter 3 on the FCRA for additional issues surrounding these forms and the exception for "truck drivers" enacted by Congress in 1998.

Any competent screening firm can provide all the necessary forms for pre-employment screening. If an employer's attorney or legal department already has forms, use those — assuming those forms fully comply with the requirements of the FCRA as well as applicable state rules. There is currently no nationally accepted set of forms for employment screening.

There are some special issues involved with these forms:

✓ The disclosures may not have excessive language that detracts from a clear understanding of the form; and
✓ Whether a form may request that an applicant waive his rights to sue the employer or CRA.

Per the FTC staff, an applicant cannot be required to waive his rights under the FCRA (See staff letter to Richard Hauxwell, January 12, 1998, at www.ftc.gov/os/statutes/fcra/hauxwell.htm). However a form may ask that an applicant waives his or her rights to the extent permitted by law. It is not clear that such waiver language however, gives a screening firm or the employer a great deal of protection against state torts such as defamation or invasion of privacy. Even if there is such a waiver, there is a problem of putting it on the disclosure form. For those reasons, some employers and CRA's will use two separate forms.

✓ First, the release form that contains the identifying information along with the waiver language, if utilized.
✓ Second, the disclosure form contains only the required language.

Employer Order Form

If the employer is faxing an order to a CRA instead of self-entry of the order into the CRA's Internet system by either the employer or the applicant, then an **Employee Order Form** is typically sent with each order. It tells the CRA what is being requested, who requested it and sending instructions. The CRA can customize the form for each employer so paperwork is minimized. The customized form will reflect the type of screening program the employer requires and the employer's name, contact person, and contact information. To ensure accuracy and to avoid delays, the employer needs to confirm that the applicant's name, Social Security Number, driver's license number, and any other data needed to fulfill the order has been provided and is legible. Any information that is incorrect or not clear will cause a delay or result in inaccurate information returned. If a screening firm is given a name that is spelled wrong or a driver's license number or Social Security Number is not legible, say, a "3" looks like an "8," the result may be either bad data or data that is delayed. If the applicant has not given the names of past employers or provided the city and state, a delay may ensue. The applicant's telephone number may be requested so the CRA may contact an applicant directly to clarify anything that is not clear on the form, however, having a screening firm contact the applicant is not always a good practice — an applicant may get concerned or confused, especially if the screening firm is calling to obtain the applicant's Social Security Number or other confidential data.

If an employer utilizes an online system to enter screening orders, the employer first needs to carefully review the application materials before placing the order online. For any material that is illegible or incomplete, the employer can contact the applicant to clarify. This not only saves time and avoids data errors, but also speeds up the screening process considerably since the screening begins as soon as the employer transmits the order electronically. If the order is faxed to the background firm, the order can be delayed pending the background firm entering the order into its computer system or by having to contact the employer to clear up any uncertainties.

Of course, all of these issues are moot with new technology that allows an applicant to receive an email and to self-enter their own data. Even more advanced technology allows employers to initiate a background check seamlessly from their Applicant Tracking System (ATS) with the click of the mouse. That can generate an email to the applicant prompting them to go online, fill out the required forms, and provide a mouse signature. In addition, real time report status, as well as a link to the final report, can be transmitted back to the employer's ATS so all processes are performed on the ATS site. By the use of a "single sign-on," an employer never needs to leave the ATS site to review progress or see the finished background report.

To the extent the employer has already collected past employment or education data from the applicant as part of the process, this data can also be seamlessly passed to the background screening firm. Thus when the applicant goes online to enter their data, employment and education information is pre-populated.

The technology to facilitate such communications and efficiencies between system and employer is made possible with widespread advances and adoption of a standard suite of software specifications that enables the automation of human resources-related data exchanges between software systems. This is called HR-XML — the human resources version of a language used to write software that facilitates communication.

Applicant Resume and/or Application

When the CRA is asked to do an employment check or educational verification, it is a good practice to send the CRA both a copy of the full application and the consent even if the employer has entered the order online. This practice assists the screening firm to identify past employers. Regardless if the employer uses a screening firm's online order entry system, many schools and past employers may require a copy of a signed release before providing information. Again, screening firms leveraging the latest technology do not face this issue because the signature can be captured by an E-sign technology that can even include a mouse signature.

3. What language should be in the employer's employment application form?

In addition to the forms supplied by a CRA, an employer should also have two recommended sections in their own employment application forms. The language relates to criminal convictions, and truthfulness and honesty in the application process. Many states have their own requirement and an employer should consult legal counsel on these. Employers may also place information about the nature of the employment relationship, such as "at will," and can also stet its anti-discrimination policy (See Chapter 7 on Application Forms.)

4. When does the applicant sign the forms?

Typically, the actual screening begins after a company has decided that an applicant is a good prospect and wants to verify that their hiring assessment is correct. However, if an employer is still using paper forms, the forms can be signed ahead of time even if an applicant is not going to be submitted for screening.

Employers can take two approaches. Many employers have all applicants sign written screening forms as part of the initial application process. There are several advantages. First, by having background forms in the standard application packet, it discourages applicants with something to hide. Second, applicants with a minor infraction in their past may still wish to apply and tend to self-disclose any negative information. This helps contribute to a very open interview. Third, employers find it much easier to administer the screening program if the candidate's necessary forms have already been signed.

The alternative approach is to have the finalist only sign the consent forms. Some firms wait until an offer has been made first. Firms use this approach if they feel a background screening may interfere with effective recruiting, although in this day and age, most job applicants understand that pre-employment screening is a standard business practice and is not a reflection upon them personally. This approach requires the HR, Security Department, or the hiring manager give the finalist the forms at a second interview. This can present administrative difficulties. Even if forms are not filled out as part of the initial application, it is suggested the applicants still be informed there will be a pre-employment background screening as a standard part of the hiring process.

Technology provides an option by allowing the applicant to fill out the forms at the point in the process where an employer believes a background screening would be appropriate. That way, an employer is not requesting or collecting a date of birth or social security number prematurely.

Utah passed a new law effective May 12, 2009 called "The Employment Selection Procedures Act." See: http://le.utah.gov/~2009S1/bills/hbillenr/hb1002.htm. The law prohibits an employer with more than 15 employees from collecting an applicant's social security number, date of birth or driver's license number before a job offer or before the time when a background check is requested. In addition, if the person is not hired, the employer will not keep the information beyond two years. The employer also may not use the information for any other purposes and must maintain a *specific policy regarding the retention, disposition, access, and confidentiality of the information.* An applicant has the right to view the policy. The idea appears to be to limit the flow of personal data before or unless it is needed and to destroy it if no longer needed. For employers using paper applications, it creates an administrative burden since the employer needs to add another step to get the data required for a background check if an applicant moves forward in the hiring process. However, electronic hiring procedures, such as the Applicant Generated Report (AGR) system solves this issue since an applicant is only asked to provide confidential data only if the employer decides to perform a background check and the information only goes to the screening firm.

5. During what step should applicants be screened and who should be screened – all applicants or just finalists?

Employers typically utilize pre-employment screening toward the end of the selection process — after the field has been narrowed down. After all, employment screening is designed generally help an employer decide who NOT to hire. Other tools in the employer's quiver of selection devices help an employer whittle down the applicant pool. Because of time and expenses involved, firms do not typically request screening on the entire applicant pool. Screening normally occurs after a company has decided that an applicant is a good prospect and wants to verify their hiring assessment is correct.

There are two directions that firms typically take. The more common approach is to have a CRA perform its screening function on a finalist or after a conditional job offer has been tendered. The purpose of pre-screening at that point is to demonstrate due diligence and to eliminate uncertainties about an applicant.

Alternatively, a firm will ask a CRA to screen the two or three finalists, then use the results in the selection process. The advantage is that a firm can make a selection with more facts. The disadvantages are:

- ✓ Multiple screens cost more;
- ✓ Adds two to four days to the selection process; and
- ✓ There are possible FCRA and EEOC implications that can be triggered.

Some employers use a system referred to as "progressive screening," where the employer may ask the screening firm to run a preliminary screen that may utilize a Social Security trace. If the preliminary screening is satisfactory, the employer may request a more detail check. The problem with "progressive" screening is that any cost savings in eliminating an applicant early before doing a full background check, may be overwhelmed by the administrative time and cost of monitoring such a process, not to mention potential delays involved with the employer having to review the initial screen and then order additional research. Even if the screening firm is requested to review the preliminary results, a screening firm can only apply the employer's criteria, and cannot make judgments on the employer's behalf. If a screening firm or employer eliminates a candidate with an automated scoring or adjudication process then this can run contrary to the EEOC rules concerning individualized consideration. For these reasons, an employer may find it more efficient and cost-effective to avoid "progressive screening" on the basis that whatever cost caving can occur on occasion are offset by the greater cost and risk involved in a "progressive" screening program.

Using pre-employment reports to choose among finalists can also arguably impact EEOC considerations when EEOC-sensitive reports such as criminal history or credit reports are used. An argument can be made that **the initial selection should be based upon the applicant's job qualifications and job fit only**; a pre-employment report is used only to eliminate an applicant with a **job-related criminal history, falsified credentials, or if negative history** is uncovered.

> **AUTHOR TIP** Under a new federal case from the Ninth Circuit, the timing of the background screening may also impact Americans with Disabilities Act (ADA). If a background report is necessary before a person becomes a finalist, then a firm may need to complete the background check before obtaining medical information or performing pre-employment physicals. The idea is that medical information should only be requested after there has been a real job offer, which means all relevant non-medical information has been evaluated. This enables an applicant to determine if there was a medical basis to a rejection, and to maintain medical privacy until later in the hiring process. See Leonel v. American Airlines, 400 F.3d 702 (9th Cir. 2005).

In addition, if any part of the selection process involves consideration of the pre-employment background report, then the "adverse action" rules apply. This means the applicant has the right to receive a copy of the report and the FCRA-compliant statement of his or her rights. Even if the information relied upon was not negative, the rejected applicant still has rights under the FCRA.

For these reasons, pre-employment screening reports are most often utilized at the very end of the selection procedure, after the company has selected a finalist.

6. Can an employer screen some finalists but not others?

Another important consideration in administering a screening program is that once a decision is made to screen for a particular opening, all finalists being considered for that opening should be screened. Selective screenings could raise an inference of discriminatory practice, particularly if the subject is a member of a legally protected group. Furthermore, all individuals who are screened should also be evaluated using the same criteria — for each position, the screening level must be the same for all candidates.

An employer may certainly have different screening requirements for different positions. A maintenance worker does not have to be screened at the same level as a bookkeeper. If there are different screening standards for different positions, an employer should be able to articulate a rational basis as to why some positions are screened differently than others. That typically revolves around the risk associated with the position. However, all maintenance workers should be screened the same way, and all bookkeepers screened the same way. For any particular opening, all candidates must be treated the same.

7. What positions should be screened and what information should be requested?

The level of pre-employment screening a firm should utilize is normally determined by the extent of the risk involved if a firm makes a bad hire. There are two primary reasons a company would perform pre-employment screening:

- ✓ To exercise due diligence in the hiring process, primarily for the protection of co-workers, innocent third parties, and the public; and
- ✓ To protect the company from the legal and financial harm stemming from a bad hire.

Decision Based Upon Due Diligence Considerations

The law requires an employer exercise reasonable care when selecting new employees. Unless a firm is regulated by a state or federal law or by accepted industry standards, there is generally no single accepted industry standard as to what level of care is required in pre-employment screening. Whether a firm meets a standard of reasonableness would, under judgment, likely be determined based upon the totality of all the circumstances and the testimony of expert witnesses. However, given the relatively modest cost of pre-employment screening compared to the harm that can be caused by a bad hire, it is likely that a jury would hold an employer to a high standard. It would be difficult to defend a company against a charge of negligent hiring when the victim's attorney can argue that if the company had spent just another $20.00 on screening, some terrible crime would not have occurred, or a problem or loss could have been avoided.

Decision Based Upon Protecting the Company

Any company needs to protect its own economic and legal interests, and companies with shareholders, in fact, have a duty to take reasonable steps to protect assets.

Employers should consider various levels of background screening that increase in depth as the risk for a bad hire also increases. Certainly an employer is not held to the standard of an FBI level check for each hire. However, given the relatively modest cost of screening compared to the protection afforded, a firm should probably error on the side of more screening than less.

Consider the following factors

1. Does the position have access to money or assets?
2. Does the position carry significant authority or fiduciary responsibility?
3. Does the position have access to members of the public or co-workers so that any propensity to violence would cause harm?
4. Does the position require the worker to go into someone's home?
5. Does the person work with a vulnerable group such as children, the elderly, or people with disabilities?
6. Would the position be difficult to replace in terms of recruitment, hiring and training?
7. Would a falsification of skills, experience, or background put the firm at risk or lower the firm's productivity?
8. Would a bad hire expose the firm to litigation or financial claims from the applicant, co-workers, customers, or the public?
9. What degree of supervision is the worker under?
10. Is the person full-time, part-time, seasonal, temporary, or a volunteer?

Using the above factors, an employer can create a risk matrix for each position. The employer needs to consider the risk inherent in the position and the amount of supervision the position needs.

8. Are there different levels to background screening?

The following are some suggested background screening levels for job candidates:

Screening Level	Recommended Searches
Basic Screening: For entry-level employees, retail, or manufacturing positions, or positions where the employer has internally checked	A full seven-year onsite criminal records check for felonies and misdemeanors, credit report or Social Security and identity check, and driver's license check. The number of counties searched depends

references. Basic Screening is the very least background screening an employer should conduct to maintain due diligence.	upon the risk factors listed above. For maximum protection, an employer may consider doing ALL counties where a person lived, worked, or studied.
Standard Screening: For more responsible positions and permanent hires.	The Basic Screening plus verification of the last three employers and references (if available), and highest post high school education
Extended Screening: For positions involving increased responsibility or supervision of others.	The Basic and Standard Screenings plus checking superior court civil cases for litigation matters that may be job related.
The Integrity Check: For any type of position involving significant responsibility, access to cash or assets, or access to sensitive data or a company's proprietary materials. Especially good for C-Level positions such as CEO & CFO.	Includes everything previously mentioned plus TEN year searches of federal court for criminal and civil cases, employment history verifications, college degrees and professional licenses checks, and for superior court civil lawsuits in the last two counties of residence.

9. What about conditional hiring based upon receipt of the background check report?

An employer can make an offer of employment or begin the employment relationship contingent upon the receipt of an acceptable background report. This may occur when an employer has a difficult position to fill and does not want to chance losing a good candidate. It is recommended that the offer letter contain the following language:

"This offer of employment is conditioned upon the employer's receipt of a pre-employment background screening investigation **that is acceptable to the employer at the employer's sole discretion**."

The suggested language specifies that the report must meet the employer's satisfaction so there can be no debate on what constitutes a satisfactory report.

10. How are orders and forms transmitted?

How an order makes it from the employer to the screening firm depends on the screening firm's technology. If the screening firm has an web system, then the employer has the ability to key in orders online. If the employer is connected in a seamless interface as described earlier, then the order's detail and data will automatically transmit without additional key-in. When paper documentation is a consideration, employers and screening companies may prefer the use of fax machines for order communications.

Even when electronic methods are used, there may still be occasion when a physical piece of paper must be handled. This occurs when a past employer, school, or DMV requires a written release form from the requestor. The screening company may need to contact the employer to obtain a physical copy of the release form. However, technologically advanced firms can provide an online solution where the applicant not only provides an electronic signature, but can use the mouse to create a "wet" signature that should generally satisfy past employers and schools.

11. How long does it take to get the report?

A 72 hour turnaround time for a background report is the general industry standard. It is sometimes expressed as three days, but that does not take into account the fact that the day the report is received may be also a day, depending upon the informant needed, time zones where the information is located, and the time of the day the request is submitted. For example, if a West Coast employer submits a request on a Monday at 4:00 pm P.S.T., and it includes a request for information from courts, schools, or employers on the East Coast, it is already 7:00 on the East Coast. That means that courts, schools and business are closed. That is why it is more accurate to express completion in terms off hours.

In addition, turnaround time can also depend upon the screening firm's technology. Advanced technology allows a screening firm to automatically full some request, such as driving records or Social Security trace reports. Even those requests that need manual fulfillment, a sophisticated system immediately puts the request in queue with no time being lost for data processing.

There can be delays beyond the 72 hours in situations where a CRA has no control. For example, it can take longer than three days if there is a potential name match in a criminal case and the court clerk must obtain records from storage. In addition, schools may be closed during Summer or holidays, or employers may not call back or may have merged, moved, or closed. If a form is unreadable, that can delay a report. Some reports take longer than three days as a matter of course, such as international checks. Sources of potential delay are discussed in the following chapters on criminal record, employment, education and international background checks.

12. How is the report sent back to the employer?

Screening firms using state-of-the-art web-based systems can make reports available to their clients in real time over the Internet. Also, Internet retrieval allows employers to have real-time access to the exact status of the report at any time in order to monitor progress or answer questions from hiring managers. If a criminal search is delayed, an online system can advise the employer about the delay and the estimated time to obtain the information. Reports can also be faxed or emailed to the employer. A CRA will generally require the fax machine be private and secured. A faxed report should have a cover sheet to warn the unauthorized against seeing confidential information.

 When a California, Oklahoma, or Minnesota applicant requests to receive a copy of his or her credit report, the CRA must provide a copy to the applicant at the same time the employer receives the report.

13. What should an employer do with the report when it comes back, and who sees the report?

Because the report contains sensitive and confidential information, all efforts must be made to keep the contents private and only available to decision-makers directly involved in the hiring process. The Report itself, along with the Release and Authorization forms signed by the applicant, should be maintained separately from the employee's personnel file. They should be kept in a relatively secured area, in the same fashion that medical files or sensitive employee matters are kept. These reports should definitely not be made available to supervisors or managers other than those in the hiring approval process. For example, during periodic performance appraisals, an employer would not want a supervisor to have access to a non-performance-related confidential background report.

For screening firms with advanced Internet systems, there is in fact no need to physically download the report since it is available online. The screening firm should be instructed to keep the report in case it may be needed later. However, an employer needs to be assured of Internet security, and the employer needs to maintain a system of strong password protections. It is important that authorized users do not share passwords with those not authorized, nor reveal the password in any manner. Some screening firms require the user to change passwords every thirty days as a security measure.

Typically, reports are returned to either Human Resources or Security Departments. Reports are reviewed for any negative information. If the report is clear, then the hiring manager is notified and the hiring proceeds. If there is a red flag or derogatory information, then the information itself is shared with the appropriate decision-makers. The physical report, however, normally stays with HR or Security. This protects against confidential information wrongfully being made known generally within the company.

14. How does an employer review, analyze and utilize the information?

How such information is utilized of course is the crux of the issue for employers. In the following chapters outlining various types of information employers may review from background screening reports, specific issues are disused. Generally however, there are areas of concern for employers:

✓ **Honesty:** If the background check reveals dishonesty on the part of the applicant that is a matter the employer must consider. A lack of honesty is normally a bar to employment. As set out in more detail in Chapter 7, if an applicant is dishonest in the manner they obtain a job, there is a strong likelihood they will demonstrate dishonesty once in the job.

Dishonesty can either be a material lie or a material omission where the applicant deceived an employer by intentionally omitting information. A material omission is not necessarily a failure to admit matters that are potentially adverse on their face, such as a criminal matter. Many employers find it equally troublesome if an applicant lies about date of employment, or gives false dates in such a way to hide a significant past employer out of concern that the past employer may respond negatively to a reference call.

When analyzing dishonesty, the two important issues are materiality and willfulness.

- **Materiality** means that the lie or omission was about something relevant and important, as opposed to a minor manner where an applicant may have simply glossed over something that did not seem relevant, such as a temporary job years ago.

- **Willfulness** means that the applicant was not confused or, misinformed or forgetful, but made a conscious decision to mislead the employer. For example, if an applicant checks a box on an employment application to indicate he has NO criminal record, and it is discovered that the applicant has a failure to appear in court to handle a traffic ticket. Or, an applicant fails to report a misdemeanor conviction and when confronted informs HR that he lawyer told her that the matter was all taken care of and she no does need to admit to anyone.   At that point, the employer needs to determine whether there was an intentional act of dishonesty The appoint may have assumed that the employer was not interested in traffic matters or the applicant did not in fact know there was a warrant for his arrest. A related issue is whether the application form was clear or was the question murky and confusing. Unfortunately, there is no surefire test for an employer, human resources or security professional to ascertain if an applicant was being willfully dishonest. It depends upon the totality of the circumstances and how the decision maker accesses the creditability of the applicant.

✓ **Lack of Credentials:** The background repot may show the applicant did not possess the job prerequisites and therefore does not qualify for the position (which may also potentially act of dishonestly).

✓ **Disbarment or Disqualification:** A background checks ma shoe that an applicant is on disbarment or sanctions list that eliminates them from consideration.

✓ **Past Conduct Inconsistent with Business Needs:** It is often observed that past conduct is the most reliable indication of future conduct, and that it is unlikely that an applicant will perform better for you than they did in the past. Of course, that is a gross generalization, and certainly is not true for everyone. Job applicants should not be forever saddled with their past or an assumption that people do not change. For example, an applicant may not have performed well in the past, but it could have been due to being a member of a dysfunctional team, led by a micromanager, where the team had no clear goals, agenda or resources. The impact of past criminal records is discussed in Chapters 14 to 16.

15. What does a CRA do about information that an employer is not supposed to have?

Some CRA's carefully monitor their reports to ensure that no information is given to an employer that violates the various rules concerning limitations on what employers can and cannot use in making employment decisions. However, this is a tricky area. A CRA is not acting as an attorney and cannot make legal decisions. On the other hand, there are clear industry accepted practices about what an employer cannot have. Firms with expertise and technology can build into software a great deal of intelligence in order to have the information needed to analyze a criminal records, for example, to determine if its reportable under generally accepted industry standards.

Some CRA's take the position they are primarily data conduits to the employer, and it is the employer's obligation to not utilize any information an employer should not have. An employer should carefully consider this issue in selecting a service provider.

An employer may not be clear how their screening firm operates on this issue and not realize if a screening firm does not do any filtering, the employer may be using information they are not supposed to possess.

16. How long should forms signed by applicants and applicant records be kept?

Record keeping requirements for employers can vary in accordance to the type of document in question. However, it is generally advisable for an employer to maintain all paperwork concerning the formation of the employment relationship for a period of at least three years from the termination of any relationship. That means if a person is hired, the report and all related screening documentation should be kept during the entire employment relationship and for three years after termination. If an applicant is screened and an employment relationship does not occur, then the reports and documents should be maintained for three years from the date of the report. The three-year period should cover any statute of limitations in the event of a claim or lawsuit.

However, as outlined in Chapter 3, the 2003 FCRA amendment changed the applicable statute of limitations for claims under the FCRA to up to five years for **records concerning pre-employment screening by a CRA**. An employer and consumer reporting agency should maintain records concerning pre-employment screening by a CRA for at least six years following a screening, based upon the five-year statue, and an extra year to reflect the amount of time states generally allow to serve a lawsuit. Employers utilizing the services of a CRA with an advanced Internet system may have the ability to archive the reports permanently.

There are two reasons why employer should also maintain the background screening authorization forms and disclosure forms as well as any other forms related to ordering a screening report for the same period of time.

1. First, they may be needed to prove that the employer had consent for a screening report and a permissible purpose under the FCRA.

2. Second, if a screening firm is audited by a data provider (such as a state motor vehicle department), the applicant's consent may be needed by both the background firm and the employer to demonstrate that the request for information was legal.

Many background firms require in their contracts with employers that all such documents will be maintained by the employer and provided to the CRA if necessary for an audit. If there is an electronic signature, then this data needs to be preserved as well.

17. What does an employer do if they decide not to hire an applicant?

If an employer decides to take any type of adverse action regarding an application for employment, based in any way upon information contained in a screening report, the provisions of the FCRA come into play. At that point, it is the employer's responsibility to first provide the applicant with a copy of the report and a statement of the consumer's rights. If the applicant does not contest the report and the decision stands, then the employer must send a second notice to the applicant under Section 615 of the FCRA notifying the applicant of a number of specific rights.

An employer does NOT need to specify exactly why an applicant was rejected. The procedures set forth in the FCRA only require the applicant have an opportunity to review the background report prior to an adverse action being taken and be given a statement of his or her rights. If the decision is made final, the applicant then receives a letter indicating the action has been made final and was based in part upon the consumer report. See Chapter 3 on the FCRA for more details and sample notices.

Some CRA's will provide all the necessary notices to the applicant. Under the rules of the FCRA, although it is the employer's responsibility to provide the pre-adverse and post-adverse action notices, that duty can be delegated to an agent such as a screening firm. If the applicant disagrees with any of the information contained in the report, then the applicant communicates directly to the CRA. The CRA has a duty under the FCRA to re-investigate within 30 days — up to 45 days under certain circumstances. The employer, however, has no obligation to keep the position open during the re-investigation period.

In addition, under the 2012 EEOC Guidance on criminal records, employers should also consider conducting an Individualized Assessment. See Chapter 16.

Extension of 30-Day Period to Reinvestigate Disputed Information

From 15 USC § 1681i - Procedure in case of disputed accuracy

(a) Reinvestigations of disputed information

(1) Reinvestigation required

(A) In general

Subject to subsection (f) of this section, if the completeness or accuracy of any item of information contained in a consumer's file at a consumer reporting agency is disputed by the consumer and the consumer notifies the agency directly, or indirectly through a reseller, of such dispute, the agency shall, free of charge, conduct a reasonable reinvestigation to determine whether the disputed information is inaccurate and record the current status of the disputed information, or delete the item from the file in accordance with paragraph (5), before the end of the 30-day period beginning on the date on which the agency receives the notice of the dispute from the consumer or reseller.

(B) Extension of period to reinvestigate

Except as provided in subparagraph (C), the 30-day period described in subparagraph (A) may be extended for not more than 15 additional days if the consumer reporting agency receives information from the consumer during that 30-day period that is relevant to the reinvestigation.

(C) Limitations on extension of period to reinvestigate

Subparagraph (B) shall not apply to any reinvestigation in which, during the 30-day period described in subparagraph (A), the information that is the subject of the reinvestigation is found to be inaccurate or incomplete or the consumer reporting agency determines that the information cannot be verified.

---

18. Is there the possibility of legal liability if an employer rejects an applicant as a result of a screening report?

When an employer follows the procedures in the FCRA, and also makes all hiring decisions utilizing legal and job related-reasons, the chances of a lawsuit from a rejected applicant are minimized. However, no employer can ever make itself immune from a lawsuit. Anyone with enough money to cover the court's filing fee can go to the court and file a lawsuit. The real issue is whether the benefits from a pre-employment screening program outweigh the risks.

If an employer intends to take adverse action based upon a background report, an applicant must first be provided with a copy of the report and a statement of his or her rights. Because of this procedure, an applicant will have the chance to correct anything in a report that is incorrect or inaccurate. If the information is inaccurate, the applicant will have the opportunity to object and to offer a correction. At that point, the employer can proceed with the hire. Under the previous system where applicants did not have to be told their reports contained negative or derogatory information, employers ran a greater risk of making hiring decisions based upon incorrect information.

19. How can a firm conduct pre-employment screening without interfering with recruitment or employee morale?

In performing pre-employment screening, it is important not to damage the bond of trust a firm seeks to develop with their employees. HR and Security departments are placed in a difficult position. The firm does not want to make bad hires, but also cannot afford to use a process that alienates its employees or interferes with recruiting. Furthermore, obnoxious background procedures will discourage good applicants. In other words, an employer does not want to diminish their "employer branding" in a way to hamper recruiting top talent or by making the employer a seemingly less desirable place to work. Some background investigators start with the proposition that all applicants are potential criminals until they prove otherwise — applicants may not want to work for a firm that treats them that way.

The solution is to make it clear to applicants that pre-employment screening is a sound business practice benefiting not only the company, but all employees as well. No one wants to work with an unqualified person who obtained the job under false pretext or with a co-worker with an undisclosed criminal record. Once an applicant understands the process is not a reflection on him or her, but is actually for their benefit as well, they will understand this is a good thing for a company to do.

Furthermore, the applicant should be assured all procedures used will respect his or her rights to privacy, all information is kept strictly confidential and is used only for employment purposes, and all legal rights are respected. Furthermore, the scope of the investigation should be clearly job-related.

20. What should go into a background screening contract?

Because of the FCRA employer certification requirement, there must be a written agreement between the background firm and the employer. An agreement between an employer and CRA contains several areas. First, there are the legally required employer FCRA certifications. There may also be required state certifications as well such as the language required by California.

Next, the agreement usually will often lay out other duties, such as an employer's duty to keep matters confidential and passwords secured (in order to ensure only those with a permissible see the reports), the duty to only utilize the report for employment screening purposes and the duty to follow all laws and regulations. An agreement will review the duties of the CRA, such as the duties to use best efforts for accuracy, to follow the FCRA and all applicable laws and regulations, and to re-investigate any disputed information. Other advisements typically include advising the employer that a CA does not give legal advice, and reminding the employer of their duty to provide adverse action notices.

There is not widely accepted national standard industry form. Some employment law firms have prepared summaries of the minimum FCRA requirements that must be in a background screening employer certification. The NAPBS Accreditation Program reviewed in Chapter 11 uses certain clauses that are considered best practices to add. See: www.napbs.com/files/public/Consumer_Education/Accreditation/NAPBS_Standard_with_Audit_Criteria_030209.pdf. These include:

- ✓ "3.1 – CRA shall have procedures in place to inform client of client's legal responsibilities when using consumer reports for employment purposes or shall have resources to direct client to this information. CRA shall advise client to consult their legal counsel regarding their specific legal responsibilities. These legal responsibilities include:
  - Having permissible purpose,
  - Disclosing to consumer,
  - Obtaining consumer authorization,
  - Following prescribed adverse action procedures,
  - Complying with all applicable state and federal law, and
  - Obtaining, retaining, using, and destroying data in a confidential manner.

✓ 3.4 – CRA shall advise client that there are legal requirements imposed by the federal FCRA and, in some instances, state consumer reporting laws, regarding taking adverse action against a consumer based on a consumer report. CRA shall advise client that they should consult their legal counsel prior to taking adverse action.

✓ 3.6 – CRA shall communicate to client that they are not acting as legal counsel and cannot provide legal advice. CRA shall communicate to client the importance of working with counsel to develop an employment screening program specific to their needs. CRA shall also communicate to client the necessity to work with counsel to ensure that client's policies and procedures related to the use of CRA-provided information are in compliance with applicable state and federal laws.

✓ A CRA shall provide information to client regarding (1) the sensitive nature of consumer reports, (2) the need to protect such information and (3) the consumer report retention and destruction practices as outlined in the federal FCRA and the DPPA (Drivers Privacy Protection Act)."

Agreements will also cover business terms with many provisions reflecting the same language appearing in any agreement with a service provider. However, there are some unique matters that often arise in background screening agreements.

Mistakes and Guarantees

An issue that often surfaces is the degree of a screening firm's liability in the event of a mistake. Screening firms will typically have language that protects them or their vendors, suppliers, officers and employees from liability from ordinary negligence. That is because a screening firm does not make or maintain the data on the record's being reported. If a court clerk or a past employer conveys incorrect information, and the background firm has used reasonable procedures, than any error is not the fault of the screening firm. (Of course, an employer may argue a screening firm should be responsible for it's own negligence.) A screening contract will also typically include a clause that in no event shall either party be liable to the other party for any special, incidental, consequential or punitive damages arising out of this agreement. This is because the screening firm is only playing one role in the entire hiring process. The screening firm typically does not have contact with the applicant and is not involved in the interview or other process. For the services charged, a screening firm cannot in effect provide any guarantee or insurance that the applicant will work out. In addition, a screening firm has no way to positively identify an applicant and cannot be responsible for identification.

Some employers require a turnaround time guarantee, sometime as part of a Service Level Agreement (SLA). However, a screening firm can only guarantee their own work. If a court clerk delays results, or a school is closed for vacation or an employer reuses to return a phone call, there is little a screening firm can do about it.

Some of larger screening firms may request a guaranteed contract period in exchange for price concessions. Employers need to judge this carefully. Screening is a professional knowledge based service in a complex legal environment. Normally, professional services are not subject to a contract period. If the service is not satisfactory, an employer may want the option to make adjustments.

Another area is a screening firm's security. Although large employers are accustomed to requesting a report called a SAS 70 audit demonstrating security procedures, or similar reports, they may not be applicable when hiring a screening service. For example, if a firm shows it is accredited by NAPBS, being PCI compliant as well as having security and data protection policies is likely more important than a formal SAS 70 audit.

AUTHOR TIP There are a number of online sites that offer all sorts of data on consumers including pre-employment background checks. If the site does not prominently mention the FCRA or require a written agreement that contains the above material, DO NOT use for employment background checks. Background checks are subject to intense legal regulation, legislation, and litigating. An employer that uses a do-it-yourself online service without the proper compliance is putting their organization at extreme risk. For an example of this risk, read the section 'FTC Fines Data Broker $800,000 Dollars to Settle Charges of Violating FCRA' in Chapter 3.

Chapter 13

A Criminal Record Primer

Inside This Chapter:

✓ Crime and Punishment – The Abridged Version

✓ State Courts

✓ Federal Crimes and Federal Courts

✓ Classifying Crimes by Seriousness

✓ Criminal Sanctions

✓ Other Important Criminal Record Terms

✓ The Million Dollar Question – How to Judge the Seriousness of a Criminal Conviction

✓ Glossary of Criminal Terms

Crime and Punishment – The Abridged Version

The following is a brief introduction to the criminal justice system for employers, human resources professionals, and security professionals who utilize criminal records. The purpose is to assist a user in understanding a potential criminal record when making an employment decision. Keep in mind that, in addition to federal law, each state and U.S. territory has its own law. Consequently, our "Abridged Version" is intended as a general introduction to criminal law and procedures only, and users need to take additional steps to understand the appropriate rules and procedures in any relevant jurisdictions.

A crime is an act or omission that is prosecuted in a criminal court by a government prosecutor and can be punished by confinement, fine, restitution and/or a forfeiture of certain civil rights. Legislative bodies such as state legislature or the U.S. Congress decide what acts or omissions are against the law. Such prohibited criminal acts are published by a legislative body as part of a "code." For example, in California, criminal acts are published primarily in the California Penal Code. However, criminal acts can be defined in other codes as well — certain drug offenses are contained in the California Health and Safety Code. Federal crimes are defined in the United States Codes.

When a person is charged with a crime, the plaintiff is the prosecuting attorney who brings the criminal case in the name of The People or the government. In a civil case, a private party brings a tort action for monetary damages.

> ### Here is an Example
>
> Assume Jack D. Ripper assaults Stewart Victim with a knife in California. Jack is caught and arrested shortly afterward. If Jack is prosecuted for the crime in state court, the case is called *"The People of the State of California vs. Jack D. Ripper."* If Stewart Victim sued Jack for damages in civil court, then that would be a TORT case. That case would be titled *"S. Victim vs. Jack D. Ripper."*

A criminal case can be brought in either a federal court or a state court. When a criminal case is brought in a **state court**, a County Prosecutor initiates it. Every county has its own state court. In some circumstances, a local law or ordinance may bring lesser charges by a city or municipal attorney. When charges are brought in **federal court**, a Federal Assistant U.S. Attorney (AUSA), who is part of the United States Justice Department, initiates it.

Some sort of **accusation** initiates a criminal charge. The accusation is typically brought by a prosecuting authority against the person arrested, either pursuant to an arrest warrant or a warrantless arrest by a law enforcement agent who had probable cause to believe a felony had been committed. In the case of a misdemeanor arrest, there is generally a requirement that it be committed in the presence of a law enforcement officer, but there are certain exceptions.

Depending upon the jurisdiction, the accusation is commenced with some sort of **charging** document. The charging document may be known by such terms as a complaint, information, or indictment. For serious charges, called felonies, there is typically a "probable cause" determination before a trial in which there is a judicial determination that there is sufficient evidence for a trial to go forward. The standard of proof is just that it is more likely than not that a crime occurred and the defendant committed the crime. This is a much lower standard than proof beyond a reasonable doubt, which is needed in order to achieve a conviction. In some jurisdictions, the probable cause determination is accomplished by some sort of hearing before a magistrate or judge, sometimes referred to as a preliminary or probable cause hearing. In other jurisdictions, and typically in federal courts, there is a **grand jury indictment**.

State courts generally have three levels — the trial courts, an intermediate appellate court, and the highest appellate court. Furthermore, in many states, trial courts are further divided into a lower court, which typically hear misdemeanor and preliminary criminal matters such as probable cause hearings and felony trial courts. Certain states also have higher and lower civil courts, divided by a monetary limit. Other states have unified the trial court system so there is no upper and lower trial court.

Federal courts also have three levels. The federal courts where trials are heard are called a **Federal District Court**. There are 94 Federal District Courts. Each state has at least one district court. Larger states will have up to four district courts. For example, New York State has four district courts – Eastern District, Northern District, Southern District, and Western District. Furthermore, district courts can have various divisions. The Southern District of New York for example has divisions in New York City and White Plains. The New York City Federal District Court only covers Bronx and Manhattan boroughs. Other boroughs are under jurisdiction of the Eastern Division which includes Queens, Kings, Richmond boroughs, and the two Long Island counties

The federal courts also have intermediate appellate courts called United States Circuit Courts. The U.S. Circuit Courts are divided into thirteen circuits. For example, the Ninth Circuit hears appeals from the nine western-most states and two territories, Guam and the Marianas Is.

The highest court in the land is the United States Supreme Court, with nine members nominated by the President for a lifetime term, approved by the United States Senate, and headed by the Chief Justice of the United States.

State Courts

If a person is convicted of a crime in STATE court, several things can happen:

✓ **Sentenced to State Prison**. A state prison is an institution that is administered by the state, as opposed to a local county jail. In other words, a state prison will accept a prisoner from any county in the state. Sometimes the prison is referred to as the "Big House," such as San Quentin Prison in California, or Sing-Sing in New York. Depending upon your generation, think James Cagney in *White Heat* or Tim Robbins in *The Shawshank Redemption*.

✓ **Sentenced to County Jail**. A county jail is run by the local sheriff and accepts prisoners from the local county. Every county, parish, or borough in the U.S. has a local jail.

✓ **Fined**. A person convicted of a crime can have a fine imposed.

There are two other important terms to consider— **Probation and Parole**.

✓ **Probation** — Probation means in exchange for not giving a defendant his or her full jail sentence, a judge has imposed terms and conditions of behavior on a convicted criminal defendant. Probation occurs on the county level at a state court. Assume for example a defendant is convicted of a drug crime that carries a potential sentence of one year in the county jail. Instead of sentencing the defendant to jail for the entire year, the judge can impose just 90 days and hold the rest of the sentence in abeyance as long as the defendant obeys the terms of his or her probation. Typical terms of probation may include:

- Violate no law or ordinance
- Participate in a drug rehabilitation program
- Pay a fine
- Pay restitution, if applicable
- Perform community service
- Submit to search and seizure upon request by a police officer without a warrant or probable cause
- Do not possess any item connected to the crime. For example, in a drug case a person will have a term and condition to not possess drugs or drug paraphernalia

If a defendant violates the probation by not adhering to the terms or conditions, then the defendant can be sentenced to jail for the remainder of the sentence. In other words, when a defendant is on probation, the unused jail time is like a reverse bank account being held in reserve — if he or she misbehaves, then the judge can impose more jail time.

✓ **Parole** — When a person is sentenced to prison, he is placed on parole when released. That is an important difference when compared to probation. If a person violates his parole, then he can be sent back to state prison.

A parole officer is employed by the state, while the local county government employs a probation officer. As a practical matter, parole is out of the hands of the county judge or prosecutor and is instead handled by the state.

The actual sentence a defendant receives in state court depends upon a number of factors. There may be minimum or maximum penalties set forth by statute. For certain crimes, a defendant is not eligible for probation and MUST go to state prison. This can occur where the crime is serious, such as certain sexual offenses or an offense using a weapon, or where by statute the person is classified as a repeat offender, such as a third strike in a three-strike case.

If a defendant is eligible for probation, a court will look a mitigating and aggravating factors of the crime and factors about the defendant to determine if probation is appropriate. If a person is sentenced to prison and a court has some sentencing discretion in terms of the length of sentence, the court again looks at mitigating and aggravating facts about the offender and the offense. A mitigating factor may be for example a lack of a record, the young age of a defendant, or the defendant's minor role in the offense. Examples of aggravating factors are:

- The defendant has a history of committing offenses,
- Committed an offense while on parole or probation,
- The offense was particularly violent.

Urban Myth: A Current License Means a Person has NO Criminal Record

A popular urban myth is that members of regulated and licensed professions, such as doctors, lawyers, CPA's, nurses or teachers do not need a background check because some governmental agency is in charge of ensuring that individuals that commit crimes or misconduct will not have a license to practice their profession. Unfortunately, nothing can be further from the truth.

Licensing is conducted by numerous state occupational licensing boards in the 50 states and territories. The system for a licensing board to discover a criminal conviction is far from perfect. It is entirely possible for an applicant with a criminal action that would forbid licensing to be licensed by the state agency, per the following:

1. Conviction data may not be sent to a licensing board immediately or at all. In addition, there can be a substantial lag time between the alleged criminal act, the arrest, and the conviction.

2. Even if the criminal conviction is discovered by the licensing board, the disciplinary process takes time. Unless the licensing board takes action to issue an immediate suspension, the licensee may be able to continue to practice while the administrative procedures drag on.

3. While the disciplinary action is pending, a licensee may simply move to another state and apply for a license, covering up the proceedings in the first state. In other words, a licensee may try to "beat the discipline" before the new state finds out about it.

4. Even if a person is suspended in one state, an employer cannot assume that all state licensing boards share information with each other. As we discovered post 9/11, we do not live in a world where the government routinely collects and shares data with other governmental entities.

5. There can even be situations where a person commits a crime that does not result in losing a license but is still important for an employer to know about. In fact, in some licensed occupations, a person may even get a "private" reprimand meaning that a check with the appropriate licensing board may not reveal anything.

The bottom line: Employers that hire a member of a licensed or regulated occupation cannot assume that they are immune from liability simply because a person appears to have a current license. Since it is possible for criminal conviction or act of misconduct to "fall through the crack," an employer still has a duty to exercise due diligence by its own independent background check.

For a listing of the numerous state agencies that license occupations including and those that offer free search capabilities, see: www.brbpublications.com/pubrecsitesOccStates.asp.

Federal Crimes and Federal Courts

Persons convicted in federal court and sentenced to prison fall under the authority of the Federal Bureau of Prisons (BOP). The BOP operates a federal prison system throughout the United States. Think of such institutions such as the old Alcatraz Federal Prison that housed such famous federal prisoners as the Birdman of Alcatraz and Al Capone, or the well-known Leavenworth Federal Penitentiary in Kansas, or "Club Fed," the popular name for the low security federal institutions where Watergate Conspiracy participants and white collar criminals like Martha Stewart have spent time.

Federal prisoners currently serve about 87% of their sentence. The remaining portion can be spent on parole, supervised by the U.S. Probation office. Federal defendants not sent to prison are supervised by the U.S. Probation office and subject to probation terms and conditions.

Similar to state systems, a federal defendant can also be sentenced to a federal version of probation. This may include "local time" on a supervised program under the direction of a federal probation officer.

The maximum and minimum sentences for federal crimes are set forth in the code section defining the crime. The factors that go into a sentence — and that serve to mitigate or aggravate a sentence — are found in the Federal Sentencing Guidelines.

Classifying Crimes by Seriousness

Criminal acts can be classified into three distinct categories based upon the potential sentence:

Felony

A Felony is a serious offense that is punishable by a sentence to a state prison. Note the use of the word punishable, as opposed to actually punished. The distinction is important because a person can be convicted of a felony but may not go to prison. How does that work? Depending upon the state and the crime, there are certain felonies wherein a judge can give a defendant felony probation. This typically occurs with a relatively less-serious felony committed by a relatively less-serious offender. An example may be a first time felony drug offender convicted of a less-serious drug offense such as possession of a small amount of drugs for sale. If a defendant receives felony probation, the court can still sentence him/her to custody but in the local county jail. If the defendant violates his/her probation, the court then has the option of sending the defendant to state prison. That obviously creates a great deal of incentive for a felony defendant to not violate probation.

Misdemeanor

A Misdemeanor is a less serious offense that is only punishable by local jail time at the county level. Typically a misdemeanor may be punishable by up to one year in the county jail in the custody of the local county sheriff and a fine up to $1,000. A court can also impose terms and conditions of probation such as discussed above. However, there are drawbacks to assuming that a misdemeanor is less serious in all cases then a felony. As noted below, misdemeanors can be extremely serious.

Infraction

An Infraction is a public offense punishable only by a fine. This is typically a traffic violation such as an illegal left turn, speeding, or seat belt not fastened.

There are two reasons that a misdemeanor can still be a very serious matter, even though it carries the possibility of a lower sentence then a felony:

Wobbler or Hybrid Crime

Criminal laws become even more complicated because there are a number of offenses that can be charged as EITHER a felony or a misdemeanor. For example, grand theft is typically a felony that involves a larger amount of money stolen than a petty theft. However, in many states, a District Attorney can choose to charge such an offense as a misdemeanor instead of a felony. In some states, a judge can also reduce a felony to a misdemeanor if the offense is a wobbler. This decision can be based upon a number of factors, including mitigating information about the accused, the alleged crime, the behavior, or the harm. For example, a person who has no record and faced some degree of provocation commits assault with the intent to commit great bodily injury could be charged with a misdemeanor offense instead of a felony.

 AUTHOR TIP For a number of real world reasons, the eventual status of a hybrid crime can have little or nothing to do with the seriousness of the crime, but instead relate to a number of unpredictable variables in the criminal justice system. Very serious conduct may end up as a misdemeanor because of court overcrowding resulting in plea bargains, critical evidence being excluded pursuant to a motion to suppress, a critical witness may be reluctant to testify, unskilled attorneys can impact the outcome, or a jury may reach a compromise verdict. The only time that an employer can assume with some level of confidence that a misdemeanor is a less serious offense is where the crime charged can only be charged as a misdemeanor offense, which means that the legislature has made a determination that in all cases, the highest punishment can only be at a misdemeanor level.

Plea Bargaining

To add to the complication, in many states, a defendant may be able to plea bargain a felony to a misdemeanor. This can happen for any number of reasons, including overcrowded court calendars, witness problems for the District Attorney, a prosecutor who is just not inclined to prosecute the case to a jury, or some equitable facts about the crime or the defendant that convinces a District Attorney to plea bargain. The importance of understanding the role of pleas escalated with the 2012 EEOC Guidance on the use of criminal records. The problem is that the eventual disposition in terms of either being a felony or misdemeanor may have nothing to do with the seriousness of the underlying conduct.

YOU NEED TO KNOW **Dispositions**

One word that appears in this chapter frequently is "disposition," which means the final outcome in a criminal case. For example, if a case is dismissed, the defendant pleads guilty, or a judge or jury finds the defendant guilty, that is the disposition of the case. The word can also be used more broadly to include the terms and conditions of a sentence, if the person is found guilty. An example of disposition may be that a "defendant was found guilty, given three years informal probation the terms and conditions of which are to serve 10 days in the county jail with 3 days credit for time served, perform 50 hours of community service, and during the three year probation period break no law or ordinance, and not use or possess alcohol or a controlled substance." Sometimes criminal lawyers will use the short hand term "dispo," such as "what was the dispo in that case?"

At the end of this chapter is a glossary of terms associated with criminal proceedings and files.

Understanding that misdemeanors can in fact reflect very serious conduct becomes important in the context of evaluating criminal matters pursuant to the EEOC updated Enforcement Guidance on the Consideration of Arrest and Conviction

Records in Employment Decisions Under Title VII of the Civil Rights Act of 1964 issued April 25, 2012. The EEOC Guidance (covered in detail in Chapter 16), the EEOC provides:

Careful consideration of the nature and gravity of the offense or conduct is the first step in determining whether a specific crime may be relevant to concerns about risks in a particular position. The nature of the offense or conduct may be assessed with reference to the harm caused by the crime (e.g., theft causes property loss). The legal elements of a crime also may be instructive. For example, a conviction for felony theft may involve deception, threat, or intimidation.115 With respect to the gravity of the crime, offenses identified as misdemeanors may be less severe than those identified as felonies.

It is noteworthy that the EEOC does recognize that misdemeanors "may" be less serious than felonies. The table below indicates how state court offenses are carried out.

State Court Offenses Table

	Sentence	Supervisor
Felony	State prison or local jail time or felony probation	If sentenced to prison – placed upon parole upon release from state prison and supervised by a parole officer. If given probation – supervised by local probation office.
Misdemeanor	Up to one year in a local county jail	If probation – supervised by local probation officer who works for the county where the sentence is imposed.
Infraction	A fine only.	No custody or supervision.

Classifying Crimes by Types

Another way to classify criminal behavior is by the type of crimes. Although there is no one accepted standard, a typical breakdown of types of crimes is shown below:

Crimes against the Person

A crime that is committed using direct harm or force against the victim is a crime against the person. These crimes are typically the most serious and include acts such as murder, robbery, child molestation, kidnapping, or rape. Because of the seriousness or potential harm, these offenses are typically felonies. However, there are a number of offenses that can be wobbler/hybrid so that they can be either a felony or misdemeanor. For example, assault crimes can vary widely in their seriousness and can be either a felony or misdemeanor depending upon factors such as the nature of the offender, the degree of harm, and the details surrounding the offenses. Some authorities place sexual offenses in a separate category.

Crimes against Property

A crime committed by damaging, destroying, or intruding on the property of another is a crime against the property victim. Example can be arson, vandalism, burglary, or trespassing. Some property crimes also carry with them elements of crimes against the person or theft. For example, a burglary committed for the purposes of harming someone inside of a house, can be both a crime against property and a person. A burglary committed with the intent to steal from inside the house, carries an element of theft. Many property crimes that only involved a threat to property, and do not involve a threat of harm or an element of theft, can be misdemeanors. Other offenses such as arson are typically classified as felonies because of the large potential dangers involved.

Theft and Fraud Crimes

Theft is the taking of another person's property without that person's permission or consent with the intent to deprive the rightful owner of it. **Fraud** is an intentional deception made for personal gain or to damage another individual. A related offense is embezzlement which is the act of dishonestly appropriating assets by one or more individuals to whom such assets have been entrusted. There are a great many such crimes, all revolving around dishonesty. These crimes are categorized as a felony or misdemeanor depending upon factors such as the value of the stolen property, the sophistication involved, the method used, and the history of the offender. A related offense is robbery, which is the taking of money or goods in the possession of another, from his or her person or immediate presence, by force or intimidation. Robbery involves elements of both theft and a crime against persons and is typically a felony. Armed robbery means a weapon was used. The difference between petty theft and grand theft is the amount taken. However some jurisdictions provide that a person with a previous petty theft can be charged with a felony if there is a second petty theft. Robbery, which is the taking of property from another using force, is classified as a felony.

Crimes against the Public Order, Health, and Morals

There are crimes based upon acts that have been determined by a legislature to be needed to preserve public order, health, and morals. Some examples include prostitution, disorderly conduct, vagrancy, public lewdness, and prostitution. Crimes against public order are generally considered misdemeanors. However, if a child is involved, crimes in the category may be considered more serious and could be a felony level offense. This is a broad catch-all category that can include traffic related offenses, as well as violation of health or licensing ordinances. A Failure to Appear (FTA) in court after an arrest including a traffic ticket may be another example.

Substance Related Crimes

Crimes relating to substances can include simple possession of drugs for personal use, possession for purposes of sale, the sale or transportations of drugs, or the manufacturing of drugs. Driving under the influence can also be included. Again, the criteria for the punishment of such crimes as a felony, misdemeanor, or infracting depends upon the crime and the alleged criminal.

National Incident-Based Reporting System (NIBRS)

Another way of breaking down crimes is by reference to the reporting structure of the **National Incident-Based Reporting System (NIBRS)**. This is a mechanism for law enforcement reporting of criminal incidents to the FBI. (See www.policeforum.org/library/nibrs/Data_Systems_for_Policing.pdf for details on how this system was developed).

It is broken down into Category A and B offenses as follows:

Group A Offenses

1. Arson
2. Assault (Aggravated, Simple, Intimidation)
3. Bribery
4. Burglary/Breaking and Entering
5. Counterfeiting/Forgery
6. Destruction/Damage/Vandalism of Property
7. Drug/Narcotic Offenses (including drug equipment violations)
8. Embezzlement
9. Extortion/Blackmail

10. Fraud (false pretenses/swindle/confidence game, credit card and ATM fraud, impersonation, welfare, and wire fraud)
11. Gambling (betting, wagering, operating/promoting/assisting gambling, gambling equipment violations, sports tampering)
12. Homicide (murder and non-negligent manslaughter, negligent manslaughter, justifiable homicide)
13. Kidnapping/Abduction
14. Larceny (pocket picking, purse snatching, shoplifting, theft and all other larceny)
15. Motor Vehicle Theft
16. Pornography/Obscene Material
17. Prostitution Offenses (prostitution, assisting or promoting prostitution)
18. Robbery
19. Sex Offenses, Forcible (forcible rape, forcible sodomy, sexual assault with an object, forcible fondling)
20. Sex Offenses, Non-forcible (incest, statutory rape)
21. Stolen Property Offenses/Fence
22. Weapon Law Violations

Group B Offenses

1. Bad Checks
2. Curfew/Loitering/Vagrancy Violations
3. Disorderly Conduct
4. Driving Under the Influence
5. Drunkenness
6. Family Offenses, Nonviolent
7. Liquor Law Violations
8. Peeping Tom
9. Runaway
10. Trespass of Real Property
11. All Other Offenses

Criminal Sanctions

There are five general purposes for criminal sanctions:

1. **Punishment.** When a person violates the rules of society, imprisonment is used for pure punishment and revenge.
2. **Deterrence of others**. By punishing an offender, there is a possibility that others will be deterred from committing criminal offenses because they can see that such behavior results in certain punishment.
3. **Deterrence of the criminal in the future**. There is also an element of personal deterrence. If a person learns that criminal activity will result in punishment, then he or she may be less likely to commit a crime in the future.
4. **Rehabilitation.** Part of any sentencing scheme can be the goal of using punishment to effect rehabilitation. With the goal of dissuading future criminal conduct, the rehabilitation can be either by means of personal

deterrence as noted above or by using some program intended to actively assist an offender to resolve problems that create criminal behavior, such as a mandatory drug program or educational program.

5. **Protecting society.** Another use of punishment is to simply warehouse offenders so they cannot harm society.

Other Important Criminal Record Terms

Arrest vs. Conviction — In discussing criminal records, it is also important to note the critical difference between an **arrest, a conviction**, and a pending mater.

An arrest is an action by a police officer in taking a person into custody on suspicion of having committed a criminal violation. An arrest does not always result in a person being taken to jail. An arrest can also be a citation to appear in court. (See Chapter 15 on the limitations of using an arrests under EEOC guidelines, and Chapter 4 concerning state laws that also limit the consideration of an arrest.)

A conviction occurs where there has been a factual adjudication of guilt. That can be done by a jury trial where 12 jurors make a finding of guilt beyond a reasonable doubt (NOTE: typically there are 12 jurors, but certain courts allow less). Or, a person can be found guilty by a judge in a court trial, where a judge makes the decision if the defendant waives the right to a jury trial. Guilt can also be judicially established where a defendant admits his or her guilt. This can occur when a defendant pleads guilty to the criminal charge. It can also occur if a defendant pleads no contest. In criminal courts, a no contest is the same as a guilty plea, but gives a defendant some protection in the event of a civil law suit.

A pending matter is where an arrest is still pending in court because the prosecuting attorney has filed a charge, but no facts have yet been adjudicated, and there is no disposition. This is a gray area status since the case has not either been terminated in favor of the defendant, but there has also been no factual adjudication by either a jury or court trial, or a guilty plea. In California, for example, Labor Code Section 432.7 appears to allow consideration of a pending case, since an essential function of any job is to show up, an unresolved criminal matter presents an issue for an employer since there is no certainty about the outcome. Of course, the more minor the charge, the less likely it is that a person will have substantial jail sentence. The 2012 EEOC Guidance mentioned previously does not appear to address this issue when discussing arrests.

Delayed Adjudication/First Offender Programs — Numerous states have case disposition rules that are somewhere between an arrest and a conviction. These can occur in a number of situations.

For example, some states have a disposition called a *Diversion Program*. This occurs where a first offender for a relatively less serious offense is literally "diverted" from the criminal justice system and allowed to escape the criminal charge if he or she participates in and successfully completes certain court assigned tasks such as a counseling program or volunteer service. One of the most famous diversion case participants is O.J. Simpson. Prior to the death of his wife, Simpson was charged with domestic violence and allowed to participate in a domestic violence diversion program.

States also have diversion programs for such offenses as petty theft or drug use. If there is a violation of the terms of the program or a new arrest, then the court may terminate the diversion and reinstate charges, and the criminal case begins again.

A variation of the diversion program is a *delayed entry of judgment program*. In that program, the defendant actually enters a guilty plea to the offense. However, the court delays entry of the judgment in order to allow the defendant to participate in a prescribed program, which may include a course of counseling and volunteer work. Upon the successful completion of the court's requirements without having any additional violations, the criminal matter is dismissed. In some jurisdictions, there are special drug courts where defendants are given the opportunity to by-pass criminal drug charges if they participate in one or various programs.

Many jurisdictions have first offender programs where a court will discharge the defendant and set aside the conviction upon completion of various conditions, as though the arrest and/or conviction had never occurred. The primary condition is often that the defendant must not get arrested again or must stay away from a particular person. This is often used as a means of dealing with less serious misdemeanor offenses.

Post-Offender Programs — Many states also have various provisions to seal, expunge, or somehow erase a criminal conviction after it occurs. Some states have procedures by which an offender can receive some sort of state pardon or a governor's pardon. There are procedures to have criminal records legally sealed, expunged, or judicially erased in some other fashion.

California has a provision called Penal Code section 1203.4, under which a misdemeanor offender who successfully completes probation can move to have his conviction set-aside and to be relieved of all penalties and dualities. Under California law, an employer may not consider the offense when making an employment decisions.

Under another California law, Labor Code Section 432.7, an employer has the following restrictions:

> *No employer, whether a public agency or private individual or corporation, shall ask an applicant for employment to disclose, through any written form or verbally, information concerning an arrest or detention that did not result in conviction, or information concerning a referral to, and participation in, any pretrial or post trial diversion program, nor shall any employer seek from any source whatsoever, or utilize, as a factor in determining any condition of employment including hiring, promotion, termination, or any apprenticeship training program or any other training program leading to employment, any record of arrest or detention that did not result in conviction, or any record regarding a referral to, and participation in, any pretrial or post trial program.*

Another type of program is called **deferred adjudication**. Texas, for example, has a system whereby a person enters a guilty plea, and a judge may defer the adjudication of guilt pending completion of a probation period. Upon completion of the deferred adjudication, the individual may request that the case be set aside. *Tex. Code Crim. Proc. art. 42.12* provides further that the dismissal and discharge under this section may not be deemed a conviction for the purposes of disqualifications or disabilities imposed by law for conviction of an offense. For additional state court procedures affecting the status of criminal convictions, see Chapter 14.

Urban Myth: Courts Destroy Criminal Records That are Set Aside or Expunged

An Urban Myth that can surprise job applicants is that after a judge vacates, expunges, sets aside, defers the adjudication or otherwise judicially erases a criminal record in some fashion, the records disappear and can never be found.

With limited exceptions, the general rule is that the government does not destroy records. In the typical scenario, even if the judge orders a set aside, the consumer's name can still be found by searching the court indexes and the case can still be viewed as a public record. As a general rule, the only way a background firm knows there has been a judicial set aside is to examine the court file where all court orders should be noted.

Of course each state is different but as a general rule, unless an applicant has been advised by an attorney that the criminal case will be sealed and physically not available anywhere, applicants need to understand that even a criminal case that they thought was erased may still show up.

Even in those situations where the court has ordered the case sealed, the damage may already be done since the record of the case may already reside in a commercial database. If a background firm locates the case in a commercial database, then the background firm has certain obligations under the federal Fair Credit Reporting Act and similar state laws. A background screening firm is required to either notify the applicant that a criminal record is being provided, or must pull and examine the actual court file to ensure accuracy. For employers who want to avoid finding out about criminal records that have been judicially set aside, the best practice it make sure to work with a screening firm that automatically pulls the court file whenever there is a database match. This will ensure sure the criminal record is complete, accurate, up to date, applies to your applicant and is reportable.

Keep in mind that usually these post conviction processes do not result in a record being physically removed from the court's computer system. Once a unit of government creates a record, it is unlikely that anyone will physically destroy or delete it. It is unlikely a clerk's office will have access to a "case delete" button. Which means in most instances the record still exists. Even if a judge orders a record to be physically sealed, there is normally going to be some sort of record of the case somewhere in the public domain — the case number and the defendant's name will remain in some computerized index, which is available to a court researcher. In those instances, the court record and the court public index will normally include documentation that there has been some sort of judicial or executive action to lessen the offense through some post-judgment procedure. If a screening firm comes across such a record, a competent screening firm should have a procedure in place to not report such a conviction. However, if an employer does his own search of the court records and comes across such a record, the employer is asked to wipe their own memory clean.

Another new wrinkle are cases involving Drug Courts. Drug courts use a post conviction procedure where a court closely monitors and supervises a defendant with a personal drug abuse problem or who is accused of a drug-related crime. The court gives a defendant the opportunity to participate in a program, and upon successful completion, the defendant is relieved from criminal sanctions.

Un-Ringing the Bell

In TV land, a lawyer makes an inflammatory statement in front of a jury, knowing it is inadmissible, prompting the other side to noisily object. The judge admonishes the jury to disregard the last comment. Of course, the jury heard it and the offending lawyer continues as though he scored some sort of victory. The TV viewer is wondering how a jury is supposed to un-remember something they just heard. Sometimes in court this is referred to as "un-ringing the bell." Once a bell has rung, it is hard to take it back. Another analogy is – how do you get a jury to not remember the word elephant after elephant is mentioned?

This happens much more on TV than in real life. In real life, judges take a dim view of lawyers who try to insert inadmissible evidence or arguments before a jury. In fact, judges have a great deal of latitude in making lawyers who do that sort of "unauthorized dramatics" regret having done so.

Employers can find themselves in a similar position. If they come across a record they cannot use or consider, how do they ignore it? If the record was located by in-house security or the HR Department, then the record should not be passed on to a hiring manager or a person with hiring authority. That of course assumes HR or internal security has received the proper training to recognize an impermissible record and that there are policies and procedures in place.

The Million Dollar Question – How to Judge the Seriousness of a Criminal Conviction

As part of the EEOC Enforcement Guidance on the Use of Arrest and Conviction Records by employers published in 2012, a great deal of emphasis is placed on understanding the criminal offense. The EEOC indicated that one of the tests to initially screen for a criminal record is the nature and gravity of the crime, which can include:

✓ The harm caused

✓ The legal elements of the crime
✓ The classification of the offense (e.g., misdemeanor vs. felony)

The EEOC indicates that if such a screening reveals an offense that may cause an employer not to hire an applicant, a best practice is for the employer to conduct an **individualized assessment** that includes:

✓ Facts or circumstances surrounding the offense or conduct;
✓ Number of offenses for which the individual was convicted;
✓ Age at the time of conviction or release from prison;
✓ Evidence that the individual performed the same type of work post conviction without any known incidents of criminal conduct;
✓ Length and consistency of employment before and after offense;
✓ Rehabilitation efforts; and
✓ Whether individual is bonded under a federal, state, or local bonding program

To minimize the risk of violating discrimination laws, it appears that an employer must analyze the offense and the offender. But that is easier said than done. The problem is that public records do not include police reports, search warrant affidavits, arrest warrants and declarations, statements of probable cause, or probation reports – all documents that provide the real details about the offender and the offense. Of course, if there is a trial by judge or jury, transcripts of the trial may be available, but they can be expensive, time consuming, difficult to obtain, and require a great deal of reading. In fact, trial transcripts are not prepared in every case but normally only when there is an appeal.

The steps an employer can take are:

1. Review the allegations in the charging documents.
2. Understand the elements of each offense. Most jurisdictions have books of jury instructions used in criminal trials that break down and define each and every element of the charges.
3. In the case of a conviction either by a guilty plea or a trial, the employer can compare the outcome to the original charges. In other words, if the applicant was fond guilty to a lesser charge, that may give insight as to the seriousness of the situation. .
4. View the court minutes or orders concerning sentencing, which are public. Often the degree of sentencing can shed light as to the seriousness of the offense or offender. For example if the person only receives probation, that is a much less serious matter than a four month jail sentence.
5. If a defendant was placed on probation, an employer can view the terms and conditions of probation. There can be conditions of probation such as counseling, stay away orders from victims, or specific order prohibiting possession of guns, drugs, alcohol, or other items related to the offense.
6. Determine if there are any orders of restitution.
7. Determine if there are any pardons, expungements, or judicial set asides.
8. If the criminal matter was a misdemeanor, analyze state law to determine if the charge was a hybrid that could be either a felony or a misdemeanor or can only be misdemeanor, which means the state has determined that it is inherently less serious than a felony.

The problem with all of these methods is it can be like reading tea leaves to attempt to interpret the underlying crimes. Crimes can be reduced to misdemeanor or counts dismissed for all sorts of reasons having nothing to do with the applicant's conduct. The reduction can relate to problems with a witness or other evidence, motions to suppress evidence, or court congestion leading to a plea bargain. Dispositions can be impacted by a number of other factors, including the quality of the defendant's lawyer, the actions of the Judge or DA, and local practices when it comes to charring, plea bargain, and sentences.

However, under the EEOC guidelines, employers need to go beyond just the name and definitions of the offense and make some good faith effort to determine the seriousness of the underlying conviction.

Conclusion — When Using Criminal Records

As the old saying goes, the devil is in the details. Although this chapter will assist employers in gaining an overall understanding of the criminal justice system, each and every case an employer encounters must be analyzed individually depending upon the state involved.

In order to analyze the meaning of a criminal record, an employer or background firm may also have to actually pull the case file to locate details. This is discussed in greater detail in Chapter 15.

Employment Screening Background Checks and Annual Criminal Statistics

Various organizations publish their annual criminal **"hit rates"** showing how many applicants subject to background screening had criminal records or other discrepancies.

On one hand, these figures are extremely valuable because they confirm an already compelling case that background checks are critical for any employer that wants to exercise due diligence and protect its workforce and the public. On the other hand, as with all statistics, these yearly reports need to be taken with a grain of salt. First, not all criminal records come as a surprise to employers. Given the number of Americans with some sort of criminal record, many employers are still willing to hire someone for an appropriate position, providing the applicant was not dishonest in the application. In fact, certain industries by nature of their workforce are more likely to draw upon a pool of potential applicants that may tend to have higher levels of past criminal conduct. Examples might be construction or firms that provide employment for entry level workers.

A statistic that would be very interesting but much harder to obtain is how many criminal records were discovered where the applicant was dishonest about past conduct. Of course, that gets complicated by the fact that an applicant may have been genuinely confused about what is or is not reportable on an application. A related issue is that not all criminal records have the same impact. A criminal record for underage drinking is not in the same league as a conviction for armed robbery.

In reviewing these types of statistics, employers also need to keep in mind that not all of the criminal records located are job related. Employers should NOT automatically deny employment to an applicant with a criminal record unless there is a business justification that takes into account the nature and gravity of the crime, the nature of the job and the age of the crime. As noted in this book, the EEOC takes the position that the overuse of criminal records without a business justification can create a disparate impact, and therefore can be discriminatory.

Finally, it is difficult to draw firm conclusions from the statistics without knowing the search methodology. Depending on how the searches were conducted, it is entirely possible in fact that such annual statistics may even understate the number of criminal records applicants had. The most accurate criminal record searches are done by accessing information directly from the county courthouse level, either by physically going the court, or by use of the court computer system that is the functional equivalent of going to the courthouse. Databases on the other hand, although much wider in scope, are not nearly as accurate, do not have all courts or jurisdiction, may not be updated, or may not contain sufficient identifiers. To the extent any searching was done by the use of databases, the numbers could potentially be understated.

The bottom line: These statistics are an excellent reminder that employers need to be careful in hiring. However, as with most statistics, there is more to the story.

Glossary of Criminal Terms

The following glossary of common criminal terms may be helpful. Some of the definitions were provided by Derek Hinton and Larry Henry, authors of *The Criminal Records Manual 3rd Edition* (Facts on Demand Press):

abstract of record: a complete history in short, abbreviated form of the case as found in the record.

acquittal: a term used in cases where a criminal defendant goes forward to trial, with the jury or judge finding the defendant not guilty of a certain crime or crimes.

administrative license suspension (ALS): a law enforcement officer may seize the driver's license of an individual believed to be driving under the influence If the person's test results show an alcohol concentration higher than the legal limit or the presence of drugs or other intoxicating substances. That individual has seven days after receiving the notice of suspension to petition the court to challenge the suspension.

Alford plea: a plea entered by a defendant while maintaining his/her innocence in order to gain the benefit of a plea agreement.

alternative dispute resolution (ADR): a process by which an independent party is asked to review the issues in dispute between two other parties in hopes of bringing the dispute to a resolution before the court is required to conduct a formal hearing or trial. This process may occur prior to the filing of the civil action or may occur after the case is filed. A judge may choose to refer a case for alternative dispute resolution.

amicus curiae: a friend of the court; one who interposes and volunteers information or argument upon some matter of law.

arraignment: the defendant is advised of the charge against him or her and the rights he or she has. Bail is set. If the charge is a misdemeanor the defendant enters a plea in the Magistrate's Division. If the charge is a felony, the defendant appears first in the Magistrate's Division, but the defendant cannot enter a plea--the defendant determines whether he or she desires a preliminary hearing. If the defendant is bound over on a felony to answer the charge in district court, the defendant enters a plea in the District Court.

arrest of judgment: the act of staying the effect of a judgment already entered.

arrest warrant: is a warrant that authorizes law enforcement to arrest an individual.

attachment: a remedy by which a plaintiff is enabled to acquire possession of property or effects of a defendant for satisfaction of judgment which a plaintiff may obtain in the future.

bail bond: an obligation signed by the accused, with sureties, to secure his presence in court. If the defendant fails to appear, the bondsman has a period of time to deliver the defendant to the court. If this is not done, the bond is forfeited.

bail bond forfeiture: the process in which the court requires the surety to pay over the amount of bail

bail bond exoneration: a process by which the bond money paid to the court to ensure an individual's appearance in court is returned to that individual, typically when the case is concluded.

bailiff: a court attendant whose duties are to keep order in the courtroom and to have custody of the jury.

banc-(bangk) bench: the place where a court permanently or regularly sits. A "sitting en banc" is a hearing with all the judges of a court, as distinguished from the sitting of a single judge.

bench warrant: process issued by the court itself, or "from the bench," for the attachment or arrest of a person.

binding instruction: one in which jury is told if they find certain conditions to be true, they must find for the plaintiff, or defendant, as the case may be.

burden of proof: the necessity or duty of affirmatively proving a fact or facts in dispute.

caption: the caption of a pleading, or other papers connected with a case in court, is the heading or introductory clause which shows the names of the parties, name of the court, number of the case, etc.

certiorari-(ser'shi-o-ra'ri): an original writ commanding judges or officers of inferior courts to certify or to return records of proceedings in a cause for judicial review. Proceedings for a writ of certiorari are not applicable in the Idaho judicial system, except as the United States Supreme Court may grant certiorari on a case decided by the Idaho Supreme Court.

change of venue: the removal of a case begun in one county or district to another, typically done for the convenience of the parties, or when the news coverage of the circumstances associated with a case make it difficult to find a jury that can put aside what they have heard about the case and judge it fairly on the evidence presented in court.

Child Protective Act: (commonly referred to as CPA) the statutory law dealing with the protection of neglected or abused children.

common law: the body of law arising from decisions made by the courts. Also called "case law".

concurrent sentence: sentences for more than one crime in which the time of each is to be served at the same time, rather than successively

consecutive sentence: a sentence, additional to others, imposed at the same time for another offense, one sentence to begin at the expiration of another.

contempt of court: any act calculated to embarrass, hinder, or obstruct a court in the administration of justice, or calculated to lessen its authority or dignity. Contempt is of two kinds: direct and indirect. Direct contempt are those committed in the immediate presence of the court; indirect contempt is the term chiefly used with reference to failure or refusal to obey a lawful order outside the presence of the Court.

corroborating evidence: evidence supplementary to that already given and tending to strengthen or confirm it.

count: In a criminal action, the distinct allegation in an indictment or information that the defendant committed a crime.

counterclaim: a claim presented by a defendant against the plaintiff.

de novo (de no'vo): anew, afresh. A "trial de novo" is the retrial of a case.

declaratory judgment: one which declares the rights of the parties or expresses the opinion of the court on a question of law, without ordering anything to be done.

default: a "default" in an action of law occurs when a party omits to plead within the time allowed or fails to appear at the trial.

default judgment: the court may enter judgment against a defendant in a civil case in his/her absence or in the event they have failed to complete the filing of required documents within a specified time.

deferred adjudication: a form of plea deal available in various jurisdictions, where a defendant pleads "guilty" or "No Contest" to criminal charges in exchange for meeting certain requirements laid out by the court within an allotted period of time also ordered by the court. Upon completion of the requirements, which may include probation, treatment, community service, or some form of community supervision, the defendant may avoid a formal conviction on their record or have their case dismissed. In some cases, an order of non-disclosure can be obtained, and sometimes a record can be expunged.

directed verdict: an instruction by the judge to the jury to return a specific verdict.

discovery: a process whereby one party to an action may be informed as to facts known by other parties or witnesses. In Idaho, the usual modes of discovery are depositions, interrogatories, requests for production of documents, and requests for admission.

dismissal: the dropping of charges by the district attorney before a jury or judge renders a verdict.

disposition: the final outcome in a criminal case.

District Attorney: also known as the Prosecutor or DA, is a government attorney responsible for overseeing the prosecution of an accused in a criminal court of law.

dockets: in a criminal case refer to the court case calendar or schedule of cases to be heard at a given time.

domicile: that place where a person has his true and permanent home. A person may have several residences, but only one domicile.

en banc: on the bench; all judges of the court sitting together to hear a cause.

enjoin: to require a person, by writ of injunction from a court to perform, or to abstain from or stop some act.

equitable action: an action which may be brought for the purpose of restraining the threatened infliction of wrongs or injuries, and the prevention of threatened illegal action.

estoppel (es-top'el): a person's own act, or acceptance of facts, which preclude that person from later making claims to the contrary.

et al.: an abbreviation for et alli, meaning "and others."

et seq.: an abbreviation of et sequentes, or et sequentia, meaning "and the following"

ex parte (ex par'te): by or for one party; done for, in behalf of, or on the application of, one party only.

ex post facto (ex post fak'to): after the fact; an act or fact occurring after some previous act or fact, but which relates back thereto. In criminal law, an ex post facto law is one that imposes or increases punishment for an act that was committed before the law was passed, such a law is forbidden by the U.S. and Idaho Constitutions.

fugitive warrant: a judge in one state may issue a warrant for the arrest of an individual being held in custody in another state. The fugitive may then be returned to the state where he is charged through the process of extradition.

Grand Jury: In some Felony cases, a Grand Jury consisting of used to establish probable cause to proceed with the criminal case.

guardian ad litem (ad li'tum): a person appointed by a court to look after the interests of a child or incompetent whose property or rights are involved in litigation.

Guilty by plea or verdict: in criminal law, a defendant admits the conduct before trial, is said to be guilty. Guilt can also be established by means of a jury or court trial.

habeas corpus (ha'be-as kor' pus): "you have the body." The name given a variety of writs whose object is to bring a person before a court or judge. In most common usage, it is directed to the official or person detaining another, commanding him to produce the body of the prisoner or person detained so the court may determine if such person has been denied liberty without due process of law.

harmless error: in appellate practice, an error committed by a lower court during a trial, but not prejudicial to the rights of the party or the outcome of the case and for which the court will not reverse the judgment.

hearsay: evidence of a statement made out of court and offered to prove the truth of the statement, e.g., "I didn't see the accident myself, but my friend told me the light was red." It should be noted that the law on hearsay is one of the more complicated areas of the law of evidence with many qualifications and exceptions.

hung jury: in a criminal trial, a hopelessly deadlocked jury in which neither side is able to prevail.

impeachment of witness: an attack on the credibility of a witness by the testimony of other witnesses or evidence.

in camera (in kam'e-ra): in chambers; in private.

indeterminate sentence: an indefinite sentence of "not to exceed" so many years, the exact term to be served being afterwards determined by parole authorities within the maximum limits set by the court or by statute.

indictment: an accusation in writing found and presented by a grand jury, charging that a person has committed a crime.

information: an accusation for a felony criminal offense which is presented by a prosecuting attorney instead of a grand jury.

Infraction: a minor offense that is not criminal in nature but rather is a civil public offense punishable by a fine only. Examples of infractions include: speeding, failure to fasten a safety belt.

injunction: a mandatory or prohibitive writ issued by a court.

instruction: a direction given by the judge to the jury concerning the law of the case.

interlocutory: provisional; temporary; not final; refers to orders and decrees of a court.

interrogatories: written questions propounded by one party and served on an adversary, who must provide written answers under oath.

jurisdiction: the power of a court to hear and determine a given class of cases; the power to act over a particular defendant. Referred to as subject matter jurisdiction (jurisdiction over the subject of the case) or personal jurisdiction (jurisdiction over the parties).

jury, grand: a jury of inquiry whose duty is to receive complaints and accusations in criminal cases, hear the evidence and return an indictment when they are satisfied that there is a probable cause that a crime was committed and the defendant committed it.

jury, petit: the ordinary jury of twelve (or fewer) persons for the trial of a civil or criminal case. So called to distinguish it from the grand jury.

Lesser included crime: generally means an alternative to the charged crime at trial where the jury is given an lesser but related charge, in case the jury feels the defendant is not guilty of the charged crime, but is guilty of a related yet less serious crime.

mandamus: the name of a writ which issues from a court commanding the performance of a particular act.

manslaughter: the unlawful killing of another without malice; may be either voluntary, upon a sudden impulse, or involuntary in the commission of some unlawful act.

misdemeanor: offenses less than felonies; generally those punishable by fine or imprisonment in a county jail, rather than in the state prison.

mistrial: an erroneous or invalid trial, a trial which cannot stand in law because of lack of jurisdiction, wrong drawing of jurors, deadlocked jury or failure of some other fundamental requisite

moot: unsettled; undecided. A moot point is one not settled by judicial decisions.

no bill: this phrase, endorsed by a grand jury on the indictment, is equivalent to "not found" or "not a true bill." It means that in the opinion of the jury, evidence was insufficient to warrant the return of a formal charge.

No contest: a type of plea in a criminal case that is the same as a guilty plea, for all purposes, including applying for jobs and background checks. The no-contest plea is utilized in criminal cases to avoid civil litigation (being sued) as a result of the criminal plea.

NOLLE PROSEQUI: An entry made on the record, by which the prosecutor or plaintiff declares that he will proceed no further.

of counsel: a phrase commonly applied to counsel employed to assist in the preparation or management of the case, or its presentation on appeal, but who is not the principal attorney of record.

order to show cause hearing: a hearing in which a person is ordered to court to show cause why they did not comply with the order of the court.

peremptory challenge: the challenge which the parties may use to reject a certain number of prospective jurors without assigning any reason.

petition: in the context of juvenile case processing, the petition is the formal document filed with the court outlining the charges against the juvenile.

pleading: the process by which the parties in a suit or action alternately present written statements of their contentions, to narrow the field of controversy.

post conviction relief: a court hearing in which a defendant convicted of a crime petitions the court set to aside the conviction or modify or reduce the sentence imposed by court.

power of attorney: an instrument authorizing another to act as one's agent or attorney.

prejudicial error: synonymous with "reversible error"; an error which warrants the appellate court to reverse the judgment before it.

preliminary hearing: a hearing held in the Magistrate's Division on a felony charge to determine if the defendant should be bound over to the District Court to stand trial. If the magistrate determines that there is probable cause to believe that an offense has been committed and that the defendant committed the offense, the case is then presented to the District Court.

pretrial hearing: a court hearing that occurs before trial in which the judge sits down with the parties to the matter to review issues associated with the case. A hearing that attempts to ensure that all proceedings and documents have been completed and efforts to resolve the matter have been exhausted.

preponderance of evidence: greater weight of evidence, or evidence which is more credible and convincing to the mind, not the greater number of witnesses.

probable cause: The amount of information needed to justify the issuance of an arrest warrant or search warrant, or to allow an officer to make an arrest without a warrant, or to permit a defendant to be bound over to the district court on a felony charge at a preliminary hearing. It is defined as facts and circumstances sufficient to allow a prudent person to believe that a person committed a crime, or that contraband or evidence of a crime is present at a particular location.

probable cause hearing: a hearing to determine if there is sufficient evidence to warrant the filing of a charge or to bind a defendant over for trial.

probation: a sentence whereby a defendant is permitted to avoid serving the full sentence under specified conditions.

probation violation: a person who has been found guilty or has admitted to committing a crime is often placed on probation by a judge. Typically, there are conditions attached to probation that if not fulfilled or violated by the defendant, may result in probation being revoked.

pro se: representing himself or herself

proximate cause: a cause which, in natural or probable sequence, produced the damage complained of. It need not be the only cause. It is sufficient if it concurs with some other cause acting at the same time, which in combination with it, causes damage.

Public Defender's Office: lawyers employed specifically to represent indigent clients in criminal court.

punitive damages: are damages in excess of those required to compensate the plaintiff for the wrong done which are imposed to punish the defendant because of the particularly wanton or willful character or his or her wrongdoing.

quash: to vacate; to annul or void

reasonable doubt: an accused person is entitled to acquittal if, in the minds of the jury, his guilt has not been proved beyond a "reasonable doubt"; that state of the minds of jurors in which they cannot say they feel an abiding conviction as to the truth of the charge.

remanded: ordered back to custody, or sent back; e.g., a defendant being remanded to the custody of the sheriff or an appeal being remanded to the lower court.

retained jurisdiction: a judge, after sentencing an individual to a correctional institution may retain jurisdiction over that individual, which typically lasts 180 days. At the end of that time, the prisoner is returned to the court where his/her progress is evaluated to determine whether the prisoner should be placed on probation or required to serve out the sentence originally imposed.

sequestration: holding a jury separate and apart from outside contact.

small claims: known as the "peoples' court," the small claims court handles disputes between people that involve monetary amounts of less than $5,000. No jury trials are available in small claims nor are attorneys allowed to represent parties in small claims court.

stare decisis (sta're de-si'sis): the doctrine that when a court has once laid down a principle of law as applicable to a certain set of facts, it will adhere to that same principle and apply it to future cases where the facts are substantially the same.

statute of limitations: the statutory provisions limiting the amount of time within which a claim must be filed.

stay: a stopping or arresting of a judicial proceeding by order of the court.

stipulation: an agreement by the opposing parties or attorney pertaining to the proceedings that is binding on the parties to the stipulation.

subpoena: a notice or process served upon a witness to compel the witness to appear and give testimony before a court or agency authorized to issue subpoenas.

subpoena duces tecum: a notice or process by which the court commands a witness to produce certain documents or records.

summons: a court document used to require a person's appearance in Court.

tort: an injury or wrong committed, either with or without force, to the person or property of another.

trial de novo (de no'vo): a new trial or retrial held in a higher court in which the whole case is heard as if no trial had been held in a lower court.

under advisement: if during the course of a hearing, a question is posed that requires the judge to give more thought or do further research before making a decision, the judge takes the matter under advisement to review the matter and to render a decision.

venire-(ve-ni're): technically, a writ summoning persons to court to act as jurors; popularly used as meaning the body of names thus summoned.

venue-(ven'u): the particular county, city or geographical area in which a court with jurisdiction may hear and determine a case.

voir dire-(vwor der): to speak the truth - the process by which potential jurors are questioned to determine if they may serve on a jury.

waiver of speedy trial: State law requires that a defendant be tried within a specified period of time. The U.S. and Idaho Constitutions also provide every defendant with the right to a speedy trial. A defendant may waive that right to allow the proceeding to continue beyond the speedy trial deadline.

with prejudice: The dismissal of an action that prevents further proceedings on the same claim.

withheld judgment: A criminal disposition in which a judge does not impose a judgment of conviction but grants probation and imposes other conditions deemed appropriate. If the defendant successfully completes the conditions as outlined by the judge, the judge will then dismiss the case, resulting in the defendant having a clean record.

without prejudice: a dismissal "without prejudice" allows a new suit to be brought on the same cause of action.

writ: an order issued from a court requiring the performance of a specified act, or giving authority and commission to have it done.

Where and How Employers Legally Obtain Accurate and Relevant Criminal Records

Inside This Chapter:

- ✓ Core Concept One — There is NO Central Location for All U.S. Criminal Records
- ✓ Core Concept Two — Accuracy and Relevancy
- ✓ Sources of Data
- ✓ County Courthouse Searches
- ✓ How to Do a County Courthouse Search
- ✓ Looking for Criminal Offenses in Counties with Multiple Courts
- ✓ The State Agency Public Databases
- ✓ Using the Centralized State Court Administration
- ✓ Using the State Criminal Record Repository
- ✓ Additional State Criminal Record-Related Databases
- ✓ Federal Courts Are a Separate System
- ✓ Private Databases — Their Value and Limitations
- ✓ Web Data Extraction and Robotic Searches
- ✓ Online Dating Website Background Checks & Criminal Databases

So, where do employers and screening firms search for criminal records? This chapter examines the "where and how" to properly access criminal records as part of any employer's Safe Hiring Program. Just as importantly, the chapter also focuses on ensuring that the criminal records are both accurate and relate to the job applicant that is the subject of the background check. In the next chapter, the subject of "relevancy" will be visited again in the context of whether or not a crime record is relevant to the job decision. However, the first step is to ensure the record belongs to the applicant.

Two Core Concepts:

There are two core concepts central to this chapter.

1. The first core concept is that there is no one magic web site, database, or service that gives complete, accurate, and up to date criminal records. Not even the FBI database does that for employers that have legal access. Finding criminal records can be very complicated and require a number of processes.
2. The second core concert is that both employers and background firms must ensure that the criminal information associated with a job applicant is **accurate** and applies to the applicant. Accuracy also means that **relevant** records are not missed. Employers and background firms must navigate between "false positives"-records that are not accurate, current, or belong to the applicant, and "false negatives,"—failing to locate relevant records that do belong to an applicant which can create a false sense of security.

Core Concept One – There is NO Central Location for All U.S. Criminal Records

Contrary to popular belief, obtaining a criminal record is not as easy as going on a computer and getting a thumbs up or a thumbs down. There are over 10,000 state and federal courthouses in the United States, spread out over some 3,300 jurisdictions, each with its own records file. There is simply no national computer database of all criminal records available to private employers. Period. End of story.

Yes, the Federal Bureau of Investigation (FBI) and state law enforcement agencies have access to a national computer database called the National Crime Information Center (NCIC). The NCIC is a computerized index of criminal justice information, such as criminal record history information, fugitives, stolen properties, and missing persons, maintained by the FBI's Criminal Justice Information Services Division in Clarksburg, West Virginia. However, it is absolutely illegal for most private companies to obtain criminal information from law enforcement computer databases without specific legal authorization. There are three situations where this information is provided to private employers.

- ✓ First, a state may pass legislation authorizing such a check. Examples are school teachers, child care, and water-treatment plant workers.
- ✓ Second, the federal government may require an FBI criminal check. Examples are nuclear plant workers, aviation, or certain other positions in transportation.
- ✓ Third, some types of employers have been given direct access to the FBI, such as banking institutions through the American Banking Association (ABA).

One difficulty for employers – if there is a "hit" on the FBI rap sheet – is the report can be very confusing. It can be difficult to determine the nature and current status of the record without going to the courthouse and examining underlying court documents. In 2004, the U.S. Congress requested the Justice Department to conduct a study on the feasibility of opening up the FBI database to private employers directly. A subsequent report issued by the Justice Department examined a host of issues involved with opening direct employer access for all private employers to the FBI criminal records. As of the printing of this book, there is still no direct employer access to the FBI criminal records to all private employers.

The report, *The Attorney General's Report on Criminal History Background Checks*, is found at: www.usdoj.gov/olp/ag_bgchecks_report.pdf. Note the previous chapter contains material on the basics of criminal records, including terminology and an overview of where records are located.

The Real Story about the FBI's Criminal Records Database

From *The Criminal Records Manual*, 3rd Edition, by Larry Henry and Derek Hinton:

The NCIC Database

The FBI database's formal name is the **National Crime Information Center (NCIC)** and is an automated database of criminal justice and justice-related records maintained by the FBI. The database includes the "hot files" of wanted and missing persons, stolen vehicles and identifiable stolen property, including firearms. Two important points about the NCIC are:

1. The NCIC is not nearly as complete as portrayed in the movies. Because of the chain of events that must happen in multiple jurisdictions in order for a crime to appear in NCIC, many records of crime do not make it.

2. The information the NCIC does have is predominantly solely arrest-related. The disposition of most crimes in NCIC must be obtained by going to the adjudicating jurisdiction. This can be an important issue to employers as will be detailed later in the federal and state legal chapters.

This national database is currently evolving due to the National Crime Prevention and Privacy Compact.

Source of the NCIC Data

The sources of the FBI's information are the counties and states that contribute information as well as the federal justice agencies. Public criminal records are found at federal court repositories (for federal crimes), state repositories, and county courthouses. As discussed earlier, private citizens and businesses — non-criminal justice agencies — cannot, as a general rule, obtain access to the national FBI database. However, because the FBI database is perhaps the most well known repository of criminal records, some discussion is in order.

Access to NCIC files is through central control terminal operators in each state. The operators are connected to NCIC via dedicated telecommunications lines maintained by the FBI. Local agencies and beat officers can access the state control terminal via the state law enforcement network. Inquiries are based on name and other non-fingerprint identification. Also, most criminal history inquiries of the Interstate Identification Index (usually referred to as "III" or the "Triple I") system are made via the NCIC telecommunications system.

Practice Hint: Occasionally someone comes to an employer with an offer that seems too good to be true—"I will get you real FBI records." This good deal may consist of a friend with some sort of access to a law enforcement agency that obtains criminal records from NCIC. The problem: it is illegal and a serious criminal matter. Access to the FBI data is tracked and monitored, and illegal users have been prosecuted.

NAPBS Report Finds Drawbacks to NCIC Database

Detailed information on the drawbacks to the NCIC is substantiated in an August 2005 report *The National Crime Information Center: A Review and Evaluation* prepared on behalf of the National Association of Professional Background Screeners (NAPBS) by Craig N. Winston under the direction of Lester S. Rosen and Michael Sankey. The stated purpose of the report was to review the National Crime Information Center (NCIC) and the Interstate Identification System (IIS) in order to evaluate its effectiveness in maintaining accurate and complete criminal history records. Some conclusions from the NAPBS sponsored study were:

✓ Many states do not report information concerning dispositions, declinations to prosecute, failure to charge after fingerprints have been submitted, and expungements.

✓ Inconsistency in the various state reporting requirements and criminal codes impacts the completeness and accuracy of the records.

✓ The timeliness of transmission by the local jurisdictions to the state criminal history repositories remains problematic.

✓ There are still significant time lags between the time information is transmitted to the state repository and entry into the criminal history records.

✓ The process used to link data to the proper individual and case is still ineffective.

✓ Serious problems remain in the process to link dispositional information to the proper case and charge.

✓ The format and terminology used by the various states creates problems of interpretation for individuals in other states who are using the information.

✓ Even when a criminal record is searched based on fingerprints instead of name matches, many of the same issues still exist.

The report shows the FBI's NCIC database, while still the gold standard for those limited employers authorized by state or federal law to access it, is still more of an arrest databases that is not as accurate or complete as people think. The report is available at: www.napbs.com/files/members/Resources/NCIC_Report.pdf.

The FBI and New York Times Discuss Database Flaws

The NCIC Database also came under fire from the New York Times as evidenced in the summary below of this article.

NY Times Editorial Focuses On Flawed FBI Background Checks

A May 27, 2010 New York Times editorial, *Check It Again,* focused on a bill in the House of Representatives at the time that would require the Federal Bureau of Investigation (FBI) to verify and correct criminal data before issuing background checks for employment purposes, thus fixing the problem of many Americans missing a chance to get hired (as if it was not hard enough to find a job these days) because the FBI background checks employers use to screen job applicants contain incomplete or inaccurate information.

According to the Times editorial, a common problem with FBI background checks is that the criminal records included in those FBI background checks fail to include the final disposition of a case, meaning that the records may only show that a job applicant was arrested but not that the charges were dismissed or that there was no conviction.

The editorial also cited a 2009 report from the National Employment Law Project (NELP) that revealed the government had mistakenly denied credentials to tens of thousands of workers "partly because of flawed background reports" after Congress required new FBI background checks for about 1.5 million people working at the nation's ports. The editorial concludes that no one – including the nearly 50 million Americans with arrest or conviction records – should be denied a job because the Government's information contained in an FBI employment background check is wrong.

The NELP report 'A Scorecard on the Post-9/11 Port Worker Background Checks' is available at: http://nelp.3cdn.net/0714d0826f3ecf7a15_70m6i6fwb.pdf.

Source: www.nytimes.com/2010/05/27/opinion/27thu3.html?_r=1&scp=1&sq=F.B.I.%20EDITORIAL&st=cse

In response to the 'Check It Again' story, the FBI sent a letter to the New York Times which the Times published on June 8, 2010. The text of the letter, titled 'Reliability of F.B.I. Data,' is as follows:

FBI Letter Responds To NY Times Editorial on Flawed Criminal Background Checks

To the Editor:

The F.B.I. takes its role as a central repository for criminal justice information very seriously, but must rely on the voluntary submissions of criminal history records supplied by local, state, tribal and federal law enforcement agencies, and the courts, for the overwhelming majority of its information.

While the F.B.I. appreciates this support, vital data often fails to get to the bureau in a timely way because of the time lag in criminal prosecutions. To help find ways to capture this information more efficiently, the F.B.I. formed an interagency task force to identify problem areas in states disposition reporting and methods to improve the system. The F.B.I. also oversees another task force to improve the flow of criminal history information from the courts to the state repositories and then to the F.B.I.

The F.B.I. is also working on internal improvements, including the Next Generation Identification program, an upgrade to the existing fingerprint identification system, which will improve disposition reporting, while a related initiative will enable efficient electronic updates.

Through advances in technology and the continued cooperation of our partners, the F.B.I. hopes to clear the way for additional improvements in the completeness of the background check information we provide.

Daniel D. Roberts

Assistant Director, Criminal Justice

Information Services Division, F.B.I.

Washington, June 2, 2010

The letter confirms the FBI only receives what criminal background check information local jurisdictions and states will give it and admits that "vital data often fails to get to the bureau in a timely way" meaning the criminal database is not completely accurate. In other words, some FBI background checks may use inaccurate or incomplete information.

A June 2006 report from the United States Department of Justice (DOJ) – 'The Attorney General's Report On Criminal History Background Checks' – found nearly 50 percent of criminal records maintained in the FBI's National Crime Information Center (NCIC) database failed to note court decisions to dismiss arrests. The DOJ report is available at: www.justice.gov/olp/ag_bgchecks_report.pdf.

Since some employers rely on the NCIC database to conduct background checks on potential hires, background screeners would welcome any strengthening of the accuracy of the FBI's criminal database by requiring the U.S. Attorney General's Office to verify that crime data used for background checks is up to date, find out the outcome of arrests whenever an employer requests a background check, and update that record in the NCIC database.

A 2010 study released in 2011 by the Bureau of Statistics for the U.S. Department of Justice reported the state criminal history record repositories had a significant backlog of non-recorded final dispositions for arrests - in fact over 1.7 million. See www.ncjrs.gov/pdffiles1/bjs/grants/237253.pdf

Core Concept Two — Accuracy and Relevancy

The second core competency relates to the accuracy of the criminal record and the need to ensure it relates to the applicant. This applies to both a background screening firm and any employer that obtains criminal records themselves without going through a background firm.

Falsely identifying a person as a criminal, or misrepresenting the criminal record, is known as a "false positive." Examples of inaccurate criminal information can include acts such as:

✓ Reporting an offense that did not in fact belong to the applicant

✓ Reporting an offense as a felony when in fact it was a misdemeanor

✓ Reporting an offense that has been judicially set aside under state law, such as an expungement, pardon, deferred adjudication, or some other provision of law

✓ Misreporting details about the offense, such as the sentence or terms of probation, that makes the offense appear more serious than it really is

✓ Reporting counts that have been dismissed, which has the potential to misrepresent again the seriousness of the matter

✓ Reporting arrests that did not result in convictions in states that do not allow such reporting (and as discussed in Chapter 16, could potentially be a violation of the EEOC Guidance)

✓ Reporting convictions that are beyond seven year in states with seven year limitations

✓ Reporting arrests that are older than seven years in violation the FCRA

✓ Reporting criminal matters inadvertently by asking questions of employers designed to determine if a matter is reportable by means of a question that reveals a criminal matter.

✓ Repetitive references to the same offense, creating a false impression of greater criminality.

Some of these types of errors were documented in a report issued by National Consumer Law Center (NCLC) called 'Broken Records: How Errors by Criminal Background Checking Companies Harm Workers and Businesses' found at: www.nclc.org/images/pdf/pr-reports/broken-records-report.pdf. Although such errors may exist, the report has been heavily criticized for taking a few incidents out of the millions of background checks conducted in order to create a false impression of widespread inaccuracies. The NCLC report also did not appear to understand the difference between data brokers and a background screening firm. The author of this book issued a detailed response to the NCLC report found at: www.esrcheck.com/articles/NCLC-Report-on-Criminal-Background-Checks-Inaccurate.php.

In the event a criminal record is reported, FCRA section 613 is also concerned about accuracy and relevancy. That section provides two options to background firms. One option involves the use of "strict procedures," and the other is to send the consumer notice at the same time the criminal matter is reported to the employer so the consumer can dispute it. FCRA section 613 states that:

(a) *In general*. A consumer reporting agency which furnishes a consumer report for employment purposes and which for that purpose compiles and reports items of information on consumers which are matters of public record and are likely to have an adverse effect upon a consumer's ability to obtain employment shall:

(1) at the time such public record information is reported to the user of such consumer report, notify the consumer of the fact that public record information is being reported by the consumer reporting agency, together with the name and address of the person to whom such information is being reported; or

(2) maintain strict procedures designed to insure that whenever public record information which is likely to have an adverse effect on a consumer's ability to obtain employment is reported it is complete and up to date. For purposes of this paragraph, items of public record relating to arrests, indictments, convictions, suits, tax liens, and outstanding judgments shall be considered up to date if the current public record status of the item at the time of the report is reported.

Congress drove this point home even further in statement of Congressional findings and statement of purpose contained in section 602:

(b) *Reasonable procedures*. It is the purpose of this title to require that consumer reporting agencies adopt reasonable procedures for meeting the needs of commerce for consumer credit, personnel, insurance, and other information in a manner which is fair and equitable to the consumer, with regard to the confidentiality, accuracy, *relevancy*, and proper utilization of such information in accordance with the requirements of this title. (*Emphasis added.*)

The use of the word "*relevancy*" in the FCRA further underscores the need for a background check firm to ensure that reasonable steps are taken to only report information relevant to the consumer.

On the other side of the coin, accuracy also means NOT missing relevant criminal information that would assist an employer in making a better hiring decision. Failure to locate criminal records that would be germane to a hiring decision can be equally devastating to innocent victims if an employer hires someone that is dangerous, dishonest, unqualified, or unfit due to the failure of a background screening firm to locate potentially relevant information. Reporting someone as clear, when in fact there is a relevant criminal record, is known as a "false negative."

Sources of Data

The remainder of the chapter examines various sources of criminal records including their worthiness and the pros and cons of using them. Sources covered include:

- ✓ State Level Crimes Housed in County Court Houses
- ✓ Statewide Court Databases and Web Sites
- ✓ State Record Repositories
- ✓ Other Criminal Record-Related Databases
- ✓ Federal Court Searches
- ✓ Privately Assembled Commercial Databases

County Courthouse Searches

The **access method most often used** is to **physically visit each relevant county courthouse and look up the record**. That is done for two good reasons.

- ✓ First, it is reliable and usually the fastest method. Indexes and records cans be viewed immediately.
- ✓ Second, if there is a potential match, the researcher can make arrangements to view the file and look at case details, finding identifiers to be certain it is indeed their person on the spot.

The First Step –Determine Where to Search

Since every county courthouse cannot be searched, the key is to choose which counties are relevant. Here are some guidelines:

- ✓ **County of Residence**: At a minimum, employers should search the county of residence or the last place where the applicant spent the most time. Although there are no conclusive studies to prove the point, many criminal justice professionals have observed that the county of residence is the most likely location for a criminal to commit a crime. Many background screening firms have found that employers get the "biggest bang for the buck" by searching the county of residence – assuming a person has not moved there recently.
- ✓ **Last Three Counties**: Some employers have a policy to search the last three counties lived in. "Three" is not based upon any court case or official government recommendation; rather, it is based upon the experience of screening firms showing that most applicants have lived in an average of 2-3 counties in a seven-year period.
- ✓ **Seven-Year Search**: A much higher degree of protection is a minimum seven-year county search of all places where the applicant lived, worked, or studied based on his or her application. Some states have forms of seven year limitations. The county names can be determined as a result of verification of past employment and all past addresses provided as part of a Social Security Trace. The Social Security Trace is discussed in detail in the next chapter. More information about how the seven year period is calculated is found in Chapter 4. Information about how far back a search should go is also a potential EEOC issue discussed in Chapter 16.

✓ **Adjacent County or Metro Searches**: An employer can go to an even higher level by also searching metro areas of adjacent counties. This search recognizes the fact that there is nothing to prevent a person with a criminal record from crossing county lines. For example, if an employer wanted to search for criminal records for a person who lived in Boston, the employer would likely check Suffolk County. However, a metro search would include Norfolk, Middlesex, and Essex Counties. Here are several other examples (the first county named is where the city is located):

- **Atlanta** – Fulton, Clayton, Cobb, Dekalb, Douglas
- **Baltimore** – City of Baltimore, Anne Arundel, Baltimore, Howard
- **Chicago** – Cook, Dupage, Kane, Lake, Will
- **Dallas** – Dallas, Collin, Ellis, Kaufman, Tarrant
- **Detroit** – Wayne, Macomb, Monroe, Oakland, Washtenaw
- **San Francisco** – San Francisco, Alameda, Contra Costa, Marin, San Mateo
- **San Jose** – Santa Clara, Alameda, San Benito, San Mateo, Santa Cruz, Stanislaus

A database of all adjoining counties in the U.S. is available through BRB Publications. The adjoining county data is available as a CD-ROM product and as part of an online subscription service. See www.brbpublications.com.

How to Do a County Courthouse Search

Since the most accurate and least complicated search is at the courthouse, employers should have an understanding of how this type of search is performed at the actual courthouse, in the clerk's records office, by human beings. Keep in mind the methods of access, retrieval, and storage can vary from court to court.

First - Determine Who Performs the Actual Search?

There are actually two questions.

1. The employer can either do the search itself or hire someone, usually called a record researcher, to do it for them.

2. It is good to know upfront if at the courthouse the courts provide a searchable index of records so the public can do their own searching or if the courts insist that all searches be performed by court personnel.

Searches Performed by Researchers. If the research is being conducted by a background screening firm, the actual court researcher is most likely not a direct employee of the screening firm. Because there are over 3200 court houses in America, most screening firms do not have employees at each and every courthouse. Instead there is an entire industry of "researchers" that services background firms to enable them to search any county in America within one to three days. Note that generally the firms or individuals who specialize in court record searching only work for ongoing business customers, such as attorneys or screening firms. In that case, researchers are asked to provide all information available, and it is the background firm that has the responsibility under the FCRA to determine if the matter is reportable. See the chapter on Role and Legal Use of Criminal Records for information on the legal requirements for accuracy in reporting criminal records. A county-by-county list of a select group of these retrievers who abide by a code of professional conduct is found at The Public Record Retriever Network (PRRN) at www.prrn.com.

Searches Performed by Court Personnel. Some courts require that the names to be search for be handed over to the court clerk who performs the actual search. Some courts have computer terminals that a researcher can view in person; the researcher may have to type in each name, or the researcher views a list of names to see if the applicant's name appears. Some courts index names in other searchable formats such as ledgers, microfiche, or microfilm, although with increased computerization, that is becoming less common.

What to Expect if an Employer Does it Itself

If an employer is hiring locally, the employer can go to the local courthouse, talk to the court clerk, learn the system, and search the records. Of course, the court clerk cannot give an employer legal advice, but he or she may be helpful in showing the employer the local record keeping system.

 Most court clerk's offices have signs that say they do not give legal advice. Court clerks are generally prohibited by law from giving legal advice. Not only that, but free legal advice is worth exactly what is paid for it.

Suppose an employer has an applicant from one county away, or from the other side of the state, or even from another state. Record checking becomes a very different process. The employer then needs to locate the courthouse for that county. Since every court is different, the employer then needs to contact the court ahead of time to find out exactly what procedures they use. The court may require a letter or fax, a consent form, or a fee. Then there is the issue of turnaround time. By the time the request is mailed, processed, and returned, weeks may have passed. If there is a potential match – a "hit" – then further communication is needed to arrange getting a copy of the file. Courts typically charge a per-page copy fee and usually require any fees to be paid in advance. However, many courts will not do a name search of criminal records, ignoring requests sent by mail or telephoned.

That is where the alternative of hiring a record searcher is advantageous. Presumably, an employer does not want to drive everywhere to check records, not to mention the value of the employer's time.

Internet services are also available but employers need to be very wary of them. These types of searches are covered later in this chapter and in Chapter 10.

Start by Doing a Name Search

The first step involves the researcher looking on an index for the applicant's name, or the absence of it. If the name is not shown, then the search is marked "clear." When the name is found, there are additional steps to follow.

The critical point in doing a name search depends upon a human being either entering data in a computer or visually reviewing a list of names. As with any human endeavor, errors are possible. Any human error in data input, or when looking at a list of names, can result in a "false negative," meaning a person who in fact has a criminal record is reported as "clear" when in fact they are not.

Names can also be missed if the applicant used a variation of his or her first name. For example, if looking for "Robert Smith" a researcher must also look for a "Rob Smith" or a "Bob Smith." If a researcher was looking for a "James Evans" and the person was arrested under "Jim Evans," then the name could be missed. If the applicant is a "Junior," a court index may list that at the very end instead of in alphabetical order. If an applicant was arrested under the name "Joe Smith, Jr.," a search under the "S" category may miss it.

One factor working in a researcher's favor is that by the time court record had been created, there normally has been some sort of process whereby a law enforcement officer, a jail official, a District Attorney, or Judge will have verified the person's true name. For example, if a consumer is arrested, a police officer will normally look at a consumer's identification in the form of a state issued driver's license or identification card. If a person is booked into custody, a jail may take fingerprints. If a district attorney decided to file a criminal charge, it is usual and customary to run a criminal history and/or driving record to determine the consumer's criminal history for purposes of making a decision on the appropriate charges. As part of the arraignment process, in court, where an accused individual makes an initial court appearance, a Court will typically inquire if the name on the charging document is the defendant's true name. The criminal justice system is very aware that a defendant may have an incentive to play games with their true identity in order to escape more serious charges stemming from past conduct or to avoid having to pay fines or comply with probation terms or conditions. Of course, as discussed in Chapter 28 "Employer Issues with IDs, ID Theft, and Privacy," the ability to positively identify everyone is not perfect. But court procedures do assist in minimizing name and ID issues with criminal records.

A researcher also faces cultural complications when it comes to naming conventions. In some cultures, a person uses both the maiden name and the family surname. For example, Spanish names are often based upon a first name, the mother's maiden name, and the family name. However, if an applicant only goes by the mother's name, a completely different search strategy is needed. If a search is conducted for the name 'Juan Garcia Hernandez,' and a person was arrested under the name 'Juan Garcia,' then there is a strong likelihood the record will be missed.

Be Aware of Alias Names

A similar problem exists with former names or aliases, which are also called AKA (Also Known As). A common former name issue is with a female applicant who has changed her last name as a result of marriage. An employment application or screening form should ask for previous names. It should also ask for the DATE of the name change. For example, if a name change was 20 years ago, and an employer is only searching back seven years, there is no reason to search under the former name. It is also important to remember that an alias search is a separate search. If an applicant now has the name of Susan Jones, and she changed her name three years ago from Susan Barry, then both names should be searched. As far as court records are concerned, Susan Jones and Susan Berry are two entirely separate people. If the court is doing the search, two fees will be involved because two names are searched. The same can hold true if a screening firm conducts the search. There is normally an extra charge for the second name or alias search since the court researcher is looking for two entirely different names in the court records.

A second name search should *not* be referred to as a "maiden name" search since that clearly indicates that an employer is obtaining information on marital status, which is a prohibited basis upon which to make an employment decision. The second name search should be referred to as a "previous name search." More information about this trap and other legal concerns stemming from discrimination laws are reviewed in Chapter 2.

The idiosyncrasies surrounding the name search make it critical for employers to understand that criminal record searching is not perfect and should only be considered as only one of many tools that are part of an overlapping system of checks. The fact that a criminal record can be missed also serves to underscore the importance of getting the applicant to be honest on his or her application and in interviews. Employers who utilize the AIR (Application-Interview-Reference) Process described in Chapters 7-9 find there is a much-reduced likelihood of hiring a criminal.

If There Is a "Hit," a Researcher Must Pull a Court File to Confirm Identity

If a researcher finds a criminal record in the name of the applicant, does that mean the applicant cannot be employed? The answer is an emphatic NO. The location of a criminal record by a name match is just the start of the process. If there is a "hit" (a name match), then the researcher or background firm needs to determine if the person located is truly the applicant.

A best practice is to utilize all information in the possession of the researcher, employer, or screening firm to determine if the criminal record found reasonably is associated with the subject of the search. A researcher needs to locate an identifier in order to match the court record to the applicant. Examples of commonly used identifiers are:

✓ Date of birth
✓ Driver's license number
✓ Social Security number

Some records may track by race. However, for reasons discussed in Chapter 2 concerning discrimination laws, race is not a helpful criteria category for private employers to use. Another potential source of identification may be physical characteristics, such as height or weight. The issue, however, is that such information may well be missing from the public records. Remember, a researcher is looking only at available public records, and that does not include items that may contain racial or other physical identifiers such as police reports, jail book photos (commonly called "mug shots), and arrest warrants, jail booking records, or similar data.

Where are the identifiers located?

That depends upon the court and the way the records are kept. In some courthouses, identifiers may be part of the index system. An identifier may be on the computerized index, microfiches, or whatever system the court uses to provide a record index. In some courts, there are limitations on identifiers in order to protect privacy. In courts that limit identifiers, criminal case research is made more difficult because a researcher only has a name match.

A "Name Match Only"

If there is a name match on an index without identifiers, then the court researcher must review each possible court file that bears the same name of the applicant, in order to determine if there is an identifier that relates to the name to the subject of the search. A researcher will typically try to match on date of birth. If it is a common name, this can become a very laborious procedure. There are times when identifiers are not available from the court. This can happen, for example, if the Court has purged its old files and the case file has been physically destroyed. At the point, the researcher only has a name match without identifiers so there is a question if that case is associated with the applicant. That situation is commonly referred to as a **"name match only."** The problem with a "name match only" is two-fold. If the screening firm fails to report a potential criminal case where there are no identifiers but only a name match, and in fact it would have led to a red flag being discovered and a workplace problem avoided, then the screening firm can be potentially liable for not providing adequate information. On the other hand, if the "name match only" leads to a consumer dispute by an applicant that maintains it is not his or her criminal record, the screening firm must under the FCRA do a re-investigation (Section 611) and remove any data it cannot verify. That potentially puts a screening firm in a Catch-22. If a background screening firms does report a result based upon a "name match only" without identifiers, it is critical for the screening firm be clear that there are no identifiers. Many screening firms however will not report a "name match only," out of concern that it does not meet the accuracy requirements of the FCRA. This again underscores that although background checks are a critical due diligence tool, there are times when there are matters beyond the control of a screening firm. That is why it is important to keep in mind that no one tool should be relied upon to conduct due diligence, and that overlapping tools and processes are critical.

What data does a researcher look at in the court files?

✓ The charging document specifies the exact law by section, that the defendant is charged with, along with other details such as the name and location of the court and the prosecution who brings the case. It may contain identifiers about the defendant.

✓ The court docket and/or clerk minutes contain the events that occurred at each court appearance. It is essentially the history of the case. The docket will include such items as the plea entered by the defendant, and in the event the defendant either pleads guilty or is found guilty, it will contain the sentence imposed as well as the exact charges for which the defendant was convicted. This file may also contain identifiers.

In order to review the case file to look for identifiers, a court researcher must typically ask court personnel to find – or pull – files. In some courts, there are limits to how many files a court clerk can pull. Further delays are possible if the file is placed in storage. Although citizens generally have a right to access public files, the speed at which a court clerk chooses to obtain the files is up to that court clerk. Even when an employer performs background checks in person, there can be delays.

Why Do Some Government Agencies Feel Compelled to Shoot Themselves in the Foot?

In some jurisdictions, court clerks have taken the position that identifiers should be masked or not be made public in order to protect privacy and to guard against identity theft. Some counties have even restricted the access to court records. When this occurs, several things happen. First, employers and job applicants are immediately penalized because background checks take much longer. Any delay in a CRA's ability to complete reports in a timely manner works to the determent of consumers and employers. Consumers want a CRA to have fast access to criminal records. Second, criminals and terrorists are arguably the primary beneficiaries since they have a better chance of avoiding detection. Finally, the courts end up becoming over-burdened because suddenly there is a much-increased workload, as employers and researchers have a greater need to pull files to search for identifiers. If a researcher finds a match for common names in the court index, the researcher will need to request and review every file to look at identifiers in an effort to determine if the case belongs to the applicant in question. That substantially increases the workload on county clerks.

Although protecting privacy and combating identity theft are important considerations, courts need to balance privacy versus public access and the public good. Perhaps the best way to achieve the balance is to leave in the date of birth identifier needed to perform an accurate check and mask out the Social Security number. This way, researchers have access to date of birth, which is the primary identifier. Privacy is protected, since typically the Social Security Number is the tool used for identity theft. Leaving a date of birth on a court record presents a small privacy risk since little harm occurs to an individual if the date of birth is used.

The Researcher Must Confirm Case Details

Assuming the criminal file is examined and identifiers are located, that still does not mean the criminal matter can be used in the consideration of the applicant's employment. There are a number of reasons a criminal record may not be legal to use — there are a number of regulatory considerations to weigh before using a criminal record.

In order to determine if the record may be used, a researcher must obtain details about the case — the nature of the offense, the offense date, future court dates, sentencing, probation terms, and whether the case is a *felony* or a *misdemeanor*.

One note of caution — in most jurisdictions, the actual **police reports** are typically not **public records** and therefore not available in the file. Police reports typically contain witness statements, a description of the offense or crime scene, the statement of the defendant if one was made, and facts upon which a prosecution is based. This information is generally not available in the court file open to the public.

Still, searching the court file is helpful. First, there may be documents in the file pertaining to some legal process of interest. For example, in a criminal case, a defendant has the opportunity to file various motions, such as a motion to suppress evidence, or a statement, or to request some other legal remedy, such as a dismissal of charges. Also, in the legal papers filed by both sides, critical facts of the case may be revealed.

Information can be gleaned just from the public documents, typically a complaint, indictment, or some sort of charging document that would normally state the basis of the charges and may reveal the victim or additional case details. The court may state certain terms and conditions in the sentencing that may shed light on the case. If the defendant was convicted of assault, and the court orders the defendant to attend a drug program, that may indicate drugs were involved.

It Can Be a Big Mistake Not to Look for Misdemeanors - If Permitted

One of the biggest mistakes an employer can make is to only ask about or search for felonies, or the job application only asks about felonies. This practice is partly because in many states there are limitations on asking about misdemeanors. However, in some states, misdemeanors can be very serious.

An employer certainly wants to know if an applicant has been convicted of:

- ✓ Resisting arrest
- ✓ Battery on a police officer
- ✓ Possession of drug paraphernalia
- ✓ Illegal gun possession
- ✓ Commercial burglary
- ✓ Assaulting a child or spouse

In many states, these violations are misdemeanors, not felonies.

In some instances, a misdemeanor case can be extremely relevant to a job and even more relevant than a felony. For example, petty theft may be a misdemeanor, but if an applicant was being considered for a bookkeeping position, that would be good information to have. Another example: a driving under the influence can be a misdemeanor but a very relevant one to any position involving driving.

It is not unusual for felony charges to be reduced to a misdemeanor through a plea bargain. When some element of the case may be hard to prove, the felony charge can be reduced to a misdemeanor by plea-bargaining. There may have been mitigating circumstances in either the crime itself or in the life of the perpetrator, so that a prosecutor feels a misdemeanor is appropriate under the circumstances. Sometimes one "bad actor" commits a crime against another "bad actor," leading to one person with a criminal record testifying against another with a criminal record after having bargained for a lesser penalty in exchange for cooperating with authorities. In large jurisdictions with more crimes to prosecute than there are resources, there may be more pressure to plea-bargain cases out of the system.

The Bottom Line: Because a misdemeanor can be the result of behavior that may otherwise have been serious enough to be considered a felony, and is only a misdemeanor due to a plea bargain, employers cannot afford to ignore misdemeanors. But in order to ask about misdemeanors, it is important for the employer to first be aware of the rules in its state.

About Court Access Fees

When court personnel must perform the search onsite there is often an **access fee** or **search fee charged**. This court fee ranges from $1.00 to $20.00. A court may also charge a copy fee for documents and a certification fee if that document needs to be certified.

Fees are often incurred as well when the record index is searched online. The highest fee for a search, $65.00, is charged by the New York State Office of Court Administration's (OCA) of its statewide Criminal History Record Search (CHRS). Although New York authorities claim that is for an entire statewide search, it is not clear that all relevant courts or all potential offense are covered.

Background firms add these court fees as a surcharge to all searches since the fee represents an actual out-of-pocket cost. Since the fees vary by courts, some background screening firms add the surcharge automatically when an employer orders a search from a particular court. Other screening firms use a pricing platform that may average in the cost of the court fees on the theory that flat fees make accounting easier. Either way, it is a real cost that is eventually passed on to employers. An employer should make sure they understand which billing/fee approach a background firm utilizes.

Be Prepared for Court Delays

A common problem for background screening firms and employers is unavoidable court delays. By now, it is clear that criminal record searches done correctly are not a matter of just sitting at a computer and pushing buttons. Researchers need to do actual work for each and every name for the most accurate record. However, there are occasions that despite the best efforts of a court researcher, a court caused delay frustrates the employer's need to have the search competed in a short time period. Unfortunately, there are some situations where even if an employer hired Sherlock Holmes, the search cannot be completed any faster.

For example:

- ✓ Some counties do not provide access to a public terminal and require that names of applicants be submitted to the court clerk. Sine this is probably not the highest court priority, there can be delays.
- ✓ If a file needs to be physically examined to find additional identifiers or to verify the details of the case, there can be delays in the court clerk pulling the physical court file. If a court file has been moved to storage, and the court clerk only drives to the storage facility once a week, there is nothing anyone can do to make a court clerk go to the storage facility any faster.
- ✓ On occasions, court is subject to slow-downs due to budget cuts and layoffs. When that occurs, updating or processing criminal records is simply not a priority.
- ✓ Some courts are behind in computerizing case files.
- ✓ Winter weather, natural disasters, power outages, or similar problems can also adversely impact court researching. In such circumstance, a court may not be able to operate normally, or researchers may be physically prevented from accessing the court.

Looking for Criminal Offenses in Counties with Multiple Courts

When using the services of background screening firms, they typically only provide court records by searching the central courthouse.

While most counties have a central court where all felony records are held, some jurisdictions have multiple lower level courts such as municipal courts or justice of the peace courts. These local courts may not report all convictions to a central court. The good news, however, is that these outlying lower courts often only handle minor cases such as town or municipal infractions. If these cases were more serious, then they would typically be sent to the central court. An example is Aiken County, SC. There is a central Circuit Court where felonies and most misdemeanors are available. There are also five Magistrate Courts with minor case offenses. In this county it is not practical for employers to go driving all over the country side in case there is a minor record in a remote lower court not reported to that central circuit court.

Therefore, it is not likely employers are missing much if they fail to check the small courts. In addition, these local courts can be difficult to search, have irregular hours of operation, or may be located in remote areas. One plus is that if the offense is driving-related, such as a driving under the influence case, it should be reported to the state motor vehicle department and should show up in a driving record. However, there are exceptions. For example, in Middlesex County, MA, the use of the central court would miss the vast majority of criminal cases, since less than 10% are filed in the "central" court and the rest filed in outlying district courts such as Concord, Lowell, or Woburn.

The bottom line is that once again criminal record searches are not perfect and some offenses can still slip through the cracks.

Federal Court Rules Unnecessary Repetition of Single Criminal Incident can be Misleading and be the Basis of an Allegation for Punitive Damages Against Background Screening Firm

A case decided by a federal district court demonstrates the need for background screening firms to exercise reasonable procedures for maximum possible accuracy in order to avoid lawsuits for punitive damages.

In this case, the plaintiff alleged among other things that his background report unnecessarily repeated information about a single criminal incident multiple times, causing the criminal record to appear much more serous then it was. The case was brought on behalf of not only the plaintiff, but also on behalf of "the thousands of employment applicants throughout the country who have purportedly been the subject of prejudicial, misleading and inaccurate background reports performed by Defendant and sold to employers."

The plaintiff complained that the repeated reference to a single incident was inaccurate under the federal Fair Credit Reporting Act (FCRA) because it was misleading in such a way and to such an extent that it could be expected to affect employment decisions.

The plaintiff contended this constituted a violation of FCRA section 607(b) which states:

> *(b) Accuracy of report. Whenever a consumer reporting agency prepares a consumer report it shall follow reasonable procedures to assure maximum possible accuracy of the information concerning the individual about whom the report relates.*

The background firm brought a motion to dismiss on the basis the plaintiff did not state a claim upon which relief could be granted. In reviewing this motion, the Court did not make any factual determination, but instead assumed the plaintiff's allegations were true for purposes of the motion. The Court then determined that if all the factors are assumed to be true, if there is a basis for a judgment in favor of the plaintiff.

The plaintiff also asked for punitive damages. The background firm requested that claim be dismissed.

The Court ruled the prevailing national rule is a claim can be made where the plaintiff alleges sufficient facts in the legal pleadings to demonstrate even an accurate report can be misleading if it presents information in such a way it is misleading or it creates a materially misleading impression. (Although the 6th Circuit has adopted a more limited rule that looks at the technical accuracy of the report, the Court noted the majority of courts have agreed on a broader definition that would include misleading information.)

It is important to note, however, that while it was still a factual issue for the trier of fact (such as jury or a judge in the case of a Court trial) as to whether the information was misleading, the mere fact that a background report may be incorrect or misleading does not prove that a background firm did not utilize reasonable procedures. In some circumstances, the error can be so egregious that the error itself demonstrates a lack of reasonable procedures. The background firm however, still has the opportunity to present evidence that even though there was an error, the firm uses reasonable procedures, and the error was not a usual occurrence.

To prevail in a claim for an erroneous, inaccurate or misleading background report, a plaintiff must generally prove that:

- ✓ There was inaccurate or misleading information in a report;
- ✓ The report was inaccurate because a screening firm failed to exercise reasonable care;
- ✓ There was harm to the consumer; and
- ✓ The harm was caused by the background firm.

The case also discussed the punitive damages allegation which the background screening firm sought to dismiss. The background firm argued, among other things, that any alleged error in the report did not rise to the level of willful recklessness under Supreme Court case of *Safeco Ins Co. v. Burr, 551 U.S. 47 (2001)*. That case arguably lowered the threshold for punitive damages against a background screening firm. Here, the background firm argued that the allegations made against it did not meet to the standards in the Safeco case.

However, the court held that the "statutory text at issue here …has a plain and clearly ascertainable meaning." Since the allegations in case were that the background firm's conduct under FCRA section 607(b) could be found to be an objectively unreasonable interpretation of the statute, the plaintiff had the right to request punitive damages.

It should be noted that the actual case is much more detailed and contains other issues. In addition, it is critical to note that the motion was decided at the stage where the court only had legal pleadings and allegations, and there have been no actual facts determined.

However, the case does have some walkway points for background screening firms:

✓ Unnecessary reporting of a single criminal event multiple times in a background report where the impact is arguably to mislead an employer into believing that the consumer's background is more serious than it really is can be the basis for a claim of inaccuracy.

✓ Given the presence of punitive damages, it is even more critical for screening firms to pay close attention to their legal obligations. Errors made in such a way that is arguably objectively unreasonable under the plain meaning of the FCRA or in violation of clearly stated authority, can raise the stakes in any litigation.

The case is at www.paed.uscourts.gov/documents/opinions/10d0473p.pdf.

This case once again underscores that background screening is far from being a data driven endeavor where employers are just given data. It is a professional endeavor that is heavily legally regulated and can be unbelievably complex. It requires the services of background firms that have a great deal of ability and knowledge when it comes to federal and state legal compliance.

The State Agency Public Databases

A public database is a database maintained by an official government body, such as a court, where records are available online to the public for name look-ups. Some public databases are free to search while others are commercial systems with fees or subscriptions required for access to be granted. There are also commercial databases operated by third parties data aggregators. Those types of database are coved in a later section.

There are two possible locations at the state level that may hold criminal record data:

1. State Criminal Record Repository
2. Centralized State Court Administration

The key to using either of these systems as a primary search is if they are equivalent to an on-site search of the court records.

The following article provides an excellent overview of these state resources of criminal records. The article was written by Michael Sankey, CEO of BRB Publications, Inc. (www.brbpublications.com). The original article appeared in the April 2012 Issue of BRB's Free Newsletter – 'The Public Record Update.'

Following this article is a closer look at each of these state resources.

The Statewide Criminal Record Databases: How Good Are They?

Criminal court records are perhaps the most widely sought public record in the U.S. The process of researching court records online can be very complicated and frustrating because of the extensive diversity of the accessibility and content. Each state has two possible online resources of criminal court record content—

1. The court administration agency that oversees the state's trial and appellate court system. This agency is usually referred to as the Administration Office of the Courts (AOC) or the State Court Administration.

2. The designated state agency holding the criminal record repository. The agency may be known by such names as the Criminal Record Bureau or State Police or Department of Public Safety, etc.

About the State Court Administrator's Records

Most states have a centralized case management system managed by this agency. In 32 states this agency offers a program for a public search of state or county court docket information. Most programs are online, but Mississippi and South Dakota offer unique, non-online statewide programs. A search in these court managed systems can be a particularly useful tool in those states – such as NY, NC, or UT – which do not permit a search from the state's criminal records repository.

Note: Overall, only 66% of the courts holding felony records provide online access. Also, many states will not sell their data in bulk electronic format. These facts make you wonder about the legitimacy of some of the so-called instant national background checks being sold on the Web.

About the State Criminal Record Repositories

As mentioned, all states have a central criminal record repository of records on individuals who have been subject to that state's criminal justice system. The repository content comes from information submitted by state, county, parish, and municipal courts as well as from local law enforcement. Information forwarded to this agency includes notations of arrests and charges, all usually with a set of fingerprints. Afterward the disposition is later forwarded as well (most of the time). 27 states offer access online to the repository.

How to Measure the Worthiness of these Online Sources

The value of a statewide criminal record search varies by state. Online researchers need to be aware of the many possible nuances and variations. For example; 1) there is no instant online statewide search in AZ since the 2nd largest county is not online, but many firms tout an "instant" online service; 2) In MN, there are cases not on the statewide online system but do appear on the courthouse terminal system. Here are five factors to consider when evaluating the online statewide sources.

1. Is the site considered to have onsite equivalency? In other words, does the public access terminal (PAT) at the courthouse provide the exact same results and content as when searching online?

2. What is the date range of the records online – meaning how far back do the records go online? Not all online sources go back 7 years.

3. How reliable is the database in terms of completeness and accuracy? Are all incidents recorded? Are all dispositions recorded? Are records updated? Are all courts reporting?

4. What identifiers are provided – do you get the full DOB in order to match the subject to the record?

5. Is the online site termed to be an Official Site or is it a Public Information site with a very distinct and strong Disclaimer?

Pluses and Minus of the Court Systems

In general, the records found at the Office of Court Administration are more likely to show arrests and have the final disposition than records found at the state repository.

Often the online search is free, but not always. The use of subscription accounts is common. A growing trend is to offer online access to information on a pay-as-you-go basis. Some agencies will give you a glimpse of the index or docket, but will charge a fee for the record copy. Some allow the record to be printed on the spot; others may only mail a document.

As accurate as the best statewide online systems may be, the fact remains there will always be stories about exceptions, errors, typos, etc. The recording of records is still a condition where humans are doing data entry - so the phrase *Garbage In, Garbage Out* is applicable to some degree.

Pluses and Minus of the State Repository Systems

The states' official criminal record repositories often only have records submitted with fingerprints. While this is helpful when identifying the correct subject of the search, these records are more apt to only have convictions (no pendings) or to be missing dispositions or delayed disposition updates. Often deferred adjudication cases that were revoked resulting in a conviction at the county court do not make it into the repository. So how widespread is the disposition problem? Per the most recent statistics released by the U.S. Department of Justice the U.S. Department of Justice, Bureau of Justice Statistic's 2010 Survey of State Criminal History Information Systems, released November 2011

- 9 states reported that 25% or more of all dispositions received could NOT be linked to the arrest/charge information in the state criminal record database.

- A total of 1,753,623 unprocessed or partially processed court disposition forms were reported by 18 states.

- 27 states reported a significant backlog for entering court disposition data into the criminal history database.

See the full report at www.ncjrs.gov/app/publications/abstract.aspx?ID=259283.

Please don't misunderstand the message here – there are certainly good reasons for performing a search of a state repository record database. A statewide search covers a wider geographic range than a county search and is certainly less expensive than a separate search of each county. Many states do have strong database systems. But having access to the complete record with the final disposition can be a problem. And state statutes often designate this agency to be the official state repository–regardless of the completeness or accuracy.

The Bottom Line

A significant factor all providers and end-users of criminal records should consider boils down to a key concept - "What if the worthiness of the database is needed to show in court? Can you justify the validity of the search of the record source?"

Many consumer reporting agencies take the approach that for proper due diligence when performing a criminal record search, the best procedure is to use a statewide search with a county on-site search. And a search from a database vendor should also be considered as a key supplementary search. This is extremely critical for employers making hiring decisions in states with legislative limitations on using criminal records without dispositions or when using misdemeanor records.

Using the Centralized State Court Administration

Nearly all states now have some level of centralized case management system managed by an Administrative Office. In 32 states, this office provides record searching capabilities to the public. Access is often online but not necessarily statewide. Overall, it has been estimated that upwards of 65% of the courts in the U.S. have some sort of online access capability, and many of these online courts are accessed via the state court administration system.

The Good News

With online access, employers can go to a court web site and do name searches to see if their candidate is listed on any index of criminal cases. If the person's name is not on the list, the person can potentially be marked "clear." That assumes of course the database is complete and up to date.

Some systems offer a statewide search.

The Bad News

Unfortunately there is much more bad news about online court web sites:

- ✓ Typically, court web site searches are only of a record index. If there is an index "hit," the site does not give the searcher the full case file information. This means that arrangements must be made to retrieve actual court records. That may require some back-and-forth correspondence with the court, plus fees, release forms, etc., as described earlier.

- ✓ Online searches can also have limitations when using first names. Some courts will only search the exact name entered and not take into account any variations or "wildcard" first. So, if the employer has a Robert Smith who was charged under the name "Rob Smith" or "Bob Smith," an employer can get a "false negative." This means the person will come back "clear" and, in fact, he or she could have a criminal record. The alternative is to pay to search for each permutation of the first name.

- ✓ Identifiers are an issue for online services. Many court online systems require a requester to submit a date of birth. As discussed earlier, there can be a problem for the employer to obtain the DOB. A related problem is that the online index may contain only names with no identifiers. If the name does not appear (assuming the correct first name was run), then the person is clear. If a common name was run and gets matches, someone is then required to go to the courthouse and pull files to determine the proper identity.

- ✓ Most courts will have a disclaimer that the online data is "as is" and may not be a true reflection of actual court records. There may even be a "prohibition against commercial use."

- ✓ Remember those TV shows where a professional stunt person would perform, and the announcer would say, "Remember, we are professionals. Do not try this at home." To avoid getting false results, there is an element of training and experience needed when using some databases. A number of the court online sites are not equivalent to an onsite search at the courthouse (such as in Minnesota). Also there are online vendors selling "instant statewide court criminal record searches" in states where not all the records are online (such as Arizona). Unless a researcher or employer knows this, searches will be incomplete.

Federal Case Illustrates Problems with Using Statewide Court Data

In a case decided by a federal court in Kentucky, the court observed the difficulties with using a statewide court repository of records as the basis of a background check. The opinion also reviewed various difficulties in reporting public records. The court first noted that the statewide criminal records maintained by the Kentucky Administrative Office of the Courts (AOC) does not contain official court records, but is only a statewide repository of official records and clearly indicates in bold type it does not provide an official court report. The court reviewed the difficulties in reading and analyzing the Kentucky AOC records in this case that could lead to a misunderstanding of the actual court records from the county where the offense occurred. See below:

> **Court Finds No Liability Though Background Check Report Inaccurate since Employer Already Decided Not to Hire**
>
> In a case that touched upon number of issues affecting background checks, a federal district court held that even though a background check report was erroneous and inaccurate, it had no bearing on the employment decision since a hospital had already decided to not hire a candidate based upon their prior knowledge of misconduct and a bad interview.
>
> In a decision from the U.S. District Court for the Western District of Kentucky, the plaintiff applied for a position as an Associate Medical Director. Before the background check report was returned, the hospital discovered that the plaintiff had been involved in criminal activity related to prescription

drugs, although not aware of the details. The plaintiff also interviewed very poorly. The decision had already been made to continue the search to fulfill that position before the background check report was returned.

The background check report, based upon a review of a statewide repository of county court records maintained by the Kentucky Administrative Office of the Courts (AOC), reported a felony for possession of controlled substance not stored in their original container.

Upon reviewing the background check report, the Plaintiff notified the background check firm that the report was wrong. Within several minutes, the background check firm contacted the county where the offense occurred and attempted to correct the background check report to show the plaintiff only had a misdemeanor conviction (although the details were still not entirely correct).

In ruling on a motion for summary judgment, the Court ruled that even assuming all of the allegations by the plaintiff were correct, the plaintiff failed to state a grounds for relief in that the hospital had already decided NOT to hire before reviewing the inaccurate background check report, and that the incorrect report "merely supported the decision they had already made." The court noted that the background check report was promptly amended, and although it was still not entirely accurate, did indicate the offense was only a misdemeanor.

The opinion also reviewed various difficulties in reporting public records. The Court first noted that the statewide criminal records maintained by the Kentucky AOC does not contain official court records, but is only a statewide repository of official records and that it clearly indicates in bold type that it is not an official court report. The Court reviewed the difficulties in reading and analyzing the Kentucky AOC records in this case that could lead to a misunderstanding of the actual court records from the county where the offense occurred. The Court noted the even after contacting the court clerk in Jefferson County, the background check firm still did not have an entirely accurate report, although it was correct insofar as the ultimate offense was a misdemeanor.

The Court also addressed the fact that there are different approaches to analyzing if a background check firm utilized reasonable procedures in reporting criminal records:

✓ The Court noted that one approach is that a background check firm is entitled to rely upon whatever is noted in the official court records, and is not obligated to go beyond that. To require more would be unduly burdensome and expensive. In addition, if there is an inaccuracy, a consumer is in the better position to note it, and can bring it to the attention of the consumer reporting agency (CRA) that can then correct it.

✓ A second approach is that a background check firm is responsible for looking beyond the notations in a court report to ensure the information is correct.

✓ A third approach is that a background check firm can report what is in a public record, provided that it believes the source is reputable and there is nothing to suggest that there are problems with the sources of information, or that the information appears implausible or inconsistent.

✓ A fourth approach is that any allegation of errors are an issue for a jury to decide, unless the issue of reasonableness is beyond question or was not the cause of an adverse hiring decision as in this case.

This case was complicated by the fact that background check firm did NOT utilize the actual county legal records, but instead relied upon on a statewide repository, which did not apparently tell the entire story. However, given that any error was not the cause of the plaintiff's failure to get the job under the unique facts of the case, but was only an "additional cumulative justification," the Court did not have to decide if the background check firm used reasonable procedures.

The case potentially creates a defense for background check firms sued for inaccurate reports, where the facts show that a decision has already been made not to hire and therefore the background check report was not a cause of any alleged damages.

In addition, the case also demonstrates potential dangers of using secondary sources of information instead of going to the actual courthouse to view the primary records. Although the court ultimately decided the case on the basis that the background check report did not cause the decision, the court discussion demonstrates once again that background checks are heavily legally regulated. Background check firms need to take precautions to ensure accuracy in reporting criminal records.

See: http://law.justia.com/cases/federal/district-courts/kentucky/kywdce/3:2008cv00272/65643/47.

Here is another example:

A Graphic Illustration of the Need for Caution in Using Court Databases

During the 2003 California recall elections, an individual made allegations of misconduct against one of the candidates. A supporter of an opposing candidate apparently went online to the Los Angeles County court system and ran the name, finding serious criminal records that certainly raised questions about the character of the accused. The problem was, according to news accounts that came out later, the criminal record belonged to someone else. So, defamation lawsuits were contemplated. This is a graphic reminder of the pitfalls of using court indexes without pulling files to look for all possible identifiers *before* making conclusions.

Using the State Criminal Record Repository

All states have a central criminal record repository of records on individuals who have been subject to that state's criminal justice system. The repository content comes from information submitted by state, county, parish, and municipal courts as well as from local law enforcement. Information forwarded to this agency includes notations of arrests and charges, all usually with a set of fingerprints. Afterward, the disposition is later forwarded as well (most of the time).

The Good News
- ✓ Usually there is no problem with identifiers.
- ✓ If fingerprints are being used, this is the place to go.
- ✓ Some states have designated these agencies as the "official source."

The Bad News
For employment purposes, accessing state-held records at the official state repository may not be as useful as might be expected due to a number of reasons including:

- ✓ Many statewide systems are only clearinghouses for those counties that choose to deposit records and are not actually the most accurate source of data. There are no guarantees that all counties are up-to-date or even participating.
- ✓ Also, other statewide databases might be put together by correctional authorities and are not complete.

- ✓ There are some counties that have their records online and some states that have online records directly from the state court – but not all.
- ✓ Some states do not even have such a resource, such as California.
- ✓ In some states offering a criminal records service, especially through a law enforcement agency, there can be substantial time delays.
- ✓ Complicating matters, the employer must make sure they utilize the appropriate form and send the required means of fee payment. Often, a release form signed by the applicant and even fingerprints are required. There is a bureaucratic delay as someone in the appropriate state office physically processes and responds to each request. If the request form is not filled out correctly, the request may be sent back.
- ✓ If there is a potential "hit," then delays can be even longer since someone at the state agency may be required to conduct a physical review of the material to determine if it is eligible for release. Reviewing criminal files quickly may not be a state employee's number one priority.
- ✓ If the state is willing to release information, the data in their computer system may be only a summary of the charges, or incomplete. Then the employer may need to request and view the actual file to determine what the case is about.

Utilizing the Best Criminal Records Alternatives and Resources

Employers and screening companies are free to use a combination of resources. In some states it may make sense to do a criminal record at both the county level and at the state level. Other employers may enhance their search results when they do a name search at the county level and also a search through PACER, which is the federal court records online system. There are also private vendor databases, state drivers' records, and jail and prison records.

Employers who use the services of pre-employment screening firms will find these screening experts will have plenty of good suggestions on which sources to search for criminal records.

For the reasons discussed above, these sources must be approached with caution and are typically not a primary source of information for employers. First, consider: In the event of a "hit" during a database search or online search, the physical files still need to be pulled for inspection, and there are a number of traps for the unwary.

A case on point is Texas:

State Audit Reveals Gaps in Criminal Records Database Affect Background Checks in Texas

A 2011 state audit in Texas has revealed that gaps in the state's criminal records database may cause criminal background checks used to screen job applicants – including teachers, doctors, nurses and daycare employees – to fail to uncover arrest records. The audit also found that the state's Department of Public Safety (DPS) Computerized Criminal History System is an unreliable source for complete information and that DPS should improve the timeliness and accuracy of its data.

According to the Fort Worth Star-Telegram, while Texas state law requires courts and prosecutors to submit information to the state within 30 days of receiving it, in 2009 prosecutors and courts failed to submit disposition records on about one of every four arrests, a slight improvement from a 2006 audit. In addition, the audit found:

✓ In November 2010, 1,634 of 21,351 offenders – 7.65 percent – admitted to jail, prison, or probation by the Texas Department of Criminal Justice did not have corresponding prosecutor and court records in the DPS system.

✓ County officials cannot submit some records because they lack required arrest incident numbers or state identification numbers (Tarrant County alone had 1,730 probation records that lacked the state identification number).

✓ Computer problems may cause county officials to receive rejection or error notices when the DPS system does not accept records they submit.

✓ The Texas Code of Criminal Procedure does not provide DPS with the ability to penalize prosecutor offices and courts for not submitting information.

✓ Criminal history background checks provided by DPS do not include probation records.

See www.star-telegram.com/2011/09/29/3406283/database-gaps-hinder-texas-criminal.html for the full story from the *Star-Telegram*.

The problem with gaps in criminal database records hindering background checks in Texas is not new. A 2004 investigation by the *Dallas Morning News* concerning inadequacies in the statewide criminal database maintained by the Texas Department of Public Safety, found that the Texas database was used over 3 million times a year but only had 69 percent of the complete criminal histories records for 2002.

The Morning News revisited the story in August 2008 and found, essentially, that nothing had changed. For 2006, the database still only had 69% of the state's criminal history. The story noted that only 106 out of Texas' 254 counties reported electronically and even then there appeared to be glitches or communication issues with various state law enforcement agencies. Other problems had to do with keeping trained personnel or officials in smaller jurisdictions that kept forgetting to report the status of a case.

These stories underscore common issues for employers performing background checks where searches of criminal databases can be problematic. Employers need to keep these problems in mind when utilizing criminal databases. The best practice is for all possible criminal "hits" on databases is to be reconfirmed at the county court level to insure the information is accurate, complete, and up to date.

Additional State Criminal Record-Related Databases

In addition to the sources already mentioned, there are other search resources available to employers. These include driving records, the local prison system, the Federal Bureau of Prisons (BOP), and sexual offender databases.

What each of these searches has in common is that, in theory, the records should have already been found. For example, a search of state and federal prisons should indicate the same record found during a court search. The driving records and sexual offender databases are compilations of a particular category of conviction that also would have generated a criminal record in the first place.

Given the limitations inherent in criminal records, checking these "secondary sources" provides an extra layer of protection. However, each of the searches has a drawback.

State Motor Vehicle Records – MVR's

As mentioned previously, matters reported on driving records are driving-related only, thus not nearly a complete resource of criminal records. On the plus side, an MVR search is a true statewide search. These records are discussed in more detail in Chapter 20.

State Sexual Offender Registers

State sexual registration requirements became mandatory on May 17, 1996 when a law, popularly now known as Megan's Law, was signed by President Clinton. This law had two primary goals:

✓ To require each state and the federal government to register sexual predators; and
✓ To provide for community notifications.

A more detailed discussion of the uses and limitations of these sex offender searches is provided in Chapter 20.

Federal Prison Locator

The Federal Bureau of Prisons (BOP) has an inmate locater on its website www.BOP.gov. The site contains information about inmates going back to 1982. However, as a research tool, the database has the same drawbacks as most other large databases of names. If an employer already has the inmate's prison number — or another government number, such as the FBI or INS number — then the look-up is easy. However, for a pre-employment inquiry, an employer presumably would not have that number. There may be an additional look-up options that allow lookup by other factors such as race, sex, and age usually within two years. Due to rules concerning the use of race as a factor in employment, it is unlikely that any employer will use that search option. In addition, many employers have the same sensitivity about age. This leaves only a name search. Any database that depends upon a name only look-up inherently has problems, plus, when information is entered into a database from numerous sources, there is increased likelihood of discrepancies. As a result, this is another database that requires a researcher to run all sorts of first name variations, including just the first letter of the target's first name.

State Prison Records

A number of states have state prisoner locator services on the Internet. Each state with a locator operates differently. Some sites contain only current prisoners, some contain those on parole, and others contain historical information. Again, as with any database, a researcher needs to fully understand the look-up logic and be prepared to run a number of name variations. There are two excellent resources to find these websites:

✓ www.corrections.com/links (Go to "Inmate Locator")
✓ www.brbpublications.com/freeresources/pubrecsites.aspx

Many of the state correctional databases are included in proprietary databases compiled by vendors, as described in a later next section.

 AUTHOR TIP One of the most comprehensive and up-to-date lists of free searchable public databases is available online at no charge. See www.brbpublications.com/freeresources/pubrecsites.aspx

For more information, including an in-depth profile of each county and state agency including procedures on how to access records, restrictions and requirements, policies and procedures, fees, and contact information is found in the Public Record Research System (PRRS). See www.brbpublications.com/products.aspx.

Federal Courts Are a Separate System

There are two entirely separate court systems in the United States – federal courts and state courts. A search of one system does not include a search of the other system, and each system operates under its own sets of rules and has its own courthouses, clerk's offices, indexes, and judges.

Federal District Courts are the trial courts that oversee criminal law cases and therefore these court records can be a critical search resource for employers.

Based on the fact that the overwhelming numbers of prosecutions are in state courts, many feel that federal searches have a relatively low rate of return. According to the Prisoners in 2010 (Revised) report from the Bureau of Justice Statistics (BJS), the federal prison population reached 209,771 prisoners by the end of 2010, up 0.8% (1,653 prisoners), the smallest percentage growth since 1980. Meanwhile, state correctional authorities had jurisdiction over 1,402,624 prisoners at yearend 2010. Approximately half (51%) of federal inmates in 2010 were serving time for drug offenses, 35% for public order defenses (largely weapons and immigration), and less than 10% each for violent and property offenses. For more information, see: http://bjs.ojp.usdoj.gov/content/pub/pdf/p10.pdf.

The decision to include a federal search, especially when hiring for a lower paid position, should take into account two other factors:

1. **The Nature of Federal Prosecutions**. The old saying, "Don't make a federal case out of it" has some relevance to the type of cases employers might find in federal court. By definition, federal courts are the place where violations of federal law are prosecuted. Although in recent years there has been a trend in congress toward "federalizing" more offenses that have traditionally been associated with state courts, federal crimes still tend to be slanted toward more serious cases, such as large drug cases, financial fraud, bank robbery, kidnappings, and interstate crimes. The majority of criminal cases in federal court are for drug violations. In 2001, of the 82,614 cases commended in federal court by the U.S. Attorney's office, 86% were for felonies. Of those, 43% were drug related. Another 14% involved immigration offenses.
2. **Federal Sentencing Procedures**. In federal courts, defendants are sentenced according to mechanical procedures set forth in the U.S. Sentencing Guidelines. This procedure has produced very long sentences, especially for drug offenders and those who commit acts of violence or crimes with weapons. In 2001 the average federal prison sentence was 57 months, with the highest sentences going to defendants convicted of violent felonies (91 months), weapons felonies (87 months), and drug felonies (74 months).

In many instances, the tip-off to a federal violation is not a court record search, but a large unexplained gap in the employment history. This underscores a key point made previously — that a past employment check can be just as critical as a criminal record check.

Because of the nature of federal crimes and sentences, many employers have seen less relevance in doing federal searches. Another reason for the lack of enthusiasm for federal record searches is the fact that a federal offense by definition can occur anywhere in the U.S. Thus, it is harder to select which jurisdictions to search, unless an employer uses the PACER system described below.

The Good and the Bad about Federal Criminal Record Checks

The "Good"

The federal courts use a centralized online system called PACER (Public Access to Court Electronic Records) that provides record searches for the public for most U.S. courts. Through PACER, a user accesses the "U.S. Party/Case Index." This index contains certain information from the court files — case numbers and the names of those involved in the case. For an employer trying to determine if an applicant has a federal criminal record, the system is beneficial since it allows one to search by name.

The PACER Case Locator is a national index for U.S. district, bankruptcy, and appellate courts for conducting nationwide searches to determine whether or not a party is involved in federal litigation. A small subset of information from each case is transferred to the PACER Case Locator each night and the system serves as a locator index for PACER.

In addition, the CM/ECF (Case Management/Electronic Case Filing) system is the Federal Judiciary's comprehensive case management system for all bankruptcy, district, and appellate courts that allows courts to accept filings and provide access to filed documents over the Internet. Some of the advantages of CM/ECF include:

✓ Keeping out-of-pocket expenses low;
✓ Giving concurrent access to case files by multiple parties;

- ✓ Offering expanded search and reporting capabilities;
- ✓ Offering the ability to immediately update dockets and make them available to users;
- ✓ Offering file pleadings electronically with the court, and
- ✓ Downloading documents and printing them directly from the court system.

The PACER website is www.pacer.gov.

The "Bad"

The "bad" part about PACER is that it typically does not provide enough identifiers to do a proper match. Date of birth or Social Security number is not part of a PACER report. If the applicant has a common name, identification can be very difficult. Under the FCRA, a screening firm may not be exercising "reasonable procedures for maximum possible accuracy" by merely reporting a "name match only." If the consumer requests a re-investigation, a screening firm may have a difficult time justifying having reported a mere name match in the first place. Often additional documents are needed.

Even if a federal court document is pulled, identifiers are typically hard to find, unlike the county level courts where there is often a date of birth. According to BRB Publication's Public Record Research System, more than 85% of the district courts show only the name on search results. The other 15% show a partial identifier such as the birth year. If there is a name match only, then other means must be used to determine if that case relates to a particular applicant. For example, if a person was found guilty of a serious offense, and the court files indicate a substantial prison sentence, but the applicant in question was employed during that time period, then the case was probably not the same person. If a conclusion cannot be reached by comparing information in the court file to information that has been confirmed by the employer, then it may be necessary to do some sleuthing, perhaps with a phone call to the AUSA (an Assistant United States Attorney who acts as the prosecutor in federal court cases) or the criminal defense attorney. Case materials will typically reveal the attorneys for both sides.

AUTHOR TIP One of the most comprehensive and up-to-date lists of free searchable public databases is available online at no charge. See www.brbpublications.com/freeresources/pubrecsites.aspx

For the rest of the story - detailed information on 20,000+ agencies including in-depth profiles of each county court, federal court, and state agency, including procedures on how to access records, restrictions and requirements, procedures, fees, and contact information see the Public Record Research System (PRRS) at see www.brbpublications.com/products.aspx.

Private Databases — Their Value and Limitations

A tool widely touted to employers is a "national database search" of criminal records. A number of vendors advertise they have, or have access to, a "national database of criminal record information." These services typically talk about having millions of records from all states. Unfortunately, this form of advertising can create an impression in an employer's mind that they are getting the real thing — access to the nation's criminal records. Nothing could be further from the truth.

These databases are compiled from a number of various state repositories, sexual offender registries, correctional, and county sources. There are a number of reasons why this database information may not be accurate or complete. It is critical to understand that these multi-state database searches represent **a research tool only, and under no circumstances are they a substitute for a hands-on search at the county level.**

Users of these databases must proceed with caution. Just because a person's name appears in one of these databases it does not mean the subject is a criminal. On the other hand, if a person's name does not appear, this likewise should not be taken as conclusive that the person is not a criminal. In other words, these databases can result in "false negatives" or "false positives;" and an over-reliance can cause one to develop a false sense of security.

Database Value and Limitation Issues

These database searches are of **value** because they cover a much larger geographical area than traditional county-level searches. By casting a much wider net, a researcher may pick up information that might be missed. The firms that sell database information can show test names of subjects that were "cleared" by a traditional county search, but criminal records were found in other counties through their searchable databases. In fact, it could be argued that failure to utilize such a database demonstrates a failure to exercise due diligence given the widespread coverage and low price.

But overall, the best use of these databases is as a **secondary or supplemental research tool**, or "lead generator" which tells a researcher where else to look.

The compiled data typically comes from a mix of state repositories, correctional institutions, courts, and any number of other county agencies that are willing to make their data public, or to sell data to private database brokers that accumulate large "data dumps" of information.

The **limitations** of searching a private database are the inherent issues about completeness, name variations, timeliness, and legal compliance.

Completeness and Accuracy Issues

The various databases that vendors collect may not be the equivalent of a true all-encompassing multi-state database.

- ✓ First, the databases may not contain complete records from all jurisdictions — not all state court record systems contain updated records from all counties. The various databases that vendors collect are not the equivalent of a true all-encompassing multi-state database. First, the databases may not contain complete records from all jurisdictions — not all state court record systems contain updated records from all counties. In California, for example, a limited number of counties allow their data to be used, and even those counties do not provide data of birth. Since most firms need to use both name and date of birth to find names, there are very few "hits" form California. If the date of birth was not used in the search, then there would be too many names returned to deal with. New York is another example. These databases only contain New York corrections records of people who have been to prison and can only be obtained by going through an official New York statewide search offered by the New York AOC for a large fee. So, when Texas is added into the mix as discussed earlier with its problems, then the three of the largest states—California, New York, and Texas—will represent insufficient coverage.
- ✓ Second, for reporting purposes, the records actually reported may be incomplete or lack sufficient detail about the offense or the subject.
- ✓ Third, some databases contain only felonies or contain only offenses where a state corrections unit is involved.
- ✓ Fourth, the database may not carry subsequent information or other matter that could render the results not reportable, or result in a state law violation concerning criminal records use. For example, in states that provide for deferred adjudication, once a consumer goes back to court and gets the record corrected, the database firm may still be reporting the old data. There is typically not a mechanism for a data broker to correct any one individual's record. Because of the issues with database as to completeness and accuracy, another issue is a false sense of security. Databases can have both false positives and false negatives. This is another reason why employers should be very cautionary.
- ✓ Finally, there are some states where a date of birth is not in the court records made public. Since databases match records by date of birth, searching when no DOB exists is of little value since no "hits" will be reported. In those situations, it is necessary to run a search in just the state in question and then individually review each name match. That can be tedious, especially if a common name is being searched.

The result is a crazy quilt patchwork of data from various sources and lack of reliability. These databases are more accurately described as "multi-jurisdictional databases."

Name and Date of Birth Match Issues

Besides the possibility of lacking identifiers as described above, an electronic search of a vendor's database may not be able to recognize variations in a subject name, which a person may potentially notice if manually looking at the index. The applicant may have been arrested under a different first name or some variation of first and middle name. A female applicant may have a record under a previous name. Some database vendors have attempted to resolve this problem with a wild card first name search (i.e. instead of Robert, use Rob* so that any variations of ROB will come up). However, there are still too many different first and middle name variations. There is also the chance of name confusion for names where a combination of mother and father's name is used. In addition, some vendors require the use of date of birth in order to prevent too many records from being returned. If an applicant uses a different date of birth, it can cause errors.

The issue comes down to technically how broad or how narrow the database provider sets the search parameters. If a database sets the search parameters on a narrow basis, so it only locates records based upon exact date of birth and last name, then the number of records located not related to the applicant would be reduced. In other words, there will be less "false positives." However, it can also lead to records being missed, either because of name variations or because some states do not provide date of birth in the records. That can lead to "false negatives." Conversely, if the parameters are set broadly to avoid missing relevant records, then there is a greater likelihood of finding criminal records relating to the applicant, but at the same time, there are likely to be a number of records that do not belong to the applicant. That can happen for example in a state where no date of birth is provided, and the database is run on a "name match only basis.

Timeliness Issues

Records in a vendor's database may be stale to some extent. The government agency selling the data often offers the data on a monthly basis. Even after a vendor receives new data, there can be lag time before the new data is downloaded into the vendor database. Generally the most current offenses are the ones less likely to come up in a database search.

Legal Compliance Issues

When there is a "hit" an employer must be concerned about legal compliance. If an employer uses a commercial database via the Internet, the employer must have an understanding of the proper use of criminal records in that state. If the employer acts on face value results without any additional due diligence research, potentially the applicant could sue the employer if the record was not about them.

If a screening firm locates a criminal hit, then the screening firm has an obligation under the FCRA Section 613 (a)(2) to send researchers to the court to pull the actual court records. This section requires that a background-screening firm must:

> "…maintain strict procedures designed to insure that whenever public record information, which is likely to have an adverse effect on a consumer's ability to obtain employment, is reported, it is complete and up-to-date. For purposes of this paragraph, items of public record relating to arrests, indictments, convictions, suits, tax liens, and outstanding judgments shall be considered up-to-date if the current public record status of the item at the time of the report is reported."

As discussed in Chapter 3, FCRA section 613(a)(1) provides an alternative procedure. Instead of going to the courthouse, a Consumer Reporting Agency (CRA) can notify the consumer that public record information is being reported by the consumer reporting agency and give name and address of the requester. However, some states arguably do not permit this alternative procedure. This is a potential compliance issue for employers who operate in states that do not allow the "notification" procedure to be used instead of the "strict procedure" method of double-checking at the courthouse.

So, unless an industry is controlled by a federal or state regulation, there are no national standards and few state standards for conducting criminal record checks by private employers (beyond FCRA). When there is a lawsuit involving wrongful use of criminal records, a jury decides whether an employer was negligent or not.

Two states, Florida and Texas, have passed some laws setting criminal records use standards. In Florida, an employer that uses the official Florida online database is presumed not to be negligent, although NOT using official state databases does not result in an employer being presumed to be negligent. Texas now requires criminal record checks on in-home workers (*V.T.C.A., Civil Practice & Remedies Code § 145.002*).

The best approach for an employer is to insist that a CRA always confirm the details of a database search by going to the courthouse to review the actual records. For a detailed discussion about the legal uses of a database, see the November 2002 report called *"National" Criminal History Databases: Issues and Opportunities in Pre-employment Screening* at www.esrcheck.com/file/NationalCriminalHistoryDatabases.pdf. Below is an excerpt from this article. Additional information about the FCRA and databases is covered in Chapters 3 and 10.

"National" Criminal History Databases: Issues and Opportunities in Pre-employment Screening

By Carl R. Ernst and Les Rosen, November 26, 2002

"...7. Conclusions

We have looked at the issues raised by the availability of online, proprietary criminal history databases from the point of view of the vendors that provide them, the CRA/pre-employment screening firms that use them, and the employers who either use them or obtain information through CRA's from them.

We have concluded that such databases are a potentially useful and legal tool for employers and their agents to use, as long as each kind of user understands:

1. The inherent limitations of the information in these databases,

2. The inherent liabilities under FCRA and other federal and state laws for misuse of information garnered from these databases,

3. The necessity of also performing actual searches in actual courts to verify criminal case information unless FCRA 613(a)(1) is invoked, and

4. The necessity of contractual provisions among vendors, CRA's and employer clients to determine how information may be reported.

Whether or not the proprietary criminal history database vendors come to grips with the issues raiseed in this article, CRA's and employers should use the information obtained from these databases with great care to assure compliance with the letter as well as the spirit of the FCRA.

The entire report is available at www.esrcheck.com/file/NationalCriminalHistoryDatabases.pdf. The paper was cited in several footnotes by the EEOC in the April 25, 2012 Guidance.

AUTHOR TIP | **Criminal Database Reports Sold Directly to Employers without Courthouse Verifications puts Entire Screening Industry in a Bad Light**

Under FCRA section 613, it is the "letter notice" option that is a significant cause of inaccurate data. Inaccurate criminal records come primarily from data aggregators that sell data over the Internet directly to businesses. These records are unfiltered by a professional CRA that has an obligation under the FCRA to provide accurate data. In California, by comparison, a background screening firm can only report a criminal conviction or other matters of public record for employment purposes if "it is complete and up to date," which is defined as checking the status at the time the matter is reported. See California Civil Code section 1786.28(b).

Some data brokers do have language that attempts to tell employers that such databases are not to be used for employment and are not FCRA compliant. However, these warnings, if even given, are often in the fine print.

Double-checking a database "hit" at the courthouse certainly affords employees, applicants, and background screening firms the most protection and the highest degree of accuracy. The duty to deal with adverse information in a public record can have an important impact when using criminal record databases.

If the goal is to increase accuracy and to prevent unsubstantiated bulk data from being provided to employer's, the obvious and most immediate remedy is to apply the California rule nationally, and to prohibit the letter option.

Concerned CRAs and the Use of Databases

Approximately 170 leading Consumer Reporting Agencies have joined 'Concerned CRAs' to publically reject the use of databases without taking the steps necessary to a ensure accuracy and completeness as required under the FCRA. The Concerned CRAs and their position statements on bulk data and offshoring can be found at their web site www.concernedcras.com.

According to the Concerned CRAs website, the organization's membership who all are committed to maintaining FCRA compliant standards are concerned that:

. . .some employment background screening firms sell "national criminal records databases" to employers without appropriate safeguards to ensure that the information they are delivering is accurate and up to date. We believe that criminal records databases are valuable sources of information if they are used in a responsible manner.

We are concerned that these practices do not appropriately protect employment applicants from avoidable harm. Likewise, employers are placed at increased risk of litigation and public relations problems when their employment background screening partners employ these practices. Ultimately, we are concerned that ongoing media coverage related to errors in background checks and the potential for litigation and overreaching legislative solutions place our profession at risk.

The Concerned CRAs statement on use of criminal databases:

Often marketed as "national" or "nationwide", criminal records databases are compiled by private companies who purchase information from a patchwork of sources: county courts, state criminal records repositories, sex offender registries, and prison systems.

Criminal records database searches are valuable because they cover a much larger geographical area than searching only the jurisdictions associated with an employment applicant's residential history. People may get into legal trouble in jurisdictions where they don't live. Because there are more than 3,200 counties in the United States, not all courts can be effectively checked on-site.

While criminal records databases are useful in identifying potential criminal records they should not be relied upon as accurate or complete for several reasons:

✓ *Most jurisdictions do not make their records available in bulk electronic format, which means that many important criminal records are missing from criminal records databases.*

✓ *Many jurisdictions remove key pieces of defendant's identifying information (such as date of birth). This often leads to criminal records being associated by the database with the wrong person. For example, an employment applicant with a common name might be confused with a registered sex offender with the same name.*

✓ *Because criminal records often change over time, databases sometime report outdated information to employers. For instance, expunged or sealed cases are sometimes found in database records. Likewise, probated cases that later turn into convictions when the defendant fails to successfully complete probation are often misreported.*

A CRA that chooses to display the "Responsible Criminal Databases" seal is self-certifying that they subscribe to the following standards when using criminal records in databases in the context of employment-related screening, exclusive of the screening of volunteers, tenants, and other non-employment relationships:

1. *Criminal records databases compiled by non-government entities will only be used as indicators of possible records. Prior to making any report about a potential or current employee to an employer about a criminal record from a database, the CRA will verify the information directly with the reporting jurisdiction. This ensures that employers make decisions based on accurate and up-to-date information.*

2. *When using these databases it is important that current or prospective employer clients are provided information about the limited nature of criminal records databases and the importance of researching each applicant's criminal history in the jurisdictions in which the applicant currently or previously has lived or worked.*

There are also specific issues with the database vendors being data brokers. While most CRAs do not store personal data of consumers, public record brokers are a separate issue. The FTC has made an effort to rein in data brokers.

FTC Privacy Report Recommends Legislation to Regulate Data Brokers

The FTC final report – 'Protecting Consumer Privacy in an Era of Rapid Change: Recommendations For Businesses and Policymakers' – recommended that Congress consider enacting data broker legislation.

In the report, the FTC calls on data brokers to make their operations more transparent by creating a centralized website to identify themselves, and to disclose how they collect and use consumer data. In addition, the website should detail the choices that data brokers provide consumers about their own information. The FTC report notes that data brokers often buy, compile, and sell highly personal information about consumers who are often unaware of their existence and to how their data is used.

To address the invisibility of – and the lack of consumer control over – the collection and use of consumer information by data brokers, the FTC supports legislation that would provide consumers with access to information about them held by data brokers. To further increase transparency, the FTC calls on data brokers that compile data for marketing purposes to explore creating a centralized website where data brokers could:

✓ Identify themselves to consumers and describe how they collect and use consumer data and

✓ Detail the access rights and other choices they provide with respect to the consumer data they maintain.

While Congress considers such privacy legislation, the FTC urges individual companies and self-regulatory bodies to accelerate the adoption of the principles contained in the privacy framework if they have not already done so. The FTC will work to encourage consumer privacy protections by focusing on greater transparency whereby companies should disclose details about their collection and use of consumer information and provide consumers access to the data collected about them.

The FTC report recommends companies to develop clear standards regarding privacy and train their employees to follow them. Trade associations and self-regulatory groups also should be more proactive in providing guidance to their members about retention and data destruction policies. Accordingly, the FTC calls on industry groups for data brokers and other sectors – including the online advertising industry, online publishers, mobile participants, and social networks – to do more to provide guidance in this area.

According to the report, data brokers are "companies that collect information, including personal information about consumers, from a wide variety of sources for the purpose of reselling such information to their customers for various purposes, including verifying an individual's identity, differentiating records, marketing products, and preventing financial fraud." However, the FTC also noted that consumers "are often unaware of the existence of these entities, as well as the purposes for which they collect and use data."

The FTC report is at: www.ftc.gov/os/2012/03/120326privacyreport.pdf.

Are There Limits to the Use of Private Databases?

Remember the story in Chapter 3 about a data broker who agreed to pay $800,000 to settle Federal Trade Commission (FTC) charges? The company, among other things, allegedly marketed online information to employers and recruiters in violation of the FCRA by failing to tell users of its consumer reports about their obligation under the FCRA, including the requirement to notify consumers if the user took an adverse action against the consumer based on information contained in the consumer report.

Some companies appear to take the position that because of the letter notice opting contained in FCRA section 613 that there are no additional duties to confirm accuracy. After all, the FCRA specifically sets out a letter option.

However, FCRA section 607(b) also set a standard for "reasonable procedures for maximum possible accuracy." Although groups such as Concerned CRA's oppose the use of the letter option, the fact remains it is still part of the law Congress passed. However, FCRA section 607(b) is also the law. A basic rule in reading a stature is that a court should "give effect, if possible, to every clause and word of a statute." See: www.fas.org/sgp/crs/misc/97-589.pdf.

The way the two statutes can be read together is to place upon a CRA the obligation to use reasonable procedures in the selection of the databases that they use. In other words, section 613 is not a blank check to send out any data a data broker or CRA can find. If the CRA or data broker have not tested the database, there can well be a 607(b) violation even if there a letter notice sent. The situation is complicated since much of the data included in criminal databases came from governmental sources. However, many governmental databases carry a clear disclaimer that errors can exist. This is probably matter that will eventually be resolved by litigation.

Web Data Extraction and Robotic Searches

As technology advances, new ways have been found to access court records. Background firms are able to electronically connect to a number of state and county databases through a variety of means. Automated processes with built in intelligence call permit screening firms to access publically available material with automated processes. Some companies have developed "screen scraping" techniques where court information may be gleaned from court web sites.

This is not new technology according to an article called *Web Data Extraction (a.k.a. screen scraping) and Online Public Records*, written by John Kloos and appearing in *The Manual to Online Public Records* (Facts on Demand Press):

"...In the public records research marketplace, this technology is often referred to as *Screen Scraping*. In fact, *Screen Scraping* is a term dating to the 1960's when programmers wrote processes to read or "scrape" text from computer terminals so that it could be used by other programs. *Web Data Extraction* is a much more sophisticated technology that incorporates the automated scheduling, extraction, filtering, transformation and transmission of targeted data available via the Internet." To say that a well-deployed *Web Data Extraction* system is performing *Screen Scraping* is like calling a modern refrigerator an ice box.

An example of a relatively simple *Web Data Extraction* application is the free service Google provides for repeatedly searching news articles on a specific topic."

Although this approach sounds good on paper, there are many practical pitfalls for the unwary. Since the key is always accuracy, the critical part is to ensure that the information obtained is the "functional equivalent" of going to the courthouse and accessing a public computer terminal or other means of locating names of defendants.

If employers and background firms use this technology to search records in thousands of counties that in fact do not have data that is complete and up to date, then there is a great deal of risk. Unless a background firm performs proper due diligence so the remote computer search renders the same detail as going to the courthouse, the employer may otherwise find they are not getting the protections they thought they were receiving.

Another issue with such remote computer access is at least one major jurisdiction, Cook County, Illinois (Chicago), does not allow such remote access for commercial use. And it use for commercial purposes may even be unlawful. See www.cookcountyclerkofcourt.org/?section=TERMSPage.

AUTHOR TIP

A Screening, a Scanning, or a Scamming?

Some background firms advertise fast turnaround times by accessing data directly from courts through some variation of screen scarping, data extraction or software connection to the court's pubic site. Here is the issue: all data is not created equally. Unless the background firm has verified that the data they are accessing for each county is the functional equivalent of going to the courthouse, then it is difficult to consider that to be a background **"screening."** If the court interface is only getting some data but not all, then employers need to understand that the screening firm is only **"scanning"** available data and is not getting the best data possible. If a screening firm reports county searches from a county where the screening firm either knew or reasonably should have known with due diligence that the data is inaccurate or incomplete, but sold it as a true background screen, then it has been suggested that such an approach more resemble a **"scamming."** That is another reason why employers need to ask plenty of questions when selecting a screening provider.

Online Dating Website Background Checks & Criminal Databases

What is information about online dating website background checks doing in a book about safe hiring?

This information is included here to illustrate a point about the problems of depending too much on criminal databases when conducting criminal background checks.

Online Dating Background Checks: Fast and Easy But Not Always Accurate?

Is Mr. Nice Guy Prince Charming or just a charming sex offender?

New technology such as online dating background checks can supposedly help users find out the answer to the question above in mere seconds and with little effort or cost. However, while these new online dating background check services appear extremely fast and easy to use, the information provided by them may not be wholly accurate or complete.

These online dating background checks allow users to instantly run background checks and search public information of people including their criminal history, property records, contact information, relatives, and neighbors. The online dating background checks may also come with an email search to find out what social networks the person uses along with online photos, websites, and blog posts.

Are these online dating background checks accurate? Users of online dating background checks may not understand their limitations and may be falsely convinced that they will never have to worry about people they meet again. In reality, such information found on instant background checks is "raw data" best used as a secondary source to lead to more detailed and accurate information.

Because of the nature of criminal databases, the appearance of a person's name in online dating background checks does not necessarily indicate that person is a criminal any more than the absence shows that person has a clean record. Any positive match must be verified by reviewing actual court records. In other words, these instant criminal databases may contain both "false positives" and "false negatives" as defined previously, but offered again below:

✓ A "False Positive" is where there is a criminal match with the person being checked, but upon further research it is not the same person.
✓ A "False Negative" is where there is not a criminal match with the person being checked, but that person is indeed a criminal.

Like a phony cure for cancer, users think they are protected when they are not, and then they fail to do the usual things to protect themselves because they have let their guard down. Background checks for online dating sites may be well intentioned but are meaningless unless a dating website specifies in detail the nature and extent of the background check. For example, was there just a database search, or did it include county court level criminal checks?

Instant online dating background checks may not even offer the protection they promise, since an unsuspecting consumer may not understand the following:

✓ The criminal databases are full of inaccuracies so that a search may be a great deal more "miss" than "hit" (i.e. an actual criminal record found).
✓ Even if there is a "hit," it is problematic to even know if the real criminal is the person being searched or merely someone with the same name.
✓ The data utilized for the so-called "living situation" and financial searches is based upon billions of public records and is often described by data experts as being a "data dump," meaning a less then useful amalgamation of public records that may or may not be accurate, complete, or relevant, or it is information easily obtained from a quick Google search.
✓ The information garnered from social networking sites can be wildly inaccurate.

In addition, online dating background check searches immediately raise privacy issues for the person being "instantly checked" and legal issues if the information found turns out to be inaccurate, incomplete, or out-of-date. The end result is that the uses and liability associated with instant online dating background checks need to be closely reviewed before consumers place any reliance on them.

Popular Online Dating Site Settles Lawsuit by Pledging to Background Check Members for Sex Offenders

In 2011, Match.com settled a lawsuit with a woman who sued the popular online dating site after she was raped by a fellow member she was linked up with for a date by pledging to perform background checks on all current and future members in order to screen out sex offenders. The woman's assailant had at least six previous sexual assault convictions before the attack on her.

The lawsuit claims the attack may have been prevented if Match.com had performed background screening by checking the names of members against public sex offender registries. The woman's attorney predicted a "domino effect" among other online dating sites to follow Match.com's background check policy, and online dating sites eHarmony and Zoosk have confirmed that they would background check members to enhance security.

Members of Match.com were also provided with the following 'Safety Tips for Meeting Offline' that warn them to always take precautions and use the following guidelines:

- ✓ Always meet in public.
- ✓ Tell a friend.
- ✓ Stay sober.
- ✓ Drive yourself to and from the first meeting.
- ✓ Don't leave personal items unattended.
- ✓ Stay in a public place.

Source: www.match.com/help/safetytips.aspx?lid=4.

Illinois Internet Dating Safety Act Requiring Disclosure of Background Check Policy Heads to Governor

Legislation in Illinois – Senate Bill 2545 (SB 2545) – that would create the "Internet Dating Safety Act" requiring Internet dating websites offering services in Illinois to disclose if they conduct criminal background checks on all their members or post warnings online that they do not conduct criminal background checks has passed both the House and Senate and now heads to Governor Pat Quinn to sign.

According to a brief synopsis on the SB 2545 status page on Illinois General Assembly website, the Internet Dating Safety Act:

- ✓ Requires Internet dating services offering services to Illinois members to provide a safety awareness notification to all Illinois members.

- ✓ Provides that if an Internet dating service does not conduct criminal background screenings on its members, the service shall disclose, clearly and conspicuously, to all Illinois members that the Internet dating service does not conduct criminal background screenings.

- ✓ Provides that an Internet service provider does not violate the Act solely as a result of serving as an intermediary for the transmission of electronic messages between members of an Internet dating service.

- ✓ Provides that the Attorney General, pursuant to the Illinois Administrative Procedure Act, shall adopt rules and regulations to effectuate the purposes of the Act.

- ✓ Amends the Consumer Fraud and Deceptive Business Practices Act.

- ✓ Provides that it is an unlawful practice under the Consumer Fraud and Deceptive Business Practices Act for an Internet dating service to fail to provide notice or falsely indicate that it has performed criminal background screenings in accordance with the Internet Dating Safety Act.

- ✓ it has a policy allowing a member who has been identified as having a criminal conviction to have access to its service to communicate with Illinois members;

- ✓ That criminal background checks are not foolproof;

- ✓ That criminal background checks may give members a false sense of security;

- ✓ That criminal background checks are not a perfect safety solution;

- ✓ That criminals may circumvent even the most sophisticated criminal search technology;

- ✓ That not all criminal records are public in all states and not all databases are up to date;

- ✓ That only publicly available convictions are included in the screening; and

✓   That criminal background checks do not cover other types of convictions or arrests or any convictions from foreign countries.

If passed, the Internet Dating Safety Act would take effect immediately. Source: www.ilga.gov/legislation/BillStatus.asp?DocNum=2545&GAID=11&DocTypeID=SB&SessionID=84&GA=97

Here is another example:

Three Leading Online Dating Websites Agree to Use Background Checks to Protect Members from Sex Offenders

In March 2012, the California Attorney General and three of the nation's leading online dating websites – eHarmony, Match.com, and Spark Networks – issued a 'JOINT STATEMENT OF KEY PRINCIPLES OF ONLINE DATING SITE SAFETY' that online dating providers should follow to help protect members from sexual predators through background checks, the California Office of the Attorney General (OAG) announced in a press release on the OAG website.

The joint statement says that online dating companies will protect their members through the use of online safety tools that included checking members against national sex offender registries to prevent registered sex offenders from using their services. Any member who was identified as a registered sex offender would not be allowed to use these services. The joint statement also ensured that the online dating service providers have rapid abuse reporting systems, which give members access to a website, email address and/or phone number to report any suspected criminal activity, including physical safety concerns.

The joint statement follows the 2010 sexual assault of a Los Angeles-area woman by a man she met through Match.com. As reported earlier on the ESR News blog, Match.com settled a lawsuit with a woman who sued the popular online dating website after she was sexually assaulted following a date with a fellow member. The woman sought a court order requiring Match.com to background check applicants for convicted sex offenders and dropped the suit after the website began background screening. The woman's assailant – who had several previous sexual assault convictions prior to the attack – pleaded no contest and was sentenced to a year in jail. He also had to register as a sex offender.

However, the joint statement also warns online dating website providers and members that screening sex offender registries for sexual predators is not a foolproof solution:

* *While sex offender screening can be a useful safety tool, such screening tools have many limitations which impact their efficacy. However, the providers will use tools and technologies to identify sexual predators, including checking sex offender registries when the providers possess the requisite information to conduct such checks, and, when identified, remove registered sexual predators from participating in fee-based services on their websites.*

* *The providers will remind members that the members are responsible for their own safety and offline activities. As noted, because there are limitations to the effectiveness of sex offender screening tools and use of such tools does not guarantee member safety, providers will not promote or publicize sex offender screening tools in a manner intended to lead members to assume that due to the providers' use of sex offender screening tools, meeting people online is any safer than meeting people any other way. The providers will disclose in the Terms of Use or User Agreements for their websites that members should not rely on sex offender screenings or other protective tools as a guarantee for safety or a replacement for following Safety Tips.*

> According to the OAG press release at http://oag.ca.gov/news/press_release?id=2647, 40 million Americans used an online dating service and spent more than $1 billion on online dating website memberships in 2011.
>
> A copy of the joint agreement, which also aims to protect online dating website members from identity theft, is available at: http://ag.ca.gov/cms_attachments/press/pdfs/n2647_agreement.pdf?.

Summary of Issues with Private Databases

✓ Multi-jurisdictional database searches are NOT official FBI database searches. FBI records are only available to certain employers or industries where Congress or a state has granted access. Searches offered by background firms are drawn from government data that is commercially available or has been made public.

✓ Multi-jurisdictional and statewide database searches are a research tool only and are not a substitute for a hands-on search at the county level under any circumstances (or the functional equivalent of a county level search). The best use is to indicate additional places to search in case a record is found in a jurisdiction that was not searched at the county court level.

✓ In addition, not all states have a database that is available to employers. In some instances, the databases that are available have limited information. Therefore, the value of these searches may be very limited in some states. That means searches in those states should be conducted by a single state search in order to locate all possible names. An employer should carefully review what information is available in their state and not merely depend upon a database search.

✓ Databases in each state are compiled from a number of sources. There are a number of reasons that database information may not be accurate or complete. Because of the nature of databases, the appearance of a person's name on a database is not an indication the person is criminal any more than the absence of a name shows he/she is not a criminal. Any positive match MUST be verified by reviewing the actual court records. Any lack of a match is not the same as a person being "cleared." However, a database is a valuable tool in helping employers cover a wider area and know where to search for more information.

✓ There are some states that make official state police records or records directly from the court available. However, even these databases have potential drawbacks. The information may not be reportable under state or federal law for various reasons. Information from these sources should be reviewed by a qualified background checking professional.

✓ The search is based upon matching last name, the date of birth, and the first three letters of the first name in order to eliminate computer matches that are not applicable. Note: In some states, there is no or limited date of birth information. The database description will indicate where the records do not contain a date of birth, which means a search of that state will have little or no value.

✓ All possible "hits" should be reconfirmed at the county court level to insure that the information is accurate, complete, and up to date at the time it is reported, per FCRA Section 613. Also keep in mind that a criminal record should not be used to automatically disqualify an applicant without taking into account the EEOC rules as to what is a job-related criminal offense.

The only way that remote computer access represents a best practice is if the information being accessed is the same as going to the court house. If it is not the functional equivalent, then an employer is not getting a real background screen. At best, they are getting a scan of what information may be available, but it is not complete or up to date. A scam is where a background firm sells such remote access as the real thing when in fact it is not. Employers selecting a background firm that advertises quick turnaround time by means of electronic courthouse connecting need to make sure they are getting a screen, and not a scam.

Another danger sign? A background firm claims they have some special or exclusive access. All public records are available to the public.

Criminal record vendors and background firms should make clear, and employers need to understand, the exact nature and limitations of any database they access. These private database searches are ancillary and can be very useful, but proceed with caution. In other words, it cannot be assumed that a search of a proprietary criminal database by itself will show if a person is or is not a criminal, but these databases are outstanding secondary or supplemental tools with which to do a much wider search.

The Role and Legal Use of Criminal Records in Safe Hiring

Inside This Chapter:

- ✓ Why Criminal Records are Important Indicators
- ✓ Bureau of Justice Statistics
- ✓ Mandatory Criminal Record Checks
- ✓ Other Legal Compliance and Discrimination Issues Associated with Use of Criminal Records
- ✓ Criminal Records and Safe Hiring Checklist
- ✓ Importance of When a Criminal Record is Discovered
- ✓ Written Employer Policies on Criminal Records
- ✓ If a Person with a Criminal Record is Hired…
- ✓ With All of These Rules, Are Criminal Records Still Worth Accessing?

As repeatedly mentioned throughout this book, it is a statistical certainty that unless an employer checks for criminal records, the employer will eventually hire someone with an unsuitable criminal record.

However, the new Equal Employment Opportunity Commission (EEOC) Guidance issued in April 2012 and its emphasis on giving ex-offenders a second chance is resulting in a closer evaluation of how to make sure there is a job for everyone, even though everyone is not suitable for every job. The new EEOC Guidance, and best practices for employers, is covered in detail in Chapter 16.

Why Criminal Records are Important Indicators

An essential element of a Safe Hiring Program is performing a criminal record check. An unsuitable criminal record may be evidence of past behavior that may be inappropriate for a particular job. Consider these true stories taken from the files of background screening companies:

- ✓ **True Story 1:** An applicant for a manufacturing job looks good in the interview, and the hiring manager is prepared to make an offer. The Human Resources Department sends the background package to a screening service for a standard background check. The background check indicates the applicant has over ten criminal convictions. The convictions range from assaulting police officers, to selling drugs, to possessing weapons, to assault on girlfriends. Except for a background check, that person would have been a member of that company's workforce. What a nightmare.
- ✓ **True Story 2:** A healthcare facility makes a job offer to a health worker. The job includes access to drugs. A standard criminal check on the worker discloses two serious drug-related convictions. That person came within an inch of having a key to the drug locker.
- ✓ **True Story 3:** A driver for an airport pick-up service takes a female passenger to a remote location and sexually assaults her. Later it is discovered the driver had recently been released from prison for a sex crime. The company claims it had done everything it could to perform a background check. In order to test that claim, a screening firm does a background check based upon the limited information in the newspaper. Within six hours, the screening company has the full story on the driver's background. For a very small amount of money – the cost of a background check – disaster would have been avoided.

These examples show why employers need the protection of a pre-employment background check that includes a criminal record check. Newspapers and law books are full of cases of employers sued for negligent hiring because a criminal record check was not performed. Failure to do even most rudimentary background checks has led to innocent people being the victims of crimes in their home or workplace, including murder, robbery, theft, child molestation, sexual assaults, and more. As noted in the Introduction, lawsuits for negligent hiring are among the fastest growing types of civil lawsuits.

In addition, an employer has a continuing responsibility after a person is hired even if there is not a criminal record at the time of the hire. An employer should have policies and procedures to govern post-hire workplace situations. Timely and attentive management of potential problem situations along with appropriate follow-through and documentation are the keys to avoiding legal claims of negligent retention and negligent supervision. The bottom line is employers are the job creators who feed and support the economy, and employers need a safe and qualified workforce in order to continue to create jobs.

For an employer, the importance of a criminal offense is not necessarily the mere fact a person committed a crime in the past. The importance can come down to a matter of character. The conduct leading to the criminal offense may demonstrate a character trait that does not bode well in terms of future workplace conduct. For example, "Thou shall not steal" is not a difficult concept. It's ingrained in our culture, as well as many other cultures. If a person decides to steal or commit an act of dishonestly, the employer's real fear is that the person revealed their true character — a willingness to take from others even though they know it is wrong.

Of course, nothing is that simple. What if the theft was minor in nature, such as a youthful indiscretion of a small amount? Or what if it was driven by a need for food due to hunger? Should that offense really bar someone from gainful employment for life? These are complicated issues that are discussed, among other issues, in the reminder of this Chapter and in Chapter 16.

Criminal Records and Repeat Offenders

In employment law, the fundamental basis of negligent hiring lawsuits is the assumption that a person with proven dangerous propensities in the past may well exhibit those in the future.

Statistics seem to bear that out. According to the U.S, Department of Justice: "Two studies come closest to providing 'national' recidivism rates for the United States. One tracked 108,580 State prisoners released from prison in 11 States in 1983. The other tracked 272,111 prisoners released from prison in 15 States in 1994. The prisoners tracked in these studies represent two-thirds of all the prisoners released in the United States for that year."

One of the studies, available at http://bjs.ojp.usdoj.gov/content/reentry/recidivism.cfm, reported:

✓ Most former convicts were re-arrested shortly after getting out of prison — 30 percent within six months, 44 percent within a year, 59 percent within two years, and 67 percent by the end of three years.

✓ Post-prison recidivism was strongly related to arrest history. Among prisoners with one arrest prior to their release, 41 percent were re-arrested. Of those with two prior arrests, 47 percent were re-arrested. Of those with three earlier arrests, 55 percent were re-arrested. Among those with more than 15 prior arrests (about 18 percent of all released prisoners), 82 percent were re-arrested within the three-year period.

✓ The 272,111 inmates had accumulated more than 4.1 million arrest charges prior to their current imprisonment and acquired an additional 744,000 arrest charges in the 3 years following their discharge in 1994 – an average of about 18 criminal arrest charges per offender during their criminal careers. These charges included almost 21,000 homicides, 200,000 robberies, 50,000 rapes and sexual assaults, and almost 300,000 other assaults.

✓ The 1994 recidivism study estimated that within 3 years, 51.8% of prisoners released during the year were back in prison either because of a new crime for which they received another prison sentence, or because of a technical violation of their parole.

Screening industry statistics also strongly suggest that without doing a screen for criminal records, there is a **statistical certainty** an employer will eventually hire a person with a criminal record that is inconsistent with safe hiring. Screening firms report a criminal "hit rate" up to ten percent, whether disclosed or non-disclosed. Keep in mind this hit ratio represents applicants who signed a background screening form telling them that background checks would be conducted.

Of course, all statistics need to be examined carefully. The "hit" statistic may include lesser offenses that are not disqualifying or offenses the applicant may have revealed. However, a ten percent hit rate is still an astounding number. The "hit rate" statistic is not that surprising in view of government studies concerning the rate of criminal convictions and incarceration in America.

Bureau of Justice Statistics

The following statistics can be found on the U.S. Department of Justice (DOJ) Office of Justice Programs (OJP) Bureau of Justice Statistics (BJS) web page located at http://bjs.ojp.usdoj.gov/index.cfm. The mission of the BJS is to collect, analyze, publish, and disseminate information on crime, criminal offenders, victims of crime, and the operation of justice systems at all levels of government to ensure justice is both efficient and evenhanded.

Total Correctional Population

According to the BJS web page, the total correctional population includes all persons incarcerated, either in prison, jail, or supervised in the community (probation or parole). The basic count for correctional population is updated annually.

The BJS report *Correctional Population in the United States, 2010 (NCJ 236319),* which presented statistics on the number of offenders under the supervision of adult correctional authorities in the U.S. at the end of 2010, found:

✓ Approximately 7.1 million people, or 1 in 33 adults, were under the supervision of adult correctional authorities in the U.S. at yearend 2010.

✓ Most offenders under correctional supervision (about 7 in 10 persons or nearly 4.9 million people) were supervised in the community on probation or parole at yearend 2010.

✓ About 3 in 10 (or nearly 2.3 million people) were incarcerated in state or federal prisons or local jails.

For more information, see: http://bjs.ojp.usdoj.gov/content/pub/pdf/cpus10.pdf.

State and Federal Prisoners

The BJS maintains several data collections on prisoners and prison facilities using administrative records maintained by the each state's department of corrections, the Federal Bureau of Prisons (BOP), and personal interviews with inmates in state and federal prisons. State and federal prisoner populations differ from the jail inmate population in terms of conviction status, offense distribution, and average length of stay.

Using information gathered from these data sources, the BJS regularly publishes reports. Highlights of the *Prisoners in 2010 (Revised)* report include:

✓ As of December 31, 2010, state and federal correctional authorities had jurisdiction over 1,612,395 prisoners, and the 2010 imprisonment rate for the nation was 500 sentenced prisoners per 100,000 U.S. residents, about 1 in 200 residents.

✓ The federal prison population increased by 0.8% (1,653 prisoners), while the number of prisoners under state authority declined by 0.5% (7,228 prisoners).

✓ During 2010, prison releases (708,677) exceeded prison admissions (703,798) for the first time since BJS began collecting jurisdictional data in 1977.

For more information, see: http://bjs.ojp.usdoj.gov/content/pub/pdf/p10.pdf.

Community Corrections (Probation and Parole)

The BJS maintains two annual data series, the *Annual Probation Survey and the Annual Parole Survey,* designed to provide national, federal, and jurisdiction-level data from administrative records of adults supervised in the community on probation or parole. Both data series also collect information on the characteristics of probationers and parolees. The BJS also maintains the annual data series, the *National Corrections Reporting Program,* designed to provide data.

Summary findings of the BJS report *Probation and Parole in the United States, 2010 (NCJ 236019)* include:

✓ At yearend 2010, there were an estimated 4,887,900 adults under supervision in the community either on probation or parole — the equivalent of about 1 out of every 48 adults in the U.S.

✓ Probationers (4,055,514) represented the majority (83%) of the community supervision population at yearend 2010, while parolees (840,676) accounted for a smaller share (17%).

✓ The rate of incarceration during 2010 (5.7%) among probationers at risk of violating their conditions supervision—the number of probationers under supervision at the beginning of the year plus the number who entered supervision during the year—remained at about the same level observed in 2000 (5.5%).

✓ Among parolees at risk of violating the conditions of their supervision, about 13% were reincarcerated during 2010, down from about 16% reincarcerated during 2000.

At the end of 2010, the BJS found:

✓ 73% of probationers were on active supervision, as were 82% of parolees. This type of supervision decreased as a percentage of all parolees, down from 85% in 2009. Active supervision requires offenders to regularly report to a probation or parole authority in person, by telephone, by mail, or electronically. A corresponding increase in the percentage of parolees on inactive status, excluded from regular reporting but still on parole, was observed between 2009 (4%) and 2010 (7%). Most of this change was related to a California law that went into effect in January 2010 that required parolees who meet specific criteria to be placed on non-revocable parole. These parolees on non-revocable parole meet BJS's definition of inactive status because they are excluded from regular reporting but are still on parole.

✓ 50% of probationers were felons, unchanged from 2009. At yearend 2010, property offenders represented 28% of the probation population, and drug offenders represented 26%. About 19% of probationers were supervised for a violent offense.

✓ Drug offenders represented a slightly smaller share of the parole population at yearend 2010 (35%) compared to 2009 (36%).Violent offenders accounted for 27% of the parole population, unchanged from 2009.

For more information, see: http://bjs.ojp.usdoj.gov/content/pub/pdf/ppus10.pdf.

Recidivism

According to the BJS, "recidivism" is measured by criminal acts that resulted in the rearrest, reconviction, or return to prison with or without a new sentence during a three-year period following the prisoner's release. The BJS special report released in June 2002, *Recidivism of Prisoners Released in 1994 (NCJ-193427*, was based upon the prison and criminal records of an estimated 272,111 discharged prisoners in 15 states. Summary findings of the report included:

✓ During 2007, a total of 1,180,469 persons on parole were at-risk of reincarceration. This includes persons under parole supervision on January 1 or those entering parole during the year. Of these parolees, about 16% were returned to incarceration in 2007.

✓ Of the 272,111 persons released from prisons in 15 states in 1994:
  • An estimated 67.5% were rearrested for a felony or serious misdemeanor within 3 years,
  • 46.9% were reconvicted,
  • 25.4% resentenced to prison for a new crime, and
  • 51.8% were back in prison, serving time for a new prison sentence or for a technical violation of their release, like failing a drug test, missing an appointment with their parole officer, or being arrested for a new crime.

✓ These offenders had accumulated 4.1 million arrest charges before their most recent imprisonment and another 744,000 charges within 3 years of release.

✓ Released prisoners with the highest re-arrest rates were robbers (70.2%), burglars (74.0%), larcenists (74.6%), motor vehicle thieves (78.8%), those in prison for possessing or selling stolen property (77.4%), and those in prison for possessing, using, or selling illegal weapons (70.2%).

✓ Within 3 years, 2.5% of released rapists were arrested for another rape, and 1.2% of those who had served time for homicide were arrested for homicide.

For more information, visit: http://bjs.ojp.usdoj.gov/content/pub/pdf/rpr94.pdf.

Based upon the numbers, it is no wonder that employers face increased exposure from negligent hiring. However, there is also research to suggest that the longer an offender is able to stay out of jail, the less likely they are to re-offend, and after three years, the risk may fall off rapidly. Issues concerning the use of criminal records as a valid predictor of future criminal behavior as well as concerns over giving ex-offenders an opportunity to re-enter society are reviewed in a report to the American Bar Association in 2007. See:

http://meetings.abanet.org/webupload/commupload/CR209800/newsletterpubs/SealRescleanRC6507alfsasFINAL.pdf.

Courts and the Relevancy of Repeat Offenders

If a person is charged with driving under the influence of alcohol, and the person has been convicted in the past of the same offense, chances are the jury will never be told about the first conviction. Why is that information kept from the jury? Is it because evidence of prior bad conduct is not relevant?

Actually, prior criminal behavior is often kept from juries because experience demonstrates it is **too relevant**. Courts all across the U.S. have recognized the basic principle that evidence of a prior criminal conviction is so powerful that it overwhelms the jury's decision-making process — that human beings jump to the conclusion the accused did it again regardless of the evidence of the actual crime in the new case. Courts recognize part of the human make-up is to assume what a person has done in the past is what they will do in the future. For that reason, in criminal cases, evidence of past misconduct is admitted under very limited circumstances, for instance, when the past arrest is specifically relevant to some disputed fact in the case. However, a prosecutor may not introduce evidence of prior criminal behavior just to show the defendant is a "bad" person; if he did it before, then he did it again.

Past Crimes

There are reasons why a prosecutor can argue that evidence of a past crime is admissible. However, because the evidence is considered so prejudicial against a defendant, there must be a justification to introduce the past bad acts. The probative value must exceed the prejudicial impact. Reasons to introduce the evidence of past crimes can include:

✓ The past crime proves some element of the new case, such as a unique method of committing a crime that provides proof of identity, motive, or means;

✓ The defendant testifies and the past act is used to impeach the defendant's credibility or to contradict the claim of defendant while testifying;

✓ The defense presents evidence of good character, and the past acts are used to impact the character witness under cross-examination;

✓ The past crime is an element of the new crime, such as a charge of a felon in possession of a gun, so that the past felony is part of the new offense;

✓ The past crime is considered by the jury as part of the penalty such as in a death penalty case.

Mandatory Criminal Record Checks

In some regulated industries, state or federal law mandates criminal record checks. It is not a matter of criminal propensities or statistics — it is the law.

All states have regulations requiring criminal background checks for jobs that involve contact with populations who are vulnerable or at risk. This may include teachers, childcare workers, health care professionals, and workers who care for the elderly or populations at risk. Another example is a professional licensing board. Per state law, these boards are state agencies that oversee the certification of certain professions. Those applicants subject to such regulations are normally aware of the criminal record check requirements through licensing procedures or industry contacts. Typical professions requiring a criminal record background check include private investigators, security guards, security brokers, insurance agents, bail bondsmen, jockeys, casino workers, and so forth.

Mandatory criminal record checks are typically done with a fingerprint check of state and federal criminal records. Usually the checks are arranged for the employer directly through the specific state licensing agency rather than using the services of a professional background screening company.

There are also federal rules for certain industries. For example, the Federal Aviation Administration (FAA) has rules for mandatory background checks for workers employed by airport operators as well as employees having unescorted access to restricted areas. Similarly, the banking industry has certain mandatory background checks.

Given the news stories surrounding negligent hiring or child abductions and child abuse in volunteer and community organizations, new laws are proposed in nearly every state every year. These laws seek to expand the number of occupations that are subject to mandatory checks. For example, in Pennsylvania, in response to the horrific murder of a guest by a hotel worker with a criminal record, a grassroots effort is under way to require hotels to conduct background checks on all employees (See http://www.nanslaw.org). The clear trend is towards the government getting into the background checking business by making criminal record checks mandatory.

Post 9/11 and Homeland Security concerns

There has also been a new impetus behind mandatory screening as a result of the Homeland Security efforts. These issues are touched upon in Chapter 22.

Survey Finds Nearly 70 Percent of Organizations Conduct Criminal Checks on All Job Candidates

Nearly seven out of ten organizations – 69 percent – conduct criminal background checks on all of their job candidates while 18 percent conduct criminal checks on select job candidates and 14 percent do not conduct criminal checks on any job candidates, according to a survey released in July 2012 titled *'Background Checking—The Use of Criminal Background Checks in Hiring Decisions'* from the Society for Human Resource Management (SHRM). Key findings include:

✓ Among organizations that conduct criminal background checks, 62 percent initiate criminal background checks after a contingent job offer and 32 percent initiate them after the a job interview. Only 4 percent initiate criminal background checks before a job interview.

✓ 52 percent of organizations conduct criminal checks on job candidates to reduce legal liability for negligent hiring while 49 percent conducted them to ensure a safe work environment for employees.

✓ 96 percent of organizations say that they are influenced not to hire convicted violent felons while 74 percent say they are influenced by non-violent felony convictions.

✓ 69 percent of organizations conduct criminal checks on job candidates for positions with fiduciary and financial responsibilities and 66 percent conduct them on job candidates who will have access to highly confidential employee information.

✓ 58 percent of organizations allow job candidates to explain the results of their criminal checks before the decision to hire or not to hire is made while 27 percent allow job candidates to explain the results after the decision is made.

✓ Larger organizations are more likely to conduct criminal background checks for all job candidates than smaller organizations: 83 percent of organizations with 2,500 to 24,999 employees and 69 percent of organizations with 100 to 499 employees conducted criminal background checks for all job candidates while only 48 percent of organizations with 1 to 99 employees performed them.

This survey from SHRM is available at:
www.shrm.org/Research/SurveyFindings/Articles/Pages/CriminalBackgroundCheck.aspx.

Other Legal Compliance and Discrimination Issues Associated with Use of Criminal Records

The following are some other compliance and discrimination issues that employers face when using criminal records of employees and job applicants for employment decisions.

Criminal Records and Safe Hiring Checklist

As has been shown, federal and state laws associated with obtaining and using a criminal record are not only overwhelming, but also very confusing. What is legal in one state to utilize for employment purposes may not be legal in another state. Employers and professional screening companies must pay strict heed to the Federal Fair Credit Reporting Act (FCRA) and the requirements of the Equal Employment Opportunity Commission (EEOC). Certain portions of these laws can apply depending on "when" the record was discovered.

If negative information is located, is there a company policy in place or procedure to follow? What are the important considerations? Below is a quick checklist guide:

✓ **Policies** — Are there written guidelines to follow?
✓ **Documentation** — are all procedures and decisions documented to file?
✓ **Review** — is there a review process, with a particular person in the organization in charge of the process?
✓ **Uniformity** — Are similarly situated applicants treated the same?
✓ **Privacy** — is there a mechanism to ensure that information remains private and secured, and only appropriate decision makers view the information? (e.g., reports with negative information are not sent through office mail to a hiring manager's desk).
✓ **Legal Compliance** FCRA — if a third party obtains information under the FCRA, is there a procedure to ensure pre-adverse action and post-adverse letters are handled as required by law?
✓ **Legal Compliance** EEOC — if the negative information is a criminal record, does the firm understand and follow the Equal Employment Opportunity Commission rules concerning the use of criminal records? Under EEOC rules, an employer may not deny employment to an ex-offender unless it is a business necessity, determined by reviewing the following three factors:
  • The nature and gravity of the offense;
  • The nature of the job being held or sought; and
  • The amount of time that has passed since the conviction or completion of sentence.

Below is a 2012 news story that reinforces the need to have the correct policies and procedures in place.

> **"Pepsi Pays Over $3 Million to Resolve EEOC Finding of Hiring Discrimination Against African Americans**
>
> In January 2012, Pepsi Beverages (Pepsi), formerly known as Pepsi Bottling Group, agreed to pay $3.13 million and provide job offers and training to resolve a charge of race discrimination filed in the Minneapolis Area Office of the U.S. Equal Employment Opportunity Commission (EEOC). The monetary settlement will primarily be divided among black applicants for positions at Pepsi, with a portion of the sum being allocated for the administration of the claims process. Based on the investigation, the EEOC found reasonable cause to believe that the criminal background check policy formerly used by Pepsi discriminated against African Americans in violation of Title VII of the Civil Rights Act of 1964.
>
> The EEOC's investigation revealed that more than 300 African Americans were adversely affected when Pepsi applied a criminal background check policy that disproportionately excluded black applicants from permanent employment. Under Pepsi's former policy, job applicants who had been arrested pending

prosecution were not hired for a permanent job even if they had never been convicted of any offense. Pepsi's former policy also denied employment to applicants who had been arrested or convicted of certain minor offenses. The use of arrest and conviction records to deny employment can be illegal under Title VII of the Civil Rights Act of 1964, when it is not relevant for the job, because it can limit the employment opportunities of applicants or workers based on their race or ethnicity.

During the course of the EEOC's investigation, Pepsi adopted a new criminal background check policy. In addition to the monetary relief, Pepsi will offer employment opportunities to victims of the former criminal background check policy who still want jobs at Pepsi and are qualified for the jobs for which they apply. The company will supply the EEOC with regular reports on its hiring practices under its new criminal background check policy. Pepsi will conduct Title VII training for its hiring personnel and all of its managers."

Source: "Pepsi to Pay $3.13 Million and Made Major Policy Changes to Resolve EEOC Finding of Nationwide Hiring Discrimination Against African Americans" www.eeoc.gov/eeoc/newsroom/release/1-11-12a.cfm.

Importance of When a Criminal Record is Discovered

An employer may uncover a criminal record at one of three different stages of the hiring or employment cycle. In each stage there are a number of considerations to what an employer legally can or should do in response to this information.

1. Legal Compliance When the Applicant Accurately Self-Reveals a Criminal Record

This may occur if an applicant accurately self-reports a criminal matter in the application, resume, or during an interview. Keep in mind the EEOC has urged employers in its 2012 Guidance to not ask about criminal records in the application. However, at some point in the process, an employer can ask questions about past criminal records, and if the applicant lies, that can be a serious issue. In the event an employer uses a background firm to ask about past criminal conduct as mentioned above, if the applicant lies to the background firm, that may also be a factor for an employer to consider.

When the applicant accurately tells an employer about a criminal record, and there is no element of dishonesty, then the issue arises as to what an employer can legally do and should do. At that point, an employer needs to be aware of their obligations under both federal and state discrimination laws.

2. Legal Compliance When the Applicant Lied and Did Not Reveal a Criminal Record

Employment applications should ask about criminal records in broad, clear language, and inform applicants that dishonesty is a basis to deny employment. If a background check locates criminal matters that an applicant misrepresented, then the dishonesty can be the grounds to deny employment.

This discovery may occur in a variety of ways. During the hiring process an employer may discover the criminal record through a past employer reference check or from the background report. A past criminal record may also come to the employer's attention after the applicant has been hired. For example, a worker may tell a co-worker about his or her criminal past and the conversation is reported to management, or an applicant may misrepresent a criminal record such as disclosing a petty theft that was in fact a robbery.

Here is a common scenario to watch out for. An employer uses an application form at some stage during the process that only asks about *felonies* (See Chapter 7 for three common mistakes employers make regarding the criminal question on an application form). The applicant's background report comes back and reveals convictions on serious misdemeanors. The employer's first reaction is to deny employment because the person lied. The applicant did not lie — the question was answered truthfully. As a result the employer must make a decision based upon the three-part EEOC test discussed earlier — are the crimes job-related?

If the question on the application was worded properly, and the employer caught the applicant in a lie, then it is the LIE that forms the basis for the termination of the hiring process. Dishonesty can always be a basis not to hire.

3. Arrests and Convictions That Occur After Employment

How the employer discovers a new criminal matter can occur in a variety of ways. Perhaps an employer may first hear about an arrest or conviction from the news media, or as a result of investigating absenteeism, or even after being contacted by the local probation office to arrange for an employee's participation in some sort of jail-release program.

An employer should review their employee manual on the subject of arrests. In Chapter 6, suggested language was offered on employment screening and safe hiring. The language below covers employees who are on the job and are arrested for a criminal act AFTER being hired.

> *In addition, in order to ensure a safe and profitable workplace, all employees are required to report to their supervisor if they are arrested, charged or convicted for any criminal offense, with the exception of minor traffic offenses unless the employee is in driving position (driving position is any position where the employee drives on company time or for the benefit of the company.)*

> *If an employee is arrested, charged, or convicted for any offense, then the employee must report the matter to their direct supervisor and submit a police report or other documentation concerning the arrest and/or charges. The report must occur within two business days of the arrest.*

> *The employer will review the underlying facts of the matter. The employer will not take any adverse action based only upon the fact of an arrest. Any action will be based upon the underlying facts of the arrest. Any action will be considered on a case-by-case basis taking into account the underlying facts and the totality of all the circumstances. At the employer's discretion actions may range from no action, to leave with or without pay, to termination.*

> *Noncompliance with the above stated requirement constitutes grounds for termination. Furthermore, misrepresentation of the circumstances of the events can serve as grounds for termination. Employees that are unavailable to report for work due to incarceration are subject to suspension or termination in accordance with the terms of the employee manual.*

Before implementing this policy, employers should contact their legal counsel concerning the laws in their state. It is important to note that the employer should not take action due to the mere fact of the arrest. That could violate the EEOC policy. The employer needs to base any decision on the underlying facts of the arrest or on the conviction. If, as a result of an arrest, a person is incarcerated, the inability to come to work may give grounds for an employer to terminate employment.

 As covered in Chapter 4, many states have their own procedural rules on the proper use of criminal records that employers and screeners must follow when obtaining and using background reports.

Also, employers need to proceed with caution before utilizing "non-criminal" offense records. Some states, such as New York and New Jersey, have created categories of minor offenses that are specifically deemed to be "non-criminal."

Be Aware of State Discrimination Laws

The states listed below have discrimination restrictions on the use of criminal records, including convictions and arrests laws similar to the EEOC rules. Some states impose rules that are more stringent than the EEOC. Even in states without a separate set of rules in this area, the federal rules would apply. Employers in the states listed below should check with their employment lawyer. Employers in states NOT listed should probably be checked as well in order to ensure there are no restrictions.

Alaska, Arizona, California, Colorado, Connecticut, Delaware, District of Columbia, Florida, Georgia, Hawaii, Idaho, Illinois, Iowa, Kansas, Louisiana, Maine, Maryland, Massachusetts, Michigan, Minnesota, Missouri, Nebraska, Nevada, New Hampshire, New Jersey, New York, North Dakota, Ohio, Oklahoma, Oregon, Pennsylvania, Rhode Island, South Dakota, Texas, Utah, Vermont, Virginia, Washington, West Virginia, and Wisconsin. (NOTE: The list of states is provided for educational purposes only, and no representation is made that this list is accurate or current.)

Written Employer Policies on Criminal Records

Given all the EEOC, FCRA, and state restrictions, what policy should an employer have regarding the use of criminal records? In Chapter 6, a sample policy template was provided along with an internal memo on procedures. Depending upon how a firm responds to the 2012 EEOC Guidance, an employer may need to modify the Policy and Practices and Procedures with a description of the actual practices followed in light of the new Guidance.

In their policies, employers make three common mistakes.

Having a Policy that Flatly Prohibits Employment of an Applicant with a Criminal Record or Employment for Persons with Certain Crimes

According to the EEOC, a flat policy against anyone with a criminal conviction is likely to have an adverse impact on members of a protected class and therefore could be contrary to the rules of the EEOC. The EEOC covers this topic in EEOC Enforcement Guidance No: N-915, "Policy Statement on the Use of Statistics in Charges Involving the Exclusion of Individuals with Conviction Records from Employment," July 29, 1987 at www.eeoc.gov/policy/docs/convict2.html. If challenged, the employer has a duty to present statistical data concerning applicant data flow to demonstrate that a flat policy against hiring anyone with a conviction would not have an adverse impact. However, the EEOC also cautions that such data could also be challenged if the applicant pool artificially limits members of the protected groups from applying in the first place. According to the EEOC notice, "if many Blacks with conviction records did not apply for a particular job because they knew of the employer's policy and they therefore expected to be rejected, then applicant flow data would not be an accurate reflection of the conviction policy's actual effect." Notice N-915 (7/29/87). (NOTE: This exact same exact language has been stated more recently in EEOC compliance Manual Section 604 "Theories of Discrimination" in the appendices – policy documents – current though August 2009.)

AUTHOR TIP

Are Flat Polices Against Criminal Offenders Inherently Unfair?

Some Security and HR professionals have suggested a flat policy against criminal offenders is inherently fairer because an employer is not required to make a distinction between candidates. They suggest further a flat policy is fair because it is applied regardless of the person.

In fact, the opposite is true. A flat policy that judges a person by his or her status or membership in a category (i.e. criminal offender) is inherently prejudicial because it denies individualized consideration. In other words, a person is being pre-judged not based upon who they are, but upon the label attached to them. The root of the word prejudice is to "pre-judge."

Of course, this means that an employer could be placed in a situation where they have two applicants with identical criminal records, but one gets a job offer and the other does not. That can happen because one applicant has engaged in substantial rehabilitation and has great references. In this decision, an employer needs to document why the two individuals are being treated differently.

> The answer is simple— although they committed the same crime, they are different people with different qualifications.

Unless an employer plans to hire a professional statistician and a team of labor lawyers and demographics experts, the best policy is to not have a flat and automatic prohibition on applicants with criminal records. Employers using criminal background checks for employment purposes should be careful not to have a "blanket policy" that excludes job applicants who are ex-offenders. Employers should follow the EEOC guidelines for conviction records under Title VII of the Civil Rights Act of 1964 that prohibits discrimination in employment based on race, gender, national origin, and other protected categories.

Having a Scoring Policy, Where a Conviction of Certain Crimes Automatically Eliminates an Applicant

Another potential mistake employers make is to have a flat prohibition on certain crimes. For example, an employer may have a flat and automatic prohibition against hiring someone with certain convictions such as theft, robbery, violence, or drugs.

Some employers go even further and have a "scoring" system whereby an employer uses the services of a screening firm to automatically eliminate an applicant. Some employers use a "traffic light system." If the applicant has no criminal records, then he or she is given a "green light." If the applicant has a disqualifying criminal record, such as a violent crime, the screening company gives the applicant a "red light." If there is a crime that is not on the employer's automatic elimination list, that person receives a "yellow" or "caution light" so that the crime can be reviewed with the employer.

The same EEOC notice mentioned above also addresses this issue. According to the Commission, past decisions were based upon national or regional statistics for crime as a whole. However, if the employer can present more narrow regional or local data on conviction rates for all crime or the specific crime showing that protected groups are not convicted at disproportionably higher rates, then the employer may be able to justify such a policy. In addition, the employer can show that the policies in fact did not result in disproportionately higher rates of exclusion. This is a tough sell for an employer.

In view of the legal exposure for discrimination and the potential high cost of defending the process, employers may consider changing the "red flag" from automatic disqualification to a policy of "strict scrutiny of the offense" pursuant to the EEOC three-part test. Now the red-flagged person will go through a special process whereby the employer reviews the details of the past offense, the applicant, the job, then reaches an individualized, documented decision.

Having no policy

As a general rule, it is a best practice for employers to have written policies on important issues. Without a policy, an employer's actions in denying employment may become harder to defend. Having no policy also subjects an employer to claims of a discriminatory practice.

 It is worth remembering that if a screening firm performs any process to carry out an employer's policies or compliance with the new EEOC Guidance, the screening firm is only acting in a "clerical" capacity carrying out the employer's policies and instructions and is not making any independent decisions, analysis or recommendations. However, screening firms should be able to build in a great deal of compliance capacity into its screening software to process the employer's particular policies.

Using a Conditional Offer of Employment

A criminal background check can take a little time — several days or weeks — depending on the government agencies involved and who is doing the check. Meanwhile, an employer may have a difficult position to fill, or have concerns about losing a good candidate who has cleared the earlier safe hiring steps and seems to be a good fit for the job. The employer may choose to make a contingent offer of employment based upon the receipt of an acceptable background report.

If a contingent offer is made, then the following language is recommended for the offer letter:

This offer of employment is conditional upon the employer's receipt of a pre-employment background screening investigation that is acceptable to the employer at the employer's sole discretion.

This suggested language specifies the report must meet the **employer's satisfaction**, so there can be no debate over what constitutes a satisfactory report. In other words, an employer will require that the background checks meet their subjective approval as opposed to some sort of reasonable standard objective criteria. Of course, even the use of subjective standards does not permit discriminating or decisions that are arbitrary and capricious, but if an employer needs to make a close judgment call, having this recommended language could potentially afford some additional protection.

If candidates have not been forthcoming up to this point, many will self-elect to decline an offer letter that is tentative, pending results.

Public Comment to EEOC on Arrest and Conviction Records as a Hiring Barrier

On July 26, 2011, the U.S. Equal Employment Opportunity Commission (EEOC) held a meeting that focused on the use of criminal records by employers for employment background checks to see if arrest and conviction records were an unfair and discriminatory hiring barrier to ex-offenders. The Commission invited members of the public to submit written comments on any issue or matters discussed at the meeting.

The author of this book submitted a letter to the EEOC, a portion of which is shown below.

Dear Member of the EEOC:

I am writing a comment in connection with the Meeting of July 26, 2011 held by the EEOC on the issue of Arrest and Conviction Records as a Hiring Barrier. I am an attorney and founder and CEO of a background screening firm, Employment Screening Resources (ESR). I am also the author of 'The Safe Hiring Manual,' a guide to employment background checks. I was also the first co-chair of the National Association of Professional Background Screeners (NAPBS). All opinions expressed in this letter are solely that of the writer of this letter.

In reviewing of some of the comments and testimony from the hearing on July 26, it appears there are some important considerations that the EEOC should consider that may not have been sufficiently addressed at the meeting. Of course, the pre-employment screening industry recognizes that unless ex-offenders receive a second chance, we stand the risk as a society of creating a class of permanently unemployed and employable individuals. The results are not only devastating to the ex-offenders and their families, but it also places a substantial strain on societal resources.

However, it is just as important to understand that innocent people have the right to be safe in their workplaces and everyday lives. The use of criminal records is a difficult issue because it involves important American values that can seem to conflict. On one hand, we value public safety and a safe workspace with honest and qualified employees. All Americans have a right to be safe and secure in their workplace. On the other hand, as a society we believe in second chances, and that a person's past should not hold him or her back forever, particularly for more minor offenses. The issue is how to draw lines that both protect innocent people and, at the same time, does not burden the taxpayers by creating a permanent class of unemployed people. Unless an ex-offender can get a job, they cannot become a taxpaying and law abiding citizen and the taxpayers end up building more prisons then they do schools or hospitals, so it is a matter of finding a good balance.

In seeking to balance these competing interests, I am hopeful that the EEOC will recognize that there are some "real world" issues that need to be considered. These include:

✓ Employers face significant risk if they hire a person that is dangerous, unfit, unqualified or dishonest.

✓ A professional background screening firm – known as a Consumer Reporting Agency or CRA – operating under the federal Fair Credit Reporting Act (FCRA) is an entirely different industry than the cheap and instant online database searches that can result in inaccurate data. A CRA preforms screenings under the strict standards of the FCRA based upon the applicant's written consent, as opposed to data aggregators that sell data to anyone with a credit card.

✓ Background screening firms are NOT the employment police, but professionals that gather relevant information so employers can make intelligent decisions. Background check reports provided by a Consumer Reporting Agency protects both employers and job applicants by providing employers with reports with much greater accuracy that filter out information that cannot be used, and providing job applicants with an immediate avenue to contest any information in the report.

✓ The background screening industry as a whole has been the primary reason why employers have become aware of the EEOC position on the overly broad or automatic use of criminal records, since background screening firms deal with a high percentage of U.S. employers and typically include client education on how to properly consider the use of criminal records.

✓ The issue of inaccurate records comes primarily from the data aggregator firms. A simple solution is to require any employer to only utilize information that has been confirmed as accurate and up to date from a primary source, such as a courthouse search.

✓ Over 140 background screening firms have joined an industry group called "Concerned CRAs" (www.concernedcras.com) that opposes the use of databases provided by data aggregators for employment purposes, without first reconfirming that the information is currently complete, accurate and up-to-date.

Summary:

It is certainly critically important to our society that everyone have a second chance. However, citizens also have a right to be free of violence and fraud in their everyday dealing, either as a member of the public, an employee or employer. In reaching these difficult decisions, it is critical that the EEOC have a full understanding of all of the facts that surround background checks and criminal records.

To my knowledge, the EEOC has not hired on its own behalf in any of its offices an applicant with a criminal record (beyond low level matters) and had to deal with the complex issues involved in considering and ultimately employing persons with criminal records. It places a substantial burden on employers to bring an individual into the workplace that represents a potential threat to co-workers, clients and the public. It is easy to support giving ex-offenders a second chance, and in fact our industry's goal is to help employers place their applicants in positions that are appropriate for them based on both their experience and background, not to exclude them from the workplace. However, if the EEOC will not even bring ex-offenders into its own workplaces, how can the Commission expect private employers to take on a risk that the EEOC will not take on its own?

I am hopeful that EEOC will undertake a fair and well-reasoned evaluation of all the issues and how its rulemaking in this area would impact all stakeholders, and not act solely on its power to make rules or to commence litigation.

Thank you for your consideration.

The entire letter from Attorney Lester Rosen to the Equal Employment Opportunity Commission (EEOC) is available at www.esrcheck.com/EEOC-and-the-Use-of-Criminal-Records-for-Employment.php.

If a Person with a Criminal Record is Hired…

If a firm decides to hire an individual with a criminal record, then it is crucial to document the reasons for the decision and the processes the firm used leading up to the decision the applicant is reasonably-suited for the job. Employers should also note any considerations made as to whether these individuals need special supervision or assistance to help them succeed — and maintain workplace safety.

Persons with Criminal Records Should Still Be Able to Find a Job

As always, there are two sides to any story. On one hand, employers have an incentive to conduct background checks because of the overwhelming evidence of the importance of criminal records in anticipating future behavior.

However, as we review criminal records, it is important to keep in mind that no one is suggesting that just because a person has a criminal past, he or she can never be hired. Unless our society wishes to create a permanent criminal class, it is critical for ex-offenders who have paid the price to society to be able to get a J-O-B. Without a job, ex-offenders can never become tax paying, law-abiding, productive citizens. Logic and statistics suggest that ex-offenders who are not able to find and keep gainful employment are likely to re-offend. Unless our society wants to spend an inordinate amount of tax money on building prisons, ex-offenders need a chance at a decent career. In fact, the law provides that a criminal record cannot be used to automatically deny a job. This is discussed in detail in Chapter 16.

A person with a criminal record does not have a big scarlet C for criminal emblazoned on their forehead so that they can never rejoin society. There are certain jobs that are just inappropriate for individuals with certain backgrounds. For example, a person with an embezzlement record may not be a good candidate to be a bookkeeper. However, such a person may do perfectly well in other jobs. There is a job for everyone, but not everyone is suitable for every job.

With All of These Rules, Are Criminal Records Still Worth Accessing?

By this time, an employer may well be scratching his or her head wondering if it is worth the trouble to do a criminal records check given all the rules and procedures involved. If the employer makes a mistake, then they risk a lawsuit from a disgruntled applicant accusing them of violating their rights. Or, an employer may be concerned about the EEOC or a state authority becoming involved if an applicant complains of discriminatory practices.

Even with these complications, experts agree that it is incumbent upon employers to check for criminal records. Here is why: The chance of being sued, much less being sued successfully by a person with a serious criminal record, is remote. As long as the employer does not engage in the automatic disqualification of applicants with criminal records and treats every applicant fairly, the chance of a lawsuit is remote.

On the other hand, according to all of the available statistics, there is a statistical certainty that unless a firm exercised due diligence, they will hire a person who is dangerous or unfit for the job. As discussed in the Introduction, "The Parade of Horribles," the legal and financial fallout can be a never-ending nightmare.

To put it another way: *The number of lawsuits from disgruntled applicants with criminal records is minimal. The potential lawsuits or harm from not doing a criminal check is enormous.*

Who Can They Sue?

Attorneys are often asked by employers, "Can they sue me?" The answer is always "YES." Anyone in the U.S., for a modest filing fee, can sue anyone else for nearly anything they want. The exception is certain people who have abused the system by filing multiple lawsuits of doubtful validity can be declared a "vexatious litigant" and not be allowed to sue without court approval.

Of course, the key term is a "successful" lawsuit. So, there is never a guarantee that a lawsuit will not be filed. The question is: "What risk is there of a successful lawsuit?"

Whether or not to use criminal records ultimately comes down to a risk management decision where an employer has to weigh the cost versus the benefit.

- ✓ **Costs:** Overall costs include the time, money, and effort spent in obtaining the criminal report, as well as the potential, though not very realistic, risks of a lawsuit from a disgruntled applicant.
- ✓ **Benefits:** The benefits can range from merely avoiding an unpleasant situation to avoiding the loss of life and the loss of the business.

On a cost-benefit basis, employers are clearly ahead by doing criminal background checks.

The EEOC Guidance on the Use of Criminal Records by Employers

Inside This Chapter:

- ✓ The EEOC Concern Over Criminal Records

- ✓ Recent Actions by State & City Governments

- ✓ The EEOC 2012 Enforcement Guidance on the Consideration of Arrest and Conviction Records in Employment Decisions

- ✓ What Does All of this Mean?

- ✓ Criticism of EEOC Guidance

- ✓ The Good, the May Be Good, and the Impossible

- ✓ EEOC and Use of "Arrest Only Records"

- ✓ The Studies Cited by the EEOC Concerning Recidivism

- ✓ Use of Criminal Records and the EEOC Guidance – An Attorney's View

- ✓ The Author's Public Comment to the EEOC About the Guidance

The EEOC Concern Over Criminal Records

Recently there has been a very noticeable legislative trend to limit the use of criminal records in the employment process. This trend and the ensuing media attention has led in part to the **U.S. Equal Employment Opportunity Commission (EEOC)** April 15, 2012 announcement on new Guidance on the use of criminal records. This chapter provides an analysis of this important development.

In order to evaluate the EEOC Guidance, it is helpful to first explore the context in which it was issued.

Study Claims 1 in 4 Adult Americans have Criminal Records

The National Employment Law Project (NELP) is a national advocacy organization for employment rights of lower-wage workers and the unemployed. A March 2011 study by NELP – *'65 Million "Need Not Apply" – The Case for Reforming Criminal Background Checks for Employment'* – estimates nearly 65 million people in the United States – more than one in four adults – have criminal records. This estimate is based on records of a 2008 Survey of State Criminal History Information Systems by the U.S. Bureau of Justice Statistics that found 92.3 million people with criminal records on file with states. The 92.3 million figure was reduced by 30 percent – 64.6 million – to account for individuals who may have records in multiple states and other factors and to arrive at a conservative national estimate. Since 232,458,335 people were over the age of 18 in 2009 according to the U.S. Census Bureau, the 64.6 million figure represents an estimated 27.8 percent of the U.S. adult population who have a criminal record on file with states.

The NELP study is part of their second chance labor project which promotes the employment rights of people with criminal records and a fairer and more accurate criminal background checks for employment. It is available at www.nelp.org/page/-/65_Million_Need_Not_Apply.pdf?nocdn=1.

The study indicates employers who use criminal background checks for employment will shut out job applicants with criminal records without considering how long ago the offense occurred, the nature of the offense, and whether the offense is job-related. This prevents millions of people from finding work and has compromised the economy and public safety.

The NELP study also claims that telling workers with criminal records that they "need not apply" lowers public safety since studies show that providing ex-convicts the opportunity for stable employment actually lowers crime recidivism rates. Ensuring that all workers have job opportunities is critical since no economy can sustain a large and growing population of unemployable workers, especially with the cost of corrections at each level of government having increased 660 percent from 1982 to 2006.

The number 65 million is taken from a footnote which extrapolates a conclusion from some government reports. The 65 million refers to anyone with a "criminal record." Depending upon the state and how it keeps records, it can also include low level misdemeanors that would present little if any barrier to employment. The number can also include dismissed cases. Technically, a traffic ticket may be considered a criminal record and it is not clear if those are included as well. In other words, a great deal more research is needed to understand the true number and what it means.

A Reality Check

'The Employment Situation – July 2012' report released August 3, 2012 by the U.S. Department of Labor's Bureau of Labor Statistics reported there were 12.8 million unemployed people in the U.S. representing an unemployment rate of 8.3 percent. If in fact there are 65 million people that "need not apply," it would seem the unemployment rate would be astronomical. The vast majority of the so-called "65 million" apparently do have employment. The report addresses the problems faced by ex-offenders. They have less opportunities to get jobs since there are employers that will slam the door in the face of anyone with a criminal record, even if it is minor, old, or not relevant to the job.

However, the NELP report did note several significant issues. First, regardless of the actual number, there is a significant social problem with ex-offenders encountering barriers in obtaining jobs. The report noted a criminal record can become a lifetime bar to employment and gave examples of a number of employers and staffing agencies who required applicants to have NO criminal record, not even a misdemeanor, for various jobs. The report also attempted to calculate the economic impact of incarceration as opposed to putting ex-offenders to work.

1997 Study Shows One Third of U.S. Young Adults Arrested by Age 23

The federal government's National Longitudinal Survey of Youth 1997 (NLSY97) "documents the transition from school to work and from adolescence to adulthood." The study found that 30.2 percent of the 23-year-olds participating in the study reported being arrested for an offense other than a minor traffic violation. This figure is noticeably higher than the 22 percent reported in an earlier NLSY study conducted in 1965.

The NLSY97 web page states the study "consists of a nationally representative sample of approximately 9,000 youths who were 12 to 16 years old as of December 31, 1996. Round 1 of the survey took place in 1997. In that round, both the eligible youth and one of that youth's parents received hour-long personal interviews. Youths continue to be interviewed on an annual basis."

According to researchers, 15.9 percent of the participants in the study reported having been arrested by the age of 18, a possible reflection of the increase in arrests for drug-related offenses, zero-tolerance policies in schools, and a more aggressive and punitive justice system. The higher numbers of arrests occurring in late adolescence and early adulthood, at a time when most people enter the workforce, are notable since employers now routinely conduct criminal background checks on job candidates.

The questions for the 'Crime, Delinquency & Arrest' section of the NLSY97 survey asked the youth respondents whether they had ever been arrested by the police or taken into custody for an illegal or delinquent offense (not including arrests for minor traffic violations) and the total number of times that it had happened. The list of possible arrest charges included: assault, burglary, destruction of property, possession or use of illicit drugs, sale or trafficking of illicit drugs, a major traffic offense, and a public order offense.

More information about The NLSY97 study may be found at www.bls.gov/nls/nlsy97.htm. More information on the 'Crime, Delinquency & Arrest' section of the NLSY97 survey is available at: www.nlsinfo.org/nlsy97/nlsdocs/nlsy97/topicalguide/crimeetc.html.

Claims of Inaccurate Background Reports

A report issued by the National Consumer Law Center (NCLC) in April 2012 entitled *"Broken Records: How Errors by Criminal Background Checking Companies Harm Workers and Business,"* suggests that inaccurate criminal background checks are widespread and makes recommendations to remedy errors that can cost jobs. The report describes a number of ways in which background screening companies make mistakes that greatly affect a consumer's ability to find employment:

- ✓ Mismatch the subject of the report with another person;
- ✓ Reveal sealed or expunged information;
- ✓ Omit information about how the case was disposed or resolved;
- ✓ Contain misleading information; and
- ✓ Mischaracterize the seriousness of the offense reported.

The NCLC report is available at: www.nclc.org/images/pdf/pr-reports/broken-records-report.pdf.

Although the NCLC report received a great deal of publicity, it also came under heavy criticism for being inaccurate, misleading, and lacking objectivity and subject matter knowledge. The report cites a handful of anecdotal stories and some court cases (out of the millions of background checks conducted yearly) where an inaccurate background check had grave consequences on a consumer's ability to get a job. In fact, based upon an objective evaluation of the claims made, given the NCLC could only find an extremely small number of erroneous reports per the millions done, the accuracy rate is actually extremely high. The report also failed to understand the difference between "data brokers" that aggregate raw data and a Consumer Reporting Agency (CRA) operating under the Fair Credit Reporting Act (FCRA). It also failed to acknowledge the horrendous harm done to victims of crimes when employers could have prevented a situation with a proper background check. It is much easier for applicants to get a job after an erroneous background report then it is for crime victims to get on with their lives after harmed as a result of negligent hiring. To read a detailed discussion by the author regarding the NCLC report, visit: www.esrcheck.com/articles/NCLC-Report-on-Criminal-Background-Checks-Inaccurate.php.

NAPBS to Release Study Affirming Accuracy of Background Checks

The National Association of Professional Background Screeners (NAPBS) announced in press release a recent study of background screening companies that affirms the accuracy of background checks and refutes a report recently issued by the National Consumer Law Center (NCLC). The NCLC accused background screeners of routinely making mistakes.

The NAPBS report, scheduled to be released to the public later 2012 after the printing of this book, found that 98 percent of background screening providers surveyed encountered consumer disputes less than 5 percent of the time out of millions of background checks performed annually, and more than 95 percent of those disputed background check reports were ultimately found to be accurate.

The NAPBS study, validated by market research agency Mathew Greenwald & Associates in Washington D.C., is a response to a report from the NCLC released April 2012, 'Broken Records: How Errors by Criminal Background Checking Companies Harm Workers and Businesses,' that examined the accuracy of background checks. The NCLC report claimed that 65 million Americans with criminal records were "forever tarnished and unemployable as a result of background checks."

The NAPBS stated that the NCLC report included "several inaccurate points" and failed "to offer critical empirical data to back up its findings." According to NAPBS, the NCLC allegation that criminal background checks make it more difficult for workers to obtain employment is not supported by the facts since the Equal Employment Opportunity Commission (EEOC) "has stepped up enforcement against employers who discriminate based on criminal history." Furthermore, the NAPBS said the Fair Credit Reporting Act (FCRA) mandates that a Consumer Reporting Agency (CRA) must follow reasonable procedures to assure maximum possible accuracy of the information in a background check report.

Source:

www.napbs.com/files/public/Learn_More/Press%20Releases/NAPBS-NCLC%20Media%20PointsXLT612F.pdf

---

Recent Actions by State & City Governments

The concern over giving ex-offenders a second chance in order to re-enter society is so acute that a number of city governments have instituted a new policy to help ex-offenders re-enter the workforce by taking out questions about past criminal conduct from the employment application. Boston, Chicago, Minneapolis, San Francisco, and St. Paul have taken the lead in trying to place ex-offenders into the workforce by not asking questions about past offenses in the initial application process that would limit ex-offenders from applying in the first place. Other jurisdictions, including Indianapolis, Los Angeles, Newark, and Philadelphia, are considering such legislation. In Boston, the law has gone further and applies to an estimated 50,000 vendors who do business with the city.

The logic behind these laws is to ensure that applicants are considered for jobs based upon their qualifications and experience before the employer searches out criminal records. In addition, such protection also encourages ex-offenders to apply in the first place. The laws are designed to address the problems faced by ex-offenders who are unable to obtain the employment necessary to become tax paying and law-abiding citizens and to reduce the high recidivism rate of ex-offenders. It can cost taxpayers over $30,000 per year to incarcerate an individual, so society has a vested interest in having ex-offenders succeed.

These laws do not mean that convicted child molesters will be getting jobs as playground supervisors. The cities and counties passing such laws allow for background checks on finalists, consistent with the EEOC guidelines on the permissible use of criminal records for employment.

An Illinois legislature act (SB 3007), effective 2005, allows for the sealing of certain non-violent felonies in order to ease ex-offender's re-entry into society by helping them get jobs without being hindered by a criminal record. According to one legislator quoted in a press story:

> "It costs us more than $25,000 a year to send someone to prison. Helping people re-integrate into society doesn't just help the individual, it helps the state. People with jobs will be less likely to turn to crime, which means fewer people in prison."

(See; www.insperityscreening.com/misc/display_news.asp?article_id=041116091304&return_link=True)

Another supporter noted that, "Most Chicago ex-offenders return to high-crime and low-employment communities. This leads to difficulties not only for the ex-offender themselves but contributes to neighborhood deterioration. Easing their transition back to pubic life will improve neighborhoods and the city as a whole."

Supporters also noted that although in Illinois African-Americans are 15 percent of the illicit drug users, they are 37% of those arrested for drug offenses and more than 75% of the total drug prisoners in Illinois.

The logic here is sealing certain criminal records will drop one of the most significant barriers in finding work. The new law allows law enforcement to access the records, and the records can still be utilized for certain high-risk occupations such a childcare or driving a school bus. The law also calls for study of recidivism rates among those with their records sealed.

See Chapter 30 for advice to job applicants with criminal records.

"Ban the Box" Movement Aims to Remove Criminal Questions on Applications

The issue of whether employers can use a job application to ask about a job applicant's criminal record is becoming more complicated. In an effort to provide fair employment opportunities for ex-convicts, some states, cities, counties, and local governments across the country are joining the "ban the box" movement. This practice removes the "box" job applicants are asked to check regarding the question on the job application which asks about past criminal arrest and conviction. The purpose is to give those applicants with criminal pasts a fair shot at obtaining employment. By removing this question, supporters claim job applicants can be sure that they will not be automatically excluded for consideration for a job because of their past mistakes.

A Resource Guide from NELP – *'Ban the Box: Major U.S. Cities and Counties Adopt Fair Hiring Policies to Remove Unfair Barriers to Employment of People with Criminal Records'* – updated in February 2012 lists the following cities and counties as having banned the box when asking applicants about felony convictions: Alameda County, CA; Atlantic City, NJ; Austin, TX; Baltimore, MD; Berkeley, CA; Boston, MA; Bridgeport, CT; Cambridge, MA; Chicago, IL; Cincinnati, OH; Cleveland, OH; Cumberland County, NC; Detroit, MI; Hartford, CT; Jacksonville, FL; Kalamazoo, MI; Memphis, TN; Minneapolis, MN; Multnomah County, OR; Muskegon County, MI; New Haven, CT; Norwich, CT; Oakland, CA; Philadelphia, PA; Providence, RI; San Francisco, CA; Seattle, WA; St. Paul, MN; Travis County, TX; Washington, DC; and Worcester, MA.

Others have since joined the "Ban the Box" movement and removed the question regarding arrests and convictions from job applications. The above mentioned Resource Guide from NELP is found at: http://nelp.3cdn.net/14047d447967924539_zcm6bz5bp.pdf.

Massachusetts CORI Reform Law Prohibits Employers from Asking About Criminal Convictions on Initial Job Applications

An overhaul of the Massachusetts Criminal Offender Record Information (CORI) that took effect November 4, 2010 means employers in Massachusetts are no longer able to ask about convictions on "initial" written job applications because of new legislation that prohibits employers from asking about criminal offender record information, which includes criminal charges, arrests, and incarceration.

The new law contained several provisions that affected the way employers use the criminal histories of prospective and current employees and impacted Massachusetts employers performing criminal background checks on job applicants and employees. While the new law does not prevent employers from obtaining criminal histories of job applicants or employees contained in the CORI database, under the CORI reform law those records will no longer contain:

✓ Felony convictions closed for more than ten years, whether convictions occurred more than ten years ago or individuals were released more than ten years ago.

✓ Misdemeanor convictions closed for more than five years.

In addition, the new law also includes the following provisions:

✓ Employers that decide not to hire applicants or take adverse actions based on criminal histories in CORI reports must first give applicants copies of the reports.

✓ Employers conducting five (5) or more criminal background checks per year must maintain a written criminal offender record information policy.

✓ Employers are prohibited from maintaining CORI records of former employees or unsuccessful job applicants for more than seven years from the last date of employment or from the date of the decision not to hire the job applicant.

For more information, visit: www.mass.gov/eopss/crime-prev-personal-sfty/bkgd-check/cori.

The EEOC 2012 Enforcement Guidance on the Consideration of Arrest and Conviction Records in Employment Decisions

Against the backdrop of concerns over the widespread use of background reports, the U.S. Equal Employment Opportunity Commission (EEOC) issued its updated *Enforcement Guidance on the Consideration of Arrest and Conviction Records in Employment Decisions Under Title VII of the Civil Rights Act of 1964* on April 25, 2012. Below are four important links regarding this Guidance:

1. The updated EEOC Guidance for criminal background checks by employers is available at www.eeoc.gov/laws/guidance/arrest_conviction.cfm.
2. A brief Q&A was also issued at www.eeoc.gov/laws/guidance/qa_arrest_conviction.cfm.
3. Materials for the EEOC public meeting held April 25, 2012 on the use of arrest and conviction records, including testimony and transcripts, are available at www.eeoc.gov/eeoc/meetings/4-25-12/index.cfm.

4. A video of the proceedings of the meeting is available online at www.eeoc.gov/eeoc/meetings/4-25-12/video.cfm.

The Guidance is not a series of rules or regulations that a court must enforce. A court will generally consider the opinion of the EEOC, but courts have in the past disregarded and overruled such guidance. An example is in the area of the Americans with Disabilities Act (ADA), see *Sutton v. United Air Lines, 130 F3d 893(10 Cir. 1997).*

It has been argued that Congress intentionally withheld rulemaking authority from the EEOC when it passed Title VII of the Civil Right Act of 1964, and it only gave the power to issue suitable procedural regulations to carry out the federal law 42 USC § 2000e–12. However, the EEOC has adopted a practice of issuing enforcement "guidance" instead. Such guidance can be issued without public comment, as this one was, because it does not have the force or effect of law. However, a large firm targeted by the EEOC under the new Guidance may need to spend substantial time, money, and effort resisting the Guidance in court. Per EEOC, the updated Guidance "builds on longstanding court decisions and guidance documents that the EEOC issued over 20 years ago" and "focuses on employment discrimination based on race and national origin." The EEOC noted previous guidance but noted that "this Enforcement Guidance will supersede the Commission's previous policy statements on this issue."

Are Small Businesses Impacted?

Title VII only applies to employers who employ 15 or more employees for 20 or more weeks in the current or preceding calendar year (42 U.S.C. § 2000e(b)). However, how employee counts are determine if the threshold is met for the application of federal laws can get complicated. If an employer is close to the 15 employee mark, they should realize the EEOC may look at "independent contractors" to see if they should also be counted as employees, if the relationship more resembles employment. The government can also look at common ownership of separate firms and lump those together if they are sufficiently integrated. See: www.eeoc.gov/policy/docs/threshold.html#2-III-B-1-a-i.

Previous EEOC guidelines include:

✓ **1987** - EEOC Policy Statement on the Issue of Conviction Records under Title VII of the Civil Rights Act of **1964**, as amended, 42 U.S.C. § 2000e et seq. (1982)(2/4/87): www.eeoc.gov/policy/docs/convict1.html

✓ **1987** - EEOC Policy Statement on the Use of Statistics in Charges Involving the Exclusion of Individuals with Conviction Records from Employment (7/29/87): www.eeoc.gov/laws/guidance/arrest_conviction.cfm#sdendnote3sym

✓ **1990** - Policy Guidance on the Consideration of Arrest Records in Employment Decisions under Title VII of the Civil Rights Act of 1964, as amended, 42 U.S.C. §2000e et seq. (1982)(9/7/90): www.eeoc.gov/policy/docs/arrest_records.html

It should be noted that the 2012 Guidelines are just internal investigation guidelines for the EEOC and are not official rules or regulations and do not have the force or effect of laws. They were passed by the EEOC on a 4-1 vote without any public preview or comment period. Until the morning of April 25, 2012, no one knew what the guidelines would say. Following passage of the guidelines, the U.S. House of Representatives voted to defund the ability of the EEOC to enforce the guidelines. However, the EEOC still has the power to investigate complaints based upon the provisions of these guidelines and to issue right to sue letters or to file lawsuits, which means that an employer takes a substantial risk in ignoring them.

The guidelines came on the heels of recent enforcement actions, the **E-RACE initiative (Eradicating Racism and Colorism in Employment)** and strategic plan to target systemic violators (e.g. Pepsi case). The findings were somewhat telegraphed in advance by means of two letters written by EEOC staff counsel. One letter was written to the Peace Corp and was critical of an open ended application form with very broad questions about past convictions and arrests. See: www.eeoc.gov/eeoc/foia/letters/2011/title_vii_criminal_record_peace_corps_application.html. (FCRA attorneys Rod Fliegel, a Shareholder in Littler Mendelson's San Francisco office, and Jennifer Morazán, Associate in the Los Angeles office, wrote a review of the letter at www.littler.com/publication-press/publication/eeoc-advisory-guidance-offers-insight-use-arrest-and-conviction-record.)

Also see: www.eeoc.gov/eeoc/foia/letters/2011/titlevii_crimial_history.html.

The EEOC's stated purpose in issuing the new guidelines was based upon statistics showing a disproportionate impact of criminal records on protected groups, including Blacks and Hispanics. The EEOC cited statistics and studies showing criminal records have a discriminatory impact on Blacks and Hispanics. At the same time, they cited a 2010 Society for Human Resources Management (SHRM) study where 92% of responding employers stated that they subjected all or some of their job candidates to criminal background checks.

See: www.shrm.org/Research/SurveyFindings/Articles/Pages/BackgroundCheckCriminalChecks.aspx.

According to the EEOC Guidance: "In the last twenty years, there has been a significant increase in the number of Americans who have had contact with the criminal justice system and, concomitantly, a major increase in the number of people with criminal records in the working-age population. In 1991, only 1.8% of the adult population had served time in prison. After ten years, in 2001, the percentage rose to 2.7% (1 in 37 adults). By the end of 2007, 3.2% of all adults in the United States (1 in every 31) were under some form of correctional control involving probation, parole, prison, or jail. The Department of Justice's Bureau of Justice Statistics (DOJ/BJS) has concluded that, if incarceration rates do not decrease, approximately 6.6% of all persons born in the United States in 2001 will serve time in state or federal prison during their lifetimes."

The EEOC further noted: "Arrest and incarceration rates are particularly high for African American and Hispanic men .African Americans and Hispanics are arrested at a rate that is 2 to 3 times their proportion of the general population. Assuming that current incarceration rates remain unchanged, about 1 in 17 White men are expected to serve time in prison during their lifetime; by contrast, this rate climbs to 1 in 6 for Hispanic men; and to 1 in 3 for African American men."

The EEOC also expressed concern about the accuracy of criminal records. The EEOC Guidance indicated: "recent studies have found that a significant number of state and federal criminal record databases include incomplete criminal records."

✓ A 2011 study by the DOJ/BJS reported that, as of 2010, many state criminal history record repositories still had not recorded the final dispositions for a significant number of arrests.

✓ A 2006 study by the DOJ/BJS found that only 50% of arrest records in the FBI's III database were associated with a final disposition.

Additionally, the EEOC cited other studies suggesting inaccuracies of criminal records:

✓ One report found that even if public access to criminal records has been restricted by a court order to seal and/or expunge such records, this does not guarantee that private companies also will purge the information from their systems or that the event will be erased from media archives.

✓ Another report found that criminal background checks may produce inaccurate results because criminal records may lack "unique" information or because of "misspellings, clerical errors or intentionally inaccurate identification information provided by search subjects who wish to avoid discovery of their prior criminal activities."

The EEOC was clear to say background checks are not eliminated. They noted some situations where there is a clear nexus between the job and the offense, and in some situations, federal or state laws eliminate certain individuals with certain offenses.

The EEOC then addressed the different considerations for an arrest as opposed to a conviction. It re-stated its long standing position that: "The fact of an arrest does not establish the criminal conduct has occurred, and an exclusion based on an arrest, in itself, is not job related and consistent with business necessity. However, an employer may make an employment decision based on the conduct underlying an arrest if the conduct makes the individual for the position in question."

The guidance noted "in contrast, a conviction record will usually serve as sufficient evidence that a person engaged in particular conduct. In certain circumstances, however, there may be reasons for an employer not to rely on the conviction record alone when making an employment decision."

To protect job applicants from discrimination, the EEOC noted: "As a best practice, and consistent with applicable laws, the Commission recommends that employers not ask about convictions on job applications and that, if and when they make such inquiries, the inquiries be limited to convictions for which exclusion would be job related for the position in question and consistent with business necessity."

This approach appears to serve two purposes:

1. This is essentially a reaction to suggestions that a criminal record is a lifetime ban on employment. If an applicant is asked to reveal their entire criminal history without regard to relevance as to the offense or the time period involved, there is a concern that large numbers of individuals with criminal records will never be allowed in the workforce.

2. It is a restatement of the "ban the box" approach. The idea is that an applicant is not asked about a criminal record on the initial application in order not to deter or "chill" otherwise qualified applicants from applying since an applicant with a criminal record may reasonably suspect that his or her chances of proceeding successfully through the employment process would be diminished. In fact, applicants with criminal records may fear that their application may immediately end up in the trash heap, regardless of their qualifications. The "ban the box" approach is to ensure that all applicants, even those with past criminal records, are initially evaluated based upon their qualifications, and at an appropriate time, an employer can then do a background check including relevant criminal records. If a criminal record is located, the employer is better able to put the criminal matter in context, having first evaluated the applicant as an individual without regard to their status as an ex-offender.

The EEOC drove home the point in a discussion of potential defenses to discrimination an employer may have in determining disparate impact. Although the Commission would assess the probative value of an employer's applicant data, the guidance quoted a Supreme Court decision that noted that an "application process might itself not adequately reflect the actual potential applicant pool since otherwise qualified people might be discouraged from applying" because of an alleged discriminatory policy or practice.

Disparate Treatment and Disparate Impact

The EEOC Guidance reviewed two types of discrimination.

✓ **Disparate Treatment:** "A violation may occur when an employer treats criminal history information differently for different applicants or employees, based on their race or national origin (disparate treatment liability)."

✓ **Disparate Impact:** "An employer's neutral policy (e.g., excluding applications from employment based on certain criminal conduct) may disproportionately impact some individuals protected under Title VII, and may violate the law if not job related and consistent with business necessity."

In determining Disparate Impact, the EEOC summarized a three-part test:

1. **Identifying the policy or practice:** The first step in disparate impact analysis is to identify the particular policy or practice that causes the unlawful disparate impact. For criminal conduct exclusions, relevant information includes the text of the policy or practice, associated documentation, and information about how the policy or practice was actually implemented. More specifically, such information also includes which offenses or classes of offenses were reported to the employer (e.g., all felonies, all drug offenses); whether convictions (including sealed

and/or expunged convictions), arrests, charges, or other criminal incidents were reported; how far back in time the reports reached (e.g., the last five, ten, or twenty years); and the jobs for which the criminal background screening was conducted. Training or guidance documents used by the employer also are relevant, because they may specify which types of criminal history information to gather for particular jobs, how to gather the data, and how to evaluate the information after it is obtained. The Guidance noted that, in addition, the "Commission will closely consider whether an employer has a reputation in the community for excluding individuals with criminal records."

2. **Determining if there is a Disparate Impact:** Per EEOC, studies that show nationally that African Americans and Hispanics are arrested in numbers that are disproportionate, supports a finding that an employer that uses criminal records to prevent employment will have a disparate in pact on groups protected by Title VII. During an EEOC investigation, the employer also has an opportunity to show, with relevant evidence, that its employment policy or practice does not cause a disparate impact on the protected group(s). At this point, these cases can become a battle of statistics as well as evidence of employer practices. For example, an employer may be able to show that within the relevant hiring area, protected groups do not face criminal charges or conviction at a greater rate than the general population.

3. **If Disparate Impact Established, Employer has the Burden:** After the plaintiff in litigation establishes disparate impact, Title VII shifts the burdens of production and persuasion to the employer to "demonstrate that the challenged practice is job related for the position in question and consistent with business necessity."

Assuming the employer meets the burden, the EEOC or applicant still has one last bite of the apple which is an argument that there was a less discriminatory alternative available that the employer did not adopt. The argument could be that different policies were needed, or perhaps even a longer time was needed for applicants to contest the decision.

Two Circumstances Where Employers Meet EEOC Approved Defense

Assuming a discrimination charge gets to the third part or stage, the key issue for employers is to meet the requirement that the "challenged practice is job related for the position in question and consistent with business necessity." The Guidance describes two circumstances in which the EEOC believes employers will consistently meet the "job related and consistent with business necessity" defense:

1. "The employer validates the criminal conduct exclusion for the position in question in light of the Uniform Guidelines on Employee Selection Procedures (if there is data or analysis about criminal conduct as related to subsequent work performance or behaviors); or

2. The employer develops a targeted screen considering at least the nature of the crime, the time elapsed, and the nature of the job."

The three-part test was issued in the 1987 "EEOC Policy Statement on the Issue of Conviction Records under Title VII of the Civil Rights Act of 1964."

Three part test dates to 1987 based *upon Green v .Missouri Pacific Railroad*, 523 F.2d 1290 (8th Cir. 1975) However, the EEOC added some additional insights to this case:

1. **Nature and Gravity of offense**
   "Careful consideration of the nature and gravity of the offense or conduct is the first step in determining whether a specific crime may be relevant to concerns about risks in a particular position. The nature of the offense or conduct may be assessed with reference to the harm caused by the crime (e.g., theft causes property loss). The legal elements of a crime also may be instructive. For example, a conviction for felony theft may involve deception, threat, or intimidation. With respect to the gravity of the crime, offenses identified as misdemeanors may be less severe than those identified as felonies."

2. **Time since the conviction and/or completion of the sentence**
   "Employer policies typically specify the duration of criminal conduct exclusion. While the Green court did not endorse a specific timeframe for criminal conduct exclusions, it did acknowledge that permanent exclusions from all employment based on any and all offenses were not consistent with the business necessity standard.

Subsequently, in El, (plaintiff was rejected for a job as a paratransit driver based on his 40-year old homicide conviction which is discussed in detail in Chapter 2) the court noted that the plaintiff might have survived summary judgment if he had presented evidence that "there is a time at which a former criminal is no longer any more likely to recidivate than the average person . . . Thus, the court recognized that the amount of time that had passed since the plaintiff's criminal conduct occurred was probative of the risk he posed in the position in question. Whether the duration of exclusion will be sufficiently tailored to satisfy the business necessity standard will depend on the particular facts and circumstances of each case. Relevant and available information to make this assessment includes, for example, studies demonstrating how much the risk of recidivism declines over a specified time."

3. **Nature of the job held or sought**
"Finally, it is important to identify the particular job(s) subject to the exclusion. While a factual inquiry may begin with identifying the job title, it also encompasses the nature of the job's duties (e.g., data entry, lifting boxes), identification of the job's essential functions, the circumstances under which the job is performed (e.g., the level of supervision, oversight, and interaction with co-workers or vulnerable individuals), and the environment in which the job's duties are performed (e.g., out of doors, in a warehouse, in a private home). Linking the criminal conduct to the essential functions of the position in question may assist an employer in demonstrating that its policy or practice is job related and consistent with business necessity because it "bear[s] a demonstrable relationship to successful performance of the jobs for which it was used.""

 The term **"Green Factors"** refers to the three-part test used by employers to determine the "business necessity" for using criminal records through three factors (nature and gravity of the offense, time since the conviction and/or completion of the sentence, and nature of the job held or sought) based upon *Green v .Missouri Pacific Railroad, 523 F.2d 1290 (8th Cir. 1975).*

Individualized Assessment

If an applicant is the subject of a targeted screen using the Green factors, the EEOC indicated that an "individualized assessment" is recommended, but not required by law. According to the EEOC:

"The employer's policy then provides an opportunity for an individualized assessment for those people identified by the screen, to determine if the policy as applied is job related and consistent with business necessity. (Although Title VII does not require individualized assessment in all circumstances, the use of a screen that does not include individualized assessment is more likely to violate Title VII)."

The EEOC Guidance described the process as follows:

"Individualized assessment generally means that an employer informs the individual that he may be excluded because of past criminal conduct; provides an opportunity to the individual to demonstrate that the exclusion does not properly apply to him; and considers whether the individual's additional information shows that the policy as applied is not job related and consistent with business necessity.

The individual's showing may include information that he was not correctly identified in the criminal record, or that the record is otherwise inaccurate. Other relevant individualized evidence includes, for example:

- The facts or circumstances surrounding the offense or conduct;
- The number of offenses for which the individual was convicted;
- Older age at the time of conviction, or release from prison;
- Evidence that the individual performed the same type of work, post-conviction, with the same or a different employer, with no known incidents of criminal conduct;
- The length and consistency of employment history before and after the offense or conduct;

- Rehabilitation efforts, e.g., education/training;
- Employment or character references and any other information regarding fitness for the particular position; and
- Whether the individual is bonded under a federal, state, or local bonding program.

If the individual does not respond to the employer's attempt to gather additional information about his background, the employer may make its employment decision without the information. The Guidance also notes even if "an employer successfully demonstrates that its policy or practice is job related for the position in question and consistent with business necessity, a Title VII plaintiff may still prevail by demonstrating that there is a less discriminatory "alternative employment practice" that serves the employer's legitimate goals as effectively as the challenged practice but that the employer refused to adopt."

State and Local Regulations Affected by the EEOC Guidance

An area of potential concern for employers is that the EEOC has also taken the position that employers subject to state or local regulations, as opposed to federal regulation, concerning background checks are not shielded from a Title VII action just because of the legal requirements, since federal law supersedes state and local law. Per the Guidance:

"States and local jurisdictions also have laws and/or regulations that restrict or prohibit the employment of individuals with records of certain criminal conduct. Unlike federal laws or regulations, however, state and local laws or regulations are preempted by Title VII if they "purport[] to require or permit the doing of any act which would be an unlawful employment practice" under Title VII. Therefore, if an employer's exclusionary policy or practice is not job related and consistent with business necessity, the fact that it was adopted to comply with a state or local law or regulation does not shield the employer from Title VII liability."

The Catch-22 for employers is they may follow state or local laws in good faith, and yet still be subject to an EEOC action. If an employer determines it needs to violate state or local laws to comply with Title VII, the employer is potentially subject to legal actions for violation of the state or local law in question.

EEOC Suggested "Best Practices" for Employers

The EEOC Guidance concluded with some suggested best practices for employers:

General

- ✓ Eliminate policies or practices that exclude people from employment based on any criminal record.
- ✓ Train managers, hiring officials, and decision makers about Title VII and its prohibition on employment discrimination.

Policy

Develop a narrowly tailored written policy and procedure for screening applicants and employees for criminal conduct.

- ✓ Identify essential job requirements and the actual circumstances under which the jobs are performed.
- ✓ Determine the specific offenses that may demonstrate unfitness for performing such jobs.
  - Identify the criminal offenses based on all available evidence.
- ✓ Determine the duration of exclusions for criminal conduct based on all available evidence.
  - Include an individualized assessment.
- ✓ Record the justification for the policy and procedures.
- ✓ Note and keep a record of consultations and research considered in crafting the policy and procedures.
- ✓ Train managers, hiring officials, and decision makers on how to implement the policy and procedures consistent with Title VII.

Questions about Criminal Records

✓ When asking questions about criminal records, limit inquiries to records for which exclusion would be job related for the position in question and consistent with business necessity.

Confidentiality

✓ Keep information about applicants' and employees' criminal records confidential. Only use it for the purpose for which it was intended.

What Does All of this Mean?

✓ First, the EEOC makes it clear that employers can certainly do background checks. That is not an issue. The issue is the fair and relevant use of criminal records so it does not create a discriminatory disparate impact.

✓ Second, the EEOC restated its long standing position dealing with automatic disqualification based upon a criminal record, reaffirming a no automatic disqualification rule
This is a critical rule when it comes to the use of criminal records: an employer cannot deny employment *automatically*. An employer needs a business justification not to hire based upon a criminal past. The United States Supreme Court ruled in *Griggs v. Duke Power CO., 401 U.S. 424 (1971)*, that a plaintiff can allege employment discrimination without a proving a discriminatory intent.

 AUTHOR TIP As a result of Griggs and ensuing cases, the EEOC has made it clear the automatic use of a criminal record without showing a business necessity can have discriminatory impact by disqualifying a disproportionate number of members of minority groups. The key term is, of course, "business necessity." Important court cases on the subject were summarized recently in *El v. Southeastern Pennsylvania Transportation Authority, 479 F.3d 232 (3d. Cir. 2007)*. See the article 'From Griggs to SEPTA: The EEOC's Increased Focus on Employment Screening' in Chapter 3.

✓ Third, the EEOC restated it reaffirmed another long standing position on the use of arrests records. Although the EEOC stated the new guidance superseded previous guidance, the 1990 Policy Guidance on the Consideration of Arrest Records in Employment Decisions went into arrest records in considerably more detail. (See additional discussion below.)

✓ Fourth, the EEOC is clearly concerned about lifetime disqualification from the job market, as well as the deterrent effect of asking about a criminal record too soon in the process, so that an otherwise qualified applicant does not have a fair chance. A key thrust of the EEOC efforts seem to be concerned that if an applicant reveals a criminal record too early, that an employer may summarily throw out the application and not even give an otherwise potentially qualified person a chance to compete.

✓ A related concern is that a broad and opened question about a person's entire criminal history can be discriminatory and that employers should only ask about criminal matters that are job related.

✓ In addition, nothing in the EEOC Guidance or the FCRA prohibits a background firm from turning over everything they find. There is no obligation for a background firm to censor any data that is otherwise not prohibited by any other state or federal laws. However, by the time a background check is ordered by an employer, the applicant is either a finalist or a semi-finalist and has clearly been considered on his or her merits. However, if a background check is returned with a criminal record, the employer clearly should apply the Green factors and if a decision is made to not hire, the Individualized Assessment.

Criticism of EEOC Guidance

The new rules of the EEOC Guidance have come under heavy criticism as evidenced below:

✓ Commissioner Constance S. Barker cast the lone dissenting vote against issuing the Guidance. Her concerns were the Guidance goes beyond the jurisdiction of the EEOC, it will negatively affect business owners, and did not receive sufficient public comment. She felt the new Guidance represented a large shift from the advice being given for 22 years, yet no one from the public actually saw the Guidance until the day of vote. It has also been suggested that the EEOC was not given authority to make rules and therefore acted in excess of its jurisdiction. *The text of Commissioner Barker's comments at the EEOC April 25, 2012 meeting is at the end of this section.*

✓ These are not regulations with the force and effect of law. These are litigation guidance only. Many experts are questioning how much credence to give them. However, if the EEOC makes an employer a test case, then the employer is exposed to a significant legal and financial challenge, even if the EEOC's position loses in court.

✓ The EEOC is clearly focused on the notion that after a period of time, the impact of a criminal record lessens, and furthermore, overtime the likelihood of re-offending is diminished. The Guidance contains citations in various footnotes to studies arguing that the predictive value of criminal records statistically diminish over time. However, the EEOC Guidance is noticeably vague on exactly what the time periods should be. A close examination of the studies shows the scope is extremely limited and certainly not advanced to the point where it can be the basis of social policy. The failure of the EEOC to even suggest time periods and to only cite very limited studies is a major shortcoming in the Guidance.

✓ On the heels of issuing the new guidance, there was an impact in Congress. The U.S. House of Representatives passed an appropriations bill (H.R. 5326) that provided funding for several agencies including the allocation of $367 million for the U.S. Equal Employment Opportunity Commission (EEOC) but also included amendments that would block implementation and enforcement of several programs including the new EEOC Guidance. As of this writing, the matter is still pending in Congress.

Practice Note: How Would EEOC or Private Parties Bring Lawsuits or Legal Actions?

The EEOC may itself investigate, mediate, or file lawsuits on behalf of employees where it is alleged there is discrimination. In fact, the EEOC recently approved its 'Strategic Plan for Fiscal Years 2012-2016' that establishes a framework for achieving the EEOC's mission to "stop and remedy unlawful employment discrimination." It includes targeted action against systemic discrimination. See: http://www.eeoc.gov/eeoc/plan/strategic_plan_12to16.cfm.

Furthermore, certain state agencies that enforce state fair employment laws can also enforce Title VII. All states have such agencies with the current exception of Arkansas and Mississippi. See: www.eeocoffice.com. Under Title VII, individuals can bring a private lawsuit. However, the individual must first file a complaint of discrimination with the EEOC within 180 days of learning of the discrimination or the individual may lose the right to file a lawsuit. The idea is that the EEOC or state agency can review the claim to determine if it will take any action in the matter. If the EEOC or state agency does not pursue the matter, that individual can obtain a "right to sue" letter. State agencies may have different time period or procedures. Such a letter does not mean the EEOC endorses the complaint and it is still up to the individual to obtain an attorney.

Recent EEOC Failed Enforcements

The EEOC has received very pubic judicial rebukes in their enforcement efforts.

In a decision ending over three years of litigation, a federal court in Michigan recently sanctioned the EEOC and ordered it to pay $751,942.48 for attorney's fees, expert fees, and court costs to a private employer,

PeopleMark, Inc., a staffing company headquartered in Kentucky.

The EEOC had filed a class action lawsuit against PeopleMark in 2008, alleging that the company violated Title VII of the Civil Rights Act by adopting a blanket policy of refusing to hire job applicants with criminal records. According to the EEOC, the policy had a "disparate impact" on minority groups such as African Americans and Hispanics.

After the EEOC was unable to prove that PeopleMark had a policy of refusing to hire job applicants with criminal record, or identify any person who had suffered discrimination as a result of PeopleMark's alleged hiring policies, and was unable to produce statistical or expert evidence to back up its claims of discrimination, the EEOC dismissed its case.

(See: www.esrcheck.com/wordpress/2011/04/08/eeoc-sanctioned-by-federal-court-and-ordered-to-pay-more-than-750000-in-fees).

More recently, in a case filed in 2010 by the EEOC against Kaplan Higher Education Corporation ("Kaplan") in federal district court in Ohio, the EEOC charged that Kaplan used credit checks for job applicants and employees, and it had an unlawful disparate impact on African American individuals in violation of Title VII of the Civil Rights Act of 1964 ("Title VII").

Kaplan's attorneys attempted to discover information from the EEOC regarding its own policies on credit checks of applicants. Kaplan argued that, "to the extent the EEOC's use of credit checks for specific positions is consistent with the practices it challenges in this lawsuit, this consistency supports Kaplan's estoppel defense." The EEOC did not want to turn over information on how it used credit checks itself and opposed the discovery request on the basis that it was overly broad, unduly burdensome, and not relevant to the case. The court however ruled that Kaplan had a right to such informant, and the EEOC had to supply information on how they used credit checks if they were using a private company for discriminatory use. The district court previously ruled in the case that the "EEOC's use of background or credit checks in its own hiring of employees was relevant to Kaplan's asserted defense of business necessity in using such check in its hiring process." See:

www.littler.com/files/press/pdf/2012_04_ASAP_DoAsISay_EEOC_DiscoveryEmploymentPractices.pdf.

- ✓ The examples given in the EEOC Guidance are not useful. They utilize extreme examples that may illustrate the points, but the extreme examples are the easy ones—in real life, decisions much more difficult and close calls often need to be made.
- ✓ The EEOC Guidance notes a study in a footnote that suggests a LACK of a background check is actually a barrier to employment by members of protected groups. Per the Guidance, "a 2006 study demonstrated that employers who are averse to hiring people with criminal records sometimes presumed, in the absence of evidence to the contrary, that African American men applying for jobs have disqualifying criminal records. Harry J. Holder et al., Perceived Criminality, Criminal Background Checks, and the Racial Hiring Practices of Employers, 49 J.L. & ECON. 451 (2006)."
- ✓ The EEOC quotes figures showing a dramatic number of individuals that are the subject of the criminal justice system:

    "By the end of 2007, 3.2% of all adults in the United States (1 in every 31) were under some form of correctional control involving probation, parole, prison, or jail. In footnote 8, the EEOC quotes a study that suggests: noting that when all of the individuals who "are probationers, parolees, prisoners or jail inmates are added up, the total is more than 7.3 million adults; this is more than the populations of Chicago, Philadelphia, San Diego, and Dallas combined, and larger than the populations of 38 states and the District of Columbia)."

The difficulty with the figures cited by the EOC is they include "probationers." For example, every person convicted of driving under the influence (DUI) would be a person that falls into the statistic quoted by the EEOC since the vast majority of all misdemeanor convictions for DUI result in a period of probation. It is elementary that in state courts, where misdemeanors can be typically be punished by up to one year in jail, a Judge will normally impose just a portion of the sentence, place the person on probation, and leave the remainder of the sentence pending the person's successful completion of probation. A misdemeanor sentence will typically include either formal probation (meaning there is an assigned probation officer) or informal (sometimes called Court probation) where there is no probation officer, but the Court's file says active, and the defendant is placed under Court orders appropriate to the case. A misdemeanor defendant for example, may be ordered to obey all laws, attend a program, not to possess or consume drugs or alcohol, or other conditions related to the conviction. If the defendant fails to satisfy these conditions, a Court has the option to impose the jail time not previously imposed.

This means the statistics cited by the EEOC for the proposition that an alarming number of Americans are involved in the criminal justice system are seriously overstated and inflated because it includes practically all misdemeanor conviction.

This illustrates why statistics can be deceiving and underscores the need for the EEOC to develop a better understanding of the criminal justice system. It also demonstrates that the EEOC's use and understanding of criminal statistics would have benefited by a comment period where the statistics could be analyzed.

✓ Another expressed concern is the new standards will create brand new industries: Professional litigants consisting of ex-offenders assisted by plaintiffs who can simply apply to any possible employer just to try to set up a lawsuit and seek damages. Also the Guidance promotes new opportunities for lawyers and experts in statistics, industrial organizations, and related topics to advise employer's on how to deal with this complex web of new rules.

✓ The EEOC Guidance appears to have the impact of nearly conferring upon ex-offenders the status of a protected group, similar to protections given on the basis of race, color, religion, sex, or national origin through Title VII of the Civil rights Act, or other laws that provide protection based upon such facts as age or physical disability. With the very complex procedures outlined by the EEOC for consideration of criminal records, it can be argued that ex-offenders may even have more rights than groups protected by Title VII, even though such status was not approved by Congress.

Commissioner Constance S. Barker's Comments at EEOC Meeting of April 25, 2012

The following text is taken from a transcript of the EEOC Meeting of April 25, 2012 - Enforcement Guidance on the Consideration of Arrest and Conviction Records in Employment Decisions under Title VII of the Civil Rights Act of 1964:

COMMISSIONER BARKER: Madam Chair, fellow Commissioners, and members of the public who have joined us today. I object to and will vote against the proposed new Guidance on criminal background checks for four fundamental reasons. First and foremost, I object to the utter and blatant lack of transparency in the approval process. The proposed revision before us today represents a major shift in the advice we have given the American public for the last 22 years. Yet, we are about to approve this dramatic shift in our interpretation of the rights of job applicants and the obligations of America's businesses under Title VII without ever circulating it to the American public for review and discussion.

There is absolutely no justification for totally excluding the American people from this process or for this blatant failure to be transparent in how we conduct our business. I am devoted to the issue of civil rights and to the work of this Commission, but if we vote to approve this guidance today, how can we expect the American people to have confidence that this Agency operates openly and with full transparency. We are public servants. We work for the American people. What could possibly justify keeping them from knowing what is in this document before we approve it?

This particular proposed new Guidance, which, in reality, is a kind of regulation, has tremendous implications for Americans. It is exactly the type of policy shift that we should share with the American people; ask them to take a look; tell us what they think. Have we forgotten anything? Have we explained things well? Or is it confusing? And most importantly, how will this impact you? But we didn't do that. Instead, the document was rapidly brought to a vote without the American people ever having a chance to see what was in it. That is just plain wrong.

There are people in the Commission room today and throughout America who have considerable expertise in the subject the Guidance addresses, yet, we are about to give final approval to this draft without ever letting any of these experts, or the public-at-large, see a single word that it contains. And we are approving it without even bothering to submit it to OMB for their expert review. That begs the question, why? Why don't we want America to see what's in this document before we make it final? We should have spent months reviewing and discussing this with the public as we have other regulatory and sub-regulatory documents. Yes, the Commission did have a meeting on background checks and did hear from stakeholders on the general subject of the pros and cons of conducting criminal background searches; but seeking general input is a far cry from sharing what is actually in the actual proposed revised Guidance. As soon as our revised Guidance was drafted, the public was shut out.

Here is my second concern. It is my understanding that the Senate Appropriations Committee, Subcommittee on Commerce, Justice, and Science, the Committee that determines our funding year to year, under the direction of Chairman Senator Barbara Mikulski and Ranking Member Senator Kay Bailey Hutchison, in the report attached to the appropriations bill, specifically addressed their concerns about the haste with which this Commission was proposing to approve changes to the current criminal background checks Guidance and specifically instructed the Commission to: A, engage stakeholders in discussion about the intended changes to the Criminal Background Checks Guidance; and B, circulate any proposed changes to the Guidance for public input for at least six months before bringing it before the Commission for a vote.

When the Senate Appropriations Committee, the Committee that controls our funding, attaches to the bill that will determine our funding, specific instructions to hold off taking any action on this revised Guidance until we have circulated a copy to the public for input for at least six months, it seems to me, we should take that seriously. So why is this even on the agenda today? Are we seriously going to ignore this directive from the Senate Committee that decides our funding, especially when, and here's the irony, there is absolutely no need to take any action on this today or anytime in the immediate future. What is the big rush to approve this Guidance? What would justify ignoring a Senate Appropriations directive and ignoring our obligation to be transparent with the American people?

There have been no changes in Title VII, no new Supreme Court decisions that would compel a single change to our current guidance. In contrast, our Guidance on the Use of Arbitration Agreements in Employment Contracts has been out of date and a misstatement of the law since the first Supreme Court decision on that subject in 1991. As far as I know, there's no effort being made to circulate any revision of that guidance or bring it before the Commission for a vote.

Thirdly, I object to the Guidance because it so obviously exceeds our authority as a regulatory commission. We are an enforcement agency. We have the authority to issue, amend, or rescind federal procedural regulations. We have no authority to make substantive changes in the law by issuing guidance that goes beyond what is contained in the statues as interpreted by the courts. Our job is to follow Congressional intent and court interpretations; not make new law.

No matter how well intentioned we may be, no matter how much a change in the law may be warranted, we simply lack the authority to make those changes through the issuance of guidances. It is Congress' job, not ours, to weigh the pros and cons of proposed new legislation and approve or disapprove it. We are not Congress. We are not part of the Legislative Branch. And it is the job of the courts to interpret the laws that Congress passes. We are not the courts. We are not part of the Judicial Branch. Our job is to explain what is already the law, not to expand it.

No matter how much some of us may want Title VII to provide additional protections, we cannot use our authority to issue guidances to create new rights and protections that Title VII does not provide. If we think Title VII should be expanded we should make our concerns known to Congress, not take it upon ourselves to do Congress' job.

Finally, I oppose the Guidance because of the real impact it will have on America's business. Last night, I tried and read the Guidance as a business owner would read it. What I came up with over and over again was that, if I were a business owner, no matter what business I was in, I would never again conduct another criminal background check on a potential employee unless I'm required to under federal law, not just state law, but federal law. I understand all of the well-intentioned reasons for drafting the revised Guidance, but I question whether it will achieve what it attempts to achieve.

I'm afraid the reality is, the only real impact the new Guidance will have will be to scare business owners from ever conducting criminal background checks. Thus, the unintended consequence will be that, even those business owners who we all agree should conduct criminal background checks, simply will not. Why should they? The Guidance tells them that they are taking a tremendous risk if they do. The Guidance tells them that, even if they are not discriminating, if they are treating all races and ethnicities equally; they could be found guilty of unintentional discrimination under a disparate impact theory.

All this new Guidance does is to put business owners between a rock and a hard place. Conduct criminal background checks to protect your employees and the members of the public you serve, and you bear the risk of having to defend your actions as discriminatory. Don't conduct the background checks, and you take the risk that an employee or a member of the public will be harmed. This is no help to America's business owners. In summary, I object to the utter lack of transparency in the development of this Guidance. I object to the inexcusable way the public has been intentionally shut out of this process. I object to the unnecessary haste at which this document has been pushed through. And I object to the burden it places on business owners. I strongly oppose the Guidance and will vote against it. Thank you.

Source: www.eeoc.gov/eeoc/meetings/4-25-12/transcript.cfm

The Good, the May Be Good, and the Impossible

As a result of the EEOC Guidance, employers may find that there is the Good, the May Be Good, and the Impossible.

The Good

✓ First, the Guidance does not prevent employers from performing a mission critical function — obtaining the highest quality of hire possible. A business is often only as good as its workers, and background checks are critical to select honest, safe, and qualified workers. In a Question and Answer page, the EEOC made it clear that the EEOC in no way is impinging upon the ability of an employer to receive background reports. Per the EEOC at www.eeoc.gov/laws/guidance/qa_arrest_conviction.cfm:

> **"2. Does Title VII prohibit employers from obtaining criminal background reports about job applicants or employees?**
>
> No. Title VII does not regulate the acquisition of criminal history information. However, another federal law, the Fair Credit Reporting Act, 15 U.S.C. § 1681 et seq. (FCRA), does establish several procedures for employers to follow when they obtain criminal history information from third-party consumer reporting agencies. In addition, some state laws provide protections to individuals related to criminal history inquiries by employers."

✓ Second, the EEOC Guidance actually gives employers additional guidance regarding the Green factors that are part of the long standing three part test. Before for example, the EEOC merely recommended an employer considers the nature of the job. The EEOC has added sensible enhancements to help employers deal with that requirement, such as the job duties, the essential functions of the job, the circumstances, and the environment of the job.

The May Be Good

Two suggestions were made in the EEOC Guidance that explicitly stated they were not required of employers. But these may be practices that employers would find useful.

✓ First, the EEOC is essentially suggesting employers treat criminal records somewhat similar to other sensitive material. The later in the process an employer waits before asking about a criminal record, the more protections an employer has against allegations of discrimination since the employer can show that they have considered the individual on his or her merits, and that they were not "knocked out" early due to their status as an ex-offender. Of course, when the criminal record is considered, it is critical that there be a business justification to not proceed further with the applicant, based on the enhanced "Green" actors.

✓ Second, the notion of the Individualized Assessment can help employers ensure that any decision about a criminal record has been well documented. Further, it provides a "safety" value against an employer acting too hastily. Although the EEOC recognized that there may be situations where such an assessment is not needed due to the "demonstrably tight nexus" between the job and crime, a better practice may be for the employer to conduct the assessment in all cases, in order to avoid allegations of discrimination based on performing the procedure for some and not others.

The Impossible

There are three aspects to the new Guidance that appear to put employers in a near impossible situation:

✓ The use of "recidivism" studies that are in their infancy.
✓ Limiting the inquiries about past criminal records to matter relevant to the position.
✓ Indicating that employers who follow state hiring requirements may not be protected under federal laws.

1. The use of "recidivism" studies that are in their infancy.

The EEOC cites studies that criminal past becomes irrelevant over time and even suggests employers consider recidivism studies when applying the Green factors revolving around the time of the offense. The problem?

First, it seems the EEOC is taking contradictory positions within the same Guidance. On one hand, when discussing validation studies, the EEOC notes: "Although there may be social science studies that assess whether convictions are linked to future behaviors, traits, or conduct with workplace ramifications, and thereby provide a framework for validating some employment exclusions, such studies are rare at the time of this drafting."

However, when discussing the Green factors the EEOC then goes onto to suggest: "Whether the duration of exclusion will be sufficiently tailored to satisfy the business necessity standard will depend on the particular facts and circumstances of each case. Relevant and available information to make this assessment includes, for example, studies demonstrating how much the risk of recidivism declines over a specified time."

The problem is that studies relating crime to future conduct are just the reverse side of the question as to the risk of recidivism. The bottom line is inquiries still revolve around predicting future dangerousness from current offenses. In other words, an employer must determine if a person's past is the prologue for future conduct. If an employer gets it wrong, they have substantial exposure for negligent hiring if a person who is dangerous, unfit, dishonest, or unqualified is employed and causes harm.

The studies cited by the EEOC concerning recidivism, although useful and a good place to start, are in the very early stages of research and are not developed to the point where such studies can form the basis of a social policy. The science of judging rehabilitation over time is in its infancy. Even the authors of one of the most often cited studies from Carnegie Mellon University concluded much more study was needed and there are substantial issues still to be addressed. The authors' characterization that the study represents a "significant step forward in area where so little is known empirically" is well-taken. Yet the EEOC seems to not only have based the April 25, 2012 Guidance on such a flimsy scientific foundation, but has urged millions of employers to consider them. It raises the question as to how small and medium businesses are supposed to deal with detailed scientific and statistical studies and draw any conclusions. (See a summary later in this Chapter concerning the studies cited by the EEOC and an in-depth analysis of the Carnegie Mellon University study.)

2. Limiting the inquiries about past criminal records to matter relevant to the position.

Another practical issue is the near impossibility in an employment process is to limit criminal inquires to relevant criminal matters as suggested by the EEOC. The EEOC suggested some best practices, such as employers having a policy or limiting inquires or questions about past criminal acts that are relevant to the job in question. The recommendation by the EEOC is: "When asking questions about criminal records, limit inquiries to records for which exclusion would be job related for the position in question and consistent with business necessity."

The purpose is to apparently prevent a lifetime ban on employment because of an old and potentially irrelevant criminal record. Yet the commission has not provided any examples of such material.

There are hundreds and hundreds of different crimes in each state. There are thousands of different types of jobs. It would be exceedingly burdensome to try to analyze every job in terms of what criminal behavior is impacted, especially for multi-state employers. It is possible to create broad categories such as "crimes against persons" or "crimes against property," but those titles are extremely wide and encompass a large range of conduct and behavior stemming from the insignificant to exceedingly relevant.

In addition, the EEOC Guidance does not take into account the realities of state criminal laws when judging the seriousness of a crime based upon the level of conviction. The Guidance suggests for example that, "With respect to the gravity of the crime, offenses identified as misdemeanors may be less severe than those identified as felonies." As noted in Chapter 13, the mere fact a case is a misdemeanor does not mean it was not serious. The only time an employer can assume with some level of confidence that a misdemeanor is a less serious offense is where the crime charged can only be charged as a misdemeanor offense. This means the legislature has made a determination that in all cases, the highest punishment can only be at a misdemeanor. Also important is to understand there is no way for an employer to even make an informed judgment as to the nature and gravity of an offense unless the employer obtains some information from the actual court file. If an employer is prevented from asking a board based criminal question at some point during the hiring process, an employer cannot exercise due diligence or ensure that it has the information to determine which counties should be searched for criminal records. When a court researcher goes to the courthouse, on behalf of either a background firm or employers, there is no mechanism to only identity "serious crimes." Court indexes do not contain the information needed to make those sorts of judgments. In some counties, court clerks do the actual search and there are no mechanisms for a court clerk to make any determinations. The bottom line is that a court case must be reviewed first.

Even assuming an employer was to analyze numerous crimes (not to mention federal crimes) in the context of numerous different jobs to determine which crimes may be relevant to a particular job, the next issue is trying to have job applicants review what could well be a very large listing of possible crimes. There are a number of real world drawbacks with following the EEOC suggestion of only asking about relevant crimes. In fact, it can be argued that the section of the EEOC Guidance suggesting employers attempt to limit their inquiries can actually have the unintended real world consequence of working against ex-offenders trying to get jobs. Consider the following:

✓ Even if only relevant crimes were determined and then listed, the crimes can have a wide range of possible seriousness. This can make it impossible for an employer to only ask about serious crimes that could impact a job decision.

✓ Even if the crimes are filtered by age with the idea that older crimes are less serious, employers need to determine whether to use the date of occurrence, the date of conviction, or the date of release from custody. Due to the workings of the criminal justice system and based in part on the past record of the offender, it is entirely possible that two offenders that commit the same crime on the same date, can have widely different dates of conviction and release.

✓ Given the complexities of the criminal justice system, job applicants historically have a difficult time recalling the exact details of a criminal disposition. An applicant may not recall exactly what he or she was charged with or the details of the eventual outcome. An applicant may not have understood that terms and conditions of his or her sentence, or their lawyer's instructions in terms of the collateral consequences of a conviction. An applicant could be forced to make difficult legal and factual determinations to ensure they are giving honest answers.

✓ If the applicant is asked a question that calls for a subjective answer or a judgment call, such as: "Have you ever been convicted of a serious theft crime," then the applicant is put into a position of having to make a very complicated legal and factual judgment of what is serious and what is not.

✓ If the applicant answers any questions about past criminal conduct inaccurately due to a lack of recollection or understanding of past events, or based upon information they believed was given by their attorney or based upon some subjective response that the employer finds unreasonable, the applicant is placed in a position where it may appear he or she is deceptive and dishonest. For example, any Human Resources professional involved in hiring has likely heard on at least one occasion an applicant with a criminal record explaining incorrect or false statements about their record by saying they thought their attorney was going to take care of it, or the attorney said not to worry because it will go away. Since an employer is never under an obligation to hire someone who lies during the hiring process, the new EEOC Guidance potentially works against the interest of ex-offenders seeking a second chance. If the applicant claims an incorrect statement about past criminal questions was a mistake or misunderstanding, it puts the employer in the difficult position of trying to determine if the ex-offender made a mistake, genuinely misunderstood, or was being intentionally dishonest and deceitful.

AUTHOR TIP The EEOC suggestions may set-up ex-offenders for failure, since an ex-offender must try to deal with very narrow questions, and many people who go through the criminal justice system really don't recall or understand the exact legal details of their offense, what their lawyer told them, or subtle differences between offenses or offense levels. So, by asking ex-offenders to thread a very difficult needle, any errors or inaccuracies can be perceived as an attempt to fabricate and is a basis not to hire. Essentially, the whole concept that an employer needs to somehow limit the criminal inquiry when made somehow based upon on the job, ends up in the real world being harmful and detrimental to ex-offenders.

This is an example of the *law of unintended consequences*.

The EEOC has not provided concrete examples of the types of questions it recommends employers ask when attempting to only ask about relevant criminal matters. Based upon court decisions in the EEOC against Kaplan Higher Education Corporation, where the court ordered the EEOC to produce information about how the EEOC itself uses credit reports in hiring, it would seem that the EEOC will shortly be ordered to turn over its own hiring procedures if the EEOC challenges what private employers are doing. At that point, the EEOC will be able to see firsthand the difficulties involved in implementing its own guidance.

3. Indicating that employers that follow state hiring requirements may not be protected under federal laws.

The EEOC states in the 2012 Guidance:

"States and local jurisdictions also have laws and/or regulations that restrict or prohibit the employment of individuals with records of certain criminal conduct. Unlike federal laws or regulations, however, state and local laws or regulations are preempted by Title VII if they "purport[] to require or permit the doing of any act which would be an unlawful employment practice" under Title VII. Therefore, if an employer's exclusionary policy or practice is not job related and consistent with business necessity, the fact that it was adopted to comply with a state or local law or regulation does not shield the employer from Title VII liability."

Thus employers can be potentially put in a Catch 22 if state or local rules require elimination from a job due to certain criminal matters. And then the EEOC threatens to pursue employers for just following the state law. Some labor attorneys are recommending that employers required to follow state rules continue to do so. Presumably, if elected state legislators and the elected governor have passed a law prohibiting individuals with certain criminal records from holding certain jobs or licenses, they must have been a factual bias for the decision. It has been suggested that the EEOC emphasis on state laws is actually aimed at encouraging states to think through such restrictions, as opposed to placing employers in an impossible situation.

The Bottom Line

Regardless what approach an employer uses, these primary points must be well understood.

- ✓ An employer should **NEVER** utilize a technique that creates automatic exclusions based upon a criminal record. That actually is not a new issue and was the subject of detailed discussions when the first edition of this book was published in 2004. However, the new Guidance makes that even clearer.
- ✓ An employer should clearly not rely on records that are so old they are no longer relevant to the job or business necessity.
- ✓ If an adverse decision is made based upon a criminal record, employers must be able to document what was done and why. It is critical to maintain all documents relating to a decision not to hire a particular applicant due to a criminal record. An employer needs to show this decision was a result of a consistent and considered process that was approached fairly and uniformly. Failure to maintain documentation can imply that such decisions were made automatically in a knee jerk reaction or in an arbitrary or capricious manner.
- ✓ The EEOC Guidance suggests appropriate steps need to be taken to protect confidential information about an applicant's criminal record. This includes both the security of data and documents, as well as limited access on a need to know basis within an organization.
- ✓ Utilize the enhanced "Green" factors to analyze the nature and gravity of the crime, the age of the offense, and the nature of the job.
- ✓ Consider the "Individual Assessment" recommendation in the event the use of the "Green" factors suggests a person should not be hired due to a criminal record.
- ✓ Consider taking the 'criminal' question out of the initial employment applicant or process. An employer may consider a **Criminal Advisement** stating that at an appropriate time a criminal check relevant to the position will be performed before a person is on boarded. The statement advises applicants the employer will conduct an appropriate background check on anyone prior to the start of employment, including a criminal record check, pursuant to all applicable state and federal laws including all discrimination laws, and that no candidate will be automatically eliminated as a result of a criminal check. Even then, an employer must be careful to ensure such a notice does not amount to a roundabout way of shutting the door to any applicant with a record by deterring or chilling their efforts to apply and by suggesting that any criminal record may disqualify them.
- ✓ Have a written policy. However, just having a policy sitting on a shelf gathering dust is meaningless. Make certain all managers are trained on the policy and are following it.
- ✓ Even if an employer decides not to have a labor law firm design a compliance program, an employer should consider review by an attorney or qualified professional such as a Human Resources consultant.

 **AUTHOR TIP** For help evaluating past criminal conduct, see Chapter 13 "The Million Dollar Question – How to Judge the Seriousness of a Criminal Conviction."

EEOC Compliance Alternatives

Assuming the current EOCC guidance continues to be the position of the EEOC, employers need an action plan to comply with the new rules. The following are potential paths employers can consider. Note these steps do NOT constitute legal advice and are offered for educational purposes only.

1. EEOC Compliance Alternative Number One:

The best protection, but most expensive, is to retain a labor law firm and appropriate statistical experts to review and develop the employer's program by analyzing every job, creating a matrix of related criminal criteria that is defensible, developing appropriate criminal questions for each position, and ensuring that its procedures are in conformity with the Guidance. A labor law firm can also write policies and procedure, do training to meet the guidelines, and can document the processes and facts used to create the policies and any matrix. Part of the reason large organizations should consider this approach is because the EEOC has already announced its plan to further its goals of implementing E-race Initiative through its Strategic Plan and large employers may well be a target. Another advantage of utilizing the services of a law firm is the employer receives some protection since any communication with the law firm is covered by attorney-client privilege and work product privilege.

2. EEOC Compliance Alternative Number Two:

For small to medium firms that wish to avoid the time and expenses of having a labor attorney and associated experts prepare an overall program, the following four steps can be taken. In addition, an employer should consider its method for asking applicants questions about past criminal records as explained below.

Step 1: Use a **"Job Class Analysis"** to analyze each job class in terms of potential risk. In order to demonstrate an even handed approach, jobs can be grouped into a classification such as "Laborer," "Administrative," "Management," "Professional," or "Executive." There may be additional subcategories such as "Driver" or "Access to Cash or Assets." An employer can further break down each job category by characteristics of the job. This where an employer considers such things as the job duties, the essential functions of the job, the circumstance under which the job is performed (such as level of supervision), and the environment of the job (such as in a factory or going into a client's home). Taking into account the EEOC factors for judging the nature of the job, an employer can analyze the importance of various job characteristics. This then becomes the basis to analyze the impact on the job of prior criminal behavior. This approach also enables an employer to avoid having a great many different protocols for inquiring about criminal behavior and instead groups jobs by risk factor.

The Job Class Analysis can also include an analysis of other screening tools relevant to the position, such as past employment, education, or special credentials. Of course, if an applicant does not possess the required qualifications, or it turns out that the background check reveals an applicant lied about their credentials, then the employer may well act upon the dishonesty and may never need to even consider any criminal records.

Step 2: Create a **"Risk Assessment Matrix"** to demonstrate how various frequently encountered criminal matters compare to each job or job groups, taking into account the age and level of the crime. For example, the crime of assault may be further divided into level of offense (such as felony or misdemeanor) and age of offense, such as 3-7 years. If based on the **Job Analysis Worksheet** and the **Risk Assessment Matrix**, the applicant would not be eliminated, and then the applicant can proceed. If based upon the job and crime and further research is needed, then the applicant goes to step 3 which is a "Stage Two Assessment" based upon "Green Factor" analysis.

Employers also need to consider other factors, such as if the time period starts from the date of the criminal act, conviction, or release. In addition, how does an employer handle someone with more than one crime where each crime represents separate acts of behavior? When considering attempted crime, a conspiracy to commit or a charge of aiding and abetting, employers would generally treat it as though the applicant committed the crimes being attempted.

The Risk Assessment Matrix can actually do double duty. It can be used before a background check to determine if a self-admitted offense is relevant. And it can be used after the background check to document how the employer proceeded in the event a criminal matter is found.

AUTHOR TIP

At first blush, an employer may be tempted to say that a great deal of work is involved. In reality, it is no more difficult than a number of other HR functions, such as creating an employee handbook, reviewing employee classification, or dealing with open enrollment for benefits. Once it's done, then the employer has an essential tool in place that only needs to be reviewed periodically.

It is also important to understand an employer does not go through this process with every single job. Because jobs can be grouped (such as "Administrative"), an employer can have a Risk Assessment Matrix that covers a number of workers. The key point, however, is that an employer needs to analyze why a particular criminal matter would eliminate someone from employment. The essential thrust of the EEOC Guidance is to eliminate a knee-jerk reaction to a past offense and instead think through what the offense actually means in terms of employment. The process of using the Job Class Analysis and Risk Assessment Matrix to whiteboard out the relationship between jobs and criminal records provides a framework for an employer to develop a plan. This can also be a powerful defense to discrimination allegations to show an employer spent time and effort to make these judgments, and the decisions about criminal records were carefully thought out and considered.

Reasonable minds may differ on the final results, but where an employer can demonstrate the use of such a process in good faith to carefully analyze jobs and crimes, it would presumably be less likely a judge or jury will try to second guess the employer's conclusions as long as they are reasonable.

Step 3: In the event a criminal record is located that potentially has a bearing on employment based upon the first two steps, the employer then goes into a "Green" factor analysis. In this step, a "Green Factors Assessment" is used based upon the "Green" factors to determine if the applicant is permitted to be considered further. If the assessment shows the applicant should not be eliminated, then the person may continue down the hiring process. If the person is eliminated, Step 4 comes into play.

Step 4: At this state, the applicant has been eliminated based upon the first three steps. However, the applicant would have the opportunity to have an individualized assessment in order to demonstrate a reason to overturn the finding of elimination. An employer can utilize an "Individualized Assessment Notification." In this step, the employer "informs the individual that he may be excluded because of past criminal conduct; provides an opportunity to the individual to demonstrate that the exclusion does not properly apply to him; and considers whether the individual's additional information shows that the policy as applied is not job related and consistent with business necessity."

Per the EEOC: "If the individual does not respond to the employer's attempt to gather additional information about his background, the employer may make its employment decision without the information. In others words, the employer does not need to chase down applicants who are being rejected. If the applicant has clearly informed that the procedure is available and declines to take advantage of it, the employer can stop at that point except for the final adverse action letter."

FCRA Key Point

In Chapter 3, we learned under the federal Fair Credit Reporting Act (FCRA), there must be a notice of pre-adverse action sent to an applicant if a Consumer Reporting agency (i.e. a background firm) is used, and the background report forms a basis in whole or in part to ask an "adverse action," which means not hiring, retaining, or promoting a consumer.

So how do the new EEOC rules on "Individualized Assessment" and the pre-adverse action rules work together? The EEOC does not address how the EEOC Guidance and the FCRA interact. It is very likely an employer would send out a pre-adverse action notice at the same time the employer informs the applicant that they can ask for an "Individualized Assessment." See Chapter 3 for information on this topic and sample language which can be used for both the pre-adverse action letter and a notice to the consumer about the "Individualized Assessment."

Dealing with the EEOC Recommendation on Questions about Past Criminal Records

An employer must also make decisions on how to deal with two related additional issues regarding Compliance Alternative Number Two. The EEOC made the following statement in the 2012 guidance that employers need to address:

"As a best practice, and consistent with applicable laws, the Commission recommends that employers not ask about convictions on job applications and that, if and when they make such inquiries, the inquiries be limited to convictions for which exclusion would be job related for the position in question and consistent with business necessity."

This raises two immediate employer issues:

1. First, an employer should decide if their application form should ask about criminal convictions.
2. Second, an employer must decide how to deal with EEOC recommendation that once applicant is asked about criminal records, they can only be asked about criminal matters "relevant" to the job that are consistent with business necessity.

Dealing with the EEOC Recommendation against Asking about Past Criminal Conduct in the Application Form

The EEOC recommendation to all private employers that questions about criminal convictions not be on the application is essentially an extension of the "Ban the Box" discussed earlier in this chapter.

One advantage to employers in removing the criminal question from the application is that it lessens the possibility of a professional litigant with criminal records applying to numerous employers just to be rejected so that a claim can be filed. Recruiters often find that at least 70% of all applications for employment received are clearly not a match for the position just based on the requirements of the job or the knowledge, skills, and abilities need. By adding a criminal question too soon, an employer may find itself defending a claim of discrimination from someone that does not even qualify based on the initial cursory screening of credentials.

Progressive Application Review

By not having the criminal question on the application, the employer must first look at other factors, such as whether the applicant has the knowledge, skills, and abilities listed to even meet job requirements. For example, does the person's past job history show they have the experience needed? What about degrees or credentials needed?

In addition, even among those that appear on a first screening to be in the running, the employer may then continue to whittle down the applicant pool to the best qualified before starting telephone screening or scheduling interviews. That part of the process is based upon facts provided by the applicant. The employer is making decisions based upon a screening for neutral (that is, non-discriminatory) factors. An employer does not need to have the criminal history to engage in an initial screen to determine if the candidate is even in the running. By having a progressive process of first looking at objective factors related directly to job qualifications, the employer does not even get to the issue of criminal records.

If it turns out that a person has the qualifications needed for the job, was invited for an interview, and then a criminal record is discovered that makes the person unsuitable for the job, the employer is in a position to evaluate the criminal record in light of having talked with the candidate. An employer may say that the interview was a waste of time. However, the employer needs to weigh and balance if an occasional wasted interview is a small price to pay for overall compliance. In other words, having a criminal question at the beginning of the hiring process that serves as an early "knock-out" punch to ex-offenders may be more trouble than it is worth. Why use a question that may invite litigation or investigation when an employer can instead use non-controversial methods to whittle down the applicant pool to qualified workers?

As part of banning the box, an employer may consider replacing the questions about past criminal conduct with an advisement that a job related criminal check will be needed before the job is finalized. If that, in fact, is part of the procedure, there is nothing in the EEOC Guidance or case law that requires an employer to hide that fact or to create a false impression of the hiring process.

By the same token, an employer can make such an advisement concerning criminal background checks provided it does not amount to a backdoor effort to keep out anyone with criminal records and does not act to deter or chill ex-offenders from applying in the first place.

By analogy to other sensitive areas, this appears to be a tried and proven path. For example, it is generally recommended that an employer not ask an applicant about citizenship or place of birth in an application or interview. However, an employer can advise an applicant that as a condition of employment, there will be a verification of the legal right to work in the U. S. Similarity an employer cannot ask about any disability until well into the process. However, a valid pre-employment inquiry is a statement that employment may be conditioned upon an employer conducting a physical exam. A third example is the EEOC position on date of birth. As discussed in Chapter 2, there is actually not a prohibition from asking about age. However, since it may tend to deter older applicants, such a request would be scrutinized closely to determine if it was made for a lawful purpose. (See, for example, sample California guidelines on proper questions at www.dfeh.ca.gov/res/docs/Publications/DFEH-161.pdf.)

Here is a sample advisement:

Sample Criminal Record Advisement

Here is a sample of what such a "criminal advisement" may contain. However, this is not legal advice and an employer should review the matter carefully with their legal counsel:

If the company determines an applicant is suitable for the position based on a job related evaluation of skills and experience that may also include an interview, prior to final selection and subsequent employment, an applicant will be subject to a background check that is appropriate to the job functions and business necessity. If related criminal records are revealed in the process, the applicant will not be disqualified automatically.

Dealing with the EEOC Recommendation "Relevant" Criminal Questions only Consistent with Business Necessity

Once an applicant has progressed further into the process to the point where they are being seriously considered by an employer, at some point the employer will likely want to ask the applicant about past criminal matters. There are two good reasons for this:

- ✓ First, rather than making an employer or a background firm play a guessing game, getting information from an applicant is a good source of data. Even if the applicant cannot recall the exact details, they should be able to generally recall such matters as an arrest and court case.
- ✓ Second, it is a valuable tool to get an applicant "on the record" on such an important issue. If the applicant is not honest, then any lack of honesty is certainly a matter for employers to consider.

The key question is how to ask such a question and be consistent with the EEOC directive that any question about past criminal conduct, when asked, meets the test of being "limited to convictions for which exclusion would be job related for the position in question and consistent with business necessity." In other words, asking for an applicant's entire criminal resume is a potential problem area for the EEOC.

There are three alternatives an employer may consider:

1. Using a **Risk Assessment Matrix** as described above, the employer can attempt to design criminal questions for each job taking into account all of the crimes that may be potentially relevant. As discussed above, given the number of possible crimes that exist, such as a course is not only challenging for an employer, but it also may not be in the best interest of ex-offenders either.

2. Instead of trying to ask about only "relevant" criminal records, an employer may instead consider appointing an in-house employee with no hiring responsibility to act as a Criminal Record Assessment Specialist.

    In order to avoid having to try to anticipate each and every criminal matter that could potentially be relevant to a particular position, an employer could continue to ask broad and open ended questions about past criminal conduct if an applicant is either a finalist or in the final pool. However, the information goes to a specially designated in-house employee who has no hiring duties and whose job is to analyze each sitting in accordance with the enhanced "Green" factors. This person must filter out those matters that are not job related so that anyone with hiring duties does not see material deemed irrelevant under the "Green" factors.

    In addition, before even reporting the criminal matter, the in-house reviewer would also go through the individualized assessment process.

    The most critical point is that a trained in-house reviewer is behind an "ethics wall," which means that other than processing the criminal records, the in-house reviewer has no hiring responsibilities. That enables any decision maker to only make decisions based upon recent information that has been processed through the four-step system suggested above.

3. The third approach presents the least difficult for an employer. Assuming an employer is working with a background firm with advanced technology, the "criminal question" can be asked by the background firm at the time the background check is requested, and the applicant only gives the information to the screening firm. That sequence would work as follows:

    a. An applicant applies for a job without being asked any question about his or her criminal record (although an employer may give a criminal record advisement).

    b. The applicant undergoes a selection process and becomes a finalist.

    c. At that point, the employer generates a request for a background check, either through the screening firm directly or through an integrated partner such as an Applicant Tracking System (ATS).

    d.   The background firm sends an email to the applicant with instructions to take the applicant to a secured online site.

    e.   On the online site, the applicant provides the personal information necessary for a background check and provides an electronic signature for the consent and disclosure.

    f.   As part of the process, the background firm requests that the applicant provide any information about past criminal records.

    g.   Critically, the applicant is advised that the information is provided solely to assist the background firm's research and the applicant's own statements are not provided to the employer.

    h.   The background firm conducts its research and passes back any results to the employer.

    i.   The employer then looks to see if any record fits into the Risk Assessment Matrix and proceeds to analyze the information as outlined above.

The advantage to the employer is an applicant is not deterred or chilled from applying. The applicant was able to proceed through the process without revealing any criminal record. The question about a past criminal record was asked at the end of the process, and was only asked by the screening firm, thereby addressing the EEOC's concern of asking an applicant open-ended questions about past criminal matters may force an applicant to reveal information about a crime not relevant to the job position. Since only the screening firm sees the answers to the questions about past criminal conduct, the employer does not need to deal with the near impossible task of asking narrowly tailored questions. The screening firm does advise applicants that their answers are kept confidential, and only public records permitted by state and federal law will be provided to an employer. As noted above, the EEOC clearly stated in its Question and Answer web page on the Guidance that a screening firm may provide a report to an employer. Under this approach, the employer need not be concerned with crafting complicated questions about a criminal record or hiring an in-house person to review records.

Another critical point is that the employer documents each time a criminal record is the basis for elimination of an applicant from further consideration. The employer can use the data to develop a "Job Analysis Worksheet" and a "Risk Assessment Matrix."

The one point of caution an employer will need to show is there is no disparate treatment or impact between those who are eliminated from consideration per the criminal records. A best practice would be for the in-house reviewer to be trained in discriminating laws.

3. EEOC Compliance Alternative Number Three:

The third option is to take the position that the 1987 EEOC Guidance has effectively prevented discrimination, and that the new EEOC Guidance is not law and is only a statement of how the EEOC plans to investigate allegations of discrimination. There is no certainty the courts or juries will require strict adherence to the recommended EEOC practices.

Even if an employer takes the position that it is not necessary to utilize a **"Job Analysis Worksheet"** and a **"Risk Assessment Matrix,"** in order to comply with all of the EEOC recommendations, an employer is still well advised to carefully review the new EEOC Guidance and to implement those portions that can give it extra protection. The most helpful suggestions may be:

1.   Extend the traditional "Green" factors to include the enhanced considerations suggested by the EEOC.

2.   Remove the criminal question from the initial application and replace it with a Criminal Record Check Advisement.

3.   Modify any questions about criminal conduct so it is asked later in the process, such as after the interview process, and also place reasonable modifications on the question so it is not broad and open ended.

4. Utilize the individual assessment approach recommended by the EEOC as the final safety valve to ensure that each applicant has been considered fairly and any decision based upon a criminal record has a business justification.
5. Review current policies to ensure that an employer does not have any blanket prohibitions that may run into conflict with an employer's Title VII obligations.
6. Conduct training for anyone involved in making hiring decisions on the issues raised by the EEOC in the new Guidance and an employer's duties under Title VII.
7. Ensure that all information about criminal records for applicants and employees are held confidential and only used for hiring purposes.

Many employers are likely already following some of the EEOC Guidance on an informal basis. For example, when an employer requests a background check that means the applicant is already a finalist or at least a semi-finalist. That also means that the employer has gone through time and effort to whittle down the applicant pool and has invested resources in the applicant, not to mention the cost of a background check. If an employer is surprised by an unexpected criminal record, the employer has a vested interest in finding out more about the applicant. In effect, a great many employers already conduct an Individualized Assessment informally. The only change is a more formalized and documented process.

AUTHOR TIP

What if an applicant is not a member of a class protected by Title VII? A frequently asked question is: Do the EEOC rules about the use of criminal records apply to applicants who are not members of a protected class?

Although if such a person were to bring a private lawsuit for discrimination, an employer could attempt to defend on the basis of a lack of a legal standing to sue, the short answer is that an employer is well advised to apply these same criminal record rules to all applicants. First, it is risky businesses for an employer to make assumptions about whether a particular applicant is a member of a protected group just based upon factors such as physical appearance or name. More importantly, if a non-covered applicant were to file a complaint with the EEOC or a state enforcement agency there would be no barrier to investigation if the case suggested a pattern and practice of the discriminatory use of criminal records. The bottom line is that treating applicants differently can create a high risk and the best approach may well be to assume the EEOC rules on criminal records apply to everyone.

EEOC and Use of "Arrest Only Records"

A critical point is the difference between an arrest and a conviction. An arrest is the process by which a criminal case is initiated by means of a police officer taking some action to initiate criminal charges. It can be a physical arrest, where the person is taken into custody, or some alternative form of custody such as a citation or order to appear in court. However, if NO CONVICTION occurs as a result of the arrest, then in terms of pre-employment screening, this action or record is considered to be an "arrest only."

If there are limitations for convictions, then it stands to reason there would be even more stringent limitations if using an arrest only record. Why? Because an arrest itself is only a police officer's opinion. An arrest only does not prove underlying conduct, and only underlying conduct may be considered.

There are many reasons an arrest may not turn into a conviction, including:

✓ A prosecuting attorney may determine there is insufficient evidence to file the charges, and a criminal charge is never filed in the courthouse.
✓ In some jurisdictions, arrestees for certain offenses are taken before a magistrate for a probable cause determination or a grand jury. At that point in the system, charges may not be filed or are dropped.

✓ In some instances, even after the charges are filed, a District Attorney may end up dropping the charges for any number of reasons, such as insufficiency of the evidence or inability to obtain witnesses.

✓ In some cases, the criminal charges may be dismissed by a court based upon motions brought by the defendant, alleging such things as illegal search and seizure or some other deficiency.

✓ Finally, a person could be found not guilty as a result of a court trial or jury trial, meaning the underlying facts of the arrest were insufficient for a determination of guilt.

In each of the first four instances, the end result was never a judicial determination on the guilt or innocence to the person arrested. Therefore, the arrest itself is only an opinion of the police officer and not facts of any conduct or behaviors. As the United States Supreme Court has ruled, "[t]he mere fact that a [person] has been arrested has very little, if any, probative value in showing that he has engaged in misconduct." *Schware v. Board of Bar Examiners, 353 US 232, 241 (1957).*

What about a **Pending Case**? A criminal case can also be in the gray area between an arrest and a conviction. This occurs in a case where an arrest has been made, a court case has been filed, and a public record as been created, but the case is still in court pending a resolution. There has been no factual determination of the truth of the charges, nor have they been dismissed. Since a case has been filed, a search of courthouse records may uncover the pending case. In California for example, an employer is specifically not prohibited from asking an applicant about an arrest for which the employee or applicant is out on bail or on his or her own recognizance pending trial (See California Labor code section 432.7). In addition, since showing up for work is normally an essential function of any job, a pending court case may have relevance since an applicant may miss work to go to court and if convicted, may not be able to come to work. There are other criminal dispositions as well, such as a deferred adjudications or diversion programs, that can fall into a gray area. It is up to the rule of each state as to whether such matters can be considered. See Chapter 13 for a discussion of a criminal disposition other than a conviction that can be subject to special state rules.

EEOC Rules on Arrest Records

Under the previous guidance issue on September 7, 1990, the EEOC went into some detail on how an arrest is to be considered. www.eeoc.gov/policy/docs/arrest_records.html. The guidance issued April 25, 2012 by its own terms superseded previous guidance. However, it would appear the 1990 guidance is still in effect due to comments made by the EEOC in its Question and Answer page where it specifically referred to this 1990 guidance. (See: www.eeoc.gov/laws/guidance/qa_arrest_conviction.cfm.) Regardless, both the 1990 and 2012 guidance make it clear that:

✓ An employer must look beyond the arrest and determine what actually happened.

✓ After determining what actually happened, the employer must then determine whether the conduct is relevant to an employment decision.

In the 1990 Guidance on arrests, the EEOC notes the following:

"Conviction records constitute reliable evidence that a person engaged in the conduct alleged since the criminal justice system requires the highest degree of proof ("beyond a reasonable doubt") for a conviction. In contrast, arrests alone are not reliable evidence that a person has actually committed a crime. *Schware v. Board of Bar Examiners*, 353 U.S. 232, 241 (1957) ("[t]he mere fact that a [person] has been arrested has very little, if any, probative value in showing that he has engaged in misconduct"). Thus, the Commission concludes that to justify the use of arrest records, an additional inquiry must be made. Even where the conduct alleged in the arrest record is related to the job at issue, the employer must evaluate whether the arrest record reflects the applicant's conduct. It should, therefore, examine the surrounding circumstances, offer the applicant or employee an opportunity to explain, and, if he or she denies engaging in the conduct, make the follow-up inquiries necessary to evaluate his/her credibility. Since using arrests as a disqualifying criteria can only be justified where it appears that the applicant actually engaged in the conduct for which he\she was arrested and that conduct is job related, the Commission further concludes that an employer will seldom be able to justify making broad general inquiries about an employee's or applicant's arrests."

If an employer locates an arrest, it can be very difficult to determine the underlying conduct. Phone calls to the local police or prosecutor may be required, and they may not be willing to cooperate. According to the 1990 guidance, an employer should not summarily dismiss the applicant's statement about the arrest. In fact, the EEOC notes in the 1990 Guidance state:

> "An arrest record does no more than raise a suspicion that an applicant may have engaged in a particular type of conduct. Thus, the investigator must determine whether the applicant is likely to have committed the conduct alleged. This is the most difficult step because it requires the employer either to accept the employee's denial or to attempt to obtain additional information and evaluate his/her credibility. An employer need not conduct an informal "trial" or an extensive investigation to determine an applicant's or employee's guilt or innocence. However, the employer may not perfunctorily "allow the person an opportunity to explain" and ignore the explanation where the person's claims could easily be verified by a phone call, i.e., to a previous employer or a police department. The employer is required to allow the person a meaningful opportunity to explain the circumstances of the arrest(s) and to make a reasonable effort to determine whether the explanation is credible before eliminating him/her from employment opportunities."

Even if the employer is able to establish the underlying conduct, the employer must then go through an analysis to determine if there is a business justification to deny the employment similar to the analysis used for a conviction. However, the EEOC notes that where the position involves security, or "gives the employee easy access to the possessions of others, close scrutiny of an applicant's character and prior conduct is appropriate where an employer is responsible for the safety and/or well being of other persons."

As a practical matter, employers need to think long and hard before using information from an arrest in the view of clear EEOC rules.

 As discussed in Chapters 3 and 4, there are FCRA and state law considerations when using arrest records.

The Studies Cited by the EEOC Concerning Recidivism

Review of Carnegie Mellon Study on "Redemption" for Purposes of Employment

One study cited by the EEOC in its guidance is a 2009 study released by researchers from Carnegie Mellon University. The study attempted to devise a model to quantify what most people assume intuitively – that the relevance of a criminal record for employment recedes over time when a person is not re-arrested. The study looks to develop a methodology to measure how much time must pass before an applicant with a criminal record is no greater risk than an applicant without a criminal record. (Blumstein, A. and Nakamura, K. "Redemption in the Presence of Widespread Criminal Background Checks," Criminology, Volume 47, Issue 2, pp 327-359 (May 2009)).

The study focused on the problems faced by ex-offenders in obtaining employment due to the perception that once a person has offended in the past, they are more likely to do so in the future. The study sought to explore empirically when a past criminal act was no longer relevant so a person could be considered to be "redeemed" for purposes of seeking employment.

The study was based upon data from the state of New York for individuals first arrested within New York State at ages 16, 18, and 20 for three specific crimes: robbery, burglary, and aggravated assault. The study was seeking to establish two values. First, the study was aimed at determining how many years must pass before the risk of re-offending was no greater than for other individuals of the same age. The second value was how many years must past before the chance of re-offending was no greater than that of the general population that never offended.

The study found that with time, a person with a criminal record was no greater threat than persons without a criminal record. Depending upon the offenses included in the study and the age at which the offenses were committed, the study suggested that after approximately 4½ to 8 years without further arrests, an offender had a minimal risk of re-offending. Of course, the more violent the offense, the longer the time would be required before a person could be considered "redeemed." Serious crimes such as murder, rape, or child molestation were not part of this particular study, but presumably more serious crimes would have a different result.

Although there is a temptation for the press to take "sound bites" from the findings, the authors were clear that much more study was needed, and there are substantial issues still to be addressed. The authors' characterization that the study represents a "significant step forward in area where so little is known empirically" is well-taken.

The study does not have nearly enough data to reach conclusions from which policy recommendations can be effectively made, and has a number of drawbacks that can affect its reliability. Many of these limitations were acknowledged by the authors.

- ✓ First, the study was based only on records from New York State. Records maintained by federal law enforcement were not available, and it is clear from the study that the authors wanted to examine federal records and those of other states as well.
- ✓ Second, the study notes a number of issues that the researchers indicated needed further consideration. For example, the researchers were unable to determine whether offenders re-offended out of state. Without access to that data, it is certain the study was not totally accurate in terms of how many re-offended, which would have skewed the result in favor of ex-offenders.

Another very critical issue raised by the researchers is that further study is needed to differentiate between arrests only and those cases that ended up with a conviction. This is most critical since overall it would appear cases resulting in a conviction would be more serious than an arrest only. Including individuals who were never convicted could significantly skew the time required for a criminal record to lose relevance to a number that is artificially low.

In addition, arrests not resulting in convictions are not generally as relevant to employment decisions, since the FCRA limits the reporting of arrests to seven years and many states prohibit reporting arrests without convictions at all. Even if arrests are considered, the EEOC cautions employers to give the arrest no weight unless the employer can ascertain the underlying facts.

Another critical area the authors indicate needs to be taken into account in further studies is the amount of time an individual spent in custody. If someone committed a serious crime five years ago and just got out of custody, it is doubtful the person could be considered "redeemed" for purposes of all types of employment.

Yet another issue is the fact more studies are needed to research a much wider range of offenses before coming to conclusions that can be used as the basis for policy recommendations.

In reviewing the study, it appears there are two unstated assumptions that need to be folded into the analysis as well. First is the apparent assumption that criminals in 1980 are the same as criminals in 2009. The problem with this assumption is there has arguably been an explosion in streets gangs, drug sales, new potent drugs, and gun violence in the past few decades. Before utilizing a study for policy changes, this question should be explored.

The second assumption is just because a person was not re-arrested that consequently he or she has stayed clean and is closer to a point of redemption. This overlooks the fact there are large numbers of unsolved crimes, and not everyone is arrested for every crime that he or she commits. It is entirely possible these individuals committed new crimes for which they were not caught. Of course, it is also possible that people with no criminal records may have committed crimes where they were never arrested as well, but one cannot assume without additional study that both groups get away with crimes at the same rate.

The bottom-line is these drawbacks suggest it is entirely possible that the actual point of redemption may well turn out to be substantially longer than suggested in this initial study. This underlines, once again, it is extremely premature to draw policy conclusions from this one study.

The study did recite in general terms why employers were concerned about hiring individual with criminal records, but perhaps not to the degree needed. When bad hiring decisions are made, horrendous harm can be done. The "Parade of Horribles" resulting from hiring an unsuitable candidate can range from workplace violence that results in death, grave harm, or other serious matters, to lawsuits that could ruin a business.

Although alluded to in the study, attention should be directed to the fact there are a substantial number of state laws which in fact protect applicants from the unfair use of past criminal records. The study reports correctly that the availability of past convictions has risen dramatically due to computerization as well as the number of background checks demanded. It is equally important to emphasize the tremendous growth in state laws that limit the use of criminal records, as well as laws that prohibit the use of criminal data not resulting in convictions or cases that were judicially set aside under state law.

Ironically, the use of a mathematical approach taking into account the type of crime and age when first committed could result in discrimination. The EEOC clearly discourages automated decision-making regarding the use of criminal records. As stated earlier, the EEOC Guidance suggests employers should not automatically reject an applicant on the basis of a conviction, but should consider whether there is a business justification by taking into account the nature and gravity of the crime, the nature of the job, and the time that has passed. Assigning a numerical value to a person based upon a mathematical formula and treating that person accordingly may not be an improvement over the current system and in fact may be a step backwards.

The study also notes that the time period can be affected by the risk that an employer is willing to tolerate. What that appears to be driving at is the notion that risk is related to the nature of the job, which is one of the EEOC factors. Jobs with higher risk may well require a greater period of time. For example, a petty theft committed three years ago would logically have little to do with a job on a refrigerator manufacturing line. It may however affect if a person should handle a cash register. In other words, the amount of time required for the point of redemption also relates to the risks associated with the job. The problem with this general area of research is that there is a lack of attention paid to studying how to assign the risk associated with all of the various jobs available in the U.S. Further research on risk factors would appear to be a requirement before policy can rationally be changed.

If anything, this study demonstrates that trying to predict a future "lack of dangerousness" is just as difficult as predicting future "dangerousness." This study is critical since this entire area of research is at an embryonic state. Much more study is needed before a broad general rule can be articulated across all situations and all jobs that after a certain time, a past criminal conviction is statistically not relevant.

The bottom line is that is it premature to contemplate policy changes based upon one study where the meaning of the data is not fully understood and where a great deal more work needs to be done. There are some policy recommendations in the study, which are consistent with a number of recommendations commonly discussed concerning this issue. However, this study is not an appropriate vehicle at this point for policy recommendations.

The policy recommendations are also rendered less effective due to an apparent lack of appreciation by the study as to how certain things actually work in "the real world." For example, the study discuses that certain sealed or expunged record that occur earlier in time and are no longer relevant need to be removed. In fact, a large number of states already prohibit the use of such records, and they are removed by background screening firms from reports. The authors discuss issues related to problems with setting aside convictions and the problems related to concealment of records. They do not appear to understand that in reality, public records are rarely physically destroyed. The records are still generally available even if there is a pardon or some other judicial set aside.

The current protections afforded to applicants are laws that either prohibit screening firms from reporting the record or prohibit employer from using them. For the most part, it is the background screening industry that protects applicants by filtering out records that are not reportable. A number of states already have some sort of seven year rule, and there are numerous restrictions as to what employers can consider. These issues underscore the need for an interdisciplinary approach which includes experts in background screening and public records to be included in these discussions.

It should be noted that most background screeners take great effort to educate employers that criminal records cannot be used automatically to prevent employment, and the screening industry's trade association has in fact donated money to programs to assist ex-offenders to re-enter society. No one denies that everyone needs a job to be a taxpaying, law-abiding citizen and that as a society, it is better to build more schools and hospitals than prisons. However, not every applicant is suited to every job, and the role of the screening industry is to advise employers of the facts so they can make intelligent selection decisions.

The study *Redemption in the Presence of Widespread Criminal Background Checks* is available at www.heinz.cmu.edu/research/233full.pdf.

 It costs an average of $47,102 per year to incarcerate an inmate in prison in California. Source: www.lao.ca.gov/laoapp/laomenus/sections/crim_justice/6_cj_inmatecost.aspx?catid=3

Other Recidivism Studies Cited in the EEOC Guidance

The following recidivism studies were cited in the updated EEOC Guidance for the use of arrest and conviction records in employment decisions. As one study notes, "these findings are but a first look at this important question. To further understand patterns of desistance, we encourage further inquiry into this issue." These studies are, at best, a first step towards creating the necessary information for informed discussion about the relative risks of offending presented by individuals with past criminal records.

These studies tend to confirm the comments made in the Carnegie Mellon University study that this is an area where very little is known empirically. As in the Carnegie Mellon University study, there are issues as to the size of the sample, whether the sample is representative, as well as unstated assumptions such as a lack of a subsequent arrest or conviction means the subject was crime free during a relevant period. At the end of the day, the best that one could rationally conclude is that depending upon the nature of the offense, the age and frequency of the offense or offenses, and the time lapse between any new offenses, that over time, in some circumstances and for some people, the relevancy of past criminal conduct in term of employment decisions diminishes. This is likely a proposition that most reasonable employers would normally accept, even in the absence of academic studies.

The real issue however is that in the real-world, employers that create the jobs that are responsible for the economy of the county need to make real decisions about real individuals, in a legal environment where even one mistake will lead to a lawsuit for negligent hiring, not to mention the legal and financial nightmare associated with a bad hiring decision. A theoretical academic construct that over time for some people in some circumstances that past criminal records may be less relevant is not very helpful. The following studies, although extremely interesting and critically important, have hardly matured to a level of scientifically tested empirical evidence upon which social policies can be decided much less serve as the basis for hiring decisions.

✓ *'The Predictive Value of Criminal Background Checks: Do Age and Criminal History Affect Time to Redemption?'* by Shawn D. Bushway, Paul Nieuwbeerta, and Arjan Blokland

- Published in Criminology, Volume 49, Issue 1, pp. 27-60 ©2011 American Society of Criminology.
- The study is available online (limited access) at http://dx.doi.org/10.1111/j.1745-9125.2010.00217.x or on the website of the Netherlands Institute for the Study of Crime and Law Enforcement (NSCR), a

research institute of the Netherlands Organization for Scientific Research, at www.nscr.nl/index.php?option=com_content&view=article&id=239%3Ahoe-lang-behouden-strafbladen-hun-voorspellende-waarde-publicatie&catid=47%3Apublicaties&Itemid=123&lang=en.

- Email coauthor Arjan Blokland at ablokland@nscr.nl to receive a copy.

✓ *'The Risk of Offending: When do Ex-Offenders Become Like Non-Offenders?'* by Keith Soothill & Brian Francis

- Available at www.docstoc.com/docs/36215747/WHEN-DO-EX-OFFENDERS-BECOME-LIKE

✓ *'Enduring Risk? Old Criminal Records and Short-Term Predictions of Criminal Involvement'* by Megan C. Kurlychek, University of South Carolina, Robert Brame, University of South Carolina, and Shawn D. Bushway, University of Maryland

- Available at http://blogs.law.columbia.edu/4cs/files/2008/11/crime-and-delinquency-racine.pdf

✓ *'Scarlet Letters and Recidivism: Does an Old Criminal Record Predict Future Offending?'* by Megan C. Kurlychek, Robert Brame, and Shawn D. Bushway.

- *Available at:* www.jjay.cuny.edu/centersinstitutes/pri/events/032406Desistance/ScarletLetter.pdf

Conclusion About the EEOC Cited Studies

In reviewing various studies cited by the EEOC, what emerges is that evaluation of the time period where an ex-offender is no more likely to re-offend than a non-offender, an employer should really be considering a whole host of factors that would absolutely run contrary to state and federal discrimination rules. For example information that is extremely useful may be matters such as the age of the first offense, the type and nature of past offenses and time on the street between offenses. Other facets affecting social stability may also have an influence, such as marital status or children. Yet, an attempt to inquire into any one of these areas of inquiry would run afoul of state and federal discrimination rules. For example the EEOC has made it clear that asking an open ended and non-job related questions about a person's entire criminal history from the beginning may be discriminatory. That of course, denies the critical information needed according to various studies. Asking about age (to determine age at time of past offenses), marital status, or children would also be problematic in many states. The end result is to deny employers the very information that may be most relevant to accomplish the EEOC's objectives.

Use of Criminal Records and the EEOC Guidance – An Attorney's View

The following article was written by Ms. Pamela Devata and Ms. Kendra Paul from the law firm of Seyfarth Shaw shortly after the EEOC Guidance was made public. Ms. Devata and Ms. Paul are widely respected authorities regarding the FCRA, EEOC and the use of criminal records. The author sincerely wishes to thank them both for permitting the inclusion of their article within this publication.

How Should Employers Use Criminal History in Employment Now That The EEOC Has Issued Enforcement Guidance?

By Pamela Devata, Seyfarth Shaw LLP and Kendra Paul, Seyfarth Shaw LLP

Introduction

Criminal history information can be a crucial tool in the employment decision process. During the past few years, federal agencies and state governments have been limiting, employers' use of criminal history information in the employment process through regulation, litigation, and legislation. The Equal Employment Opportunity

Commission ("EEOC") recently issued new guidance in an effort to limit employers' options with respect to their use of this tool. The EEOC's new *Enforcement Guidance on Consideration of Arrest and Conviction Records in Employment Decisions Under Title VII of the Civil Rights Act of 1964* (the "Guidance") passed today by a 4-1 vote of the EEOC's Commissioners. See http://www.eeoc.gov/eeoc/newsroom/release/4-25-12.cfm.

This new Guidance's roots can be traced back to the Unites States Supreme Court's 1971 opinion in *Griggs v. Duke Power Company* and the more recent EEOC E-RACE (Eradicating Racism and Colorism in Employment) Initiative, which seeks, among other things, to address "21st century manifestations of discrimination" under Title VII of the Civil Rights Act of 1964. According to the EEOC, studies reveal that people of certain races, colors, and national origins are arrested more frequently than others outside of those groups. In 2011 alone, 50,060 charges of discrimination alleging race/color/national origin-based discrimination were filed with the EEOC, which accounted for 50% of the charges filed that year. See http://www.eeoc.gov/eeoc/statistics/enforcement/charges.cfm. The new Guidance also supports its reasoning by citing studies finding that criminal history information is often incomplete and inaccurate.

The EEOC's Unilateral Move

The EEOC did not release a draft of this new Guidance for public notice and comment before finalizing it. Based on this unilateral move, many industry groups have protested against the issuance of new Guidance. It remains to be seen how far such challenges will go.

Some employer guidance was gleaned during a recent March 2012 conference where EEOC Commissioner Victoria Lipnic cautioned employers to avoid blanket policies on their use criminal history information (e.g., policies that prohibit individuals who have committed certain crimes from even being considered for employment). According to Commissioner Lipnic, employers with blanket policies will be targeted by the EEOC for investigation and even litigation. This statement was confirmed in the EEOC Guidance. Although not every EEOC investigation results in a lawsuit, an investigation alone can exhaust an employer's time, energy, and finances. This is especially true given that Commissioner Ishimaru stated in his remarks at the public meeting that the EEOC was currently investigating hundreds of cases where employers illegally used criminal history information in employment decisions. Most notably, on May 9, the United States House of Representatives passed an appropriations bill seeking to limit funding to the EEOC for "enforcement or administration" of the EEOC Guidance. Employers should consider to monitor what, if any, effect this will have on the EEOC's investigation of employers using criminal records

The EEOC's History Of Enforcement

Because the EEOC did not allow for public comment, it is unclear whether or not the EEOC's new Guidance will be upheld by the courts. Unlike Congress, the EEOC does not have the authority to create statutes or issue non-procedural regulations under Title VII. Regardless, however, the EEOC can make it difficult and costly for employers that choose not to follow this new Guidance through its investigations, enforcement actions and subsequent litigation. Either employers will face substantial costs in following the new Guidance or fighting it in court. At the very least, if any of the non-legal challenges are upheld, employers now have the EEOC's "playbook" to investigations involving the use of criminal history. As part of its E-RACE Initiative, the EEOC has already filed several lawsuits against companies it believes use criminal history information in a manner that creates a disparate impact on race, color, or national origin. For example:

- In January 2012, the EEOC entered into a conciliation agreement with a beverage company for $3.13 million based on allegations that the company racially discriminated against African American applicants based on their criminal history information. According to its press release, the EEOC stated that its investigation revealed that the Company had a policy of not hiring applicants with pending criminal charges that had not resulted in convictions; and failed to hire applicants with arrests or minor conviction records.

- In September 2009, the EEOC filed a complaint against Freeman Companies (Case No. 09-CV-2573) in the District of Maryland alleging that the company's use of credit histories and criminal backgrounds as selection criteria has a "significant disparate impact on [African American] applicants and that [the company's] use of criminal history information has an adverse impact on Hispanic and male applicants." This is a nationwide class action lawsuit under Title VII that is still pending.

- In September 2008, the EEOC filed a complaint against Peoplemark, Inc. (Case No. 08-CV-0907) in the Western District of Michigan alleging that the company maintained a blanket no-hire policy that denied hiring or employment to any person with a criminal record and that such policy had a disparate impact on African American applicants. This was a nationwide class action lawsuit under Title VII. After many months of expensive discovery, it became clear that the EEOC did not have a statistical expert to rebut Peoplemark, Inc.'s expert, so the case was voluntarily dismissed in March 2010, and thereafter, sanctions were imposed against the EEOC.

State And Local Laws Addressing Criminal History Information

Many states have their own laws concerning "job relatedness" requirements for an employer's use of criminal history information, including Hawaii, Kansas, Missouri, New York, Pennsylvania, and Wisconsin. Other states do not even permit employers to inquire about criminal history information on the initial written application form, subject to a couple of narrow exceptions. Although most of these states (California, Connecticut, Hawaii, Massachusetts, Minnesota, and New Mexico) apply this prohibition to public employers, both the Hawaii and Massachusetts (and the city of Philadelphia) laws also cover private employers. Some 27 cities and counties in California, Connecticut, Florida, Illinois, Maryland, Massachusetts, Michigan, Minnesota, Ohio, Oregon, Pennsylvania, Rhode Island, Tennessee, Texas, and Washington also have this prohibition. Again, while these local laws apply mostly to public employers, private employers in cities in Connecticut, Massachusetts and Philadelphia are also impacted. Some of these state and local laws, such as Hawaii's law, also prohibit employers from inquiring about an applicant's criminal history information until after a conditional offer of employment is made. Additional states, cities, and counties have similar legislation currently pending.

The New EEOC Guidance

The EEOC's new Guidance consolidates and supersedes the EEOC's 1987 and 1990 policy statements concerning employers' use of criminal history information. The following are the key highlights of the new Guidance.

What An Employer Can Ask

The EEOC recommends as a best practice that employers not ask about criminal history on applications. As such, employers should evaluate if asking such a question later in the process may mitigate their risk. According to the EEOC, inquiries about criminal history, if made, should be limited only to those that are job-related. Many employers currently ask about convictions in a blanket fashion or with minimal exclusions required by state or local laws. Per the new Guidance, employers should review their job applications and pre-employment inquiries. Even when considering convictions to determine job-relatedness, however, it is very difficult for an employer to establish whether a given conviction is job-related, and employers may need to rely on outside experts to make such an analysis. Employers may also want to consider the scope of their criminal history question as it relates to time of conviction or release from incarceration or specific types of crimes.

Arrest Records

The Guidance makes clear that use of arrest records "is not job related and consistent with business necessity," but goes on, however, to state that an employer may make a decision on the underlying conduct if the conduct makes the individual unfit for a position. Such an analysis will require additional investigation and at the very least will require a credibility determination by the employer. As such, employers should consider how, if at all, they want to use arrest records. The new Guidance does not specifically discuss whether pending records are different from arrests, which may cause additional difficulty for employers. The Guidance does state person can be placed on an unpaid administrative leave while an employer investigates the underlying facts.

Factors To Consider When Evaluating Criminal History Information

It is no surprise that the EEOC reinforced its earlier guidance that bright line policies relating to the use of criminal history information will be unlawful. The good news is that the new Guidance does not contain any rule specifically limiting how far back in time an employer may consider recent criminal history information, or only a specified list of offenses—which many thought would be contained in the new Guidance. Rather, the new Guidance gives more insight into the factors that were originally set forth in the EEOC Policy Statement on the Issue of Conviction Records Under Title VII, http://www.eeoc.gov/policy/docs/convict1.html, as well as adding some additional factors to be considered. Based on the new Guidance, employers should consider the following factors when evaluating criminal history information and making an individualized assessment to determine:

- The nature and gravity of the offense or offenses (which the EEOC explains may be evaluating the harm caused, the legal elements of the crime, and the classification, i.e., misdemeanor or felony);

- The time that has passed since the conviction and/or completion of the sentence (which the EEOC explains as looking at particular facts and circumstances and evaluating studies of recidivism); and

- The nature of the job held or sought (which the EEOC explains requires more than examining just the job title, but also specific duties, essential functions, and environment).

Individualized Assessment

One of the biggest areas of change in the new Guidance is that the EEOC recommends that an "individualized assessment" can help employers avoid Title VII liability. Reading between the lines, although the new Guidance states that "Title VII does not necessarily require individualized assessment in all circumstances," employers may be challenged by the EEOC or private litigants if they do not do so. But, according to Commissioner Lipnic's opening statement at the public meeting yesterday, there may be instances "when particular criminal history will be so manifestly relevant to the position in question that an employer can lawfully screen out an applicant without further inquiry. A day care center need not ask an applicant to "explain" a conviction of violence against a child, nor does a pharmacy have to bend over backward to justify why it excludes convicted drug dealers from working in the pharmacy lab."

The EEOC sets forth a number of individual pieces of evidence that an employer should review when making an individualized determination including:

- The facts or circumstances surrounding the offense or conduct;

- The number of offenses for which the individual was convicted;

- Age at the time of conviction, or release from prison;

- Evidence that the individual performed the same type of work, post-conviction with the same or a different employer, with no known incidents of criminal conduct;

- The length and consistency of employment history before and after the offense or conduct;

- Rehabilitation efforts, e.g., education/training;

- Employment or character references and any other information regarding fitness for the particular position; and

- Whether the individual is bonded under a federal, state, or local bonding program.

This is perhaps the most concerning area of the new Guidance. Clearly, this list is extremely burdensome and will cause employers to spend time and resources in evaluating criminal history information. One saving grace is the new Guidance indicates if the applicant does not respond to the employer's attempt to gather data, the employer can make the determination without the additional information. Employers will need to evaluate if there are any criminal offenses that have a "demonstrably tight nexus to the position in question" such that an individualized assessment may be circumvented. These will likely be in rare instances. In all other cases, employers should consider both when and how to provide an applicant the opportunity to respond to criminal history and when to conduct the individualized assessment.

Compliance With Other Laws

The new Guidance acknowledges that compliance with "federal laws and regulations" disqualifying convicted individuals from certain occupations is a defense to charges of discrimination. For example, convictions of theft and fraud that disqualify in the financial services industry. Also recognized as a defense in the new Guidance: denying employment based on failure to obtain a federal security clearance—if the clearance is required for the job. However, the EEOC opines that compliance with state and local laws and regulations will not shield employers from Title VII liability due to Title VII pre-emption of state and local laws. Employers should therefore evaluate whether other laws on which they may be relying as a defense to run specific criminal history or eliminate an applicant/employee are preempted by Title VII.

Next Steps For Employers

Based on the new Guidance, employers should evaluate their pre-employment and hiring practices. Because the EEOC will be enforcing Title VII with this new Guidance in mind, employers are well advised to consider adjusting their use of criminal history information in accordance with it. Whether or not the EEOC prevails in any of its enforcement actions or lawsuits, the employers in these actions will be forced to spend substantial financial resources to defend and resolve them. The new Guidance itself sets forth a few employer "best practices:"

- Employers should eliminate policies or practices that exclude people from employment based on any criminal record.

- Employers should train managers, hiring officials, and decision-makers about Title VII and its prohibition on employment discrimination.

- Employers should develop a narrowly tailored written policy and procedures for screening for criminal history information. The policy should: (i) identify essential job requirements and the actual circumstances under which the jobs are performed; (ii) determine the specific offenses that may demonstrate unfitness for performing such jobs (i.e., identify the criminal offenses based on all available evidence); (iii) determine the duration of exclusions for criminal conduct based on all available evidence (i.e., include an individualized assessment); (iv) record the justification for the policy and procedures; and (v) note and keep a record of consultations and research considered in crafting the policy and procedures.

- Employers should train managers, hiring officials, and decision-makers on how to implement the policy and procedures consistent with Title VII.

- When asking questions about criminal history information, employers should limit inquiries to records for which exclusion would be job related for the position in question and consistent with business necessity.

- Employers should keep information about applicants' and employees' criminal history information confidential and only use it for the purpose for which it was intended.

The Author's Public Comment to the EEOC About the Guidance

Below is a letter of public comment sent by the author of this book, Lester Rosen, to the EEOC. Mr. Rosen is an attorney and is Founder and CEO of Employment Screening Resources (ESR).

Dear Commission:

I am submitting a public comment on the April 25, 2012 meeting where the U.S. Equal Employment Opportunity Commission (EEOC) issued its Enforcement Guidance on the Consideration of Arrest and Conviction Records in Employment Decisions Under Title VII of the Civil Rights Act of 1964 available at http://www.eeoc.gov/laws/guidance/arrest_conviction.cfm.

I believe I have a unique perspective on the issues involved. I am the founder and CEO of a nationwide background check firm, Employment Screening Resources (ESR), an accredited Consumer Reporting Agency. I was the chairperson of the committee that founded the National Association for Professional Background Screeners (NAPBS), and served as its first co-chair. I am also the author of the first comprehensive book on background checks, 'The Safe Hiring Manual.' I have qualified and testified as an expert witness on safe hiring in California, Arkansas, and Florida and I have spoken at numerous national and regional human resources and security conferences. This letter, however, is written strictly in my capacity as a business owner and is not intended to represent the view of any other organization.

Before entering the background screening industry, I retired from a career as a criminal trial attorney. I spent nearly 20 years practicing criminal law, the majority of time as a defense lawyer, and approximately four years as a deputy District Attorney. For a number of years I was recognized by the State Bar of California as a certified specialist in criminal law. In my capacity as a defense attorney, I have represented a large number of people accused of criminal acts, ranging from misdemeanors such as driving under the influence and petty theft all the way to homicide, serious sexual assaults, child molestation and crimes of violence. My jury trials have also included complex federal drug cases, sex crimes, murder and death penalty cases and a wide variety of other cases associated with a criminal practice. I have had the opportunity to work with numerous offenders and their families very closely and often assisted offenders in gaining employment as part of an effort to present the best case at sentencing.

I fully embrace the EEOC objective of ensuring that ex-offenders are not the subject of unfair treatment. In my career, this is not an abstract concept but a goal that involves large numbers of people I have known and worked with personally and closely. America is a country of second chances, and if a person has committed a crime and done the time, he or she needs need a job in order to become a law abiding and a tax-paying citizen. As a society, we cannot afford to build more prisons then schools or hospitals. In fact, I have written a widely distributed article titled 'Criminal Records and Getting Back into the Workforce: Six Critical Steps for Ex-offenders Trying to Get Back into the Workforce' which is available at http://www.esrcheck.com/articles/Criminal-Records-and-Getting-Back-into-the-Workforce.php.

However, I have also seen the devastating results first hand when the wrong person is put in the wrong job. I have been involved in cases, both as an attorney and an expert witness, where children have been molested, woman subjected to serious sexual assaults in their own homes, and people murdered in their own homes, all because appropriate due diligence was not exercised. I am a firm believer that there should be a job for everyone, but not everyone is entitled to every job.

For those reasons, I believe the recently updated EEOC Enforcement Guidance is very troubling. In my view, the Guidance has the unintended consequences of hurting ex-offenders, while at the same time, making it harder for millions for employers to provide jobs during this period of economic recovery. To the extent that the

Commission hinders job creation, everyone is impacted, including members of groups protected under Title VII. Below are the reasons that I would urge the Commission to withdraw or modify the Guidance.

1. The statistics cited in the EEOC Guidance to show the number of Americans involved in the criminal justice system are overstated and inflated.

The EEOC quotes figures showing a dramatic number of individuals in this country are the subject of the criminal justice system:

*By the end of 2007, 3.2% of all adults in the United States (1 in every 31) were under some form of correctional control involving probation, parole, prison, or jail.

*In a footnote 8, the EEOC quotes a study that notes that "when all of the individuals who are probationers, parolees, prisoners or jail inmates are added up, the total is more than 7.3 million adults; this is more than the populations of Chicago, Philadelphia, San Diego, and Dallas combined, and larger than the populations of 38 states and the District of Columbia."

The difficulty with the figures cited by the EEOC is that they include "probationers." That means the statistics cited by the EEOC for the proposition that an alarming number of Americans are involved in the criminal justice system are seriously overstated and inflated because it includes practically all misdemeanor convictions.

For example, every person convicted of driving under the influence (DUI) would be a person that falls into the statistic quoted by the EEOC since the vast majority of all misdemeanor convictions for DUI result in a period of probation. It is elementary that in state courts, where misdemeanors can be typically be punished by up to one year in jail, a Judge will normally impose just a portion of the sentence and place the person on probation, and leave the remainder of the sentence pending the persons successful completion of probation. A misdemeanor sentence will typically include either formal probation (meaning there is an assigned probation officer) or informal (sometimes called Court probation) where there is no probation officer, but the Court's file says active and the defendant is placed under Court orders appropriate to the case. A misdemeanor defendant, for example, may be ordered to obey all laws, attend a program, or not to possess or consume drugs or alcohol, or other conditions related to the conviction. If the defendant fails to satisfy these conditions, a Court has the option to impose the jail time not previously imposed.

This illustrates why statistics can be deceiving and underscores the need for the EEOC to develop a better understanding of the criminal justice system. It also demonstrates that the EEOC's use and understanding of criminal statistics would have benefited by a comment period where the statistics could be analyzed.

2. The EEOC Guidance gives ex-offenders the status of a "protected group" similar to groups based on race, religion, or national origin.

The EEOC Guidance appears to have the impact of conferring upon ex-offenders the status of a protected group, similar to protections given on the basis of race, color, religion, sex or national origin through Title VII of the Civil rights Act, or other laws that provide protection based upon such facts as age or physical disability. With the very complex procedures outlined by the EEOC for consideration of criminal records, it can be argued that ex-offenders may even have more rights than groups protected by Title VII, even though such status was not approved by Congress.

3. The recidivism studies cited in the EEOC Guidance are still in the early stage and should not be the basis of social policy.

The EEOC cites studies that an ex-offender's criminal past becomes irrelevant over time, and even suggests employers consider recidivism studies when applying the "Green factors" (from *Green v. Missouri Pacific Railroad, 549 F.2d 1158 (8th Cir. 1977)*, in which the court found a complete bar on employment based on most criminal activity unlawful under Title VII) revolving around the offense:

* The nature and gravity of the criminal offense(s);

* The time that has passed since the conviction and/or completion of the sentence; and

* The nature of the job held or sought.

In addition to the Green factors, where arrest records show no conviction, the EEOC's 1990 Guidance requires the employer to evaluate whether the arrest record reflects the applicant's conduct. The problem?

First, it seems the EEOC is taking contradictory positions within the same guidance. On one hand, when discussing validation studies, the EEOC notes:

Although there may be social science studies that assess whether convictions are linked to future behaviors, traits, or conduct with workplace ramifications, and thereby provide a framework for validating some employment exclusions, such studies are rare at the time of this drafting.

However, the EEOC then goes on to suggest when discussing the Green factors that:

Whether the duration of exclusion will be sufficiently tailored to satisfy the business necessity standard will depend on the particular facts and circumstances of each case. Relevant and available information to make this assessment includes, for example, studies demonstrating how much the risk of recidivism declines over a specified time.

The problem is that studies relating crime to future conduct are just the reverse side of the question as to the risk of recidivism. The bottom line is that the inquiries still revolve around predicting future dangerousness from current offenses. In other words, an employer must determine if a person's past is the prologue for future conduct. If an employer gets it wrong, they have substantial exposure for negligent hiring if a person is dangerous, unfit, dishonest, or unqualified if employed, and causes harm.

The studies cited by the EEOC concerning recidivism, although useful and a good place to start, are in the very early stages of research and have not developed to the point where such studies can form the basis of a social policy. The science of judging rehabilitation over time is in its infancy. Even the authors of one of the most often cited studies from Carnegie Mellon University concluded that much more study was needed and that there are substantial issues still to be addressed. The authors' characterization that the study represents a "significant step forward in area where so little is known empirically" is well-taken. Yet the EEOC seems to not only have based the April 25, 2012 Guidance on such a flimsy scientific foundation, but has urged millions of employers to consider them. It raises the question as to how small and medium businesses are supposed to deal with detailed scientific and statistical studies and draw any conclusions.

4. The new EEOC Guidance will create brand new industries of "professional litigants" and advisors on complex new rules.

Another concern that had been voiced is the sheer complexity of the new standards will create brand new industries of "professional litigants" consisting of ex-offenders assisted by plaintiffs lawyers who can simply apply to any possible employer just to try to set up a lawsuit and seek damages, as well as vast new opportunities for lawyers and experts in statistics, industrial organizations, and related topics, to advise employer's on how to deal with this complex web of new rules.

5. The EEOC Guidance limiting criminal inquiries only to "relevant criminal matters" to a job is nearly impossible for employers to carry out.

Another practical issue is the near impossibility of an employment process that limits criminal inquires to relevant criminal matters as suggested by the EEOC. The EEOC suggested some best practices such as employers having a policy or limiting inquires or questions about past criminal acts that are relevant to the job in question. Yet the commission has not provided any examples of how to carry that out.

The problem is that there are thousands of crimes in each state. It is exceedingly burdensome to try to analyze every job in terms of what criminal behavior is impacted. It is possible to create broad categories such as "crimes against persons" or "crimes against property," but those titles are extremely wide and encompass a large range of conduct and behavior stemming from the insignificant to exceedingly relevant.

In addition, the EEOC Guidance does not take into account the realities of state criminal laws when it comes to judging the seriousness of a crime based upon the level of conviction. For example, the Guidance suggests that: "With respect to the gravity of the crime, offenses identified as misdemeanors may be less severe than those identified as felonies."

However, as the old saying goes, the devil is in the details. Many crimes can be classified as a "wobbler" or hybrid crime that can be either a felony or a misdemeanor. For example, there can be felony or misdemeanor grand theft, or crimes of violence. For a number of real world reasons, the eventual status of a hybrid crime as a felony or misdemeanor can have little or nothing to do with the seriousness of the crime, but instead relate to a number of unpredictable variables in the criminal justice system. Very serious conduct may end up as a misdemeanor because of court over overcrowding resulting in plea bargains, critical evidence being excluded pursuant to a motion to suppress, a critical witness may be reluctant to testify, unskilled attorneys can impact the outcome, or a jury may reach a compromise verdict. The only time that an employer can assume with some level of confidence that a misdemeanor is a less serious offense is where the crime charged can only be charged as a misdemeanor offense, which means that the legislature has made a determination that in all case, the highest punishment can only be at a misdemeanor level.

6. The EEOC Guidance of employers limiting inquiries can have the unintended consequence of working against ex-offenders trying to get jobs.

Even assuming that an employer were to analyze thousands of state crimes (not to mention federal crimes) to determine which crimes may be relevant to a particular job, the next issue is trying to have job applicants review what could well be very large listing of possible crimes. There are a number of real world drawbacks with following the EEOC suggestion of only asking about relevant crimes. It can be argued that in fact the section of the EEOC Guidance that suggests employers attempt to limit their inquiries can actually have the unintended consequences in the real world of working against ex-offenders trying to get jobs:

*Even if only relevant crimes were determined and then listed, the crimes can have a wide range of possible seriousness, making it impossible for an employer to only ask about serious crimes that could impact a job decision.

*Even if the crimes are filtered by age with the idea that older crimes are less serious, employers need to determine whether to use the date of occurrence, the date of conviction, or the date of release from custody. Due to the workings of the criminal justice system and based in part on the past record of the offender and a number of intangible factors related to the operation of the criminal justice system, it is entirely possible that two offenders that commit the same crime on the same date, can have widely different dates of conviction and release.

*Given the complexities of the criminal justice system, job applicants historically have a difficult time recalling the exact details of a criminal disposition. An applicant may not recall exactly what he or she was charged with or the details of the eventual outcome. An applicant may not have understood that terms and conditions of his or her sentence, or their lawyers instructions in terms of the collateral consequences of a conviction.

*If the applicant is asked a question that calls for a subjective answer or a judgment call, such as, "Have you ever been convicted of a serious theft crime," then the applicant is being put into a position of having to make a very complicated legal and factual judgment of what is serious.

*If the applicant answers any questions about past criminal conduct inaccurately due to a lack of recollection or understanding of past events, or based upon information they believed was given by their attorney or based upon some subjective response that the employer finds unreasonable, the applicant is placed in a position where it may appear her or she is deceptive and dishonest. For example, any Human Resources professional involved in hiring has likely heard on at least one occasion an applicant with a criminal record explaining incorrect or false statements about their criminal record by saying they thought their attorney was going to take care of it, or the attorney said not to worry because it will go away. Since an employer is never under an obligation to hire someone who lies during the hiring process, the new EEOC Guidance potentially works against the interest of ex-offender seeking a second chance. If the applicant claims an incorrect statement about past criminal questions was a mistake or misunderstanding that puts the employer in the difficult position of trying to determine if the ex-offender made a mistake or genuinely misunderstood was being intentionally dishonest and deceitful.

7. The EEOC Guidance of limiting inquiries on criminal records means employers cannot make informed decisions if they do not view actual court case files.

It is also important to understand that there is no way for an employer to even make an informed judgment as to the nature and gravity of an offense unless the employer obtains some information from the actual court file. If an employer is prevented from asking a board based criminal question at some point during the hiring process, an employer cannot exercise due diligence or ensure that it has the information to determine which counties should be searched for criminal records. When a court researcher goes to the courthouse, on behalf of either a background screening firm or employers, there is no mechanism to only identity "serious crimes." Court indexes do not contain the information needed to make those sorts of judgments. In some counties, court clerks do the actual search, and there are no mechanisms for a court clerk to make any determinations. The bottom line is that a court case must be reviewed first.

Essentially, the whole concept that an employer needs to somehow limit the criminal inquiry when made based upon on the job, ends up in the real world being harmful and detrimental to ex-offenders. This is an example of "the law of unintended consequences."

The EEOC has not provided concrete examples of the types of questions it recommends employers ask when attempting to only ask bout relevant criminal matters. Based upon Court decisions in the EEOC case currently pending against Kaplan Higher Education Corporation, where the Court ordered the EEOC to produce information about how the Commission itself uses credit reports in hiring, it would seem that the EEOC will shortly be ordered to turn over its own hiring procedures if they challenge what private employers are doing. At that point, the EEOC will be able to see the difficulties involved first hand in implementing its own guidance.

I hope this information is useful. I am available to the Commission and its staff to provide any assistance on these complex matters.

Sincerely,

Attorney Lester S. Rosen

Founder and CEO, Employment Screening Resources (ESR)

Source: www.esrcheck.com/Les-Rosen-Public-Comment-on-EEOC-Criminal-Guidance.php.

Credit Reports and Social Security Number Traces

Inside This Chapter:

✓ Employers and Credit Reports

✓ Why Employers Use Credit Reports in Employment Decisions

✓ What are the Legal Limits in Obtaining a Credit Report?

✓ The FTC and Use of Credit Reports by Employers

✓ The EEOC, Employment Credit Checks & Discrimination

✓ What Other Credit Reporting Rights do Job Applicants Have?

✓ State Limitations on Credit Report Use by Employers

✓ Conclusion – Employers Need Clear 'Business Justification' for Credit Report Checks

✓ Complying with FTC Identity Theft "Red Flag" Rules

✓ The Social Security Trace

✓ Privacy and the Social Security Number

Employers and Credit Reports

A credit report can be a useful screening tool to evaluate a candidate and to exercise due diligence in the hiring process. However, job applicants may feel the use of a credit report is discriminatory, an invasion of privacy, or a violation of their rights. Of all the potential tools available to the employer to make safe hiring decisions, a credit report comes closest to invading a perceived zone of privacy since it directly reflects where and how we spend money in our personal lives. A credit report can indicate where you shop and the amount you spend.

When a credit reports is ordered for employment purposes, the credit bureaus a customized reported referred to as an **employment credit report**. And contrary to misstatements sometimes found in news stories, an employment credit report does <u>NOT</u> contain a credit score. This is because there is no evidence of a connection between a credit score and employment.

 This chapter is focused on credit reports from the point of view of employers. For a discussion of credit reports from the applicant's viewpoint, see Chapter 30.

The theme of this section? Employers should approach credit reports with caution, making sure they are used only for valid business-related reasons and only using information that is fair, recent, and relevant.

What is on an Employment Credit Report?

The personal credit report used for employment purposes typically contains four types of information:

✓ Identifying data such as name, Social Security number, and past addresses.
✓ Payment and credit data that shows how persons pay their debts such as credit cards and personal loans and indicates if there are car payments, student loans, and mortgage payments. It also shows how much credit a person has been given, how much they currently owe, and whether debts have been paid late, were delinquent, or sent for collection.
✓ Records of others who have requested the credit report. When used for employment, requesting a credit report does NOT affect a person's credit score.
✓ Public records are reported such as court judgments, liens, and bankruptcies. Negative information will stay on a report for seven years and bankruptcies for 10 years (there are limitations to using a bankruptcy in an employment decision).

Job applicants have substantial legal protection concerning the use of credit reports for employment. In fact, an employer cannot obtain a credit report without an applicant's written permission and cannot use it to deny a job until the applicant has had the chance to review the report.

What is NOT on an Employment Credit Report?

As mentioned above, a common misperception is that "credit scores" are used for employment purposes. There is a difference between credit reports used to obtain financing and reports used for employment purposes. The three major credit bureaus use a special reporting format that leaves out actual credit card account numbers, credit risk scoring, and age. Credit reports used for employment purposes will have a credit history showing, for example, if a person misses payments, but an employment credit report does not contain a credit score. Even though there is research suggesting that credit scores can have a discriminatory impact, credit scores are simply NOT used for employment purposes. That is an urban myth.

Other important differences between a credit report used for employment and a credit report used for credit granting purposes are:

✓ An employment credit report does NOT contain a person's age or date of birth, in order to prevent age discrimination.

✓ Although the source and type of credit is listed, such as the store name or loan holder, specific account numbers are not included on a credit report for employment purposes.

✓ The generation of an employment credit report generally does not have any impact on a credit score. Any time an "Inquiry" is made on a credit report; it must be listed so a consumer knows who is viewing their report. However, an employment inquiry is listed separately from an inquiry that may be made for the purpose of applying for a loan or credit cards. When a credit report is related to a credit transaction, there is the possibility that a consumer's credit score is impacted, since an act to obtain more credit may be relevant to the credit score. However, if the inquiry is for employment purposes, generally speaking there is no impact on a credit score.

✓ In order to even have access to an employment credit report, the employer itself must essentially undergo a background check. Credit Bureaus, concerned about the sensitive and confidential nature of credit information, have required background screening firms to undertake an extensive vetting process of any employer requesting a credit report. For example, part of the process includes a physical onsite inspection of the employer's business to ensure the employer requesting the report is a legitimate business and is not on a list of businesses that cannot obtain credit reports from credit bureaus.

How is Credit Information Accumulated?

Credit reports are based upon millions of records being gathered in a variety of methods all over the United States. Records are obtained directly from furnishers of credit such as credit card companies, gas companies, or department stores that issue credit cards. Data is also obtained from court runner services that go to courts daily across the U.S. to obtain public records including judgments, liens, and bankruptcies. Add to the mixture the fact there are a number of competing credit organizations in the U.S. There are the three major national credit bureaus, as well as local or regional organizations that gather credit data and may be associated with one of these national bureaus.

What Should Employers Take Into Account Before Using a Credit Report?

Employers should approach the use of credit reports with caution; having policies and procedures in place to ensure the use of credit information is both relevant and fair. An employer should first determine if there is a sound business reason to obtain a credit report. Many employers limit credit reports to management and executive positions, or to positions that have access to cash, assets, company credit cards, or confidential information. Employers are well advised to run credit reports on bookkeepers or others who handle significant amounts of cash.

Unless the information in a credit report is directly job related, its use can be considered discriminatory. For example, running a credit report for an entry-level person with low levels of responsibility or no access to cash is probably not a good practice. Unnecessary credit reports can discourage applicants from applying, and running mass credit reports on all applicants, regardless of the position, can have the effect of discriminating against certain protected classes. Although an employer may want to run credit reports on perspective cashiers, for example, most employers do a drawer count at night, and if money is missing, an employer will know almost immediately.

In addition, employers should avoid making negative hiring decisions on credit report information that is old, relatively minor, or has no relevance to job performance. For example, poor credit caused by medical bills may have nothing to do with employment. Or, a consumer may have refinanced a home and, for a brief period, both the old mortgage and the new mortgage may show on the credit report giving a false impression of greater indebtedness. For those reasons, an employer needs to ensure that the information is accurate. In order to protect a consumer's rights, and guard against error, an employer must carefully follow the requirements of the federal Fair Credit Reporting Act and any applicable specific state rules.

Are There Mistakes in Credit Reports?

Mistakes are always possible. Although credit bureaus make efforts to be accurate, credit reports are based upon millions of pieces of data assembled by human beings and computers.

According to screening expert Dennis L. DeMey, author of *Don't Hire a Crook:*

"Keep in mind that there may be mistakes. Also, different credit bureaus can have different information. One credit bureau may have extensive information on the subject whereas another may have very little. Lenders do not necessarily utilize and/or communicate with every bureau. Consequently, one bureau may be more up-to-date than another in a specific region. In instances where such a search is critical, it is wise to verify using more than one bureau."

How Frequently are Mistakes Made?

A 2003 study released by the Consumer Federation of America and the National Credit Reporting Association demonstrates why employers need to be careful using credit reports. The study found discrepancies in more than one-third of consumer reports. Any inaccuracies in a credit report could adversely affect employment for those employers who utilize credit reports in making employment decisions. The study also dealt with consumer credit scoring, which does not appear in a credit report used for employment purposes. In response to the study, the credit bureaus countered that the discrepancies were not errors but only a reflection of the fact that the three major bureaus may report items differently. Perhaps, but not always. This report underscores the fact that use of credit reports must be approached with caution. This possibility of error is a big reason why employers need to move cautiously when it comes to the use and analysis of credit reports.

Why Employers Use Credit Reports in Employment Decisions

Employers seek credit reports on job applicants for a variety of reasons. However, currently there is no mathematical model that attempts to "score" a credit report for employment purposes. Such a scoring would face substantial challenges to prove it is a valid and non-discriminatory predictor of job performance. As a result, the use of credit reports tend to be "judgment calls," where the credit report is utilized in conjunction with all other available information.

Some employers take the position that a credit report shows whether an applicant is responsible and reliable by looking at the way that applicant handles his or her personal affairs. The logic is that a person who cannot pay their own bills on time or make responsible personal financial decisions may not be the best fit for a job that requires handling the company's funds or making meaningful decisions.

Employers may request credit reports to alert them about applicants whose monthly debt payments are too high for the salary involved. The concern is if a person is under financial stress due to a monthly debt that is beyond their salary, then that can be a "red flag." One of the common denominators in cases of embezzlement is a perpetrator in debt beyond his or her means or has excessive financial pressure due to personal debt. See Chapter 24 on Dealing With Fraud, Embezzlement, and Integrity.

You Never Know What You Will Find

An interesting story is told by a private investigator who obtained a credit report during an in-depth background investigation. In reviewing the credit report, the investigator looked at the section concerning inquiries. This is the list of entities that previously requested a credit report on the individual. One requestor was the United States Probation Office. A little further research revealed that the U.S. Probation Office requested a credit report because the applicant was in fact on federal probation for a federal crime and had been ordered to pay restitution. This story demonstrates that doing a background investigation sometimes requires more effort than merely buying data. It is important to look at the whole person and to "connect the dots" by looking at a number of factors and performing appropriate follow-ups.

Employers hiring sales positions may require that a salesperson utilize a personal credit card. A credit report may help to indicate a potential candidate's ability to use a credit card wisely. There have been employers who discovered months into the employment relationship the reason a salesperson was not making their quota was the person was not able to fly or travel due to an inability to cover advance travel expenses.

Credit reports also help verify identity. The top part of a credit report, often referred to as the "credit header," contains personal data about the applicant such as past addresses. However, an employer does not order an entire credit report just to obtain the credit header.

A separate search, called a "Social Security Trace," provides an employer with information to help confirm identity. A discussion on this important tool for employers follows later in this chapter.

The Items an Employer Can Look for in a Credit Report

In reviewing a credit report, an employer is typically looking at the following:

- ✓ What are the person's total monthly payments? How does it compare to the projected salary and benefits?
- ✓ How many negative items are listed, such as late payments, collection actions, defaults, or accounts closed?
- ✓ Are there negative public records and are they related to employment? For example a tax lien may indicate someone has not paid attention to their affairs or is under financial stress. If there is a bankruptcy in the credit report, the employer should NOT utilize the bankruptcy without talking to the attorney. It can be a form of discrimination to deny employment based upon an applicant taking advantage of their legal right to start over and get a fresh start through bankruptcy proceedings. Federal law expressly prohibits a private employer from discrimination solely on the basis of a person exercising their rights under the bankruptcy laws (See 11 U.S.C. § 525).
- ✓ Are there any alerts from the credit agencies? Some bureaus issue fraud alerts based upon a variety of criteria if there is suspicion of fraud or abuse.

Survey Shows Credit Background Checks <u>Not</u> Used by Over 50 Percent of Organizations

A July 2012 survey from the Society for Human Resource Management (SHRM), "Background Checking — The Use of Credit Background Checks in Hiring Decisions," found that more than half of the responding organizations – 53 percent – do not conduct credit background checks on any of their job candidates, a noticeable increase from 40 percent in 2010 and from 39 percent in 2004. Key findings include:

- ✓ While 53 percent of organizations did not conduct credit background checks on any job applicants, 34 percent did conduct them for select job candidates and 13 percent conducted them on all candidates.
- ✓ Of the organizations that did conduct credit background checks, 58 percent initiate a credit background check after a contingent job offer while 33 percent initiate them after a job interview. Only 2 percent initiate credit background checks before a job interview.
- ✓ As to why organizations conduct credit background checks, 45 percent conduct credit background checks to reduce/prevent theft and embezzlement while 22 percent said it was to reduce legal liability for negligent hiring.
- ✓ Of the organizations that conduct credit background checks, 80 percent reported that they have hired a job candidate with a credit report containing information that reflected negatively on his or her financial situation while 64 percent allow job candidates to explain the results of the credit checks before the decision to hire or not to hire is made.
- ✓ Of the organizations that conduct credit background checks, 87 percent conduct credit background checks on job candidates applying for positions with financial responsibilities, 42 percent on candidates applying

for senior executive positions, and 34 percent for positions with access to highly confidential employee information.

In addition, the survey also found the three most important factors that influence the final decision to hire a particular candidate over another are previous work experience, a good fit with the job and the organization, and specific expertise needed for the job.

The SHRM survey "Background Checking — The Use of Credit Background Checks in Hiring Decisions" is available at: www.shrm.org/Research/SurveyFindings/Articles/Pages/CreditBackgroundChecks.aspx.

What are the Legal Limits in Obtaining a Credit Report?

First and foremost, the job applicant must provide written authorization before an employer can request a credit report. Under the federal Fair Credit Reporting Act, an applicant has a series of additional rights. If an employer intends not to hire someone based upon information in the credit report, then the applicant must first receive a copy of the report and a statement of rights. The applicant has a right to review the credit report and to dispute any information believed to be inaccurate or incomplete. This right applies even if the employer has additional reasons not to hire the person or if an applicant has excellent credit and even if there are other concerns such as a reported high debt level. For example, an employer may be concerned that an applicant's debt level is higher than what the job pays even though the applicant has a perfect payment record. It may be that the applicant has refinanced their home and the credit report is erroneously showing the old mortgage to still be outstanding. If the employer did not give the applicant their right under the FCRA to review the credit report for errors, then the applicant would have been unfairly eliminated. If a final decision is made, then an applicant is entitled to a second confirming letter. In California and certain other states, job applicants must also be given the opportunity to request a free copy of a report originally obtained by an employer.

Before utilizing negative information found in a credit report, the employer should consider:

- ✓ Is the negative information a valid predictor of job performance?
- ✓ Is the information current and correct?
- ✓ Is there negative information reported outside the applicant's control such as the result of a disputed bill, medical bills, dissolution of marriage, or some other problem?
- ✓ Is there any reason not to consider the negative information? (For example, an employer generally should not consider a bankruptcy.)
- ✓ Is the employer consistent in the use of negative information? i.e.: have other applicants been hired with the same type of negative information and, if so, is there a rational reason why it was overlooked for others? Is there a company hiring policy or some documentation put in the file to demonstrate that the employer is consistent?
- ✓ Has any decision or conclusion been documented?
- ✓ Is the applicant being afforded all of his or her legal rights?

AUTHOR TIP To prevent the misuse of credit reports, the credit bureaus have significantly increased safeguards. Before a background firm may issue a credit report to an employer, the background firm must essentially conduct a background check on the employer. This includes an on-site inspection to ensure the employer is a legitimate business with a proper and permissible purpose for using an employment credit report.

The FTC and Use of Credit Reports by Employers

The Federal Trade Commission (FTC) published an article for employers on the proper use of credit reports. Here is an excerpt every employer should read if they use credit reports for employment decisions:

> **"In Practice...**
>
> You advertise vacancies for cashiers and receive 100 applications. You want just credit reports on each applicant because you plan to eliminate those with poor credit histories. What are your obligations?
>
> ✓ You can get credit reports — one type of consumer report — if you notify each applicant in writing that a credit report may be requested and if you receive the applicant's written consent. Before you reject an applicant based on credit report information, you must make a pre-adverse action disclosure that includes a copy of the credit report and the summary of consumer rights under the FCRA. Once you have rejected an applicant, you must provide an adverse action notice if credit report information affected your decision.
>
> You are considering a number of your long-term employees for a major promotion. You want to check their consumer reports to ensure that only responsible individuals are considered for the position. What are your obligations?
>
> ✓ You cannot get consumer reports unless the employees have been notified that reports may be obtained and each has given their written permission. If the employees gave you written permission in the past, then you need only make sure that the employees receive or have received a 'separate document notice' that "reports may be obtained during the course of their employment." No more notice or permission is required. If your employees have not received notice and given you permission, you must notify the employees and get their written permission before you get their reports.
>
> In each case where information in the report influences your decision to deny promotion, you must provide the employee with a pre-adverse action disclosure. The employee also must receive an adverse action notice once you have selected another individual for the job.
>
> A job applicant gives you the okay to get a consumer report. Although the credit history is poor and that's a negative factor, the applicant's lack of relevant experience carries even more weight in your decision not to hire. What's your responsibility?
>
> ✓ In any case where information in a consumer report is a factor in your decision — even if the report information is not a major consideration — you must follow the procedures mandated by the FCRA. In this case you would be required to provide the applicant a pre-adverse action disclosure before you reject his or her application. When you formally reject the applicant, you would be required to provide an adverse action notice.
>
> The applicants for a sensitive financial position have authorized you to obtain their credit reports. You reject one applicant whose credit report shows a debt load that may be too high for the proposed salary, even though the report shows a good repayment history. You turn down another, whose credit report shows only one credit account, because you want someone who has shown more financial responsibility. Are you obliged to provide any notices to these applicants?
>
> ✓ Both applicants are entitled to a pre-adverse-action disclosure and an adverse action notice. If any information in the credit report influences an adverse decision, then the applicant is entitled to the notices — even when the information isn't negative.
>
> **Non-compliance**
>
> There are legal consequences for employers who fail to get an applicant's permission before requesting a consumer report, or who fail to provide pre-adverse-action disclosures and adverse action notices to

unsuccessful job applicants. The FCRA allows individuals to sue employers for damages in federal court. A person who successfully sues is entitled to recover court costs and reasonable legal fees. The law also allows individuals to seek punitive damages for deliberate violations. In addition, the Federal Trade Commission, other federal agencies, and the states may sue employers for noncompliance and obtain civil penalties."

For the entire article, including a summary of how to comply with the FCRA, see www.bbb.org/us/article/ftc--using-consumer-reports-what-employers-need-to-know-4533.

For the information that the FTC provides for employers, see http://business.ftc.gov/documents/bus08-using-consumer-reports-what-employers-need-know.

The EEOC, Employment Credit Checks & Discrimination

If the use of credit reports for employment decisions results in the unfair exclusions of applicants with poor credit, it may have Equal Employment Opportunity Commission (EEOC) implications. Even though a credit report may appear neutral on its face, if its use results in a "disparate impact" upon members of protected groups, a claim can be made that the use of credit reports is in fact discriminatory.

The EEOC held a public meeting in October of 2010 on the 'Employer Use of Credit History as a Screening Tool' that explored the growing use of credit histories of job applicants as selection criteria during employment background screening to see if the practice was discriminatory. The EEOC – the agency of the United States Government that enforces the federal employment discrimination laws – heard testimony from representatives of various groups to help the Commission ensure that the workplace is made free of all barriers to equal opportunity.

As a result of high unemployment forcing more people into the job market, an increasing number of job applicants are exposed to employment background screening tools such as credit checks that could unfairly exclude them from job opportunities. Critics of using credit histories for employment purposes said the practice can have a disparate and discriminatory impact on protected groups, including people of color, women, and the disabled. They can also be inaccurate and are not valid predictors of job performance.

Another concern expressed was that the use of credit histories creates a "Catch-22" situation for job applicants during the current period of high unemployment and high foreclosures, both of which have negative impacts on credit. Many job seekers are caught in a situation where they cannot pay their bills because they do not have a job but cannot get a job because of bad credit since they cannot pay their bills.

Representatives from the business community told the EEOC that the use of credit histories is permissible by law, limited in scope, predictive in certain situations of reliability, and credit histories were only utilized by a few companies for every job opening. Some of the testimony tried to clear up common misperceptions about employment credit reports, including the falsehood that these types of credit reports include a credit score. They do not. The statements of October 2010 meeting can be found on the EEOC website at www.eeoc.gov/eeoc/meetings/10-20-10/index.cfm.

In 2008, the EEOC has an initiative called E-RACE (Eradicating Racism and Colorism From Employment.) According to the EEOC, the use of credit, although it appears facially neutral, can have a discriminatory impact. See www.eeoc.gov/eeoc/initiatives/e-race/.

SHRM Tells EEOC Credit Checks Legitimate Background Screening Tool

A November 2010 news story on the Society for Human Resource Management (SHRM) website, "Credit Checks Are Legitimate Screening Tool," reported how a representative for SHRM – the world's largest association devoted to human resource management – told the EEOC during the October 2010 public hearing on the use of credit reports for employment purposes that the federal government should not eliminate an employer's use of credit histories to help make decisions about job candidates.

The representative said that "SHRM believes there is a compelling public interest in enabling our nation's employers – whether that employer is in the government or the private sector – to assess the skills, abilities, and work habits of potential hires." In addition, the representative said credit history is one of many factors – including education, experience, and certifications – that employers use "to narrow that applicant pool to those who are most qualified."

The SHRM representative also pointed out Human Resources typically conducts a background check on the job finalist or group of finalists before making a job offer, and that background check might include checking personal references, criminal history, and credit history depending on the employer and the position to be filled. Citing the Fair Credit Reporting Act (FCRA) of 1970 and the Civil Rights Act of 1964, the representative said SHRM believes "employees already have significant federal protection for the misuse of background checks."

The article is available at: www.shrm.org/about/news/Pages/LegitimateScreeningTool.aspx.

Opinions from Other Entities

According to an interview with SHRM magazine in April 2007 with an EEOC official, unnecessary credit reports can end up being a subtle form of discrimination and are best utilized when there is a legitimate business need. See: www.shrm.org/Publications/HRNews/Pages/CMS_020975.aspx.

Statistics by the **Texas Department of Insurance** seemed to suggest that members of protected groups do have lower credit scores. Even though an employment credit report does not provide a credit score, the credit history is included.

The state of **Washington** has addressed these concerns through a new law passed in 2007 that prohibits employers from obtaining a credit report as part of a background check unless the information is: "substantially job related and the employer's reasons for the use of such information are disclosed to the consumer in writing"; or required by law. (See RCW 19.182.020 http://apps.leg.wa.gov/rcw/default.aspx?cite=19.182.020.)

A 2004 study reported by the **Society for Industrial and Organizational Psychology (SIOP)** questioned whether credit checks have any validity in predicting the job performance of employees. According to the report, two Eastern Kentucky University researchers studied credit reports of nearly 200 current and former employees working in the financial service areas of six companies. The results suggested that a person's credit history is not a good predictor of job performance or turnover. The study is found at: www.newswise.com/articles/view/502792/.

 It is possible that the EEOC will come out with a guidance on the use of credit reports by employers. It will be critical for any organization utilizings credit reports to carefully monitor the EEOC's actions on this issue.

What Other Credit Reporting Rights do Job Applicants Have?

If job applicants are concerned about their credit reports, then they should first contact all three major credit bureaus and request a copy. Typically, there is a fee not exceeding $8.00, but in some circumstances reports are free. Under new federal law that took effect in 2004, the FACT Act (discussed in Chapter 3), applicants have a right to a free credit report once a year from each of the "big three" credit bureaus: Equifax, Experian, and TransUnion. See: www.annualcreditreport.com/cra/index.jsp. Credit reports, as well as information on costs and procedures to dispute information, can be obtained from the following sources, also known as the "Big Three" national consumer reporting agencies:

- ✓ Equifax:
    - Website: www.equifax.com
    - Phone: 888-532-0179
- ✓ Experian:
    - Website: www.experian.com
    - Phone: 800-972-0322
- ✓ Trans Union:
    - Website: www.transunion.com
    - Phone: 800-888-4213

If there is an error or explanation the applicant cannot resolve with the creditor, then the applicant should write a detailed letter to the three credit bureaus, which have thirty days to investigate and resolve the dispute. If the report is corrected, the applicant may request the agencies to notify anyone who has received the report for employment in the past two years. If the dispute is not resolved to the applicant's satisfaction, the applicant has a right to place a brief statement on his or her credit report. All of these rights are explained in detail on the Federal Trade Commission website at www.ftc.gov/bcp/menus/consumer/credit.shtm which oversees the credit industry.

If a job applicant has bad credit and wants to clear it up, there are excellent credit-counseling services available. The National Foundation for Consumer Credit is a non-profit organization that has over 1,400 affiliates throughout the United States who provide this service, see www.nfcc.org. Unfortunately, there also are scam artists who make false or misleading claims; the Federal Trade Commission issues warnings about these scams and provides information for consumers on the FTC website.

According to an interview with SHRM magazine in April 2007 with an EEOC official, unnecessary credit reports can end up being a subtle from of discrimination and are best utilized when there is a legitimate business need. See: www.shrm.org/Publications/HRNews/Pages/CMS_020975.aspx.

State Limitations on Credit Report Use by Employers

Currently, eight states – **California, Connecticut, Hawaii, Illinois, Maryland, Oregon, Vermont, and Washington** – have passed laws regulating the use of employment credit reports of job applicants and current employees that have impacted the way employers conduct background checks. Below is an overview of each bill and requirements.

California Assembly Bill 22 (AB 22)

Signed into law by Governor Jerry Brown in October of 2011, **California Assembly Bill 22 (AB 22)** – which took effect January 1, 2012 – amended Section 1785.20.5 of the Civil Code and added Chapter 3.6 (commencing with Section 1024.5) to Part 2 of Division 2 of the Labor Code, relating to employment. AB 22 prohibits most employers and prospective employers in the state – with the exception of certain financial institutions – from obtaining consumer credit reports for employment purposes unless the position of the person for whom the report is sought is one of the following:

- ✓ A managerial position;
- ✓ A position in the state Department of Justice;
- ✓ A sworn peace officer or other law enforcement position;
- ✓ A position for which the information contained in the report is required by law to be disclosed or obtained;
- ✓ A position that involves regular access to specified personal information for any purpose other than the routine solicitation and processing of credit card applications in a retail establishment;
- ✓ A position in which the person is or would be a named signatory on the employer's bank or credit card account, or authorized to transfer money or enter into financial contracts on the employer's behalf;
- ✓ A position that involves access to confidential or proprietary information; or
- ✓ A position that involves regular access to $10,000 or more of cash.

In addition, AB 22 also requires written notice informing the person for whom a consumer credit report is sought for employment purposes to also inform that person of the specific reason for obtaining the report.

However, the new California credit report check law restricting the use of credit report checks by employers for employment purposes is unnecessary and confusing for employers since the law essentially standardizes best practices for background checks that employers across the country should be following already.

One potential problem with the new California law is that the categories created are very ambiguous, and it is unclear who falls into what category. In addition, some of the categories are arguably so large that it makes the law meaningless because so many positions can qualify, such as any employee with access to confidential or proprietary information. The law could have simply stated that the employer must state a good reason to run a check. AB 22 standardizes or establishes what many already consider to be a best practice, which is credit reports ought to be used sparingly and only in those situations where there is a nexus or a correlation to the job.

To read California Assembly Bill 22 (AB 22), visit: http://leginfo.ca.gov/pub/11-12/bill/asm/ab_0001-0050/ab_22_bill_20110920_enrolled.pdf.

Connecticut Senate Bill 361 (S.B. 361)

A law passed in Connecticut – **Senate Bill No. 361 (S.B. 361)** – prohibiting certain employers from using credit reports in making hiring and employment decisions regarding existing employees or job applicants took effect in October 1, 2011. The law applies to all employers in Connecticut with at least one employee.

Exceptions to S.B. 361 are employers that are financial institutions as defined under law, credit reports required to be obtained by employers by law, and credit reports "substantially related to the employee's current or potential job." These "substantially related" reports are allowable if the position:

- ✓ Is a managerial position that involves setting the direction or control of a business, division, unit or an agency of a business;
- ✓ Involves access to personal or financial information of customers, employees or the employer, other than information customarily provided in a retail transaction;
- ✓ Involves a fiduciary responsibility to the employer, as defined under the law;
- ✓ Provides an expense account or corporate debit or credit card;
- ✓ Provides access to certain confidential or proprietary business information, as defined under the law; or
- ✓ Involves access to the employer's nonfinancial assets valued at $2,005 or more, including, but not limited to, museum and library collections and to prescription drugs and other pharmaceuticals.

The full text of Connecticut Senate Bill 361 (CT SB 361) is available at: www.cga.ct.gov/2011/ACT/PA/2011PA-00223-R00SB-00361-PA.htm.

Hawaii House Bill 31 S.D. 1 C.D. 1

The Hawaiian legislature – over the Governor's veto – passed a law that took effect on July 1, 2009 that put limits on the use of employment credit history or credit reports unless it "directly related to a bona fide occupational qualification" or falls under another exception. **Hawaii House Bill 31 S.D. 1 C.D. 1** amended the Hawaiian Fair Employment Practices Act by making it an unlawful discriminatory practice for any employer to refuse to hire or employ, continue employment or to bar or discharge from employment, or otherwise to discriminate against any individual in compensation or in the terms, conditions, or privileges of employment of any individual because of the individual's credit history or credit report, unless the information in the individual's credit history or credit report directly relates to a bona fide occupational qualification.

The law also indicated that in terms of hiring in the first place, the employer can only inquire into the credit history or credit report on a prospective employee only after there has been a conditional job offer, and only if the information is directly related to a bona fide occupational qualification. The law makes exceptions for employers that are expressly permitted to inquire into credit history or a credit report by federal or state law, and financial institutions that are insured by a federal agency or to managerial or supervisory employees. The law sets out a specific definition of what constitutes a "Managerial" or "Supervisory" employee.

The full text of Hawaii House Bill 31 SD1 CD1 is available at: www.capitol.hawaii.gov/session2009/bills/HB31_CD1_.pdf.

Illinois House Bill 4658 – "Employee Credit Privacy Act"

Illinois House Bill 4658, was signed by Governor Pat Quinn and created the **"Employee Credit Privacy Act"** which prohibits employers in the state from discriminating based on the credit history of job seekers or employees. The law took effect January 1, 2011 and prohibits employers from inquiring about or using an employee's or prospective employee's credit history as a basis for employment, recruitment, discharge, or compensation. Employers who violate the new law can be subject to civil liability for damages or injunctive relief.

However, under the new law, employers may access credit checks under limited circumstances, including positions that involve:

- ✓ Bonding or security per state or federal law;
- ✓ Unsupervised access to more than $1,000;
- ✓ Signatory power over businesses assets of more than $100;
- ✓ Management and control of the business; and
- ✓ Access to personal, financial or confidential information, trade secrets, or state or national security information.

To full text of the "Employee Credit Privacy Act" (House Bill 4658) is available at: http://e-lobbyist.com/gaits/text/21025.

Maryland "Job Applicant Fairness Act" (House Bill 87)

Maryland's **"Job Applicant Fairness Act" (House Bill 87),** which took effect October 1, 2011, enacted legislation placing restrictions on credit checks by employers who use the credit report or credit history of job applicants or employees for employment decisions. Along with prohibiting an employer from using the credit report or credit history of an employee or job applicant for employment purposes, the Act specifically prohibits most employers from using credit checks to determine whether to:

- ✓ Deny employment to a job applicant;
- ✓ Discharge an employee;
- ✓ Decide compensation; or
- ✓ Evaluate other terms and conditions of employment.

While the Act applies to Maryland employers of any size, some employers are excluded from the Act's prohibitions, including financial institutions and employers required under federal or state law to inquire into the credit history of job applicants or employees. In addition, the Act also allows exceptions for employers to request or use credit history information if the data is related to "a bona fide purpose that is substantially job–related," an exception that generally applies to:

- ✓ Jobs such as managerial positions involving handling money or confidential duties;
- ✓ Employees with expense accounts or corporate credit cards; and
- ✓ Employees with access to confidential business information.

The Act also requires that employers wishing to request or use credit information of job applicants and employees for a bona fide purpose must disclose the intent to do so in writing to the job applicant or employee.

The full text of the Maryland "Job Applicant Fairness Act" (House Bill 87) is available at: mlis.state.md.us/2011rs/chapters_noln/Ch_29_hb0087T.pdf.

Oregon Senate Bill 1045 (SB 1045)

Oregon prohibited the use of credit history of job applicants for employment decisions by issuing new rules with **Oregon Senate Bill 1045 (SB 1045)** which took effect in February 2010. SB 1045 prohibits the use of credit histories of job applicants in making employment-related decisions including hiring, discharge, promotion, and compensation.

However, SB 1045 provides exceptions for financial institutions, public safety offices, and other employment if credit history is job-related and use is disclosed to applicant or employee. The exceptions to the law include the following circumstances:

- ✓ Employers that are federally insured banks or credit unions;
- ✓ Employers that are required by state or federal law to use individual credit history for employment purposes;
- ✓ The employment of a public safety officer, or
- ✓ Employers that can demonstrate that the information in a credit report is substantially job-related AND the employer's reasons for the use of such information are disclosed to the employee or prospective employee in writing.

To full text of Oregon Senate Bill 1045 is available at: www.leg.state.or.us/10ss1/measpdf/sb1000.dir/sb1045.a.pdf.

Vermont Act No. 154 (S. 95)

Effective July 1, 2012, **Vermont Act No. 154 (S. 95)** prohibits employers in the state, subject to various exceptions, from using or inquiring into credit reports or credit histories of job applicants and employees in the employment context and further prohibits discriminating against individuals based on their credit information.

The Act pertains to "credit history" that includes any credit information obtained from any third party, not only information contained in a credit report. The Act sets forth exemptions based on the type of employers at issue and the position or responsibilities of applicants or employees. Employers are exempt and may obtain and use credit information if they meet one or more of these conditions:

- ✓ The information is required by state or federal law or regulation.
- ✓ The position of employment involves access to confidential financial information.
- ✓ The employer is a financial institution or credit union as defined by state law.
- ✓ The position of employment is that of a law enforcement officer, emergency medical personnel, or a firefighter as defined by state law.
- ✓ The position of employment requires a financial fiduciary responsibility to the employer or a client of the employer, including the authority to issue payments, collect debts, transfer money, or enter into contracts.
- ✓ The employer can demonstrate that the information is a valid and reliable predictor of employee performance in the specific position of employment.
- ✓ The position of employment involves access to an employer's payroll information.

However, even exempted employers that seek to obtain or act upon the credit information of an applicant or employee are prohibited by the Act from using credit report or credit history as the sole factor in making any employment decision. In addition, the Act requires employers to first obtain the written consent of the employee or applicant to the disclosure of the credit information and must also disclose in writing its reasons for accessing the report. If an employer intends to take an adverse employment action based on any contents of the credit report, the employer must notify the applicant or employee in writing of its reasons for doing so and also offer the subject an opportunity to contest the accuracy of the credit report or credit history.

The full text of Vermont Act No. 154 (S. 95) is available at: www.leg.state.vt.us/docs/2012/bills/Passed/S-095.pdf.

Washington Chapter 19.182 (RCW)

New restrictions were placed on the use of credit reports when Washington passed a law in 2007 stating employers could not obtain a credit report as part of a background check unless the information was substantially job related and the employer's reasons for the use of such information were disclosed to the consumer in writing. Under the amended **Revised Code of Washington (RCW),** employers cannot obtain a credit report as part of a background check unless the information is:

- ✓ Substantially job related and the employer's reasons for the use of such information are disclosed to the consumer in writing; or
- ✓ Required by law.

Employers in the state of Washington utilizing employment credit reports needed to change their forms, carefully review any job position where a credit report is requested, and communicate to job applicants the reason a credit report is substantially related to a particular job.

The full text of **"RCW 19.182.020 (Consumer report — Furnishing — Procuring)"** is available at: http://apps.leg.wa.gov/rcw/default.aspx?cite=19.182.020.

Conclusion – Employers Need Clear 'Business Justification' for Credit Report Checks

While credit report checks are one tool available as part of a background check, employers are not encouraged to perform routine credit checks on all candidates since credit checks may contain errors, may not be job related, can feel like an invasion of privacy, or may violate federal and state laws.

A professional background check provider should proceed with extreme caution when using applicant and employee credit histories in the background screening process. Employment credit reports should not be used unless they can articulate a clear "business justification," which normally means that that the job applicants or current employees have or will hold "sensitive" positions in which they may handle money or have access to personal data. In fact, with many states recently passing laws limiting the use of credit checks for employment purposes, employers need to be careful when, to whom, and how they perform credit checks on prospective job applicants.

Complying with FTC Identity Theft "Red Flag" Rules

The following is provided as general information solely for the education of the reader and for no other purpose or use. It is not intended to be exhaustive or all-inclusive and is not to be construed as legal advice. It is strongly recommended that you get the advice of legal counsel prior to initiating any of the programs, polices or procedures referenced below.

FTC Identity Theft Red Flag Rules

These rules in large part affect **employers who receive consumer reports for employment purposes** that contain a notice of address discrepancy from a nationwide consumer reporting agency i.e. one of the three major credit bureaus. Below is an example of the special message that employers may see as a "red flag":

SPECIAL MESSAGES:

ADDRESS ALERT: CURRENT INPUT ADDRESS DOES NOT MATCH FILE ADDRESS(ES)*

The rules will also affect **creditors or financial institutions**. Please note, the FTC has defined "creditor" very broadly to include any entity that has a continuing relationship and offers deferred payments to covered accounts (accounts for family, household, or personal purposes). Thus, utility companies, automobile dealerships, cell phone companies, healthcare institutions, landlords, or anyone else who issues credit with payments over time may fall into this category.

The new rules were written by various federal agencies as a result of provisions in the 2003 Fair and Accurate Credit Transactions Act of 2003 (FACTA), designed to combat identity theft when "Red Flags" were raised in credit reports. Although employers are affected, the rules go well beyond employment and also regulate financial institutions and creditors. Although implementation of the rules for some institutions have been delayed, it would appear that the rules affecting employers are now in effect.

It is important to note that this FTC rule does not apply to addresses returned with an SSN trace, but only applies when a notice of address discrepancy is included in a credit report.

1. Most employers who need to comply will fall under the definition of "User".
    a. **"User"** is defined as: Any end-user or entity that uses a consumer report and that receives a notice from a nationwide CRA (Consumer Reporting Agency) that there is an address discrepancy.
    b. **A Nationwide CRA** is a CRA who also maintains credit information—i.e., a credit bureau (TransUnion, Equifax, Experian).
2. Users for other than credit granting purposes (employment purposes for example) are required to put into place **a written policy** to respond to a notice of address discrepancy.
    a. Each "user" is required to develop written policies and procedures to comply with the FCRA's Identity Theft Provisions when it receives a notice of address discrepancy in a credit report.
    b. The purpose is to "form a reasonable belief that the user knows the identity of the person to whom the consumer report pertains"; and to ensure that the Nationwide CRA is subsequently reporting accurate information.
    c. Users are obligated to have a written policy in place to verify the address and identity of the subject of the credit report when an address mismatch notice is returned. These notices are clearly labeled and appear within the report itself informing the user that there is a "substantial difference" between the address provided to the Nationwide CRA when the consumer credit report was requested and the address that the Nationwide CRA has on file for that consumer.
    d. The regulations provide examples of address confirmation methods users can employ:
        i. The user can verify the address with the consumer;
        ii. The user can review its own records, such as employment applications;
        iii. The user can verify the address through third party sources; or
        iv. It can use other reasonable means to verify the address.
3. Creditors with covered accounts and financial institutions **must develop a written identity theft program** to identify, detect, and mitigate possible red flags in setting up covered accounts and existing covered accounts. Creditors and financial institutions may also be considered "users" under the FTC regulations.
    a. **The term "Creditor" has a broad definition.** Creditor is defined as: *"any person who regularly extends, renews, or continues credit; any person who regularly arranges for the extension, renewal, or continuation of credit; or any assignee of an original creditor who participates in the decision to extend, renew, or continue credit."* It includes lenders such as banks, finance companies, automobile dealers, mortgage brokers, landlords, utility companies, and telecommunications companies.
        i. Does the organization have continuing relationships with people (i.e., customers, renters, students, patients, etc.)?
        ii. Does the organization offer extended/deferred payment plans?
        iii. Does the organization extend credit to employees?
        iv. Does the organization extend loans/credit to students?

4. If the organization answered yes to (i) along with at least one of (ii), (iii) or (iv), it is likely that organization is a creditor with some covered accounts.

5. **"Covered Account"** is defined as: An account (a continuing relationship established by a person) that a creditor offers or maintains primarily for personal, family, or |household purposes, that involves or is designed to permit multiple payments or transactions, such as a credit card account, mortgage loan, real property lease, automobile loan, margin account, cell phone account, utility account, checking account, or savings account.

   a. Creditors must develop and implement a written program with policies and procedures to "detect, prevent, and mitigate identity theft in connection with the opening of a covered account or any existing covered account."

6. Such a program must include reasonable policies to:

   i. Identify relevant Red Flags for the covered accounts that the financial institution or creditor offers and incorporate those Red Flags into its Program;

   ii. Detect Red Flags that have been incorporated into the Program;

   iii. Respond appropriately to any Red Flags that are detected to prevent and mitigate identity theft; and

   iv. Ensure that the Program is updated periodically.

   The obligations and requirements of Financial Institutions and Creditors are not insignificant. If you fall into this category, you should be sure to engage appropriate counsel to help you create a compliant program.

AUTHOR TIP

It is also important to keep in mind that for employment purposes, these regulations only apply to information from a national credit bureau, which will mean, as a practical matter it is limited to only those applicants where an employer requests a credit report. Other types of background reports, such as criminal records, driving records, past employment, or educational verifications are not impacted.

The important point for employers is that the address discrepancy notices are not likely to be a significant burden on employers or Human Resources professionals. Employers would expect to receive such notices primarily in two situations:

First, if an applicant has moved to a new address that has not been picked up by credit bureaus, such a notice may be generated.

Second, an employer may get a notice where there is a case of identity theft with an applicant impersonating someone else. In that event, employers will benefit from the new rules.

Simple as 1-2-3

Employers may have questions as to what to do with the "RED FLAG ADDRESS MISMATCH" alerts. The resolution is as **Easy as 1, 2, 3**.

1. First, have a written policy in place at your office on how you will deal with this issue. Specifically the issue is that the address the applicant listed differs from the address that the Credit Bureau has on record. ESR has written up a sample policy that you can adopt.

2. Second, contact the applicant and ask him/her to send you or show you some documents that indicate the new address. Any "official" document will do – driver's license, apartment lease, utility bill, etc. (The attached sample policy includes the full list of the items that will adequately prove the new address.) Once you review the evidence of the new address and you're satisfied with it, that's all you need to do.

3. Third, if the applicant is concerned that the Credit Bureau doesn't have the new address, you can give him/her a document that ESR will provide that explains how to make the change with them.

TO RECAP – You'll want to create a written policy for your company as soon as you can. You'll want to watch your Background Reports to note whether the Credit Report is Red Flagged. And you'll want to take the easy address verification steps with your applicant if there is a different address on the Credit Report and the Background Report. As simple as 1, 2, 3.

Sample Employer Policy on Use of Credit Reports

Below is a sample policy. The policy generally incorporates the type of practices that many employers already use to ensure that applicants are really who they say they are. In the event of a "Red Flag Address Alert," the sample policy explains what to do. The policy needs to be in place but does not need to be given to the applicant.

ABC Company Policy Regarding Order Credit Reports

In order to help curb identity theft and to comply with 15 U.S.C. §1681c(h) this Company will give special attention to the addresses that applicants provide to us. When ordering a credit report, we will take steps to accurately transmit the current address that the applicant provides to us. If the credit bureau advises us that the address we have provided for an individual substantially differs from the address that the credit bureau has on its records for that individual, "SPECIAL MESSAGES ***ADDRESS ALERT", this company will conduct an investigation to either confirm the address we provided to the credit bureau or obtain verifiable information that this is the applicant's new address. Upon receiving such a "SPECIAL MESSAGES ***ADDRESS ALERT" notification, the following steps will be taken:

The ABC Company will first review all documentation received from the individual and any Consumer Reporting Agency regarding the individual's current street address to determine whether an error was made when the address was transmitted to the credit bureau by us. If this review establishes such an error and our documentation support an address in the report from the credit bureau, then the investigation will be concluded.

However, if the review does not resolve the discrepancy, then the individual will be contacted to present proof of his/her address and determine why discrepancies may exist in the address provided by the individual and the address(es) furnished by the credit bureau. Such a review may include contacting the Consumer Reporting Agency to conduct a search to locate and verify the individual's current address;

Alternatively, we may obtain and review one or more of the following:

a. A current photo ID/drivers license with the individual's current address;

b. Current utility bill;

c. Current voter registration card;

d. Current mortgage payment book;

e. Current residential lease;

f. If applicant has a landline telephone at his/her current address that can be used for a reverse look up at sites such as: www.anywho.com, www.reversephonedirectory.com, or www.whitepages.com/reverse_address; and

g. Verify that the address is a legitimate address.

The Social Security Trace

A standard verification tool used by nearly every pre-employment screening firm is the "Social Security Trace." In cases where an employer does not have a sound business reason to obtain a credit report, obtaining the Social Security Trace can provide information about a person's past addresses and will help to uncover any identity fraud issues. The Social Security Trace is also used as a critical research tool by screening firms to assist in locating jurisdictions to search that may be relevant to the candidate. However, as noted below, there is a growing trend among screening firms to not provide the details of the Social Security Trace since it is primarily a "locator" tool containing information that cannot be easily verified in the screening process.

The Social Security Trace is a "Credit Header"

The Social Security Trace report contains the same information as a credit report about names and addresses associated with a Social Security number, but the Social Security Trace does not include any of the financial information. The information is taken from the top portion of a credit report; ergo this report is referred to as a "credit header."

This top portion of a credit report is compiled from identifying information obtained by credit bureaus when individuals apply for credit cards, provide a change of address to a credit card company, or engage in any transaction that is credit-related. For example, anytime a person applies for a credit card, the data (including the person's SSN as well as a name and address) goes into large computer databanks kept by the major credit bureaus. If two years later a person moves and submits a change of address card, then that new data also goes into the computer memory.

The Social Security Trace Helps Verifies Social Security Numbers

A Social Security Trace report will assist an employer in determining if their applicant is in fact associated with the Social Security number submitted. Depending on the date issued, it can also reveal other data such as state and approximate date of issue. Remember though: not all employers want date of issue or date of birth due to discrimination problems associated with knowing an applicant's age (as discussed in Chapter 5).

About the Social Security Number and How Numbers are Issued

A Social Security number (SSN) is a nine-digit number issued by the U.S. Social Security Administration (SSA), the federal agency with responsibility to administer various Social Security programs. Until June 24, 2011, this is how the make-up of a SSN worked. The first three digits of the SSN indicate in which state the number was issued. The middle two digits, known as "group numbers," indicate the range of years when this group of SSNs was issued. Thus by using the methodology behind these two sets of numbers, an employer used to be able determine the state of issue and the approximate year of issue. For example, using the master table one would know the Social Security Number 212-51-xxxx was issued in Maryland in 1997. The 212 is associated with Maryland. The 52 group was issued in 1997. The last four digits belong uniquely to the individual.

Changes to the Issuance of the Social Security Number

As mentioned, until June 24, 2011, one could verify the state and date range when the number was issued as described above. Since that date, all unassigned numbers have been placed a pool and are now assigned randomly. Below is an article, written by Michael Sankey of BRB Publications, which provides an overview of these changes.

> ### SSN Issuance and Randomization
>
> June 24th, 2011 was the last day the Social Security Administration (SSA) assigned a Social Security Number (SSN) based on the numeric order within a state's allocation of the first 5 digits. All unassigned numbers within the numeric sequence have now been placed in a random pool. Effective June 27, the assignment of a new SSN is much like a lottery; a random number is drawn from the unassigned pool of 420 million numbers available for assignment.

For example, the Series of 048-15-xxxx was assigned to CT and was used to issue new SSNs. Effective June 27, all of the possible unassigned numbers within that Series have been assigned to the random pool. Therefore someone in any state or an immigrant coming into the country could be assigned an SSN in the 048-15 series this year or any year in the future. There are 755 Series groups that were in the process of being assigned as of June 2011. There are over 75,000 groups have had all possible numbers within the group previously assigned.

Previously unassigned areas numbers (the first three digits of the SSN) that are still excluded from assignment in the pool include 000, 666, and 900-999.

For years employers, investigators and background screening firms have used software with the assigned SSN groups and corresponding state/date range to validate the state and year of issuance an SSN. The fact that the SSA will no longer provide the ability to validate newly issued numbers has upset quite a few businesses and employers. However, these validations will still be useful, although they will diminish in value over time. Most people entering the workforce were assigned an SSN well before June 27, 2011. The primary people entering the workforce with a new randomly assigned SSN will be immigrants.

The Social Security Administration will continue to provide opportunities for direct name based SSN verification. Internet based verification services include:

The Social Security Number Verification Service (SSNVS) (www.ssa.gov/employer/ssnv.htm) which is free to use for wage reporting purposes.

E-Verify (www.ssa.gov/employer/ssnv.htm)

Consent-Based SSN Verification Service (SBSV) (www.ssa.gov/employer/ssnv.htm)

There are stipulations. For example, the cost for SBSV is $5,000 to sign-up and $5.00 per verification. For questions about the randomization process, email ssn.randomization@ssa.gov or visit www.ssa.gov/employer/randomization.html.

The Social Security Trace Shows Past Addresses

Past addresses are critical because it helps employers determine where to search for criminal records. Since there is no true national criminal database available for private employers, and there are over 10,000 courthouses in America, a social trace can help employers narrow down which courts to search.

In addition, there may be occasions when there are names or addresses incorrectly associated with a SSN. This can occur for a variety of reasons. For example, if a data entry clerk for a credit card company accidentally switched two numbers in a Social Security Number while entering a change of address form, the credit bureau records may link the wrong name and addresses to a Social Security number. Sometimes, members of the same family may have their credit history intertwined. For example, if a father and son have similar names, the databases can end up "merging" their data, causing confusion. Also, with the increase in identity theft, confusing numbers can also cause confusing results.

What a Social Security Trace is Not

Many employers mistakenly believe these searches are an "official review" of government records. The Social Security Trace information is NOT being accessed directly from government records and is therefore not an official verification of a Social Security number. A Trace report may contain supplemental information from the Social Security Administration's list of deceased individuals, but usually the report is created from data found in the databases created by private firms and in credit headers. When a screening firm reports a trace result and indicates the Social Security number it appears to be a valid and also indicates a state and date it was issued, that does NOT mean the screening firm actually checked with the Social Security Administration (SSA) and found information about the particular applicant. Rather, the screening firm is advising an employer that based upon information the SSA provides to the public on how to interpret the numbering sequence prior to June 2011, the number appears valid. However, as time passes the information of year and state of issue will only be applicable to numbers assigned prior to 2011, the value of this service will diminish.

In addition, it is critical to understand that a Social Security Trace report is NOT an official registry of current or past addressees. Nor is it an identity or address valuation tool. Current and past addresses will not appear on a trace report if the applicant never used those addresses in any dealings of interest to the major credit bureaus. On occasion, there may be no names or addresses associated with an SSN. This can occur when a person has never applied for credit, is too young to be in the credit bureau records, or is new to this country and have recently obtained a Social Security Number.

An employer should never make a direct hiring decision based upon the absence of an address in a Social Security Trace. Although Trace reports can be helpful for identity purposes and for determining where to search for criminal records, they are not positive proof of identify or the validity of a Social Security number. However, the information in a trace report can be the basis for further research of an applicant.

Do Only Dangerous and Nefarious People have AKAs?

The author of this book went into a major department store to purchase some items and was told the store had a promotion whereby the author could get a 10% discount on purchases if he signed up that very day. It only required a SSN and driver's license to get an instant credit card and the discount. Seeing no downside, he went ahead and did it.

It turned out that the young employee behind the cash register was not very experienced and managed to misspell the author's first name as "Lesler" instead of Lester. Signing up for a credit card is a "credit event" since the Social Security number is involved. The usual procedure is for the SSN used in the credit application, along with the name and address associated with the number, to be forwarded by the store to one or more national credit bureaus. Because of the clerical error, the author's name in some reports could read that he has an Also Known As (AKA), in that he sometimes goes by the alternate name of "Lesler." Of course, not only dangerous and nefarious people trying to hide something have "AKAs."

This story shows the margin for error when millions of SSN's are being recorded every day into credit bureau databases and public record databases.

Because of the possibility of human error, a Social Security Trace is used as a helpful tool in a background report but is not considered an "official report." If an applicant is concerned about any such discrepancy, then they can contact all three major credit bureaus to review their files.

Using Social Security Trace To Cross Check Applicants

A Social Security Trace report or verification showing numerous different names can indicate the applicant is using a fraudulent SSN. Clarify this by asking the applicant to contact the Social Security Administration to demonstrate it is genuinely his or her number. In the alternative, if a person's address history starts, for example, just five years ago, and the person is of an age where they would reasonably have a longer address history, an employer can also be concerned. For example, if a consumer was just released from prison, there can be a hole in past address information. Of course, given that the social trace information is gathered and assembled by private firms and is not an official government record, such inferences should be taken with a grain of salt, since it could lead to inaccurate conclusions.

Examples of Social Security Number Trace "Macros"

Below are examples of "macros" screening firms may use to explain results of a Social Security Trace to employers:

✓ **Possible Invalid SSN Reported**

The SSN appears to be an invalid number based on criteria the SSA provides to the public on how to interpret the number sequence for numbers issued prior to June 25, 2011. Numbers beginning with 000, 666, and 900-999 will never be assigned.

✓ **ALL DIFFERENT Names Reported – SSN is Valid**

The SSN appears to be a valid issued number based on criteria the SSA provides to the public on how interpret the number sequence but for "ALL" Social Security Trace result(s) returned - different name(s) than the applicant provided name are being reported. The applicant provided name is NOT returned in any of the results.

✓ **No Names Reported – SSN is Valid**

The SSN appears to be a valid issued number based on criteria the SSA provides to the public on how interpret the number sequence but there appear to be no names and/or addresses associated with this number. This situation of no names and/or addresses associated with this number can occur when a person is very young and has not yet used their SSN for commercial purposes or is new to the country and has just recently been assigned their SSN.

✓ **SSN Trace is Un-Performable.** No matching records found in the underlying database that is assembled and maintained by non-governmental sources. This not a definitive indicator of the validity of SSN in question.

In each instance, it can also be helpful pass along this information to the employer:

"For additional information on this topic please visit the Social Security Administration website at www.socialsecurity.gov. As an employer if you are concerned about a SSN not being valid for a particular applicant you can access the Social Security Number Verification Service (SSNVS) at www.socialsecurity.gov/employer/ssnv.htm or call 800-772-1213. Your Employer Identification Number (EIN) is required."

Obtaining a Social Security Trace through a Background Screening Firm

With the applicant's signed release, the Social Security Trace can be obtained directly from major credit bureaus or through pre-employment screening firms. Background screening firms have introduced new searches that enhance the Social Security Trace search with name and address information gathered from a number of additional sources; the information is gathered by private organizations and comes from multiple sources, including billions of public and private records.

Should a Background Screening Firm Even Report the Details of a Social Security Trace to an Employer?

Actually a growing trend among screening firms is not report to employers the details of the social trace. There are a number of reasons. Since the social trace information is not an official government record and is based on data gathered by private firms from a large number of sources, it is difficult to defend the accuracy of any information in the trace report. Under the FCRA, a screening firm must use "reasonable procedures for maximum possible accuracy." Since the data comes from so many different sources and is assembled by private firms, it is difficult to make the case the information is accurate.

The best use of the trace report is as a "location" tool to assist a screening firm in determining other places to search for possible criminal records. Given that there are over 3,000 courthouses in America and employers cannot search all of them, the social trace provides valuable information as to where to search. However, employers cannot and should not make any hiring decisions based upon past addresses reported, or whether the trace report validates the Social Security number or not.

In addition, if a screening firm reports that a social security number is valid, an employer must also keep in mind that only means the SSN appears to be a valid issued number based on criteria the SSA provides to the public on how interpret the number sequence. The Social Security Trace information is NOT being accessed directly from government records, and is therefore not an official verification of a Social Security number. The Social Security Trace information is drawn from multiple proprietary databases – well over 400.

If there is a no name match result it does not mean the applicant has lied. A no match can also mean a person is very young and has not yet used their SSN for commercial purposes, or is new to the country and was recently assigned a SSN, or a clerical error has occurred.

Identity Verification from the Social Security Administration

Legal authority for SSN verification is found in the Freedom of Information Act (FOIA), the Privacy Act at 5 U.S.C. § 552a (b), section 1106 of the Social Security Act, codified at 42 U.S.C. § 1306, and SSA regulation at 20 C.F.R. § 401.100.

There are three methods to verify the social security number of an applicant or new employee through official records of the Social Security Administration (SSA):

✓ Pre-Hire: Consent Based Social Security Number Verification Service (CBSV).

✓ Post-Hire: Social Security Number Verification Services (SSNVS).

✓ Post-Hire: E-Verify check through the U.S. Citizenship and Immigration Services (USCIS), the government agency that oversees lawful immigration to the United States which accesses both the SSN data and the Department of Homeland Security (DHS), and done in conjunction with an I-9 Employment Eligibility Verification Form. This method is described fully in Chapter 29.

1. Consent Based Social Security Number Verification Service (CBSV)

The Consent Based SSN Verification System (CBSV) allows private businesses and government entities to verify that the name and SSN obtained from a customer matches or does not match the data in SSA's records. The information is matched against SSA's Master File of Social Security Numbers (SSNs), using Social Security number, name, date of birth, and gender code (if available)

With the consent of the SSN holder, enrolled users may utilize CBSV to verify whether the SSN holder's name and Social Security Number (SSN) combination match SSA's records. CBSV returns a "yes" or "no" verification indicating that the submission either matches or does not match our records. If records show that the SSN holder is deceased, CBSV returns a death indicator. CBSV verifications do not verify an individual's identity. CBSV is typically used by companies who provide banking and mortgage services, process credit checks, provide background checks, satisfy licensing requirements, etc.

Costs include a $5,000 initial enrollment fee and a per-SSN verification transaction fee of $1.05, paid in advance. Detailed information about CBSV can be found at www.socialsecurity.gov/cbsv/ including a sample User Agreement, Web Service technical documents, and a User Guide.

AUTHOR TIP ICBSV is designed to provide only a "yes" or "no" verification if the submitted SSN matched SSA records. CBSV does not verify identity, citizenship, employment eligibility, nor does it interface with the Department of Homeland Security (DHS) verification system. CBSV verifications do not satisfy DHS's I-9 requirements. Also, an employer must have an Employer Identification Number (EIN) to enroll in CBSV.

CBSV could have Uncovered Airport Security Supervisor Who Used Dead Man's ID for 20 Years

In May 2012, authorities arrested a longtime New Jersey airport security supervisor known by his co-workers as "Jerry Thomas" on a charge of impersonating someone else to hide his illegal immigrant status. The suspect was carrying the identity of a victim in an unsolved murder case 20 years earlier.

The Port Authority of New York and New Jersey said "Jerry Thomas" had worked at Newark's Liberty International Airport for about 20 years and had passed background checks by using the name Jerry Thomas since 1992, the year Thomas was killed in New York City.

The use of CBSV would have revealed the Social Security number of a deceased person used by a new hire or existing employee who are unauthorized workers.

The identities of nearly 2.5 million deceased Americans were used improperly to apply for credit products and services each year, according to a new study released today from ID Analytics' ID:A Labs. This is the first study to examine the extent of fraudsters improperly using a deceased person's identity to establish credit accounts.

The study compared the names, dates of birth (DOB) and Social Security numbers (SSNs) on 100 million applications during the first three months of 2011 to data in the Social Security Administration's Death Master File (DMF) to find which applications used personally identifiable information (PII) associated with deceased individuals.

The study found:

✓ Identity Theft of the Dead – Nearly 800,000 deceased Americans' identities are intentionally targeted for misuse on applications for credit products and cell phone services by fraudsters each year.

✓ Inadvertently Misusing SSNs of the Deceased – In approximately 1.6 million applications annually, an identity manipulator inadvertently used the SSN of a deceased person.

✓ Identity Theft of the Dying – Several hundred thousand potential misuses of dying people's identities each year.

Sources:

www.foxnews.com/us/2012/05/14/longtime-security-supervisor-arrested-at-nj-airport-for-using-dead-man-id/ and www.prnewswire.com/news-releases/identities-of-nearly-25-million-deceased-americans-misused-each-year-148491305.html

2. Social Security Number Verification Services (SSNVS)

The Social Security Administration's Social Security Number Verification Service SSNVS is an option to include as part of the new employee in-take procedures. The service is free, but registration is required. While the service is available to all employers and third-party submitters, it can only be used to verify current or former employees and only for wage reporting (Form W-2) purposes. A background screening firm or employer cannot use this service prior to an offer of employment being made. Employers typically call after a person has been hired as part of the new hire paperwork.

Requesters will be told if the name and DOB match what the SSA has on file. Once registered, employers have two options:

1. Verify up to 10 names and SSNs (per screen) online and receive immediate results. This option is ideal to verify new hires.

2. Upload overnight files of up to 250,000 names and SSNs and usually receive results the next government business day. This option is ideal if you want to verify an entire payroll database or if you hire a large number of workers at a time.

The registration process takes approximately 14 days. During that time, the SSA will provide verifications over the telephone. For more information, visit www.ssa.gov/employer/ssnv.htm.

The Social Security Administration has also posted a Legal Use Policy, which is shown below.

Legal Policy – Don't Discriminate or Misuse SSNVS

"SSA will advise you if a name/SSN you submitted does not match our records. This does not imply that you or your employee intentionally provided incorrect information about the employee's name or SSN. It is not a basis, in and of itself, for you to take any adverse action against the employee, such as termination, suspending, firing, or discriminating against an individual who appears on the list. SSNVS should only be used to verify currently or previously employed workers. Company policy concerning the use of SSNVS should be applied consistently to all workers, e.g. if used for newly hired employees, verify all newly hired employees; if used to verify your database, verify the entire database. Any employer that uses the information SSA provides regarding name/SSN verification to justify taking adverse action against an employee may violate state or federal law and be subject to legal consequences. Moreover, this makes no statement about your employee's immigration status."

The toll-free Social Security Administration telephone number is 1-800-772-6270 and is open weekdays from 7:00 a.m. to 7:00 p.m. EST. An employer will also be asked for the company name and federal Employer Identification Number (EIN). More information is available at www.ssa.gov/employer/ssnv.htm.

Privacy and the Social Security Number

The Social Security number has been getting a great deal of attention in the media recently due to the growing problems involved in identity theft. The ability of identity thieves to obtain Social Security numbers in order to commit fraud has become a national issue (See Chapter 28 on Identity Theft). The issue of privacy and Social Security numbers is being looked at carefully in Washington DC, as well as in various states. Part of the concern expressed by privacy advocates is the proliferation of Internet websites that sell data on consumers.

For the purposes of a Safe Hiring Program, any time information is obtained by an employer or a screening firm, it is always done with the expressed consent of the applicant for the expressed purpose of employment. In addition, if a third party firm is used, such as a background screening firm, then the requirements of the Fair Credit Reporting Act kick in as well, adding additional layers of protection and privacy for the applicant.

Changes to the FCRA effective in 2004 also addressed privacy concerns and the use of the Social Security number. The FCRA requires that screening firms, upon request from a consumer, must truncate the Social Security number on a background report. When a Social Security number is truncated, only the last four digits display such as xxx-xx-1234. The reason for the truncation requirement is that, often, identity theft occurs at the consumer's mailbox, where background reports mailed to the consumer can be stolen. By truncating the SSN, the consumer has some protection if the screening report falls into the wrong hands.

At least one state, California, has already passed strong legislation to protect the confidentiality of Social Security numbers, which includes controlling the use of SSNs by employers. California Civil Code § 1798.85 places numerous limitations on the use of SSNs including restrictions on anything mailed to the consumer. There is an exception in the law for any document whereby state or federal law requires the SSN to be on the document. Another California law also requires that California residents have an opportunity to check a box so they can receive a copy of any screening report, which is typically sent by mail. They are entitled to the same report the employer receives, which includes the applicant's SSN. To comply with these various California requirements, some screening firms have taken the position that the best practice is to truncate the SSN on any report sent to a California resident, revealing only the SSN's last four digits.

AUTHOR TIP Identity theft is also a significant issue in the workplace. Employers who obtain background reports may wish to consider having a paperless system. Background reports can be electronically restricted only to those with a need-to-know and it prevents the possibility of paper reports "floating" around the office or sitting on desks. Another solution is to require a screening firm to put a security page on the front of each report with only the applicant's name and no identifiable data. Another option is to truncate the SSN on any printed version of a screening report.

Another attempt by the federal government to protect the privacy of a Social Security number is the Financial Modernization Act of 1999, also known as the "Gramm-Leach-Bliley Act" or GLB Act. The law was passed in order to protect consumers' personal financial information held by financial institutions. However, since pre-employment screening is done in a consensual matter, the GLB has not had an impact on the use of the Social Security number for safe hiring purposes, especially when screening is conducted by an outside agency under the Fair Credit Reporting Act. More information is available at the Federal Trade Commission website at http://business.ftc.gov/privacy-and-security/gramm-leach-bliley-act.

As mentioned earlier in this chapter, another post-hire tool involving the Social Security number is an E-Verify check. This search confirms the work eligibility of newly hired employees by comparing information from the employee's Form I-9 to the information in U.S. Department of Homeland Security (DHS) and Social Security Administration (SSA). This procedure is described in detail in Chapter 29.

Education and Credentials Verifications

Inside This Chapter:

- ✓ The Need for Verification of Education Credentials

- ✓ The Verification Process

- ✓ How to Verify if a School is Accredited

- ✓ The Use of Fake Diplomas is a Real Problem

- ✓ About Distance Learning (Online) Schools

- ✓ Verifying High School and GED Diplomas

- ✓ Occupational Licensing and Vocational Verifications

- ✓ Conclusion — Educational Credentials Checking

- ✓ Additional Education Verification Resources

The Need for Verification of Education Credentials

The verification of educational credentials is an important part of an employer's decision making process in hiring. Educational achievement tells an employer a great deal about an applicant's ability, qualifications, and motivation. Many employers feel that educational qualifications are a critical factor in predicting success on the job. For many positions, education is a prerequisite in terms of subject matter knowledge or for obtaining the appropriate license for the position.

However, surveys that examined resumes and application forms suggest that as many as 30% of all job applicants falsify information about their educational backgrounds. The falsifications can include outright fabrications such as making up degrees from legitimate schools the applicant never attended or valueless degrees from non-accredited schools, many of which are often referred to as *diploma mills*.

According to the **Oregon Office of Degree Authorization**, the definition of diploma mills or degree mills is:

> *Diploma mills – or degree mills – are substandard or fraudulent "colleges" that offer potential students degrees with little or no serious work. Some are simple frauds, a mailbox to which people send money in exchange for paper that purports to be a college degree. Others require some nominal work from the student but do not require college-level course work that is normally required for a degree.*

See www.osac.state.or.us/oda/diploma_mill.html.

An applicant can also falsify his or her educational achievements based upon some semblance of fact, such as claiming degrees from schools the applicant actually attended but did not obtain the degree claimed. Typically a candidate turns their months or weeks of attendance into an AA degree or claims a BA or an advanced degree even if they did not complete the course work or fulfill all graduation requirements.

CEO Leaves Company after Discrepancy in Academic Credentials Revealed

In May 2012, Yahoo! Inc. announced that recently hired Chief Executive Officer Scott Thompson had left the company soon after it was revealed there was a discrepancy in his academic credentials included in online biographies and filings with the Securities and Exchange Commission. Not only did Thompson's record contain incorrect information, but it was also revealed the Chairwoman of the Search Committee who hired him also had a discrepancy in her academic credentials.

Read more about the story at: http://pressroom.yahoo.net/pr/ycorp/233946.aspx.

The above incident of fraud underscores the need to do research on the educational qualifications of candidates. Confirming diplomas, degrees, or certificates, along with dates of attendance, verifies applicants' education and skills is an indication of their ability to do the job. Confirmation also supports their honesty by substantiating claims made on an application. To an employer, the value of diplomas, degrees, or certificates also depends upon the quality of the degree-granting institution. The issue of accreditation is important for employers attempting to determine if a degree translate into knowledge, skills, or experience that will be of benefit in the workplace.

AUTHOR TIP

What about Schools that are Licensed but Not Accredited?

Another related issue is that in the U.S., there are schools that are not accredited, but may still be licensed by a state agency. One example is trade or vocational school. More problematic for employers is there are some schools that have obtained a state license, but are not accredited yet are offering "academic" degrees. Such a school may still be essentially a "degree mill" offering substandard education or worthless degrees. Or, a school may be in the process of applying for accreditation. Another situation arises where a school has lost their accreditation but is still licensed, and was accredited when the applicant graduated. The bottom-line is that being licensed is not the same as being accredited. A license does not necessarily inform an employer about the quality of the school or the value of the degree in terms of skills and education needed for employment. In the case of a licensed but unaccredited school, an employer will need to conduct its own due diligence to determine the value of the degree in terms of the applicant's qualifications and the requirements of the job. All of this underscores the complexities of academic accreditation in the U.S. and the need for employers to exercise caution when evaluating a degree from an unfamiliar school they.

The Verification Process

There are four primary pieces of information needed to verify one's education history and qualifications:

1. The school attended does exist.
2. The school is accredited by an approved accrediting body (or in the least state licensed).
3. The subject attended the school during the time period claimed.
4. A degree was actually granted to the subject as claimed.

Also, if the position involves proof of course-taking, then:

1. The subject completed the courses of study for any degree granted and are shown on an official copy of their school transcripts.

Verifying Attendance or Degree Via the School

Traditionally, a verification request is sent by mail, email, or fax to the school's Registrar office. Few accept phone calls to verify prior attendance. Some schools now provide online, interactive request forms. Some schools require a signed release from the student to be included with the request. Verifications are usually free but not always. Confirmations may be faxed back although you may ask to school to confirm their results via phone. Requests should include a DOB, SSN, and the name used during attendance. Gender and approximate or exact years of attendance should be mentioned, and always be concise about where verification results should be returned – your address, phone, company name, etc. If you mail a request, be sure to include a SASE.

 One suggestion to help employers is to include the following language on the employment application:

"Please list all degrees or educational accomplishments that you wish to be considered by the employer in the employment decision."

This statement has the advantage of putting the burden on the applicant to determine if they want to report a degree or educational accomplishment. The applicant is on notice that any degree they report can be used by the employer for the employment decision. If the applicant chooses to report a worthless degree, or a degree not earned, they can hardly complain if an employer uses that to deny employment, even if the degree was not a requirement of the job.

Verifying Attendance or Degree Via the National Student Clearing House

Nearly 33% of schools have outsourced verification duties to a non-profit, third-party vendor – The National Student Clearing House (NSCL). But these schools represent over 80% of the students attending an accredited post-secondary degree granting institution. So chances are most verifications will need to be done using the NSCL. This outsourcing ostensibly takes the tasks out of the hands of cost-conscious registrar offices. Fees are involved and requesters must generally provide the subject's signed release. NSCL can be found at www.nslc.org.

Acquiring Transcript Copies

If you do need to obtain a copy of a transcript, this data is considered private and can only be obtained with a signed release of the student. Per the Family Educational Rights and Privacy Act (FERPA), the education records of students are not public record unless used as general directory information.

Most schools charge a fee for each transcript copy; fees vary from $1.00 to $20.00 each but usually around $5.00. Often transcription request forms are found online at the schools webpage. Credit card payment may be allowed. A number of schools offer Unofficial Transcripts as a cost-saving measure, the benefit being that an unofficial copy can be returned by fax or email. Official copies are usually mailed back.

A number of schools outsource their transcript fulfillment duties to a 3rd party vendor, including NSCL.

Closed private institutions such as military or seminary schools are a different story. Their records may have been transferred to another school, a nearby same-denomination school, or simply held by a surviving alumnus.

Finding Records from a Closed School

The applicant's resume reads "Attended 'Aakers' Business College in Fargo, ND." But when one seeks to verify the applicant's attendance there, the school is found to be closed. Perhaps the applicant is claiming they attended there but didn't, knowing that verifications there might be hard to come by.

Closed schools within a state are registered through an education-related state agency. The records may be maintained by the agency or the agency may know who does and have some mechanism in place to help you either 1) identify the current location of the closed school's student records, or 2) the agency may perform the record check for you. This is also true for transcript requests, but, depending on the state, transcripts and student attendance/degree information may not always be found at the same place. Knowing of the difficulty and urgency of your search request, the state agency can usually handle phone requests or is quick to instruct you how to correctly submit your request.

Visit http://wdcrobcolp01.ed.gov/CFAPPS/FSA/closedschool/searchpage.cfm for an excellent search site dealing with finding closed schools.

How to Verify if a School is Accredited

How are employers supposed to avoid diploma mills or worthless degrees? The first line of defense is to see if a school is accredited by a recognized accrediting agency. Sometimes this is referred to as confirming that a school is on a "white" list of accredited and legitimate schools.

Accreditation is a complicated process of peer and self-assessment aimed at improving academic quality and demonstrating the quality of an institution to the public. A legitimate accreditation can give the employer a greater comfort level in the legitimacy and quality of an applicant's degree.

Adding to the challenge of employers detecting education fraud, some diploma mills have even created fake accreditation agencies to falsely vouch for the phony schools. To combat diploma mills in the United States, schools are generally accredited by private organizations that are recognized as legitimate accreditors.

Unlike most of the rest of the world however, accreditation in the United States is not done directly by the government. In the United States, numerous private organizations can provide accreditation to a school. The recognized U.S. accrediting organizations all have one thing in common— the accrediting agencies are in turn accredited by one of two nationally recognized agencies.

1. The U.S. Department of Education (DOE). According to the Department of Education: "The goal of accreditation is to ensure that education provided by institutions of higher education meets acceptable levels of quality." For an overview, see www.ed.gov/admins/finaid/accred/accreditation.html#Overview.

    The Department of Education limits their accreditation activities to institutions that receive federal money such as financial aid. The U.S. Department of Education has provided an internet listing of organizations that it has accredited to be an accrediting agency. See www.ed.gov/admins/finaid/accred/accreditation_pg4.html.

    The Department of Education has also created a website with a Database of Accredited Postsecondary Institutions and Programs at www.ope.ed.gov/accreditation/search.aspx.

2. The Council for Higher Education Accreditation (CHEA) found online at www.chea.org is the other accepted organization that can accredit the accreditors. CHEA is a successor to two previous organizations that also fulfilled this function — the Commission on Recognition of Postsecondary Accreditation (CORPA) and the Council on Postsecondary Accreditation (COPA). At the CHEA website, employers can find not only the names and contact information for each recognized organization but can also do a look-up by state that gives a link to every school accredited. The Department of Education website states, "CHEA is currently the entity that carries out a recognition function in the private, nongovernmental sector." For more information on the function of CHEA, see www.ed.gov/admins/finaid/accred/accreditati on_pg2.html.

CHEA and the U.S. Department of Education classify accrediting institutions into three types of organizations:

1. **Regional accreditation organizations.** There are six regional associations that accredit public and private schools, colleges, and universities in the United States. In the list at the end of this chapter, eight such organizations are listed. Two have two branches reflecting a division for "colleges and universities" and a division for "other types of institutions." A list with details about these regional accreditations organizations is located at the back of this chapter and also at:
    *   www.chea.org/Directories/regional.asp
    *   www.ed.gov/admins/finaid/accred/accreditation_pg5.html
2. **Single purpose national accreditation organizations.** These organizations accredit a particular type of school. At the end of the chapter are the names of eleven such national organizations, of which only six are recognized by CHEA. All are recognized by the U.S. Department of Education. The six national accreditation agencies recognized by CHEA are located at:
    *   www.chea.org/Directories/national.asp
    *   Additional agencies accredited by the U.S. Department of Education are listed at www.ed.gov/admins/finaid/accred/accreditation_pg6.html.
3. **Specialized and professional accrediting organizations.** These academic programs are administratively located in degree or non-degree granting institutions. These bodies range from acupuncture (Accreditation Commission for Acupuncture and Oriental Medicine) to veterinary medicine (American Veterinary Medical Association, Council on Education). For lists, see:
    *   www.chea.org/Directories/special.asp
    *   www.ed.gov/admins/finaid/accred/accreditation_pg6.html#aom

The Use of Fake Diplomas is a Real Problem

Apparently that act of earning a college diploma apparently no longer requires years of hard work, taking tests, paying tuition, or even reading a book. Why bother going through the formalities when all a person needs is a credit card and a web browser in order to buy an authentic looking diploma that mimics real colleges, universities, and even high schools across the U.S. Go to any search engine and run keywords such as "fake diploma" and anyone can instantly "graduate" from nearly any school in America with a very handsome and authentic looking diploma suitable for hanging.

The earlier example of the false education credentials presented by the CEO of Yahoo! is not merely an isolated incident. The use of "genuine fake diplomas" is definitely on the rise. The following recent news stories indicate how widespread the problem of diploma mills and education fraud has become in the U.S.:

✓ In December 2011, a New York Times investigation found that the Yale head football coach had never been a Rhodes Scholar candidate or applicant, even though his résumé and Yale website biography indicated otherwise. The Coach resigned – see http://thequad.blogs.nytimes.com/2011/12/21/yale-football-coach-resigns/.

✓ In a December 2011 article 'Cops bust caretakers for bogus credentials,' The Miami Herald reported a crackdown called 'Operation Cardiac Arrest' on a diploma mill in Florida that gave customers fake certificates for health workers for training in CPR, infection control, and care for people with special needs. The phony certificates helped unqualified and untrained caretakers to get jobs at assisted living facilities with elders and mentally ill. To read the full article, visit: www.miamiherald.com/2011/12/07/2536436/cops-bust-caretakers-for-bogus.html.

✓ In November 2011, the new Chief Information Technology (IT) Officer of the State of Kansas resigned after reports in the Topeka Capital-Journal raised questions about his college degree from an unaccredited school linked to diploma mills. The newspaper reported that the newly hired chief IT officer resigned from the $150,000-a-year position following the disclosure that his college degree in business administration was acquired from the University of Devonshire, an unaccredited school linked to a consortium of diploma mills in the University Degree Program, a company viewed as "one of the most prolific diploma-production enterprises." See   http://cjonline.com/news/2011-11-08/kan-it-chief-resigns-over-questions-about-degree   and http://cjonline.com/news/2011-11-07/state-it-chiefs-degree-unaccredited-college.

✓ In what may be one of the largest cases of a possible 'diploma mill' handled by federal agents, a two-year investigation by the U.S. Immigration and Customs Enforcement's (ICE) Homeland Security Investigations (HSI) resulted in the arrest of the President of an alleged 'sham' university – Tri-Valley University in Pleasanton, California – on charges that include student visa fraud, money laundering, and alien harboring. According to a May 2011 ICE news release, the Tri-Valley University President engage in a "scheme to defraud the Department of Homeland Security (DHS) by submitting phony documents in support of Tri-Valley University's applications to admit foreign nationals on student visas." In addition, an indictment also alleged that after obtaining approvals, the President issued fraudulent visa-related documents to the estimated enrollment of 2,500 student aliens in exchange for "tuition and fees." The defendant also allegedly engaged in money laundering totaling over $3.2 million. See: www.ice.gov/news/releases/1105/110502oakland.htm.

✓ An audit report of Dickinson State University (DSU) in North Dakota released in March 2012 described the school as a "diploma mill" for foreign students that awarded hundreds of unearned degrees to students mostly from China who did not complete their course work while also enrolling students who did not have qualifying grades.   The audit is available at www.ndus.edu/uploads/reports/96/dsu-internal-review-ddj-final-draft1-020912.pdf.

The rise of diploma mills is further evidenced by **Accredibase**, a recognized global leader in investigating diploma mills.

Report Reveals 48 Percent Increase Worldwide in Diploma Mills in 2010

The second annual Accredibase™ Report for 2011 from Accredibase Limited, a recognized global leader in investigating diploma mills, revealed an astounding 48 percent increase worldwide in the number of known, fake diploma mills in 2010. According to the report, the United States was the world's fake college capital and saw a 20 percent increase in known diploma mills with the number rising from 810 to 1,008.

The top ten states and areas in the U.S. with the highest number of diploma mills – which the report described as "largely online entities whose degrees are worthless due to the lack of valid accreditation and recognition" – were:

- California – 147 diploma mills.
- Hawaii – 98 diploma mills.
- Washington – 91 diploma mills.
- Florida – 84 diploma mills.
- Texas – 68 diploma mills.
- New York – 55 diploma mills.
- Arizona – 44 diploma mills.
- Louisiana – 42 diploma mills.
- Delaware – 37 diploma mills.
- District of Columbia – 33 diploma mills.

The United Kingdom (U.K.) by far remained Europe's bogus university capital with a 25 percent increase in known diploma mills, with the number rising from 271 to 339, and also accounting for 57 percent of European diploma mills. The number of diploma mills in Europe rose from 454 to 593, an increase of 31 percent.

Accredibase™ runs a proprietary database of diploma and accreditation mills, and has identified approximately 6,000 suspect educational institutions and accreditors. In addition to the 2,810 confirmed diploma mills known to Accredibase™, more than 3,000 suspect institutions are currently under investigation for inclusion in the database. The second annual Accredibase™ Report for 2011 is available at www.accredibase.com/report.

How to Spot a Diploma Mill

The problem with these lists of diploma mills is that the mills are moving targets. They can change their names overnight and new ones can sprout up as easily as a scam artist can put up a new Internet site. There are literally hundreds of websites that offer fake degrees, diplomas, or certificates.

Here are some of the spins used in their advertisements:

- ✓ Here is an opportunity to get ahead.
- ✓ University diplomas.
- ✓ Obtain a prosperous future, money earning power, and the admiration of all.
- ✓ Diplomas from a prestigious university.
- ✓ Based upon your present knowledge and life experience.
- ✓ No required tests, classes, book or interview.
- ✓ Bachelors, Master's, MBA, and doctorate (PhD) diplomas available in your field of choice.
- ✓ No one is turned down.
- ✓ Confidentiality assured. Call now to receive your diploma within days.

Of course, these schools have no classes, no faculty, no course catalog, and typically a single point of contact such as email address or P.O. Box, but these schools typically do have really impressive websites with outstanding testimonials and wonderful pictures of campus life. They also provide wonderful looking diplomas, which any good graphic artist and print shop can produce.

Other Warning Signs that Help Identify of Diploma Mills

The second annual Accredibase™ Report for 2011 also identified the following "red flags" – or warning signs – that may help identify of diploma mills:

✓ The institution does not have authority to operate or grant degrees from the education authorities where it claims to be based.

✓ Degrees are delivered in a short space of time – sometimes a few days.

✓ Degrees are granted based entirely on work or life experience.

✓ Contact details are limited to email addresses and vague about the institution's location.

✓ The institution allows students to choose their own course titles and specify graduation years on the certificate.

✓ Sample certificates, transcripts, or verification letters are available on the website.

✓ The institution's name is similar to that of a recognized and respected education institution.

✓ The institution's Internet domain names are misleading.

✓ The institution's website is poorly designed, has poor spelling and grammar, or plagiarizes from other institutions.

Fake Accreditation Scams

The scam artists that sell fake credentials have figured out that it helps to be accredited. Therefore, the diploma mill and fake diploma industry has developed a fake accreditation industry. There are even fake agencies with names similar to authenticated agencies. The bottom line — just because a school says they are accredited does not mean they are.

According to the State of Oregon, here are some "fake" accreditation agencies:

✓ Accrediting Commission International.

✓ American Association of International Medical Graduates.

✓ Association for Online Academic Excellence.

✓ Association of Christian Colleges and Theological Schools.

✓ Central States Council on Distance Education.

✓ Distance Graduation Accrediting Association.

✓ Distance Learning Council of Europe.

✓ European Council for Distance & Open Learning.

✓ International Association of Universities and Schools.

✓ International University Accrediting Association.

✓ Office of Degree Authorization.

✓ Southern Accrediting Association of Bible Institutes and Colleges.

✓ United Congress of Colleges.

✓ US-DETC.*

✓ Virtual University Accrediting Association.

✓ World Association of Universities and Colleges.

* NOTE: US-DETC is not to be confused with the legitimate DETC or Distance Education and Training Council, based in Washington DC. DETC is recognized by both the Department of Education and CHEA.

The situation with fake degrees got so out of hand that in 2004 the United States Department of Education announced the development of a "positive list" of accredited institutions of higher education. This announcement was in response to a series of incidents of federal workers found holding worthless credentials issued by "diploma mills." The government became concerned about diploma mills when a senior director in the Department of Homeland Security was placed on administrative leave following an allegation that his degree came from Hamilton University, allegedly a diploma mill that operated out of a refurbished hotel in Evanston, Wyoming. A memo issued April 2004, by the Federal Office of Personnel Management (OPM) reported other abuses including a computer specialist who claimed both a Bachelors and Master's degree in computers obtained only four months apart and a police officer who submitted his resume online to a diploma mill and received a degree based upon life experiences.

 One may now do a search of an institution or an accrediting agency at: http://ope.ed.gov/accreditation/Search.aspx.

Keep in mind that even if an employer reviews the accreditation resources, things can still slip through the cracks. Here is why:

✓ A school may have changed names.
✓ A website may not have been updated.
✓ A school may have lost accreditation.
✓ A school may be accredited, but since the last accreditation, the quality has fallen.
✓ The so-called accreditation was by a non-accredited accreditation agency (See below).

Other Resources for Locating Degree Mills and Bogus Accrediting Agencies

If an employer is unable to locate a school on a "white" list, an employer does have the option of viewing several free listings of known diploma mills or paying for detailed information.

1. States Education Agencies

There are four states – Hawaii, Maine, Oregon, and Texas – that tracks the authenticity of college degrees and provide lists.

✓ **Oregon:** The Oregon Office of Degree Authorization (ODA) at www.osac.state.or.us/oda/unaccredited.aspx. This agency generally considered the most well-known of the group.
✓ **Hawaii:** Hawaii.gov - Unaccredited Degree Granting Institutions (UDGI): http://hawaii.gov/dcca/ocp/udgi
✓ **Maine**: Department of Education State of Maine – Non-Accredited Colleges & Universities: www.maine.gov/education/highered/Non-Accredited/a-am.htm
✓ **Texas:** Texas Higher Education Coordinating Board - Enforcement Actions Against Institutions Violating the Texas Education Code: www.thecb.state.tx.us/apps/consumerinfo/Enforcement.cfm

NOTE: The Michigan Civil Service Commission previously published a list of schools whose degrees had been found to not satisfy educational requirements indicated on job specifications for state classified positions. The Commission now offers the following guidance on the acceptance of degrees to meet educational requirements for positions in the Michigan state classified service:

"Degrees issued by institutions that are accredited by an accrediting body recognized in the database maintained by the Council on Higher Education Accreditation (www.chea.org) are typically accepted. Please note that individual degree programs that have not been accredited by the recognized, programmatic accrediting body might not be accepted. Degrees issued by foreign colleges and universities may be accepted if an applicant or employee presents evidence to demonstrate that the degree represents education equivalent to similar studies at an accredited university."

2. The Publication Degree Mills by Ezell and Bear

The most recent 2012 edition of *Degree Mills: The Billion-dollar Industry That Has Sold Over A Million Fake Diplomas'* written by Allen Ezell and John Bear 'shows how much money can be made while running an unaccredited school that awards unearned degrees.

Here is a description of the first edition book from its Amazon.com page: www.amazon.com/Degree-Mills-Billion-dollar-Industry-Diplomas/dp/159102238X:

> "Need a degree from Harvard, Yale, Stanford, or MIT! No problem. Send us a check! Do you know where your doctor, lawyer, or clergyman earned his or her degree? In 1986, a congressional committee report concluded that: more than 500,000 working Americans have a fraudulent degree. The media hardly noticed. The public yawned. The academic world buried its head in the sand. And things have gotten much, much worse since then. Allen Ezell, who specialized in degree fraud during his 35 years with the FBI, and John Bear, prolific author and expert witness on the subject in federal and state courts, reveal the shocking dimensions of this growing scam in this thoroughly researched expose. They show how degree mills operate, offer detailed warning signs that a school might be fake, tell how to check up on anyone's degree, and what to do when a fake degree is discovered. Also provided are information and links to useful lists of bad and fake schools. This is an invaluable reference book for personnel departments in business and academia, as well as for the average consumer."

The following excerpt comes from an article by Mr. Bear, who has written numerous articles on educational issues:

> "There are more than 300 unaccredited universities now operating. While a few are genuine start-ups or online ventures, the great majority range from merely dreadful to out-and-out diploma mills — fake schools that will sell people any degree they want at prices from $3,000 to $5,000.

> "It is not uncommon for a large fake school to "award" as many as 500 Ph.D.s every month.

> "The aggregate income of the bad guys is easily in excess of $200 million a year. Data show that a single phony school can earn between $10 million and $20 million annually.

> With the closure of the FBI's diploma mill task force, the indifference of most state law enforcement agencies, the minimal interest of the news media, and the growing ease of using the internet to start and run a fake university, things are rapidly growing worse."

Mr. Bear's web page is at www.degree.net.

3. The White List and Diploma Mill List at BRB Publications

BRB Publications has an inexpensive subscription product which provides not only detailed information about schools, but also includes over 800 known diploma mills in its searchable database. The data available about each school includes:

- ✓ Degree levels granted
- ✓ The Accrediting Agency
- ✓ The state government agency that gives authority to operate in a state
- ✓ If verifications are performed by the school or if a requester must contact the National Student Clearing House
- ✓ A cross-reference list of over 2,000 schools that have closed or have had name changes.

4. Accredibase

Accredibase is the recognized global leader in tracking and investigating diploma mills. The number of diploma mills monitored in their database goes well beyond the other lists mentioned. While the number of "publically known mills" totals about 800, Accredibase has at least 2,810 confirmed mills and another 3,322 under investigation. The content Accredibase provides to its subscribers also includes addresses, logos, website screenshots, sample certificates and transcripts to help you identify if the institute is the same as the one you are researching. Furthermore, Accredibase provides copies of press articles, legal documents and much more, all of which help its clients build a clearer picture of the activity of each institution in question and the people and organizations that run them.

AUTHOR TIP

The Role of a Background Screening Firm in Finding "Diploma Mills"

According to the NAPBS Accreditation Standards (discussed in detail in Chapter 11), Standard 5.3 "Diploma Mills" requires that a background screening firm have a reasonable procedure in place to advise clients if a degree came from a known or suspect diploma mill. A CRA should have procures in place to access the "white" lists and "black" lists outlined in this chapter. The difficulty is a Consumer Reporting Agency cannot necessarily offer an opinion that a school is offering worthless degrees. That potentially creates legal liability for the screening firm. On the other hand, there is a duty to put an employer on notice that there is an issue as to the worth of the claimed degree. If a screening firm determines a school is not on any list of known accredited schools, or is on a list of known degree mills, the screening report may note that the firm is unable to verify the school is accredited and may even note the presence of the schools name on a blacklist. That will put an employer on notice that more research is necessary.

About Distance Learning (Online) Schools

Diploma mills should not be confused with legitimate schools that offer valuable distance-learning programs over the Internet. If an employer is not familiar with a school, the employer should review the school's website to check out the accreditation, curriculum, faculty, and graduation requirements.

The Accrediting Commission of the Distance Education and Training Council (DETC) at www.detc.org is a legitimate, recognized accrediting agency for schools that provide their curriculum via online learning. But there are many agencies that are unrecognized as a legitimate accrediting body for distance learning, as shown below.

Unrecognized and Fake Agencies for Online College Accreditation

Here is the official list of 30-plus distance learning accrediting agencies that claim to oversee a variety of online college and university degree programs from **Get Educated** (www.geteducated.com). Most "accredit" diploma mills or degree mills. NONE of these accrediting agencies are recognized as college accreditors in the U.S. by the Council on Higher Education Accreditation or the U.S. Department of Education. Colleges claiming "accreditation" by these agencies are not accepted as valid providers of online education or degrees and should be approached with great caution:

- Accreditation Council for Distance Education (ACTDE).
- Accreditation Council for Online Academia (ACOHE).
- Accreditation Council of Online Education (ACOE).
- Accreditation Panel for Online Colleges and Universities (APTEC).
- Accrediting Commission International (ACI).
- American Accrediting Association of Theological Institutions.
- American Council of Private Colleges and Universities.
- American Association of Drugless Practitioners (ADP).
- Association of Accredited Bible Schools.
- Association of Distance Learning Programs (ADLP).

- Association of Private Colleges and Universities.
- Association for Online Academic Accreditation.
- Association for Online Excellence.
- Association for Online Academic Excellence.
- Board of Online Universities Accreditation (BOUA).
- Council for Distance Education.
- Council of Online Higher Education.
- Central States Consortium of Colleges & Schools.
- Distance and Online Universities Accreditation Council (DOUAC).
- Distance Learning International Accreditation Association (DEIAA).
- Global Accreditation Bureau (GAB).
- Global Accreditation Commission for Distance Education (GACDE).
- International Commission for Higher Education.
- International Accreditation Agency for Online Universities (IAAOU).
- International Accreditation Association for Online Education (IAAFOE).
- International Accreditation Commission (IAC).
- International Accreditation Commission for Online Universities (IACOU) (Kingston).
- International Accreditation Organization (IAO).
- International Council on Education (ICE).
- International Education Ministry Accreditation Association.
- International Online Education Accrediting Board (IOEAB).
- National Academic Higher Education Agency (NACHE).
- National Academy of Higher Education.
- National Accreditation and Certification Board (NACB).
- National Board of Education (NBOE).
- National College Accreditation Council (NCAC).
- National Commission of Accredited Schools (NCAS).
- National Distance Learning Accreditation Council (NDLAC).
- New Millennium Accrediting Partnership for Educators Worldwide.
- Organization for Online Learning Accreditation (OKOLA).
- Transworld Accrediting Commission Intl. (TAC).
- United Christian College Accreditation Association (UCCAA) (Divine Heart).
- United Nations Council.
- United States Distance Education & Training Council of Nevada*.
- Universal Accreditation Council (UAC).
- Universal Council for Online Education Accreditation (UCOEA).
- World Association for Online Education (WAOE)**.
- World Association of Universities and Colleges (WAUC).
- World Online Education Accrediting Commission (WOEAC).
- World-Wide Accreditation Commission of Christian Educational Institutions (WWAC).

- Worldwide Higher Education Accreditation Society (WHEAS).

Remember: Most diploma mills and degree mills are accredited – but only by the fake or phony agencies the degree mills owned and operated by themselves!

*__IMPORTANT NOTE 1__: A similarly titled agency, the Distance Education & Training Council (DETC), of Washington, D.C.—http://www.detc.org—is a VALID and RECOGNIZED online learning accreditation agency) NOTE: US-DETC is not to be confused with the legitimate DETC or Distance Education and Training Council, based in Washington DC. DETC is recognized by both the Department of Education and CHEA.

** __IMPORTANT NOTE 2__: WAOE is a real, esteemed professional agency for educators. It is a discussion group of teachers who are experimenting with computer mediated methods of teaching in their own schools, colleges, and universities around the world. WAOE does not condone the use of its name as an accrediting agency by any online college. Any online college using the WAOE name as a college accrediting agency does so without the consent of WAOE and in contradiction to the organization's mission. For more on the WAOE and its valuable mission uniting educators involved in computer-mediated education visit WAOE online at www.waoe.org.

Source: www.geteducated.com/diploma-mills-police/college-degree-mills/204-fake-agencies-for-college-accreditation.

AUTHOR TIP

It's A Moving Target

Part of the problem with keeping up with diploma mills and fake accreditation scams is that it can seem like a game of "Whac-A-Mole." As soon as one scam is discovered, another can pop up almost instantly. It does not take much to start a fake school or accreditation agency beyond having a computer. The lesson for employers again is that if you are not familiar with a school, extreme caution is advised. Employers that utilize the services of a professional Consumer Reporting Agency have an advantage since a CRA can access resources that help distinguish between legitimate schools and degree mills.

Verifying High School and GED Diplomas

Searching for high school records can be a difficult task. Of course this is easily done if the employer is hiring from a local familiar area, provided the employer understands that during summer vacation and school breaks there may not be anyone at school offices to answer the phone. When employers hire from outside their locale, there are practical problems. First, it is not always easy to locate a particular high school. Over the years, schools can close, merge, or be renamed. A high school name can be misspelled or not quite remembered. Most states have a website or an office that provides school lists. If a student received his or her high school degree by testing, such as GED, then there can be delays in obtaining those through the appropriate state or district office.

There are several excellent websites that provide comprehensive lists and data pertaining to high schools as well as junior highs and elementary schools.

The site maintained by Council of Chief State School Officers at www.schoolmatters.com provides detailed information on each school including the school's address, telephone number, total students, and also very detailed comparisons on performance matters. At press time the site is undergoing changes and promises to be up shortly, merged with SchoolDataDirect.

Also, check out the subscription site at www.schoolinformation.com. Designed for entities marketing products to schools, this resource is valuable if extensive searching or due diligence is required. Also, a Google search will reveal a number of state lists. Of course, an on-site visit of a school is a good way to view a yearbook to find pictures and activity information about individual students.

General Education Diplomas (GED)

Not everyone graduates from a high school. But later a person may pass a high school equivalency test and receive a General Education Diploma (GED). A database of GED recipients is maintained at the state level by the agency that oversees adult education. A GED record search will verify if someone truly received a GED certificate for high school education equivalency. Many of these state agencies will verify over the phone the existence of a GED certificate or give a "yes-no" answer by fax. Copies of transcripts or diplomas usually require a fee and a signed release. Search requirements include the name of the student at the time of the test and a general idea of the year and test location. GED records are not useful when trying to locate an individual.

BRB's Public Record Research System provides detailed information on each state's GED office with record searching requirements.

Occupational Licensing and Vocational Verifications

Not all vocational or trade schools are accredited by recognized accrediting organizations. Each state has an agency in charge of certifying state-approved educational programs. If there are questions about the legitimacy of a vocational or trade school, then an employer should contact the appropriate authority in their state. There are numerous distance learning programs available on the internet as well. The same verification rules apply. An employer should determine what accreditation or recognition they have and then evaluate the value of the degree. It is the employer's job to evaluate how a degree or coursework from a vocational or trade school or distance learning program translates into a person's ability to perform a given job. An employer needs to view the school's literature or website to find out about the quality of the facilities and faculty, the course of study required, and other factors that go into determining the value of the education to the job position.

For helpful information on evaluating non-accredited but otherwise licensed schools, see a publication by the Federal Trade Commission. The document summarizes some factors that potential students and employers may find beneficial to review: www.ftc.gov/bcp/edu/pubs/consumer/products/pro13.shtm.

For confirming the status of a license or credential needed to legally practice a profession, there are literally thousands of governmental boards that have control over licenses and professional certification. There are also private organizations that issue certifications.

Examples? Hospitals may need to verify the license status of a doctor, nurse, radiologist, or physical therapist. An employer may want to confirm that a person claiming to be an accountant is, in fact, licensed by the state board that licenses accountants. In order to verify a license an employer needs to require that the applicant provide key information:

- ✓ The name or type of license.
- ✓ The issuing agency.
- ✓ The state AND date of issuance.
- ✓ Current status and date of expiration.

Nearly every governmental licensing organization can be contacted by telephone. Many agencies have Internet sites where verifications can be done immediately. An extensive listing of agency websites offering a free public search of a licensee or licensee list is available at www.brbpublications.com/freeresources/pubrecsitesOccStates.aspx.

 During the verification process, an employer will also want to know if the agency reports any actions against the license or derogatory information about the applicant. That helps to determine if the applicant's license is in good standing.

Confirmation of certifications issued by private organizations. Certificates issued by private organizations are typically difficult to verify. Unless the certification was conducted through an accredited school, such as a community college, it is a substantial challenge to verify it. These can include items such as any kind of "Certificate of Good Work" and a number of different computer and software-related certificates provided by a number of organizations, legitimate or otherwise.

Conclusion — Educational Credentials Checking

When it comes to education credentials — employers beware! If an employer is not familiar with the school, check it out. Do not be fooled by a slick looking website with pretty pictures of a campus and academic scenes and glowing testimonials. The existence of a very academic looking diploma does not mean anything; fake schools are capable of producing some very convincing worthless diplomas. A common sense approach is a valuable tool in evaluating the worth of a degree. Look first to see if it is accredited by a recognized accreditation agency, then take reasonable steps as necessary to confirm the value of the degree such as examining the curriculum, the qualifications and reputation of the faculty members, the facilities, the qualifications of the institution's president, or graduation requirements.

Additional Education Verification Resources

List of Regional Accrediting Organizations

The following Regional Accrediting Organizations are recognized by both CHEA and DOE:

- ✓ **Middle States Association of Colleges and Schools** – www.msache.org
  - Delaware, the District of Columbia, Maryland, New Jersey, New York, Pennsylvania, Puerto Rico, and the U.S. Virgin Islands, including distance education programs offered at those institutions.
- ✓ **New England Association of Schools and Colleges** – www.neasc.org
  - Connecticut, Maine, Massachusetts, New Hampshire, Rhode Island, and Vermont.
- ✓ **North Central Association of Colleges and Schools** – www.ncahigherlearningcommission.org
  - Arizona, Arkansas, Colorado, Illinois, Indiana, Iowa, Kansas, Michigan, Minnesota, Missouri, Nebraska, New Mexico, North Dakota, Ohio, Oklahoma, South Dakota, West Virginia, Wisconsin, and Wyoming.
- ✓ **Northwest Commission on Colleges and Universities** – www.nwccu.org
  - Alaska, Idaho, Montana, Nevada, Oregon, Utah, and Washington.
- ✓ **Southern Association of Colleges and Schools** – www.sacscoc.org
  - Alabama, Florida, Georgia, Kentucky, Louisiana, Mississippi, North Carolina, South Carolina, Tennessee, Texas, and Virginia.
- ✓ **Western Association of Schools and Colleges, Accrediting Commission for Senior Colleges and Universities** – www.wascweb.org
  - California, Hawaii, the United States territories of Guam and American Samoa, the Republic of Palau, the Federated States of Micronesia, the Commonwealth of the Northern Mariana Islands and the Republic of the Marshall Islands.

National Accrediting Organizations

The following National Accrediting Organizations are recognized by both CHEA and the DOE:

- ✓ **Accrediting Association of Bible Colleges (AABC) Commission on Accreditation** – www.aabc.org
- ✓ **Accrediting Commission of the Distance Education and Training Council (DETC)** – http://www.detc.org
- ✓ **Accrediting Council for Independent Colleges and Schools (ACICS)** – www.acics.org
- ✓ **Association of Advanced Rabbinical and Talmudic Schools (AARTS)** – 212-363-1991 (Web: N/A)
- ✓ **Association of Theological Schools in the United States and Canada (ATS)** – www.ats.edu
- ✓ **Transnational Association of Christian Colleges and Schools Accreditation Commission (TRACS)** – www.tracs.org

The following National Accrediting Organizations are recognized only by the DOE:

- ✓ **Accrediting Bureau of Health Education Schools**
- ✓ **Accrediting Commission of Career Schools and Colleges of Technology**
- ✓ **Accrediting Council for Continuing Education and Training**
- ✓ **Council on Occupational Education**
- ✓ **National Accrediting Commission of Cosmetology Arts and Sciences, Inc.**

For listings of Specialized and Professional Accrediting Organizations, see:

- ✓ www.ed.gov/admins/finaid/accred/accreditation_pg4.html
- ✓ www.chea.org/Directories/special.asp

Chapter 19

Social Media Background Checks

Inside This Chapter:

✓ The Social Media Explosion

✓ Research Shows How Employers Use Internet for Screening

✓ Landmines and Traps with Social Media Background Checks

✓ Legal Risks for Employers Using Social Media for Employment Screening

✓ Solutions if Using Social Media Background Checks

- Solutions for Employers

- Solutions for Recruiters

- Solutions for Job Applicants

✓ Bottom Line with Social Media Background Checks: Proceed with Caution

✓ Setting a Company Policy

The Social Media Explosion

This chapter provides an informative introduction for both employers and recruiters using Internet search engines like Google and social networking sites such as Facebook for recruitment and employment screening background checks. The chapter examines the possible legal risks faced when conducting such "social media background check" screening, as well as potential solutions to avoid legal issues.

No discussion on employment screening background checks these days is complete without an analysis of how social media is used for uncovering information about job candidates. In what is often referred to as **Web 2.0** – which, generally speaking, refers to the evolution of the web where social interactions and conversations can occur as opposed to Web 1.0 pages that viewers simply viewed. Recruiters and employers can harvest information from a variety of social networking sites like Facebook, Google+, and Twitter, and numerous other places where applicants may reveal themselves ranging from blogs and YouTube videos to business connection sites such as LinkedIn and search engines like Google. Many employers have focused with laser-like intensity on using the plentiful amount of information found online.

AUTHOR TIP This chapter discusses the use of social media only in the context of employee selection. However, employers also need to recognize that the use of social media, along with related privacy issue such as ownership of email and computers, are critical issues post-hire. Post-hire social media policies are beyond the scope of this book. However, since they are so critical in today's online world, every employer needs one. A starting place for employers to build a social media policyis the valuable information contained on the website for the National Labor Relations Board (NLRB) at http://mynlrb.nlrb.gov/link/document.aspx/09031d4580a22fc3.

The following are some of the more popular social media websites currently:

Most Popular Social Media Websites

Social Media Website	Estimated Users*
Facebook.com	900+ million
Twitter.com	500+ million
Google+	250+ million
LinkedIn.com	150+ million

* Statistics from Wikipedia.org as of July 2012

Employers have uncovered what appears to be a treasure trove of job applicant information on the Internet. Using search engines and social networking sites, they believe they are effectively able "to look under the hood" and try "to get into an applicant's head." Unlike traditional hiring tools such as interviews and contacting past employers, social networking sites hold out the promise of revealing the "real" job applicant. Statistics from various surveys and anecdotal evidence confirm there is an increased use of social media to screen candidates.

Firms providing this service may offer to go online for the employer and filter out any information that is either potentially discriminatory or not job related. This may be done by live researchers, or perhaps by automation, based upon key words and phrases. The advantage is that a third party firm undertakes the burden of looking for relevant information and at the same time relieves employers from the legal liability of viewing materials that are inappropriate. Of course, questions can arise as the ability of either human or computer software to actually evaluate what is real or relevant and to give each employer material that may be of particular relevance to them. These "social network background checks" will search social networking sites mentioned above and anywhere else on the Internet for information about job applicants, including things they may have put online years ago and completely forgotten about.

For employers, this can appear to be a valuable service. Failure to utilize these social networking sites when a search could have revealed relevant information could expose an employer to claims of negligent hiring. The argument is also made that many employers are already doing such searches informally and may not be following best practices to prevent potentially unlawful use of these sites. By outsourcing to a third party, an employer is shielding themselves from allegations of discrimination since they are not viewing potentially discriminatory or irrelevant information.

Are There Potential Legal Ramifications?

However, companies providing social network background checks present a number of challenging questions that HR professionals and recruiters will need to deal with. What is overlooked in the rush to use social media for employment screening background checks is a question that needs to be asked: **What are the legal risks for employers using the social media for employment screening?**

That question is hard to answer since another challenge for employers is the lack of certainty as to the boundaries and scope of legal use. As we will discuss in this chapter, the phenomenon of social networking sites has progressed much faster than case law or legislative action. It takes time for cases to develop and for legislatures to act. Not only that, but the websites themselves can modify access or even terms of use without notice, leading to further uncertainty.

Research Shows How Employers Use Internet for Screening

Below are examples of how employers are currently using social media sites.

Microsoft Study

On Data Privacy Day in January 2010, Microsoft released a commissioned research study that outlined the ways human resources professionals worldwide used personal, yet publicly available, online information when screening job candidates. Twelve hundred interviews were conducted for the study in the United States, United Kingdom (U.K.), Germany, and France. Some of the results raised eyebrows.

For example, 79 percent of HR professionals surveyed in the U.S. reported reviewing information found on the Internet when examining job candidates. In addition, 84 percent of the HR professionals surveyed in the U.S. categorized online reputation information as one of the top two factors they considered when reviewing a comprehensive set of candidate information.

The Microsoft study also found that employers were not only reviewing the information, they were acting on it, as 70 percent of those surveyed in the U.S. had rejected a candidate based on online information, with the top factor for rejection being unsuitable photos and videos online. The study revealed that HR professionals are regularly using information about candidates found on the Internet, which could have significant repercussions.

CareerBuilder.com Study

A 2012 survey conducted by job networking site CareerBuilder.com of more than 2,000 hiring managers revealed 37 percent of employers used social networking sites to research candidates. The survey also revealed 15 percent of the employers who did not research candidates on social media said their company prohibited the practice. In addition, 11 percent reported they did not currently use social media to screen but planned to start.

When hiring managers and human resource professionals were asked why they used social media to conduct background research, they survey found

- ✓ 65 percent said to see if the candidate presents himself/herself professionally.
- ✓ 51 percent said to see if the candidate is a good fit for the company culture.

- ✓ 45 percent said to learn more about the candidate's qualifications.
- ✓ 35 percent said to see if the candidate is well-rounded.
- ✓ 12 percent said to look for reasons not to hire the candidate.

As for whether social media was helping or hurting job candidates, more than one third – 34 percent – of survey respondents currently researching candidates via social media said they have found information, ranging from evidence of inappropriate behavior to information that contradicted their listed qualifications, which caused them not to hire a candidate

Source: http://cb.com/HQUCWt.

Journal of Applied Social Psychology

A February 2012 study in the Journal of Applied Social Psychology – *'Social Networking Websites, Personality Ratings, and the Organizational Context: More Than Meets the Eye?'* – claims that a quick review of social networking website (SNW) profile pages of job applicants on sites such as Facebook can be a better predictor of job success than standardized tests currently used by many human resources departments.

The authors of the study – Donald H. Kluemper (Department of Management, Northern Illinois University), Peter A. Rosen (Schroeder Family School of Business Administration, University of Evansville), and Kevin W. Mossholder (Department of Management, Auburn University) – examined the psycho-metric properties of the 'Big Five' personality traits assessed through social networking profiles in two studies of SNW users. The 'Big Five' traits examined were:

- ✓ Extraversion.
- ✓ Agreeableness.
- ✓ Conscientiousness.
- ✓ Emotional stability.
- ✓ Openness.

The study involved trained "raters" who spent five to ten minutes evaluating 274 Facebook pages of job candidates and answering questions related to personality. The researchers followed up six months later for performance reviews from the supervisors of 69 of the job candidates – approximately 25 percent of the original group – and found that the quick Facebook evaluations more accurately predicted success than standard tests. An excerpt from the study explains more:

> "Those high in agreeableness are trusting and get along well with others, which may be represented in the extensiveness of personal information posted. Openness to experience is related to intellectual curiosity and creativity, which could be revealed by the variety of books, favorite quotations or other posts showing the user engaged in new activities and creative endeavors. Extroverts more frequently interact with others, which could be represented by the number of SNW (social networking websites) friends a user has."

Source: http://onlinelibrary.wiley.com/doi/10.1111/j.1559-1816.2011.00881.x/pdf.

SHRM Survey Finds Employers Wary of Using Social Media Background Checks

An August 2011 survey from the Society of Human Resource Management (SHRM) – 'SHRM Survey Findings: The Use of Social Networking Websites and Online Search Engines in Screening Job Candidates' – found that, contrary to popular belief, only roughly one-quarter (26 percent) of organizations indicated they used online search engines such as Google to screen job candidates during the hiring process while even fewer organizations (18 percent) used social networking sites like Facebook for that purpose.

Conversely, the SHRM survey found that close to two-thirds (64 percent) of organizations had never used online search engines to screen job candidates or used them in the past but no longer did so, while more than two-thirds (71 percent) of organizations had never used social networking websites to screen job candidates or used them in the past but no longer did so. The reasons why some organizations did not use social networking websites to screen job candidates included the following:

- ✓ Two-thirds (66 percent) of organizations indicated they did not use social networking websites due to concerns about the legal risks/discovering information about protected characteristics such as age, race, gender, and religious affiliation.
- ✓ Nearly one half (48 percent) of organizations did not use these sites because they could not verify with confidence the information from the social networking website pages of job candidates.
- ✓ Another 45 percent of organizations indicated that the information found on the social networking sites may not be relevant to a job candidate's work-related potential or performance.

The survey also revealed a significant increase in the prevalence of formal or informal policies regarding the use of social networking websites to screen candidates over the past three years. While 72 percent of organizations had no formal or informal policies regarding the use of social networking websites for job screening in 2008, this figure has dropped to 56 percent in the more recent survey. In addition, 29 percent of organizations plan to implement a formal policy in the next 12 months, up from 11 percent in 2008.

As for how many organizations disqualified candidates based on information found by online search engines or social networking websites, of the small percentage of organizations that used such information only 15 percent of this group indicated that they used online search engine information to disqualify job candidates while 30 percent indicated they used social networking information to disqualify job candidates.

The SHRM survey 'The Use of Social Networking Websites and Online Search Engines in Screening' is at: www.shrm.org/research/surveyfindings/articles/pages/theuseofsocialnetworkingwebsitesandonlinesearchenginesinscreeni ngjobcandidates.aspx.

Landmines and Traps with Social Media Background Checks

This section takes an in-depth look at each of the potential risks when using these social media sites for screening job applicants.

1. Too Much Information (TMI) – Discrimination Allegations

Employers can find themselves in hot water when utilizing Internet search engines and social networking sites for screening due to allegations of discrimination. This issue is sometimes referred to as Too Much Information or TMI. The problem surfaces once an employer is aware an individual is a member of a protected group. It is difficult to claim the employer can "un-ring" the bell and forget the information. All hiring decisions need to be based upon information that is non-discriminatory and is a valid predictor for job performance.

When using the Internet for employment screening, recruiters could be accused of discrimination by disregarding online profiles of job candidates who are members of protected classes based on prohibited criteria. A job candidate may reveal information that reflects race, creed, color, nationality, ancestry, medical condition, disability (including AIDS), marital status, sex (including pregnancy), sexual preference, age (40+), or other facts an employer may not consider under federal law or state law. There may even be photos showing a physical condition that is protected by the Americans with Disabilities Act (ADA) or showing someone wearing garb suggesting their religious affiliation or national origin. All of these protected aspects of applicants may be revealed by a search of the Internet.

Of course, the analysis is complicated by the fact that the aggrieved job applicants may have placed the information on the web themselves. However, it would be challenging to suggest that a person somehow consented to discrimination by placing material on the web that was then used illegally by employers. Until Courts rule on these issues, employers can only try to apply established legal concepts to their online recruiting efforts.

A related issue is whether a firm is treating all applicants in a similar fashion. If employers are performing Internet searches on a hit or miss basis, with no written policy or standard approach, an applicant that is subject to adverse action as a result of such a search can potentially claim to be a victim of discrimination. Also problematic is that on social network sites, an employer may view photos, personal data, discussion of personal issues and political beliefs, behavior at parties, and other information that an applicant may not have intended for the world to see. If a site shows that an applicant has a tattoo or a piercing, employers may need to ask themselves whether having a tattoo is really a good reason not to hire someone.

The bottom line is once an employer is aware that an individual is a member of a protected group, they may be exposed to "failure to hire" law suits based upon discrimination or Equal Employment Opportunity Commission (EEOC) claims.

2. Too Little Information (TLI)

On the other hand, a failure to utilize all the available resources could potentially expose employers to lawsuits for negligent hiring if a victim could show that information was easily accessible online that could have prevented a hiring a person that was dishonest, unfit, dangerous, and unqualified, and it was foreseeable that some harm could occur. In other words, employers that do NOT use such websites can potentially be sued for not exercising due diligence. This is a case of Too Little Information (TLI).

For example, if an organization is hiring for a position that involves access to children, and a simple web search may have revealed the applicant belongs to a group or has written blogs that approve of inappropriate relationships with children, the employer could be at risk for a lawsuit by failing to go on a computer and locate the material. If the employee harms a child, and a lawsuit results, the victim's attorney could argue that the employer failed to exercise reasonable care given the fact that children are very vulnerable, and the employer should have known the applicant was inappropriate for the job.

Another related issue to the use of Web 2.0 and TLI is the ease with which less scrupulous job seekers can utilize the Internet to obtain worthless college diplomas from degree mills, as well as totally fabricated job histories. Job seekers use elaborate scams where fake accreditation agencies and live operators "verify" the fake information, or elaborate websites are set up to create fake past employers, as discussed in the chapter on Education Verifications. This can be a case of Too Little Information (TLI). The result is that employers may be placed in a "Catch-22" situation where they are in trouble if they do use such websites and are also in trouble if they do not.

The Ideal Job Candidate?

Stories from recruiters and Human Resources show why these sites are so enticing. One recruiter recounts how she had found "The Ideal Candidate" for a prestigious consulting firm. Then, just out of curiosity, she ran the applicant's phone number on a search engine, and up popped some rather explicit ads for discreet adult services that the applicant was apparently providing at night. Another recruiter tells the story of finding an applicant's MySpace page, where the intern had demonized his firm, his boss, and his coworkers in considerable detail and by name.

3. Credibility, Accuracy, and Authenticity Issues

Another issue is whether the information found on the Internet about job applicants is even credible, accurate, and authentic – in other words, true. How does the employer know it is true or just a matter of some people being silly with their friends? The authenticity issue can be that the person said it, but it was not true, or the applicant was not even the source or subject of the online information.

Employers should keep in mind that the idea behind social network sites is friends talking to friends, and users of these sites have been known to embellish. Employers may have to consider what a person says on their site and if true, whether it would be a valid predictor of job performance or whether it would be employment related at all. After all, people have been known to exaggerate or make things up. They may believe they are just having fun or spoofing their friends.

When using the Internet for employment screening, how do employers know for sure what is "real" on the Internet? How do employers know that the "name" they found is their applicant's name? They don't.

Even trickier is the issue of third party references to a candidate. If a recruiter or employer goes beyond material that appears to be authored by the applicant and begins relying upon blogs or pictures posted by others about the applicant, the employer is entering even more uncertain territories. A third party statement about an applicant is clearly "hearsay" in nature and is inherently subject to greater scrutiny. When a photograph that is problematic is posted of someone, there is an issue of whether there was permission to post and is it even your applicant.

If a CRA were to utilize third party comments, then another section of the FCRA comes into play. **FCRA section 606(d)(4)** requires extra precautions when a third party provides adverse information. In such a case, a CRA must either takes steps to insure that the source of information was the best source, or use reasonable procures to obtain an additional source of information from an additional source with independent direct knowledge. If a search of the Internet shows a criminal record, the CRA must also consider if **FCRA Section 613** applies, which also has special requirements.

4. "Computer Twins" & "Cyber-slamming"

With more than 300 million Americans today, most people have "computer twins," people with the same names and even a similar date of birth. There is also the question of how does a recruiter even know for sure the applicant actually wrote the item or authorized its posting?

Employers need to make sure what they see online actually refers to the applicant in question. There are anecdotes on the Internet of false postings under another person's name – a sort of "cyber identity theft."

If anonymous information is posted in a chat room, this may be the new phenomena of "Cyber-slamming," where a person can commit defamation without anyone knowing their real identity. Cyber-slamming is online smearing usually done anonymously and includes derogatory comments on websites or setting up a fake website that does not belong to the supposed owner.

For example, with practically no time or effort and at no cost, anyone can set up a blog masquerading as someone else and say anything they want. Short of filing a lawsuit against the Internet Service Provider (ISP) that hosts the blog, in order to obtain records showing the unique IP address of the computer, it is nearly impossible to trace down the person who actually posted the item. Even armed with the IP address, it is extremely difficult as a practical matter to then associate that IP address with a specified account or address, which may even require a second lawsuit.

Employers need to be careful that the site they are looking at actually refers to the applicant. In other words, if negative information about a candidate is found on the Internet or a social networking site, how is the employer supposed to verify that the information is accurate, up-to-date, authentic, and if it even belongs to or applies to the candidate in question?

5. Privacy Issues

Another problem with Internet background checks yet to be fully explored by the courts is privacy. Contrary to popular opinion, everything online is not necessarily "fair game" for employers.

On the other hand, if users do not adjust the privacy setting so their social network site is not easily available to an Internet search, those users may have a more difficult time arguing that there is a reasonable expectation of privacy.

In addition, the terms of use for many social network sites prohibit commercial use, and many users literally believe that their social network site is exactly that, a place to freely socialize. The argument would be that it is the community norm, and a generally accepted attitude, that social media sites are off limits to unwelcome visitors even if the door is left open. After all, burglars can hardly defend themselves on the basis that the front door to the house they stole from was unlocked so they felt they could just walk in.

The conventional wisdom, however, is that anything online is "fair game" because any reasonable person must understand the whole world has access to the Internet. Even though they communicate and share photos in a forum which can be public, there is sense that what goes on in social networking sites like MySpace or Facebook stays there and should stay there. This argument is buttressed by the fact that in order to enter some social networking sites, a user must agree to "terms of use" and to get details of another site member, the new user must set up their own account. Also, these types of websites have "terms of use" that typically do not allow "commercial" uses, which can include screening candidates. Since a user must jump through some hoops, it can be argued there is an expectation the whole world won't be privy to confidential information.

On the other hand, employers can argue that the routine "terms of use language" where someone simply hits the "I agree" button is not much of a privacy barrier. In addition, if an applicant fails to utilize the privacy controls provided by the website, this alone undercuts any reasonable belief that what was on the website would remain confidential.

One reason the use of social networking sites presents a risk stems from their original purpose. In the beginning, users intended to limit access to friends or members of their own network, arguably creating a reasonable expectation of privacy. It's like a "cyber high school," but instead of people seeing friends near lockers, they can see friends and make contacts all over the world. Younger workers in particular may regard invading their social network sites in the same way older workers may regard someone that crashes a private dinner party uninvited – a tasteless act that violates privacy.

This issue is far from being settled. The bottom line is that the question of whether an applicant has a reasonable expectation of privacy can depend upon the specific facts of the case being litigated, and the issue is far from settled. Frankly, it could be decided either way.

Until the courts sort this out, one thing does seem certain: If an employer uses subterfuge, such as creating a fake online identity to penetrate a social network site, the privacy line has probably been crossed.

6. Requiring Applicants to Provide Facebook or Other Social Media Passwords

One prime example of a privacy issue that has made news headlines recently is the practice by some employers of asking job applicants to provide login information such as usernames and passwords for their Facebook page and other social media websites. News stories have appeared concerning background checks in the digital age where prospective businesses, government agencies, and colleges are increasingly curious about the online life of potential workers and students. Below is one example.

Example of Privacy Issue

In 2009, Bozeman, Montana made international headlines when local media reported that the city government's background check had requested that job candidates provide their usernames and passwords for social networking sites for a few years. The background check form stated: *"Please list any and all current personal or business websites, web pages or memberships on any Internet-based chat rooms, social clubs or forums, to include, but not limited to: Facebook, Google, Yahoo, YouTube.com, MySpace, etc."*

Although the city said the information was not actually sought until a conditional job offer, overwhelmingly negative reactions to the city's policy raised privacy and free speech concerns for job applicants. A poll indicated 98 percent of respondents believed the city's policy had amounted to an invasion of privacy. The City of Bozeman later dropped the requirement until it conducted a more comprehensive evaluation of the practice. According to a press release: *"The extent of our request for a candidate's password, user name, or other internet information appears to have exceeded that which is acceptable to our community. We appreciate the concern many citizens have expressed regarding this practice and apologize for the negative impact this issue is having on the City of*

Bozeman." Although this is an evolving area of law, employers need to tread carefully in the area of social media background checks since they may open themselves up to discrimination claims if the social network site reveals an applicant's membership in a protected group such as race, nationality, ethnicity, religious afflation, marital status, and medical condition. Employers should also formulate clear policies and procedures to ensure they are looking for factors that are valid predictors of job performance. *(Sources: 'Want a job? Give Bozeman your Facebook, Google passwords' http://news.cnet.com/8301-13578_3-10268282-38.html & 'Bozeman to job seekers: We won't seek passwords' http://news.cnet.com/8301-13578_3-10269770-38.html).*

While it is common for some employers to review *publically available* Facebook, Twitter, and other social networking websites to learn about job candidates, many users have their social media profiles set to *'private'* which makes them available only to selected people or certain networks and more difficult for employers to view.

Although online privacy is an evolving area of law, employers need to tread carefully in the area of social media background checks since they may open themselves up to discrimination claims if the social network site reveals an applicant's membership in a protected group such as race, nationality, ethnicity, religious afflation, marital status, and medical condition. Employers should also formulate clear policies and procedures to ensure they are looking for factors that are valid predictors of job performance.

Unless an applicant is applying for a position that requires a security clearance, or public safety is involved, such as law enforcement, employers need to be very careful in asking applicants for their Facebook or other social media passwords. It is difficult to see how turning over such information is voluntary in the context of a job interview, where the choice is to hand it over or not get the job. If a lawsuit is filed, an applicant can allege an invasion of privacy by intrusion into private and personal information where an applicant had a reasonable expectation of privacy. The employer would then have the burden to demonstrate both that such a request was justified and that a less intrusive means to make the employment decision was not available. That could be a difficult standard for an employer to meet given all of the hiring tools at an employer's disposal.

Facebook Warns Employers Asking Job Applicants for Social Media Passwords May Expose Businesses to Legal Liability

Responding to an increase in reports of employers seeking to gain "inappropriate access" to social network profiles of job applicants, online social media giant Facebook issued a warning to employers in a recent blog posted on the company website – 'Protecting Your Passwords and Your Privacy' – that the practice of asking job applicants for their social media passwords "undermines the privacy expectations and the security of both the user and the user's friends" and could potentially expose businesses to "unanticipated legal liability."

In a blog dated March 23, 2012, Erin Egan, Facebook's Chief Privacy Officer, responded to recent news reports of employers "seeking to gain inappropriate access" to the social media profiles of job applicants and employees. She also said that Facebook would "take action to protect the privacy and security" of users and consider "initiating legal action" where appropriate. The entire blog is below:

"Protecting Your Passwords and Your Privacy

In recent months, we've seen a distressing increase in reports of employers or others seeking to gain inappropriate access to people's Facebook profiles or private information. This practice undermines the privacy expectations and the security of both the user and the user's friends. It also potentially exposes the employer who seeks this access to unanticipated legal liability.

The most alarming of these practices is the reported incidences of employers asking prospective or actual employees to reveal their passwords. If you are a Facebook user, you should never have to share your password, let anyone access your account, or do anything that might jeopardize the security of your account or violate the privacy of your friends. We have worked really hard at Facebook to give you the tools to control who sees your information.

As a user, you shouldn't be forced to share your private information and communications just to get a job. And as the friend of a user, you shouldn't have to worry that your private information or communications will be revealed to someone you don't know and didn't intend to share with just because that user is looking for a job. That's why we've made it a violation of Facebook's Statement of Rights and Responsibilities to share or solicit a Facebook password.

We don't think employers should be asking prospective employees to provide their passwords because we don't think it's right the thing to do. But it also may cause problems for the employers that they are not anticipating. For example, if an employer sees on Facebook that someone is a member of a protected group (e.g. over a certain age, etc.) that employer may open themselves up to claims of discrimination if they don't hire that person.

Employers also may not have the proper policies and training for reviewers to handle private information. If they don't—and actually, even if they do–the employer may assume liability for the protection of the information they have seen or for knowing what responsibilities may arise based on different types of information (e.g. if the information suggests the commission of a crime).

Facebook takes your privacy seriously. We'll take action to protect the privacy and security of our users, whether by engaging policymakers or, where appropriate, by initiating legal action, including by shutting down applications that abuse their privileges.

While we will continue to do our part, it is important that everyone on Facebook understands they have a right to keep their password to themselves, and we will do our best to protect that right.

– Erin Egan, Chief Privacy Officer, Policy"

The blog is available at: www.facebook.com/notes/facebook-and-privacy/protecting-your-passwords-and-your-privacy/326598317390057.

Can Employers Demand to See Employees' and Applicants' Facebook Pages?

By Stephen J. Hirschfeld, Curiale Hirschfeld Kraemer LLP, CEO Employment Law Alliance &

Kristin L. Oliveira, Curiale Hirschfeld Kraemer LLP

It has been reported that some employers are requiring job applicants to disclose their login information and passwords in order to access Facebook and other private information housed on social media. It has long been known that interviewers troll the Internet to obtain publicly-available information about a candidate as part of a background check. But now, as more people are making their social media profiles private, employers are requesting login information from prospective candidates in order to see their profiles. Some hiring managers are directing candidates to access their private accounts on the employer's computer and then "shoulder-surfing" the candidate's photographs, posts, and "tweets."

Motivations for Accessing Private Social Media Accounts

Why are some employers now resorting to reviewing social media sites or searching the Internet as part of their background check on applicants?

Most employers today are reluctant to provide meaningful references for fear of being sued for defamation. For example, California prohibits employers from intentionally interfering with former employees' attempts to find jobs by giving false or misleading references. While the law in most states permits an applicant to sue for defamation if the statements made by his or her former employer as part of a job reference are false and contributed to the candidate not receiving the position, the reality is that very few such lawsuits have been filed across the country. However, many employers resort to providing only 'name, rank and serial number' for former employees or simply say "no comment." Consequently, future employers have little meaningful data about an employee's performance or workplace demeanor to make an informed hiring decision.

Second, many employers are concerned about being held liable for failing to conduct a full and complete background check out of fear that one of their applicants – who had a history of misconduct that wasn't uncovered during the background check – repeats that conduct once again after being hired. These "negligent hiring" lawsuits, however, are still relatively rare. The theory behind these claims is based upon the notion that had the employer conducted a sufficient background check, it could have prevented later harm by never hiring the applicant in the first place.

The question of whether an employer could actually be held liable for failing to insist upon reviewing password-protected social media accounts is far from settled leaving many with legitimate concerns.

Finally, the sad reality is that resume fraud appears to be on the rise. Many employers have come to realize that applicants whom they have already hired have either fabricated work experience or education or greatly exaggerated/embellished credentials. Employers are seeking new ways to combat this trend.

The Legal Consequences of Requiring Access to Private Social Media Accounts

Numerous legal issues are triggered when employers require applicants to provide access to this information. Discrimination claims are one of the biggest concerns. For example, an employer might learn information about an applicant (such as their marital status, religion, sexual orientation or ethnicity) which might later allow that individual, if they are not hired, to contend said information is the reason why they weren't ultimately hired. Learning that a candidate either recently became pregnant or is planning to – whether held against that individual or not – can form the basis of a discrimination claim. Once the employer is on notice of a trait or characteristic learned from social media, they subject themselves to the very same claim that would be brought if identical information had been learned during an interview. The major difference – one that could be viewed very differently by a trier of fact – is that this information will have been obtained involuntarily by requiring Facebook credentials as opposed to perhaps voluntarily disclosed by the candidate.

Employers also subject themselves to claims that the applicant's right of privacy was invaded. Some states such as California afford a constitutional right of privacy that applies to private entities. Although it has not been tested in the Facebook context, a California applicant may have a viable claim that requiring the disclosure of a confidential password – which allows access to private, personal information – constitutes an invasion of privacy. Other states may allow such a claim to proceed based upon some type of common law invasion of privacy cause of action. Regardless of the type of claim, a court will first look at whether the applicant had a reasonable expectation of privacy. The only possible way to lower and perhaps eliminate that expectation, and potentially avoid such a claim, is to be explicit in places like job advertisements and applications that disclosure and access to private social media sites is a condition of being considered for hire.

In addition, some states have laws that prohibit employers from making adverse decisions based on off-duty lawful conduct. For instance, under New York law, employers cannot refuse to hire an individual based on his off-duty recreational activities, certain political activities, and the use of legal consumable products. While there does not appear to be a court decision directly on this point, it does not seem far-fetched that an applicant may pursue a claim under this or other similar statutes.

An employer's request for access to personal electronic accounts clearly violates one state law. On May 2, 2012, Maryland became the first state to outlaw such a practice with the "User Name and Password Privacy Protection Act." Effective in October of this year, that new law will prohibit an employer from requesting or requiring that "an employee or applicant disclose any user name, password, or other means for accessing a personal account or service through an electronic communications device." It precludes an employer from discharging or otherwise penalizing any employee who refuses to provide this information with some exceptions.

Finally, there is legal authority for the proposition that coercing employees to divulge passwords violates an existing federal statute – the Stored Communications Act (SCA). The SCA is violated when one intentionally accesses electronic information without authorization. The Ninth Circuit Court of Appeals recently found that an employee had a cognizable legal claim under the SCA when his employer accessed a secure website that contained criticisms of management using someone else's login information. *Pietrylo v. Hillstone Restaurant Group d/b/a Houston's*, 2009 U.S. Dist. LEXIS 88702 (D.N.J., September 25, 2009).

In March, Senators Charles Schumer and Richard Blumenthal asked the Department of Justice (DOJ) to investigate whether employers who ask for Facebook passwords are violating the SCA or the Computer Fraud and Abuse Act (CFAA). The CFAA makes it a crime for current or former employees to intentionally access a protected computer issued or owned by their employer "without authorization" or in a manner that "exceeds authorized access," resulting in damage and loss. The DOJ has not yet issued an opinion. Nonetheless, employers face a risk of violating the SCA or CFAA if they request confidential social media credentials and use that information to login into secure websites.

State And Federal Legislative Actions To Watch

In addition to Maryland, 12 other states, including California and New York, have moved to limit employers' rights to access social media. Illinois stands to be the second state to bar employers from seeking social media passwords with its pending "Right to Privacy in the Workplace Act."

Congress has also moved swiftly to respond to this practice. Recently, House Democrats introduced "The Password Protection Act of 2012" and Senator Blumenthal introduced a companion bill in the Senate with identical prohibitions. These bills would amend the Computer Fraud and Abuse Act and prohibit employers from:

✓ Forcing prospective or current employees to provide access to their own private account as a condition of employment;
✓ Discriminating or retaliating against a prospective or current employee because that employee refuses to provide access to a password-protected account; and
✓ Engaging in an adverse employment action as a consequence of an employee's failure to provide access to his/her own private accounts.

The Password Protection Act of 2012, as currently written, preserves the rights of employers to:
✓ Permit social networking within the office on a voluntary basis;
✓ Set policies for employer-operated computer systems; and
✓ Hold employees accountable for stealing data from their employers.

Both bills establish what may be viewed as a right of workplace privacy, prohibiting employers access to private employee data under any circumstances, even if the employer uses its own computers to access that data.

Another piece of proposed federal legislation in the House is the "Social Networking Online Protection Act" offered in April. This would prohibit employers and schools from requiring or requesting that employees and certain other individuals provide a user name, password, or other means for accessing a personal account on any social networking website.

Several states are moving forward with legislative measures. Delaware is considering "The Workplace Privacy Act." It would make it unlawful for employers to mandate that an employee or applicant disclose password or account information that would grant the access to their social networking profile or account. It would also prohibit employers from requesting that employees or applicants log onto their respective social networking profiles or accounts to provide the employer direct access.

California is considering a ban on requests for social media information. Assembly Bill 1844, introduced in February, would bar an employer from requiring an employee or applicant to disclose a username or account password to access a personal social media account that is exclusively used by the employee or prospective employee. California is also considering the "Social Media Privacy Act." In this proposed bill, public and private employers (as well as postsecondary educational institutions) are precluded from threatening an individual with or taking specified pecuniary actions (e.g., discharge, discipline, or otherwise penalize) for refusing to disclose permissibly requested information related to their personal social media account. Employers may request, but not require, an employee to provide access to a personal social media account to aid in an investigation concerning allegations of harassment, discrimination, intimidation or potential violence.

Practical Considerations and Conclusion

Employers have legitimate concerns as to whether they are obtaining the information they need to make a fully informed decision about candidates they are interested in hiring. At the same time, they need to be mindful that there are legal risks if they attempt to obtain information from password protected social media sites. Beyond this, employers need to seriously consider what these actions say about their corporate culture. Given the proliferation of social media usage in this country and in light of how important the new entrants into the workforce feel about their ability to communicate and express themselves this way, an employer may be hindering its ability to attract the best and brightest applicants by using these methods.

Employers need to decide if already existing procedures for conducting extensive, legal background checks are sufficient methods for obtaining needed information, or if more aggressive means need to be employed.

Stephen J. Hirschfeld is a founding partner at Curiale Hirschfeld Kraemer LLP and the CEO of the San Francisco-based Employment Law Alliance – a network of more than 3,000 labor and employment attorneys worldwide. Kristin L. Oliveira is Of Counsel at Curiale Hirschfeld Kraemer LLP. They can be reached at shirschfeld@chklawyers.com and koliveira@chklawyers.com respectively, or via the firm's website: http://www.chklawyers.com.

7. Legal "Off Duty" Conduct

Yet another issue is legal off-duty conduct. If a social media search reveals legal off duty conduct, a candidate can claim they were the victims of illegal discrimination. A number of states protect workers engaged in legal off-duty conduct and have prohibitions limiting use of private behavior for employment decisions. However, employers do have broader discretion if such behavior would damage a company, hurt business interests, or be inconsistent with business needs.

8. What is "Fair Game" on the Internet?

Employers should not simply assume that anything on the web is "fair game" and freely available without consequence. One area where an employer would be flirting with particular trouble is if information from Facebook or MySpace is obtained by manipulating the sites. This could be done by creating multiple identities or by using "pretexting," which can include pretending to be someone else or something you are not.

For example, Facebook allows greater access into sites within the user's own network. If an employer were to violate Facebook rules and create fake identities just to join a network belonging to a job applicant, that would likely cross over into the realm of employer behavior that is overly intrusive and invades too deeply into private matters.

Example of "Fair Game" Issue

Suppose a recruiter or HR professional attended a convention, and after a long day of listening to speakers or walking the trade show, the recruiter has drinks with colleagues from different firms. Soon the talk turns to professional subjects, such as how they like their co-workers, their boss, or their company. Of course, at such an informal conversation, no one has signed a Non-disclosure agreement and everyone is talking in a public place. Then suppose one of the recruiter's professional acquaintances proceeds to take what the recruiter considered a private exchange of information between professionals and placed the recruiter's more colorful and derogatory comments on a blog for the world to see. Would the recruiter be offended?

Yes. Most reasonable people under such a circumstance would be appalled. Generally accepted standards of normal behavior would dictate that the conversation was meant to be private, even though there was no agreement not to make the information public, even though the conversation took place in a public place. Many people feel the same about their statements made on Internet social media sites. Not everything online is "fair game."

Legal Risks for Employers Using Social Media for Employment Screening

The use of social networking sites to obtain deeper levels of information on job applicants is not without legal risk. Such efforts can potentially raise issues of discrimination, invasion of privacy, improper use of legal off duty conduct, as well as issues relating to authenticity and accuracy.

Uncertainty Abounds as Courts and Legislators have not Caught Up with Social Media

Part of the risk of using social media is because the area is so new that courts and legislators have not yet entered into the act. Ground rules can change at any time without notice. This has created a feeling of uncertainty for employers and labor lawyers.

At the time this book was written, there is very little in the way of court cases on point. There are cases in the education arena revolving around tenure and academic freedom where information on a social networking site was involved and cases involving current employees. However, there are no court decisions yet on the exact issue of the use of the Internet for applicant recruiting and selection. It takes time for an aggrieved party to first file a lawsuit, and then the lawsuit has to go before an appellate court on some issue in order to get a ruling. Of course, each case is very fact specific, so the outcome of a particular case may or may not have broad implications.

Neither Congress nor state legislatures, with the exception of Maryland (see below), have taken any official action on this issue either. The last time Congress passed a law that arguably impacts this area was in 1986 with the Stored Communications Act (SCA), back in the days of dial up modems and well before the advent of the World Wide Web as we currently know it.

Senators' Letter About Business Practices

In September 2011, the dangers of using social networking sites was recognized by two members of the United States Senate – Senator Richard Blumenthal (D-Connecticut) and Senator Al Franken (D-Minnesota) – in a letter sent to a background screening firm that specializes in reviewing and storing social networking data for employment background checks.

Senators Blumenthal and Franken requested information about the business practices of the company as they relate to personal privacy and were concerned that the company's collection of online and social media information about job applicants and distribution of that information to potential employers. Their letter addressed concerns if the firm's services could contain inaccurate information, invade consumers' right to privacy online, violate the terms of service agreements of the websites from which the company culls data, and infringe upon intellectual property rights.

The Senators were also concerned that there are numerous scenarios under which a job applicant could be unfairly harmed by the information the company provides to an employer.

The questions the Senators asked in their letter are shown below. They provide an excellent set of criteria for employers to consider.

Accuracy of Information

1. How does your company determine the accuracy of the information it provides to employers?
2. Does your company have procedures in place for applicants to dispute information contained in the reports your company produces? If so, what are these procedures?
3. Is your company able to differentiate among applicants with common names? How?
4. Is your company able to determine whether information it finds on a website is parody, defamatory, or otherwise false? How?
5. Does your company accord less weight to certain sources of information that may be inaccurate, such as community-edited websites like Wikipedia?
6. Search engines like Google often provide archived versions of websites; these cached web pages may contain false information that was later updated. Search engines also provide "mirrors" of websites, like Wikipedia or blog articles; these mirrored pages may be archives of inaccurate information that has since been corrected. Is your company able to determine whether information it is providing is derived from an archived version of an inaccurate website? How?

Consumers' Right to Online Privacy

1. Does your company require the consent of a job applicant before conducting a background check on the applicant? If so, who requests the applicant's consent: your company, or the potential employer? Based on your experience with employers, does an applicant's refusal to consent to a background check by your company damage his or her eligibility for a job?
2. Does your company specify to employers and/or job applicants where it searches for information—e.g., Facebook, Google, Twitter?
3. Is the information that your company collects from social media websites like Facebook limited to information that can be seen by everyone, or does your company endeavor to access restricted information, for example by creating a Facebook profile with the same city and/or alma mater of an applicant, in an attempt to see information restricted by geographical or university network? Has your company ever endeavored to access a user's restricted information by joining the user's network of "friends" on sites like Facebook?
4. Companies like Google and Facebook have faced scrutiny in the past for making public portions of their users' information that the users had set as private, often without the consent of users. This has resulted in previously private information, such as pictures, being made publicly available against the wishes of the users. Users are then required to opt out of sharing information they had previously thought to be private. Does your company include such information in its reports?
5. If your company conducts multiple background checks on an applicant, to what extent does it reuse information it has collected in previous checks? If your company were to gain access to private information in a manner contemplated in the previous question, and found that it no longer had access to such information in a subsequent search, would it include the previously accessed information in subsequent reports?

Terms of Service and Intellectual Property Violations

1. The reports that your company prepares for employers contain screenshots of the sources of the information your company compiles. One publicly available report contains pictures of a user's Facebook profile, LinkedIn profile, blog posts for a previous employer, and personal websites. These websites are typically governed by terms of service agreements that prohibit the collection, dissemination, or sale of users' content without the consent of the user and/or the website. LinkedIn's user agreement, for example, states that one may not "rent, lease, loan, trade, sell/re-sell access to LinkedIn or any information therein, or the equivalent, in whole or in part." Your company's business model seems to necessitate violating these agreements. Does your company operate in compliance with the agreements found on sites whose content your company compiles and sells? If so, how?

2. More troubling than the apparent disregard of these websites' terms of service are what appear to be significant violations of users' intellectual property rights to control the use of the content that your company collects and sells. Your company includes pictures in its background reports; example reports have included a picture depicting the subject holding a gun to illustrate alleged "potentially violent behavior." These pictures, taken from sites like Flickr and Picasa, are often licensed by the owner for a narrow set of uses, such as noncommercial use only or a prohibition on derivative works. Does your company obtain permission from the owners of these pictures to use, sell, or modify them?"

The full text of the letter is available at: www.blumenthal.senate.gov/newsroom/press/release/blumenthal-franken-call-on-social-intelligence-corp-to-clarify-privacy-practice

The FCRA and Use of Social Media Sites

Employers should realize that background firms using social media information must follow the federal Fair Credit Reporting Act (FCRA) rules regulating the collection, dissemination, and use of consumer information. A June 2011 blog on the Federal Trade Commission (FTC) website, 'The Fair Credit Reporting Act & Social Media: What Businesses Should Know,' indicated that background checks using information found with online search engines and on social networking sites must follow the same FCRA rules that apply to the more traditional information that FCRA compliant background screening firms and employers have used in the past.

The FTC blog (available at business.ftc.gov/blog/2011/06/fair-credit-reporting-act-social-media-what-businesses-should-know) includes the following paragraph to remind users of Internet background checks of their duty to comply with the FCRA:

> *Employment background checks can include information from a variety of sources: credit reports, employment and salary history, criminal records – and these days, even social media. But regardless of the type of information in a report you use when making hiring decisions, the rules are the same. Companies providing reports to employers – and employers using reports – must comply with the Fair Credit Reporting Act.*

Under the FCRA section 603(f), a CRA can be a third party firm that engages in the "assembling or evaluation" of consumers for employment. When a firm is reviewing the Internet to create a report about a job applicant's online information for purpose of employment, this is clearly a background report (also known as a "consumer report") under the FCRA. This means that these types of services are essentially background checking firms with all of the same legal duties and obligations of any other background check firm. Therefore, such sites need to have full FCRA compliance, including client certifications under FCRA section 604 as well as adverse action notices and numerous other obligations such as re-investigation upon request. Background checking is subject to heavy legal regulation.

Although employers may request background screening firms perform this function, there are a number of drawbacks.

1. First, a background screening firm does not have the same in-depth knowledge the employer has of the details of the position.

2.   If a social network background check is done by a background screening firm, the search falls under the federal Fair Credit Reporting Act (FCRA) which requires a background screening firm to maintain reasonable procedures for maximum possible accuracy.

3.   If a website is searched by a background screening firm on behalf of an employer, then consent and certain disclosures are mandated under the federal Fair Credit Reporting Act (FCRA).

4.   A background screening firm performing the search falls under the Accuracy and Relevancy requirements of the FCRA.

FCRA Section 607(b) sets forth in no uncertain terms the duty of a CRA to be accurate. The section reads:

(b) *Accuracy of report*. Whenever a consumer reporting agency prepares a consumer report it shall follow reasonable procedures to assure maximum possible accuracy of the information concerning the individual about whom the report relates.

That section means that the accuracy requirement applies to both the information reported and the duty to ensure it is being reported about the right person. Congress drove this point home even further in statement of Congressional findings and statement of purpose contained in section 602:

(b) *Reasonable procedures*. It is the purpose of this title to require that consumer reporting agencies adopt reasonable procedures for meeting the needs of commerce for consumer credit, personnel, insurance, and other information in a manner which is fair and equitable to the consumer, with regard to the confidentiality, accuracy, *relevancy*, and proper utilization of such information in accordance with the requirements of this title. (Emphasis added.)

The use of the word *relevancy* in the FCRA further underscores the need for a background check firm to ensure that reasonable steps are taken to only report information relevant to the consumer.

The issue is that it is inherently difficult for a background check firm to know if the information online was authored or authorized by the applicant or applies to the applicant.

Another issue is if a consumer disputes an item on a social networking site was authored by the applicant, the Consumer Reporting Agency would have barriers in the dispute process.

5.   Under FCRA Section 611, any consumer can dispute the accuracy contents of a consumer report. The CRA then has 30 days (and no more than 45 if a consumer provides supplemental information) to either verify the accuracy of the data or, if unable to do so, remove it. If a consumer disagrees with information from a social networking site, the question arises as to how a CRA can verify that such material belongs to the applicant. Trying to locate what is "real" in the cyber world is very tricky. Although every computer has an "IP" address, as a practical matter it is very difficult to locate the precise location of an actual computer short of issuing subpoena as part of a lawsuit. Even if the actual computer is found, there can be an additional issue of who was using it if it was at public location.

As a result, a CRA may end up having to remove the material from the social networking report if there is dispute because of the difficulty of proving it was the consumer who made the entry.

A strong argument can be made that a CRA that inserts information in a consumer report that it knows, or reasonably should know, cannot withstand a request for re-investigation and would have to be removed, would be a violation of the FCRA's accuracy requirements. In other words, a CRA should not place in a report anything it cannot defend if a request for a re-investigation is made.

Because a background screening firm has no way of knowing if the online information is accurate, authentic, or even belongs to the job applicant in question, it is difficult for background screening firms to perform this service consistent with the FCRA. In other words, due to the FCRA, background screening firms may not be best suited to perform these types of 'social network background checks.'

Employers should carefully consider the pros and cons of outsourcing this task to a background screening firm. The solution may be that employers should do the search in-house utilizing approaches and techniques outlined later in this chapter.

The Fine Print

There is limited law or statutes governing the use of social media cites for pre-employment screening. There is the federal Stored Communications Act (SCA), a federal law enacted as part of the Electronic Communications Privacy Act (See: 18 U.S.C. §§ 2701 to 2712), which deals with voluntary and compelled disclosure of "stored wire and electronic communications and transactional records" that are stored by third-party Internet service providers (ISPs). However, that law was passed in 1986 when computer users were still utilizing dial up modems.

When a new area of law develops, it takes time for legal precedent to be developed. Lawsuits must first be filed, and then litigated with a losing party taking an appeal to a higher court. That takes time.

Another issue is that human resources and labor law issues are heavily regulated by state laws, so when court cases begin to appear or legislation is enacted, it may turn out to be a patchwork of various state rules.

It's also worth noting that some of the issues in play in this area rely upon the terms of use of various websites. So if a social media site indicated that the site is for non-commercial use, it can affect the calculus of piracy unless it is shown that such a restriction is just boilerplate and not enforced in any way. Of course, terms of use can change at a moment's notice, adding another level of complexity.

At this point, given there is little in the way of legal precedent or legislative mandate, the best that can be done is to take known existing laws and legal principals and project them forward to determine how and where they may apply to using social networking for recruiting and hiring. However, this is an area that needs to be followed closely as any day, a new court case can be handed down that may significantly alter our view of how to proceed in this area.

But Maryland has drawn first blood.

Solutions if Using Social Media Background Checks

Solutions for using the Internet for background checks fall into three categories:

1. Solutions for Employers
2. Solutions for Recruiters
3. Solutions for Job Applicants

1. Solutions for Employers

The considerations for employers using the Internet are different than recruiters.

For employers who want to use social network sites to screen a candidate and do not want to use a background screening firm, the safest path is to obtain consent from the candidate first and only search once there has been a conditional job offer to that candidate. This procedure helps ensure that impermissible information was not considered before the employer evaluates a candidate using permissible tools such as interviews, job-related employment tests, references from supervisors, and a background check. In other words, it demonstrates that an employer used permissible criteria that were objective and neutral as to protected classes.

At that point, after using permissible screening tools, the reason for employers to search social networking sites would be to ensure there is nothing that would eliminate the person for employment.

This approach is also is consistent with the Americans with Disabilities Act of 1990 (the "ADA") and similar state laws. Under the ADA, an employer may only inquire about medically related information once there has been a real job offer. Per the EEOC:

A job offer is real if the employer has evaluated all relevant non-medical information which it reasonably could have obtained and analyzed prior to giving the offer. (From: www.eeoc.gov/policy/docs/preemp.html)

By analogy, waiting until there has been a job offer helps to guard against an inference that an employer was using impressible criteria in deciding who was finalist.

Reasons for an employer eliminating an applicant for employment or withdrawing the job offer would then need to be based upon the use of social networking and Internet searches which showed an applicant engaging in behavior that damages the company, hurts business interests, or is inconsistent with business needs.

Example of such behavior could include matters such as:

✓ Disparaging a co-worker or supervisor during past employment;
✓ Engaging in online harassment;
✓ Admitting illegal conduct;
✓ Information showing dishonest behavior;
✓ Information showing falsehoods in the application or interview process; or
✓ Information on the web that shows poor judgment or communication skills.

This is not a complete list, but what all of these factors have in common is that there is a clear nexus between what is found online and the job. In other words, there is a rational and articulable business justification.

Another method employers may use is to have a person in-house not connected to any hiring decisions review social network sites in order to ensure impermissible background screening information is not given to the decisions maker. The in-house background screening should also have training in the non-discriminatory use of background screening information, knowledge of the job description, and use objective methods that are the same for all candidates for each type of position.

That way only permissible information is transmitted to the person that is making the decision. Again, this is best done post-offer but pre-hire and with consent. An employer may be looking for online information concerning job suitability. For example, did the potential employee say derogatory things about past employers or co-workers or demonstrate that he or she is not the best candidate for the job.

To minimize the risks of using the Internet for background checks, employers should take the following steps when considering using search engines or social network sites for screening:

✓ Using the Internet to screen candidates is not risk-free, especially when it comes to social networking sites. News travels fast on the web, and employers who rely too much upon social networking sites may find that job applicants are not as eager to look at their firm.
✓ If an employer uses social media searches, they should first consult their attorney in order to develop a written policy and fair and non-discriminatory procedures designed to locate information that is a valid predictor of job performance and non-discriminatory. Employers should focus on objective criteria and metrics as much as possible.
✓ Employers should have written job descriptions that contain the essential functions of the job, as well as the knowledge, skills, and ability (KSA) required for the job.
✓ The employer should have ongoing and documented training on how to avoid discriminatory hiring practices.
✓ As a general rule, the later in the hiring process social media searches are used, the less open an employer may be to suggestions that matters viewed on the Internet were used in a discriminatory fashion. The most conservative approach is to not use the Internet for a social media search until AFTER there has been a conditional job offer to demonstrate that all applicants were considered utilizing legal criteria.
✓ Employers need to be concerned if information found online is potentially discriminatory to job candidates who are members of protected classes based on prohibited criteria such as: race, creed, color, sex (including

pregnancy), ancestry, nationality, medical condition, disability, marital status, sexual preference, or age (40+). All of these protected criteria may be revealed by a social media search.

✓ Employers need to be concerned if information found on the Internet violates state laws concerning legal "off duty" conduct.

✓ For legal protection, the most conservative approach is to perform a social media search only after consent from the job applicant and a job offer is made contingent upon completion of a background check that is satisfactory to the employer.

✓ Employers should not use any fake identities or engage in "pretexting" to gain access to information online.

✓ Whatever an employer's policy is regarding social media searches, it should be written. For employers that recruit at college, there is a trend to require employers to notify students ahead of time as to their policy for searching the Internet for an applicant's online identity.

✓ Employers should also consider the use of a person in-house not connected to hiring decisions to review social media sites in order to ensure impermissible or discriminatory information is not given to decision makers. The in-house reviewer should also have training in the non-discriminatory use of online information, knowledge of the job description, and use objective methods that are the same for all job candidates for each type of position. That way only permissible information is transmitted to the person making the decision. The person in-house conducting the review is on the other side of an "ethics" wall from any decision maker and helps prevent allegations that impermissible information was used in the hiring process.

✓ As an additional protection, an employer may consider having the in-house reviewer first contact the applicant with any potential information found online before it is passed along to the decision maker in order to allow the applicant the opportunity to dispute the accuracy or applicability of the information.

2. Solutions for Recruiters

If recruiters use social media for background screening, they should realize that much of the 'new media' available to them for background screening is still covered by current employment regulations.

Recruiters in the sourcing stage may want to consider having a clear internal policy and documented training that Internet sourcing is not being used in violation of federal and state discrimination laws and only factors that are valid predictors of job performance will be considered, taking into account the job description, and the Knowledge, Skills, and Abilities (KSA) required for the position. It also helps to have objective and documented methods and metrics on how to source and screen on the Internet.

Recruiters considering using social media in the sourcing stage may want to consider some of the following:

✓ Ensure each position has a detailed job description written for that specific position that clearly lays out the essential functions of the job and the knowledge, skills, and abilities (KSA) required for the position.

✓ Have a clear internal policy that Internet sourcing is NOT being used in violation of federal and state discrimination laws and only factors that are a valid predictor of job performance will be considered, taking into account the job description and the KSA required for the job.

✓ Have documented training on legal recruiting techniques. The training should include clear information on what would constitute a discriminatory practice.

✓ Have a clear procedure that outlines key words, criteria, and methodology for sourcing, so recruiters can demonstrate that they are searching for objective requirements to be considered as part of the pool. Even better is if the criteria being used can be measured or have a metric attached.

✓ If someone meets the objective requirements but is not placed in the pool of potential candidates for other reasons, a recruiter may want to note why the exception is being made. For example, if the social networking website demonstrated behavior inconsistent with business interests, that should be noted.

Recruiters can also argue that if a passive job candidate not actively looking for work is passed over because of discriminatory criteria revealed on a social network site, the candidate is not harmed since they did not even know they were disregarded and are none the wiser. The problem with that approach is three-fold.

✓ First, discrimination and civil rights laws would likely still apply, even in recruiting passive candidates.

✓ Second, there are few secrets in the world. If a firm is using discriminatory criteria, a member of the recruiting team who feels uncomfortable about such a practice may well say something – either publicly on the web or within the organization.

✓ Third, it can be argued that discriminatory criteria were being used if it turns out that the entire workforce happens to be homogeneous and does not include members of protected classes. Such a statistical anomaly could suggest a pattern of discrimination.

3. Solutions for Job Applicants

For job applicants, the advice is simple: Don't be the last to know what a web search about you would reveal. If job applicants do not want employers looking at their social networking site, then they should set the privacy parameter to "restricted use only." Savvy applicants can even go on the offense and create an online presence that helps them get a job. More information in this subject can be found in Chapters 30 and 31.

Social Network Screening by Employers May Make Companies Unattractive to Job Applicants

Employers that implement online screening practices such as social networking searches through social media sites like Facebook may be unattractive or reduce their attractiveness to job applicants and current employees alike, according to research from a study conducted on the effects of social media screening in the workplace presented at the 27th Annual Society for Industrial and Organizational Psychology (SIOP) Conference in San Diego in April 2012.

In the study by North Carolina State University (NCSU) coauthors Will Stoughton, Lori Foster Thompson, and Adam Meade: *"175 students applied for a fictitious temporary job they believed to be real and were later informed they were screened. Applicants were less willing to take a job offer after being screened, perceiving the action to reflect on the organization's fairness and treatment of employees based on a post-study questionnaire. They also felt their privacy was invaded."*

Stoughton, a doctoral candidate in industrial and organizational psychology at NCSU, said that studies show nearly two out of three employers – sixty-five percent – screen job applicants through social networking websites. While organizations may practice social network screening to find the best applicants, the study found that *"the social network screening process actually reduces an organization's attractiveness for the applicant and likely the incumbent worker."*

Stoughton said while employers typically look on sites like Facebook or Google for pictures of alcohol or drug-related use and remarks about previous employers or co-workers to weed out bad job applicants, screening social networks doesn't always accomplish the intended goal: "By doing this, you assume the applicants that organizations end up choosing are more conscientious, but no studies show that these individuals are any better," he said. "They could actually be eliminating better applicants."

For more information, read the article 'Judging a Facebook by Its Cover' on the SIOP website at www.siop.org/article_view.aspx?article=991.

Bottom Line with Social Media Background Checks: Proceed with Caution

Employers need to be very careful when it comes to harvesting information about job candidates from the web's social media. Employers need to know how to protect themselves against allegations of discrimination and issues with authenticity, accuracy, credibility, and privacy if no further action is taken after the discovery on the Internet that a person is a member of a protected class or when finding negative information. How and when an employer obtains such information is critical.

At this point in the evolution of social networking, there are no published cases yet on point. Lawsuits take time to work their way through the courts until an appellate court is finally called upon to issue an opinion. However, it is all but certain that someday an employer will land in court being sued on allegations of discrimination or a violation of privacy for making use of a social networking site in the hiring process. The bottom line: Before using the Internet to screen candidates, or using third party services, see your labor attorney.

Setting a Company Policy

So far, this chapter has addressed the use of the Internet and social network sites for recruiting and making hiring decisions and has NOT covered employer concerns AFTER a person is hired. That is another topic entirely. However, every employer needs to have an "Internet Policy" regarding use of social media in the Information Age. What follows is a brief summary of this subject. The NLRB (see below) has also issued additional reports on the topic.

NLRB Acting General Counsel Releases Report on Social Media Cases

In August 2011, the National Labor Relations Board's (NLRB) Acting General Counsel released a report detailing the outcome of investigations into 14 cases involving the use of social media and employers' social and general media policies. The NLRB hoped that this report will be of assistance to practitioners and human resource professionals.

Each case was submitted by regional offices to the NLRB's Division of Advice in Washington, DC, and the results were detailed as follows:

- ✓ In four cases involving employees' use of Facebook, the Division found that the employees were engaged in "protected concerted activity" because they were discussing terms and conditions of employment with fellow employees.
- ✓ In five other cases involving Facebook or Twitter posts, the Division found that the activity was not protected.
- ✓ In one case, it was determined that a union engaged in unlawful coercive conduct when it videotaped interviews with employees at a nonunion jobsite about their immigration status and posted an edited version on YouTube and the Local Union's Facebook page.
- ✓ In five cases, some provisions of employers' social media policies were found to be unlawfully overly-broad. A final case involved an employer's lawful policy restricting its employees' contact with the media.

The NLRB report presented recent case developments arising in the context of today's social media that includes various online technology tools that enable people to communicate easily via the Internet to share information and resources and can encompass text, audio, video, images, podcasts, and other multimedia communications. The report also presented emerging issues concerning the protected and/or concerted nature of employees' Facebook and Twitter postings, the coercive impact of a union's Facebook and YouTube postings, and the lawfulness of employers' social media policies and rules. This report discusses these cases, as well as a recent case involving an employer's policy restricting employee contacts with the media. The NLRB report is available at: www.nlrb.gov/news/acting-general-counsel-releases-report-social-media-cases.

Social Media/Internet Policy for Employees

It is crucial for any business with employees to have a social media policy in today's Information Age to manage and monitor what is being said about the company and how social media is used. To put it simply, a company's social media policy outlines guidelines of communicating in the online world for employees.

Here is a list of subjects that social media strategists suggest companies should consider covering in their social media policies for both personal and corporate usage:

- ✓ Blogs
- ✓ Comments
- ✓ Email
- ✓ Facebook
- ✓ LinkedIn
- ✓ Online Communications
- ✓ Passwords
- ✓ Postings
- ✓ Social Networks
- ✓ Twitter
- ✓ YouTube
- ✓ Web pages
- ✓ Wikis (Wikipedia)

AUTHOR TIP A social media policy for current employees needs to address issues such as: Who owns the company computer and what right of privacy does an employee have (i.e. can an employer monitor Internet use and e-mails)? What is acceptable blogging/posting for employees? What happens if an employee posts a derogatory comment about the employer or reveals confidential information? If the employers are unionized, how does that affect the social media policy?

The Social Media Governance website has most complete listing of social media policies with an online database of nearly 200 social media policies referenced by the world's largest brands and agencies is available at: http://socialmediagovernance.com/policies.php.

In addition, an excellent example of how and when to write a social media policy is provided in *Inc. Magazine* at: www.inc.com/guides/2010/05/writing-a-social-media-policy.html.

Chapter 20

Other Background Screening Tools for Employers

An employer may consider any number of sources of information on applicants. This chapter examines driving records, workers' compensation records, civil court records, judgments, liens, bankruptcies, sex offender registries, security clearances, military records, merchant databases, and the National Wants and Warrants list.

Inside This Chapter:

- ✓ Driving Records

- ✓ Workers' Compensation Records

- ✓ Using Civil Court Case Files

- ✓ Judgments, Liens & Bankruptcies

- ✓ Sexual Offender Databases

- ✓ Military Records

- ✓ Security Clearances

- ✓ Merchant Databases

- ✓ National Wants and Warrants

- ✓ Specialty Databases - Government

- ✓ Specialty Databases - Private

Driving Records

The employment screening industry often refers to driving records as "MVRs." Many employers simply call them driver records and utilize them as a safe hiring tool whether the position applied for involves driving America's highways and byways or not. It is important to note that each state has its own database of drivers' records — there is no national database. Typical information on an MVR might include full name, address, Social Security Number, physical description, and date of birth along with conviction and accident history. Also, there is license type, restrictions, and endorsements which can provide useful background data on an individual. However, while there is some consistency, the data appearing on a MVR record may vary from state-to-state. Also, the specific access requirements will vary by state depending on individual state privacy laws and administrative rules. Sometimes the version of the MVR provided to employers by a background screening firm will contain the applicant's name and driving record, but with personal data — date of birth, address, physical characteristics, etc. — removed.

Outcomes of Driving Records Searches

There are thousands of vehicle code violations among the 50 states. Driving records are flagged when something other than a good standing is returned from the Department of Motor vehicles. Some examples of good standing are: Valid, In Force, Eligible, not suspended, Active, Privileges in Good Standing, Licensed (valid DL). There are 6 common outcomes for an "employment" DMV/MVR check.

1. Valid license without any violations

2. Valid license with violations

3. License has been suspended, revoked, or expired

4. License status "pending"

5. ID card only (in California): no license.

6. No license or ID card.

If the driving record is relevant to the job position, then employers ALWAYS need to review the DMV/MVR record. Remember that for employment purposes, the DMV only provides 3 years' worth of records. Your insurance carrier can pull more extensive records for an applicant.

Consideration When Driving for an Employer

For a person who is driving a company vehicle or is in a "driving position" for the company, such a check is a necessity. However, in most jurisdictions, "driving for work" is very broadly defined. The question is: When is an employee driving for work? The term "driving for work" can cover any employee behind the wheel of a vehicle for the employer's benefit.

For example, an employee who drives to the office supply store during lunch or between branches of the same firm or attends classes that are paid for by the company, can be considered "driving for work." If an accident occurs in any of those situations, an employer may be sued.

The one time an employer likely has no responsibility for an employee's driving is for an employee who only drives to work and drives home. This is referred to as the "Going and Coming Rule" — a worker driving to work and driving home does not drive for the employer in-between work and home.

For positions that involve driving, an employer can review the applicant's driving history and verify a license's status. A check of the driving record may also give insight into the applicant's level of responsibility. Just having moving violations may not relate to the ability to perform the job, but if an applicant has a history of failing to appear in court or pay fines, that can be a telling indicator about their level of responsibility.

Statewide driving records databases may be the first place where difficulties with drugs or alcohol are revealed — there may be "driving while impaired" violations. However, there are restrictions on the use of this information under the federal Americans with Disabilities Act (ADA), plus anti-discrimination law in certain states. The employer must determine whether the information is job-related and should exercise discretion when using it to the detriment of the applicant.

Record Access Restrictions and Signed Releases

The state laws governing the release of motor vehicle data to the public and to employers must comply with the Driver's Privacy Protection Act (DPPA), which was signed into law by President Clinton in 1997. States differentiate between requesters who are permissible users (14 permissible users are designated in DPPA) and those who are casual requesters to determine who may receive a record and/or how much personal information is reported on the record. For example, if a state DMV chooses to sell a record to a "casual requester," the record can only contain personal information (address, gender, etc.) unless written consent of the subject is presented.

Does the permissible user designation apply to employers obtaining driving records on applicants? No, unless the employer is hiring a licensed commercial driver such as truckers of 18-wheelers, etc. This means that employers must obtain a signed release from a prospective applicant before access to the record is granted (except for commercial drivers' records).

The Record Ordering Process

This is how the ordering process works.

✓ Employers usually obtain MVRs through the services of an employment-screening firm. A screening firm can typically obtain a driving record in one or two business days. Most states permit the release forms to be on file with the screening company rather than require a paper release submitted with each request.

✓ Screening companies, in turn, usually utilize the services of an MVR vendor. These vendors obtain and supply records nationwide in a timely manner for a very low service fee. The MVRs are delivered electronically, are uniform in appearance, and are reliable in content. There are a limited number of national and regional driving record vendors. Many of the national vendors limit their clientele to permissible users, such as the insurance industry, but there are vendors who will process requests from employers and background screening companies, providing the employer or company complies with state regulations.

Some states' DMVs offer a notification program for employers who hire a large number of drivers. The employer is notified if a driver has activity or a moving violation. There is typically a modest fee paid to register each driver, then a fee when activity is shown. More information about these programs can be obtained from state DMVs.

Idea! Have Applicants Obtain Their Own Records

Some employers who hire for a position that requires a driver's license require all applicants to bring a certified driving record to the job interview. Applicants must visit their local DMV office and request an official copy of their own license with a "certification" stamp showing it is authentic. To obtain your own records, there is usually a minimal fee charged by the DMV

There are two reasons that employers engage in this process. First it makes the application process go more efficiently by eliminating those without a satisfactory driving record.

Second, some employers feel that by requiring an applicant to bring in a certified license, an employer can eliminate from consideration applicants who are unable or unwilling to accomplish that small task. By requiring an applicant to jump through a "small hoop," the employer eliminates anyone who is unable or unwilling to complete a simple task.

At least one employer has reported a potential "scam" in the process. An applicant with a poor driving record found a friend with a "clean record." Both the applicant and the friend went to the DMV and got their records. The applicant then took the bottom half off the friend's clean record, added the top part of his record with his name, and then copied the fake record. He then presented what looked like a clean record to the employer. Fortunately, the applicant's ingenuity was not matched by his artistic skills. He created a suspicious document that caused the employer to look deeper and uncover the deception.

Readers interested in extensive, detailed information about state driving records, access restrictions and procedures, and violation codes, may refer to BRB Publications' *The MVR Access and Decoder Digest*. See www.mvrdecoder.com.

Workers' Compensation Records

Employers have become very aware of the high costs of compensation claims. The loss to American business from both fraudulent claims and re-injury causes many employers to want to know whether a job applicant has a history of filing workers' compensation claims.

At the same time, the Federal Americans with Disabilities Act (ADA), as well as numerous state laws, seek to protect job seekers from discrimination in hiring as a result of filing valid claims. The ADA also seeks to prevent the discrimination against workers who, although suffering from a disability, are nevertheless able to perform essential job functions as long as there are reasonable accommodations.

Before the ADA was introduced in 1990, employers had little legal limitations when it came to asking job applicants about their medical history or past workers' compensation claims. Now there are numerous legal restrictions that must be observed closely. The bottom line is that an employer cannot request workers' compensation records in order to have a policy of not hiring anyone who has made a claim. It is discriminatory to penalize a person who has exercised a lawful right and filed a valid claim.

Employers are well-advised to contact a labor lawyer before seeking to obtain workers' compensation records. A labor law expert can assist an employer in preparing company policies, job descriptions, and forms and procedures necessary to comply with the ADA, such as a conditional job offer and medical review form.

Obtaining and Using Workers' Compensation Records

The following brief summary describes the major points involved in obtaining and using workers' compensation records.

✓   There are wide variations between the states in the availability of these records. In a few states, the records are not available to the public, period. In some states, there are special requirements before obtaining the records such as a notarized release. Because they are familiar with state regulations, background screening firms can assist employers in obtaining these records.

✓   Under the ADA, an employer may not inquire about an applicant's medical condition or past workers' compensation claims until a conditional job offer has been extended. A conditional job offer means that a person had been made an offer of employment, subject to certain conditions such as a job-related medical review. The conditions must be fulfilled prior to coming on-site for employment.

✓   When it comes to matters controlled by the ADA, the job offer must be "real," meaning there are no other conditions left to fulfill.

✓   Any questioning in a job interview must be restricted to whether the person can perform the essential job functions with or without reasonable accommodation.

✓   If a candidate discloses a disability, then there should not be any follow-up. Questioning should be limited to whether that applicant can perform the job.

✓   Only after a conditional job offer has been extended may an employer inquire about past medical history, require a medical exam, or inquire about workers' compensation claims.

✓ The better procedure is to have an applicant fill out a written medical review form that reviews their medical condition and workers' compensation claims history and provides consent as well. Firms that utilize medical examinations as part of their procedures should have a written medical review policy.

✓ The procedure should be administered uniformly. If one worker in a job category is the subject of such an investigation, then all applicants must be treated the same. However, an employer may treat different job categories differently. Not all employees must be sent for a medical exam.

✓ If a history of filing workers' compensation claims is found, then the offer may only be rescinded under very limited circumstances:

    a. The applicant has lied usually during a medical examination about a workers' compensation history or medical condition;

    b. The applicant has a history of filing false claims;

    c. In the opinion of a medical expert, the past claims demonstrate the applicant is a safety or health threat to himself or others; and

    d. The past claims demonstrate the applicant is unable to perform the essential functions of the job even with a reasonable accommodation.

✓ If the applicant has lied on the medical questionnaire, then the employer may be justified in rescinding the job offer based upon dishonesty. If an applicant has a history of multiple claims that have been denied, then an employer may be justified in rescinding the offer. The recession is based upon an inference of fraud, not disability. However, even individuals with false claims will usually not have multiple false claims. Rescinding the job offer based upon reasons (b) and (c) however, does require a medical opinion.

Some firms contend that a workers' compensation record may also be used to determine the truthfulness of information on a job application on the theory that an applicant may try to hide a past employer where a claim was filed. However, even with this justification, if used, the best practice may be to review the records post-hire only. Also keep in mind in those states that release records, sometimes it can take two to three weeks for the agency to fulfill the order.

 The most important walkaway point about workers compensation records is that under the ADA and similar state laws, they cannot be ordered until there has been a conditional job offer, which means there has been a real offer of employment, and that the workers' compensation record check or other medical procedure are performed as the very last condition of hiring before the start date.

Case Affects Timing of Background Checks and Pre-employment Physicals

A Ninth Circuit federal case has a potential impact on employers who conduct both pre-employment background checks as well as job-related medical tests. In *Leonel v. American Airlines, 400 F.3d 702 (9th Cir. 2005)*, the plaintiffs were seeking jobs with a major airline. They were issued conditional offers of employment contingent upon passing both their background check and medical examination. Their blood was drawn prior to the background checks being completed. According to the case, the airline then discovered a medical condition, and rescinded the job offers on the basis the applicants did not disclose the medical condition during the medical exams.

The plaintiffs sued for a violation of both the federal Americans with Disability Act (ADA) and also under the California law governing employment discrimination, the California Fair Employment and Housing Act (FEHA). The plaintiffs alleged that under federal law and California law, before a medical test can be performed, there must first be a "real" job offer on the table. Since the background check was not yet completed before the medical information was obtained, the plaintiffs argued that the employer had not met federal and state standards and had conducted a medical test before there was a job offer.

The court accepted the argument, ruling that in order to conduct a "post-offer" medical exam, the employer must have first evaluated all relevant and available non-medical information. Where the employer still has non-medical information to evaluate, such as a background check, it is premature to request a medical exam because there has been no job offer. The rule has two benefits for job applicants. First, it allows a job applicant to determine if they were rejected for medical reasons or some non-medical reason obtained in the background report. Secondly, it safeguards the applicant from having to reveal personal medical information prematurely. If the applicant is not offered the job, then they are not put in to a position of providing personal medical information for no reason.

The argument that the medical examination and blood sample were collected but not utilized until AFTER the background check was completed was rejected. The Court held that applicants have a right to not undergo a medical examination at all until there is a "real" job offer first. Both federal and state law allows an applicant to shield their confidential medical information until they know that if they meet the medical requirements, they have the job.

This case has a potential impact on any employer that conducts a medical examination post-offer but before actual employment begins. For example, an employer who conducts pre-employment physicals should consider waiting until the background check is successfully completed before performing a physical or any other medical procedure

Source: www.ca9.uscourts.gov/datastore/opinions/2005/04/27/0315890.pdf.

Using Civil Court Case Files

Another screening tool for employers involves using civil court records. A civil case occurs when one party sues another. Unlike a criminal case, which is brought by the government and a defendant can face jail time, a civil case is typically about money. There are some lawsuits that seek remedies other than money, such as a request for an injunction, which is where a party seeks to have another party ordered to do or not do some physical act. Lawsuits brought in family court or probate courts are also considered civil lawsuits. Civil cases can be for torts or contracts.

A contract case is when one party sues another for a violation or enforcement of an agreement. A tort case is when one party sues another for an injury in civil court for actions other than breach of contract. Tort cases can involve both intentional conduct and unintentional conduct. An unintentional tort is typically a negligence action, such as an auto accident. An intentional tort can be such causes of action as assault, intentional infliction of emotional distress, or some intentional wrong. Although the same conduct could also form the basis of a criminal case as well, a criminal case is only brought by the government. Tort cases can involve injury to the person (assault and battery or infliction of emotional distress), injury to property (trespass, theft, conversion), injury to reputation, or some business advantage (slander and liable).

AUTHOR TIP **A Familiar Illustration of Civil and Criminal Cases**

When O.J. Simpson was prosecuted for murder, the case was brought in the criminal courts by a prosecuting attorney. The case was called "The People vs. Simpson." However, Simpson was also sued in civil court by private attorneys hired by plaintiffs who were the family members of the victims. That case name had the title of the parties to the case: Sharon Ruffo, et al. vs. Simpson.

The fact that Simpson was found not guilty in the criminal case but guilty in the civil court also illustrated the difference between civil and criminal cases. In a criminal case, a prosecutor must convince all twelve jurors unanimously, beyond a reasonable doubt, the defendant is guilty. On the other hand, in a civil case, a plaintiff only needs to prove the case by a preponderance of the evidence, which is a much lesser standard. That standard means that it is more likely than not the plaintiff proved the case. Sometimes it is described as a standard whereby the plaintiff must prove the case by 51%. In civil cases, a plaintiff only needs nine jurors to agree, not all twelve.

The following table illustrates the differences between civil and criminal cases:

Subject	Criminal Case	Civil Case
Who brings the case	A government prosecutor	A private party normally though their attorney
Name of case	People vs. Smith (if state court) or the United States of America vs. Smith (if federal court)	Adams vs. Smith (the names of the parties)
Outcome if Plaintiff successful	Criminal sanctions including imprisonment, fine, and probation terms	Monetary damages. In some lawsuits the plaintiff may be seeking injunctive relief.
Jurors who must agree with the plaintiff	All twelve-unanimous verdict	Nine jurors out of 12
Standard of proof	Government must overcome the presumption of innocence by proving guilt beyond a reasonable doubt.	Plaintiff only needs to show their side is more convincing, so that it is more probable they are right.

How to Obtain Civil Case Records

Obtaining civil records is similar to obtaining criminal records but with many more complications. Similar to criminal records, civil records are located at the county courthouse level in state court. Researchers locate records for civil lawsuits in the same fashion they search for criminal records. However, unlike criminal records that have a connection to where a defendant has lived or worked, civil records can be more diverse geographically. The rules for jurisdictions are somewhat broader for civil cases. For example, in a lawsuit for breach of contract, the suit can be brought where the contract was formed or breached. An applicant may not have lived in any of those places. Therefore, civil record searches can take on a "needle in a haystack" quality. Published appellate cases where the lawsuit was appealed can also be searched. However, published appellate opinions represent an extremely small fraction of all civil cases.

Locating Identifiers

The next big problem is that civil records have very few identifiers. The initial search is by name match only, a similar problem to searching for federal criminal records, as explained previously. For example, if an Adam Smith is prosecuted for a crime in state court, there is likely going to be a date of birth, a Social Security Number, or a driver's license somewhere in the court file. However, if Adam Smith is involved in a civil lawsuit as either a defendant or a plaintiff, there are no reasons that any identifiers are necessarily present in the file.

In order to determine if a civil record belongs to the job applicant, it is necessary to look for clues in the files. In most civil lawsuits, the allegation will contain a description of the party that is related to the reason for the legal action. So, if there is a lawsuit for medical malpractice, and the applicant is not a doctor, it is not likely a legal action involving your applicant. The complication occurs when a court researcher goes to the courthouse; the researcher normally does not have the knowledge to determine from the lawsuit or other information in the file if the lawsuit pertains to your applicant. The researcher normally must ask the court clerk for a copy of the file. However, civil files can be very large and also very expensive to copy. Before getting surprised with a large bill for court clerk copies, an employer needs to determine how many pages are necessary. Usually the first five or so pages will set out the identities and relationship of the parties. There may be other means in the court file to identify the parties, such as information on a summons or proof of service of the lawsuit, reference to employment, or data found in exhibits attached to the civil complaint.

Another option is to call an attorney involved with the case and ask for help on identification.

Utilizing Civil Records in Employment Decisions

The third issue is to determine if a civil lawsuit has any relevance to the position. Many civil lawsuits are clearly not job related. For example, if an applicant is a plaintiff (the person bringing the action against the defendant) in a personal injury lawsuit, this would not likely have bearing on job performance (unless the applicant was suing a past employer and had a custom and practice of doing that). A civil search may uncover a case of dissolution of marriage. Often such lawsuits will have a detailed description where the parties are bringing out all the dirty laundry. As interesting as that might be to read from a human-interest point of view, it likely to have little bearing upon employment.

Employers are likely looking for lawsuits that have some rational relationship to the job or workplace performance. These lawsuits can be directly job-related, such as an harassment suit by a former employee or character traits that may be involved in workplace behavior, such as lawsuits for violence or dishonest behavior.

Of course, as we have seen over and over again, nothing is as simple as it seems when it comes to public records. Every lawsuit has some sort of caption that indicates the court where it was filed, the parties involved, and the type of lawsuit. However, lawsuits in state or federal courts usually only have a rather cursory description of the nature of the action in the caption. The lawsuit may only be described as a "Suit for Damages." That tells a researcher nothing at all. In order to determine the underlying nature of the litigation, it is again necessary for the court researcher to request that the court clerk copy the first few pages where the essential thrust of the allegations of the lawsuit is usually recounted. The file could indicate, for example, if a person was being sued for harassment in the workplace, whether the defendant was the employer or manager.

Judgments, Liens & Bankruptcies

Databases of judgment, liens, and bankruptcy records can be other valuable data resources.

Judgments are typically a final decision in court cases where the judge or jury awards monetary damages against the defendant. Often, the party who wins the judgment will record the judgment with the county records clerk. Information provider firms have assembled national databases consisting of these judgments. The purpose is to allow employers to know an applicant has been sued. As with civil records, employers must approach this type of information with caution when using the records for employment purposes. First, the employer must make sure the judgment is valid. Next, the employer needs sufficient data to conclude that the judgment pertains to their applicant. Third, the employer must determine if the judgment is relevant to a job. Another problem is that judgment databases can have errors and be missing judgment records. In addition, the great majority of civil lawsuits are settled out-of-court, so there may not be a judgment entered.

Another search that some employers use is a search for **tax liens**. When a person or business owes delinquent, unpaid taxes to a government agency, the agency can record a tax lien that gives the government priority to collect upon the proceeds from the sale of real property. Like judgments, tax liens must be taken with a grain of salt. An employer must determine 1) if that tax lien data applies to the applicant, 2) if the data is accurate, and 3) if used for employment purposes, is it relevant and fair? Tax liens are generally found in the same state database that records Uniform Commercial Code (UCC) filings.

The third category is **bankruptcies**. All bankruptcy cases are heard in a federal court. The information is easily accessible; however, employers should exercise extreme caution in attempting to utilize these records. The argument against using bankruptcy for employment is that if a person went into bankruptcy to re-arrange their life but cannot get a job because of the bankruptcy, then that person could never get ahead. He or she would be placed in a new form of debtors' prison, unable to break the debt cycle.

Federal Court Case

The argument has been made that federal bankruptcy law prohibited the use of bankruptcy records for pre-employment because it prevented a person from having a "fresh start." A decision by the United States Court of Appeals for the Third Circuit in 2010 clarified the issue of whether a private employer can legally consider a job applicant's bankruptcy under U.S bankruptcy law in making an employment decision. The Court ruled that Congress intentionally only protected current employees from discrimination under bankruptcy law, and job applicants were not protected. In that case, the plaintiff applied for employment at a retail store, and it appeared he would be hired. However, after a bankruptcy was discovered, the employer refused to hire him due to the bankruptcy. The job applicant filed a lawsuit on the basis that under federal bankruptcy law, a consumer filing bankruptcy was entitled to a fresh start, and an employer could not discriminate against him based upon a bankruptcy.

The Court noted that there were two sections of federal law concerning bankruptcy and employment. Under 11 U.S.C. Section 525(a), Congress specifically stated that a governmental unit could not deny employment based upon a bankruptcy. (Note: U.S.C. stands for United States Codes, where federal laws are found. They are divided into titles, with Title 11 covering bankruptcy).

Congress later added a section 525(b) covering private employers that read:

(b) No private employer may terminate the employment of, or discriminate with respect to employment against, an individual who is or has been a debtor under this title…"

The section concerning private employers did not specify that a private employer could not deny employment due to bankruptcy. The job applicant argued that the term "discriminate with respect to employment" was board enough to protect job applicants as well as current employees. In addition, even though section 525(b) does not refer specifically to job seekers, such an interpretation is consistent with the reasoning of the section which intends to give someone a fresh start and not let the bankruptcy prevent employment. The applicant further argued the omission of the verbiage concerning denial of employment when it came to private employers was just an error in drafting.

The Court disagreed and noted that Congress clearly wrote the law so that the government may not "deny employment," but specifically declined to add the same language to the section concerning private employers. The Court reasoned that if Congress wanted to extend the same protections to consumers seeking jobs with private employers, then Congress could have used the same language used it used in section 525(a) in regards to government employment.

The Court noted that the United States Supreme Court has established a rule of statutory interpretation that "where Congress included particular language in one section of a statute but omits it in another section of the same Act, it is generally presumed that Congress acts intentionally and purposely in the disparate inclusive or exclusion."

In other words, Congress is presumed to know what was in 525(a) and could have used the same language in 525(b) in regards to private employers but chose not to. The Court ruled that where the language is clear, a Court's duty is to enforce a statute according to its language.

However, this case should not be seen as opening the floodgates for widespread use of bankruptcy information. A bankruptcy should still be used with caution. The case was litigated on just the basis that the actions were discriminatory under bankruptcy law. A job applicant could potentially file a claim of discrimination under Title VII if it can be shown that the use of bankruptcy creates a disparate impact on the basis of race, creed, color, nationality, sex, or some other prohibited criteria.

As with all pre-employment screening tools and assessments, bankruptcy should only be used if there is a business justification, meaning essentially that the tool is a valid predictor of job performance and does not have a discriminatory impact. Employers should still approach the use of bankruptcy with caution. A number of states have or are in the process of limiting the use of credit reports for employment due to concerns that it is being used unfairly. Such concerns can also arise if bankruptcies are used unfairly in a way not related to employment or that has the impact of treating members of protected groups unfairly. Employers may want to consider whether a bankruptcy is related to a bona fide occupational qualification BFOQ.

The case can be found at http://caselaw.findlaw.com/us-3rd-circuit/1548259.html.

Sexual Offender Databases

Another tool available to employers is the use of sexual offender databases. State sexual registration requirements, popularly known as Megan's Law, were signed into law by President Clinton on May 17, 1996. The law had two primary goals. The first goal was to require each state and the federal government to register sexual predators. The second goal was to provide for community notifications by the local police.

These state databases were the subject of a 2003 news story centered on a survey of the fifty states by a child advocacy group. The group found literally tens of thousands of offenders who should have been registered but were "lost" in the system. Either the sexual offenders did not register or the state did not know where the registrants were located.

The group – Parents for Megan's Law – contacted all fifty states by telephone. According to news accounts, the study showed that states, on average, were unable to account for twenty-four percent of sex offenders who were supposed to be in the databases. Eighteen states said they were unable to track how many sex offenders were failing to register, or simply did not know.

According to ABCnews.com (October, 2003)

"The extent of the problem was dramatized this summer in California when a state audit of the sex offender registry found that some 23,000 people on the list were unaccounted for because their records had not been updated in at least one year. The records of 14,000 of those had not been updated in at least five years.

"That audit was carried out after the state had mounted a concerted effort to locate missing sex offenders, after a report in January by The Associated Press that California law enforcement had lost track of about 39 percent of the more than 70,000 people on the list."

FAQs about Sexual Offender Registration Searches

How does a sexual offender search differ from a criminal search?

Both searches are looking for criminal records, but a sexual offender search is limited to violations that require a person to register with a central authority. The state registry is a compilation of records of offenses that are sexual in nature and taken from counties across the state. Of course, a criminal search is looking at all criminal records regardless of nature or gravity.

How does an employer locate sexual offender records?

Three sources for sexual offenders lists exist. The most accurate sources are the lists maintained directly by states and counties. However, not all jurisdictions provide sufficient detail to identify or locate an offender.

The U.S. Department of Justice provides a searchable website www.nsopr.gov. The database supplies what each state reports to it. The *use notes* for each state should be carefully reviewed. In addition, unlike commercial databases, the state lists that are reported through the U.S. Department of Justice database may drop an offender's name when the registration period is over.

In addition, there are information provider firms that have assembled large national databases composed of data from various state and local sources. These national sexual offender databases are an excellent secondary or supplemental tool to perform a broader search that is national in nature. However, some of the national database providers are unable to produce a date of birth or other identifier for all states, so an employer can be stuck with a name match only which would have to be confirmed by going to a more specific state database or pulling a court record.

What are the advantages of a sexual offender search?

In theory, a sexual offender search includes the entire state so that it is less subject to the limitations of a county search. A person may have been convicted of a sexual offense in a county where an employer or background firm may not know to look. For example, a person may not list the county where the sexual offense occurred, and it may not come up on a SSN Trace.

Are sexual offender searches subject to accuracy issues?

Yes. There are a number of problems with the accuracy and completeness of the data, similar to the issues described in Chapter 14 for criminal databases. There can be both false positives and false negatives. A "false positive" is where there is a match, but upon further research it is not the same person as the job candidate. A "false negative" is where a sexual offender is not located, but in fact the person is a sexual offender. That is one reason why searchable websites, including those maintained by states, have disclaimers warning that records can be missed.

What are the reasons for a "false negative?"

False negatives can occur for several reasons. First, if the person should have registered but did not, and the state did not track him or her down, then the current information may not be on the list. Second, if a sexual offender leaves a jurisdiction and goes elsewhere and does not register, the offender will not show up on the appropriate sex offender registry. That person may roam free unless a law enforcement agency happens to encounter them and runs them through a computer that identifies them as a sex offender. Some jurisdictions are discussing ways to monitor the movements of sex offenders, such as electronic bracelets, which can be an expensive proposition if it works at all.

The difficulty with these registries is that each state does things its own way, and not all states do it as well as others. As seen from the ABC News stories above, many states have large holes in their databases. It is an immense task requiring substantial resources to track all offenders and a difficult challenge when law enforcement budgets are tight. Perhaps a person may have committed a number of crimes, including a sex crime, and pursuant to a plea bargain, the sex crime may have been dismissed resulting in the person not being required to report.

A false negative can also occur because less severe offenses may not be reportable. Nearly all states place some access limits based on the severity of the offense. For example, most states divide offenses into three levels and will only report the more serious offenses, such as level 3 only, or levels 2 and 3.

Also, the date the database "began" can affect a search. In reviewing state databases, it is important to know when the database was started. Many states began their databases after 1997. Another reason for false negatives is that registration is not necessarily permanent. Depending upon the state, the offense, and the offender, registration requirements can be removed.

The manner in which records are kept by the state can also contribute to an error rate. Each state's central repository must collect data from local courts. If a county is late or inaccurate, then there can be errors. Also, not every state makes their central repository available to the public — a researcher would need to check county by county for a complete sex offender record search.

These reasons underscore the basic message— searches, although valuable, are far from perfect and should just be one element in the background screening process.

What are the reasons for "false positives?"

As in all public records, identifiers are critical before assuming that a criminal record belongs to a particular applicant. With approximately 300 million people packed into 50 states in the U.S., the statistical likelihood of people with the same name and same date of birth is higher than one might imagine. For this reason, an employer should never assume that an applicant is a sexual offender without the positive proof of an ID match or pulling the underlying court record.

What should an employer do if a sexual record is located?

The same rules apply as to any criminal records. First, the employer must ensure that they have positive ID so that they know the record belongs to their applicant. Next, the employer needs to determine if the applicant lied about a criminal record by reviewing the application and what was said in the interview. This is where the AIR Process discussed earlier proves so valuable. Third, the employer or volunteer group should pull a copy of the court file from the courthouse to ensure that the information is accurate and up to date and to ascertain the details. Finally, the employer must also consider if, under EEOC rules, there is a "business justification" for disqualifying the applicant based on the criminal conviction. For example, in California it is illegal to use the sexual offender information unless there is an identifiable group at risk, meaning that there must be a job-related reason to utilize sexual offender data.

More on California Sex Offender Search Employment Screening Background Check

The use of the California Sexual Registration listing, commonly known as Megan's Law, is widespread among employers. **However, there is a little known provision in California that may actually limit an employer's legal use of this information in certain situations.**

The Megan's Law was first passed in 1996. Originally, information on sex offenders that register under California Penal Code Section 290 was only available by personally visiting police stations and sheriff's offices, or by calling a 900 number. The website at www.meganslaw.ca.gov was established by the California Department of Justice pursuant to a 2004 California law for the purpose of allowing the public for the first time to use their personal computers to view information on sex offenders required to register with local law enforcement under California's Megan's Law.

The purpose of Megan's law is summarized on the web site:

California's Megan's Law provides the public with certain information on the whereabouts of sex offenders so that members of our local communities may protect themselves and their children. Megan's Law is named after seven-year-old Megan Kanka, a New Jersey girl who was raped and killed by a known child molester who had moved across the street from the family without their knowledge. In the wake of the tragedy, the Kankas sought to have local communities warned.

The California site allows anyone to search the database by a sex offender's specific name, obtain ZIP Code and city/county listings, obtain detailed personal profile information on each registrant, and use a map application to search their neighborhood or anywhere throughout the State to determine the specific location of any of those registrants on whom the law allows us to display a home address.

Megan's law contains a provision which prohibits the information to be used when it comes to insurance, loans, credit, employment, education, housing or accommodation or benefits or privileges provided by any business.

California Penal Code Section 290.4(d) (2).

However, there is an exception. According to California law, a person is authorized to use information disclosed pursuant to this section only to protect a person at risk. California Penal Code Section 290.4(d) (1).

The problem for employers that want to use this information is that there is no legal definition for the term "a person at risk." Neither the California Penal code, the legislative history of the section or the Megan's law website defines a "person at risk." Until a court provides a definition, employers are well advised to apply a common-sense approach by looking at risk factors associated with the nature of the job. For example, there is a widespread industry agreement that vulnerable individuals are at risk, such as the young, the aged, the infirmed, or the physically or mentally disabled. In addition, people inside their own home are likely to be at greater risk, since it is harder to obtain help, so home workers may be considered a population that works with people at risk. Another category is workers that operate under some sort of badge or color of authority or who wears a uniform. In that situation, a person may let their guard down. Until a court makes a clear decision, employers should make an effort to determine if there is a good faith belief that it is reasonably foreseeable that a member of a group at risk could be negatively impacted if a sexual offender was hired.

Of course, if the underlying criminal record is discovered and otherwise meets the many complicated rules governing the reporting and use of criminal records in California, then the at "risk" analysis may not be needed, and the employer can handle it like any other criminal record.

There are two other challenges for California employers using the Megan's law website:

✓ First, it is possible that a person may be registered as a sex offender, but their crime is beyond the 7 year California reporting provisions that restrict what a Consumer Reporting Agency can report. Although not yet tested in the Courts, the industry standard is for a screening firm to report the listing, on the basis that the background firm is reporting on the offender's current status as a registered sexual offender.

✓ The other issue is that there are large numbers of sex offenders that either do not register or abscond from the jurisdiction(s), or do not re-register. Some studies suggest a significant number of sex offenders did not have current registration and authorities have lost track of their whereabouts.

A California case also ruled a background screening firm has a constitutional right to report that an applicant has appeared on the Megan's Law website (MLW) as a registered sex offender. See: *Mendoza v. ADP Screening and Selection Services, Inc.*, (2010) 182 Cal.App.4th 1644.

The bottom line: When an employer is hiring an applicant for a position where it is foreseeable that there would be contact with members of groups at risk, then the sexual offender database search can be valuable. However, employers should keep in mind that there are limitations that have yet to be fully defined by courts or the legislature, and the databases may not be up-to-date or 100% accurate.

What if he underlying criminal case is too old to be reported or used, but the person is still registers?

The standard industry advice is that the offender's current status as a registered sex offender is reportable, since it is accurate and up to date public information, even if the underling crime is too old to report. However, if there is doubt about a particular state, it may be advisable to get a lawyer's opinion.

Sex Offender Records — Conclusion

A sexual offender database search, both nationwide and using state and local websites, is an extremely valuable tool. It is especially valuable when the position involves access to a group-at-risk such as children or the elderly. However, employers and volunteer groups need to understand that these databases are not primary tools but supplemental tools subject to some degree of error and should be utilized with some caution and in conjunction with other safe hiring procedures.

Military Records

Another record that some employers may want to verify is a military service record. With the national focus on the military after the events in Iraq and Afghanistan, it is likely that employers will receive applications from those with military experience. Many employers realize applicants with military service provide critical skills and training which are extremely valuable in the workforce.

The standard way to verify military records is to ask an applicant for a copy of his or her DD-214. This is the common term for the document given to all members of the military who are discharged from the U.S. Navy, Army, Air Force, Marine Corp, or Coast Guard. The "DD" stand for Department of Defense. The short name is "discharge papers."

For employers who want more than a cursory confirmation of military service, the story goes much deeper. There are actually a number of different copies of the DD-214 with different pieces of information. A discharged service person receives copy 1, which has the least information. The copy with the codes that gives the nature of the discharge, i.e. General, Honorable, Dishonorable, etc. – and details of service is actually on copy 4. The codes characterize the service record of a veteran. The codes are known as SPD (Separation Program Designator), SPN (Separation Program Number), and RE (Re-Entry) codes. Other issues with access and use of the DD-214 are listed below.

- ✓ For a discharged service person to get copy 4, the person must actually ask for it.
- ✓ If a person did not ask for the copy 4 or wants to hide some embarrassing fact, then the person may only present copy 1 to an employer.
- ✓ If the employer wants copy 4, and the applicant does not have it, then there can be a problem acquiring and understanding the copy. The employer can have the applicant sign a Form 180 and send it to the National Personnel Records Center (NPRC) in St. Louis, Missouri. However, there can be a wait — up to six months. Some records are no longer available due to a very destructive fire at the St. Louis facility in 1973. Although the government has reconstructed some of the records by use of other military documents. For details about these military records, see www.archives.gov/research_room/obtain_copies/veterans_service_records.html.
- ✓ A note of caution. Even after getting a copy 4, there is the issue of translating the military codes. There are websites that provide a complete list of the codes and definitions. However, should civilian employers use these codes for hiring decisions, since the codes were meant for internal military use only? The various codes may represent items that have no foundation or were the result of clerical errors, or are simply not related to job performance.

When making hiring decisions, employers should be very careful before attempting to draw conclusions from various codes on the DD-214. Using the codes on the DD-214 to infer conduct in order to make hiring decisions could result in claims of discrimination or decisions being made based upon irrelevant or unsubstantiated criteria. The situation can be further complicated if the employers insist that an applicant first obtains a complete DD-214 and then rejects the applicant. That record request could potentially be viewed as evidence of discrimination.

An employer should also exercise caution in using a discharge as a basis of an employment decision. There are four common types of military discharges: honorable, general, undesirable, and dishonorable. Of these, only a dishonorable discharge is given as a result of a factual adjudication equivalent to a criminal trial. In order to avoid potential EEOC claims, an employer should treat a dishonorable discharge in the same fashion as a criminal conviction, taking into account the various factors reviewed in Chapter 14. A general discharge or undesirable discharge may or may not have any bearing on employment and generally should not be the basis of an employment decision.

The best advice may be to use the basic DD-214 to confirm a person was in fact in the military, then ask for the names of references from their military service to obtain job-related information that would be relevant to an employment decision.

Security Clearances

On occasion an employer may want to verify that a person had a security clearance in the past. This will occur when an employer receives an application indicating, as part of past qualifications, the applicant had a security clearance. The employer wants to confirm that the person is being truthful. Some employers will ask if a person has ever had a security clearance, if they had been refused one, and details about the last clearance held, including granting agent, level, date granted, and date expired. Details about security clearance, including various levels and how they are obtained, are beyond the scope of this book.

If the current job requires a security clearance, then there is already an established process in place. Entities who have security clearance needs, such as private employers used by government, will have an authorized designatee in charge of a process called the Special Security Officer (SSO). Security clearances stay with the entity and do not travel with the individual. If the individual leaves a position, the person no longer has a clearance. When a person leaves one employer that requires a clearance to go to another position that also requires a clearance, then the SSO at each entity arranges for the appropriate transfers.

If an applicant is applying for a job that does not require a security clearance, and the employer wants to verify the past claim, then the best procedure is for the employer or screening firm to contact the past employer and request the name and mailing address of the SSO. If a copy of a release is provided, then the SSO may verify that there was some level of clearance but may not go into detail.

Merchant Databases

Some firms offer a product commonly referred to as a merchant database which is typically used by large retailers who hire a large sales staff. These databases are created from data supplied by retail stores who contribute information about employees who have admitted to theft, whether or not a criminal case occurred. The databases may also contain other information such as records from various state criminal databases and Social Security Number information. These searches are relatively inexpensive, which is an advantage for employers. Since retail positions are often filled by lower-paid employees with high turnover rates, there is pressure on retailers to keep background screening as low cost as possible.

The difficulty with using these databases is the underlying reliability of the data. The databases will include information on individuals who were never prosecuted. The information is often based upon a report from a store loss-prevention employee concerning an interrogation where a person admitted they committed the theft in exchange for not being prosecuted. Since the matter did not go to court, there would not be a court file, police report, or any sort of adjudication in any factual matter.

Given the nature of these databases, there are two obvious problems with their use. First, use of such a database may run contrary to the EEOC rules, as explained in Chapter 3. An applicant may be the victim of a negative decision without any underlying factual determination. Considering the EEOC is concerned about the use of arrest records on the basis that an arrest is not a factual determination, unsubstantiated reports of a confession to store personnel are potentially troublesome.

The second issue is whether these databases are in fact FCRA compliant. Under the FCRA, a Consumer Reporting Agency (CRA) must take reasonable procedures to ensure accuracy. If information from a merchant database is a reported confession with no judicial findings, a CRA may have difficulty justifying the negative information unless it independently contacts the person performing the interview to confirm the facts. Otherwise, a person denied a job on the basis of a merchant database could claim a lack of reasonable procedures. The difficulty with relying upon confessions is that there is a large body of research that shows that false confessions are a significant issue in interrogations. Without other evidence such as recovery of stolen items or eyewitness confirmation, relying on confessions of theft as a basis for entry into a merchant theft database can be problematic. For more information, see *"Dangerous Confessions: The Psychology Behind False Confessions"* by Susan Davis, *California Lawyer*, April, 2005.

National Wants and Warrants

Until 2001, there was one portion of the FBI's National Crime Information Center (NCIC) database that was available to employers through pre-employment screening firms. The portion of the database available to employers was known as the National Wants and Warrants. The data contained information on fugitives wanted on federal warrants, also state warrants when a state was willing to extradite an offender back to the issuing state.

By allowing access to this database, law enforcement did not have to rely entirely on the strategy of "chance encounter" to apprehend wanted individuals. The primary method for apprehending wanted individuals in the United States is this strategy of **"chance encounter."** Most warrants sat patiently in the system in the hope that someday the wanted person will come back into the grips of law enforcement on some chance encounter such as a traffic stop. Unfortunately, it is also possible the person will come to the attention of law enforcement for a new crime. Because of budget restrictions and a host of other priorities, very little law enforcement resources are spent looking for individuals who are the subject of an arrest warrant.

However, in 2001 the FBI decided to close access to background screening firms who at the time were provided this useful information to employers.

According to Version 2.0 of the CJIS Security Policy issued in 2001, under the section title "Dissemination of State or Federal Hot File Records," and with the subject "Commercial Dissemination," the FBI Policy is as follows:

> "The commercial dissemination of state or federal hot file records obtained from NCIC (CJIS Systems) is prohibited. Information derived for other than law enforcement purposes from national hot file records can be used by authorized criminal justice personnel only to confirm the status of a person or article, i.e., wanted or stolen. Any advertising of services providing 'data for dollars' is prohibited. The request for bulk data is prohibited. Authorized agencies are allowed to charge a processing fee for disseminating data for authorized purposes."

Then, under Commentary Section, the CJIS Security Policy further states:

> "The wholesale marketing of data for profit is not permitted, as in the example of a pre-employment screening or background checking company requesting that wanted person checks from NCIC be conducted on individuals for various non-criminal justice employments."

Although the NCIC is not available, some private firms are able to gather extensive wants and warrants information directly from various local and state jurisdictions and make this data available. In addition, as of the printing of this book, at least one state will provide the names of jurisdictions where wants and warrants may be outstanding, but no other details.

A Few Thoughts from Author Les Rosen

From the point of view of both law enforcement and the public, making this database available to background screening firms was a tremendous advantage to public safety. Background firms would routinely run numerous names through this database that law enforcement and the FBI would not have the tracking resources to do. In addition, when an employer ran the name through the screening firm, the screening firm had the current address for the person being run. If there was a "hit," then law enforcement had the opportunity of getting a wanted and potentially dangerous person off the street.

Given the Justice Department statistic that the recidivism rate can be as high as 67% for a person released from prison within three years, it would seem that executing arrest warrants would be a big public safety priority. A screening firm's use of the "Wants database" would certainly seem to further the goals intended of the NCIC database.

According to the website for the FBI Criminal Justice Information Services (CJIS), the organization with responsibility for the NCIC database, part of the CJIS mission is to:

> "Reduce terrorist and criminal activities by maximizing the ability to provide timely and relevant criminal justice information to the FBI and to qualified law enforcement, criminal justice, civilian, academic, employment, and licensing agencies concerning individuals, stolen property, criminal organizations and activities, and other law enforcement related data."

(See additional CJIS information at www.fbi.gov/hq/cjisd/about.htm.)

By shutting down access to wants and warrants, the "chance encounter approach" is more institutionalized than ever. However, according to a June, 1999 investigative report by the San Francisco Chronicle, this chance approach is very troubling. The article indicated there was a backlog of 2.5 million warrants in California alone. The article noted a number of drawbacks to the "chance encounter" methodology of serving warrants:

✓ The current system has cost the lives of police officers who had "chance encounters" with felons having no intention of risking custody. For example, one of the most potentially dangerous situations for a police officer is making a routine traffic stop or having some other sort of contact with a person who has an outstanding warrant. The felon does not know if the police officer knows about the warrant, leading to instances where felons not wanting to take a chance of going back to prison will shoot police officers.

✓ An individual who remains at large subjects the public to the risk of new offenses. A significant amount of crime is committed by criminals-at-large with outstanding warrants.

✓ The chance encounter may never occur, leaving the wanted person at large.

✓ Even if there is a chance encounter, the individual may be using a false identity, or the computer check may not reveal the warrant.

✓ The criminal justice system is downgraded, since accused offenders know if they ignore a want or warrant, there is a significant chance nothing will ever happen to them.

According to the article, one judge familiar with the crisis described it as a "Cataclysmic breakdown of the law enforcement system."

Allowing screening firms access to the wants and warrants would seem to be a much better solution than relying on "chance encounters."

Specialty Databases – Government

Another series of tools used by employers and screening firms are specialty databases with various disbarment or sanctions lists. Below is a summary of some of the more frequently utilized databases. The list is by no means exhaustive and is not presented here as an endorsement or recommendation, but used only to illustrate that such additional sources of informant exist.

OIG/GSA Name Search

The OIG/GSA Name Search is vital for most healthcare industries. Together, the OIG (Office of the Inspector General) Excluded List and GSA (General Services Administration) Sanctions Report search the U.S. Department of Health and Human Services and OIG databases for individuals and businesses excluded or sanctioned from participating in Medicare, Medicaid, and other Federally funded programs.

Expanded healthcare searches cover disciplinary actions taken by federal agencies as well as those taken by licensing and certification agencies in all 50 states. This is the most comprehensive search method available. See http://exclusions.oig.hhs.gov.

FACIS® (Fraud and Abuse Control Information Systems)

FACIS® (Fraud and Abuse Control Information Systems) is a database search of records containing adverse actions against individuals and entities sanctioned in the healthcare field. This includes information on disciplinary actions ranging from exclusions and debarments to letters of reprimand and probation. There are three levels, each with same day turnaround in most cases:

✓ Level 1 searches against the OIG and GSA and other federal agency sources of information.
✓ Level 2 searches those sources included in Level 1 plus agencies operating in one selected state.
✓ Level 3 searches all state and federal sources included in the FACIS® database.

A Level 3 search is the most robust search option to conduct a search of disciplinary actions taken by federal agencies as well as those taken by licensing and certification agencies in all 50 states. The FACIS® database contains information from 800+ source agencies and their databases. This information covers all 50 States on individuals who have been the subject of state licensing board and certification agency sanctions including FRA debarment. This information is helpful in assisting healthcare companies avoid other potential liabilities and risks of employing or contracting with individuals who have been subject to performance of behavior problems elsewhere. It is not possible to obtain a definitive list due to the proprietary nature of the database. However, we are able to confirm or deny inclusion of a source on a specific state and or federal list via request. For high-risk individuals and contractors, or those who are directly involved in patient care such as physicians, nurses, physical therapists, etc., there are 800+ source agencies searched.

SAM and the Excluded Parties List System

The Excluded Parties List System (EPLS) is provided as a public service by General Services Administration (GSA) and includes information regarding entities debarred, suspended, proposed for debarment, excluded or disqualified under the non-procurement common rule, or otherwise declared ineligible from receiving Federal contracts, certain subcontracts, and certain Federal assistance and benefits, pursuant to the provisions of 31 U.S.C. 6101, note, E.O. 12549, E.O. 12689, 48 CFR 9.404, and each agency's codification of the Common Rule for Non-procurement suspension and debarment. For more information, visit www.epls.gov/.

At the end of July 2012, access to the Excluded Parties List System (EPLS) was taken over by a new system. EPLS, along with Federal Agency Registration (FedReg), the Central Contractor Registration (CCR), and the Online Representations and Certifications Application (ORCA), were migrated into the new System for Award Management also known as SAM. For more information, please visit www.SAM.gov.

The Financial Industry Regulatory Authority (FINRA) Search

The Financial Industry Regulatory Authority (FINRA) Search will check the professional background of current and former FINRA registered securities firms and brokers through the Central Registration Depository (CRD®), the securities industry online registration and licensing database, as reported on industry registration/licensing forms which brokers, brokerage firms, and regulators complete. Additionally this will also check for information about Investment Adviser (IA) firms through the Investment Adviser Registration Depository (IARD®), regulated by, and electronically registered with, the Securities and Exchange Commission (SEC) or state regulators. (NOTE: Central Registration Depository (CRD) or Investment Adviser Registration Depository (IARD) number required to insure exact match.)

Financial Institution Sanctions Search (FISS)

The following Federal government databases are searched for enforcement actions and orders against institutions or their affiliated parties:

✓ Board of Governors of the Federal Reserve System (FRB)

✓ Federal Deposit Insurance Corporation (FDIC)
✓ National Credit Union Administration (NCUA)
✓ Office of the Comptroller of the Currency (OCC)
✓ Office of Thrift Supervision (OTS)

Securities and Exchange Commission (SEC) Sanctions

Search by company name for SEC documents regarding Enforcement, Litigation, and Regulatory Actions. (NOTE: The Central Index Key (CIK) number if provided will insure a more accurate search.)

MIB (Medical Information Bureau)

MIB Group, Inc. (formerly The Medical Information Bureau Inc.) is the only insurance consumer reporting agency in North America and operates a database of medical information on some individuals who have previously applied for health insurance, life insurance, disability insurance, critical illness insurance, and long-term care insurance. According to the Federal Trade Commission (FTC), MIB's member companies account for 99 percent of the individual life insurance policies and 80 percent of all health and disability policies issued in the United States and Canada. Under the FCRA, the MIB is categorized as a "nationwide specialty consumer reporting agency" and must provide annual disclosure of credit reports to all consumers who request their files. See www.mib.com/.

The Data Bank

The Data Bank, consisting of the National Practitioner Data Bank (NPDB) and the Healthcare Integrity and Protection Data Bank (HIPDB), is a confidential information clearinghouse created by Congress to improve health care quality, protect the public, and reduce health care fraud and abuse in the United States. See: www.npdb-hipdb.hrsa.gov/

National Practitioner Data Bank (NPDB)

The National Practitioner Data Bank (NPDB) was established by Title IV of Public Law 99-660, the Health Care Quality Improvement Act of 1986, as amended (Title IV). Final regulations governing the NPDB are codified at 45 CFR Part 60. In 1987 Congress passed Public Law 100-93, Section 5 of the Medicare and Medicaid Patient and Program Protection Act of 1987 (Section 1921 of the Social Security Act), authorizing the Government to collect information concerning sanctions taken by state licensing authorities against all health care practitioners and entities. Congress later amended Section 1921 with the Omnibus Budget Reconciliation Act of 1990, Public Law 101-508, to add "any negative action or finding by such authority, organization, or entity regarding the practitioner or entity." Responsibility for NPDB implementation resides with the Bureau of Health Professions, Health Resources and Services Administration, U.S. Department of Health and Human Services (HHS).

Healthcare Integrity and Protection Data Bank (HIPDB)

The Secretary of HHS, acting through the Office of Inspector General (OIG) and the U.S. Attorney General, was directed by the Health Insurance Portability and Accountability Act of 1996, Section 221(a), Public Law 104-191, to create the Healthcare Integrity and Protection Data Bank (HIPDB) to combat fraud and abuse in health insurance and health care delivery. The HIPDB's authorizing statute is more commonly referred to as Section 1128E of the Social Security Act. Final regulations governing the HIPDB are codified at 45 CFR Part 61. The HIPDB is a national data collection program for the reporting and disclosure of certain final adverse actions taken against health care practitioners, providers, and suppliers. The HIPDB collects information regarding licensure and certification actions, exclusions from participation in Federal and State health care programs, health care-related criminal convictions and civil judgments, and other adjudicated actions or decisions as specified in regulation.

Specialty Databases – Private

DAC Reports

The DAC employment report is a detailed summary of a trucker's work history in the trucking industry. Most trucking companies today participate in sharing this information about truckers. HireRight (DAC Services) has a proprietary database of employer-contributed employment histories of commercial truck drivers. This assists trucking companies in fulfilling their DOT reference check requirements when hiring drivers. In addition, member truck driving schools contribute their students' performance to the database.

RentBureau®

Experian® RentBureau® collects updated rental histories from property management companies nationwide every 24 hours and makes that information available immediately to the multifamily industry. RentBureau provides property management companies and resident screeners a more accurate and complete picture of residents, leading to improved leasing decisions. To learn more, visit www.experian.com/rentbureau/renter-credit.html.

ChexSystems

ChexSystems is an eFunds check verification service and consumer credit reporting agency like Experian, Equifax, and TransUnion. While most credit reporting agencies broker data about how a consumer handles credit relationships, ChexSystems provides data related to how a consumer has handled deposit accounts at banking institutions. See: https://www.consumerdebit.com/consumerinfo/us/en/index.htm.

Chapter 21

International Background Checks

Due to the mobility of workers across international borders in a global economy, it is no longer adequate to conduct these background screening checks solely in the United States. Background screening also must be done internationally since an increasing number of workers have spent time living, working, and attending school abroad.

Inside This Chapter:

✓ Introduction

✓ Statistics Supporting the Use of International Background Screening

✓ Two Types of International Background Checks: Screening vs. Investigation

✓ Why Employers Cannot Assume Government Screens Workers from Abroad

✓ The Basic Components and Challenges of International Background Screening

✓ Additional Challenges Specific to International Criminal Checks

✓ International Education Verifications

✓ International Employment Verifications

✓ Other Resources and Tips for International Screening Due Diligence

✓ Legal Implications for Employers Doing International Background Checks

✓ Privacy and Data Protection in International Background Screening

✓ A Comparison of Privacy Laws in the U.S. and the EU

✓ About Canada's Strict Privacy Laws — PIPEDA

✓ Recommendations for International Background Screening Programs

✓ Additional Resource Links

Introduction

A need for international background screening can occur in several situations:

✓ **Applicant Born Abroad**: An American company is considering a job applicant who was born abroad and is either coming directly to the U.S. from another country or has not been in the United States long enough for the employer to rely solely upon checking American references and records. It is important employers never identify applicants as "applicants born abroad" since it may be discriminatory under Equal Employment Opportunity Commission (EEOC) regulations.

✓ **Applicant Spent Time Abroad**: An American company is considering a job applicant who spent relevant time abroad in another country, and the employer wants to obtain data for that time period.

✓ **Applicant from Other Country will Work in that Country:** An American company is hiring an individual in another country to work in that country. For example, a U.S. company may open an office in India or they are hiring an outside sales representative.

This chapter provides an informative introduction to international background screening, the risks employers conducting such screenings should be aware of, the many ways background screening overseas differs from background screening in the United States, and the solutions that employers may use to help with international background checks.

AUTHOR TIP Due to the perceived difficulty in performing international employment screening, some employers may be tempted to skip verifying international credentials or perform foreign criminal checks. However, the mere fact that information may be more difficult to obtain from outside of the U.S. does not relieve employers from their due diligence obligation associated with hiring.

Employers cannot simply take the position it is harder to exercise due diligence because the research is international. Nor can employers simply assume the U.S. government has conducted background checks if the worker was issued a visa. After the events of September 11, 2001, the U.S. has increased checks on foreign visitors and on workers on government "watch lists." However, the government checks are generally not aimed at verifying credentials or checking for criminal records for employment purposes.

If an employer hires a worker without verifying his or her international background and the employer is sued for negligent hiring when it turns out that a due diligence check would have uncovered important facts, what is the defense? If a victim has been hurt or injured, then the employer's testimony will sound very hollow when they did nothing because international screening was too difficult or they did not know how. Although international searches come with their own unique challenges and obstacles, employers do have a number of options to exercise due diligence.

Statistics Supporting the Use of International Background Screening

The following statistics show how many people in the U.S. were born or have spent time abroad. They can be broken down into four categories: 1.) Foreign Born U.S. residents, 2.) Legal Permanent Residents (LPRs), 3.) Unauthorized Immigrants, and 4.) U.S. Citizens that spend much time abroad. Together, these four categories make up a surprisingly large amount of the current U.S. population:

✓ **Foreign Born U.S. Residents:** Based on the 'Place of Birth of the Foreign-Born Population: 2009' report from the U.S. Census issued in October 2010 that presents data on the foreign born population using the 2009 American Community Survey (ACS), there are 38.5 million foreign-born U.S. residents, representing 12.5

percent of the population. The foreign-born population of the United States has continued to increase in size and as a percent of the total population: from 9.6 million or 4.7 percent in 1970, to 14.1 million or 6.2 percent in 1980, to 19.8 million or 7.9 percent in 1990, and to 31.1 million or 11.1 percent in 2000. Also, more notable than the growth of the foreign born population is the change in the distribution of origin countries over time.

✓ **U.S. Legal Permanent Residents (LPRs):** According to the report 'U.S. Legal Permanent Residents: 2009' (April 2010) from the Office of Immigration Statistics (OIS), a total of 1,130,818 persons became Legal Permanent Residents (LPRs) of the United States in 2009, up from 1,107,126 in 2008, a 2.1 percent increase in legal immigration. A LPR or "green card" recipient is defined by immigration law as a person who has been granted lawful permanent residence in the United States. Permanent resident status confers certain rights and responsibilities. LPRs may live and work permanently anywhere in the United States, own property, and attend public schools, colleges, and universities. They may also join certain branches of the Armed Forces and apply to become U.S. citizens if they meet certain eligibility requirements.

✓ **Unauthorized Immigrants:** The Department of Homeland Security (DHS) Office of Immigration Statistics (OIS) report 'Estimates of the Unauthorized Immigrant Population Residing in the United States: January 2009' (January 2010) provides estimates of the number of unauthorized immigrants residing in the United States as of January 2009. According to the OIS report, the unauthorized immigrant population living in the United States reached an estimated 10.8 million in January 2009 and grew 27 percent between 2000 and 2009. The unauthorized resident population is the remainder or "residual" after estimates of the legally resident foreign-born population – legal permanent residents (LPRs), asylees (individuals who travel to the U.S. and apply for grants of asylum), refugees, and non-immigrants – are subtracted from estimates of the total foreign-born population.

✓ **U.S. Citizens That Spend Much Time Abroad:** No reliable statistics exist regarding the number of U.S. citizens that spend a considerable amount of time abroad and outside of the United States. Suffice to say, while many U.S. citizens have travelled outside the country on vacation, some of them have lived, worked, or attended school in another country for a considerable amount of time. These people would warrant an international background screening by their employers.

Two Types of International Background Checks: Screening vs. Investigation

There are two types of international background checks employers may utilize. The first type is an "international employment screening" while the second type is an "international investigation."

For most U.S. employers, **international employment screening** involves verifications of supplied information by an applicant who has given express written consent to the screening. In a screening, an employer will have already obtained from an applicant the names, addresses, and phone numbers of previous employers or schools. Also, the employer will have obtained a rough list of locations where an applicant has lived, worked, or studied. A typical international background screen will consist of contacting the employers and schools that have been supplied and conducting a criminal check to the extent possible in that country. A screening may also include, if available, a driving record and credit report. If more information is needed, such as the applicant's school identification number or some other data, then the applicant can be asked to supply the needed data. The applicant will help the employer obtain the information since the applicant has signed a consent form and wants to be hired. The overall cost of international background screening, although greater than a typical U.S. screening, is considerably less expensive than an international investigation.

An **international investigation** typically involves a trained and experienced investigator working in the country where the investigation is being conducted. (In contrast, when an employer utilizes a firm to conduct an international screen, there is not necessarily an agent on the ground in the country where the information is being obtained. The background screening may be conducted by phone or email contact with courts, employers, and schools. The person available to assist in the foreign country may be a humble court runner as opposed to an experienced investigator.) Typically, an international investigation is considerably more expensive than background screening since international investigations may involve a different level of qualifications of personnel on the ground in the foreign country — doing in-person interviews or obtaining records — and the cost can be thousands of dollars. If an employer is filling a highly sensitive position or is conducting a due diligence investigation of a potential business partner, then the services of a qualified investigative firm may be needed. When the stakes are high, there is no substitute for having a trained investigator who knows the country, the language, the customs, and laws. If an employment screening firm only conducts background screening and an investigation is required, that employment screening firm can assist the employer in obtaining qualified professional assistance.

International Screening vs. Global Screening

International screening should not be confused with "global screening." International screening occurs when a U.S. firm hires someone in the U.S. for a U.S. based position, but part of the relevant work experience was outside of the U.S. In this situation, a U. S. based background screening firm is typically utilized to make international inquiries. By comparison, when a U.S. employer opens an office or facility outside of the U.S. and wants to screen employees in that foreign county, this is known as "global screening." The U.S. employer may contact a screening firm with expertise in that particular country.

Why Employers Cannot Assume Government Screens Workers from Abroad

Employers may be tempted to rely on the U.S. Government screening conducted for the work visa instead of conducting their own background screen. This is not appropriate, as the depth of screen conducted for the visa and the types of searches conducted may not be equal to the requirements of the U.S. background screen. Also, accessing information for one purpose and using it for another may not be allowed in some countries. Just as we saw in the chapters about the FCRA and DPPA, the "permissible use" is important when considering the ability to access a search for international background screens. Some sources only allow their data to be used for a non-employment purpose, such as for a visa or adoption purpose.

There are essentially two legal ways for individuals to come to the U.S. to work or live:

1. Apply for an immigrant visa
2. Apply for a non–immigrant visa. (An example of a non-immigrant visa is an H1-B visa. This visa is issued for an initial three-year period to applicants with specialized professional skills to obtain permission to work in the U.S.)

Here is the crux of the matter for employers:

1. Employers cannot assume the U.S. government has performed a background check that relieves employers of their due diligence obligation to conduct their own screening. Government efforts are not foolproof nor are they geared toward the same type of due diligence required for employment decisions. After the events of September 11, 2001, the U.S. Government has certainly increased checks on foreign visitors and workers. However, these checks are primarily aimed at keeping terrorists and international fugitives from entering the U.S. or deporting those non-citizens that commit crimes in the U.S. or overstay their visas. The efforts the government makes, although vital, do not substitute for what an employer needs to do. The government efforts are not aimed at lesser convictions that may be relevant to job performance or verifications of credentials.
2. Information obtained for visa purposes may not always be allowed for use in employment decisions.

The Problem with Police Certificates in the Visa Process in Lieu of a Criminal History Search for Employment Purposes

One difficulty of International background screening is when a person applies for either an immigration visa or a non-immigration visa, there are potential holes in the criminal background check process. Criminal checks are done in different ways, depending on the type of visa. For non-citizens applying for an immigration visa in order to immigrate to the U.S. to live and to receive a "green card," there is a "police certificate" requirement. The applicants must obtain a police certificate from "appropriate police authorities" in their home countries. The applicants must include any prison records. That sounds good in theory, but in practice there are three main problems with police certificates:

1. The first problem is that the time period for issuing police certificates may allow a person with a criminal record to evade detection. Under the State Department rules, the police certificate comes from a country, area, or locality where the alien has resided for six months. However, if a person has frequently moved around inside that country, criminal records can be missed, depending on how the records are kept. Recent offenses may not be reported. If a person has lived in other countries, then the relevant time period is one year, so records can be missed if the person was in the country for a short period of time or left after committing an offense. The consular officer — a State Department officer assigned to a local U.S. Consulate — may require a police certificate from additional jurisdictions regardless of length of residence in any country if the officer has reason to believe a criminal record exists.

2. The second problem is that police certificates differ all over the world in terms of reliability, timeliness, and completeness. Police certificates are still only as good as the efforts, resources, and abilities of the local law enforcement authorities in each country, so even when a police certificate is available, the completeness of the data can still be an open question. In addition, a number of countries do not even have police certificates available, or police certificates are too difficult to obtain and not available as a practical matter.

3. Some jurisdictions have strict limitations on the purposes for which a police certificate is issued. It may be a violation to obtain a police certificate for employment purposes in some areas. Or some areas may provide different information on a police certificate that is issued for employment purposes than what is found on a certificate issued for visa purposes. Singapore is a good example. "To apply for a COC, the applicant is required to produce documents from the relevant authority to substantiate that a foreign country requires the COC for a specific purpose." Source: www.ifaq.gov.sg/spf/apps/fcd_faqmain.aspx.

The U.S. State Department recognizes these as important issues. The State Department maintains the Visa Reciprocity and County Document Finder, an international listing by country of issues involved in obtaining necessary visa documents. For more information, visit: http://travel.state.gov/visa/reciprocity/. Visa applicants can visit the website to find out how to obtain police certificates and court records from their own country.

The State Department also recognizes the need to continuously update the availability of each country's criminal records information. The State Department Foreign Affairs Manual and Handbook is available online. According to the State Department rules:

Consular officers should periodically discuss with the host government the availability and quality of police clearance information, as well as the procedures to be followed for visa applicants to obtain clearances both within and outside the country. Posts should provide information concerning the degree of automation and centralization of records, as well as any purge procedures followed by the host country. Posts should also determine how criminal records are indexed in their nation. The use of a unique national identification number as opposed to nonstandard spellings of names is also significant. Posts should provide background to the Department (abbreviations omitted) as well as draft language for inclusion in Appendix C (the Visa Reciprocity and County Document Finder.) Posts should coordinate with like-minded foreign embassies as appropriate.

A second type of visa application occurs when a person applies for a non-immigration visa. In other words, he or she is not applying to live permanently in the U.S. but to stay temporarily. An example is the H1-B visa. Another potential hole is that an applicant may come to the U.S. on a student visa and then change to an H1-B visa. In that case, it is not clear exactly what is being checked and by whom.

In the situation of a non-immigrant visa, the applicant is asked about a criminal record on the non-immigrant visa form called a DS-156. Pursuant to 22 CFR 41.105(a) (4), a consular officer may request a police certificate if they have reason to believe a criminal record exists. Therefore, the police certificate is only required by the U.S. Consulate office on a per-case review. If an applicant coming to the U.S. decides to lie, and the U.S. Consulate does not have reason to challenge the lie, then a criminal record could exist, and a person with a disqualifying criminal record could obtain a non-immigrant visa.

In addition, for some visas such as the H1-B, an applicant's past employment and education is a critical part of the visa process. However, given the fact that several high ranking Government officials were found to have fake degrees from diploma mills ('U.S. Officials Sport Fake Degrees,' Wired Magazine, 05.13.04), this raises the question of how effective credentials verification can be when done for large numbers of applicants from all over the world by the Government. International degree fraud is an ongoing issue. Employers need to take steps to confirm past education and past employment.

The essential lesson is there are statistically a significant number of potential job applicants where the relevant background information will come from outside of the United States. An employer cannot depend upon the visa process as protection. That means U.S. employers should consider what they can and should do internationally in the area of safe hiring and employment screening.

The Basic Components and Challenges of International Background Screening

To exercise due diligence in hiring, employers should – at a minimum – consider screening internationally to match the same screens as they do in the U.S. Primary searches for consideration are:

- ✓ Criminal records,
- ✓ Employment records,
- ✓ Education records,
- ✓ Publicly available terrorist lists and international databases, and
- ✓ Other methods such as driver's licenses, media searches, and – in some countries – credit reports.

Keeping in Mind the How Different the Rest of the World Is

Each and every country is completely different when performing international background screening. Techniques, information, and availability of public records that are taken for granted here in the United States are often times not available abroad. Each country has its own laws, customs, and procedures for background screenings.

With respect to the availability of criminal records or other types of background checks outside of the U.S., employers must realize there may be restrictions on availability based on the use of this information for employment purposes. In some countries, access to searches such as criminal or credit history for employment purposes is not allowed at all or may be restricted to very specific positions. In other countries, there may be no reliable method to obtain this information.

Here are some of the special challenges and practical difficulties employers may face when performing international background screening.

- ✓ **Each and every country is unique with differences in courts and legal systems:** Techniques and information that are taken for granted in the United States are often times not available abroad. Outside of the United States, there is often limited access to public records and the types of information needed for background screening. Each country has its own laws, customs, and procedures for background screenings and its own legal codes, definition of crimes, and court system. Employers should keep this in mind when searching international courts.

International criminal checking requires an understanding of each country's court system, how criminal records are created and maintained, where searches should be conducted, the type of records available, and what the records mean.

✓ **Privacy and data protection**: This is a crucial issue. Many countries have strict data privacy regulations that require detailed notice to the individual about the purposes of the data collected, information about who will see the personal information, and restrictions on the use of the data. The EU's privacy rules place strict restrictions on transferring personal information out of the EU and impact any data transfers to the U.S. The U.S. Department of Commerce offers a Safe Harbor program to allow for the legal flow of personal information between the U.S. and E.U. Many U.S. background screening firms that do international searches have signed up to participate in this voluntary program. (http://export.gov/safeharbor/)

✓ **Name variations:** The issue of name variations when expressing foreign names in the English alphabet is extremely complicated for two reasons. First, many cultures have naming conventions that are entirely different than the U.S. Some cultures may start the name with the family or clan name, where other cultures may utilize the mother's name as an integral part of the naming mechanism. Many cultures do not have the concept of a middle name. The second difficulty has to do with expressing a foreign name in an English format. For the languages that utilize the English alphabet — such as names in Italian, German, and Spanish — the expression of names is somewhat easier, though keeping in mind that Spanish names can have cultural variations. When it comes to expressing names that utilize a different alphabet, there is room for error and confusion. There is no easy way to translate Chinese, Korean, Arabic, or Japanese names into English. The two techniques used to render names in foreign alphabets into English are transliteration and phonetic transcription.

- Transliteration into English is based upon using a representation of the characters in the original language with English characters so that certain characters in one language always translate into English by use of agreed upon letters. It is analogous to using a codebook. Transliteration means mapping a name from one language into another. An example is Iraq, where the Q is pronounced as English CK.
- Phonetic transcription – or "transcribing" – is based upon taking the sounds of a foreign name and attempting to associate the same sounds to the sounds of the English alphabet. With either method there can be any number of variations. For example, "Osama bin Laden" can be represented as both "Laden" with an "e" or "Ladan" with an "a." First name variations can be "Usama" or "Osama."

✓ **Time differences:** Communicating with researchers, past employers, or schools around the world must take into consideration time differences. This can add lag time to the reporting process and can be very inconvenient. For employers attempting to conduct international past employment verification themselves, it is often necessary to have an employee wake up in the middle of the night to complete a call. There can be delays due to time differences when communicating with researchers, past employers, or schools around the world.

✓ **Means and cost of communications:** Each country will have different means of communication. Although email would be preferable, not all countries have reliable email delivery. Communications can also be done by fax machine. Of course, an employer wants to be careful about simply picking up the phone and dialing international numbers. Without having an international calling card or an international phone plan, the employer may suddenly receive a very high phone bill. And before any personally identifiable information is processed, the employer should make sure the information will be provided to the appropriate source and adequately protected.

✓ **Different forms:** Before submitting a request for international background screening, employers should check which forms are needed. For some searches there may be very specific forms or consent language required. Additional documentation may also be required, such as a copy of the diploma. In India, for example, most education verifications require a copy of the diploma which includes the seat number. In certain counties, employers need forms with the person's name in the language of that country, or may need the mother's or father's name. Before submitting an international background check, employers should check to see if a country has any specific form needed to comply with the rules or the situation in that country, or with privacy and data protection laws.

✓ **Calendar:** Employers should keep in mind each country has its own holidays. Since each country has its own holidays, sometimes communications are delayed because of a country's calendar. And on the topic of dates, be aware that many countries list the dates in a format different than we do in the U.S. It is not uncommon to see dates outside of the U.S. listed as DD/MM/YYYY rather than the U.S. method of listing MM/DD/YYYY.

✓ **Fraud awareness:** International screening carries an inherent risk of fraud, just as it does in the U.S. There is no guarantee that a past employer is a legitimate firm. In addition, just as the U.S. has a significant problem involving phony "degree mills" and fake degrees, there can be similar issues abroad. Although some steps can be taken to mitigate the possibility of fraud, firms that rely upon screening still face a risk. Engaging an investigator or background screening firm who is familiar with the foreign country is likely to provide the best information.

✓ **Costs:** International background screenings are normally more expensive when compared to background screening in the United States. Outside of the U.S. there are few databases available for background screening use. Searches are usually manually processed. Since an employment screening normally consists of verifying supplied information, the costs can be kept more reasonable. However, even verifying supplied information can be expensive for the reasons indicated earlier. In some countries, a translation fee is involved. In many countries, criminal searches must be conducted in each relevant location where a person has lived, worked, or studied. In many countries, there are search options that are national in scope. Although the system for international criminal checks is not perfect, making the effort allows an employer to demonstrate due diligence. Checking records also discourages applicants with something to hide.

✓ **Payments:** Fees and other payments are often required to be in local currency. If an investigator is used, many will require some or all of the fees be paid in advance. Employers who do their own background verifications and contract with an international investigator may find they need to have their bank do an international money transfer by wire (perhaps taking two weeks or more) or purchase a money order in the target country.

This chapter does not attempt to cover each country in the world. There are 192 members of the United Nations. See www.iso.org/iso/country_codes/iso_3166_code_lists/country_names_and_code_elements.htm for a list of 249 "country-like" entities. Some of the entities may be affiliated with another country but have characteristics that set it apart. While this chapter is a summary of the entire international area and not intended as a country by country view, there are several lists worthy of mention.

Top 20 Foreign Countries for International Screening

A recent list compiled by a leading international screening company shows the *Top 20 Foreign Countries* for international education verifications and international employment verifications in alphabetical order: Australia, Brazil, Canada, Chile, China, France, Germany, India, Ireland, Israel, Japan, Malaysia, Mexico, Nigeria, Pakistan, Philippines, Russia, Singapore, South Africa, and United Kingdom (U.K.).

"Red Zone" Countries

Red Zone countries are those dealing with war, political unrest, unreliable communications infrastructure, lack of standardized procedures, bureaucracy, or ambivalence toward America and/or background checks. Red Zone countries have unpredictable turnaround times and many closed businesses and schools. Local assistance and surcharges may be required. Current "red zone" countries include (list subject to change) but are not necessarily limited to: Afghanistan, Burma/Union of Myanmar, Cameroon, Chad, China, Congo (Democratic Republic of the Congo), Cote D'ivoire (Ivory Coast), Eritrea, Ethiopia, Haiti, Iran, Iraq, Kenya, Kosovo, Liberia, Libya, Nigeria, Northern Mariana Islands, Papua New Guinea, Rwanda, Saint Kitts & Nevis, Senegal, Sierra Leone, Somalia, Sudan, Syria, Uganda, Zambia, and Zimbabwe.

The next portion of this chapter examines the challenges to the specific components used in international background screening. This is followed by additional information on legal implications and privacy of data.

Additional Challenges Specific to International Criminal Checks

The problem of how to obtain international criminal records today is very similar to the situation employers and screening professionals faced in the U.S. in the 1980's. One can imagine how these issues are magnified, given the potential number of countries where a search may occur and all of the different laws, languages, cultures, and access issues, each adding to the puzzle.

Below are specific issues that employers should be cognizant of when dealing with international criminal records:

- ✓ **The Criminal Record Sources:** Outside the United States there is less access to public records and the types of information needed for background screening. Each country has its own laws, customs, and procedures for background screenings. Records may be obtained from courts, police agencies, or other government agencies depending upon the location and job involved. Access to criminal history is rarely computerized as it is in the U.S. In some countries, there is confusion about the availability of searches and the legality of obtaining records. As a rule, employers should analyze any claim that a particular country does not allow criminal background checks. Some countries consider it illegal for the police to provide the criminal record information to a private firm, while a similar criminal record disclosure may be available from courts or criminal records bureaus. Police records are typically broader and may include arrests for which there is no conviction. When the police are prohibited from providing such records, the courts are the next alternative. Employers should distinguish when a complete prohibition on obtaining criminal records exists versus a lack of availability versus limitations in the manner and means of obtaining and utilizing criminal records. (Note: The EU Privacy Laws and the FCRA for the data privacy rules in effect for European Union members are covered in a later section of this chapter.)
- ✓ **Employment Restrictions:** Even in cases where criminal records are available, they may be only available for non-employment proposes. The question becomes if a country does not allow the use of criminal records for employment inside the country, should a U.S. firm be accessing the records for use in the U.S. for employment purposes?
- ✓ **The State Department List of Countries:** A useful tool to determine what criminal records are generally available in a country is found at the U.S. Department of State web site at Travel.State.Gov which has list called "Visa Reciprocity and County" at http://travel.state.gov/visa/fees/fees_3272.html. The site advises immigrants and visitors coming to the U.S. on the availability of required visa documents. Although the information on the website is aimed at assisting individual visa applicants, it is useful for employers and screening firms to determine what information is available from what source. If an individual can obtain his or her own records, it may be possible for an employer or screening firm to obtain these records from abroad, with consent. Note, though, that just because a criminal record certificate may be available for visa or adoption purposes, there may be restrictions on availability or use for employment purposes. For each country listed, the web site describes the availability of police certificates and court records.
- ✓ **Scope of International Searches and Fees:** Typically, searches for criminal records quote per court in a country and not for the entire country. Unless specifically noted, foreign searches are conducted in each locale where an applicant lived or worked. Not every country has a "national" criminal search available to private employers. A criminal check may require multiple searches. For example, if an applicant merely indicated a certain foreign city, a background firm may search the main criminal court in that city, but the main court may cover very little of the actual jurisdiction of the area, and records can be missed. Before ordering an international criminal record, an employer should carefully specify how many areas will be searched since the average price of an international criminal search can exceed $100 per location.
- ✓ **Foreign Identifiers:** In order to identify the person, an employer will need to supply the proper type of identification needed for each country. Identifiers can include:
    - Full name and date of birth.
    - A national ID number, if a country provides one.

- Mother's maiden name.
- Father's name.
- Applicant's name in the primary language of that country.
- Each state or city where a person has lived. Some countries only maintain criminal records by a single jurisdiction.
- A legible copy of passport or picture identification card.
- A copy of a consent for screening, signed (click electronic signatures are not accepted)

✓ **American Rules May Apply Abroad:** Employers obtaining criminal records from foreign countries need to be careful how it is done. The one thing that no American firm wants to do is pay money to a foreign official to obtain criminal records where the rules of the country do not permit such records to be released. Such actions could conceivably be prosecuted in the United States under the federal Foreign Corrupt Practices Act of 1977 (FCPA), 15 U.S.C. §§ 78dd-1, et seq.

✓ **Turnaround Time:** The response time for a report can vary greatly depending upon the country. The average Turnaround Time (TAT) for international criminal searches is more than 7 business days. In some extreme situations, the time period may be measured in terms of weeks or even months. Courts in certain countries may take longer for the same reasons as in the U.S. — often the court is located in a remote or less-populated region.

✓ **Translation of Court Documents:** If there is a criminal "hit," then the foreign criminal record must be translated into English. Remember, too, that British, Australian, and other nations with English as the primary language use different law terms that must be matched to the equivalent in the U.S. to allow understanding of the facts of an offense.

✓ **Level of Offenses:** For most counties, the search is for felony or major type offenses. However, some courts do allow researchers to obtain records for misdemeanors or lesser offenses.

✓ **Audit Trail and No Record Found:** In the U.S., when court records are searched and there is no record found, there is typically no document provided by the court clerk. Court clerks do not normally confirm a lack of a finding. A "no record" is normally reported by the researcher, indicating they made the appropriate effort and there were no results found. The same is true in doing court searches throughout most of the world. If the criminal record search is at a court and no record is found, there is not likely going to be a document or paper trail that says "No Record." To have a confirmation that there is, in fact, no record, an employer may need to have the applicant obtain a police certificate. That process can be subject to long delays.

Focus On India

In India, data protection laws are in place. There are no country specific releases required, and a general release is acceptable. Normally, a local criminal record search conducted through the police districts are based on a candidate's residential address. Although in some areas there are databases available. Court searches may also be available depending upon the state or city in question. The India court system is very fragmented and paper driven. There is no standardization of how information is entered into the local district court systems. Education verifications require a copy of the degree and can have extended time service for some universities with out of pocket fee required. Falsified degrees are common, and diploma mills are fairly abundant.

Focus On United Kingdom (U.K.)

Criminal records are available for employment purposes in the United Kingdom (U.K.) – which includes England, Scotland, Wales, and Northern Ireland. Three levels of criminal records "Disclosure" exist: Basic, Standard, and Enhanced. The level of Disclosure allowed is dependent upon the job duties. Each level contains a different mix of information. The source of the Disclosure depends on the location where the subject will be working. The three primary sources are: Disclosure Scotland, Criminal Records Bureau (CRB), and Access Northern Ireland (AccessNI). The most commonly requested is the "Basic Disclosure" from Disclosure Scotland. The Basic Disclosure is also available from AccessNI. This Disclosure discloses all convictions which are not spent under the Rehabilitation of Offenders Act and covers all of the UK; it is not limited to Scotland or Northern Ireland. The results will list all unspent convictions or the result will indicate there are no convictions. This Basic Disclosure is available for any position in any industry, as long as there is job-relatedness to the search. It is the most commonly used type of disclosure from the UK. This search requires a special release signed by the applicant before the search can be submitted. Additionally, the employer must provide copies of requested identity and address documents along with the special release. The typical turnaround time for a Basic Disclosure is five (5) working days. If the person works in the Republic of Ireland, it is a different country. If the candidate is a resident outside of U.K., the only available Disclosure is the Basic Disclosure.

Disclosure Scotland: http://disclosurescotland.co.uk/

CRB: www.homeoffice.gov.uk/agencies-public-bodies/crb/

AccessNI: www.dojni.gov.uk/accessni

Focus On Japan

Employers may be able to utilize a Japanese Criminality Search (JCS). JSC is a proprietary database containing criminality information sourced from government records, Japanese media, Japanese courts, public records, independent anti-organized crime associations, and privately held information of individuals and companies with known connections to unlawful associations such as organized crime and right-wing organizations. It is important to note that the JCS is a database search and NOT a search at the courthouse. This search requires a signed release that includes the name of the individual in Japanese characters (kanji), date of birth, and address. While it is not possible to legally conduct a comprehensive criminal record check in Japan, the JCS is the most comprehensive resource available in the country covering organized crime and criminality information. The Japanese Criminality Search (JCS) can provide comprehensive and actionable information in a cost effective manner. The typical turnaround time for background screening in Japan is three (3) business days.

International Education Verifications

Verification of an educational degree earned abroad is critical to verify credentials and to avoid fraud. Statistics show that education fraud can run as high as 20 percent. An employer needs to determine if an applicant attended the school claimed and received the degree claimed. The employer also needs to determine if the school is accredited and authentic. The world is awash with phony schools, fake degrees, and worthless diplomas. If the employer is not familiar with a school, research should be conducted. A legitimate school will often have an e-mail address or phone number so that they can be easily contacted to verify a degree.

Manila Information, Please

One international firm reports being asked to verify a high school degree in Manila in the Philippines. The school had a name similar to "Immaculate Heart" in its title. The exact school phone or address was not provided so the firm dutifully researched, found, and contacted the high school. The school indicated the person never attended much less graduated. The applicant insisted she absolutely had graduated and supplied contact information and a copy of the diploma. Upon further investigation, the screening firm learned that there were numerous schools throughout Manila with similar names. The lesson — screening internationally requires very precise information.

Be prepared to pay additional fees. The amount of additional fees (if any) will depend on the institution. Requests for additional fees from a background screening firm may contain the actual fee amount as well as a small administration fee. If there is a wire transfer fee, they will include that amount as well. All amounts are converted and requested in U.S. dollars. There is also the issue of additional fees that some schools charge to provide the verification. Most employers do an excellent job of providing copies of degrees and mark sheets in advance to the background screener once they understand the reasoning behind the request.

Problems with Applicant Provided Documents

This is probably the #1 question international background screening firms are asked: "If the applicant provides the document, why do we need you?" The answer is fraud. In order for legitimate schools to combat fraud, they need documents to cross check and reference. It helps the international background screening firm to identify the school. Here are the main reasons why the end client should not accept a document from the applicant as the definitive verification and why the background screening firms ask for the degree, mark sheets, or additional documentation:

✓ **Name confirmation:** The degree copy helps to clearly identify the name, in local language, under which the degree was granted.

✓ **Record Archiving Systems:** Some schools overseas need the degree/mark sheet/roll number in order to know exactly which of their systems to check. Some schools have two for the most part: the paper trail system or the updated computerized system.

✓ **Fraud Prevention:** In India alone, this is a multi-million rupee business. Companies go to H1-B visa hopefuls and write their whole resume giving false credentials on the resume. The subject of the scam sometimes was and sometimes wasn't "aware" of the issue. The other side of the fraud was schools back in early 2000 were actually involved in "Fraudulent Degree Rings." People high up in the institutions in Registrar offices were being paid to confirm a degree when none existed. Fast forward to the present, and schools will now sometimes ask for: Copy of Degree, Seat Number, Roll Number, Mark Sheets, Father's Full Name/Mother's Full Name, Place of Birth, and a copy of the applicant's photo. The reason for this is that all or part are used now to deter fraud. If a school receives a copy of the degree and something from that degree is off according to their records, the school will ask for the next document/piece of information and so on until they cross checked them all and are satisfied. Another reason why a background screening company may ask for a copy of the degree is if they have reasonable suspicion that there may be fraud. They will maintain on file copies of previously provided degrees from schools – both confirmed frauds and legitimate. If the background screening company does suspect fraud, they will always forward the actual document to the school and obtain their official response as the authenticity in writing for their customers.

✓ **Location Assistance:** A background screening firm will ask for a copy of the degree from the customer in order to help locate the school. The applicant may advise that he or she attended Leningrad State University, but the degree will show Saint Petersburg State University. They are both the same but their name changed back and forth then back again. For schools in countries with dramatic government changes (i.e., fall of Communism in Russia), most higher education institutions changed their name to reflect the new government. In Russia, the fall of Communism spurred the change from Leningrad to Saint Petersburg.

Tips on Performing Education Verification of International Schools

The verification process has three parts:

1. **Determine if applicant in fact attended the school claimed and received the degree claimed:** Did the applicant actually attend the listed school and receive the degree claimed? Verification can be done by an employer or by a screening firm. Internet resources offering lists of schools around the world are available. If the applicant presents a diploma or some other document, it should be sent to the issuing school for verification. Typically, schools can be contacted by phone or by email. Of course, challenges to overcome are language and time differences. Despite these handicaps, there is no question that the verification can certainly occur. Before performing the verification, it is helpful to obtain as much information as possible from an applicant. An employer needs to obtain the applicant's full name used while attending school, the exact spelling in the language utilized by the school, the dates the person attended the school, and any student ID number that was used. A copy of the degree or other documentation may be needed. It is helpful to obtain as much information as possible, such as school web site and email.

2. **Determine if the school is accredited and authentic:** While it is important to establish that a school is accredited and authentic, employers should never assume that accreditation automatically equals a real school since there are many fake accrediting bodies and also real schools that are not accredited. Some public schools may lose their accreditation due to mismanagement or be on probation. So the lack of accreditation, while problematic, may or may not be the deciding factor in deciding if a school is real. There is a significant problem with fake schools abroad. Employers in the United States have a difficult time detecting fraudulent degrees in America, let alone on an international scale. To resolve the authenticity issue, there are numerous resources that can assist an employer. For an example of the size of the problem of diploma mills, an online story in the Khaleej Times in India on May 13, 2004 proclaimed 'Fake India Degrees Flood Middle East Market.' "India churns out brilliant graduates by the thousands every year. Unfortunately, it also churns out fake degrees by the thousands. Manufacturing fake certificates is a money-minting industry that has never stopped churning business for the people involved in it. The effect of such fakes is being felt globally." Many agents also say it is quite difficult to spot a fake degree nowadays as it resembles an original one in every way — from the texture of the paper to the university stamp. The story noted that not only are people claiming degrees they did not earn, but job applicants are also making up fake schools. As a result, the process of obtaining actual verifications from schools can be time consuming and can cause harm to a real graduate who must take extra steps to prove his or her education credentials are genuine.

3. **Determine the equivalency of a foreign degree in terms U.S. employers can understand:** Understanding the equivalency of a foreign degree in terms U.S. employer can understand is not an easy task. However, there are several agencies offering services that provide an equivalency analysis. For example, for information about degrees issued by foreign medical schools, there is a well-established mechanism to make that determination: the National Committee on Foreign Medical Education and Accreditation (NCFMEA) was established under the Higher Education Amendments of 1992.

International Employment Verifications

International employment verifications have similar challenges as faced by employers in the United States, augmented by all the problems associated with working internationally. To obtain background screening information, employers may need to schedule calls for the middle of the night, locate foreign phone numbers, and overcome language barriers.

To conduct an international verification efficiently, it is important to have the applicant provide as much information as possible. It is not practical for an American firm to attempt to call a foreign country to locate the past employer's phone number. When a better phone number is required, an international screening agency may need permission to contact an applicant directly to ask for better information. A background screening firm will typically need permission to contact the applicant directly in order to obtain any additional necessary information.

There are three essential keys to successful international employment verifications:

- ✓ **No Such Thing as Too Much Information:** Obtain as much information as possible from the applicant. Since locating past employers in a foreign county is difficult, the applicant should be asked to provide as much information as possible. Of course, there is always the possibility of a "set-up" or fake reference. Whenever possible, effort should be made to independently verify the existence and authenticity of past employers.
- ✓ **Use Local Languages for Verifications:** In order to obtain the best results, employment and educational verifications should be conducted in the primary language of that country. Even though there are international translation services, communicating with employers and schools in their native language improves the chances of completing a verification task.
- ✓ **Be Careful when Providing PII:** If utilizing researchers or firms outside of the U.S. to obtain employment (or even education) verification, be very careful about providing any personally identifiable information (PII), such as date of birth, passport number, or similar information. The best practice is to only utilize researchers outside

of the U.S. to the extent possible to obtain contact information, but only provide PII directly to the employer or school.

Employers using international background screening for past employment and credentials verifications may also encounter fake experience certificate issues in India and other countries. This whole fake employment system is a growing problem for employers. For example, a number of stories have appeared recently concerning fake CVs in India. C.V. stands for Curriculum Vitae. When people refer to CVs they are usually talking about a biographical résumé. Some recent articles about the India fake CVs include:

✓ 'Fake certificate racket busted' (The Times of India 9/26/2008): http://timesofindia.indiatimes.com/city/hyderabad/Fake-certificate-racket-busted/articleshow/3529134.cms
✓ 'Fake CVs Nightmare for Employers' (Daily News & Analysis 2/2/2011): www.dnaindia.com/money/report_fake-cvs-proving-to-be-a-real-nightmare-foremployers_1502008-all.
✓ 'India Inc grapples with rash of fake CVs' (Hindustan Times 7/20/2008): www.hindustantimes.com/storypage/Print.aspx?Id=f56c6187-c09c-4bc5-8638-059e4d8b92df
✓ 'India Inc hit by lying job seekers' (IndianExpress.com 1/24/2011): www.expressindia.com/latest-news/India-Inc-hit-by-lying-job-seekers/741670/
✓ 'IT Firms in Pact to Banish Fake CVs' (Business Standard 8/24/2009): www.business-standard.com/india/news/it-firms-in-pact-to-banish-fake-cvs/306440/
✓ 'Over 51K fake degrees issued in state' (The Times of India 10/28/2010): http://timesofindia.indiatimes.com/articleshow/6825330.cms?prtpage=1
✓ 'Private eye on false resume' (The Telegraph, Calcutta, India 5/6/2010): www.telegraphindia.com/1100506/jsp/others/print.html

Other Resources and Tips for International Screening Due Diligence

In addition to the screening tools already mentioned, there are other steps an employer can take for performing due diligence when hiring a person who has spent time abroad that include:

✓ **Domestic Background Checks:** Even though the person's time in the U.S. could be limited, do whatever background checking is possible based upon their time in the U.S. This effort demonstrates due diligence by documenting the fact employers did what they could do.
✓ **Domestic Personal References:** Even if a person is relatively new to this country, ask for the names of personal references in the U.S. Be sure to document the relationship between the reference and the applicant. Although this is not a perfect solution, as with domestic background checks, an employer demonstrates due diligence by making and documenting an attempt to do a screening.
✓ **Disclosure of International Background Checks:** If hiring a number of applicants from abroad, then state in the release forms that you will also conduct background investigations in any countries where an applicant has lived in the past seven to ten years. This can at least have the effect of discouraging an applicant with something to hide. However, this should be worded carefully so that an employer does not imply that any hiring decisions are being made based upon country of origin or ethnicity.

AUTHOR TIP In order not to run afoul of Equal Employment Opportunity Commission (EEOC) rules, never refer to a screening in a foreign country as a search of "country of origin" or any other reference that implies that nationality or ethnicity is a consideration. Instead, employers may indicate that "a search abroad" is simply a search in other countries where an applicant has lived or worked.

U.S. Terrorist Watch Search Lists

Other due diligence tools include the various terrorist databases available to the public, such as the Office of Foreign Assets Control ("OFAC") list maintained by the U.S. Department of the Treasury. Such lists are readily available but there are limitations as well, such as working with name matches only when no additional details are available. See Chapter 20.

International Sanctions Search

Below are recommended resources.

✓ **Global Sanction List (GSL) – Sanctioned Entities:** The Global Sanction List (GSL) contains information from the most important sanction lists from around the world, which are then aggregated and grouped into one category. The GSL offers close to 20,000 profiles of individuals and companies of the highest risk rating. Covered lists include:

- Bank of England,
- Bureau of Industry and Security,
- Department of State,
- EU Terrorism List,
- FBI Top Ten Most Wanted,
- Interpol Most Wanted,
- OCC Shell Bank List,
- Office of Foreign Assets Control (OFAC) Sanctions and SDN & Blocked Entities,
- Treasury PML List,
- SECO List,
- UN Consolidated List,
- WorldBank Debarred Parties List,
- CBI List, and
- ICE List.

✓ **Global Politically Exposed Persons (PEP) List:** PEPs – or "Politically Exposed Persons" – are considered high risk people, and employers require enhanced due diligence when conducting business with Politically Exposed Persons, particularly in Private Banking. Financial institutions that have conducted business with PEPs without following adequate Know Your Customer procedures and enhanced due diligence processes have been hit with heavy fines. Since the events of September 11, 2001 over 100 countries have changed their Anti Money Laundering laws to fight against corruption. There has also been greater emphasis and cooperation between nations to enforce the Foreign Corrupt Practices Act. While there exists no global definition for a PEP, the Financial Action Task Force (FATF), U.S. Patriot Act, and the European Union (EU) Directive use similar definitions and guidelines in which the term Politically Exposed Person was typically defined by the following:

- Local legislations like officials in the executive, legislative, administrative, military, or judicial branch of a foreign government (elected or not).
- A senior official of a major foreign political party.
- A senior executive of a foreign government owned commercial enterprise.
- An immediate family member – spouse, parents, siblings, children – of such individuals.
- Any individual publicly known to be a close personal or professional associate.
- While the interpretation of these guidelines varies from country to country, and there might be slight variations, the expectations for organizations doing business with Politically Exposed Person are universally similar. The following process is international standard:
  - Identify the "Politically Exposed Persons" amongst clientele.
  - Make sure that funds managed by an organization on behalf of the Politically Exposed Person do not derive from a corrupt source.

✓ **Global Enforcement List (GEL) – Enforcement Agencies:** The Global Enforcement List, or GEL, consists of information received from regulatory and governmental authorities that list the content of warnings and actions against individuals and companies. The GEL lists narcotic-traffickers, money launderers, fraudsters, human traffickers, fugitives, and other criminals to provide the most comprehensive protection to clients.

✓ **Global Adverse Media List (GAL) – News Media:** The Global Adverse Media List (GAL) is an extensive proprietary database comprised of the results of public domain news. The GAL has more than 20,000 newspapers and magazines in over 10 languages that are monitored for risk relevant information to provide impressive protection from risk entities.

International Screening Database Information

International screening database information comes from many resources, sources, and media searches. However, all international screening database information needs to be taken with a grain of salt, due to name similarity. Employers also need to make sure not to discriminate as well on the basis of national origin of job applicants. For foreign countries, employers need to realize that information in some countries is better than in others. Although there may be limited information available from a country such as Afghanistan, for example, it is nowhere near to being complete and up-to-date.

Legal Implications for Employers Doing International Background Checks

It is important to stay within legal guidelines that are applicable in both the U.S. and the foreign country. When obtaining information from an applicant about past employment or education abroad, it is important not to refer to the country as their country of origin. That would likely be a form of discrimination since such a statement can imply that the employer is considering ethnicity or country of origin as a factor of employment. Instead of using the phrase "country of origin," an employer should refer to any screening outside of the U.S. as simply an "international screening." It is also important not to perform any type of check that would be an invasion of privacy or contrary to the laws of either the U.S. or the foreign country. For example, employers who only conduct background checks on a person's history in the U.S. could potentially be discriminatory in their actions towards individuals who have been long time U.S. residents. For example, if an applicant has lived in the U.S. all of his or her life, the criminal search could be for 7 years or for 10 years of history. If the employer only screens U.S. history on an applicant who just immigrated to the U.S., this second person will get a criminal search for a much shorter period of time. In this example, employers are holding U.S. citizens to an inconsistent and potentially higher standard.

Thus, the legal implications of international background screening can be very complex and involve the intersection of U.S. domestic law and the operation of foreign law. Furthermore, international screening and the flow of information across borders is a relativity new and developing area of law.

Below is a discussion of some of the more significant considerations involved. Employers must be aware of how the data is obtained, transmitted, and utilized.

1. **Obtaining Foreign Data:** The essential rule for any employer in the U.S. is that information should be obtained in a manner consistent with the laws of the country where the data originated. If it is not legal in a particular country to obtain a criminal record from the police, then a U.S. employer should not do so either. A U.S. firm could be exposed to liability for obtaining foreign records that would be prohibited in the foreign country if the employer somehow obtained the records by illegal means in the applicant's home country. If a lawsuit arises, an applicant can claim an invasion of privacy or other violation of rights based upon the illegally obtained records. A complaint could be filed in the foreign country, and the U.S. employer could face a lawsuit in the U.S. or the foreign country. A key element in legally obtaining data is, of course, the applicant's written consent. In the context of employment screening, the assumption is made that the applicant has not only consented, but wants to assist the employer in obtaining records in order to facilitate the employment decision.

2. **Transmitting Foreign Records:** The concept of data transmittal has to do with data privacy protection rules in effect for many countries. Data that may be obtained legally from a source may become improper to use if privacy rules are not followed.

3. **Utilization of Foreign Records:** Utilization refers to rules that determine if and how a criminal record can be used in an employment decision. The first issue is whether the record was obtained legally. The next issue is whether a U.S. employer may legally consider information obtained from a foreign country for employment, especially in the context of criminal records. If the job and the applicant are both in a foreign country, then it is likely the rule of the foreign country applies. As the old saying goes, "When in Rome, do as the Romans." In this situation the employer is best advised to consult legal counsel in the host country and follow the rules used in that country for any type of pre-employment screening. If the job and the applicant are in the U.S., then the best practice for the U.S. employer is to apply at the minimum the same rules they would to information obtained in the U.S. This means to follow the EEOC rules concerning the use of criminal data. This also means a screening firm has the same obligations for accuracy and re-verification when it locates a criminal record in the U.S. For example, under FCRA section 607(b), there is an obligation to utilize reasonable procedures to assure maximum possible accuracy. If a record is found, then there is an obligation under FCRA section 613 to either utilize strict procedures to ensure the record is up-to-date or to give the applicant notice. Other specific adverse action notice procedures also apply. However, when obtaining the data, employers should also take into account any privacy and data protection laws that exist in the country where the information is located. If the job is in the U.S. but the applicant is living abroad, and if there is a law in the foreign country that prohibits the use of criminal records in that country, then the employer needs to make a risk-management decision. The U.S. employer needs to exercise due diligence before bringing the worker to the U.S. Failure to exercise due diligence would leave the employer vulnerable in case the applicant committed some sort of harm or if the employer had to defend hiring practices in court. On the other hand, an employer does not want to be in the position of violating a foreign law. An employer may take the position that the use of the criminal record is regulated under U.S. law, since the employment is to be performed in the U.S. and that is where the employer stands the greatest chance of being sued. In addition, any criminal record obtained abroad is done so with express authorization of the applicant under the FCRA. Under general privacy principles, a valid consent goes a long way to protect an employer from a complaint that the employer violated an applicant's rights. In the interest of enforcing a consistent policy worldwide, an employer may also decide to operate under U.S. rules when considering how to utilize foreign criminal records on applicants who will be working in the U.S. However, this is still an emerging area of law.

When conducting background screening conducted on residents of foreign countries, the employer must also be aware of other regulations that may protect that individual's rights, in addition to privacy laws. Some of these will be Human Rights Codes, Labor Laws, or Consumer Protection laws. Know that these regulations, just as the privacy regulations, may be national and/or localized. Just as in the U.S., it is recommended to consult with counsel to make sure your company is following the local requirements. It is also important to consult with counsel knowledgeable about foreign laws.

Privacy and Data Protection in International Background Screening

Because the background screening process involves collecting and transferring personally identifiable data of the applicant, the process will fall under a country's data privacy regulations, among other regulations. As discussed in other chapters of this book, the primary privacy regulation in the U.S. impacting background screening is the FCRA. Additional regulations are GLB and DPPA, as well as state specific regulations. Outside of the U.S., privacy regulations, when they exist, are often comprehensive, covering an entire country. These privacy regulations will cover how the personal information is obtained, transmitted, and utilized. A U.S. based employer may legally obtain information from a foreign country and use the information in a legal manner, but yet still run afoul of the source country's privacy laws.

Privacy regulations that are most often impacted by U.S. employers are those dealing with the European Union (EU) and Canada. Other country's privacy laws have similar elements to the EU and Canadian laws and requirements are based upon the OECD (Organization for Economic Cooperation and Development) Guidelines. A good resource for understanding these basic principles, as well as for requirements for moving personal data across a country border is the OECD Guidelines on the Protection of Privacy and Transborder Flows of Personal Data web page: www.oecd.org/document/18/0,3343,en_2649_34255_1815186_1_1_1_1,00.html. Remember, there are over 100 countries in the world with privacy regulations either in force or being developed. Since there are only 27 EU Member States, this leaves many other countries with their own privacy regulations that need to be adhered to. A useful website called Privacy International outlines privacy rights and status in many countries is found at: www.privacyinternational.org/index.shtml.

A Look at European Union (EU) Privacy Laws

The following article, written by Mr. Robert R. Belair, is an excellent analysis of the differences in privacy laws affecting employment screening in the U.S. and EU. The author sincerely thanks Mr. Belair for granting permission to include herein.

Employment Background Screening – A Comparison of Privacy Laws in the U.S. and the EU

By Robert R. Belair, Attorney at Law, Arnall Golden Gregory LLP

Setting the Scene

This article highlights the differences – and the similarities – in employment screening privacy law between the U.S. ("U.S."") and nations in the European Union ("EU").[1]

In the U.S., employment screening is governed principally by the federal Fair Credit Reporting Act ("FCRA")[2] and, to a lesser extent, by other federal statutes, including Title V of the Gramm Leach Bliley Act ("GLBA")[3]; the Driver's Privacy Protection Act ("DPPA")[4]; Title VII of the Civil Rights Act of 1964[5]; and Section 5 of the Federal Trade Commission Act ("FTC Act"). Statutes and regulations adopted by individual states can also be important and frequently take the form of consumer reporting statutes; uniform deceptive acts and practices statutes; criminal history record information laws; Freedom of Information Act and Open Records Act laws; and various state employment rights laws.[6] These laws are mostly enforced by the Federal Trade Commission (and now, in certain limited circumstances, the Consumer Financial Protection Bureau established in the Dodd-Frank Act ("Dodd-Frank"))[7]; state attorney generals and state offices of consumer protection; and through a variety of private rights or actions.

---

[1] There are currently 27 European Union member nations: Austria, Belgium, Bulgaria, Cyprus, the Czech Republic, Denmark, Estonia, Finland, France, Germany, Greece, Hungary, Ireland, Italy, Latvia, Lithuania, Luxembourg, Malta, the Netherlands, Poland, Portugal, Romania, Slovakia, Slovenia, Spain, Sweden and the United Kingdom.

[2] 15 U.S.C. § 1681 et seq.

[3] 15 U.S.C. § 6801-6809

[4] 18 U.S.C. § 2721-2725

[5] 42 U.S.C. § 2000e et seq.

[6] *E.g.*, Arizona § 41-1401 et seq.; California Government Code §§ 12900-12926; Ohio § 4113.02 et seq.; and Virginia § 2.2-3900 et seq.

[7] Pub.L. 111-203, Title X

In the EU, the laws governing employment background screening are based upon the 1995 EU Data Privacy Directive ("EU Directive")[8]; national laws incorporating and, in many cases, enhancing the provisions in the EU Directive and adopted in all 27 EU nations; provincial privacy laws adopted in some EU nations (such as by the German "Lander"); and directives issued by the various national data privacy authorities established in all EU nations. In addition, most EU nations have adopted various labor and employment laws, as well as freedom of information type laws, that can significantly impact employment background screening.

Similarities

The U.S. and EU employment screening laws rest on a foundation of comprehensive and fundamental similarities – both approaches rely on a requirement that applicants and employees are provided with comprehensive fair information practice privacy protections.

A comparison of key fair information practice standards applicable under both U.S. and EU law tells the story.[9]

Fair Information Practice Provision	United States	EU Nations
Notice to Applicants and Employees that a background screen will be conducted	Yes; Section 604(b)(2)(A)(i) and 604(b)(1)(B) of the FCRA	Yes; Article 10 of the EU Directive
Consent by the applicant or employee required for background screening	Yes; Section 604(b)(2)(A)ii	Yes; Article 7(f)
Access by the Applicant or Employee to a copy of their background screen report	Yes; Section 609 of the FCRA	Yes; Article 12(1)
Dispute and correction by the applicant or employee	Yes; Section 611	Yes; Article 12(2)
Data quality protections – accuracy and timeliness	Yes; Sections 605; 607; and 613	Yes; Article 6(1)
Confidentiality	Yes; Section 604(a)	Yes; Article 7(f)
Data Security	Yes; Section 607	Yes; Article 17(1)
Enforcement	Yes; Sections 616; 617; 621	Yes; Articles 23; 24; and 28

Differences

The similarities, while numerous and important, do not mean that the laws governing background screening in the U.S. and the EU nations are, by any means, identical. Four differences are especially important.

1. Registration of Background Screeners and Background Screening Activities. In most EU nations, commercial entities collecting, maintaining, using or disclosing personally identifiable information ("PII") (dubbed "controllers" under Article 2 of the EU Directive) must file a registration application with their national data protection authority describing the proposed data processing activity. These registration requirements vary significantly among the 27 EU nations and also vary depending upon the exact nature and purpose of the processing. (Article 19 of the EU Directive).

2. Restrictions on Types and Amounts of PII That May Be Collected. Article 8 of the EU Directive restricts the "processing" of sensitive categories of PII, including information relating to racial or ethnic origin; political

---

[8] Within the next few years, the EU Data Privacy Directive is expected to be replaced by a comprehensive privacy regulation adopted by the European Parliament. Directive 95/46/EC.

[9] In the United States, if an employer does not use a consumer reporting agency to conduct the background screening, many of the fair information practice standards embodied in the FCRA may be limited or may not be available at all. In the EU, the availability of fair information practice protections is unaffected by whether the employer conducts a background screening directly or outsources the screening to a professional background screening company.

leanings; religious affiliations; trade union memberships; and information about health or sexual behavior. In addition, some EU countries – France, for example – restrict the use of financial information or credit history information in employment background screenings. The collection and use of criminal history record information, to a lesser extent, is also restricted in background screening products in some EU nations.

3. <u>Restrictions on TransBorder Data Flows</u>. Article 25 of the EU Directive restricts the transfer of PII outside of the EU to nations that fail to ensure an "adequate level of protection." The United States is a nation that falls into this unwelcome category. As a result, a background screen compiled in the EU (even if about a U.S. citizen) cannot be communicated to a location in the U.S. unless one of several protections applies, including using EU approved model contractual protections or adopting "binding corporate rules" or participating in the EU/U.S. Safe Harbor Registration Program.

In July of 2000, the U.S. and the European Commission entered into a "Safe Harbor Accord" in order to facilitate PII transfers from the EU to the U.S. Domestic background screening companies wishing to participate in the Safe Harbor program must file an application with the U.S. Commerce Department, self-certifying that they are in compliance with the seven Safe Harbor principles (a set of fair information practice standards); that they commit to cooperate with investigations of privacy violations conducted by the EU relevant national data protection authority; and that they commit to notify the Commerce Department and the European Commission of such violations.

Safe Harbor membership will usually provide sufficient authority for the transfer.

4. <u>Restrictions on the Use of Consent for Employment Screening</u>. Another type of restriction on the transfer of PII from EU nations to the U.S. is the uncertainty surrounding the use of consent as a basis for the transfer. (Article 25(1)(a)). The EU Article 29 Working Party charged with developing guidelines and recommendations for the application of the EU Directive, has expressed reservations about the extent to which a consent obtained from an applicant or an employee is, in fact, voluntary.[10] Because the EU Directive requires that the consent to transfer PII from the EU to the U.S. must be explicit and unambiguous and almost always in writing, the Article 29 Working Party guidelines have cast doubt on the use of consent alone as a basis for transfers. According to Article 29 Working Party, individuals applying for employment or hoping to keep their employment are highly likely to consent to whatever data processing an employer or its agent, a consumer reporting agency, may request.

Recommendations

In view of all this, a U.S.-based background screening company performing a background screen investigation in one of the 27 EU nations and planning to share the results of the screen with an employer in the U.S., should be mindful of the following strategies.

- Make sure that your company understands the EU Directive and the national privacy laws thereunder in every EU country in which your company will be conducting background screens. Bear in mind that many EU citizens or residents (or for that matter, U.S. citizens working in the EU) have resided in multiple EU countries. This will mean that the details of applicable privacy laws may differ substantially.

- Pay special attention to "relevance." The relevance of information obtained and placed in a background screen is becoming an enhanced consideration in the U.S. thanks to several factors, including the recent

---

[10] Article 29 Data Protection Working Party, Opinion 15/2011, on the definition of "consent", 0197/11/EN, WP187, adopted on July 13, 2011 (expressing concern that consent is not "freely given" if "the data subject is under the influence of the controller, such as an employment relationship").

EEOC Guidance.[11] Relevance, however, has been a major concern in the EU for many years. Data that is collected and placed in a background screen must be relevant to the job for which the individual is applying and the amount of data collected must not be "excessive." Article 6(1)(c).

- Before conducting EU governed background screens, make sure that you have reviewed your company's Fair Credit Reporting Act compliance. If your company is based in the U.S., your company will already need to be in compliance with the FCRA. In doing so, you can be confident that your company will meet many (but not all) of the EU Directive's fair information practice requirements.

- Understand the workings of the data privacy supervisory authority in those countries from which you will be obtaining data, including the rulings and guidance published by that authority. These requirements vary significantly. In some EU countries, prior approval from the data privacy authority for any data processing, including preparation of background screening reports, is necessary. In other EU countries, notice may be required, but authorization from the authority is customarily not required prior to conducting the background screen.

- Be mindful if your company will be collecting "sensitive PII" as defined in Article 8 of the EU Directive. Insofar as practicable, avoid collecting this type of data.

- Always obtain an applicant or employee's consent in writing and be sure that the consent is unambiguous, explicit and specific. Having said this, do not rely on consent as a basis for transmitting the report to the U.S. Always have another legal basis on which to rely in transmitting the report to the U.S. This means that your company should have adopted a workable transborder data flow strategy, as discussed earlier.

- Finally, make certain that your company has implemented a plan for monitoring and periodic updating of your EU strategies. The EU Parliament, as noted earlier, is considering a comprehensive regulatory approach to privacy, replacing the EU Directive. In addition, national privacy laws change frequently. Ruling and interpretations from the national data privacy commissions change even more frequently.

Conclusion

If a U.S. company is planning to employ an EU national or, for that matter, a U.S. citizen who has been a long-time EU resident, it is frequently important to conduct appropriate, EU sourced background screens. As a background screening company, your company may need to obtain advice from European counsel, particularly those that are familiar with the data privacy commission in the country in which you will be obtaining information.

At a minimum, U.S. consumer reporting agencies and employers need to be thoughtful about obtaining the requisite legal authority to conduct EU sourced background screens and thoughtful about an appropriate strategy for transferring the information from that screen to a U.S. based employer.

Introduction to the European Union (EU) Data Protection Directive (*Directive 95/46/EC of the European Parliament and of the Council of 24 October 1995*)

Protection of an individual's personal data is a fundamental right in the EU. The EU rules went into effect in 1998 and they impact the transmissions of "personally identifiable data" (PII) from the EU countries to the U.S. Each EU Member Country is required to have data protection laws which must be equal or more stringent than the EU Data Privacy

---

[11] Equal Employment Opportunity Commission ("EEOC") Enforcement Guidance on the Consideration of Arrest and Conviction Records in Employment Decisions, No. 915.002 (April 25, 2012).

Directive. The list of countries in the European Union is found at: http://europa.eu/. Information about the EU Directive is at: http://ec.europa.eu/justice/data-protection/index_en.htm. The EU Data Protection Directive is the baseline for privacy regulations in the EU.

Protection of Personal Data in the European Union (EU)

The EU Data Protection Directive outlines the following basic enforceable rights for individuals who have their personal data is processed:

✓ The right to be informed that your personal data is being processed in a clear and understandable language;

✓ The right to have access to your own data;

✓ The right to rectify any wrong or incomplete information;

✓ The right, in some cases, to object to the processing on legitimate grounds;

✓ The right not to be subjected to an automated decision intended to evaluate certain personal aspects relating to you, such as your performance at work, creditworthiness, reliability, and conduct; and

✓ The right to receive compensation from the data controller for any damage you suffer, etc.

In addition, the organization responsible for processing an individual's personal data (the "data controller") has certain obligations:

✓ To ensure that your rights are observed (i.e. inform you, give access to your data);

✓ To ensure that data are collected only for specified, explicit and legitimate purposes, that they are kept accurate and up to date and for no longer than is necessary;

✓ To ensure that the criteria for making data-processing legitimate are observed, for example, when you give your consent, sign a contract, or have legal obligations, etc.;

✓ Confidentiality of the processing;

✓ Security of the processing;

✓ Notification to the data protection authority, in some cases; and

✓ To ensure that, when a transfer of data occurs to countries outside the EU, these countries guarantee an adequate level of protection.

Source: 'Protection of Personal Data in the European Union' at http://ec.europa.eu/justice/data-protection/files/eujls08b-1002_-_protection_of_personnal_data_a4_en.pdf

---

Firms that process data on individuals from EU member countries without compliance with the EU rules can be in violation of EU law. This can have a serious impact on international firms or firms that do business in an EU country. American firms under the general jurisdiction of the FTC or DOT have the option of joining a "Safe Harbor" offered by the U.S. Department of Commerce as one means to process information from the E.U. This is a voluntary program that involves self-certification regarding the mechanisms to protect confidential personal data.

Note that the Safe Harbor principles have different requirements than the individual EU country data privacy requirements. The Safe Harbor requirements are relevant when the organization intends to transfer information from the EU to the U.S. under the Safe Harbor regime. Organizations that are processing data in an EU member country will need to abide by that country's privacy regulations, which contain other requirements.

Introduction to the "Safe Harbor"

According to the U.S. Department of Commerce:

"The European Commission's Directive on Data Protection went into effect in October, 1998, and prohibits the transfer of personal data to non-European Union nations that do not meet the European 'adequacy standard' for privacy protection."

While the United States and the European Union (EU) share the goal of enhancing privacy protection for their citizens, the United States takes a different approach to privacy from the approach of the European Union. The United States uses an approach that relies on a mix of legislation, regulation, and self-regulation. The European Union, however, relies on comprehensive legislation that requires creation of government data protection agencies, registration of databases with those agencies and, in some instances, prior approval before personal data processing may begin. Generally, the EU considers the U.S. as not having adequate privacy protections. As a result of these different privacy approaches, the Directive could have significantly hampered the ability of U.S. companies to engage in many trans-Atlantic transactions.

"In order to bridge these different privacy approaches and provide a streamlined means for U.S. organizations to comply with the Directive, the U.S. Department of Commerce, in consultation with the European Commission, developed a 'safe harbor' framework. The safe harbor — approved by the EU in July of 2000 — is an important way for U.S. companies to avoid experiencing interruptions in their business dealings with the EU or facing prosecution by European authorities under European privacy laws. Certifying to the safe harbor will assure that EU organizations know that your company provides 'adequate privacy protection,' as defined by the Directive."

A background screening firm or employer can become Safe Harbor certified by following the guidelines listed at the Department of Commerce web site at www.export.gov/safeharbor/.

A listing of firms on the Safe Harbor list appears at https://safeharbor.export.gov/list.aspx.   Note that Safe Harbor Certification is not the only mechanism by which a U.S. company can transfer personal information from the EU. The key is that the company has identified a means of conducting this transfer legally. Simply transferring information, even with the consent of the subject, will not make it legal.

Safe Harbor Privacy Principles

In order to self-certify compliance with Safe Harbor, an organization must agree to comply with seven principles which correspond to the EU Data Protection Directive requirements. For employers in the U.S., these principles line up with existing requirements in the FCRA.

✓ **Notice:** Individuals must have clear notice that personally identifiable information is being collected. Notice is typically given in a consent form. Employers in the U.S. are familiar with a notice requirement, since consents are required by the Fair Credit Reporting Act (FCRA) when screening is done through a CRA for employment purposes. One difference between the U.S. and other countries is with the details of what is required in the consent. The content of the Notice (aka consent) may need to be more detailed in some countries than is required in the U.S.

✓ **Choice:** Choice is closely linked with Notice and is typically exercised with the Consent. The individual must be given a clear notice that details how their information will be processed in order for that individual to be able to exercise their choice in having their data processed or to opt-out of processing by a third party if they wish to do so. The FCRA in the U.S. requires employers to obtain consent prior to screening with a CRA. If the subject does not wish to consent (or wants to "opt out" of the process), then the employer may not proceed with this screening process. Choice in the EU is more difficult, since unambiguous and freely given consent are required for a consent to be valid. (However, in the EU, the concept of consent as a means to exercise choice in the employment context is not thought of as being "freely given" due to the subservient nature of the employment relationship. Some in the EU consider that consent in the employment process can never be freely given, due to inherent coerciveness of the employer – applicant relationship.) Choice also impacts the potential re-use of data for purposes other than the purpose the data was originally collected for. This is one reason why so few databases exist outside of the U.S.

✓ **Onward Transfer:** The EU laws deal with issues of how the data is protected when it is forwarded to other parties. Transfer must be done to third parties with appropriate security controls and contracts in place to require the same level of protection of the data with the third party as the original recipient is required to maintain.

✓ **Access:** The EU privacy rules are concerned with an individual's ability to access his or her data and to correct information. Under the FCRA, individuals have extensive rights to know what is being said about them and to contest the contents of consumer reports through the Adverse Action process and also through the FACT Act.

✓ **Security:** The EU rules also address the issue of security. Under the FCRA, there is an obligation to utilize data only for permissible purposes which means only those with a need to know may view and use data. U.S. screening firms are very pro-active in providing state-of-the-art security for employment screening data.

✓ **Data Integrity:** The EU rules are concerned with the use of the data for the intended purpose. The data should also be current and accurate. Under the FCRA, employment data can only be used for the permissible FCRA purpose it was collected. The FCRA also stipulates accuracy and currency requirements.

✓ **Enforcement:** For any regulations to have merit there must be a body providing enforcement. The EU rules address enforcement of privacy rules and individual recourse. In the U.S., employment screening under the FCRA is regulated by the Federal Trade Commission (FTC). In order to become Safe Harbor certified, the organization must generally be under the jurisdiction of the FTC or the DoT (U.S. air carriers and ticket agents). Background screening companies in the U.S. are under the jurisdiction of the FTC. Screening firms must also agree to an independent recourse mechanism. As example of such a mechanism is the service offered by the Council of Better Business Bureau's BBB OnLine® Privacy Program or TRUSTe.

These principles are outlined in more detail at www.export.gov/safeharbor/.

About Canada's Strict Privacy Laws — PIPEDA

Canada has a complicated system of Federal and Provincial privacy and data protection laws which has an impact on employment screening. The Personal Information Protection and Electronics Document Act, or PIPEDA, went into effect on January 1, 2004. PIPEDA privacy rules have a much broader application than just employment screening. For employment purposes, the law broadly applies to not only firms involved in a federal undertaking (such as governmental corporations or private firms involved in fields such as telecommunications, aeronautics, banks, communications, or transportation) but has been extended to nearly all employers engaged in commercial activity unless their province has substantially similar privacy protections in place. Currently, British Colombia, Alberta, and Quebec have laws substantially similar to the federal Canadian law. Under PIPEDA, employers can still conduct pre-employment background screening, but only with some stringent privacy controls.

PIPEDA identifies ten principals for privacy, which employers need to understand and take into account in their screening.

✓ **Accountability:** Employers are responsible for the personal information under their control, and must designate someone who is accountable for compliance with the Act.

✓ **Identifying purposes:** Employers must specify why they are collecting personal information from employees at or before the time they do so.

✓ **Consent:** The employee's knowledge and consent is required for the collection, use, or disclosure of personal information.

✓ **Limiting collection:** Employers may only collect the personal information necessary for the purpose they have identified and must collect it by fair and lawful means.

✓ **Limiting use, disclosure, and retention:** Unless they have the consent of the employee, or are legally required to do otherwise, employers may use or disclose personal information only for the purposes for which they collected it, and they may retain it only as long as necessary for those purposes.

✓ **Accuracy:** The employees' personal information must be accurate, complete, and up-to-date.

✓ **Safeguards:** All personal information must be protected by appropriate security safeguards.

✓ **Openness:** Employers must make their personal information policies and practices known to their employees.

✓ **Individual access:** Employees must be able to access personal information about themselves and be able to challenge the accuracy and completeness of it.

✓ **Challenging compliance:** Employees must be able to present a challenge about the employer's compliance with the Act to the person that the employer has designated as accountable.

Some helpful links for employers to use to better understand PIPEDA and the substantially similar Provincial regulations are:

✓ Office of the Privacy Commissioner of Canada: www.priv.gc.ca

✓ Office of the Information and Privacy Commissioner for Alberta: www.oipc.ab.ca

✓ Office of the Information and Privacy Commissioner for British Columbia (B.C.): www.oipc.bc.ca

✓ Commission d'accès à l'information du Québec: www.cai.gouv.qc.ca

More information about the Privacy laws can be found at www.privcom.gc.ca/fs-fi/02_05_d_18_e.asp

As with the EU Data Privacy Directive, the Canadian rules are similar to the FCRA. Both rules require notice, applicant consent, accuracy requirements, limitations on use of data, and the ability of consumers to know what is said about them and to contest it.

However, there are some important differences. First, under the Canadian rules as well as the E.U., there is a concept of not retaining information longer then needed. Under the FCRA, data is generally retained for six years in order to meet the FCRA statute of limitation requirement, as well as an extra year that a party may have to actually serve the lawsuit. (See the FCRA material at Chapter 3).

The Canadian rules also require a posted privacy policy and the designation of an individual to be in charge of privacy matters. In the U.S., these are best practices but not mandates.

U.S. employers with offices or facilities in Canada need to review their compliance with PIPEDA and the provincial laws not only for employment screening purposes, but also for numerous other aspects of their businesses.

Canadian Criminal Records

A search of the Canadian Police Information Centre (CPIC), managed by the Royal Canadian Mounted Police (RCMP), is often conducted. A search of the CPIC requires a special release signed by the applicant. If the results of the CPIC are unclear, meaning a record may exist, then fingerprints are required before any conviction history is provided. Additionally, the employer needs to verify and provide copies of two (2) photo identification documents and sign the special release as well. The typical turnaround time for a CPIC search is three (3) working days or less. However, while the turnaround time for CPIC may be short for cursory results, the actual turnaround time for more detailed results requiring fingerprints is far longer, and employers need to be aware of the situation.

Addition problems with the CPIC search is that it does not cover all offenses. Lesser offenses (summary offenses) are not included. Also, as of this printing, there is a substantial backlog of criminal records not entered into CPIC. According to some knowledgeable firms, the authorities may be as much as two and a half years behind.

Some employers opt for a local search which can be done through the courts. This local search may cover an entire province. No special consent is needed and summary results are provided.

Recommendations for International Background Screening Programs

Although international background screening can be challenging, it is not impossible. Employers can find themselves in hot water if they assume that international screening is too difficult or expensive and simply bypass the process. While international background screening is challenging, the mere fact that information is more difficult to obtain from outside of the U.S. does not relieve employers from their due diligence obligation associated with hiring.

Under the Fair Credit Reporting Act (FCRA), both employers and background screening firms still have certain obligations regarding international screening. If the task of international screening is outsourced to a screening firm, that firm has an FCRA obligation to take reasonable procedures to insure accuracy. If there is a negative public record, such as a criminal record "hit," then the firm must make certain the information is correct and up-to-date, and supplied in a way that does not violate any data or privacy protection rules.

Employers should implement an international background screening program that best fits their needs and follows these recommendations:

- ✓ Employers should not assume that just because a person has spent time outside of the U.S., that an international check is not possible.
- ✓ Employers should perform international background screening in a legally compliant manner.
- ✓ Employers should use the broadest criminal search allowed in each country.
- ✓ Employers should find verification of, at the very least, the highest education that the applicant attained and the last employment where the applicant worked.
- ✓ Employers should use proper consent forms meeting country and search specifics.
- ✓ Employers should include international credit reports and driving records when available in some countries and when the information is job related.

The bottom-line very simply is that the rest of the world is not like the United States. Processes that are taken for granted here in terms of due diligence may not exist in other counties. The U.S. standards of due diligence before hiring is not shared around the world, such as in time is not always of the essence as it is in the U.S. These are factors employers need to keep in mind in performing international screening.

Additional Resource Links

Below are more links to pages not mentioned previously, but may be helpful:

World Information Center:
- ✓ Criminal Justice Systems of the World: www.bjs.gov/content/pub/html/wfcj.cfm
- ✓ Directory of Cities and Towns in the World: www.fallingrain.com/world
- ✓ Freedom of Information and Access to Government Records Around the World: www.privacyinternational.org
- ✓ Holidays and Celebrations Around the World: www.earthcalendar.net/index.php
- ✓ The CIA World Fact Book: www.cia.gov/library/publications/the-world-factbook/index.html
- ✓ The Official US Time: www.time.gov
- ✓ The World Clock - Time Zones: www.timeanddate.com/worldclock

Other Resources:

- ✓ Canada Data Privacy Commissioner: www.priv.gc.ca/index_e.asp
- ✓ Disclosure Scotland Case Studies: www.disclosurescotland.co.uk/pdf/CASE%20STUDY%20-%20BASIC%20-%20SCOTTISH%20POWER.pdf and www.disclosurescotland.co.uk/pdf/CASE%20STUDY%20-%20BASIC%20-%20MANPOWER.pdf
- ✓ Estimates, Unauthorized Immigrant Population Resident in the U.S.: January 2009 (January 2010): www.dhs.gov/xlibrary/assets/statistics/publications/ois_ill_pe_2009.pdf
- ✓ EU Directive on Data Protection: http://ec.europa.eu/justice/data-protection/index_en.htm
- ✓ 'Fake India Degrees Flood Middle East Market' (*Khaleej Times* May 13, 2004): www.khaleejtimes.com/DisplayArticle.asp?xfile=data/theuae/2004/May/theuae_May323.xml&section=theuae
- ✓ Place of Birth of the Foreign-Born Population: 2009 (October 2010): www.census.gov/prod/2010pubs/acsbr09-15.pdf
- ✓ Privacy International: www.privacyinternational.org/index.shtml
- ✓ Safe Harbor Information: www.export.gov/safeharbor
- ✓ U.S. Legal Permanent Residents: 2009 (April 2010): www.dhs.gov/xlibrary/assets/statistics/publications/lpr_fr_2009.pdf
- ✓ 'U.S. Officials Sport Fake Degrees' (*Wired Magazine*): www.wired.com/politics/law/news/2004/05/63436

Terrorist Database Searches and The Patriot Act

Inside This Chapter:

✓ The Post 9/11 World and Terrorist Search Procedures for Employers

✓ Terrorist Searches and U.S. Vital Industries

✓ Terrorist Databases — the Good and the Bad

✓ Use All the Tools

✓ Past Employment Verification — The Key to Protecting Vital Industries from Terrorists

✓ Conclusion

The Post 9/11 World and Terrorist Search Procedures for Employers

Prior to the events of September 11, 2001, the topic of how not to hire terrorists was not on the radar of most employers. Although most Americans would have acknowledged — if asked before 9/11 — that we live in a dangerous world, the danger had not significantly impacted American life to the extent it has after the attack on the United States.

Certainly employers with defense and other sensitive government contracts have long been involved in dealing with security clearance (See Chapter 20 section on Security Clearances). However, outside of security clearances, most employers were not focused on safe hiring from the point of view of keeping the U.S. safe from terrorists' harm. Employers in sensitive industries or sectors involved with the country's basic infrastructure have become concerned, post-9/11, with the potential risk that just one terrorist can have in their workplace. For example, a terrorist act could be aimed not only at airlines, but food and water supplies, transportation of hazardous materials, nuclear and other energy facilities, transportation, and a host of other vital industries.

As demonstrated by the events after 9/11, even small and medium employers that do not consider themselves involved in vulnerable sectors may need to be more alert in the future.

According to a 12/10/2003 article in the *Washington Times*:

> "U.S. authorities said sleeper cells also operate in at least 40 states from Florida and New York to California and Washington state – living low-profile lives, often in ethnic communities. The September, 2002 arrest of seven members of a terrorist cell in Lackawanna, N.Y., just south of Buffalo, was a first major clue to their existence.

> Between 2,000 and 5,000 terrorist operatives are said to be in the United States, many of whom are hiding in ethnic communities throughout the country, populated by millions of foreign immigrants, including illegal aliens for which the U.S. government cannot account."

Source: www.washingtontimes.com/news/2003/dec/9/20031209-114319-3699r/?page=all

It is difficult to verify these types of estimates. Even if the number was much smaller, it could still mean there is a high probability a terrorist with malicious designs toward the American way of life may well be applying to work at firms in the United States. A terrorist may apply for employment either with intent to do that firm harm in the future or to earn a livelihood while awaiting the orders to take some action against the U.S.

Part of the problem is identifying who is a terrorist. Terrorists applying for jobs with U.S. employers are going to take measures to hide their true intentions and possibly their true identity. There is not a single accepted definition of the term *"terrorist."* For purposes of American employers, the following definition from the Code of Federal Regulations is helpful. Terrorism is defined as:

> "...the unlawful use of force and violence against persons or property to intimidate or coerce a government, the civilian population, or any segment thereof, in furtherance of political or social objectives." *(See 28 C.F.R. § 0.85(l) which describes one of the general functions of the FBI within the Department of Justice)*

The FBI further describes terrorism as either domestic or international, depending on the origin, base, and objectives of the terrorists. For example:

- ✓ Domestic terrorism is the unlawful use, or threatened use, of force or violence by a group or individual based and operating entirely within the United States or Puerto Rico without foreign direction committed against persons or property to intimidate or coerce a government, the civilian population, or any segment thereof, in furtherance of political or social objectives.
- ✓ International terrorism involves violent acts or acts dangerous to human life that are a violation of the criminal laws of the United States or any state, or that would be a criminal violation if committed within the jurisdiction of the United States or any state. These acts appear to be intended to intimidate or coerce a civilian population, influence the policy of a government by intimidation or coercion, or affect the conduct of a government by

assassination or kidnapping. International terrorist acts occur outside the United States or transcend national boundaries in terms of the means by which they are accomplished, the persons they appear intended to coerce or intimidate, or the locale in which the perpetrations operate or seek asylum.

In 2005, the National Counterterrorism Center (NCTC), adopted the definition of "terrorism" that appears in 22 USC § 2656f(d)(2), "premeditated, politically motivated violence perpetrated against noncombatant targets by subnational groups or clandestine agents."

Source: www.nctc.gov/witsbanner/docs/2010_report_on_terrorism.pdf.

Although employers currently tend to think of terrorists as being connected to events in the Middle East, the definition can be much broader. Another definition of terrorism from an online dictionary states:

"...the systematic use of terror or unpredictable violence against governments, publics, or individuals to attain a political objective. Terrorism has been used by political organizations with both rightist and leftist objectives, by nationalistic and ethnic groups, by revolutionaries, and by the armies and secret police of governments themselves."

Identifying terrorists and keeping them out of the workspace is a significant task for employers. It would be made easier, of course, if employers could assume the efforts by the federal government to keep terrorists out of the U.S. in the first place were 100% effective. The U.S. government is taking a number of measures to track terrorists in the U.S. and to prevent their entry in the first place. However, given the enormous numbers of people who are in the U.S. illegally, as well as the fact the U.S. has two very long borders — 4,121 miles with Canada and 1,940 miles with Mexico — employers cannot simply assume terrorists will not be in the U.S. applying for jobs. Even the biometric databases being deployed at airports and seaports for foreign visitors, and the US-VISIT program, will likely have a margin of error due to the unruly nature of larger scale databases. See "The Bad News" section later in this chapter.

Employers, especially those in vulnerable and critical industries, have no real choice but to consider the importance of terrorism in their hiring program.

The Patriot Act and Financial Institutions

In the aftermath of the events of 9/11, Congress passed the U.S. Patriot Act. Its official title is **"Uniting and Strengthening America by Providing Appropriate Tools Required to Intercept and Obstruct Terrorism (USA PATRIOT) Act of 2001."** To read the full text of the Patriot Act, visit www.epic.org/privacy/terrorism/hr3162.pdf.

President George W. Bush signed this complicated, 342 page bill into law on October 26, 2001. The law gave sweeping powers to both domestic law enforcement and international intelligence agencies. For employers, it created the need to deal with a wide range of issues such as access to business records by governmental agencies that have the power to request a judicial order to review records. The Act also provided procedures for the federal government to tap phones and internet use and seize voicemail or emails, which raises additional workplace issues.

The Patriot Act also addressed the ease with which the September 11 terrorists were able to utilize holes in U.S. financial regulations to bring large sums of money into the U.S. to finance terrorists operations. According to reports following September 11, terrorists were able to transfer large sums to the U.S., including opening an account with a bank in Florida using false Social Security numbers.

The use of documents such as foreign passports, visas, along with numerous variations of the spelling of last names can help terrorists slip through the cracks. Given the size and volume of financial transactions and records in the U.S., searching for suspicious transactions and looking for links and patterns is like looking for the proverbial needle in the haystack. The U.S. Internal Revenue Service (IRS) tracks suspicious transactions through forms that certain financial institutions must file, as well as cash transactions over $10,000, but the data must still be analyzed (of course, foreign terrorists are likely aware of this $10K ceiling). To help combat these problems, The Patriot Act in part created a system whereby banks and financial institutions were also forced to take much greater care to know their customers and to report information to a central source.

Financial institutions were especially regulated under the Patriot Act with respect to controlling money laundering. The Act was aimed at controlling money used to finance terrorists' activities. Many financial institutions had already been the subject of regulation when it comes to financial crimes. The Act increased these obligations. The Act also created an obligation to report suspicious activities with the Federal Financial Crimes Enforcement Network (FinCEN) at http://www.fincen.gov. The goal was to create a large database of information shared between the financial industry and law enforcement to help combat money laundering.

One of the most critical aspects of the Patriot Act was the definition of a financial institution, which was considerably enlarged. The definition had included traditional institutions such as banks, mutual funds, credit card systems, and SEC registered securities brokers. The Act also defined other institutions as financial, such as travel agencies, sellers of boats, planes, cars, precious metals, and even casinos.

According to the Act, financial institutions include an insured bank; a commercial bank or a trust company; a private banker; an agency or branch of a foreign bank in the United States; any credit union; a thrift institution; a broker or dealer registered with the SEC under the Securities Exchange Act of 1934; a broker or dealer in securities or commodities (whether registered with the SEC or not); an investment banker or investment company; a currency exchange; an issuer, redeemer, or cashier of traveler's checks, checks, money orders, or similar instruments; an operator of a credit card system; an insurance company; a dealer in precious metals, stones, or jewels; a pawnbroker; a loan or finance company; a travel agency; a licensed sender of money or any other person who engages as a business in the transmission of funds, including any person who engages as a business in an informal money transfer system or any network of people who engage as a business in facilitating the transfer of money domestically or internationally outside of the conventional financial institutions system; a telegraph company; a business engaged in vehicle sales, including automobile, airplane and boat sales; persons involved in real estate closings and settlements; the United States Postal Service; an agency of the United States Government or of a State or local government carrying out a duty or power of a business described in the definition of a "financial institution"; a state-licensed or Indian casino with annual gaming revenue of more than $1,000,000; and certain other businesses designated by Treasury (collectively "Financial Institutions"). See 31 USC 5312(a)(2)(A) – (Z).

A key requirement of the Act dealing with fighting suspicious activity and money laundering is Section 326. This section centers on identifying customers and putting the obligation on financial institutions to match customer names against published lists of terrorists and terrorist organizations. Section 326 of the Act requires that:

> "(l) IDENTIFICATION AND VERIFICATION OF ACCOUNTHOLDERS-
> (1) IN GENERAL- Subject to the requirements of this subsection, the Secretary of the Treasury shall prescribe regulations setting forth the minimum standards for financial institutions and their customers regarding the identity of the customer that shall apply in connection with the opening of an account at a financial institution.
> (2) MINIMUM REQUIREMENTS- The regulations shall, at a minimum, require financial institutions to implement, and customers (after being given adequate notice) to comply with, reasonable procedures for—
> (A) verifying the identity of any person seeking to open an account to the extent reasonable and practicable;
> (B) maintaining records of the information used to verify a person's identity, including name, address, and other identifying information; and
> (C) consulting lists of known or suspected terrorists or terrorist organizations provided to the financial institution by any government agency to determine whether a person seeking to open an account appears on any such list."

The substantive requirements of Section 326 are codified as Part of the Treasury's regulations in 31 CFR Part 103. Rather than impose the same list of specific requirements on every financial institution, the regulation requires all institutions to implement a Customer Identification Program (CIP) appropriate given the institution's size, location, and type of business. The regulation requires an institution's CIP to contain the statutorily proscribed procedures, describe the procedures, and detail certain minimum elements that each of the procedures must contain. The CIP must be written and approved by the institution's board of directors or a committee of the board, highlighting the responsibility of the board of directors to approve and exercise general oversight over the institution's CIP.

See: www.bankersonline.com/aml/326whitepaper.pdf and www.sec.gov/about/offices/ocie/aml2007/67fr9874-78.pdf.

While each financial institution must develop a CIP that is individually tailored, the rule requires four minimum elements:

1. **Identity Verification Procedures.** First, the customer must provide certain identifying information. Second, the financial institution must verify the accuracy of the information provided.
2. **Verification Record-Keeping.** The minimum identifying information provided by the customer must be retained for five years after the account is closed.
3. **Government List Comparison.** The CIP must have procedures for determining whether a customer appears on any list of known or suspected terrorist organizations issued by the federal government.
4. **Notice to Customers.** A CIP must include procedures for providing customers with adequate notice that the financial institution is requesting information to verify their identities.

Prudent risk management would suggest that any firm the Patriot Act requires to exercise due diligence in identifying customers would also fall below a standard of care if they did not take the same precautions with their own employees. For example, financial institutions must perform due diligence on customers because of the harm customers can cause the U.S. if precautions are not taken. It is logical that financial institutions should know at least as much about their employees as they are required to know about their customers.

The current due diligence standard for financial institutions is that employees of financial institutions actually control the instrumentalities of commerce Congress has found to be vulnerable to abuse by terrorist, international drug dealers, and others who would harm the U.S. If the government is concerned that financial institution customers can adversely affect national security, then certainly the backgrounds of employees who run the institutions are just as critical.

To some extent, a criminal record check is already part of the hiring process for some financial institutions. For example, the Federal Deposits Insurance Corporation (FDIC) mandates insured banks may not hire, without the FDIC's consent, a person convicted of certain offenses involving dishonesty or breach of trust, money laundering, or drug trafficking (See Section 19 of the Federal Deposit Insurance Act: www.fdic.gov/regulations/laws/rules/5000-1300.html). Financial institutions covered by the Patriot Act without specific statutory duties to conduct criminal checks should also consider implementing a pre-employment screening program.

Terrorist Searches and U.S. Vital Industries

A growing trend by the federal government is to protect America's vital interests and infrastructure by requiring background checks in sensitive industries.

Food and Drug Administration Guidelines

In 2002 the U.S. Food and Drug Administration (FDA) issued voluntary guidelines on workplace safety and security, urging virtually every business in the food industry – from "farmer to table" – to adopt more aggressive measures to protect the nation's food supply. The FDA's suggestions included asking employers to obtain and verify work references, addresses, and phone numbers, and to consider performing criminal background checks. In 2003, the FDA updated its guidance and suggested that various industries involved in the food chain should also follow the guidelines. Additional dates were issued in 2007.

Although these guidelines are not mandatory, the FDA indicated the guidelines help minimize the possibility that items:

"…under their control will be subject to tampering or other malicious, criminal, or terrorist actions. It does not create or confer any rights for or on any person and does not operate to bind FDA or the public."

FDA recommends that operators of food importing establishments consider:

"1. Screening (pre-hiring, at hiring, post-hiring): examining the background of all staff (including seasonal, temporary, contract, and volunteer staff, whether hired directly or through a recruitment firm) as appropriate to their position, considering candidates' access to sensitive areas of the facility and the degree to which they will be supervised and other relevant factors."

(For more information, see Food Security Preventive Measures Guidance at www.fda.gov/Food/GuidanceComplianceRegulatoryInformation/GuidanceDocuments/FoodDefenseandEmergencyResponse/ucm078978.htm#hestaff.)

Further suggestions include obtaining and verifying work references, addresses, and phone numbers, having a criminal background check performed by local law enforcement or by a contract service provider, and participating in one of the pilot programs managed by the Immigration and Naturalization Service and the Social Security Administration.

These pilot programs provide electronic confirmation of employment eligibility for newly hired employees. For more information, call the INS SAVE Program toll free at 1-888-464-4218, fax a request for information to 202-514-9981, or write to: US/INS, SAVE Program, 425 I Street, NW, ULLICO-4th Floor, Washington, DC 20536.

The FDA recommended that screening procedures should be applied equally to all employees regardless of race, national origin, religion, and citizenship, or immigration status. For more information about these guidelines, see: www.fda.gov/Food/GuidanceComplianceRegulatoryInformation/GuidanceDocuments/FoodDefenseandEmergencyResponse/ucm078978.htm#hestaff.

The same guidelines issued to importers of food were also issued to operators of cosmetics establishments, including firms that process, store, repack, re-label, distribute, or transport cosmetics or cosmetics ingredients.

Purpose and Scope of FDA Laws to Thwart Terrorism

This summary of materials is on the U.S. Food and Drug Administration (FDA) website at: www.fda.gov/RegulatoryInformation/Guidances/ucm125340.htm.

The draft guidance document entitled 'Retail Food Stores and Food Service Establishments: Food Security Preventative Measure Guidance' is designed as an aid to operators of retail food stores and food service establishments (i.e., for example, bakeries, bars, bed-and-breakfast operations, cafeterias, camps, child and adult day care providers, church kitchens, commissaries, community fund raisers, convenience stores, fairs, food banks, grocery stores, interstate conveyances, meal services for homebound persons, mobile food carts, restaurants, and vending machine operators).

It identifies the kinds of preventative measures that operators may take to minimize the risk that food under their control will be subject to tampering or other malicious criminal or terrorist actions. Operators of retail food store, food service, and cosmetics establishments are encouraged to review their current security procedures and controls in light of the potential for tampering or other malicious, criminal, or terrorist actions and make appropriate improvements.

Implementation of these measures requires commitment from both management and employees to be successful and, therefore, both should participate in development and review.

The draft guidance documents, when finalized, will represent the agency's current thinking on appropriate measures that retail food store, food service, and cosmetics establishments may take to minimize the risk of foods or cosmetics under their control will be subjected to tampering or other malicious, criminal or terrorist actions. They do not create or confer any rights for or on any person and do not operate to bind FDA or the public.

Food Safety and Inspection Guidelines

The Food Safety and Inspection Service of the United States Department of Agriculture (USDA) has also issued safety and security guidelines The guidelines are the FSIS Safety and Security Guidelines for the Transportation and Distribution of Meat, Poultry, and Egg Products. According to the FSIS, "The second section of the guidelines deals specifically with security measures intended to prevent the same forms of contamination due to criminal or terrorist acts." Here is an example of one USDA guideline:

USDA Asks to Screen & Educate Employees

Screen all potential employees, to the extent possible, by conducting background and criminal checks appropriate to their positions, and verifying references (including contract, temporary, custodial, seasonal, and security personnel). When this is not practical, such personnel should be under constant supervision and their access to sensitive areas of the facility restricted. See www.fsis.usda.gov/oa/topics/transportguide.pdf.

Bioterrorism and the Nation's Water Supply

Similar contamination concerns exist for the nation's water supply. On June 12, 2002, President Bush signed the Public Health Security and Bioterrorism Preparedness and Response Act of 2002 – "The Bioterrorism Act". This act enhances federal and state efforts to prepare for and respond to the threat of bioterrorism and other public health emergencies. The act requires all community water systems serving a population greater than 3,300 to conduct a vulnerability assessment and provide a written copy of the assessment to the U.S. Environmental Protection Agency (EPA) administrator. One of the areas of inquiry under the act is the security screening of employees or contractor support services.

See www.fda.gov/RegulatoryInformation/Legislation/ucm155780.htm for SEC. 1433. (42 USC 300i-2) Terrorist and other intentional acts.

These examples show federal agencies have put focus on background checks as weapons in the fight against terrorists. The list of affected industries is likely to increase.

Terrorist Databases — the Good and the Bad

The Good News

For employers without access to non-public government terrorist data, the most frequently used tool is a list provided by the U.S. Treasury Office of Foreign Assets Control (OFAC). The OFAC publishes a list of individuals and companies owned or controlled by, or acting for or on behalf of, targeted countries. Also listed are individuals, groups, and entities such as terrorists and narcotics traffickers designated under programs that are not country-specific. Collectively, such individuals and companies are called Specially Designated Nationals or SDNs. Their assets are blocked and U.S. persons are generally prohibited from dealing with them. The OFAC list also has other designations, such as SDGT, standing for "Specially Designated Global Terrorist." There are approximately 3,000 names on the list.

According to the OFAC website at www.treasury.gov/resource-center/faqs/sanctions/pages/answer.aspx:

"Prohibited transactions are trade or financial transactions and other dealings in which U.S. persons may not engage unless authorized by OFAC or expressly exempted by statute. Because each program is based on different foreign policy and national security goals, prohibitions may vary between programs."

There are public information provider firms who specialize in obtaining all the data that is publicly available from organizations that keep terrorist lists and then assemble all the information into a proprietary database. These databases are useful search tools for employers since they contain the OFAC list and many of the public "most wanted lists" issued by various organizations and generally available on websites.

Below is a list of elements that could be found in a typical vendor's terrorist database:

- OFAC Specially Designated Nationals (SDN) & Blocked Persons
- OFAC Sanctioned Countries, including Major Cities & Ports
- Non-Cooperative Countries and Territories
- Department of State Trade Control (DTC) Debarred Parties
- U.S. Bureau of Industry & Security (formerly BXA)
- Unverified Entities List
- Denied Entities List

- Denied Persons List
- FBI Most Wanted Terrorists & Seeking Information
- FBI Top Ten Most Wanted
- INTERPOL Most Wanted List
- Bank of England Sanctions List
- OSFI - Canadian Sanctions List
- United Nations Consolidated Sanctions List
- Politically Exposed Persons List
- European Union Terrorism List
- World Bank Ineligible Firms

As a practical matter, an employer may want to consider at least searching the following databases, which are easily available either online or through information or software providers:

- ✓ OFAC List. See: http://sdnsearch.ofac.treas.gov.
- ✓ Denied Persons List — This is a list supplied by the United States Commerce Department and indicates individuals and entities restricted from exporting from the United States. See: www.bis.doc.gov/dpl/default.shtm.
- ✓ OSFI List — This list supplied by the Canadian Office of the Superintendent of Financial Institutions contains names of individuals and organizations subject to the Regulations Establishing a List of Entities made under the Criminal Code or the United Nations Suppression of Terrorism regulations. See: www.osfi-bsif.gc.ca/osfi/index_e.aspx?ArticleID=2523.
- ✓ EU and UN Terrorist Lists — Lists supplied by HM Treasury: www.hm-treasury.gov.uk/fin_sanctions_index.htm.

Interpol also publishes a web page to check international wants and warrants at: www.interpol.int/Wanted-Persons.

The Not So Good News

It would be an easy procedure for businesses to avoid hiring or dealing with terrorists just by going online and looking up the OFAC list. Unfortunately, searching this list is easier said than done for the following reasons:

- ✓ The online database is difficult for private employers to access efficiently. The OFAC data is maintained at http://sdnsearch.ofac.treas.gov/. Anyone can access it. However, as a practical matter, most private employers find the search difficult and time consuming. As alternatives, there are a number of private firms who provide Patriot Act compliance services that regularly assemble the OFAC data and make it available to employers and businesses through various web-based and computerized solutions.
- ✓ The OFAC search, although valuable, does not include other "terrorist search" tools from other organizations and governments. For example, the Commerce Department maintains separate lists for the purposes of the programs it administers. Their Denied Persons List consists of individuals and companies that have been denied export and re-export privileges by the BIS. Their Entity List consists of foreign firms who pose an unacceptable risk of diverting U.S. exports and technology to alternate destinations for the development of weapons of mass destruction. Accordingly, U.S. exports to those entities may require a license. The two lists are maintained

separately because the BIS Entity List has a purpose different than the OFAC list. Some software firms that provide Patriot Act compliance services merge the two lists.

✓ Positive identification can be difficult. The OFAC search provides as much data as possible, but it is not always sufficient. The names are often of Middle Eastern origin and the identifiers are not always sufficient to make a determination as to identity. Typically, international terrorists on the OFAC list do not have valid Social Security numbers.

OFAC provides a Frequently Asked Questions webpage and outlines steps to take in the event of a possible match. The FAQ that follows tell financial institutions what to do if there is a "hit." The information is very useful for employers as well.

OFAC Frequently Asked Questions

If you are calling about an account:

Step 1. Is the "hit" or "match" against OFAC's SDN list or targeted countries, or is it "hitting" for some other reason, (i.e., "Control List" or "PEP," "CIA," "Non-Cooperative Countries and Territories," "Canadian Consolidated List (OSFI)," "World Bank Debarred Parties," or "government official of a designated country") or can you not tell what the "hit" is?

✓ If it is hitting against **OFAC's SDN list or targeted countries**, continue to Step 2 below.

✓ If it is hitting for some other reason, you should contact the "keeper" of whichever other list the match is hitting against. For questions about:

✓ **The Denied Persons List and the Entities List**, please contact the Bureau of Industry and Security at the U.S. Department of Commerce at 202-482-4811.

✓ **The FBI's Most Wanted List** or any other FBI-issued watch list, please contact the Federal Bureau of Investigation. (www.fbi.gov/contact/fo/fo.htm)

✓ **The Debarred Parties List**, please contact the Office of Defense Trade Controls at the U.S. Department of State, 202-663-2700.

✓ **The Bank Secrecy Act and the USA PATRIOT Act**, please contact the Financial Crimes Enforcement Network (FinCEN), 1-800-949-2732.

✓ If you are unsure whom to contact, then you should contact your interdict software provider which told you there was a "hit."

✓ If you can't tell what the "hit" is, you should contact your interdict software provider which told you there was a "hit."

Step 2. Now that you've established that the hit is against OFAC's SDN list or targeted countries, you must evaluate the quality of the hit. Compare the name of your accountholder with the name on the SDN list. Is the name of your accountholder an individual while the name on the SDN list is a vessel, organization or company (or vice-versa)?

✓ If yes, you do not have a valid match.*

✓ If no, please continue to Step 3 below.

Step 3. How much of the SDN's name is matching against the name of your account holder?

Is just one of two or more names matching (i.e., just the last name)?

✓ If yes, you do not have a valid match.*

✓ If no, please continue to Step 4 below.

Step 4. Compare the complete SDN entry with all the information you have on the matching name of your accountholder. An SDN entry often will have, for example, a full name, address, nationality, passport, tax ID or cedula number, place of birth, date of birth, former names, and aliases. Are you missing a lot of this information for the name of your accountholder?

✓ If yes, go back and get more information and then compare your complete information against the SDN entry.

✓ If no, please continue to Step 5 below.

Step 5. Are there a number of similarities or exact matches?

✓ If yes, please call the hotline at 1-800-540-6322.

✓ If no, then you do not have a valid match.*

* If you have reason to know or believe that processing this transfer or operating this account would violate any of the Regulations, you must call the hotline and explain this knowledge or belief. [08-22-07]

Also see: www.treasury.gov/resource-center/faqs/sanctions/pages/answer.aspx.

FCRA, EEOC, and Terrorist Searches

All employment screening is conducted under the federal Fair Credit Reporting Act (FCRA), which requires the use of reasonable procedures to assure maximum accuracy. A terrorist search may contain many common names and not provide the sufficient identifiers to determine if a match belongs to an applicant. As indicated in Step 5 above, OFAC also has a hotline to assist employers in the event of a possible match where there are insufficient identifiers on the search results.

In addition, employers need to be aware that a large number of names may be of Middle Eastern origin. Under the FCRA, a background screening may not be used in violation of any state or federal anti-discrimination laws. As a result, it is important that all efforts be made to determine if there is a positive match before taking any adverse action. This can prevent an employer from being the subject of a complaint for discrimination in hiring based upon national origin or ethnicity.

The EEOC issued a press release on this topic following the September 11, 2001 terrorist attacks:

EEOC Chair Urges Workplace Tolerance in Wake of Terrorist Attacks

WASHINGTON - In the wake of this week's tragic events, Cari M. Dominguez, Chair of the U.S. Equal Employment Opportunity Commission (EEOC), called on all employers and employees across the country to promote tolerance and guard against unlawful workplace discrimination based on national origin or religion.

"We should not allow our anger at the terrorists responsible for this week's heinous attacks to be misdirected against innocent individuals because of their religion, ethnicity, or country of origin," Chair Dominguez said. "In the midst of this tragedy, employers should take time to be alert to instances of harassment or intimidation against Arab-American and Muslim employees. Preventing and prohibiting injustices against our fellow workers is one way to fight back, if only symbolically, against the evil forces that assaulted our workplaces Tuesday morning."

EEOC encourages all employers to do the following:

✓ Reiterate policies against harassment based on religion, ethnicity, and national origin;

✓ Communicate procedures for addressing workplace discrimination and harassment;

✓ Urge employees to report any such improper conduct; and

✓   Provide training and counseling, as appropriate.

Ms. Dominguez exhorted all individuals to heed the words of President Bush, who said yesterday: "We must be mindful that as we seek to win the war [against terrorism] we treat Arab-Americans and Muslims with the respect they deserve."

EEOC enforces Title VII of the Civil Rights Act of 1964, which prohibits discrimination in employment on the basis of race, color, religion, national origin, sex, and retaliation for filing a complaint. For example, Title VII precludes workplace bias based on the following:

✓   Religion, ethnicity, birthplace, culture, or linguistic characteristics;

✓   Marriage or association with persons of a national origin or religious group;

✓   Membership or association with specific ethnic or religious groups;

✓   Physical, linguistic or cultural traits closely associated with a national origin group, for example, discrimination because of a person's physical features or traditional Arab style of dress; and

✓   Perception or belief that a person is a member of a particular national origin group, based on the person's speech, mannerisms, or appearance.

"Our laws re-affirm our national values of tolerance and civilized conduct. At this time of trial, these values will strengthen us as a common people," Ms. Dominguez said. "The nation's workplaces are fortified by the enduring ability of Americans of diverse backgrounds, beliefs, and nationalities to work together harmoniously and productively."

The EEOC press release is online at: www.eeoc.gov/eeoc/newsroom/release/9-14-01.cfm.

The Bad News

When private employers utilize publicly available lists for terrorist searches, there are four areas of "bad news."

✓   As discussed in detail in Chapters 13 and 14, any criminal record database has inherent limitations. There are *issues as to timeliness, accuracy, and completeness*. Since the names on the lists are by necessity a judgment call, the list is certainly not complete or comprehensive. There is no way to know how long it takes for a name to be "approved" to be entered onto the list. In addition, the mechanics of a government agency making a decision that a person is a terrorist is not generally public information. Names can fall through the cracks.

✓   *Terrorists can circumvent the databases*. If a person is a terrorist, then this person probably knows that he or she may be on a government watch list. A terrorist attempting to obtain employment at an American facility will have a fake name, driver's license, Social Security card, or other false identification. As a result, the bad news is that a determined terrorist may figure out a way around a terrorist database search. For a more detailed discussion on the problems associated with identity fraud, see Chapter 28.

✓   Employers need to understand a terrorist database is subject to a high rate of *false positives and false negatives*. As explained previously, a false positive means someone is incorrectly identified (as a terrorist or criminal). A false negative is when a person who should have been identified as a risk and stopped for further inquiry was not and was allowed through. This can happen for a number of reasons. Terrorist databases may have a number of name variations and spellings that can lead to names being mixed. Since many names on the terrorist lists are from other countries, there is the issue of translating the person's name into an English version. Terrorists may purposely alter spellings of their name. Since the terrorist may have false ID's or foreign ID's, the number that appears may not be a number consistent with numbering scheme of legitimate ID's — the terrorist's ID would be a false document. On the other end of the spectrum, it is entirely possible to have "computer twins," where two different people have the same names and the same birthday, which means at least one false positive.

✓   A terrorist database search can potentially create a false sense of security if employers do not fully understand the *inherent limitations in a terrorist database*. As in a criminal database, just because a name is not in the database does not mean the applicant is not a threat. At the same time, just because a person's name is in a database does not mean it is that person. A database search is only one tool and is most beneficial when used as part of a series of overlapping hiring tools.

Use All the Tools

As with all safe hiring techniques, no one tool is the complete answer. Besides using the terrorist databases and lists such as OFAC as a measure of safety against hiring terrorists, an employer should use the various employment screening procedures suggested in this book.

- ✓ A strong AIR (Application /Interview /Reference checking) Process.
- ✓ A minimum seven-year criminal check for all jurisdictions where an applicant has lived, worked, or studied. Include both federal and state criminal convictions.
- ✓ A national criminal index search as described in Chapter 14.
- ✓ A Social Security trace (or an address information manager search) that utilizes a number of databases including credit bureaus' files for a list of all names and addresses associated with a particular Social Security number. This is particularly important to guard against fake identification documents. It is also critical to review the times that addresses were reportedly used in conjunction with the SSN to look for unexplained gaps in a person's whereabouts. (However, as discussed in Chapter 17, the trend for screening firms is not to provide the address information due to accuracy concerns under the federal Fair Credit Reporting Act.)
- ✓ Verification of employment for the past five to ten years.
- ✓ Verify education and any special credentials.
- ✓ A driver record search.
- ✓ Complete the I-9 process.

The I-9 Process

If a person is made a conditional offer of employment, then it is also critical to make sure the I-9 process is completed. This process, by which an employer verifies a person's eligibility to work in the U.S., is done pursuant to rules prepared by the Immigration and Naturalization Service. This also provides an employer a great deal of protection against someone who may be using a fake identity. As part of the I-9 process, the employer can also contact the Social Security Administration and verify the Social Security number. See Chapter 17 on how employers can contact the Social Security Administration after a conditional job offer has been made.

Consent Based Social Security Number Verification Service (CBSV)

With the consent of the Social Security number (SSN) holder, enrolled users may **utilize Consent Based Social Security Number Verification Service (CBSV)** as part of a pre-employment screening program to verify whether the SSN holder's name and Social Security number (SSN) combination match Social Security Administration (SSA) records. CBSV returns a "yes" or "no" verification indicating that the submission either matches or does not match our records. If SSA records show that the SSN holder is deceased, CBSV returns a death indicator. CBSV verifications do not verify an individual's identity.

For more information on CBSV, read the CBSV section in Chapter 24 'Dealing with Fraud, Embezzlement, and Integrity,' or visit the CBSV page on the Social Security Administration at www.ssa.gov/cbsv.

Past Employment Verification — The Key to Protecting Vital Industries from Terrorists

Of all the available tools an employer can use, verifying past employment is probably the most critical. As noted in Chapter 9 on References, this screening tool could have most likely raised a red flag had any of the 9/11 terrorists applied for employment in a critical industry.

Chapter 28 discusses the nature of identity. When determining who a person really is and what history to attach to them, the least meaningful source of information is what the person says about himself. However, as you check public records, the reliability factor increases. Validations from past employment and education checks give the employer more confidence that a person is who he says he is — and has the history he claims.

The problems with spotting a potential terrorist, however, are as follows:

✓ They are more likely than most to attempt to thwart safe hiring techniques by misrepresenting themselves and attempting to conceal their true identities and purpose.
✓ They are more likely to be presenting false identification information and documents.
✓ There is likely to be less info about the terrorist in the normal domestic database searches.
✓ Terrorist databases can be circumvented.

The government has warned about "sleeper" terrorists, potential terrorists who have fit into American society and are waiting to be told to take some course of action. If a "sleeper" terrorist applies for a job not requiring a security clearance, then he or she may well be a perfectly honest applicant with nothing to indicate a secret mission. If the government with their resources cannot identify them, then employers are at a distinct disadvantage.

As a result, it is arguably more difficult for employers to prevent the hiring of terrorists than someone with an unsuitable criminal record or falsified credentials. Even though there are substantially less terrorists likely to apply to a vital infrastructure employer, the harm can be substantial.

The key is past employment calls. By calling to verify past jobs for the past five to ten years, an employer verifies the applicant's general whereabouts and general accuracy of his or her job history.

 Since information from applicants and databases may not be trusted sources, where can employers turn? The ultimate key to verification of identity and history stems from obtaining information from a "trusted source." For more information about the **"trusted source rule"** see Chapter 28.

Where does this trusted source come in? A researcher doing a past employment check has the ability to access a directory assistance, a printed phonebook, or some other source of information that is generally considered reliable and would be extremely difficult to for an outsider to manipulate. By utilizing a telephone listing independently obtained and calling that past employer, it can be confirmed that the past employers exists and the phone number in fact belongs to a legitimate firm.

Although it may sound like a slender thread, the possibility of terrorists, such as the 9/11 hijackers, setting up a five to ten year employment history just to weasel their way into a job in a sensitive industry is remote. It is not impossible, but it would require considerable effort.

To avoid such a possibility, employers in sensitive industries may consider the following certain steps. Once the information is obtained, the researcher should then review the confirmed information, matching it to data known about the applicant — developing a pattern for looking for consistencies or inconsistencies. The employer should develop a protocol to crosscheck applicants and other screening materials. For example:

✓ Does the job history match the address and the Social Security trace? The Social Security trace shows address and name associated with an applicant. If an applicant has a long job history, then the dates and locations should correspond to the information on the trace. The dates must be viewed as a whole to see if it is inherently consistent. In other words, the employer needs to see if the dots connect and all the information makes sense.

✓ A person claiming to have been self-employed for the past five to ten years creates additional challenges, requiring verifications from trusted sources in the information path. The recommended procedure is to contact customers of the applicant's businesses, and verifying the existence directly by phone. Even more important is to develop references. Call the references supplied by the applicant, and ask those supplied references if they know other clients of the self-employed applicant who can confirm if he was in business.

✓ With enough resources, know how, and planning, it is possible for a would-be terrorist to set-up an elaborate ruse. A person would need to start a company for the purpose of being in the phonebook, and then an accomplice posing as a legitimate reference would have to stand by to deliver a credible reference when the new prospective employer should happen to call. Of course, when calling past employers, a researcher needs to use common sense and be on the alert for conversations that do not sound businesslike and correct.

A suspected terrorist could set up an elaborate ruse to pass the reference check, and this underscores the inherent difficulty faced by private employers. If the government, with all of its resources, did not detect the terrorist in the United States in the first place, then private employers are certainly at a disadvantage. However, employers can place as many barriers as possible in the way of potential terrorists in order to undermine their efforts, or to force would be terrorists to foul-up in their efforts to hide their identity or true purpose.

Credit Report Case Demonstrates Challenges in Reporting OFAC Terrorist Information in a Background Screening Report

A case involving a consumer credit report used in an automobile purchase demonstrates the potential dangers of terrorist database searches commonly used by background firms. This appears to be the first case in the nation dealing with use of terrorist databases by credit bureaus under the federal FCRA and provides guidance for the use of such information by Consumer Reporting Agencies (CRAs), which includes both credit bureaus and background screening firms.

In a case handed down by the United States Court of Appeals for the Third District on August 13, 2010, a consumer tried to purchase a car. She obtained her own credit report which showed a score of 760. She was born in Chicago, stated she had never been out of the Unites States, and was living in Colorado when she tried to purchase her car.

Unknown to the consumer, the automobile dealership ran their own credit report, and it included information that was not available to the consumer, including an alert that stated that "OFAC ADVISOR ALERT - INPUT NAME MATCHES NAME ON THE OFAC DATABASE."

As the court explained, the Treasury Department – through the Office of Foreign Asset Control (OFAC) – maintains various lists since it "administers and enforces economic and trade sanctions based on U.S. foreign policy and national security goals against threats to the national society, foreign policy, or economy of the United States." These OFAC resources include lists of terrorists and narcotic traffickers, that are called "Specially Designated Nationals or "SDNs." The OFAC list, in conjunction with numerous other terrorist lists, is often used by background screening firms as part of a background check as well.

In this case, the consumer was asked questions about whether she ever lived outside this country. She was asked to wait in an office for several hours. When she asked to leave, she was told to wait since the FBI was being called. She finally left the dealership.

Although she went back that night and finally got her car, she described other events relating to the OFAC information, such as emotional distress, the need to take medication, and having to confront the same issue when trying to rent.

After that, she described a number of efforts to have the credit bureau remove the information from any credit report relating to her. She contacted the credit bureau several times and got nowhere. She reviewed the OFAC alerts posted on the internet and apparently found a name close to hers but still different, that also reflected a different date of birth. She demanded that the alerts be removed.

She later discovered that although there were no alerts on the copy of the credit reports she obtained, the alerts in fact were not removed when sent to users of credit reports. She eventually filed a lawsuit under the FCRA.

Per the Court's opinion, the jury found that:

- ✓ The credit bureau failed to follow reasonable procedures to assure maximum possible accuracy in producing the credit report (which is required by the FCRA);
- ✓ The credit bureau willfully failed to reinvestigate the consumer's disputes after she had demanded it (which is required by the FCRA);
- ✓ The credit bureau willfully failed to note the consumer's dispute on subsequent credit reports as required by the FCRA; and
- ✓ The credit bureau willfully failed to provide the consumer all of the information in her file despite requests.
- ✓ The jury awarded $50,000 in actual damages and $750,000 in punitive damages; they were lowered by the trial court to $100,000.

It should be noted that the above grounds used by the jury are duties placed upon any Consumer Reporting Agency (CRA), regardless of whether it supplies employment background reports or credit reports.

The credit agency attempted to defend on the basis that the OFAC information was not subject to the FCRA. The court quickly dispensed with that defense, pointing out that argument would require a court to disregard the clear language of the law and conclude that the Congress did not mean what it said.

Although the case was in the context of a credit report, under the FCRA, it equally applies to a background check for employment. The case ran some 91 pages and covered detailed areas of credit reports and federal law, but the lessons for background screening firms are clear:

- ✓ A screening firm cannot automatically report the results of an OFAC or other terrorist search without following some reasonable procedures to assure maximum possible accuracy. In the case of an OFAC potential match, there is substantial information on the U.S. Treasury web site on how to attempt to determine if a possible match belongs to the target of the report, including a phone number to call for assistance. What is clear is that just passing on the information is not a defensible practice.
- ✓ If a consumer requests a re-investigation, a CRA has an absolute responsibility to conduct the re-investigation, normally within 30 days.

This case once again underscores the fact that employment screening background checks are not a mere data service, but a highly regulated professional service that must be conducted by firms that have an understanding of the laws controlling background checks and the immense impact that an incorrect report can have on both employers and consumers.

The case is found at: http://caselaw.findlaw.com/us-3rd-circuit/1534956.html.

Conclusion

The bottom line — American employers must do what they are able to do to protect the United States.

Chapter 23

Drug Testing in the U.S.

Inside This Chapter:

- ✓ Introduction

- ✓ Studies Show Drugs in Workplace Cost Employers Billions

- ✓ The ABC's of Drug Testing

- ✓ Setting Drug Testing Policies and Procedures

- ✓ What is Tested? – DOT Drug Tests and Non-DOT Drug Tests

- ✓ How Does the Drug Test Work?

- ✓ Pros and Cons of Testing Methods

- ✓ Drug Testing Costs

- ✓ Legal Issues and Drug Testing

- ✓ Is Drug Testing Covered by the Fair Credit Reporting Act?

- ✓ Recommended Drug Testing Information Resources

Introduction

Drug testing in the workplace is fast becoming a fact of life for many employers. Although the drug testing practice was initially adopted by the Fortune 500 companies, pre-employment drug testing is gaining increasing acceptance in all sizes of businesses looking to keep their workplaces safe and their costs down.

According to a study by the U.S. Department of Labor, drug use in the workplace costs an estimated $75 billion to $100 billion in lost time, absenteeism, accidents and on the job injuries, health care, and workers' compensation claims each year. Sixty-five percent of all accidents on the job are related to drugs or alcohol, and substance abusers utilize 16 times as many health care benefits and are six times more likely to file workers compensation claims then non-abusers.

A 2010 survey of illicit drug use by the U.S. Substance Abuse and Mental Health Services Administration (SAMHSA) estimates that approximately 22.6 million Americans, or 8.9 percent of the population aged 12 or older, were considered to be "current illicit drug users" in 2010. By SAMHSA's definition, "current" drug use means use of an illicit drug during the month prior to the survey interview.

The National Institute on Drug Abuse reports that nearly 75 percent of drug users are employed. Using the above figure supplied by SAMHSA, it figures there are nearly 17 million (22.6 million x 0.75) illicit drug users participating in the American workforce. See: www.drugabuse.gov/publications/drugfacts/workplace-resources.

Human Resources and Safety professionals consider drug testing an important safety issue in the workplace to lessen the impact from drug abuse in the workplace, including:

Absenteeism	Crime	Theft
Accidents	Decreased productivity	Turnover
Attitude problems	Tardiness	Violence

Employers have turned to pre-employment drug testing as a tool to try to minimize the impact of drug use by employees.

In 1987, a national testing laboratory, SmithKline Beecahm, found that 18.1 percent of all workers tested had positive results. By 1997, that figure was down to 5.4 percent. In 2008, it was down to 3.6 percent. See: http://ir.questdiagnostics.com/phoenix.zhtml?c=82068&p=irol-newsArticle_print&ID=1285206&highlight=. Drug experts debate whether this means drug use has fallen, or drug abusers simply avoid employers that test and instead apply at firms that do not test. Either way, most HR and Safety professionals have found that drug testing can be a valuable and cost-effective deterrent and a risk management tool.

Studies Show Drugs in Workplace Cost Employers Billions

In addition to the examples quoted above, statistics show that a majority of drug and alcohol abusers in the United States were employed either full or part time as of 2006: 75 percent of illicit drug users over 18, nearly 80 percent of binge and heavy drinkers, and 60 percent of adults with substance abuse problems. These statistics are from Substance Abuse and Mental Health Services Administration (SAMHSA) 2006 (www.tresearch.org/headlines/2009Nov_SUD_Fact_Sheet.pdf) and the 'Working Partners' National Conference Proceedings Report sponsored by the DOL, the Small Business Administration (SBA), and the Office of National Drug Control Policy (www.tn.gov/labor-wfd/dfwp.html#thecost).

According to the Institute on Health Care Costs and Solutions, each year, substance abuse costs the United States billions of dollars in expenditures for health care, workplace injuries, disability payments, and productivity losses. Nationwide, health care costs stemming from alcohol abuse alone are estimated at 26.3 billion, while productivity losses are estimated at 134.2 billion. A large share of these costs is borne by employers, because most adults who have problems with alcohol or drug use are in the workforce. See: www.wbgh.org/pdfs/substance_brief.pdf.

The 'Working Partners' Report found the loss of money connected to drugs in the workplace occurs mainly for the following reasons:

✓ **Workers Compensation:** 38 percent to 50 percent of all workers' compensation claims are related to substance abuse in the workplace; as substance abusers file three to five times as many workers' compensation claims.

✓ **Medical Costs:** Substance abusers incur 300 percent higher medical costs than non-abusers.

✓ **Absenteeism:** Substance abusers are 2.5 times more likely to be absent eight or more days a year.

✓ **Lost Productivity:** Substance abusers are 1/3 less productive.

✓ **Employee Turnover:** It costs a business an average of $7,000 to replace a salaried worker.

While some employers and researchers may question or challenge the statistics or the actual costs of drugs in the workplace, and many of these studies are based on estimates using various models, it does appear from the majority of statistics cited that substance abuse costs businesses money and has a real impact on bottom lines. According to various studies over the past two decades, workplace drug abuse is estimated to drain somewhere between $60 billion to well over $200 billion from American businesses:

✓ The National Institutes of Health reported that alcohol and drug abuse cost the economy $246 billion in 1992, while in 1990 problems resulting from the use of alcohol and other drugs cost American businesses an estimated $81.6 billion in lost productivity (See: www.dol.gov/elaws/asp/drugfree/benefits.htm).

✓ A 1996 paper from three professors at Virginia Tech cites studies indicating the loss can be from $60 billion to $99 billion (See: http://6aa7f5c4a9901a3e1a1682793cd11f5a6b732d29.gripelements.com/pdf/vol-717.pdf).

Although there is no way to know the exact figure, drug use in the workplace still appears to be a significant issue and is a growing concern for employers since many drug users, heavy drinkers, and people with substance use disorders are employed. A 2008 study from the U.S. Department of Health and Human Services, Substance Abuse and Mental Health Services Administration (SAMHSA) Office of Applied Studies (See: http://oas.samhsa.gov/nsduh/2k7nsduh/2k7results.cfm) – which included results from the 2007 National Survey on 'Drug Use and Health: National Findings' – revealed the following information about substance use and abuse among American workers:

✓ Of the 17.4 million current illicit drug users age 18 and over, 13.1 million (75.3 percent) were employed.

✓ Among 55.3 million adult binge drinkers, 44.0 million (79.4 percent) were employed.

✓ Among 16.4 million persons reporting heavy alcohol use, 13.1 million (79.6 percent) were employed.

✓ Of the 20.4 million adults classified with substance dependence or abuse, 12.3 million (60.4 percent) were employed full-time.

Small Businesses Employ More Drug Users but Drug Test Less

According to statistics of businesses from the U.S. Census Bureau, smaller businesses were most vulnerable to drug use and particularly disadvantaged by worker substance use and abuse in the workplace but drug tested less than larger businesses. While roughly half of all U.S. workers worked for small and medium sized businesses with fewer than 500 employees, the 2007 report 'Worker Substance Use and Workplace Policies and Programs' from SAMHSA (See: http://oas.samhsa.gov/work2k7/work.pdf) found:

✓ About nine in ten employed current illicit drug users and almost nine in ten employed heavy drinkers worked for small and medium sized firms.

✓ About nine in ten full-time workers with alcohol or illicit drug dependence or abuse worked for small and medium size firms.

However, this report from SAMHSA also found smaller firms were generally less likely to drug test for substance use and to have drug test programs in place to combat the problem. The report also noted that individuals who could not adhere to a drug-free workplace policy sought employment at firms that did not have a drug test policy. The cost of one error caused by an impaired employee could devastate a smaller company.

Furthermore, studies have found the impact of employee substance use and abuse is a problem that extends beyond the substance-using employee, as there is evidence that co-worker job performance and attitudes are negatively affected.

Workers have reported being put in danger, having been injured, or having had to work harder, to re-do work, or to cover for a co-worker as a result of a fellow employee's drug use.

SHRM Study Finds More than Half of Employers Favor Drug Testing

A recently released study examining the use of drug testing programs by employers conducted by the Society for Human Resource Management (SHRM) and commissioned by the Drug and Alcohol Testing Association (DATIA) found that more than half of employers (57 percent) conduct drug tests on all job candidates.

According to the poll released in September 2011 that surveyed 1,058 randomly selected Human Resource professionals, 69 percent of employers who drug test job candidates have done so for seven years or more while 12 percent have used drug tests for five to six years. The study also found that:

✓ 71 percent of large organizations with 2,500 or more employees required all job applicants to take a pre-employment drug test.
✓ 62 percent of medium-sized businesses with 500 to 2,499 employees reported that they required drug testing.
✓ 56 percent of businesses with 100 to 499 employees required pre-employment drug testing.
✓ 39 percent of small businesses with fewer than 100 employees had a drug-testing policy for job candidates.

In addition, two thirds of all businesses polled (66 percent) did not conduct drug testing for any of its contract employees, while almost three-quarters (72 percent) of multinational businesses reported that they used the same drug testing policies in operations outside the United States. For more information about the SHRM study:

✓ See the article 'SHRM Poll: Drug Testing Applicants Favored by More than Half of Employers' at www.shrm.org/Publications/HRNews/Pages/DrugTestingFavored.aspx (Only available to SHRM members).
✓ To see the SHRM and DATIA poll, visit the SHRM site at: www.shrm.org/Research/SurveyFindings/Articles/Pages/lDrugTestingEfficacy.aspx.

Pre-Employment Screening at Missouri Hospital Includes Drug Test for Nicotine

A hospital in Cape Girardeau, Missouri no longer hires smokers who fail a drug test for nicotine as part of a pre-employment background screening program beginning January 1, 2011. The "Current Openings" page (http://careers.sfmc.net/CurrentOpenings.htm) of the Saint Francis Medical Center website contains the following message under the heading **'Nicotine-free hiring policy'** for prospective job candidates:

"Because it is important for healthcare providers to promote a healthy environment and lifestyle, effective January 1, 2011, Saint Francis Medical Center has a nicotine-free hiring policy. Applicants will be tested for nicotine as part of a pre-employment screening. **I understand that my application will not be considered if I use tobacco products.***"

Cost/Benefit of Drug Testing

Pre-employment drug testing programs can be set up with a minimal amount of effort. Firms that operate from a single location can usually turn to a local medical clinic for tests. For firms with multiple locations, or who have applicants from various areas, programs can be set-up through drug testing agencies to allow testing at locations convenient to the job applicant throughout the United States.

Most employers find that a drug-testing program will eliminate people with problems, but not good applicants. Drug tests for small to medium employers generally cost in the $50-$70.00 range and include a collection of the sample, laboratory analysis, services of a Medial Review Officer (MRO), and communications of the results in the manner most convenient to the employer. Compared to the cost of even one employee with a substance abuse problem, most firms find eliminating the problem in the first place is well worth the time and money involved in a drug-testing.

The ABC's of Drug Testing

Do I Need to Test My Employees?

Although drug testing laws vary from state to state — in some cases, from county to county — only a handful of employers are mandated by law to screen their employees for illicit substances. The majority of these employers are in the transportation industry, and they tend to know who they are. For the remainder not bound by federal guidelines, the decision as to whether or not to drug test is up to the employer subject to the type of legal limitations discussed below.

Many positions pose considerable risk to property, personnel, or the public. In these instances, drug or alcohol screening is often considered to be a necessary measure for preventing or mitigating potential mishaps.

Mandatory Screening

Employers are legally required to screen employees for drugs and alcohol in certain cases, for example, truck drivers are regulated by the Department of Transportation (DOT) and must be tested if they drive a Commercial Motor Vehicle with a gross combination weight rating of over 26,001 pounds, or if the vehicle is designed to transport 16 or more passengers or hazardous materials. Testing requirements exist for workers in other regulated and safety sensitive industries such as aviation, rail, transit, maritime, and pipeline industries.

Another example centers on employers who operate under federal contracts and are subject to mandatory rules for a Drug Free Workplace. That applies to employers who do business with the federal government and have contracts in excess of a set minimum dollar amount.

Recommended Screening

Employers not legally required to test for drugs or alcohol sometimes choose to require the procedure anyway, especially employers with workers in particularly safety-sensitive positions, such as any employee who:

- ✓ Works closely with children, the elderly, or the disabled.
- ✓ Has extensive, unsupervised contact with the public.
- ✓ Is required to operate a vehicle or heavy machinery.
- ✓ Works in or has access to private residences and businesses.
- ✓ Handles money or valuables.
- ✓ Has access to weapons, drugs, or dangerous substances.
- ✓ Works in a supervisory position.

 If an employer determines that a drug screening program is necessary, then screening should be implemented universally in order to avoid problems with discrimination.

Pre-Employment and Post-Employment Drug Screens

Pre-employment drug screens are the most common tests used by employers. Courts have consistently upheld the legality of requiring a drug test as a condition of being considered for employment. Employers should consult their attorneys concerning any legal issues involved with drug testing.

Many employers utilize a single drug screen 'on the way in' to satisfy their requirement for demonstrating due diligence. For the most part, this is true. Screening a job applicant once prior to making a hiring decision does demonstrate that efforts have been made to prevent individuals with substance abuse problems from entering the workplace. However, maintaining a screening program that excludes existing employees from testing makes a potentially fatal presumption that employees' lives do not change past the moment of hire. Factors in any employee's life can change at a moment's notice and bad habits develop quickly. A drug test administered to a new hire on the way in is accurate only up to the moment that specimen was produced.

The decision to screen should be made considering all employees, not just candidates for the job.

How is drug testing conducted?

Most drug testing is done by sending an applicant to a collection site, where a urine sample is obtained and sent to a certified laboratory for analysis. Negative results are normally available within 24 hours. There are instant test kits on the market. These are similar to home pregnancy tests and require the employer to manipulate a urine sample. Although these tests are considered accurate for immediate screening, they are useless in the event of a positive result, since that requires laboratory confirmation and retention of a sample for retesting by the subject. In addition, they are not that much less expensive then laboratory tests.

 Most employers will insist that a job applicant give the urine sample within a specific period of time to prevent a drug user from waiting until the drugs leave the system. Some drug experts consider a drug test to be an IQ test—taking a test knowing there are drugs in the system is not a good sign. Laboratories and collection sites also have ways to determine if the applicant has attempted to alter the test sample.

What About Consent?

Prior to the hire, express written consent should be obtained for a pre-employment drug test. When doing post-hire screening, the consent is often covered in the form of workplace rules and policies. Therefore, it is imperative for any firm intending to conduct post-accident testing or probable-cause testing to have written policies and procedures in place before attempting to conduct post-hire drug tests.

Setting Drug Testing Policies and Procedures

A drug-testing program should not be implemented without first establishing policies and procedures. An effective, comprehensive program covering post-hire testing should address such issues as:

✓ Communicating to the workforce about the need and advantages of a drug testing program – a safe workplace, lower health costs, improve productivity, etc.

✓ A well-written policy that has been reviewed by legal counsel.

✓ Proof that all employees have received and are familiar with the policy.

✓ Confidentiality of medical records.

✓ The company's stance on workplace drug or alcohol use (i.e., Zero Tolerance).

✓ The events or times at which testing takes place.

✓ What constitutes a passed or failed drug test.

✓ Having a policy on what to do in the event of a positive test, such as allowing the employee to explain or retest the sample.

✓ Procedures involved if a person is suspected of violating the policy.

✓ The consequences of a violation of the policy.

✓ Options for treatment, counseling and rehabilitation, and other employee assistance.

✓ Supervisor training in drug testing procedures and policies.

✓ Using medically approved tests and procedures.

✓ Keeping all tests confidential and maintained separate from the personnel file.

✓ Considering use of a Medical Review Officer (MRO) – mandatory for certain types of testing.

Keep in mind that employers of certain size are subject to the rules and regulations of the Federal Americans with Disabilities Act (ADA) as well as similar state rules. Although the current use and abuse of drugs or alcohol is not considered to be a disability – and therefore not protected by the ADA – post-hire drug testing can be a very complicated legal area. Any employer looking to implement a post-hire screening program should first consult an attorney specializing in labor practices.

Rules for Testing Other than for Pre-employment?

There may be times when an employer is required by legal obligations or employee behavior to conduct drug testing post-hire. The three major categories of testing other than pre-employment are suspicion-less (or random) testing, post-accident testing, and reasonable suspicion testing. Following are some points to consider.

Suspicion-less Testing	✓ Applies to safety sensitive positions. ✓ Normally government mandated, such as truck drivers, railroad workers, custom workers, security clearance, nuclear workers, jockeys, airline personnel, gas pipeline workers. ✓ For example, Department of Transportation (DOT) has extensive rules and regulations including contacting past employers, random pools, special rules for testing, and the use of Medical Review Officers (MRO).
Post-accident Testing	✓ Announce the program in advance as part of company policy. ✓ Offer counseling or treatment without fear of reprisal. ✓ Will test safety sensitive positions. ✓ Tested only after a serious accident. ✓ Less intrusive testing possible, e.g. urine instead of blood test.
Reasonable Suspicion Testing	✓ Employer may test if there is observable phenomena such as direct observation of drug use, or physical symptoms, pattern of abnormal conduct or erratic behavior, arrest for drug related offense, or information provided by credible sources. ✓ Best practice is to have a drug policy in place and have supervisors formally trained to recognize signs of drug use. ✓ On the issue of off-duty conduct justifying drug test—does it raise suspicion of on-duty impairment?

What is Tested? – DOT Drug Tests and Non-DOT Drug Tests

For the most part, drug screens are separated into two categories — DOT (Department of Transportation) screens and Non-DOT screens (also called "forensic" or "non-regulated" screens). The two screens vary by criteria.

✓ In DOT screens, a limited panel of drugs can be tested for only in urine or breath testing with federally-mandated "cutoff levels" at specific times within the employee's time with the company.

✓ In non-DOT screens, employers are free to select the specimen to be tested — blood, breath, saliva, urine or hair — the panel of substances to be tested against, the cutoff level, and the times or circumstances at which the test may be taken.

Drug Testing for DOT Employers

DOT regulations require that employers test employees for a specific, limited panel of substances, under specific circumstances:

✓ Pre-employment.
✓ Random selection.
✓ Reasonable suspicion/cause.
✓ Post-accident.
✓ Return-to-duty.
✓ Follow-up

Typically a "5 panel" NIDA (National Institute of Drug Abuse) test and DOT tests include:

✓ Marijuana (THC).
✓ Cocaine.
✓ Phencyclidine (PCP).
✓ Opiates such as codeine, heroin, and morphine.
✓ Amphetamines, including methamphetamine.

Nearly every testing facility and vendor in the testing industry refers to these five substances as their "basic 5-panel test." When facilities and vendors refer to "panels," they mean the number of substances for which they are screening, i.e. "5-panel" meaning a test for five substances, "10-panel" for ten substances.

Non-DOT drug tests do not satisfy DOT regulations, but the same laws governing privacy and disclosure still apply to these tests. Non-DOT tests can screen for more and different substances than DOT tests, including:

✓ Barbiturates.
✓ Benzodiazepines.
✓ Methadone.
✓ Propoxyphene.
✓ Methaqualone (Quaaludes).
✓ Hallucinogens (LSD, psilocybin).
✓ Designer drugs.

Drug Testing for Non-DOT Employers

While there are all varieties of illicit substances to be found in most major metropolitan areas — and just about anywhere else — most employers screen their applicants for the five most common "street drugs" using the "5 panel" screen. Some employers may replace the PCP screen with a screen for methamphetamines such as Ecstasy.

Many additional tests are available on the market, including tests for prescription medications or "designer" drugs. A typical ten-panel screen may test for THC (marijuana), cocaine, PCP, opiates, methamphetamines (including Ecstasy), methadone, amphetamines, barbiturates, benzodiazepines, and tricyclic antidepressants (TCAs).

However, the standard five-panel screen serves its purpose – it weeds out those applicants found to have those substances in their systems, deters many more potentially problematic candidates from applying, and demonstrates due diligence in the event that an applicant with a substance-abuse problem slips through.

What Happens if there is a Positive Test or Abnormal Test?

Testing labs have extensive procedures to re-confirm a positive test before reporting it. If a sample tests positive in the initial screening procedures, then the sample is subjected to testing by a gas chromatography/mass spectrometry (GC/MS). This is considered the state-of-the-art science for the definitive testing of drugs.

Most drug testing programs also utilize the services of an independent physician called a Medical Review Officer (MRO) to review all test results. In the case of a positive result, the MRO will normally contact the subject to determine if there is a medical explanation for the positive results.

There can also be tests that are "negative' but show an abnormal result, such as a "low creatine level," which can indicate an applicant attempted to dilute the sample by the excessive drinking of water or some other form of alteration. That is also a result that a MRO would examine. A specific gravity test can be conducted to measure the concentration of particles in urine, which can indicate an applicant's attempt to mask drugs by drinking excessive fluids.

If the positive test is confirmed, the subject should have the right to pay for a retesting of the sample they gave at a laboratory of their choice. Urine samples for all positive tests are retained for that purpose. Merely taking a new test is not helpful since the drugs may have left the system. Reputable and certified laboratories will stand behind their results and provide expert witnesses, although the chances of a false positive are practically nil.

If a current employee tests positive, then the employer must follow the policies and procedures they have put into place. Some employers will utilize an Employee Assistance Program (EAP), which can arrange for professional assessment and treatment recommendations. All drug-testing results should be maintained on a confidential basis separate from an employee's personnel file.

How Does the Drug Test Work?

As drugs are processed by the user's system, they produce metabolites – substances produced as a byproduct of the user's body metabolizing or "digesting" the drug. While a drug will pass relatively quickly through the user's system, chemical traces of the metabolites produced by the person's body in processing the substance can remain afterwards for days or weeks. In general, drug tests do not screen for the drugs themselves, but instead test the user's system for the metabolites that were derived as a result of the drug passing through the user's system. In other words, drug tests don't test for drugs, instead for what the drugs leave behind.

When looking for evidence of illegal drug use, labs test bodily fluids (usually urine, but sometimes blood or saliva) or hair for traces of drugs or drug metabolites. Alcohol can be detected in blood but is generally tested for in the breath.

Drug Detection

Although each drug and each person is different, most drugs will stay in the system about two to four days. As mentioned above, chronic users of certain drugs such as marijuana or PCP may have results detected for up to fourteen days and sometimes much longer.

The following chart illustrates the average detection window in which traces of drug use can be found in a user's system. While there is some "wiggle room" on either side of the specified time frames, this chart reflects the average retention periods of the average user.

Drug	Detection Window
Marijuana	3 – 15 days
Cocaine	1 – 3 days
Opiates	1 – 2 days

Methadone	2 – 3 days
Phencyclidine	Up to 7 days
Amphetamines	2 – 4 days
Barbiturates	Up to 14 days
Benzodiazepines	Up to 14 days

Due to the limited detection windows of most drugs, one would think that the savvy drug user would seek to avoid detection by simply cleaning up for a few weeks prior to an anticipated test. Typically, this is not the case. Instead, a whole industry has surfaced purveying cheats, gimmicks, and products designed to help users defeat drug screening devices.

Laboratories and collection sites have countered this wave of anti-detection innovation with their own methods to determine whether or not the applicant has attempted to alter or replace the test specimen. The table below indicates the most common cheats and the most common countermeasures.

Cheat	Countermeasure
System dilution (drinking excessive water, "flushing" the system)	Specific gravity tests measure the concentration of particles in urine. A significantly reduced result indicates tampering.
Specimen substitution (substituting clean urine from another individual or reconstituted "powdered" urine)	Measuring the specimen's temperature immediately can indicate whether or not the specimen was produced prior to or at the time of testing.
Prosthetic delivery devices	A firsthand witness is required to successfully prove that an individual used a prosthetic device to administer a false specimen. A possible giveaway is the "clunk" sound the device makes when it contacts the specimen cup.
Additives (doping the sample)	Doping the specimen to be tested only results in a polluted specimen, requiring a re-test.
Refuting results	An applicant refuting the results of a drug test is entitled to prove his or her innocence by having the specimen re-tested at the laboratory of choice. However, applicants typically are not allowed to retake a test since that simply gives time to clear out the system.

Cutoff Levels

The amount of a substance detected during the initial screen is important. The Mandatory Guidelines for Federal Workplace Drug Testing Programs published by SAMHSA (the Substance Abuse and Mental Health Services Administration) indicates a specific cutoff level for each drug. This is the set ratio of drug or drug metabolite to volume of liquid in the specimen that must be found in order for the specimen to legitimately qualify for positive detection. This applies to an initial screen and in a confirmatory screen. In urine analysis, cutoff levels are measured in nanograms per milliliter (ng/mL) – that is, billionths of a gram of the substance per thousandth of a liter of urine, more quantitatively translated into millionths of a gram per liter — in any case, not very much is required for a positive result. Employers held to DOT regulations must follow the SAMHSA cutoff levels for the most commonly tested-for drugs.

What are the Cutoff Concentrations for Drug Tests?

A laboratory must use the cutoff concentrations displayed in the following table for initial and confirmatory drug tests. All cutoff concentrations are expressed in nanograms per milliliter (ng/mL). If an initial urine screen shows marijuana metabolites evidenced in the amount of 26 nanograms per milliliter, and the cutoff level for marijuana metabolites is 50 ng/mL, the initial screen would come back negative for use of marijuana. Basically, the more frequently a substance is used, the higher the volume will be seen in the specimen in ng/mL. In order to suit the company's needs, "acceptable standards" may be established by any private employer. The Federal Workplace standards are not mandatory.

Initial Test Analyte	Initial Test Cutoff Concentration	Confirmatory Test Analyte	Confirmatory Test Cutoff Concentration
Marijuana metabolites	50 ng/mL	THCA[1]	15 ng/mL
Cocaine metabolites	150 ng/mL	Benzoylecgonine	100 ng/mL
Opiate metabolites			
Codeine/Morphine[2]	2000 ng/mL	Codeine	2000 ng/mL
		Morphine	2000 ng/mL
6-Acetylmorphine*	10 ng/mL	6-Acetylmorphine*	10 ng/mL
Phencyclidine	25 ng/mL	Phencyclidine	25 ng/mL
Amphetamines[3]			
AMP/MAMP[4]	500 ng/mL	Amphetamine	250 ng/mL
		Methamphetamine[5]	250 ng/mL
MDMA[6]	500 ng/mL	MDMA	250 ng/mL
		MDA[7]	250 ng/mL
		MDEA[8]	250 ng/mL

[1] Delta-9-tetrahydrocannabinol-9-carboxylic acid (THCA).

[2] Morphine is the target analyte for codeine/morphine testing.

[3] Either a single initial test kit or multiple initial test kits may be used provided the single test kit detects each target analyte independently at the specified cutoff.

[4] Methamphetamine is the target analyte for amphetamine/methamphetamine testing.

[5] To be reported positive for methamphetamine, a specimen must also contain amphetamine at a concentration equal to or greater than 100 ng/mL.

[6] Methylenedioxymethamphetamine (MDMA).

[7] Methylenedioxyamphetamine (MDA).

[8] Methylenedioxyethylamphetamine (MDEA).

* The heroin metabolite is known as 6-acetylmorphine or 6-monoacetylmorphine. Because it rapidly metabolizes into morphine, it is rarely found during a screening.

Source: http://edocket.access.gpo.gov/2010/pdf/2010-20095.pdf.

DOT Amends Procedures for Transportation Workplace Drug Testing

The U.S. Department of Transportation (DOT) amended procedures for transportation workplace drug and alcohol testing program. This was part of an effort to create consistency with many new requirements established by the U.S. Department of Health and Human Services (HHS). Full details of the final rule – which took effect October 1, 2010 – are available at http://edocket.access.gpo.gov/2010/pdf/2010-20095.pdf.

Some of the changes affect the training of and procedures used by Medical Review Officers (MROs). Highlights of these changes include the following:

✓ DOT began requiring drug testing for Ecstasy (Methylenedioxymethamphetamine or MDMA). The initial screening cut-off concentration for MDMA is 500 ng/ml, and the confirmatory cut-off concentration is 250 ng/ml for MDMA, as well as Methylenedioxyamphetamine (MDA) and Methylenedioxyethylamphetamine (MDEA), drugs that are chemically similar to Ecstasy;

✓ The drug test cutoff concentrations for cocaine were lowered. The initial screening test cutoff dropped from 300 ng/ml to 150 ng/ml, and the confirmatory test cutoff concentration was lowered from 150 ng/ml to 100 ng/ml;

✓ The drug test cutoff concentrations for amphetamines were lowered. The initial screening test cutoff was lowered from 1,000 ng/ml to 500 ng/ml, and the confirmatory drug test cutoff concentration from 500 ng/ml to 250 ng/ml; and

✓ Initial drug testing for 6-acetylmorphine ("6-AM," a unique metabolite of heroin, considered to be definitive proof of heroin use) is now required. Specific rules were added to address the way in which Medical Review Officers ("MROs") analyze and verify confirmed positive drug test results for 6-AM, codeine, and morphine.

Pros and Cons of Testing Methods

The table below gives an excellent description of the pros and cons of the five most common test methods used by employers.

Method	How it Works	Pros	Cons
Urine sample at third party collection site	Applicant is sent to a third party collection site and is given a Chain of Custody (COC), or one is provided at site. Employers can use one of the national firms (including Quest, Lab Corp, etc.), a regional firm, or a local drug-testing lab. The labs should be certified by the Substance Abuse and Mental Health Services Administration (SAMHSA)	There are over 20,000 third party collection sites. The test does not require the employer or HR to be involved in the physical collection procedures. Normally, negatives are returned in 24 hours.	Some employers feel it is unduly intrusive to have applicants provide a urine sample. The test window is only 2 to 4 days for some substances such as cocaine, opiates, and amphetamines.

On-site instant kits	The employer collects the urine sample at the job. A 're-agent" is introduced into the sample, creating an instant result by some sort of color change.	Instant results. Relatively inexpensive.	If a positive, then the best practice is to send sample or applicant for a test where the results can be analyzed in a lab. Employers should not use a positive as an indication of drug use without further testing. Requires special care for the operator who handles body fluids.
Instant oral test	The applicant places receptor in mouth under tongue (which is basically the size of a Q-tip). The operator then manipulates the device in order to place saliva onto a regent pad to view any color change.	Like the on-site instant kit, an instant oral kit is very accurate but less intrusive.	If a positive, then the best practice is to send sample or applicant for a test where results can be analyzed in a lab. Employers should not use a positive as an indication of drug use without further testing. Requires special care for the operator who handles body fluids. Of limited use past measurement
Laboratory salvia test	Applicant handles entire procedure, from opening sealed applicator to sealing in a bag, to shipping to a lab.	No handling of body fluids by operators. Much less intrusive than a urine sample. Laboratory testing ensures accuracy.	Slow due to delay in mailing to lab. Not DOT approved as of 01/04.
Hair testing	A sample of hair is taken from the crown of hair and mailed to laboratory.	Extremely accurate and not subject to contamination or efforts to mask the results. Goes back 90 days.	Some people find it an invasion of privacy to cut hair. Test needs sample from the crown of the head, about the size of pencil eraser. Mailing and testing takes longer than other tests and is more expensive.

Drug Testing Costs

Most small employers should expect to be able to get a standard, run-of-the-mill, 5-panel screen from a third-party vendor for somewhere in the $40.00 to $60.00 range or, for slightly more money, directly from the detection lab where third parties often receive volume discounts. The fee usually includes the handling and processing of the sample as well as monitoring chain-of-custody — tracking the specimen to ensure at no point is it possible for the specimen to be "switched" — and providing medical review services.

The availability of "home testing" kits — also called "quick and dirty" tests — from the web is increasing. These products generally cost between $5.00 and $10.00 each, are usually sold by the box, and often allow the employer to "mix and match" the panel of substances for which the applicants will be tested.

These home testing kits, while a little cheaper, do have their drawbacks. First, they are non-DOT compliant, meaning the detection cutoff levels do not have to match those governed by the DOT. Second, the results cannot be confirmed. Positive results cannot be re-tested to confirm the presence of a substance, and negative results cannot be tested for tampering. The biggest drawback to these tests is the employer is required to manipulate the specimen, not to mention also witness the "donation" process in order to discourage cheating.

Legal Issues and Drug Testing

The most common type of drug testing program is for pre-employment purposes. Courts have consistently upheld the legality of requiring a pre-employment drug test as a condition of employment. It is a best practice to obtain consent and to clearly indicate drug testing is a requirement for employment.

Although the Americans with Disabilities Act (ADA) and similar state laws provide protection for people who are in rehabilitation for a drug addition, the ADA does not protect people currently abusing drugs.

The following are some leading cases and current legal issues impacting drug testing. At the end of the chapter are resources that will assist employers in all 50 states.

The Conflict between California Medical Marijuana and Federal Law

The California Compassionate Use Act of 1996 is a California law which allows patients with a valid doctor's recommendation to possess and cultivate marijuana for personal medical use. However, in *Ross v. RagingWire Telecommunications, Inc. (2008) 42 Cal.4th 920*, the California Supreme Court determined that an employee authorized to use marijuana for medical purposes could not state a cause of action for wrongful termination. The Court's opinion emerged from a collision among principles of California law, Federal law, and public policy.

In Ross, the employee was directed by his physician to use marijuana to treat chronic pain. He was then fired when a pre-employment drug test required of new employees revealed his marijuana use. The employee alleged that the company violated the California Fair Employment and Housing Act (FEHA) by discharging him and failing to make reasonable accommodation for his disability. The court concluded that The Compassionate Use Act did not require California companies to accommodate the use of marijuana and reaffirmed that the company could take illegal drug use into consideration in making employment decisions.

Job Applicants May be Required to Undergo a Pre-Employment Drug Test

In *Loder v. City of Glendale (1997) 14 Cal.4th 846*, the City of Glendale, CA, implemented a drug testing program for all newly hired or promoted city employees. Loder, a taxpayer, sought to enjoin the drug testing program as an invasion of privacy. The court held that, under the California constitution, employers may require and conduct pre-employment testing for illegal drugs and may take illegal drug use into consideration if making employment decisions.

The California court, however, also found that drug testing of current employees without any individualized suspicion of drug use or other special circumstances would violate the employees' privacy rights. Under *Loder,* current employees enjoy greater privacy protection than "applicants." The rationale for the difference is that, with a current employee, an employer "can observe the employee at work, evaluate his or her work product and safety record, and check employment records to determine whether the employee has been excessively absent or late," an opportunity the employer lacks with a job applicant. The applicant also has a reduced expectation of privacy because they must provide information to an employer, and the applicant expects to answer questions about their suitability for a particular job.

A person may continue to be an "applicant" and not considered a "current employee" after several days of working a job. In *Pilkington Barnes Hind v. Superior Court, 66. Cal. App. 4th 28 (1998)*, the court ruled that after several days of working, the applicant had not performed any substantive work, and the employer had insufficient opportunity to observe and determine if he had performance problems that might be related to substance abuse. Therefore the employee, who had delayed submitting to the pre-employment drug testing until after the start of employment, was not allowed to evade the employer's testing requirement on the grounds he was a current employee and immune from such testing.

It is not constitutionally permissible, however, for an employer to require drug testing of an employee who applies for promotion to another position. According to *Loder*, the reasonableness of testing in promotion situations must turn upon the nature and duties of the position in question.

Loder was decided in the context of a governmental employer; however, it has been extended to California private-sector employers as well. *See Kraslawsky v. Upper Deck Co., 56 Cal.App.4th 179 (1997).*

"One Strike" Rules

A California employer had a "one-strike" rule for applicants: fail the drug test, and you're permanently ineligible for hire. An applicant applied for a job as a longshoreman and was rejected because he failed his mandatory drug test. After the rejection, the applicant entered rehab and, while still in the program, re-applied for a position. The employer again rejected him, citing its "one-strike" rule. The employee sued, claiming the rule violated the Americans with Disabilities Act (ADA) protections for recovering addicts. The Ninth Circuit upheld the "one-strike" rule, holding that the company's rule was not intended to exclude past addicts but to ensure a safe workforce. It also noted that the rule applied to all candidates, not just addicts, and therefore didn't discriminate based on addiction under the ADA or California's FEHA. As the court stated, the "one-strike rule bars applicants based on conduct, testing positive for illegal drugs, regardless of whether their failed test was attributable to recreational drug use or an addiction." See: Lopez v. Pacific Maritime Association, __ F.3d __, 2011 WL 711884 (9th Cir. March 2, 2011).

In conclusion: if a company's "one-strike" drug testing policy is consistently applied to all employees, then it's likely legal under the ADA and California's FEHA.

"Suspicionless" Random Testing

At the federal level, Department of Transportation (DOT) employers are responsible for conducting random, unannounced drug and alcohol tests. The goal of random testing is to discourage substance use by making testing unpredictable. The selection must be made by a random, scientifically valid method, like selection by a computer, and all employees covered by the rule must have an equal chance of being tested. The total number of random tests required each year varies between agencies.

State law may limit or prohibit random suspicionless testing of employees unless the position warrants such testing, such as in "safety sensitive positions." For example, California has upheld an Irrigation District's random drug-testing program for employees who perform safety-sanative work. See *Smith v. Fresno Irrigation District, 72 Cal.App.4th 147* (1999). In Smith, a ditch tender and maintenance worker employed by the District was terminated after testing positive for illegal substances in a random drug-test. The appellate court found that the District had a legitimate interest in protecting its employees from a substantial and real risk of injury. It also noted that the employer had distributed a written substance abuse policy ahead of time, had informational meetings, and encouraged employees to seek assistance before testing began.

The court rejected the idea that only individuals who worked in positions affecting public safety could be subjected to random testing and held it was enough if holding a work position in which an impairment could pose a real threat to the employee or his coworkers. Whether a particular position is safety-sensitive is determined by "the degree, severity and immediacy of the harm posed" by the drug impaired performance of the duties of the position. Where there is a hazardous work environment or hazards in the work itself, the position is likely to be considered safety-sensitive.

Recently in Florida, the random testing of state employees was found to be unconstitutional where there was not a compelling enough reason to do so. The Florida rule ordered random drug testing for about 80,000 state employees. The federal court ruling held that there was no evidence of a large-scale problem and no urgent reason to mandate drug tests. See: www.nytimes.com/2012/04/27/us/court-rules-florida-governors-drug-testing-order-unconstitutional.html.

Other states including Connecticut, Delaware, Maine, Massachusetts, Minnesota, New Jersey, New York, and West Virginia limit random testing to workers in safety-sensitive positions. Vermont prohibits random testing altogether.

There are also local restrictions on random drug testing. Employers in San Francisco and Berkeley, California, for example, must comply with local laws that further restrict drug testing. Under San Francisco's ordinance, any drug testing requires reasonable grounds and a clear and present physical danger to the employee, co-worker, or a member of the public – thereby prohibiting random testing.

Reasonable-Suspicion Testing

Reasonable suspicion testing is used when a trained supervisor or employer has reasonable suspicion to believe that an employee has used a controlled substance. A reasonable suspicion of drug use must generally be based on actual facts and logical inferences, such as:

- ✓ Direct observation of drug use,
- ✓ Direct observation of physical symptoms of drug use, including slurred speech, agitated or lethargic demeanor, uncoordinated movement, and inappropriate responses to questions,
- ✓ A pattern of abnormal conduct,
- ✓ Erratic behavior while at work,
- ✓ Arrest for drug-related offense,
- ✓ A significant deterioration in work performance,
- ✓ A report of drug use provided by a reliable and credible source that has been independently corroborated,
- ✓ Evidence the employee has tampered with current drug test results,
- ✓ Information that the employee has caused or contributed to an accident at work, or
- ✓ Evidence the employee has used, possessed, sold, solicited, or transferred drugs while working or at work.

A California executive secretary at a company with a reasonable suspicion drug testing program was observed by her senior manager slumped over her desk. When she did not move, the manager asked her what was wrong and she did not answer. The human resources director then observed that the employee's speech was slurred, her demeanor was lethargic, she was swaying, she was unable to maintain eye contact, and her answers seemed to be controlled and very deliberate. However, neither the senior manager nor the human resources director had received formal training on detecting substance abuse. The employee was also allowed to drive herself to a lab for drug testing. For a California jury, these facts implied that the employer did not truly believe she was impaired at the time and the employee was allowed to proceed with a lawsuit for invasion of privacy and wrongful termination. See *Kraslawsky vs. Upper Deck Company, (1997) 56 Cal.App.4th 179.*

In conclusion, the best practice is to have a drug testing policy in place and to conduct formal supervisor training on how to recognize the signs of drug use.

The ADA Does Not Protect Current Illicit Drug/Alcohol Use

In general, a person with a drug addiction who is currently in a drug rehabilitation program or has successfully completed rehabilitation and has not used drugs illegally for some time is covered by the Americans with Disabilities Act (ADA). The ADA makes it unlawful to discriminate against qualified people with disabilities in employment.

Persons who are currently illegally using drugs, however, are not protected under the ADA. The illegal use of drugs includes the use of illegal drugs and the misuse of prescription drugs that are "controlled substances". An employer may refuse to hire an applicant or discharge or discipline an employee based upon a test result that indicates illegal use of drugs. An employer has no obligation toward individuals who are currently using illegal drugs, regardless of whether such individuals are addicts or casual users of drugs, and regardless of whether the illegal drug use impacts upon the individuals' behavior or job performance.

Is Drug Testing Covered by the Fair Credit Reporting Act?

The answer is: it depends.

The Fair Credit Reporting Act (FCRA) requires, among other things, that employers provide disclosure and obtain consent before securing a "consumer report." The definition of "consumer report" is broad and includes information about an individual's "character, general reputation, personal characteristics, or mode of living." Additionally, to be covered by the FCRA, a report must be prepared by a consumer reporting agency (CRA). See FCRA § 603(d)(1).

Regarding the applicability of the FCRA to drug tests, the Federal Trade Commission (FTC) takes a circumstance specific approach. In a letter from William Haynes dated June 11, 1998 ("Haynes – Islinger letter"), the FTC states:

> *When a drug lab provides the results directly to the employer, the test is not a "consumer report" under the FCRA. When an intermediary does so, a detailed factual analysis is needed to determine the answer. When a CRA provides the test results, it is clearly making a "consumer report" to the employer.*

When a Drug Lab Provides Results Directly to Employer it is NOT a Consumer Report

The Haynes-Islinger letter explains that "[d]rug tests do bear on an individual's character, general reputation, personal characteristics, or mode of living," however, FCRA § 603(d)(2)(A)(i) excludes from the definition of "consumer report" any report "containing information solely as to transactions or experiences between the consumer and the person making the report." Since drug tests constitute reports based on the experience of the laboratory, these reports fall into the exception and are not covered by the FCRA when they are provided directly to the employer by the laboratory.

Likewise, the Fifth Circuit has concluded that drug test reports are included in the general definition of a "consumer report." See *Hodge v. Texaco, Inc., 975 F.2d 1093* (5th Cir. 1992). However, the Fifth Circuit ultimately found that the drug report in question fell within the "transactions or experiences" exclusion of FCRA § 603(d)(2)(A)(i) ("any report containing information solely as to transactions or experiences between the consumer and the person making the report"). The Fifth Circuit held that this exclusion "exempts from coverage any report based on the reporter's first-hand experience of the subject." Therefore, a laboratory's report to the employer fell within this exclusion and the report did not constitute a "consumer report" for purposes of the FCRA.

More recently, the United States District Court Northern District of Texas affirmed that workplace drug test reports are not categorically excluded from coverage in *Martinets v. Corning Cable Systems, 237 F.Supp.2d 717* (N.D. Tex. 2002). Again, however, the court found that following the administration of a breathalyzer test on an employee, the laboratory prepared a report that was based on information that it derived as part of its own analysis of the test, which purported to measure the alcohol level in the employee's system. Since the report was a direct result of a transaction and experience between the employee and the laboratory, the court concluded that the report also fell within the "transactions or experiences" exclusion and did not constitute a "consumer report"

When testing is conducted first hand by a credible facility such as a laboratory that provides testing results directly to an employer rather than relying on another facility's results, the testing facility is not a "consumer reporting agency" and the FCRA does not apply.

When an Intermediary Provides the Results to the Employer

Where an intermediary reports the results of a test done by a lab, the issue of whether the communication is a "consumer report" requires a detained review of the facts. The answer depends on whether the intermediary is a "consumer reporting agency" (CRA). "Consumer reporting agency" is defined in FCRA § 603(f) as a party that "regularly engages … in the practice of assembling or evaluating … information on consumers for the purpose of furnishing consumer reports to third parties."

According to the Haynes-Inslinger letter, if an intermediary contributes to, or takes any action that determines the content of the information conveyed to an employer, it is "assembling or evaluating" the information and the intermediary qualifies as a CRA. If, however, the intermediary does nothing more than perform mechanical functions, such as arranging for a laboratory to conduct a drug test, collecting samples, forwarding them to the laboratory, and transmitting the test results to the employer, it probably will not be a CRA making a "consumer report." The letter states, by way of example that:

> *"... an intermediary that retains copies of tests performed by drug labs and regularly sells this information to third parties for a fee is a CRA whose reports of drug test results are "consumer reports" covered by the FCRA....If a drug test is provided by a party that is indisputably a CRA because of the general nature of its business (e.g. a credit bureau or employment screening service), the report would clearly be a "consumer report" because the communication is made by a CRA..."*

When employers conduct background checks using the service of a background firm, the firm is "assembling or evaluating" information for a consumer. In this case, any drug test results included in the reporting services would likely be considered a consumer report and FCRA guidelines must be followed.

In conclusion, if an employer obtains drug testing information directly from a drug testing lab, it is less likely to be considered a "consumer report" and subject to the FCRA. If, however, if an employer obtains drug test results as part of a background firm's reporting services, it is likely that the drug test **will** be considered a "consumer report."

The Hayes – Islinger letter may be found at: www.ftc.gov/os/statutes/fcra/islinger.shtm.

Recommended Drug Testing Information Resources

This chapter was intended as a brief introduction to employment drug testing. A great deal more information is available from these government or non-profit websites.

- ✓ www.samhsa.gov — Sponsored by the Substance Abuse and Mental Health Services Administration (SAMHSA), an agency of the U.S. Department of Health and Human Services.
- ✓ www.nida.gov — Sponsored by the U.S. National Institute of Drug Abuse.
- ✓ www.dot.gov — U.S. Department of Transportation site, covering tests mandated by that department, commonly referred to as DOT testing.
- ✓ http://store.samhsa.gov/home — The national clearinghouse for drug and substance abuse information, sponsored by SAMHSA.
- ✓ www.drugfreeamerica.org — Information concerning drug abuse and prevention.
- ✓ www.drugfreeworkplace.org — Sponsored by the Institute for a Drug-Free Workplace.
- ✓ www.datia.org — Drug and Alcohol Testing Industry Association.

Links to drug test stats used in chapter:

- ✓ www.tn.gov/labor-wfd/dfwp.html#thecost
- ✓ www.dol.gov/elaws/asp/drugfree/benefits.htm
- ✓ http://6aa7f5c4a9901a3e1a1682793cd11f5a6b732d29.gripelements.com/pdf/vol-717.pdf
- ✓ http://oas.samhsa.gov/nsduh/2k7nsduh/2k7results.cfm
- ✓ http://oas.samhsa.gov/work2k7/work.pdf
- ✓ http://edocket.access.gpo.gov/2010/pdf/2010-20095.pdf

Chapter 24

Dealing With Fraud, Embezzlement, and Integrity

Inside This Chapter:

✓ Screening for Honesty and Morality

✓ Eight Tools to Encourage Future Honesty

✓ How to Avoid Hiring an Embezzler

✓ Corporate Fraud and Sarbanes-Oxley

✓ Psychological Testing for Honesty and Integrity

Screening for Honesty and Morality

Corporate fraud and dishonesty have recently been major news topics. The media has focused on a variety of stories ranging from corporate fraud — Enron, MCI, and others — to the resume fibs of sports coaches. These stories all have one thing in common — applicants either lied to get their position or committed acts of dishonesty in the job, or employers were lax about hiring or exercising sound controls over unethical behavior.

How do firms hire honest employees? Of course, honesty and morality are not easy traits to screen. There is no magic scanning machine that can read an applicant's soul or heart, or the synapses of the brain, declaring that an honest person is applying. Most often, in the hiring process, a firm is only able to look for manifestations of past or current dishonesty. These can include:

- ✓ Casting oneself in a false light by submitting an application that contains material lies or omissions. It is estimated from various sources that up to one out of three applications and resumes contain material falsehoods or omissions, typically involving past education or employment.
- ✓ Lying in an interview, as discussed in Chapter 8.
- ✓ Having committed a criminal act which demonstrates dishonesty or a willingness to commit fraud or some other act of moral turpitude, or such an act that results in a civil lawsuit.

An additional complication is the very nature of honesty itself. For example, an applicant may be the type of person who tells a socially polite "little white lie," e.g. "that was delicious, but I am full" when the meal did not taste very good. However, no one would suggest this person is dishonest for purposes of employment.

The bigger issue is predicting future behavior. Honesty has multiple dimensions. One issue is "what standards and moral values does a person have and to what level are they ingrained in a person?" The past is often prologue. If a person had been honest in the past or is being honest now, then there is a very good chance he or she will be honest in the future. Will an employer be able to predict what guides a person's moral compass in the future under a variety of temptations? Some situations can be predicted since they are part of the job. For example, a bookkeeper will have access to assets and money. Can the new hire with no drug abuse history resist sampling the products at the pharmaceutical warehouse? Other situations cannot be predicted. In the future, a person may undergo sudden life changes or stress that may tempt dishonesty, or a supervisor may ask an employee to participate in a questionable act, such as document shredding — an act with an element of coercion or an implicit threat they would lose their job if they do not cooperate. Part of the complication is to discover ahead of time how a person may react when ordered to do something dishonest.

How does an employer know in advance if applicants will be influenced towards dishonesty if put into a situation where they feel an element of coercion if they do not go along or are tempted by greed or succumb to life's pressures? People's ability to resist life stress and act in an honest an ethical fashion may well depend upon their internal level of ethical development. However that is extremely difficult to test.

ACFE 2012 Report to the Nations Finds Fraud Costs Organizations Five Percent of Revenues Each Year

The *2012 Report to the Nations on Occupational Fraud and Abuse* from the Association of Certified Fraud Examiners (ACFE) estimates that the typical organization loses five percent of its revenues to occupational fraud each year and that this figure translates to a potential projected global fraud loss of more than $3.5 trillion applied to the estimated 2011 Gross World Product. The study also found that the median loss caused by the occupational fraud cases was $140,000, and more than one-fifth of these cases caused losses of at least $1 million. The ACFE 2012 Report to the Nations is available at: www.acfe.com/RTTN/.

"We are proud to say that the information contained in the original Report and its successors has become the most authoritative and widely quoted body of research on occupational fraud..." ACFE President & CEO James D. Ratley, Certified Fraud Examiner (CFE), wrote in an excerpt from a 'Letter from the President & CEO' in the report. "As in previous years, what is perhaps most striking about the data we gathered is how consistent the patterns of fraud are around the globe and over time. We believe this consistency reaffirms the value of our research efforts and the reliability of our findings as truly representative of the characteristics of occupational fraudsters and their schemes."

Since the inception of the initial report in 1996, the ACFE has released six updated editions – in 2002, 2004, 2006, 2008, 2010, and 2012 – based on detailed case information provided by Certified Fraud Examiners (CFEs). The ACFE *2012 Report to the Nations on Occupational Fraud and Abuse* is based on data compiled from a study of 1,388 cases of occupational fraud that occurred worldwide between January 2010 and December 2011. The fraud cases in the study came from 94 nations — providing a truly global view into the plague of occupational fraud.

Some Key Findings and Highlights of the ACFE 2012 *Report to the Nations* include:

✓ **Fraud Detection:** The frauds reported lasted a median of 18 months before being detected. Occupational fraud is more likely to be detected by a tip than by any other method, with the majority of tips reporting fraud come from employees of the victim organization.

✓ **Victims of Fraud:** Small businesses suffered the largest median losses due to occupational fraud since they typically employ fewer anti-fraud controls than their larger counterparts, which increased their vulnerability to fraud. The industries most commonly victimized in our current study were the banking and financial services, government and public administration, and manufacturing sectors. Nearly half of victim organizations – 49 percent – had not recovered any losses that they suffered due to fraud at the time of the survey.

✓ **Perpetrators of Fraud by Age/Sex:** Approximately 54 percent of all fraudsters were between the ages of 31 and 45. Fraud losses, however, tended to rise with the age of the perpetrator. For example, the 50–55 year range had a median loss of $600,000, nearly two-and-a-half times higher than the median loss in any other age range. Males tended to account for roughly two-thirds of all fraud cases, and male fraudsters tended to cause losses that were more than twice as high as the losses caused by females. In the 2012 study, the median loss in a scheme committed by a male was $200,000 while the median loss for a female was $91,000.

✓ **Perpetrators of Fraud by Length of Employment:** Approximately 42 percent of occupational fraudsters had between one and five years of tenure at their organizations. Meanwhile fewer than 6 percent of perpetrators committed fraud within the first year on the job. Tenure at a job has a strong correlation with fraud losses. Individuals who worked at an organization for a longer period of time often enjoy more trust from their supervisors and co-workers, which can mean less scrutiny over their actions. Their experience can also give them a better understanding of the organization's internal controls, which enables them to more successfully carry out and conceal their fraud schemes.

✓ **Perpetrators of Fraud by Position/Department:** Perpetrators of fraud with higher levels of authority tended to cause much larger losses. The median loss among frauds committed by owner/executives was $573,000, the median loss caused by managers was $180,000, and the median loss caused by employees was $60,000. More than three out of four fraud cases in the study – 77 percent – were committed by individuals working in one of six departments: accounting, operations, sales, executive/upper management, customer service, and purchasing.

✓ **Perpetrators of Fraud by Past Criminal Record:** Most occupational fraudsters are first-time offenders with clean employment histories, with 87 percent of occupational fraudsters having never been charged or convicted of a fraud-related offense and 84 percent having never been punished or terminated by an employer for fraud-related conduct.

✓ **"Red Flags" Indicating Fraud:** In the majority of cases – 81 percent of cases – the fraudster displayed one or more behavioral red flags that are often associated with fraudulent conduct: living beyond means (36 percent of cases), financial difficulties (27 percent of cases), unusually close association with vendors or customers (19 percent of cases), and excessive control issues (18 percent of cases). 65 percent of employees who committed insider intellectual property theft had accepted a new job with a competing company or started their own company at the time of the theft. About 20 percent were recruited by an outsider who targeted the data and 25 percent gave the stolen IP to a foreign company or country. Over 50 percent stole data within a month of leaving.

The ACFE 2012 *Report to the Nations* also includes these Conclusions & Recommendations:

✓ The nature and threat of occupational fraud is truly universal, as many trends and characteristics were similar regardless of where the fraud occurred around the globe.

✓ Fraud reporting mechanisms, such as hotlines, should be set up to receive tips from both internal and external sources and should allow anonymity and confidentiality since providing individuals a means to report suspicious activity is a critical part of an anti-fraud program. Management should actively encourage employees to report suspicious activity.

✓ External audits should not be relied upon as an organization's primary fraud detection method, since the study found they detected only 3 percent of the frauds reported and their usefulness as a means of uncovering fraud is limited.

✓ Targeted fraud awareness training for employees and managers is a critical component of a well-rounded program for preventing and detecting fraud since employee tips are the most common way occupational fraud is detected and our research shows organizations that have anti-fraud training programs experience lower losses and shorter frauds.

✓ Small businesses are particularly vulnerable to fraud since these organizations typically have fewer resources than their larger counterparts, which translated to fewer and less-effective anti-fraud controls. In addition, because they have fewer resources, the losses experienced by small businesses tend to have a greater impact than they would in larger organizations.

✓ Managers, employees, and auditors should be educated on the common "red flag" behavioral patterns and traits exhibited by most fraudsters and encouraged to consider them to help identify patterns that might indicate fraudulent activity.

✓ Proactive measures to prevent fraud are critical since the cost of occupational fraud — both financially and to an organization's reputation — can be damaging with nearly half of victim organizations were unable to recover their losses. Management should continually assess the organization's specific fraud risks and evaluate its fraud prevention programs.

The ACFE 2012 Report to the Nations is available at: www.acfe.com/RTTN/.

Statistics Show Why Honesty is Critical

The reasons that honesty and ethics are critical issues are demonstrated by the following facts and statistics drawn from various industry sources:

✓ Employee dishonesty alone causes 30% of all business failures.

✓ Employee theft amounts to 4% of food sales at a cost in excess of $8.5 billion annually. 75% of inventory shortages are attributed to employee theft, according to the National Restaurant Association.

✓ Employee theft costs between 1/2%-3% of a company's gross sales. Even if the figure was only 1%, it would still mean that employees steal over a billion dollars a week from employers.

According to the AFCE *2012 Report to the Nations* mentioned earlier:

✓ Survey participants estimated that the typical organization loses 5% of its revenues to fraud each year. Applied to the estimated 2011 Gross World Product, this figure translates to a potential projected global fraud loss of more than $3.5 trillion.

✓ The median loss caused by occupational fraud in the cases in the study was $140,000. More than one-fifth of the cases caused losses of at least $1 million.

✓ Occupational fraud is a significant threat to small businesses. The smallest organizations in the study suffered the largest median losses. These organizations typically employ fewer anti-fraud controls than their larger counterparts, leading to their increased vulnerability to fraud. In 81% of cases, the fraudster displayed one or more behavioral red flags that are often associated with fraudulent conduct: Living beyond means (36% of case); financial difficulties (27%); unusually close association with vendors or customers (19%); and excessive control issues (18%).

According to statistics from the American Society of Employers:

✓ Businesses lose 20% of every dollar to employee theft.

✓ The U.S. Retail Industry loses $53.6 billion a year due to employee theft.

According to statistics from Jack Hayes International, Inc. 2007 Survey:

✓ In 2007, one in every 28.2 employees in the U.S. was apprehended for theft from their employer.

✓ In 2007, 82,648 employees were apprehended from 24 large U.S. retail chains, up 17.57% from 2006.

According to the U.S. Chamber of Commerce:

✓ Estimates that 75% of all employees steal at least once, and half of these employees steal again and again.

✓ Reports that one of every three business failures are the direct result of employee theft.

According to David J. Lieberman's book *Executive Power: Use the Greatest Collection of Psychological Strategies to Create an Automatic Advantage in Any Business Situation*, (John Wiley & Sons, March 9, 2009):

✓ Embezzlement costs organizations somewhere between $450 and $600 billion every year.

✓ More than 50 percent of all business bankruptcies are attributed to employee theft.

✓ Each year, employee theft will cause 20 percent of existing businesses and 30 percent of new businesses to fail.

✓ Security industry experts estimate that 30 percent of all employees steal from their employers and another 60 percent would steal, given sufficient motive and opportunity.

According to Lisa Guerin's book, *The Essential Guide to Workplace Investigations: How to Handle Employee Investigations* (Nolo, July 12, 2010):

✓ Retailers lose more to their own employees than to shoplifters.

✓ Up to one-third of small business closures and bankruptcies are due to employee theft.

✓ 66% of employees would steal if they saw others getting away with it and 13% would steal regardless.

The above figures do not take into account the fallout from employee embezzlement, dishonesty, and fraud. The fallout can include destruction of a firm's reputation, the inability to stay in business, the damage to employee morale, and the time and energy taken from productive projects to deal with dishonesty. For a small business, the personal loss experienced by the owners can be devastating when a trusted employee is discovered to have been an embezzler or thief.

New Research Reveals Warning Signs of Intellectual Property Theft Committed by Corporate Insiders

Corporate insider intellectual property (IP) thieves are usually males under 40 holding technical positions, have a new job ready at the time of the theft, and steal information they were authorized to access, according to the findings of a new report "Behavioral Risk Indicators of Malicious Insider Theft of Intellectual Property: Misreading the Writing on the Wall" from leading information security solutions provider Symantec.

Since the Commerce Department estimates the theft of intellectual property costs U.S. businesses more than $250 billion annually, the research paper – authored by experts in the fields of psychological profiling and employee risk management – helps employers learn about insider theft profiles, key risk indicators and factors, and steps to take to defend against intellectual property theft. The report also addresses the high level of organizational anxiety surrounding potential theft of intellectual property by employees and also describes the people and organizational conditions contributing to this risk.

Based on a review of empirical research, the report identifies the following key behaviors and indicators that contribute to intellectual property theft by corporate insiders:

✓ The majority of insider intellectual property theft is committed by current male employees averaging about 37 years of age in technical positions that include engineers, scientists, managers, and programmers. Many IP thieves had signed IP agreements, indicating that policy without effective enforcement is ineffective.

✓ Approximately 65 percent of employees who committed insider intellectual property theft had accepted a new job with a competing company or started their own company at the time of the theft. About 20 percent were recruited by an outsider who targeted the data, and 25 percent gave the stolen IP to a foreign company or country. Over 50 percent stole data within a month of leaving.

✓ Three out of four employees – 75 percent – who committed insider intellectual property theft stole information they were authorized to access since they knew and worked with the data and often felt entitled to it in some way.

✓ The most common type of intellectual property stolen by corporate insiders was Trade secrets (52 percent of cases), followed by business information and other administrative data (30 percent), source code (20 percent), proprietary software (14 percent), customer information (12 percent), and business plans (6 percent).

The report also revealed that key patterns and common problems preceded inside intellectual property theft. These warning signs contributed to the motivation of corporate insider thieves and included perceived professional setbacks and unmet expectations that fast-tracked insiders into stealing IP. These signals of impending intellectual property theft showed the role of personal psychology and stressful events as indicators of insider risk.

The report features recommendations for employers concerned with intellectual theft risk that include building a team to fully address insider theft, evaluating risk factors, creating effective policies and practices, training and education, and using pre-employment screening to make informed decisions and mitigate the risk of hiring a "problem" employee.

This free report is available at www.symantec.com/about/news/release/article.jsp?prid=20111207_01.

Eight Tools to Encourage Future Honesty

Along with pre-employment screening of new hires, listed below are eight tools firms can use to help foster an environment that promotes and encourages future honesty.

1. **Establish Clear Policies Regarding Conduct**

   According to the U. S. Declaration of Independence, "some truths are self-evident." That may be true, but an employer should still have a clear written policy that theft, dishonesty, or unethical conduct will not be tolerated, no matter when discovered. Those negative behaviors are grounds for discipline, up to and including termination.

2. **Have Adequate Internal Controls and Auditing in Place**

One of the most critical parts of preventing fraud is having internal controls in place. Having controls is useless if supervisors and management are asleep at the wheel, or the controls only exist on paper. As a general rule, an organization only accomplishes those things that are measured, audited, and rewarded. The same applies to controls in an organization to protect against dishonest or unethical behavior. If the job involves handling of cash or assets or reporting of financial activity in any way, then there are a number of controls that can be put into place. One of the main thrusts behind the Sarbanes-Oxley Act is an environment of control, discussed later in this chapter.

3. **Immediate and Appropriate Response to Dishonest or Unethical Conduct**

Employers need to make it clear that dishonest behavior is not tolerated and will be the subject of swift and certain response by the employer.

4.   **Continuing Education on Success, Ethics, and Honesty**

A continuing effort is critical to institutionalize honest and ethical dealing and to remind all members of the team these concepts are essential to the firm's success and an individual's success. This can be accomplished through continuing education, staff meetings, videotapes, and other visible reminders of the firm's position.

5. **Atmosphere and Corporate Culture**

The development of a corporate culture often starts at the top. If the leaders of an organization demonstrate honest and ethical dealings in both words and deed, then it should flow down throughout the entire organization.

6.   **Anonymous Tip Hotline**

The establishment of such a hotline is one of the provisions of the Sarbanes-Oxley Act. Experts agree that the ability of employees to give anonymous tips without fear of reprisals is a highly-effective, low-cost best practice.

7.   **Ethics and Honesty Advisory Hotline**

When a good employee is faced with a situation that falls into the category of dishonest or unethical conduct, the employee may simply have no one to talk to. Providing a safe haven for discussion — or where an employee can seek advice — is a best practice.

8. **Psychological Testing for Honesty and Ethics**

The use of such tests is an attempt to predict who will act in an honest and ethical fashion in the future. These tests and their effectiveness are discussed later in this chapter.

How to Avoid Hiring an Embezzler

Embezzlement is an equal opportunity crime. It affects employers of all sizes as well as profit and non-profit firms.

At the root of embezzlement is a violation of trust. By definition, **embezzlement** is a crime where a person legally uses or possesses property belonging to the employer, then permanently converts this property to his or her personal use. Embezzlement differs from theft, where the culprit has no right to possession in the first place. Embezzlement is considered more serious and harder to detect.

Embezzlement can range from simply stealing cash from the cash drawer to more elaborate schemes such as writing checks to oneself or to ghost employees, setting up and making payments to fake vendors, paying phony expense reimbursements, or giving oneself a pay increase. Embezzlement typically occurs when there is a combination of motive, opportunity, and means. The opportunity and means portion is usually a result of a lack of proper internal controls. If an embezzler or thief has a co-conspirator, then the act becomes more difficult to guard against.

For purposes of safe hiring, the critical task is to look for a person who may have a motive for theft or a history of past financial misconduct.

How to Spot an Embezzler

When embezzlement occurs, typically one or more of the following situations are true:

✓ The business did very little, if any, due diligence when hiring the embezzler. The firm did not determine if the applicant may be motivated to steal or had stolen in the past. Not following the rules of Safe Hiring, the employer made the decision based primarily upon the interview and subjective impression of the applicant. In a great number of embezzlement cases even the slightest due diligence could have revealed the danger signals. Often times, employers merely need to look deeper instead of handing over the keys to someone who had created a favorable impression during their hiring interview.

✓ The employer typically had very little, if any, internal controls in place. "Internal controls" typically refers to a system of cross checks so that no one person runs the company's finances. To accomplish embezzlement, a criminal needs to control most, if not all, aspects of the firm's financial life: writing the checks, making deposits, reconciling bank statements, and/or opening mail. If any of these functions are interrupted by external controls or cross checks, then the ability of an embezzler to steal is diminished.

✓ Embezzlers often come disguised as the hard-working "perfect employee." They are perceived as hardworking and loyal. They never seem to take a vacation. They arrive first, leave last, and always volunteer to get the mail. Embezzlers put on their show for two reasons. First, since embezzlement is fundamentally a violation of an employer's trust, embezzlers need to earn that trust in order to have the opportunity to embezzle — employers are more likely to delegate responsibility and access to cash and assets to someone who is considered hardworking and loyal. Second, embezzlers need to control their environment as much as possible to accomplish their embezzlement and to hide their activities from others. Should an embezzler take a day off, then someone else could answer a call from an unpaid vendor, perhaps prompting the replacement to ask why bills are not being paid. Or, if the embezzler does not get to the mail first, incriminating letters cannot be intercepted. To keep the scheme going, an embezzler needs complete control.

There is no one profile of an embezzler. Embezzlers can be young or old, male or female, well-educated or high school dropouts. Disguised as perfect employees, embezzlers are very difficult to detect. However, there are some common traits:

✓ An embezzler is completely self-focused on one's own needs, wants, and desires. He or she is not overly concerned with betraying a trust or hurting co-workers — or the employer or company.

✓ If they are prosecuted, embezzlers are more focused on their own pain caused by the prosecution and being put into an embarrassing position. There is often a mental disconnect between the fact that they violated trust and stole and the position they find themselves in. "In denial" is the popular term.

✓ The embezzler almost immediately begins to blame the victim; their reasoning may be:
  • I needed the money more than they did.
  • I worked hard and they did not treat me right.
  • I deserved the extra money.
  • They made me take it — if they had treated me right, it would not have happened.

✓ Embezzlers often do not want to give up even one cent of their ill-gotten gains. Even if it would keep them out of jail, embezzlers and white collar criminals are so focused on the money they will try to do anything to not have to pay it back.

✓ Many times the embezzled money is simply squandered. It is not uncommon for the stolen money to have already been wasted on clothes, travel, or general high living. Once the person is prosecuted or sued, little can be recovered for purposes of victim restitution.

There is always the possibility that the motivating event could be something totally out of the embezzler's control, such as the sudden illness of a family member requiring an expensive operation. However, this is unusual. More often, motivation for embezzlement is a need to have something the embezzler cannot otherwise afford. Quite often, the signs of this covetous attitude are spotted before the first time the person embezzles.

Also, the motivating factor can be an outgrowth of some personality trait of the embezzler, such as a drug habit or gambling habit. The problems caused by such habits may be discovered during a standard background check. A credit report may show a debt level incompatible with the salary for their position. Perhaps a past employment check reveals the applicant was habitually late to work, which can be associated with a problem employee profile.

As mentioned above, once an employer is a victim, there often is no ability to obtain restitution. An embezzler may have little left in the way of assets. Court proceedings often prove ineffective at returning property. It is not usual for an employer to attempt to resolve the matter by working out an agreement for restitution that calls for the employer not to contact the police. The result, of course, is that an embezzler is free to move on to yet another victim.

Of course, the best defense for an employer is to not hire the embezzler in the first place. To accomplish that, an employer needs to utilize all of the tools in their Safe Hiring Program.

From the Courts: A Sobering Tale for Employers

A recent state court case in Iowa concerned a local office of a national staffing firm. The firm supplied an employer with a bookkeeper who turned out to have a criminal record for felony fraud and who also misrepresented her educational background. The worker embezzled $138,350.

The employer sued the staffing firm for their losses. The employer based the lawsuit on the fact that the staffing firm represented they would send a qualified candidate. It turned out the candidate had a criminal conviction for felony fraud as well as false educational claims. However, according to the court decision, since the employer did not specify the staffing firm should do a background check, and the staffing firm never claimed that they would perform a check, the employer's claims were dismissed.

Most employers would probably assume that they would not have to specifically request a staffing professional not send someone convicted of felony fraud who also faked educational claims to handle their books. However, staffing firms should not assume, based upon this decision, that the failure to perform background checks is always legally defensible. Even though the staffing firm won this case, it is not clear that all courts would ultimately dispense the same decision. In addition, given the negative publicity and potential harm to reputation, a background check would have been very cheap by comparison. At a minimum, clearly specifying the staffing firm's policy on background checks would also have been a best practice.

The employer in this case also apparently had a lack of internal financial controls. As the court noted, the embezzler had access to signed blank checks, was the sole person to review the general ledger, handled cash, and had complete access to the employer's bank accounts. However, staffing professionals are generally well acquainted with the fact the small businesses often cannot afford the type of internal controls needed to prevent embezzlement, which is another reason that staffing firms need to be careful when they place people in sensitive positions.

The walkway point: Employers need to be very careful about who they put in charge of their money, and at the same time, have good internal controls in place.

Corporate Fraud and Sarbanes-Oxley

When the Sarbanes-Oxley Act was signed into law on July 30, 2002, over 15,000 publicly held companies were given a new set of rules regarding corporate ethics. This far-reaching law radically changed the landscape of corporate governance, controls, audits, and financial disclosures as follows:

- ✓ Chief executive officers and chief financial officers must personally attest to the accuracy of earnings reports and other financial statements.
- ✓ Curtailment of non-auditing consulting services must be provided by outside auditors.
- ✓ Whistle-blowers should receive protections.
- ✓ Criminal penalties are increased, including fines and jail terms for misdeeds by executives.
- ✓ Investment firms must take steps to improve the objectivity of reports performed by securities analysts.
- ✓ A Public Company Accounting Oversight Board was established to oversee the audits of companies that are subject to securities laws.
- ✓ The relationship between executives and directors to outside auditors was regulated.

Among the many critical provisions is Section 404 which requires public firms establish and maintain financial controls and processes. Public corporations are also required to conduct periodic evaluations of their current controls. Also under Section 404, merely having financial controls is inadequate — one of the most important provisions of Section 404 is that external auditors must also attest to the effectiveness and adequacy of the controls in the annual report.

Sec. 404. Management Assessment of Internal Controls

"SEC. 404. MANAGEMENT ASSESSMENT OF INTERNAL CONTROLS. (a) RULES REQUIRED.—The Commission shall prescribe rules requiring each annual report required by section 13(a) or 15(d) of the Securities Exchange Act of 1934 (15 U.S.C. 78m or 78o(d)) to contain an internal control report, which shall— (1) state the responsibility of management for establishing and maintaining an adequate internal control structure and procedures for financial reporting; and (2) contain an assessment, as of the end of the most recent fiscal year of the issuer, of the effectiveness of the internal control structure and procedures of the issuer for financial reporting. (b) INTERNAL CONTROL EVALUATION AND REPORTING.—With respect to the internal control assessment required by subsection (a), each registered public accounting firm that prepares or issues the audit report for the issuer shall attest to, and report on, the assessment made by the management of the issuer. An attestation made under this subsection shall be made in accordance with standards for attestation engagements issued or adopted by the Board. Any such attestation shall not be the subject of a separate engagement."

Under Sarbanes-Oxley, the Securities and Exchange Commission (SEC) issued rules on how Section 404 must be implemented. To ensure honesty and ethical dealings, public companies must have an ongoing effort aimed at instituting and documenting corporate controls.

There are a number of important tasks a public firm must do to be in compliance. Appearing on any list of 404 compliance tasks is the use of background checks. Experts agree that part of insuring that a firm engages in honest and ethical dealings is to hire honest and ethical people. Hence background screening has become a part of Sarbanes-Oxley compliance. The need for background checks was confirmed with the November, 2003 publication of a white paper by PricewaterhouseCoopers titled K*ey Elements of Antifraud Programs and Controls*. The PricewaterhouseCoopers white paper outlined very specific steps a public firm should take when creating the critical control environment needed within the overall framework of internal oversight roles for individuals with direct access to company assets or information systems. The paper was published in conjunction with the Committee of Sponsoring Organizations of the Treadway Commission (COSO). That organization authored *Internal Control – Integrated Framework,* widely accepted as a framework by which management and auditors evaluate internal controls.

The PricewaterhouseCoopers white paper with its specific recommendations for background screening is available at: www.pwcglobal.com/Extweb/NewCoAtWork.nsf/docid/D0D7F79003C6D64485256CF30074D66C/$file/PwC_Antifrau d_Final.pdf.

The standards being compiled by the Open Standards and Ethics Group (OCEG) also support employment background screening as a key business practice. OCEG was formed by a multi-industry, multi-disciplinary coalition that saw the need to integrate the principles of effective governance, compliance, risk management, and integrity into the practice of everyday business. See: www.oceg.org.

The need for background checks as part of Section 404 requirements is not limited to new employees. According to an article in the *CareerJournal*:

> "To meet new corporate governance requirements mandated by last year's Sarbanes-Oxley Act, legions of companies are also more rigorously investigating current employees via detailed background checks."

(Source: www.careerjournal.com/recruiters/jungle/20030827-jungle.html - *CareerJournal* published by the *Wall Street Journal*).

The Association of Certified Fraud Examiners (ACFE) also suggests steps for the prevention of corporate fraud and for compliance with Sarbanes-Oxley. According to an article by ACFE, part of a program of establishing a fraud detection process should include conducting background checks on all potential employees. (See www.cfenet.com/media/releases/021203.asp.)

Psychological Testing for Honesty and Integrity

Another useful tool to help find honest employees is psychological testing. An internet search will reveal a great number of firms offering testing that not only measures attitude, skills, and compatibility for a job, but also purports to measure if a person can be reasonably anticipated to act in an honest and ethical fashion. Generally, an honesty test relies upon three different categories of questions. First, it looks for admissions by an applicant of prior acts of dishonesty. Second, it tests an applicant's attitudes toward dishonest behavior. Third, it explores other personal characteristics of a person that may have a bearing on the potential for dishonest behavior. For example, some test vendors believe a person who feels alienated may be more likely to steal.

For Safe Hiring purposes, an honesty test is a written test designed to identify individuals applying for work who have a relatively high propensity to steal money or property on the job or are likely to engage in counterproductive behavior. Chapter 8 describes "Integrity Interviews" where an applicant is asked point-blank questions about his or her past and habits. However, these interviews are conducted by professionally trained interviewers, and results are not scored or evaluated using psychological measurements and are not subject to the validity studies discussed below.

Honesty tests utilize two types of questions. **"Direct questions"** explore a person's own past dishonest acts. An example is "Describe what you have stolen in the past from an employer." Similar questions may explore an applicant's attitude toward theft or dishonesty such as "If you knew someone was stealing, would you report it to your supervisor?" or "Have you associated with employees who you knew stole from their employers?"

The second type is called **"indirect questions."** These indirect questions seek to discern attitudes or behavior that may have a bearing upon dishonesty. Sample questions include "Do you feel lonely even when with others?" or "How often do you make your bed?" or "Do you feel most people steal at least a few small things from their employer?"

Well-designed honesty tests have generally been shown to have a high degree of accuracy. In addition to using the tests as hiring tools, they can help improve a firm's current culture when, for instance, the tests are combined with leadership development training.

Issues Surrounding Honesty Testing

Employers should be aware of certain issues associated with honesty tests.

1. **Honesty is inherently a difficult character trait to nail down, since it can be situational**

    The basic premise behind a personality test is that it can help predict future behavior. The difficulty with predicting future honesty is that honesty may not be a permanent trait but can be situational. It can be argued that everyone has told "little white lies." In some social situations, it would be considered rude not to lie when the truth would be unnecessary and hurtful. A dinner guest may say the soup is fine when in fact they dislike it. That does not mean this person would not be a good candidate for a job. On the other hand, if a person is dishonest about things that are more critical, this could have a bearing on how he or she will behave in the future. Factors that need to be considered when a lie is told are 1) the motive for the lie; 2) who is being lied to; 3) the methodology of the lie; 4) how effective the person is at lying; and perhaps the most critical, 5) the harm done to others by the consequences of telling the lie.

2. **Too similar to a polygraph**

    Employers must be aware if their honesty testing comes too close to polygraph testing. Although legal in most states, most states do prohibit any test "similar to a polygraph," without defining what that means. Per the passage of the Employee Polygraph Protection Act of 1988, the use of polygraphs was barred for most employment-related situations. As a result, the number of firms offering some sort of honesty testing instrument has increased. An employer should consult legal counsel for the current law in the jurisdiction where the new hire will be employed.

3. **Reliability**

    Reliability is simply a way of stating that if the test is repeated a short time later with the same group, the results would be consistent. In other words, a test is reliable if there is "consistency of measurement." If the same test on the same group produced widely different results, then the testing instrument would come under question.

4. **Validity**

    A valid test is one which measures what it is truly stated. In the context of an employment test, validity means the test actually predicts who is going to be honest. However, if the test does not give job-related information, the test is not valid. The firm that prepares and sells the testing must convince the employer that their instrument is a valid predictor of future job honesty. The subject of demonstrating test validity is extremely complex and beyond the scope of this book, however, good advice to follow is that an employer should not use any test unless the developer is able to produce a substantial body of data as to the validity of the test.

5. **EEOC considerations**

    Another critical consideration is whether the testing instrument is discriminatory and violates the rules of the Equal Employment Opportunities Commission (EEOC). Even if the test is not discriminatory on its face, an employer needs to be aware that a test can have the effect of being discriminatory by the manner in which it is applied. Recall the discussion about the use of criminal records in Chapters 5 and 11 — The EEOC has ruled that the use of criminal records can have an adverse effect on certain protected groups. The short answer for employers is that firms selling the test instrument are responsible to provide the employer with documentation as to the Title VII implications associated with the test.

6. **Americans With Disabilities ACT (ADA)**

    A related issue is the Americans with Disabilities Act implications. A test for honesty will rarely contain a reference to a disability. However, the employer should require a vendor to document that vendor is not asking any questions that indirectly require an applicant to reveal or discuss a disability or in some way discourage an applicant with a disability from applying.

7. Faking or distortion issues

A major issue with the validity of honesty tests is when applicants try to outsmart the test and give fake answers based upon what they believe the test makers are looking for. Employers should review with testing vendors if psychologists have devised any methods that take such a distortion into account. Perhaps the test taker notices that for every question the best answer is always the third question.

8. Administration of test

Any employer using these tests will want its administration to be as quick and easy as possible. Even though there are pencil and paper tests, tests are also available over the internet and by phone. The costs for these tests are also very reasonable, as low as $10 or less per test for an off the shelf instrument. However, the development of a custom instrument is very expensive, such as those based upon modeling a firm's best current employee.

9. Security of results and privacy

Of course, it is critical for an employer to ensure all results are confidential and that the privacy of an applicant is maintained. The vendor should demonstrate that their system is properly secured, and all results are returned in a manner that protects privacy and confidentiality.

10. Analysis and use of results

Employers must be very careful using off-the-shelf instruments to make a hiring decision based upon a resulting numerical score. Psychological tests for honesty can be very complicated; a cookie cutter analysis can be deceptive. It is important to note certain cut-off points can be set while making sure not to hire any dishonest workers. For example, in order to make sure all of the potential "crooks" are eliminated, it is possible that some good candidates are eliminated along with the bad. The tests can also be prejudiced against an honest person. Perhaps one applicant may honestly admit he or she once took a pen home, but another applicant may consider that too trivial to report.

The lesson here is to very carefully review the instrument and the manner in which it is scored before using it to make any decision. Many experts suggest the results of an honesty test not be the sole deciding factor but rather they be used as just one of the factors. However, there are employers who have found these tests are highly accurate and do place a great deal of faith in them.

11. Who is tested

Another aspect of honesty testing is that they are typically used for hiring lower paid, hourly workers. Retail and manufacturing firms that hire unskilled or semi-skilled labor often use these tests; the tests are not typically used to the same degree for "white-collar" positions. However, given the emphasis on corporate honesty and ethics, a firm may want to consider using these tests for its salaried workers and professionals. The use of these tests serves to underscore the importance of honesty as well as possibly protect a firm from a bad hire in the executive offices.

12. Possible negative consequences of honesty tests

There are a number of negative consequences employers must consider and address before administering a testing program. These include:

- *False Sense of Security* — These tests could create a false sense of security among employers.
- *Hardship among Honest Workers* — If workers are denied employment based upon a test, there can be an inability to find a job. These tests can limit honest workers in an effort to find employment if they are unfairly tagged as not having passed a test.
- *Invasion of Privacy* — Lawsuits have been filed based upon unfair or intrusive questions appearing on tests. An employer should review all questions carefully to ensure the tests do not offend applicants.
- *The Employer-Employee Relationship* — It is important that applicants do not develop a negative first impression of a company due to a badly worded phrase, test item, or poor overall test. Typically,

applicants receive indirect questions better than direct ones. Direct questions have been shown to offend a greater number of honest applicants. The goal of a test is to ultimately increase the odds of identifying those applicants that have more honest tendencies than others.

Do Honesty Tests Really Work?

Yes. Below is an article by Dr. John Schinnerer. The author sincerely thanks Dr. Schinnerer for permitting this article to be included herein.

Elevating Corporate Behavior One Test at a Time

By John Schinnerer, PhD, Executive Coach and Founder of Guide to Self, Inc.

Honesty and integrity tests have been used ever since the polygraph, or lie detector, test was outlawed. The question that many people have is, "Do these tests really work?"

The short answer is "Yes, they do work." The proof that they work has been demonstrated by two concepts known as validity and reliability.

Validity is demonstrated when a test measures what it purports to measure, in this case – honesty and integrity. Most validity studies for honesty tests are done with two groups of people – an average group of people and a group of prison inmates. The idea being that prisoners have already demonstrated antisocial behaviors such as theft, assault, and deceit. The results from these two groups are then used to look at the items individually and collectively.

The major yardstick of honesty tests is predictive validity – a test's ability to predict who is more likely to have honest tendencies. The EEOC has set forth validity guidelines as to the usefulness of tests. These guidelines state that a validity of .21 to .35 is likely to be useful while anything above .35 is highly useful. On average, honesty tests have a validity of .41 (Ones, Chockalingan, & Schmidt, 1993) which has a great benefit to those looking to reduce shrinkage, theft of data, or other counterproductive behaviors.

The majority of these tests rely on very similar questions. These questions have been used over and over on different people (and occasionally the same person) over time. Certain questions have been shown to repeatedly and consistently differentiate between individuals with antisocial tendencies and those who tend to obey the rules of society.

This brings us to the second concept, that of reliability. Reliability occurs when a test measures a concept, such as integrity, similarly in the same individual over time. A reliable integrity test should be able to consistently identify a felon as having more antisocial ideas today as well as one year from now.

Assuming we have a test that is reliable and valid, many people ask, "How do these questions work?" There are two main types of items in integrity and honesty tests – direct and indirect. Direct questions ask test-takers about their past behaviors in a direct manner. For example, "How many times in the past six months have you taken office supplies from your employer?" The answer choices for this question include "Zero", "Once or twice", "Three to five times", "Six to ten times", or "More than ten times."

Indirect items get at the same information in a more discrete manner. These items rely on a psychological concept known as projection. Projection is what humans do in an attempt to normalize their own behaviors. The assumption is that an individual will project his or her characteristic mode of responding into the question. These items are more or less disguised as to their true intent, thereby reducing the chances that the test-taker can deliberately create a desirable impression. An example of an indirect item is the following statement, "Borrowing office supplies from your employer is okay if you plan to replace them later." The test-taker is asked to what extent they agree with the statement above on a 1 to 5 scale. The greater the degree to which they agree with the statement, the more likely it is they are engaging in stealing or "borrowing" office items.

Another tool that test creators use is that of repetition. Most honesty tests will include similar items worded in different ways. Honesty is measured by the degree to which individuals remain consistent between these different items. This is one way to minimize our tendency to manage the impressions that other people have of us. To allow for this, most honesty tests are over 150 items in length to allow the test-taker adequate time and space to forget previous items measuring the same behavior (e.g., employee theft) that are worded differently.

While honesty tests have been shown to be valid, they are also situational. In other words, honesty is applied differently in different situations depending on the importance one places on the situation. Situations that are deemed important are more likely to be handled in an honest manner. For this and other reasons, honesty tests should never be used as the sole hiring criteria.

Honesty tests should be used as part of a battery of tests in an attempt to look at the entire applicant, not merely their honesty. Success on the job is comprised of much more than honesty. Success is usually a result of motivation, emotional intelligence, traditional intelligence, knowledge and honesty.

Sources: Ones, D., Chockalingan, V., & Schmidt, F. "Comprehensive Meta-Analysis of Integrity Test Validities Findings and Implications for Personnel Selection and Theories of Job Performance" from Journal of Applied Psychology , 78.4 (1993): 679 – 703.

John Schinnerer, Ph.D. is Executive Coach and Founder of Guide to Self, Inc., a coaching company founded in the San Francisco Bay Area in 2005. Dr. Schinnerer received his doctorate in educational psychology from U.C. Berkeley. His areas of expertise range from positive psychology to leadership development to anger management. He has consulted with companies such as Pixar, Sutter Health, Kaiser Permanente and UPS. Contact by email at john@guidetoself.com; the website is www.guidetoself.com.

Chapter 25

Workplace Violence

Inside This Chapter:

- ✓ What is Workplace Violence?

- ✓ Examples and Studies of Violence in the Workplace

- ✓ The Economic Cost of Workplace Violence

- ✓ What Causes Workplace Violence?

- ✓ Defining the Circumstance

- ✓ Three Severity Levels of Workplace Violence Behavior

- ✓ Preventing Workplace Violence

- ✓ Other Important Resources for Workplace Violence

What is Workplace Violence?

The U.S. Occupational Safety and Health Administration (OSHA) is charged with assuring safe and healthful working conditions for working men and women by setting and enforcing standards and by providing training, outreach, education and assistance. OSHA defines **"workplace violence"** as:

"..any act or threat of physical violence, harassment, intimidation, or other threatening disruptive behavior that occurs at the work site and can range from threats and verbal abuse to physical assaults and even homicide."

Workplace violence is a major concern for all businesses since it can affect and involve employees, clients, customers, and visitors. OSHA estimates nearly **2 million American workers report having been victims of workplace violence each year**. However, many cases of workplace violence – which can strike anywhere and at any time – go unreported.

Examples and Studies of Violence in the Workplace

Here are a few examples of workplace violence that took place in different types of work environments and were perpetrated by men and women of varying age and race:

✓ January 2010: A male employee at a manufacturing company in Missouri involved in a lawsuit filed against the company allegedly killed three people and then shot himself.

✓ February 2010: A female professor was accused of killing three colleagues and wounding three others during a faculty meeting after being denied tenure at a university in Alabama. In an interview on ABC's Good Morning America, two family members of one victim said they hoped the shooting would lead to more thorough background checks for the school's faculty after learning about the accused killer's allegedly violent past.

✓ March 2010: A female supermarket worker in Florida fired for threatening to kill a coworker returned to work and made good on her threat.

✓ August 2010: In the wake of the tragic shooting spree on November 5, 2009 in which an Army psychiatrist allegedly opened fire at Fort Hood, Texas and took the lives of 13 military personnel and wounded 32 others, the Department of Defense called for more education about workplace violence as part of its final review of the recommendations from the independent report 'Protecting the Force: Lessons Learned from Fort Hood.' Specifically, "Recommendation 2.6 a, b: Update Policies to Address Workplace Violence" states the Independent Review found "guidance concerning workplace violence" is insufficient and that these programs "may serve as useful resources for developing more comprehensive workplace violence prevention."

✓ August 2010: A truck driver in Connecticut who purportedly stole from his company and resigned reportedly killed eight people and then shot himself with a handgun.

✓ September 2010: After being suspended from her job, a woman allegedly killed coworkers at a baking plant in Philadelphia.

✓ March 2011: After being confronted by a co-worker about stolen merchandise in her bag, an employee at a Maryland athletic clothing shop reacted by beating her co-worker to death and then attempting to cover up the crime.

✓ July 2011: After a yearlong dispute, a man shot his supervisor before taking his own life at a dispatch facility in Kentucky.

✓ October 2011: A trucker at a rock quarry in California opened fire on co-workers killing three and wounding seven.

Obviously, the above incidents remind employers they should have education and policies on how to help prevent workplace violence, including training on how to recognize and deal with the warning signs of workplace violence.

All workers are not necessarily susceptible to the same degree of a workplace violence incident. Research has identified these factors that may increase the potential risk and likelihood of workplace violence for some workers at certain worksites:

- ✓ Exchanging money with the public.
- ✓ Working with volatile and unstable people.
- ✓ Working alone or in isolated areas.
- ✓ Providing services and care.
- ✓ Working where alcohol is served.
- ✓ Working late at night or in areas with high crime rates.

According to OSHA, among employees with an increased risk of workplace violence are workers who exchange money with the public, delivery drivers, healthcare professionals, public service workers, customer service agents, law enforcement personnel, and those who work alone or in small groups.

The OSHA Workplace Violence website is located at www.osha.gov/SLTC/workplaceviolence/index.html. Also see the OSHA Workplace Violence Fact Sheet at: www.osha.gov/OshDoc/data_General_Facts/factsheet-workplace-violence.pdf.

Homicides in the Workplace

According to the final 2010 National Census of Fatal Occupational Injuries (CFOI) program conducted by the U.S. Bureau of Labor Statistics released in the spring of 2012, of the 4,690 fatal workplace injuries that occurred in the United States in 2010, 518 deaths were caused by workplace homicides. These figures mean approximately **11 percent of workplace deaths – more than one out of ten – were attributed to homicide**. Homicide is also the leading cause of death for women in the workplace.

Results from the **2010 Census of Fatal Occupational Injuries (CFOI)** regarding fatal occupational injuries resulting from homicides by occupation in the U.S. found that sales related occupations such as sales supervisors, salespeople, and cashiers were the most vulnerable to workplace homicide:

Top Five Occupations Most Vulnerable to Workplace Homicide in 2010

Occupation	Workplace Homicides
Sales Related (Sales Supervisors, Salespeople & Cashiers)	134
Protective Service (Police Officers & Security Guards)	97
Transportation & Moving (Truck Drivers & Taxi Drivers)	83
Management (Executives & Managers in Various Industries)	55
Food & Beverage Serving (Cooks, Bartenders & Fast Food Workers)	24

The final 2010 National Census of Fatal Occupational Injuries (CFOI) is available at www.bls.gov/iif/oshwc/cfoi/cfoi_revised10.pdf.

Along with the attributed 518 workplace deaths to homicide in 2010, final data from the 2010 National Census of Fatal Occupational Injuries (CFOI) program also found:

✓ Although workplace homicides declined 7 percent in 2010 to the lowest total ever recorded by the CFOI, and workplace homicides incurred by men were down by 10 percent, workplace homicides that involved women increased by 13 percent.

✓ Workplace homicides made up 17 percent of multiple fatality incidents in 2010.

✓ Of the 518 deaths from workplace homicides in 2010, 423 of the victims were men while 95 were women.

✓ Of the 518 workplace homicides in 2010, 405 were homicides by shooting, and 113 were other homicides.

✓ 432 of the 518 workplace homicides in 2010 – over 80 percent – occurred in private industry.

✓ A higher percentage of fatal work injuries involving women resulted from homicides compared to men, 26 percent for women to 10 percent for men.

The 2010 Census of Fatal Occupational Injuries (CFOI) is at: www.bls.gov/iif/oshcfoi1.htm.

Report from the National Council on Compensation Insurance, Inc. (NCCI)

A January 2012 report *Violence in the Workplace* by the National Council on Compensation Insurance, Inc. (NCCI) shows that while work-related homicides and injuries due to workplace assaults remain well below levels observed in the mid-1990s, homicides committed by "work associates" (a Bureau of Labor Statistics category of both co-workers and customers) have increased.

In the report, NCCI states that the "reality of workplace violence is markedly different from popular opinion" and that workplace homicides – which account for 11 percent of workplace fatalities in private industry – "are not crimes of passion committed by disgruntled coworkers and spouses, but rather result from robberies." In addition, the majority of workplace assaults are committed by healthcare patients. Key Findings of the report "Violence in the Workplace" include the following:

✓ Work-related homicides and injuries due to workplace assaults remain well below levels observed in the mid-1990s, consistent with the patterns of declines in rates of homicide and aggravated assaults reported for the country. The rate of workplace homicides fell 59 percent from 1993 to 2009, while the overall rate of homicides fell 47 percent during the same period, according to NCCI.

✓ Homicides account for 11 percent of workplace fatalities. Homicides due to robberies and similar criminal acts fell markedly over the late 1990s but still make up 69 percent of all homicides.

✓ Homicides committed by "work associates" – a BLS category made up of both coworkers and customers – have increased to about 21 percent, mostly reflecting an increase to 9 percent in violent acts by customers while the share of workplace homicides due to coworkers has remained steady at about 12 percent. The actual number of such homicides has been in the 50 to 60 range in recent years.

✓ Healthcare workers experience remarkably high rates of injuries due to assaults by patients, especially in nursing homes and other long-term care facilities. In fact, 61 percent of all workplace assaults are committed by healthcare patients.

To view the complete report, visit: https://www.ncci.com/documents/Workplace_Research.pdf.

Survey Finds Half of Emergency Nurses Experienced Workplace Violence

An August *2010 Emergency Department Violence Surveillance Study* from the Emergency Nurses Association (ENA) Institute for Emergency Nursing Research revealed that more than half of the nurses surveyed by ENA – a mean of 54.8 percent – reported experiencing either physical or verbal abuse at work in the past seven days. These findings mean that every week in the U.S., between approximately eight and 13 percent of emergency department nurses are victims of incidents of physical workplace violence.

In addition, the survey found that 15 percent of emergency nurses who reported experiencing physical violence said they sustained a physical injury as a result of the incident and that, in nearly half of the cases (44.9 percent), no action was taken against the perpetrator of workplace violence. Furthermore, almost three out of four emergency nurses (74.4

percent) who were victims of workplace violence reported the hospital gave them no response regarding that workplace violence.

The survey also found emergency nurses working at hospitals with policies regarding workplace violence reported experiencing fewer incidents of physical or verbal violence. For example:

✓ Hospitals with zero-tolerance reporting policies had an 8.4 percent workplace violence rate.
✓ Hospitals with a non-zero-tolerance policy had a 12.3 percent workplace violence rate.
✓ Hospitals with no policy had an 18.1 percent workplace violence rate.

Based on quarterly surveys of a total of 3,211 emergency nurses across the country from May 2009 to February 2010, *The Emergency Department Violence Surveillance Study* also found that:

✓ Patients and their relatives were the perpetrators of the workplace violence abuse in nearly all incidents of physical violence (97.1 percent) and verbal abuse (91 percent).
✓ The majority of incidents of physical violence occurred in patients' rooms (80.6 percent).
✓ The most frequently reported activities that emergency nurses were involved in when they experienced workplace violence were triaging a patient (38.2 percent), restraining or subduing a patient (33.8 percent), and performing an invasive procedure (30.9 percent).
✓ Male nurses reported higher workplace violence rates than female nurses (15 percent versus 10.3 percent).
✓ Workplace violence rates were higher in large urban areas (13.4 percent) than in rural areas (8.3 percent).

As a result of the Surveillance Study findings, ENA has urged OHSA to make its guidelines for preventing workplace violence into mandatory standards that to which all hospital and health care centers must adhere. See the Emergency Department Violence Surveillance Study at www.ena.org/IENR/Documents/ENAEDVSReportAugust2010.pdf.

The Economic Cost of Workplace Violence

The cost of workplace violence to America is staggering not only in personal terms, but in economic loss as well. The National Institute for the Prevention of Workplace Violence issued a paper *The Financial Impact of Workplace Violence* that includes some historical data on the cost of workplace violence.

✓ In 1992 the Department of Justice estimated that the cost of workplace violence to employers was approximately $6.2 million dollars.
✓ In September of 1993, the National Safe Workplace Institute released a study pegging the cost of workplace violence at $4.2 billion annually. They estimated that in 1992 111,000 violent incidents were committed in work environments resulting in 750 deaths.
✓ In 1995 the National Council of Compensation Insurance found $126 million in workers' compensation claims for workplace violence.
✓ A study released by the Workplace Violence Research Institute in April 1995 showed that workplace violence actually resulted in a $36 billion annual loss.
✓ According to the Bureau of Justice Statistics, about 500,000 victims of violent crime in the workplace lose an estimated 1.8 million workdays each year. This presents an astounding $55 million in lost wages for employees, not including days covered by sick and annual leave and a loss of productivity that has direct consequences for an employer's bottom line.
✓ The Bureau's statistic further state that domestic violence causes employees to miss over 175,000 day of paid work annually and 66 percent of Fortune 1000 senior executives recently surveyed said that financial performance of their company would benefit from addressing the domestic violence experienced by employees.

✓ Lawsuits in the area have been impacting cost substantially. The average out-of-court settlement for this type of litigation approaches $500,000.00 and the average jury award of $3 million. A few awards have reached as high as $5.49 million. (Campbell and Karin, Workplace Violence Reporter).

✓ For six to 18 weeks after an incident happens there is a 50 percent decrease in productivity and a 20 to 40% turnover in employees according to Duane Frederickson, Detective, Minneapolis Police Department.

See *The Financial Impact of Workplace Violence* at www.workplaceviolence911.com/docs/FinancialImpactofWV.pdf.

Another document by the National Institute for the Prevention of Workplace Violence, Inc. is the *2011 Workplace Violence Prevention Fact Sheet* which reflects an increased cost to employers.

✓ The economic cost of workplace violence nationwide is around $121 billion a year.

✓ Nonfatal workplace assaults alone result in more than 876,000 lost workdays and $16 million in lost wages.

✓ The overall impact and cost to a business of reacting after an incident occurs can be staggering versus the cost of focusing on preventing an incident from occurring in the first place. One report indicates that the cost of reacting after a serious incident has occurred is 100 times more costly than taking preventative actions.

The 2011 Workplace Violence Prevention Fact Sheet is available at: www.workplaceviolence911.com/.

What Causes Workplace Violence?

Acts of workplace violence can come from two sources. First, the acts can be caused by external parties, such as robbery in the workplace by a stranger. In those circumstances, employers have certain duties to maintain a safe and secured workplace. The second source is existing employees. For purposes of this chapter, the concerns over workplace violence center on workplace violence carried out by existing employees.

Types of workplace violence incidents are usually broken down into two categories – **"Opportunity-motivated incidents"** and **"Stress-based incidents"**:

✓ **Opportunity-motivated incidents** occur when an employee feels that he or she can get away with something. The motivation behind the action can vary from rationalization such as "I earned a little bonus, and besides, the boss won't miss $20 from the till" to desperation, "I'm way behind on my rent, and the landlord's going to evict me." With a rationale like that, you have an employee who is willing to steal money, equipment, or goods from the employer. This type of action is seldom pre-meditated, occurring usually when the employee has unsupervised access to cash or materials.

✓ **Stress-based incidents** are usually the result of frustration with work-related issues such as problems with management, co-workers, procedures, etc. These problems are often compounded by external stresses, including marital trouble, issues with sick or dependent family members, or substance abuse problems.

Most employees who commit acts of stress-related workplace violence are not typically "bad employees." Violent employees in fact can be dedicated, devoted individuals who take their jobs seriously. They can react violently to any perceived threat to work or employment. In a nutshell, their jobs are their life. Therefore, employment-related issues are elevated to "life and death" decisions. As a result, workplace violence often can be caused by the perpetrator's belief that some form of injustice has been inflicted, and the violence is an attempt to regain a perceived loss of control or an attempt to get even for the perceived injustice or unfair treatment. If an employee defines their self-worth by their job, then a perceived mistreatment by the employer can amount to their devaluation as a human being. The resulting stress that leads to violence can be driven by an intense need to defend their self against what they perceive as such personal devaluation. Obviously, violence is not an acceptable response to stress, and employers must take appropriate measures to identify and protect against any employees who turn to violence.

A particularly sensitive area is termination. Losing a job can be a traumatic experience for anyone. For those people whose work is their life, termination can potentially set-off a lethal explosion of workplace violence even if the person being terminated has been warned and knows it is coming. As a result, every termination must be handled carefully, taking into account the potential for an outburst. Part of preventing workplace violence is a well thought out termination policy, which can be compiled with assistance from a labor attorney or a human resources consultant.

Defining the Circumstance

Workplace violence can take place anywhere employees are required to carry out a business-related function. The type of incident liable to occur varies by circumstance but generally breaks down in the following manner:

Event or incident	Where it Occurs	Perpetrated by
Anger-related incidents Arguments Arson Bullying/intimidation Bringing a hand-gun on premises, and using it to intimidate, threaten or bully Harassment Murder Physical assaults (biting, hitting, kicking, etc.) Pranks Property damage Psychological trauma Pushing Rape Robbery Rumors Sabotage Suicide Swearing Theft Vandalism Verbal abuse Written threats	At the traditional workplace (office, job site) Off-site at a business-related function (conference, trade show, etc.) At a social event related to work In customer or client homes Away from work but resulting from work (such as threats made by clients to employees at their residences)	An outsider with no legitimate relationship to the victim or workplace A customer or someone who is a recipient of a service provided by the affected victim or workplace. A current or former employee who has an employment-related relationship with the workplace victim. Employee-related outsider who is a current/former spouse/lover, relative, acquaintance, etc. who has a dispute involving an employee of the workplace. Domestic violence can become workplace violence

While the definition at the start of this chapter covers a fair degree of actions, a better interpretation should be used by employers in order to create an effective, defensible policy. For example, a company policy should account for the type of offense, circumstance — where and when an incident occurs, and whether it is considered to be "on-the-job" — and party or parties involved. This includes examining the severity levels of workplace violence.

Three Severity Levels of Workplace Violence Behavior

A case where a cashier is caught stealing from the register must be looked at differently than a case where an employee beats up a co-worker. Therefore, it becomes necessary to add a level of criteria to define the degree of severity of a behavior or action. Most experts on the subject classify workplace violence behaviors into three severity levels.

Level One: Low-level workplace violence acts or behaviors not severe enough to require disciplinary action but which indicate that a problem may exist. This type of problem may not result in any significant damage to person or property, but acts as a warning sign that education or intervention may be necessary. Level One behavior is most frequently seen in an employee's attitude. This type of behavior includes:

- ✓ Argumentative or confrontational behavior. Consistently moody, caustic, or mean behavior when dealing with co-workers or customers.
- ✓ Uncooperative or arrogant behavior. Consistent refusal to cooperate with co-workers or supervisors.
- ✓ Inappropriate behavior. Consistent use of profanity, spreading rumors, or comments of an off-color or sexual nature.

Level Two: Moderate level workplace violence actions that may merit Level Two behavior indicates that a problem exists and must be dealt with before it can escalate into more serious behavior. This includes:

- ✓ Outbursts or "acting out." Expressing a desire or intent to hurt others, slamming doors, punching walls, vandalism, verbal or written threats, etc.
- ✓ Disobedience. Open and intentional disregard of company policies and procedures.
- ✓ Non-mutual displays of affection. Persistent romantic overtures that are clearly one-sided and unwelcome, up to and including light sexual harassment.
- ✓ Theft

Level Three: Severe acts of workplace violence against person or property that merit Level Three may include:

- ✓ Minor physical assault. Hitting, fights, etc.
- ✓ Major physical assault. Murder, rape, etc.
- ✓ Strong-arm or armed robbery
- ✓ Arson or major destruction of property

A person acting inappropriately and violently may encounter a cycle of violence where he or she goes through a progression. As the outbursts increase in intensity, the cycle can occur more quickly, and the outbursts can become more pronounced. It is critical to deal with signs and symptoms of workplace violence as early as possible before it escalates into a heartbreaking statistic.

Preventing Workplace Violence

Unfortunately, there is no cure-all to eliminate the threat of violence. The unpredictable nature of human behavior makes it necessary for employers to keep a close watch on conditions and events in the workplace in order to ensure the safety and security of employees and customers.

This does not mean that employers are powerless to prevent workplace violence – far from it. The Safe Hiring Program (SHP) described in this book includes a range of tools, techniques, and services available to help employers mitigate the risk of hiring or retaining a potentially dangerous employee. The goal is to ensure that hiring managers company-wide follow procedures and pay attention to safe hiring.

Many employers consider background checks and reference checks to be the cornerstone of a Safe Hiring Program, effectively "weeding out" most potentially troublesome employees. By having a policy in place that lets job applicants know the information they provide to the company will be independently verified — and past employers will be contacted and criminal records checks may be conducted to search for any indication of violence in the past — the employer lets the applicant know that the company is serious about preventing problems in the workplace. Those applicants with a history of violent behavior may be considered ineligible for consideration based on past offenses or just simply dissuaded from applying in the first place.

Some employers go so far as to require that employees submit to a psychological profile to be considered eligible for hire. While this practice might indeed identify that an employee may have some obsessive tendencies or a propensity for violent or aggressive behavior, the number of faults with this type of screening immediately outweighs the benefits in all but the most extreme circumstances. For example, a negative hiring decision based on a psychological profile instead of an actual event or offense would be difficult to defend — the report may potentially identify the person as having a 'disability,' thus invoking the ADA which explicitly prohibits not hiring someone unless there is a preponderance of current medical or other evidence indicating the person is a direct threat. In addition, the sheer cost of a psychological profile quickly puts the process beyond most employers' budgets. If psychological assessments are used, they should be only a part of all the factors considered among an array of selection processes determining a person's employability.

For the most part, the elements of a Safe Hiring Program are relatively basic, inexpensive, and easy-to-implement steps that, as a whole, can be instrumental in minimizing the potential for problems in the workplace. The typical elements of such a program include development of policies, procedures, and guidelines as well as employee training, policy implementation, and process evaluation. Without a program in place, the employer is subject to the Negative Hiring Doctrine.

Workplace Violence and the Negligent Hiring Doctrine

Under the Negligent Hiring Doctrine, the employer is largely liable for any problems that occur in the workplace under the Negligent Hiring Doctrine.

The Negligent Hiring Doctrine dictates that employers can be held liable for damages if they knowingly employ persons known to pose a potential threat to co-workers or the public. The Doctrine even goes so far as to state that if the employer should have known the employee was a threat, the employer is responsible.

That said, the question arises— how can an employer identify a potentially problematic employee?

Here is the problem. There is no magic formula that tells an employer in advance who will and will not be violent. Predicting future violence is a matter of considerable controversy.

However, experts have found some factors that are present in many cases of workplace violence. One important factor is a history of past violence. For that reason, properly done pre-employment background checks are widely regarded as an effective screening procedure. As discussed in previous chapters, contacting past employers to ask about incidents of past violence may be difficult given the reluctance of many past employers to give any information beyond dates of employment and job title. This is why performing a check for past criminal acts is a critical step.

However, there is more to preventing workplace problems than screening at the door.

Factors in employees' lives change. A person who checked out in an initial screen may over time develop the traits or behaviors indicative of a potentially violent employee. It is up to the employer to maintain a constant eye on conditions and events in the workplace — to stay aware of employee attitudes and concerns in order to ensure the safety and security of everyone involved.

Setting a Workplace Policy

One critical task is to have a clear workplace violence policy that everyone acknowledges and understands. In this way, employees have a clear understanding the employer has a commitment to a safe workplace and enforces a policy that includes training for supervisors and consequences for failing to follow the policy.

An employer establishing a SHP should also assemble a team responsible and accountable for the process. The team should be comprised of employees and professionals from different functional areas to ensure all possible considerations are taken into account regarding the scope of establishing and implementing the program. The team will be responsible for administering the program, including the development and implementation of policy and practices, communicating the policies to all employees within the organization, and training employees in identifying and responding to problems. When or if a crisis occurs, they serve as the employer's response and intervention team.

Sample Policy - Establishment of Team

Team members can include:

- ✓ Human Resources.
- ✓ Security.
- ✓ Attorney.
- ✓ Psychologist or outside expert on violence.

Team members will need to address the following subjects:

1. Policies, Procedure, and Guidelines:

- ✓ Establish a detailed, precise definition of workplace violence, citing examples.
- ✓ Clearly define the company's response to violence, both actual and threatened.
- ✓ Identify and address all potential problem areas, including security elements currently missing and existing methods of dealing with incidents.
- ✓ Assess which areas of security should be outsourced to a third-party vendor versus what can be done with the company's existing resources.
- ✓ Have a termination policy, including policies on how a person is evaluated and terminated and the physical termination process.

2. Implementation:

- ✓ Make appropriate changes to the application/interview/hiring process — background or reference checks, requiring signed applications, etc.
- ✓ Communicate all necessary policy and procedural changes to all employees verbally, as a memo, and in the company manual.

3. Employee Training:

- ✓ Train employees in recognizing and responding to situations.
- ✓ Create an environment where employees are encouraged to report potential workplace violence issues, including a guarantee of confidentiality.
- ✓ Train employees in prevention of possible volatile situations.
- ✓ Provide an Employment Assistance Program (EAP) to encourage employees with personal problems to seek help.
- ✓ For employees who are victims of violence or threats, EAP may assist in obtaining stay away orders from the court or police (such as in stalking or domestic violence cases).

4. Evaluation:

- ✓ Periodically audit all employees involved in the hiring process to ensure their adherence to the program.
- ✓ Evaluate elements involved in physical security, such as:

1) Making sure public areas are set up to protect employees and to make them visible. This protects employees from external violence.

2) Consider physical barriers, controlling the number of entrances, controlling access, protective fencing, and adequate lighting and alarms.

5. Crisis Response:

✓ Prepare a crisis response plan taking into account issues of physical security and premises evacuation. The crisis teams should include professionals to assess the stress, security expert to implement an immediate response, and HR and legal assistance to assess what action to take.

Recommendations from OSHA

OSHA recommends that the best protection employers can offer is to establish a zero-tolerance policy toward workplace violence against or by their employees. The employer should establish a workplace violence prevention program or incorporate the information into an existing accident prevention program, employee handbook, or manual of standard operating procedures. It is critical to ensure that all employees know the policy and understand that all claims of workplace violence will be investigated and remedied promptly. In addition, employers can offer additional protections that include the following:

✓ Provide workplace violence education for employees so they know what conduct is not acceptable and what to do if they witness or are subjected to workplace violence.

✓ Secure the workplace by installing video surveillance cameras, extra lighting, and alarm systems and minimize access by outsiders through identification badges, electronic keys, and guards.

✓ Limit the amount of cash on hand by keep a minimal amount of cash in registers during evenings and late night hours.

✓ Equip staff with cellular phones and hand-held alarms or noise devices if necessary and keep employer provided vehicles properly maintained.

✓ Conduct background checks on all staff members to help ensure a safe and secure workplace.

Workplace Violence: An Attorney's Prospective

Preventing and Addressing Workplace Violence in the Workplace – A Lawyer's Perspective

By Ron S. Brand, Esq., Fisher & Phillips LLP

The tragic headlines of violence in the workplace are, unfortunately, all too common. There are more than 30,000 violent incidents on the job every year. According to various studies, including ones conducted by the National Institute of Occupational Safety and Health and the U.S. Bureau of Labor Statistics, homicide is the third highest work-related cause of death in the United States. This tragedy is compounded by the fact that many incidents of workplace violence are preventable. There are a variety of steps employers can take to significantly reduce the chance of violence occurring in their workplace, and to increase the safety and welfare of their employees.

The first step toward prevention of violence in the workplace is to avoid, from the beginning, hiring a troubled individual who may be prone to acts of violence. A comprehensive safe hiring program, including having a criminal background check completed in accordance with the Fair Credit Report Act and any applicable state laws, will significantly increase the likelihood that a troubled employee will be weeded out.

Second, employers should institute a comprehensive, zero tolerance policy against violence in the workplace. The policy should be contained in an employee handbook or as a stand-alone document signed by the employees. The policy should address threats of violence and fighting, as well as acts of violence. It should prohibit the bringing of weapons to work and announce that searches of employees' lockers, toolboxes, desks and vehicles may be conducted. Employees who violate this policy should be disciplined, or, when necessary, terminated before things get out of control. Along with instituting a workplace violence policy, employers may want to consider providing workplace violence education for employees so they know what conduct is unacceptable, and what to do if they witness or are subjected to workplace violence.

Third, supervisors and co-workers should be alert for warning signs of a troubled employee who may be prone to acts of violence. Such warning signs include talking about weapons and violence, making threats to supervisors or co-workers, anger management problems, substance abuse, and inappropriate behaviors such as stalking others or the habitual use of racial epithets. The employee's personal life should be taken into account as well; perpetrators of workplace violence tend to be loners, or have severe marital, financial and/or emotional difficulties. Supervisors should be trained on how to appropriately intervene in situations when potential violence enters the workplace.

Fourth, employers should consider sending troubled employees to an employee assistance program (EAP). An EAP is intended to help employees deal with personal problems that might adversely impact their work performance, health, and well-being. While an EAP may provide valuable assistance to a troubled employee, some state laws (like California) prohibit an employer from forcing an employee to get help. Generally speaking, the EAP must remain a voluntary option. It should be noted that the Americans with Disabilities Act permits an employer to require an employee who appears to present a direct threat to the safety and welfare of other employees to undergo a "fitness for duty" mental examination, but this is often an incomplete solution. The better approach is to treat threatening and violent conduct as a disciplinary matter rather than as an issue for therapy.

Fifth, employers should take reasonable steps to secure the workplace. Such steps may include installing video surveillance cameras, extra lighting, and alarm systems, and minimizing access by outsiders through identification badges, electronic keys and, when appropriate, guards.

Sixth, should a troubled employee have to be terminated, some advance preventive planning is essential. Many local police departments offer assistance in threat assessment and will provide uniformed or plainclothes officers as necessary to assist with the termination of a potentially violent employee. A private security consultant may also provide valuable assistance. Prior to the termination meeting, the employee's access to company databases should be barred. Furthermore, the employee's final paycheck should be prepared and arrangements made for the employee to remove all personal effects at the time of termination so that he or she will have no need to return to the workplace. Following a termination of a violent individual, it may be wise to have surveillance done on the ex-employee, or to post security personnel around the workplace for a few days in case the ex-employee should attempt to return with the intent of committing acts of violence.

Restraining orders are available where an employee has exhibited a pattern of threatening or violent conduct, but such orders should be used with caution. An irrational and angry individual with a genuine propensity for violence may well just be further incited by a restraining order. A careful analysis of the likely effect of such an order on the employee and the level of threat the employee poses should be conducted before such an order is obtained. Often, less confrontational methods are preferable.

Should an employer follow these basic steps, the chances of yet another tragic headline of workplace violence will be significantly reduced.

Sample Workplace Violence Policy

By Ron S. Brand, Esq., Fisher & Phillips LLP

The Company has a zero tolerance for violent acts or threats of violence against our employees, applicants, customers or vendors.

We do not allow fighting, threatening words or threatening conduct. Weapons of any kind are strictly prohibited and not permitted on Company premises.

No employee should commit or threaten to commit any violent act against a co-worker, applicant, customer or vendor. This includes discussions of the use of dangerous weapons, even in a joking manner.

Any employee who is subjected to or threatened with violence by a co-worker, customer or vendor, or is aware of another individual who has been subjected to or threatened with violence, is to report this information to his/her supervisor or manager as soon as possible.

All threats should be taken seriously. Please bring all threats to the attention of your supervisor or the Human Resources Department so that we can deal with them appropriately.

All threats will be thoroughly investigated, and all complaints which are reported to management will be treated with as much confidentiality as possible.

<u>Employee Acknowledgment of Receipt of Workplace Violence Policy</u>

This will acknowledge that I received a copy of the Workplace Violence Policy and that I will comply with its requirements.

PRINT FULL NAME_____

SIGNED_____

DATE_____

(RETAIN IN EMPLOYEE'S PERSONNEL FILE)

Ron Brand, Fisher & Phillips LLP, Attorneys at Law, www.laborlawyers.com.

Other Important Resources for Workplace Violence

There are many excellent websites to assist employers in dealing with issues related to workplace violence. Resources listed below lead to voluminous research and materials on preventing workplace violence:

- ✓ www.osha.gov/SLTC/workplaceviolence/ –Workplace violence resources and sites from OSHA
- ✓ www.ccohs.ca/oshanswers/psychosocial/violence.html – The Canadian Centre for Occupational Health and Safety has assembled a list of examples of factors and situations that increase the potential for risk of workplace violence.
- ✓ www.opm.gov/employment_and_benefits/worklife/officialdocuments/handbooksguides/workplaceviolence/index.asp – Dealing with Workplace Violence, A Guide for Agency Planners by the Federal Office of Personnel Management
- ✓ www.atapworldwide.org – Association of Threat Assessment Professionals
- ✓ www.workplaceviolence911.com – The National Institute for Prevention of Workplace Violence
- ✓ www.asisonline.org – American Society for Industrial Security

✓   www.opm.gov/employment_and_benefits/worklife/officialdocuments/handbooksguides/WorkplaceViolence/p1-s3.asp#pre-emp. This U.S. Office of Personnel Management web page 'Dealing with Workplace Violence: A Guide for Agency Planners'* contains the following paragraph under the heading 'Pre-employment Screening':

   "Pre-employment screening is an important part of workplace violence prevention. Prior to hiring an employee, the agency should check with its servicing personnel office and legal office, if necessary, to determine what pre-employment screening techniques (such as interview questions, background and reference checks, and drug testing) are appropriate for the position under consideration and are consistent with Federal laws and regulations."

Chapter 26

Additional Issues and Trends for Employers

Inside This Chapter:

- ✓ Employers Come in All Sizes

- ✓ Frequently Asked Questions about Small Business

- ✓ Special Challenges Faced by Small Businesses

- ✓ Large Employer Issues

- ✓ Special Problems with Large Hourly, Seasonal, Temporary Contract Workforces

- ✓ Using Instant Online Databases for Quick Hiring Decisions

- ✓ Special Issues When Hiring in a Labor Shortage

- ✓ Special Issues with Safe Hiring and Job Boards

- ✓ Special Issues with Safe Hiring and Recruiters

- ✓ Electronic Signatures and Applicant Consents

- ✓ Candidates Presenting Their Own Verified Credentials

- ✓ Looking Toward the Future – Background Screening and the Creation of a Human Capital Database

- ✓ Top Ten Trends in Background Checks for 2012

- ✓ Useful Human Resource Sites for Employers

Employers Come in All Sizes

The latest Statistics of U.S. Businesses (SUSB) Annual Data from the U.S. Census Bureau provides a breakdown of U.S. employers by number of paid employees. The study also shows the total number of persons employed by firms within a specific size range.

In 2009 (the most recent year available), of the nearly 6 million employer firms with more than 114 million paid employees, only 17,509 firms – less than one percent – had 500 employees or more. The total number of paid employees at firms with 500 employees or more, 58,228,123, made up approximately half the total amount of paid employees.

The study thus underscores the importance of small businesses – which the Office of Advocacy of the Small Business Administration (SBA) defines for research purposes only by industry, size, and income as an independent business having fewer than 500 employees – since statistics show small businesses make up over 99 percent of all firms and about 50 percent of all paid employees.

Employment Size of Employer Firms, 2009*

Size of Firm	Number of Firms	Paid Employees
1-4 employees	3,558,708	5,966,190
5-9 employees	1,001,313	6,580,830
10-19 employees	610,777	8,191,289
20 to 99 employees	495,673	19,389,940
100 to 499 employees	83,326	16,153,254
500 to 749 employees	5,854	3,563,852
750 to 999 employees	2,777	2,399,250
1,000 to 1,499 employees	2,834	3,458,407
1,500 to 1,999 employees	1,446	2,497,868
2,000 to 2,499 employees	916	2,043,085
2,500 to 4,999 employees	1,795	6,236,581
5,000 to 9,999 employees	956	6,594,104
10,000 employees or more	931	31,434,976
Total	**5,767,306**	**114,509,626**

*Statistics about Small Business from the Census Bureau: www.census.gov/econ/susb/.

Frequently Asked Questions about Small Business

The Office of Advocacy of the Small Business Administration (SBA), the voice of small business in government, provides a 'Frequently Asked Questions' PDF updated in January 2011 at www.sba.gov/sites/default/files/sbfaq.pdf.

What is a small business?

The Office of Advocacy defines a small business as an independent business having fewer than 500 employees. (The definition of "small business" used in government programs and contracting varies by industry; see www.sba.gov/size.)

How important are small businesses to the U.S. economy?

Small firms (defined by Small Business Administration (SBA) endorsed sizing criteria as a business with no more than 500 employees for most manufacturing and mining industries and no more than $7 million in average annual receipts for most nonmanufacturing industries):

- ✓ Represent 99.7 percent of all employer firms.
- ✓ Employ about half of all private sector employees.
- ✓ Pay nearly 43 percent of total U.S. private payroll.
- ✓ The net job gains of small businesses matched those of large businesses during the last half of 2010, and the gross job gains of small businesses outpaced those of large businesses by about 3 to 1, including virtually all the job gains from new businesses.
- ✓ Create 46 percent of the nonfarm private Gross Domestic Project (GDP).
- ✓ Hire 61 percent of scientific and professional jobs.

Source: *U.S. Dept. of Commerce, Census Bureau and Intl. Trade Admin.; Advocacy-funded research by Kathryn Kobe, 2012* (*www.sba.gov/sites/default/files/rs390tot_0.pdf*) *and CHI Research, 2003* (*http://archive.sba.gov/advo/research/rs225tot.pdf*); *U.S. Dept. of Labor, Bureau of Labor Statistics.*

How many small businesses are there?

In 2009, there were 27.5 million businesses in the United States, according to Office of Advocacy estimates. The latest available Census data shows that there were 5.7 million firms with employees in 2009 and 21.0 million without employees in 2009. Small firms with fewer than 500 employees represent 99.9 percent of the total (employers and non-employers), as the most recent data shows there were 17,509 large businesses in 2009.

Source: *Office of Advocacy estimates based on data from the U.S. Dept. of Commerce, Census Bureau, and trends from the U.S. Dept. of Labor, Bureau of Labor Statistics, Business Employment Dynamics.*

What is small firms' share of employment?

Small businesses employ about half of U.S. workers. Of the 120.9 million nonfarm private sector workers in 2008, small firms employed 59.7 million, and large firms employed 61.2 million. About half of small firm employment is in second-stage companies (10-99 employees) and half is in firms that are 15 years or older. Small firms' share of employment in rural areas is slightly higher than in urban areas; their share of part-time workers (22 percent) is similar to large firms' share (19 percent). Small firms' employment share remains steady since some small firms grow into large firms over time.

Source: *U.S. Dept. of Commerce, Census Bureau: Statistics of U.S. Businesses, Current Population Survey, and Business Dynamics Statistics; and the Edward Lowe Foundation (http://youreconomy.org).*

What net share of new jobs do small businesses create?

Small firms accounted for 65 percent (or 9.8 million) of the 15 million net new jobs created between 1993 and 2009. Much of the job growth is from fast-growing high-impact firms, which represent about 5–6 percent of all firms and are on average 25 years old.

Source: *U.S. Dept. of Labor, Bureau of Labor Statistics, Business Employment Dynamics; Advocacy-funded research by Zoltan Acs, William Parsons and Spencer Tracy, 2008* (http://archive.sba.gov/advo/research/rs328tot.pdf).

Special Challenges Faced by Small Businesses

Because small businesses operate with fewer employees, a single bad hire arguably has an even greater impact on small employers. Even though small businesses employ over 50% of all employees, and the impact of a bad hire is significant, it is amazing that small businesses do not take meaningful precautions to know exactly whom they are hiring. There are several reasons why small businesses may not perform background checks:

✓ Safe hiring is focused on problem avoidance in the future. If a firm has not had a bad experience, then efforts at a Safe Hiring Program can seem like a waste of time and money. It is human nature to base future action on past experience; if a business has not had the issue arise, it's not a priority.

✓ Some small firms have the ability to hire people that are known to the firm. Firms operating in a small community often hire individuals recommended by current employees. Hiring individuals who are known to the firm helps reduce the firm's risk of hiring a bad employee.

✓ Some firms are so busy growing they simply do not take time to re-organize their processes as they expand. For a firm to initiate components of a Safe Hiring Program, someone in management must recognize that safe hiring is a core business practice and take the initiative to make it happen.

✓ As firms get bigger, they hang onto methods that worked well when they were smaller. These methods often include "flying by the seat of the pants" hiring methods. As a firm matures, it should recognize that more methodical procedures are needed.

✓ As a small business gets bigger, it will eventually hire a human resources professional to handle the many tasks necessary to hire and maintain a large workforce. The number of tasks placed on a new HR is immense, particularly if HR is a department of one. By the time a firm reaches fifty employees, an HR position probably is a necessity. Prior to that, someone who holds the position of "office manager" and/or "payroll" typically handles the HR functions.

Why Safe Hiring is a Challenge for an HR Department of One

When a small business hires an HR professional, as described throughout this book there are a myriad of tasks an HR professional must address about background screening and safe hiring.

✓ **Compliance.** A new HR practitioner must first ensure that a firm is in legal compliance with a number of federal and state regulations, including I-9 compliance, proper classification of employees into exempt or non-exempt status, leave of absences including maternity and family leaves, ADA, harassment, and numerous other legal issues. Failure to address these issues leaves a firm with tremendous financial and legal exposure.

✓ **Employee Manual.** Institute a handbook outlining formal practices and procedures.

✓ **Employee Files.** A new HR practitioner must typically review existing employee files, assuming those exist. Every employee should have a file that includes at least an application form or resume, a W-2 form, performance reviews, and basic employee data such as start date, salary, dates of promotions, and changes in status.

✓ **Payroll.** An HR practitioner must review how payroll is performed and determine if the best procedure is to do it in-house or outsourced.

✓ **Benefits.** Very complicated for an HR department of one! A new HR practitioner needs to review benefit concerns. Typical issues include selection of benefits to offer, cost control, selecting a benefits broker, reviewing enrollment periods, and dealing with employee complaints concerning benefits.

✓ **New Client Orientation.** In a growing firm, an HR practitioner will also need to implement a new employee orientation, including explanations of company policies and benefits. The orientation should typically include a new hire checklist with various new hire forms such as I-9 compliance or tax forms.

✓ **Compensation Review.** When a small firm hires an HR practitioner, the person must review the current compensation system. As a firm grows, a compensation strategy is necessary to make sure a firm is competitive and consistent.

✓ **Job Descriptions.** Often a small business grows without ever having prepared job descriptions. Descriptions are vital in helping an employer hire employees with the right skill sets, to perform job performance appraisals, and to comply with the ADA by identifying essential job functions.

✓ **Performance Appraisal System.** Most small businesses do not have a formalized performance appraisal system in place. Appraisals can be a critical factor to determine the proper compensation rate, to implement improvement plans for an employee, or to determine areas where additional training or supervision may be necessary to help an employee succeed.

✓ **Information Mechanism for Employees.** Another important function of a new HR department is to institute a system for keeping employees informed of such things as changes in benefits, new laws, harassment training, and even the company holiday schedule.

✓ **Training.** A growing small business may not have sufficient training in place. This includes not only training specific for a job, but also training for managers and workers in areas such as sexual harassment control.

✓ **Recruiting and Hiring.** A new HR practitioner may be asked to help the "employer effort" to recruit, interview, hire, and train new employers.

✓ **HR Software.** Another task often assigned to a new HR department is to consider automation procedures and software available to help the firm manage the employment aspects of a growing business.

The good news is that even a small employer can implement a Safe Hiring Program at very low cost. The AIR Process, described earlier in this book, costs next to nothing to implement. A small business that hires negligently would be hard pressed to defend itself on the basis that it is too small to practice safe hiring. That defense has not proven successful. Although a small business may not be expected to perform at the same level as a Fortune 500 firm, the fact is that safe hiring can be performed at little or no cost. There is no reason why any small business has to hire blindly.

Large Employer Issues

On the other side of the employment spectrum are large enterprises. While there is no generally accepted formula for what constitutes middle market and large or enterprise level employers, when an employer reaches a level of 1,000 employees, a whole new set of concerns and challenges develops. A discussion of some special considerations that large employers face would include the following:

1. Large Employers Face Legal Complexities by Hiring in Multiple States

A major challenge for large employers operating in a number of states is legal compliance. The complexity of compliance surfaces in two significant areas.

✓ **Use of criminal records by employers.** Many states have their own rules concerning the use of criminal records; some of these rules are reviewed in Chapters 6 and 11. These restrictions are typically set forth in a state's rules on discrimination in employment such as state fair employment guidelines. Some states have restrictions enacted by statutes. For example, in California it is a misdemeanor for an employer to:

"...seek from any source whatsoever, or utilize, as a factor in determining any condition of employment including hiring, promotion, termination, or any apprenticeship training program or any other training program leading to employment, any record of arrest or detention that did not result in conviction, or any record regarding a referral to, and participation in, any pretrial or post trial diversion program." Cal. Labor Code § 432.7(a).

Individual state rules can affect any aspect of the hiring process including the language on applications, proper interview questions, and the ability of employers to obtain and use screening information on applicants. Operating in multiple states requires knowledge of the rules for each.

✓ **State FCRA Laws.** As discussed in Chapter 6, there are a number of states with unique laws controlling background screening by third party professional background firms. An employer that intends to hire and screen in multiple state locations must be aware of the applicable laws. Also, employers must utilize the forms and procedures appropriate for each state. In California, using forms and procedures that work in the other 49 states could expose an employer to substantial damage awards in a civil lawsuit. (California has set its own legal requirements. See the article in the Appendix.)

✓ **Understanding which state law to apply.** Operating in multiple states also creates complicated issues of which laws apply. Assume a firm incorporated in Delaware hires a Connecticut resident for a job in New York, and a screening firm in Atlanta improperly reports a criminal conviction when the applicant went to school in California, and the case was brought into federal court in New York alleging violations of a New York state law that protect employees. This is an actual case. The case was *Obabueki v. International Business Machines Corp.*, 145 F. Supp.2d 371 (S.D.N.Y. 2001). There were follow-up cases as well. A detailed discussion of the facts and legal issues involved are beyond the scope of this book. However, the general principles involved in considering which state's law to apply are summarized in Chapter 6 on the FCRA.

A new innovation is the ability of a software system to incorporate necessary legal forms and state specific requirements on an online application system. Such a system can also automatically be updated any time there is a change in state or federal law. By asking for certain information, the system will know which states are impacted and if specific forms are required

2. Large Employer Issues with Consistency in the Organization

An issue for large multi-state employers is maintaining consistency within the organization. Assume for example that an employer has a facility in Arizona that is performing in-depth background reports and utilizing the safe hiring techniques reviewed in previous chapters. Also assume the same firm has a facility in Ohio that is not doing nearly as much to ensure safe hiring. If a person is injured as a result of workplace violence in the less vigilant Ohio facility, then the injured party's attorney could use the practices and procedures at the more vigilant facility against the employer. The argument would be the employer knew how to hire safely but chose not to follow the higher standard in that particular facility. In other words, an employer may be held to the standard in the facility that exercises the greater degree of due diligence. As a result, management must be sensitive to the need to have a consistent company-wide policy when it comes to safe hiring and employment screening.

The same considerations come into play when utilizing negative information. If the Ohio facility hired an applicant with previous criminal records to be employed, then the Arizona facility could be accused of discrimination if a similarly situated person with a similar record is denied employment.

3. Large Employer Issues with Automation, Integration with HRS, and Applicant Tracking

Another consideration for large enterprise level firms is the automation and integration of the pre-employment process with their Human Resources Information Systems, or HRIS. Some firms will manage all of the human resources with some enterprise level application such as PeopleSoft, Oracle, or SAP. Other firms may coordinate background screening with an applicant tracking system, or ATS.

An ATS system is a database that is used to manage applicant information in a firm's hiring process. The software manages the receipt of resumes and applications (including online applications) as well as correspondence and contact between applicants and the firm. The software can track open positions, engage in some sort of matching process, and track the progress of each applicant. There are at least 100 providers of this service in a market that is estimated at somewhere between $250-500 million; each ATS software provider touting any number of different bells and whistles. ATS software providers meet the needs of small, medium, large, and enterprise employers.

There are many systems to choose from with many features. Employers need to determine if they will really use all of the whistles and bells. A new trend is to develop an ATS that accomplishes an employer's goal without overburdening the business with unneeded complication. For example, see Newton Software at www.newtonsoftware.com.

One advantage of having a direct business-to-business (B2B) connection with a screening firm is the time saved by eliminating double data entry — since the applicant's name, Social Society number, and data of birth are already in the employer's computer system, there is no need to visit the background screening firm's website to manually re-enter the same data. With a seamless B2B integration, employers can instantly send the required data electronically to the screening firm, and the data is automatically populated in the screening firm's HRIS or ATS system. The B2B seamless interface can also communicate the types of searches the employer is ordering. While the order is being processed, the employer can receive updates or status reports.

 One big advantage of a system described above is the employer does not need to collect a date of birth or social security number. That can be done on the background firm's online system. Nor does the ATS or HRIS need to store background reports. The screening firm can also do that.

Although the technology involved in seamless B2B connections was complex and expensive at one time, the general rule that technology becomes less expensive and more readily available certainly applies to background screening processes for large firms.

4. Large Employers and the Impact of HR-XML

The ability of background firms to develop software that will work with a number of HRIS and ATS systems has been furthered by the advent of the HR-XML Consortium. This industry group is developing a common communications framework for employers and suppliers of HR services. Here is an overall description of what they do (from http://www.hr-xml.org/?page=About):

✓ The HR-XML Consortium is an independent, non-profit organization dedicated to the development and promotion of a standard suite of XML specifications to enable e-business and the automation of human resources-related data exchanges.

✓ The mission of the HR-XML Consortium is to lead the ongoing development of robust, extensible, global HR interoperability standards enabling easy-to-implement, time- and cost-effective integration of business applications within the HR community; expand and engage the community to share experiences and expertise for the betterment of the community; to collaborate with other identified standards organizations to ensure interoperability and business alignment.

In August 2011, the consortium released standards for pre-employment screening. The HR-XML schemas are not universally implemented. However, the schema set the stage for a kind of universal translator between software systems used by employers to manage their human capital and the suppliers of various services.

5. Large Employer Issues with Managing Privacy and Reports across Organizational Lines

With multiple facilities and/or multiple divisions and hiring managers, a large employer needs to be concerned about how privacy and confidentiality are maintained. Unless precautions are taken, reports may be viewed by co-workers, administrative staff, or others who are not involved in the hiring process and do not have a need to review the reports. A screening report does not contain secret information. However, it does contain information confidential in nature that should not be made available to anyone who is not directly involved in the hiring decision. An argument can be made that even a hiring manager should not view a background screening report but should only be advised by Security or Human Resources if there is a problem that needs to be addressed.

A solution would be a system whereby reports go only to one contact person in charge of reviewing the information. Also, the contact person should maintain the reports. If a firm utilizes an online system for reports, then only the contact person should have access to the online system. Most screening firms offer online systems where an employer can easily manage the process. There is typically a screen that indicates the status of all current reports and the degree of completion. An online system can also route reports to the right office.

Screening firms can set-up accounts that use parent-child relationships so a supervisor can view all reports, but only the appropriate office or person can view the reports that pertain to them. This also allows a screening firm to set up sub-accounts for an organization so that management reports and billing can be provided to the correct branch or office.

6. Large Employer Issues with Training Hiring Managers across the Organization

Another issue in large organizations is training the various hiring managers to consistently follow the organization's safe hiring procedures. This is especially an issue for organizations that hire for a large number of branches, such as banks, hotels, or sales offices. Consistency and training are important for a number of reasons especially for documenting that a firm, in fact, follows safe hiring procedures, and it also helps protect the firm against allegations of discrimination.

The best tool is the S.A.F.E. Program outlined in Chapter 6, including a Safe Hiring Checklist, which outlines the essential steps in a Safe Hiring Program. The hiring manager fills out the checklist as new hires are finalized. The checklist gives clear directions on what has to be done and enables an organization to audit, measure, and reward hiring managers for following the safe hiring procedures.

7. Large Employers Contracting for Safe Hiring Services Based Primarily on Price

One trend among large firms is to have purchasing or procurement departments involved in the selection of service providers, including background-screening services. Recently, some organizations have even taken to awarding contracts based upon online auctions, where the finalists bid against each other in an effort to obtain the lowest possible price.

The difficulty for large employers with this approach is purchasing a professional service on a purely price-driven model leaves the organizations vulnerable in the event the low cost provider fails to adequately perform. If a firm utilizes the auctions approach, the firm must recognize they are making a calculated risk-management decision that spending the minimum is sufficient. If the low cost provider fails to perform, and the firm gets sued, then the employer would face a substantial challenge in attempting to prove they exercised due diligence.

The biggest variable factor in screening is the cost of labor. The raw cost of data has a relatively narrow margin. Shortcuts can include using untrained clerical workers to produce screening reports or utilizing incomplete databases for criminal searches. What if court researchers enter criminal information directly into the computer, and there is no review prior to viewing by the employer? The employer sees data not reviewed for accuracy, completeness, or legality by a screening professional. Another way large employers obtain cheap pricing is to utilize a service that offers screening services essentially as a "loss leader" in order to sell other HR products. Firms using auctions may also attract screening firms that are purely data houses willing to sell at or near cost to increase their volume or willingly take a smaller profit per transaction as long as they can keep their costs down. Again, since the largest item of overhead is trained staff, a large employer who is driving down the price through an auction cannot count on having the level of professional service the task requires.

Firms using the auction method would probably not do so for finding and hiring other professional services such as a corporate attorney or an auditor. When using an auction for screening and safe hiring services, a large employer is essentially relegating safe hiring to a commodity product, ignoring the professional services aspect.

One employer found out the hard way. In Kay v. First Continental Trading, Inc., 976 F.Supp. 772,774 (N.D.Ill. 1997), a federal court ruled an expert witness could give his opinion that a screening firm could not have effectively conducted a proper investigation for the low price it charged the employer. The end result is employers who focus solely on price may find themselves paying more later. As the saying goes, "You get what you pay for."

Special Issues with Hiring the Non-Traditional Workforce

According to a 1999 U.S. Department of Labor report *Futurework, Trends and Challenges for Work in the 21st Century*:

✓ "The age of 'just in time' production has given rise to 'just in time' workers—employees whom a business can hire on a moment's notice to fill a moment's need.

✓ Roughly one in ten workers fits into an *alternative arrangement*. Nearly four out of five employers use some form of non-traditional staffing arrangement.

✓ America's *alternative workers* number 13 million and are a mixed group. The majority (8.5 million) are independent contractors. A growing number (1.3 million) are *agency temporary workers*."

Of course, not every independent contractor or non-traditional worker prefers that status. Even though a non-traditional job provides greater flexibility, at the same time it does not afford the same benefits or salary that a full time employee may typically enjoy.

The recent economic downturn beginning in 2008 caused many people to have to take part time jobs. During the ongoing recovery, employers wary of adding too many full-time employees are also opting to add only temporary help. Still, these part-time workers need to be screened.

The non-traditional workforce raises special considerations when practicing safe hiring. Past employment history is harder to pin down when the applicant has had a number of positions.

When hiring a non-traditional worker, employers need to exercise the same safe hiring precautions they would for any other job applicant. If an employer decides to save costs by not attempting to verify every past work assignment in the past five to ten years or search every past county in the past seven years for criminal records, then utilizing the AIR Process (as outlined in previous chapters) is even more important. In determining how much effort, money, and energy to put into background screening non-traditional workers, an employer should consider two factors:

✓ **Use consistency.** The same level of screening used for similar positions should be used for a position that is to be filled by a non-traditional worker or else the firm may be subject to allegations of disparate treatment of similarly situated people.

✓ **The duty to hire with due diligence.** This basic rule still applies. An employer is negligent if they hire someone who the employer either knew or should have known, in the exercise of reasonable care, was dangerous, unfit, or not qualified for the position.

 Free Agent Nation and Corporate Me

The role of non-traditional workers was popularized during the internet bubble from 1990 to 2002. One book, *Free Agent Nation: The Future of Working for Yourself* popularized the notion of a "free agent nation" based upon the premise that a person is no longer defined by their job or job title. Instead, the new workers really work for themselves. They are their own corporation with their own brands. When they are on someone else's payroll, they are really "consultants," and every job should be an opportunity to increase their value. www.amazon.com/Free-Agent-Nation-Working-Yourself/dp/0446678791).

Special Problems with Large Hourly, Seasonal, Temporary Contract Workforces

Industries with large hourly, seasonal, or temporary contract workforces typically include hospitality and tourism, manufacturing, service, retail, food and restaurants, drug and groceries stores, and call centers. Compounding their hiring problems are multiple locations and large turnovers.

Unicru was an employment assistance firm that specialized in total workforce acquisitions solutions for specific industries, including industries with large hourly workforces. According to a 2002 special report by Unicru (which was acquired by Kronos in 2006):

"In the United States, over 90 million workers – more than 80 percent of the labor pool – are hourly or front-line employees. On an annual basis, large companies will hire far more hourly workers than salaried or professional staff.

The mechanics of hiring from these two segments are vastly different. Hiring cycles for salaried personnel are longer than for hourly workers. The former tend to apply to positions and/or organizations in large numbers, while the latter tend to apply in much smaller numbers to locations within five miles of their homes. Psychologically, hourly workers feel much more pressure to find work quickly and tend to be on the market for only a few days, while a salaried candidate's shelf life is measured in months. A manager of salaried staff will typically interview only three candidates for a position and hire one person or less per year, but a location or store manager will hire more than 15 people per year, interviewing an average of five applicants per position. In the salaried workforce, turnover is less than 10 percent; it is 6 to 10 times that among hourly employees."

The challenge is greater if the firm is engaged in providing services that have a greater degree of risk to third parties. For example, resorts hiring seasonally have greater exposure since children are present during their peak seasons. If temporary or seasonal employees are involved in higher risk activities in roles as lifeguards, ski instructors, or other similar jobs, then the stakes are higher.

So, how do industries with significant turnover — or with large numbers of hourly, seasonal, temporary or contract workers — protect themselves in a cost-effective and efficient manner? Employers are under pressure to reduce the time and cost per hire by minimizing those costs and delays associated with pre-employment screening. A cost-effective solution is to devise a mechanism that incorporates the elements of the S.A.F.E. Hiring program and the AIR Process described in previous chapters in an assembly line fashion.

At a minimum, run a basic public records search. It is essential to run a Social Security trace and at least one county criminal record check. If any driving is involved, then a driving record should also be run. Of course, if it is a driving position regulated by the Department of Transportation or for any other position that is regulated by federal or state rules, then all applicable laws must be followed.

Even though the cost of background checks can add up for large hiring programs, employers are still held to a standard of due diligence hiring for hourly, temporary, or seasonal employees. If sued, an employer might assert the defense that imposing the requirement of doing background checks was too costly of a burden to place on employers, but such a defense is not likely to succeed. Courts have taught employers that the cost of safe hiring is minor when compared to the possible harm not performing the check could cause. As explained in Chapter 5, the cost of litigation and attorney fees alone from one bad new-hire can negate the money saved on cutting corners.

CEOs and CFOs who take the position that safe hiring and pre-employment screening are not important or are too expensive need to carefully review the true economics of their firm and the risk factors involved from a single bad hire.

More about Hiring Juveniles

Hiring young workers or juveniles presents special problems. Juvenile records are typically not "public records," and criminal records are difficult to acquire unless the juvenile was tried as an adult. In addition, juvenile workers and young workers may not have a significant employment history. Employers, however, can require that they provide at least two letters of recommendation from non-family members or teachers who know them. This procedure helps eliminate those applicants without the initiative to obtain such letters and helps an employer show some due diligence in hiring. Parental consent and state child labor laws are also issues; if an employer is only obtaining public records, verifying past employment information or school attendance, parental consent is probably not required, in the absence of a specific state law. These procedures are not intrusive and there are FCRA protections. However, if parental consent is available, it does add extra protection.

Using Instant Online Databases for Quick Hiring Decisions

Another trend is the emergence of web pages with the instant background check. These websites offering employers so called "instant searches" often include the following sample language:

> *Human resource professionals can conduct extensive national pre-employment background checks in real time! Within seconds our system can reveal the following:*
>
> ✓   *Positively identify your candidate.*
> ✓   *Validate their SSN's.*
> ✓   *Secure all addresses the candidate used for the past 7-15 years.*
> ✓   *Reveal their relatives and associates.*
> ✓   *Determine if the applicant has been involved in litigation, bankruptcy, or has tax liens.*
> ✓   *Confirm property ownership.*
> ✓   *Verify the candidate's driver's license information (available in some states).*
> ✓   *Scan for any criminal records or sex offender listings.*

Unfortunately, this type of instant search does not provide as much coverage and protection as employers may believe. One reason is because instant databases are supplemental in nature (remember the fact that only 66% of court records are even online). They are best used as a lead generator by screening firms.

"Instant results" are essentially "data-dumps" based upon an automated search through billions of records. Criminal or sexual offender searches are subject to the database problems since a database search is not necessarily complete, up-to-date, or accurate.

Some types of records sold by instant information vendors are not valid predictors of job performance. For example, a search that focuses on finding out if someone has declared bankruptcy could violate a consumer's rights. Consideration of whether a person owns property is not likely to be a valid predictor of job performance and can be discriminatory by creating a disparate impact on certain groups. Obtaining names and addresses of "relatives and associates" could be a violation of discrimination laws and an invasion of privacy.

Employers using information obtained from the instant web background check sites can violate the federal Fair Credit Reporting Act (FCRA) and state and federal discrimination laws, as explained in previous chapters. These instant internet sites can lead an employer to believe that all they need is a credit card to obtain data. The employer must obtain consents, provide authorizations, and abide by the FCRA or face a serious threat of litigation. Many of these internet services are only giving lip service to FCRA requirements, if mentioned at all.

The value and limitation of private databases is examined in detail in Chapter 14. Please refer to that chapter. Below are summaries of two studies and details of a recent court case that may have great impact on this topic.

Interesting Results from Two Studies

An April 11, 2004 article in the *Chicago Tribune* featured a story about a University of Maryland Associate Professor of Criminology who ran a test on an online database service. According to the article, Professor Bushway obtained the criminal records of 120 parolees in Virginia and submitted these names to the popular online background check company. According to the article, sixty names came back showing no criminal record. Many other reports were so jumbled that the offenses were tough to pick out. See Chapter 15 for a more detailed explanation of why database searches can miss names.

The same article reported that the *Chicago Tribune* had conducted its own study. The *Tribune* selected an online data service and submitted the names and birthdates of 10 Illinois offenders whose sentences were in the media for crimes ranging from drunken driving and fraud to possession of child pornography. The online statewide search found no criminal records for any of the names. The search flagged only one person as a sex offender but provided little additional useful information.

The source of these articles is http://articles.chicagotribune.com/2004-04-11/news/0404110512_1_background-checks-criminal-records-offenders.

Recent Class Action Lawsuit Regarding Instant Database Searches

Any firm that sells instant database material directly to employers should follow this case closely since it can have far ranging impact. See below for examples of lawsuits concerning instant database searches and also read the section 'FTC Fines Data Broker $800,000 Dollars to Settle Charges of Violating FCRA' in Chapter 3.

Class Action Complaint Filed Against Consumer Reporting Agency for Allegedly Violating Fair Credit Reporting Act with Instant Database Searches

A class action complaint filed against a Consumer Reporting Agency (CRA) on April 16, 2012, alleged the Defendant reported inaccurate criminal data obtained from an "instant" criminal record search without courthouse confirmation and also that there was allegedly no notice to the consumer who was the subject of the search. The suit also alleged that such acts were in violation of the federal Fair Credit Reporting Act (FCRA) that protects consumers from inaccurate or irrelevant information and failed to meet the standard of accuracy and fairness mandated by the FCRA.

The Plaintiff claimed the Defendant – a CRA that collects consumer information and sells "consumer reports" that are also known as background checks – failed to meet the standard of accuracy and fairness mandated by the FCRA, which requires all CRAs that report criminal conviction and other information to employers adopt and implement procedures that "assure maximum possible accuracy of the information concerning the individual about whom the report relates."

The Plaintiff claimed when she applied for a job, the CRA:

✓ Reported to two different employers that used their "instant" database that the Plaintiff had been arrested and charged with felony offenses in Los Angeles County but failed to report the felony charge had been dismissed and a misdemeanor conviction had been legally expunged;

✓ Provided her potential employer with outdated, incomplete, and inaccurate information regarding her alleged criminal record;

✓ Failed to provide timely notice that such information had been reported; and

✓ Caused Plaintiff to be denied valuable employment opportunities.

Despite the requirements of FCRA, the complaint alleged the CRA:

✓ Twice failed to notify Plaintiff contemporaneously of the fact that public record information about her was being reported;

✓ Failed to maintain strict procedures designed to insure such information was complete and up-to-date; and

✓ Failed to utilize reasonable procedures to assure maximum possible accuracy of the adverse information it reported to her potential.

The complaint also claimed the CRA failed to ensure accurate and timely reporting of convictions and other consumer information due to a promise of instant results. According to the complaint filed in the Alameda County Superior Court in California:

"Some or all of [Defendant's] unlawful conduct is attributable to its promise of "instant" results, which are incompatible with the accuracy requirements imposed on credit reporting agencies by the FCRA. Plaintiff is informed and believes, and on that basis alleges, that rather than conducting an individualized investigation of a consumer's criminal record at the time a background check is requested, [Defendant] responds to its employer clients' requests on the basis of information collected in internal databases. This

information does not and by definition it cannot include the most timely and accurate information, as the FCRA requires."

The complaint noted that individuals with criminal records have difficulties getting employment, and rehabilitation is even more difficult when expunged criminal records are "illegally and incorrectly reported."

The complaint indicated that because of the impact of the CRA's wrongful practices, the Plaintiff is suing on behalf of consumers throughout the country who have been the subject of similar prejudicial, misleading, and inaccurate background check reports prepared by the Defendant. Since the suit alleges that the CRA's non-compliance was willful, the Plaintiff and class members are entitled to statutory damages provided by the FCRA. Under FCRA section 616, the potential penalties for willful noncompliance can be $100 to $1,000 per victim plus attorney's fees and punitive damages.

The case was brought on behalf of JANE ROE, individually and on behalf of all others similarly situated, Alameda County (CA) Superior Court, Case No: RG12625923. The Attorneys for the Plaintiff JANE ROE and the Proposed Class are Nance F. Becker and Christian Schreiber of Chavez & Gertler LLP in Mill Valley, CA; Devin H. Fok of The Law Offices of Devin H. Fok in Alhambra, CA; and Joshua E. Kim of A New Way of Life Reentry Project in Los Angeles, CA.

Keep in mind these are only allegations, which is the way a lawsuit is initiated. However, these allegations do touch upon important issues.

A background screening firm has separate obligations under the FCRA when reporting criminal records. First, as a general rule under section 607(b), a background screening firm "shall follow reasonable procedures to assure maximum possible accuracy of the information concerning the individual about whom the report relates."

In addition, if there is a criminal record likely to adversely impact employment, FCRA Section 613 requires that the background screening firm shall:

- ✓ At the time such public record information is reported to the user of such consumer report, notify the consumer of the fact that public record information is being reported by the consumer reporting agency, together with the name and address of the person to whom such information is being reported; or
- ✓ Maintain strict procedures designed to insure that whenever public record information which is likely to have an adverse effect on a consumer's ability to obtain employment is reported it is complete and up to date. For purposes of this paragraph, items of public record relating to arrests, indictments, convictions, suits, tax liens, and outstanding judgments shall be considered up to date if the current public record status of the item at the time of the report is reported.

The impact is that the background screening firm can send a letter notice if criminal information is reported to an employer. However, even with a letter, use of a database may not meet the general obligation of "reasonable procedures" if the database had stale information that was not updated.

It appears that the single biggest source of allegations of inaccurate records comes from reporting database results directly to the end-user employer without taking steps to ensure the record is complete, accurate, and up-to-date and belongs to the consumer. However, a great many screening firms do not report database hits directly until the information is confirmed.

The fallout from reporting inaccurate criminal database information to an employer potentially creates a risk to the whole screening industry. The tremendous value of databases as a research tool is well recognized, but if CRAs provide incomplete or inaccurate data directly to employers without vetting, it may well eventually cause a legislative over-reaction.

FCRA section 613 does allow the so-called 'letter-notice' option, but that needs to be read in conjunction with FCRA Section 607(b) that mandates "reasonable procedures for maximum possible accuracy." Although the 613 letter option is part of the law, a CRA cannot ignore the general duty to proceed with reasonable procedures, which can mean that using a database that is inherently flawed by a failure to update, can potentially result in an FCRA violation even if a letter notice is sent.

The bottom line is that the 613 letter option does not open the flood gates to allow a CRA to report anything that comes up in a database as long as a letter is sent to the consumer. If a CRA knows or reasonably should know for example, that a database is not updated, and reports it anyways, that could potentially be a violation of 607(b) even if a letter is sent.

In summary, employers need to be very careful about using online instant data brokers. Not only can there be issues with the accuracy, completeness, and applicability of the data, but there are also a number of FCRA, discrimination, and privacy considerations.

Special Issues When Hiring in a Labor Shortage

Although the current economic environment has relatively high unemployment, experts tell us that the future will be very different. The news media reports that once the recession is over, the real story will be a worker shortage, especially for jobs requiring higher education. If and when a shortage occurs, the pressure on employers and recruiters to fill positions is much greater. Delaying a new hire to wait for a background report could result in a good candidate being hired elsewhere.

However, when employers and recruiters become less selective and take a gamble, they can end up with new hires they may wish they could have avoided. During a labor shortage an employer may wish to consider the following guidelines:

- ✓ Resist the temptation to hire as fast as possible. Do not dispense with the fundamentals of a Safe Hiring Program. Shortcuts in hiring can come back to haunt the firm, the recruit, and the hiring manager in the future.
- ✓ Understand that if a firm makes a bad hire, the "perceived need for speed" will likely not make much of an impact in front of a jury if the employer is sued.
- ✓ If time is of the essence, then make sure the no-cost suggestions made in this book about Applicant/Interview/Reference (AIR Process) checking practices are followed. This helps to minimize problematic hires.
- ✓ If the situation demands the applicant be hired without delay, then be certain to provide a written offer letter stating the new hire is conditional based upon receipt of a background report that is satisfactory to the employer.

Special Issues with Safe Hiring and Job Boards

Although it is debated how many jobseekers actually find employment from online services, there is no question that millions of Americans use the internet to look for job opportunities. Some of the websites most visited by job seekers looking for work online currently include the list below. Indeed, the world's largest job search site as of February 2012, had 60 million monthly unique visitors and one billion job searches. (Source: http://articles.businessinsider.com/2012-02-21/tech/31081848_1_indeed-com-job-mobile-app.)

Popular Online Job Websites

Online Job Website	Web Address
Indeed	www.indeed.com
CareerBuilder	www.careerbuilder.com
Monster.com	www.monster.com
Simply Hired	www.simplyhired.com
Linkedin	www.linkedin.com
Craigslist	www.craigslist.com

Understanding the Job Board and Recruitment World

There are two useful websites that assemble, categorize, and analyze the various job boards, including recruiting and employment-related sites on the internet. Peter Weddles is a veteran of the online job world. He publishes guides to employment websites for recruiters and jobseekers. His recruiting guide has data on over 40,000 career-related sites. See www.weddles.com. Another service is offered by CareerXroads, publisher of a yearly book that reviews job and employment-related sites. See www.careerxroads.com. The best cyberspace resource to follow major developments in the online employment scene is www.interbiznet.com. This site offers a daily newsletter for the recruiting industry, special employment reports, and a daily column by John Sumser who is widely considered the leading source of analysis for the electronic recruiting industry.

Verification of Resumes Found on Job Boards

One difficulty with the millions of resumes on job boards is verification. Resumes are not verified by a trusted third party. Although numerous job boards claim they "screen" candidates, the use of the word "screened" in the job board context is typically a process used to perform some sort of preliminary evaluation of candidate qualifications, at least on cyber-paper. The purpose is to eliminate unqualified candidates and guide employers to candidates more likely qualified. The catch is that job board screening tools are based on the premise that what people say about themselves is true.

 Do not be confused by the use of the word "screened" on job boards. Unless the employer knows for a fact the screening included safe hiring steps and verifiable background screening, the employer must take the same steps with job board candidates as they would with any other. Using proper safe hiring steps will also keep you in compliance with equal opportunity laws.

If job boards independently verified facts on resumes, it would be immensely valuable. Employers could hire with a great deal more accuracy and confidence.

Consequently, the value of job boards is only as a tool for employers and jobseekers to find each other in the first place. Job boards, from the smallest local niche board to the biggest boards, are still essentially the electronic equivalent of a local supermarket bulletin board or the want ads in the newspaper. Using a job board does not relieve an employer of their safe hiring obligations — employers still have the same legal duty to exercise due diligence regardless of the source of the candidate.

An excellent resource comes from The Privacy Rights Clearinghouse which published a special report by Pam Dixon, author and investigative researcher for the World Privacy Forum. The report is titled *Fact Sheet 25: Privacy Tips for Online Job Seekers* and is on the Privacy Rights Clearinghouse website at https://www.privacyrights.org/fs/FS25-JobSeekerPriv.htm.

BBB Warns Job Seekers about Bogus BBB Job Posting Aimed to Scam the Unemployed

In July 2011, the Better Business Bureau (BBB) serving Upstate New York warned job seekers about a bogus 'BBB Data Entry Opportunity' on a popular job board website that the BBB did <u>not</u> post. The bogus job posting directed applicants to sign up for a 'banking institution' to receive their pay via direct deposit.

Since it is common for the unemployed to use social networking sites and online postings to look for jobs, the BBB offers the following tips when finding a job through online searches:

- ✓ Exercise Caution.
- ✓ Guard Your Resume.
- ✓ Start with Trust.
- ✓ Never Pay Upfront Fees.
- ✓ Protect Personal Information.
- ✓ Be Careful of the "Perfect Offer."
- ✓ Avoid Work-at-Home Offers.
- ✓ Report Fraud.

For more information on finding a job and to check the reliability of any company, visit www.bbb.org.

Source: www.buffalo.bbb.org/article/bbb-warns-job-seekers--28308.

Special Issues with Safe Hiring and Recruiters

Recruiters are a source of applicants for employers. Recruiters are called upon to find highly qualified candidates appropriate for a particular job description. Employers use recruiters to economically and quickly find applicants interested in long-term job situations. Recruiters find applicants from a number of different venues, from job boards to cold calling to networking. Recruiters can be independent or work for a particular employer on an in-house basis.

The fees and reputations of independent recruiters and recruiting firms depend largely on the qualifications of the candidates they present. Although some recruiters may do some past employment checks themselves, the act of recruiters doing pre-employment screening before presenting candidates does not appear to be a wide spread practice. When balancing the relatively low cost of a screening report with the fees a recruiter can receive with the negative impact of just one bad candidate, it would seem to be an ideal due diligence service to have recruiters make a practice of screening all candidates.

Under the Fair Credit Reporting Act, there is no barrier to a recruiter obtaining a background report. A recruiter will need to follow the FCRA in terms of obtaining written authorization and providing the candidate with a disclosure of their rights. A screening firm can provide the necessary documents to the recruiter. There are two special considerations:

- ✓ In the release form for a background screening, the recruiter should add a provision indicating the candidate also releases the information to an employer who may wish to view the report. This allows the recruiter to share the background report with a potential employer.
- ✓ There are restrictions in obtaining credit reports. The recruiter is not the end user of credit reports, and the credit bureaus require the actual end-user be identified and to show a permissible purpose. However, there are no restrictions on other basic screening tools such as checking past employment or education or searching for criminal records.

In-house recruiters have different issues. Hiring managers will typically assign an in-house recruiter to fill a certain number of job positions. While the Human Resources or security department dictates the safe hiring protocol for the employer — the background screening process that the firm may use — in-house recruiters typically are under pressure to complete the hiring quickly. As discussed in previous chapters, the process used for background screening usually takes up to three days. For large firms, even a one-day delay can have an impact since many employers have a preset new employee orientation schedule. If a new hire misses the start date, then the new hire may have to wait a week or more before the next new employee classes begin.

In-house recruiters can help speed up the process in several ways:

✓ First, the recruiter must understand the process can be delayed if screening firms are sent incomplete information or forms that are not legible or completely filled out. Screening firms often face difficulty in deciphering an application in order to identify and locate past employers, but having a recruiter review and correct all candidates' applications before sending those applications to a screening firm will help eliminate delays. This is simply a good practice for any employer or recruiter.

✓ Second, an in-house recruiter needs to communicate with hiring managers so there are not unrealistic expectations. A hiring manager may not understand, for example, that criminal records are searched at each relevant courthouse or that delays can occur if there is a potential match that needs to be verified. Hiring managers must also be advised that employment and education verifications can be delayed for the all reasons discussed in Chapters 9 and 14. If there is a delay in receiving a completed screening report, the recruiter should examine the source of the delay.

✓ Third, if a recruiter is working with a screening firm that has an online ordering system, the process is considerably faster and with greater accuracy. Even faster is new technology that allows a seamless and paperless integration between an Applicant Tracking System (ATS) and a background screening firm.

Finally, there are times when a recruiter may determine that even though the screening firm has not been successful in obtaining all of the information, enough data is available to make a hiring decision. Typically, delays happen when verifying previous employment, and past employment oldest in time is the most difficult to obtain, though the oldest employment may be the least relevant. If the applicant, for example, worked in a fast food restaurant six years ago after getting out of school, and the fast food place will not call back, then there may be no reason to delay the hiring decision if the screening firm has obtained the most recent and presumably more relevant job verifications.

An Emerging Tool – Use of Employment Kiosks

Another method for employers to find candidates is using job kiosks. Job kiosks are small, mobile, ATM type devices that jobseekers may use for applying online. Kiosks are usually controlled and operated by staffing firms or particular employers seeking employment applications. Employment kiosks, also known as "job" kiosks or "hiring" kiosks can be found in many places currently, including larger retail stores as well as many major supermarkets.

Employment Application Kiosks and Sites

The text below is taken from a 2003 Job Search Privacy Study conducted by Pam Dixon and published by the World Privacy Forum at www.worldprivacyforum.org/applicationkiosks.pdf:

"In place of a resume, many of the employment kiosks that researchers studied requested that job seekers supply SSNs, date of birth, and the answer to detailed skills and personality questions. Some kiosks also facilitated an instant SSN check and instant background check.

The kiosks are usually equipped with a miniature keypad, phone, mini computer screen, and secure connection. But all too frequently, the kiosks do not come equipped with the most important thing of all: a privacy policy that discusses how a job seekers' SSNs, dates of birth, and questionnaire data are stored, handled, and deleted, among other things.

As such, the rapid deployment and adoption of kiosk technology in the retail sector as the de facto means of applying for work represents some risk to the affected job seekers."

An important issue in the process for applying for a job by kiosk or an online system is the applicant's consent for a background check. A kiosk will typically request private and sensitive data to process the request, which can include a

Social Security number and possibly date of birth. The use and storage of this information involves a myriad of compliance issues mentioned throughout this book.

Electronic Signatures and Applicant Consents

A source of frustration for recruiters in the hiring process is obtaining the paperwork necessary for the background check and then entering data into an online screening system. Typically, recruiters struggle to obtain a "wet signature," meaning that they need to have the applicant sign an actual piece of paper containing the background consent and disclosure, and physically get that to the screening firm. If the recruiter utilizes an online background screening system, then the data must be entered on the background firm's system.

However, by using electronic signatures with the latest technology, sophisticated background firms can now offer "paperless" online background checking systems, where the applicant fills out the online information and signs an online consent.

Such a process is permissible due to a law enacted on June 30, 2000 that went into effect in October 2000 called the **Electronic Signatures in Global and National Commerce Act (ESIGN)**. Section 101(a) of the act provides that:

"(a) . . . Notwithstanding any statute, regulation, or other rule of law (other than this title and title II), with respect to any transaction in or affecting interstate or foreign commerce

(1) a signature, contract, or other record relating to such transaction may not be denied legal effect, validity, or enforceability solely because it is in electronic form..."

In addition, 47 states have adopted the **Uniform Electronic Transactions Act (UETA)**. This was a uniform standard formatted by the National Conference of Commissioners on Uniform State Laws (NCCUSL). The goal was to create uniform state rules that address issues related to electronic contracts and electronic agreement. Through these laws, a traditional "wet signature" where the applicant physically signs a piece of paper is replaced by an electronic signature.

The subject of which law, ESIGN or UETA, applies to which transaction is very complex. As a general proposition, the federal ESIGN law governs in the absence of a state law or where states have made modifications to UETA that are inconsistent with ESIGN.

Electronic Signatures and the FTC

The Federal Trade Commission initially took the position that a mouse click was insufficient to meet the standards of the Fair Credit Reporting Act (FCRA) when written consent is required. (See the *Landever letter*, issued October 12, 1999 at www.ftc.gov/os/statutes/fcra/landever.htm.)

FCRA Section 604(b)(2)(A)(ii) specifically requires that:

"the consumer has authorized in writing (which authorization may be made on the document referred to in clause (i)) the procurement of the report by that person."

The FTC revisited the issue of electronic authorization in the Zalenski letter issued May 24, 2001, after the passage of the federal ESIGN law

The FTC concluded that in view of the ESIGN Act, it was possible to use electronic signatures for authorization for a background check. After reviewing the statues, the FTC stated that:

Therefore, electronic signatures, contracts, or other records relating to transactions are not unenforceable or invalid solely based on their electronic format. Moreover, with respect to the reach of this provision, under Section 106(13) of the ESIGN Act, the term "transaction" is defined as "an action or set of actions relating to the conduct of business, consumer, or commercial affairs between two or more persons . . ." This broad definition of "transaction" appears to include the scenario described in the letter where a business that needs a consumer report on an individual includes in a contract or application form clear authorization by the individual to obtain his or her consumer report. Thus, under the ESIGN Act, a consumer's electronic authorization may not be denied legal effect solely based on its electronic nature.

The FTC also indicated that whether or not the electronic signature is valid depends on the specific facts of each situation. Specifically:

- ✓ The electronic signature must clearly convey the consumer's instructions.
- ✓ The FTC stated that as specified by Section 101(e) of the ESIGN Act, that consumer's electronic authorization "must be in a form that can be retained and retrieved in perceivable form." In other words, there must be a clear and reproducible record showing the electronic consent.

To view the letter, visit: www.ftc.gov/os/statutes/fcra/zalenski.htm.

Best Practices on Electronic Signatures

In legal terms, the concept of authorization or consent means "an agreement to do something" or to "allow something to happen," and made voluntarily with complete knowledge of all relevant facts such as the risks involved or any available alternatives.

Neither ESIGN nor UETA provide any specifically required wording or specifies exact steps or process that automatically validates the electronic signature procedure. However, the laws do provide a framework for the use of electronic signatures and records in government or business transactions. This framework gives employers and screening firm a basis to design legally complaint procedures for electric online signatures. In addition, since some background screening authorizations carry state law requirements, it is arguable that both federal and state rules must be considered.

Based upon a reading of ESIGN and UETA, some of the best practice steps should include provisions such as the following:

- ✓ Notice of and agreement to an electronic transaction.
- ✓ Paper based alternative made available to those who decline the electronic transaction.
- ✓ Method to determine an electronic signature is attributable to a specific person.
- ✓ Method to correct errors before signing.
- ✓ Method for subject to print or store the electronic record.
- ✓ A clear explanation of what is being consented to.
- ✓ An option to discontinue the process at each step and before final agreement.
- ✓ Clear instructions on how to withdraw consent in the future.

If the electronic signature is done by mouse click, a potential issue is created when a past school or employer requests an actual signed document. A screening firm may have to track down the applicant and ask for a written release. Another option is to provide the past employer or school with sufficient assurances that there was an electronic release. However, an organization is not legally required to accept an electronic signature.

New technology however allows a screening firm to capture an actual signature by use of a mouse or other software, making the whole process paperless. If requested, the screening firm can forward an actual although electronically produced signature.

Additional Links

- ✓ Text of UETA: www.law.upenn.edu/library/archives/ulc/fnact99/1990s/ueta99.pdf
- ✓ Test of ESIGN: www.gpo.gov/fdsys/pkg/PLAW-106publ229/html/PLAW-106publ229.htm
- ✓ States that have passed UETA: www.ncsl.org/issues-research/telecom/uniform-electronic-transactions-acts.aspx

Candidates Presenting Their Own Verified Credentials

A new development is the concept of applicants proving their own credentials. A candidate self-credentialing website permits applicants to purchase a "verified" screening report.

One of the first websites to offer this service was MyJobHistory.com – now called MyESRcheck.com. Since the site was introduced, similar services have become available. Large job boards such as Monster.com and Careerbuilder.com also provide such services through partners. The value of such a site is to help employers sort through a sea of resumes and focus on those candidates who are willing to have their qualifications scrutinized.

Even if an employer hires an applicant that has a verification statement from such a website, an employer should still conduct whatever due diligence they normally perform — to take their normal steps to make sure a person is a good fit for the job and organization, including conducting a criminal record check.

Applicant-supplied criminal checks create a number of potential issues. First, the employer should decide where to conduct the search and how extensive it should be, not an applicant. An applicant with a criminal record may well decide to not request a criminal record check for that specific jurisdiction. Second, a criminal search is only good up until the day it is conducted. When an applicant supplies the criminal search, there is no way to know if the data is still current.

One website attempts to remedy that by only making the search available for ninety days. However, that still does not address the issue of applicants providing their own report, creating the potential for an applicant to hide his or her past. Another website provides a so-called "national database" search. However, for the reasons reviewed in that chapter, such a search is only a secondary research tool and not a true criminal search.

There is one additional note of caution— an employer should not place a condition for employment upon the jobseeker to pay for such a report. Such a policy could be construed as discriminatory. In addition, charging an application fee may violate state law. For example, California Labor Code 450 can make it a criminal act to require an application fee.

Looking Toward the Future – Background Screening and the Creation of a Human Capital Database

The ideal situation for an employer would be to have the ability to visit to a website, put in an applicant's name and Social Security number, and instantly get a thumbs up or thumbs down — to hire or not to hire. Such a database does not exist and is not likely to for some time.

Conversely, from the point of view of a job applicant, life would be good if he or she could visit a website, input their unique "profile," and instantly find the perfect job at the right location and salary.

In such a perfect world, where there was perfect information about job opportunities and applicants, employers and employees could find each other instantly. There would be a true labor market, where market forces would operate in such a way to instantly match the right person with right job at the right time, with a minimum of delay or transaction costs. There would essentially be a "just in time" system of employment.

Part of the reason there is not such a labor market in the United States is that markets operate on information. Part of what is lacking in the U.S. is a database of extensive pre-verified applicant information.

Of course, background screening is only one part of such a database. Additional applicant information would be needed, including data as to "job fit." Verification of credentials and information about a criminal record would certainly be a major component of any such database.

The term used to describe this type of applicant data is a Human Capital Database. There are many definitions of "human capital." One definition is:

The set of skills which an employee acquires on the job, through training and experience, and which increase that employee's value in the marketplace.

Additional definitions are provided by John Sumser at www.interbiznet.com/ern/archives/040601.html.

The future of safe hiring may well involve the creation of these large human capital databases, offering the ability to use the information intelligently and fairly. However, all sorts of issues arise from building a human capital database, including how to score, model, profile, and predict without discriminating. Equally important is privacy and the ability of a consumer to fairly access, control, and contest what is in the database. However, for the long run the future appears to be heading towards massive databases to facilitate employment.

Top Ten Trends in Background Checks for 2012

For the past five years, the author has compiled a list featuring emerging and influential trends in employment screening background checks. In 2012, the use of criminal background checks of job applicants by employers coming under greater scrutiny of the U.S. Equal Employment Opportunity Commission (EEOC) topped the list. The list is posted on the author's company web page at www.esrcheck.com/ESR-Top-10-Trends-in-Background-Checks-for-2012.php. Portions of the *2012 Top Ten Trends in Background Checks* are presented below.

Trend Number 1 - Criminal Background Checks of Job Applicants by Employers Coming Under Greater Scrutiny by EEOC

With a recent survey showing nine out of ten employers conduct criminal background checks on some or all job candidates, the Equal Employment Opportunity Commission (EEOC) held a public meeting in July 2011 examining the use of arrest and conviction records by employers for criminal background checks to determine if the practice was an unfair and discriminatory hiring barrier to job seeking ex-offenders. The EEOC's actions, coupled with the growing "Ban the Box" movement seeking to remove the criminal history question from job applications, shows that employer use of criminal records is under fire now more than ever. *(NOTE: Information about the updated EEOC Guidance for criminal background checks passed on April 2012 is available in Chapter 16).*

Trend Number 2 - Credit Report Background Checks of Job Applicants by Employers Increasingly Regulated by State Laws

In recent years, several U.S. states have passed laws regulating the use of employment credit reports of job applicants and current employees that have impacted the way employers conduct background checks. Seven states – California, Connecticut, Hawaii, Illinois, Maryland, Oregon, and Washington – currently have laws that limit the use of credit report checks by employers for employment purposes, with the most recent law, California Assembly Bill 22 (CA AB 22), taking effect January 1, 2012. Other states, and the U.S. Equal Employment Opportunity Commission (EEOC), are considering further restrictions on credit checks by employers. *(NOTE: Information about the credit reports is available in Chapter 17).*

Trend Number 3 - Social Media Background Screening Checks of Job Applicants Becoming More Prevalent and More Controversial

Employers and recruiters have discovered a treasure trove of information about potential job applicants on social media sites such as Facebook, LinkedIn, and Twitter, and so-called 'social media background checks' are becoming more popular and prevalent than ever. However, the use of social media background checks for job applicants has become controversial and can present legal risks. Failure to utilize social media resources can arguably be the basis of a negligent hiring claim if an unfit person was hired for a position where a search of the internet may have raised a "red flag." Conversely, employers face numerous landmines and pitfalls that can include privacy, discrimination, and accuracy issues. Lawsuits and developments in this area will likely be an ongoing topic in 2012. *(NOTE: Information about social media background checks is available in Chapter 19).*

Trend Number 4 - Automation in Employment Background Screening Leads to Both Increased Efficiency and Increased Risks

In recent years, employment background screening has gone from a costly and time consuming task reserved for selected job applicants to an increasingly automated and technology driven business necessity in a global economy where employers expect fast, accurate, and inexpensive results from screening providers. However, both employers and background screeners are finding with increased efficiency comes increased risks, especially when it comes to the use of unfiltered information going directly to employers from criminal database or inaccurate information obtained by "screen scrapping or automated robotic searches." *(NOTE: Information about automation is available in this chapter, Chapter 26).*

Trend Number 5 - Background Screening Accreditation Program Proof of Increased Emphasis on Professionalism in Industry

When the National Association of Professional Background Screeners (NAPBS®) was formed in 2003 as a professional trade association for the background screening industry, the idea of an accreditation process was a central driving force in order to demonstrate that background screening was a professional endeavor. Currently, NAPBS accreditation is quickly becoming a requirement of many employers when considering a background screening provider since it is the only practical means of third party verification of the professionalism and competency of a particular screening firm. *(NOTE: Information about NAPBS Accreditation is available in Chapter 11).*

Trend Number 6 - Diploma Mills Offering Fake Degrees and False Credentials Likely to Increase in Tight Job Market

A 2011 report from Europe's leading background screening firm revealed an astounding 48 percent increase worldwide in the number of known fake diploma mills in the previous year, and the number of what the report describes as "largely online entities whose degrees are worthless due to the lack of valid accreditation and recognition" is likely to increase in the coming year as desperate job applicants knowingly – and unknowingly – do business with companies that offer fake degrees and false credentials for a price. *(NOTE: Information about diploma mills is available in Chapter 18).*

Trend Number 7 - Employment Screening Lawsuits Increase as Attorneys and Consumers Become Familiar with FCRA Laws Regulating Background Checks

Consumers and attorneys are looking more closely at background check reports and laws governing employment screening and filing more lawsuits against employers. On one hand, employers are being sued by victims that alleged the employer failed to perform adequate screening. On the other, employers and background screening firms also face lawsuits from job applicants complaining about the accuracy of background reports or failure to meet the guidelines of the federal Fair Credit Reporting Act (FCRA). In a number of cases, class action suits are being utilized as the vehicle to bring legal actions against employers. *(NOTE: Information about FCRA lawsuits is available in Chapter 3).*

Trend Number 8 - New E-Verify Laws Create Complex Web of Federal and State Rules for Employers

While federal law mandates that federal contractors and subcontractors in all states must use the otherwise voluntary electronic employment eligibility verification system known as E-Verify, several U.S. states – including Alabama, Arizona, California, Georgia, and North Carolina – recently enacted laws mandating the use (or non-use) of E-verify, a free web-based system that allows employers to verify the legal work authorization status of newly hired employees, creating a complex and confusing web of laws and regulations. *(NOTE: Information about E-Verify is available in Chapter 29).*

Trend Number 9 - Offshoring Personally Identifiable Information Outside of US Increases Concern Over Privacy and Identity Theft

A new California law that took effect January 1, 2012 – Senate Bill 909 (SB 909) – appears to be one of the first in the nation that addresses the growing concerns over the controversial practice of "offshoring" personally identifiable information (PII) collected during background checks of job applicants by sending the data outside of United States and its territories and beyond the protection of U.S. privacy and identity theft laws. *(NOTE: Information about offshoring is available in Chapters 2 and 28).*

Trend Number 10 - Self Background Checks Proactively Conducted by Job Seekers to Help Verify Accuracy of their Public Information

If jobseekers want to get hired for a job these days, they will probably have to undergo a background check. And if they have to undergo a background check, it would be in their best interest to make sure the information found on the background check is accurate, up-to-date, and complete. As a result, some jobseekers are taking matters in their own hands by proactively conducting "self" background checks on themselves to verify the accuracy of their public information. *(NOTE: Information about self background checks is available in Chapter 30).*

Useful Human Resource Sites for Employers

The websites listed below are extremely useful for employers, and will link to other websites.

✓ **HR.com**— Aims to bring together experts and resources as a one-stop site for all Human Resources needs. www.HR.com

✓ **SHRM**— The Society for Human Resource Management's home page. www.shrm.org

✓ **Workforce Online Magazine**—HR Trends and Tools for Business Results. www.workforce.com

✓ **HR Guide**— A selection of resources, separated into categories, including an HR guide to numerous websites as well as HR software, consultants, and resources. www.hr-guide.com

Screening Temps, Vendors, Consultants, Independent Contractors & Volunteers

Inside This Chapter:

- ✓ Screening Essential Non-Employees

- ✓ The Duty of Due Diligence

- ✓ Screening and Special Issues Concerning Independent Contractors

- ✓ Screening Staffing Firms and Temporary Workers

- ✓ Screening Volunteers

- ✓ Screening Home Workers

Screening Essential Non-Employees

Up to this point, *The Safe Hiring Manual* has emphasized that when hiring employees, employers are sitting ducks for expensive litigation, workplace violence, negative national publicity, and economic loss if they do not take measures to conduct pre-employment screening and exercise due diligence in hiring.

However, many employers do not realize they potentially face the same exposure from vendors, independent contractors, or temporary employees from staffing vendors. Employers' risk management controls often do not take into account the "need to know" about these workers who are not on their payroll but are on their premises, with access to computer systems, clients, co-workers, and assets.

Non-employees are typically described as a contingent workforce that is not on the businesses' payroll, and do not receive a W-2 form. A contingent worker may be engaged for particular project or for a specific time period. A contingent worker may be paid by a third party agency, such as a staffing firm, a Professional Employer Organization (PEO), or firms that specialize in managing contingent workers. A contingent worker can also be paid directly by the business if they are a consultant or independent contractor; but instead of being paid with a paycheck resulting in a W-2 at the end of the year, the worker receives a 1099 form and no benefits (vacation, medical, sick pay, etc.).

Examples of a contingent worker are:

- ✓ A temporary worker supplied by a staffing firm for a limited time or project and paid by the staffing firm.
- ✓ A worker sent on a "temp to perm" basis where the worker starts as a temporary worker, and after a specified period of time, hours, or a fee, can be converted to employee status.
- ✓ A full time worker on the payroll of PEO or "leased" to a business through a staffing agency where they are on the payroll of the third party vendor.
- ✓ A "freelancer" or independent contractor hired for a period or job that is paid by the employer for services but is not considered an employee.

In the situations where the worker is paid by a third party agency, but the worker is under the direction or control of the business, a situation can arise called "co-employment." Co-employment means there are two different entities (the staffing vendor and the workplace) with control over a worker. Both organizations have legal rights, duties, and risks with respect to the worker. Although the typical situation involves a worker that is on the business worksite, a contingent worker can create liability for remote job assignments.

A vendor, by comparison, is an independent business that provides services to another business. When vendors have direct physical contact with a business (by coming on site), due diligence becomes an issue.

The Duty of Due Diligence

The law is absolutely clear if a non-employee working on behalf of a business harms a member of the public or a co-worker, the business can be just as liable as if the person were on the business' payroll. All of the rules of due diligence discussed in Chapter 1 apply with equal force to vendors, temporary workers, or independent contractors. A business can be liable if, in the exercise of reasonable care, the business should have known that a vendor, temporary worker, or independent contractor was dangerous, unqualified, or otherwise unfit for employment. An employer has an absolute obligation to exercise due diligence not only in whom they hire on payroll, but in whom they allow on premises to perform work. (See e.g. a compilation of cases throughout the U.S. annotated in 78 ALR3d 910).

In addition, many employers have found out the hard way that using unscreened workers from a vendor or staffing firm or hired as an independent contractor can also cause damage. When an employer is the victim of theft, embezzlement, or resume fraud, the harm is just as bad regardless of whether the worker is on their payroll or someone else's payroll. No employer would dream of walking down the street and handing the keys to the business to a total stranger, yet many businesses across America essentially do exactly that every day when engaging the services of vendors and temporary workers.

For example, firms routinely hire night time janitorial services without appropriate due diligence. The fast food industry routinely hires suppliers and service firms that come into their restaurants to clean or deliver supplies. Without knowing who has the keys to facilities, an employer is giving total strangers unfettered access to his or her business — and is totally exposed to the risk of theft of property, trade secrets, or damages.

Employers do have challenges in ensuring they have exercised due diligence regarding contingent workers, vendors, and independent contractors. The practical issue is fortunately, there are a number of cost-effective avenues available. For example, employers can insist in any contract for any service that any time a worker comes on premises, that worker has been the subject of a background screening. This has become a practice gaining widespread acceptance in American businesses. An employer must have a hard and fast rule — no worker supplied by a third party is allowed to work unless the worker has a background check.

The following steps can help in administering the process:

- ✓ Make it clear to all service providers and independent contractors that the business has a policy of maintaining a safe and qualified workforce, the company has a background checking policy for its own employees, and the same policies apply to all workers that perform work for the company, regardless of their status as a contingent worker, independent contractor, or vendor.
- ✓ Subject independent contractors to the same screening and safe hiring practices as would be done with a W-2 employee. Some employers may wish to alter the consent form in order to clarify that the individual being screened is an independent contractor, and the screening procedure does not alter the nature of the relationship.
- ✓ When using a temporary worker from a staffing firm, require the staffing agency or Professional Employer Organization (PEO) to conduct a background check. As an extra precaution, an employer can request that the FCRA release extend to the employer's workplace. Under the FCRA, as long as the applicant consents to this, it is perfectly acceptable for both the staffing firm and the employer of the workplace to review the background report. Again, ensure that there is language in the FCRA release to the effect that the business where the consumer is performing the assignment can review a background report, and that does not create an employment relationship.
- ✓ A vendor must certify there has been a background check that is acceptable under the employer's criteria. If there is a question about the suitability of a particular worker, a business is within its rights to require a review of the background report to ensure that it meets the business policy. Again, as long as there is consent, under the doctrine of "co-employment," a business would have a "permissible purpose" under the FCRA to do such a review without altering the fact that the contingent worker is on the payroll of the third party staffing vendor.
- ✓ The staffing vendor must provide the business with the name and identity of the firm performing the background check and a statement that the firm performing the background checks is experienced and suitable for the assignment. A good practice is to have the same firm that does the background checks for the business also perform the vendor's background checks. Another best practice is to ensure that any provider of background screening service is a member of and even accredited by the National Association of Profession Background Screeners (NAPBS). See Chapter 11.
- ✓ For extra precaution, require the vendor to provide the employer with a "Certification of Compliance." This certification should indicate the following:
  - The name, identity, and qualifications of the firm that provided the vendor's background checks.
  - A statement that vendor has advised their background service of the criteria required.
  - Only workers who pass the background check are allowed on your premises.
  - In the event there is something negative in the worker's background, the vendor has thoroughly investigated the issue and has determined the matter does not otherwise disqualify the worker from going onto your premises.

- In the event there is negative material, then the business may ask to review it as well to determine if the worker meets the business's criteria. The best practice is to require the vendor to have the worker sign a release permitting that process.

Businesses may be concerned if these policies are illegal and will make it more difficult to find vendors and suppliers of services. The answer is a resounding NO to both concerns. An employer has an absolute right to exercise, and even the obligation, to follow the same due diligence in selecting workers and vendors that they would use in selecting their own employees. As long as the screening requirements are fair, non-discriminatory, and validly job-related, there is no legal reason why a business cannot protect itself.

 Employers need to be careful to make sure the vendor, staffing firm, or PEO does more than go through the motions. Reports must be ordered, tracked, documented. The employer must require that the vendor certify that they have reviewed the screening reports looking for any red flags and they took appropriate steps. Although this may seem obvious, it is worth clarifying who has the responsibility to review background reports and determine eligibility to work.

In this way, staffing vendors and suppliers also demonstrate that safe hiring and due diligence are critical parts of their business as well as their commitment to supplying quality workers. Any vendor not willing to engage in pre-employment screening is not likely to be a good choice anyway. Although there may be a slight increase to the vendor in terms of expenses, a vendor should be willing to pay necessary costs to obtain good workers and to satisfy the needs of the employer-clients.

The bottom line — there is no reason for employers not to require vendors and independent contractors undergo background checks.

 The new EEOC Guidance issued April 25, 2012 on the use of criminal records can potentially impact staffing vendors as well. Staffing vendors may want to review Chapter 16 to become familiar with the EOCC Guidance in order to take appropriate measures.

Screening and Special Issues Concerning Independent Contractors

The law is clear that classifying a worker as an independent contractor does not shield a business from liability if it fails to exercise due diligence in the selection process.

When reviewing issues related to independent contractor's classification, there are two considerations:

1. Is the worker even an independent contractor? Misclassifying a worker as an independent contractor when in fact they should be an employee on payroll creates a large potential liability.
2. Even if a worker is truly an independent contractor under various tests, it is still a best practice to treat them as though the Fair Credit Reporting Act (FCRA) applies.

In addition to # 2 above, the Federal Trade Commission (FTC) has suggested that the FCRA applies to situation where a consumer has an employment-like relationship regardless of the label. FTC staff-issued letters of opinion following the 1997 amendment to the FCRA — although the letters do not have the force of law — are considered highly persuasive. In the Mr. Herman L. Allison letter dated February 23, 1998, the FTC staff was asked if the FCRA rules concerning disclosures and releases applied in the case of a certain trucking company who employed independent owner-operators. The truck drivers were not on the payroll as employees, but "owned and operated their own vehicles."

The FTC rejected the position that there was not an employment relationship. The FTC cited a Fourth Circuit Court of Appeals case [*Hoke v. Retail Credit Corporation,* 521 F.2d 1079, 1082 (4th Cir. 1975), *cert. denied,* 423 U.S. 1087 (1976)] that the broad purposes of the FCRA required that "employment" not be strictly defined in traditional terms, but would include independent contractor relationships. As a result, the application of the FCRA does not depend upon whether a worker receives a W-2 tax form as an employee or a 1099 as an independent contractor. The essential factor is the employment-like nature of the relationship. Keep in mind, if an employer has classified a worker as an independent contractor, it is critical to adjust the background screening consent form to take out any reference to employment in order to not change the independent contractor status. An employer can utilize wording referring to an "engagement" instead.

A Different Point of View

A Magistrate Judge in a federal district court case for the Eastern District of Wisconsin took a different approach and rejected the FTC position. In *Lamson vs. EMS Energy Marketing Service, Inc.*, the plaintiff was hired for a sales position as an independent contractor according to the agreement between the parties. As a result of a background report, the plaintiff was terminated. He filed a lawsuit on the basis that the FCRA required that he receive a notice of pre-adverse action and a statement of his rights. The plaintiff argued that regardless of the agreement he signed, he in fact had the legal status of an employee, because he was hired to sell one product and was under the control of the company. He argued that even if he was an independent contractor, the FCRA still applied. In a decision that did not appear to be very persuasive, a magistrate judge applied a common law test and determined that the plaintiff was not misclassified. The magistrate judge then additionally held that the FCRA, through a literal reading, applied to employees and not independent contractors.

Employers should be hesitant to read too much into this one case. First, it was just one case from one district court, and it was only from a magistrate judge, who is not a judge appointed by the President but a person hired by the local court. There are no other cases cited for the proposition that the FCRA does not apply to independent contractors. Also the issue was the plaintiff's claim that his rights were violated. It has no bearing on claims that may be brought for negligent hiring if an independent contractor harms a third party. In addition, since this appears to be an "unpublished" case in terms of being included in the official report of cases for the federal district courts, it carries much less authority than a published case. Employers would be well advised to continue to apply the FCRA to independent contractors. Unless and until there are other opinions on the subject, the magistrate's opinion appears to be an "outlier" that would be risky to follow.

See: www.employerlawreport.com/uploads/file/Lamson.pdf.

Avoiding the Trap of Misclassifying of Workers

There are obvious financial and tax advantages to classifying home workers as independent contractors instead of employees. This situation even exists in the background screening industry, as covered in Chapter 12 concerning the use of at-home operators.

By classifying a worker as an independent contractor, an employer avoids the payroll costs associated with employees, such as paying workers' compensation insurance premiums, unemployment insurance, withholding taxes, or paying the employer share of payroll taxes. An employer can also save money by not paying benefits, such as paid holidays, vacation, health, or retirement. In addition, firms seek to achieve economic savings by having a flexible workforce.

The issue is whether these so-called "independent" workers are really that independent. In reality, an independent contractor may only be providing services to just one firm. An independent contractor, such as an at-home worker, typically does not have business cards, their own insurance, yellow page ads, a business license, or any of the other attributes of a true independent business.

Simply put, the advantages enjoyed by a business in classifying a worker as an independent contractor are **disadvantages** for the Internal Revenue Services (IRS) and state agencies that administer tax collection programs. The IRS has an interest in businesses putting workers on payroll to better ensure the collection and withholding of payroll taxes. States want employers to pay workers' compensation premiums and unemployment insurance. As a result, the IRS and the states have a big stake in ensuring that businesses do not **misclassify** a worker as an "independent contractor" when in fact they should be on payroll.

The IRS and state agencies have the authority, which they do exercise, to conduct extensive audits of a business to determine if the classification was correct. If the IRS or state agencies determine that workers should have been classified as employees, then the business can be subject to fines, penalties, back taxes, and lawyer's fees.

How does the independent contractor or at-home worker trigger an employer being the subject of an IRS or state audit? There are a number of ways:

- ✓ The worker gets injured and files for workers' compensation benefits. The business claims that the worker was in fact an independent contractor. At that point, the claim can trigger an audit of all business practices related to independent contractors. Failure to have workers' compensation in place is unlawful and has extremely serious consequences for businesses.
- ✓ An at-home worker decides to resign, files for unemployment insurance benefits, and lists the firm as the last employer. When the state shows no record of employer contributions, an audit may be triggered.
- ✓ An at-home worker files a discrimination claim.
- ✓ An at-home worker feels they are doing the same work as employees but without the benefits, and they file a claim or even a lawsuit for benefits. This happened to Microsoft, when so-called independent contractors sued because they were doing the same work as employees, but not getting benefits or stock options.

Thus, if the relationship goes sour for any reason, a business is essentially at the mercy of their former worker who can trigger a very expensive audit that can have significant financial repercussions.

The IRS formerly used what was known as the "20 Factor Test" as part of its audit. However, the IRS recently consolidated the twenty factors into eleven main tests and organized them into three main groups. Per the IRS web page:

"Facts that provide evidence of the degree of control and independence fall into three categories:

1. **Behavioral:** Does the company control or have the right to control what the worker does and how the worker does his or her job?

2. **Financial:** Are the business aspects of the worker's job controlled by the payer? (these include things like how worker is paid, whether expenses are reimbursed, who provides tools/supplies, etc.)

3. **Type of Relationship:** Are there written contracts or employee type benefits (i.e. pension plan, insurance, vacation pay, etc.)? Will the relationship continue and is the work performed a key aspect of the business?"

See www.irs.gov/businesses/small/article/0,,id=99921,00.html.

A number of jurisdictions, courts, and state agencies often use variations of the IRS test or various other tests. When applying the various tests, there are three things to keep in mind:

1. First, the most important consideration is whether the at-home worker is truly an "independent" person running their own business or just an employee in disguise. The courts focus on the degree of control. For a worker to be classified as an independent contractor, he or she must be both physically and economically autonomous of the employer.

2. The second consideration is that the independent contractor test is not a mechanical application of the rules— some employers make the mistake of reviewing the list as a scorecard and coming to the wrong conclusion. It can be extremely difficult to predict what the IRS or state will conclude in any given situation. The law of proper

classification of workers is very complex and normally requires the assistance of a lawyer, Human Resources consultant, or CPA.

3. Finally it is irrelevant what the parties chose to call themselves. Courts, the IRS, and state agencies are not influenced at all by a written piece of paper that some worker signed alleging they are independent.

What happens if the audit or test results find a business was essentially "cheating" by misclassifying workers as independent contractors instead of employees? The consequences can be substantial. The IRS or state may flag the business for an audit of how it classifies all of its independent contractors. The auditing process can be extremely time consuming and expensive. Some employers have had the experience of government auditors literally setting up shop for extensive periods of time in their offices during the auditing process. If the audit reveals that there were others who were wrongly classified, the financial consequence could be enormous. A firm can potentially face:

✓ Liability for all federal and state payroll taxes that should have been paid for all misclassified workers.

✓ Interest, fines and penalties to the IRS or state. Penalties can be substantial.

✓ Costs, and attorney's fees, and compensatory and punitive damages if litigation is involved.

✓ Benefits the workers would have received if classified as employees, including vacation, health, paid holidays and retirement.

✓ Overtime pay under the Fair Labor Standards Act and comparable state laws if the hours he or she provided to the contracting party in the past exceeded the standard workweek.

✓ Unemployment claims.

✓ Extending any stock option plan the worker would have had if they were properly treated as employees.

✓ Liability and potential penalties for not paying into state workers compensation fund.

The bottom line is that an employer attempting to justify classifying an at-home worker as an independent contractor faces a substantial uphill challenge and considerable risks.

Screening Staffing Firms and Temporary Workers

An area where employers can be blindsided is when working with temporary ("temp") or staffing agencies. Employers would not intentionally bring people on the premises with criminal records, unsuitable for a particular job. Yet employers consistently hire temporary workers and independent contractors from staffing agencies with no idea as to the background or qualifications of those hired. Given the sensitive information found on business computer systems, even one bad temp could do substantial damage. Even though workers may be on the payroll of a staffing agency, since the workers perform duties at an employer's place of business, the employer can be liable for harm a worker causes.

The unfortunate reality is many staffing firms simply do not routinely perform due diligence checks before supplying workers. That reluctance is for two reasons. First, staffing firms are exceptionally cost conscious and given the large volume of workers they handle, the cost of background checks, such as criminal checks, can have a significant impact on their bottom line. Second, staffing firms must work on an extremely tight time line. Staffing firms need to place workers as soon as possible. Every hour of delay is lost revenue to a staffing firm. In addition, if a potential new worker is told to wait a day or two for a background check, that worker may go down the street to another staffing firm.

Staffing firms often advertise that they carefully "screen" all applicants but without stating the extent or nature of the screening. A business utilizing staffing services needs to be very specific when asking a staffing firm exactly what screening is done. Unless the staffing firm specifically tells the employer a criminal check is being done, an employer should assume that no criminal check is being conducted. An employer is well advised to require some of the steps suggested in the previous pages in order to confirm exactly what is being done in terms of a criminal background check. Issues regarding screening and criteria should be specifically addressed in any contract between a business and the staffing vendor.

A business needs to carefully document what a staffing firm is doing because employers can have a "co-employment relationship" with temporary workers. Co-employment has been defined as a legal relationship in which more than one employer has legal rights and obligations with respect to the same employee or group of employees. Both the Internal Revenue Service and various courts have found that a temporary worker of a supplier working at the customer's work site — even though paid and treated as an employee of the supplier — may still be considered an employee of both the supplier and the customer for legal purposes. The employer sets the specific duties, the duration of the assignment, and the level and types of skills required even though the staffing firm is responsible for recruitment, placement, and pay rates.

AUTHOR TIP

It's a sobering thought, but every time a recruiting professional makes a placement, there is the possibility that new hire can put them out of business.

Why? Because if a dangerous, unqualified, unfit, or dishonest candidate is placed in a job and harm occurs, a staffing vendor faces the possibility of a lawsuit. Perhaps just as important, a bad placement can result in loss of business and damage to a professional reputation that may have been years in the making.

If it gets to the point of a lawsuit, the heart of the staffing professional may sink when those dreaded words echo across the courtroom: "Ladies and Gentleman of the Jury." In a lawsuit, a staffing professional would need to show, for example, whether credentials and education were verified, whether past employment was checked, and whether a criminal background check was done.

A staffing professional accused of negligence in making a placement can be sued by a number of parties, including the business entity that relied upon the professional judgment of the recruiter or staffing firm. Certainly, a co-worker or member of the public who was injured by the bad hire can sue for damages. The worst case scenario would be that the bad hire resulted in the death of a fellow worker, and the victim's family is suing for wrongful death. This is just what happened in a highly publicized case in California. A 28-year-old female winery worker was stabbed to death by a co-worker who was a convicted murderer and had been placed at the winery by a temp agency. The agency did NOT conduct a background check. The jury awarded the family $5.5 million.

If a recruiter is sued, it may well be an uphill battle to win in court. The jury will hear evidence that the staffing vendor recruited, recommended, or placed the offender. In most cases, the staffing professional probably makes representations about the quality of their services. The staffing professional's website and sales literature may suggest that they provide only the best candidates who are carefully screened. However, in the world of recruiting, "screening" really only means that resumes have been reviewed to determine a good fit for the job opening as opposed to "background screening" for criminal records and verification of facts represented on the resume.

The employer, hoping to lay the blame onto someone else, will of course claim that they relied upon the professional abilities of the staffing professional to send them qualified and safe candidates. There would likely be evidence that the recruiting or staffing firm made a fee on the placement. In the end, the attorney for the injured or deceased employee would ask jury members, "Didn't the staffing professional have not only the resources and opportunity, but also the duty to conduct employee screening on the potential employee before approving their introduction into the workplace?"

The bottom line is that due diligence and background checks go to the very integrity of the product being sold by recruiting and staffing professionals – workers who are qualified and fit for the job. If a staffing firm does not exercise due diligence, it is like playing Russian Roulette with each candidate that is sent out. Which one of these candidates will land you in court or on the front page of the newspaper? Staffing and search professionals have traditionally focused on Sourcing and Sales. Staffing professionals can protect their own business, their clients, and the public by shifting their focus from just Sourcing and Sales to Sourcing, Verifying, and Sales.

What Can Staffing Companies Do?

Staffing vendors and third party recruiters may want to consider the following best practices:

- ✓ Carefully consider the cost of doing background checks versus the risk of not performing them. Preventing even one embezzler or violent offender from being sent to a client can be worth the cost in the long run in terms of avoiding litigation, lost clients, and a loss of professional reputation.
- ✓ Carefully review any marketing materials, representations on your website, and sales presentation to ensure that clients are accurately informed about your practices. Do not imply that your firm "carefully screens" or only "sends the best" if in fact you are not doing adequate background checks.
- ✓ Be careful doing in-house criminal record checks. That can trigger application of the FCRA.
- ✓ Be careful of using commercial low-cost databases for all of the reason described Chapter 15. The use of databases may also trigger the FCRA.
- ✓ Utilize the Safe Hiring Program outlined in this book and document all steps taken.
- ✓ Make sure that your contracts with clients accurately describe what, if any, background checks you will be doing. Consider:
  - Depth and level of screening.
  - Who reviews reports, what criteria is used, and who makes decisions on eligibility.
  - Who selects the screening firms?
  - Adequacy of consent issue – the consent form needs to release information to both the staffing firm and employer where the worker may be sent.

AUTHOR TIP Where there is going to be a joint use of the report by both staffing vendor and the business where the work is to be performed, it is important for purposes of the Fair Credit Reporting Act (FCRA) to ensure that only individuals with permissible purpose are reviewing a report and that the consumer has consented. Here is an example of language for that issue:

> *I agree, authorize, and consent to the release and disclosure of any and all information including but not limited to the above to [COMPANY] and to [CRA], and to a related third party entity only where I am being considered for direct or temporary Engagement with or by them. In no event does consideration for Engagement create an employment relationship.*

The last sentence is important in order to prevent any confusion about who the consumer is working for and to clarify that by viewing the report, the business where the consumer is actually providing service does not become the employer.

Court Rules Staffing Firm that Outsources Background Checks Cannot be Sued under FCRA

A staffing firm that places individuals in temporary positions with independent employers cannot be sued under the federal Fair Credit Reporting Act (FCRA) when a background check firm hired by the staffing firm delivers a background check report that is inaccurate or erroneous.

In a case from the United States District Court for the Eastern District of Tennessee, a staffing firm retained an employment screening firm to provide a background check report. The background check report indicated that the plaintiff had been convicted of a felony and misdemeanor, had served jail item, was serving probation, and had made restitution for theft and assault.

According to the lawsuit, the problem with the background check report was that it was false and erroneous. As a result, the plaintiff lost an opportunity to become a permanent employee at the location where she was assigned and was also terminated from working for the staffing firm.

Among other rulings, the Court dismissed the allegations that the staffing firm violated the FCRA for the simple reason that when a staffing firm hires a background check firm (CRA), the staffing firm is not considered to be a Consumer Reporting Agency (CRA) under federal law. In this case, the staffing firm outsourced that function to a background check firm. The Court held that the staffing firm clearly did not qualify as a CRA because it was not engaged in conducting background checks as defined by the FCRA.

However, this does not mean that staffing firms are always in the clear. Although not alleged in this case, a staffing firm could still potentially be the subject of litigation for "negligent" selection of a background screening firm if a consumer can show that the staffing firm fell below an acceptable standard of care in choosing a background screening firm, and that firm produced an inaccurate background check report.

See: http://dockets.justia.com/docket/tennessee/tnedce/3:2010cv00280/57912/

Another court came to a different conclusion. In *Adams v. National Engineering Svc Corp, et al* U.S. district Court, District of Connecticut, a staffing firm that outsourced background checks was also sued, as was a background firm. In that case, there were allegations of incorrect criminal records leading to lost job opportunities. The court held that the staffing firm was a Consumer Reporting Agency and could be sued for FCRA violations. The ruling has been citified for being superficial, and the case resulted in a jury verdict in favor of both the staffing agency and the background firm.

One area where an employment agency can assemble and evaluate consumer information is calling past employers for a reference check. Staffing firm very often do not want to outsource calling past employers because it is an opportunity to not only obtain information, but also for prospecting for new business as well.

FCRA Section 603(o) provides an exemption for communications that would otherwise be an investigative consumer report when past employment reference check are made by a firm that is regularity engaged in "procuring an opportunity for a natural person to work for the employer." However, to qualify for this exception, an employment agency must engage in additional steps. First, the consumer must consent in writing. (A consumer can give a verbal consent initially but it must be followed up with a written consent within three days.)

In addition, the FCRA provides that the staffing agency must notify the consumer in writing of their right to have disclosure of what the staffing firm learns. If the consumer makes that request, the staffing firm must respond in five days and provide that nature and substance of the information, except that it does not need to reveal the source. The staffing firm discloses in writing to the consumer who is the subject of the communication, no later than 5 business days after receiving any request from the consumer for such disclosure, the nature and substance of all information in the consumer's file at the time of the request, except that the sources of any information that is acquired solely for use in making the communication and is actually used for no other purpose, need not be disclosed other than under appropriate discovery procedures in any court of competent jurisdiction in which an action is brought;

and any information obtained can only be for the purposes of employment and the staffing firm cannot use the information in violation of any state of federal discrimination law.

As a result, staffing vendors should ensure that have procedures in place to comply with the FCRA rule.

However, if a staffing firm performs any other types of checks, such as accessing criminal records, then the staffing firm would be a Consumer Reporting Agency, and have all of the duties and obligations required under the FCRA.

AUTHOR TIP The most critical point for a staffing firm is to not simply go through the motions when doing a background check. A background screening veteran tells the story of an employer that utilized a temporary worker from a staffing firm following what the employer thought was a successful background check. Six months later, the employer decided to make the worker a permanent employee and conducted their own background check only to discover a very serious criminal conviction that the staffing firm failed to mention. When confronted with the issue, the staffing firms said, "We were told to do background check, but no one ever told us to read it."

The walkaway point – a staffing firm or business cannot simply go through the motions. A well thought out program needs to be in place for everyone's protection.

Screening Volunteers

Unfortunately in today's world, the fact remains that sex offenders and deviants exploit volunteer, youth, and faith-based organizations to gain access to potential victims. Doing background checks help protect children and the vulnerable from criminals. The good news is over the past few years, there has been a substantial increase in volunteer groups, youth organizations, and churches performing background checks. Checks for criminal records have become standard procedures for organizations like the Little League or Scouts. The increased emphasis on these checks has been fueled by numerous news stories and lawsuits about children being the victim of criminal conduct, especially sexual abuse. The whole issue of exploitation of children received national attention in 2011 with the allegations of sexual abuse inside athletic facilities at Penn State.

There are numerous organizations involved with helping youth. These organizations rely in large part on volunteers in addition to paid staff, who will have extensive contacts with young people in a variety of situations. These can include:

- ✓ Faith-based organizations.
- ✓ Youth Sports Leagues (Little League, youth soccer, etc.).
- ✓ Youth organization's (Boy Scouts and Girl Scouts or Big Brothers and Big Sisters).
- ✓ Volunteer groups that work with youth at risk.
- ✓ Sporting associations with youth training.
- ✓ Camps and other similar organizations designed for children.

Sexual predators utilize the opportunity to volunteer in these groups to gain access to children to commit sexual crimes. Although "stranger abduction" most often makes the news, the most prevalent form of child sexual abuse is actually perpetrated by someone who knows the child. A predator attempts to exploit a position of trust to not only "groom" a child for sexual abuse in a way that manipulates the child into not telling anyone about it, but to also insulate himself or herself from apprehension by ingratiating themselves inside of the organization so that responsible adults have a hard time believing anything like that could happen. The big problem is that an abuser in a youth organization may appear on the surface to be a wonderful asset. To gain access to the child, the abuser must gain the trust of both the organization and the victim. The situation is aggravated because parents and children believe that they are in a safe environment designed for children, which can lead to a false sense of security. Many organizations have difficulty believing that such a thing could happen in their group and even when a molester is revealed, organization leaders or other adults may have difficulty believing the child.

A predator intent on grooming a child will pick their victim very carefully. Although there is not one single profile of a potential victim, there are common traits. A predator is looking for vulnerabilities, such as a child who is a loner, has self-esteem or confidence issues, has been abused previously, is emotionally needy, or comes from a family where there is domestic conflict or parental neglect. As the groomer builds trust, he or she (and yes, there are women offenders) will introduce physical contact into the relationship and will push the boundaries towards sexual acts. The groomer will attempt to maintain control over the relationship in a number of ways, including guilt, threats of what will happen if the secret is revealed, or threatening the child with the loss of the relationship.

AUTHOR TIP — There are a number of articles and studies available on the internet that review how predators work and the "grooming" process in detail. According to one well-known expert, Forensic psychiatrist Dr. Michael Welner, **"grooming"** is a process consisting of six stages where a sex offender draws a victim into a relationship that becomes shrouded in secrecy and leads to sexual molestation. To learn more, read the article *'Child Sexual Abuse: 6 Stages of Grooming'* at www.oprah.com/oprahshow/Child-Sexual-Abuse-6-Stages-of-Grooming#ixzz21lJ3BOD6.

Of course, the long term harm to a child that is victimized by sexual abuse is incalculable. In addition, the efforts of organizations that are dedicated to helping children can be undermined by lawsuits, negative publicity, and a crisis of confidence from parents, contributors, and other stakeholders that cannot understand how an organization designed to support children could have left them unprotected.

A common observation by experts in this field is that child molesters are looking for "soft targets," in the form of organizations that have lower barriers to entry, less supervision, and less attention to the problem. A molester may avoid groups that take precautions such as a careful volunteer selection process, establishment of clear rules and boundaries (such as no child is ever alone with an adult), or training volunteers and children to recognize signs of improper behavior.

To assist youth-serving organizations in dealing with this critical issue and to adopt policies and procedures to safeguard children, the **Centers for Disease Control and Prevention (CDC)** has developed a guide that identifies six key components of child sexual abuse prevention for organizations. It also references a number of excellent resources. The publication is *Preventing Child Sexual Abuse Within Youth-serving Organizations: Getting Started on Policies and Procedures* and is available at www.cdc.gov/violenceprevention/pdf/PreventingChildSexualAbuse-a.pdf#page=1.

The Guide identifies these six areas where youth organizations need to focus energy:

1. Screening and selecting employees and volunteers
2. Guidelines on interactions between individuals
3. Monitoring behavior
4. Ensuring safe environments
5. Responding to inappropriate behavior, breaches in policy, and allegations and suspicions of child sexual abuse
6. Training about child sexual abuse prevention

> **AUTHOR TIP** Training is a key element of any Safe Environment program by training adults who interact with children, youths, and elders how to recognize, report, and prevent abuse. It is essential for volunteers and organizational leaders as well as employees that work with children. Although everyone has an ethical responsibility to prevent child abuse and protect children, certain professionals are mandatory reporters and are legally required to report child abuse and neglect, and failure to report is a crime in many states. In addition, another key part of a training program is to train children as well on such topics as appropriate boundaries and what to do if they feel something inappropriate is happening. A leading national firm in this area is Shield the Vulnerable by LawRoom. See www.shieldthevulnerable.org.

Under screening and selecting employees and volunteers, the Guide examines a number of options including education about the organization and its policies, written applications, personal interviews, reference checks, and background checks.

The following text is taken from pages 7 and 8 of the CDC's *Preventing Child Sexual Abuse Within Youth-serving Organizations: Getting Started on Policies and Procedure.*

Criminal Background Checks

Criminal background checks are an important tool in screening and selection. However, they have limitations. Criminal background checks will not identify most sexual offenders because most have not been caught. When this report was published, an efficient, effective, and affordable national background screening system was not available.

- Use background checks as one part of child sexual abuse prevention efforts. Using back-ground checks alone may give your organization a false sense of security.
- Save time and resources by delaying criminal background checks until the end of the screening and selection process. Applicants who do not make it through the written applications, personal interviews, and reference checks will not need a criminal background check.
- Obtain permission from applicants before beginning a criminal background check.
- Determine the type and level of check required for each applicant. Types of checks include name, fingerprint, sex offender registries, and social security number. Checks may be implemented at county, state, and national levels. Records are not always linked or comprehensive, so a thorough search may be needed to address concerns about an applicant. For example, if an applicant has moved frequently, checks in multiple states may be necessary.
- Plan for the time and financial resources needed to conduct background checks.
- Decide which offenses to examine in the background checks and which offenses will dis-qualify applicants. For child sexual abuse, absolute disqualifiers include violent behavior and child sexual abuse perpetration history. Depending on the risk of the situation or the mission of your organization, drug and driving offenses may also be disqualifiers. Arrest data are not grounds for disqualification; only offenses resulting in convictions may be used.
- Develop procedures to keep the results of criminal background checks confidential. Select a secure storage location and limit access to the files.
- Ensure that your organization's process for conducting criminal background checks is legally sound. Consult county, state, and national laws and regulations, as well as your organization's attorney and insurance company, as needed.

The critical point is that background checks are a powerful tool when used with a number of other approaches to protect children, but alone will not guarantee the safety of children. Just having a background check program shows an organization is not a soft target. Statistics do seem to show that many child predators have never been caught and therefore would not have a criminal record. However, a background check program is a critical part of an overall due diligence program in conjunction with a host of other tools to discover molesters looking for easy opportunities.

AAU Implements Background Check Program for Staff & Volunteers to Ensure Safety of Youth Athletes

In June 2012, the national Amateur Athletic Union (AAU) released a comprehensive report from two independent task forces – *'Recommendations to the Amateur Athletic Union from the Youth Protections and Adult/Volunteer Screening Task Forces'* – and announced actions to implement steps to protect the wellbeing of hundreds of thousands of young athletes that include requiring that all adults involved in AAU activities – including coaches, staff, and volunteers – undergo detailed background checks.

The report released by the AAU – one of the largest non-profit volunteer sports organizations in the United States – also calls for adopting clear policies and procedures designed to ensure that young athletes are never left alone with individual adults and requiring all AAU volunteers and staff to report any incidents of suspected child abuse to law enforcement and AAU officials. In the report, the task forces – the Youth Protection Task Force and the Adult/Volunteer Screening Task Force – were made up of nationally recognized experts in child protection and law enforcement and offered 42 recommendations for changes in AAU policies, procedures, and protocols that covered six broad subject areas: culture, protocols, screening, participation, training, and reporting:

✓ **Culture:** The AAU should establish and foster a culture that clearly and explicitly makes child protection an overarching value and priority. This includes requiring all adult volunteers, staff, parents, and other youth to report questionable behavior.

✓ **Protocols:** The AAU should adopt clear policies, procedures, and protocols to protect children from abuse and exploitation to the fullest extent possible, including policies to prevent adults from being alone with children and eliminating other opportunities for abuse to occur.

✓ **Screening:** The AAU should implement significant initial and ongoing screening procedures for all adults who participate in AAU activities to help identify and exclude individuals who may pose a threat to youth participants.

✓ **Participation:** Anyone who is prohibited from participating in an organization that serves youth or who violates the AAU's child protection policies should be barred from participating in AAU activities, even if they have not been convicted of a crime.

✓ **Training:** The AAU should educate staff, adult volunteers, parents/guardians, and youth participants on safety protocols, appropriate vs. inappropriate behaviors and other information they need to keep children safe while participating in AAU activities.

✓ **Reporting:** All AAU volunteers and staff should be considered mandatory reporters and should be expected to report suspected child abuse to appropriate law enforcement authorities and child abuse hotlines, as well as to AAU authorities.

The full 31-page report *'Recommendations to the Amateur Athletic Union from the Youth Protections and Adult/Volunteer Screening Task Forces'* is available at http://image.aausports.org/dnn/pdf/TFreportfinal.pdf.

 **Is this Any Way to Treat a Loyal Volunteer?**

Some organizations report that volunteers, especially those who have been volunteering for some time, sometimes find it objectionable that they are suddenly subject to a background check. Having donated countless hours, volunteers can be miffed since in their mind their integrity and honesty is now being questioned. That is why the rollout of a volunteer screening program is so important. Volunteers need to appreciate a background check is for the good of the organization overall and for the protection of the very people the organization is trying to protect. It is certainly no reflection on an individual volunteer. By submitting to the background check, the volunteer is showing support for the organization and its missions and goals. Volunteers need to understand that it is not personal or aimed at them, but is an essential tool for the organization.

How to Check? Fingerprints or Private Background Screening Firms

One issue for youth organizations is how to do the checks. There are two options—fingerprints through state or federal authorities or private background firms.

Depending upon the organization and the mission, agencies may have access to the FBI database. Certain states have legislation permitting organizations to take advantage of state fingerprinting or criminal record programs. On October 9, 1998, President Clinton signed the Volunteers for Children Act into law – Public Law 105-251 – amending the Nat'l Child Protection Act of 1993. Organizations and businesses dealing with children, elderly, or the disabled may now use national fingerprint-based criminal history checks to screen out volunteers and employees with relevant criminal records.

The Wisconsin Attorney General's Office has produced an excellent brochure describing not only their state program, but also the Federal Act and how to obtain FBI background checks; see the online version at www.doj.state.wi.us/dles/cib/forms/brochures/vol_children.pdf.

The same office also provides a website listing state sites where volunteer organization can obtain fingerprint information. See www.doj.state.wi.us/dles/cib/sclist.asp.

Some organizations, however, find the use of fingerprints (or sometimes referred to as "Livescan") does not meet their needs. Volunteers must either go to a law enforcement office or a printing location to have their prints taken and there are fees for that. There are the pros and cons for each approach:

Fingerprint Checks:

✓ Pros:

- Much broader and wider search then private databases utilizing FBI and state Department of Justice databases.
- May be necessary to satisfy state law for certain positions, such as teachers.

✓ Cons:

- More expensive since fees imposed for "rolling" fee (including Livescan) when volunteers go to a law enforcement agency or use private services.
- FBI/State databases are not perfect and can miss cases since FBI database is primarily an arrest database, and both the FBI and state databases must rely upon local courts or law enforcement to report data.
- Reports can be difficult to read or understand.
- If there is a positive result, organizations still need to have records pulled to understand status, nature, and gravity of offense.
- The organization is responsible for tracking the status of all volunteers who need fingerprints and to coordinate periodic checks if needed.

Checks by Private Background Firms:

✓ Pros:

- Less costly.

- Less of an imposition on volunteers; no traveling to printing locations.

- Screening firm can manage the process to ensure all volunteers are getting screened.

- Screening firm can assist on FCRA and legal compliance.

- Report is typically more readable.

- By combining screening with a training program, such as Shield the Vulnerable by LawRoom (www.shieldthevulnerable.org), training and background check can be conducted in one program, providing an organization with a tool to know who has been screened and when, when rescreening is due, and can also be used to create a list of past findings so a molester cannot go from one location to another.

✓ Cons:

- Certain positions, such as teaching staff, may be required to use fingerprints.

- Private background checks are NOT official FBI or state criminal record checks, and in some states are spotty at best. Best practice is to review each state for completeness of database information and to supplement if needed by local jurisdictions searches.

Also, using the criminal offender databases described in Chapter 12 provides low-cost and instant searches of some sexual offender database information.

 One question that arises is whether a screening on a volunteer needs to be conducted under the Fair Credit Reporting Act (FCRA) since the volunteer is not paid. The best practice is to still operate under the FCRA, even for volunteers. There is no requirement under the FCRA that a person is only employed if they are paid in monetary form. Also, as noted earlier, the FTC takes the position that the FCRA is given broad interpretation to protect consumer's rights. Conclusion— an organization should not assume the FCRA does not apply just because a person is a volunteer. That also means that volunteers should receive pre and post adverse action notices.

Screening Home Workers

There are numerous horror stories about innocent and unsuspecting people who opened their doors to home service providers or workers and became the victims of serious crimes, including murder, right in their own homes. Routinely, many people casually allow workers in their homes to deliver appliances or furniture, act as nannies or caregivers, clean carpets, make home improvements, perform household repairs such as plumbing or electrical, kill pests, and a multitude of other tasks.

Unfortunately, people are particularly vulnerable in their own homes. Good help is harder to get, and if there are children, senior citizens, or a disabled person at home, the risks are even greater. Yet, no state except Texas currently requires background checks on workers who enter homes. Results are tragic. See a recent Study by the Northwestern University School of Medicine, posted at www.feinberg.northwestern.edu/news/2012/07/dangerous_caregivers.html. The Study determined many agencies recruit and place unqualified caregivers in homes of the elderly.

U.S. Courts have held employers liable for negligence when their workers committed crimes in the home. An employer obviously does not send a worker into the home in order to steal, murder, or sexually assault. Certainly, criminal action was not in the scope and course of the employee's duties, however, employers are held to a higher standard of care in view of the inherent risks involved in sending workers into homes. Employers can be found negligent for not only hiring someone who they should have known was dangerous, unqualified, or unfit, but also for failure to supervise, train, or properly assign workers. If an employer was on notice that a current worker was unsafe, and retained the person anyway, then that employer can be sued for negligent retention. See ALR5th 21 for an article entitled, *Employer's Liability for Assaults, Theft or Similar Intentional Wrong Committed by Employee at Home or Business of Customer.*

AUTHOR TIP — **Should a Background Firm Check a Babysitter, Nanny, or a Caregiver for an Elderly Parent for a Family?**

Background screening firms are sometimes asked to do background checks for sensitive family situations such as when hiring a babysitter, nanny, or perhaps a caregiver for an elderly parent. Since these are high risk positions, due diligence is needed when hiring.

But is hiring a background screening firm the best route for the family to take? If a family hires a background screening firm (a Consumer Reporting Agency or "CRA"), then all the compliance issues described in this book are triggered. For example, the hiring procedure must include the same paperwork and compliance items required at both the state and federal level as well the vetting of the "employer" to insure there is a permissible purpose and the request is legitimate. If the worker is to be paid under the table can add to the complexity of vetting the family to see if it has a permissible purpose

Another issue for a CRA is the cost factor of setting up an account for persons who likely will not place very many future requests.

However, the biggest issue is that a background check by a screening firm may be legally taken as an "approval" of the candidate. A screening firm is providing a public records search. Even if the screening firm calls past employers, this check is still not the type of in-depth interview process needed to decide if an applicant should be in close personal contact with a family member. The danger is a family may develop a false sense of security if using a background report meant for employers for sensitive positions. The point here is even if the screening firm found no negative information on a public records check this is not the same as clearing a candidate to work inside a home with high risk groups.

The best approach for these highly sensitive personal positions may very well be to utilize the services of a licensed private investor. An investigator can conduct in-person and in-depth personal and professional references. Most investigators are experienced interviewers and having a professional interview of candidate for a sensitive home position is certainly warranted. An investigator can also follow-up on leads. Hiring an investigator may be more expensive, but considering the stakes, this procedure should be considered when family safety is involved.

The Nine Million Dollar Service Call

According to a news article by the Daytona Beach News-Journal Online, a civil case was settled for nine million dollars when a well-known air conditioner repair firm sent a worker who was a twice convicted sex offender to a home, and he killed the home owner. According to the June 1, 2004 article, the repairman cleaned the air ducts and then returned six months later and raped and murdered the victim. According to the news study, a criminal background check would have revealed the repairman's criminal past. The victim's family has started an organization called the Sue Weaver CAUSE (Consumer Awareness of Unsafe Service Employment) to raise awareness that not all contractors can be trusted. The case underscores the heightened responsibilities of employers who send workers into people's homes.

If you hire employees to work in peoples' homes, do not skimp on background checks!

C.A.U.S.E. Shows Background Checks Needed To Uncover Unsafe Service Employees Working In Homes

When hired workers enter homes to perform services, do the homeowners who requested the services know to whom they are opening their doors?

Background checks are needed to uncover unsafe employees working in and around homes of other people, and can help people avoid tragedies like the one experienced by Lucia Bone, the founder of 'Sue Weaver CAUSE (Consumer Awareness of Unsafe Service Employment).'

In 2001, Sue Weaver, Lucia Bone's sister, was raped and beaten to death in her Florida home by a worker who had previously entered her home for a job. Six months before her death, Weaver had contracted with a major department store to clean the air ducts in her home. Both workers sent to her house had criminal records. One was a twice-convicted sex offender on parole who returned to the home where he had once worked to commit a crime.

Sadly, Weaver's murder is not an isolated case, since many consumers are robbed, assaulted, and murdered each year by workers with jobs that allow them access into homes. Because of this, Bone started Sue Weaver CAUSE to both honor her sister and to fight for standardized background checks of all in-home service employees. Through consumer awareness and legislation, Bone wants to ensure that big, reputable retail companies and others perform thorough criminal background checks on the contractors and sub-contractors they send into homes.

Since there are currently no federal or state laws requiring companies to do criminal background checks on contractors or sub-contract workers sent into homes, Sue Weaver CAUSE is demanding legislation for CAUSE Certification compliance. When interviewed for the article on HuffingtonPost.com, Bone said the CAUSE Certification would require annual background checks following CAUSE minimum screening standards on all employees, contractors, and subcontractors. Bone added that these standards were determined from survey results from questions asking background screening professionals what minimum screening should be conducted on workers going into homes of elderly mothers, pregnant wives, and people with special needs.

According to Bone, the minimum requirements for CAUSE Certification are:

✓ Social Security Number (SSN) Address Trace;

✓ County-Level Criminal Check (Search records for past seven years in counties where applicant lived, worked, or attended school);

✓ Multi-jurisdictional/"National" Criminal Database, and;

✓ National/State Sex Offender Registry.

In addition, Bone says consumers "never think about (criminal background checks for in-home service workers)" and automatically assume the company they hire would not send criminals into their homes. She advises consumers to be proactive and not assume companies properly screen workers sent to homes. "Bonded and insured is not a background check."

The Sue Weaver CAUSE website is located at www.sueweavercause.org.

Source: www.huffingtonpost.com/janet-kinosian/could-you-or-a-loved-one_b_559526.html.

Employer Issues with IDs, ID Theft, and Privacy

Inside This Chapter:

- ✓ The Problem of 'Who is Really Who'

- ✓ Identity in America

- ✓ Identification Criteria Used by Employers

- ✓ Tools Employers Can Use to Avoid Fraudulent Identification in the Workplace

- ✓ Identity Verification Before or After the Hire

- ✓ Employee Privacy Rights

- ✓ Privacy and Data Protection in Background Check Screening Reports

- ✓ FTC Report on Protecting Consumer Privacy Recommends Businesses Adopt Best Privacy Practices

The Problem of 'Who is Really Who'

America is undergoing an identity crisis. Identity theft is one of the fastest growing crimes in the United States.

For employers however, the difficulties associated with ID theft goes well beyond credit card fraud and other financial losses. Firms can be the victims of ID theft by hiring someone with a false or fraudulent identity, with serious consequences. Employers do need to be concerned about whom they are really hiring since criminals and terrorists have been known to fake their identities.

Since 9/11/2001 there have been a number of initiatives to use modern technology to firmly establish who is who in our society. However, there is still a widespread ability for one person to steal the identity of another — or create a new identity — and masquerade as someone else. Numerous agencies and private firms are working on biometric identifiers for a variety of reasons. The use of biometric data has become a critical element in Homeland Security efforts, particularly at airports and essential industries and services. There is a national debate over national ID cards, including the privacy and social implications of the government assigning every individual a unique number or identity. Should we collect biometric data and continue building large information databases?

These issues affect the lives of every American and should be the topic of discussion in a free citizenry. Let us review what employers need to know and what to do in our current environment to protect the workplace.

Identity in America

What is a person's identity? Identity has many different meanings. Use of the word by a psychologist would be very different than use by a teenager, a philosopher, a police officer, a scientist, or a privacy advocate. A popular dictionary, gives this definition of identity:

1. The collective aspect of the set of characteristics by which a thing is definitively recognizable or known.
2. The set of behavioral or personal characteristics by which an individual is recognizable as a member of a group.
3. The quality or condition of being the same as something else.
4. The distinct personality of an individual regarded as a persisting entity; individuality.

For our purposes, we are looking at identity in the bureaucratic sense of the word, utilizing the third definition — the quality or condition of being the same as something else.

Real Identity

Society has an interest in keeping everyone straight when it comes to financial transactions between each other, transactions with various levels of government from the IRS all the way down to getting a speeding ticket, and especially employment. This is a person's "real identity." Putting aside any philosophical implications — and for the purpose of safe hiring — real identity is the process of matching up the past history with the present.

A key element of a Safe Hiring Program is to know what a person has done in the past. That is not to say that a person is defined solely by the past, or that every past act can be, or legally should be, considered relevant to employment decisions. However, past acts that are in the public domain for the world to see are what an employer needs to have. Now the employer needs to verify the public history of the applicant is not only factual, but also is the history that belongs to that person. By knowing a person's real identity, an employer can match up the employment history, education, credentials, or past court records. The real identity is also needed for a number of governmental functions effecting labor regulation such as various tax withholdings.

Positive Identity

Employers are less concerned with the concept of "Positive Identity." Positive identity means that you are the same person that was part of an original transaction, so that you have the right to be a part of the new transaction. For example, if you went to a website in the past and signed up for a service, the site would need positive ID that you are the same person coming back for another transaction. It is irrelevant to the website that you may have initially used a different or even a false identity. As far as the website is concerned — provided there is no fraudulent financial transaction — you are you as long as you now know the password, i.e. you have the unique identifier that only you would know.

Consider this— a person creates or steals an identity and is hired by a firm under the false name. If that firm engages in some biometric identification procedures, such as identity badges, then each time the person comes into the workplace, his or her positive identity is confirmed. The employer knows this is the person presenting the badge. However, there is the possibility that the badge was gained because of a false "real" identity in the first place.

Negative Identity

Another type of identity is "Negative Identity." This means that you are NOT a particular someone. For example, when you get on an airplane, an important consideration is that you are not a terrorist or a wanted criminal. However, as a practical matter, the most efficient way of showing you are not someone is to show who you really are.

In the Employee/Employer Relationship, Correct Identity is the Employer's First Concern

For employers, the primary concern is real identity. The problem is how to accurately track, in a cost-effective manner that does not unduly invade our privacy, the identities of not only 300 million U.S. citizens, but also the people from around the world who apply for jobs here.

Identification Criteria Used by Employers

There are different identification criteria possible, each with their own set of considerations:

Name

A **person's name** is only one part of one's identity. Under English Common Law, people can change their name and be known by anything they want as long as they are not trying to deceive. Not only can people change names, but also they can use all sorts of variations of their first, middle or last names. In some traditional cultures, a woman may, upon marriage, take the family name of the husband. Many cultures have different protocols with names, such as variations of the family name or mother's maiden name. There is also an issue of non-English names, especially in those countries where a non-familiar alphabet is used, and there are numerous English variations of the same name.

Finally, in any large database of people, there is bound to be a great many duplicate names. It is surprising for people who believe their names are unique to go on an internet phone directory and find many others across North America with identical matching first and last names.

The bottom line— name identification by itself is practically worthless for the purpose of real identification. It is necessary to have other identifiers as well. As a matter of both math and logic, the more identifiers associated with an individual, the more likely a job applicant can be identified as a "real identity."

Date of Birth

Date of birth is probably the next most used identifier. The initial date used for date of birth comes from the applicant. However, if an applicant gives a different date of birth, a search for criminal records could be thrown off. To guard against this, a screening firm or investigator should review the records for all name matches even if the date of birth does not match. However, this creates a significant issue for a court researcher if the name is common.

Date of birth is subject to regulation due to laws concerning age discrimination, as discussed in Chapter 2. These laws present barriers for employers or screening firms from requesting the date of birth.

Another difficulty, given the sheer size of the American population, is just name and date of birth can result in "computer twins." "Computer twins" are two people with identical names and dates of birth. The problem is created when two different people are possibly identified as the same person.

Social Security Number (SSN)

The nine digit **Social Security number (SSN)** is an assigned number developed for the purpose of administering the U.S. Social Security program. As a practical matter, the SSN is treated as a de facto national identification number. It is widely used as a unique identifier and is commonly required for any number of transactions — practically any financial transaction will require the Social Security number.

Until June 2011, issuance of numbers followed a pattern. The first three numbers represented the state of issue. The second set of numbers was related to the date the card was issued. As a result of the changes to the issuance of SSNs, as described in Chapter 17, all numbers are now issued randomly, with no pattern. But it is still possible to tell the state and date of issue from the SSN, if issued prior to June 2011.

Also as discussed in Chapter 17, an employer will typically obtain a Social Security Trace Report, also known as a "credit header." The report gives the employer additional information such as other names and addresses associated with the SSN and possibly the date of birth.

There are problems with using the Social Security number as an identifier. The SSN was never intended to act as a national identification number, and when issued, it is not part of a national ID system that systematically records biometrics to uniquely match a SSN to a particular person. For example, there is no fingerprint or other definite biometric measurement that is permanently associated with a particular SSN. On the other hand, government computers can eventually track if a number is being misused. For example, if an identity thief steals a Social Security number and uses it for employment, the government may eventually note another use of the same number for tax withholding purposes.

Motor Vehicle Driver's License

Each state issues its own **driver's license (DL)** that entitles the name on the card to legally operate a motor vehicle. In fact, the driver's license has become a national identification card since it is the only widespread and easily recognized official government card issued with a photo for identification. The DL is used for such purposes as cashing checks, entering the security area in an airport, and anything else that requires a proof of identify. Among the 50 states, there are not necessarily strict security controls over the issuance of the license. There have been instances of criminals using false identity papers to obtain a driver's license under a false name. In addition, a search on Google of a "fake driver's license" reveals a number of websites that sell books and resources on how to make a fake driver's license and other ID's. A person on the East Coast could potentially create a fake driver's license from a state in the West and hope that a lack of familiarity will allow the document to pass.

Congress passed the REAL ID Act of 2005, Pub.L. 109-13, 119 Stat. 302, enacted May 11, 2005. The law was intended, among other things, to standardize procedures for issuance of state driving licenses and state issued identification cards. However, the bill has proved controversial and many states have not implemented its provisions. Bills have also been introduced to repeal this act as well.

Physical Characteristics

Identifying **physical characteristics** may be reported on a government identity form such as a driver's license. The most common physical features are height, weight, sex, hair, and eye color. When photo identification is used, a physical identifier will also include facial features depicted in a photograph. It can also refer to race, although that is typically not used as an identifier because of concerns over discrimination.

There are two immediate problems with these physical identifiers. First, the identifiers can change. A person's weight or hair color shown on a driver's license tends to become inaccurate as time goes by. Second, there can be a question as to the integrity of the data in the first place. When the data appears on a driver's license, for example, there is an assumption that a government official verified the data, so the data has verified authenticity. However, the situation is different if the document was forged or obtained under false pretense, as discussed below.

Unique Biometric Characteristics

Biometric characteristics are biological measurements. The notion behind biometrics is to provide a basis for personal authentication. Methods of recognizing a person are based upon physical characteristics such as fingerprints, eye scans of the iris, or retinal scans. Other types of measurements being studied are based upon the physical features of the face or geometric features of the human hand and voice print. There is also a study of biometrics based upon handwriting. A biometric measure relates to a particular individual as opposed to a password or a document that someone carries.

The challenge with a biometric identification is to ensure that the biometric identity is properly associated with the appropriate person when the measurement is first made. Unless the original identification can be trusted, subsequent identifications based upon the biometric have little value. If a criminal, terrorist, or imposter successfully obtains a false biometric identity, then that person essentially has a future "free pass" — unless the error is somehow detected and corrected.

With its U.S.-VISIT program, the United States has introduced biometric measurements at airports and seaports for visitors from certain countries. The biometric measurements include digital imaging of a visitor's face and a digital fingerprint (See: www.dhs.gov/dhspublic/interapp/content_multi_image/content_multi_image_0006.xml).

Other Government-issued Documents

Identification can also be based upon other documents issued by state or local governments. A United States passport can be the basis for identification. Various governmental agencies may also issue identification of workers, for those in law enforcement or public safety identification. Other government issued identities can involve the issuance of "smart cards" that workers performing certain duties may be required to carry. These cards can contain embedded computer chips that allow identity verification and authorization to perform certain tasks or allow access to certain areas.

Past Data Associated with an Applicant

Another means of identification is to compare the applicant to public records contained in large information databases. There are a number of companies with access to literally billons of public records. One company claims that it has information on nearly 98% of the adult population and data entries relating to approximately 205 million individuals in the United States. Of course, access to the most extensive databases will cost money. There are two excellent websites that list links to literally thousands of free searchable public records databases; see www.searchsystems.net and www.brbpublications.com/freeresources/pubrecsites.aspx.

In addition to the criminal records databases discussed in Chapter 15 and the Social Security Trace information discussed in Chapter 17, there are numerous other records maintained in proprietary databases. Available record types can include:

- ✓ Property ownership records
- ✓ Bankruptcies, liens, and judgments
- ✓ UCC filings
- ✓ Ownership of boats or planes
- ✓ Professional licenses

Use of Private Documents for Identifying

Another source of identity documents are those issued by private firms. Examples are credit cards and membership cards. These documents are far from ideal identifiers. Applicants with something to hide can attempt to manipulate the drawbacks on these forms of identities and create false identities. Who would want to do that? Individuals who do not want their true names or intentions divulged! These may be people simply wanting privacy, or they may be criminals or even terrorists.

Tools Employers Can Use to Avoid Fraudulent Identification in the Workplace

While it may be beyond our purpose here to review the many ways that identity can be stolen or created, employers do need to be aware there are a great many ways a determined criminal or terrorist can steal or create an identity for the purpose of entering the workplace under false pretenses. Identity theft can run from simple and amateurish attempts, such as simply using another name, to attempting to obtain false identification such as a Social Security number or driver's license, all the way to sophisticated schemes involving document forgery and creation of an entirely fictitious person.

It can be a challenge for employers to identify a well-financed and sophisticated scheme to create a false identity. Although not impossible to do, it is still difficult to create a false identity. Employers do have substantial protections by taking some common sense precautions, mainly by conducting a background check.

To help prevent someone with a stolen identity from coming to your workplace, use the following tools. Keep in mind that use of these tools by themselves or even in combination are not guaranteed to protect an employer. Use of these tools goes a substantial way to discouraging applicants with something to hide. These tools demonstrate due diligence in the workplace.

Screening Discourages False Applicants

The best protection for an employer is to not have the issue of a false ID arise in the first place. Perhaps the first and best approach is to make it very clear to all job applicants that your firm does engage in a Safe Hiring Program. All finalists are subject to background checks. As a general rule, criminals and terrorists are looking for "soft" and easy targets. Why risk exposure at a firm that will perform a background check if they can go down the block to some organization who is not as particular about whom they hire? An applicant with a false identity may not know the extent of the employer's background checks, but an imposter may not be willing to take the risk.

An employer can take the following steps:

- ✓ In the newspaper ad or job announcement, indicate that the employer does background checks. In looking at the "classified' section in any newspaper, it is common to see employers state that applicants must undergo drug testing and background checks.

- ✓ Clearly state that in the application process a screening will occur, and obtain consent for it.

- ✓ Utilize the six critical questions outlined in Chapter 8 that demonstrate the employer's commitment to safe hiring.

As the hiring process begins, some employers utilize the Social Security trace tool as an initial identity tool. If the applicant's identity does not check out then the time and effort of a further background check is saved. However, a Social Security trace is only a limited tool, and the entire screening process is helpful to verify identity, along with post-hire procedures discussed later in this chapter and the next.

The Trusted Source Rule — Third Party Verification

When America was made up of small towns, farms, and villages, everyone knew each other. There was no question who was who. This is obviously no longer the case. The best method for knowing what we know is still based on what people we know say, assuming we give those people credibility.

The Google search engine works in a similar manner. It does not matter to Google what a website says about itself as much as what others say about it, in terms of linking to it; the more third party sites that validate a website by linking to it, the higher the rating. It is a form of third party verification. The same rule applies to safe hiring as well. As we have seen throughout this book, what is important is not what an applicant states, but what can be independently verified.

In employment, the old adage "it is not what you know but who you know" reflects the obvious truth — that employers would prefer to hire a known quantity. If an employer actually knows the applicant, the applicant stands a better chance of being hired. The next best thing is to be recommended by a hiring manager or current worker. That is why firms place so much emphasis on employee-based recruiting. These are all variations of the basic premise of this chapter— that employers prefer to use a trusted source of information.

If every business owner could only hire candidates they either knew personally, or were known personally by people they knew, then there would be less time and effort spent managing and dealing with employee problems. To prevent a person with a false identity from entering your workforce, at some point your knowledge of an applicant must be tied to a trusted source. The trusted source may be another HR manager or a security professional you know and trust.

As seen throughout this book, reliance on public data or criminal databases alone is not advisable. A determined criminal, terrorist, or imposter may be able to steal an identity and pass such a test, or a database may give a "false negative," meaning the person is erroneously cleared when they should not be. Furthermore, just trusting a person's word for who they are is obviously insufficient.

The key is a trusted source that can independently verify that the person sitting in front of you for an interview is the same person who has the history they claim. This is best done by **past employment verification**. Verifying past employment allows the employer to detect and hopefully eliminate any red flags caused by unexplained employment history gaps, or discover the resume/application is false. Thus the employer breaks the chain of relying upon what people say about themselves, relying upon documents that can easily be forged, or relying on databases that can contain errors.

If an employer is contacting someone they do not know, then the trusted source may turn out to be the telephone book or directory assistance or some similar online service to validate the authenticity of a past employer's telephone number. Having a listed telephone number provides at least some assurance that the past employer is a legitimate business that qualified for a phone number and directory assistance. Past employers can also be "Googled" or researched from other databases.

If the applicant claims self-employment, then it is more difficult to find an independent verification source. In this case, the approach is to ascertain from the applicant the names of past clients and then verify through directory assistance or some trusted source that the client is for real.

A warning — there are a number of well-meaning attempts being made to create databases, cards, or other schemes to validate identity. The basis of these efforts is some mechanism to perform some sort of "clearance," then the individual is tied into some sort of biometric measure. However, the so-called "clearance" appears to be based upon simply searching public records and government databases. Any reliance on any database is problematic. The drawbacks are multiplied when a criminal, terrorist, or imposter manages to obtain such a card, then it can be used to help conceal their identity in the future.

So a recommended best practice to validate identity for purposes of employment, safety, or other type of security concern is to include an element of third party verification from a trusted source. Although contacting a trusted source is a manual task, and not nearly as quick or inexpensive as using databases, it is critical if there is to be any confidence in an identity validation or "clearance" program.

Confirmation of Facts

Confirmation of facts is covered in a number of previous chapters. As the old saying goes, "trust but verify." Using the tools in this book, it is critical to verify facts and to utilize the various screening tools available, including a Social Security trace, past employment checks, verifying education and professional licenses, and a criminal records check.

Look for Internal Consistency or Inconsistency

Another tool that goes hand-in-hand with the trusted source rule is looking to see if there is a pattern of consistency — or "applicant congruence." Congruence means "agreement, harmony, conformity, or correspondence."

Employers, hiring managers, human resources professionals or security professionals must ask themselves, "Does the total package make sense?" An employer needs to look at the applicant as a whole and, based upon the application and interview, be sensitive to anything that does not add up or make sense. For example:

✓ If a person claims to have a degree in computer science, does the person appear to have the appropriate knowledge in their interview?

✓ Does the employment history make sense for what the person did, where, and for how long?

✓ Are the educational accomplishments and past employment consistent with the person's knowledge, skills, and abilities?

✓ Are the job descriptions consistent with the person's knowledge, skills, and abilities?

✓ Are there unexplained gaps in employment?

✓ Did the applicant give specifics in the interview when discussing past jobs, knowledge, skills and experience, or did the person only give vague generalities?

In other words, does the person at the interview seem to match the history shown on the application? If something does not "add up," red flag!

Cross-Referencing Accumulated Data

Based upon all the data the employer obtains, the next step is to cross reference the known facts to determine if everything makes sense. For our purposes, cross-referencing is a process of not relying upon just one fact, but on a combination of accumulated facts obtained both from the applicant and other sources. Information from one source is compared to others to determine if the applicant is factual about their claimed identity and history. Keep in mind that use of massive databases for employment purposes does have some legal limitations as discussed in Chapter 15. Another issue is how to effectively utilize large databases containing literally billions of records. A developing technology is data mining of large databases and specialized software to "connect the dots" to see trends and connections.

Again, another valuable tool is the Social Security trace. As described in Chapter 17, the Social Security trace is based upon information obtained by the three major credit bureaus — names and addresses associated with a particular Social Security number. If an employer is working with a screening firm, then the employer may receive data that is also based upon a number of other public record databases. This should help you create a useful address history. It is important to understand that these reports are not an official list of past residences, and there can be errors and variation. However, for purposes of cross-referencing, it is a tool that employers should use. For example, if a person claimed employment as a production supervisor in Chicago from 1998-2002, but the trace report indicated two different addresses in Los Angeles during the same time period, that would be a red flag.

Identity Theft Tops Federal Trade Commission List of Complaints for 2011

For the 12th year in a row, identity theft topped the list of consumer complaints released by the Federal Trade Commission (FTC) for 2011. Of more than 1.8 million complaints filed in 2011, 279,156 – or 15 percent – were identity theft complaints, and nearly 25 percent of those identity theft complaints were related tax- or wage-related fraud. For more information about the FTC's Top Complaint Categories for 2011, visit: www.ftc.gov/opa/2012/02/2011complaints.shtm.

The FTC – the government agency working for consumers to prevent fraudulent, deceptive, and unfair business practices – enters complaints into the Consumer Sentinel Network (CSN), a secure online database of millions of consumer complaints available to more than 2,000 civil and criminal law enforcement agencies in the United States and abroad. In addition to storing complaints received by the FTC, the CSN also includes complaints filed with federal, state, and non-governmental organizations.

The CSN report breaks out complaint data on a state-by-state basis and also contains data about the 50 metropolitan areas reporting the highest per capita incidence of fraud and other complaints. In addition, the 50 metropolitan areas reporting the highest incidence of identity theft are noted. According to the FTC, the top ten complaint categories for 2011 were:

✓ Identity Theft: 279,156 Complaints (15 percent)

✓ Debt Collection: 180,928 Complaints (10 percent)

✓ Prizes, Sweepstakes, and Lotteries: 100,208 Complaints (6 percent)

✓ Shop-at-Home and Catalog Sales: 98,306 Complaints (5 percent)

✓ Banks and Lenders: 89,341 Complaints (5 percent)

✓ Internet Services: 81,805 Complaints (5 percent)

✓ Auto Related: 77,435 Complaints (4 percent)

✓ Imposter Scams: 73,281 Complaints (4 percent)

✓ Telephone and Mobile Services: 70,024 Complaints (4 percent)

✓ Advance-Fee Loans and Credit Protection/Repair: 47,414 Complaints (3 percent).

Begun in 1997 to collect fraud and identity theft complaints, the CSN now has more than 7 million complaints, including those about credit reports, debt collection, mortgages, and lending, among other subjects. Between January and December 2011, the CSN received more than 1.8 million consumer complaints, which the FTC has sorted into 30 complaint categories. For more information about the Consumer Sentinel Network, visit www.FTC.gov/sentinel.

The FTC guide 'Taking Charge: What to Do if Your Identity is Stolen' is available at www.ftc.gov/bcp/edu/pubs/consumer/idtheft/idt04.pdf.

Identity Verification Before or After the Hire

A tool that is available to employers pre-employment is the Consent Based Social Security Number Verification Service, known as CBSV (www.ssa.gov/cbsv/). CBSV can be obtained through background screening firms. However, it requires special documentation above and beyond forms applicants normally sign so here are additional administrative steps (See Chapter 17 for a discussion of this program).

There are also two post-hire processes an employer can utilize:

1. Part of the "intake" of a new employee is to verify that the Social Security number provided by the new employee is valid. The Social Security Administration provides several services to employers to verify the SSN. Refer to Chapter 17 for details on the Social Security Number Verification Service (SSNVS)
2. Other "after the hire" government programs to validate the identity and the SSN of a new employer include Form I-9 and E-Verify. These programs are examined in detail in Chapter 29.

Employee Privacy Rights

Beth Givens, Director of the Privacy Rights Clearinghouse (www.privacyrights.org) prepared the following summary of what an employer should and must do to protect identity.

Reprinted here with permission, the original article is available at the Privacy Rights Clearinghouse website at www.privacyrights.org/ar/PreventITWorkplace.htm. For resources on responsible information handling practices, see www.privacyrights.org/ar/SDCountyIT.htm.

What Employers Can Do to Protect the Privacy Rights of Employees

By Beth Givens

Experts in identity theft report that an increasing number of cases can be traced back to dishonest employees in the workplace or computer hackers who obtain Social Security numbers (SSNs) of employees and customers, then disclose that information to individuals involved in crime rings or other identity theft schemes.

One of the keys to preventing identity theft, therefore, is to safeguard sensitive personal information *within the workplace*, whether that workplace is a government agency, private business, or nonprofit organization. Everyone must get involved in protecting personal information such as SSNs, financial account numbers, dates of birth – in other words, any information used by identity thieves to impersonate individuals in the marketplace.

Workplace Information-Handling Practices

The Privacy Rights organization makes these suggestions for the responsible handling of information. Although these recommendations are based upon California law, they comprise "best practices" for employers and institutions in all states:

✓ **Adopt a comprehensive privacy policy** that includes responsible information-handling practices. Appoint an individual and/or department to be responsible for the privacy policy, one who can be contacted by employees and customers with questions and complaints.

✓ **Store sensitive personal data in secure computer systems.** Store physical documents in secure spaces such as locked file cabinets. Data should only be available to qualified persons.

✓ **Dispose of documents properly**, including shredding paper with a cross-cut shredder, "wiping" electronic files, destroying computer diskettes and CD-ROMs, and so on. Comply with California's document destruction law, Civil Code 1798.80-1798.84. The FACT Act passed in 2003 also added provisions in section 628 about the proper manner to dispose of consumer reports under the FCRA. The FTC has prepared regulations. A summary may be found at http://business.ftc.gov/documents/alt152-disposing-consumer-report-information-new-rule-tells-how. Also, see chapter 29 on "After the Hire" issues.

✓ **Build document destruction capabilities into the office infrastructure**. Place shredders around the office, near printers and fax machines, and near waste baskets. Make sure dumpsters are locked and inaccessible to the public.

✓ **Conduct regular staff training**, including new employees, temporary employees, and contractors.

✓ **Conduct privacy "walk-throughs"** and make spot checks on proper information handling. Reward employees and departments for maintaining "best practices."

✓ **Put limits on data collection to the minimum information needed.** For example, is SSN really required? Is complete date of birth needed, or would year and month be sufficient?

✓ **Put limits on data display and disclosure of SSN.** Do not print full SSNs on paychecks, parking permits, staff badges, time sheets, training program rosters, lists of who got promoted, on monthly account statements, on customer reports, etc. Unless allowed by law, do not print SSN on mailed documents or require that it be transmitted via the internet. In compliance with California law, do not use SSN as customer number, employee ID number, health insurance ID card, etc. Comply with California Civil Code 1798.85-86 and 1786.6.

- ✓ **Restrict data access to staff with a legitimate need to know.** Implement electronic audit trail procedures to monitor who is accessing what. Enforce strict penalties for illegitimate browsing and access.
- ✓ **Conduct employee background checks**, especially for individuals who have access to sensitive personal information. Screen cleaning services, temp services, contractors, etc.
- ✓ **Safeguard mobile computers**, laptops, PDAs that contain files with sensitive personal data.
- ✓ **Notify customers and/or employees of computer security breaches** involving sensitive personal information, in compliance with California law Civil Code 1798.29 and 1798.82-1798.84, including security breaches involving paper records.

Other Suggestions for Employers

It should be noted that ID theft now has even more opportunity. With the adoption of so many mobile devices and increasing technology, theft of sensitive data can occur more often. Internet access can even be stolen from wireless systems with readily available equipment that can be purchased at retail stores. Targets for identity thieves include SSNs, driver's license numbers, financial account numbers, PINs, passcodes, and dates of birth.

Other helpful suggestions include:

- ✓ **Implement a written Identity Theft Prevention Program** to detect the warning signs – or "red flags" – of identity theft. A "how-to" guide for companies that are considered a "low risk" for identity theft is provided by the Federal Trade Commission.

...work is protected with the proper security settings

...than strip-shredders

...Credit Reporting Act (FCRA) has a provision on

...**onsumer report information and records**.).

...y breach notice laws. Also notify individuals when ...outside the scope of most laws. **Develop a crisis** ...mployee or customer data is lost, stolen, or acquired ...nstructions to prevent identity theft if SSNs and/or ...gitimately.

...nation-handling practices and privacy policies.

Privacy ... d Check Screening Reports

Because bac... be made to l... process.

...s sensitive and confidential information, efforts must ...able to decision-makers directly involved in the hiring

The Report... separately fr... medical files... or managers... employer wo...

...ms signed by the applicant, should be maintained ...in a relatively secured area, in the same fashion that ...hould definitely not be made available to supervisors ...example, during periodic performance appraisals, an ...mance-related confidential background report.

For screening firms with advanced internet systems, there is no need to physically download the report. It is available online. However, an employer needs to be assured that the screening firm has appropriate internet and data security, and the employer needs to maintain a system of strong password protections. It is important that authorized users do not share passwords with those not authorized, nor reveal the password in any manner. Some screening firms require the user to change passwords periodically as a security measure and to sign security agreements.

Typically, reports are returned to either Human Resources or Security Departments. Reports are reviewed for any negative information. If the report is clear, then the hiring manager is notified, and the hiring proceeds. If there is a red flag or derogatory information, then the information itself is shared with the appropriate decision-makers. The physical report, however, should normally stay with HR or Security. This protects against confidential information wrongfully being made known generally within the company if reports are transmitted between departments either by means of a paper copy or electronically.

The question arises as to how long records and documents should be maintained after separation. Unlike Canada where privacy laws encourage the destruction of confidential data when no longer needed, there are no U.S. requirements that materials related to background screening be destroyed. In fact, there are a number of state and federal laws that control document retention, and labor attorneys will typically advise employers on how long various documents must be retained. However, for purposes involving safe hiring and background screening, the recommendation by ESR is six years. The FCRAÂ was amended in 2003 to lengthen the statute of limitations under the act to as long as five years. In addition, state laws often allow a one-year period to file and serve a lawsuit. As a workable general rule, a six-year retention period should serve employers, with the six years running from the termination of employment or, if not hired, from the time the decision was made not to hire the applicant.

Many screening firms now store reports indefinitely, and if the applicant used an online system, the consent and disclosure can also be retained indefinably. However, if an employer downloads any data, or used a paper based consent and disclosure, then consider six years as the minimum. Although technically there is no maximum period under federal law, it is still a best practice to periodically purge old data in order to minimize the amount of Personal and Identifiable Information (PII) that is available in the work environment. After all, most identity theft occurs in the workplace.

If disposing of any information in a consumer report, it is important to follow regulations set out by the FTC pursuant to FCRA Section 628. Paper or electronic reports must be destroyed, pulverized, or erased so it cannot be read or reconstructed. An employer must show due diligence when a shredding firm is hired.

Also, review the best practice the recommendations from the Privacy Rights Clearinghouse described in the previous section.

Trend Towards Mandated Privacy and Data Protection – Massachusetts Regulations Require Businesses to Have Information Security Program to Protect Personal Information

The increased emphasis on data and information protections can be demonstrated by strict new privacy rules put in place by Massachusetts, described as the toughest data protection and privacy rules in the nation. The Massachusetts Offices of Consumer Affairs and Business Regulations (OCABR) passed regulations that went into effect March 1, 2010 and are aimed at safeguarding the personal information of Massachusetts residents by requiring a business to have a Written Information Security Program (WISP) to protect personal information.

The new rules cover any business that "receives, stores, maintains, processes, or otherwise has access to personal information in connection with the provision of goods or services or in connection with employment."

The rules defines personal information as a Massachusetts resident's name combined with a Social Security number, driver's license number or state-issued ID card, or a financial account number or credit/debit card number. The regulations also apply to third parties and require that there be contracts to ensure that the regulations are implemented and maintained, although the contracts did not need to be updated before March 1, 2012. It appears that Massachusetts takes the position that the rules apply to out of state firms that handle personal information as well.

A business that is regulated by these rules must have and implement a comprehensive WISP. The rules do not specify exact policies but provides minimum requirements and indicate that a business should take a certain number of factors into account such as the kind of records it maintains and the risk of identity theft.

Some of the things a business must do include a review of foreseeable internal and external risks, evaluation and improvement of safeguards, policies for employee access outside of the business, implementing security measures such as password control and up to date firewall, employee training, ensuring that terminated employees cannot access confidential data as well as disciplinary measures for violations of the regulations.

A text of the new regulations 201 CMR 17.00: STANDARDS FOR THE PROTECTION OF PERSONAL INFORMATION OF RESIDENTS OF THE COMMONWEALTH can be viewed at: www.mass.gov/ocabr/docs/idtheft/201cmr1700reg.pdf.

FTC Report on Protecting Consumer Privacy Recommends Businesses Adopt Best Privacy Practices

In March 2012, the Federal Trade Commission (FTC) issued a report – *'Protecting Consumer Privacy in an Era of Rapid Change: Recommendations For Businesses and Policymakers'* – outlining best practices for businesses to protect the privacy of American consumers and give them greater control over the collection and use of their personal data, according to an FTC press release. The FTC also recommended that Congress consider enacting general privacy legislation, data security and breach notification legislation, and data broker legislation.

The FTC report also called on businesses handling consumer data to implement recommendations for protecting privacy that include:

✓ **Privacy by Design** – Businesses should build in privacy protections for consumers at every stage in developing their products, including reasonable security for consumer data, limited collection and retention of consumer data, and reasonable procedures to promote data accuracy;

✓ **Simplified Choice for Businesses and Consumers** – Businesses should give consumers the option to decide what information is shared about them, and with whom, and should include a 'Do-Not-Track' mechanism to provide a simple and easy way for consumers to control the tracking of their online activities.

✓ **Greater Transparency** – Businesses should disclose details about their collection and use of personal information of consumers and provide consumers access to the data collected about them.

As the nation's chief privacy policy and enforcement agency, the FTC urges individual business to accelerate the adoption of the principles contained in the privacy framework. The FTC has indicated it will encourage consumer privacy protections by focusing on the following five action items:

✓ **Do-Not-Track** – The FTC commends the progress made by browser vendors that have developed tools to allow consumers to limit data collection about them, and will work with these groups to complete implementation of an easy-to-use, persistent, and effective Do Not Track system.

✓ **Mobile** – The FTC urges companies offering mobile services to work toward improved privacy protections, including disclosures, and will host a workshop on May 30, 2012 to address how mobile privacy disclosures can be short, effective, and accessible to consumers on small screens.

✓ **Data Brokers** – The FTC calls on data brokers to make their operations more transparent by creating a centralized website to identify themselves, to disclose how they collect and use consumer data, and to detail the choices that data brokers provide consumers about their own information.

✓ **Large Platform Providers** – The FTC cited heightened privacy concerns about the extent to which platforms, such as Internet Service Providers, operating systems, browsers and social media companies, seek to comprehensively track the online activity of consumers. The FTC will host a public workshop in the second half of 2012 to explore issues related to comprehensive tracking.

✓ **Promoting Enforceable Self-Regulatory Codes** – The FTC will work with the Department of Commerce to develop industry-specific codes of privacy conduct, and when companies adhere to these codes, the FTC will take that into account in its law enforcement efforts. If companies do not honor the codes they sign up for, they could be subject to FTC enforcement actions.

Recognizing the potential burden on small businesses, the report concludes that the privacy framework should not apply to businesses that collect and do not transfer only non-sensitive data from fewer than 5,000 consumers a year. The FTC report, *'Protecting Consumer Privacy in an Era of Rapid Change: Recommendations For Businesses and Policymakers,'* is available at: www.ftc.gov/os/2012/03/120326privacyreport.pdf.

In a Dissenting Statement released along with the report, FTC Commissioner Thomas Rosch dissented from the issuance of the Final Privacy Report and voiced his concerns with the proposed reforms. Rosch warned the reforms, which were approved by a vote of 3-1, would install "Big Brother" as the watchdog over online and offline privacy practices and go "well beyond what Congress has permitted the commission to do." The Dissenting Statement is available at www.ftc.gov/speeches/rosch/120326privacyreport.pdf.

Form I-9, E-Verify, and "After the Hire" Issues

Inside This Chapter:

- ✓ Introduction to "After the Hire" Issues
- ✓ "Form I-9" Employment Eligibility Verification Compliance
- ✓ "E-Verify" Electronic Employment Eligibility Verification
- ✓ Employment "At Will" and Probationary Periods
- ✓ Confidentiality Agreements and Ethics Policy
- ✓ Maintaining Employment Screening Records
- ✓ Employees May Have the Right to Inspect Their Personnel Files
- ✓ Screening Current Employees
- ✓ "Continuous Screening" or "Re-Screening"
- ✓ If Screening Results Lead to Possible Termination Issues
- ✓ Employee Misconduct Issues
- ✓ Ongoing Training
- ✓ Performance Reviews and Ongoing Monitoring
- ✓ Responding to Employee Complaints
- ✓ Termination Procedures
- ✓ Exit Interviews
- ✓ Maintaining Documents after Separation
- ✓ E-Verify History and Milestones

Introduction to "After the Hire" Issues

A Safe Hiring Program does not stop once the candidate goes on the payroll. Lawsuits for negligent retention have put employers on notice that due diligence extends well beyond the hiring stage. In fact, employers have a continuing obligation during the entire employment relationship to exercise due diligence for protecting co-workers, the public, customers, and investors.

The laws governing employment relationship are complicated, involved, and covered by scores of outstanding books and resources. The purpose of this chapter is to focus on areas unique to safe hiring and due diligence.

The Offer Letter

Making a formal offer letter in writing is generally considered a best practice. The offer letter will verify the basic terms agreed upon by the employer and the applicant — the salary, job title, start date, and benefits.

If the employer makes the offer prior to the completion of the background report, then the offer letter serves another vital purpose: it explains to the applicant that the hiring decision is conditioned upon the employer's receipt of "a background screening report that is satisfactory to the employer." This is important language. First, the offer letter protects the employer in the event the screening is not yet completed. By specifying the background report must be satisfactory to the employer, it limits a future debate over what is or is not an objectively satisfactory report. The idea is to create a subjective standard. This does not give an employer the right to make judgments that are discriminatory, arbitrary, or capricious, but it does give some measure of protection if something is discovered after the offer is made.

Importance of Well-Written Job Description

A well-written and detailed job description is normally the basis of any effort to recruit new employees. An employer needs to define precisely what the job requires and what reasonable accommodation will help the employee carry out the job. Job descriptions are used to determine the requirements for the position, identifying responsibilities, and setting compensation. While an offer letter will set out the knowledge, skills, and abilities needed to be successful on the job, a well-written job description will specify the essential functions of the job. This is critical in the event an applicant files a claim under the Americans with Disabilities Act (ADA). From a legal perspective, a well-written job description also assists an employer in defending against claims of discrimination. For the purposes of a Safe Hiring Program, the specification of qualifications is critical.

New Employee Orientations

Another critical step for new hires is the new employee orientation. The orientation starts the employment relationship off on the right track by letting new employees know what role they play in the company and how their contributions are important. Typically, the first few days on the job are stressful for any new employee. Experienced managers know that taking the time to go through a well-planned orientation can lessen the anxiety considerably and contribute to a new employee's success. As a practical matter, the new employee orientation also serves as an opportunity to convey necessary information to that employee on such practical matters as the physical layout of the premises and introduction to co-workers, and to a review of employment terms such as compensation and benefits.

From a Safe Hiring Program perspective, the new employee orientation also serves as a valuable opportunity to impress upon new employees the importance the firm places on safety and employees. It is an opportunity to underscore the firm's commitment to a workplace with zero tolerance for drugs, dishonesty, or violence.

Employee Manual

An employee manual is a mission critical item for any organization. A manual spells out the terms and conditions of employment so there is no misunderstanding. From a legal viewpoint, labor lawyers have long taught employers that a manual is one of the most effective defenses an employer has for defending themselves against employment lawsuits. For example, if an employee violates a work rule, an employer has a much better chance of defending discipline or termination if the work rule was in a manual that the employee received and signed. If an employer has a sexual harassment or discrimination policy in their manual, this also gives increased protection.

An employee manual is invaluable as part of as Safe Hiring Program because it sets out policies in several important areas:

✓ **Workplace Violence** – It is a critical part of any effort to prevent workplace violence to clearly set out a policy that states the employer maintains a safe workplace; that there is a zero-tolerance policy for violence, threats, or intimidation; that all employees are expected to assist in the effort.

✓ **Drugs** – An employee manual is an essential aspect of any program to deal with employment related drug abuse.

✓ **Background Screening** – A best practice is to have information about safe hiring and references about screening in the employee manual.

✓ **"At Will" Basis** – The employment is "at will," which means there is no employment contract and either side can terminate the relationship.

Identity Verification

There are several tools provided by the Social Security Administration designed to halt the use of fake or stolen Social Security numbers. See Chapter 17 for details on these programs.

Part of the "intake process" of a new employee includes the use of certain government identity verification programs, one of which is mandatory for an employer to use. The next portion of this chapter reviews the Form I-9 and E-verify programs.

"Form I-9" Employment Eligibility Verification Compliance

The Immigration Reform and Control Act (IRCA) of 1986 makes it "unlawful for a person or other entity… to hire, or to recruit or refer for a fee, for employment in the United States an alien knowing the alien is an unauthorized alien." Employers violating that prohibition may be subjected to federal civil and criminal sanctions. The IRCA also requires employers to take steps to verify an employee's eligibility for employment. Per federal law, every employer is obligated to utilize a procedure to insure that a person has a right to work in the U.S.

The form used in this procedure is called the 'Form I-9, Employment Eligibility Verification' or simple "Form I-9." The completion of the I-9 Form is done after a person is hired and gives the employer another layer of protection against employing a person with a false identity.

The Form I-9 program is under the authority of the U.S. Citizenship and Immigration Services (USCIS) within the Department of Homeland Security (DHS). That department was formerly known as the Immigration and Naturalization Service (INS). The most recent version of the Form I-9 OMB No. 1615-0047, which expires August 31, 2012, is available on the USCIS.gov web site at www.uscis.gov/files/form/i-9.pdf.

For more additional information on Form I-9 visit www.uscis.gov/i-9 and click on "I-9 Central" or call 800-870-3676.

The Form I-9 Process

In the I-9 procedure the employer is required to physically view documents concerning identity and list eligibility. The Form I-9 process defines and utilizes three classes or lists of documents—A, B, and C.

List A includes documents that confirm both identity and the right to work. For U.S. citizens, the easiest means of proof is a U.S. passport. For individuals who are citizens of other countries, there are various documents they can provide, such as cards issued by the USCIS.

List B includes documents that show identity, such a driver's license or various other government ID cards.

List C documents show an eligibility to work, and can include a certified birth certificate or a card issued by the Social Security Administration.

There are two important rules to keep in mind:

1. Employers must review and verify by examining one document from List A OR examine one document from List B and one from List C.

2. If a person does not have a List A document, then one document from List B and one from List C must be provided.

Below are the acceptable documents for each List. All documents must be unexpired.

List A - Documents that Establish Both Identity and Employment Authorization

1. U.S. Passport or U.S. Passport Card
2. Permanent Resident Card or Alien Registration Receipt Card (Form I-551)
3. Foreign passport that contains a temporary I-551 stamp or temporary I-551 printed notation on a machine-readable immigrant visa (MRIV)
4. Employment Authorization Document that contains a photograph (Form I-766)
5. In the case of a nonimmigrant alien authorized to work for a specific employer incident to status, a foreign passport with Form I-94 or Form I-94A bearing the same name as the passport and containing an endorsement of the alien's nonimmigrant status, as long as the period of endorsement has not yet expired and the proposed employment is not in conflict with any restrictions of limitations identified on the form
6. Passport from the Federated States of Micronesia (FSM) or the Republic of the Marshall Islands (RMI) with Form I-94 or Form I-94A indicating nonimmigrant admission under the Compact of Free Association Between the United States and the FSM or RMI

List B - Documents that Establish Identity

1. Driver's license or identification (ID) card issued by a state or outlying possession of the United States, provided it contains a photograph or information such as name, date of birth, gender, height, eye color and address
2. ID card issued by federal, state or local government agencies or entities, provided it contains a photograph or information such as name, date of birth, gender, height, eye color and address
3. School ID card with a photograph
4. Voter's registration card
5. U.S. military card or draft record
6. Military dependent's ID card
7. U.S. Coast Guard Merchant Mariners Document (MMD) Card
8. Native American tribal document
9. Driver's license issued by a Canadian government authority

Acceptable List B Documents for persons under age 18 who are unable to present a document listed above:

10. School record or report card
11. Clinic, doctor or hospital record
12. Day-care or nursery school record

Note: For minors under the age of 18 and certain individuals with disabilities who are unable to produce any of the listed identity documents, special notations may be used in place of a List B document.

List C - Documents that Establish Employment Authorization

1. Social Security Account Number card other than one that specifies on the face that the issuance of the card does not authorize employment in the United States
2. Certification of Birth Abroad issued by the U.S. Department of State (Form FS-545)
3. Certification of Report of Birth issued by the U.S. Department of State (Form DS-1350)
4. Original or certified copy of a birth certificate issued by a state, county, municipal authority or outlying possession of the United States bearing an official seal
5. Native American tribal document
6. U.S. Citizen ID Card (Form I-197)
7. Identification Card for Use of Resident Citizen in the United States (Form I-179)
8. Employment authorization document issued by the Department of Homeland Security (DHS)

Note: Some employment authorization documents issued by DHS include but are not limited to the Form I-94 issued to an asylee or work-authorized nonimmigrant (e.g., H-1B nonimmigrants) because of their immigration status, the unexpired Reentry Permit (Form I-327), the Certificate of U.S. Citizenship (Form N-560 or N-561), or the Certificate of Naturalization (Form N-550 or N-570). Form I-797 issued to a conditional resident may be an acceptable List C(8) document in combination with his or her expired Form I-551 ("green card"). For more information about DHS-issued documents please contact customer support.

Of course, a determined individual may find a way around this procedure. As reported on the official USCIS website, "Employers are not required to be document experts. In reviewing the genuineness of the documents presented by employees, employers are held to a reasonableness standard."

However, the I-9 verification process is one of the most powerful tools an employer has. At a minimum, it puts up roadblocks that may deter, or detect persons using fraudulent identification.

The U.S. Citizenship and Immigration Services (USCIS) I-9 Procedures

The procedures for the I-9 process can be found online. Here is a description of the procedures taken from the UCCIS website at www.uscis.gov.

Employee's Responsibility Regarding Form I-9

A new employee must complete Section 1 of a Form I-9 no later than close of business on his/her first day of work. The employee's signature holds him/her responsible for the accuracy of the information provided. The employer is responsible for ensuring that the employee completes Section 1 in full. No documentation from the employer is required to substantiate Section 1 information provided by the employee.

Employer's Responsibility Regarding Form I-9

The employer is responsible ensuring completion of the entire form. No later than close of business on the employee's third day of employment services, the employer must complete section 2 of the Form I-9. The employer must review documentation presented by the employee and record document information of the form. Proper documentation establishes both that the employee is authorized to work in the U.S. and that the employee who presents the employment authorization document is the person to whom it was issued. The employer should supply to the employee the official list of acceptable documents for establishing identity and work eligibility. The employer may accept any List A document, establishing both identity and work eligibility, or combination of a List B document (establishing identity) and List C document (establishing work eligibility), that the employee chooses from the list to present (the documentation presented is not required to substantiate information provided in Section 1). The employer must examine the document(s) and accept them if they reasonably appear to be genuine and to relate to the employee who presents them. Requesting more or different documentation than the minimum necessary to meet this requirement may constitute an unfair immigration-related employment practice. If the documentation presented by an employee does not reasonably appear to be genuine or relate to the employee who presents them, employers must refuse acceptance and ask for other documentation from the list of acceptable documents that meets the requirements. An employer should not continue to employ an employee who cannot present documentation that meets the requirements.

Questions About Genuineness of Documents

Employers are not required to be document experts. In reviewing the genuineness of the documents presented by employees, employers are held to a reasonableness standard. Since no employer which is not participating in one of the employment verification pilots has access to receive confirmation of information contained in a document presented by an employee to demonstrate employment eligibility, it may happen that an employer will accept a document that is not in fact genuine – or is genuine but does not belong to the person who presented it. Such an employer will not be held responsible if the document reasonably appeared to be genuine or to relate to the person presenting it. An employer who receives a document that appears not to be genuine may request assistance from the nearest Immigration field office or contact the Office of Business Liaison.

Discovering Unauthorized Employees

It occasionally happens that an employer learns that an employee whose documentation appeared to be in order for Form I-9 purposes is not actually authorized to work. In such case, the employer should question the employee and provide another opportunity for review of proper Form I-9 documentation. If the employee is unable to provide satisfactory documentation, then employment should be discontinued. Alien employees who question the employer's determination may be referred to an Immigration field office for assistance.

Discovering False Documentation

False documentation includes documents that are counterfeit or those that belong to someone other than the employee who presented them. It occasionally happens that an employee who initially presented false documentation to gain employment subsequently obtains proper work authorization and presents documentation of this work authorization. In such a case, U.S. immigration law does not require the employer to terminate the employee's services. However, an employer's personnel policies regarding provision of false information to the employer may apply. The employer should correct the relevant information on the Form I-9.

Photocopies of Documents

There are two separate and unrelated photocopy issues in the employment eligibility verification process. First is whether an employer may accept photocopies of identity or employment eligibility documents to fulfill I-9 requirements. The answer is that only original documents (not necessarily the first document of its kind ever issued to the employee, but an actual document issued by the issuing authority) are satisfactory, with the single exception of a certified photocopy of a birth certificate. Second is whether the employer may or must attach photocopies of documentation submitted to satisfy Form I-9 requirements to the employee's Form I-9. The answer is that this is permissible, but not required. Where this practice is undertaken by an employer, it must be consistently applied to every employee, without regard to citizenship or national origin.

I-9 Audits of Employers

The U.S. Immigration and Customs Enforcement (ICE) – the principal investigative arm of the U.S. Department of Homeland Security (DHS) – performs inspections to determine if employers in the United States are violating employment laws by hiring unauthorized workers. ICE has the authority to issue a Notice of Inspection (NOI) to employers to give notice the agency is conducting inspections for compliance of proper use of the Form I-9s. Businesses undergoing I-9 audits must hand over all Form I-9s for ICE to inspect, and these audits may result in the firing of illegal workers found on a company's payroll and civil and criminal penalties for employers ranging from fines to criminal charges.

ICE issued 2,238 I-9 inspection notices in the fiscal year that began October 1, 2010, part of the government's "quiet immigration raid" policy to crackdown on employers of illegal immigrants. Statistics over the past few years show that ICE has been focusing more and more on targeting the employers that hire illegal workers through the use of Form I-9 audits and investigations. Below is a news story about one recent audit.

Company Forfeits $2 Million to DHS for Hiring Illegal Workers and Agrees to Use E-Verify

In May 2012, the U.S. Immigration and Customs Enforcement (ICE) – the largest investigative arm of the Department of Homeland Security (DHS) – announced in a press release that a Houston, Texas-based tree trimming company has avoided criminal prosecution for employing illegal workers by agreeing to forfeit $2 million to the DHS related to revenue derived from the employment of illegal workers. The company has also agreed to adhere to revised immigration compliance procedures that include the use of E-Verify, a free electronic employment eligibility verification system run by the U.S. government.

According the press release, ICE Homeland Security Investigations (HSI) agents began investigating the tree trimming company in 2008 following complaints that a significant portion of the company's employees were undocumented aliens. HIS agents reviewed the Employment Eligibility Verification Forms – known as "Form I-9" – and other documentation for approximately 2,500 employees at the company. As of the second quarter of 2009, the inspection had revealed that "a significant number of employees" – about 30 percent of the workforce – consisted of undocumented aliens who had presented invalid personal identification information when hired.

In March 2010, HSI agents executed a federal search warrant at the company's Houston headquarters and seized employment and personnel records. The government's investigation revealed the company "ignored federal law by falsely attesting on I-9s that work authorization documents presented by new hires appeared genuine" and received notices from the Social Security Administration known as "no-match letters" indicating employee names and Social Security numbers did not match SSA records. Since approximately $2 million in revenue was derived from using an illegal workforce, the figure represents the amount of money that the company forfeited under its non-prosecution agreement with the government.

Since the investigation, the company has "imposed significant immigration compliance measures" that includes the use of E-Verify, an Internet-based system that allows employers to verify the legal work authorization status of newly hired employees to work in the United States by checking information on the Employment Eligibility Verification Form I-9 that all newly hired employees in the U.S. are required to complete against DHS and Social Security Administration (SSA) databases. The company also has introduced "new policies concerning the proper completion, retention, and auditing of I-9s and for responding to SSA No Match letters" and has terminated hundreds of undocumented workers.

Source: www.ice.gov/news/releases/1205/120518houston.htm.

One way to be prepared for an audit is to utilize solutions that provide an electronic online verification process. A number of private firms offer commercial solutions.

"E-Verify" Electronic Employment Eligibility Verification

As indicated in the previous news story, in addition to filling out the paper Form I-9 Form, employers can also utilize the Electronic Employment Eligibility Verification Process known as E-Verify. This program run by the federal government allows employers to verify the employment eligibility of prospective employees through the Social Security Administration and the DHS.

E-Verify is an Internet-based system that compares information from an employee's Form I-9 to data from U.S. Department of Homeland Security and Social Security Administration records to confirm employment eligibility. It is operated by the U.S. Citizenship and Immigration Services (USCIS), part of the Department of Homeland Security (DHS), and is the government agency that oversees lawful immigration to the United States. It utilizes both Homeland Security and Social Security Administration (SSA) data.

The program is voluntary except the federal government requires that all federal contractors and sub-contractors use E-Verify to verify that their newly hired workers are legally eligible to work in the United States. In addition, a number of U.S. states have enacted laws mandating the use of E-Verify. A table of these states is proved later in this chapter.

In order to participate in the program, an employer must execute a Memorandum of Understanding (MOU). Background screening firms may also act as an employer's authorized 'Designated E-Verify Employer Agent.'

For information on how the E-Verify program operates, visit: www.dhs.gov/e-verify.

There has been much debate as to the accuracy and completeness of the databases used, and if a worker is not verified, then there are a number of steps an employer must go through to complete the process. Note that in early 2007, the federal government significantly increased the penalty on employers who employ workers with fake Social Security numbers.

E-Verify For Federal Contractors

The following information is found on the 'For Federal Contractors' pages on the USCIS web site:

"Executive Order 12989 Amendment

On June 11, 2008, President George W. Bush amended Executive Order 12989 to direct all executive departments and agencies to require contractors to electronically verify employment authorization of employees performing work under qualifying federal contracts. U.S. Department of Homeland Security (DHS) designated E-Verify as the electronic employment eligibility verification system that all federal contractors must use to comply with the amended Executive order 12989.

Employment Eligibility Verification, Federal Acquisition Regulation (FAR)

On November 14, 2008, the Civilian Agency Acquisition Council and the Defense Acquisition Regulations Council published a Federal Acquisition Regulation (FAR) final rule (FAR case 2007-013, Employment Eligibility Verification) that implements amended Executive Order 12989. FAR is a set of rules and regulations used to manage the way the federal government acquires supplies and services for appropriated funds. The FAR final rule, known as the E-Verify federal contractor rule, directs federal agencies to require many federal contractors to use E-Verify to electronically verify the employment eligibility of certain employees. For more information about FAR, visit: http://edocket.access.gpo.gov/2008/E8-26904.htm.

The Federal Contractor Rule and E-Verify

The final rule became effective September 8, 2009 and requires certain federal contractors, through language inserted into their contract, to begin using E Verify to verify their new and existing employees. For additional information see the E-Verify Supplemental Guide for Federal Contractors manual at: www.uscis.gov/USCIS/Verification/E-Verify/E-Verify%20from%20Controlled%20Vocabulary/FAR_Supplemental_Guide_REVISED_FINAL.pdf.

E-Verify Federal Contractor List

In accordance with the E-Verify Memorandum of Understanding, U.S. Department of Homeland Security posts the E-Verify Federal Contractors List - a list of contractors who currently use E-Verify on the Federal Acquisition Regulation clause. The list contains: business name (the name which was used during registration with E-Verify, whether the legal name of the business or individual, a trade name or abbreviation), contact address used at registration, workforce size, employee verification (all new hires or entire workforce), and query volume. You can access by going to the Federal Contractors List page. The list may take several minutes to download."

U.S. States with Laws Requiring E-Verify Use

As mentioned, use of E-Verify is voluntary, other than those employers affected by the federal law mandating use for federal contractors and subcontractors in all states. However, a number several U.S. states have enacted laws mandating the use of E-Verify for all employees. The table below provides details about these state laws. A current E-Verify Legislation Map is also available at www.trackercorp.com/everify-legislation-map.php.

U.S. States with Laws Requiring Mandatory E-Verify Use as of February 2012*

State	E-Verify Law(s)	Effective Date(s)
Alabama	**HB 56 – Beason-Hammon Alabama Taxpayer and Citizen Protection Act:** Passed in 2011, HB 56 is regarded as many as the nation's toughest immigration enforcement law passed at the state level. HB 56 requires all businesses, public and private, to begin using E-Verify by April 2012. The penalty for businesses not complying with the E-Verify mandate is a suspension of its business license.	**April 1, 2012**
Arizona	**HB 2779 – Arizona Fair and Legal Employment Act:** Passed in 2007, HB 2779 prohibits employers from knowingly hiring undocumented workers and requires all employers to use E-Verify, effective January 1, 2008. It was followed up in 2008 with **HB 2745**, which prohibits government contracts to any businesses not using E-Verify, effective May 1, 2008.	**January 1, 2008 & May 1, 2008**
Colorado	**HB 1343:** Passed in 2006, HB 1343 prohibits state agencies from entering into contract agreements with contractors who knowingly employ illegal aliens and requires prospective contractors use E-Verify to ensure legal work status of all employees. In 2008, SB 193 was passed requiring contractors with state contracts to use E-Verify. The effective date for SB 193 was August 6, 2008.	**August 6, 2008**
Florida	**Executive Order 11-02:** Executive Order 11-02 requires all Florida state agencies under the direction of the Governor to use E-Verify to confirm the employment eligibility of all current and prospective employees (including subcontractors) assigned to perform work pursuant to a state agency contract, effective January 4, 2011. **Executive Order 11-116**, issued on May 27, 2011 provides some clarification. The requirement for state contractors to use E-Verify applies to "all contracts for the provision of goods and services to the state in excess of nominal value" in which there is an express requirement for such use.	**January 4, 2011**
Georgia	**SB 529:** Passed in 2006, SB 529 requires public employers, contractors and subcontractors with 500 or more employees to participate in E-Verify for all new employees, effective July 1, 2007. Public employers, contractors and subcontractors with more than 100 employees (but less than 500) must use E-Verify on or before July 1, 2008 and public employers, contractors and subcontractors with fewer	**July 1, 2007** **July 1, 2008** **July 1, 2009** **July 1, 2011** **July 1, 2013**

	than 100 employees must use E-Verify on or before July 1, 2009. **HB 87 – The 'Illegal Immigration Reform and Enforcement Act of 2011':** Passed in 2011, HB 87 requires all private businesses with more than 10 employees to use E-Verify. The phase-in began on July 1, 2011 and runs through July 1, 2013.	
Idaho	**Executive Orders:** In May 2009, Gov. Butch Otter signed **Executive Order 2009-10** requiring all state agencies and contractors to use E-Verify if they wanted a share of the state's $1.24 billion from the economic stimulus bill. In December 2006, Governor Jim Risch also issued **Executive Order 2006-40**, with immediate effect, requiring that state agencies participate in the E-Verify system.	**May 2009 December 2006**
Indiana	**SB 590:** Passed in 2011, SB 590 requires state and local agencies and state and local contractors to use E-Verify. The bill also requires private employers to use E-Verify in order to qualify for certain tax credits on their state income taxes.	**2011**
Louisiana	**HB 342/HB 646:** Passed in 2011, **HB 342** requires all state and local contractors to use E-Verify. **HB 646** requires private employers to either use E-Verify or check multiple forms of identification from the new hire, which must be kept on file. The bill states that employers that chose to use E-Verify to check the status of new hires have acted in "good faith" and are protected from prosecution.	**2011**
Mississippi	**SB 2988:** Passed in 2008, SB 2988 requires public and private employers to participate in E-Verify with full participation by July 2011.	**July 2011**
Missouri	**HB 1549:** Passed in 2008, HB 1549 requires all public employers to use E-Verify. If a court finds that a business knowingly employed someone not authorized to work, the company's business permit and licenses shall be suspended for 14 days. Upon the first violation, the state may terminate contracts and bar the company from doing business with the state for 3 years. Upon the second violation, the state may permanently debar the company from doing business with the state.	**2008**
Nebraska	**L 403:** Passed in 2009, LB403 requires state and local governments and contractors to use E-Verify effective October 1, 2009. The bill also includes incentives for private employers to use E-Verify.	**October 1, 2009**
North Carolina	**SB 1523:** Passed in 2006, SB 1523 requires all state agencies, offices, and universities to use E-Verify. The law applied to all employees hired after January 1, 2007 except for local education agencies which was March 1, 2007. **HB 36:** Passed in 2011, HB 36 requires all employers with more than 6 employees to use E-Verify. The phase-in period begins in October 2012 and runs through July 2013. Seasonal workers are not required to be verified through E-Verify.	**January 1, 2007 March 1, 2007 October 2012 - July 2013**
Oklahoma	**HB 1804 'Oklahoma Taxpayer and Citizen Protection Act':** Passed in 2007 and made effective on November 1, 2007, HB 1804 requires public employers, contractors and subcontractors to participate in E-Verify and requires income tax withholding for independent contractors who do not have valid Social Security numbers.	**November 1, 2007**

South Carolina	**HB 4400:** Passed in 2008, HB 4400 requires the mandatory use of E-Verify for all employers by July 1, 2010. All public employers, private employers with more than 100 employees and public contractors with more than 500 employees were required to comply by January 1, 2009. All private employers must comply by July 1, 2009 and all other all businesses by January 1, 2010.	**January 1, 2009** **July 1, 2009** **January 1, 2010** **July 1, 2010**
Tennessee	**HB 1378:** Passed in 2011, HB 1378 requires all employers with at least 6 employees to use E-Verify. The phase-in begins in January 2012 and runs through January 2013. Companies that utilize legal guest workers do not have to use E-Verify.	**January 2012 - January 2013**
Utah	**SB 0251:** Passed in 2010, SB 0251 requires all employers with more than 15 employees to begin using E-Verify July 1, 2011. Companies that utilize legal guest workers do not have to use E-Verify. **SB 81:** Passed in 2008 and made effective on July 1, 2009, SB 81 requires public employers, public contractors and subcontractors to E-Verify and makes it illegal to discharge a lawful employee while retaining an unauthorized alien in the same job category.	**July 1, 2009** **July 1, 2011**
Virginia	**HB 737:** Passed in 2010, HB 737 requires all state agencies to begin using E-Verify by December 1, 2012. **HB 1859/SB 1049:** Passed in March 2011, the bill requires all state contractors with at least 50 employees and a contract worth at least $50,000 to use E-Verify.	**December 1, 2012**

*Source: Information Obtained from NumbersUSA.com & www.ncsl.org/issues-research/immigration/e-verify-faq.aspx

The article below details a ruling by the U.S. Supreme Court that upheld Arizona's E-Verify law.

U.S. Supreme Court Ruling Upholds Mandatory Arizona E-Verify Law

In a 5-to-3 decision in May of 2011, the U.S. Supreme Court ruled states can punish employers who violate mandatory E-Verify laws by upholding a 2007 Arizona law that requires employers to enroll in the voluntary federal E-Verify program which checks the legal status of workers by comparing information on their Employment Eligibility Verification Form I-9s against Department of Homeland Security (DHS) and Social Security Administration (SSA) databases.

In the majority opinion for the Court, Chief Justice John Roberts wrote that Arizona enforces its E-Verify employment verification requirement through licensing laws:

> "Arizona's procedures simply implement the sanctions that Congress expressly allowed the States to pursue through licensing laws. Given that Congress specifically preserved such authority for the States, it stands to reason that Congress did not intend to prevent the States from using appropriate tools to exercise that authority… We hold that Arizona's licensing law falls well within the confines of the authority Congress chose to leave to the states and therefore is not expressly preempted."

The U.S. Chamber of Commerce had sued the state of Arizona over a 2007 law that suspends licenses of businesses if they fail to use E-Verify to check the eligibility of all new hires, arguing that immigration enforcement is exclusively the purview of the federal government. Arizona was the first state in the country to pass a mandatory law requiring mandatory use of the E-Verify electronic employment eligibility verification system by employers. Mississippi and South Carolina have also passed mandatory E-Verify laws, while many other states have passed laws requiring E-Verify use by some businesses. The full Supreme Court ruling on the case is available at: www.supremecourt.gov/opinions/10pdf/09-115.pdf.

U.S. States with Laws Prohibiting Mandatory E-Verify Use

While many U.S. states have passed laws requiring the use of E-Verify, other states have passed *laws prohibiting the mandated use of E-Verify.*

California:

✓ **AB 1236 – The Employment Acceleration Act of 2011:** In October 2011, Governor Jerry Brown signed AB 1236 into law. The law prohibits the state, or a city, county, city and county, or special district, from requiring an employer other than one of those government entities to use an electronic employment verification system except when required by federal law or as a condition of receiving federal funds. The law took effect January 1, 2012.

Illinois:

✓ **HB 1774:** HB 1744 bars Illinois companies from enrolling in any Employment Eligibility Verification System until accuracy and timeliness issues are resolved.

✓ **HR 1743:** Illinois also enacted HB 1743, which creates privacy and antidiscrimination protections for workers if employers participating in E-Verify don't follow the program's procedures.

✓ **S1133:** On August 24, 2009, Illinois enacted S1133 prohibiting the state or localities from requiring employers to use an employment eligibility verification system.

Washington:

✓ **HB 2568 (Proposed Jan. 2012):** A proposed bill in the Washington State House of Representatives, House Bill 2568, would prohibit the state and municipalities from requiring that a private employer use the E-Verify program, unless required by the federal government.

GAO Report Notes Improvements in Accuracy of E-Verify

According to a December 2010 report from the United States Government Accountability Office (GAO), the U.S. Citizenship and Immigration Services (USCIS) bureau has taken steps to improve the accuracy and efficiency of the E-Verify electronic employment eligibility verification system used to check if workers are legally eligible to work in the country.

The report – GAO-11-146 Employment Verification (http://www.gao.gov/new.items/d11146.pdf) – found that USCIS had boosted the E-Verify system's accuracy by expanding the number of databases consulted to determine the legal status of a new hire and by establishing new quality control procedures that included making employers double-check information for employees found unauthorized to work in the U.S. and allowing E-Verify to automatically correct clerical errors.

More improvements to the E-Verify system mean that more eligible workers are being approved immediately. E-Verify immediately confirmed nearly 97.5 percent of 8.2 million new hires entered into the system during fiscal year 2009, while another 0.3 percent successfully contested their "tentative nonconfirmation" status. In addition, GAO found that the USCIS had taken more precautions to protect the personal information of employees.

Despite these improvements, GAO cautioned that "E-Verify remains vulnerable to identity theft and employer fraud." Nevertheless, E-Verify – a free, web-based system that compares employee information on the Employment Eligibility Verification Form I-9 against records in the Department of Homeland Security (DHS) and Social Security Administration (SSA) databases – is currently being used by at least 243,000 employers that ran more than 16 million queries in fiscal 2010, according to USCIS.

In December 2011, E-Verify reached a milestone. Employers are now using E-Verify at more than one million worksites.

Designated E-Verify Employer Agents

Employers may choose to have a Designated E-Verify Employer Agent assist them in maintaining compliance with the Form I-9 and E-Verify process and can help virtually eliminate I-9 form errors, improve the accuracy of their reporting, protect jobs for authorized workers, and help maintain a legal workforce.

Employment "At Will" and Probationary Periods

A critical issue for employers is the nature of the employee-employer relationship. Employers typically hire on an "at will" basis, meaning there is no employment contract and either side can terminate the relationship. Of course, nothing is that simple. Employers are normally advised to be very clear in all stages of the recruiting, interviewing, and hiring procedure that no promises or contracts are made, either expressed or implied, that modify the at-will arrangement. Again, nothing is that smooth. An applicant may argue that, by certain employer's actions or deeds, there is an implied promise of future employment that can only be terminated "for cause" as opposed to "at will."

Examples of instances where an employee may argue they are no longer "at will" are listed below:

- ✓ Language in an interview that says "if a person does well, the company will take care of them," or other similar promise of special treatment on the part of the employer.
- ✓ Language in the employee manual that creates a "probationary period." The implication is that if a person passes the probationary period, they have vested or obtained a more secure status and there must be "good cause" to terminate rather than a right to terminate "at will."
- ✓ Employee manual language that sets out a series of progressive disciplinary steps where an employee has a chance to improve performance. The implication is if they meet the standards, then the person is no longer "at will."
- ✓ A listing of actions or omissions that are grounds for discipline or termination. The argument is if one of these enumerated acts or omissions is not committed, then the employer needs cause to terminate.
- ✓ When an employee has been with the employer for a period of time and has received promotions, regular pay increases, and good performance reviews, the employee can argue he or she is no longer at will.

Along with appropriate statements in the application, the employee manual is also a critical tool to reinforce the "at will" nature of employment.

It is also necessary to insure that everyone with hiring responsibilities is trained not to make statements that imply a commitment beyond "at will." There are also other exceptions to the "at will" status, such as civil service employment, collective bargaining agreements, or public policy exceptions to "at will" status.

From the perspective of a Safe Hiring Program, maintaining the "at will" relationship can be vital to an employer in the event issues arise related to workplace violence or misconduct, or it is later discovered the employee made material misstatements or omissions during the hiring process. Even though an employer may have grounds to terminate based upon the misconduct or misrepresentation, the "at will" status will assist the employer's position.

Confidentiality Agreements and Ethics Policy

Another best practice is to obtain a confidentiality and ethics agreement as part of the employment relationship. Some firms place the language in the employee manual. However, having it as separate document may give additional emphasis. Although the specific language may vary for a particular industry, the essential thrust is to establish that honest and ethical dealings are part of the firm's culture, and an essential element of the duties and responsibilities of every employee. Although some employers may assume that some truths are self-evident and that it goes without saying that honest and ethical behavior is required, saying so serves as a valuable reminder.

Maintaining Employment Screening Records

Record keeping and maintaining personnel files are always important issue for employers. Files should contain information regarding the employment application, and qualifications for employment, as well as all personnel actions such as compensation, promotions, transfers, demotions, discipline, and terminations.

In reality, an employer maintains multiple files on an employee. In addition to the "official" personnel file, supervisors or managers may maintain files. In addition, there are matters normally kept in a separate and secured file. These files are normally stored in an area only accessible to Human Resources personnel or those who are authorized. These files contain matters that are confidential or sensitive in nature, thus widespread publication could constitute an invasion of personal privacy. These files should NOT be accessible by supervisors during performance appraisals.

Confidential matters contained in these files can include:

- ✓ Background reports.
- ✓ Letter of reference.
- ✓ Verification of right to work (Employment Eligibility Verification "Form I-9").
- ✓ Workers' compensation claims.
- ✓ Medical information.
- ✓ Documents concerning employee status as a disabled person, veteran, or other status.
- ✓ Defamatory information.
- ✓ Information unrelated to the job.

Supervisors may also keep files reflecting such things as notes or memos of discussions for issues or problems that have arisen. These notes may indicate what was discussed, when, and who was present. These notes may be used during performance evaluations.

Employees May Have the Right to Inspect Their Personnel Files

Keep in mind that, in many states, employees have a right to inspect their own personnel file.

Files should be maintained where the employee reports to work. Employers may generally impose reasonable restrictions such as setting up appointments during regular business hours or on the employee's own time, limiting the frequency, or require an employer representative to be present, but the employer cannot set arbitrary time limits. If there is an inspection, then the employer should keep a history of the request and the response.

The right to inspection may not include:

- ✓ A record of investigation of possible criminal offense.
- ✓ Letters of reference, unless steps are taken to safeguard the identity of the authors.
- ✓ If a file contains other confidential data, then the identity of persons can be removed, i.e. the employer should protect the privacy of third persons.

An example is California Labor Code Sec. 1198.5(a) that provides that every public and private employee has a right to inspect his or her personnel files except for public safety offenses and certain employees' subject to the Information Practices Act of 1977. The right to inspect includes files with information used to determine employee qualifications, promotion, compensation, termination, or other disciplinary action. Failure to allow inspection is a misdemeanor, punishable by a fine up to $100 and imprisonment for 30 days.

Screening Current Employees

When reviewing background-checking policies, a question often arises about whether current employees should be screened, or whether the background check policy should apply to new applicants only.

The need to screen current employees can be necessitated by a new contract with a customer who requires all workers performing the contract have a background check. It can also occur when a firm "acquires" another workforce through a merger or acquisition. There can also be situations where an employer is concerned about some type of workplace misconduct or wrongdoing such as theft or harassment.

There are two factors to consider in screening current employees— legal and practical.

It is perfectly legal to screen current employees as long as all their rights are respected. (Keep in mind if an employer is unionized, there may be special workplace rules.) A current employee is entitled to the same legal rights as a new applicant, and if there is a union involved, perhaps even more rights. Under the Federal Fair Credit Reporting Act, if the background check is performed by a third party service provider, then current employees are entitled to the same rights as new applicants, which includes a disclosure of rights and written consent. Some states have additional rules that employers must be mindful to follow. As previously mentioned in Chapter 3, if an existing employee is screened for allegations of wrongdoing or misconduct, then his or her consent may not be needed under the FACT Act amendment to the FCRA.

The practical consideration is whether the employer wants to ask existing employees to consent to a background check. The issue is one of corporate culture—not alienating employees who have been hardworking and loyal by performing background checks.

If an employer decides it is necessary to screen current employees, it is recommended that HR explain screening is "a business necessity for the good of the entire organization" and not directed to any one employee. This will increase employee "buy-in." Equally critical is for employees to understand all their rights are being respected, and nothing will occur as a result of a background check until the employee has an opportunity to discuss any negative findings with the employer. Problems can arise if an employee feels powerless in the process, concerned about an adverse action without an opportunity to be heard. It is crucial to tell all employees they may come to Human Resources to privately discuss the procedure. An employee may start off talking about privacy concerns, when in fact there is something of concern in the person's background.

Another consideration occurs when an existing employee may not sign a consent form. If employees have a clear understanding of how this policy helps both the employer and the employee, then there is typically good employee "buy-in." However, in a worst case scenario where an employee absolutely refuses to consent, an employer can take the following position – let the employee know that they have the right not to consent. On the other hand, just as the employee has a right not to consent, the next time the employee is up for a pay raise or promotion, the employer equally has the right not to promote or give a raise. This tactic may be considered if a current employee refuses to sign a consent form before the employer takes the more difficult track of termination.

Kelchner v. Sycamore Manor Health Center

In the first court case to address the issue of an employee not consenting, a Federal District Court in Pennsylvania decided that an employer can terminate a current employee who refused to sign a consent for a background check. In *Kelchner v. Sycamore Manor Health Center*, 2004 U.S. Dist. Lexis 2942 (M.D. Pa. 2004), the employer required all employees to sign a consent to a consumer report. A worker with 19 years on the job refused to sign and was terminated. The Court held that the plain language of the statute as well as Congressional intent demonstrated that employers had the right to require such a consent and could terminate if an employee refused, just as an employer could refuse to hire an applicant who did not consent in the first place.

"Continuous Screening" or "Re-Screening"

A new evolving practice called "Continuous Screening," "Infinity Screening," or "Re-Screening" is aimed at running periodic criminal records checks, such as every two weeks or monthly, on employees. These periodic checks have the potential to identify criminal cases that occur after the person was hired. Although the argument is made that the employer would likely be aware of a crime committed by a current worker because the worker did not show up to work, there are many serious offenses where a worker can be bailed out and serve a sentence with work furlough, weekend jail, volunteer hours, or some other alternative to actual incarceration. Such ongoing searches are seen as a way to continue to demonstrate due diligence and to protect the workplace.

While these continuous searches can be a valuable risk-management tool, an employer needs consider a number of factors:

✓ False Sense of Security. Remember, employers sometimes use databases that contain errors.
✓ Consent Issue. Does the employee know he or she will be re-screened?
✓ What to do if a Record is Found. Will the applicant be put on probation or fired?
✓ EEOC Considerations. Make sure the re-screening is not discriminatory under Title XII.
✓ Impact on Workforce. Will morale of employees suffer?

One possible solution for employers considering continuous screening is to use a random pool for re-screening similar to DOT regulated drug testing and perform searches at the local county courthouse.

Continual Re-Screening on Current Employees Carries Risks

The verdict on whether or not the advantages of periodic background checks of current employees outweigh the disadvantages is: "the jury is still out."

Even though periodic criminal screening of current employees may have some apparent advantages, the jury is still out on whether it is a cost-effective tool or even if the advantages outweigh the disadvantages. Here are some points to consider:

✓ There is no empirical evidence that shows that such checks have resulted in any advantage to employers. There are no studies to suggest on a cost-benefit basis, such checks produce results.
✓ If such checks are done, the next issue is how. If databases are used, then there is the possibility of both false positives and false negatives since databases available to private employers are not always complete or up to date. In large states like California, New York, and Texas, such database searches have very limited value.
✓ If there is a periodic check, it should be done ideally on the courthouse level in addition to any databases, which increases the cost.
✓ There is also the consent issue. Under the federal Fair Credit Reporting Act (FCRA), periodic checks must be done with consent (unless there is a specific investigation for suspicion of misconduct or wrongdoing), Although most consent forms contain "evergreen" language that makes the consent valid indefinitely or until revoked (usually in writing), at some point, an employee can either withdraw the consent or claim it has become stale over time. In California, it is arguable that a new consent is needed each and every time.
✓ If an employee withdraws consent, the question arises if the employee can be terminated for refusal to consent. It is clear that employers have much more discretion in requiring pre-employment testing, based upon the fact that they do not have experience with the applicant. For that reason, courts have granted wider latitude pre-hire. However, once someone is employed, the necessity argument is less convincing since the employer now has a history with the worker. Therefore, it is not clear that an employee can be terminated for a refusal to consent to an ongoing criminal check, absent some explicit employer policy. The employer could argue that since employment is "at will," failure to consent to an ongoing background check can constitute grounds for termination. The problem is that as time goes on, the "at will" relationship can become murky depending upon the facts of the employment relationship.

✓ The issue becomes more complicated if the refusing employee is a member of a protected class. That raises potential discrimination issues.

✓ In addition, a firm needs a well laid out policy in an employee manual as to how they will deal to a new criminal record that may be uncovered during a periodic check. At a minimum, any action must be based upon some business justification, taking into account the nature and gravity of the offense, the nature of the job, and how long ago it occurred. In addition, the pre-adverse action notice requirements of the federal Fair Credit Reporting Act (FCRA) would come into play.

✓ There are also the cultural considerations. What type of message does it send the workplace if workers are constantly suspected of criminal activity. What type of workplace stress is created if an otherwise long time and loyal employee feels they are subject to dismissal at any time for a minor offense that may or may not bear upon their suitably as an employee. If the employer is unionized, then union rules can also play a role.

✓ One possible solution for employers that have determined that continual screening is necessary is to conduct it in a similar fashion to random drug testing done for certain drivers that are controlled the Department of Transportation. Random pools can be set up.

Having noted the disadvantages, the case can well occur where an employer is sued for a failure to check current employees, if such a failure to check was the proximate cause of workplace violence or some other harm that arguably could have been prevented.

The bottom line is that this is an issue that will be worked out in court decision in the coming years. In the meantime, employers contemplating such periodic checks should approach it with caution and seek the advice of their attorney.

If Screening Results Lead to Possible Termination Issues

What if the screening of a current employee results in a decision to terminate? If the screening reveals the applicant had a criminal conviction not indicated on the application, then an employer could choose to terminate for dishonesty. However, keep in mind that the exact wording of the criminal question on the employment application is critical. If the employer only asked about felonies, then an undisclosed misdemeanor — even a serious misdemeanor — may not be grounds to terminate for dishonesty. An employee may give other reasons why failure to disclose was not an act of dishonesty. An employee may claim that they did not realize it was a conviction or claim they did not understand what the judge or their lawyer told them. Some defendants enter a plea of "nolo" or "no contest." Although that may give a criminal defendant some protection if they are later sued in a civil court, a "nolo" or "no contest" plea has the same effect as pleading guilty.

Suppose the screening of existing employees reveals a criminal record that was not mentioned in the application or interview process. This is potential grounds for termination, providing the employer's application form put an applicant on notice that any material misstatement or omission is grounds for termination no matter when discovered. (See the discussion about application forms in Chapter 7.) The situation becomes difficult when the employee claims he/she did inform the manager of past difficulties, but the manager failed to inform human resources. The solution is to ensure that all pre-hire procedures are followed and documented, and all managers are trained in the hiring procedures.

In addition, if the screening discloses an offense that occurs AFTER employment, the employer may decide to take action. However, the Equal Employment Opportunity Commission (EEOC) rules apply. The employer must take into account the nature and gravity of the offense, how long ago it occurred, and whether it is job-related in order to determine if there is a business necessity to deny continued employment.

An employer should also document any decision NOT to terminate in case the employer has to defend a decision to terminate some employees with criminal records and not others. If the employer has a written policy that requires employees to inform the employer if a criminal conviction occurs after employment begins, then an employer can take position that the termination is a result of a violation of a written company policy. As a practical matter, an employer would likely be aware of any serious criminal matter after employment commences, since an employee may not show up to work or need time off for court appearances. If an employee is arrested and not able to come to work, then an employer should examine the employee manual to determine the company's rule for unexcused absences.

If termination is considered, then the employer needs to be mindful of the FCRA requirements for pre-adverse action. An employee cannot simply be brought into the office and given their final check. The FCRA requires a pre-adverse action notice, giving the employee has a meaningful opportunity to review, reflect, and respond to the consumer report if the employee feels it is inaccurate or incomplete. One method is to meet with the employee, explain that a matter of concern came up in the screening report, and to provide the employee with a copy of the report and a statement of their rights prepared by the FTC, which the screening firm can provide. The employee should also be provided a letter advising that he or she should respond to the employer or the screening firm as soon as possible if there is anything the employee wishes to challenge or explain.

Since by definition the employer notice is pre-adverse action, an employer may consider placing the employee on three days paid administrative leave with instructions to either contact the employer in three days if the employee plans to contest the consumer report, or the leave turns into a termination. If the employer does not hear back, then the employee is terminated. See the Termination Procedures section below for special considerations on terminations.

If the applicant notifies the employer of plans to contest the report, then the employer can make a case-by-case judgment to either continue the employment, place the employee on unpaid leave, or terminate pending resolution of the re-investigation with a right to reapply. The FCRA does not require the employer keep a job open or keep an employee on paid leave during the re-investigation period, but only requires a meaningful opportunity to receive notice of pre-adverse action and deal with the report before the adverse action is taken. If the decision to terminate becomes final, then the employee is entitled to the second FCRA post-adverse action letter. The decision to place on leave can also be affected by the provisions of the employee manual or the existence of union contracts.

Employee Misconduct Issues

Another situation where a background check may be warranted involves workplace misconduct, such as theft, harassment, or threats of violence. Prior to the 2003 amendments to the FCRA, these types of investigations presented substantial legal issues when background checks were conducted by professional third party investigators. For example, if the investigation centered on suspected criminal activities such as theft, drug dealing, or workplace violence, it would be difficult to conduct an undercover investigation and obtain witness identities if consent had to be obtained first. A number of court decisions undercut the FTC's position. The matter was finally laid to rest with the passage of the Fair and Accurate Credit Transactions Act (FACT) in 2003, with amendments to the FCRA becoming effective in 2004. The amendments allow investigation of current employees to take place without FCRA consents, subject to some requirements, such as if an adverse action was taken that there be disclosure.

Ongoing Training

Ongoing training is also another critical aspect to employers. Training can cover a wide variety of topics; an employer should include issues related to safety and security.

Training should have an emphasis on supervisors, having them trained to recognize, report, and deal appropriately with workplace misconduct. In addition, supervisors must be properly trained and educated regarding the employer's liability for negligent hiring, supervision, retention and, promotion.

Performance Reviews and Ongoing Monitoring

Periodic performance appraisals as well as ongoing review of performances are additional mission critical tasks for employers. For purposes of ongoing safe hiring, the concern is whether the firm conducts periodic performance reviews of workers that include issues related to workplace conduct.

It is especially important that supervisors be evaluated on compliance with the duty to record, report, and address workplace misconduct. Supervisors must also understand they are evaluated in part upon monitoring workplace misconduct. Without proper documentation an employer may lack evidence later.

Advantages of Performance Reviews

According to Dennis L. DeMey in his book *Don't Hire a Crook* (©2001 BRB Publications, Tempe, AZ), performance reviews are an excellent way to maintain quality employment. As mentioned earlier, the job description informs the employee of the company's expectations of him or her. The performance review is the follow-up.

Performance reviews give employers the opportunity to examine employee performance and let them know areas where they need to improve. Oftentimes, a performance evaluation is conducted in conjunction with a salary review, then used to determine if a pay increase should be given and, if so, how much.

There are many times when a review may be conducted. Here are a few reasons:

✓ The employee has reached the end of his or her probationary period.
✓ The employee is being considered for promotion.
✓ The employee has exhibited unsatisfactory performance.
✓ Company policy requires that a review be documented annually.
✓ The employee has performed exceptionally well.

Performance reviews are yet another means of good communication between employee and employer. Likewise, it is a step that should be documented. By documenting performance reviews, two goals are accomplished:

✓ The employee has a written copy of areas that need improvement, and therefore may refer back to it; and
✓ The employer has a document that can be used to illustrate a history of problems, if that is the case.

Responding to Employee Complaints

Employees concerned about violence, dishonesty, or fraud should have the opportunity to lodge complaints. Timely and attentive management of potential problem situations along with appropriate follow-through and documentation are the keys to avoiding legal claims of negligent hiring/supervision.

To accomplish these goals, employers must have a mechanism for employees to report instances of workplace misconduct, such as violence, dishonesty, or fraud. The mechanism should also include the ability to report acts of harassment, discrimination, or other incidents that create a hostile work environment, but without fear of retaliation or reprisals, especially if the subject of the complaint is a supervisor or someone in authority. Under Sarbanes-Oxley, a whistleblower hotline may also be established.

In fact, in the employee policy manual an employer can even require that in the event of harassment or other misconduct, there is a duty to report it to management so the employer can investigate and take remedial action.

Also, the employer must have a mechanism in place to fairly and promptly investigate complaints and to have demonstrated a commitment to take appropriate actions in response to the results of the investigation. Being able to document these procedures is critical should an employer be sued for negligent retention or supervision.

Termination Procedures

Termination of employees presents numerous challenges and consideration for any organization. Numerous legal and human resources materials are available to employers on dealing with termination. The fear of being sued over a termination is always a key consideration.

However, employers should also consider the possibility of being sued over the failure to terminate. Employers who fail to take action, including termination, where they have actual or constructive knowledge that a current employee is dangerous or unqualified for a position, can risk litigation for negligent retention, negligent supervision, or even negligent promotion.

Method of Termination

The method of termination is very critical and there exists numerous resources and checklists of how to go about the process. The reason an employee seeks the assistance of a lawyer in order to explore bringing legal action is often because, at some fundamental level, the employee feels mistreated or somehow demeaned as an individual. Therefore it is critical that an employee be treated in a fair, impartial, and dignified way in the termination process. At the same time, the employer needs to protect the organization and co-workers. Below are some points to consider:

✓ When an employee is called in for the meeting with human resources or security about a consumer report or termination, a best practice is to do so at the end of the day to minimize embarrassment to the employee and disruption in the workplace. Many employers prefer to terminate at the beginning of the week rather than a Friday. Thus a terminated employment does not stew while still on the job and the workweek does not end on a sour note.

✓ A best practice is to have two employer representatives at the meeting so there is no question afterwards as to what was said.

✓ When the employee leaves the meeting, often a manager will accompany the employee to the employee's desk or to the exit in order to avoid disruption and to keep the situation calm.

✓ Depending upon the potential for violence or disruptions, some firms will have security service available for assistance.

✓ As part of the termination process, the employer must arrange to block passwords and access to the computer system and to change building entrance codes. If the employee has business material at his desk such as customer lists or phone numbers, then the material should also be secured by the employer.

✓ There are wage requirements to meet, such as giving the terminated employee a final paycheck that accounts for all wages, vacations, and any other time that is owed.

✓ The manner in which a termination occurs, when the person is escorted off premises or to their work areas to retrieve personal items, is also important. Employers have been sued for causing undue embarrassment and emotional distress in the way termination was handled.

✓ Many employers will take appropriate precautions to ensure that the reasons for the termination remain confidential.

✓ Consider if an offer of a severance agreement is appropriate. Such an agreement typically provides an employee with severance pay (such as two weeks) in exchange for a waiver of any claims the employee may feel he or she has against the employer. An employer should contact an attorney to determine what rules apply in their state. Some of the critical aspects include a fair payment to the employee ("adequate consideration" in legal terms), adequate time for the employee to consider all options, a very clearly drafted agreement so the employee cannot later claim a lack of understanding to any rights given up, and the ability to rescind the agreement within a certain time period.

Exit Interviews

Exit interviews are an often overlooked opportunity for employers to exercise due diligence in protecting their workplace and third parties — an opportunity to locate potential landmines in an organization. Employees may have more information on what is actually occurring in an organization than managers and supervisors. An employee who is leaving may be willing to tell an employer what is really going on in the organization. For example, employees who have been terminated may be a source of information for acts of misconduct they have witnessed.

If the separation is involuntary, then the employer should still attempt an exit interview. There have been occasions, for example, where terminated employees used the exit interview to talk about how unfair the termination was in light of what others are doing who have not been terminated.

A sample Exit Interview Form is provided in the Appendix.

IRS Launches Voluntary Classification Settlement Program (VSCP) for Worker Misclassification Amnesty

In September 2011, in a move designed to increase tax compliance and provide past payroll tax relief to employers, the Internal Revenue Service (IRS) launched a new Voluntary Classification Settlement Program (VCSP) that enabled employers to resolve past worker classification issues and achieve certainty under the tax law at a low cost by voluntarily reclassifying their workers, according to a news release from the IRS website.

Part of a larger "Fresh Start" initiative at the IRS to help taxpayers and businesses address their tax responsibilities, the VCSP will allow employers the opportunity to get into compliance by making a minimal payment covering past payroll tax obligations rather than waiting for an IRS audit. Under the program, eligible employers can obtain substantial relief from federal payroll taxes they may have owed for the past, if they prospectively treat workers as employees.

The VCSP is available to businesses that currently – and erroneously – treat their workers as nonemployees or independent contractors, and now want to correctly treat these workers as employees. To be eligible for the program, an applicant must:

✓ Consistently have treated the workers in the past as nonemployees.

✓ Have filed all required Forms 1099 for the workers for the previous three years.

✓ Not currently be under audit by the IRS.

✓ Not currently be under audit by the Department of Labor or a state agency concerning the classification of these workers.

✓ Jobs where by statute, there is particular sensitivity. An example can be safety sensitive positions such as workers at nuclear plants. Sarbanes-Oxley compliance is another area where that may create a higher duty of care.

Interested employers may apply for the program by filing Form 8952, Application for Voluntary Classification Settlement Program (VCSP), at least 60 days in advance of treating the workers as employees. Form 8952 is available at www.irs.gov/formspubs/article/0,,id=242970,00.html.

(Source: www.irs.gov/newsroom/article/0,,id=246203,00.html).

Maintaining Documents after Separation

The question arises as to how long records and documents should be maintained after separation. There are a number of state and federal laws that control document retention, and labor attorneys will typically advise employers on how long various documents must be retained. However, for purposes involving safe hiring and background screening, the recommendation is six years. The FCRA was amended in 2003 to lengthen the statute of limitations under the act to five years. In addition, state laws often allow a one-year period to file and serve a lawsuit. As a workable general rule, a six-year retention period should serve employers — the six years run from the termination of employment or, if not hired, from the time the decision was made not to hire the applicant.

If disposing of any information in a consumer report, it is important to follow regulations set out by the FTC pursuant to FCRA Section 628. Paper or electronic reports must be destroyed, pulverized, or erased so it cannot be read or reconstructed. An employer must show due diligence when a shredding firm is hired. See: http://business.ftc.gov/documents/alt152-disposing-consumer-report-information-new-rule-tells-how.

 Employers, HR professionals, and security professionals are not finished with their due diligence obligations when an offer of employment is made. Considerations exist during the entire employment relationship and even after the employment relationship has ended, thus the need for maintaining accurate employment and hiring history records.

E-Verify History and Milestones

The final part of this chapter is a chronological summary of the most important milestones of the E-Verify Program taken from the 'History and Milestones' page of the USCIS website.

Year	Description of E-Verify History and Milestone	# of Employers Using E-Verify
1986	**The Immigration Reform and Control Act of 1986 (IRCA) Enacted:** The Immigration Reform and Control Act (IRCA) of 1986 required employers to examine documentation from each newly hired employee to prove his or her identity and eligibility to work in the United States. This act led to the Form I-9, Employment Eligibility Verification, requiring employees to attest to their work eligibility, and employers to certify that the documents presented reasonably appear (on their face) to be genuine and to relate to the individual.	
1996	**Illegal Immigration Reform and Immigrant Responsibility Act of 1996 (IIRIRA) Enacted:** The Illegal Immigration Reform and Immigrant Responsibility Act (IIRIRA) of 1996 required the then Immigration and Naturalization Service (INS) – which became part of the U.S. Department of Homeland Security in 2003 – to conduct three distinct pilot programs: Basic Pilot, the Citizen Attestation Pilot, and the Machine-Readable Document Pilot. These pilots were used to determine the best method of verifying an employee's employment verification.	
1997	**Basic Pilot Program Launched:** The INS, in conjunction with the Social Security Administration (SSA), implemented the Basic Pilot Program in California, Florida, Illinois, Nebraska, New York and Texas. The Basic Pilot Program was voluntary and allowed employers to confirm the work eligibility	

	of their newly hired employees. The Basic Pilot Program used information from the employee's Form I-9 and compared it to the information in INS and SSA records. To verify information with SSA, employers were required to call SSA. Once the SSA information was confirmed by phone, the employer entered I-9 data into a computer program which transmitted the data to INS via a modem connection.	
1998	**Basic Pilot Program Integrates SSA Verification:** Employers were able to complete both the SSA and INS portion of the verification case by entering I-9 data into a computer program which transmitted the data to INS and SSA via modem.	
1999	**Designated Agent Basic Pilot Launched:** INS, in conjunction with the Social Security Administration (SSA), implemented the Designated Agent Basic Pilot Program. The Designated Agent Basic Pilot Program was voluntary and allowed employers to use a third-party agent to confirm the work eligibility of their newly hired employees.	
2003	**Basic Pilot Program Extension and Expansion Act of 2003 Enacted:** Congress enacted the Basic Pilot Program Extension and Expansion Act of 2003. This extended the Basic Pilot Program to November 2008. The new law also required the expansion of the Basic Pilot Program to all 50 states no later than December 1, 2004.	2,144
2007	**Basic Pilot Improved and Renamed E-Verify:** The Basic Pilot Program was renamed E-Verify. Along with the new name, the program added more features including an automatic flagging system that prompts employers to double-check the data entered into the web interface for those cases that are about to result in a mismatch. This change reduced data entry errors and initial mismatches by approximately 30 percent. The launch of E-Verify also marked the addition of photo matching. Photo matching is the first step in incorporating biometric data into the web interface. Photo matching was developed for employees presenting a Permanent Resident Card or Employment Authorization Document, and allows the employer to match the photo on an employee's document with the photo in USCIS records. State workforce agencies were encouraged to use E-Verify to confirm the employment eligibility of any worker referred to an employer in response to an H-2A job order.	24,463
2009	**Congress authorizes a three year extension of E-Verify until the end of September 2012 & Federal Contractor Regulation Goes into Effect:** On September 8, 2009, the "Federal Contractor Regulation" went into effect. The new rule implements Executive Order 12989, as amended on June 6, 2008. Executive Order 12989 directs federal agencies to require many federal contractors entering into new contracts to use E-Verify on all new employees, and on existing employees working on covered federal contracts.	156,659
2011	**DHS Introduces E-Verify Self Check for Workers:** E-Verify Self Check ("Self Check") is a voluntary, fast, free and simple service that allows individuals to check their employment eligibility in the United States. If any mismatches are found between the information provided and Department of Homeland Security or Social Security Administration records, Self Check explains how to correct those mismatches. USCIS is releasing E-Verify Self Check in phases. Initially, the service is offered only to users that maintain an address and are physically located in Arizona, Idaho, Colorado, Mississippi, or	302,529

		Virginia. **Self Check is now available in Spanish and has expanded to residents of 21 states and the District of Columbia.** Self Check allows workers to check their own employment eligibility status online. Self Check is now available to individuals who maintain addresses in: Arizona; California; Colorado; Idaho; Louisiana; Maine; Maryland; Massachusetts; Minnesota; Mississippi; Missouri; Nebraska; Nevada; New Jersey; New York; Ohio; South Carolina; Texas; Utah; Virginia; Washington; and the District of Columbia.	
2012		**Self Check Expands Nationwide:** In February, USCIS announced the nationwide expansion of Self Check allowing workers anywhere in the U.S. to check their own work eligibility. This expansion is also available in Washington D.C., Puerto Rico, Guam, the U.S. Virgin Islands, and the Commonwealth of the Northern Mariana Islands. In March, USCIS redesigned the Self Check Webpages.	353,822* *as of March 31 2012

Source:
www.uscis.gov/portal/site/uscis/menuitem.eb1d4c2a3e5b9ac89243c6a7543f6d1a/?vgnextoid=84979589cdb76210VgnVCM100000b92ca60aRCRD&vgnextchannel=84979589cdb76210VgnVCM100000b92ca60aRCRD.

Chapter 30

Job Seeker Questions and Concerns about Background Checks

Inside This Chapter:

- ✓ Introduction

- ✓ A Job Seeker's Guide to Background Checks

- ✓ Job Applicants and Credit Reports

- ✓ Criminal Records and Getting Back Into the Workforce — Six Critical Steps for Ex-Offenders Trying to Get a Job

- ✓ Background Check Mobile Phone Apps and Instant Background Check Web Sites: Fast and Easy, But Are They Accurate?

Introduction

Chapter 30 and Chapter 31 are written from the point of view of a Job Applicant. Why is this information contained in a book written for employers?

- First, job applicants often have questions about the procedures. It is in the interest of employers that these questions be answered.
- Second, while many applicants shrug off background checks as just another part of the process, employers do not want to discourage otherwise good applicants just because an applicant may be unaware of the details of the procedures or their rights in the process.
- Third, with the advent of what has been called Web 2.0, the web has become more interactive and is now a primary source of recruiting. An essential element for successful recruitment of the best talent is employer "branding." In order to have a successful online brand for recruiting purposes, employers need to be aware of the applicant experience since that can impact the success of a firm's recruiting efforts. Part of that online branding extends to the applicant experience when it comes to background checks.

For job seekers, it is critical to understand that employers are increasingly turning to background screenings of job applicants as a way of minimizing legal and financial exposure. Concerns about workplace violence, negligent-hiring lawsuits, wrongful termination and other problems are leading many employers to be more careful about who is hired in the first place.

Of course, a background screening is not a full-fledged FBI-type investigation. Screening companies are typically looking for red flags indicating potential problems or resumes that are not factual or omit important information.

In many cases, a background check is considered a prerequisite for eligibility in the application process. Many applicants understand, in this post-9/11 world, that background checking is a new fact of life.

BBB Warns Jobseekers of Job Scams Involving Background Checks and Credit Reports

In September 2010, the Better Business Bureau (BBB) issued a warning to jobseekers about scammers taking advantage of the current weak economy by targeting unemployed people desperate to work, scams including false background checks and unnecessary credit report checks.

Since not thoroughly researching a job opportunity can result in jobseekers losing money instead of gaining employment because of job-related scams, the BBB has identified common job scam "red flags" to help jobseekers to protect themselves while they search for a job. The BBB recommends jobseekers look out for the following seven red flags:

✓ **The employer asks for money upfront for a background check or training:** The BBB has heard about jobseekers that paid phony employers upfront fees for supposedly required background checks or training for jobs that didn't exist.

✓ **The employer requires check of a credit report:** The BBB warns that employers that ask job applicants to check their credit reports before they get work may be attempting to get the jobseekers to divulge sensitive financial information.

✓ **The employer offers the opportunity to become rich without leaving home:** The BBB advises jobseekers to be use extreme caution when considering a work-at-home offer and always research the company with BBB at www.bbb.org.

✓ **The employer offers salary and benefits that seem too-good-to-be-true:** The BBB uses an old adage – "If the deal sounds too good to be true, it probably is." – to demonstrate how phony employers lure unsuspecting job hunters into their scam.

    ✓ **The employer's e-mails have many errors in grammar and spelling:** The BBB warns that online fraud is often done by scammers outside the U.S. and English is not their first language, as evidenced by poor grammar and misspelling of common words.

    ✓ **The employer asks for personal information too quickly:** The BBB warns that job applicants should never give out their Social Security Numbers or bank account information over the phone or by email until they confirm the job is legitimate.

    ✓ **The employer requires money wire transactions or dealing of goods:** The BBB also warns jobseekers about cashing checks sent by companies and wiring a portion of the money to another entity or receiving and mailing suspicious goods.

Job scams targeting jobseekers, especially those involving background checks and credit reports, are on the rise during the recent economic troubles. For more information about the Better Business Bureau, visit www.bbb.org.

Source: www.bbb.org/us/article/scammers-target-job-hunters-in-weak-economy-21901.

Job Applicants Have Protection

However, for some applicants, background screening can create an uneasy feeling of mistrust from the start — or "Big Brother is watching." The fact is however, that applicants have a great deal of protection regarding background checks. Such checks are normally conducted by third party background firms. If an employer utilizes a third party service, the Fair Credit Reporting Act (FCRA) requires an employer to obtain the applicant's express written consent to perform a background or reference check, and the employer is also required to give certain legal disclosures.

The fact is, background screenings of job applicants benefit employers and employees alike, and with the recent changes to the FCRA, job applicants now have a greater legal protection. In fact, it can be argued that the pendulum has clearly swung in favor of job applicants given the protections afforded under the FCRA.

For applicants, the advantages of working for a company that requires screening shows efforts have been made to ensure co-workers have the qualifications and credentials they say they have. Who wants to work in a situation where someone with a fake employment or education history is making the same salary but got the job by cheating? Or, who wants to work in an unsafe environment? In addition, employers typically screen out those with criminal record that are suitable for the job, especially involving violence or dishonesty.

The following questions and answers cover most concerns an applicant might have regarding a pre-employment background check or drug screen — so they can understand the importance of this process and how their rights are protected.

A Job Seeker's Guide to Background Checks

Why is a background check necessary?

A background check is more than keeping the employer out of trouble. Employers who screen their employees demonstrate a commitment to keeping employees safe on the job. In addition to the safety and well-being of their employees, employers are held responsible for the safety of their customers and anyone who may be affected or harmed by the actions or negligence of an on-duty employee.

It doesn't stop there. Employers can be held liable for damages if a court determines the employer should have known an employee posed a potential risk to people or property. Failing to make sure an employee is "safe" can land an employer in hot water as well as put innocent people at risk.

Are background checks legal?

It is legal for an employer to perform a background check on an employee or job applicant. An employer has the right to select the most qualified applicant for a position, providing the employer is basing the decision on non-discriminatory factors that are valid predictors of job performance.

However, the employer must follow the guidelines set in the Federal Fair Credit Reporting Act (FCRA). Under the FCRA, when an employer uses a background screening company to prepare a report, several steps must occur:

✓ The employer must clearly disclose to the applicant that a report is being prepared. This disclosure must be a separate, stand-alone document and cannot be buried in the fine print of an application form.

✓ The employer must obtain the applicant's express written consent in order to obtain records such as criminal convictions or pending criminal cases, driving records, credit reports, past employment data, or educational credentials.

✓ An additional notice is required when a background firm checks references, such as asking previous employers about job performance.

✓ If an employer intends to deny employment based upon information in the report, the job applicant must receive a copy of the report and a notice of his or her legal rights.

✓ If the decision to deny employment is made final, an applicant is entitled to some additional information.

Employers are strictly bound by any state and local laws governing background checks. These laws vary from state to state and may place additional limits on the background checking process.

Why do the same laws apply to credit reports and background checks?

Even though the name of the Fair Credit Reporting Act uses the term "credit," this is actually misleading because the FCRA applies to much more than just credit applications. A credit report is just one type of consumer report governed by the FCRA. The FCRA defines a consumer report as any written, oral, or other communication of any information by a consumer reporting agency bearing on a consumer's "credit worthiness, credit standing, credit capacity, character, general reputation, personal characteristics, or mode of living which is used or expected to be used or collected in whole or in part" for various listed purposes, including credit, employment, or the underwriting of insurance.

Any employer or organization obtaining an applicant's driving records, employment records, or criminal records directly from a third party assembling this information into a consumer report is subject to the FCRA. A professional, third party background screening firm that gathers and assembles this information is called a Consumer Reporting Agency (CRA). Employers who fail to comply with the FCRA may be liable for damages or subject to other penalties.

 The Federal Trade Commission (FTC) issued an FTC Facts for Consumers notice in May 2010 titled 'Employment Background Checks and Credit Reports' that included details about key employment provisions such as Notice and Authorization, Pre-Adverse Action Procedures, and Adverse Action Procedures, as well as an Annual Credit Report Request Form. The FTC notice is available at www.ftc.gov/bcp/edu/pubs/consumer/credit/cre36.pdf.

What information gets checked, and where does it come from?

A background check is not a full-scale investigation into someone's private life. Instead, the process is used to confirm the information provided on an application and that all relevant licenses, certifications, and degrees are in good standing. Previous employers and colleagues may also be contacted to confirm past employment and education. Employers and other references may be asked about job performance as well. A search may be conducted for criminal conviction records that may indicate that a person is unsuitable for a particular job. For example, if a person has a history of violent behavior, this tendency could possibly put employees, customers, or the business at risk. An applicant with a conviction for theft or fraud may not be suitable for a job that requires handling money or assets.

Some employers may attempt to collect this information themselves. Employers may contact past employers or schools. However, in order to access much of the information needed by employers, specialized search skills, knowledge, or resources are required. For that reason, many employers seek screening assistance from Consumer Reporting Agencies.

For the most part, background checks collect and verify information from state and federal agencies, credit bureaus, private institutions, and businesses. This information falls into two categories— public records checks and references/verifications.

Public Records Checks

- Social Security Number (SSN) Trace is a check of names and addresses that are associated with a Social Security number found in the databases maintained by the national credit bureaus. These checks may also include a check of other databases as well.
- Criminal records checks search for pending criminal cases or records of criminal convictions. Under federal law, the check for a conviction has no age limit, although some states do put a limit on how far back a screening firm may search. Criminal records are typically obtained from the relevant courthouse where the cases are held, and records must be manually retrieved by a researcher or clerk. Although there are some "canned" databases of criminal records available from vendors, records directly from the source are the most accurate and up-to-date.
- Driving records are typically accessed for up to three years of history and cover accident history and driver's license status. The driving records obtained for employment purposes come from the databases of individual states' Department of Motor Vehicles. Additionally, some trucking and transportation agencies will provide information about driver accidents.
- Workers' Compensation claims provide details about past injuries and Workers' Compensation claims filed by an individual. When an employee's claim goes through a state system or a Workers' Compensation Appeals Board (WCAB), the case becomes public record. An employer may only use this information for hiring purposes if an injury might interfere with one's ability to perform required duties AFTER there has been a conditional job offer. This rule is per under the Americans with Disabilities Act (ADA) and many similar state laws.
- Credit reports retrieve a seven-year credit history, including high-low balances, trade lines, loans, mortgages, liens, bankruptcies, judgments, collections, and summaries of the individual's payment patterns. Credit checks can reveal information such as fraudulent use of a Social Security number or general credit history, as well as provide current and previous addresses. (More information about credit reports is found later in this chapter).

References and Verifications

- Employment verifications confirm dates of employment, title, salary, and eligibility for rehire with each employer listed on the application. The information is verified with a supervisor or payroll/HR representative within the company.
- Education or degree verifications confirm dates of enrollment, programs of study, and degrees held. Generally, the information comes directly from the school attended or a licensed third-party records service, usually National Student Loan Clearinghouse. Some information, such as GED records, must be obtained from state agencies.

What can my former employer say about me?

Potential employers often contact an applicant's past employers for qualitative references. Contrary to popular misconception, employers are at liberty to provide information about a previous employee's performance and ability, provided the information is truthful, job-related, and accurate. However, in this litigious society, most employers have opted to implement a policy to only confirm dates of employment, job title, and in some cases, salary. Many employers are concerned that, if they give information beyond name, rank, and serial number, they could potentially be sued for defamation. Many large employers, in fact, have deposited past employment information on a telephone service, limiting new employers to hearing a computerized voice verifying just employment dates and job title.

About Past Employer References

The reluctance of employers to give information may actually work to the detriment of an applicant, making it more difficult to get a letter of recommendation. Applicants still have many avenues available to communicate about their past successes to new employers, even if past employers will not give a reference. The key is to plan ahead and to remember the importance of promoting your own career by obtaining the materials necessary to successfully market yourself:

✓ When leaving a job, clarify the past employer's policy on references and try to determine what will be said if a new employer calls.

✓ Before leaving a job, try to obtain personal letters of recommendation. Even if the firm does not give references, a supervisor or co-worker may be willing to write a favorable letter on the theory that it is a personal recommendation.

✓ Seek a letter of recommendation from someone no longer at the firm, who can verify your job performance.

✓ Keep copies of outstanding performance appraisals, or keep an example of your work to show at an interview, provided it was proper to retain it, i.e. not protected as a trade secret or by a non-disclosure agreement.

✓ Try to have references give specific examples. General statements like "great team player" are not nearly as strong as examples of behavior or performance in specific situations.

✓ Retain pay stubs and other documents as a means of verifying past employment. When firms merge, go out of business, or move, it can be difficult to confirm past employment.

✓ If the previous employment involved a contract with an outside agency or was through an employee-leasing firm, then the actual workplace may not have records of you.

✓ It is also very important to accurately summarize the job duties and title for previous jobs on a resume. Although everyone wants a resume to shine, a resume that over-reaches can raise questions about your honesty.

In many states, employees have a right to review their own personnel files and make copies of documents they have signed. The personnel files of state or federal employees are protected under various state laws or the federal Privacy Act of 1974, and can only be disclosed under limited circumstances.

Most jobs involving the freight and transportation industries are regulated by the federal Department of Transportation. Employers are required to accurately respond to any inquiry from a prospective employer about whether an employee took a drug test, refused a drug test, or tested positive in a drug test while with the former or current employer.

What if the information is wrong?

Despite the best efforts of record keepers and modern information storage systems, mistakes sometimes occur. Out of the millions of background checks done yearly, it would appear the error rate is extremely low. However, for the applicant (also called the consumer) who is subject of an error, that is of little consolation. However, applicants who genuinely are the victims of mistaken identity or bureaucratic errors are given the opportunity to know what is being said about them and to dispute errors or discrepancies that might otherwise unfairly deny them opportunity or eligibility for a position. Because of the rise of identity theft crimes, some applicants receive a very unpleasant surprise when a background check is conducted — they may discover that someone using their identity is the subject of a criminal record. If a person is arrested and uses your name, you become a double victim when a warrant for your arrest is issued after he fails to show up in court. Of course, since you – the applicant – was not the one arrested, you have no idea a warrant for your arrest is outstanding. There are even cases where the criminal stealing the identity pled guilty to a criminal charge using the stolen identity, creating a criminal conviction record for some unsuspecting ID theft victim. At that point, a job applicant must somehow correct the mess left by the identity thief. For more information on identity theft, see Chapter 28.

Other sources of errors can be courts that do not update their files to show that an offense had been set aside, or a past employer's records are incorrect. Many applicants discover these issues for the first time when a background check is performed and are able to correct the underlying issue so it does not happen again.

Unfortunately, sometimes errors can be caused due to the feature of a background firm to excise best practices under the Fair Credit Reporting Act when it comes to accuracy. A discussion of the accuracy obligations of a background firm is found in Chapter 3. However, if a background firm chooses to take shortcuts, such as using dates instead of the most current and up to date information, errors can occur.

Fortunately, there is an escape valve so applicants have the right to find out if there are errors, and a procedure to correct them. Under federal law, an employer intending to use information from the consumer report for an adverse action — such as denial of a job or promotion or terminating the employee — must take the steps outlined below.

1. Before the adverse action is taken, the employer must give the applicant a "pre-adverse action disclosure," including a copy of the report and an explanation of the applicant's rights under the FCRA.

2. After the adverse action is taken, the individual must be given an "adverse action notice." This document must contain 1) the name, address, and phone number of the employment screening company, 2) a statement that the employer, not the background screening company, is responsible for making the adverse decision, and 3) a notice that the individual has the right to dispute the accuracy or completeness of any of the information in the report.

3. A background checking company is required to remove or correct inaccurate or unverified information, usually within thirty days of notification.

Lesson on How a Consumer should NOT React to an Inaccurate Background Check

A federal District Court decision issued in August of 2009 in the Western District of Arkansas contains a valuable lesson for a consumer who believed that a background check was inaccurate. In that case, a Court held it was the consumer's own behavior after the background check that caused the job loss and not an inaccuracy caused by human error that was quickly corrected.

The plaintiff in the case was seeking employment at a college to teach courses on psychology and domestic violence. During her background check, the court research firm made a clerical error that falsely labeled the plaintiff ironically as a person who was convicted of assault and family violence in Texas. The case was before the court on motions for summary judgment, which is a procedure where a party asserts that even if the evidence was viewed in a light most favorable to the other party, there is insufficient evidence as a matter of law for a jury to find against them.

The facts showed the college utilized the services of a background screening firm (called a Consumer Reporting Agency or CRA) to conduct a background check, including a check for criminal records, and the CRA in turn used other researchers. Due to simple human error, the court researcher made a clerical mistake, resulting in mixing up someone else's criminal records with the plaintiff's, who in fact had no record.

Three days later the Plaintiff learned that the background report was negative and reported a criminal conviction. The plaintiff immediately contacted the college and the CRA. The screening report was promptly corrected and the plaintiff received a 'clear' report. The college indicated they were ready to proceed with the hire.

However, even though the report was quickly corrected and she was going to get the job, the plaintiff was still apparently unhappy. In a conversation with college personnel, the consumer talked about how the college had put her through hell, they had put her family through stress, and that (the college) had tarnished her reputation. The plaintiff also indicated she had interviewed elsewhere. The college then decided not to hire her based upon her demeanor after the matter was cleared up and took the position that this decision was not related to the initial report. The plaintiff also claimed emotional distress even though the report was promptly corrected.

The Court dismissed the claim for loss of employment because the evidence clearly showed the incorrect report was not the reason she lost the job. The job loss was due to how she reacted to the situation. Given that the report was promptly corrected and the college was intending to hire her, she could not blame the screening firms for her own behavior. The court did find however, she was entitled to continue with her claims for emotional distress based upon the brief period of time before the report was corrected, and it was a jury issue as to whether the screening firms involved exercised an appropriate level of care.

This case demonstrates the old adage of the reaction to events is sometimes more important than the event itself. Even though screening firms go to great lengths to ensure every report is accurate, as with anything that involves human beings, errors can occur. That is why under the federal Fair Credit Reporting Act (FCRA) there are extensive provisions for re-investigating and correcting reports. It is certainly understandable that an applicant that teaches about domestic violence would be upset at being inaccurately portrayed as a violator. However, the mistake was caused by human error, and the report was promptly corrected. It was only the consumer's own reaction that caused the job loss.

What can I do to prepare?

Applicants who anticipate changing jobs in the near term can take several steps to ensure the information to be gathered is correct, and all precautions have been taken in the event contradictory information surfaces, or records cannot be located. The following tips are excerpted with permission from the Privacy Rights Clearinghouse, 'Fact Sheet 16: Employment Background Checks: A Job Seeker's Guide' available online at www.privacyrights.org/fs/fs16-bck.htm.

Privacy Rights Clearinghouse – How to Prepare for a Background Check

Note: If you are concerned about whether a previous arrest, probation, or conviction will show up on a background check, visit: www.privacyrights.org/fs/FS16c-FAQ-BkgChk-060928.htm#4

When you know you are going to be on the job market, take the following steps to reduce the chances that you and/or the potential employer will be "surprised" by information found in the background check process:

Order a copy of your credit report.

If there is something you do not recognize or that you disagree with, dispute the information with the creditor and/or credit bureau before you have to explain it to the interviewer. Another individual's name may appear on your credit report. This happens when someone mistakenly writes down the wrong Social Security number on a credit application causing that name to appear on your file. Or you might be a victim of identity theft. (See PRC Fact Sheet 6 on your credit reporting rights, www.privacyrights.org/fs/fs6-crdt.htm, and Fact Sheet 17a on identity theft, www.privacyrights.org/fs/fs17a.htm.)

Check court records.

If you have an arrest record or have been involved in court cases, go to the county where this took place and inspect the files. Make sure the information is correct and up to date.

Reporting agencies often report felony convictions when the consumer truly believes the crime was reduced to a misdemeanor, or that it was reported as a misdemeanor conviction when the consumer thought the charge was reduced to an infraction. Court records are not always updated correctly. For example, a signature that was needed to reduce the charges might not have been obtained or recorded by the court. Don't rely on what someone else may have told you. If you think the conviction was expunged or dismissed, get a certified copy of your report from the court. For an explanation of expungement, visit www.epic.org/privacy/expungement.

It is always a good idea to keep certified copies of any papers filed in court, especially the judge's order or other document that disposes of the case. If you later learn the court record is inaccurate but do not have a certified copy, first contact the clerk of court where the matter was heard. If you cannot correct the problem at this level, it may be necessary to petition the court yourself or hire an attorney to act on your behalf.

Check DMV records.

Request a copy of your driving record from the Department of Motor Vehicles, especially if you are applying for a job that involves driving.

Many employers ask on their application if you were ever convicted of a crime. Or they might word the question to ask whether you have ever been convicted of a felony or misdemeanor. Typically, the application says you do not have to divulge a case that was expunged or dismissed, or that was a minor traffic violation.

Don't be confused. A DUI (driving under the influence) or DWI (driving while intoxicated) conviction is not considered a minor traffic infraction. Applicants with a DUI or DWI who have not checked "yes" on a job application may be denied employment for falsifying the form -- even when the incident occurred only once or happened many years before. The employer perceives this as dishonesty, even though the applicant might only have been confused by the question.

Do your own background check.

If you want to see what an employer's background check might uncover, hire a company that specializes in such reports to conduct one for you. That way, you can discover if the data bases of information vendors contain erroneous or misleading information. (Consult the Yellow Pages under "Investigators.") Or, you can use one of the many online search services to find out what an employer would learn if conducting a background check in this way.

Ask to see a copy of your personnel file from your old job.

Even if you do not work there anymore, state law might enable you to see your file. Under California law, you can access your file until at least a year from the last date of employment. And you are allowed to make copies of documents in your file that have your signature on them. (California Labor Code §432.) You may also want to ask if your former employer has a policy about the release of personnel records. Many companies limit the amount of information they disclose.

Read the fine print carefully.

When you sign a job application, you will be asked to sign a consent form if a background check is conducted. Read this statement carefully and ask questions if the authorization statement is not clear. Unfortunately, jobseekers are in an awkward position, since refusing to authorize a background check may jeopardize the chances of getting the job.

Note: Notice of a background check has to be on a separate form. The only other information this form can include is your authorization and information that identifies you. Neither the notice of a background check nor any other form should ask questions like "race," "sex," "full date of birth," or "maiden name." Such questions violate the federal Equal Employment Opportunity laws. And, you should not be asked to sign any document that waives your right to sue a screening company or the employer for violations of the law.

Tell neighbors and work colleagues.

Tell neighbors and work colleagues, past and present, that they might be asked to provide information about you. This helps avoid suspicion and alerts you to possible problems. In addition, their prior knowledge gives them permission to disclose information to the investigator. Forewarning others speeds up the process and helps you get the job faster.

Clean up your "digital dirt."

Conduct a search on your name -- in quotation marks -- in the major search engines such as Google and Yahoo. If you find unflattering references, contact the Web site to learn if and how you can remove them. If you have created profiles in popular social networking Web sites such as MySpace and Facebook, review, and if necessary, edit what you have posted to make sure that an employer would not be offended.

Do not underestimate the power of your online reputation to sway potential employers. A report commissioned by Microsoft, Inc., issued in January 2010, found that only 15% of consumers surveyed thought what they posted online had any effect on their job prospects. In sharp contrast, the report found that 75% of the recruiters surveyed reported formal policies that required online research of applications. To read the full Microsoft report, go to www.microsoft.com/en-us/news/features/2010/jan10/01-26dataprivacyday.aspx.

Some employers are turning to third-party screening companies such as Social Intelligence to monitor and report on a potential employee's social networking activity. Understand that if employers themselves monitor your Internet activity, you do not have rights under the Fair Credit Reporting Act.

The Federal Trade Commission investigated Social Intelligence. In a letter dated May 9, 2011 the agency announced that the investigation was closed but made it clear that such companies are subject to the FCRA and that consumers have the same rights as with more traditional background screening conducted by third-party screeners.

To read the FTC's letter closing the investigation into Social Intelligence, See: http://privacyblog.littler.com/uploads/file/FederalTradeCommissionLetterReSocialIntelligenceCorporation.pdf.

For further discussion see: Workplace Privacy Counsel blog, "Social Checks" Come of Age: What Does it Means for Employers?," posted July 11, 2011. http://privacyblog.littler.com/2011/07/articles/background-checks/social-checks-come-of-age-what-does-it-mean-for-employers/#more.

Do you blog? Re-read your entries from the perspective of a potential employer. Remove or edit postings that could harm your job seeking efforts. But don't necessarily remove Web content that shines a light on your positive achievements. A personal Web site or blog that highlights your good deeds could benefit you. You can read more about cleaning up your "digital dirt" at www.abilitiesenhanced.com/digital-dirt.pdf.

Request previous background check reports.

If you have been the subject of a background check covered by the FCRA, you may be entitled to receive a copy of your "file" from the employment screening company. If you do not know the name of the screening company, ask the employer who requested the check. For more on your right to get a free employment report, see PRC Fact Sheet 6b. www.privacyrights.org/fs/fs6b-SpecReports.htm

Order a copy of your credit report. If there is something you do not recognize or that you disagree with, dispute the information with the creditor and/or credit bureau before you have to explain it to the interviewer. Another individual's name may appear on your credit report. This happens when someone mistakenly writes down the wrong Social Security Number on a credit application causing that name to appear on your file, or you might be a victim of identity theft (See PRC Fact Sheet 6 on your credit reporting rights online at www.privacyrights.org/fs/fs6-crdt.htm and Fact Sheet 17a on identity theft online at www.privacyrights.org/fs/fs17a.htm).

Check court records. If you have an arrest record or have been involved in court cases, go to the county where this took place and inspect the files. Make sure the information is correct and up to date. Reporting agencies often report felony convictions when the consumer truly believes the crime was reduced to a misdemeanor, or that it was reported as a misdemeanor conviction when the consumer thought the charge was reduced to an infraction. Court records are not always updated correctly. For example, a signature that was needed to reduce the charges might not have been obtained or recorded by the court. Don't rely on what your attorney may have told you. If you think the conviction was expunged or dismissed, get a certified copy of your report from the court.

Check DMV records. Request a copy of your driving record from the Department of Motor Vehicles, especially if you are applying for a job that involves driving. Many employers ask on their application if you were ever convicted of a crime. Or they might word the question to ask whether you have ever been convicted of a felony or misdemeanor. Typically, the application says you do not have to divulge a case that was expunged or dismissed, or that was a minor traffic violation. Don't be confused. A DUI (driving under the influence) or DWI (driving while intoxicated) conviction is not considered a minor traffic infraction. Applicants with a DUI or DWI who have not checked "yes" on a job application may be denied employment for falsifying the form – even when the incident occurred only once or happened many years before. The employer perceives this as dishonesty, even though the applicant might only have been confused by the question.

Do your own background check. If you want to see what an employer's background check might uncover, hire a company that specializes in such reports to conduct one for you. That way, you can discover if the databases of information vendors use contain erroneous or misleading information. Consult the Yellow Pages under "Investigators," of you may use one of the many online search services to find out what an employer would learn if conducting a background check online.

Ask to see a copy of your personnel file from your old job. Even if you no longer work there, state law might enable you to see your file. Under California law, you can access your file until at least a year from the last date of employment, and you are allowed to make copies of documents in your file that have your signature on them (California Labor Code §432). You may also want to ask if your former employer has a policy about the release of personnel records. Many companies limit the amount of information they disclose.

Read the fine print carefully. When you sign a job application, you will be asked to sign a consent form if a background check is conducted. Read this statement carefully and ask questions if the authorization statement is not clear. Unfortunately, jobseekers are in an awkward position, since refusing to authorize a background check may jeopardize the chances of getting the job. Notice of a background check has to be on a separate form. The only other information this form can include is your authorization and information that identifies you. Neither the notice of a background check nor any other form should ask questions on race, sex, full date of birth, or maiden name. Such questions violate the Federal Equal Employment Opportunity laws. You should not be asked to sign any document that waives your right to sue a screening company or the employer for violations of the law.

Tell neighbors and work colleagues, past and present, that they might be asked to provide information about you. This helps avoid suspicion and alerts you to possible problems. In addition, their prior knowledge gives them permission to disclose information to the investigator. Forewarning others will speed up the overall process and help you get the job faster.

Source: www.privacyrights.org/fs/fs16-bck.htm#9

Job Applicants and Credit Reports

The following is the complete text of the White Paper *The Use of Credit Reports in Employment Background Screening— An Overview for Job Applicants*. The paper was researched and written by Kerstin Bagus and Lester Rosen.

The Use of Credit Reports in Employment Background Screening—an Overview for Job Applicants

If you are looking for a job today there is a good chance a background check will be conducted before or shortly after you are hired. Employers and volunteer organizations, conduct background checks to verify the information provided on an application and to conduct due diligence. These background checks protect the employer and volunteer organization in many ways, primarily by making sure the information they were given on the job application is accurate and that the organization is not hiring someone that is inappropriate for the position. This protects the organization as well as their workers, customers, and sometimes the general public.

Most often this background check will review criminal record history. Other commonly checked areas are identification information, the education, professional license, and employment history provided by the applicant. If driving is involved, driver's license status and history are often verified. Some employers will also check a person's credit history during the application process.

The subject of using credit reports in the job application process has been in the news lately. Concern has been raised that when credit reports are part of a background check, the information on the credit report may be used unfairly against the job applicant. The following information is intended to assist job applicants in understanding the role that a credit report may play in a background check and to explain the differences between a credit report used in the job application process versus a credit report a lender may see.

The first thing to know is that there are different types of credit reports depending on the purpose of the report. A credit report viewed by an employer or volunteer agency is called an Employment Credit Report and does not contain the same information as is found on a credit report available to lenders or even the credit report you get when you exercise your rights to view your own credit report from a credit bureau. The employment version of a credit report does provide information about your credit and payment history, just like other versions of a credit report. However there are many things that are different in this version of a credit report:

- A credit score is not available to employers. It is recognized by credit bureaus, credit scoring companies, and background screening companies that a credit score has no relationship to job performance and is simply not provided to employers. Unlike the copy of the credit report available to you, the employer cannot even pay extra to see a credit score.

- Account numbers are not listed on the Employment Credit Report. The source and type of credit is listed, such as the store name or loan holder. But specific account numbers are not on the employment version of a credit report.

- Your age is not listed nor is your year of birth.

- The Inquiry is different and is not calculated in a credit score. An Inquiry is the listing of who requested at your credit report. This must be listed on every person's credit history and is one of the things used in determining a person's credit score. There are different types of Inquiries and they have different impact on a credit report and a credit score. When an employer or volunteer agency orders an Employment Credit Report, a special type of Inquiry is listed on the person's credit history that is not used in the credit scoring process. In some cases, this Employment Inquiry may not be visible to other organizations who request your credit report – it may only be visible to you and the credit bureau. (This may not be the case for all Employment Credit Reports and depends on how the specific credit bureau treats these Employment Inquiries.)

Second, employers are not running credit reports in order to find ways to deny jobs to applicants. Background checks cost employers money and time. Employers run background checks, including credit reports, **AFTER** they have gone through the time, cost and effort to find the right candidates, usually from a large field of applicants. An employer does not invest money in a background report just to find ways not to hire. When an employer orders a background check, it is because they are interested in hiring the applicant and are conducting due diligence to make sure there is no business related reason not to hire that person.

Third, employers have obligations they must follow before not hiring someone as a result of any part of a background check obtained from a Consumer Reporting Agency (a company that provides these types of background checks), including a credit report. Employers, and the background screening firms that provide these reports, do not take these obligations lightly. There are serious penalties if the employer fails to follow through with their obligations. (See the FTC's web site at www.ftc.gov for more information.) More on how this affects you as a job applicant is below.

What should a job applicant do regarding credit reports and job hunting?

First, understand that if you get to the point where an employer is running a background check, that is great news. It means you made it through the preliminary stages of the hiring process so that you are most likely one of the final candidates being considered for the job.

Secondly, if you are concerned that a background check may include a credit report, do not be the last to know what your credit report may say. As a consumer (that is the term used to identify a person whose report is being viewed), you are entitled to a free credit report every 12 months from each of the credit bureaus, and more often in some states and under certain circumstances. Go to https://www.annualcreditreport.com/cra/index.jsp for information on how to get your free credit report. If you see some sort of error, it would be a good idea to get that corrected as soon as possible. There is a well established procedure for contacting the credit bureaus to bring an error to their attention and request it be corrected. The FTC has excellent information about the use of credit reports and credit on their website at www.ftc.gov/bcp/menus/consumer/credit.shtm.

Third, if you are concerned that your credit history may reflect negatively, have a discussion ahead of time with the hiring manger or Human Resources about your credit reports. As most experienced Human

Resources professionals can tell you, information honestly disclosed by an applicant has much less impact than information the employer discovers for themselves.

Also keep in mind that hiring professionals understand that people have to deal with the realities of life. For example if a person was undergoing economic stress due to the recession, and relied on credit cards, or there was a medical issue that caused bills, let Human Resources or the hiring manager know. Also keep in mind that the only reason you are having this discussion is that the firm is seriously considering hiring you, and has gone through allot of time and effort to make that decision, including reviewing numerous other resumes.

Fourth, applicants need to keep in mind that they have rights. Under the federal Fair Credit Reporting Act (FCRA), a credit report is only obtained after the applicant has given consent and after a legally required disclosure on a standalone document has been given. Before the employer utilizes the credit report in any way not to hire, an applicant is entitled to a copy of their credit report in what is known as a pre-adverse action notice. You are also required to receive a document called a Statement of Rights, which will list your rights and also information on how to correct information on the report.

The bottom-line: If an employer feels a credit report is job related, keep in mind that the employer has made you a finalist, and therefore has an interest in hiring you. You were evaluated without the employer having any idea of what was in the credit report. Protect your credit history. Think of it as one piece of your reputation. Know what is in your credit report and correct errors. If there are negative entries, be prepared to share it before the credit report is run.

Consumer Resources:

www.ftc.gov

www.ftc.gov/bcp/menus/consumer/credit.shtm

www.annualcreditreport.com/cra/index.jsp

Criminal Records and Getting Back Into the Workforce — Six Critical Steps for Ex-Offenders Trying to Get a Job

Employers have become increasingly concerned about knowing if an applicant has an undisclosed criminal record and are conducting pre-employment background checks for criminal records. Employers have been the subject of large jury verdicts for *negligent hiring* in cases where they hire a person with a criminal record who harms others, especially when the harm could have been avoided by a criminal record check. Employers have a legal duty to exercise *due diligence* in the hiring process, and that duty can be violated if an employer hires someone who they "either knew or should have known" in the exercise of reasonable care was dangerous or unfit for a job. The concern from the employer's point of view is that a person with a criminal past may have a propensity to re-offend in the future.

On the other hand, society also has a vested interest in helping people with a past criminal record obtain and maintain employment. It is difficult for an ex-offender to become a law abiding, taxpaying citizen without a job. Unless society wants to continue to spend its tax dollars on building more and more jails and prisons, ex-offenders need the opportunity to rejoin the workforce.

For an ex-offender, a job search can become a frustrating "Catch-22" situation. Nearly every employment application will ask, in some fashion, if a person has a criminal record. If a person lies, then the person is always at risk of being terminated for lying upon such a criminal record being discovered. If a person is honest and admits the past misconduct, there is a risk of not getting the job.

Studies demonstrate what ex-offenders already know — it is significantly harder to get a job with a criminal record. According to a study conducted at Georgetown University in Washington DC and quoted in the *USA Today* (11/21/2003), only twenty percent of employers surveyed indicated a willingness to hire an ex-offender. Employers were most willing to hire ex-offenders for jobs that had little customer contact, such as in the construction or manufacturing industries.

The problem is getting worse. With the surging prison population, there are a substantial number of people released from jails prisons every year. Studies show that ex-offenders with jobs are less likely to re-offend. Society has a vested interest in keeping released prisoners from re-offending and going back into custody. Yet ex-offenders have the toughest time getting jobs, especially in a down economy.

There is no perfect answer. A person with a criminal record is going to face greater challenges in getting employment. However, **challenging** is not the same as **impossible**. The key is the right attitude and getting and keeping that first job so as time goes by, a person develops a successful job history that will outweigh past problems.

Here are six approaches a person with a past criminal record can take to help obtain a job.

1. Understand Your Rights

A person who has a criminal record and is looking for employment must understand his or her rights. There are instances where an applicant can legally and ethically answer NO to a question about a past offense. This may occur in some of the following situations:

- ✓ In many states, there is no obligation to report arrests not resulting in a conviction or arrests with results not currently pending.
- ✓ There are limitations on reporting pre-trial adjudications where the conduct by statute is not considered a criminal offense. Some states have pre-trial diversion or delayed entry of judgment.
- ✓ There may be restrictions on the use of minor drug offense records. In California, for example, an employer may not ask about a minor marijuana offense for personal use older than two years.
- ✓ Some states have procedures to judicially "erase" a criminal offense. In another California example, if the matter is a misdemeanor and a person goes back to court and receives a certificate of rehabilitation under Penal Code 1203.4, the incident is not reportable.

Also, keep in mind most employment applications contain language stating the conviction of a crime will not automatically result in a denial of employment. Automatic disqualification could be a violation of state and federal discrimination laws. However, an employer may deny employment if the employer can establish a business-related reason for the refusal to hire.

2. See an Attorney

This is critical. Make sure you understand your rights. An attorney will help determine if you are eligible to get your conviction sealed, expunged, or legally minimized. An employer may not legally ask about or consider certain offenses. Each state has different rules on this, but all states have a mechanism for going back to court to try to seal or expunge certain offenses. Make sure you explore your options. The attorney who represented you or the local Public Defender or Probation Office should be able to assist.

3. Seek Professional Assistance

There are also organizations that assist past offenders. Some of these organizations have relationships with employers who are willing to give an ex-offender a chance. In addition, these organizations can help a person prepare a resume and practice interview techniques to deal honestly with the past offense. This helps a job applicant put his best foot forward by explaining why the applicant can perform the job and why the employer should hire him. Various re-entry or training programs will help ex-offenders develop new skills or teach job search techniques.

4. Honesty is the Best Policy

When applying for a job, honestly is always the best policy. A criminal matter honestly explained during an interview may have much less negative impact than hiding it and having an employer discover it later. If an employer discovers an applicant is dishonest, the denial of a job could be based upon a lack of honesty, regardless of the nature of the criminal offense. However, a person who has made a mistake and is now motivated to do well at a job may be of great interest to some employers.

5. Rebuild Your Resume

The rebuilding of a resume is done one step at a time even if it involves taking a job that is not perfect. All employers know the best indicator of future job performance is past job performance. If a person with a criminal record can obtain whatever job he or she can, hold that job, and do well, the next job becomes much easier to obtain. It is the building block approach — one block at a time.

It is critical to seek employment that can help rebuild your resume. You should first seek employment with people you know; they are more likely than a stranger to give you a chance. Ask everyone you know to recommend someone who might be willing to hire you. Yes, mention your conviction, but stress your professional strengths and how much "you have learned from your past."

You have to consider starting at the bottom. However, a few months of good work in an entry-level position can yield a good reference which can start your career upward.

According to career coach Marty Nemko, an entry level-job can be a launch pad and a foot in the door. Do a great job, build up relationships with higher ups, and express interest in moving up, and before long, you many find yourself promoted.

Mr. Nemko also gives the following advice: "If you take an entry-level job in order to rebuild your resume, be sure it is one in which people with the power to promote you can observe the quality of your work. Avoid taking a job off-site or in a remote location. If you enjoy working for the organization, then ask questions, learn skills, and let them know you are interested in moving up."

There are certain industries in real need of workers. A fast food job, for example, may not be the job you want, but it is an example of a job that is widely available and allows a person to rebuild credentials and show what he or she can do.

The key point is that whatever you do, with determination you can set yourself apart. It's not the job that is important but the way you do it and the attention you give that will get you recognized and create more opportunities.

Eventually, what a new employer sees is a person with great recommendations and an excellent job history. As the criminal conviction gets older, and the job history become stronger, a person who has made a mistake in the past will eventually find the criminal record is less of an issue.

It cannot be stressed enough — the best way to get a great job in the future is to get any job you can right now and perform well.

6. Take the Long-Term View

This is the most difficult advice to follow. An ex-offender is anxious to get back into the workforce to start making a living. Ex-offenders may also be anxious to have their old life back, yet the deck is stacked against a person with a criminal record. The jobs available may not be the ones you want. You may be qualified for something a great deal better. Doors may slam in your face. You may be subject to unfair assumptions. The frustration level could easily build with each disappointment encountered.

It comes down to this— ex-offenders need to take the long view and have the faith and patience that the criminal matter will eventually be put behind them. As frustrating as it is, the basic rule still applies — a person must rebuild a resume over time. As time goes by, the criminal offense becomes less of a factor in a person's life — but it is going to take time.

Even if it takes five years to rebuild your resume and get the job you want, five years will still go by. Five years later, what would you rather have — a new life with a good job or still living in frustration because you could not get what you wanted right away? Here are three case studies to consider:

✓   **Case Study One:** A schoolteacher was convicted of a misdemeanor offense that disqualified her from teaching. The person had dedicated her life to teaching, and suddenly it was no longer an option. She was very depressed and upset that she could no longer do what she loved and knew how to do so well. In order to qualify for a work-furlough program, she obtained a job with a friend in a retail store. It turned out she had a talent for the new job, became very successful and happy with it, and found a new and satisfying career.

✓ **Case Study Two:** A medical professional committed an offense that disqualified him from practicing his profession. He could not imagine not being employed in medicine. His career in medicine had been the most important aspect of his life and defined who he was. Over a long period of adjustment, he was very depressed and unhappy about how unfair it was he could not do what he did best. Out of necessity, he found a job in construction. It turned out he had a talent for this temporary job. He loved the hours and the freedom the job gave him. He also realized the pressures he had put himself under were the root cause of the criminal conduct. A few years later, when he would have been eligible to attempt to regain his license, he decided he enjoyed his new life and did not want to go back into medicine.

✓ **Case Study Three:** A young woman became involved in the wrong crowd at an early age. She was convicted of drug offenses and spent time in prison. In prison she obtained her GED. Upon release, she found a job in a fast food place. It was not the best job, but she worked hard and made herself the best worker there. She was always on time, cared about her job, respected her co-workers and supervisors, and she showed a real interest in succeeding. Since employers need that kind of worker, she was eventually promoted to the management trainee program. She then turned for assistance to a program that helped women get jobs, and was able to find a well-paying administrative job in a growing firm. It took time, but she did everything right.

These case studies have one critical element in common— the individuals could not have been more depressed and frustrated with their situations. By being patient, taking the long view, and believing things could improve, eventually their lives went in new and better directions.

 "Self" Background Checks

Since many jobseekers will probably undergo a some form of background check to gain employment, it would be in their best interest to make sure the information found during the background check is accurate, up-to-date, and complete. As a result, some jobseekers are taking matters in their own hands by proactively conducting "self" background checks on themselves to verify the accuracy of their public information.

By conducting self background checks similar to those conducted by professional and accredited background screening companies, job seekers may discover that they have fallen victim to some of the following situations that have popped up during real background checks, situations that could hinder their attempts to find employment:

* A job seeker is the victim of identity theft.

* Someone with the same name as a job seeker has committed a crime.

* Some minor or old criminal matter that the job seeker thought was judicially set aside or was too old to matter still pops up.

* Some past employer or school does not have the job seeker's record under the proper name so that a background check may be inaccurate.

* A school may have a job seeker under a different name or may not have officially given the job seeker the degree due to not paying a final bill.

* A driving record check may reveal an old ticket that the job seeker thought was taken care of but went to a warrant for failure to appear.

Background Check Mobile Phone Apps and Instant Background Check Web Sites: Fast and Easy, But Are They Accurate?

Job seekers should be warned that a <u>real</u> "self" background check should <u>not</u> consist solely of using a cheap and instant online database search through "apps" (applications) and websites.

According to a 2011 white paper – *'Background Check Mobile Phone Apps and Instant Background Check Web Sites: Fast and Easy, But Are They Accurate?'* – co-authored by Lester Rosen and Kerstin Bagus, users of mobile phone apps and Web sites offering so-called "instant" background checks should be aware that while these services are cheap and easy to use, they may not provide entirely accurate information.

The white paper examined background check apps and sites that allow users to perform instant background checks on anyone anytime from their mobile phones and computers by searching publicly available records and checking social networking sites such as Facebook, YouTube, Twitter, and LinkedIn. While this kind of information is viewed as a lead source for further review by professional investigators or researchers, in the hands of the average person the data can lead to hasty and dangerous conclusions. Some of the dangers of using instant background checks offered by mobile phone apps and web sites include:

✓ Reporting inaccurate information that can include outdated results or can show no criminal history when one actually does exist.

✓ Returning information for the wrong person with the same name since these services do not generally require identifiers such as dates of birth.

✓ Creating a false sense of security when a "clear" background check result assumes the person being searched has no criminal record.

✓ Privacy issues for the person being checked since the average person is not knowledgeable about proper usage of public records and there are no privacy controls in place.

✓ Reputational injuries to the individual being searched if the information is not correct.

✓ Misuse of information for employment purposes since employers who use results from these sites can find themselves in a legal and financial nightmare due to intense legal regulation surrounding the use of information for employment purposes from the FCRA as well as numerous state laws.

The white paper noted that unsuspecting users of background check apps or Web sites may not understand that it is not easy to get a complete picture of an individual's background, particularly their criminal history, due to the following considerations:

✓ No nationwide criminal record database exists that contains all criminal record convictions in the United States.

✓ If criminal information is found on an individual, it does not mean that the information is current, the criminal record resulted in a conviction, or the information belongs to the person being searched.

✓ If no criminal record is found, it does not mean the person being searched does not have a record since the app or Web site can easily miss a criminal record.

✓ Some of the information returned is based upon a "data dump" of billions of public records.

✓ The information pulled from social networking sites can be wildly inaccurate.

The white paper also discusses how to select apps, social networking data, criminal record databases, and special issues for employers and volunteer agencies. The complimentary white paper *'Background Check Mobile Phone Apps and Instant Background Check Web Sites: Fast and Easy, But Are They Accurate?'* is available at: www.esrcheck.com/Download/.

What Job Seekers Can Do about Identity Theft

Inside This Chapter:

- ✓ The Extent of the Identity Theft Problem

- ✓ What is Identity Theft?

- ✓ Consumer Advice From the FTC

- ✓ How to Protect Yourself and What to Do If You Are a Victim

- ✓ Helpful Resources in the Fight against Identity Theft

The Extent of the Identity Theft Problem

In Chapter 28, identity and identify theft are discussed from the point of view of the employer. Because identity theft can have an impact on background checks, this chapter revisits identity theft but from the perspective of the consumer.

According to the *2012 Identity Fraud Report: Social Media and Mobile Forming the New Fraud Frontier* from Javelin Strategy & Research, identity fraud increased by 13 percent and more than 11.6 million adults became victims of identity theft in the United States in 2011. Also per the report, much of this increase in identity theft and fraud was due to the usage of social media and smart phones.

> **2012 Identity Fraud Report finds Identity Theft Rose 13 Percent to Victimize 11.6 Million Americans Due to Social Media, Smart Phones & Data Breaches**
>
> Fueled in part by the rise in the use of smart phones and social media by consumers, as well as a large number of data breaches, identity theft incidents in the United States increased by 13 percent in 2011 to affect 11.6 million Americans, according to the '2012 Identity Fraud Report: Social Media and Mobile Forming the New Fraud Frontier' survey released by Javelin Strategy & Research.
>
> However, while the number identity theft incidents increased, the dollar amount stolen remained steady. In addition, consumer out-of-pocket costs from identity theft have decreased by 44 percent since 2004, mostly due to improved prevention and detection tools. Other key findings of the survey include:
>
> ✓ **Social media behaviors put consumers at risk of identity theft:** The survey found certain social media behaviors had higher incidence rates of identity theft than all consumers. Despite warnings that social media networks are a great resource for identity theft, consumers still share a significant amount of personal information frequently used to authenticate a consumer's identity. Specifically, 68 percent of people with public social media profiles shared their birthday information, 63 percent shared their high school name, 18 percent shared their phone number, and 12 percent shared their pet's name – all examples of personal information a company would use to verify an individual's identity.
>
> ✓ **Smart phone owners experienced greater incidences of identity theft:** The survey found seven percent of smart phone owners were victims of identity fraud, a one-third higher incidence rate compared to the general public. Part of this increase may be attributed to consumer smart phone behavior, as 32 percent of smart phone owners did not update to a new operating system when it became available, 62 percent did not use a password on their home screen – enabling anyone to access their information if the phone is lost – and 32 percent saved login information on their device.
>
> ✓ **Data Breaches increased causing more damage from identity theft:** The survey found another likely contributing factor to the rise in identity theft was the 67 percent increase in the number of Americans impacted by data breaches in 2011 compared to 2010. Victims of data breaches were 9.5 times more likely to be a victim of identity theft than consumers who did not receive a data breach letter.

The Javelin Strategy & Research survey is the nation's longest-running study of identity theft, which they define as the unauthorized use of another person's personal information to achieve illicit financial gain. The 2012 Identity Fraud Report: Social Media and Mobile Forming the New Fraud Frontier from Javelin Strategy & Research is available at: https://www.javelinstrategy.com/brochure/239.

More Proof of Identity Theft on the Rise

Additional proof of identity is theft is also evident when figures from recent surveys such as the 2012 Fraud Report from Javelin are compared with surveys from with the past decade. According to 'The Federal Trade Commission – 2006 Identity Theft Survey Report,' results of the survey suggested that approximately 8.3 million U.S. adults discovered that they were victims of some form of identity theft in 2005. The survey is available at: www.ftc.gov/os/2007/11/SynovateFinalReportIDTheft2006.pdf

Along with the large human toll, there is a financial as well, as victims try to dig out from underneath the economic damage. Repairing identity theft can take months of frustrating calls to police, merchants, financial institutions, and credit bureaus. Although technology has made this process quicker, the FTC's '2003 Identity Theft Survey Report' available at www.ftc.gov/os/2003/09/synovatereport.pdf found:

> "Victims of ID Theft also spend a considerable amount of their own time resolving the various problems that occurred because of the misuse of their personal information. On average, victims reported that they spent 30 hours resolving their problems. On average, victims of the "New Accounts and Other Frauds" form of ID Theft spent 60 hours resolving their problems. This suggests that Americans spent almost 300 million hours resolving problems related to ID Theft in the past year, with almost two-thirds of this time – 194 million hours – spent by victims of "New Accounts and Other Frauds" ID Theft."

The damage caused by identity theft has multiple dangers to employers. A business loses productivity when one of its employees is sidetracked by serious personal financial worries. A business also faces liability if they are adjudged as the cause of the identify theft. Businesses have obligations not only to their customers but also their employees in terms of safeguarding the confidentiality of private information.

Most studies have found that early detection is the key to lessening the impact of identity theft. The economic losses were much smaller and the damage to individuals in both out-of-pocket costs and time spent resolving the problem were substantially smaller the sooner the victim discovered the theft.

GAO Report Reveals Huge Jump in Tax-Related Identity Theft Incidents Identified by IRS

The United States Government Accountability Office (GAO) issued a report in May 2011 titled *'TAXES AND IDENTITY THEFT – Status of IRS Initiatives to Help Victimized Taxpayers'* that revealed a huge jump in the number of tax-related identity theft incidents identified by Internal Revenue Service (IRS). Primarily refund or employment fraud attempts, the IRS identified 248,357 tax-related identity theft incidents in 2010, nearly five times the amount of such incidents reported in 2008.

The GAO report found that identity theft harmed innocent taxpayers through employment and refund fraud and that both the IRS and taxpayers may not discover refund or employment fraud until after legitimate tax returns are filed. The report also showed that the number of tax-related identity theft incidents identified by the IRS, such as refund or employment fraud, has grown rapidly in the past three years:

✓ 51,702 tax-related identity theft incidents in 2008.

✓ 169,087 tax-related identity theft incidents in 2009.

✓ 248,357 tax-related identity theft incidents in 2010.

In **refund fraud**, an identity thief uses a taxpayer's name and Social Security number (SSN) to file for a tax refund, which IRS discovers after the legitimate taxpayer files. Refund fraud delays the refunds of innocent taxpayers.

In **employment fraud**, an identity thief uses a taxpayer's name and SSN to obtain a job. When the thief's employer reports income to IRS, the taxpayer appears to have unreported income on his or her return. Employment fraud exposes innocent taxpayers to enforcement actions for unreported income.

The report *'TAXES AND IDENTITY THEFT – Status of IRS Initiatives to Help Victimized Taxpayers'* from GAO – known as "the investigative arm of Congress" and "the congressional watchdog" – is at www.gao.gov/new.items/d11674t.pdf.

What is Identity Theft?

According to the 'About Identity Theft' section of the Federal Trade Commission (FTC) Identity Theft website at www.ftc.gov/bcp/edu/microsites/idtheft/:

"Identity theft occurs when someone uses your personally identifying information, like your name, Social Security number, or credit card number, without your permission, to commit fraud or other crimes.

The FTC estimates that as many as 9 million Americans have their identities stolen each year. In fact, you or someone you know may have experienced some form of identity theft. The crime takes many forms. Identity thieves may rent an apartment, obtain a credit card, or establish a telephone account in your name. You may not find out about the theft until you review your credit report or a credit card statement and notice charges you didn't make—or until you're contacted by a debt collector.

Identity theft is serious. While some identity theft victims can resolve their problems quickly, others spend hundreds of dollars and many days repairing damage to their good name and credit record. Some consumers victimized by identity theft may lose out on job opportunities, or be denied loans for education, housing or cars because of negative information on their credit reports. In rare cases, they may even be arrested for crimes they did not commit."

How do Identity Thieves Steal an Identity?

The FTC Identity Theft web site describes a variety of methods skilled identity thieves may use to get hold of your personally identifying information (PII) such as name, Social Security number, credit card numbers, or other financial account information:

1. **Dumpster Diving.** Identity thieves rummage through trash looking for bills or other paper with your personal information on it.
2. **Skimming.** Identity thieves steal credit/debit card numbers by using a special storage device when processing your card.
3. **Phishing.** Identity thieves pretend to be financial institutions or companies and send spam or pop-up messages to get you to reveal your personal information.
4. **Changing Your Address.** Identity thieves divert your billing statements to another location by completing a change of address form.
5. **Old-Fashioned Stealing**. Identity thieves steal wallets and purses; mail, including bank and credit card statements; pre-approved credit offers; and new checks or tax information. They steal personnel records, or bribe employees who have access.
6. **Pretexting.** Identity thieves use false pretenses to obtain your personal information from financial institutions, telephone companies, and other sources.

Types of Identity Theft

Fundamentally, identity theft occurs when someone passes himself or herself off as someone else in order to gain a fraudulent advantage. Identity theft typically occurs when the thief gains access to another person's personal information, such as Social Security number, bank or credit card account numbers, then uses them to commit fraud or theft. Here are three examples of identity theft:

1. The first type is **"account takeover."** This occurs when a criminal literally takes over another person's existing accounts and makes purchases using a victim's credit cards.

2. The second type is what experts refer to as **"true name fraud"** or **"application fraud."** This involves a thief creating brand new accounts using someone else's personal information such as the Social Security number. For example, a criminal may use the data to open a new American Express account.

3. A third type of identity theft is **"impersonation,"** where an identity thief takes over another person's identity — by utilizing the victim's identification, the thief obtains documents to enable them to pass themselves off as the victim. If the ruse is successful, the ID thief has the ability to commit more sophisticated "application fraud," ranging from getting a job under the false name, to creating a whole life using someone else's identity. Another variation is "criminal identity theft" where a person who has stolen an identity is arrested and even convicted under the false identity. The victim of identity theft now has a criminal record in his or her name!

Identity Theft Tops Federal Trade Commission List of Complaints for 2011

For the 12th year in a row, identity theft topped the list of consumer complaints released by the Federal Trade Commission (FTC) for 2011. Of more than 1.8 million complaints filed in 2011, 279,156 – or 15 percent – were identity theft complaints, and nearly 25 percent of those identity theft complaints were related tax- or wage-related fraud.

The FTC – the government agency working for consumers to prevent fraudulent, deceptive, and unfair business practices – enters complaints into the Consumer Sentinel Network (CSN), a secure online database of millions of consumer complaints available to more than 2,000 civil and criminal law enforcement agencies in the United States and abroad. In addition to storing complaints received by the FTC, the CSN also includes complaints filed with federal, state, and non-governmental organizations.

The CSN report breaks out complaint data on a state-by-state basis and also contains data about the 50 metropolitan areas reporting the highest per capita incidence of fraud and other complaints. In addition, the 50 metropolitan areas reporting the highest incidence of identity theft are noted. According to the FTC, the top ten complaint categories for 2011 were:

✓ Identity Theft: 279,156 Complaints (15 percent)

✓ Debt Collection: 180,928 Complaints (10 percent)

✓ Prizes, Sweepstakes, and Lotteries: 100,208 Complaints (6 percent)

✓ Shop-at-Home and Catalog Sales: 98,306 Complaints (5 percent)

✓ Banks and Lenders: 89,341 Complaints (5 percent)

✓ Internet Services: 81,805 Complaints (5 percent)

✓ Auto Related: 77,435 Complaints (4 percent)

✓ Imposter Scams: 73,281 Complaints (4 percent)

✓ Telephone and Mobile Services: 70,024 Complaints (4 percent)

✓ Advance-Fee Loans and Credit Protection/Repair: 47,414 Complaints (3 percent)

Begun in 1997 to collect fraud and identity theft complaints, the CSN now has more than 7 million complaints, including those about credit reports, debt collection, mortgages, and lending, among other subjects. Between January and December 2011, the CSN received more than 1.8 million consumer complaints, which the FTC has sorted into 30 complaint categories.

For more information about the Consumer Sentinel Network, visit www.FTC.gov/sentinel. For more information about the FTC's Top Complaint Categories for 2011, visit: www.ftc.gov/opa/2012/02/2011complaints.shtm.

Criminal identity theft is especially worrisome. There have been numerous horror stories of innocent, law-abiding citizens arrested and tossed into jail for no apparent reason, only to find they have been the victims of identity theft. Someone who stole their identity committed some act resulting in a criminal charge or warrant, and gave the stolen name and information — your name, your information.

Report on Child Identity Theft Reveals 1 in 10 Children Targeted by Identity Thieves

It may be hard for most parents to imagine that their children could have homes in foreclosure or huge bills in collection before they are even old enough to apply for student loans for college, but a new report released by Carnegie Mellon University's CyLab – *'Child Identity Theft: New Evidence Indicates Identity Thieves are Targeting Children for Unused Social Security Numbers'* – reveals that one in ten 10 children scanned for the report had someone else using their Social Security number (SSN) to commit identity theft and fraud.

Based on scans of over 42,000 U.S. child IDs by an identity theft protection company, the report found that 4,311 of the children in the report – or 10.2 percent – had someone else using their Social Security number to purchase homes and automobiles, open credit card accounts, secure employment, and obtain driver's licenses. Other key findings include:

✓   The largest identity theft fraud ($725,000) was committed against a 16-year-old girl.

✓   303 identity theft victims were under the age of five years.

✓   The youngest victim of identity theft was five months old.

The report offers glimpses into the real life threat of identity theft to the financial security of families, articulate vital concerns, and raises public awareness about identity theft. For more information and to download the full report, visit www.cyblog.cylab.cmu.edu/2011/03/child-identity-theft.html.

Consumer Advice From the FTC

In January 2012, the Federal Trade Commission (FTC), the nation's consumer protection agency, prepared a Guide – 'Taking Charge: What To Do If Your Identity Is Stolen' – to help consumers repair the damage that identity theft can cause and reduce the risk of identity theft happening to them. The Guide has tips, worksheets, blank forms, and sample letters to guide consumers through the recovery process. The content below is taken from this Guide which is located at www.ftc.gov/bcp/edu/pubs/consumer/idtheft/idt04.pdf. The FTC's Identity Theft website is located at: www.FTC.gov/idtheft.

How can identity theft victims tell that someone has stolen their information?

✓   They see unexplained withdrawals from bank accounts.

✓   They don't get bills or other mail.

✓   Merchants refuse their checks.

✓   Debt collectors call about debts that are not theirs.

✓ They find unfamiliar accounts or charges on their credit reports.

✓ Medical providers bill them for services they did not use.

✓ Their health plan rejects legitimate medical claims because records show they reached benefits limit.

✓ The Internal Revenue Service (IRS) notifies them that more than 1 tax return was filed in their name or they have income from an employer they did not work for.

✓ They get notice that their information was compromised by a data breach at a company where they do business or have an account.

✓ They are arrested for a crime someone else allegedly committed in their name

What steps should consumers take if they are a victim of identity theft?

If a consumer's wallet, Social Security card, or other personal, financial, or account information is lost or stolen, the immediate steps should include:

✓ Contact the credit reporting companies and place an initial fraud alert on credit file.

✓ Check bank and other account statements for unusual activity.

✓ Exercise legal right to a free copy of credit report.

✓ Check for other rights under state law.

✓ Create an Identity Theft report

Another useful FTC document is its annual publication titled *ID Theft: When Bad Things Happen to Your Good Name.* . Here is an excerpt from that document.

How Identity Thieves Use Your Personal Information

✓ They call your credit card issuer and, pretending to be you, ask to change the mailing address on your credit card account. The imposter then runs up charges on your account. Because your bills are being sent to the new address, it may take some time before you realize there is a problem.

✓ They open a new credit card account using your name, date of birth, and Social Security Number. When they use the credit card and don't pay the bills, the delinquent account is reported on your credit report.

✓ They establish telephone or wireless service in your name.

✓ They open a bank account in your name and write bad checks on that account.

✓ They file for bankruptcy under your name to avoid paying debts they've incurred under your name, or to avoid eviction.

✓ They counterfeit checks or debit cards and drain your bank account.

✓ They buy vehicles by taking out auto loans in your name.

✓ They give your name to the police during an arrest. If they are released from police custody, but do not show up for their court date, then an arrest warrant is issued in your name.

How to Protect Yourself and What to Do If You Are a Victim

The immediate economic damages to a victim of identity theft are generally limited. A victim may not be liable for any amount greater than the first $50.00, if that. However, the damage can go further. Debit card users have less protection against fraud since their checking accounts wiped out and they could be liable for the total amount of the loss depending on how quickly they report the loss to the financial institution. (Electronic Funds Transfer Act, 15 USC sec. 1693) For more about credit card and debit card laws, read the Federal Reserve's Consumer Handbook, www.federalreserve.gov/pubs/consumerhdbk.

The text below is an excerpt of a guide from the Privacy Rights Clearinghouse website 'Fact Sheet 17: Coping with Identity Theft: Reducing the Risk of Fraud. This document, which is available www.privacyrights.org/fs/fs17-it.htm provides excellent advice on how consumers can take to reduce their risk of fraud.

For true victims of identity theft, or those people with lost or stolen wallets or Social Security numbers, read their 'Fact Sheet 17a: Identity Theft: What to Do if It Happens to You' at www.privacyrights.org/fs/fs17a.htm.

Steps to Reduce Your Risk of Becoming a Victim of identity Theft

From the Fact Sheet 17: Coping with Identity Theft: Reducing the Risk of Fraud

www.privacyrights.org

Credit cards, debit cards, and credit reports:

✓ Reduce the number of credit and debit cards you carry in your wallet. We recommend that you do not use debit cards because of the potential for losses to your checking account (see above). Instead, carry one or two credit cards and your ATM card in your wallet. Nonetheless, debit cards are popular. If you do use them, take advantage of online access to your bank account to monitor account activity frequently. Report evidence of fraud to your financial institution immediately.

✓ When using your credit and debit cards at restaurants and stores, pay close attention to how the magnetic stripe information is swiped by the waiter or clerk. Dishonest employees have been known to use small hand-held devices called skimmers to quickly swipe the card and then later download the account number data onto a personal computer. The thief uses the account data for Internet shopping and/or the creation of counterfeit cards.

✓ Do not use debit cards when shopping online. Use a credit card because you are better protected in case of fraud. See our online shopping guide, www.privacyrights.org/fs/fs23-shopping.htm.

✓ Keep a list or photocopy of all your credit cards, debit cards, bank accounts, and investments – the account numbers, expiration dates and telephone numbers of the customer service and fraud departments – in a secure place (not your wallet or purse) so you can quickly contact these companies in case your credit cards have been stolen or accounts are being used fraudulently.

✓ Never give out your SSN, credit or debit card number or other personal information over the phone, by mail, or on the Internet unless you have a trusted business relationship with the company and you have initiated the call. Identity thieves have been known to call their victims with a fake story that goes something like this. "Today is your lucky day! You have been chosen by the Publishers Consolidated Sweepstakes to receive a free trip to the Bahamas. All we need is your Social Security number, credit card number and expiration date to verify you as the lucky winner."

✓ Always take credit card receipts with you. Never toss them in a public trash container. When shopping, put receipts in your wallet rather than in the shopping bag.

✓ Never permit your credit card number to be written onto your checks. It's a violation of California law (Civil Code sec. 1725) and laws in many other states, and puts you at risk for fraud.

✓ Watch the mail when you expect a new or reissued credit card to arrive. Contact the issuer if the card does not arrive.

✓ Order your credit report at least once a year. Federal law gives you the right to one free credit report each year from the three credit bureaus: Equifax, Experian, and TransUnion. If you are a victim of identity theft, your credit report will contain the tell-tale signs – inquiries that were not generated by you, as well as credit accounts that you did not open. The earlier you detect fraud, the easier and quicker it will be to clean up your credit files and regain your financial health. We recommend that you stagger your requests and obtain one report each four months. That way, you can monitor your credit reports on an ongoing basis. But if you are in the market for credit or are a victim of identity theft, order all three at one time. For more information on your free credit reports, visit the Federal Trade Commission web site at www.ftc.gov/bcp/edu/microsites/freereports/index.shtml. How to order your free annual credit report: By telephone: (877) 322-8228; Online: www.annualcreditreport.com; By mail – Print out the order form here: https://www.annualcreditreport.com/cra/requestformfinal.pdf.

✓ Residents in seven states can obtain free annual credit reports under state law, in addition to the free reports available under federal law. These states are: Colorado, Maine, Massachusetts, Maryland, New Jersey, Vermont, and Georgia (two free reports per year in Georgia). If you live in one of these states, be sure to order both your free reports under federal law as well as state law each year – enabling you to even more effectively monitor your credit files on an ongoing basis.

✓ Individuals nationwide are able to "freeze" their credit reports with Equifax, Experian, and TransUnion. By freezing your credit reports, you can prevent credit issuers from accessing your credit files except when you give permission. This effectively prevents thieves from opening up new credit card and loan accounts. In most states, security freezes are available at no charge to identity theft victims and for a relatively small fee for non-victims. The California Office of Privacy Protection provides a guide on security freezes for Californians, www.privacy.ca.gov/consumers/cis10english.pdf. For state-by-state information on security freezes, visit this Consumers Union web page: www.consumersunion.org/campaigns//learn_more/003484indiv.html.

✓ Many companies, including the three credit bureaus, offer credit monitoring services for an annual or monthly fee. They will notify you when there is any activity on your credit report, thus alerting you to possible fraud. We do not endorse credit monitoring services because we believe that individuals should not have to pay a fee to track their credit. If you decide to subscribe, be sure to choose a service that monitors all three credit reports on an ongoing basis. You can create your own credit monitoring strategy at no cost by ordering one of your free credit reports each four months, as explained above. For more information about monitoring services, see PRC *Fact Sheet 33, Identity Theft Monitoring Services.*

✓ There are many identity theft insurance products available to consumers. We do not recommend them unless they are available as a free or low-cost rider on an existing insurance policy. For more information on such insurance products, visit www.iii.org/individuals/other/insurance/identitytheft (no endorsements implied).

Passwords and PINS:

✓ When creating passwords and PINs (personal identification numbers), do not use the last four digits of your Social Security number, mother's maiden name, your birthdate, middle name, pet's name, consecutive numbers or anything else that could easily be discovered by thieves. It's best to create passwords that combine letters and numbers. Here's a tip to create a password that is strong and easy to remember. Think of a favorite line of poetry, like "Mary had a little lamb." Use the first or last letters to create a password. Use numbers to make it stronger. Use both upper and lower case. For example, MhALL, or better yet MhA2L!. The longer the string, the harder it is to crack.

✓ Ask your financial institutions to add extra security protection to your account. Most will allow you to use an additional code or password (a number or word) when accessing your account. Do not use your mother's maiden name, SSN, or date or birth, as these are easily obtained by identity thieves. If asked to create a reminder question, do not use one that is easily answered by others.

✓ Memorize all your passwords. Don't record them on anything in your wallet.

✓ Shield your hand when using a bank ATM machine or making long distance phone calls with your phone card. "Shoulder surfers" may be nearby with binoculars or video camera.

Social Security numbers:

✓ Protect your Social Security number (SSN). Release it only when absolutely necessary (like tax forms, employment records, most banking, stock and property transactions). The SSN is the key to your credit and banking accounts and is the prime target of criminals. If a business requests your SSN, ask if it has an alternative number that can be used instead. Speak to a manager or supervisor if your request is not honored. Ask to see the company's written policy on SSNs. If necessary, take your business elsewhere. If the SSN is requested by a government agency, look for the Privacy Act notice. This will tell you if your SSN is required, what will be done with it, and what happens if you refuse to provide it. If your state uses your SSN as your driver's license number, ask to substitute another number. If possible, do not provide the SSN on job applications. Offer to provide it when you are interviewed or when a background check is conducted. (Read PRC Fact Sheet 10 on SSNs, www.privacyrights.org/fs/fs10-ssn.htm.)

✓ Do not have your SSN or driver's license number printed on your checks. Don't let merchants hand-write the SSN onto your checks because of the risk of fraud.

✓ Do not say your SSN out loud when you are in a public place. And do not let merchants, health care providers, or others say your SSN out loud. Whisper or write it down on a piece of paper instead. Be sure to retrieve and shred that paper.

✓ Do not carry your SSN card in your wallet except for situations when it is required, the first day on the job, for example. If possible, do not carry wallet cards that display the SSN, such as insurance cards, except when needed to receive healthcare services. A California law places restrictions on the display and transmission of SSNs by companies. It is being phased in through 2005. For more information, read the California Office of Privacy Protection guide on SSN "recommended practices," at www.privacy.ca.gov/consumers/ssn_rec.pdf. If you feel you must carry your health insurance or Medicare card with you at all times, try this. Photocopy the card and cut it down to wallet size. Then remove or cut out the last four digits of the SSN. Carry that with you rather than the actual card. But be sure to carry your original Medicare card with you the first time you visit your healthcare provider. They are likely to want to make a photocopy of it for their files.

✓ It is a violation of federal law for state motor vehicles departments to use the Social Security number as the driver's license (DL) number. (Intelligence Reform and Terrorism Prevention Act of 2004, implemented December 17, 2005) If you are carrying an older driver's license containing your SSN that is not yet ready for renewal, contact the motor vehicles agency in your state and request to have your DL replaced before the actual renewal date. This way, you are not carrying a document in your wallet that contains your SSN.

Internet and computer safeguards:

✓ Install a firewall on your home computer to prevent hackers from obtaining personal identifying and financial data from your hard drive. This is especially important if you connect to the Internet by DSL or cable modem.

✓ Install and update virus protection software to prevent a worm or virus from causing your computer to send out files or other stored information.

✓ Password-protect files that contain sensitive personal data, such as financial account information. Create passwords that combine 6-8 numbers and letters, upper and lower case. In addition, encrypt sensitive files.

✓ When shopping online, do business with companies that provide transaction security protection, and that have strong privacy and security policies. For more online shopping tips, read PRC Fact Sheet 23, www.privacyrights.org/fs/fs23-shopping.htm.

✓ Before disposing of your computer, remove data by using a strong "wipe" utility program. Do not rely on the "delete" function to remove files containing sensitive information.

✓ Never respond to "phishing" email messages. These appear to be from your bank, eBay, or PayPal. They instruct you to visit their web site, which looks just like the real thing. There, you are told to confirm your account information, provide your SSN, date of birth and other personal information. Legitimate financial companies never email their customers with such requests. These messages are the work of fraudsters attempting to obtain personal information in order to commit identity theft. Visit www.antiphishing.org.

✓ Be aware that file-sharing and file-swapping programs expose your computer to illegitimate access by hackers and fraudsters. If you use such programs, make sure you comply with the law and know what you are doing.

Install and update strong firewall and virus protection. Many file-sharing programs are downloaded by youngsters without the knowledge of their parents. There are software programs available that identify file sharing software and locate shared files on home computers. For more information on safe surfing for families, visit www.getnetwise.org.

Check Your own Credit Report Periodically

The best defense against suspected identify fraud is to obtain and review your credit report on a regular basis. The reports from all "Big Three" credit bureaus – Equifax, Experian, and TransUnion – should be reviewed each year. Consumers can contact all three bureaus and request reports. The contact numbers are listed at the end of this chapter.

The three credit bureaus also created a centralized service for consumers called AnnualCreditReport.com at www.annualcreditreport.com. AnnualCreditReport.com provides consumers with the secure means to request and obtain a free credit report once every 12 months from each of the three nationwide consumer credit reporting companies in accordance with the Fair and Accurate Credit Transactions Act (FACT Act).

In addition, a consumer is entitled to a free credit report if he or she is a victim of identity theft, has been denied credit, receives welfare benefits, or is unemployed.

 A substantial source of stolen personal data used for identity theft is information taken from businesses. Employers should help safeguard data concerning their employees and clients by adhering to responsible information handling practices, as discussed in Chapter 28.

How to Repair the Damage

If a person is the victim of identity theft, then it can be a tremendous amount of work to unravel the damage. The topic of how to respond can be a book in itself. A number of websites give detailed advice on what to do. Some of these websites are listed as resources at the end of this chapter.

- ✓ Report the theft to the three major credit bureaus immediately. Obtain a copy of your credit report and if necessary, place a fraud alert in your files.
- ✓ Report the theft to the police immediately. Depending upon the state where a consumer lives, there may be helpful things the police can do. At a minimum, make a police report and get a copy of the report.
- ✓ Review your credit report and credit card statements carefully for signs of fraudulent activity.
- ✓ Get complete details on any fraudulent new account or any fraudulent use of an existing account.
- ✓ If an identification document is stolen, contact the issuing agency immediately. For example, if your driver's license is stolen or lost, go to your state Department of Motor Vehicles. If your mail is stolen, report it to the U.S. Postal Inspector office. If your passport is stolen, check with the State Department at the address at the end of this chapter.
- ✓ If you are wrongly accused of a crime because a thief used your identity, check to see what program or procedures are available in your state to set the record straight. In California, for example, there is a special statewide repository where identity theft victims can register. You may need to contact your local police departments and courts to find out how to have any records corrected. Correcting the problem may involve having your fingerprints taken so that you can be eliminated as a suspect in a pending case.
- ✓ If a bill collector contacts you, indicate you are a victim of identity theft and the debt is not yours. However, do not stop there. Write letters to bill collectors and creditors immediately —no later than 30 days — with all of the relevant information. Include as much documentation as possible in the letter, including your police report and identity theft affidavit. You have rights under federal law to stop a bill collector from bothering you.

Helpful Resources in the Fight against Identity Theft

Credit Reporting Companies

Equifax:
PO Box 105069
Atlanta, GA 30348
www.equifax.com
1-800-525-6285

TransUnion:
PO Box 6790
Fullerton, CA 92834
www.transunion.com
1-800-680-7289

Experian:
PO Box 9532
Allen, TX 75013
www.experian.com
1-888-397-3742 (1-888-EXPERIAN)

(Ask each company for the email or postal mail address for sending dispute or blocking requests.)

Federal Government

Federal Communications Commission
For help with telephone service:
www.fcc.gov/cgb
1-888-225-5322
1-888-835-5322 (TTY)

Federal Financial Institutions Examination Council
To locate the agency that regulates a bank or credit
union: www.ffiec.gov/consumercenter

Federal Trade Commission
To report identity theft:
www.ftc.gov/complaint
FTC identity theft website:
www.ftc.gov/idtheft
1-877-438-4338
1-866-653-4261 (TTY)
Taking Charge: What To Do If Your Identity Is
Stolen:
www.ftc.gov/bcp/edu/pubs/consumer/idtheft/idt04.pdf

Internal Revenue Service
Identity Protection Specialized Unit
To report identity theft:
www.irs.gov/identitytheft
1-800-908-4490

Legal Services Programs
To locate a legal services provider:
www.lsc.gov/local-programs/program-profiles

Social Security Administration
To report fraud:
Go to www.socialsecurity.gov and type "Fraud" in the
Search box.
1-800-269-0271

U.S. Department of Education
To report fraud:
www.ed.gov/about/offices/list/oig/hotline.html
Or go to www.ed.gov and type "OIG Hotline" in the
Search box.
1-800-647-8733

U.S. Department of Justice
To report suspected bankruptcy fraud:
www.justice.gov/ust/eo/fraud
Or send email to:
http://USTP.Bankruptcy.Fraud@usdoj.gov

U.S. Postal Inspection Service
To file a complaint:
https://postalinspectors.uspis.gov/contactUs/filecompl
aint.aspx
1-877-876-2455

U.S. Postal Service
To place a hold on mail:
www.usps.com/holdmail
To locate a post office:
www.usps.com
1-800-275-8777

U.S. Securities and Exchange Commission
To report fraud:
www.sec.gov/complaint/tipscomplaint.shtml
1-800-732-0330

U.S. Department of State
To report a lost or stolen passport:
www.travel.state.gov/passport
1-877-487-2778
1-888-874-7793 (TDD/TTY)

Other Resources

American Bar Association
To locate state and local bar associations:
www.americanbar.org/groups/bar_services/resources/state_local_bar_associations.html

AnnualCreditReport.com
To order a free annual credit report:
www.annualcreditreport.com
1-877-322-8228

Certegy
To ask about a declined check:
www.askcertegy.com
81-800-437-5120

ChexSystems, Inc.
To report checking accounts opened in your name:
www.consumerdebit.com
1-800-428-9623

Identity Theft Resource Center (ITRC)
www.idtheftcenter.org
1-888-400-5530

Identity Theft Survival Kit
www.identitytheft.org
1-800-725-0807

National Association of Attorneys General
To find a State Attorney General:
www.naag.org
1-202-326-6000 (Not a toll-free number)

National Association of Regulatory Utility Commissioners
To get contact information for a state utility commission:
www.naruc.org/commissions
1-202-898-2200 (Not a toll-free number)

Opt Out
To opt out of prescreened offers of credit or insurance:
www.optoutprescreen.com
1-888-567-8688

Privacy Rights Clearinghouse
www.privacyrights.org
619-298-3396
Identity Theft IQ Test:
www.privacyrights.org/itrc-quiz1.htm

TeleCheck Services, Inc.
To report check fraud:
www.firstdata.com/telecheck
1-800-710-9898

Chapter 32

Take the Safe Hiring Audit Test

Employee Problems, Problem Employees

Everything covered in this book comes down to one sentence:

> *Most employee problems are caused by problem employees, and most of those problems can be avoided in the first place with a Safe Hiring Program.*

If a firm does not practice a Safe Hiring Program, then they can suffer what lawyers like to call the "Parade of Horribles." These "Horribles" are examples of the bad things an employer may encounter, and let us hope you will not encounter many of these situations. In fact, through luck or good fortune some employers may not as of yet have encountered any. However, without a Safe Hiring Program, eventually a problem will occur.

If Your Firm is Sued, Can You Show Due Diligence?

If your firm is sued, the question before a jury is: "Did your firm take appropriate steps in your hiring practices to protect the public, co-workers, or others at risk?"

Every employer has a legal duty to exercise due diligence in hiring. Firms that fail to exercise due diligence in their hiring also have a litigation exposure. **An employer can be sued for negligence if they hired someone they knew, or in the exercise of reasonable care should have known, who was dangerous or unfit for that particular job**.

Employers are at a disadvantage in litigation. A lawsuit for negligent hiring is typically brought as a result of serious injury to an employee or member of the public. In an extreme case involving a murder in the workplace, it can be the surviving spouse or family members who may be suing, claiming essentially the employer was responsible. Not only is the jury hearing evidence of a serious loss, but also in these cases, the evidence will show that the employer had greater ability and resources to prevent harm through safe hiring. After all, it is the employer who has a legal duty of care as well as the resources to have prevented a hiring mistake.

A jury decides if an employer is negligent by using the mythical "reasonable person" standard. That standard leaves a great deal of latitude for a jury to decide that with a little more effort, an employer could have prevented the harm. Jurors are often employees themselves. They may be more likely to identify with an injured victim or family than an employer who was too lazy, cheap, or unconcerned to exercise due diligence procedures. Unless an employer has a really good reason why the injury, sexual assault, or other harm was not their fault, employers lose the majority of cases.

So, for employers, here is the Big Question. If your firm is sued, can you demonstrate due diligence?

AUTHOR TIP **Other Advantages of an Audit**

As can be seen from previous chapters, it is not only individual plaintiffs who can bring legal actions against an employer. The EEOC and FTC areis stepping up enforcement as well. An audit can also help protect an employer against governmental investigations.

Audit Your Hiring Program

Below is a two-part **Safe Hiring Audit Test** for employers – a Safe Hiring Report Card. This exercise allows you to see how your organization measures up in case you have to defend your firm's hiring practices in court or in a deposition before trial.

What is a Deposition?

A deposition is a device used in a civil lawsuit where each side is allowed to question potential witnesses under oath. All information is recorded by a court reporter. This is part of what is called the "Discovery Process" when each side is allowed to discover facts that may be relevant to the case before the trial. A witness is put under oath by the court reporter and testifies as though the person was in court, but there is no judge or jury. Whatever a witness says is transcribed into a written booklet and can be referred to in court. There are other discovery devices as well, depending upon the jurisdiction (state or federal). For example, each side can send written questions to each other that must be answered. They are called "Interrogatories." Parties can also send a demand to each other requesting they admit or deny certain items of information, called a "Request for Admission." Demands can also be made to provide documents, or to allow an inspection of premises.

Part One: Start with a Benchmark Exercise

Trial attorneys often take a "test drive" to identify the fundamental thrust of a case. A test drive can range from something as sophisticated as presenting their case to a "mock jury" to simply running the facts by non-lawyers to get their response. To determine how your firm may do in a negligent hiring lawsuit, let us create a hypothetical scenario and ask what you would tell a jury when called upon to defend your firm's safe hiring procedures. This "test drive" will establish a benchmark and you will be auditing your firm's hiring program.

Assume your organization hired an accounting clerk who falsified his or her credentials and later attacked and injured a co-worker during an argument over the clerk's numerous professional errors. The co-worker was hurt and cannot work, and consequently sues your firm for negligent hiring. Describe:

✓ **What your firm did to exercise due diligence.** To merely say you had a background screening firm do a check is not sufficient.

✓ **What due diligence was exercised in selecting the background firm.** Include the pre-hire steps taken in the application, interview, and reference checking process before the background check.

Part Two: Take the Audit

After you have compiled and written your response to this exercise, take the Safe Hiring Audit that begins on the following page.

The goal is to perform a self-assessment audit of your firm's procedures used in the hiring process. The audit will identify your present hiring program's strengths and weaknesses — to find areas needing improvement or where your compliance may be weak.

Note of Caution

The Safe Hiring Audit is for educational purposes only. Do not create a document that could be construed as a company policy analysis; it could be used against your organization in court. If your organization decides to conduct a formal audit, a best practice would be to have an attorney perform the audit so it would be protected by work product or attorney-client privilege.

AUTHOR TIP When performing the audit, it is worth recalling the discussion on Policies, Practices, and Procedures:

- A **Policy** is a general statement of a principle according to which a company performs business functions.

- A **Practice** is a general statement of the way the company implements a policy. Best practices support policy.

- A **Procedure** documents an established practice. Documentation is the KEY. In a lawsuit, documentation is a very critical factor. For example, it is not sufficient to simply have a training session. Can you document who attended, when, if they stayed for the entire time, what was taught, if there was any follow-up or testing of skills learned? Everything needs to be documented in writing.

A firm cannot score high on this audit without documentation.

Take the Safe Hiring Audit

The Safe Hiring Audit consists of 25 questions dealing with safe hiring practices. For each of the 25 questions, test takers should score their organizations on a 0-4 point scale.

- ✓ **0 = Doing nothing or out of compliance (equivalent to an F on a report card).**
- ✓ **1 = Taking some steps but falling short of what an employer should do (D).**
- ✓ **2 = Taking some measures but need to improve (C).**
- ✓ **3 = Taking strong measures; have some but not all documentation (B).**
- ✓ **4 = Yyour operation could be a model for other firms; all documentation is verified as legal (A).**

There are 100 possible points for a perfect score to the Safe Hiring Audit (25 Questions X 4 Points = 100). Once you have completed all 25 questions, add the scores for the **total score** and then divide by 25 for the **average score per question**. For example, if the total score is 75, the average score per questions would be 3 (75 ÷ 25 = 3). This will give you a general idea of the quality of your Safe Hiring Program.

The Safe Hiring Audit

The Safe Hiring Audit consists of 25 questions. Each question includes "Best Practice" information to help test takers calculate their scores.

1.   Does your organization have written policies, practices, and procedures for safe hiring? SCORE: _____

Best Practice:

How would you rate your company's written policies as far as demonstrating a commitment to safe hiring, such as found in your employee manuals or operations manuals?

How accurately are specific practices documented?

How well will written forms and procedures stand up to an audit?

Do your written policies also cover the need for data protection and confidentiality as well as the need to limit the use of information to hiring and selection purposes?

Case in Point:

Although a firm had an "understanding" between managers to hire safe, qualified workers, the hiring procedure is done on the basis of "oral tradition." This would be a "0" – not compliant.

2. **Are the safe hiring policies, practices, and procedures reviewed and updated every year for legal compliance? SCORE: _____**

Best Practice:

Review your Policies, Practices, and Procedures for legal compliance:

Federal Fair Credit Reporting Act (FCRA) followed if third party firms involved.

In compliance with EEOC and state equivalent rules, especially the EEOC Guidance on criminal records issued April 25, 2012.

ADA and state ADA rules followed.

Specific state laws obeyed (i.e., California regulates both third-party screening AND internal employer investigations through the Investigative Consumer Reporting Agencies Act).

Privacy Protection and Defamation-avoidance procedures in place.

3. **Are the organization's policies and procedures on safe hiring communicated effectively to the workforce and managers? SCORE: _____**

Best Practice:

Are the company's policies and procedures on safe hiring communicated effectively to the workforce and managers?

Procedures:

Can you document how frequently policies and procedures are communicated?

If you are in a deposition, how can you document communication of your policies?

If so, what are the details? Hint — written documentation detailing dates and times works best.

4. **Is there documented organizational responsibility for safe hiring with consequences of not following program spelled out? SCORE: _____**

Best Practice:

Is there a position specifically responsible for safe-hiring practices;

i.e. are safe hiring responsibilities in someone's job description?

If safe hiring is decentralized in hiring departments, are there documented procedures in place across the organization, including training and audit of performance?

5. **Are tools and training in place to ensure hiring managers follow a Safe Hiring Program? SCORE: _____**

Best Practice:

Is there training for hiring managers, HR, etc.?

Procedures:

How is the training conducted?

Frequency of training?

How is training success monitored and measured?

Is an identifiable person responsible to analyze, implement, and evaluate the training program?

How is compliance documented?

Case in Point:

The school district had great policies, but managers failed to follow practice guidelines, which permitted a teacher with a questionable history to be hired. Also, the managers failed to document the results of background checking done on the teacher.

6. Is a procedure in place to audit all the safe hiring practices? SCORE: _____

<u>Best Practice:</u>

Is there a documented audit procedure to ensure safe-hiring practices are followed?

…i.e. can you prove someone was auditing procedures to see if it was followed?

<u>Procedures:</u>

How is the completed audit information maintained?

How frequently does auditing occur?

Who conducts the audit process?

Does the audit trail go to the TOP; i.e. local managers checked by regional managers, etc.

7. Are all hiring policies and practices reviewed for legal compliance? SCORE: _____

<u>Best Practice:</u>

Are there consequences/penalties if the hiring manager, HR personnel, etc. fail to implement or follow the plan?

<u>Procedures:</u>

Can employer document that anyone not following procedures is adversely impacted?

8. Is the Fair Credit Reporting Act (FCRA) followed if third-party firms are involved in screening? SCORE: _____

<u>Best Practice:</u>

Make sure screening service is in compliance with FCRA.

<u>Procedures:</u>

Obtain applicant's written release/disclosure on a stand-alone document.

Pre-adverse action -copy of report and statement of rights so applicant can object if information inaccurate or incomplete.

Second letter sent to applicant if decision is made final.

Employer must also certify law will be followed, i.e. not discriminate, use for employment purposes only.

If forms provided by screening firm, review for legal compliance.

Be aware many states have their own rules on screening.

9. Are there procedures to place applicants on notice that your organization engages in "Best Practices" for hiring? SCORE: _____

<u>Best Practice:</u>

Is there notice in the job announcement, bulletin, classified advertisement, internet site, etc. that you perform background checks?

<u>Reason:</u>

Discourages applicants with something to hide and encourages applicants to be truthful.

<u>Procedures:</u>

Is there a notice on the application form that a prospective candidate receives?

Do applicants sign a release for a background check?

10. Does your firm use an application form? SCORE: _____

<u>Best Practice:</u>

Utilize application forms, not resumes.

Reasons:

Resumes are often not complete or clear.

To applicant, a resume is a marketing tool.

Applications ensure uniformity.

Also, requires applicant to provide all necessary information, prevents employer having impermissible info, and gives places where applicants sign certain statements.

If no application process, is there a supplemental form with necessary language?

11. Does the application form have all necessary and correct language? SCORE: _____

Best Practice:

Depending on how an employer chooses to implement the April 25, 2012 EEOC Guidance on criminal records, does your firm address the issue of when it asks about past criminal history? For example, does your firm provide an advisement that an appropriate inquiry will be made at an appropriate time in the hiring process?

Does the application contain a statement that fraudulent statements or material omissions are grounds to terminate the process, or employment, no matter when discovered?.

12. Are completed applications reviewed for potential "red flags" including employment gaps? SCORE: _____

Procedures:

Review applications for potential "red flags" from applicant such as:

Does not sign application

Does not sign release

Leaves criminal questions blank (This depends upon how an employer implements the 2012 EEOC Guidance on criminal records.)

Applicant self-reports offense

Fails to identify past employers

Fails to identify past supervisors

Fails to explain why left past jobs

Excessive cross-outs and changes

Unexplained employment gaps

Explanations for employment gaps or leaving past jobs do not make sense

13. Are the six critical questions used in a structured interview? SCORE: _____

Best Practice:

Since they have signed consent and believe you are doing checks, job applicants have a powerful incentive to be truthful.

1. "Our firm has a standard policy of conducting background checks on all hires before an offer is made or finalized. You have already signed a release form. Do you have any concerns about that?"

(Good applicants will shrug this question off.)

2. "We also check for criminal convictions for all finalists. Do you have any concerns about that?"

(Make sure question reflects updated EEOC Guidance for use of arrest and conviction records and what employer may legally ask in your state.)

3. "When we talk to your past employers, what do you think they will say?"

(This tells applicants past employers will be contacted and provides an incentive to be accurate.)

4. "Will your past employers tell us that there were any issues with tardiness, meeting job requirements, etc.? e.g., applicant was tardy, did not perform well, etc.?"

(Questions must be on job-related issues only.)

5. "Can you tell me about any unexplained gaps in your employment history?"

(Where gaps in the employment history are not explained, it is critical to ask this question.)

6. "Is everything in the application and everything you told us in the hiring process true, correct, and complete?"

(The critical final question that sends a clear message to applicants that the employer takes the process seriously, and they need to be completely open, honest, and truthful.)

14. Are interviewers trained in legal compliance? SCORE: _____

Best Practice:

Train all interviewers to:

Question all applicants in a similar fashion

Not ask illegal questions, i.e., questions that are discriminatory or prohibited by law

Respond when an applicant volunteers impermissible information

Not to make statements to an applicant such as promises about the job

Not mark or make notes on resume

Procedure:

Document the interviewer's training and audit results.

15. Does the firm check past employment, education credentials, and references? SCORE: _____

Best Practice:

Critical to find out where applicant lived, worked, and went to school in past 7 years to get an idea of where to look for criminal records.

Verify employment to determine where a person has worked even if you only get dates and job title.

Verify academic credentials to avoid embarrassing situations later (See Yahoo CEO who had to leave company and cases of doctors practicing without licenses.)

Reasons:

Biggest mistake employer can make is not contact past employers — this is just as critical as criminal checks.

Looking for unexplained gaps.

To target locations to search for criminal records.

If able to verify person gainfully employed last five-ten years, they are less likely to have spent time in custody for serious offense.

Just attempting/documenting demonstrates due diligence.

Check academic records to see if degree is from "diploma mill" (fake college).

Case in Point:

See the example of the Yahoo CEO who had to leave company after discrepancy found on academic credentials. Also see case of murderous carpet cleaner or the case of the state sponsored computer school.

16. Does the firm look for "employment gaps"? SCORE: _____

Best Practice:

Critical to verify employment to determine where a person has been even if you only get dates and job title.

Looking for unexplained gaps.

Procedures:

Document that interviewer reviewed application for gaps and asked applicant.

If can verify person gainfully employed last five-ten years, then less likely spent time in custody for serious offense.

17. Is the firm conducting an appropriate search for criminal records? SCORE: _____

Best Practice:

Understand EEOC rules for use of criminal records based upon business necessity:

The nature and gravity of the offense

The amount of time that has passed since the conviction or completion of sentence

The nature of the job being held or sought

(Also be aware of updated EEOC guidance for criminal records as of April 2012.)

Special rules considering arrests only.

Did the applicant lie in the application?

Criminal information was verified and information is current, belongs to applicant, employer has understanding of information, and there is no prohibition on the information's use.

18. Does the firm understand the appropriate uses and the limitations on criminal record databases? SCORE: _____

Best Practice:

Use criminal databases only as a secondary tool in connection with county court level criminal searches since databases may contain inaccurate and incomplete information.

Verify possible criminal "hits" from databases with a county court level search since databases may contain "false positives."

19. Are the firm's policy and procedures for the use of negative criminal information legal and compliant with federal and state laws? SCORE: _____

Best Practice:

Policies – are there written guidelines to follow?

Documentation – are all procedures and decisions documented to file?

Individualized review – flat policy can be discriminatory.

Uniformity – are similarly situated applicants treated the same?

Legal compliance – if third party utilized under the FCRA, have a procedure to ensure pre-adverse action and post-adverse letters?

20. Does the firm use other screening tools and, if so, is the information used in accordance with safe hiring guidelines? SCORE: _____

Best Practice:

Take these additional steps as necessary if related to job:

Criminal record checks

Civil records if relevant

Social Security trace

Education and past employment credentials

Credit report (if appropriate and if policies are in place to ensure that use of credit information is recent, relevant, and fair)

Driving record

21. Are the mechanics of your screening program documented? SCORE: _____

Best Practice:

Document all procedures.

Process to send requests to screening company, track progress, receive reports, maintain privacy, and restrict results to only authorized persons.

Track the stages in the hiring process for screening

(Typically only the finalists are subject to screening.)

Degree of screening for each position

(Not every position needs to be screened at the same level.)

Uniform screening procedures – similarly situated applicants treated in the same non-discriminatory manner.

Storage and retention of reports separately from personnel files.

22. If screening is outsourced to a third-party firm, can the employer demonstrate Due Diligence and show procedures are in compliance with the FCRA? SCORE: _____

Best Practice:

If background check failed due to screening firm, then employer may be liable if he or she failed to exercise due diligence in selection of firm.

Factors:

Expertise/knowledge of the service provider

Legal compliance — FCRA and state law compliance

Personal service and consulting — providing professional consulting services

Training/consulting services available

References

Pricing of secured internet order/reporting options.

23. Are procedures in place if a person with negative information is hired? SCORE: _____

Best Practice:

Firm has examined the type of support, supervision, and structure needed to improve the chances of success within the organization.

Firm has considered the nature of the job and the circumstances of the past offense to take appropriate measures to protect the firm, co-workers, and the public from harm.

Firm has documented decision-making factors.

24. Are procedures in place if employment is offered before a background check is completed?   SCORE: _____

Best Practice:

If employment begins before completion of a background check, is there a written statement that employment is conditioned upon receiving a report that is satisfactory to the employer?

Does policy eliminate a possible debate over what is an acceptable background report?

Issue:

May need to escort the person off premises if background check is negative.

25. Does the organization have written policies, practices, and procedures for screening employees post-hire?
SCORE: _____

Best Practice:

Safe hiring also extends to retention, supervision, and promotion.

Procedures:

Are supervisors periodically trained and educated regarding the employer's liability for negligent retention, supervision, or promotion?

Are supervisors trained to recognize, report, and deal appropriately with workplace misconduct?

Are there procedures to investigate workplace misconduct?

Is there a mechanism for workers or managers to report and record workplace misconduct?

Is it part of written job descriptions for supervisors to record, report, and address workplace misconduct and part of performance appraisal?

Does firm audit and review entire Safe Hiring Program each year?

SAFE HIRING AUDIT TOTAL SCORE: _____

Conclusion — How Do Your Safe Hiring Practices Measure Up?

After taking the Audit and assessing your practices, you should begin a program of improving those areas where there is potential litigation exposure. If there are areas where your firm needs improvement, utilize the resources in this book.

If your overall score is less than 75 points and your average score per question is lower than 3 points –

You have to do some work to improve your safe hiring program.

If your score is above 75 points –

Good job but there still may be some room for improvement.

❖

If your score is 100 points –

Congratulations!

Appendix

Inside The Appendix:

FCRA Mandated Forms

Before January 1, 2013

According to regulations from the Consumer Financial Protection Board (CFPB), three essential forms mandated by the federal Fair Credit Reporting Act (FCRA) used in the background screening process must be modified by January 1, 2013. The primary change is that the forms must be changed to reflect that consumers can obtain information about their rights under the FCRA from the CFPB instead of the Federal Trade Commission (FTC). The three forms in use currently indicate that the FTC is the agency consumers can contact with questions at www.ftc.gov/credit.

Below are links to FCRA mandated forms from the FTC that can be used until January 1, 2013:

✓ **A Summary of Your Rights Under the Fair Credit Reporting Act**

www.ftc.gov/bcp/edu/pubs/consumer/credit/cre35.pdf

The prescribed form for this summary is a disclosure that it substantially similar to the Commission's model summary with all information clearly and prominently displayed. The list of federal regulators that is included in the Commission's prescribed summary may be provided separately so long as this is done in a clear and conspicuous way. A summary should accurately reflect changes to those items that may change over time (e.g., dollars amounts, or telephone numbers and addresses of federal agencies) to remain in compliance. Translation of this summary will be in compliance with the Commission's prescribed model, provided that the translation is accurate and that it is provided in a language used by the recipient consumer.

✓ **Notice to Furnishers of Information: Obligations of Furnishers Under The FCRA**

www.ftc.gov/os/2004/11/041119factaappg.pdf

The prescribed form for this disclosure is a separate document that is substantially similar to the Commission's model notice with all information clearly and prominently displayed. Consumer reporting agencies may limit the disclosure to only those items that they know are relevant to the furnisher that will receive notice.

✓ **Notice to Users of Consumer Reports: Obligations of Users Under the FCRA**

www.ftc.gov/os/2004/11/041119factaapph.pdf

The prescribed form for this disclosure is a separate document that is substantially similar to the Commission's notice with all information clearly and prominently displayed. Consumer reporting agencies may limit the disclosure to only those items that they know are relevant to the furnisher that will receive notice.

Until January 1, 2013, for more information about additional rights, go to www.ftc.gov/credit or write to: Consumer Response Center, Room 130-A, Federal Trade Commission, 600 Pennsylvania Ave. N.W., Washington, D.C. 20580.

FCRA Mandated Forms
Starting January 1, 2013

1. "A Summary of Your Rights Under the Fair Credit Reporting Act"

Appendix K to Part 1022—Summary of Consumer Rights: The prescribed form for this summary is a disclosure that is substantially similar to the Bureau's model summary with all information clearly and prominently displayed. The list of Federal regulators that is included in the Bureau's prescribed summary may be provided separately so long as this is done in a clear and conspicuous way. A summary should accurately reflect changes to those items that may change over time (e.g., dollar amounts, or telephone numbers and addresses of Federal agencies) to remain in compliance. Translations of this summary will be in compliance with the Bureau's prescribed model, provided that the translation is accurate and that it is provided in a language used by the recipient consumer.

Para informacion en espanol, visite <u>www.consumerfinance.gov/learnmore</u> *o escribe a la Consumer Protection Financial Bureau, 1700 G Street N.W., Pennsylvania Ave. N.W., Washington, DC 20006.*

A Summary of Your Rights Under the Fair Credit Reporting Act

The federal Fair Credit Reporting Act (FCRA) promotes the accuracy, fairness, and privacy of information in the files of consumer reporting agencies. There are many types of consumer reporting agencies, including credit bureaus and specialty agencies (such as agencies that sell information about check writing histories, medical records, and rental history records). Here is a summary of your major rights under the FCRA. **For more information, including information about additional rights, go to** <u>www.consumerfinance.gov/learnmore</u> **or write to: Consumer Protection Financial Bureau, 1700 G Street N.W., Pennsylvania Ave. N.W., Washington, DC 20006.**

- **You must be told if information in your file has been used against you.** Anyone who uses a credit report or another type of consumer report to deny your application for credit, insurance, or employment – or to take another adverse action against you – must tell you, and must give you the name, address, and phone number of the agency that provided the information.

- **You have the right to know what is in your file.** You may request and obtain all the information about you in the files of a consumer reporting agency (your "file disclosure"). You will be required to provide proper identification, which may include your Social Security number. In many cases, the disclosure will be free. You are entitled to a free file disclosure if:
    - a person has taken adverse action against you because of information in your credit report;
    - you are a victim of identity theft and place a fraud alert in your file;
    - your file contains inaccurate information as a result of fraud;
    - you are on public assistance;
    - you are unemployed but expect to apply for employment within 60 days.

  In addition, all consumers are entitled to one free disclosure every 12 months upon request from each nationwide credit bureau and from nationwide specialty consumer reporting agencies. See www.consumerfinance.gov/learnmore for additional information.

- **You have the right to ask for a credit score.** Credit scores are numerical summaries of your credit-worthiness based on information from credit bureaus. You may request a credit score from consumer reporting agencies that create scores or distribute scores used in residential real property loans, but you will have to pay for it. In some mortgage transactions, you will receive credit score information for free from the mortgage lender.

- **You have the right to dispute incomplete or inaccurate information.** If you identify information in your file that is incomplete or inaccurate and report it to the consumer reporting agency, the agency must investigate unless your dispute is frivolous. See www.consumerfinance.gov/learnmore for an explanation of dispute procedures.

- **Consumer reporting agencies must correct or delete inaccurate, incomplete, or unverifiable information.** Inaccurate, incomplete or unverifiable information must be removed or corrected, usually within 30 days. However, a consumer reporting agency may continue to report information it has verified as accurate.

- **Consumer reporting agencies may not report outdated negative information.** In most cases, a consumer reporting agency may not report negative information that is more than seven years old, or bankruptcies that are more than 10 years old.

- **Access to your file is limited.** A credit reporting agency may provide information about you only to people with a valid need – usually to consider an application with a creditor, insurer, employer, landlord, or other business. The FCRA specifies those with a valid need for access.

- **You must give your consent for reports to be provided to employers.** A consumer reporting agency may not give out information about you to your employer, or a potential employer, without your written consent given to the employer. Written consent generally is not required in the trucking industry. For more information, go to www.consumerfinance.gov/learnmore.

- **You may limit "prescreened" offers of credit and insurance you get based on information in your credit report.** Unsolicited "prescreened" offers for credit and insurance must include a toll-free phone number you can call if you choose to remove your name and address from the lists these offers are based on. You may opt-out with the nationwide credit bureaus at 1-888-5-OPTOUT (1-888-567-8688).

- **You may seek damages from violators.** If a consumer reporting agency, or, in some cases, a user of consumer reports or a furnisher of information to a consumer reporting agency violates the FCRA, you may be able to sue in state or federal court.

- **Identity Theft victims and active duty military personnel have additional rights.** For more information, visit www.consumerfinance.gov/learnmore.

States may enforce the FCRA, and many states have their own consumer reporting laws. In some cases, you may have more rights under state law. For more information, contact your state or local consumer protection agency or your state Attorney General. For more information about your Federal rights, contact:

TYPE OF BUSINESS:	CONTACT:
1.a. Banks, savings associations, and credit unions with total assests of over $10 billion and their affiliates.	a. Bureau of Consumer Financial Protections 1700 G Street NM Washington, DC 20006
b. Such affiliations that are not banks, savings associations, or credit unions also should list, in addition to the Bureau.	b. Federal Trade Commission: Consumer Response Center - FCRA Washington, DC 20580 (877) 382-4357
2. To the extent of not included in item 1 above: a. National banks, federal savings associations, and federal branches and federal agencies of foreign banks.	a. Office of the Comptroller of the Currency Customer Assistance Group 1301 McKinney Street, Suite 3450 Houston, TX 77010-9050
b. State member banks, branches and agencies of foreign banks (other than federal branches, federal agencies, and insured state branches of foreign), commercial lending companies owned or controlled by foreign banks, and organizations operating under section 25 or 25A of the Federal Reserve Act.	b. Federal Reserve Consumer Help Center P.O. Box 1200 Minneapolis, MN 55480

c. Nonmember Insured Banks, Insured State Branches of Foreign Banks, and insured state savings associations.	c. FDIC Consumer Response Center 1100 Walnut Street, Box #11 Kansas City, MO 64106
d. Federal Credit Unions	d. National Credit Union Administration Office of Consumer Protection (OCP) Division of Consumer Compliance and Outreach (DCCO) 1775 Duke Street Alexandria, VA 22314
3. Air carriers	Asst. General Councel for Aviation Enforcement & Proceedings Department of Transportation 400 Seventh Street SW Washington, DC 20423
4. Creditors Subject to Surface Transportation Board	Office of Proceedings, Surface Transportation Board Department of Transportation 1925 K Street NW Washington, DC 20590
5. Creditors Subject to Packers and Stockyards Act	Nearest Packers and Stockyards Administration area supervisor
6. Small Business Investment Companies	Associate Deputy Administrator for Capital Access United States Small Business Administration 409 Third Street, SW, 8th Floor Washington, DC 20416
7. Brokers and Dealers	Securities and Exchange Commission 100 F St NE Washington, DC 20549
8. Federal Land Banks, Federal Lank Bank Associations, Federal Intermediate Credit Banks, and Production Credit Associations	Farm Credit Administration 1501 Farm Credit Drive McLean, VA 22102-5090
9. Retailers, Finance Companies, and All Other Creditors Not Listed Above	FTC Regional Office for region in which the creditor operates or Federal Trade Commission: Consumer Response Center – FCRA Washington, DC 20580 (877) 382-4357

2. "Notices to Furnishers of Information: Obligations of Furnishers Under the FCRA"

Appendix M to Part 1022—Notice of Furnisher Responsibilities: The prescribed form for this disclosure is a separate document that is substantially similar to the Bureau's model notice with all information clearly and prominently displayed. Consumer reporting agencies may limit the disclosure to only those items that they know are relevant to the furnisher that will receive the notice.

All furnishers subject to the Federal Trade Commission's jurisdiction must comply with all applicable regulations, including regulations promulgated after this notice was prescribed in 2004. Information about applicable regulations currently in effect can be found at the Consumer Financial Protection Bureau's Web site, www.consumerfinance.gov/learnmore.

NOTICE TO FURNISHERS OF INFORMATION:
OBLIGATIONS OF FURNISHERS UNDER THE FCRA

The federal Fair Credit Reporting Act (FCRA), 15 U.S.C. 1681-1681y, imposes responsibilities on all persons who furnish information to consumer reporting agencies (CRAs). These responsibilities are found in Section 623 of the FCRA, 15 U.S.C. 1681s-2. State law may impose additional requirements on furnishers. All furnishers of information to CRAs should become familiar with the applicable laws and may want to consult with their counsel to ensure that they are in compliance. The text of the FCRA is set forth in full at the Bureau of Consumer Financial Protection's website at www.consumerfinance.gov/learnmore. A list of the sections of the FCRA cross-referenced to the U.S. Code is at the end of this document.

Section 623 imposes the following duties upon furnishers:

Accuracy Guidelines

The banking and credit union regulators and the CFPB will promulgate guidelines and regulations dealing with the accuracy of information provided to CRAs by furnishers. The regulations and guidelines issued by the CFPB will be available at www.consumerfinance.gov/learnmore when they are issued. Sections 623(e).

General Prohibition on Reporting Inaccurate Information

The FCRA prohibits information furnishers from providing information to a CRA that they know or have reasonable cause to believe is inaccurate. However, the furnisher is not subject to this general prohibition if it clearly and conspicuously specifies an address to which consumers may write to notify the furnisher that certain information is inaccurate. Sections 623(a)(1)(A) and (a)(1)(C).

Duty to Correct and Update Information

If at any time a person who regularly and in the ordinary course of business furnishes information to one or more CRAs determines that the information provided is not complete or accurate, the furnisher must promptly provide complete and accurate information to the CRA. In addition, the furnisher must notify all CRAs that received the information of any corrections, and must thereafter report only the complete and accurate information. Section 623(a)(2).

Duties After Notice of Dispute from Consumer

If a consumer notifies a furnisher, at an address specified by the furnisher for such notices, that specific information is inaccurate, and the information is, in fact, inaccurate, the furnisher must thereafter report the correct information to CRAs. Section 623(a)(1)(B)

If a consumer notifies a furnisher that the consumer disputes the completeness or accuracy of any information reported by the furnisher, the furnisher may not subsequently report that information to a CRA without providing notice of the dispute. Section 623(a)(3)

The federal banking and credit union regulators and the CFPB will issue regulations that will identify when an information furnisher must investigate a dispute made directly to the furnisher by a consumer. Once these regulations are issued, furnishers must comply with them and complete and investigation within 30 days (or 45 days, if the consumer later provides relevant additional information) unless the disputer is frivolous or irrelevant or comes from a "credit repair organization." The CFPB regulations will be available at www.consumerfinance.gov/learnmore. Section 623(a)(8).

Duties After Notice of Dispute from Consumer Reporting Agency

If a CRA notifies a furnisher that a consumer disputes the completeness or accuracy of information provided by the furnisher, the furnisher has a duty to follow certain procedures. The furnisher must:

- Conduct an investigation and review all relevant information provided by the CRA, including information given to the CRA by the consumer. Sections 623(b)(1)(A) and (b)(1)(B).

- Report the results to the CRA that referred the dispute, and, if the investigation establishes that the information was, in fact, incomplete or inaccurate, report the results to all CRAs to which the furnisher provided the information that compile and maintain files on a nationwide basis. Sections 623(b)(1)(C) and (b)(1)(D).

- Complete the above steps within 30 days from the date the CRA receives the dispute (or 45 days, if the consumer later provides relevant additional information to the CRA). Section 623(b)(2).

- Promptly modify or delete the information, or block its reporting. Section 623(b)(1)(E).

Duty to Report Voluntary Closing of Credit Accounts

If a consumer voluntarily closes a credit account, any person who regularly and in the ordinary course of business furnishes information to one or more CRAs must report this fact when it provides information to CRAs for the time period in which the account was closed. Section 623(a)(4)

Duty to Report Dates of Delinquencies

If a furnisher reports information concerning a delinquent account placed for collection, charged to profit or loss, or subject to any similar action, the furnisher must, within 90 days after reporting the information, provide the CRA with the month and the year of the commencement of the delinquency that immediately preceded the action, so that the agency will know how long to keep the information in the consumer's file. Section 623(a)(5)

Any person, such as a debt collector, that has acquired or is responsible for collecting delinquent accounts and that reports information to CRAs may comply with the requirements of Section 623(a)(5) (until there is a consumer dispute) by reporting the same delinquency date the FCRA previously reported by the creditor. If the creditor did not report this date, they may comply with the FCRA by establishing reasonable procedures to obtain and report delinquency dates, or, if a delinquency date cannot be reasonably obtained, by following reasonable procedures to ensure that the date reported precedes the date when the account was place for collection, charged to profit or loss, or subject to any similar action. Section 623(a)(5).

Duty of Financial Institutions When Reporting Negative Information

Financial Institutions that furnish information to "nationwide" consumer reporting agencies, as defined in Section 603(p), must notify consumers in writing if they may furnish or have furnished negative information to a CRA. Section 623(a)(7). The Federal Reserve Board has prescribed model disclosures, 12 CFR Part 222, App. B.

Duty When Furnishing Medical Information

A furnisher whose primary business is providing medical services, products, or devices (and such furnisher's agents or assignees) is a medical information furnisher for the purposes of the FCRA and must notify all CRAs to which it reports of this fact. Section 623(a)(9). This notice will enable CRAs to comply with their duties under Section 604(g) when reporting medical information.

Duties When ID Theft Occurs

All furnishers must have in place reasonable procedures to respond to notifications from CRAs that information furnished is the result of identity theft, and to prevent refurnishing the information in the future. A furnisher may not furnish information that a consumer has identified as resulting from identity theft unless the furnisher subsequently knows or is informed by the consumer that the information is correct. Section 623(a)(6). If a furnisher learns that it has furnished inaccurate information due to identity theft, it must notify each consumer reporting agency of the correct information and must thereafter report only complete and accurate information. Section 623(a)(2). When any furnisher of information is notified pursuant to the procedures set forth in section 605B that a debt has resulted from identity theft, the furnisher may not sell, transfer, or place for collection the debt except in certain limited circumstances. Section 615(f).

The Consumer Financial Protection Bureau's website, www.consumerfinance.gov/learnmore, has more information about the FCRA.

---

3. "Notice to Users of Consumer Reports: Obligations of Users Under the FCRA"

Appendix N to Part 1022—Notice of User Responsibilities: The prescribed form for this disclosure is a separate document that is substantially similar to the Bureau's notice with all information clearly and prominently displayed. Consumer reporting agencies may limit the disclosure to only those items that they know are relevant to the user that will receive the notice.

All users of consumer reports must comply with all applicable regulations, including regulations promulgated after this notice was prescribed in 2004. Information about applicable regulations currently in effect can be found at the Consumer Financial Protection Bureau's Web site, www.consumerfinance.gov/learnmore.

NOTICE TO USERS OF CONSUMER REPORTS:
OBLIGATIONS OF USERS UNDER THE FCRA

The federal Fair Credit Reporting Act (FCRA), 15 U.S.C. 1681-1691y, requires that this notice be provided to inform users of consumer reports of their legal obligations. State law may impose additional requirements. The text of the FCRA is set forth in full at the Consumer Financial Protection Bureau's website at www.consumerfinance.gov/learnmore. At the end of this document is a list of United States Code citations for the FCRA. Other information about user duties is also available at the Bureau's website. **Users must consult the relevant provisions of the FCRA for details about their obligations under the FCRA.**

This first section of this summary sets forth the responsibilities imposed by the FCRA on all users of consumer reports. The subsequent sections discuss the duties of users of reports that contain specific types of information, or that are used for certain purposes, and the legal consequences of violations. If you are a furnisher of information to a consumer reporting agency (CRA), you have additional obligations and will receive a separate notice from the CRA describing your duties as a furnisher.

I. OBLIGATIONS OF ALL USERS OF CONSUMER REPORTS

A. Users Must Have a Permissible Purpose

Congress has limited the use of consumer reports to protect consumers' privacy. All users must have a permissible purpose under the FCRA to obtain a consumer report. Section 604 of the FCRA contains a list of the permissible purposes under the law. These are:

- As ordered by a court or a federal grand jury subpoena. Section 604(a)(1).

- As instructed by the consumer in writing. Section 604(a)(2).

- For the extension of credit as a result of an application from a consumer, or the review or collection of a consumer's account. Section 604(a)(3)(A).

- For employment purposes, including hiring and promotion decisions, where the consumer has given written permission. Sections 604(a)(3)(B) and 604(b).

- For the underwriting of insurance as a result of an application from a consumer. Section 604(a)(3)(C).

- When there is a legitimate business need, in connection with a business transaction that is initiated by the consumer. Section 604(a)(3)(F)(i).

- To review a consumer's account to determine whether the consumer continues to meet the terms of the account. Section 604(a)(3)(F)(ii).

- To determine a consumer's eligibility for a license or other benefit granted by a governmental instrumentality required by law to consider an applicant's financial responsibility or status. Section 604(a)(3)(D).

- For use by a potential investor or servicer, or current insurer, in a valuation or assessment of the credit or prepayment risks associated with an existing credit obligation. Section 604(a)(3)(E).

- For use by state and local officials in connection with the determination of child support payments, or modifications and enforcement thereof. Sections 604(a)(4) and 604(a)(5).

In addition, creditors and insurers may obtain certain consumer report information for the purpose of making "prescreened" unsolicited offers of credit or insurance. Section 604(c). The particular obligations of users of "prescreened" information are described in Section VII below.

B. Users Must Provide Certifications

Section 604(f) prohibits any person from obtaining a consumer report from a consumer reporting agency (CRA) unless the person has certified to the CRA the permissible purpose(s) for which the report is being obtained and certifies that the report will not be used for any other purpose.

C. Users Must Notify Consumers When Adverse Actions Are Taken

The term "adverse action" is defined very broadly by Section 603 of the FCRA. "Adverse actions" include all business, credit, and employment actions affecting consumers that can be considered to have a negative impact as defined by Section 603(k) of the FCRA – such as denying or canceling credit or insurance, or denying employment or promotion. No adverse action occurs in a credit transaction where the creditor makes a counteroffer that is accepted by the consumer.

1. Adverse Actions Based on Information Obtained From a CRA

If a user takes any type of adverse action as defined by the FCRA that is based at least in part on information contained in a consumer report, Section 615(a) requires the user to notify the consumer. The notification may be done in writing, orally, or by electronic means. It must include the following:

- The name, address, and telephone number of the CRA (including a toll-free telephone number, if it is a nationwide CRA) that provided the report.

- A statement that the CRA did not make the adverse decision and is not able to explain why the decision was made.
- A statement setting forth the consumer's right to obtain a free disclosure of the consumer's file from the CRA if the consumer requests the report within 60 days.
- A statement setting forth the consumer's right to dispute directly with the CRA the accuracy or completeness of any information provided by the CRA.

2. Adverse Actions Based on Information Obtained From Third Parties Who Are Not Consumer Reporting Agencies

If a person denies (or increases the charge for) credit for personal, family, or household purposes based either wholly or partly upon information from a person other than a CRA, and the information is the type of consumer information covered by the FCRA, Section 615(b)(1) requires that the user clearly and accurately disclose to the consumer his or her right to be told the nature of the information that was relied upon if the consumer makes a written request within 60 days of notification. The user must provide the disclosure within a reasonable period of time following the consumer's written request.

3. Adverse Actions Based on Information Obtained From Affiliates

If a person takes an adverse action involving insurance, employment, or a credit transaction initiated by the consumer, based on information of the type covered by the FCRA, and this information was obtained from an entity affiliated with the user of the information by common ownership or control, Section 615(b)(2) requires the user to notify the consumer of the adverse action. The notice must inform the consumer that he or she may obtain a disclosure of the nature of the information relied upon by making a written request within 60 days of receiving the adverse action notice. If the consumer makes such a request, the user must disclose the nature of the information not later than 30 days after receiving the request. If consumer report information is shared among affiliates and then used for an adverse action, the user must make an adverse action disclosure as set forth in I.C.1 above.

D. Users have Obligations When Fraud and Active Duty Military Alerts are in Files

When a consumer has placed a fraud alert, including one relating to identity theft, or an active duty military alert with a nationwide consumer reporting agency as defined in Section 603(p) and resellers, 605A(h) imposes limitation on users of reports obtained from the consumer reporting agency in certain circumstances, including the establishment of a new credit plan and the issuance of additional credit cards. For the initial fraud alerts and active duty alerts, the user must have reasonable policies and procedures in place to form a belief that the user knows the identity of the applicant or contact the consumer at a telephone number specified by the consumer; in the case of extended fraud alerts, the user must contact the consumer in accordance with the contact information provided in the consumer's alert.

E. Users Have Obligations When Notified of an Address Discrepancy

Section 605(h) requires nationwide CRAs, as defined in Section 603(p), to notify users that request reports when the address for a consumer provided by the user in requesting the report is substantially different from the addresses in the consumer's file. When this occurs, users must comply with regulations specifying the procedures to be followed, which will be issued by the Consumer Financial Protection Bureau and the banking and credit union regulators. The Consumer Financial Protection Bureau regulations will be available at www.consumerfinance.gov/learnmore.

F. Users Have Obligations When Disposing of Records

Section 628 requires that all users of consumer report information have in place procedures to properly dispose of records containing this information. The Consumer Financial Protection Bureau, the Securities and Exchange Commission, and the banking and credit union regulators have issued regulations covering disposal. The Consumer Financial Protection Bureau regulations may be found at www.consumerfinance.gov/learnmore.

II. CREDITORS MUST MAKE ADDITIONAL DISCLOSURES

If a person uses a consumer report in connection with an application for, or a grant, extension, or provision of, credit to a consumer on material terms that are materially less favorable than the most favorable terms available to a substantial proportion of consumers from or through that person, based in whole or in part on a consumer report, the person must provide a risk-based pricing notice to the consumer in accordance with regulations prescribed by the Consumer Financial Protection Bureau.

Section 609(g) requires a disclosure by all persons that make or arrange loans secured by residential real property (one to four units) and that use credit scores. These persons must provide credit scores and other information about credit scores to applicants, including the disclosure set forth in section 609(g)(1)(D)("Notice to the Home Loan Applicant").

III. OBLIGATIONS OF USERS WHEN CONSUMER REPORTS ARE OBTAINED FOR EMPLOYMENT PURPOSES

A. Employment Other Than in the Trucking Industry

If information from a CRA is used for employment purposes, the user has specific duties, which are set forth in FCRA Section 604(b). The user must:

- Make a clear and conspicuous written disclosure to the consumer before the report is obtained, in a document that consists solely of the disclosure, that a consumer report may be obtained.

- Obtain from the consumer prior written authorization. Authorization to access reports during the term of employment may be obtained at the time of employment.

- Certify to the CRA that the above steps have been followed, that the information being obtained will not be used in violation of any federal or state equal opportunity law or regulation, and that, if any adverse action is to be taken based on the consumer report, a copy of the report and a summary of the consumer's rights will be provided to the consumer.

- **Before** taking an adverse action, the user must provide a copy of the report to the consumer as well as the summary of the consumer's rights. (The user should receive this summary from the CRA.) A Section 615(a) adverse action notice should be sent after the adverse action is taken.

An adverse action notice also is required in employment situations if credit information (other than transactions and experience data) obtained from an affiliate is used to deny employment. Section 615(b)(2).

The procedures for investigative consumer reports and employee misconduct investigations are set forth below.

B. Employment in the Trucking Industry

Special rules apply for truck drivers where the only interaction between the consumer and the potential employer is by mail, telephone, or computer. In this case, the consumer may provide consent orally or electronically, and an adverse action may be made orally, in writing, or electronically. The consumer may obtain a copy of any report relied upon by the trucking company by contacting the company.

IV. OBLIGATIONS OF USERS OF INVESTIGATIVE CONSUMER REPORTS

Investigative consumer reports are a special type of consumer report in which information about a consumer's character, general reputation, personal characteristics, and mode of living is obtained through personal interviews by an entity or person that is a consumer reporting agency. Consumers who are the subjects of such reports are given special rights under the FCRA. If a user intends to obtain an investigative consumer report, Section 606 requires the following:

- The user must disclose to the consumer that an investigative consumer report may be obtained. This must be done in a written disclosure that is mailed, or otherwise delivered, to the consumer at some time before or not later than three days after the date on which the report was first requested. The disclosure must include a statement informing the consumer of his or her right to request additional disclosures of the nature and scope of the investigation as described below, and the summary of consumer rights required by Section 609 of the FCRA. (The summary of consumer rights will be provided by the CRA that conducts the investigation.)

- The user must certify to the CRA that the disclosures set forth above have been made and that the user will make the disclosure described below.

- Upon the written request of a consumer made within a reasonable period of time after the disclosures required above, the user must make a complete disclosure of the nature and scope of the investigation. This must be made in a written statement that is mailed, or otherwise delivered, to the consumer no later than five days after the date on which the request was received from the consumer or the report was first requested, whichever is later in time.

V. SPECIAL PROCEDURES FOR EMPLOYEE INVESTIGATIONS

Section 603(x) provides special procedures for investigations of suspected misconduct by an employee or for compliance with Federal, state or local laws and regulations or the rules of a self-regulatory organization, and compliance with written policies of the employer. These investigations are not treated as consumer reports so long as the employer or its agent complies with the procedures set forth in Section 603(x), and a summary describing the nature and scope of the inquiry is made to the employee if an adverse action is taken based on the investigation.

VI. OBLIGATIONS OF USERS OF MEDICAL INFORMATION

Section 604(g) limits the use of medical information obtained from consumer reporting agencies (other than payment information that appears in a coded form that does not identify the medical provider). If the report is to be used for an insurance transaction, the consumer must give consent to the user of the report or the information must be coded. If the report is to be used for employment purposes – or in connection with a credit transaction (except as provided in regulations issued by the banking and credit union regulators) – the consumer must provide specific written consent and the medical information must be relevant. Any user who receives medical information shall not disclose the information to any other person (except where necessary to carry out the purpose for which the information was disclosed, or as permitted by statute, regulation, or order.)

VII. OBLIGATIONS OF USERS OF "PRESCREENED LISTS"

The FCRA permits creditors and insurers to obtain limited consumer report information for use in connection with unsolicited offers of credit or insurance under certain circumstances. Sections 603(l), 604(c), 604(e), and 615(d). This practice is known as "prescreening" and typically involves obtaining from a CRA a list of consumers who meet certain pre-established criteria. If any person intends to use prescreened lists, that person must (1) before the offer is made, establish the criteria that will be relied upon to make the offer and to grant credit or insurance, and (2) maintain such criteria on file for a three-year period beginning on the date on which the offer is made to each consumer. In addition, any user must provide with each written solicitation a clear and conspicuous statement that:

- Information contained in a consumer's CRA file was used in connection with the transaction.

- The consumer received the offer because he or she satisfied the criteria for credit worthiness or insurability used to screen for the offer.

- Credit or insurance may not be extended if, after the consumer responds, it is determined that the consumer does not meet the criteria used for screening or any applicable criteria bearing on credit worthiness or insurability, or the consumer does not furnish required collateral.

- The consumer may prohibit the use of information in his or her file in connection with future prescreened offers of credit or insurance by contacting the notification system established by the CRA that provided the report. The statement must include the address and the toll-free telephone number of the appropriate notification system.

In addition, the Consumer Financial Protection Bureau has established the format, type size, and manner of the disclosure required by Section 615(d), with which users must comply. The relevant regulation 12 CFR 1022.54.

VIII. OBLIGATIONS OF RESELLERS

A. Disclosure and Certification Requirements

Section 607(e) of the FCRA requires any person who obtains a consumer report for resale to take the following steps:

- Disclose the identity of the end-user to the source CRA.
- Identify to the source CRA each permissible purpose for which the report will be furnished to the end-user.
- Establish and follow reasonable procedures to ensure that reports are resold only for permissible purposes, including procedures to obtain:
  1. the identity of all end-users;
  2. certifications from all users of each purpose for which reports will be used; and
  3. certifications that reports will not be used for any purpose other than the purpose(s) specified to the reseller. Resellers must make reasonable efforts to verify this information before selling the report.

B. Re-investigations by Resellers

Under Section 611(f), if a consumer disputes the accuracy or completeness of information in a report prepared by a reseller, the reseller must determine whether this is a result of an action or omission on its part and, if so, correct or delete the information. If not, the reseller must send the dispute to the source CRA for reinvestigation. When any CRA notifies the reseller of the results of an investigation, the reseller must immediately convey the information to the consumer.

C. Fraud Alerts and Resellers

Section 605(f) requires resellers who receive fraud alerts or active duty alerts from another consumer reporting agency to include these in their reports.

IX. LIABILITY FOR VIOLATIONS OF THE FCRA

Failure to comply with the FCRA can result in state government or federal government enforcement actions, as well as private lawsuits. Sections 616, 617, and 621. In addition, any person who knowingly and willfully obtains a consumer report under false pretenses may face criminal prosecution. Section 619.

The Consumer Financial Protection Bureau Web site, www.consumerfinance.gov/learnmore, has more information about the FCRA.

EEOC Enforcement Guidance

Number: 915.002 **Date:** 4/25/2012

1. **SUBJECT**: Enforcement Guidance on the Consideration of Arrest and Conviction Records in Employment Decisions Under Title VII of the Civil Rights Act of 1964, *as amended*, 42 U.S.C. § 2000e *et seq.*

2. **PURPOSE**: The purpose of this Enforcement Guidance is to consolidate and update the U.S. Equal Employment Opportunity Commission's guidance documents regarding the use of arrest or conviction records in employment decisions under Title VII of the Civil Rights Act of 1964, as amended, 42 U.S.C. § 2000e *et seq.*

3. **EFFECTIVE DATE**: Upon receipt

4. **EXPIRATION DATE**: This Notice will remain in effect until rescinded or superseded.

5. **ORIGINATOR**: Office of Legal Counsel.

Consideration of Arrest and Conviction Records in Employment Decisions Under Title VII of the Civil Rights Act of 1964

Table of Contents

I. Summary

- An employer's use of an individual's criminal history in making employment decisions may, in some instances, violate the prohibition against employment discrimination under Title VII of the Civil Rights Act of 1964, as amended.

- The Guidance builds on longstanding court decisions and existing guidance documents that the U.S. Equal Employment Opportunity Commission (Commission or EEOC) issued over twenty years ago.

- The Guidance focuses on employment discrimination based on race and national origin. The Introduction provides information about criminal records, employer practices, and Title VII.

- The Guidance discusses the differences between arrest and conviction records.

  - The fact of an arrest does not establish that criminal conduct has occurred, and an exclusion based on an arrest, in itself, is not job related and consistent with business necessity. However, an employer may make an employment decision based on the conduct underlying an arrest if the conduct makes the individual unfit for the position in question.

  - In contrast, a conviction record will usually serve as sufficient evidence that a person engaged in particular conduct. In certain circumstances, however, there may be reasons for an employer not to rely on the conviction record alone when making an employment decision.

- The Guidance discusses disparate treatment and disparate impact analysis under Title VII.

  - A violation may occur when an employer treats criminal history information differently for different applicants or employees, based on their race or national origin (disparate treatment liability).

  - An employer's neutral policy (e.g., excluding applicants from employment based on certain criminal conduct) may disproportionately impact some individuals protected under Title VII, and may violate the law if not job related and consistent with business necessity (disparate impact liability).

    - National data supports a finding that criminal record exclusions have a disparate impact based on race and national origin. The national data provides a basis for the Commission to investigate Title VII disparate impact charges challenging criminal record exclusions.

- Two circumstances in which the Commission believes employers will consistently meet the "job related and consistent with business necessity" defense are as follows:

    - The employer validates the criminal conduct exclusion for the position in question in light of the Uniform Guidelines on Employee Selection Procedures (if there is data or analysis about criminal conduct as related to subsequent work performance or behaviors); or

    - The employer develops a targeted screen considering at least the nature of the crime, the time elapsed, and the nature of the job (the three factors identified by the court in *Green v. Missouri Pacific Railroad*, 549 F.2d 1158 (8th Cir. 1977)). The employer's policy then provides an opportunity for an individualized assessment for those people identified by the screen, to determine if the policy as applied is job related and consistent with business necessity. (Although Title VII does not require individualized assessment in all circumstances, the use of a screen that does not include individualized assessment is more likely to violate Title VII.).

- Compliance with other federal laws and/or regulations that conflict with Title VII is a defense to a charge of discrimination under Title VII.

- State and local laws or regulations are preempted by Title VII if they "purport[] to require or permit the doing of any act which would be an unlawful employment practice" under Title VII. 42 U.S.C. § 2000e-7.

- The Guidance concludes with best practices for employers.

II. Introduction

The EEOC enforces Title VII of the Civil Rights Act of 1964 (Title VII) which prohibits employment discrimination based on race, color, religion, sex, or national origin.[1] This Enforcement Guidance is issued as part of the Commission's efforts to eliminate unlawful discrimination in employment screening, for hiring or retention, by entities covered by Title VII, including private employers as well as federal, state, and local governments.[2]

In the last twenty years, there has been a significant increase in the number of Americans who have had contact[3] with the criminal justice system[4] and, concomitantly, a major increase in the number of people with criminal records in the working-age population.[5] In 1991, only 1.8% of the adult population had served time in prison.[6] After ten years, in 2001, the percentage rose to 2.7% (1 in 37 adults).[7] By the end of 2007, 3.2% of all adults in the United States (1 in every 31) were under some form of correctional control involving probation, parole, prison, or jail.[8] The Department of Justice's Bureau of Justice Statistics (DOJ/BJS) has concluded that, if incarceration rates do not decrease, approximately 6.6% of all persons born in the United States in 2001 will serve time in state or federal prison during their lifetimes.[9]

Arrest and incarceration rates are particularly high for African American and Hispanic men.[10] African Americans and Hispanics[11] are arrested at a rate that is 2 to 3 times their proportion of the general population.[12] Assuming that current incarceration rates remain unchanged, about 1 in 17 White men are expected to serve time in prison during their lifetime;[13] by contrast, this rate climbs to 1 in 6 for Hispanic men; and to 1 in 3 for African American men.[14]

The Commission, which has enforced Title VII since it became effective in 1965, has well-established guidance applying Title VII principles to employers' use of criminal records to screen for employment.[15] This Enforcement Guidance builds on longstanding court decisions and policy documents that were issued over twenty years ago. In light of employers' increased access to criminal history information, case law analyzing Title VII requirements for criminal record exclusions, and other developments,[16] the Commission has decided to update and consolidate in this document all of its prior policy statements about Title VII and the use of criminal records in employment decisions. Thus, this Enforcement Guidance will supersede the Commission's previous policy statements on this issue.

The Commission intends this document for use by employers considering the use of criminal records in their selection and retention processes; by individuals who suspect that they have been denied jobs or promotions, or have been discharged because of their criminal records; and by EEOC staff who are investigating discrimination charges involving the use of criminal records in employment decisions.

III. Background

The contextual framework for the Title VII analysis in this Enforcement Guidance includes how criminal record information is collected and recorded, why employers use criminal records, and the EEOC's interest in such criminal record screening.

A. Criminal History Records

Criminal history information can be obtained from a wide variety of sources including, but not limited to, the following:

- Court Records. Courthouses maintain records relating to criminal charges and convictions, including arraignments, trials, pleas, and other dispositions.[17] Searching county courthouse records typically provides the most complete criminal history.[18] Many county courthouse records must be retrieved on-site,[19] but some courthouses offer their records online.[20] Information about federal crimes such as interstate drug trafficking, financial fraud, bank robbery, and crimes against the government may be found online in federal court records by searching the federal courts' Public Access to Court Electronic Records or Case Management/Electronic Case Files.[21]

- Law Enforcement and Corrections Agency Records. Law enforcement agencies such as state police agencies and corrections agencies may allow the public to access their records, including records of complaints, investigations, arrests, indictments, and periods of incarceration, probation, and parole.[22] Each agency may differ with respect to how and where the records may be searched, and whether they are indexed.[23]

- Registries or Watch Lists. Some government entities maintain publicly available lists of individuals who have been convicted of, or are suspected of having committed, a certain type of crime. Examples of such lists include state and federal sex offender registries and lists of individuals with outstanding warrants.[24]

- State Criminal Record Repositories. Most states maintain their own centralized repositories of criminal records, which include records that are submitted by most or all of their criminal justice agencies, including their county courthouses.[25] States differ with respect to the types of records included in the repository,[26] the completeness of the records,[27] the frequency with which they are updated,[28] and whether they permit the public to search the records by name, by fingerprint, or both.[29] Some states permit employers (or third-parties acting on their behalf) to access these records, often for a fee.[30] Others limit access to certain types of records,[31] and still others deny access altogether.[32]

- The Interstate Identification Index (III). The Federal Bureau of Investigation (FBI) maintains the most comprehensive collection of criminal records in the nation, called the "Interstate Identification Index" (III). The III database compiles records from each of the state repositories, as well as records from federal and international criminal justice agencies.[33]

The FBI's III database may be accessed for employment purposes by:

- the federal government;[34]

- employers in certain industries that are regulated by the federal government, such as "the banking, nursing home, securities, nuclear energy, and private security guard industries; as well as required security screenings by federal agencies of airport workers, HAZMAT truck drivers and other transportation workers";[35] and

- employers in certain industries "that the state has sought to regulate, such as persons employed as civil servants, day care, school, or nursing home workers, taxi drivers, private security guards, or members of regulated professions."[36]

Recent studies have found that a significant number of state and federal criminal record databases include incomplete criminal records.

- A 2011 study by the DOJ/BJS reported that, as of 2010, many state criminal history record repositories still had not recorded the final dispositions for a significant number of arrests.[37]

- A 2006 study by the DOJ/BJS found that only 50% of arrest records in the FBI's III database were associated with a final disposition. [38]

Additionally, reports have documented that criminal records may be inaccurate.

- One report found that even if public access to criminal records has been restricted by a court order to seal and/or expunge such records, this does not guarantee that private companies also will purge the information from their systems or that the event will be erased from media archives.[39]

- Another report found that criminal background checks may produce inaccurate results because criminal records may lack "unique" information or because of "misspellings, clerical errors or intentionally inaccurate identification information provided by search subjects who wish to avoid discovery of their prior criminal activities."[40]

Employers performing background checks to screen applicants or employees may attempt to search these governmental sources themselves or conduct a simple Internet search, but they often rely on third-party background screening businesses.[41] Businesses that sell criminal history information to employers are "consumer reporting agencies" (CRAs)[42] if they provide the information in "consumer reports"[43] under the Fair Credit Reporting Act, 15 U.S.C. § 1681 *et seq.* (FCRA). Under FCRA, a CRA generally may not report records of arrests that did not result in entry of a judgment of conviction, where the arrests occurred more than seven years ago.[44] However, they may report convictions indefinitely.[45]

CRAs often maintain their own proprietary databases that compile information from various sources, such as those described above, depending on the extent to which the business has purchased or otherwise obtained access to data.[46] Such databases vary with respect to the geographic area covered, the type of information included (e.g., information about arrests, convictions, prison terms, or specialized information for a subset of employers such as information about workplace theft or shoplifting cases for retail employers[47]), the sources of information used (e.g., county databases, law enforcement agency records, sex offender registries), and the frequency with which they are updated. They also may be missing certain types of disposition information, such as updated convictions, sealing or expungement orders, or orders for entry into a diversion program.[48]

B. Employers' Use of Criminal History Information

In one survey, a total of 92% of responding employers stated that they subjected all or some of their job candidates to criminal background checks.[49] Employers have reported that their use of criminal history information is related to ongoing efforts to combat theft and fraud,[50] as well as heightened concerns about workplace violence[51] and potential liability for negligent hiring.[52] Employers also cite federal laws as well as state and local laws[53] as reasons for using criminal background checks.

C. The EEOC's Interest in Employers' Use of Criminal Records in Employment Screening

The EEOC enforces Title VII, which prohibits employment discrimination based on race, color, religion, sex, or national origin. Having a criminal record is not listed as a protected basis in Title VII. Therefore, whether a covered employer's reliance on a criminal record to deny employment violates Title VII depends on whether it is part of a claim of employment discrimination based on race, color, religion, sex, or national origin. Title VII liability for employment discrimination is determined using two analytic frameworks: "disparate treatment" and "disparate impact." Disparate treatment is discussed in Section IV and disparate impact is discussed in Section V.

IV. Disparate Treatment Discrimination and Criminal Records

A covered employer is liable for violating Title VII when the plaintiff demonstrates that it treated him differently because of his race, national origin, or another protected basis.[54] For example, there is Title VII disparate treatment liability where the evidence shows that a covered employer rejected an African American applicant based on his criminal record but hired a similarly situated White applicant with a comparable criminal record.[55]

Example 1: Disparate Treatment Based on Race. John, who is White, and Robert, who is African American, are both recent graduates of State University. They have similar educational backgrounds, skills, and work experience. They each pled guilty to charges of possessing and distributing marijuana as high school students, and neither of them had any subsequent contact with the criminal justice system.

After college, they both apply for employment with Office Jobs, Inc., which, after short intake interviews, obtains their consent to conduct a background check. Based on the outcome of the background check, which reveals their drug convictions, an Office Jobs, Inc., representative decides not to refer Robert for a follow-up interview. The representative remarked to a co-worker that Office Jobs, Inc., cannot afford to refer "these drug dealer types" to client companies. However, the same representative refers John for an interview, asserting that John's youth at the time of the conviction and his subsequent lack of contact with the criminal justice system make the conviction unimportant. Office Jobs, Inc., has treated John and Robert differently based on race, in violation of Title VII.

Title VII prohibits "not only decisions driven by racial [or ethnic] animosity, but also decisions infected by stereotyped thinking . . . ."[56] Thus, an employer's decision to reject a job applicant based on racial or ethnic stereotypes about criminality - rather than qualifications and suitability for the position - is unlawful disparate treatment that violates Title VII.[57]

Example 2: Disparate Treatment Based on National Origin. Tad, who is White, and Nelson, who is Latino, are both recent high school graduates with grade point averages above 4.0 and college plans. While Nelson has successfully worked full-time for a landscaping company during the summers, Tad only held occasional lawn-mowing and camp-counselor jobs. In an interview for a research job with Meaningful and Paid Internships, Inc. (MPII), Tad discloses that he pled guilty to a felony at age 16 for accessing his school's computer system over the course of several months without authorization and changing his classmates' grades. Nelson, in an interview with MPII, emphasizes his successful prior work experience, from which he has good references, but also discloses that, at age 16, he pled guilty to breaking and entering into his high school as part of a class prank that caused little damage to school property. Neither Tad nor Nelson had subsequent contact with the criminal justice system.

The hiring manager at MPII invites Tad for a second interview, despite his record of criminal conduct. However, the same hiring manager sends Nelson a rejection notice, saying to a colleague that Nelson is only qualified to do manual labor and, moreover, that he has a criminal record. In light of the evidence showing that Nelson's and Tad's educational backgrounds are similar, that Nelson's work experience is more extensive, and that Tad's criminal conduct is more indicative of untrustworthiness, MPII has failed to state a legitimate, nondiscriminatory reason for rejecting Nelson. If Nelson filed a Title VII charge alleging disparate treatment based on national origin and the EEOC's investigation confirmed these facts, the EEOC would find reasonable cause to believe that discrimination occurred.

There are several kinds of evidence that may be used to establish that race, national origin, or other protected characteristics motivated an employer's use of criminal records in a selection decision, including, but not limited to:

- <u>Biased statements</u>. Comments by the employer or decisionmaker that are derogatory with respect to the charging party's protected group, or that express group-related stereotypes about criminality, might be evidence that such biases affected the evaluation of the applicant's or employee's criminal record.

- <u>Inconsistencies in the hiring process</u>. Evidence that the employer requested criminal history information more often for individuals with certain racial or ethnic backgrounds, or gave Whites but not racial minorities the opportunity to explain their criminal history, would support a showing of disparate treatment.

- <u>Similarly situated comparators (individuals who are similar to the charging party in relevant respects, except for membership in the protected group)</u>. Comparators may include people in similar positions, former employees, and people chosen for a position over the charging party. The fact that a charging party was treated differently than individuals who are not in the charging party's protected group by, for example, being subjected to more or different criminal background checks or to different standards for evaluating criminal history, would be evidence of disparate treatment.

- <u>Employment testing</u>. Matched-pair testing may reveal that candidates are being treated differently because of a protected status.[58]

- <u>Statistical evidence</u>. Statistical analysis derived from an examination of the employer's applicant data, workforce data, and/or third party criminal background history data may help to determine if the employer counts criminal history information more heavily against members of a protected group.

V. Disparate Impact Discrimination and Criminal Records

A covered employer is liable for violating Title VII when the plaintiff demonstrates that the employer's neutral policy or practice has the effect of disproportionately screening out a Title VII-protected group and the employer fails to demonstrate that the policy or practice is job related for the position in question and consistent with business necessity.[59]

In its 1971 *Griggs v. Duke Power Company* decision, the Supreme Court first recognized that Title VII permits disparate impact claims.[60] The *Griggs* Court explained that "[Title VII] proscribes . . . practices that are fair in form, but discriminatory in operation. The touchstone is business necessity. If an employment practice which operates to exclude [African Americans] cannot be shown to be related to job performance, the practice is prohibited."[61] In 1991, Congress amended Title VII to codify this analysis of discrimination and its burdens of proof.[62] Title VII, as amended, states:

An unlawful employment practice based on disparate impact is established . . . if a complaining party demonstrates that an employer uses a particular employment practice that causes a disparate impact on the basis of race, color, religion, sex, or national origin and the respondent fails to demonstrate that the challenged practice is job related for the position in question and consistent with business necessity. . . .[63]

With respect to criminal records, there is Title VII disparate impact liability where the evidence shows that a covered employer's criminal record screening policy or practice disproportionately screens out a Title VII-protected group and the employer does not demonstrate that the policy or practice is job related for the positions in question and consistent with business necessity.

A. Determining Disparate Impact of Policies or Practices that Screen Individuals Based on Records of Criminal Conduct

1. Identifying the Policy or Practice

The first step in disparate impact analysis is to identify the particular policy or practice that causes the unlawful disparate impact. For criminal conduct exclusions, relevant information includes the text of the policy or practice, associated documentation, and information about how the policy or practice was actually implemented. More specifically, such information also includes which offenses or classes of offenses were reported to the employer (e.g., all felonies, all drug offenses); whether convictions (including sealed and/or expunged convictions), arrests, charges, or other criminal incidents were reported; how far back in time the reports reached (e.g., the last five, ten, or twenty years); and the jobs for which the criminal background screening was conducted.[64] Training or guidance documents used by the employer also are relevant, because they may specify which types of criminal history information to gather for particular jobs, how to gather the data, and how to evaluate the information after it is obtained.

2. Determining Disparate Impact

Nationally, African Americans and Hispanics are arrested in numbers disproportionate to their representation in the general population. In 2010, 28% of all arrests were of African Americans,[65] even though African Americans only comprised approximately 14% of the general population.[66] In 2008, Hispanics were arrested for federal drug charges at a rate of approximately three times their proportion of the general population.[67] Moreover, African Americans and Hispanics were more likely than Whites to be arrested, convicted, or sentenced for drug offenses even though their rate of drug use is similar to the rate of drug use for Whites.[68]

African Americans and Hispanics also are incarcerated at rates disproportionate to their numbers in the general population. Based on national incarceration data, the U.S. Department of Justice estimated in 2001 that 1 out of every 17 White men (5.9% of the White men in the U.S.) is expected to go to prison at some point during his lifetime, assuming that current incarceration rates remain unchanged.[69] This rate climbs to 1 in 6 (or 17.2%) for Hispanic men.[70] For African American men, the rate of expected incarceration rises to 1 in 3 (or 32.2%).[71] Based on a state-by-state examination of incarceration rates in 2005, African Americans were incarcerated at a rate 5.6 times higher than Whites,[72] and 7 states had a Black-to-White ratio of incarceration that was 10 to1.[73] In 2010, Black men had an imprisonment rate that was nearly 7 times higher than White men and almost 3 times higher than Hispanic men.[74]

National data, such as that cited above, supports a finding that criminal record exclusions have a disparate impact based on race and national origin. The national data provides a basis for the Commission to further investigate such Title VII disparate impact charges. During an EEOC investigation, the employer also has an opportunity to show, with relevant evidence, that its employment policy or practice does not cause a disparate impact on the protected group(s). For example, an employer may present regional or local data showing that African American and/or Hispanic men are not arrested or convicted at disproportionately higher rates in the employer's particular geographic area. An employer also may use its own applicant data to demonstrate that its policy or practice did not cause a disparate impact. The Commission will assess relevant evidence when making a determination of disparate impact, including applicant flow information maintained pursuant to the Uniform Guidelines on Employee Selection Procedures,[75] workforce data, criminal history background check data, demographic availability statistics, incarceration/conviction data, and/or relevant labor market statistics.[76]

An employer's evidence of a racially balanced workforce will not be enough to disprove disparate impact. In *Connecticut v. Teal*, the Supreme Court held that a "bottom line" racial balance in the workforce does not preclude employees from establishing a prima facie case of disparate impact; nor does it provide employers with a defense.[77] The issue is whether the policy or practice deprives a disproportionate number of Title VII-protected individuals of employment opportunities.[78]

Finally, in determining disparate impact, the Commission will assess the probative value of an employer's applicant data. As the Supreme Court stated in *Dothard v. Rawlinson*, an employer's "application process might itself not adequately reflect the actual potential applicant pool since otherwise qualified people might be discouraged from applying" because of an alleged discriminatory policy or practice.[79] Therefore, the Commission will closely consider whether an employer has a reputation in the community for excluding individuals with criminal records. Relevant evidence may come from ex-offender employment programs, individual testimony, employer statements, evidence of employer recruitment practices, or publicly posted notices, among other sources.[80] The Commission will determine the persuasiveness of such evidence on a case-by-case basis.

B. Job Related For the Position in Question and Consistent with Business Necessity

1. Generally

After the plaintiff in litigation establishes disparate impact, Title VII shifts the burdens of production and persuasion to the employer to "demonstrate that the challenged practice is job related for the position in question and consistent with business necessity."[81] In the legislative history of the 1991 Civil Rights Act, Congress referred to *Griggs* and its progeny such as *Albemarle Paper Company v. Moody*[82] and *Dothard*[83] to explain how this standard should be construed.[84] The *Griggs* Court stated that the employer's burden was to show that the policy or practice is one that "bear[s] a demonstrable relationship to successful performance of the jobs for which it was used" and "measures the person for the job and not the person in the abstract."[85] In both *Albemarle*[86] and *Dothard*,[87] the Court emphasized the factual nature of the business necessity inquiry. The Court further stated in *Dothard* that the terms of the exclusionary policy must "be shown to be necessary to safe and efficient job performance."[88]

In a case involving a criminal record exclusion, the Eighth Circuit in its 1975 *Green v. Missouri Pacific Railroad* decision, held that it was discriminatory under Title VII for an employer to "follow[] the policy of disqualifying for employment any applicant with a conviction for any crime other than a minor traffic offense."[89] The Eighth Circuit identified three factors (the "*Green* factors") that were relevant to assessing whether an exclusion is job related for the position in question and consistent with business necessity:

- The nature and gravity of the offense or conduct;[90]
- The time that has passed since the offense or conduct and/or completion of the sentence;[91] and
- The nature of the job held or sought.[92]

In 2007, the Third Circuit in *El v. Southeastern Pennsylvania Transportation Authority*[93] developed the statutory analysis in greater depth. Douglas El challenged SEPTA's policy of excluding everyone ever convicted of a violent crime from the job of paratransit driver.[94] El, a 55 year-old African American paratransit driver-trainee, was terminated from employment when SEPTA learned of his conviction for second-degree murder 40 years earlier; the conviction involved a gang fight when he was 15 years old and was his only disqualifying offense under SEPTA's policy.[95] The Third Circuit expressed "reservations" about a policy such as SEPTA's (exclusion for all violent crimes, no matter how long ago they were committed) "in the abstract."[96]

Applying Supreme Court precedent, the *El* court observed that some level of risk is inevitable in all hiring, and that, "[i]n a broad sense, hiring policies . . . ultimately concern the management of risk."[97] Recognizing that assessing such risk is at the heart of criminal record exclusions, the Third Circuit concluded that Title VII requires employers to justify criminal record exclusions by demonstrating that they "accurately distinguish between applicants [who] pose an unacceptable level of risk and those [who] do not."[98]

The Third Circuit affirmed summary judgment for SEPTA, but stated that the outcome of the case might have been different if Mr. El had, "for example, hired an expert who testified that there is a time at which a former criminal is no longer any more likely to recidivate than the average person, . . . [so] there would be a factual question for the jury to resolve."[99] The Third Circuit reasoned, however, that the recidivism evidence presented by SEPTA's experts, in conjunction with the nature of the position at issue - paratransit driver-trainee with unsupervised access to vulnerable adults - required the employer to exercise the utmost care.[100]

In the subsections below, the Commission discusses considerations that are relevant to assessing whether criminal record exclusion policies or practices are job related and consistent with business necessity. First, we emphasize that arrests and convictions are treated differently.

2. Arrests

The fact of an arrest does not establish that criminal conduct has occurred.[101] Arrests are not proof of criminal conduct. Many arrests do not result in criminal charges, or the charges are dismissed.[102] Even if an individual is charged and subsequently prosecuted, he is presumed innocent unless proven guilty.[103]

An arrest, however, may in some circumstances trigger an inquiry into whether the conduct underlying the arrest justifies an adverse employment action. Title VII calls for a fact-based analysis to determine if an exclusionary policy or practice is job related and consistent with business necessity. Therefore, an exclusion based on an arrest, in itself, is not job related and consistent with business necessity.

Another reason for employers not to rely on arrest records is that they may not report the final disposition of the arrest (e.g., not prosecuted, convicted, or acquitted). As documented in Section III.A., *supra*, the DOJ/BJS reported that many arrest records in the FBI's III database and state criminal record repositories are not associated with final dispositions.[104] Arrest records also may include inaccuracies or may continue to be reported even if expunged or sealed.[105]

> **Example 3: Arrest Record Is Not Grounds for Exclusion.** Mervin and Karen, a middle-aged African American couple, are driving to church in a predominantly white town. An officer stops them and interrogates them about their destination. When Mervin becomes annoyed and comments that his offense is simply "driving while Black," the officer arrests him for disorderly conduct. The prosecutor decides not to file charges against Mervin, but the arrest remains in the police department's database and is reported in a background check when Mervin applies with his employer of fifteen years for a promotion to an executive position. The employer's practice is to deny such promotions to individuals with arrest records, even without a conviction, because it views an arrest record as an indicator of untrustworthiness and irresponsibility. If Mervin filed a Title VII charge based on these facts, and disparate impact based on race were established, the EEOC would find reasonable cause to believe that his employer violated Title VII.

Although an arrest record standing alone may not be used to deny an employment opportunity, an employer may make an employment decision based on the conduct underlying the arrest if the conduct makes the individual unfit for the position in question. The conduct, not the arrest, is relevant for employment purposes.

> **Example 4: Employer's Inquiry into Conduct Underlying Arrest**. Andrew, a Latino man, worked as an assistant principal in Elementary School for several years. After several ten and eleven-year-old girls attending the school accused him of touching them inappropriately on the chest, Andrew was arrested and charged with several counts of endangering the welfare of children and sexual abuse. Elementary School has a policy that requires suspension or termination of any employee who the school believes engaged in conduct that impacts the health or safety of the students. After learning of the accusations, the school immediately places Andrew on unpaid administrative leave pending an investigation. In the course of its investigation, the school provides Andrew a chance to explain the events and circumstances that led to his arrest. Andrew denies the allegations, saying that he may have brushed up against the girls in the crowded hallways or lunchroom, but that he doesn't really remember the incidents and does not have regular contact with any of the girls. The school also talks with the girls, and several of them recount touching in crowded situations. The school does not find Andrew's explanation credible. Based on Andrew's conduct, the school terminates his employment pursuant to its policy.
>
> Andrew challenges the policy as discriminatory under Title VII. He asserts that it has a disparate impact based on national origin and that his employer may not suspend or terminate him based solely on an arrest without a conviction because he is innocent until proven guilty. After confirming that an arrest policy would have a disparate impact based on national origin, the EEOC concludes that no discrimination occurred. The school's policy is linked to conduct that is relevant to the particular jobs at issue, and the exclusion is made based on descriptions of the underlying conduct, not the fact of the arrest. The Commission finds no reasonable cause to believe Title VII was violated.

3. Convictions

By contrast, a record of a conviction will usually serve as sufficient evidence that a person engaged in particular conduct, given the procedural safeguards associated with trials and guilty pleas.[106] However, there may be evidence of an error in the record, an outdated record, or another reason for not relying on the evidence of a conviction. For example, a database may continue to report a conviction that was later expunged, or may continue to report as a felony an offense that was subsequently downgraded to a misdemeanor.[107]

Some states require employers to wait until late in the selection process to ask about convictions.[108] The policy rationale is that an employer is more likely to objectively assess the relevance of an applicant's conviction if it becomes known when the employer is already knowledgeable about the applicant's qualifications and experience.[109] As a best practice, and consistent with applicable laws,[110] the Commission recommends that employers not ask about convictions on job applications and that, if and when they make such inquiries, the inquiries be limited to convictions for which exclusion would be job related for the position in question and consistent with business necessity.

4. Determining Whether a Criminal Conduct Exclusion Is Job Related and Consistent with Business Necessity

To establish that a criminal conduct exclusion that has a disparate impact is job related and consistent with business necessity under Title VII, the employer needs to show that the policy operates to effectively link specific criminal conduct, and its dangers, with the risks inherent in the duties of a particular position.

Two circumstances in which the Commission believes employers will consistently meet the "job related and consistent with business necessity" defense are as follows:

- The employer validates the criminal conduct screen for the position in question per the Uniform Guidelines on Employee Selection Procedures (Uniform Guidelines) standards (if data about criminal conduct as related to subsequent work performance is available and such validation is possible); [111] or

- The employer develops a targeted screen considering at least the nature of the crime, the time elapsed, and the nature of the job (the three *Green* factors), and then provides an opportunity for an individualized assessment for people excluded by the screen to determine whether the policy as applied is job related and consistent with business necessity.

The individualized assessment would consist of notice to the individual that he has been screened out because of a criminal conviction; an opportunity for the individual to demonstrate that the exclusion should not be applied due to his particular circumstances; and consideration by the employer as to whether the additional information provided by the individual warrants an exception to the exclusion and shows that the policy as applied is not job related and consistent with business necessity. *See* Section V.B.9, *infra* (examples of relevant considerations in individualized assessments).

Depending on the facts and circumstances, an employer may be able to justify a targeted criminal records screen solely under the *Green* factors. Such a screen would need to be narrowly tailored to identify criminal conduct with a demonstrably tight nexus to the position in question. Title VII thus does not necessarily require individualized assessment in all circumstances. However, the use of individualized assessments can help employers avoid Title VII liability by allowing them to consider more complete information on individual applicants or employees, as part of a policy that is job related and consistent with business necessity.

5. Validation

The Uniform Guidelines describe three different approaches to validating employment screens.[112] However, they recognize that "[t]here are circumstances in which a user cannot or need not utilize" formal validation techniques and that in such circumstances an employer "should utilize selection procedures which are as job related as possible and which will minimize or eliminate adverse impact as set forth [in the following subsections]."[113] Although there may be social science studies that assess whether convictions are linked to future behaviors, traits, or conduct with workplace ramifications,[114] and thereby provide a framework for validating some employment exclusions, such studies are rare at the time of this drafting.

6. Detailed Discussion of the *Green* Factors and Criminal Conduct Screens

Absent a validation study that meets the Uniform Guidelines' standards, the *Green* factors provide the starting point for analyzing how specific criminal conduct may be linked to particular positions. The three *Green* factors are:

- The nature and gravity of the offense or conduct;
- The time that has passed since the offense, conduct and/or completion of the sentence; and
- The nature of the job held or sought.

a. The Nature and Gravity of the Offense or Conduct

Careful consideration of the nature and gravity of the offense or conduct is the first step in determining whether a specific crime may be relevant to concerns about risks in a particular position. The nature of the offense or conduct may be assessed with reference to the harm caused by the crime (e.g., theft causes property loss). The legal elements of a crime also may be instructive. For example, a conviction for felony theft may involve deception, threat, or intimidation.[115] With respect to the gravity of the crime, offenses identified as misdemeanors may be less severe than those identified as felonies.

b. The Time that Has Passed Since the Offense, Conduct and/or Completion of the Sentence

Employer policies typically specify the duration of a criminal conduct exclusion. While the *Green* court did not endorse a specific timeframe for criminal conduct exclusions, it did acknowledge that permanent exclusions from all employment based on any and all offenses were not consistent with the business necessity standard.[116] Subsequently, in *El*, the court noted that the plaintiff might have survived summary judgment if he had presented evidence that "there is a time at which a former criminal is no longer any more likely to recidivate than the average person . . . ."[117] Thus, the court recognized that the amount of time that had passed since the plaintiff's criminal conduct occurred was probative of the risk he posed in the position in question.

Whether the duration of an exclusion will be sufficiently tailored to satisfy the business necessity standard will depend on the particular facts and circumstances of each case. Relevant and available information to make this assessment includes, for example, studies demonstrating how much the risk of recidivism declines over a specified time.[118]

c. The Nature of the Job Held or Sought

Finally, it is important to identify the particular job(s) subject to the exclusion. While a factual inquiry may begin with identifying the job title, it also encompasses the nature of the job's duties (e.g., data entry, lifting boxes), identification of the job's essential functions, the circumstances under which the job is performed (e.g., the level of supervision, oversight, and interaction with co-workers or vulnerable individuals), and the environment in which the job's duties are performed (e.g., out of doors, in a warehouse, in a private home). Linking the criminal conduct to the essential functions of the position in question may assist an employer in demonstrating that its policy or practice is job related and consistent with business necessity because it "bear[s] a demonstrable relationship to successful performance of the jobs for which it was used."[119]

7. Examples of Criminal Conduct Exclusions that Do Not Consider the *Green* Factors

A policy or practice requiring an automatic, across-the-board exclusion from all employment opportunities because of any criminal conduct is inconsistent with the *Green* factors because it does not focus on the dangers of particular crimes and the risks in particular positions. As the court recognized in *Green*, "[w]e cannot conceive of any business necessity that would automatically place every individual convicted of any offense, except a minor traffic offense, in the permanent ranks of the unemployed."[120]

Example 5: Exclusion Is Not Job Related and Consistent with Business Necessity. The National Equipment Rental Company uses the Internet to accept job applications for all positions. All applicants must answer certain questions before they are permitted to submit their online application, including "have you ever been convicted of a crime?" If the applicant answers "yes," the online application process automatically terminates, and the applicant sees a screen that simply says "Thank you for your interest. We cannot continue to process your application at this time."

The Company does not have a record of the reasons why it adopted this exclusion, and it does not have information to show that convictions for all offenses render all applicants unacceptable risks in all of its jobs, which range from warehouse work, to delivery, to management positions. If a Title VII charge were filed based on these facts, and there was a disparate impact on a Title VII-protected basis, the EEOC would find reasonable cause to believe that the blanket exclusion was not job related and consistent with business necessity because the risks associated with all convictions are not pertinent to all of the Company's jobs.

Example 6: Exclusion Is Not Job Related and Consistent with Business Necessity. Leo, an African American man, has worked successfully at PR Agency as an account executive for three years. After a change of ownership, the new owners adopt a policy under which it will not employ anyone with a conviction. The policy does not allow for any individualized assessment before exclusion. The new owners, who are highly respected in the industry, pride themselves on employing only the "best of the best" for every position. The owners assert that a quality workforce is a key driver of profitability.

Twenty years earlier, as a teenager, Leo pled guilty to a misdemeanor assault charge. During the intervening twenty years, Leo graduated from college and worked successfully in advertising and public relations without further contact with the criminal justice system. At PR Agency, all of Leo's supervisors assessed him as a talented, reliable, and trustworthy employee, and he has never posed a risk to people or property at work. However, once the new ownership of PR Agency learns about Leo's conviction record through a background check, it terminates his employment. It refuses to reconsider its decision despite Leo's positive employment history at PR Agency.

Leo files a Title VII charge alleging that PR Agency's conviction policy has a disparate impact based on race and is not job related for the position in question and consistent with business necessity. After confirming disparate impact, the EEOC considers PR Agency's defense that it employs only the "best of the best" for every position, and that this necessitates excluding everyone with a conviction. PR Agency does not show that all convictions are indicative of risk or danger in all its jobs for all time, under the *Green* factors. Nor does PR Agency provide any factual support for its assertion that having a conviction is necessarily indicative of poor work or a lack of professionalism. The EEOC concludes that there is reasonable cause to believe that the Agency's policy is not job related for the position in question and consistent with business necessity. [121]

8. Targeted Exclusions that Are Guided by the *Green* Factors

An employer policy or practice of excluding individuals from particular positions for specified criminal conduct within a defined time period, as guided by the *Green* factors, is a targeted exclusion. Targeted exclusions are tailored to the rationale for their adoption, in light of the particular criminal conduct and jobs involved, taking into consideration fact-based evidence, legal requirements, and/or relevant and available studies.

As discussed above in Section V.B.4, depending on the facts and circumstances, an employer may be able to justify a targeted criminal records screen solely under the *Green* factors. Such a screen would need to be narrowly tailored to identify criminal conduct with a demonstrably tight nexus to the position in question. Title VII thus does not necessarily require individualized assessment in all circumstances. However, the use of individualized assessments can help employers avoid Title VII liability by allowing them to consider more complete information on individual applicants or employees, as part of a policy that is job related and consistent with business necessity.

9. Individualized Assessment

Individualized assessment generally means that an employer informs the individual that he may be excluded because of past criminal conduct; provides an opportunity to the individual to demonstrate that the exclusion does not properly apply to him; and considers whether the individual's additional information shows that the policy as applied is not job related and consistent with business necessity.

The individual's showing may include information that he was not correctly identified in the criminal record, or that the record is otherwise inaccurate. Other relevant individualized evidence includes, for example:

- The facts or circumstances surrounding the offense or conduct;
- The number of offenses for which the individual was convicted;
- Older age at the time of conviction, or release from prison; [122]

- Evidence that the individual performed the same type of work, post conviction, with the same or a different employer, with no known incidents of criminal conduct;
- The length and consistency of employment history before and after the offense or conduct; [123]
- Rehabilitation efforts, e.g., education/training; [124]
- Employment or character references and any other information regarding fitness for the particular position; [125] and
- Whether the individual is bonded under a federal, state, or local bonding program. [126]

If the individual does not respond to the employer's attempt to gather additional information about his background, the employer may make its employment decision without the information.

Example 7: Targeted Screen with Individualized Assessment Is Job Related and Consistent with Business Necessity. County Community Center rents meeting rooms to civic organizations and small businesses, party rooms to families and social groups, and athletic facilities to local recreational sports leagues. The County has a targeted rule prohibiting anyone with a conviction for theft crimes (e.g., burglary, robbery, larceny, identity theft) from working in a position with access to personal financial information for at least four years after the conviction or release from incarceration. This rule was adopted by the County's Human Resources Department based on data from the County Corrections Department, national criminal data, and recent recidivism research for theft crimes. The Community Center also offers an opportunity for individuals identified for exclusion to provide information showing that the exclusion should not be applied to them.

Isaac, who is Hispanic, applies to the Community Center for a full-time position as an administrative assistant, which involves accepting credit card payments for room rentals, in addition to having unsupervised access to the personal belongings of people using the facilities. After conducting a background check, the County learns that Isaac pled guilty eighteen months earlier, at age twenty, to credit card fraud, and that he did not serve time in prison. Isaac confirms these facts, provides a reference from the restaurant where he now works on Saturday nights, and asks the County for a "second chance" to show that he is trustworthy. The County tells Isaac that it is still rejecting his employment application because his criminal conduct occurred eighteen months ago and is directly pertinent to the job in question. The information he provided did nothing to dispel the County's concerns.

Isaac challenges this rejection under Title VII, alleging that the policy has a disparate impact on Hispanics and is not job related and consistent with business necessity. After confirming disparate impact, the EEOC finds that this screen was carefully tailored to assess unacceptable risk in relevant positions, for a limited time period, consistent with the evidence, and that the policy avoided overbroad exclusions by allowing individuals an opportunity to explain special circumstances regarding their criminal conduct. Thus, even though the policy has a disparate impact on Hispanics, the EEOC does not find reasonable cause to believe that discrimination occurred because the policy is job related and consistent with business necessity. [127]

Example 8: Targeted Exclusion Without Individualized Assessment Is Not Job Related and Consistent with Business Necessity. "Shred 4 You" employs over 100 people to pick up discarded files and sensitive materials from offices, transport the materials to a secure facility, and shred and recycle them. The owner of "Shred 4 You" sells the company to a competitor, known as "We Shred." Employees of "Shred 4 You" must reapply for employment with "We Shred" and undergo a background check. "We Shred" has a targeted criminal conduct exclusion policy that prohibits the employment of anyone who has been convicted of any crime related to theft or fraud in the past five years, and the policy does not provide for any individualized consideration. The company explains that its clients entrust it with handling sensitive and confidential information and materials; therefore, it cannot risk employing people who pose an above-average risk of stealing information.

Jamie, who is African American, worked successfully for "Shred 4 You" for five years before the company changed ownership. Jamie applies for his old job, and "We Shred" reviews Jamie's performance appraisals, which include high marks for his reliability, trustworthiness, and honesty. However, when "We Shred" does a background check, it finds that Jamie pled guilty to misdemeanor insurance fraud five years ago, because he exaggerated the costs of several home repairs after a winter storm. "We Shred" management informs Jamie that his guilty plea is evidence of criminal conduct and that his employment will be terminated. Jamie asks management to consider his reliable and honest performance in the same job at "Shred 4 You," but "We Shred" refuses to do so. The employer's conclusion that Jamie's guilty plea demonstrates that he poses an elevated risk of dishonesty is not factually based given Jamie's history of trustworthiness in the same job. After confirming disparate impact based on race (African American), the EEOC finds reasonable cause to believe that Title VII was violated because the targeted exclusion was not job related and consistent with business necessity based on these facts.

C. Less Discriminatory Alternatives

If an employer successfully demonstrates that its policy or practice is job related for the position in question and consistent with business necessity, a Title VII plaintiff may still prevail by demonstrating that there is a less discriminatory "alternative employment practice" that serves the employer's legitimate goals as effectively as the challenged practice but that the employer refused to adopt.[128]

VI. Positions Subject to Federal Prohibitions or Restrictions on Individuals with Records of Certain Criminal Conduct

In some industries, employers are subject to federal statutory and/or regulatory requirements that prohibit individuals with certain criminal records from holding particular positions or engaging in certain occupations. Compliance with federal laws and/or regulations is a defense to a charge of discrimination. However, the EEOC will continue to coordinate with other federal departments and agencies with the goal of maximizing federal regulatory consistency with respect to the use of criminal history information in employment decisions.[129]

A. Hiring in Certain Industries

Federal laws and regulations govern the employment of individuals with specific convictions in certain industries or positions in both the private and public sectors. For example, federal law excludes an individual who was convicted in the previous ten years of specified crimes from working as a security screener or otherwise having unescorted access to the secure areas of an airport.[130] There are equivalent requirements for federal law enforcement officers,[131] child care workers in federal agencies or facilities,[132] bank employees,[133] and port workers,[134] among other positions.[135] Title VII does not preempt these federally imposed restrictions. However, if an employer decides to impose an exclusion that goes beyond the scope of a federally imposed restriction, the discretionary aspect of the policy would be subject to Title VII analysis.

> **Example 9: Exclusion Is Not Job Related and Consistent with Business Necessity.** Your Bank has a rule prohibiting anyone with convictions for any type of financial or fraud-related crimes within the last twenty years from working in positions with access to customer financial information, even though the federal ban is ten years for individuals who are convicted of any criminal offense involving dishonesty, breach of trust, or money laundering from serving in such positions.
>
> Sam, who is Latino, applies to Your Bank to work as a customer service representative. A background check reveals that Sam was convicted of a misdemeanor for misrepresenting his income on a loan application fifteen years earlier. Your Bank therefore rejects Sam, and he files a Title VII charge with the EEOC, alleging that the Bank's policy has a disparate impact based on national origin and is not job related and consistent with business necessity. Your Bank asserts that its policy does not cause a disparate impact and that, even if it does, it is job related for the position in question because customer service representatives have regular access to financial information and depositors must have "100% confidence" that their funds are safe. However, Your Bank does not offer evidence showing that there is an elevated likelihood of committing financial crimes for someone who has been crime-free for more than ten years. After establishing that the Bank's policy has a

disparate impact based on national origin, the EEOC finds that the policy is not job related for the position in question and consistent with business necessity. The Bank's justification for adding ten years to the federally mandated exclusion is insufficient because it is only a generalized concern about security, without proof.

B. Obtaining Occupational Licenses

Title VII also does not preempt federal statutes and regulations that govern eligibility for occupational licenses and registrations. These restrictions cover diverse sectors of the economy including the transportation industry,[136] the financial industry,[137] and import/export activities,[138] among others.[139]

C. Waiving or Appealing Federally Imposed Occupational Restrictions

Several federal statutes and regulations provide a mechanism for employers or individuals to appeal or apply for waivers of federally imposed occupational restrictions. For example, unless a bank receives prior written consent from the Federal Deposit Insurance Corporation (FDIC), an individual convicted of a criminal offense involving dishonesty, breach of trust, money laundering, or another financially related crime may not work in, own, or control "an insured depository institution" (e.g., bank) for ten years under the Federal Deposit Insurance Act.[140] To obtain such FDIC consent, the insured institution must file an application for a waiver on behalf of the particular individual.[141] Alternatively, if the insured institution does not apply for the waiver on the individual's behalf, the individual may file a request directly with the FDIC for a waiver of the institution filing requirement, demonstrating "substantial good cause" to grant the waiver.[142] If the FDIC grants the individual's waiver request, the individual can then file an application directly with the FDIC for consent to work for the insured institution in question.[143] Once the institution, or the individual, submits the application, the FDIC's criminal record waiver review process requires consideration of mitigating factors that are consistent with Title VII, including evidence of rehabilitation, and the nature and circumstances of the crime.[144]

Additionally, port workers who are denied the Transportation Workers Identification Credential (TWIC) based on their conviction record may seek a waiver for certain permanently disqualifying offenses or interim disqualifying offenses, and also may file an individualized appeal from the Transportation Security Administration's initial determination of threat assessment based on the conviction.[145] The Maritime Transportation Security Act, which requires all port workers to undergo a criminal background check to obtain a TWIC,[146] provides that individuals with convictions for offenses such as espionage, treason, murder, and a federal crime of terrorism are permanently disqualified from obtaining credentials, but those with convictions for firearms violations and distribution of controlled substances may be temporarily disqualified.[147] Most offenses related to dishonesty are only temporarily disqualifying.[148]

> **Example 10: Consideration of Federally Imposed Occupational Restrictions.** John Doe applies for a position as a truck driver for Truckers USA. John's duties will involve transporting cargo to, from, and around ports, and Truckers USA requires all of its port truck drivers to have a TWIC. The Transportation Security Administration (TSA) conducts a criminal background check and may deny the credential to applicants who have permanently disqualifying criminal offenses in their background as defined by federal law. After conducting the background check for John Doe, TSA discovers that he was convicted nine years earlier for conspiracy to use weapons of mass destruction. TSA denies John a security card because this is a permanently disqualifying criminal offense under federal law.[149] John, who points out that he was a minor at the time of the conviction, requests a waiver by TSA because he had limited involvement and no direct knowledge of the underlying crime at the time of the offense. John explains that he helped a friend transport some chemical materials that the friend later tried to use to damage government property. TSA refuses to grant John's waiver request because a conviction for conspiracy to use weapons of mass destruction is not subject to the TSA's waiver procedures.[150]

Based on this denial, Truckers USA rejects John's application for the port truck driver position. Title VII does not override Truckers USA's policy because the policy is consistent with another federal law.

While Title VII does not mandate that an employer seek such waivers, where an employer does seek waivers it must do so in a nondiscriminatory manner.

D. Security Clearances

The existence of a criminal record may result in the denial of a federal security clearance, which is a prerequisite for a variety of positions with the federal government and federal government contractors.[151] A federal security clearance is used to ensure employees' trustworthiness, reliability, and loyalty before providing them with access to sensitive national security information.[152] Under Title VII's national security exception, it is not unlawful for an employer to "fail or refuse to hire and employ" an individual because "such individual has not fulfilled or has ceased to fulfill" the federal security requirements.[153] This exception focuses on whether the position in question is, in fact, subject to national security requirements that are imposed by federal statute or Executive Order, and whether the adverse employment action actually resulted from the denial or revocation of a security clearance.[154] Procedural requirements related to security clearances must be followed without regard to an individual's race, color, religion, sex, or national origin.[155]

E. Working for the Federal Government

Title VII provides that, with limited coverage exceptions, "[a]ll personnel actions affecting employees or applicants for employment . . . shall be made free from any discrimination based on race, color, religion, sex, or national origin."[156] The principles discussed above in this Guidance apply in the federal employment context. In most circumstances, individuals with criminal records are not automatically barred from working for the federal government.[157] However, the federal government imposes criminal record restrictions on its workforce through "suitability" requirements for certain positions.[158] The federal government's Office of Personnel Management (OPM) defines suitability as "determinations based on a person's character or conduct that may have an impact on the integrity or efficiency of the service."[159] Under OPM's rules, agencies may bar individuals from federal employment for up to three years if they are found unsuitable based on criminal or dishonest conduct, among other factors.[160] OPM gives federal agencies the discretion to consider relevant mitigating criteria when deciding whether an individual is suitable for a federal position.[161] These mitigating criteria, which are consistent with the three *Green* factors and also provide an individualized assessment of the applicant's background, allow consideration of: (1) the nature of the position for which the person is applying or in which the person is employed; (2) the nature and seriousness of the conduct; (3) the circumstances surrounding the conduct; (4) the recency of the conduct; (5) the age of the person involved at the time of the conduct; (6) contributing societal conditions; and (7) the absence or presence of rehabilitation or efforts toward rehabilitation.[162] In general, OPM requires federal agencies and departments to consider hiring an individual with a criminal record if he is the best candidate for the position in question and can comply with relevant job requirements.[163] The EEOC continues to coordinate with OPM to achieve employer best practices in the federal sector.[164]

VII. Positions Subject to State and Local Prohibitions or Restrictions on Individuals with Records of Certain Criminal Conduct

States and local jurisdictions also have laws and/or regulations that restrict or prohibit the employment of individuals with records of certain criminal conduct.[165] Unlike federal laws or regulations, however, state and local laws or regulations are preempted by Title VII if they "purport[] to require or permit the doing of any act which would be an unlawful employment practice" under Title VII.[166] Therefore, if an employer's exclusionary policy or practice is *not* job related and consistent with business necessity, the fact that it was adopted to comply with a state or local law or regulation does not shield the employer from Title VII liability.[167]

Example 11: State Law Exclusion Is Job Related and Consistent with Business Necessity. Elijah, who is African American, applies for a position as an office assistant at Pre-School, which is in a state that imposes criminal record restrictions on school employees. Pre-School, which employs twenty-five full- and part-time employees, uses all of its workers to help with the children. Pre-School performs a background check and learns that Elijah pled guilty to charges of indecent exposure two years ago. After being rejected for the position because of his conviction, Elijah files a Title VII disparate impact charge based on race to challenge Pre-School's policy. The EEOC conducts an investigation and finds that the policy has a disparate impact and that the exclusion is job related for the position in question and consistent with business necessity because it addresses serious safety risks of employment in a position involving regular contact with children. As a result, the EEOC would not find reasonable cause to believe that discrimination occurred.

Example 12: State Law Exclusion Is Not Consistent with Title VII. County Y enforces a law that prohibits all individuals with a criminal conviction from working for it. Chris, an African American man, was convicted of felony welfare fraud fifteen years ago, and has not had subsequent contact with the criminal justice system. Chris applies to County Y for a job as an animal control officer trainee, a position that involves learning how to respond to citizen complaints and handle animals. The County rejects Chris's application as soon as it learns that he has a felony conviction. Chris files a Title VII charge, and the EEOC investigates, finding disparate impact based on race and also that the exclusionary policy is not job related and consistent with business necessity. The County cannot justify rejecting everyone with any conviction from all jobs. Based on these facts, County Y's law "purports to require or permit the doing of an[] act which would be an unlawful employment practice" under Title VII.

VIII. Employer Best Practices

The following are examples of best practices for employers who are considering criminal record information when making employment decisions.

General

- Eliminate policies or practices that exclude people from employment based on any criminal record.
- Train managers, hiring officials, and decision makers about Title VII and its prohibition on employment discrimination.

Developing a Policy

- Develop a narrowly tailored written policy and procedure for screening applicants and employees for criminal conduct.
  - Identify essential job requirements and the actual circumstances under which the jobs are performed.
  - Determine the specific offenses that may demonstrate unfitness for performing such jobs.
    - Identify the criminal offenses based on all available evidence.
  - Determine the duration of exclusions for criminal conduct based on all available evidence.
    - Include an individualized assessment.
  - Record the justification for the policy and procedures.
  - Note and keep a record of consultations and research considered in crafting the policy and procedures.
- Train managers, hiring officials, and decision makers on how to implement the policy and procedures consistent with Title VII.

Questions about Criminal Records

- When asking questions about criminal records, limit inquiries to records for which exclusion would be job related for the position in question and consistent with business necessity.

Confidentiality

- Keep information about applicants' and employees' criminal records confidential. Only use it for the purpose for which it was intended.

Approved by the Commission:

/s/

_____

Chair Jacqueline A. Berrien

4/25/2010

_____

Date

 The EEOC Guidance is available online. The online verison shows all endnotes. See this document at www.eeoc.gov/laws/guidance/arrest_conviction.cfm

Interview Forms and Questions

#1 - Telephone Interview Form

For uniformity of treatment, all applicants should be asked the same questions, and the form filled out.

Applicant:

Date/Time called:

Caller:

Telephone Script—

Hello I am calling about a resume in sent us in response to our ad in the (*name of newspaper*) for (*job title*). Do you have a few minutes to talk on the phone?

1. Can you tell me why you applied for this position and what interests you about it?

2. May I ask you why you are looking for new employment?

3. Can you describe your best five[1] skills?

4. We are located in (*your town or city*) — is that convenient for you and can you get here?

   May I ask you what your salary history is in your current position?

#2 - Phone Interview Form

1. What hours are you available to work?

2. May I ask you what your salary history is in your current position?

3. If we would like to go into more detail and schedule an interview, what would be the best time and date for you?

If the person sounds acceptable, schedule an interview for as soon as possible.

If the person does not appear to be a good fit, but further discussion with them may be an option, say—

Thank you for your time. We need to review this information with the hiring manager, and if it looks like this is a match, we will call you back.

(*It is okay to give your phone number if the person requests it, but stress that* "we will call them.")

Interview Rating and Impressions—

__ Excellent potential for position — *Interview is a priority*
__ Could be a good candidate — *Interview would be helpful*
__ *No further action necessary*

---

[1] number of skills asked for can vary

Additional Interview Questions to Ask a Past Employer

1. In what areas did the applicant show need for improvement?

2. How did the applicant get along with supervisors and managers?

3. Did the applicant exhibit any tendency towards violence or inappropriate conduct/behavior that was workplace related? (this may include use of drugs, alcohol, or dishonesty)

4. How did the candidate compare to the person now doing the job?

5. Can you identify specific jobs this applicant would be better suited for?

6. How did the candidate respond when confronted with an urgent assignment?

7. Do you have any additional comments regarding this applicant?

8. Why didn't you try to rehire or induce him/her to stay?

Employment Verification and Reference Worksheet

Name Of Applicant	
Social Security Number	
Previous Employer Name	
City/State	
Phone Number	
Fax Number	
Contact Name	
Relationship To Candidate	
Title And Department	

	Applicant Reported	**Employer Reported**
Start Date		
End Date		
Starting Position		
Ending Position		
Ending Salary		
Reason For Leaving		
Eligible For Rehire?		

Will Employer give reference? YES   NO   If yes, see last page for reference information

Call History

Date	Time	Who Called	Results	Notes

1. Please record all efforts made to obtain a verification and reference for this applicant
2. Please note any changes in phone numbers or special instructions needed to obtain a reference on this applicant
3. If unsuccessful and no response to voicemail, contact the main number and send a fax to the employer. *Note time and date the fax request is sent.*

EMPLOYMENT REFERENCE for: _____ **page 2**

If reference is given by a source different than above, please note

Reference Name	
Phone Number	
Relationship To Candidate	
Title And Department	
Current Employer (If Different)	

1. What were the applicant's job and the nature of his/her duties?

2. Is the applicant's resume description of their duties accurate and consistent?

3. Can you describe or give examples of the applicant's strengths?

4. What could the applicant do to improve his/her job performance?

5. How would you describe the quality of his/her work? Can you give examples?

6. Can you describe how he/she got along with others? …teamwork, relationship to supervisors, etc.

7. Can you give examples of times when the applicant demonstrated leadership characteristics?

8. How would you describe the applicant's communication skills?
   (If the applicant was a supervisor, describe how he/she supervised others)

9. How did the applicant show initiative or leadership on the job?

10. Were there any problems with attendance or punctuality?

11. Were there any work-related problems with this applicant?

12. On a scale of 1-10 (10 being the highest), overall, how would you rate
    the applicant's performance?

13. If you were responsible for the hiring process, would you consider him/her eligible for rehire?

14. Do you have any additional comments regarding this applicant?

Exit Interview Report

EXIT INTERVIEW REPORT

ALL ANSWERS ARE HELD STRICTLY CONFIDENTIAL

Employee's Name: _____ Employee #: _____

Department: _____ Position: _____

Dates of Employment: From _____ To _____

Supervisor: _____

Reason for leaving Company: _____

Return of:

_____ keys   _____ company documents   _____ uniform

_____ I.D. card   _____ safety equipment   _____ tools

_____ credit card   _____ other company property   _____ company auto

Employee informed of restriction on:

_____ trade secrets   _____ employment with competitor (if applicable)

_____ patents   _____ removing company documents

_____ other data   _____ other _____

Employee exit questions:

1.   Did management adequately recognize employee contributions? _____

_____

2.   Do you feel that you have had the support of management on the job? _____

_____

3.   Were you adequately trained for your job? _____

_____

4.   Did you find your work rewarding? _____

_____

(Continued)

EXIT INTERVIEW REPORT **PAGE 2**

5.   Do you feel you were fairly treated by the company? _____

_____

6.   Were you paid an adequate salary for the work you did? _____

_____

7.   Were you content with your working conditions? _____

_____

8.   Do you feel your supervision was adequate? _____

_____

9.   Did you understand company policies and the reasons for them? _____

_____

10.   Have you observed incidences of theft of company property? _____

_____

11.   How can the company improve security? _____

_____

12.   How can the company improve working conditions? _____

_____

13.   What are the company's strengths? _____

_____

14.   What are the company's weaknesses? _____

_____

15.   Other comments: _____

_____

_____

_____

USE ADDITIONAL SHEETS FOR FURTHER COMMENTS

Turnover Cost Calculator Form

Separation Costs—	
Cost of time required to terminate the employee	$
Cost of exit interviewer's time	$
Employee's separation/severance pay	$
Increase on unemployment taxes	$
Termination-related administrative costs	$
	$
Vacancy Costs—	
Cost of overtime required of workers covering the vacancy	$
Cost of any directly-hired temporary help in covering the vacancy	$
Cost of any agency-based temporary help (agency costs and contracts)	$
Replacement Costs—	
Pre-employment administrative expenses	$
Cost of attracting applicants (recruitment advertising)	$
Cost of entrance interviews	$
Screening/testing (aptitude/skills test, drug screens, background/reference checks)	$
Hiring-related travel expenses	$
Moving or relocation expenses	$
Post-employment medical exams	$
Post-employment information gathering and dissemination costs (payroll, benefits, policies and procedures, time required to enter the individual into all relevant systems/programs, etc.)	$

Turnover Cost Calculator Form (page 2)

Training Costs—	
Costs of informational literature (manual, employee handbook, brochures, policies)	$
Formal training costs (classroom, instructor or specialty trainer)	$
Informal training costs (supervisor, on-the-job training)	$
Any overtime required by employee as s/he learns the job	$
Additional overtime required of co-workers as new employee learns the job	$
Opportunity Costs—	
Cost of difference in productivity between former employee and replacement	$
Anticipated learning curve (time at which productivity returns to former standard)	$
Cost of any customers or accounts lost in conjunction with loss of employee	$
Supervisory and Staff Costs—	
Cost of first-line supervisors addressing turnover (problem solving, mentoring, troubleshooting)	$
Total Cost →	

Description of Pre-Employment Screening Tools

Type of Information	What It Will Tell	Reason You Need This Information	Limitations/Notes on Using This Information
Criminal Record Search (County Courts)	Felony and Misdemeanor convictions and pending cases, usually including date and nature of offense, sentencing date, disposition and current status. Generally goes back seven years. May also search federal court records. It is critical to search both for felonies and misdemeanors in state court, since many serious job-related violations can be classified as misdemeanors.	Critical information to protect your business and employees. Protects employer from negligent hiring exposure and helps reduce threat of workplace violence, theft, disruption and other problems. Failure to honestly disclose a prior criminal conviction can also be the basis not to hire. For the maximum protection, all jurisdictions where an applicant has lived, worked or studied in the past seven years should be checked.	Some restrictions on having certain information (such as arrests not resulting in convictions), or certain minor offenses.[2] Employment cannot be automatically denied based upon a criminal record, but must show some sound business reason per EEOC Guidance (See Chapter 16). Criminal records are not available by computer nationwide. Check public records at county courthouses[3] in locations where applicant resided or worked. Be careful in using databases– if there is a "hit" then court file should be reviewed for identifiers and details.
Driver's License Search	Driving history for three years. Verification of driving privilege, and operator restrictions that might indicate the applicant's ability to perform job tasks.	Helps verify identity. Gives insight on level of applicant's responsibility. Determine if applicant keeps commitments to appear in court or pay fines, has a drug/alcohol problem, and current license status. "Driving for work" is very broadly defined in most jurisdictions and is not limited to driving positions.	This information can be accessed by an outside agency on the employer's behalf. Background firms can also help interpret the DMV record. An alternative is having applicants go to the DMV to obtain their own records, which is not practical and is subject to fraud. DMV may has a program for firms that would like record updates.

[2] for instance, in New York state, misdemeanors cannot be considered — and all misdemeanors could not be found as there are over 1200 courts handling some sort of misdemeanor records in New York

[3] there can be delays when a court clerk pulls a file. Some courts charge a court search fee, copy fee, cert fee.

Type of Information	What It Will Tell	Reason You Need This Information	Limitations/Notes on Using This Information
Social Security Number Trace/Check	Provides names and addresses associated with the applicant's Social Security Number and may indicate fraudulent use. Helps verify other applicant information.	Helps verify that applicants are who they say they are, critical to ensure employer not the victim of a fraudulent application by someone with something to hide. Can show where to search for criminal records.	Where employer does not have a sound business reason to obtain a business credit report, the Social Security trace gives information to help confirm identity and may uncover fraud.
Credit Report	Credit history and public records such as judgments, liens, and bankruptcies. May include previous employers, addresses, and other names used.[4]	Helps determine whether an employee is suitable for a position involving handling cash or the exercise of financial discretion. A possible way to gauge trustworthiness and reliability.	A credit report should only be requested when it is specifically relevant to a job function, and the employer has appropriate policies and procedures in place to ensure that the use of credit reports are relevant and fair. State law can impact the use of credit reports.
Employment Verification	Basic verification includes dates of employment, job title, and reason for leaving. Some employers will verify salary. Usually obtained from HR, personnel, or payroll dept. Some employers provide reference information recorded on a 900 service.	This information confirms applicant's resume, and verifies their previous job history. Helps eliminate any *unexplained gaps* in employment, which ensures that appropriate jurisdictions have been checked for criminal records, reducing likelihood of incarceration for a serious offense.	Employers are often hesitant to give recommendations and may limit prior employment checks to release of basic information only. Limited results if— not allowed to contact current employer, employer will not return call, past employer is out of business or cannot be located, or if employee was working through an agency.
Employment Reference Check	This is a more in-depth reference check that seeks job duties, performance, salary history, strengths and weaknesses, eligibility for rehire, and other detailed information.	Allows an employer to have a realistic assessment of a candidate from former employers. It promotes a better "fit," confirms the hiring opinion, and protects the expensive hiring investment.	Although most employers would like references, few past employers give them due to concerns over legal liability. Always attempt to obtain verifications and references in order to demonstrate due diligence.

---

[4] an employment credit report differs from commercial credit report-employment version. The employment version does not have age, credit scoring, or account numbers of credit cards.

Type of Information	What It Will Tell	Reason You Need This Information	Limitations/Notes on Using This Information
Personal Reference Check	Contact personal references to ascertain additional information about your applicant concerning fitness for the job in question.	Personal references can provide valuable information as to a person's character as it relates to the job opening.	Inquire about the applicant's relationship to the reference and how long they have known each other in order to judge the usefulness of the information provided. Contact "developed references" for a better picture of the applicant.
Education Verification	Will confirm degrees, diplomas or certificates, and dates attended.	Confirms that applicant has educational experience and professional ability to do the job.	Industry sources show that 30% of all job applicants falsify information about educational background. Expect to pay a fee for transcripts, but verifications generally free. Some schools require a verification fee, or only fax back documents to an 800 number.
Professional Licenses	The type of license, whether currently valid, dates issued, state licensing authority.	Confirms whether an applicant has the required credentials or licenses for the position.	There is a high rate of job applicants making up or falsifying licenses or credentials.
Civil Records (includes Litigation, Judgments, and Tax Liens)	Date of filing, case type, case number or file record, jurisdiction and, if available, identity of parties involved.	Discover whether your applicant has sued former employers or has been sued for reasons that are relevant to employment.	An employer should use this information where it is relevant to job performance. Have standard policies and procedures for civil records use.
Workers' Compensation Records	Information about Workers' Compensation claims and previous injuries to determine if the person can perform the essential functions of the job or is a health and safety threat to themselves or others.	This information allows the employer to conduct *post-job offer* reviews in compliance with strict standards of the Americans with Disabilities Act. It is highly recommended an employer seek legal advice before requesting this sensitive information.	Federal and state laws regulate how and when these records can be obtained and used. Cannot be used for the purpose of eliminating any applicant who has filed a legal claim and who can perform the essential functions of the job with or without reasonable accommodation. Have policies and procedures in place before requesting or utilizing Workers' Comp records.

Index

About the Author Lester S. Rosen

Attorney at Law Lester S. Rosen is Founder and CEO of **Employment Screening Resources (ESR)** – www.ESRcheck.com – a nationwide accredited background screening company located in Novato, California. He is the author of "The Safe Hiring Manual," the first comprehensive guide to background checks, and "The Safe Hiring Audit." A recognized background check expert, his speaking appearances have included numerous national and regional conferences, as well as international conferences. See: www.esrcheck.com/Newsletter/ESR-Speaks. He has been quoted in web sites, newspapers, and trade journals across the United States and the world.

In 1997, Mr. Rosen founded Employment Screening Resources with a mission to promote safe workplaces for employers, employees, and the public. ESR – 'The Background Check Authority[SM]' – provides accurate and actionable information, empowering clients to make informed safe hiring decisions. ESR is accredited by the National Association of Professional Background Screeners (NAPBS®) Background Screening Credentialing Council (BSCC) for successfully proving compliance with the Background Screening Agency Accreditation Program (BSAAP).

Mr. Rosen was the chairperson of the steering committee that founded the NAPBS, the professional trade organization for the background screening industry, and also served as the first co-chairman. He has testified as an expert witness on employment screening and issues surrounding safe hiring and due diligence in California, Florida, and Arkansas.

Mr. Rosen is a former deputy District Attorney and criminal defense attorney and has taught criminal law and procedure at the University of California Hastings College of the Law. His jury trials have included murder, death penalty, and federal cases. He graduated UCLA with Phi Beta Kappa honors and received a J.D. degree from the University of California at Davis, serving on the Law Review. He holds the highest attorney rating of A.V. in the national Martindale-Hubbell listing of U.S. Attorneys.

Mr. Rosen resides with his wife and daughter in Tiburon, California. To contact him for a speaking engagement, story information, or professional consultation, please email lsr@esrcheck.com.